D0212162

ENCYCLOPEDIA OF THE PALESTINIANS

Edited by Philip Mattar

Facts On File, Inc.

Encyclopedia of the Palestinians

Copyright © 2000 by Philip Mattar
Maps on pages 124, 138, 194, 200, 210, 211, 239, 245, 295, 309, 318, 320, 344, 426, 437, and 438 by Dale Williams;
© Facts On File, Inc.

All rights reserved. No part of this book may be reproduced or utilized in any form or by any means, electronic or mechanical, including photocopying, recording, or by any information storage or retrieval systems, without permission in writing from the publisher. For information contact:

Facts On File, Inc.
11 Penn Plaza
New York NY 10001

Library of Congress Cataloging-in-Publication Data

Encyclopedia of the Palestinians/edited by Philip Mattar.
p. cm.
Includes bibliographical references and index.
ISBN 0-8160-3043-X
1. Palestinian Arabs Encyclopedias. I. Mattar, Philip, 1944– .
DS113.6.E53 2000
909'.049274'003—dc21 99–23510

Facts On File books are available at special discounts when purchased in bulk quantities for businesses, associations, institutions, or sales promotions. Please call our Special Sales Department in New York at 212/967-8800 or 800/322-8755.

You can find Facts On File on the World Wide Web at http://www.factsonfile.com

Cover design by Cathy Rincon
Text design by Evelyn Horovicz

Printed in the United States of America

VB FOF 10 9 8 7 6 5 4 3 2 1

This book is printed on acid-free paper.

CONTENTS

For
Christina

PREFACE

The aim of this encyclopedia is to respond to the need for a comprehensive one-volume compendium of knowledge about modern Palestinian history and society that is at once wide in scope, intermediate in size, authoritative, and readable. That is not a task for one person, which is why I gathered a team of forty-eight scholars, most of whom were Americans, Palestinians, and Israelis.

The encyclopedia covers three broad periods in modern times: the late Ottoman era from the brief Egyptian occupation (1831–40) until British conquest of Palestine; British rule from 1917 until 1948; and the years since the 1948 war. The third period, because of the dispersion of Palestinians after 1948, can be subdivided into several periods and topics, such as Israeli Palestinians since 1948, the West Bank and Gaza Strip (1948–67, 1967–present), diaspora communities since 1948, Palestine Liberation Organization (PLO) since 1964, and the peace process since 1991. While this work includes all three major periods, it is weighted in favor of the twentieth century, when the major events that shaped Palestinian history and society occurred and about which we know much more than the nineteenth.

There was no easy way to select some four hundred entries, and to assign length to each from a few words to thousands of words. I drew up a list based on numerous general and specialized books, and sent it to eight scholars for comments. Their suggested additions and deletions—and, in the case of biographies, the overlaps in their selections—helped finalize the overall list. Ultimately, the selection process is subjective, especially the biographies, which constitute a third of the entries. I chose individuals who exerted a significant impact on Palestinian society and politics for a period of time, and about whom readers would expect to find entries in a work such as this. In addition, while the selection of each entry and the assignment of length are determined by the significance of topic and the length of period covered, it is also prescribed by the amount and quality of information available.

Even though more has been written about modern Palestine and the Palestinians than about many Middle East countries and societies, we know little about long periods of Palestinian history and other disciplines, such as Palestinian archaeology and historical geography. Much of the writing has focused on the political struggle over Palestine between Arabs and Jews since 1882. The history of Palestine is frequently subsumed under studies of the Palestine problem, which, after 1948, became known as the Arab-Israel conflict, a branch of study that emerged in conjunction with Middle Eastern studies in the late 1940s in Britain, and in the mid-1950s in the United States. In much of the literature about Palestine, there was little about the Palestinian people during a period of rapid developments.

It was not until the early 1970s that Palestinian studies emerged as a separate field. Two major reasons account for the increased interest in Palestinian affairs. First, the Palestinian national movement, which was active during British rule but dormant after 1948, reemerged in the form of the Palestine Liberation Organization in 1964, at a time of heightened tension over the Arab-Israeli conflict and increased involvement of the United States and the Soviet Union in the Middle East. Second, the opening of materials in major archives—such as the Public Records Office (PRO) near London, Israel State Archives (ISA) and the Central Zionist Archives (CZA) in Jerusalem, and the National Archives (NA) in Washington, D.C.—enabled a young and better trained generation of scholars to consult literally millions of documents.

Scholarship on the Palestinians is limited in scope and quality. Indeed, much of it focuses on the political and diplomatic history of six and one-half out of seventeen decades of Palestine in the modern period. There are very few works on the period prior to the 1830s, despite the availability of the massive Ottoman archives in Istanbul that cover Palestine from 1516–1917, and the abundance of court records and memoirs. Only two periods—British rule from 1917 to 1948 and post-1964—are developed well enough to constitute a critical mass. And, like the history of the Arab-Israeli conflict from which it grew, the history of the Palestinians lacks the quality not only of older fields of history but also of more recent ones, such as East Asian history. There is no college or university department specializing exclusively in Palestinian studies. There is no Palestinian national archive, no viable oral history program, no bibliography, no quality dictionary or scholarly encyclopedia, and no adequate general textbook or even comprehensive textbook on Palestinian history of the nineteenth century or on other relevant disciplines. Naturally, this state of underdevelopment is partly due to the nascent stage of a field that has not yet had the time to grow in breadth and depth, and to Palestinian exile and dispersion. Yet neither of these explain why so much has been written that is so limited in scope and quality.

A major reason for the narrow focus and lower standards by Israelis and Palestinians and their supporters is the fusion of ideology and scholarship. Like the history of the conflict, Palestinian historiography is one of the most polarized and politicized of any historical craft. The field is dominated by partisans, Israelis, and Palestinians and their supporters (many of whom are amateurs lacking professional skills), who have used scholarship and journalism to galvanize their people, to gain world support, and as a weapon against each other in their struggle over historic Palestine.

Many Israeli and Zionist scholars, who dominate the field and have contributed to most of the distortion, are seemingly qualified to write about the Palestinians. That is, many have acquired the basic academic knowledge of Palestinian history, politics, society, religion, and of Arabic. Yet most are unable or unwilling to empathize (not sympathize) with the Palestinian people they are studying, even though empathy is indispensable, considering the cultural, religious, and political divide between them and the Palestinians. Consequently, they are locked out, unable to fully understand and explain.

Israeli domination of the field is partly due to the small numbers of Palestinian scholars. Whereas the Jewish people were in the forefront of European education since the Renaissance, and the historical craft for two centuries, and came to Palestine with scholarly standards and methodology, the Palestinians were an underdeveloped people until the Mandate period (1922–48). Even by the end of the Mandate, there were few Palestinian college graduates and fewer professional scholars. They lacked a scholarly tradition based on archival research and critical inquiry, not to mention self-criticism.

After 1948, education became a prized asset, yet most talented Palestinians gravitated to careers outside of academia. In Israel, Palestinian education was underfunded and few Palestinians found jobs, yet the superior Israeli education produced a number of capable Palestinian historians. In the West Bank and Gaza Strip, Palestinian universities were poorly funded for almost two decades of Jordanian and Egyptian rule, respectively, and for almost three decades of Israeli occupation. The Israeli military occupation—accompanied by university closures, censorship, confiscation of documents, and massive arrests—and the Palestinian national reaction to it, consumed and disrupted academic life. In addition, Palestinian scholars lacked a support system, especially research funding, that is essential for intellectual pursuits and productivity, a situation that continued to exist under the rule of the Palestinian Authority.

Despite a more conducive environment in the diaspora, Palestinian scholars there have not been much more productive, either in their writings in or in institution building. Indeed, some of the better-known scholars in the Arab world and the West have written little, and most have not written a book on Palestine and the Palestinians that can be considered a major work. I suggest that they were diverted by several factors. First, they had to make a living, and the field of Palestinian studies was too narrow to sustain them. Second, many of them volunteered in the 1970s and 1980s to serve the Palestinian national movement as activists, championing the Palestinian cause. In the 1990s, some of the best and brightest were commandeered for the peace process, as negotiators or advisers. A few were productive despite other preoccupations, and a handful even benefited by their involvement in the national struggle and the peace process because it enriched their writing and work. This is true for Rashid Khalidi, who wrote about Palestinian identity, Yezid Sayigh, who wrote about the Palestinian national movement since 1948, and Camille Mansour, who established Bir Zeit University's legal center. It is particularly true of Walid Khalidi, who, besides his direct and indirect involvement in the peace process and his leadership of the Institute for Palestine Studies, wrote and edited a number of major studies. Yet for most, every hour they spent on making a living, on political activity, and on the peace process was an hour lost to scholarship. Since the pool of professional scholars was already small (a few dozen by world standards), the output of capable scholars was very little.

Israeli and Palestinian scholars are so overwhelmed by emotional and ideological considerations, be it antipathy or sympathy, that they are unable to write objectively. Their research and analysis are motivated, whether consciously or not, by a political stake in the outcome rather than a rigorous intellectual curiosity and honesty. And they write with the full moral and financial backing of their institutions and communities for a receptive audience that does not seem to require higher standards.

The consequence has been the development of a Zionist and Israeli narrative and a Palestinian narrative of Palestinian history that is closer to the official positions than to the historical record. There is hardly an issue or event in the history of the Palestinians that these narratives (especially the Zionist and Israeli), often dressed in academic garb, have not distorted or mythologized. Most often this is done by focusing on that part of the story that supports their case and ignoring the part that does not, by selecting the sources and tailoring facts to fit their thesis, by reading into history more or less than the data warrants, and above all, by subtly condemning or exonerating.

Yet, these works are useful as much for their footnotes that may lead the researcher to primary sources as for their information, however imbalanced. Indeed, many partisan works are indispensable, especially those about areas that are understudied or those written by authors who lived in the period about which they are writing. For example, no one working on the history of the Mandate can ignore the works, no matter how partisan, of such Zionist authors as Norman Bentwich, Richard Meinherzhagen, and Albert Hyamson, and such Palestinian writers as Muhammad Izzat Darwaza, Ihsan al-Nimr, and Subhi Yasin.

Fortunately, some Western, Palestinian, and Israeli scholars, relying on archival and other primary sources, armed with scholarly tools of research and analysis and knowledge of the original languages, and dedicated to scholarly standards and integrity, have produced some fine works since the early 1970s. These scholars are relatively few and have not written enough about most periods and fields. Yet, they have written pioneering studies that have filled in some of the gaps in the scholarship on the Palestinians, and set new standards for future generations to follow. It is from this group of scholars that I selected most of the authors of this encyclopedia, such as Ann M. Lesch, Laurie Brand, Mark Tessler, Muhammad Muslih, Neil Caplan, Julie Peteet, Rashid Khalidi, Don Peretz, and Salim Tamari, among others. This group also includes a few scholars—such as Benny Morris, Avi Shlaim, and Ian Lustick—who have gone a step further by producing revisionist, often called "new," history that has challenged a few, mainly Zionist but also Palestinian, distortions and myths.

The authors of this work are diverse. Their interpretations and even data are not always consistent. Morris and Nur Masalha, for example, agree that an expulsion took place in 1948 but not about why and how many were expelled. Throughout the work there are inconsistencies regarding basic data, especially numbers of population, refugees, and casualties. I have tried neither to reconcile inconsistencies nor to get between my colleagues. The variety of voices and interpretations is not only reflective of the scholarship in the field, it enriches it and stimulates further research and writing. Ultimately, the contributions will not fill in the gaps nor challenge every distortion (it would take decades of scholarship to remedy these flaws) but they represent some of the finest scholarship in the past three decades and make this encyclopedia the most reliable, balanced, and scholarly reference work on modern Palestinian history and society to date.

ACKNOWLEDGMENTS

I am very grateful to the authors who invested their scholarship and time in this project. They were patient and generous despite delays beyond their control and repeated requests for revisions. Most of them revised their entries in light of one to three readers' comments, revised again based on editorial comments, and, because of delays, updated their entries. Some of them wrote more than one article, and some provided invaluable advice. I am also grateful to the many readers of the long entries for their valuable comments.

One of the authors, Michael R. Fischbach, stands out. Besides several long articles, Fischbach wrote most of the short entries, the chronology, and the glossary. He also proofread the manuscript and compiled the index. I am deeply grateful to Fischbach for his substantial help, enthusiastic interest, and judicious advice.

I wish to thank the Ford Foundation for a grant to assist with the administrative and editorial work. I am grateful to Steve Fergus, Lindsey Austin, Michele Kjorlien, and Sinan Antoon for their help with administration and research at various stages of the project. I owe a debt of gratitude to Eric Hooglund for his substantive editing of many of the long articles.

This work would not have been possible without the support of a few people at Facts On File, Inc. I am grateful to Drew Silver, who persuaded me to undertake this work, for the enthusiastic support he gave me, and for helping with the formative stage of the work. I am also grateful to Laurie E. Likoff, editorial director, for her judicious leadership in overseeing the project, and for her confidence and support. I am deeply grateful to Mary Kay Linge, senior editor, who took over the project after a delay, and brought her considerable talents to bear on the last and most difficult stage, until its successful completion. Linge gave me intelligent advice and much support. I wish to thank her assistant, Cynthia Yazbek, who was prompt, efficient, and productive. I wish to also acknowledge the intelligent copyediting of the manuscript by Rachel Kranz, Susan Thornton, and Michael G. Laraque. Finally, I want to thank my dear wife Evelyn for her patience, understanding, and moral support.

—Philip Mattar

A NOTE ON TRANSLITERATION AND ORGANIZATION

The system used in this encyclopedia is a modified form of that used by the *International Journal of Middle East Studies.* Yet I chose to be inconsistent for several reasons. Many place-names and historical personalities are familiar to the English reader by their English rather than their Arabic or Hebrew names, e.g., Jerusalem rather than al-Quds or Yerushalayim. Others are transliterated inaccurately, such as Beirut for Bayrut. In both cases, I chose to use what is familiar to the English reader. Arabs and Jews often adopted spellings of their names that are inconsistent with a scholarly transliteration system, such as Nuseibeh instead of Nusayba. I have used Nuseibeh since that is how the owner of the name wants to spell it. When the spelling is not known, I have used the scholarly spelling, which in this case renders the diphthong "ay" not "ei" and the *ta marbuta* "a" not "eh." In many cases, alternate spellings of the name were provided, as well as a nom de guerre, if applicable. No diacritical marks—mainly dots and dashes above and below certain letters—were used, because they mean little to anyone who does not know Arabic. For the same reason, I have excluded both the *'ayn* (') and *hamza* (') from the beginning and at the end of a word. But I retained them, in most cases, in the middle, to give clear distinction between letters on either side of the *'ayn* and *hamza.* In general, particularly because this work is for the general reader and not the specialist, I sacrificed scholarly accuracy and consistency for ease of use.

The encyclopedia is arranged alphabetically, though the definite article al- or el- is not taken into account. Cross-references to related topics are in small capital letters. Foreign words are provided in italics.

Abbas, Mahmud

Abu Mazin; activist, politician
1935– Safad

Mahmud Abbas left Palestine for Syria in 1948. Thereafter, he studied in Egypt and became active in the General Union of Palestinian Students. He eventually received a Ph.D. in Israeli studies at Moscow University. In 1957, he moved to Qatar, where he rose to a high position in the nation's department of education and began organizing Palestinian nationalists.

Abbas, known by the nom de guerre Abu Mazin, rose to become a senior figure in the Palestinian national movement. He was a founding member of FATAH in the early 1960s, was a long-time member of the group's central council, and later held high positions in the PALESTINE LIBERATION ORGANIZATION (PLO), including head of its national department and membership on the executive committee.

Abbas became a leading expert on Israeli and Jewish issues within the PLO. His seniority and expertise led to his assumption of the PLO's important Occupied Territories portfolio on the death of KHALIL AL-WAZIR (Abu Jihad) in 1988.

Abbas was also a major figure in the PLO's attempts to resolve the Arab-Israeli conflict through negotiations. He coordinated indirect secret talks with Israeli officials through Dutch intermediaries in the Netherlands in 1989. With the onset of Arab-Israeli peace talks beginning in October 1991, Abbas was placed in charge of the PLO's behind-the-scenes coordination of the Palestinian team negotiating with Israel. He remained one of the main high-level PLO supporters of continuing negotiations when Palestinian dissatisfaction with the talks mounted.

In the winter and spring of 1993, Abbas was one of four PLO officials engaged in direct secret talks with representatives of the Israeli government in Norway, talks that were actually carried without the knowledge of the Palestinian negotiating team. The result of these talks was the Israeli-PLO Declaration of Principles (DOP), signed in Washington by Abbas and Israeli foreign minister Shimon Peres on September 13, 1993, known as the OSLO AGREEMENTS. Abbas later headed the Israeli-Palestinian liaison committee, which began meeting in Cairo that October, leading negotiations with Peres over the Israeli withdrawal from Gaza and Jericho.

Abbas returned to Jericho in September 1994. He continued to lead negotiations, although he was not always content with their course. At meetings of Fatah's central council and the PLO executive committee in March 1995, for example, Abbas denounced the concept of a phased Israeli withdrawal, which the PLO and Israel were then negotiating. However, Abbas continued to work with Yasir ARAFAT and the PALESTINIAN AUTHORITY (PA). He headed the central elections committee, formed in December 1995 to oversee elections for the PA's PALESTINIAN LEGISLATIVE COUNCIL, and was himself elected to the council in January 1996. He was also appointed secretary of the PLO executive committee.

Abbas's book, *Tariq Uslu,* which appeared in English as *Through Secret Channels: The Road to Oslo: Senior PLO Leader Abu Mazen's Revealing Story of the Negotiations with Israel* (Reading, England: Garnet, 1995), created a stir, with its revelations of the details of PLO-Israeli talks.

Michael R. Fischbach

Abbas, Muhammad

Abu al-Abbas; guerrilla leader
1941?, 1947?– Galilee

Also known by the nom de guerre Abu al-Abbas, Muhammad Abbas fled Palestine in 1948 for Syria, where he studied English and Arabic literature at the University of Damascus. In the late 1960s, Abbas joined the POPULAR FRONT FOR THE LIBERATION OF PALESTINE (PFLP), but later he left that organization. Then, in 1973, he joined the POPULAR FRONT FOR THE LIBERATION OF PALESTINE–GENERAL COMMAND (PFLP-GC) and rose to become the group's spokesman. Abbas and other PFLP-GC militants disagreed with the pro-Syrian organization's decision not to oppose Syrian intervention against PALESTINE LIBERATION ORGANIZATION (PLO) forces in Lebanon in 1976 and left the group to form their own group, the PALESTINE LIBERATION FRONT (PLF), in 1977. In November 1984, Abbas joined the PLO executive committee.

In October 1985, four PLF members commandeered the Italian cruise ship *Achille Lauro* off the Egyptian coast and killed an elderly disabled Jewish-American passenger, Leon Klinghoffer. Abbas was involved in the four men's surrender to Egyptian authorities. While Abbas and the hijackers were flying to Tunisia aboard an Egyptian aircraft, U.S. jets intercepted the plane and forced it to land in Italy, where the five were taken into Italian custody, but Abbas was soon released.

Another violent PLF exploit created considerable problems for the PLO. The United States, already angry about Abbas's role in the *Achille Lauro* affair, suspended the dialogue it had established with the PLO in December 1988 after a foiled landing by PLF commandos on a beach near Tel Aviv in May 1990, claiming that the PLO had not censured Abbas for the raid. As a result, Abbas left the PLO executive committee in October 1991.

In April 1996, Israel allowed Abbas to enter the areas under the control of the PALESTINIAN AUTHORITY to attend the meeting of the PALESTINE NATIONAL COUNCIL that voted to amend the Palestinian National Charter. On that occasion, Abbas apologized for the 1985 murder of Leon Klinghoffer.

Michael R. Fischbach

Abd al-Baqi, Ahmad Hilmi

banker, politician
1882–1963 Sidon, Lebanon

Born in LEBANON of a father serving in the Ottoman military, Abd al-Baqi later moved with his family to NABLUS, where he pursued his studies. He later worked with the Ottoman Agricultural Bank in the city and with the Ottoman government in Iraq.

Abd al-Baqi became involved in Arab nationalist politics, joining the secret al-Fatat organization and later the ISTIQLAL PARTY. He briefly served in the administration of Faysal bin Husayn in Syria from 1919 to 1920 and later in the government of Transjordan.

Abd al-Baqi returned to Palestine in 1926, whereupon he worked as general inspector of the Islamic *waqf* (Islamic endowments) until 1930. He later helped found the Arab Bank and the Agricultural Bank and was active in a number of other financial organizations, especially those dedicated to extending credit to Palestine's peasants. These included the Arab Nation's Bank, the Industrial Bank, and the Arab National Fund. He also played important roles in the Arab Chamber of Commerce in Jerusalem, the ARAB LEAGUE's Economic Committee, and other business groups, as well as charitable organizations like the Institute for the Sons of the Arab Nation.

Abd al-Baqi was involved in Palestinian nationalist politics as well. He was a member of the ARAB HIGHER COMMITTEE (AHC), formed in April 1936, and was exiled along with other AHC members by mandatory authorities to the Seychelles Islands in October 1937. Abd al-Baqi later served on the fourth AHC, which was reconstituted by the Arab League at the BLUDAN CONFERENCE of June 1946.

When the first Arab-Israeli war broke out in May 1948, Abd al-Baqi was the sole remaining member of the AHC in Palestine. He served on the Defense Committee in Jerusalem. Abd al-Baqi was then chosen as prime minister in the short-lived ALL-PALESTINE GOVERNMENT in September and October 1948. He continued to represent Palestine at the Arab League in Cairo thereafter.

In 1963, Abd al-Baqi left Cairo for medical treatment in Lebanon. He died in the village of Suq al-Gharb and was buried in Jerusalem.

Michael R. Fischbach

Abd al-Hadi, Awni

lawyer, politician
1889–1970 Cairo

Awni Abd al-Hadi studied in Istanbul and later at the law faculty of the University of Paris. While in Paris, he became a leading member of the Arab nationalist movement, helping to establish the al-Fatat organization in 1911. He also was a member of the DECENTRALIZATION PARTY, which sought to decrease the centralizing policies of the Committee of Union and Progress after 1908, and he attended an ARAB CONGRESS held in Paris in June 1913.

After World War I, Abd al-Hadi served as secretary to Amir Faysal bin Husayn and was legal adviser to the Hijazi delegation representing Faysal's father, Sharif Husayn bin Ali, at the 1919 Paris peace conference. He later worked with Faysal's short-lived Arab government in Damascus and joined the ISTIQLAL [Independence] PARTY that emerged out of al-Fatat in 1918. After Faysal's defeat at the hands of the French in 1920, Abd al-Hadi attended the Cairo conference of March 1921 with Faysal's brother Emir Abdullah and served him briefly after the British established him as prince of Transjordan.

Upon returning to Palestine, Abd al-Hadi practiced law. He maintained his pan-Arab orientation even as he was elected to the ARAB EXECUTIVE—the leading nationalist body among the Palestinians in the 1920s and early 1930s—at the Fifth, Sixth, and Seventh Arab Congresses (1922, 1923, and 1928, respectively). Abd al-Hadi advocated dialogue with British authorities even as he pushed for Palestinian political demands that ran contrary to British policy. He was among the Palestinians attending several significant conferences, including the London Conference of 1930 and the Islamic Conference in JERUSALEM in 1931. He also presented Palestinian viewpoints before the SHAW COMMISSION, which was investigating the 1929 WESTERN (WAILING) WALL DISTURBANCES. Abd al-Hadi was able to continue Palestinian nationalist activities even though Zionist land purchasing agencies used his legal services in the famous Wadi Hawarith land deal of 1929, in which they acquired 30,000 *dunums* (30,000,000 square meters) of land.

By 1932, however, Abd al-Hadi had adopted a more militant response to the British. That year, he was among several former members of the Istiqlal who decided to reactivate the party in Palestine; he eventually rose to the post of secretary-general. The Istiqlal not only challenged British rule but also offered a forum for militant anti-British, anti-Zionist activism outside the context of the bitter rivalry between the HUSAYNI FAMILY and the NASHASHIBI FAMILY that had plagued Palestinian politics during the PALESTINE MANDATE, a rivalry criticized by the Istiqlal as divisive.

Abd al-Hadi was appointed general secretary of the ARAB HIGHER COMMITTEE, which was formed in April 1936 to coordinate the general strike among Palestinians. Placed under arrest from June to October 1936, he later appeared before the PEEL COMMISSION in January 1937. He remained in exile from 1937 to 1941, during which time he attended the LONDON CONFERENCE in 1939, which issued the famous White Paper limiting British support for ZIONISM. After his return to Palestine in 1941, Abd al-Hadi helped revive the Arab Higher Committee.

After the 1948 war, Abd al-Hadi was given a position in the ALL-PALESTINE GOVERNMENT that was formed in Gaza under Egyptian sponsorship, but he never served. He later became the Jordanian ambassador to Egypt from 1951 to 1955, a minister in several Jordanian cabinets, and a member of the Jordanian senate from 1955 to 1958. Abd al-Hadi moved to Egypt in 1964 and died there in 1970.

Michael R. Fischbach

Abd al-Hadi Family

One of the most influential families in central Palestine, the Abd al-Hadis of NABLUS were the most prominent of this large family's several branches. However, numerous members of all branches occupied government positions during Ottoman, British, and Jordanian rule.

Amin (politician) A former Ottoman parliamentarian, Amin was appointed by British authorities to a proposed ADVISORY COUNCIL in May 1923, although he and other appointees refused to serve for political reasons. In 1929 he was appointed a member of the SUPREME MUSLIM COUNCIL, the power base of the HUSAYNI FAMILY councilists, but he supported the rival NASHASHIBI-led opposition.

Fakhri (?–1943; guerrilla leader) Born in Arraba, in the West Bank, Fakhri was one of the top guerrilla commanders in central Palestine during the Arab Revolt of 1936–38, rising to become the second in command to the paramount guerrilla leader FAWZI AL-QAWUQJI. After a period of exile outside Palestine, he joined the Nashashibi-led opposition in the fall of 1938. He thereafter worked against guerrillas backed by the Husayni faction as a top commander of the "Peace Gangs," a self-defense force established to combat guerrilla attacks directed against opposition figures. Fakhri was assassinated in 1943.

Ruhi (1885–1954; administrator) After studying in Istanbul at the Lycée Imperial and Istanbul University, Ruhi served in the Ottoman foreign office for fifteen years. After his return to Palestine following World War I, he was appointed district officer of JERUSALEM by the British in 1921 and eventually became the senior assistant secretary of the Palestine government in 1944. He later served in the Jordanian government as foreign minister in 1949 and from 1952 to 1953.

Michael R. Fischbach

Abd al-Hadi, Mahdi

academic, activist
1944– Nablus

Mahdi Abd al-Hadi studied law at the Damascus University School of Law, obtaining the LL.B. in 1970. He then returned to the WEST BANK to take up a career in journalism and academia. From 1972 to 1974, he edited the Jerusalem-based newspaper *al-Fajr.* Later, he served as director of public relations and information for BIR ZEIT UNIVERSITY from 1977 to 1980. His interests in the future of higher education and scholarly research in the West Bank were also reflected in his service to the West Bank Council for Higher Education (1977–80) and in his establishment of the Palestinian Academic Society for the Study of International Affairs (PASSIA) in 1987.

One of Abd al-Hadi's greatest contributions to intellectual life in the West Bank was the ARAB THOUGHT FORUM, which he helped establish in 1977 and of which he served as president from 1977 to 1980 and as a member of the board of trustees from its inception. In addition to sponsoring research on development issues, the forum created an important nationalist coordinating group, the NATIONAL GUIDANCE COMMITTEE, in 1978.

After resuming graduate study and receiving a Ph.D. from Bradford University's School of Peace Studies in Britain in 1984, Abd al-Hadi moved to Jordan, where he became a member of the Jordanian–Palestinian Joint Committee in the early 1980s. He later served as special adviser to the Jordanian ministry of occupied lands affairs from 1985 to 1986. Since 1987, he has been president of PASSIA, which holds seminars, conducts research, and publishes studies on Palestinian policy.

Michael R. Fischbach

Abd al-Shafi, Haydar

physician, activist
1919– Gaza

Haydar Abd al-Shafi, son of a graduate of al-Azhar University in Cairo and *waqf* (Islamic endowment) custodian in Gaza and Hebron during the PALESTINE MANDATE, studied medicine at the American University of Beirut, graduating in 1943. Upon returning to Palestine, he worked for the government hospital in Jaffa until 1945. He also served as a medical officer in the Transjordanian Arab Legion from 1943 to 1945 and as a member of the Arab Medical Society in Palestine beginning in 1945.

Following years of private practice in Gaza after the 1948 war, Abd al-Shafi served in the Egyptian administration in the GAZA STRIP as head of the health department from 1958 to 1960. He was also active in politics as head of the Gaza legislative council in 1962 and 1964. In 1964, he represented Gaza at the Palestinian conference in East Jerusalem that led to the creation of the PALESTINE LIBERATION ORGANIZATION (PLO).

After the Israeli occupation of Gaza in 1967, Abd al-Shafi was jailed briefly in 1969 and deported in 1970, but he was eventually allowed to return. Associated with the PALESTINE COMMUNIST PARTY, he was one of the main nationalist figures in Gaza and throughout the Occupied Territories by the 1980s. He also maintained his interest in medical issues throughout, serving as president of the PLO-affiliated Palestine RED CRESCENT Society in Gaza from 1972 until the present.

Despite his age, Abd al-Shafi became identified with a new generation of activists in the Occupied Territories that emerged during the INTIFADA ("to be shaken off"; the Palestinian uprising against Israel's occupation, 1987–93). Although affiliated with PLO organizations, these figures represented a new indigenous leadership that was not content merely to execute the policies adopted by the PLO in exile but wanted to shape them as well. The fact that the Western media soon amplified these figures' growing prestige was demonstrated in April 1988, when Abd al-Shafi was one of four activists from the Occupied Territories who participated in an American television program on the *Intifada* along with Israeli government officials and legislators.

Abd al-Shafi's stature as a leading nationalist figure in Gaza was confirmed by the PLO in 1991, when it chose him to head the Palestinian component of the joint Jordanian-Palestinian delegation to the MADRID PEACE CONFERENCE. He continued to serve as head of the Palestinian delegation throughout the negotiations with Israel from 1991 to 1993.

After two years of negotiations, Abd al-Shafi became increasingly frustrated both with Israeli intransigence at the negotiating table and with PLO chairman YASIR ARAFAT's autocratic style of leadership. He and other members of the delegation were thoroughly surprised by the 1993 PLO-Israel Declaration of Principles that had been secretly negotiated in OSLO. Dissatisfied with the concessions made by the PLO, especially with its agreement to defer important issues like refugees and Jewish settlements until final status talks, Abd al-Shafi resigned from the delegation shortly after the accords were made public in August 1993.

Abd al-Shafi thereafter became increasingly vocal in his opposition to the Israeli-Palestinian autonomy agreement and to Arafat's leadership of the PALESTINIAN AUTHORITY (PA), which emerged from that agreement. Nevertheless, he refused to work actively to sabotage either the agreement or the PA. Before the January 1996 elections for the PA's PALESTINIAN LEGISLATIVE COUNCIL, he founded a political movement called the National Democratic Coalition and was elected to the council after receiving more votes than any other candidate. Increasingly critical of PA authoritarianism and frustrated with the council's inability to affect PA decisions, Abd al-Shafi resigned his council seat in October 1997.

Michael R. Fischbach

Abd Rabbo, Yasir

Adib Abd Rabbo, Abd Rabbih;
resistance leader, politician
1944–

Yasir Abd Rabbo was active in the pan-Arab Movement of Arab Nationalists and later in the POPULAR FRONT FOR THE LIBERATION OF PALESTINE (PFLP). He and other leftist PFLP activists, such as NAYIF HAWATIMA, left the front and in 1968 established the Popular Democratic Front for the Liberation of Palestine, later known simply as the DEMOCRATIC FRONT FOR THE LIBERATION OF PALESTINE (DFLP).

Abd Rabbo rose to become a member of the DFLP's politburo and its second most powerful figure. He was the leading DFLP member to serve on executive bodies of the PALESTINE LIBERATION ORGANIZATION (PLO). He headed the PLO's information department from 1977 to 1994, during which time he grew close to PLO chairman YASIR ARAFAT. As a result, he represented the PLO during the U.S.-PLO dialogue in Tunisia from December 1988 through May 1990.

By the early 1990s, serious differences had emerged between Abd Rabbo and Hawatima. In part, these stemmed from disagreements over the extent to which the DFLP should maintain its traditional involvement in the political process in Jordan, Hawatima's homeland. Another source of tension was Abd Rabbo's embrace of Arafat's diplomatic efforts to end the Arab-Israeli conflict, a process criticized by Hawatima. Violence between Abd Rabbo's and Hawatima's factions erupted, and Abd Rabbo finally broke with Hawatima in 1991, although both factions continued to use the name DFLP until 1993, when Abd Rabbo's group changed its name to the Palestinian Democratic Union, known by the backward Arabic acronym *FIDA*.

Abd Rabbo cautiously supported the 1993 PLO-Israel OSLO accords. In May 1994, he was appointed minister of culture and arts in the PALESTINIAN AUTHORITY.

Michael R. Fischbach

Abdullah ibn Husayn See KING ABDULLAH AND THE ZIONISTS.

Abu al-Abbas See ABBAS, MUHAMMAD.

Abu Ala See QURAY, AHMAD.

Abu Ammar See ARAFAT, YASIR.

Abu-Amr, Ziad

Ziyad Abu Amr; academician, legislator
1950– Gaza

Abu-Amr received a B.A. in English language and literature from Damascus University. He obtained an M.A. in Arab studies from Georgetown University in 1980 and a Ph.D. in comparative politics from Georgetown in 1986. Abu-Amr was a schoolteacher in Syria, Bahrain, and Oman during the 1970s, at Georgetown University from 1979 to 1983 and from 1990 to 1991, and at BIR ZEIT UNIVERSITY from 1988 to 1989 and 1993 to the present.

Abu-Amr has also served with several research institutions and academic associations. Since 1987 he has been on the executive committee of the Arab Organization for Political Science, and he was a member of the Brookings Working Group on Arab-Israeli Peace in 1990 and 1991. Since 1991, Abu-Amr has been a member of the executive committee of the Center for Policy Analysis on Palestine in Washington and a senior fellow at the CENTER FOR PALESTINE RESEARCH AND STUDIES in NABLUS, since 1993.

Abu-Amr has also been involved in elections and the legislative process in the PALESTINIAN AUTHORITY. In 1994, he was deputy chairman of the Independent Group for Palestinian Elections and was elected to the PALESTINIAN LEGISLATIVE COUNCIL (PLC) during the February 1996 balloting. He currently chairs the PLC's political committee.

Abu-Amr has written numerous scholarly articles on the Arab-Israeli conflict and Islamic fundamentalism and is the author of *Islamic Fundamentalism in the West Bank and Gaza* (1994).

Michael R. Fischbach

Abu Ayyash, Radwan

journalist, activist
1950– Askar refugee camp, Nablus

Radwan Abu Ayyash began working as a journalist for the JERUSALEM newspaper *al-Sha'b* in 1975. After receiving a B.A. in English from BIR ZEIT UNIVERSITY in 1982, he worked with the Palestine Press Service, editing the group's magazine *al-Awda* from 1982 until Israeli authorities closed it in 1986. Abu Ayyash quickly rose to become a leading figure in media circles in the Occupied Territories, heading the Arab Journalists Association from 1985 to 1991. The association played a crucial role during the INTIFADA ("to be shaken off"; the Palestinian uprising against Israel's occupation) by accrediting the foreign journalists who flocked to the territories to cover the uprising. He has also directed the Arab Media Center from 1988 until the present.

Affiliated with FATAH, Abu Ayyash was one of a group of activists who emerged as the nucleus of a leadership cadre in the Occupied Territories during the Intifada. In 1991, he was chosen to head the fourteen-member advisory committee of the Palestinian delegation to the MADRID PEACE CONFERENCE, a committee that made recommendations to the delegation's steering committee. Abu Ayyash left the negotiating process after the initial round of peace talks in Madrid.

Abu Ayyash later chaired the Palestinian coordinating committee of nongovernmental organizations at the United Nation in 1991 and was asked by PLO chairman YASIR ARAFAT to head the Palestinian Broadcasting Corporation, which began operating in the PALESTINIAN AUTHORITY.

Michael R. Fischbach

Abu Iyad See KHALAF, SALAH.

Abu Jihad See AL-WAZIR, KHALIL.

Abu-Lughod, Ibrahim

academic
1930–

Abu-Lughod received a Ph.D. from Princeton University in 1957. He taught political science at Northwestern University in the 1970s and 1980s. In 1979–80, he headed the United Nations Educational, Scientific and Cultural Organization team carrying out the Palestine Open University Feasibility project. He was president of the Association of Arab-American University Graduates. In the early 1990s he moved to the West Bank, where he became vice president and instructor at Bir Zeit

University. He is editor of *Transformation of Palestine* (1971) and is coeditor of *Settler Regimes in Africa and the Arab World: The Illusions of Endurance* (1974).

Michael R. Fischbach

Abu Marzook, Musa

Abu Marzuq; Islamic militant
1951– Gaza

Abu Marzook was the head of the HAMAS political bureau during the early 1990s. A resident of the United States since 1982, he was arrested by U.S. authorities in July 1995 on his arrival in New York from a trip to the United Arab Emirates and charged with TERRORISM. He remained imprisoned in New York for nearly two years while the United States studied the legal bases for extraditing him to Israel to face charges of terrorism. Israel ultimately declined to seek his extradition, whereupon he was deported to Jordan in May 1997 with the permission of the Jordanian government.

While in detention, Abu Marzook was replaced by Khalid Mash'al in the Hamas hierarchy in Jordan.

Michael R. Fischbach

Abu Mazin

See ABBAS, MAHMUD.

Abu Middayn, Furayh

Freih Abu Middein; lawyer, politician
1944– Gaza

Born in Gaza, Abu Middayn hails from a BEERSHEBA family and is the grandson of the first mayor of that town. He obtained an LL.B. in 1971 from Alexandria University in Egypt, after which he returned to Gaza to practice law. He served as a member of the Gaza Council of Law and chaired the Gaza Bar Association beginning in 1989.

Associated with FATAH, Abu Middayn was a member of the Palestinian delegation to the MADRID PEACE CONFERENCE in 1991. Upon the formation of the PALESTINIAN AUTHORITY (PA) in 1994, he was appointed to serve as its first minister of justice. He was elected to the PA's PALESTINIAN LEGISLATIVE COUNCIL in February 1996 as well.

Michael R. Fischbach

Abu Nidal

Sabri al-Banna; dissident leader
1937– Jaffa

Al-Banna is mostly known by his nom de guerre Abu Nidal or ("father of stuggle" in Arabic). He has become one of the most infamous Palestinians in the world because his organization, the Fatah Revolutionary Council, has perpetrated notorious acts of aimless violence.

Little is known about Abu Nidal's childhood except that he was born to a wealthy father in JAFFA. His family was displaced when Israel was established in 1948 and had to relocate to a refugee camp in the GAZA STRIP before moving again to NABLUS, in the WEST BANK. Abu Nidal never completed secondary education. He worked as an electrician in Jordan, where he joined the Ba'ath Party in the mid-1950s.

Abu Nidal was not known as a strong advocate of any particular ideology, although his activities against the Jordanian government landed him in jail. Abu Nidal later worked in Saudi Arabia but was expelled in 1967. He then returned to Amman, where he joined the Fatah movement and rose in its ranks. In 1969, Abu Nidal was appointed the Fatah representative in Sudan. He went on to his most important appointment, as the movement's representative in Iraq, where he established strong ties with the Ba'thist intelligence apparatus and the Iraqi leadership.

Abu Nidal supported the "rejectionist" position of the Iraqi government, which opposed any peaceful settlement of the ARAB ISRAEL CONFLICT. Then, in 1974, the PALESTINE LIBERATION ORGANIZATION (PLO), under the leadership of YASIR ARAFAT's Fatah, implicitly accepted the "two-state solution." Al-Banna accused his former comrades of treason and defected from the PLO to form his own organization, Fatah Revolutionary Council. Meanwhile, Fatah sentenced Abu Nidal in absentia to death for plotting to kill a PLO leader.

The birth of Abu Nidal's organization was revealed through a series of spectacular violent acts that showed no concern for civilians. Although Abu Nidal's name is associated in the West with anti-Israeli violence because of strikes in Rome, Vienna, Istanbul, and London, his targets have been mainly Arab: Palestinians, Syrians, Saudis, and Lebanese. His organization targeted and killed a number of the PLO's diplomats in key

European countries because they were involved in talks with Jewish and Israeli personalities. Not all of his killings have been ideological; he has been a hired gun for a variety of clients over the years, including both Iraq and Libya.

Abu Nidal's relationship with the Iraqi Ba'thist regime began long before his defection from Fatah. Abu Nidal was loyal to Iraqi interests, killing many of Iraq's enemies around the world. He maintained his headquarters in a secret location in Baghdad while organizing cells in the Arab world and Europe. The relationship lasted until 1983, when he found the Iraqi regime too eager to please the West and the Arab oil regimes so that they could acquire financial and military help in their war against Iran. Reports about Abu Nidal's cooperation with former Soviet bloc countries remain unconfirmed.

Between 1981 and 1985, Abu Nidal based his headquarters in Damascus despite his violent record against Syrian interests. (Syria wanted to take advantage of Abu Nidal's services to punish its regional enemies.) In 1982, his men shot and severely injured the Israeli ambassador in London, Shlomo Argov, an act that was used by the Israeli government as the pretext for its massive invasion of Lebanon. Syria tolerated Abu Nidal's presence until 1985, when Western pressure finally led Syria to expel him. His whereabouts after 1986 are unknown, although he was publicly received by Libyan leader Muammar al-Qadhafi in the late 1980s. He also made sure to bolster his organizational structure in the refugee camps of Lebanon, where fear of government crackdowns was minimal during the civil war (1975–1990). After years of boycotting the media for fear of threats to his life, he opened an office in Beirut to deal with the press.

Abu Nidal's organization is run on terror and intimidation. No members are allowed to leave once they join, and the official organ of his movement, *Filastin al-Thawra,* regularly carried announcements of the execution of "traitors" within the movement. In Palestinian popular circles, Abu Nidal is considered a dangerous terrorist who has done more harm to the Palestinian cause than to Israel, and his influence has always been limited to a couple of hundred followers at most.

In 1989, the chief spokesperson of Abu Nidal's movement, Atif Abu Bakr, defected from Fatah Revolutionary Council along with 150 members who had become disenchanted with Abu Nidal's methods of operation. In the early 1990s, Abu Nidal tried to wrest control of the refugee camps in Sidon from Yasir Arafat, but he failed, and that failure led to the almost total dissolution of his organization in Lebanon and to the defection of more of his aides to Fatah. In 1996, the Fatah Revolutionary Council was dormant. In the summer of 1998, he was reported to be ill and under arrest in Egypt. In early 1999, newspapers reported that Abu Nidal had moved, yet again, to Iraq as the marriage of interest between Saddam Husayn's regime and Abu Nidal resurfaced. His organization is no longer capable of posing a threat to any regime.

As'ad AbuKhalil

BIBLIOGRAPHY

Melman, Yossi. *The Master Terrorist.* New York: Adama Books, 1986.

Miller, Aaron David. "Sabri Khalil Al-Banna." In Bernard Reich, ed., *Political Leaders of the Contemporary Middle East and North Africa: A Biographical Dictionary.* Westport, Conn.: Greenwood Press, 1990.

Seale, Patrick. *Abu Nidal: A Gun for Hire.* New York: Random House, 1992.

Steinberg, Matti. "The Radical Worldview of the Abu Nidal Faction." *Jerusalem Quarterly* 48 (Fall 1988): 88–104.

Abu Sharif, Bassam

PLO moderate

1946– Jerusalem

Bassam Tawfiq Abu Sharif, known as Abu Umar, was born in the Old City of JERUSALEM on August 9, 1946, to upper-middle-class Sunni Muslim parents. He was raised in Jordan, where his family had been residing since 1943, when his father, previously an announcer in the Arabic section of the Palestine Broadcasting Service, joined the staff of the Arab Bank.

The younger Abu Sharif attended secondary school in Irbid, Jordan. Although he never completed secondary studies, he enrolled at The American University of Beirut (AUB) in 1963; he graduated in 1967.

A committed Nasirist during his youth, Abu Sharif joined the Movement of Arab Nationalists (MAN), led by Dr. GEORGE HABASH, shortly after he enrolled at AUB, and he became a prominent cadre. Deported to Jordan in 1966 for his political activities, he returned to Beirut the following year and participated in the December 11, 1967, founding conference of the POPULAR FRONT FOR THE LIBERATION OF PALESTINE (PFLP). A member of its central committee from 1968, Abu Sharif was elected in 1972 to the PFLP politburo. In July 1969, he became deputy editor of the newly established official PFLP weekly *al-Hadaf* (The Target).

During the late 1960s and early 1970s, Abu Sharif gained international prominence as a PFLP spokesperson during the height of its campaign of "international operations." Among his activities, he helped recruit the Venezuelan militant Ilyich Sanchez Ramirez ("Carlos") to the PFLP and forged links with the radical German Red Army Faction. On July 25, 1972, shortly after a Japanese Red Army attack on Tel Aviv's Lod airport conducted on behalf of the PFLP that left twenty-six dead, Abu Sharif was severely injured and permanently disfigured by a parcel bomb sent in his name to the *al-Hadaf* offices in Beirut by the Israeli external intelligence service, Mossad. Because *al-Hadaf* editor and chief PFLP spokesperson GHASSAN KANAFANI had been assassinated by a Mossad car bomb on July 8, 1972, Abu Sharif assumed Kanafani's posts after his recuperation. He became secretary of the General Union of Palestinian Writers and Journalists in 1972 and vice-president of the International Organization of Journalists in 1974; he was awarded the Lenin Prize (1980), the German Golden Pen (1981), and similar prizes for his journalism.

During much of the 1970s, Abu Sharif led a powerful faction within the PFLP that advocated closer ties with the Palestine National Liberation Movement (FATAH) within the PALESTINE LIBERATION ORGANIZATION (PLO) and with Iraq within the Arab world. Steeped in public relations and diplomacy but lacking a military background, Abu Sharif also argued for a greater emphasis on political rather than military struggle. At the 1981 PFLP general congress, however, the more militarist, pro-Syrian, and anti-Fatah faction led by Abu Ali Mustafa succeeded in removing him from both the politburo and the editorship of *al-Hadaf*.

Demoted to head the PFLP's external relations department (he briefly regained his former posts in 1985–86), Abu-Sharif became increasingly disenchanted with the organization when it relocated to Damascus as a result of the 1982 Israeli invasion of Lebanon. He meanwhile drew increasingly close to PLO chairman YASIR ARAFAT. In the fall of 1987, Abu Sharif was expelled from the PFLP for meeting with Egyptian president Husni Mubarak; he was immediately thereafter appointed special adviser by Arafat (although he joined neither Fatah nor the PLO bureaucracy). There is a general consensus that he would eventually have jumped had he not been pushed and that Arafat had actively promoted this split.

In his new capacity, Abu Sharif played a leading role in the Palestinian diplomatic offensive that accompanied the popular uprising INTIFADA ("to be shaken off"; the Palestinian uprising against Israel's occupation) of 1987–93 in the Palestinian OCCUPIED TERRITORIES. Precisely because he could not be called to account in the same manner as a Fatah cadre or PLO bureaucrat and because, when necessary, he could be presented by his sponsor as a loose cannon, he participated in numerous forums and published several articles (the best known of which is his June 1988 "Prospects for Peace in the Middle East: The Two-State Solution") in which it is generally accepted he elaborated Arafat's real views as much as his own.

With some justification, Abu Sharif has claimed responsibility for Palestinian participation in the October 1991 MADRID PEACE CONFERENCE and the secret negotiations that resulted in the September 1993 Israeli-Palestinian Declaration of Principles on Interim Self-Government Arrangements. Soon after this document was signed, however, he virtually disappeared from public view and his relationship with Arafat cooled noticeably. Based in Amman, Abu Sharif engaged in private business ventures with his numerous contacts, at one point mediating the feud between the Egyptian al-Fayid brothers and the German tycoon Tiny Rowland over ownership of London's Harrods department store.

In January 1996, Abu Sharif received permission to return to the Palestinian Occupied Territories and announced his intention to reside there.

Muin Rabbani

BIBLIOGRAPHY

AbuKhalil, As'ad. "Internal Contradictions in the PFLP: Decision Making and Policy Orientation." *The Middle East Journal* 41 (1987): 361–378.

Abu-Sharif, Bassam, and Uzi Mahnaimi. *Best of Enemies: The Memoirs of Bassam Abu-Sharif and Uzi Mahnaimi.* Boston: Little, Brown and Co., 1995.

Abu Zayyad, Ziyad

journalist, lawyer
1940– Ayzariyya (Bethany)

Ziyad Abu Zayyad received a degree in law from Damascus University in 1965. He worked thereafter in the Jordanian department of immigration and passports in Jerusalem. After the Israeli occupation of his native WEST BANK, Abu Zayyad worked for the newspaper *al-Quds* before editing a Hebrew-language edition of *al-Fajr* in 1977. Beginning in 1986, he founded a Hebrew-language newspaper, *Gesher,* designed to familiarize the Israeli public with Palestinian thinking.

Abu Zayyad also used his legal training to assist Palestinians arrested by Israeli occupation authorities. He was arrested on several occasions by the Israelis.

In 1991, Abu Zayyad was chosen to head the fourteen-member advisory committee of the Palestinian delegation to the MADRID PEACE CONFERENCE, which offered recommendations to the delegation's steering committee. He also headed a Palestinian working group at the multilateral negotiations and chaired the FATAH-oriented Political Committee of Jerusalem, which tried to rally Palestinian support for the peace process.

Michael R. Fischbach

Acre

Arabic, Akka; Hebrew, Akko

Acre was one of Palestine's two major seaports (the other was JAFFA) until the twentieth century and was a fortified town of significant political import throughout Palestine's history.

Lying at the foothills of Galilee on the northern end of the Gulf of Acre, the city's location has given it a vital strategic importance for both defenders and potential conquerors. Acre's current walls date from the ninth century. In 1104, Acre fell to Crusaders and became the main seaport for the Latin Kingdom of Jerusalem. After changing hands several times, the city became the last Crusader stronghold in Palestine to fall, in 1291. In 1799, it earned the distinction of resisting Napoleon's conquest of Egypt and Palestine.

Acre was a major seaport and trade center for Greater Syria. The Ottoman sultan Sulayman the Lawgiver (the Magnificent) allowed the French king Francis I to station French traders in the city. In the seventeenth century, the regional ruler Fakhr al-Din II undertook many construction projects in the city, which was benefiting from the rise in European trade with the eastern Mediterranean. The Palestinians of Acre flourished during the rule of Zahir al-Umar in the third quarter of the eighteenth century, and so they undertook more rebuilding during the rule of the Ottoman governor Ahmad Jazzar Pasha. By the Ottoman era, Acre was a major port for the export of grain, which arrived from Hawran in southern Syria via camel caravan.

During the late Ottoman era, Acre's trade position began to suffer. The establishment of a railroad link between Damascus and the port of Beirut in 1895 led to the halving of Acre's trade. Its remaining trade was hurt in 1904 when the Syrian hinterland was connected with nearby HAIFA via railroad. However, the city's population doubled during the PALESTINE MANDATE, from some 6,420 in 1922 to 12,300 by 1944, one-sixth of whom were Christian Palestinians within a Muslim majority.

Acre contains several notable religious institutions. The Jazzar Mosque, built in 1781, includes relics from the Prophet Muhammad. Baha'ullah, the Iranian founder of the Baha'i faith, arrived in Acre in 1868 and was buried north of the town in 1892. The Islamic school for training *ulama* ("men of religion"), established during the Palestine Mandate in the Jazzar Mosque, was the only one of its kind in Palestine.

During the ARAB-ISRAEL WAR OF 1948, Acre was once again coveted for its vital strategic location. The Jewish Haganah captured the city on May 17, 1948, and all but some 3,200 of its inhabitants were expelled. The old quarters of the city, within the walls, soon disintegrated into slum districts. By 1953, 12,000 Jewish immigrants were settled in Acre. The city's population in 1987 stood at 37,200 Jews and 8,200 Palestinians.

Michael R. Fischbach

Advisory Council

In October 1920, British high commissioner Sir Herbert Samuel created the Advisory Council in Palestine until such time as a legislative body could be established. The council consisted of twenty persons appointed by Samuel, ten of whom were government officials. Of the remainder, seven were Palestinians (four Muslims and three Christians) and three were Jews. Palestinian leaders partly accepted the council because they viewed it as a temporary measure and the seven figures appointed by Samuel stated that service on the council did not imply their representation of the Palestinian community at large.

In August 1922, Samuel announced his intention to replace the council with a legislative council in accordance with a new constitution for promoting self-government in Palestine. Whereas the Jewish community reluctantly accepted the proposals, Palestinian leaders rejected them, arguing that participation in a legislature implied their acceptance of the Mandate's commitment to the BALFOUR DECLARATION. Palestinian leaders boycotted legislative council elections held in February 1923. The boycott prompted Samuel to abandon his plan, whereupon he created a new advisory council composed of eleven government officials (including him), ten Palestinians (eight Muslim and two Christian), and two Jews. Despite initially accepting nomination, seven of the ten Palestinian council members later resigned in May 1923 after Samuel associated the advisory council with the proposed legislative council.

Samuel finally abandoned the concept of self-government and governed Palestine directly in consultation with an advisory council that comprised government officials only.

Philip Mattar

Aghazarian, Albert

academic
1950– Jerusalem

A member of the Armenian community of Jerusalem, where he was born August 18, 1950, Albert Aghazarian earned a B.A. in political science at the American University of Beirut in 1972 and an M.A. in history from Georgetown University in 1979. He edited the newspaper *al-Quds* from 1973 to 1975 before teaching at BIR ZEIT UNIVERSITY from 1979 to 1989. (The Israeli authorities closed the university in 1988.) In 1989, Aghazarian began working as Bir Zeit's director of public relations. In 1991, he headed the Palestinian press center during the MADRID PEACE CONFERENCE.

Michael R. Fischbach

al-Aker, Mamdouh

Mamduh al-Aqr; physician, politician
1943– Nablus

Al-Aker completed medical school at Cairo University in 1969. After working in Kuwaiti hospitals from 1970 to 1973, he returned to the WEST BANK. Later he left there and was associated with the Royal College of Surgeons in Edinburgh, Scotland, in 1977. Al-Aker completed urological training at Kings College Hospital in London in 1981. He returned to the West Bank and worked at al-Maqasid Hospital in JERUSALEM and other hospitals during the 1980s.

Al-Aker has also been involved in Palestinian political and cultural life. He joined the pan-Arab Movement of Arab Nationalists while a teenager in the West Bank and was briefly active in one of its successor movements, the POPULAR FRONT FOR THE LIBERATION OF PALESTINE, from 1967 to 1970. He helped found the Mandela Institute for Palestinian Political Prisoners. Al-Aker has served on the board of trustees for the al-Hakawati theater group and was a member of the Palestinian delegation to the MADRID PEACE CONFERENCE in 1991. He continued to represent the Palestinians during the bilateral Israeli–Palestinian talks that followed.

Michael R. Fischbach

al-Alami Family

One of the most prominent landowning families from JERUSALEM, the Alamis produced many religious scholars and officials during the Ottoman and Mandate periods.

Musa (1881; official) Musa was a member of the administrative council for the Jerusalem governorate during the Ottoman period, and mayor of Jerusalem in the 1870s.

Faydi (1865–1924; official) Son of Musa Al-Alami (d. 1881), Faydi served the Ottoman government in Palestine as a tax official and judge before being appointed district director of BETHLEHEM in 1902. He was mayor of Jerusalem from 1906 to 1909 before serving on the administrative council for the Jerusalem governorate. From 1914 to 1918, he was the Jerusalem governorate's representative to the Ottoman parliament.

Michael R. Fischbach

al-Alami Family

The following are members of this prominent family of landowners and businessmen in Gaza.

Yusuf (1897–1939; Gaza; businessman) Yusuf was a member of the Gaza municipal council and a prominent figure in southern Palestine during the PALESTINE MANDATE. A supporter of the councilist faction, he was assassinated in April 1939.

Samih (1921–1997; Gaza; physician) Samih, the son of Yusuf al-Alami, obtained a B.A. from The American University of Beirut (AUB) in 1952, an M.A. from the University of Texas in 1955, and an M.D. from the University of Oklahoma in 1960. After practicing in the United States, Samih was director of the medical laboratory at AUB in the 1970s and remained involved with AUB's hospital until his death. He was one of the founders of the Palestine RED CRESCENT Society.

Sami (1924– ; Jerusalem; banker) Son of Yusuf, he received a B.A. in business administration (1944) and an M.A. in economics (1946) from The American University of Beirut (AUB) in 1944. After the ARAB-ISRAELI WAR OF 1948, Sami taught at the Commercial College in Baghdad and worked for the Arab Bank, beginning in 1950, rising to head its Beirut branch in 1953. He remained with the Arab Bank until 1985.

Sami began his Palestinian nationalist activities as a volunteer for the PALESTINIAN NATIONAL FUND in the late 1940s and later worked with the Arab Office in Jerusalem beginning in 1947. Since 1968 he has served on the board of directors of the INSTITUTE FOR PALESTINE STUDIES. He also advised PALESTINE LIBERATION ORGANIZATION chairman YASIR ARAFAT on financial matters.

Michael R. Fischbach

al-Alami, Musa

prominent official, independent politician
1897–1984 Jerusalem

Musa al-Alami was an official during the British PALESTINE MANDATE and subsequently a leading independent politician. He was born in Jerusalem into a family that had played a central role in Jerusalem's civil and religious life since the twelfth century C.E. His grandfather had been mayor of Jerusalem and his father was elected to the Ottoman parliament in Istanbul in 1914. Drafted into the Ottoman army in 1917, al-Alami hid in Damascus in 1918; there he contacted Arab nationalists. Subsequently, he studied law at Trinity College, Cambridge University (until 1922), and, after returning to Palestine, worked as junior legal adviser to the British administration (1925–29). His career flourished as he moved from assistant government advocate (1929–32) to private secretary to the HIGH COMMISSIONER FOR PALESTINE (1932–33), a post from which he tried to persuade British officials to balance Arab and Jewish interests. However, the World Zionist Organization launched a campaign against him, causing his demotion to government advocate (1933–37).

David Ben-Gurion, chair person of the Jewish Agency Executive Committee, met with al-Alami in 1934 and 1936. Ben-Gurion wanted Palestinian support for an eventual Jewish majority and statehood, whereas al-Alami hoped those discussions would moderate Ben-Gurion's stance so that he would accept a canton solution short of statehood and a ceiling below 50 percent for the Jewish proportion of the population. Given their antithetical objectives, al-Alami concluded that the Zionists would not compromise substantively. In June 1936, he circulated a petition among the senior Arab officials, which all 137 of them signed. The petition called on the British government to accept the demands made by the Arab general strike. Those demands included the temporary suspension of Jewish immigration, a possibility he also discussed privately with Zionist officials, to no avail.

Al-Alami was fired from the legal department in October 1937, after the PEEL COMMISSION report recommended his replacement by a British advocate. He lived in exile in Beirut and then Baghdad (1937–42), serving during that time as an independent delegate to the LONDON CONFERENCE (1939). He then sought unsuccessfully to broker a compromise agreement between the British and Palestinians. Al-Alami was the sole Palestinian delegate to the conference that founded the ARAB LEAGUE in 1944; he subsequently headed the league-funded Information Office in London. Al-Alami sought to retain his independence from the ARAB HIGHER COMMITTEE (AHC), controlled by the HUSAYNI FAMILY, even though his brother-in-law was JAMAL AL-HUSAYNI (Jamal Husayni). However, the Information Office and related Constructive Scheme came under the AHC's control in 1945.

Al-Alami lost considerable property during the 1948–49 war, including his home in Jerusalem. Afterward, he transformed the Constructive Scheme into the Arab Development Society (ADS), which by 1967 ran a forty-thousand-acre farm with twenty-six irrigating wells. The ADC operated an orphanage and vocational and secondary training center for refugee boys near JERICHO, graduating up to two hundred boys each year. The project sold dairy and poultry products abroad, despite the harsh environmental conditions and periodic criticism for accepting foreign funds from the Swedish, Norwegian, and U.S. governments and the Ford Foundation. Most ADS residents fled to Jordan during the 1967 war, but the project continued to function on a limited basis despite the Israeli occupation.

Ann M. Lesch

BIBLIOGRAPHY

Caplan, Neil. *Futile Diplomacy*. Vol. 2. *Arab-Zionist Negotiations and the End of the Mandate.* London: Frank Cass, 1986.

Furlonge, Geoffrey. *Palestine Is My Country: The Story of Musa Alami.* London: John Murray, 1969.

Hurewitz, J. C. *The Struggle for Palestine.* 1950. Reprint, New York: Schocken Books, 1976.

Kolinsky, Martin. *Law, Order and Riots in Mandatory Palestine, 1928–35.* New York: St. Martin's Press, 1993.

Porath, Yehoshua. *The Palestinian Arab National Movement 1929–39: From Riots to Rebellion.* London: Frank Cass, 1977.

al-Ali, Naji

Ali Naji al-Azami; cartoonist
1936? 1937?–1987 al-Shajara

Born in the Galilee, al-Ali fled with his family to southern Lebanon during the ARAB–ISRAELI WAR OF 1948 and spent his youth in the Ayn al-Hilwa refugee camp. He began drawing cartoons on the walls of Lebanese prisons during the late 1950s and was later encouraged to publish his cartoons by the famous Palestinian writer GHASSAN KANAFANI. Al-Ali later moved to Kuwait in the early 1960s. Returning to Lebanon in 1971, al-Ali served on the editorial board of the prominent Lebanese newspaper *al-Safir* and also contributed cartoons to other prominent Arab newspapers.

Al-Ali's cartoons were often biting commentaries on life in the Middle East. Each cartoon featured a young boy, Hanzala, as spectator. Fiercely independent, al-Ali sought to defend what he believed was the common Arab man and woman and alienated a host of regimes and political movements in the process. Al-Ali left Lebanon in 1983 for Kuwait out of fear for his life; however, he was expelled in 1985 under pressure from neighboring Saudi Arabia and moved to London. He was shot by an unknown assailant on July 22, 1987, and died on August 30 of the same year.

Al-Ali was posthumously awarded the International Federation of Newspaper Publishers' Golden Pen Award in 1988 to recognize his contributions to freedom of expression.

Michael R. Fischbach

All-Palestine Government

On September 15, 1948, the ARAB LEAGUE approved the establishment by the ARAB HIGHER COMMITTEE, headed by al-Hajj AMIN AL-HUSAYNI, the mufti of Jerusalem, of the All-Palestine Government. The decision could have led to the creation of a Palestine state, not in all Palestine as the Palestinians had intended, but in part of the area allotted to the Palestinians by the United Nations partition resolution of November 29, 1947. But even this limited goal was doomed from the outset.

The mufti, who had rejected the partition resolution, had appealed to the Arab League a number of times before May 14, 1948, when British troops were to leave Palestine, to form a Palestinian government that would establish a state in all of Palestine. In October 1947 he asserted that such a government would forestall partition. A few weeks before mid-May 1948 he argued that a government would fill in the political and military vacuum resulting from British departure, even while Palestinian fighters were being thoroughly defeated by Zionist forces. The mufti's support within the Arab League was dependent on the interests and rivalries of its members. Whereas Egypt, Syria, and Saudi Arabia were for establishing a limited form of government, a local administration, Iraq and Transjordan were opposed to it. Support for the mufti was not so strong as to risk a crisis within the league or an independent action by Transjordan's king ABDULLAH, who, as a result of secret agreements with the Jewish Agency, sought to share Palestine with the Zionists. The mufti's pleas, therefore, were ignored.

The Arab armies entered Palestine on May 15, inaugurating the first phase of the ARAB-ISRAELI WAR OF 1948. By the first truce on June 11, the Israelis controlled areas beyond those allotted by the U.N. PARTITION PLAN to the Jewish state. The land still in Arab hands was held mainly by Transjordan, with smaller sections controlled by Iraq and Egypt. Given the situation on the ground and British persuasion, Count FOLKE BERNADOTTE, the U.N. mediator, recommended on June 27 that the areas assigned to the Arab state under the partition plan should fall under Abdullah's control.

To counter Abdullah and prevent him from simply annexing what remained of Arab Palestine, the Political Committee of the Arab League decided on July 8, 1948, to establish a temporary civil administration in Palestine directly responsible to the league. Dependency on the league and a temporary civil administration was not what the mufti wanted, and he therefore had reservations about the proposal. Although the civil administration was not actually established, for lack of funds, it survived on paper.

At the next meeting of the Political Committee of the league from September 6–16 in Alexandria, the proposal for transforming the idea of a temporary civil administration into a government for all Palestine was at the top of the agenda. Transjordan still had reservations, but it was under considerable public pressure. Suspicion of Abdullah, fueled by the Bernadotte proposal, had continued to grow in the Arab world, where he was accused of making a deal with the British and Zionists and thought to be the villain behind efforts to annex Palestinian territory, especially after his overt claim that Transjordan, not the Arab Higher Committee, represented the Palestinians. At all events, JAMAL AL-HUSAYNI visited Arab capitals to enlist support for the Palestine government proposal. Despite reservations, the proposal was passed.

The Arab Higher Committee announced on September 22 the establishment of an All-Palestine Government in Gaza headed by AHMAD HILMI ABD AL-BAQI. Ahmad Hilmi was a military governor of JERUSALEM and well liked and respected among the Palestinians. Besides, the Egyptian prime minister had strongly advised the mufti against making himself head of the Palestinian Arab state because, having sided with the Nazis, he "would never be accepted by the Western Powers." Ahmad Hilmi sent telegrams to Azzam and members of the Arab League stating as follows:

> I have the honor to inform you that the inhabitants of Palestine, in the exercise of their natural right to determine their own fate and in accordance with the discussions and decisions of the Political Committee [of the Arab League], have decided to declare all of Palestine, within the frontiers that were established when the British mandate ended, an independent state ruled by a government known as the Government of Palestine, based on democratic principles. I take this opportunity to express the desire of my Government to strengthen the bonds of friendship and mutual assistance between our countries.

The new government set about issuing Palestinian passports and sought recognition from the international community, including sending a delegation to the United Nations. Meanwhile, Abdullah was repeatedly asserting that the new government had been established against the will of the Palestinians. To counter these accusations, the All-Palestine Government decided to convene in Gaza on September 30 the Palestine National Council, to which 150 representatives from the chambers of commerce, trade unions, political parties, local councils, and national committees were invited.

The prime mover behind the government was, of course, the mufti, who had been prevented from leaving Cairo by the Egyptian authorities. But with the help of the pro-mufti Egyptian officers (Muslim Brethren and Free Officers) he secretly arrived in Gaza on September 28, 1948—the first time that he had stepped on the soil of Palestine in eleven years. His popularity had remained intact, especially among the refugees, and the streets of Gaza were crowded when the mufti and Ahmad Hilmi entered the city accompanied by motorcycles and armored cars.

The Palestine National Council convened on September 30, 1948. Because of the difficulties of travel, only seventy-five to ninety attended. They quickly elected the mufti as president of the council. The Palestine Declaration of Independence issued on October 1, 1948, included the following: "Based on the natural and historical right of the Palestinian Arab people for freedom and independence . . . [we declare] total independence of all Palestine . . . and the establishment of an independent, democratic state whose inhabitants will exercise their liberties and rights." The council passed a vote of confidence in the government, which consisted of prominent Palestinians. Ahmad Hilmi Abd al-Baqi was confirmed as prime minister, Jamal al-Husayni as foreign minister, Raja'i al-Husayni as defense minister, Michael Abcarius as finance minister, and Anwar NUSAYBA as secretary of the cabinet. Others included AWNI ABD AL-HADI, AKRAM ZU'AYTIR, Dr. HUSAYN AL-KHALIDI, Ali Hasna, Yusif Sahyun, and Amin Aqil.

The council declared that the capital of Palestine was to be Jerusalem and its flag was that of the 1916 Arab revolt, with black, white, and green stripes and a red triangle. The government was to consist of a higher assembly, a defense assembly, and a national council.

In practice, however, the government had no territory of its own, as Gaza had been entirely under Egyptian control. It had no administration, no money, no army beyond what remained after the Israeli defeat of the Jaysh al-Jihad al-Muqaddas, the irregular force that had been crushingly defeated by Jewish forces in April. The rest of the area allotted to the Palestinians was in the hands of the mufti's mortal enemies, the Hashemites backed by Britain. The fact that the mufti should declare a government in such circumstances attests to his unrealistic expectations in the face of the formidable forces arrayed against him.

The Arab regimes, under considerable pressure from the British not to recognize the government, equivocated, but their actions were clear. Iraq, which held large portions of Palestine, could have allowed the government to extend its authority there but did not. The Egyptians were no more forthcoming. Within days of the declaration of the All-Palestine Government in Gaza, the Egyptian prime minister and defense minister ordered the mufti back to Cairo, ostensibly because Gaza was a military zone.

The real reason, according to the Egyptian prime minister, Nuqrashi, is that the Egyptian army "would not tolerate his having any military command in their region and they wished to restrict his political activity." When ordered to come quietly to Cairo, the mufti asked, "Is this at the wish of the King Abdullah or of the British?" This was reported to King Faruq, who was so angered that he said he would have nothing further to do with him. Eight days after his triumphant entry into Gaza, the mufti was unceremoniously escorted by military police out of the city and back to Cairo, where he was put under police surveillance. Soldiers were placed around his residence, presumably so he could not perform yet another disappearing act.

Meanwhile, Abdullah was alarmed by the establishment of the government and sought to legitimize his own leadership in Palestine by convening in Amman, on the very day (October 1) the council convened in Gaza, the first Palestinian Congress. Several thousand Palestinians attended, either on their own initiative or because they were bribed or summoned by Transjordanian military governors. The congress swore allegiance to Abdullah, denounced the Gaza government, and declared that Transjordan and Palestine were indivisible.

Abdullah next ordered the British commander of the Arab Legion, Glubb Pasha, to dismantle Jaysh al-Jihad al-Muqqadas. When Arab officers were reluctant to perform the task, British officers swiftly carried it out on October 3.

The British applied considerable pressure on the Arab regimes not to recognize the new government. Their representatives were instructed to use the following argument:

> a. that a separate Arab State in Palestine would not be covered by any of our existing treaties with Arab states.
>
> b. that, in view of the ex-mufti's association with the new "Government", we should be most unlikely to enter into treaty negotiations with it, and
>
> c. that under existing circumstances a Palestine-Arab State could not be economically viable and its absorption by Jews would sooner or later be inevitable.

The Arab regimes equivocated for days despite strong public support for the new government. Meanwhile, the Israelis broke the second truce on October 15 in an action against the Egyptian army, which retreated along the GAZA STRIP. The territory under the government's nominal authority was thus reduced. Yet it was at this juncture, in mid-October, that the Arab regimes—Egypt, Iraq, Syria, Lebanon, and Saudi Arabia—finally recognized the All-Palestine Government. It was obviously an empty gesture designed to pacify the Arab masses. At the same time, Egypt forced Ahmad Hilmi and members of his cabinet to leave Gaza city, still in Egyptian hands. They were never to return. In Cairo, they were unable to perform their duties. The Arab League shunned them and refused to give them financial assistance. No wonder that the British Foreign Office, which had focused its pressure on Egypt and the Arab League, congratulated itself on November 2 for having "achieved our object . . . of reducing the Mufti's influence." Within weeks, the members of the cabinet, most of whom were educated and talented professionals, took up positions in various Arab countries. The government became nothing more than a department of the Arab League.

The All-Palestine Government was doomed by inter-Arab rivalry, by strong opposition from three powers with strategic interests in Palestine—Transjordan, Britain, and Israel—and by Palestinian weakness and ineptness.

Philip Mattar

BIBLIOGRAPHY

Mattar, Philip. *The Mufti of Jerusalem: Al-Hajj Amin al-Husayni and the Palestinian National Movement.* New York: Columbia University Press, 1992.

Shlaim, Avi. "The Rise and Fall of the All-Palestine Government of Gaza." *Journal of Palestine Studies* 77 (Autumn 1990): 37–53.

Amiry, Suad

Su'ad Amiri; academician

1951– Damascus

Amiry studied at the American University of Beirut and the University of Michigan before obtaining a Ph.D. in architecture at the University of Edinburgh. In addition to teaching at BIR ZEIT UNIVERSITY and the University of Jordan, Amiry wrote *Palestinian Rural Settlements and Architecture* (1983) and coauthored *The Palestinian Village Home* (1989).

Amiry has also been active in the Palestinian national movement and participated in the Palestinian–Israeli peace talks in the early 1990s. Since the OSLO AGREEMENTS, she has worked with the Committee on Regional Planning for the Palestinian Economic Council for Development and Reconstruction (PECDAR) and the Palestine Housing Council. She serves as director general of the Ministry of Culture, Art and Information in the PALESTINIAN AUTHORITY.

Michael R. Fischbach

Anglo-American Commission

1945–1946

In October 1946, the British government proposed the formation of a joint Anglo-American commission to investigate the plight of Jewish refugees from the Holocaust in Europe. The twelve-member commission, made up of six Britons and six Americans, was officially called the Anglo-American Commission of Inquiry Regarding the Problem of European Jewry and Palestine. It interviewed witnesses in the United States, Britain, Europe, and the Middle East; Jewish, British, and Arab leaders addressed its sessions. During the commission's sessions in Palestine, Palestinians also offered testimony; among them was JAMAL AL-HUSAYNI of the reconstituted ARAB HIGHER COMMITTEE, who argued against further Jewish immigration into Palestine.

The commission issued its report on May 1, 1946. It proposed that the solution for Jewish refugees in Europe was emigration to Palestine and suggested that PALESTINE MANDATE authorities immediately allow 100,000 Jews into the country. It also urged a continuation of the Mandate, an end to limits on Jewish land purchases, and some kind of future unified Palestine, as opposed to partitioning of Palestine into Jewish and Palestinian states.

Whereas the American government accepted the commission's report and its recommendation for the immediate admission of 100,000 Jewish refugees, the British government did not. Zionist leaders in Palestine such as David Ben-Gurion also condemned the report, objecting to the idea of a future unified Palestine. The American and British governments established the MORRISON-GRADY Commission shortly thereafter to discuss future arrangements for Palestine.

Michael R. Fischbach

Antonius, George

educator, politician

1893–1942 Cairo

George Antonius was of Greek Orthodox background, born in Cairo of Lebanese origin. Educated at Cambridge University (1911–14), he served as deputy chief censor of the press in Alexandria during World War I. His father-in-law, Dr. Faris Nimr, was proprietor of *al-Muqattam,* a Cairo newspaper.

During the 1920s, Antonius served in the civil service in Palestine as senior inspector of schools, then assistant director of education, and finally assistant chief secretary in the Secretariat. He assisted British diplomats by participating in missions to Arabia, Yemen, Iraq, and India in the mid-1920s and received the Commander of the Order of the British Empire (C.B.E.). Nonetheless, he resigned from that post in 1930 after concluding that the British government would not adopt an evenhanded policy toward the Zionist movement and the Palestinian community.

Antonius met with David Ben-Gurion and other Zionist leaders in 1934 and 1936, seeking unsuccessfully to moderate Zionist ambitions for a Jewish state with a Jewish majority. Antonius apparently considered advocating a Jewish canton within a Palestine that would federate with other Arab states, an idea that he abandoned as impracticable by 1938.

Antonius assisted MUSA AL-ALAMI in circulating the June 1936 petition of senior Arab officials that supported the demands of the Palestinian general strike and called for a temporary suspension of Jewish immigration. In 1938, with the support of the Institute of Current World Affairs (New York), he wrote *The Arab Awakening,* a seminal analysis of the rise of Arab nationalism in the late Ottoman period and the denial of self-determination by the British and French at the end of World War I. The book published for the first time the texts of the HUSAYN-MCMAHON CORRESPONDENCE (1915–16), which, Antonius argued, proved that Palestine was included in the Arab area promised independence by Britain.

He participated in the Palestinian delegation to the LONDON CONFERENCE, 1939, in which he also served as secretary for the five delegations from Arab states. He served on the special Arab-British committee that examined the Husayn-McMahon correspondence and published the authoritative texts. However, the conferees failed to agree on Palestine's inclusion or exclusion from the area promised independence. Antonius remained in London after the conference to hold private discussions with British officials in the hope of reaching an acceptable compromise. He helped to persuade them to include in the White Paper (May 1939) provisions that Jewish immigration would require Arab approval after five years as well as a qualified promise of independence after ten years. Disappointed when the ARAB HIGHER COMMITTEE rejected the White Paper, Antonius continued to seek Arab-British reconciliation and hoped that, once the Jewish community lost its special privileges, the Palestinian Arab and Jewish residents could live together as ordinary citizens.

Ann M. Lesch

BIBLIOGRAPHY

Antonius, George. *The Arab Awakening.* New York: Capricorn Books, 1946 (originally published 1938).

——. Private Paper Collection, Middle East Centre, St. Antony's College, Oxford.

Caplan, Neil. *Futile Diplomacy.* Vol. 2. *Arab-Zionist Negotiations and the End of the Mandate.* London: Frank Cass, 1986.

Hattis, Susan Lee. *The Bi-National Idea in Palestine During Mandatory Times.* Haifa: Shikmona, 1970.

Lesch, Ann Mosely. *Arab Politics in Palestine, 1917–1939: The Frustration of a Nationalist Movement.* Ithaca, N.Y.: Cornell University Press, 1979.

Porath, Yehoshua. *The Palestinian Arab National Movement 1929–1939: From Riots to Rebellion.* London: Frank Cass, 1977.

Aqqad, Umar

businessman, philanthropist
1927– Gaza

A prominent Palestinian businessman, Umar Aqqad has directed a number of financial institutions in the Middle East, including the Saudi British Bank, the Saudi Bank, and the Arab Investment Company of Luxembourg and Switzerland. He also heads the Aqqad Group in Saudi Arabia.

In 1995, PALESTINIAN AUTHORITY president YASIR ARAFAT appointed Aqqad head of a group to develop telephone service in the WEST BANK and the GAZA STRIP. The same year, Aqqad announced the formation of the Arab Palestinian Investment Company, designed to promote investment and create jobs in the Palestinian Authority.

Aqqad is also involved in a number of philanthropic activities.

Michael R. Fischbach

Arab Agency

In October 1923, the cabinet committee on Palestine in London proposed creation of the Arab Agency in Palestine, by which the Palestinian community could represent itself to Mandatory authorities. This proposed agency was intended to provide Palestinians with a body comparable to the Jewish Agency created by Article 4 of the PALESTINE MANDATE to represent the interests of Jews in Palestine. (The role of Jewish agency was filled at the time by the Palestine Zionist Executive, which was subordinated to the World Zionist Organization in London.)

The Arab Agency's members would be appointed by the British HIGH COMMISSIONER FOR PALESTINE. They would advise the high commissioner on social and cultural matters relating to the Palestinian community only. Under such terms, the British could curb the agency's ability to discuss political matters dealing with the Jewish community, such as Jewish immigration.

High Commissioner Herbert Samuel explained the proposal to a group of twenty-six Palestinian leaders as part of an October 1923 speech in which he discussed Britain's international commitment to help the establishment of a national home for Jews in Palestine under the terms of the BALFOUR DECLARATION and the Mandate. MUSA KAZIM AL-HUSAYNI, head of the ARAB EXECUTIVE, speaking for the assembled notables, stated that the group unanimously refused to form such an agency because it failed to satisfy Palestinian aspirations for independence. Palestinian nationalists believed that acceptance of the proposal would signify acceptance of the Mandate and its commitment to ZIONISM. Furthermore, al-Husayni and the others refused to place the Palestinians—the overwhelming majority (some 90 percent) of the population at the time—on the same legal footing as the Jewish minority.

Palestinian refusal to accept the concept of the Arab Agency came at the same time as similar refusals to participate in elections for a legislative council and to sit on an advisory council. These refusals all indicated Palestinian rejection of the Mandate as long as it included references to Zionism.

Michael R. Fischbach

Arab Club

Arabic, al-Nadi al-Arabi

The Arab Club was established in 1918 in Damascus by Palestinians from NABLUS. A JERUSALEM branch of the club was also established in 1918; it was dominated by younger members of the HUSAYNI FAMILY of Jerusalem, and AL-HAJJ AMIN AL-HUSAYNI was its president.

The Arab Club in Palestine opposed ZIONISM and supported the short-lived Arab kingdom of Syria, headed by Faysal bin Husayn of the Hashemite family. It ceased functioning with the demise of the Syrian kingdom at the hands of the French in 1920.

Michael R. Fischbach

Arab College

Arabic, al-Kulliyya al-Arabiyya fi'l-Quds

One of the two best public secondary schools in Mandatory Palestine and one of the foremost educational institutions in Palestinian history, the Arab College was established by British authorities as the Teacher Training Academy for boys near Jerusalem's Herod's Gate (*Bab al-Zahira*) in 1918. In 1936, the school moved to new, permanent buildings near Government House on Jabal al-Mukabbir (Hill of Evil Counsel) in a southern suburb of Jerusalem.

Early on, the academy was a haven for Palestinian nationalist activities. Several of the academy's teachers during the early PALESTINE MANDATE were ardent nationalists. In 1925, British authorities closed the academy for several weeks after students staged a strike protesting Lord Arthur Balfour's (see BALFOUR DECLARATION) announced trip to the inauguration of the Hebrew University of Jerusalem.

The academy, renamed the Arab College in 1927, rose, under the direction of its third principal, Ahmad Samih al-Khalidi (see KHALIDI FAMILY), to become a major Arab secondary school in Palestine rather than merely a teacher training academy. It recruited the brightest boys from Palestine's elementary schools on the basis of rigorous admission standards (including intelligence tests) rather than relying on their family or regional connections, and it instructed them in Western and Arabo-Islamic subjects in both Arabic and English. Students generally studied free of charge thanks to donations, although beginning in 1939, the waiving of fees was linked to a student's performance in school. In 1930, eighty-two boys were studying at the college. Throughout its history, the Arab College typically admitted more boys from village than city backgrounds.

The Arab College underwent several changes in the 1940s. In 1941, sixth grade was added. Students thereafter took either the Palestine intermediate examination or the intermediary examination of the University of London. Students concentrated in one of two tracks: scientific or literary. Studies in the scientific track included chemistry and physics; those in the literary track included philosophy, logic, and Latin. By the 1945–46 school year, eighty-eight students were enrolled in the college. Eventually, the college offered a two-year postmatriculation course of study in the literary and scientific tracks to prepare students for teaching in Palestine or for traveling abroad to attend Arab and foreign universities. In the 1945–46 year, nineteen students were enrolled in the postmatriculation course.

A number of noted scholars and educators served as academy principal over the years. The academy's first principal was KHALIL AL-SAKAKINI (1919–22), followed by Khalil Tawtah until 1925 and al-Khalidi from 1926 until the college ceased functioning after the ARAB-ISRAELI WAR OF 1948. Many scholars, writers, and other noted Palestinians graduated from the college over the decades, including GEORGE ANTONIUS, Ahmad TUQAN, Irfan Shahid, and WALID KHALIDI. The college's academic influence was also demonstrated through its publications, including a quarterly cultural and scholarly journal, beginning in late 1927.

Michael R. Fischbach

Arab Congresses

The Arab Congresses were countrywide events initially organized at the initiative of the Jerusalem and Jaffa MUSLIM-CHRISTIAN ASSOCIATIONS (MCAs) to formulate Palestinian national demands. Seven such congresses were organized between 1919 and 1928.

The First Congress The First Congress (Jerusalem, 1919) brought together, for the first time, Palestinian politicians from all around the country in an attempt to formulate a program to be presented at the Paris Peace Conference. Two views were expressed, one favoring complete Palestinian independence and the other stressing Syrian–Palestinian unity. The latter view prevailed. The congress also demanded that Palestine remain an integral part of an independent Syria. It rejected the BALFOUR DECLARATION and approved acceptance of British assistance in the development of the country on condition that such aid did not compromise Palestinian independence.

The Second Congress The MCA proposed to hold a second Palestinian congress in Jerusalem in May 1920 to protest the confirmation of the British PALESTINE MANDATE and the incorporation of the British Balfour Declaration of sympathy with Zionist aspirations (November 2, 1917) into the instrument of the Mandate. The British military administration in Palestine refused to allow the MCAs to hold the meeting, but the MCAs considered it to have actually occurred and designated it as the second congress.

The Third Congress The Third Congress was held in Haifa in December 1920. By that time, the balance has shifted in favor of those who preferred Palestinian independence to Syrian-Palestinian unity. Two factors led to this development: the institution of civilian administration in Palestine under a British Zionist, Sir Herbert Samuel, in July 1920, and the fall in the same month of the Damascus-based Faysal ibn al-Husayn's Arab government, which had been a major source of support for the advocates of Syrian-Palestinian unity. This congress called for the establishment of a "national government responsible to a representative assembly" under British supervision and guidance if need be. The congress also elected a Jerusalem-based executive committee—known as the ARAB EXECUTIVE—to run the day-to-day activities of the Palestinian national movement. The program of the congress defined Palestinian political objectives in distinct Palestinian terms, thus helping to develop Palestinian nationalism.

The Fourth Congress The Fourth Congress was held in Jerusalem in 1921. It was occupied mainly with the selection of a Palestinian delegation that would go to Britain to work toward convincing the British government to annul or drastically modify its Balfour Declaration policy and stop Jewish immigration to Palestine. In June 1921, the congress elected the first Palestinian delegation to London, under the leadership of MUSA KAZIM AL-HUSAYNI; there it spent almost eleven months (August 1921–July 1922) in unsuccessful negotiations with the British authorities.

The Fifth Congress The Fifth Congress was convened in Nablus in 1922 after the failure of the mission of the first delegation. It resolved, among other things, to reject the Balfour Declaration policy, to boycott the LEGISLATIVE COUNCIL elections, and to establish an information office in London.

The Sixth Congress The Sixth Congress was held in Jaffa in 1923. It focused on two issues of immediate concern to the Palestinians: the proposed Anglo-Hijazi Treaty and elections in Palestine for the proposed Legislative Council. The two main resolutions of the congress were (1) the boycott of Legislative Council elections because the proposed council rested on the Mandate, including the Balfour Declaration; (2) the rejection of the Anglo-Hijazi Treaty on the grounds that it recognized the Mandate system and, by implication, the Balfour Declaration, in return for Britain's support for an Arab confederation that would comprise the Hijaz, Iraq, and Transjordan.

The Seventh Congress The Seventh Congress met in Jerusalem in 1928 after five years of political lull in Palestine, and at a time when the Palestinian national movement suffered from internal divisions and inaction. Its resolutions called for the establishment of a representative government and complained about the increasing number of British employees in the Palestine government. Although the congresses were no longer in existence after 1928, the main principles outlined in their programs continued to govern the Palestinian national movement until the 1948 disaster.

Muhammad Muslih

BIBLIOGRAPHY

Ingrams, Doreen. *Palestine Papers, 1917–1922.* New York: George Braziller, 1973.

Lesch, Ann Mosely. *Arab Politics in Palestine, 1917–1939.* Ithaca, N.Y.: Cornell University Press, 1979.

McTague, John J. *British Policy in Palestine, 1917–1922.* Lanham, Md.: University Press of America, 1983.

Muslih, Muhammad Y. *The Origins of Palestinian Nationalism.* New York: Columbia University Press, 1988.

Porath, Yehoshua. *The Emergence of the Palestinian-Arab National Movement, 1918–1929.* Vol. 1. London: Frank Cass, 1974.

Arab Executive

The Arab Executive led the Palestinian national struggle from 1920 to 1934. The initial nine-member Arab Executive was elected at the Third Arab Congress, convened in HAIFA in December 1920; in 1921 it was expanded to twenty-four and in 1928 to forty-eight persons. MUSA KAZIM AL-HUSAYNI, former mayor of JERUSALEM, was elected chair and retained that position until he died in March 1934. The original Arab Executive included two Christian merchants as well as leading Muslim urban and landowning politicians. JAMAL AL-HUSAYNI headed the permanent secretariat.

The Arab Executive played a vital role in articulating Palestinian grievances from 1920 to 1923. Its leaders met with British officials and sent delegations abroad to plead the Palestinian case and to denounce the plans for the British PALESTINE MANDATE, which would accord preferential status to the Jewish community. In July 1922 the Arab Executive led a two-day protest against the Mandate, which included nonviolent demonstrations and shop closures. The Arab Executive also galvanized opposition to elections for a legislative council in 1922–23.

When the Arab Executive failed to prevent the promulgation of the Mandate in 1923 and to block the Zionist movement, Palestinians experienced an internal crisis and became severely factionalized. The Arab Executive lost its function as an umbrella organization and increasingly represented the HUSAYNI FAMILY camp. In 1928 the Seventh Congress established an enlarged Arab Executive that included diverse groups, including twelve Christians. Musa Kazim al-Husayni retained the presidency, but the two vice presidents (one of them Greek Orthodox) favored his NASHASHIBI FAMILY rivals. The three secretaries were Jamal al-Husayni, pro-Nashashibi Protestant Mughannam Ilyas Mughannam, and pan-Arab AWNI ABD AL-HADI. The executive was charged with elaborating a plan to reorganize the national movement in order to end factional splits as well as to demand parliamentary government.

The formation of the revitalized Arab Executive coincided with renewed Arab-Jewish tension, centered on conflicting claims to the Western Wall. Riots in August 1929 undermined its efforts to negotiate with the British. (See WESTERN [WAILING] WALL DISTURBANCES.) Octogenarian Musa Kazim al-Husayni headed the fourth delegation to London (1930), which pressed for representative government, but the Arab Executive was increasingly bypassed by radicals who demanded demonstrations, strikes, and even tax-withholding campaigns. As Jewish immigration and LAND purchases escalated, the Arab Executive endorsed public demonstrations in 1933. The Arab Executive held its final meeting in August 1934, shortly after Musa Kazim al-Husayni died. By then, several political parties had been formed. In 1936, the Arab Executive was superseded by the ARAB HIGHER COMMITTEE, which led the six-month general strike.

The Arab Executive had provided an overarching structure through which the Palestinian community expressed its grievances and sought coordinated action. It linked Muslims and Christians in one national movement. By the early 1930s, however, Palestinians viewed its methods of petition and pacific protest as outdated. Its efforts failed to stem Jewish immigration and land purchases and failed to achieve Palestinian self-government. Its weakness was due in part to the refusal of the British government to recognize the Arab Executive as the Palestinians' official representative and in part to its composition. The increasingly elderly and relatively cautious politicians in the Arab Executive hoped that the British would engineer a settlement that would acknowledge Palestinian rights, but this never happened.

Ann M. Lesch

BIBLIOGRAPHY

Lesch, Ann Mosely. *Arab Politics in Palestine, 1917–1939: The Frustration of a Nationalist Movement.* Ithaca, N.Y.: Cornell University Press, 1979.

Mattar, Philip. *The Mufti of Jerusalem: Al-Hajj Amin al-Husayni and the Palestinian National Movement, 2nd ed.* New York: Columbia University Press, 1992.

McTague, John J. *British Policy in Palestine, 1917–1922.* Lanham, Md.: University Press of America, 1983.

Muslih, Muhammad Y. *The Origins of the Palestinian Nationalism.* New York: Columbia University Press, 1988.

Porath, Yehoshua. *The Emergence of the Palestinian-Arab National Movement 1918–1929.* London: Frank Cass, 1974.

Arab Higher Committee

Arabic, al-Lajna al-Arabiyya al-Uliya

The Arab Higher Committee (AHC) was established on April 25, 1936, to coordinate the nationwide general strike undertaken by Palestinians that eventually led to the Arab revolt of 1936–39. The AHC consisted of representatives of the six leading Palestinian political parties at the time: the ARAB PARTY, the NATIONAL DEFENSE PARTY, the REFORM PARTY, the NATIONAL BLOC PARTY, the ISTIQLAL PARTY, and the Youth Congress. It had three other members and a secretary as well.

The AHC became the main nationalist organization among Palestinians in 1936, not least because it included the leading Palestinian nationalist politicians among its members. Its president was the mufti of Jerusalem and president of the SUPREME MUSLIM COUNCIL, AL-HAJJ AMIN AL-HUSAYNI. The AHC organized the nationwide boycott of the Jewish economy, pushed for an end to Jewish immigration and LAND purchases, and advocated replacing the Mandate with a representative Palestinian government.

By October 1936, following harsh British security measures against Palestinian guerrillas of the Arab revolt and the subsequent intervention of leaders of several Arab states, the AHC called off the strike. The AHC later testified before the PEEL COMMISSION but rejected the commission's June 1937 recommendation that Palestine be partitioned between Arabs and Jews. Factional disputes between the Opposition led by the NASHASHIBI FAMILY and its party, the National Defense Party, and the Husayni-led Councilists and their Arab Party led the National Defense Party to withdraw from the AHC in July 1937.

British authorities banned the AHC in October 1937 after a renewal of the Arab revolt. Four of its members were arrested and exiled to the Seychelles, while al-Husayni and the rest escaped to surrounding Arab countries, where they attempted to direct the revolt from exile.

A new twelve-member AHC (in Arabic, al-Hay'a al-Arabiyya al-Uliya li-Filastin, "Higher Arab Organization for Palestine") was reconstituted through

ARAB LEAGUE intervention in November 1945; it was headed by al-Husayni. Continued intraparty conflicts, including the formation of a third AHC, led the Arab League to intervene once again, at its June 1946 conference at BLUDAN, Syria, and a new (fourth) five-member AHC headed by al-Husayni was created.

In September 1948, the AHC formed the ALL-PALESTINE GOVERNMENT in Egyptian-controlled Gaza. In part because of the rapid demise of the government, the AHC continued to exist in name only for several decades. Clearly, it had lost all relevance to Palestinian politics.

Michael R. Fischbach

Arab-Israeli Conflict

The term *Arab-Israeli Conflict* refers to a condition of belligerency between the Arab states and Israel. This condition began when the proclamation of the state of Israel on May 14, 1948, was followed by attacks by EGYPT, JORDAN, SYRIA, and elements from the Iraqi and Lebanese armies.

The Arab-Israeli conflict is a direct outgrowth of the Palestinian question. Zionist refusal to acknowledge political rights of Palestinians in their homeland had led Arab politicians from other countries to represent Palestinian interests to Great Britain during the later 1930s and in 1946–47. These two conflicts, the Arab-Israeli and the Palestinian-Israeli, have frequently been intertwined, and the question of the fate of the Palestinians has been a major factor in Arab-Israeli tensions, although expressed in different ways according to the period examined.

Throughout the Arab-Israeli conflict, the various aspects—military, political, economic, and diplomatic—can rarely be separated from the question of the Palestinians.

1948–1967: From the Creation of Israel to the 1967 War Great Britain handed over responsibility for Palestine to the UNITED NATIONS in February 1947, setting the stage for the General Assembly's partition decision of November. Fighting quickly erupted between Zionist forces and Palestinians, aided by some Arabs from surrounding Arab countries. Zionist military superiority enabled Jewish forces to gain control of the territory awarded them in the 1947 PARTITION PLAN, resulting in the declaration of Israeli independence on May 14, 1948. The attack by Egypt, Jordan, Syria, and elements of the Iraqi and Lebanese armies on Israel that immediately followed this declaration of independence indicated rejection of that claim. Nevertheless the Arab states were not united in their objectives. Most backed the creation of a Palestinian state to be led by the former mufti of Jerusalem, AL-HAJJ AMIN AL-HUSAYNI, who then lived in Egypt. Transjordan, to become the Hashemite Kingdom of Jordan in 1949, opposed Palestinian self-determination, as did the Zionists, and accepted the idea of partition, hoping to divide Palestine with the new state of Israel. Jordan's Arab Legion fought mainly to preserve control of already occupied territory and clashed with Israeli forces only when challenged for control of the old city of Jerusalem, which the Jordanians retained. Jordan's King Abdullah was assassinated in 1951 because of his negotiations with Zionists over the partition of Palestine.

Excluding Transjordan, the apparent agreement on the political objectives of their attack among other Arab states masked disagreement as to who should control Palestine and the mufti. This disarray, accentuated by the lack of Arab military coordination, led to defeat. Israel and the combatant Arab states signed armistice agreements between January and June 1949, but a state of war still existed and the Arab-Israeli conflict took shape.

Arab states refused to recognize Israel, which they regarded as an illegal entity. They established economic boycotts and Egypt forbade Israeli ships to transit the Suez Canal, although it permitted passage of foreign ships destined for Israel. Between 1948 and 1956, tensions were strong, with frequent clashes between Israel and its neighbors, Syria, Jordan, and Egypt. Most were instigated by Israel in retaliation for border crossings by individual Palestinians who had lived in what was now Israel. This strife was particularly intense along the Jordanian-Israeli frontier until 1955; Jordan was unable to control its Palestinian refugees but was held responsible by Israel for their incursions.

During 1955 the focus of Arab-Israeli animosity shifted from the Jordanian front to the Egyptian, influenced by rivalries among the great powers and the inauguration of cold war competition between the Soviet Union and the West, of paramount importance in the region. Egypt was seen as the logical lynchpin of a Middle Eastern alliance by Washington and London, but its military leaders, led by Jamal Abd al-Nasir who had taken over in a coup in July 1952, espoused the doctrine of neutrality or nonalignment with the cold war rivals.

In February 1955, Israel undertook a massive raid into Gaza that resulted in major Egyptian casualties. The raid proved to be a landmark in the Arab-Israeli conflict within the cold war context. Concerned about Egyptian military weakness, Nasir signed an arms pact with the Soviet Union in September 1955, causing Israel to seek more arms from its supplier, France. The ensuing tensions involved Britain and the United States as well as France because of Anglo-American refusal in July 1956 to finance the building of the Aswan Dam. Nasir retaliated for this act by nationalizing the Suez Canal the same month. As a result, Britain, France, and Israel, for different reasons, collaborated in an attack on Egypt.

The Suez war of late October 1956, a major stage in the Arab-Israeli conflict, ended in political failure for France and Great Britain despite the military defeat suffered by the Egyptians. Nasir's reputation as a defender of Arab nationalism was bolstered by his resistance against the attacks of European imperial powers allied with Israel. The war brought Israel ten years of peace on the Egyptian frontier, with open passage for Israeli shipping into the Gulf of Aqaba. United Nations Emergency Forces (UNEF) were stationed in the Sinai to serve as buffers between Israel and Egypt.

The Suez crisis was the last Middle Eastern war in which former imperial powers were involved as combatants striving to retain an imperial presence. Henceforth, the Arab-Israeli conflict would involve only regional forces, although the United States and the Soviets, along with European countries, were heavily involved in supplying Arab states and Israel with arms. The Suez crisis also was the Arab-Israeli confrontation that did not involve the Palestinians directly or include the Palestinian question as an issue to be considered in the peace settlement.

In contrast to the causes of the Suez crisis, the preliminaries to the 1967 Arab-Israeli war directly involved Palestinian factions; Palestinians served competing Arab state interests while seeking to define their own objectives. The war's aftermath introduced a new stage in the Arab-Israeli conflict: Israeli occupation of the West Bank and control over a large Palestinian population.

The 1967 War and the Question of the Palestinians After its secession from the United Arab Republic (1958–61), Syria strove to impugn Nasir's Arab nationalist credentials by accusing him of evading further confrontation with Israel. These charges and countercharges became a staple of Egyptian-Syrian invective, as did similar accusations hurled by Jordan's King Husayn; both leftist and conservative governments used the same propaganda, inspired at times by Egyptian claims of being in the vanguard of the confrontation with Israel. The symbols of Nasir's supposed evasion of conflict with Israel were the United Nations Emergency Force (UNEF) contingents stationed in the Sinai as a buffer to prevent a recurrence of tensions that had led to the Suez war of 1956. Syria especially referred to the UNEF forces because of increased Syrian-Israeli tensions in 1963 over Syrian development of a water diversion system that Israel attacked and destroyed.

Palestinians and a focus on the Palestinian question became embroiled in these inter-Arab disputes. At an ARAB LEAGUE meeting in Cairo in January 1964 that had been called to discuss Syrian-Israeli clashes, Egypt's Nasir agreed to back the formation of an official organization that represented the Palestinians: the PALESTINE LIBERATION ORGANIZATION (PLO). Nasir saw the PLO as a body that would focus Palestinian attention on political concerns under Egyptian control. Backing the PLO in propaganda and organizational efforts also would defuse Syrian charges of Egyptian indifference to Israel and the Palestinians.

Syria, on the other hand, was determined to incite tensions with Israel, if only to bolster its own Arab nationalist image. With Egypt controlling the PLO, Syria decided to back a small revolutionary group dedicated to the destruction of Israel. This was FATAH, founded in 1959 in Kuwait by young Palestinians, including YASIR ARAFAT, who wanted to create a Palestinian liberation movement independent of Arab state control. They began planning attacks on Israel intended to liberate all of former Palestine, attacks that did not reach fruition until Syria began to sponsor Fatah's efforts in 1965. Fatah was a revolutionary society with no links to the PLO, which Fatah leaders saw as a conservative organization. Fatah raids, which frequently originated in Jordan, not Syria, increased Arab-Israeli and inter-Arab tensions throughout 1966 and into 1967, setting in motion the path to war.

In May Israel warned Syria of possible retaliation, leading the Soviets to inform Nasir that Israel was amassing troops on the Syrian border, information later judged to be false. Nasir responded by sending Egyptian troops into the Sinai Peninsula on May 14, 1967. They ousted UNEF forces from Sharm al-Shaykh, which controlled the Straits of Tiran, and finally reimposed a blockade of those straits to Israeli shipping. Nasir thus recreated the circumstances that prevailed before the Suez war of 1956. Egypt's actions, motivated primarily to demonstrate its primacy in Arab affairs against Syrian claims, established a casus belli for Israel, which, after the Suez war, had declared that any reimposition of such a blockade would justify military retaliation.

Israel attacked Egypt on June 5, 1967, after receiving information that Egypt was not going to attack but was going to try to extricate itself from the Sinai with a propaganda victory. With the entrance of Jordan and Syria into the war, Israel erased the 1948 armistice lines separating them as well. The war resulted in Israel's conquest and occupation of the GAZA STRIP, the Sinai Peninsula, the WEST BANK, and the Golan Heights. East Jerusalem, formerly under Jordanian control, was immediately annexed to Israel with the declaration that it would remain unified and the capital of the Israeli state. Hundreds of thousands of West Bank and Gaza Palestinians now fell under Israeli rule, including many who had settled there after fleeing or being evicted from Palestine by Israeli troops in 1948.

The consequences of the 1967 war have defined the parameters of negotiations to resolve the Arab-Israeli conflict to the present. Israel declared that it would return territories in exchange for full peace agreements, leaving the extent of the lands involved unspecified. Arab countries, meeting at Khartoum, Sudan, in August 1967, issued a document calling for full Israeli withdrawal through diplomatic means but without entering negotiations with that country. It also "[insisted] on the rights of the Palestinian people in their own country."

The contradictions found in the Khartoum declaration reflected those found in the Arab alliance on the eve of the 1967 war. Nasir favored a diplomatic resolution of the crisis and sided with Jordan's King Husayn in seeking international intervention via the United Nations. However, broader Arab acquiescence to the Khartoum declaration appeared only within the context of Israeli withdrawal without Arab recognition of or negotiations with Israel. This stance reflected the Syrian and Palestinian positions.

Syrian refusal to consider negotiations was consistent with Syrian hostility to Israel prior to the 1967 war. For the Palestinians, however, whether in Fatah or the PLO, the situation was more complicated. To have had Arab states recognize Israel would have meant acceptance of refugee status for Palestinians, a condition in which there was no Palestinian political entity. A settlement of the Arab-Israeli conflict as one between states only meant for Palestinians an acceptance of the reality of 1948, when Israel and Jordan divided Palestine between them.

In 1967, Palestinian acceptance of peace was contingent on the regaining of pre-1967 Israel or former Palestine. This position was laid out in the modified 1968 PLO charter that referred to the attainment of this goal by "armed struggle." Palestinian groups and the PLO, with Yasir Arafat as its head from 1969 on, consistently opposed international efforts to resolve the results of the 1967 war unless the Palestinian political objective—self-determination—would be considered. This strategy involved the Palestinians in conflicts with Arab states as well as with Israel and the United States as all sides sought to attain their own terms for resolving the Arab-Israeli dilemma.

1967–1979: From the 1967 War to the Egyptian-Israeli Peace Treaty The focus of Palestinian opposition after the 1967 war was precisely the document that became the basis of international diplomacy to resolve the results of the 1967 war, UNITED NATIONS SECURITY COUNCIL RESOLUTION 242 (SCR 242). The resolution, passed by the United Nations in November 1967, called for the Arab-Israeli settlement of the consequences of the war. Its deliberate ambiguity led to conflicting interpretations at the Arab-Israeli state level, but none at all for the Palestinians. Although condemning "the acquisition of territory by war" and calling for all states "to live in security," SCR 242's key statement was its clause stating that Israel should withdraw "from territories occupied in the recent conflict"; this expression deliberately excluded the article *the* before the word *territories.* Israel insisted on this exclusion to ensure that it would not be required to withdraw from *all* the territories it had occupied. Israel argued that the resolution's statement that all states should live "within secure and recognized boundaries" required that it retain *some* territories acquired in the war in order to establish those secure boundaries. Reference to "*the* territories" would have meant withdrawal from all the lands Israel occupied in 1967.

Arab signatories were assured by American diplomats that boundary modification under their formula would be slight. Israel envisioned more radical changes: Various Israeli groups and politicians immediately moved to establish settlements in the newly occupied lands, especially in the West Bank and the Golan Heights, to block calls for their return.

As for the Palestinians, they were referred to in SCR 242 solely as refugees; resolution of this refugee question was to occur in the context of future Arab-Israeli state negotiations. As they had feared, the Palestinians were not considered to be a people with legitimate political aspirations. The PLO from this time onward strove to block any settlement that enshrined their refugee status while working to modify SCR 242 to permit Palestinian access to negotiations as a people with acknowledged political rights.

In the aftermath of the 1967 war Arab states worked to recover lands taken by Israel in that conflict by both military and diplomatic means. Their strategies differed according to their perceptions of their interests. Egypt undertook a war of attrition from 1968 to 1970, fighting Israel across the Suez Canal. Although the victor in terms of arms superiority, Israel achieved a triumph that was marred by significant casualties and ultimate setback. Its military advantage, especially air superiority, led Israel to attempt to cause Nasir's downfall by bombing targets inside Egypt, not just on the canal, raids designed to humiliate the Egyptian leader and discredit him. Instead these attacks brought the Soviet Union more directly into the Arab-Israeli conflict. Nearly fifteen thousand Soviet troops and pilots were shifted to Egypt to bolster its defenses. This massive Soviet presence altered drastically the cold war equation in the Arab-Israeli conflict. It also encouraged the United States to support United Nations efforts to institute a cease-fire between Israel and Egypt, achieved in August 1970, that opened the way for U.N.-sponsored negotiations.

The Palestinians also opposed diplomatic plans for Mideast peace because any possible settlement under SCR 242 would deny them political recognition. Although Arafat was now head of the PLO, he could not dominate that organization. He was challenged by groups such as the POPULAR FRONT FOR THE LIBERATION OF PALESTINE (PFLP), headed by GEORGE HABBASH, and the POPULAR DEMOCRATIC FRONT FOR THE LIBERATION OF PALESTINE (PDFLP), led by NAYIF HAWATIMA. Both called for the overthrow of conservative Arab regimes as a precondition for an assault on Israel, whereas Arafat and Fatah focused on Israel and endeavored to distance the PLO from Arab state politics. Following the Israeli-Egyptian August 1970 cease-fire, the Popular Front for the Liberation of Palestine and the Popular Democratic Front for the Liberation of Palestine attempted to overthrow King Husayn of Jordan as the first step in creating a more radical Arab front that would challenge Israel. This decision led to the Jordanian civil war of September 1970, in which Palestinian forces were overwhelmed and a major Arab-Israeli crisis barely averted.

These Palestinian-Jordanian clashes of August–September 1970 had a major impact on Arab state involvement in the Arab-Israeli conflict.

The Palestinian defeat, and subsequent Palestinian losses in later engagements with Jordanian forces, forced the PLO to move its command structure in 1971 from Jordan to LEBANON. From that time onward, PLO actions against Israel engaged Lebanon more directly in the Arab-Israeli conflict and became a major factor in instigating a Lebanese civil war in the mid-1970s.

The Jordanian civil war had another casualty: Nasir of Egypt died shortly after negotiating a cease-fire. He was succeeded by Anwar al-Sadat, who endeavored to gain American support for negotiations with Israel and Israeli withdrawal from the Sinai Peninsula. From 1971 to 1973, Sadat sought unsuccessfully to negotiate with Israel and to induce Israel to withdraw from the Sinai, preferably through United Nations mediation.

In 1973 Egypt and Syria entered into talks aimed at establishing the basis for an assault on Israel if no new diplomatic initiatives were forthcoming. Moreover, Moscow decided to issue offensive weapons systems to Egypt and Syria from February onward, allowing implementation of attacks if desired. Expectations that the diplomatic stalemate would continue were furthered when Israel decided unilaterally to annex a large area of the Sinai in defiance of SCR 242. Moshe Dayan proposed this plan as a condition of his remaining part of the Labor Party (formed in 1968) in forthcoming elections.

Egypt and Syria attacked Israel on October 6, 1973, opening the 1973 Arab-Israeli war. Israeli forces fell back in the Golan Heights but ultimately stopped the Syrians. Egyptian troops crossed the Suez Canal and overwhelmed the Israeli defenses, advancing into the Sinai before being checked. Initial Egyptian successes were thwarted by Israeli counterattacks that led to Israeli forces' crossing the canal and occupying the west bank of the Suez Canal. Technically, Israel had won the war against Egypt, but Egyptian forces held out in pockets in the Sinai against fierce Israeli efforts to oust them and to restore the status quo ante.

The 1967 war had completely overturned the political-military parameters of the Arab-Israeli conflict that had existed since 1948. The 1973 war created the framework within which resolution of the changes wrought by 1967 might be attained. Henry Kissinger, by now U.S. secretary of state as well as national security adviser, intervened in October 1973 to broker a cease-fire between Israel and Egypt that left Egyptian forces in the Sinai, creating a situation that required negotiations. Kissinger believed that limited agreements among Israel, Syria, and Egypt, involving minor withdrawals from lands occupied by Israel, could create a climate of confidence and trust whereby more extensive agreements and possibly full peace treaties might ensue. Kissinger negotiated Israeli pullback accords with both Egypt and Syria during 1974, pursuant to UNITED NATIONS SECURITY COUNCIL RESOLUTION 338, passed on October 22, 1973, the last day of the war; it called for full implementation of SCR 242.

Ever more eager to pursue talks and to recover the Sinai, Sadat agreed to a second limited agreement with Israel in September 1975 without coordinating his decision with Syria. To Hafiz al-Asad and other Arab leaders, this suggested Egypt's willingness to seek a separate agreement. Such a possibility had also occurred to Israeli politicians. Yitzhak Rabin had succeeded Golda Meir as prime minister in the summer of 1974. Rabin, like most Israeli leaders, was primarily concerned with retaining the Golan Heights and the West Bank for Israel regardless of the principles of SCR 242. A separate peace with Egypt, from this perspective, would not signify the first step toward a total resolution of the Arab-Israeli conflict by diplomacy. It would mean that Egypt would be removed from the military equation of the Arab-Israeli conflict, enabling Israel to concentrate its forces against Syria and Jordan in order to impose its terms on them. Here Rabin was reassured by Kissinger that the United States would not push for any limited withdrawal agreements between Israel and Jordan. The American-sponsored peace efforts of 1974–75 and Israeli disinterest in any agreement with Jordan over the West Bank had important repercussions for Palestinians and the PLO within the framework of the Arab-Israeli conflict.

Jordan's King Husayn had been humiliated by his exclusion from the pullback agreements of 1974, the product of Israel's refusal to negotiate over the West Bank. He had anticipated that his inclusion would reaffirm Jordan's right to rule the West Bank and to represent the Palestinians living there. A pullback agreement would have been the first step toward ultimate restoration of most of the West Bank to Jordan, thereby undercutting PLO calls for Palestinian self-determination and PLO claims to represent all Palestinians.

Further humiliation awaited Husayn. In October 1974, Arab heads of state met in Rabat, Morocco. There they recognized

> the right of the Palestinian people to establish an independent national authority under the command of the Palestinian Liberation Organization, the sole legitimate representative of the Palestinian people, in any Palestinian territory that is liberated.

The Rabat declaration remains a landmark in the history of Palestinian efforts for self-determination within the framework of the Arab-Israeli conflict. Its terms insisted that Husayn and Jordan had no right to represent Palestinian interests in any international forum, undercutting Jordanian aspirations to recoup their 1967 losses. Husayn appeared to accept this decision, which acquired international recognition when Arafat spoke at the United Nations General Assembly in November 1974 and the PLO was awarded observer status over the strong objections of Israel and the United States.

Henceforth, advocates of a diplomatic resolution of the Arab-Israeli conflict were divided. Most countries, including America's European allies, called for inclusion of the PLO in any negotiations based on SCR 242, and recognition of Palestinian political rights as an issue for consideration in any talks between Israel and its Arab neighbors. In contrast, the United States and Israel rejected inclusion in talks of the PLO, calling it a terrorist organization. As for the PLO, it hoped to amend SCR 242 to include reference to Palestinian self-determination.

The election of Jimmy Carter as U.S. president in November 1976 initiated a new approach to the Arab-Israeli conflict. Carter abandoned Kissinger's scheme of limited agreements and decided to seek a comprehensive Arab-Israeli accord. In addition, he believed that the Palestinian question had to be considered and that the PLO should be invited to an international conference if it accepted SCR 242. In this context, Carter was for a time willing to amend resolution SCR 242 to disclaim the limitation of discussion on the Palestinians to that of their refugee status.

Carter failed to gain his objectives. The CAMP DAVID ACCORDS of September 1978 between Egypt and Israel was a last-gasp effort to salvage something out of his search for a comprehensive peace. There were many reasons for Carter's inability to achieve his broader objectives. The Arab states who might have attended such a conference based on SCR 242 had no common policy agenda. Moreover, Israel's opposition to negotiations involving territory was now intransigent. Menachem Begin had succeeded Rabin as prime minister of Israel in June 1977. As a pillar of revisionist ZIONISM, he had proclaimed from 1948 to 1967 the need for Israel to invade and capture the West Bank (ancient Judea and Samaria) to fulfill the Zionist goal of governing ancient Israel. As prime minister, he sought to reinterpret SCR 242 to apply only to the Sinai Peninsula and not to the Golan Heights or to the West Bank.

Palestinian participation was also in question. Israel rejected the idea. Jordan's King Husayn called for PLO inclusion because he had to adhere to the Rabat declaration's principles, but he opposed the PLO goal, Palestinian sovereignty on the West Bank. Husayn therefore proposed that Palestinians outside the PLO be included in the Jordanian delegation, hoping to counter PLO demands for a state with his own assertion of rights, backed by his own Palestinians. Sadat claimed to represent Palestinian interests but hoped to discount specific promises if he had a chance for a separate peace with Israel. Arafat saw the Carter initiative as an opportunity. He persuaded the PALESTINE NATIONAL COUNCIL (PNC) to approve a statement in March 1977 calling for creation of a Palestinian state in "the territories from which Israel withdraws." This statement appeared to accept Israel's existence in its pre-1967 boundaries, although critics charged that it was a tactic designed as a first step to retain all Palestinian lands. Arafat hoped to use this declaration to gain access to any international conference that was held.

A final obstacle to an international conference was Israel's opposition to the inclusion of the Soviet Union, which had cooperated with the Carter administration in seeking to bring Arab countries to the peace table. Carter's willingness to include the Soviets contradicted the Nixon/Kissinger policy of isolating them to ensure American domination of Arab-Israeli peace efforts, an approach Israel had backed. Washington and Moscow agreed on a joint communiqué in October 1977 that referred to the "legitimate rights" of the Palestinians, as opposed to their "national rights," the formula that Moscow had espoused earlier. Designed to lessen opposition to Palestinian participation, the compromise gained Sadat's approval but infuriated Israel and its American supporters, forcing Carter to retreat.

Carter's about-face on full Soviet representation led Sadat to conclude that further attempts to convene an international conference might prove fruitless. He decided to approach Israel on its own terms, those of a separate peace, which could serve his interests. Peace should bring economic development to Egypt in the form of Western, especially American, assistance. On November 9, 1977, Sadat announced to the Egyptian National Assembly, with Arafat in the audience, that he would go to Jerusalem in search of peace if invited, leading to his visit to that city the same month. The search for an Egyptian-Israeli peace had been set in motion.

Sadat and Begin had contradictory assumptions of the significance of any treaty they might sign. Although willing to sign a separate peace, Sadat sought to include reference to the political future of the Palestinians, an idea Begin rejected. In the agreement hammered out in September 1978, Begin agreed to mention the "legitimate rights of the Palestinian people," interpreting these words to refer only to nonpolitical rights of the Palestinians living under Israeli occupation. Carter and Sadat assumed that this phrase referred to both the PLO and Palestinian political rights as well.

Beyond this, major disputes arose over the procedures outlined for negotiating the autonomy of the West Bank and Gaza. Sadat and Carter assumed that Begin had committed Israel to refrain from creating new settlements in the territories during the period required to negotiate such autonomy, possibly five years. Begin insisted that he had not committed Israel to any restrictions on settlements beyond a three-month span. Palestinian "autonomy" meant to Begin control over local municipal affairs under permanent Israeli sovereignty; in his view, "the Sinai had been sacrificed but Eretz Israel had been won," referring to "the greater Israel" that included the West Bank.

The most tangible result of the Camp David accords was the Egyptian-Israeli peace treaty of March 1979, the first peace treaty between an Arab state and Israel and, consequently, a milestone in the history of the Arab-Israeli conflict. But the Egyptian-Israeli peace treaty did not suggest any progress toward resolution of the broader conflict by further negotiation. Sadat's willingness to conclude a separate peace led to Egypt's being ostracized from the Arab League, whose headquarters were transferred from Cairo to Tunis. Arab censure of Sadat seemed justified by the official interpretation of the agreements: consolidation of Israel's hold over the other Occupied Territories and greater Israeli military freedom to confront Arab opposition and impose its will. The task now was to establish firmer control over the West Bank and to prove to the one million Palestinians living there that they had no hope of true self-determination.

From Camp David to the White House Lawn, 1978–1993 During the 1980s, Israeli efforts seemed to have prospects of success, as Likud governments promoted settlements in the territories, especially the West Bank. Moreover, the eight years of Ronald Reagan's presidency, 1980–88, saw the United States committed to a stark cold war perspective in which Israel was seen as a vital ally and sentiments against Israeli settlement policy were muted. Finally, the gradual breakup of the Soviet Union, declared in December 1991, appeared to create conditions suited to unilateral American imposition of terms for resolution of the Arab-Israeli conflict, Washington's long-standing goal. This Framework also appeared to favor Israeli objectives, especially with respect to the Palestinians.

In fact, precisely the opposite occurred. The demise of the Soviet Union coincided with the Palestinian INTIFADA, which erupted in December 1987. This explosion of Palestinian outrage against Israeli repression brought heavy Israeli retaliation but also greater world sympathy for Palestinian aspirations, if not for the PLO and Arafat. A second unforeseen event with a major impact on Arab-Israeli questions was Saddam Husayn's invasion of Kuwait in August 1990. Yasir Arafat's support of Saddam at a time when all other Arab leaders condemned him appeared to undermine PLO prestige, but in the aftermath of the GULF CRISIS, 1990–1991, international negotiations began under American sponsorship that for the first time included Palestinians, though not PLO members. In short, unforeseen events impacted upon the Arab-Israeli deadlock in a manner impossible to anticipate by those who deemed themselves the victors of the cold war in the Middle East. These developments placed the Palestinians at the center rather than the periphery of the peace process.

Lebanon, Palestinians, and Israel The roots of these developments can be found in PLO circumstances in the aftermath of Camp David and the Egyptian-Israeli peace treaty, when the PLO intensified attacks on Israel from Lebanon. Lebanon had long been an unwilling base for PLO operations against Israel, dating to the latter 1960s. The shift of the PLO command structure to camps outside Beirut after 1971 further exacerbated the situation and led to the formation of Maronite Catholic militias determined to thwart PLO assaults. PLO factions found themselves involved in local political tensions as well because Muslim and leftist resentment at Maronite dominance spilled over into civil war in the mid-1970s. Once a truce was achieved in Lebanon, the PLO resumed its assaults against Israel from the south.

Israel had invaded southern Lebanon in March 1978 in retaliation for a terrorist attack. In the wake of the Camp David accords (September 1978) and the Egyptian-Israeli peace treaty (March 1979), Prime Minister Menachem Begin and his chief adviser, Ariel Sharon, reconsidered their strategy regarding the PLO. The treaty with Egypt seemed to ensure Israeli domination of the West Bank. What then to do with the allegiance of most West Bank Palestinians to the PLO? Destruction of the PLO command in Lebanon would both relieve Israel of border strife and, in Likud's view, remove any hope among West Bank Palestinians that they could escape or resist Israeli rule. Israeli ambitions meshed with those of Bashir Jumayyil, leader of the Phalange, the premier Maronite militia. He hoped to oust if not destroy the PLO in Lebanon in order to remove a major challenge to Maronite preeminence. An alliance with Israel, which had trained Maronite militias since the mid-1970s, would place him in power and ensure Maronite political control of Lebanon despite the group's minority status.

These calculations resulted in the Israeli invasion of Lebanon in June 1982. The Israeli army succeeded in reaching Beirut, where repeated bombings of its suburbs caused many civilian casualties but did not destroy the Palestinian community or command. International intervention resulted in the PLO's agreeing to leave Lebanon for Tunisia with guarantees that the Palestinians who remained would be protected. Once the PLO left Lebanon, American military contingents were also withdrawn. Almost simultaneously, Bashir Jumayyil was assassinated. As a result the Israeli army permitted Maronite Phalangists to enter the SABRA AND SHATILA refugee camps, where nearly a thousand Palestinians were slaughtered.

The massacre in the camps brought the return of American forces, who remained until 1984. Intended to be a neutral presence, American troops found themselves caught up in Lebanese affairs as U.S. policy seemed to favor the Maronites. When Washington ordered naval bombardments of Druze positions, over the strong objections of the U.S. Marine commander in Beirut, opposition forces retaliated with the suicide bombing of the Marine barracks in October, causing 241 deaths. After a further show of force, Reagan ordered the withdrawal of American troops in February 1984, leaving Lebanon to its regional competitors. The Lebanese-Israeli frontier remained a zone of conflict where Lebanese Shi'ites, often members of the Iranian-backed Hizballah ("Party of God") forces, undertook assaults against Israeli troops and client forces.

The Intifada: Its Background and Significance

The 1982 Israeli invasion of Lebanon proved in retrospect to be an undertaking whose short-term triumphs masked long-term liabilities, in particular the incitement of Lebanese Shi'ite hostility to Israel. Nevertheless, these difficulties did not deter Israeli Likud politicians, Menachem Begin and later Yitzhak Shamir, from pursuing the real goal of the Lebanese venture, consolidation of the Israeli position in the West Bank. The 1980s saw the vast expansion of Israeli settlements in the area, sponsored by Likud in the hope of creating a fait accompli that would bar any future Israeli withdrawal. At the same time, Israeli occupying troops were ordered to treat Palestinians who protested these policies more harshly, especially from 1985 onward, when Yitzhak Rabin became defense minister in a coalition government. No major change in the diplomacy of the Arab-Israeli conflict occurred until December 1988, when the United States finally agreed to talk to the PLO, satisfied that it had renounced terrorism and accepted Security Council Resolution 242.

The American decision, taken with more reluctance than enthusiasm, proved to be a major stepping-stone toward resolution of issues within the framework of the broader Arab-Israeli conflict. But the impetus for the decision had nothing to do with diplomacy. It reflected a new situation created by an uprising of Palestinians on the West Bank and especially in the Gaza Strip who had rebelled against Israeli occupation. The rebellion, known as the INTIFADA, began in December 1987. The intensity of Palestinian protests and the brutality of the Israeli response forced international attention to focus on the nature of Israel's role as occupiers of these lands and ultimately called into question the future of the territories.

The Intifada contradicted the basic assumptions of Israeli policy since the Camp David accords and the 1982 Israeli invasion of Lebanon. That policy assumed that with the PLO in disarray if not vanquished, Israel could act with impunity to impose its will on the Palestinians in the territories. The Intifada gave legitimacy, if only indirectly, to PLO claims to represent them. But American agreement to discuss matters with Arafat did not mean a willingness to negotiate with him; the Jordanian solution remained the favored option. Matters remained stalemated with Likud, guided by Yitzhak Shamir, ever more determined to resist pressures to compromise, despite American pressures to do so.

From the Gulf War to the Oslo Accords The catalyst for a breakthrough toward resolution of Arab-Israeli matters was not a factor directly related to the Arab-Israeli conflict. Rather, it was the decision of Saddam Husayn to invade Kuwait in August 1990 and the counterdecision of President George Bush that the United States would forge a military coalition that included Arab armies to drive Iraqi forces out of that country. These developments, coupled with the continuing disintegration of the Soviet Union, removed the cold war justification of American-Soviet rivalry for control of Arab-Israeli negotiations. Arab states such as Syria, long a recipient of Soviet aid but a foe of Iraq, now had incentives to join an American-led force. These incentives were not limited to defeat of an Arab rival; they included American promises to seek to broaden Arab-Israeli negotiations at the conclusion of the war and to confront more directly the militancy of Yitzhak Shamir.

Herein lay the basic irony of the Gulf war. Frustrated by the blockage of progress for inclusion of the PLO in talks after December 1988, Arafat had sided with Saddam Husayn in the latter's invasion of Kuwait, interpreting it in light of Saddam's more militant defense of Palestinian rights against Israel in the months preceding the invasion. Arafat's stance made him a pariah in Arab capitals. Yet, the ultimate beneficiary of the Gulf war was to be Arafat, and with him the PLO.

The reasons for this chain of events stemmed from American determination to gain agreement for an international conference on the Arab-Israeli conflict in the aftermath of the Gulf war. With the United States now in full command of the direction of Arab-Israeli talks, it behooved Washington to pressure Israel in order to force talks, fulfilling promises made to Arab leaders to gain their inclusion in the coalition against Saddam Husayn. Secretary of State James Baker's efforts resulted in an international conference in Madrid, convened in October 1991. The Arab states represented were Syria, Jordan, and Lebanon. In addition, the Palestinians were for the first time permitted to attend such a conference, although the PLO was excluded and the Palestinian delegation was, officially, part of the Jordanian contingent.

The MADRID PEACE CONFERENCE, which included several rounds of negotiations from October 1991 to the summer of 1993, were another landmark in the history of the Arab-Israeli conflict. Arab states and Israel negotiated directly for the first time, as did Israelis and Palestinians. Although no formal agreements emerged during these talks, their atmosphere introduced incentives for further discussion, stymied primarily by the intransigence of Yitzhak Shamir's Likud cabinet in Israel. Further progress awaited Israeli elections in June 1992, which saw Yitzhak Rabin's election as prime minister.

Rabin's election was hailed as a major shift in Israel's posture regarding SCR 242 and its applicability to the territories. He promised to halt settlements he defined as nonessential to security and to pursue more energetically talks with Palestinians. Moreover, there were major outbursts of violence in the territories and increasingly in pre-1967 Israel, primarily the result of assaults by Islamic groups, HAMAS and ISLAMIC JIHAD. These attacks and Israeli reprisals led to mounting casualties on both sides, but they also created greater awareness of Palestinian resentment of Israeli rule, evidenced in the Intifada. Despite Israeli suppression of the Intifada, Palestinian anger had been reinforced by the appearance of inactivity in achieving any tangible gains at the Madrid talks. Stalemate inspired a resurgence of resistance activity fueled primarily by Islamist groups who decried Arafat's passivity. Also, they called for reclamation of all of former Palestine, meaning the eradication of Israel, whereas Arafat now clearly supported compromise and the gaining of the West Bank and Gaza only.

Ultimately it was a combination of these factors that led to the historic events of August–September 1993 where the PLO and Israel signed letters of mutual recognition and agreed to negotiate the status of the territories. The specter of continued violence and the increased prestige of Islamic groups among Palestinians made a weakened Arafat more attractive to Israeli leaders. For beleaguered Arafat, inclusion in talks as leader of the Palestinians and acceptance in the international arena transformed him from a somewhat isolated head of the PLO to a position as acknowledged head of the Palestinians.

To be sure, this was not an agreement among equals. The PLO recognized Israel's right to exist as a sovereign state. Israel in return recognized the PLO as the representative of the Palestinian people. However, Rabin made no mention of a state and left the door open for stopping talks if he so decided.

Despite this imbalance, the OSLO AGREEMENTS remain a turning point in the history of the Arab-Israeli conflict as well as the Palestinian–Zionist/Israeli conflict. For the first time a settlement of the Palestinian question involving the political rights of the Palestinians was acknowledged to be part of the resolution of the Arab-Israeli conflict. As part of the initial accords, the Palestinians were to be granted self-governing authority in most of the GAZA STRIP and in Jericho on the West Bank. Israel and the PLO established a timetable for negotiations intended to provide for Israeli troop withdrawals from other areas on the West Bank that would be handed over to the Palestinian authority. Once a Palestinian authority was established with an elected PALESTINIAN LEGISLATIVE COUNCIL, most requisites defined for the interim stage of the accord would be completed. At that point, negotiations were supposed to begin on the final stage, which included delicate issues deliberately omitted from the initial accord as too difficult to resolve; these included the status of Jerusalem, the fate of Israeli settlements in the territories, and resolution of the Palestinian REFUGEE problem.

The Israeli-Palestinian Accord and the Future of the Arab-Israeli Conflict The Israeli-Palestinian accord had significance beyond the scope of Israeli-Palestinian relations. It legitimized Jordan's right to reach its own peace treaty with Israel, long a goal of King Husayn. The treaty, signed in October 1994, created within a few months more normalization of relations than that achieved in the sixteen years spanned by Israel's treaty with Egypt. But the Jordanian-Israeli peace treaty also had implications that might prove ominous for Jordanian-Palestinian relations. Israel acknowledged Jordan's special right to protect and administer the Muslim holy places in Jerusalem, a prerogative the Palestinians reserve for themselves.

As for Syria, talks were undertaken over the future of the Golan Heights with a peace treaty the final goal, but an impasse resulted because of diametrically opposed approaches to the negotiations. Syria wanted assurances that there would be a full Israeli withdrawal in return for any treaty. Israel sought to negotiate security arrangements without committing itself to a full withdrawal. No agreement has been reached.

With respect to Israel and the PLO, the implementation of the interim agreements stemming from the 1993 accord involved tortuous negotiations as Israel strove to hold on to as much authority as possible. While the PLO envisioned a Palestinian state as the ultimate outcome of the accord, Rabin contemplated a far more limited arrangement and repeatedly rejected the idea of a Palestinian state. Moreover, the atmosphere of negotiations was severely affected by the extraordinary violence that followed the 1993 agreement. Groups on both sides opposed the pact because it rejected maximalist goals of Arab and Jewish militants: either recovering all of former Palestine from the Arab perspective, or retaining all of the land of Israel, from the Jewish perspective. Major acts of violence included Palestinian bomb attacks on Israeli buses and the massacre of more than forty Palestinians by an Israeli settler in HEBRON.

The beginning of 1995 saw talks nearly suspended because of the distrust inspired on both sides by the violence that had occurred. But the talks continued and, quietly, began to include items initially set aside to the final stage—Jerusalem, the settlements, and the refugees—even though the interim stage had not yet been implemented. There were three major reasons for these developments: first, a desire to speed up talks to show progress and mute Palestinian violence and despair; second, on the Israeli side, a goal of establishing a record of accomplishment that could not be overturned if Likud came to power in future elections; finally, Arafat's cracking down on the Palestinian extremists, aided by the fact that the political factions in Hamas appeared amenable to a compromise.

It was precisely this confluence of factors that led to the assassination of Yitzhak Rabin in November 1995 by an Israeli student of Orthodox beliefs, militantly opposed to territorial compromise. As initial lack of progress had sustained Palestinian anger at Arafat's apparent inability to gain his goals, his later success and Israeli willingness to reach agreement on more withdrawals from land inflamed Israeli opponents of the Oslo accords. In particular the reaching of the Oslo II accord in September 1995, portending future handing over of more land to the Palestinians, aroused great anger among right-wing Israelis. Likud party head Benjamin Netanyahu condemned Rabin as going against the Jewish tradition. Rabin was assassinated by a right-wing extremist who thought he was abandoning sacred Jewish land.

Rabin's successor, Shimon Peres, pursued a contradictory policy. He encouraged Arafat to reach an accommodation with Hamas political wings, as had Rabin. But he also ordered his intelligence service to assassinate a member of Hamas identified as the mastermind behind previous bombings. This killing in January 1996 ended a tacit six-month truce between Hamas and Israel and resulted in several Palestinian suicide bomb assaults in Israel that caused over sixty deaths and temporary suspension of the peace process. These suicide bombings enabled Netanyahu to portray Peres as weak on security, helping him to win the election as prime minister in May 1996 by the narrowest of margins.

Netanyahu would govern as prime minister for three years until defeated in elections in May 1999 by Ehud Barak of Labor who formed a broad coalition of parties to establish a basis for further peace initiatives. Netanyahu's tenure as prime minister had been marked by violent opposition to further concessions to the Palestinians under the Oslo agreements and a great expansion of settlements in the territories to forestall further abdication of control. From an ardent revisionist background that advocated retention of all of ancient Israel, Netanyahu had declared his willingness to accept the established terms of the Oslo accords but to go no further. His tenure as prime minister saw increasing tensions with Arab neighbors, including Jordan, whose king Husayn had been close to Rabin. Husayn's own death from cancer in early 1999 marked another transition point within the history of the Arab-Israeli conflict.

✦ ✦ ✦

The Palestinian question is still distinct from that of resolving Arab state relations with Israel. But more than ever it is a crucial component of the manner in which a final settlement of all issues is reached. Indeed, various aspects of the Arab-Israeli conflict have been altered significantly as a result of the Israeli-Palestinian accords. There is no longer an economic boycott of Israel. Some Arab states and Israel entered discussions regarding economic pacts and trading arrangements during the Rabin premiership, although these were suspended after Netanyahu assumed office. Further wars cannot be discounted, but it would appear that the military aspect of the conflict has ended. In short, the Palestinian question has proved to be a key component of the ability and willingness of Arabs and Israelis to settle their broader differences.

Of the unresolved issues, perhaps nothing will prove more difficult than the status of Jerusalem. Israeli insistence on a unified Jerusalem as the capital of Israel, declared in the aftermath of the 1967 war, leaves little apparent room for agreement on Palestinian governance in the city and for part of Jerusalem to be the seat of a Palestinian government. This question, given the sacredness of Jerusalem to Muslims as well as to Jews and to Christians, ultimately may determine whether the political rapprochement now under way between the Arabs and Israel can be sustained in its more peaceful forms of exchanges, such as trade, tourism, and open borders.

A final matter affecting Palestinians and Arab states as well as Israel will be the question of Palestinian refugees who live outside Israel and the territories: how many might be permitted to return to these regions; whether those who remain in Arab states would be recognized as subjects of a Palestinian entity, possibly a state, or would be accepted as citizens of the state in which they reside. This question itself may depend on whether a peaceful conclusion of the Arab-Israeli conflict includes the achievement of Palestinian self-determination. Will there be a Palestinian state, or will there be a Palestinian entity in confederation with Jordan? Resolutions of these matters will be linked to one another and, ultimately, to the resolution of the status of Palestine in the settlement of the Arab-Israeli conflict.

Charles D. Smith

BIBLIOGRAPHY

Abu-Amr, Ziad. *Islamic Fundamentalism in the West Bank and Gaza*. Bloomington: Indiana University Press, 1994.

Brand, Laurie A. *Palestinians in the Arab World: Institution Building and the Search for State.* New York: Columbia University Press, 1988.

Garthoff, Raymond L. *Detente and Confrontation: American-Soviet Relations from Nixon to Reagan.* Washington, D.C.: Brookings Institution, 1985.

Gerges, Fawaz A. *The Superpowers and the Middle East: Regional and International Politics, 1955–1967.* Boulder: Colo.: Westview Press, 1994.

Golan, Galia. *Yom Kippur and After: The Soviet Union and the Middle East Crisis.* Cambridge, England: Cambridge University Press, 1977.

Hunter, F. Robert. *The Palestinian Uprising: A War by Other Means,* 2d ed. Berkeley: University of California Press, 1993.

Kerr, Malcolm. *The Arab Cold War: Gamal Abd al-Nasir and His Rivals, 1958–1970.* New York: Oxford University Press, 1971.

Kyle, Keith. *Suez.* New York: St. Martin's Press, 1991.

Lebow, Richard Ned, and Janice Gross Stein. *We All Lost the Cold War.* Princeton, N.J.: Princeton University Press, 1994.

Louis, W. Roger. *The British Empire in the Middle East, 1945–1951: Arab Nationalism, the U.S., and Postwar Imperialism.* Oxford: Oxford University Press, 1984.

Morris, Benny. *The Birth of the Palestinian Refugee Problem, 1947–1949.* Cambridge, England: Cambridge University Press, 1988.

——. *Israel's Border Wars, 1949–1956: Arab Infiltration, Israeli Retaliation, and the Countdown to the Suez War.* New York: Oxford University Press, 1994.

Quandt, William B. *Peace Process: American Diplomacy and the Arab-Israeli Conflict Since 1967.* Washington, D.C.: Brookings Institution, 1993.

Sayigh, Yezid. *Armed Struggle and the Search for State: The Palestinian National Movement, 1949–1993.* Institute for Palestine Studies series. Oxford: Oxford University Press, 1997.

Seale, Patrick. *The Struggle for Syria: A Study of Post-War Arab Politics, 1945–1957.* Oxford: Oxford University Press, 1966.

Sela, Avraham. *The Decline of the Arab-Israeli Conflict: Middle East Politics and the Quest for Regional Order.* Albany: State University of New York Press, 1998.

Shlaim, Avi. *Collusion Across the Jordan: King Abdullah, the Zionist Movement, and the Partition of Palestine.* Oxford: Clarendon Press, 1988.

Smith, Charles D. *Palestine and the Arab-Israeli Conflict,* 3d ed. New York: St. Martin's Press, 1995.

Tessler, Mark. *A History of the Israeli-Palestinian Conflict.* Bloomington: Indiana University Press, 1994.

Arab-Israeli War of 1948

The war of 1948 actually began with the explosion of intercommunal violence triggered by passage of the United Nations Partition Resolution of November 29, 1947. That resolution called for the division of Palestine into sovereign Arab and Jewish entities and the internationalization of the greater JERUSALEM area. Both the ARAB LEAGUE and the newly reconstituted ARAB HIGHER COMMITTEE (AHC), representing the Palestinians, refused to accept the validity of the resolution. With one exception, the Arab parties were determined that there should be no Jewish state in any part of Palestine. The exception was King Abdullah of Jordan, who was publicly part of the anti-Zionist coalition but who, in secret negotiations with the Zionist leaders (see KING ABDULLAH AND THE ZIONISTS), had agreed not to send Transjordanian forces into areas the United Nations (U.N.) might assign to the Jews. The Zionists, for their part, accepted the resolution publicly, but David Ben-Gurion and other leaders of the *yishuv* (Jewish community) saw partition as only a step on the way to redemption of a much larger Israel. From early in the conflict, Jewish forces largely ignored the lines of the proposed partition.

The Arab ability to mount credible resistance to the much smaller Jewish community was hampered by deep internal divisions at many levels. These divisions existed among Palestinians, between Palestinians and surrounding Arab states, and among the Arab states themselves.

The Arab Higher Committee Palestinian society, although it had shown signs during early years of the British PALESTINE MANDATE of evolving into a national community, remained highly segmented along geographic, class, religious, and especially familial and clan lines. The Anglo-Zionist repression of the Palestinian revolt of 1936–39 had enhanced some of those divisions, exposed new fissures in the society, discredited much of its leadership, and, through default, made rulers of the surrounding Arab states the chief spokesmen for the Palestinian cause by the 1940s. The AHC, reconstituted in 1946, continued to be dominated by the HUSAYNI FAMILY, alienating significant segments of the Palestinian upper and middle classes not related to them; at the same time, the ability of this leadership to relate to and mobilize the predominantly peasant masses of Palestinian villages was extremely limited. The fact that not more than one or two members of the AHC resided on Palestinian soil further restricted its effectiveness. It largely failed to prepare Palestinians for the termination of the Mandate or to build effective political, organizational, or military structures.

The AHC's attempts to set up a workable military system centered on organization of the Jihad al-Muqaddas (Sacred Jihad), headed by Abd al Qadir al-Husayni in the JERUSALEM region. The core was a mobile striking force of several hundred men armed and paid by the AHC. These were surrounded by a reserve force to assist the core units when needed; villages were to organize local militias to deal with local military challenges. This broad pyramidal structure remained largely theoretical, however, and ultimately, Palestinian leaders failed to turn the various organizations into a force capable of functioning harmoniously under a central command.

The Arab League The Arab League, which came into existence in 1945, found itself as time went on increasingly in conflict with AL-HAJJ AMIN AL-HUSAYNI and the AHC. Conflict arose partly because the latter was often more intransigent on negotiations regarding the fate of Palestine than the established states with their important British and other European connections felt comfortable with and partly because Hashemite Transjordan, usually seconded by its kinsmen in Iraq, was adamantly opposed to the emergence of a sovereign Palestine. Essentially, Palestinian nationalists could count on the support only of Egypt, Syria, and Saudi Arabia, and much of this support grew out of these states' opposition to the territorial ambitions of the Hashemites and their claims to leadership within the emerging Arab system, rather than sympathy for Palestinian claims to sovereignty. At an October 1947 meeting of the Arab League Council convened at Alayh, Lebanon, the assembled ministers determined to recruit a fighting force within the league countries to deal with the eventuality of the U.N.'s imposing a partition of Palestine. Al-Hajj Amin al-Husayni, who had attended the meeting uninvited, argued in vain for the appointment to command of this force of his kinsman Abd al-Qadir al-Husayni. Instead, the league gave command to FAWZI AL-QAWUQJI, a Lebanese Muslim with a long but checkered military career in the Middle East. He presided over organization and training, at a camp near Damascus, of the force that came to be known as Jaysh al-Inqadh al-Arabi, the ARAB LIBERATION ARMY. It eventually mobilized some 5,000 fighting men but engaged in periodic conflict with the Palestinian forces of Jihad al-Muqaddas.

Phases of the War It is common to divide the war of 1948 into five phases: (1) November 29, 1947, through May 14, 1948—from the passage of the partition resolution to the end of the Mandate; (2) May 15 to June 11, 1948, from the Arab states' military intervention to the first U.N.-brokered truce; (3) July 8 to 18, the ten-day Israeli offensive; (4) the October phase; (5) the final phase, December 21, 1948, to January 7, 1949.

The first phase involved the juxtaposition of Jewish forces (primarily the mainline Haganah but also those of the Irgun Zvai Leumi) with those of the Jihad al-Muqaddas, who were most active in the Jerusalem area and, increasingly, units of the Arab Liberation Army in the north and center of the country. More or less independent village and town militias were also involved on both sides. As the British pulled back from one position after another, competing Jewish and Arab units moved to seize advantage and both sides targeted isolated enemy communities. Through February, Arabs were moderately successful in hindering Jewish communications, particularly in the northern part of the coastal plain and between JAFFA and Tel Aviv and Jerusalem. By March, combat became more violent and the stakes higher. Haganah forces began implementing Plan Dalet, which called for systematic eradication of Palestinian population centers deemed a threat within areas assigned to the Jewish state and for opening of secure routes to Jewish communities that were slated to lie outside it. This period also saw the massacre at the village of DAYR YASIN west of Jerusalem and Jewish occupation of most of eastern Galilee in mid-April and of Haifa on April 21. Attacks on JAFFA beginning on April 25 resulted in early May in the expulsion of most of that city's population. Palestinian forces of Abd al-Qadir al-Husayni, however, had considerable success in limiting access to West Jerusalem, and the Kfar Etzion Jewish settlements on the Hebron road fell to the Arabs. When Abd al-Qadir was killed in hand-to-hand combat on April 17, he was replaced by his second-in-command, Hasan Salama, but it is significant that when

Hasan Salama in turn died on June 2, he was not replaced. Leadership of the struggle had by then clearly passed to non-Palestinians.

When the British Mandate ended on May 15 and Ben-Gurion had proclaimed the state of Israel, armies from Egypt, Transjordan, Iraq, Syria, and Lebanon moved rapidly into Palestine. During this second phase of the war, Arabs were successful in securing most of the predominantly Arab areas of the country and in isolating several Jewish settlements in the south. The Arab Legion was able to drive Jewish forces from several places to the north and south of the Old City of Jerusalem and, on May 28, to force the evacuation of the ancient Jewish Quarter itself. Although the Israelis had not lost a great deal of territory, they were feeling very much on the defensive and very vulnerable.

The second phase of the war ended on June 11, when all sides agreed to a U.N. negotiated truce of four weeks. Both sides took advantage of the truce to strengthen and upgrade their military hardware, but the Israelis improved their position significantly by the acquisition of large quantities of ammunition and small arms as well as armor, some artillery, and military aircraft.

Whereas Israel agreed to prolong the truce beyond its July 8 termination, Arab leaders, apparently sensitive to various pressures generated by popular impressions that Arabs had the Jews on the run, refused to continue it. The ten days that followed brought staggering successes for the Jews, who took Nazareth and a considerable part of central Galilee and also seized the strategically located Arab cities of Lydda and Ramla, forcibly expelling in the process all of their populations of 60,000 or more.

During the second truce, Count FOLKE BERNADOTTE began promoting a revised version of an earlier peace plan that would give all of the Galilee to Israel, which already occupied most of the eastern and western sections, in exchange for most of the Negev for the Arabs. Jerusalem would still be internationalized. So completely had Palestinian claims been discounted by this time that the Bernadotte plan proposed simply ceding the Arab regions to Transjordan. It was in order to prevent such a victory for the Hashemites that the Political Committee of the Arab League proposed an ALL-PALESTINE GOVERNMENT in the Egyptian-occupied GAZA STRIP, which came into existence in September. Most Israelis had not been happy with the Bernadotte proposals either, and in the same month, members of LEHI (the Stern Gang) assassinated the U.N. mediator in West Jerusalem.

The fourth, or October, phase of the war saw the Israelis' completing their conquest of the Galilee by driving al-Qawuqji's forces out of the north-central regions they still held. Before this the Israelis had attacked Egyptian positions in the south, seizing control of southern Judea and of most of the northern Negev, thus isolating the new all-Palestine Government from the rest of the country. Barely a month after its foundation, the Egyptians ordered the Palestine government officials to evacuate Gaza and establish themselves on Egyptian soil. The Arab Legion had not moved to assist the Egyptians during the Israelis' Negev offensive, and on November 30 Transjordan was the first Arab state to agree to what became a permanent cease-fire with the Jews. The next day, in JERICHO, the Transjordanians convened a congress of Palestinian dignitaries that denounced the Gaza government, expressed nonconfidence in the AHC, and formally requested the inclusion of Arab Palestine in the Hashemite kingdom. These resolutions provided the legal basis for the annexation of the WEST BANK and East Jerusalem to JORDAN in 1950.

The fifth and final phase of the war was launched by the Israelis late in December. Called Operation Ayin, it aimed at clearing the Egyptians out of the Negev and had almost succeeded in capturing Rafah and al-Arish when finally, on January 7, 1949, the Egyptians asked for a cease-fire, formally ending the War of 1948.

By the time all of the Arab states had signed armistices with Israel, the new state occupied 78 percent of what had been Palestine. Jordan had transformed the major part of the hill country and East Jerusalem into its own West Bank, and Egypt occupied the Gaza Strip.

✦ ✦ ✦

Whereas popular Israeli narrative stresses the smallness of the Israeli population of 600,000 relative to the 1.2 Arab Palestinians and especially to the populations of the surrounding nations that sent armies against the Jews, careful analysis indicates that population disparities did not, during this war, translate into comparable troop disparities. The better organized and more completely mobilized Israelis always outnumbered the combined forces of the Arabs. During the May–June phase the total number of Arab forces, including the Arab Liberation Army, probably stood at about 40,000, and those of the Israeli forces were closer to 60,000. As the year went by, the armies on both sides grew in numbers but the relative strengths remained about the same. After some initial conflicts between Haganah leaders and those of the Revisionist Irgun Zvai Leumi, the Israelis also benefited from a centralized command structure, which the Arabs never archieved. Even more importantly they shared a vision and a firmness of purpose that neither Palestinian SOCIETY nor the broader Arab system at this point in history was able to replicate. The 1948 war between Arabs and Jews in Palestine resulted in the disappearance of Palestine as a political entity, the emergence of the state of Israel, and the beginning of the Palestinian diaspora through the occasionally voluntary but largely forced flight of about 725,000 Palestinians.

John Ruedy

BIBLIOGRAPHY

Flapan, Simha. *The Birth of Israel, Myths and Realities.* London: Croom Helm, 1987.

Kurzman, Dan. *Genesis 1948: The First Arab-Israeli War.* New York: Signet, 1972.

Louis, William, Roger, and Robert W. Stookey, eds. *The End of the Palestine Mandate.* Austin: University of Texas Press, 1988.

Morris, Benny. *The Birth of the Palestinian Refugee Problem, 1947–1949.* New York: Cambridge University Press, 1987.

Pappé, Ilan. *Britain and the Arab–Israeli Conflict, 1948–51.* New York: St. Martin's Press, 1988.

——. *The Making of the Arab–Israeli Conflict, 1947–1951.* New York: I.B. Tauris, 1994.

Shlaim, Avi. *Collusion Across the Jordan: King Abdullah, the Zionists Movement, and the Partition of Palestine.* New York: Columbia University Press, 1988.

Tamari, Salim, ed. *Jerusalem 1948: The Arab Neighborhoods and Their Fate in the War.* Jerusalem: Institute for Jerusalem Studies and Badil, 1999.

Arab-Israeli War of 1967

The June 1967 war between Israel and Egypt, Syria, and Jordan was the third major conflict between Israel and its Arab neighbors. It led to Israel's occupation of the GAZA STRIP and the WEST BANK, two areas of greatest Palestinian population, as well as the Golan Heights and the Sinai Peninsula. The war also caused a second mass exodus of Palestinians from Gaza, Arab East Jerusalem, and the West Bank. Gaza had been occupied by Egypt since the 1948 war; East Jerusalem and the West Bank had been annexed by Jordan in 1950. The war precipitated a renewal of Palestinian national consciousness and formation of several new Palestinian nationalist groups.

Failure to resolve the Palestine problem was one of the principal causes of the 1967 war. The 1948 Palestinian refugee problem; the continued dispute over Jerusalem, which was divided between Israel (West Jerusalem) and Jordan (East Jerusalem); and growing political unrest among Palestinians intensified tensions between Israel and the neighboring Arab states. Palestinian infiltration into Israel from Gaza in the south and from Jordan in the east and, after 1965, raids by Palestinian (fedayeen) organized by Syria, Egypt, and Palestinian organizations such as FATAH led to massive retaliation by Israel. The resulting escalation of border conflict climaxed in the 1967 war.

Palestinian paramilitary units fighting alongside the Egyptian army in Gaza were overrun by Israeli forces within a few hours after the war broke out. Gaza and the Sinai Peninsula were occupied by Israel within two days. Most fighting in Jerusalem and the West Bank occurred between Israeli and Jordanian forces, with only peripheral participation by armed Palestinians. Few Palestinians were involved in the battles between Israel and Syria in the Golan Heights.

During the war and in the three months following the fighting there was a major exodus of Palestinians, many from refugee camps established after the 1948 war. Of the approximately 300,000 who fled, about 120,000 had been refugees from the 1948 war. As a result of the war, some 650,000 Palestinians in Jerusalem and the West Bank and about 350,000 in Gaza fell under Israeli occupation. Both Gaza and the West Bank thereafter were governed by Israeli martial law, each region under a different military governor.

The loss of the West Bank and Jerusalem was a serious blow to Jordan's economy. Palestinians in the Occupied Territories had accounted for 38 percent of Jordan's total gross domestic product, including 55 percent of services, 47 percent of transportation, 43 percent of wholesale and retail trade, more than 50 percent of agricultural produce, and 48 percent of industrial establishments. These Palestinians constituted 37 percent of Jordan's work force. Two important sources of Jordan's income—tourism in Palestine and remittances from abroad—declined about 85 percent and 50 percent, respectively. Loss of the Bethlehem-Jerusalem tourist center, previously a mainstay of Jordan's economy, meant about a 25 percent loss in foreign currency earnings.

The influx into Jordan of nearly 400,000 Palestinians from the West Bank and Gaza increased the East Bank population by about a third, greatly straining already overtaxed food, shelter, and basic service resources. Since most of the newly added Palestinian refugee population was unskilled and impoverished, it took several years before many could find employment; to the present a large part of the refugee population is still unemployed.

Israel's imposition of martial law in the Occupied Territories began a period of abnormal life for the Palestinian inhabitants. Civilian law was replaced by military courts; civil liberties such as habeas corpus were suspended; Palestinian political organizations were banned; scores of Palestinian political leaders, including the mayor of Jerusalem and president of BIR ZEIT UNIVERSITY, were deported without trial; school texts were subject to military censorship; several thousand Palestinians were imprisoned without civilian trials; and scores of Palestinian homes were destroyed in punitive actions by the Israeli army.

From June 1967 until 1977, Israel's policy in the Occupied Territories was determined by the Labor-dominated government. This regime restricted Jewish settlement in the West Bank primarily to the Jordan Valley and the area of former Jewish settlement near Hebron. After Likud took control of the government in 1977, most restrictions on Jewish settlement in the territories were removed and settlements were set up throughout the West Bank and Gaza, many of the adjoining Palestinian cities, towns, and villages. Tension between the Jewish settlers and the indigenous Palestinian population became a major source of conflict and was one of the causes of the Palestinian INTIFADA (uprising) in December 1987.

According to Meron Benvenisti, a leading Israeli authority on occupation policy, Israeli strategy sought to

> improve conditions as far as possible within the framework of existing resources, without any essential changes. . . . Palestinian agriculture was allowed to develop only insofar as it would not affect Israeli agriculture, and on condition that its development would not involve a fiscal or economic drain on the Israeli economy or government. West Bank agriculture has been made to fit into the Israeli system and adjust itself to the demands of the "common market" created after the occupation. Naturally, the stronger and more developed economy gained the advantage over the weak and undeveloped one. (*The West Bank Handbook*, p. 2)

Most economic life in the Occupied Territories was subject to Israel's control or supervision. Israel also took control of the land and water resources. Transportation networks and the electricity grid were integrated into the Israeli systems.

An integral component of the "common market" imposed by Israel on the Occupied Territories was employment of over 100,000 Palestinians, mostly as unskilled workers, at the bottom of the wage scale in Israel. About a third of the Palestinian labor force in the occupied areas was employed in Israel before the Intifada, although this estimate did not reflect the large number of Palestinians employed "unofficially." The largest numbers worked in agriculture, construction, and services, occupations that were largely shunned by Jewish workers.

Conditions under the occupation regime imposed by Israel on Palestinians in the West Bank and Gaza after the 1967 war eventually led to the Intifada, which erupted in December 1987.

Don Peretz

BIBLIOGRAPHY

Abu-Lughod, Ibrahim, ed. *The Arab-Israeli Confrontation of June 1967: An Arab Perspective*, 2d ed. Evanston, Ill.: Northwestern University Press, 1987.

Benvenisti, Meron, Ziad Abu-Zayed, and Danny Rubinstein. *The West Bank Handbook: A Political Lexicon.* Boulder, Colo.: Westview, 1986.

Lesch, Ann Mosley. *Israel's Occupation of the West Bank: The First Two Years.* Santa Monica, Calif.: Rand, 1970.

Peretz, Don. *Intifada: The Palestinian Uprising.* Boulder, Colo.: Westview, 1990.

——. *The West Bank: History, Politics, Society, and Economy.* Boulder, Colo.: Westview, 1986.

Arab-Israeli War of 1982

An Israeli invasion of Lebanon that developed into a costly war, Israel invaded Lebanon on June 6, 1982, to destroy the military and political structure of the PALESTINE LIBERATION ORGANIZATION (PLO) there. Israeli Defense Minister Ariel Sharon was instrumental in convincing other government figures, particularly Prime Minister Menachem Begin, Foreign Minister Yitzhak Shamir, and army Chief of Staff Rafael Eitan, that destroying the PLO would enable Israel to negotiate directly with Palestinians in the WEST BANK and GAZA STRIP over a limited autonomy plan and forestall the creation of a Palestinian state. The Israelis also hoped the invasion would lead to the formation of a new Lebanese government controlled by the Phalange Party, with which Israel then maintained friendly relations.

Israel's stated reason for invading Lebanon was the threat of PLO attacks against Israel from southern Lebanon. However, U.S. emissary Philip Habib had arranged an Israeli-PLO cease-fire agreement in July 1981 that held until June 1982. On June 3, however, Israel's ambassador to Britain was shot and seriously injured by the anti-PLO Palestinian faction of ABU NIDAL. Israel stated that this constituted a violation of the cease-fire, despite the fact that PLO officials were also on the Abu Nidal group's hit list.

Diplomatically, Israel's move came at an advantageous time. The 1979 Israeli-Egyptian peace treaty removed the threat posed by Israel's most powerful enemy. The administration of U.S. President Ronald Reagan was highly supportive, to the extent that Secretary of State Alexander Haig reportedly gave Sharon the "green light" to proceed with the invasion.

Sharon stated that the invasion, called operation Peace for Galilee, was targeted at PLO forces in a zone twenty-five miles north of the Israeli-Lebanese border and south of the Litani River. Israel's action might have been accepted as a self-defense move had not Sharon and Eitan quickly ordered the Israel Defense Force (IDF) to proceed northward toward Beirut, pushing PLO forces back into the city. The invasion quickly developed into a full-fledged war. Israeli forces engaged Syrian troops and aircraft, inflicting heavy losses and causing wide-scale damage to Palestinian refugee camps and Lebanese towns like Tyre and Sidon. By mid-June, the IDF had linked up with its Phalange allies, surrounded PLO fighters and leaders in West Beirut, and begun a seven-week siege that included heavy air and artillery bombardment.

The siege, which resulted in heavy civilian losses, turned international opinion increasingly against Israel. Televised images of death and destruction caused consternation in the West, even within the Reagan administration. Following Haig's resignation and in an attempt to halt the siege, Reagan dispatched Philip Habib to broker an agreement by which the PLO could withdraw from West Beirut. The resulting accords led to a PLO withdrawal under the supervision of a multinational force, including U.S. Marines, who would also safeguard the now undefended Palestinian refugee camps. By September 1, some 14,420 PLO fighters and officials had been evacuated and had departed for Arab countries, whereupon the PLO established its new headquarters in Tunisia. Some 3,000 Syrian troops also left the city, as did the multinational troops shortly after the evacuation was completed.

Also on September 1, the United States announced the so-called REAGAN PLAN for Middle East peace. Rejecting both an Israeli annexation of the occupied West Bank and Gaza and the establishment of a Palestinian state, the Reagan Plan called for Palestinian autonomy in the Occupied Territories in association with JORDAN as well as for a freeze on Israeli settlement building. Israel, the PLO, and some of the Arab states all rejected the plan, however.

By early September, Sharon seemed to have realized his goals for the invasion. The PLO was gone, and the late August election of Bashir Jumayyil as president of Lebanon augured well for Israel's post invasion plans for Lebanon's political future. But the situation quickly changed. Jumayyil resisted Israel's call for a Lebanese-Israeli peace treaty and refused Israel's demand that its proxy in southern Lebanon, the forces of Major Sa'd Haddad, remain under Israeli authority. Then, when Jumayyil was assassinated on September 14 in a bombing that some linked to SYRIA, Sharon and Eitan ordered the IDF into West Beirut in violation of the evacuation plan arranged by the United States. While in the city, the IDF allowed the anti-Palestinian Phalange to enter the Palestinian refugee camps of Sabra and Shatila. The Phalange massacred between more than 900 Palestinian and Lebanese civilians in the two camps on September 16–18. (See SABRA AND SHATILA MASSACRE.)

The massacres outraged public opinion both worldwide and in Israel. By late September, the IDF had withdrawn from West Beirut and been replaced by the returning multinational troops. Israel established the Kahan Commission to investigate Israeli complicity. The commission determined that Israeli officials, particularly Sharon and Eitan, were indirectly responsible for the Sabra and Shatila Massacre. An international commission headed by former United Nations assistant secretary-general Sean MacBride declared Israel to be directly responsible because of its position as the occupying power and because of its allowing of the Phalange into the camps.

The three months of war proved costly to all involved. Lebanese authorities estimated that 17,825 Palestinians and Lebanese were killed, over 84 percent of whom were civilians. Israel lost about 600 troops. The war bitterly divided Israeli public opinion: some 400,000, or 8 percent of the entire population, demonstrated against the war. Even the United States suffered setbacks as it became increasingly involved in Lebanese politics. Secretary of State George Shultz, Haig's replacement, oversaw an Israeli-Lebanese security agreement signed on May 17, 1983, which ignored Syrian security needs, upheld Israel's continued occupation of southern Lebanon, and aligned the United States with Lebanon's Maronite-dominated government. Consequently, Lebanese Muslim militants bombed the U.S. embassy in Beirut. A far more serious attack occurred, after the U.S. Navy bombarded Druze villages, when a suicide bomber destroyed the Marines' barracks in Beirut and killed 241 troops in the process. The Marines were withdrawn four months later. Similar attacks took place against the French and the Israelis, who finally retreated from Lebanon after establishing a six-mile security zone in southern Lebanon garrisoned by Haddad's militia.

Philip Mattar

BIBLIOGRAPHY

Khalidi, Walid. *Conflict and Violence in Lebanon: Confrontation in the Middle East.* Cambridge, Mass.: Harvard University Press, 1979.

Schiff, Ze'ev, and Ehud Ya'ari. *Israel's Lebanon War.* New York: Simon & Schuster, 1984.

Smith, Charles D. *Palestine and the Arab-Israeli Conflict.* New York: St. Martin's Press, 1988.

Tessler, Mark. *A History of the Israeli–Palestine Conflict.* Bloomington: Indiana University Press, 1994.

Arab League

The League of Arab States (Arab League) was established, at least in part, as a response to mounting Arab concerns over Palestine. The league was also designed to facilitate cooperation among Arab nations, to foster regional integration, and to further Arab policies internationally. In 1944 representatives from the then seven independent Arab nations met in Egypt to establish the league. By 1999 it had twenty-one members, including the PALESTINE LIBERATION ORGANIZATION. The Alexandria Protocol of October 7, 1944, under which the league was created, specifically declared Arab "support of the cause of the Arabs of Palestine and its willingness to work for the achievement of their legitimate aim and the safe-guarding of their just rights." MUSA AL-ALAMI, a moderate Palestinian nationalist, who attended the Alexandria meeting as a full representative, stressed the gravity of the situation to league members. Annex 1 of the League Pact, signed on March 22, 1945, provided for Palestinian representation on the League Council; until the Palestinians had achieved full independence, this representative was to be selected by the council.

During the extraordinary session held at the BLUDAN CONFERENCE in Syria, in 1946, the members of the league dissolved two competing Palestinian political groups that emerged and reestablished a unified ARAB HIGHER COMMITTEE to represent the Palestinians. This committee had originally been created in 1936 under the leadership of the mufti (Islamic law expert) of Jerusalem, AL-HAJJ AMIN AL-HUSAYNI. Although the league members recognized the new committee as the official Palestinian representative, King Abdullah of Jordan, who had his own territorial ambitions in Palestine, sought to undermine the authority of both the mufti and the committee. (See KING ABDULLAH AND THE ZIONISTS.)

As tensions in Palestine mounted, the league sent notes to Great Britain urging the cessation of Jewish TERRORISM in Palestine and to the UNITED STATES attesting that its interference in Palestine was resented by the Arabs. At the same time, the league affirmed that Palestine was a vital part of the "Arab motherland." The league also rejected the U.N. PARTITION PLAN for Palestine. During the December 1947 meeting, members debated the policy of military action in Palestine but agreed that unless the United States and Great Britain interfered militarily, the Arab governments would not become involved. Subsequently, a Syrian plan for collective security was discussed.

Reactions After the 1948 War After protracted debate and extensive political maneuvering among competing Arab regimes, the Arab Higher Committee agreed to install the ALL-PALESTINE GOVERNMENT under AHMAD HILMI ABD AL-BAQI as the Palestinian government in September 1948; by this time much of historic Palestine had already been lost to the new Israeli state. Based in the GAZA STRIP, the new Palestinian government was recognized by all league members except JORDAN. Reflecting the political rivalries among the Arab nations, especially between Jordan and Iraq, both of which were ruled by kings of the Hashemite family who could trace their lineage back to the Prophet Muhammad, and Egypt under the monarchy of King Faruq, the league was unable to agree on which Palestinian group to support. Thus the league refused to support either an independent government for all Palestine or a government under the mufti. In fact, the league actually shunned the All-Palestine Government in the aftermath of the 1948 defeat and the loss of two thirds of historic Palestine to ISRAEL.

After the 1948 war, the league did affirm the policy of repatriation of the REFUGEES to Palestine and the nonrecognition of Israel. It also called for the "liberation, not conquest" of Palestine. This essentially meant that although nations supported Palestinian demands for national independence, the league would not use military force to achieve Palestinian statehood.

Finally, the league agreed to cooperate with the United Nations Relief and Works Agency (UNRWA) in its efforts to provide social services and relief for the refugees. In 1957, the league rejected proposals that the Palestinian refugees be resettled permanently in surrounding Arab nations and, after postponing a decision several times, reaffirmed the right of the Palestinians to return to their homes.

Once the highly charismatic Jamal Abd al-Nasir came to power in Egypt in 1952, Egypt increasingly took the leading role in championing the Palestinian cause within the league, which was headquartered in Cairo. In fact, Egypt monopolized the position of secretary-general from 1945 to 1978. A strong supporter of Arab nationalism and Palestinian rights, Nasir pushed the league to adopt a resolution in 1959 to prohibit individual member states from signing separate peace settlements with Israel. This resolution also encouraged unanimity among Arab nations regarding the Palestinian cause. Ironically, it was as a result of this resolution that Egypt's membership in the league was suspended in March 1979 after the signing of the CAMP DAVID ACCORDS and Egypt's separate peace treaty with Israel. At this time, the league headquarters was moved from Cairo to Tunis in North Africa. Egypt was readmitted in 1989 and the league moved back to Cairo.

In 1963, responding to mounting Palestinian militancy and pressure from the United Arab Republic, the league confirmed AHMAD SHUQAYRI, formerly assistant secretary of the league, as the Palestinian delegate to the council. With strong support from Egypt, a proposal for an independent "Palestinian entity" and the creation of the PALESTINE LIBERATION ARMY (PLA) stationed in Sinai, as well as Iraq and Syria, under a joint Arab command was also accepted in 1964.

From its inception, the league attempted to coordinate the responses of Arab governments to the ongoing crisis in Palestine and to the subsequent Israel/Palestine/Arab conflict. The league also sought to act as the legal representative of Palestinian Arabs in international debate and to sponsor a Palestinian delegate to the United Nations.

Economic and Political Policies League support for the Palestinians and opposition to Israel took two main forms: economic and political. The Arab boycott was the major economic weapon in the struggle against Israel. In 1945, the league council agreed to boycott all goods produced by the Zionists in Palestine. After the establishment of Israel in 1948, the boycott was expanded to ban trade both between Arab states and Israel and with companies involved in trade with Israel. A virtual blacklist of banned companies, films, books, and a variety of other products was developed. An office financed by the league, operating under the secretary-general and based in Damascus, was established in 1951 to oversee the boycott. By the 1970s, the league had promulgated some forty different articles defining the terms of the boycott. However, individual Arab governments were responsible for the implementation of boycott regulations within their own borders. Consequently, the enforcement of the boycott was always haphazard and varied from state to state. Although the boycott became a political issue in the United States, particularly in the 1970s, when pro-Zionist organizations launched a full-scale concerted campaign against it, U.S. officials generally argued that the boycott had little negative impact on Israel's economic development.

On the political and diplomatic front, the league consistently supported the Palestinian case in international organizations, where they either pushed for Palestinian membership or provided the umbrella for Palestinian representation. A press and information office disseminated materials on the Palestinian cause around the world. Throughout the 1970s and 1980s, the league provided support to the PALESTINE LIBERATION ORGANIZATION (PLO) in its struggle for international recognition. With some success, the league also sought to gain support for the Palestinian cause among third world nations, particularly in Africa. In 1952, the league strongly opposed the Luxembourg Treaty whereby Germany agreed to provide reparations to Israel. During the 1950s and 1960s, the league issued statements regarding the diversion of the Jordan River and established committees to study and make recommendations regarding the utilization and diversion of the river.

Divisions After the Gulf Crisis The GULF CRISIS, 1990–91, precipitated a serious split within the league. Although league members opposed the Iraqi invasion of KUWAIT, they were divided over the use of force and the allied military response. Whereas the PLO under YASIR ARAFAT supported Iraq and Saddam Husayn, most other league members, either directly or indirectly, supported the joint military intervention led by the United States. This split resulted in a major shift in the league's unanimous support for the Palestinians.

From the league's inception, its members generally unanimously—at least in public—opposed Israel and supported the Palestinian cause. Egypt's separate peace treaty with Israel in 1979 was a major exception to this general policy. However, Arab governments often disagreed over how best to achieve Palestinian self-determination. Many of the league's failures to respond effectively to Palestinian demands reflected the internal political divisions among its members.

On the league's fiftieth anniversary in 1995, members managed unanimously to agree to issue a communiqué demanding Israel sign the Nuclear Nonproliferation Treaty (NPT). However, the members remained divided and lacked consensus regarding the Palestine question. This lack of consensus, at least in part, stemmed from continued resentment, particularly by Kuwait and other Gulf States, over Palestinian support for Iraq during the Gulf Crisis. The league's failures to react quickly and strongly against Israeli provocations in JERUSALEM and the HARAM AL- SHARIF under the hawkish Likud government of Benjamin Netanyahu in 1996 were further indications of the disarray and continued divisions among Arab regimes.

In spite of lingering rivalries, most Arab states supported the peace process begun at Oslo in 1993 and continued in the 1998 Wye Plantation agreement and in the negotiations between the PLO and the government of Ehud Barak. Rather than taking a leadership role in pushing forward the Palestinian cause, the league members increasingly simply acquiesced to whatever policies the PLO under Arafat adopted.

Janice J. Terry

BIBLIOGRAPHY

Hasou, Tawfig Y. *The Struggle for the Arab World: Egypt's Nasser and the Arab League.* London: Kegan Paul, 1985.

Khalil, Muhammad. *The Arab States and the Arab League.* Beirut: Khayats, 1962.

MacDonald, Robert W. *The League of Arab States: A Study in the Dynamics of Regional Organization.* Princeton; N.J.: Princeton University Press, 1965.

Miller, Aaron. *The Arab States and the Palestine Question: Between Ideology and Self-Interest.* Westport, Conn.: Greenwood Publishing Group, 1986.

Arab Liberation Army

Volunteer force of Arab soldiers and officers formed in 1947 to oppose the U.N. partition plan

After Britain declared its intention to turn the question of Palestine over to the United Nations, the ARAB LEAGUE convened a conference in Alayh,

Lebanon, in October 1947. Among the topics of discussions were the military steps that the Arab states could take to help the Palestinians defeat ZIONISM. One of the measures adopted was a call for volunteers, both military and civilian, from member states to form an Arab army to frustrate the U.N. partition plan, which was finally adopted in November 1947.

Dozens of officers from Arab armies, particularly from Syria and Iraq, resigned their commissions in the fall of 1947 to serve in what came to be called the Arab Liberation Army (in Arabic, Jaysh al-Inqadh, or "Army of Salvation"). These officers were eventually joined by some ten thousand volunteers from Syria, Lebanon, Iraq, Jordan, Egypt, Saudi Arabia, and Yemen, as well as a few non-Arabs, including Britons.

Beginning in December 1947, the army was led by FAWZI AL-QAWUQJI, a Lebanese who had served in the Ottoman and Iraqi armies. In August 1936, he had recruited several hundred Arab volunteers to fight alongside Palestinian guerrillas in the Arab revolt in Palestine.

Only some forty-six hundred of those who volunteered for the Arab Liberation Army ever entered Palestine. The first contingent crossed from southern Lebanon in early December 1947 under the command of the Syrian Adib al-Shishakli (who later ruled as president of Syria, 1953–54). All the army's units that did enter Palestine were eventually concentrated in northern and central regions of the country. The Arab Liberation Army never cooperated with the Army of the Holy Struggle (Jaysh al-Jihad al-Muqaddas), a local Palestinian military organization, led by Abd al-Qadir al-HUSAYNI.

The army's first action took place in January 1948 at the Battle of Jiddayn in northwestern Galilee. Never very effective on the battlefield, the army failed to save Galilee from falling to Zionist forces in the spring of 1948 and eventually was ordered to evacuate by the regular Arab armies that entered Palestine in May 1948. Some units remained and provided assistance to Jordanian and Iraqi forces before withdrawing into southern LEBANON in the summer of 1948. The army was officially disbanded in March 1949.

Michael R. Fischbach

Arab Liberation Front

The Arab Liberation Front (ALF) was established in 1969 by the Iraqi wing of the pan-Arab nationalist Ba'th Party to counter AL-SA'IQA, the group sponsored by the rival Syrian wing of the party. The ALF counted Zayd Haydar and the Jordanian Munif al-Razzaz among its early leaders. Its most recent leaders have included Abd al-Rahim Ahmad and Mahmud Isma'il.

The ALF has maintained membership in the governing bodies of the PALESTINE LIBERATION ORGANIZATION (PLO), although it also joined the Iraqi-backed REJECTION FRONT in 1974 and opposed the PLO-Israeli peace process that culminated in the 1993 OSLO AGREEMENTS.

The ALF's clear deference to Iraqi interests and its small size have limited its influence among Palestinians.

Michael R. Fischbach

Arab Party

The Arab Party was established by the HUSAYNI FAMILY camp, known as al-Majlisiyyun (Councilists), in March 1935 to counter the NASHASHIBI FAMILY, known as al-Mu'aridun (Opposition), who had already established their own party (the NATIONAL DEFENSE PARTY) in December 1934. The titular president of the party was JAMAL AL-HUSAYNI (1892–1982), the cousin and intimate aide of the mufti of Jerusalem, AL-HAJJ AMIN AL-HUSAYNI. Allied with the party were the Scouts' movement, the Youth Congress, the workers' societies in JERUSALEM and HAIFA, in addition to several mayors and activists from the defunct ARAB EXECUTIVE. Also known as the Husaynis, the Arab Party could mobilize grass-roots support through the *hamula* (extended family) structure of Palestinian Arab society as well as through a network of Christian and Muslim supporters who had a considerable number of followers in their local communities.

The most important source of support for the party was the mufti himself, who by 1935 had emerged as the most preeminent Arab leader in Palestine. Al-Hajj Amin did not formally assume the leadership of the party because he did not want to alienate the British authorities and thus run the risk of losing his official position as head of the SUPREME MUSLIM COUNCIL (SMC). In reality, however,

Al-Hajj Amin was the real force behind the Palestine Arab Party, using the SMC as an adjunct.

The Palestine Arab Party adopted a national pact that restated the basic national demands, including the repudiation of the BALFOUR DECLARATION, the end of the PALESTINE MANDATE, the full stoppage of Jewish immigration, the prohibition of LAND sales to Jews, and the immediate granting of complete independence to the Palestinians. The party continued al-Hajj Amin's policy of avoiding anti-British agitation in the hope that nonviolent pressure tactics could induce the British government to change its pro-Zionist policy. A series of events culminating in the PEEL COMMISSION's partition recommendation of July 7, 1937, forced al-Hajj Amin to change his course and to foment active opposition to the British.

Like other Arab parties in Palestine, the Husayni party became almost moribund after the 1936 strike. Its ability to organize was seriously hampered by Al-Hajj Amin's flight to Lebanon in July 1937 and by the British-imposed ban on political organizing. Later attempts to revive the party by Jamal al-Husayni, who was allowed to return to Palestine in 1946, met with little success. Its leadership was in exile, many of its hard-core activists were at odds with each other, and the balance of forces was decisively in favor of the Zionist movement and its British sponsors.

Muhammad Muslih

BIBLIOGRAPHY

Lesch, Ann Mosely. *Arab Politics in Palestine, 1917–1939: Frustrations of a National Movement.* Ithaca, N.Y.: Cornell University Press, 1979.

Porath, Yehoshua. *The Emergence of the Palestinian-Arab National Movement, 1918–1929.* Vol. 1. London: Frank Cass, 1974.

——. *The Palestinian-Arab National Movement, 1929–1939: From Riots to Rebellion.* Vol. 2. London: Frank Cass, 1977.

Arab Studies Society

The Arab Studies Society was established in 1979 by FAYSAL AL-HUSAYNI, its first chair, and by six other persons who served on the founding committee. Located in ORIENT HOUSE in East Jerusalem, the society is one of the largest research organizations in the WEST BANK. It conducts research into numerous facets of Palestinian life, including education, sociology, science, and politics, and publishes the resulting studies. The society also translates articles from English and Hebrew into Arabic and maintains a library and an archive containing newspapers and documents.

The society has served as an important base of operations for its chair, Faysal al-Husayni, the senior FATAH figure in the West Bank. Among other activities, the society drafted a plan in the mid-1980s for Palestinian independence in the territories. During the INTIFADA, it quickly ran afoul of Israeli occupation authorities, who closed the society for several years beginning in July 1988, just one month after they released al-Husayni from prison.

Michael R. Fischbach

Arab Thought Forum

The Arab Thought Forum was developed by Palestinian professionals and activists in East Jerusalem in 1977. The academic MAHDI ABD AL-HADI was a leading figure in its creation, as was the engineer IBRAHIM DAKKAK, who headed the forum from 1977 to 1991.

The forum was one of the first Palestinian institutions that addressed the question of WEST BANK development as a way to combat Israeli authority. Formerly, intellectuals and professionals had shunned development projects for fear that such projects would imply Palestinian recognition of the Israeli authorities, with whom Palestinians would necessarily have to cooperate. It did so by providing an "official" pro–PALESTINE LIBERATION ORGANIZATION (PLO) covering for such activities. As part of its development activities, the forum collected statistics and information on the West Bank agricultural sector. The forum's interests also extend beyond development; in the realm of the arts, for instance, it sponsored one of the first LITERATURE festivals in the West Bank. It has also held symposia and conferences and publishes the results of research into a variety of aspects of Palestinian life.

On a political level, the forum helped create the influential pro-PLO NATIONAL GUIDANCE COMMITTEE in the Occupied Territories in November 1978 after the signing of the CAMP DAVID ACCORDS. Both the committee and the forum reflected the growing influence of indigenous leaders in the Occupied Territories who were attuned to local concerns and not merely spokespersons for the external PLO factions.

Michael R. Fischbach

Arab World

Before 1948, Palestinians who lived in the Arab world included a number of merchant families who lived in Egypt, Syria, Transjordan, and Lebanon; cadres of civil servants whom the British had recruited for service in Transjordan; and a handful of teachers who had been requested by the emir of Kuwait to assist in building the Kuwaiti educational system. The Arabs of Palestine also had extensive family and commercial ties in the surrounding countries. However, not until the Palestine war of 1947–49 and the expulsion or flight of over 700,000 Palestinians from their homes did the numbers of Palestinians living outside their homeland become significant politically, economically, and socially.

Where Palestinians took refuge in 1947–49 was determined primarily by family connections and geographic proximity. By 1949, 100,000 Palestinians were in Lebanon; 75,000 in Syria; 70,000 on the East Bank (Jordan); 7,000 in Egypt; and 4,000 in Iraq. Of those who took refuge in other parts of Palestine, 190,000 joined the nearly 90,000 original inhabitants of a truncated Gaza district, and some 280,000 REFUGEES joined the 440,000 original inhabitants of what subsequently came to be called the WEST BANK.

During 1948 and 1949, the Arab states bore the primary burden of providing refugee relief. When the United Nations Relief and Works Agency for Palestine Refugees in the Near East (UNRWA) was established in May 1950, less than 30 percent of the refugees lived in refugee camps. However, as Palestinians exhausted the savings they had brought with them, many were forced to move to UNRWA camps. UNRWA gradually took responsibility for a range of social welfare projects in the camps, which were established in the GAZA STRIP, the West Bank, the East Bank, Lebanon, and Syria. Health care and food rations were provided on presentation of a refugee card. Education, vocational training, and a program of small-scale loans for development projects were also sponsored by UNRWA, all aimed at achieving the international community's apparent goal for the refugees: development directed toward their gradual integration into the Arab states to which they had been expelled.

Regionally, however, the Palestinian refugees' presence was viewed quite differently. With the exception of Jordan, the Arab states were not interested in absorbing the Palestinians: they insisted that the refugees had been expelled illegally, that they had a right to return, and that nothing was to be done to compromise this right, including acquiescing in resettlement proposals or granting citizenship. Likewise, although Palestinians sought fair treatment by Arab host states, they too rejected the idea of resettlement and continued to insist on their right to return.

Varying Conditions Palestinians' lives differed dramatically, depending on the Arab state in which they had taken refuge. Jordan was the one state that annexed a part of Palestine—the West Bank—and, contravening ARAB LEAGUE calls, it extended citizenship to all of its new Palestinian residents. However, the extension of citizenship brought with it a denial of a separate Palestinian identity, and the pro-Western orientation of King Abdullah and his grandson Husayn further alienated many of the kingdom's new subjects. The "special relationship" that gradually unfolded between Jordan and the Palestinians was unique in the Arab world: Palestinians had become full citizens—indeed a majority—in a system to which they felt no attachment and for which many actually felt resentment. Gradually, some achieved economic success in the kingdom and embraced or at least acquiesced in a Jordanian identity along with their sense of belonging to Palestine. Hence, over time, Palestinian and Jordanian identities have grown increasingly blurred, indicating both the gradual integration of the two communities as well as the continuing contradictions between them.

In Syria, Palestinians had access to education, health care, and union membership, as well as the obligation of military service. Syria did not offer citizenship, but neither did it attempt to suppress expressions of Palestinian identity. For the more than 4,000 Palestinians who had gone to Iraq, the situation was similar. They carried special travel documents but enjoyed most of the other benefits of regular citizenship.

Conditions were worst for the Palestinians of Lebanon and the Gaza Strip. In Lebanon, the influx of 100,000 (mostly Muslim) Palestinians threatened the fragile confessional balance in the country. Hence, with the exception of several thousand Palestinian Christians who were able to buy citizenship, Lebanon did not even contemplate extending citizenship to Palestinians; nor did it consider providing any other services. By law, Palestinians were not permitted to work; those who did, did so illegally and often under exploitative conditions. For external travel, they were issued laissez-passers by the government, but to travel from one refugee camp to another, they were required to obtain permission from the Lebanese authorities. The refugees' health and educational needs were taken care of not by the government but by UNRWA, and the Lebanese security forces maintained a heavy hand in the camps.

The Gaza Strip, on the other hand, was administered by the Egyptian military. The refugees there received special travel documents from the Egyptian government, but their health and educational needs were taken care of by UNRWA. The travel documents were very restrictive, and Cairo did its best to prevent Gaza Palestinians from entering Egypt proper. Because of Gaza's location as a buffer between Egypt and Israel, the Egyptians were particularly concerned about any kind of independent Palestinian political activity there. Hence, Egyptian intelligence prevented any overt Palestinian organizing activity until 1960, when Cairo sponsored a Gaza extension of the Arab Socialist Union and subsequently allowed the emergence of several Palestinian labor unions. In Egypt itself, the small Palestinian community did not begin to have privileges similar to those it enjoyed in Syria until after the 1952 revolution. Palestinians were not granted citizenship, but they were also never subject to military service, and they did have access to government health and educational facilities.

The no-work restriction in Lebanon and the depressed economic conditions in the Gaza Strip and the West Bank led many Palestinians to look elsewhere to build their futures. The displacement from Palestine had come at virtually the same time as the reinvigoration of oil production in the wake of World War II. The Arab oil producing states were in need of laborers to help build their modern governmental and economic infrastructures. Kuwait was the first state to engage in active recruitment of Palestinians. This initially took place in the public sector, as the Kuwaiti government sought the seconding of teachers, bureaucrats, and managers of various sorts, generally from Jordan. As time went on, however, the Kuwaiti private sector also became involved.

Labor migration to the Gulf involved a fairly steady flow of Palestinians (as well as other Arabs, especially from Egypt and the Levant), and large Palestinian communities developed, especially in Kuwait and Saudi Arabia. In 1967, the Israeli occupation of the West Bank and Gaza Strip led to the out-migration of many families whose male heads of household had previously gone to the Gulf unaccompanied. With the arrival of families, the communities in the Gulf acquired a greater sense of permanence.

Nonetheless, those who went to the Gulf did so with the understanding that they were going for employment, not possible future citizenship. Although Palestinians in Kuwait enjoyed greater political leeway than did other expatriate communities in the emirate or other Palestinian communities elsewhere in the Gulf, they were still subject to numerous restrictions. For example, they could not own immovable property, and they were allowed to work and reside in the country only as long as they had a sponsor (*kafil*). Once their work contracts ended or were terminated, they were required to leave the country. Moreover, there was no official provision for an expatriate's retiring in the Gulf.

Through years of work in the Gulf, many Palestinians were able to lift themselves and their families out of poverty. The financial success they achieved, as well as the economic and managerial positions they reached, gave them clear, if unofficial, influence in these states. Just as important, those who became successful in the Gulf also came to form a transnational Palestinian bourgeoisie, which not only reinforced the important economic role of Palestinians in the Arab world, but also helped fill the coffers of the PALESTINE LIBERATION ORGANIZATION.

Jordan and Lebanon Palestinians' relations with Arab host states have largely been shaped by the nature of ties between the respective state and the Palestine Liberation Organization (PLO), which was established in 1964. Initially, the founding of the PLO created most difficulty for the Palestinians in Jordan because Jordan was the only Arab state that had enfranchised them. As a result, King Husayn was concerned about the question of dual loyalty as well as the prospect that the PLO might seek to liberate the West Bank, that part of Palestine that had become a part of Jordan. Relations between the PLO and Jordan were tense until the 1967 war. The war led to the defeat of the Jordanian army; to the displacement from the West Bank to the East Bank of some 265,000 Palestinians, most of them second-time refugees; to the Israeli occupation of the West Bank; and to the discrediting of the Jordanian regime. At this point, it became difficult for King Husayn to repress the leadership and organizational activity of the various Palestinian guerrilla organizations, which ultimately wrested leadership of the PLO from the old guard in 1969.

From 1967 to 1970, the numbers of PLO recruits multiplied, and so did their activities in Jordan, which served as their primary base at the time. In addition to military training, a variety of sociopolitical institutions began to emerge—all dependent on the protective umbrella of the PLO. As the resistance organizations grew in strength, they began to flout Jordanian law, and some guerrilla leaders even called for the overthrow of the Hashemite monarchy. In mid-September 1970, the king decided to confront the resistance militarily. The first few battles lasted twelve days and forced the resistance out of the capital, Amman, to the northwest of the country. The Jordanian army's final assault in July 1971 drove the rest of the resistance forces out of the country. Competition between the king and the PLO for the loyalty of East and West Bank Palestinians was renewed in the mid-1970s and has continued in various nonmilitary forms over the years.

By spring 1969, resistance groups had also become active in Lebanon. After a series of confrontations with the Palestinian guerrillas in refugee camps in the south, the Lebanese government effectively ceded sovereignty over the camps to the Palestinian resistance movement through the Cairo Agreement, partly in response to the increasing support for the Palestinians from various sectors of Lebanese society. The Palestinians then began gradually to engage in the same kind of economic and sociopolitical organizing that they had undertaken in Jordan. However, as the Lebanese state crumbled in the mid-1970s, these activities became far more intensive and wide-reaching than anything that had ever developed in Jordan. Palestinians were also drawn into what became the Lebanese civil war, fighting on the side of the Lebanese national movement, and thus were both part of and subject to the violence that convulsed the country. Nonetheless, from 1976 to 1982, Beirut developed into a virtual political and cultural capital for Palestinians.

Thus, the Israeli invasion of Lebanon in 1982 marked a major turning point for the Palestinian national movement. Not only was the Palestinian community visited with unparalleled death and destruction, the PLO was effectively expelled from the country, leaving the community vulnerable; that vulnerability led to the SABRA AND SHATILA MASSACRE.

Conditions for the Palestinians in Lebanon worsened throughout the 1980s. Various Lebanese Christian forces were determined to prevent the return of the PLO and sought to force as many Palestinians as possible out of Lebanon. By late 1983, Syrian-Palestinian hostilities had grown, triggered in part by Syrian attempts to control a crippled PLO and in part by inter-Palestinian dissension unleashed by the 1982 defeat. The hostilities with Syria led in turn to intra-Palestinian fighting in Tripoli, Lebanon. Relations deteriorated further, and in 1985 Syria unleashed its ally, the Shi'ite Amal militia, to initiate both war and siege on the camps, raising the specter of starvation among the refugees. The camps did not surrender, however, and Amal finally used the pretext of offering support for the Palestinian uprising to end the assaults in early 1988.

King Husayn's disengagement from the West Bank in July 1988 sent shock waves through the Palestinian communities on both banks. But no development since 1982 had such traumatic effects on the Palestinians as did the 1990 Iraqi invasion of Kuwait. Most of the country's 350,000 Palestinians fled the country. After the war, the Kuwaitis, resentful of the PLO's pro-Iraqi stance, expelled, arrested, and even murdered some of those who remained.

Over the years, Arab states have provided refuge and various forms of support to Palestinian communities. At the same time, however, Palestinians have been subject to the vagaries of Arab domestic and regional politics over which they have had no control. Lacking citizenship—except in Jordan—they have had no state to protect them, and the PLO's influence has depended on its own ties with each regime.

Uncertain Future The establishment of the PALESTINIAN AUTHORITY in the West Bank and Gaza and the concomitant reduction in the power and profile of the PLO have left the communities in the Arab world in a disturbing limbo. Most are 1948 refugees whose return to live under a Palestinian authority is by no means assured, their own leadership has tended to reject the existing peace accords, and most of their host states have made little progress in their own negotiations with Israel. Nor have those countries expressed a willingness to consider enfranchising them. Although Palestinians of the West Bank and Gaza increasingly carry Palestinian passports, it is the continuing statelessness of most communities in the Arab world that best exemplifies the Palestinian experience since 1948.

Laurie A. Brand

BIBLIOGRAPHY

Brand, Laurie A. *Palestinians in the Arab World: Institution Building and the Search for State.* New York: Columbia University Press, 1988.

——. *Jordan's Inter-Arab Relations: The Political Economy of Alliance Making.* New York: Columbia University Press, 1995.

Buehrig, Edward H. *The UN and the Palestinian Refugees.* Bloomington: Indiana University Press, 1971.

Al-Filastiniyyun fi al-Watan al-Arabi: Dirasat fi Awda'ihim al-Dimughrafiyya wa al-Ijtima'iyya wa al-Iqtisadiyya wa al-Siyasiyyah (Palestinians in the Arab world: Studies of their demographic, social, economic and political situation). Cairo: Ma'had al-Buhuth wa al-Dirasat al-Arabiyya, 1978.

Ghabra, Shafeeq. *Palestinians in Kuwait: The Family and the Politics of Survival.* Boulder, Colo.: Westview, 1987.

Hasan, Bilal. *Al-Filastiniyyun fi il-Kuwayt* (The Palestinians in Kuwait). Beirut: PLO Research Center, 1974.

Mishal, Shaul. *West Bank/East Bank: The Palestinians in Jordan 1949–1967.* New Haven, Conn.: Yale University Press, 1978.

Nakhleh, Khalil and Elia Zuriek, eds. *The Sociology of the Palestinians.* London: Croom Helm, 1980.

Plascov, Avi. *The Palestinian Refugees in Jordan, 1948–1957.* London: Frank Cass, 1981.

Sayigh, Rosemary. *Palestinians: From Peasants to Revolutionaries.* London: Zed Press, 1979.

Smith, Pamela Ann. *Palestine and the Palestinians, 1876–1983.* New York: St. Martin's Press, 1984.

"Summary of the Final Report on the Economic and Social Situation and Potential of the Palestinian Arab People in the Region of Western Asia," Beirut, Doc. Ref. No. TEAM/F.R./SUM. 1983.

UNRWA. *UNRWA: A Brief History, 1950–1983.* Vienna: UNRWA, 1983.

Arafat, Fathi

Husayn Arafat; physician
1933–   Cairo

Husayn Arafat was given the name Fathi in 1949 while receiving guerrilla training with the Muslim Brotherhood in Gaza.

Fathi, the younger brother of PALESTINE LIBERATION ORGANIZATION (PLO) chairman YASIR ARAFAT, completed his medical training at King Fu'ad University (now Cairo University) in Egypt. After working in KUWAIT, he helped to found and headed the medical services branch for FATAH in 1968. The organization, later renamed the Palestine RED CRESCENT Society, was headed by Arafat into the 1990s.

Michael R. Fischbach

Arafat, Yasir

Abu Ammar ("father of Ammar"), chair of the PLO since 1969 and president of the Palestinian Authority since 1996
1929–   Cairo

Yasir Arafat has been the leading figure in the Palestinian struggle for national independence since February 1969, when he was elected chairman of the Executive Committee of the PALESTINE LIBERATION ORGANIZATION (PLO), a position that also entitled him to command the PALESTINE LIBERATION ARMY (PLA) units in Egypt, SYRIA, and Iraq. In November 1988, the nineteenth PALESTINE NATIONAL COUNCIL (PNC), the PLO's parliament, chose him as president of a newly declared Palestinian state; in January 1996, he was elected as president of the PALESTINIAN AUTHORITY (PA) in the GAZA STRIP and the WEST BANK.

Early Years Arafat was born in Cairo, spent some of his childhood years in JERUSALEM, and grew up in the tumultuous final decades of British and French colonial rule in the Arab East. His father, Abd al-Ra'uf, a wholesale merchant, belonged to the Qudwa family of Gaza and Khan Yunis, a less prominent clan of the Jerusalem-based Husayni family. His mother, Zahwa, hailed from the family of Abu al Sa'id, a distinguished family who claimed direct descent from the Prophet Muhammad. Arafat plunged into politics at the age of ten, participating in Egyptian demonstrations against the British practice of forming children of his age into groups and having them march and drill. He fought in Gaza with the Ikhwan al-Muslimun (Muslim Brethren) during the 1948 Palestine war, after which he fled to Egypt, where he showed concern for the Egyptian nationalist cause. In the years between 1948 and 1956, two predominant transnational political forces in the Arab world were the Ikhwan and the communists. A Muslim in education and tradition, Arafat preferred the ecumenism of the Ikhwan to the dialectical materialism of the communists. What increased the appeal of the Ikhwan was its commitment to the cause of Palestine.

While in Egypt, Arafat was active in the Palestinian Students Union (PSU), a body set up in the early 1950s by Palestinian students residing in the country. The PSU brought together Palestinian students of various political persuasions, including Muslim Brothers, Ba'thists, communists, and independents. In 1952, Arafat was elected president of the PSU on a platform of Palestinian identity and self-reliance. Through the PSU and his other activities in student politics, Arafat met KHALIL AL-WAZIR, SALAH KHALAF, and FARUQ AL-QADDUMI, political activists who later (1959) founded FATAH and constituted its core leadership. Arafat's organizing skills made him the logical choice for the important task of representing Palestinian students in international student gatherings, such as the Warsaw Youth Festival of July 1954, in which the PSU participated as part of an Egyptian delegation. At the end of 1956, Arafat began to debate with his colleagues the future direction of their student organization. Arafat's approach was governed by his preference for independent Palestinian political and military action. He and Khalil al-Wazir were thinking primarily of how to organize and arm the Palestinians.

In early 1957, Arafat left Egypt after receiving his engineering degree from Cairo University and after discovering that his political activities there no longer were welcomed. He went to KUWAIT with some friends and found work in this booming oil city, which for approximately eight years served as the main setting for Arafat's political career. He first worked as an engineer for the Kuwaiti Public Works Department and then as an owner of a profitable construction and contracting company. In Kuwait the conditions for political activity were easier than in Egypt, because Kuwait lacked the large intelligence and other government apparati of the Egyptian state. Arafat was determined to use the possibilities of political action available to him. He mobilized Palestinian recruits and exercised leadership over the underground network that he created. His aim was not so much to overturn the existing Arab political order as to bring about a change of Arab policy toward Israel. As an organizer, Arafat understood that he could succeed only if he adopted a gradualist approach. To mobilize successfully, Arafat relied, first, on the clandestine network of Fatah; second, on the General Union of Palestinian Students (GUPS), which was established in 1959 by representatives of Palestinian students residing in Egypt; and third, on an underground monthly Palestinian publication called *Filastinuna: Nida al-Hayat* (*Our Palestine: The Call to Life*), which began publication in 1959 and helped win recruits for Fatah. Arafat also relied on support from Algeria and China, and on loyal colleagues, primarily Khalil al-Wazir.

In his seeking to exercise leadership, Arafat's tactics were dictated, to a great degree, by internal Palestinian factors. When the first Central Committee of Fatah was formed in the winter of 1963, Arafat was only one of ten in a collective leadership. With respect to strategy, he was in the minority: his preference for immediate military action against Israel was rejected by a majority of his colleagues. Arafat also sought to launch his program of armed struggle against Israel, but its implementation required a favorable balance of power within Fatah, and a more suitable moment. That moment came when an Arab summit conference, with the strong endorsement of Egyptian president Jamal Abd al-Nasir, formed the PLO in January 1964.

The creation of the PLO provided Arafat with the opportunity to consolidate his position within Fatah. Using his tactical skills, he threatened to split Fatah and go his own way if his position of early military action were not adopted. After a month of debate Arafat prevailed. His skeptical colleagues were now convinced that the only way to keep Fatah alive and to demonstrate that the Palestinians could play a real role in decisions related to their future was to embark on armed struggle without delay. Thus the stage was set for the launching of Fatah's first raid into Israel in January 1965. The operation was carried out under the name AL-ASIFA ("the Tempest"), the title of the military arm of Fatah. The raid took place at a time when the Palestinians had become increasingly frustrated by Arab inaction toward Israel. The Fatah raid evoked a powerful fascination in the Palestinian masses across the diaspora. However, the reaction of key Arab governments to Fatah's raids was hostile because they feared Israeli reprisals and opposed Palestinian action that was not under their control. As a result, the skeptics inside Fatah were quick to remind Arafat that, in order to prevent a confrontation with the Arab governments, especially the government of Nasir, Fatah had to reduce its military activities against Israel. After failing to convince Arafat, the central committee suspended his membership in Fatah and cut off funds in the summer of 1966 in the hope of depriving him of the means to continue the armed struggle. With the help of HANI AL-HASAN, who collected funds from Palestinian student organizations in West Germany and elsewhere, Arafat overcame his financial problems and thus kept the military option alive.

Arafat's other problem was to find an Arab state that would allow him to mount operations against Israel from its territory. His only realistic option was SYRIA. Arafat already had contacts with General Ahmad al-Suwaydani, who in 1966 became Syria's chief of staff and also was a supporter of the team of Salah Jadid, the Syrian leader who advocated using Palestinian guerrillas as a weapon in Syria's contest with Israel. Israel's escalatory policy against Syria in the summer of 1966 worked in Arafat's favor. Hafiz al-Asad, then acting defense minister, supported the cross-frontier forays of Fatah guerrillas as a way of taking up the Israeli challenge, although he expected the guerrillas to accept the limitations imposed by Syria. Determined to maintain his independence and pursue his strategy of triggering a general Arab–Israeli war, Arafat tried to throw off Syria's restraints. In retaliation, Asad locked up Arafat in the Mezza prison for over a month in the summer of 1966. This episode marked the beginning of an intense personal enmity between Arafat and Asad.

Rise to Power The period following the ARAB-ISRAELI WAR OF 1967 witnessed the emergence of Arafat as the leader of the Palestinian national movement. By discrediting the Arab regimes, the 1967 Arab defeat put Arafat on the path of implementing Fatah's strategy, "Revolution Until Victory." In Arafat's view, revolution did not mean an organized movement with an ideology aimed at changing the socioeconomic order but rather a movement dedicated to armed struggle until the total liberation of Palestine was achieved. Arafat's strategy of armed struggle put him on a collision course with the governments of Jordan and Lebanon. Initially, however, he focused on the Palestinian territories occupied by Israel in June 1967, moving secretly to the West Bank to determine whether conditions were ripe for the kind of guerrilla activities he had in mind. He had to start almost from scratch because there was no existing organizational infrastructure on which to build. While Arafat was in the West Bank, one of the first steps he took was to set up an organizational base in the old quarter of NABLUS, a West Bank town with a long history of nationalist struggle. Immediately after the war of June 1967, Arafat tried to organize a popular armed revolution in the Israeli-occupied West Bank and Gaza. However, the Palestinians in the Occupied Territories were not ready for a revolution. They put their trust in the Arab governments, hoping that these governments would be able to liberate the Occupied Territories. Also the Israeli military government took extreme measures against suspected Fatah guerrillas and their sympathizers, demolishing their houses, imposing curfews, and in many instances torturing them. Thus, by the early part of 1968, Arafat was compelled to flee the West Bank and turn east to Jordan, where he embarked on establishing operational bases for recruiting guerrillas and mounting hit-and-run raids against Israel.

In Jordan, Palestinian refugee camps proved to be Arafat's main source of recruits. Thanks primarily to camp volunteers, there were by 1970 a total of between 30,000 and 50,000 Palestinian guerrillas in Jordan, most of whom were Fatah loyalists and therefore under the command of Arafat. One event in particular provided Arafat an opportunity to win large numbers of recruits. On March 21, 1968, the Israelis launched a major attack against al-Karama, a Jordanian village where Arafat established the core of Fatah's command network. Supported by the Jordanian army, Fatah's defense of al-Karama put Arafat and Fatah on the political map of the Middle East. Arab governments began to pay more attention to Arafat, who was named as Fatah's spokesman in the spring of 1968. In recognition of Arafat's new authority, Nasir included him as part of an Egyptian delegation that visited the SOVIET UNION in the summer of 1968.

Fatah's soaring popularity after the battle of al-Karama entailed other benefits for Arafat. Significantly, at the February 1969 session of the PNC, Fatah and other Palestinian guerrilla groups used their new power and prestige to oust the old-guard politicians, discredited by their inaction and subordination to Arab regimes. Arafat was elected chairman of the Executive Committee, a PLO policy-making body that wielded de facto power since its full-time members were elected by the PNC. As a result, the PLO was then under the control of the guerrilla organizations. A new era in the Palestinian struggle for national independence had dawned, and Arafat was its principal figure.

With Arafat's new leadership came serious challenges, such as uniting the various guerrilla groups that were inclined to take decisions independently of the PLO, sometimes even contrary to its policy. Arafat recognized this diversity and preferred to create a broad front that would incorporate these groups. Thanks primarily to his efforts and to the efforts of the Fatah leadership, the PLO became by the late 1960s the apparatus that brought together various Palestinian guerrilla groups. Although Arafat never was able to unite all these groups, he succeeded in putting together a coalition of forces that was strong enough to take charge of various aspects of Palestinian life in the diaspora. His charisma and his bargaining skills were among his strongest assets. He galvanized the Palestinian masses, and, with the help of his political skills, he achieved consensus among diverse political forces. The consensus was never permanent, but for many years it helped maintain a reasonable degree of stability and equilibrium within the PLO.

Arafat convinced the PNC to adopt the core ideology of Fatah, namely, the belief that the Palestinians had to articulate their own vision of their political future. This was the thrust of the political program of the fourth PNC, which convened in Cairo, Egypt, in July 1968. Arafat was also instrumental in strengthening Fatah's hold on the PLO and its political organs, including the Executive Committee, the Central Council, the Palestine Liberation Army, and the Palestine Armed Struggle Command (PASC), a military police organization originally created in Jordan in 1969. A key ingredient of the PLO strategy was to knit together diaspora Palestinians and mobilize them behind the struggle for national independence.

Meanwhile Arafat had to prevent a military confrontation between the Palestinian guerrillas and the Jordanian regime. The activities of radical Palestinian organizations, particularly GEORGE HABASH'S POPULAR FRONT FOR THE LIBERATION OF PALESTINE (PFLP), put Arafat and the PLO on a collision course with the Jordanian government. With bases in Jordan after the 1967 war, the guerrillas became a state within a state, and radical Palestinian organizations challenged the Jordanian government, even calling for the overthrow of the Hashemite monarchy. The PFLP in the early part of September 1970 hijacked international airliners, including TWA and Swissair jets, and forced them to land at Dawson's Field, a strip of desert in Jordan. Also the PLO organized, with Arafat's approval, spectacular demonstrations in Jordan to protest the Egyptian and Jordanian acceptance of U.S. secretary of state William Rogers's 1970 peace plan, which called for the implementation of UNITED NATIONS SECURITY COUNCIL RESOLUTION 242 of November 1967. These developments created a crisis in the relations between the guerrilla groups and the Jordanian government. A bloody civil war, known as Black September (Aylul al-Aswad), ensued in September 1970, causing a major crisis for Arafat and the PLO leadership.

The PLO guerrillas were soundly defeated, and Arafat was forced to flee Jordan disguised in a Kuwaiti robe given to him by the crown prince of Kuwait, Shaykh Sa'd Abdullah al-Salim al-Sabah. Later, the Palestinian guerrillas who survived the Black September conflict left Jordan for Jabal al-Shaykh (Mount Hermon) in Syria. From there, they went to Lebanon after a series of crackdowns launched by the Jordanian state during 1971. Playing the TERRORISM card was one side of Arafat's response to the defeat in Jordan. The most striking example of the terror weapon was Arafat's tolerance for or endorsement of the sensational terrorist activities of the BLACK SEPTEMBER organization, which was a Fatah offshoot. Black September carried out the assassination of Wasfi al-Tall, the Jordanian prime minister, in Cairo on November 28, 1971, and the kidnapping and killing of members of the Israeli Olympic team in Munich, Germany, on September 5–6, 1972.

Arafat stayed in Lebanon between 1970 and 1982, where he organized Arab and international support for the PLO. In October 1974, the Rabat Summit Conference of Arab heads of state recognized the PLO as the sole legitimate representative of the Palestinian people. In November of the same year, the PLO was granted observer status at the United Nations. It later became a member of the nonaligned movement and of the Conference of Islamic States. By the end of the 1970s, the PLO was recognized as the legitimate representative of the Palestinian people by more than one hundred countries worldwide, with Arafat always playing the leading role in its diplomatic activities. While in Beirut, Arafat consulted his senior colleagues, particularly Salah Khalaf (Abu Iyyad) and Khalil al-Wazir (Abu Jihad). The presence of this trio created an informal system of checks and balances within the PLO decision-making process, thereby providing a sense of equilibrium. Within the context of this process, Arafat exchanged ideas with his colleagues, although he had the final say. He made decisions on the basis of his reading of the common denominator that held the different Palestinian groups together. Although Arafat was a leader who had mastered the art of consensus building, he was still subject to criticism for tolerating corruption and for selecting advisers on the basis of loyalty rather than merit. Over the years, patronage and tolerance for corruption proved to be among Arafat's principal instruments of political control and co-optation.

In his early days in Jordan and Lebanon, Arafat's outward appearance made a statement about his revolutionary credentials. He dressed in rumpled fatigues. He rarely shaved, arguing that shaving would take time and that he preferred to devote that time to the Palestinian cause. Arafat also wore his *kufiyya* (headdress) in a distinctive style that created the outline of the map of Palestine. When he addressed the General Assembly of the United Nations in November 1974, he removed his pistol but insisted on wearing his gun belt. To project an ascetic image, Arafat claimed that he was married to the cause of Palestine, and he always found it gratifying to be given names that suggested a revolutionary role, including the traditional Islamic Abu Ammar and characterizations like "Commander of the Palestinian Revolution," "Commander of the Striking Palestinian Forces," and "Chairman of the PLO Executive Committee." The image that Arafat's outward appearance was intended to project also reflected the Palestinian state of mind. In those years, many Palestinians saw liberation as coming out of the barrel of a gun. Thus, for them, Arafat's revolutionary image promised a remaking of their state of dispersal, a settling of the great score with Israel, and a revenge for the injuries inflicted on them since 1948.

From Armed Struggle to Diplomacy In the first decade of the post-1967 era, Arafat took two of the most important decisions of his life, decisions that represented the first phase of an evolution toward pragmatism in his attitude toward Israel. One was his endorsement in mid-1968 of the idea of a secular democratic state in Palestine in which all citizens, Jewish, Christian, and Muslim, would live together on the basis of the nonsectarian principles of democracy, equality, and mutual respect. The second decision was his adoption of a policy of "stages" (*marhaliyya*), that is, the policy of establishing a Palestinian state in the West Bank and Gaza as an interim solution pending the realization of the PLO objective of creating a secular democratic state. This new policy was first introduced in the twelfth PNC program of June 1974. Although the policy of "stages" was ambiguous with respect to ultimate PLO goals, it represented the first phase in the movement away from the earlier Revolution Until Victory strategy to one that employed diplomatic as well as military means to achieve less ambitious goals. To show his readiness for a negotiated settlement, Arafat in the autumn of 1973 sent signals both to the United States and to Israel through two senior aides, first through Dr. SA'ID HAMAMI, the PLO representative in London, and later through Dr. ISAM SARTAWI, a leading Palestinian activist. These signals, however, did not bring about a change in the position of the U.S. or Israeli governments, both of whom continued to reject the idea of dealing with the PLO.

Arafat also tried to gain Arab and international support for a political settlement with Israel. His first major success came at the Arab summit in Rabat, Morocco, in October 1974, which asserted the Palestinian people's right to establish their own independent state and recognized the PLO as the sole legitimate representative of the Palestinians. Arafat's second success was his participation in the U.N. General Assembly in New York in November 1974, the result of the collective efforts of the Arab and other developing nations, as well as of Western Europe, China, Japan, and the Soviet-led East European bloc. To register the international community's recognition of Arafat and the PLO, the U.N. General Assembly adopted in the fall of 1974 Resolution 3236, which recognized the right of the Palestinians to national independence and sovereignty, and Resolution 3237, which invited the PLO to participate in the sessions and work of the General Assembly as an observer.

Arafat's moderation put him at odds with a number of radical Palestinian organizations, particularly George Habash's PFLP. In the mid-1970s, Habash spearheaded the formation of the REJECTION FRONT to challenge Arafat's policy of accommodation with Israel. Arafat prevailed, thanks primarily to his charisma and the dominance of Fatah within the PLO. By the end of the 1970s, the Rejection Front was in disarray, divided by internal differences and by external Arab states who favored Arafat's preference for a diplomatic settlement.

In the Lebanese Quagmire The civil war that engulfed Lebanon in 1975 was perhaps Arafat's biggest challenge in the second half of the 1970s. Arafat found himself caught between the pressures of moderate Palestinians who wanted him to take a neutral stand and radical Palestinians who wanted Fatah to intervene in the internecine conflict. In the end, Arafat threw his weight behind the Lebanese Muslim and leftist alliance, thus shifting the balance in favor of the leftist forces in Lebanon. As a result, Syria, which traditionally had backed Fatah and the Lebanese left, intervened in Lebanon in the summer of 1976, launching an offensive against the Palestinian-leftist alliance, partly to prevent this alliance from toppling the existing Lebanese regime and thus giving Israel a pretext for intervention, but partly also to control the PLO and the Lebanese left. During the Palestinian-Syrian confrontation, right-wing Lebanese militias unleashed in June 1976 a massive assault against the Palestinian refugee camps at Tall al-Za'tar and Jisr al-Basha. After a brutal siege that lasted for nearly two months and resulted in the killing of at least fifteen hundred camp residents, Tall al-Za'tar fell, with the Syrian army sitting idle on the hilltops surrounding the camp. In these circumstances, Arafat's forces could do little to save the camp, which became a symbol of horror visited on Palestinian refugees in Lebanon. By October 1976, Arafat's military encounter with the Syrian forces in Lebanon ended through the efforts of Arab summits held in Riyadh and Cairo in the same month with the aim of ending the Lebanese civil war.

The civil war did not deflect Arafat's attention from the goal of consolidating the institutional presence of the PLO in Lebanon. Under his leadership, the PLO created a highly developed infrastructure that incorporated social, educational, and informational institutions responsible for dealing with the daily concerns of the Palestinian people in exile. Arafat was also instrumental in transforming the PLO fighters into a standing army outfitted with heavy weapons provided by the Soviet Union and the Eastern European bloc, as well as by Egypt, Syria, and a number of other Arab countries. Despite the PLO's involvement in the Lebanese civil war, Arafat continued his pursuit of a diplomatic settlement with Israel. He welcomed Soviet president Leonid Brezhnev's peace proposal of February 1981, which called for a comprehensive peace, a Palestinian state, and security guarantees for all states in the region, including Israel. Arafat also welcomed the August 1981 peace plan of Saudi crown prince Fahd (later King Fahd) who proposed an eight-point peace plan that called for the establishment of a Palestinian state in the West Bank and Gaza and implicitly recognized Israel within its pre-1967 borders.

The event that created overwhelming problems for Arafat and the PLO was the Camp David agreement of 1978, which culminated in the Egyptian-Israeli peace treaty of 1979. Arafat and the PLO strongly opposed the treaty because it led to the withdrawal of Egypt from the Arab confrontation front, thus weakening the Palestinians by weighting the balance of power more heavily in favor of Israel. The treaty helped make it possible for Israel to invade Lebanon in 1982, an invasion that resulted in the destruction of the PLO infrastructure in the country.

At the height of the war, Arafat led the defense of Beirut during an Israeli siege of eighty-eight days. Throughout the siege, Arafat gathered about himself the secretary-generals of the non-Fatah guerrilla groups to help him make critical decisions, including the most painful and difficult decision of August 1982 to evacuate Beirut. Arafat and his group of Palestinian colleagues felt they had no alternative but to leave the Lebanese capital. The resources at their disposal were no match for those of the Israeli military, who threw into the battle of Beirut one of the world's most sophisticated military machines against an overwhelmingly civilian population whose defenders wielded only hand-held weapons. Thus, by September 1, 1982, Arafat was leading the evacuation of about 10,000 Palestinian fighters from Beirut to Yemen, Sudan, and elsewhere in the Arab world. Arafat himself went to Tunis, where he set up his new headquarters. Despite this setback, and despite the subsequent massacre of hundreds of Palestinian refugees in the Sabra and Shatila camps, Arafat's leadership of the battle of Beirut enhanced his prestige within the Palestinian resistance movement and among the Palestinians in general (see SABRA AND SHATILA MASSACRE).

The most serious problem to emerge after the Lebanon war was the trouble between Arafat and the Syrian government, partly over the PLO's criticism of what it saw as Syria's insufficient participation in the Lebanon battles, but more importantly, over Arafat's insistence on maintaining the PLO's independence, as demonstrated by his efforts to coordinate his diplomatic moves with Jordan and Saudi Arabia. These moves inspired Syria's fears that it might be left out of whatever diplomatic steps might be taken to bring about an Arab-Israeli settlement. Many pro-Syrian members of the PLO, including Nimr Salih, a cofounder of Fatah and a member of its Central Committee, expressed similar fears, arguing that Arafat might strike a deal with Israel in cooperation with Jordan, a country whose government the Syrians mistrusted.

Against this background, Fatah dissidents in Lebanon rebelled against Arafat with Syrian backing in May 1983, accusing him of failing to make the necessary military preparations during the Israeli invasion. One month later, the Syrian government expelled Arafat from Damascus. This stiffened Arafat's resolve to assert PLO independence vis-à-vis Syria and to discredit the pro-Syrian dissidents who had rebelled against him. In December 1983, after regrouping his supporters in Lebanon, Arafat traveled in disguise to Tripoli, Lebanon, via Cyprus, risking being captured or killed by the Israeli gunboats patrolling the area. Outgunned by the Fatah dissidents who enjoyed Syrian support, Arafat left Tripoli in December 1983 after refusing to accept Syrian dominance of the PLO and after discrediting the Fatah rebels, who were viewed by most Palestinians as tools of the Syrian state.

In the aftermath of these events, Arafat revised his diplomatic strategy in the hope of achieving a breakthrough with Israel. The essence of the new strategy was rapprochement with Egypt and Jordan, a diplomatic process that intensified the animosity between Arafat and Syrian president Hafiz al-Asad. Thus, upon his forced departure by sea from Tripoli on December 20, 1983, Arafat stopped in Egypt, where two days later he met with Egyptian president Husni Mubarak. This was Arafat's first visit there since 1977, when Egyptian president Anwar al-Sadat had embarked on a diplomatic course that led to formal peace between Egypt and Israel. From Arafat's perspective, the rapprochement with Egypt made sense at this point. Egypt had supported Arafat during 1982 and 1983; strategically, moreover, the move toward Egypt was consistent with Arafat's desire to formulate a common peace strategy with Jordan's King Husayn, a strategy aimed at reaching a peaceful settlement with Israel.

The Jordanian component of Arafat's revised strategy was the culmination of a move toward pragmatism that had gathered momentum in September 1982, when Arafat accepted the Fez peace plan articulated by the Arab heads of state. The Fez plan called for the creation of a Palestinian state and for Israeli withdrawal from all the Arab territories occupied in 1967. Although borders were not explicitly delineated, a Palestinian state limited to the West Bank and Gaza was clearly implied in the

Fez plan. In line with his efforts to strengthen ties with Jordan, Arafat focused on achieving the sanction of popular legitimacy for a new relationship with King Husayn. Toward that end, Arafat tried to work within the framework of the PNC. In its seventeenth session of November 1984, the PNC called for an independent Palestinian state in confederation with Jordan.

In one important sense, Arafat's strategy toward Jordan was meant as a concession to both Israel and the United States, given King Husayn's acceptability to the two governments as a negotiating partner. It was also a concession to Egypt, which had been encouraging Jordanian-Palestinian coordination and which had become a strategic ally of Arafat in the wake of Israel's invasion of Lebanon. The Jordanian dimension of Arafat's strategy, however, did not yield the desired results; in February 1986, King Husayn abrogated the 1985 Amman Agreement, which had called for a joint Jordanian-Palestinian delegation in peace talks.

Arafat's policies after his expulsion from Lebanon were unacceptable in some Palestinian circles. For example, the Fatah rebels, grouped together in the National Alliance, as well as the Palestinian groups organized into a coalition known as the Democratic Alliance (most notably the groups of George Habash and NAYIF HAWATIMA), openly challenged Arafat. Reconciliation with the Egyptian government at a time when most of the Arab world ostracized it because of its separate peace treaty with Israel was unacceptable to Arafat's critics. So was reconciliation with Jordan, since many Palestinians were still alienated from King Husayn as a result of his crackdown against the Palestinian resistance in 1970–71.

Thus, one consequence of the 1982 war was the polarization of Palestinian relations. On one side stood the more powerful group led by Arafat and the core group in the Fatah Central Committee; on the other stood the anti-Arafat Fatah rebels and their supporters in other radical Palestinian groups. Arafat, who had a decisive political lead and who exercised exclusive control over PLO finances, was now more inclined to abandon the principle of consensus in favor of majority rule. In one sense, this was a positive development, because it signified a movement away from the immobility of the pre-1982 era, when a minority in the framework of the PLO could paralyze the decision-making process by opposing a proposed policy. In another sense, the majority-rule approach meant Arafat's willingness to abandon the coalition tactics of the past and move toward concentrating all decision-making powers in his own hands.

After he was forced to leave Beirut, Arafat's operational base became his suitcase and a small executive plane put at his disposal by some friendly Arab state, such as Egypt or Saudi Arabia. For this reason, he was nicknamed "the modern Bedouin"; he and his close associates frequently described themselves as "revolutionaries on a flying carpet." In addition, leaving Beirut caused Arafat's focus to shift gradually from diaspora Palestinians to the Gaza and West Bank Palestinians, whose overriding priority was to get rid of Israeli occupation and establish a ministate in their Occupied Territories. In contrast, the main aspiration of diaspora Palestinians was to return to those parts of Palestine that had been seized by Israel in 1948. In this context, Arafat had to weigh the differing needs and outlooks of the two elements of his constituency. The fact that he made the West Bank and Gaza the core ingredient of his diplomatic strategy put him on the defensive vis-à-vis diaspora Palestinians. At the same time, however, Arafat's new approach had far broader support among the Palestinians living in Gaza and the West Bank, as was made clear in the victories won by his supporters in student council and union elections in the Occupied Territories in the mid-1980s and thereafter.

Several factors sustained Arafat after 1982, enabling him to stay at the helm as a symbol of Palestinian nationalism, an indication of the will to continue the struggle. The Palestinians needed a leader, and Arafat's charisma, revolutionary past, and tactical skills helped him maintain his primacy within the PLO leadership. Besides evading the long arm of the Israeli Mossad and other hostile intelligence services, Arafat survived an Israeli air raid on the PLO headquarters in Tunis in October 1985 and a plane crash in the Libyan desert in April 1992.

At the same time, in the five years following the Israeli invasion of Lebanon, Arafat and the Palestinian cause were relegated to a secondary status in regional and international politics. This was exemplified by the Arab summit conference held in

Amman in November 1987. The summit came as a rude shock to the Palestinians, not only because of the somewhat offhand treatment of Arafat by the Arab leaders but because, for the first time in Arab summit history, the Palestine question was virtually ignored. Instead, Arab leaders focused their attention on the Iran-Iraq war, specifically on helping Iraq win the war and contain Iran.

The Intifada Scarcely a month later, the Palestinian uprising (INTIFADA) against the Israeli occupation began on a mass scale in the West Bank and Gaza. The uprising changed the political equations and catapulted Arafat to the forefront of regional and international politics. Consequently Arafat followed a two-pronged strategy. On the one hand, he moved to make the uprising an arm of the PLO. The PLO outside the West Bank and Gaza provided the strategic framework for the resistance in the Occupied Territories, while grass-roots activists in the territories coordinated the day-to-day activities of the uprising. These activists, represented by the United National Leadership of the Uprising (UNLU), accepted Arafat's leadership. On the other hand, Arafat adopted a more moderate position, hoping to set the stage for a dialogue with the United States with the goal that such a dialogue would lead to negotiations with Israel.

In this regard, a number of steps stand out as significant aspects of Arafat's strategy. In November 1988, he mobilized all resources at his disposal to convince the nineteenth PNC to adopt the Palestinian Declaration of Independence. The declaration, together with the political program that accompanied it, explicitly spelled out the principle of Palestinian statehood, whose source of legitimacy was the U.N. General Assembly Partition Resolution 181 (II) of 1947. This principle, as understood by Arafat in 1988, implied a peaceful settlement with an Israel contained within its pre-1967 borders: that is, the territory of the Palestinian state that Arafat conceived would be confined to Gaza and the West Bank. On December 13, 1988, the U.N. General Assembly convened a special session in Geneva to hear Arafat's address, after the U.S. State Department had refused him a visa the previous month, and thus prevented him from addressing the Assembly at the U.N. headquarters in New York.

The day after his speech in Geneva, Arafat stated more explicitly his acceptance of U.N. Security Council Resolution 242 and reaffirmed his renunciation of terrorism and his acceptance of the right of Israel to exist. On the same day, the U.S. government authorized the opening of a "substantive dialogue" with the PLO. Since 1975, the U.S. government had pledged to Israel that it would not recognize or negotiate with the PLO unless the PLO acknowledged Israel's right to exist and accepted Resolution 242. By accepting the U.S. condition, Arafat demonstrated the flexibility that enhanced his position as a key player in Middle Eastern politics, thus disappointing once again those who wrote his political obituary in 1982. Therefore, by the end of the 1980s, Arafat's leadership of the PLO was reconsolidated. His acceptance of a Palestinian state alongside Israel, not as a transitional stage, but as a final goal, was now explicit and complete. The Revolution Until Victory strategy was a thing of the past.

Despite his dominance, Arafat was hesitant to press his advantage as leader in critical moments. For example, in the spring of 1990, the PALESTINE LIBERATION FRONT (PLF) of MUHAMMAD ABBAS (Abu al-Abbas), technically a member of the PLO, mounted an abortive seaborne attack on Israel in violation of the PLO's December 1988 commitment not to engage in terrorism. Arafat chose not to discipline Abu al-Abbas, thus causing the U.S. government to suspend its dialogue with the PLO. This was a serious diplomatic setback for Arafat, who had worked so hard to secure at least the appearance of a de facto recognition by the United States.

Arafat's management of Palestinian politics after Iraq's seizure of Kuwait on August 2, 1990, also demonstrated his hesitancy during critical events. Although Arafat did not condone the occupation of Kuwait, he supported Iraq, a serious miscalculation, because it caused the isolation of the PLO and the dispossession of the Palestinian community in Kuwait. In one sense, Arafat's support for Iraq was a function of his frustration with the U.S. government, his belief that the concessions he had made in November and December of 1988 had not changed the U.S. and Israeli positions on the Palestinian question: indeed, it seemed that no matter what position he might take toward Iraq, the U.S. and Israeli policies would remain unchanged.

In a more important sense, however, Arafat's support for Iraq was shaped by the popular enthusiasm for Iraq among the Palestinian masses. In this important matter, Arafat was a follower, not a leader, of public opinion. Although Arafat's pro-Iraq policy resulted in the loss of critical financial and diplomatic support for the PLO, he managed to reemerge in late 1991.

Peace Process When the MADRID PEACE CONFERENCE began under the administration of President George Bush in October 1991, Arafat showed the flexibility needed to get the Palestinians included in the process despite the opposition of the Israeli prime minister, Yitzhak Shamir. To circumvent Shamir's opposition, Arafat dropped his previous insistence on the right of the PLO to participate directly in a Middle East peace conference, allowing the Palestinians to be represented by non-PLO delegates from Gaza and the West Bank, excluding East Jerusalem. These delegates were technically half of a Jordanian-Palestinian delegation, but Arafat was involved directly in their selection. Arafat also micromanaged the delegates' negotiations with Israel from his headquarters in Tunis.

Shortly after Yitzhak Rabin became Israel's prime minister in the summer of 1992, the Israeli Knesset repealed the ban on contacts with the PLO, and the first round of secret Israeli-PLO talks was held in Sarpsborg, Norway, with Rabin's consent. Arafat directed the Palestinian team that conducted the secret talks, in the process exchanging letters with Rabin via Israeli officials and PALESTINIAN CITIZENS OF ISRAEL. After eight rounds of secret talks, the last five of which were held in Oslo, Norway, the Israeli and Palestinian negotiators agreed to the Declaration of Principles (DOP) or the OSLO AGREEMENTS. The DOP, unanimously approved by the Israeli cabinet on August 30, 1993, was followed ten days later by letters of mutual recognition between Arafat and Rabin. On September 13, 1993, Arafat and Rabin shook hands at the DOP signing ceremony on the White House lawn. This watershed in the history of the Palestinian-Israeli conflict, hailed by most observers as an unprecedented breakthrough, alienated some Palestinians from Arafat. The alienation did not spring so much from opposition to peace with Israel as from what was seen as Arafat's growing tendency to make individual rather than collective decisions. Arafat's critics were particularly angered by the secrecy with which he negotiated the DOP, without the involvement or even the knowledge of PLO policymaking bodies.

Other aspects of Arafat's strategy were also a source of unhappiness, especially for diaspora Palestinians. By making the West Bank and Gaza the central focus of his agreement with Israel, Arafat lost standing among diaspora Palestinians, who believed that their role and their interests had been ignored. The DOP was followed by other agreements, most notably the Cairo agreement of May 1994, the agreement of August 1995 on the expansion of Palestinian self-rule in the West Bank, the HEBRON protocol in January 1997, and the Wye Plantation memorandum of October 1998. Arafat's critics inside and outside the West Bank and Gaza asserted that these agreements flatly contradicted the principle of Palestinian self-determination, that Arafat was making unreciprocated concessions to Israel, and that he was making unnecessary sacrifices to curry favor with Israel and the United States.

After entering the West Bank town of JERICHO in June 1994 to start the process of transition to Palestinian self-rule, Arafat had to develop a framework for economic and political governance. Although Arafat was instrumental in the launching of a parastatal government known as the PALESTINIAN AUTHORITY (PA) in the summer of 1994, he did not have a clearly defined approach to self-government. Four factors account for this: (1) his lack of experience in building state institutions since he had spent most of his life working with structures to promote national independence; (2) the organizational requirements of the postliberation phase, which were drastically different from those of the revolutionary phase; (3) the limited resources available to the PA, especially the debilitated physical, legal, and administrative infrastructures that Arafat inherited from the Israeli occupation authorities; and (4) the failure of Israel to provide the PA with the necessary information on the existing civil administration that the Israeli occupation authorities had created in the West Bank and Gaza. Despite these constraints, Arafat and the managers of the PA set up a number of functioning institutions, such as the police, the security apparatus, and the Ministry of Education.

To a great degree, the PA institutions that Arafat helped create were dominated by his trusted followers. In the post-DOP period, Arafat continued to put a particularly high premium on political loyalty, and the top elite group from among whom he filled senior PA positions were largely Fatah people loyal to him. Loyalty also determined the selection process. Thus it was difficult for the best-qualified Palestinians to reach the top political and administrative posts. Moreover, many of Arafat's appointees were corrupt. Arafat also concentrated power in his own hands, isolating himself in the process from talented Palestinians whose expertise could have enabled him to run the PA more effectively. He often used underhanded procedures, misleading assertions, and harsh language as instruments of political manipulation and control. Occasionally, he was moody and prone to angry outbursts. Further, Arafat tolerated corrupt practices and human rights violations in the areas that came under his control. As a result, the question of political reform became a top priority for Palestinian intellectuals and political activists.

Three factors account for Arafat's increasing reliance on an individual style of leadership after 1982: (1) the loss of Beirut as a political base had led to the dispersal of the PLO leadership and its institutions, thus eliminating the structures that had mitigated Arafat's natural propensity toward autocracy; (2) the informal system of checks and balances of the 1970s and 1980s was destroyed with the assassinations of PLO military leader Khalil as-Wazir in April 1988 and political leader Salah Khalaf in January 1991, two major figures who provided an equilibrium in the PLO's decision-making process; (3) Arafat's desperate search for opportunities to create a deal with Israel in the aftermath of the GULF CRISIS, 1990–91, led him to bypass PLO institutions and ignore the variety of views within the organization.

✦ ✦ ✦

Taken together, the episodes in Arafat's life reveal something about the man. Arafat was a Palestinian patriot in an age of pan-Arabism, a dreamer who wanted to liberate all of Palestine when the Arab states, whose support he needed, were looking for ways to reach a compromise settlement with Israel, a pragmatist in a period during which the forces of radicalism were on the rise, and an autocrat in a society with democratic aspirations. To look at Arafat's record is to come to terms with the drama, and ultimately with the limits, of Arafat's journey. The personal dimension looks impressive: from the military cell of armed resistance to participation in pompous ceremonies at the White House lawn; from a long and bitter war with Israel to sharing of the Nobel Peace Prize with Israeli prime minister Yitzhak Rabin and foreign minister Shimon Peres in December 1994; from marriage to the Palestine cause to marriage in 1990 to Suha al-Tawil, an urbane Christian Palestinian woman who was almost thirty-five years his junior and with whom he had a daughter, Zahwa, in 1995.

In the latter part of the 1990s, the dream of creating an independent Palestinian state was still far from being realized. The status of Palestinian refugees was still in limbo. The Palestinian economy deteriorated even further in the aftermath of Oslo, primarily as a result of Israeli-imposed closures of the West Bank and Gaza and Israeli economic protectionism. Israeli settlements in the West Bank were expanding.

These developments led many observers to argue that Arafat had very few concrete results to show for over four decades of Palestinian struggle and sacrifice. Yet, Arafat believed in Palestinian nationalism and fought for it. He inspired and directed the reawakening of this nationalism. He helped transform the Palestinians from a community of scattered refugees dependent on Arab governments to a people determined to rely on its own limited resources in the struggle for national independence. He was also instrumental in attracting many Palestinians to the path of armed struggle, thus enabling the PLO to become a principal contestant after the 1967 Arab defeat.

One result was that Palestinian nationalism became an established fact whose legitimacy was acknowledged by the international community, including a large number of Israelis. Despite its shortcomings, the peace offensive launched by the PLO under Arafat's leadership led in the mid- and late 1990s to at least one important result: the acquisition of a territorial base, small as it was, for the advancement of the goals of Palestinian nationalism. By firmly entrenching the PLO's presence in Gaza and the West Bank, this development also led to the virtual elimination of Jordan's influence in the Palestinian territories. Using the carrot and the stick, Arafat weakened the infrastructure of

Palestinian groups opposed to his peace strategy—curtailing as a result their ability to expand their base of support.

Arafat was a strong believer in the right of the Palestinians to make their own decisions in matters pertaining to their future. He was careful to cultivate relationships in Arab countries with different political systems and political orientations. This delicate balancing act was rendered feasible by his ideological moderation, and it did help him cope with some difficult challenges, for example, the 1970 showdown with the Jordanian government and the showdown with the Syrian government in Lebanon six years later.

Arafat was a statesman. When he realized in the aftermath of the 1973 Arab-Israeli war that a radical change in Palestinian policy toward Israel was a national necessity, he led and directed a Palestinian peace offensive that made possible the Oslo breakthrough of 1993. Arafat responded to the need for change and gave the change his own color and style, always moving in a gradual manner, partly to scrutinize the political fallout after every gesture that he made to Israel, and partly to prepare the Palestinians for painful compromises.

Muhammad Muslih

BIBLIOGRAPHY

Abu Iyad (Abu Iyyad) with Eric Rouleau. *My Home My Land.* New York: Times Books, 1981.

Brand, Laurie A. *Palestinians in the Arab World: Institution Building and the Search for State.* New York: Columbia University Press, 1988.

Brynen, Rex. *Sanctuary and Survival: The PLO in Lebanon.* Boulder, colo.: Westview Press, 1990.

Cobban, Helena. *The Palestinian Liberation Organization: People, Power and Politics.* Cambridge, England: Cambridge University Press, 1984.

Growers, Andrew Walker, Tony. *Behind the Myth: Yasir Arafat and the Palestinian Revolution.* London: Corgi Books, 1990.

Hart, Alan. *Arafat: Terrorist or Peacemaker?* Bloomington: Indiana University Press, 1984.

——. *Arafat: A Political Biography.* Bloomington: Indiana University Press, 1989.

Hirst, David. *The Gun and the Olive Branch.* London: Faber and Faber, 1977.

Kelman, Herbert. "Talk to Arafat." *Foreign Policy* 49 (Winter 1982–1983).

Khalidi, Rashid. *Under Siege: P.L.O. Decision Making during the 1982 War.* New York: Columbia University Press, 1986.

Khalidi, Walid. *Conflict and Violence in Lebanon: Confrontation in the Middle East.* Cambridge, Mass.: Harvard University Press, 1979.

Kiernan, Thomas. *Arafat: The Man and the Myth.* New York: W.W. Norton, 1976.

Lesh, Ann Moseley. *Political Perceptions of the Palestinians on the West Bank and the Gaza Strip.* Washington, D.C.: Middle East Institute, 1980.

Mahran, Rashida. "*Arafat, a Key Personality*" (published in series form in Arabic). Kuwait, *Al-Ra'i al-Amm,* January 1987.

Makovsky, David. *Making Peace with the PLO: The Rabin Government's Road to the Oslo Accord.* Washington, D.C.: The Washington Institute for Near East Policy, 1996.

Mattar, Philip. "The PLO and the Gulf Crisis." *The Middle East Journal* 48(1) (winter 1994): 31–47.

Muslih, Muhammad. *Toward Coexistence: An Analysis of the Resolutions of the Palestine National Council.* Washington, D.C.: The Institute for Palestine Studies, 1990.

Rubinstein, Danny. *The Mystery of Arafat.* South Royalton, Vt.: Steerforth Press, 1995.

Sayigh, Rosemary. *Too Many Enemies: The Palestinian Experience in Lebanon.* London: Zed Books, 1994.

Wallach, Janet, and John Wallach. *Arafat: In the Eyes of the Beholder.* New York: Lyle Stuart, 1990.

Ya'ari, Ehud. *Strike Terror: The Story of Fatah.* New York: Sabra, 1970.

Archaeology

Palestine has almost unlimited cultural resources, most of which are preserved underground. These resources are uncovered and made available through archaeology, an academic discipline that begins with the systematic excavation of the primary data, which often reflect the thought and action of ancestors. All over the world this nonrenewable resource is controlled and protected by governments as public property, because it documents the past lifeways of the descendant population. In a word, it tells the story of the country.

At least four forces have contributed to the version of the Palestine story generally accepted by most Westerners today. First, the biblical tradition, as interpreted by Western Christian nations to educate their youth in the Judeo-Christian heritage, has shaped the canonical Palestine story for the Anglo-American and European world. Second, European rivalry for control of the Levant in general and Palestine in particular generated a considerable knowledge of the region in order to serve

Western military, economic, and cultural needs; the data gathered to this end have been used to amplify the canonical story. Third, the decimation of the native Palestinian population in order to provide a home for Jewish refugees from European persecution lent further support to the canonical story, although leading Palestinian intellectuals forcefully reject that story as a justification of their ejection from their homeland. Fourth, the concealment of the Palestinian patrimony (material evidence) through the confiscation of Arab cultural resources by Israelis (such as the large library of Dr. Tawfiq Canaan in 1948, and the Palestine Archaeological Museum and its library in JERUSALEM in 1967), as well as the destruction of cultural property in the form of entire villages in 1948–49, have been undertaken to destroy Palestinians' claims on the past while further supporting the Western Judeo-Christian version of history. This last is particularly crucial, since the Palestinians' link to their past is largely through the villages, towns, and cities that predominated in their land during the last thirteen centuries.

Clearly the fact that much of the archaeological activity in Palestine has been carried out by Western scholars in search of evidence to support and illustrate the Bible has had significant ramifications. In effect, one of the primary resources of the country has been exploited to construct, support, or embellish the "history" of Palestine—in other words, the "archaeological record" has been selectively used to document and sometimes defend the version of the past required by Christian and Jewish Zionists to justify the occupation of Palestine. One result of this Western dominance of the archaeology of Palestine—continued by the Israelis, for whom the thirteen centuries of Arab presence and cultural impress are peripheral—has been the alienation of the native Muslim and Christian Palestinians from their own cultural past. As a consequence, it has been difficult for the Palestinians to encourage archaeologists and historians to generate an unabridged story to include an account of the Arab contribution to the cultural history of Palestine.

The Archaeology of Palestine as a Construction of Western Christians Several intellectual traditions have converged to form the study of the past that we today call archaeology. One powerful stimulus was the Renaissance revival of the Greco-Roman classical tradition in the plastic arts and architecture. A second source was the eighteenth- and nineteenth-century development of the science of geology, out of which three concepts important for archaeology emerged: stratigraphy, prehistory, and uniformitarianism. The association of stone tools and "human" remains in sealed deposits led to the discovery of the antiquity of hominids, and thus prehistory. This inevitably led to the view that the natural forces that created the sediments forming the landscape we know today are still at work, so that an understanding of today provides the key for interpreting the natural events of the past.

Applying this rule to cultural change is far more difficult than applying it to natural change. Nevertheless, early attempts to understand the parallel existence of preliterate and literate societies, farmers, and hunter-gatherers grew out of uniformitarian assumptions. All of these developments in the field of archaeology occurred in Europe at a time when the people of Palestine were suffering the consequences of Ottoman weakness. The "Arab awakening" did not occur until the late nineteenth century. Thus from the beginning, archaeology was shaped by European assumptions.

With its basic intellectual components established by the beginning of the nineteenth century, archaeology moved to the Middle East. European nations, particularly England and France, explored their own cultural origins through the search for biblical connections to the Holy Land while vying for position in the collapsing Ottoman Empire. The process began in 1798 with Napoleon Bonaparte's failed expedition to Egypt, which included a host of savants who published the monumental *Description de l'Égypte* in nineteen massive folio volumes (1809–28). The process continued in Mesopotamia with the collection of what turned out to be Assyrian art treasures from mounds in the Mosul area by Paul Emile Botta (1802–70) and Austin Henry Layard (1817–94). In the course of these expeditions, Europe discovered evidence of the several high cultures in the Middle East, many predating biblical history.

By the end of the nineteenth century, the ancient Near East was divided into numerous specialized fields of study dealing with the language, literature, and archaeology of each area. The physical remains of Arab cultures were often expropriated by Europeans; the assumption was that the living populations of Mesopotamia, Anatolia, and Egypt were not sufficiently educated to appreciate their own heritage. Indeed, Westerners laid claim to ancient Near Eastern cultural treasures as *their* heritage rather than that of the peasants and town dwellers of the nineteenth-century Middle East. This was particularly ironic since by then, European scholars saw that Europe was a cultural cross between Athens and Jerusalem and that the foundations of Athens and Jerusalem had been laid by the high cultures of the ancient Near East.

Not surprisingly then the archaeology of Palestine has been dominated by what has been called "biblical archaeology." British, American, German, and French archaeological involvement there had been generated by the Bible. Most archaeologists were biblical scholars, except the British, for whom the Bible was the "national epic": since the geography of the Bible was more familiar to them than that of Europe, no special training was required. When one examines the journals devoted to the archaeology of Palestine, most of them beginning in the late nineteenth century, the clear emphasis is on biblical background and interpretation. This emphasis continues: since 1967 Jerusalem has become the center of biblical archaeology. The first International Congress on Biblical Archaeology was held there in 1984, celebrating the seventieth anniversary of the Israel Exploration Society (formerly the Jewish Palestine Exploration Society).

Once established, archaeology began to collect masses of new data that, in Palestine at least, began to be confused. Indeed, it has not been easy to define the boundaries of the rather amorphous study of "biblical archaeology" since the seminal work of W. F. Albright (1891–1971), who saw the biblical world as encompassing virtually the entire Middle East. Albright incorporated many disciplines, thus cementing his all-encompassing view of biblical archaeology.

For example, in his publication of the Tall Bayt Mirsim excavation (1932–43), Albright put order into the sequence of pottery types by a rigorous application of topological methods. But it was not until 1952, when Kathleen Kenyon (1906–78) introduced into Palestine stratigraphic methods for excavating natural deposits, that it was possible to order with confidence the layers of tells in Palestine. Since that time there have been constant refinements in field methods and recording. But these developments have had little bearing on the motivations for excavation in Palestine, which remained for the most part tied to biblical connections.

Five foreign schools of archaeology operated in Jerusalem prior to World War I: French, American, German, British, and Italian. It was the British, however, who dominated the archaeology of Palestine. In the fifty years between 1864 and 1914, the British were responsible for ten excavations and two important surveys; the Germans were responsible for six excavations, and the Americans only one. Of these, the most important—important insofar as they developed the fundamental procedures of fieldwork that were later refined and have endured—was probably the work of Flinders Petrie at Tall al-Hasi in 1890 and George Reisner at Sebastia between 1908 and 1910.

During this period, Palestine was a province of the Ottoman Empire. Permission to excavate required a *firman* (decree) from the sultan in Istanbul. In the judgment of one of Palestine's early excavators, "the principle under which Turkish permits were issued was based on the sound principle . . . that national monuments must not be removed from the country . . . their possession must remain with the people of the country whose they are." In view of the Ottomans' demonstrated lack of interest in the population of Palestine, this statement requires many qualifiers. Nevertheless, when compared to what happened to Palestine and its past under Britain's PALESTINE MANDATE, some small virtue may yet be reserved for Ottoman rule.

British Rule 1917–1948 After World War I, the story of archaeology in Palestine was similar to that in other parts of the colonized Middle East—with one significant difference. In Iraq, Syria, and Jordan the Arabs gained independence from the British and French. In these countries, government agencies had been established during the Mandates to preserve, excavate, publish, and exhibit the material cultural remains of national pasts. These agencies, as well as the governments themselves, were staffed by Arabs. It was, to say the least, anomalous that a similar pattern did not occur in Palestine. To be sure, there was a Department of Antiquities, established in 1920 just prior to the Mandate, which was staffed by Britons, Palestinians, and Jews. But—and this is a significant difference—there was no serious effort by Mandate authorities to train and encourage Palestinian archaeologists to become professionals. The burden of the Mandate was the commitment to encourage such circumstances as would facilitate the creation of a Jewish national home.

Jewish immigrants to Palestine, many of whom had received part or all of their education in Europe, where archaeology had evolved, found the discipline of archaeology intellectually congenial and, from a nationalistic point of view, essential to establishing their right to the land. In archaeology, as in other domains, development within the Jewish community was handled by the Jews themselves, and Jews maintained their own separate institutions. Thus, the Jewish Palestine Exploration Society had been founded in 1914 by Nahum Slouschz; the society's first excavation took place in 1921–22, at Hammath-Tiberias. By 1928, E. L. Sukenik was head of the Archaeology Department of Hebrew University, which had opened its doors in 1925.

For the Palestinian population, still a three-quarters majority, there was no association or institution supporting archaeology. The only possibilities for Arabs to influence this study of their homeland lay in the British Mandate's Department of Antiquities and the British School of Archaeology in Jerusalem, and these possibilities were slim indeed. As early as 1920, the latter institution was already "making active preparation for the training of archaeologists. . . . No modern religious or political question will be allowed to affect the policy of the School . . . which is conceived on the broadest lines in an organized effort to cope with the existing national need." The "national need" must have been British, however: no Arab students benefited from this educational opportunity.

That the British were deeply interested in the archaeology of Palestine is evident from the immediate organization, as early as 1919, of a British School of Archaeology in Jerusalem and a Department of Antiquities for Palestine. These two organizations occupied the same building until 1930, though by 1926 the directorates were separated. From 1930 until after World War II, the British School of Archaeology was housed with the American School of Oriental Research. As for the Department of Antiquities, the director as well as the Advisory Board were appointed by the high commissioner from the British, French, American, and Italian schools of archaeology in Jerusalem. Two Palestinians and two Jews were also appointed to represent the interests of Muslim and Jewish cultural heritage. The department was organized into five subunits: inspectors, a records office and library, a conservation laboratory, a photographic studio, and the Palestine Museum. This last, the building of which was dedicated in 1938, had been established through a gift of $2 million (half for the building and half for the endowment) received by the Department of Antiquities in 1928.

It is instructive to look into the positions and contributions of Palestinians and Jews in the Mandate organizations devoted to the archaeology of Palestine. Of the ninety-four persons on the payroll of the Department of Antiquities on March 31, 1947, six were British Christians, six were Armenians, twenty-two were Palestinian Christians, fifty-one were Palestinian Muslims, and nine were Jews. Although the Palestinian employees greatly outnumbered the others (not surprising given their overwhelming numerical superiority on the ground), by and large they served in noninfluential, lower-status jobs: as guardians at sites around the country, museum guards and attendants, messengers, and cleaners. Only a fraction of the seventy-three Palestinians employed by the department held higher positions: three of the six inspectors commonly mentioned were Palestinians (D. Baramki, S.A.S. Husseini, and N. Makhouly), and a Palestinian (the self-taught scholar Stephan H. Stephan) worked in the library. Although only two of these four had a university education (Baramki had a bachelor's degree from London at the time and Husseini one from Beirut), six of the nine Jewish employees had university degrees, including three doctorates, one master's, and two bachelor's degrees. The preceding points up a further difference, which is the extent to which the foundations of archaeology as a discipline in the Israeli or Jewish community were laid in Europe: Among the Palestinians who could be classified as archaeologists in the pre-1948 period, only Dimitri Baramki, as mentioned, had studied in Europe.

Contemporary with the founding of the Department of Antiquities was the formation of the Palestine Oriental Society in 1920, thanks largely to the energy of Professor A. T. Clay of Yale University, who was annual professor at the American School of Oriental Research in Jerusalem that year. The membership of the society had always been dominated by foreigners, most nonresident. In 1932, for example, of 191 members, 10 were resident Palestinians, 22 were resident Jews, 42 were resident foreigners, and 117 were nonresidents. Palestinian membership fluctuated from a high of nineteen in 1926 to a low of five in 1934. A preliminary comparison of resident Palestinian and Jewish scholars indicates that, again, almost all the Jewish scholars had received a doctorate in Europe or America before or after immigrating to Palestine. To my knowledge, the Palestinians were all born in Greater Syria before World War I, and only one (Tawfiq Canaan) had a doctorate, a medical degree from The American University of Beirut.

The Department of Antiquities and the Palestine Oriental Society each sponsored a publication: the former put out the *Quarterly of the Department of Antiquities of Palestine (QDAP)* and the latter the *Journal of the Palestine Oriental Society (JPOS).* The difference in purposes between the two publications (and the organizations that issued them) is important. The *QDAP,* the scholarly voice of the Department of Antiquities, was a Mandate government publication dedicated to reporting excavations sponsored by the department as well as research dealing with the collection in the Palestine Archaeological Museum. Of necessity, then, it was dominated by the British, though both Palestinians and Jews published there as well. Of the total of 163 articles published between 1932 and 1950, 33 were contributed by 6 Palestinian scholars (the brothers Dimitri and Jalil Baramki, S. Husseini, N. Makhouly, N. G. Nassar, and S. H. Stephan) and 39 were contributed by 6 Jewish scholars, all of whom became, at one time or another, professors at Hebrew University.

By contrast, the Palestine Oriental Society—and hence *JPOS*—was open to anyone with a scholarly interest in what may broadly be called "Palestinology." The broader scope of the society's publication is reflected in the fact that Stephan's articles in the *QDAP* dealt mostly with Arabic and Turkish inscriptions or texts, whereas his articles in *JPOS* were mainly on folklore. In general, the Palestinians in the Palestine Oriental Society focused on living cultural traditions (Palestinian folklore, architecture, the social context of the village house, Muslim shrines, et cetera) in Palestine, whereas Jewish scholars there researched the topography of biblical sites and the interpretation of difficult biblical texts. Concerning the national breakdown of the authors, of the 335 articles published in the *JPOS* from 1921 to 1948, 50 were by 7 Palestinian scholars (most of them by Dr. Tawfiq Canaan and Stephan Hanna Stephan) and 92 were by 26 resident Jewish scholars. Not reflected in *QDAP,* but clear in *JPOS,* is that Jewish immigration had a significant impact on the growing weight in numbers of Jewish scholars in archaeology, while the number of Palestinians remained relatively stable and then declined. In the first two volumes of *JPOS* (1921, 1922), Arabs contributed eight articles; in the last two volumes (1946, 1948), none, reflecting the increasing Judaization of scholarship on and from Palestine.

Palestinian Archaeology After 1948 From material published by Palestinians in both *JPOS* and *QDAP,* it seems clear that there were learned Palestinians capable of dealing with both the archaeology and ethnography of Palestine. Of the many reasons they did not flourish after the 1948 foundation of Israel, two seem to be paramount: first, the turmoil resulting from the influx of REFUGEES inside a sealed border now one third of the former Palestine, and second, the lack of local academic institutions supporting scholarship in the Arab community. With Jordan's annexation of the West Bank that followed the 1948 debacle, the Department of Antiquities was reorganized with its headquarters in the Roman Theater in Amman. Since the dismissal of the department's British director and all the other British holdovers from the Mandate period in 1956, the emphasis on the East Bank of the Department of Antiquities (of Jordan) has been very clear.

The one center of archaeological activity that might have provided a base for Palestinian archaeologists was the Palestine Archaeological Museum in Jerusalem, which was under the control not of Jordan but of trustees made up of the directors of the several foreign schools of archaeology in the city. It is therefore not clear why Palestinians like Dimitri Baramki did not continue their work as archaeologists employed by the Palestine Museum. In any event, Jordan nationalized the museum only months before the June 1967 war, enabling the Israelis to claim it as theirs by right of conquest.

After 1967, there were a number of Palestinians living in Jordan who had earned archaeology degrees in Europe and the United States, but none in the Occupied Territories, where there was no university having an archaeology department. In recent times the Israeli Department of Antiquities has been willing to hire, at best, a not-too-ambitious Palestinian B.A. Moreover, those Palestinians who did enter archaeology drank from the well of Euro-American scholarship, assuming it to be objective reality. For the Palestinians, the missing element was the intellectual connection with Islamic tradition, in part because the most active Palestinian archaeologists came from Christian backgrounds and in part because, even for the Muslims, there had been no eighteenth- or nineteenth-century precursor to suggest that in the search for the past one could well begin with views of history generated by Arab scholars such as Ibn Khaldun.

There have been two primary consequences of these developments for archaeology in Palestine. First, Palestinians educated in the West have adopted the Western agenda for archaeological research, where the emphasis has been on proto- and prehistory, the Bronze and Iron Ages, and sometimes the Hellenistic and Roman periods. Certainly, biblical archaeology has continued to prevail in the area for non-Palestinians. After 1948, the Jewish Palestine Exploration Society became the Israel Exploration Society, which sponsored major excavations at such biblical sites as Dan, Hazor, and BEERSHEBA. Even in the West Bank, where Jordan was in control, the momentum of biblical archaeology brought foreign excavations to Tall Balata (Shechem), Tall al-Tall (Ai), Tall Ta'annak (Taanach), and Tall al-Sultan (JERICHO). Arab participation in these predominantly American expeditions was limited to representatives of Jordan's Department of Antiquities assigned to each of the foreign excavations to monitor the excavations and gain field experience. Two of these persons became leading archaeologists—Muawiya Ibrahim, later trained in Berlin, who participated in the Tall Ta'annak excavation, and Fawzi Zayadine, later trained in Paris, who worked at Sebastia. Both are accomplished students of traditional archaeology, now focusing their attention on Jordan, where they live and work. Though neither concentrates on the Bible, they have also not been able—or have not thought it necessary—to change the direction of archaeological research. This may in part be due to the fact that they are not working in and for Palestine as a geographical and national entity.

A second consequence is that, in the field of Islamic archaeology, Arab scholars, following their Western instructors, have focused on its art-historical aspects. This emphasis on fine arts in Islamic archaeology appeals to Arabs because it reveals the remarkably advanced technical skills of craftspeople and architects during the flowering of Islam. It is a heritage that elicits pride. But for the serious study of Palestine, this focus is a disaster, because it concentrates on Jerusalem to the exclusion of 95 percent of the land occupied by towns and villages, many of them of considerable importance. The villages of Palestine are ignored and thus the real character of Palestine has yet to be studied.

Third, since archaeological sites can be expropriated by the government and since the Palestinians have not been permitted a state, landowners fear archaeologists. The need for a benevolent Palestinian state is imperative if there is to be freedom to explore the Arab past of Palestine. In Palestine a serious problem arises from the density of evidence of the past on the landscape and from the antiquities law, which allows the state to expropriate land registered as a historical site. Since for Palestinians the state is an imposed "legality," and since the state has in the past used as much "law" as is available to expropriate land, they tend to be unwilling to encourage the identification of archaeological sites. It is evident, however, that even the existence of a Palestinian state will not automatically solve the problem. What is required will be a policy that will allow the growth and development of the built environment while preserving the subterranean cultural resources.

Steps Toward Independence: A Palestinian Archaeology The resources required to tell the Arab story have not been properly collected or preserved. Nor has evidence of the material culture been adequately protected or, where possible, restored. On the contrary, since the foundation of Israel, these resources have suffered calculated decimation. Whole villages have been destroyed, libraries and documents have been confiscated, and unique agricultural installations have been dislodged by force to be incorporated in Israeli museums.

Increasingly there is public awareness among Palestinians in Israel and the Occupied Territories that symbols of the past must somehow be preserved, if only to keep the memory of a rich past alive for the next generation. Private museums have been organized in some towns; collections of regional costumes have been published; domestic architecture has been described.

Most of the differences between the archaeological agenda inherited from the Western Christian and Jewish scholars and an archaeological agenda generated with a view to the interests of the Palestinian population relate not to technical questions but to substance. These substantive differences, which reflect sensitivities derived from both education and the explicit issues of cultural identity raised by the Palestinian community, are critical to the nature of Palestinian archaeology. Adaptations of this list of research interests can be found in many other nations of the world.

The first difference involves focusing on a distant past, as opposed to reaching the distant past through delving into recent times, or indeed the present. Beginning with the present can be supported by both national and methodological arguments. Where continuity of the present with the past is a reasonable assumption, elements of the deeper past are still alive in traditional village settlement patterns, architecture of domestic and public buildings, subsistence systems, and social organization. In order to understand the changes that have occurred it is necessary and possible to move backward through time. For the living population who are heirs to that tradition, it is logical to begin the process of exploring the past with the immediately preceding period, which in Palestine is the period of Ottoman rule. This, then, is the most significant difference between the foreign focus on "biblical archaeology" and the Arab version, Palestinian archaeology.

There are several implications of this difference. In countries where archaeology is a serious government program, the first task is to make an intensive survey of existing physical remains of the past. It has become a required feature of archaeological surface surveys not only to collect evidence of the remains of past human activities but also to gather from local oral tradition place-names and the known function of buildings and installations, at least in secondary use. The Israeli government has an ambitious survey program. Maps are being produced at a scale of 1:20,000. The area inside the Green Line will be covered in 267 volumes. The first volume published covered fifty-six square kilometers along the coast south of Haifa in the area of Atlit. Two villages destroyed in 1948, Ayn Hawd and al-Mazar, were included. The pottery on both sites is read as Byzantine and Arab. Of the 145 sites covered, 55 are said to have "no antiquities." These sites include many lime kilns, caves, ruins of buildings, wells, and other evidence of human activity. Amazingly, 110 of the 145 sites have no names, even though Palestinians traditionally have a name for every plot of land, hill, spring, and unusual feature on the landscape. These toponymies are often part of the local oral tradition not found on published maps. In Palestine, the oral tradition has gone with the expelled native population. One of the gaps in the understanding of Palestine that will forever remain a lacuna in the knowledge of the land arises from the expulsion of the populations of hundreds of villages in 1948.

A second significant difference in agenda arises from the difference between the inherited perspective and that of the inhabitants of Palestine. It has been a common assumption that Palestinian culture is borrowed, largely from the great centers of urban culture in Egypt and Mesopotamia. This is based on the assumption that the population of Palestine was nonurban and unsophisticated. Thus, for example, it has been assumed that the *terre pise* mounds that surrounded the city defenses in the second quarter of the second millennium B.C.E. were brought to the land by the Hyksos, and that the casemate defense systems and ashlar construction were innovations introduced in the tenth century B.C.E. from Anatolia via Phoenicia. We know that none of these construction techniques was imported from abroad, that in fact all these systems were native to Palestine. Against the hyperdiffusionist perspective, the one that sees virtually all features of Palestinian archaeology as imported, the Palestinian archaeologist will search for the evidence for the adaptive systems engineered by the native inhabitants in the different ecological zones of the land. Archaeology is then a tool that can be used to identify the specific forms of cultural expression linking the present with the past.

The two different agendas discussed—using the present or recent past as a starting point, and throwing off inherited preconceptions about early Palestinian cultures—can be well met by focusing on the Palestinian village. There are, however, a number of important obstacles to village study.

First, more than half of all the Arab villages in Palestine were destroyed by the Israelis between 1948 and 1950. Second, many of the house-by-house plans of all of the villages drawn up during the British Mandate are not now accessible. Third, the population of the West Bank today is suspicious of the motives of anyone collecting information about their villages. They find it difficult to believe that such study can be of value to them. More likely, in their view, the researcher will provide the occupation authorities with information that could be used to their disadvantage. Fourth, village study requires a team composed of an anthropologist, an architect, an archaeologist, a photographer, and a historian. Such a team would require a permit, which would be difficult to obtain. Fifth, such a project would be long-term and expensive, though its benefits would extend far into the future. Finally, however desirable the excavation of a destroyed village would be, receiving a permit would be virtually impossible because of Israeli fears that such an endeavor would generate adverse nationalistic publicity among the Palestinians.

Another human settlement type on the recent landscape of Palestine deserves the archaeologist's attention, namely, refugee camps, some of which in the Jericho region are virtually abandoned. Traces of refugees' presence can easily be bulldozed from the surface of the land, but refugee archaeology is a research subject that would make a significant contribution to understanding the real world of Palestine today.

Until recently, the archaeology of Palestine can be said to have focused largely, if not exclusively, on biblical archaeology, a segment of the past reconstructed to support Jewish claims to Palestine. One could claim that a "Palestinian archaeology" is but the other side of the coin, an archaeology with an equally political intent. This claim would have merit if a Palestinian archaeology involved an effort to efface the record relating to the Jews, Jerusalem in the tenth and second centuries B.C.E., or synagogues in the fifth and sixth centuries C.E., for example. But this is not the case. Palestinian archaeology, assuming the general veracity of written records, acknowledges the polytechnic nature of Palestinian cultural history. Indeed, research into the distinctive features of ethnic diversity is an important feature on the research agenda of Palestinian archaeology. "As in all good science, we do not favor one answer or the other. We will test for multicultural indicators as a hypothesis—no more than that—to determine the probability of its truth."

As Palestinians gain a hold on their own history—a process still under duress and having varied degrees of success since the 1993 Oslo accords—some encouraging progress should be recognized:

First, education and awareness in the field of archaeology are being fostered by the Palestinian universities. Three major universities presently offer courses and field training. Effort is being made by the universities and the appropriate ministries of the PALESTINIAN AUTHORITY to sensitize elementary and secondary school students regarding their archaeological and cultural heritage and its importance. Alternative tourism is developing itineraries that highlight archaeological remains of the recent as well as the ancient past, while also introducing visitors to living traditions that bridge the past to the present in Palestinian villages and towns.

Second, the Department of Antiquities of the Palestinian Authority has been given an extensive mandate: to set the appropriate priorities and standards for all archaeological activity; to regulate and enforce the protection of all archaeological resources through the creation of fair and enforceable laws and regulations; to control the efficient use of funding; and to coordinate and evaluate all aspects of the national archaeological effort. The long-term neglect and abuse of archaeological resources occasioned by occupation, followed by the recent surge of construction in both urban and rural areas, have highlighted the urgency of conducting and publishing a comprehensive survey of all historic resources. This is being addressed in the field under the joint auspices of the Ministry of Culture and the Department of Antiquities.

Third, several archaeological investigations have already begun to devote close attention to the recent past, especially to the Ottoman and Islamic periods. Currently, BIR ZEIT UNIVERSITY excavations have been notably fruitful in this respect. Projects being undertaken by AL-QUDS UNIVERSITY and by the Department of Antiquities are also redressing the previous neglect of these later periods.

Fourth, one excavation that has been undertaken has been conducted as the conscious model for the archaeological investigation of a present-day village. This study may provide a new theoretical approach that begins the search for the past in the present. Core personnel have been trained in history and anthropology as well as in refined approaches in archaeology.

Fifth, the investigation of more than four hundred "disappeared" Palestinian villages within the present state of Israel is subject to political considerations that may prevent on-site archaeology any time soon. However, the ongoing collection of data from oral history interviews of refugees, as well as photographs and other documentation, are providing a substantial resource base for such future efforts in the creation of an indigenous Palestinian historical archaeology.

Finally, a growing corps of qualified Palestinians are earning advanced degrees, including doctorates in specialized fields of archaeology. This academic achievement, coupled with their local expertise, provides a core of professionals who are capable and fully equipped to lead the fieldwork and research, both within existing Palestinian institutions and in conjunction with international colleagues. Recent joint projects at Tall Bellahem and Tall al-Sultan demonstrate the beginning of this potential in action.

Albert Glock

BIBLIOGRAPHY

Aharoni, Y. *The Archaeology of the Land of Israel.* London: SCM Press, 1978.

Ahlstrom, G. W. *The History of Ancient Palestine from the Paleolithic Period to Alexander's Conquest.* Sheffield, England: JSOT, 1993.

Albright, W. F. *Archaeology of Palestine,* New York: Pelican, 1949.

Beek, Gus Van. "W. F. Albright's Contribution to Archaeology." In *The Scholarship of William Foxwell Albright: An Appraisal,* ed. by Gus Van Beek. Atlanta: Scholars Press, 1989, pp. 61–73.

Bowerstock, G. W. "Palestine: Ancient History and Modern Politics." In *Blaming the Victims: Spurious Scholarship and the Palestine Question,* ed. by E. Said and C. Hitchens. London/New York: Verso, 1988.

Dever, W. *Recent Archaeological Discoveries and Biblical Research.* Seattle: University of Washington Press 1990.

Elon, Amos. "Politics and Archaeology." *New York Review of Books,* September 22, 1994, pp. 14–18.

Kenyon, Kathleen. *Archaeology in the Holy Land,* 4th ed. London: Methuen, 1979.

Luke, H. C., and E. Keith-Roach. *The Handbook of Palestine and Trans-Jordan.* London: Macmillan, 1930.

Macallister, R. A. S. *A Century of Excavation in Palestine.* London: The Religious Tract Society, 1925.

Silberman, Neil. *Digging for God and Country: Exploration, Archaeology, and the Secret Struggle for the Holy Land, 1799–1917.* New York: Alfred A. Knopf, 1982.

al-Arif, Arif

administrator, historian
1892–1973 Jerusalem

After completing his university studies in Istanbul, Arif al-Arif served in the Ottoman foreign ministry and became a member of the Arab nationalist organization the LITERARY SOCIETY. He was an officer in the Ottoman army during World War I, was captured on the Caucasian front by the Russians in 1915, and was imprisoned for two years in Siberia until he escaped during the 1917 Russian revolution.

Al-Arif returned to Palestine and worked with the Arab nationalist paper *Suriyya al-Janubiyya.* In the wake of the al-Nabi Musa disturbances of April 1920, he was arrested by British authorities. Sentenced to prison, he fled into exile in Damascus before his prison term began and attended the Syrian National Congress in March 1920. He later left for Transjordan after the French occupied Syria. Pardoned by the British as a gesture to Transjordanian leaders shortly thereafter, al-Arif returned to Palestine, where he served in the administration of a number of districts until the end of the PALESTINE MANDATE. From 1926 to 1928, he was seconded to the Transjordanian government, where he was the chief secretary.

Upon Jordanian control of the WEST BANK, al-Arif was appointed military governor of the RAMALLAH governorate and from 1949 to 1955 served as mayor of East Jerusalem. In 1967, he was appointed director of the Palestinian Archaeological Museum (Rockefeller Museum) in East Jerusalem.

A historian as well as an administrator, al-Arif produced a major seven-volume history of Palestine, *al-Nakba* (The disaster). He also wrote *Ta'rikh Ghazza* (The history of Gaza), and *Ta'rikh Bi'r al-Sab wa Qaba'iliha* (The history of Beersheba and its tribes), as well as several books on Jerusalem, notably *al-Mufassal fi Ta'rikh al-Quds* (A detailed history of Jerusalem).

Michael R. Fischbach

Art

For centuries, the mythical and historical events of Palestine have been a major inspiration for generations of European painters. Palestinians themselves, however, did not develop a visual art tradition before the second half of the twentieth century. Since then, however, the uniqueness and diversity of Palestinian creativity have been expressed by the studio arts. Therefore, in the following essay, the term *Palestinian art* refers only to the studio arts of drawing, painting, and printmaking.

The history of Palestinian art may be divided into three phases. In the first phase (1885–1955), icon painting was developed as one of the country's earliest traditions of picture making. The possibility of an indigenous art was aborted as a result of the uprootedness of Palestinian society, leading to the second phase (1955–65), in which pioneers, mainly raised among the refugee population, forged a new Palestinian art. The third phase (1965–95) includes art created both in exile and on native soil.

Palestinian artists came from Christian, Muslim, and Druze backgrounds. Some received academic training; others remained self-taught. Trained and untrained artists both contributed to the creation of a national Palestinian art. The nature and quality of each artist's contribution were frequently determined by the individual's proximity to political confrontation.

Characterized by fragmentation and discontinuities, the leading innovations in Palestinian art were created by men and women who were destined to be dispersed. In their exile, artists were mostly unaware of the other art created by their generation, and yet work by each artist attempts to repair the damage done by national disinheritance.

The First Phase: Beginners (1855–1955) Icon painting, derived from the Byzantine tradition, was the major form of visual art practiced by Palestinians. A distinguished iconographic style had been elaborated as early as the eighteenth century. The first practitioners commonly associated with the Jerusalem School were probably apprenticed to Greek and Russian monks serving in the Holy Land. The tradition was later perpetuated by Palestinian adherents of the Orthodox church.

Icons produced by the JERUSALEM School painters found an eager market. Small icons were originally sought by pilgrims as portable relics for their distant homes. Larger icons were usually commissioned to commemorate a site in one of the country's many sanctuaries. The reputation of the Jerusalem School painters spread throughout nineteenth-century SYRIA and LEBANON, where their icons continue to adorn remote monasteries.

Although these icons followed the Byzantine tradition, details developed by the Jerusalem School suggest naturalization: the almond-shaped eyes and rounded facial features of one patron saint recall the characteristic features of the Arab folk hero in the popular miniatures of the period. The saddle of Saint George's horse, usually painted in a plain red, turns in the hands of a Jerusalem painter to a crimson gilded in delicate stars and crescents befitting the turban of an Ottoman sultan. At times, Greek may be the alphabet used to identify the icon's liturgical title; all other words, however, were usually painted in Arabic.

The tradition of associating the icon painter's name with Jerusalem appears to have been established by a certain Hanna al-Qudsi, whose signature was composed of his first name, Hanna, followed by his title, *al-Qudsi,* meaning "the Jerusalemite." Later painters followed suit by adding to their full names "the Jerusalemite." Icon painters who continued this tradition through the second half of the nineteenth century included Mikha'il Muhanna al-Qudsi, Yuhanna Saliba al-Qudsi, Nicola Tiodoros al-Qudsi, and Ishaq Nicola al-Urushalimi. At the turn of the century, the remaining apprentices carrying on the tradition included the Jerusalem natives Nicola al-Sayigh (d. 1930), Khalil al-Hakim (d. 1963), and Khalil Halaby (1889–1964).

During the early decades of the twentieth century, as Palestine slipped out of Ottoman control, its cultural life gradually began to fall under Western hegemony. Easel painting as practiced for centuries in Europe was imported by a steady influx of veteran travelers. Under the British Mandate, easier access was granted to newcomers. In addition to the transforming presence of the British, a growing number of Westerners associated with Christian missionaries or with Jewish colonies began to secure for themselves a more permanent residence in Palestine. Many of these resident communities hosted painters who were commonly seen with their portable studio equipment painting in the open air. After the 1906 establishment of Bezalel, the first Jewish art school in Jerusalem, the settler community's public premises began to host exhibitions that displayed genre paintings alongside traditional handicrafts.

In the meantime, a few Palestinians exposed to the new method of painting began to dabble with the imported media. Unlike their peers in neighboring Arab countries, who had had access to Cairo's prestigious Fine Arts Academy since 1908 or to that of Beirut since 1937, the few Palestinians who embarked on painting were mainly self-taught. Two leading talents developed their own style by using the new tools for their customary method of painting; the icon painter Khalil Halaby and the HAIFA traditional craftsman of Islamic art Jamal Badran (b. 1905). Using photographs for their models, Halaby and Badran painted landscapes of their respective hometowns.

As admission to the local school of Bezalel was denied to non-Jews, most of the younger generation of untrained students learned by observation and crude experiments. These untrained artists included the JAFFA artists Jamal Bayari, Khalil Badawiyya, and Faysal al-Tahir:

Two young women belonging to this generation did manage to attain a limited art education. Both from Jerusalem, they were Nahil Bishara (d. 1997) and Sophie Halaby (d. 1997). Through the intervention of a British official, Bishara was allowed to attend a limited number of classes at Bezalel, where this young cousin of an icon painter received a grant to pursue her art education in France. Her paintings mainly depicted genre figures in native robes. Halaby, by contrast, depicted vacant landscapes of stormy skies and olive groves dotting the Jerusalem countryside.

As the embryonic stages of a Palestinian art were gradually evolving in urban centers, violence between Jewish and Arab forces was escalating, ultimately leading to the war that sundered the country. Growing affiliations among the few local artists were abruptly suspended. With the establishment of Israel, Palestinian artists found themselves facing the predicament of their own people, who were now either reduced to a minority in their country of birth or herded into refugee camps in neighboring countries. Under these conditions, promising talents aspiring to careers in art were thwarted.

For example, the naive painters Badawiyya and Tahir were killed in the battle for Jaffa. By the late 1950s, the young Bayari, who had created memorable paintings of Jaffa's neighborhoods after the Arab exodus, died at home, a penniless man. His colleague, Hanna Ibrahim Hanna from Rayna, whose exhibitions were thronged by his compatriots, lost hope of making a living in Israel. He emigrated to the UNITED STATES, where he died a few years after his arrival. A number of painters abandoned their vocation altogether. The self-taught JABRA IBRAHIM JABRA (1920–94), from BETHLEHEM, and GHASSAN KANAFANI (1936–73), from ACRE, continued to paint even after Jabra settled in Iraq and Ghassan in Lebanon; each, however, made his true career in writing.

The earliest signs of a resumption of Palestinian painting did not appear until a full decade after the country's fall. The main trends were shaped by those few painters who found themselves refugees in neighboring Arab countries. Unlike their predecessors, most of them did succeed in attaining some form of art education and elaborating a personal style. Tempered by the experience of exile, some refugee artists strove to recapture the memory of a place; others addressed themselves to the visual heritage of Palestinian culture. A few were recognized as major contributors to the wider movement of contemporary Arab art, and some of their works were sought by museums in the region and abroad.

The Second Phase: Pathfinders (1955–1965)

The two decades after Palestine's fall were characterized by radical political and cultural changes in the Arab world. The visual arts enjoyed an unprecedented presence in the cultural arena, which had traditionally been dominated by the oral arts. Baghdad and Cairo witnessed a boom in the state patronage of artists, but it was in Beirut, which became the region's cosmopolitan art center, that major refugee artists from Palestine made their debut.

The earliest artist to claim Beirut's critical attention was Paul Guiragossian (1926–93). Born in Jerusalem to a blind Armenian fiddler, Guiragossian was taken up at the age of three by Catholic missionary institutions. The cloistered experience of being raised by monks and of serving as an apprentice to Italian icon painters exerted a profound influence on Guiragossian's art. After the fall of Palestine, Guiragossian settled in Beirut. Over four decades, during which he became a Lebanese celebrity, Guiragossian's work reflected a relentless struggle to summon the images of his formative years in Jerusalem.

From his early academic canvases portraying intimate relations to his latest abstract paintings reducing body details to vigorous slashes of thick paint, Guiragossian's figures emerge from the repertoire of Christian iconography. Series of his paintings depicting frontal groups of upright figures recall icons honoring Christ's apostles. Huddled together, Guiragossian's people convey the artist's efforts to integrate his Armenian identity and his Palestinian experience. Recurring themes of exodus and exile were borrowed from biblical sources to elucidate the artist's personal world, a world in which disinherited Palestinians shared Armenian destitution.

Two other Palestinian artists living in Beirut also delved into their personal memories to restructure the world they lost: Juliana Seraphim (b. 1934) and Ibrahim Ghannam (1931–84). Born in Jaffa, Seraphim was fourteen when she fled by boat with her family to Sidon. She ultimately settled in Beirut, where she worked in refugee relief and attended art classes with a Lebanese painter. Years later, Seraphim was awarded grants to study in Madrid, Florence, and Paris.

Seraphim's paintings teem with evocative elements of fantasy. They bring to life imaginary orchards in which sculpted buds and wild petals swirl alongside seashells and winged beings. The translucency of her visionary landscape uncovers sensuous forms that suggest a personal paradise. Recalled from a lost childhood once enjoyed between seashore and orange grove, Seraphim's curvilinear forms are transformed into erotic objects. Glistening fragments of nature on the beach become interchangeable with the ultimate features of a woman's body. In colloquial Arabic, *jaffa* means "bride"; in Seraphim's painting, the bridal features of an ethereal woman dominate the landscape, boldly suggesting the artist's face.

Unlike Guiragossian and Seraphim, both refugees from urban centers, Ibrahim Ghannam was born and raised in the coastal village of Yajur. After he arrived in Beirut's Tall al-Za'tar refugee camp and after polio confined him to a wheelchair, Ghannam resumed his childhood hobby. Thanks to an UNRWA (United Nations Relief and Works Agency for Palestine Refugees in the Near East) nurse who provided him with painting supplies, Ghannam could vividly depict images of the countryside his bare feet had once walked.

Ghannam painted a splendid visual narrative of life in Yajur. Living on a rationed subsistence of canned foods, in a cubicle overlooking open sewers, Ghannam painted golden fields of harvest, thriving orange groves, and jubilant peasants at work. Painted with the meticulous precision of an Islamic miniaturist, all details within his frame claimed equal attention. Through his naive vision, Ghannam laboriously preserved for a generation born in the camp the legends of one of the villages demolished after the Palestinian exodus.

Two artists of Ghannam's generation who were outsiders to the cultural mainstream of their immediate environment are Abdallah al-Qarra (b. 1936) and Ibrahim Hazima (b. 1933). Al-Qarra's work evolved at home; Hazima's in exile.

Born in Daliyat al-Karmil, al-Qarra was introduced to painting when he was working as a gardener for a community of Israeli artists who had settled in the neighboring village of Ayn Hawd. After its people had been evicted, Ain Hawd was preserved to accommodate an art center. Patronized by leading Israeli artists, al-Qarra won grants to study art in Paris and later to reside for extended periods in New York.

Living on the borders of Jewish art circles, al-Qarra in his art expressed his groping for his Druze (a medieval offshoot of Shi'a Islam) identity. His earliest works were improvisational ink drawings whose delicate birds and miniature patterns were reminiscent of the decorative motifs ornamenting Palestinian Druze garments. Years later, his large canvases, composed of coarse interlaced brush strokes, repeatedly portrayed vultures devouring blood-stained prey and the obscure face of a man cloaked with a mask.

In a world no less alien, Ibrahim Hazima molded images exalting his own cultural roots. Born in Acre, Hazima was fifteen when he fled by boat to Latakia. For years, he worked as a docker in the Syrian port city to help support his refugee family. Hazima's talent for painting won him a grant to study in Leipzig, where he decided to stay and work on his art.

Indifferent to the German realist art admired in Leipzig, Hazima employed glowing imagery that abounded with lyrical metaphors and pastoral references. Painted in autumn colors with childlike simplicity, his works repeatedly depicted the upright figures of slender women peasants carrying cup-shaped baskets on their heads, their solitary bodies echoing the nearby parasol pines and olive trees scattered among frail village dwellings. In Hazima's iconography, vertical and curved details representing flesh and stone seem to be visually interchangeable. They seem to allude to Palestinian folk poetry, in which the tree is often addressed as a person and the homeland is visualized as a betrothed woman.

Whereas Hazima's visual metaphors may have recalled poetic imagery, other Palestinian artists assumed the conventional role of the political poet and employed visual expression to refurbish political rhetoric: Isma'il Shammut (b. 1930), Mustafa al-Hallaj (b. 1938), and NAJI AL-ALI (1937–87). All three were reared in refugee camps. Shammut settled in a Gaza refugee camp after journeying on foot from his LYDDA home. Al-Hallaj and al-Ali ended up in camps in Damascus and Sidon after their respective home villages of Salma and Shajara were demolished. Both Shammut and al-Hallaj received study grants to Egypt; al-Ali was self-taught.

Among the three, Shammut won the highest official recognition for assimilating conventional verbal allegories into visual images. Color reproductions of his didactic paintings became household icons within refugee camps and Palestinian institutions. Al-Hallaj's lithographs were more personal. Surreal images of men, women, and beasts imaginatively communicated elusive narratives. To reach people throughout the Arab world, al-Ali turned to the satirical art of political cartoons, in which he could actually use words. His remarkable twenty-five-year career was abruptly ended when he was assassinated on a street in London.

The Third Phase: Explorers (1965–1995) In the wake of the 1967 war, many Palestinians were displaced and entire segments of the population fell under Israeli military occupation in the West Bank and Gaza. Over the next three decades, despite a protracted struggle for self-determination, Palestinians' national aspirations remained unfulfilled. Wherever they lived, emerging Palestinian artists sought to articulate their personal predicament in relation to the collective dream of regaining their homeland.

Palestinian artists of this era lived primarily in four regions: Arab countries; the West Bank and the Gaza Strip, which were under Israeli military occupation; Galilee and the Triangle (a predominantly Palestinian region of north-central Israel), which had been incorporated into Israel; and in exile beyond the Middle East.

Palestinian artists who grew up in Arab countries generally remained on the periphery of local cultures. After the establishment of the Union of Palestinian Artists in 1969, group exhibitions of works by Palestinian artists traveled throughout the Arab world and abroad. Photo silkscreens by Layla Shawwa (b. 1940), stylized engravings by Abd al-Rahman Muzayyin (b. 1943), and experimental paintings by Imad Abd al-Wahhab (b. 1950) represented the leading innovative trends.

Jordan, which was the haven for several consecutive waves of Palestinian refugees, was a home for a number of Palestinian artists whose work also helped mold the character of Jordanian art: Fatima Muhib (b. 1931), Ahmad Nawash (b. 1934), Afaf Arafat (b. 1938), Samia Zaru (b. 1940), Mahmud Taha (b. 1942), Suha SHOMAN (b. 1944), Aziz Amura (b. 1945), and Fu'ad Mimi (b. 1949).

After the West Bank and the Gaza Strip fell under military occupation, the region turned into a cultural ghetto. Insulated from the Arab world, a new generation of artists, both trained and untrained, emerged: Karim Dabbah (b. 1937), Taysir Sharaf (b. 1937), Nabil Anani (b. 1943), Kamil Mughanni (b. 1944), Vera Tamari (b. 1945), Fathi Ghabin (b. 1947), Isam Badr (b. 1948), Sulayman Mansur (b. 1948), Taysir Barakat (b. 1959), Fatin Tubasi (b. 1959), Samira Badran (b. 1959), and Yusif Duwayk (b. 1963). In 1973 the group established the League of Palestinian Artists, whose exhibitions were the first group manifestation of Palestinian art on native soil.

Under military occupation, such exhibitions constituted a new form of political resistance. Located in schools, town halls, and public libraries, art exhibitions had a transformative effect, becoming a community event that drew ever-larger crowds from all segments of society. Because Palestinian art was an expression of collective identity, Israeli authorities began to impose military censorship on all exhibitions. Even the combined use of the four colors that made up the Palestinian flag was banned, and an attempt to establish a local gallery was aborted. Unauthorized exhibitions were stormed by troops, with the public ordered to leave and paintings confiscated. Palestinian artists were often subjected to interrogation and arrest. The harsher the measures enforced, the more politically empowered the artists became. Eventually their plight aroused the protest of some Israelis and numerous international nongovernmental groups.

The untutored Fathi Ghabin is one of the artists whose paintings made him a political celebrity within his community. Born in Gaza, Ghabin painted as an intuitive by-product of his daily involvement with community activities protesting the state of siege. Full of popular cultural symbols, Ghabin's narrative art led to his repeated incarceration. His painting of his seven-year-old nephew, who was shot dead at a demonstration, caused Ghabin to spend six months in jail for having painted the child dressed in the forbidden colors of the Palestinian flag. Upon his release, Ghabin painted the image of a mass demonstration. Above the demonstrators, the sky is framed by two raised arms from which hang broken chains. Between the raised arms, a white horse, wrapped in the flag, gallops into the sky. Among the miniature faces of the demonstrators is the face of Ghabin himself.

Whereas Ghabin's work represents a vernacular art, the work of Taysir Barakat, another Gaza artist, expresses a more personal narrative. Barakat was born and raised in a refugee camp and went on to study in Alexandria. He paints in pastel shades hazy forms that evoke a web of allegorical associations. A rooster announces sunrise to a violet sky; the sun turns into a golden ball for camp playmates; the moonlight casts bluish tones on the flesh of a slender woman, her chaste bosom recalling the lilac sand dunes appearing in the distance; fledgling doves nap in their nest, with a barefoot child flying at twilight over the camp's barren earth.

The devastating effects of military occupation and the systematic policies of repression were central to the works of a Palestinian woman who received her art education in Alexandria and Florence. Samira Badran was born in Tripoli, where her refugee father, master craftsman Jamal Badran, went to teach Islamic crafts. Two years after the family reentered the West Bank, the region was invaded by Israel. Badran's imagery is inspired by apocalyptic visions. Spread with whirling flames in lush colors, Badran's painting is full of odd machinery pieces, twisted steel cogs, spikes, barrels, and clogged wheels. The fragmentary debris and inanimate objects of destruction are scattered among dismembered human limbs. The only living beings are caged, strapped, or muzzled. In the distance, the scaffolding of blown-up buildings reaches out metallic skies.

Sulayman Mansur was born in Bir Zeit. A leading Palestinian artist, he was the only well-known artist of his nationality to study at Bezalel. Mansur's work oscillates between photographic realism and quasi-abstract style. In either case, it is full of metaphoric imagery. For example, in one figurative work, a rainbow pours through the bars of a prison window; once inside, the rainbow breaks into the colors of the national flag. Another work shows bent prison bars and a checkered dove with flaming wings dashing into the sun. Mansur's abstractions explore color and earthy textures. Their titles reveal that they represent traces of the ancestral villages that were demolished and whose names were wiped off Israeli maps.

A new generation of artists also arose among PALESTINIAN CITIZENS OF ISRAEL: Abid Abidi (b. 1942), Walid Abu Shaqra (b. 1946), Khalil Rayyan (b. 1946), As'ad Azi (b. 1954), Da'ud al-Hayik (b. 1955), Kamil Daw (b. 1956), Bashir Makhul (b. 1963), and Ibrahim Nubani (b. 1964).

Born in Haifa, Abidi worked as a blacksmith and illustrated Arabic publications that appeared in Israel. After studying in Dresden, Abidi became the first Palestinian to build monumental art on native soil. His allegorical monuments in Galilee, honoring human fortitude and resistance, include a narrative mural depicting Elijah's defiance and survival and a bronze monument dedicated to six Palestinians who were shot on Land Day.

In contrast to the urban Abidi, Abu Shaqra—born in Umm al-Fahm, and a London art graduate—was possessed by his rural background. His engravings depict landscapes haunted by human absence and native displacement: an uprooted olive tree lying in the sun; a ploughed field in the moonlight; bushes, thorns, and wildflowers growing in cracks of the remains of abandoned homes; cactus that once defined village borders, outlasting the villages that have been erased.

As Abu Shaqra expressed his closeness to the land, exiled Palestinian painters were creating an abstract art that represented their distance from it. These exiles include Jumana al-Husayni (b. 1932), Samia Halaby (b. 1936), Sari Khoury (1941–98), Vladimir Tamari (b. 1942), Kamal Boullata (b. 1942), Munira NUSSAYBA (b. 1942), Samir Salama (b. 1944), Nasir al-Sumi (b. 1948), and Nabil Shehadeh (b. 1951).

Despite minimal contact, Halaby, Khoury, Tamari, and Boullata all share visual concerns that recall their common experience of exile. All four artists were born in Jerusalem. After Palestine's fall, Halaby and Khoury emigrated to the United States with their families. After each completed an art education there, Halaby settled in New York and Khoury in Michigan. After Jerusalem's annexation, Tamari, who had studied in Beirut and London, established his residence in Tokyo, and Boullata, who had studied in Rome and Washington, D.C., continued living in the American capital.

Halaby's early abstractions explored the visual interplay of spatial ambiguities. Her paintings might be composed of cyclical helices or of repeated bands of straight diagonal lines. Color is applied in linear monochromatic stripes in precise transitional gradations. Contrasting areas of light and dark are elaborately interwoven. Undulations from each extremity meet and gradually fade into each other. Spatial ambiguity is created by the way foreground and background appear ceaselessly interchangeable. Later she portrayed two squares whose position appeared to shift diagonally. Halaby's spatial ambiguities suggest Islamic arabesques. Her work questions the notions of order and continuity.

Sari Khoury's work, by contrast, explores discontinuities, suggesting motion impeded within an ethereal void in which geometric forms abruptly break away or float off the picture's edge. These forms often allude to fragments of familiar shapes—a hint of sky, a window, a flying bird, a sleek highway, an obscure corner. Each fragment is tapered in smooth, angular shape; their interrelation appears as a dance of visual allegories anchored in a substanceless field of vision. Khoury's fusion of abstract forms and fragmented familiar shapes sometimes suggests a state of suspended animation; often it alludes to the passage between interior and exterior space, between the borders of captivity and deliverance.

Tamari's pastels and watercolors offer fluid layers of gleaming transparencies. Fading into a background often composed of improvisational spreads of paint, Tamari's amorphous forms recall the haphazard patterns of ancient walls. Prismatic colors filtering through his angular shapes glow with poignant contrasts that are reminiscent of being within a sanctuary and looking out through stained glass. Textured areas are generated by short, delicate brush strokes that emulate the manner in which Byzantine icon painters molded stylized form. Tamari's abstractions allude to the landscape, often presented in the form of a cross. As it highlights the dynamic opposition between vertical and horizontal, Tamari's cross simultaneously suggests Golgotha and his own personal home.

Halaby, Khoury, and Tamari all grew up in homes adorned by Byzantine icons. Likewise, Boullata's early apprenticeship with Jerusalem icon painter Khalil Halaby had a marked effect on his development. For years, he was fascinated by the square, geometric rendering of Arabic script. He composed fragments of text from Christian and Muslim sources in translucent colors and angular shapes, creating mandalas of Arabic in which reading becomes interchangeable with seeing. In his later acrylics, all association with script disappeared. Geometric compositions, still based on the square, were generated by doubling and dissecting quadrangles. Oppositional color contrasts heighten the ambiguity of seeming symmetries, and the fragmentation of angular forms reveals prismatic refractions. Colors thrusting forward and backward in shifting sequences traverse illusionary distance. The eye-crossing demarcations between inside and outside transcend simple reciprocities. Through geometry—whose Greek roots mean "measurement of land"—the exiled artist, half a world away from

Jerusalem, relentlessly charts the transition from memory to imagination.

From the Jerusalem School of icon painters to the Jerusalem painters in exile, bridges connect Palestinian works of art, transcending the distance separating the artists. Discontinuities notwithstanding, Palestinian art in many locations continues to interweave the artist's memory of place with the inspiring images retained from a communal culture: The vernacular art created by Ghabin in Gaza completes the narrative picture painted by Ghannam in Lebanon, just as Badran's dark world of the West Bank reveals the other side of the same world Seraphine remembered in Beirut. Similarly, Barakat's metaphoric allusions mirror those implied by Hazima, while Mansur's allegorical imagery suggests the iconography popularized by Shammut. In the same way, Abu Shaqra's landscapes tracing the remains of Arab villages in Israel become the natural sequel of Sophie Halaby's haunting landscapes of Jerusalem, as Guiragossian's Beirut abstractions prefigure the modern icons Tamari created in Tokyo.

Despite these profound connections, the orchestral fullness of Palestinian art has never been seen under one roof. The complete story of this cultural journey has yet to be written.

Kamal Boullata

BIBLIOGRAPHY

The Jerusalem School of Icon Painters

Agemian, Sylvia. "Les Icones Melkites." In *Icones: Grecques, Melkites, Russes* (Collection Abou Adal), ed. by Virgil Candea. Geneva: Editions Skira, 1993, pp. 169–285.

Candea, Virgil, et al. *Icones Melkites.* Beirut: Nicolas Sursock Museum, 1969.

General

'Abidi, 'Abid. "Ma'alim Tatawwir al-Fann al-Tishkili al Filastini fi al-Bilad" (Landmarks in the development of fine arts in the country: 1948–1988). In *Filistiniyyun* (The Palestinians), ed. by Khalid Khalifa. Shafa Am: Dar al-Mashriq, 1988, pp. 205–216.

Boullata, Kamal. "Al-Fan al-Tashkili al-Filastini Khilal Nisf Qarn: 1935–1985" (Half a century of Palestinian painting: 1935–1985). In *Al-Mawsu'a al-Filastiniyya* (Encyclopaedia Palaestina), Vol. 4. Damascus-Beirut, 1989, pp. 869–930.

——. "Facing the Forest: Israeli and Palestinian Artists." *Third Text* 7 (summer 1989): 77–95.

Shammut, Isma'il. *Al-Fann fi Filastin* (Art in Palestine). Kuwait City: Qabas, 1989.

Palestinian Art in the Arab World

Ali, Wijdan, ed. *Contemporary Art from the Islamic World.* London: Scorpion Publishing Co., 1989.

Bahnasi, Afif. *Al-Fann al-Hadith fi al-Bilad al-Arabiyya* (Modern Art in Arab Countries). Beirut: UNESCO, 1980.

Art in Gaza and the West Bank

Ankori, Gannit. "The Other Jerusalem: Images of the Holy City in Contemporary Palestinian Painting." *Jewish Art* 14 (1988): 74–92.

Boullata, Kamal. "Palestinian Expression Inside a Cultural Ghetto." *Middle East Report* 159 (July–August 1989): 24–28.

Murphy, Jay. "The Intifadah and the Work of Palestinian Artists." *Third Text* 11 (summer 1990): 122–130.

Shinar, Dov. *Palestinian Voices: Communication and Nation Building in the West Bank.* Boulder, Colo.: Lynn Rienner Publishers, 1987, pp. 132–150.

Sillem, Maurits. "Opening and Closure: Gallery 79 and the Occupied Territories of the West Bank and Gaza Strip." In *Tales of the Unexpected.* London: Royal College of Art, pp. 47–50.

Palestinian Art in Exile

Boullata, Kamal. "The View from No-Man's Land." *Michigan Quarterly Review* (fall 1992): 578–590.

Burnham, M. Anne. "Three from Jerusalem." *Aramco World* (July–August 1990): 15–21.

Halaby, Samia A. "Reflecting Reality in Abstract Picturing." *Leonardo,* 20, no. 3 (1987): 241–246.

Van Assche. *Mona Hatoum.* Paris: Centre Georges Pompidou, 1994.

Palestinian Children's Art

Boullata, Kamal. *Faithful Witnesses: Palestinian Children Recreate Their World.* Brooklyn: Interlink, 1990.

Aruri, Naseer

scholar

1934– Jerusalem

Naseer Aruri is a leading Palestinian-American scholar. Born to a family with roots in the WEST BANK towns of Arura and Burham, Aruri spent his early years in Jerusalem but fled with his family during the ARAB-ISRAELI WAR OF 1948. He came to the United States for his university education and has lived in the United States since the mid-1950s. He obtained a Ph.D. in 1967 from the University of Massachusetts, where he has been professor of political science.

Aruri writes and lectures extensively on the Palestinian situation. He has been particularly active in human rights organizations, serving on the board of Amnesty International, USA, from

1984 to 1990 and of Middle East Watch from 1990 to 1992. He has been a founding member and/or board member of several Arab human rights organizations, and since 1994 he has served on the board of commissioners of the Palestinian Independent Commission for Citizens' Rights, a Palestinian human rights monitoring organization based in the West Bank. Among his other activities, Aruri was a founding member and twice served as president of the Association of Arab-American University Graduates. In 1991, he was named to the PALESTINE NATIONAL COUNCIL.

Aruri has been highly critical of the Declaration of Principles signed in September 1993 by Israel and the PALESTINE LIBERATION ORGANIZATION (PLO). He believes that the PLO did not have a serious negotiating strategy and was willing to accept any Israeli offer simply to obtain an agreement.

Kathleen Christison

BIBLIOGRAPHY

Aruri, Naseer. *Jordan: A Study in Political Development, 1921–1965.* The Hague: Martinus Nijhoff, 1972.

——. *The Obstruction of Power: The U.S., Israel and the Palestinians.* Monroe, Maine: Common Courage Press, 1995.

——. *Occupation: Israel over Palestine.* 2d ed. Belmont, Mass.: Association of Arab-American University Graduates Press, 1983.

Ashrawi, Hanan Mikha'il

academic, activist
1946– Nablus

Born to a Christian family, Hanan Mikha'il was living in TIBERIUS at the time of the ARAB-ISRAELI WAR OF 1948, and she fled the fighting with her family to Amman. After eventually settling in RAMALLAH, her father, Da'ud Mikha'il, became an important organizer for Sulayman al-Nabulsi's leftist National Socialist Party in the WEST BANK in the 1950s. While pursuing higher education at the American University of Beirut in the 1960s, she herself grew interested in politics and became associated with FATAH, participating in the General Union of Palestinian Students from 1967 to 1970 and the General Union of Palestinian Women from 1967 to 1972. She worked in the Palestinian Information Office from 1968 to 1970.

Hanan Mikha'il received B.A. and M.A. degrees in English literature in 1968 but was unable to return to the West Bank because she had been away when it was occupied by Israel in 1967. As a result, she went to the United States to pursue doctoral studies at the University of Virginia, where she obtained a Ph.D. in English literature in 1971.

After returning to the West Bank in 1972 (with the permission of the Israelis), she taught English at BIR ZEIT UNIVERSITY, beginning in 1974, and she married Emile Ashrawi in 1975. She served as dean of arts from 1986 to 1990. While at Bir Zeit, she maintained her interest in the plight of Palestinians under occupation and was a founding member and director of the university's Legal Aid Committee, established in 1974 to hire lawyers and pay fines for students arrested by occupation authorities.

The INTIFADA revealed the existence of a new generation of influential activists in the Occupied Territories. Many became highly effective spokespersons for Palestinian national aspirations through their ability to articulate Palestinian aspirations to the Western journalists who flocked to cover the uprising. As an educated woman with flawless and forceful English, Ashrawi in particular was courted by the press and was one of four Palestinians who participated with Israeli officials in an American television program on the Intifada in April 1988.

A rising star among West Bank Palestinians, Ashrawi helped establish a political committee in 1988 that tried to muster support for the diplomatic moves of the PALESTINE LIBERATION ORGANIZATION (PLO). Beginning in April 1991, she served on a team of Palestinians who carried out a PLO-approved dialogue with U.S. Secretary of State James Baker as part of an American peace initiative that eventually led to the convening of the Arab-Israeli discussions at the MADRID PEACE CONFERENCE in October 1991. As the holder of a Jerusalem identity card, Ashrawi was not permitted by Israel to sit on the joint Jordanian-Palestinian delegation. However, she was one of seven members of the delegation's steering committee, which coordinated the negotiations in consultation with the PLO, and she served as the delegation's spokesperson.

Ashrawi continued in this capacity until the revelation that the PLO had reached an agreement with Israel in Oslo without prior consultation with the Palestinian delegation. After a political crisis within the PLO over whether Palestinians from inside or outside the Occupied Territories should take the lead in negotiations with Israel, Ashrawi was appointed to the PLO's Higher Committee for the Peace Talks in Tunis. Despite being nominated to head the PLO's Washington office, she resigned from all PLO posts in December 1993 to pursue independent political activities. She then founded the Palestinian Independent Commission for Citizens' Rights, whose goal was to place civil liberties on the Palestinian agenda; Ashrawi headed the group until the summer of 1995. She was elected to the PALESTINIAN LEGISLATIVE COUNCIL, established in the areas under the control of the new PALESTINIAN AUTHORITY (PA), in January 1996. In May 1996, she was appointed minister of higher education in the PA's executive authority.

Michael R. Fischbach

BIBLIOGRAPHY

Ashrawi, Hanan Mikha'il. *This Side of Peace: A Personal Account.* New York: Simon & Schuster, 1996.

Victor, Barbara. *A Voice of Reason: Hanan Ashrawi and Peace in the Middle East.* New York: Harcourt Brace, 1994.

el-Asmar, Fouzi

Fawzi al-Asmar; journalist, poet
1937– Haifa

After attending school in Israel, Fouzi el-Asmar studied in the United States and later obtained a Ph.D. from the University of Exeter in Britain. A journalist in the United States, he worked as managing editor of *al-Sharq al-Awsat,* as bureau chief for the United Arab Emirates news agency, and as correspondent for *al-Riyadh,* a daily newspaper in Saudi Arabia.

He has written *To Be an Arab in Israel,* which has been translated into eight languages.

Michael R. Fischbach

B

Baily Committee
1941

The Baily Committee Report on Village Administration examined ways to bolster the position of traditional Palestinian village leaders.

Michael R. Fischbach

Balfour Declaration
1917

The Balfour Declaration affected the modern history of Palestine to an extent matched by perhaps no other document. During World War I, the British cabinet allowed Zionist leaders to draft the statement, which it then revised and passed along to Foreign Secretary Lord (Arthur) Balfour. Balfour transmitted the declaration that later bore his name on November 2, 1917, to the British philanthropist and Zionist leader Lord (Walter) Rothschild, who had in fact helped write the document. The entire statement reads as follows:

> His Majesty's Government view with favor the establishment in Palestine of a national home for the Jewish people, and will use their best endeavors to facilitate the achievement of this object, it being understood that nothing shall be done which may prejudice the civil and religious rights of the existing non-Jewish communities in Palestine, or the rights and political status enjoyed by Jews in any other country.

Britain issued the declaration to facilitate a variety of goals related to the war. It needed the help of American Jews to hasten American entry into the war; the United States had declared war on Germany in April 1917 but had not yet sent troops in large numbers. Britain also needed Russian Jews' assistance in keeping Russia in the war, given the revolution shaking that country in 1917. Last, Britain's war cabinet sought Jewish financial support and wanted to make an appeal to world Jewry before Germany did.

The declaration was one of several contradictory promises Britain made during the war. Seeking an Arab uprising against the Ottoman Empire, Britain pledged to support the creation of an independent Arab nation after an Ottoman defeat, a pledge made in the HUSAYN-MCMAHON CORRESPONDENCE, 1915–16, named for the sharif of Mecca, Husayn, and Henry McMahon, British high commissioner in Egypt. The Arabs understood this state to include Palestine. At the same time, Britain and France agreed in the 1916 Sykes-Picot agreement to rule the region directly, along with their other allies, after the war.

The public atmosphere in England at the time was well disposed toward ZIONISM. Some fundamentalist Christians favored establishment of a Jewish state in Palestine as a way of realizing biblical prophecy, even though some were themselves anti-Semites. Other Britons, including Balfour and Prime Minister David Lloyd George, felt that the West should support Zionism because of past injustices suffered by the Jewish people. Furthermore, Jews exerted a significant influence on many levels of British society despite their small numbers. For example, Sir Herbert Samuel was a philosopher and several-time member of the British cabinet who later served as Britain's first HIGH COMMISSIONER FOR PALESTINE. Chaim Weizmann, head of the World Zionist Organization, was a chemistry professor in Britain whose inventions helped the British munitions industry. Through advocates such as Samuel and Weizmann, the war cabinet came to believe the claims that support for a Jewish state or commonwealth allied with Britain would be advantageous for Britain after the war.

The drafters of the Balfour Declaration were careful in selecting its phraseology. They employed the term *national home* to please anti-Zionist Jews, who feared that creation of a Jewish state in Palestine might threaten their own assimilated status in other countries. Balfour offered the following explanation of the phrase *national home,* a new term without precedent in international law, two days before he issued the declaration: "It did not necessarily involve the early establishment of an independent Jewish State, which was a matter of gradual development in accordance with the ordinary laws of political development."

The Balfour Declaration offered little mention of the indigenous Palestinian population, a population whom many Europeans considered inferior. Although Palestinians constituted 90 percent of Palestine's population at the time it was issued, the declaration refers to the Palestinian population as the "non-Jewish communities in Palestine." The declaration did state that Palestinians' civil and religious rights as "non-Jews" would be upheld, and the British later did allow Palestinian Muslims and Christians to maintain much of their religious and social practice.

Britain's support for the Zionist endeavor was crucial. The declaration was incorporated into the Mandate to govern Palestine that the League of Nations eventually granted to Britain. This support facilitated Zionist immigration so that the Jewish population in Palestine rose from 50,000 in 1917 to over 600,000 by 1947, allowing the Zionists to establish the political and military infrastructure of a future state. Fearing domination or even expulsion by the Zionists, Palestinians offered resistance that escalated into political violence in 1920, 1921, 1929, and 1933. Although these episodes were quickly contained by British forces, the Palestinian uprising from 1936 to 1939 took considerably longer for the British to suppress and only then with Zionist assistance. Thereafter, the Palestinians remained weak and unable to challenge either Britain or Zionism. Ultimately, the Balfour policy paved the way for the establishment in 1948 of the state of Israel and the exodus of some 726,000 Palestinians, who either fled the fighting or were expelled by Zionist forces.

Philip Mattar

BIBLIOGRAPHY

Hurewitz, J. C. *The Middle East and North Africa in World Politics: A Documentary Record,* 2d rev. ed. Vol. 2. *British-French Supremacy, 1914–1945.* New Haven, Conn.: Yale University Press, 1979.

——. *The Struggle for Palestine.* New York: Greenwood Press, 1968.

Jeffries, Joseph Mary Nagle. *Palestine: The Reality.* New York: Longmans, 1939.

Monroe, Elizabeth. *Britain's Moment in the Middle East.* Baltimore: Johns Hopkins University Press, 1963.

Stein, Leonard. *The Balfour Declaration.* New York: Simon & Schuster, 1961.

Weizmann, Chaim. *Trial and Error.* Philadelphia: Jewish Publication Society of America, 1949.

Banna, Sabri al-

See ABU NIDAL.

Baramki, Gabriel

academic

1929– Jerusalem

Gabriel Baramki studied at The American University of Beirut, where he obtained B.Sc. (1949) and M.Sc. (1953) degrees in chemistry. In 1959, he obtained a Ph.D. in physical organic chemistry from McGill University.

Vice-president of BIR ZEIT UNIVERSITY near RAMALLAH, Baramki assumed the post of acting president from November 1974 through May 1993 during the exile of the university's president, HANNA NASIR, whom Israeli authorities had deported. Baramki served in this post during difficult times in the university's existence, including its long closure during the INTIFADA (January 1988–July 1992).

Michael R. Fischbach

Barghuthi Family

The Barghuthi family has produced several figures active in various public spheres:

Umar Salih (1894–1965; Jerusalem; lawyer, scholar, politician). A proponent of Arab nationalism during the Ottoman period, Barghuthi deserted the Ottoman army during the First World War. Upon his return to Palestine, he was sentenced to internal exile in ACRE. He later received a law degree from the Government Law School in Jerusalem in 1924 and taught there from 1933 to 1948. During the PALESTINE MANDATE, Barghuthi supported the NASHASHIBI FAMILY–led Opposition and was a founding member of the Palestinian Arab National Party in 1923. He was appointed to the Jordanian senate in 1952, and in 1954 he was elected to the chamber of deputies.

Among his other works, Barghuthi cowrote a textbook, *Ta'rikh Filastin* (The History of Palestine), in 1922.

Bashir (1931– ; activist) Secretary-general of the Palestinian People's Party (formerly the PALESTINE COMMUNIST PARTY) in the WEST BANK and editor of the Communist weekly *al-Tali'*, Barghuthi was appointed minister without portfolio in the PALESTINIAN AUTHORITY executive authority in May 1996.

Marwan (1959– ; activist) Imprisoned by Israeli authorities in the WEST BANK for six years, he was later deported in 1987. In exile, he became a member of FATAH's revolutionary council. Upon his return to the West Bank in 1994, he became secretary of Fatah's Higher Council in the West Bank.

Mustafa (1954– ; physician) Mustafa chairs the Union of Palestinian Medical Relief Committees in the West Bank.

Michael R. Fischbach

Beersheba

Arabic, Bi'r al-Sab; Hebrew, Bershev'a

Beersheba is the capital of the large Naqab (Negev) desert region of southern Palestine. Situated as it is on the borders of the desert to the south, the coastal plain to the west, and the mountains to the north, Beersheba's location has made it a major markettown and meeting place for both Bedouin (nomads) and townspeople.

The Ottomans established the modern town a short distance from its ancient location in 1900 in order to create a political presence for themselves in the southern regions of Palestine near the border with semi-independent Egypt. They also sought to improve tax collection among the Bedouin tribes of the desert and to encourage their settlement. Beersheba was designated as the center of an administrative subprovince bearing its name and connected with the rest of Palestine by railroad. The town's population grew from some three hundred persons in 1902 to approximately one thousand in 1915.

Beersheba has been a point of convergence for the caravan trade since ancient times. In addition to its central marketplace, an open-air Bedouin market operates one day a week just east of the town. Agriculture is also an important dimension of the town's economy, including in this century production of rain-fed field crops and fruits. Beersheba is the most important center for the barley market in Palestine, and the town and its environs raise tens of thousands of camels, goats, and sheep.

Beersheba's location has lent it a vital strategic importance throughout this century. It was a major staging ground for Ottoman forces facing the British army during World War I and in fact fell to the British in October 1917. It remained the administrative center for the Mandatory province bearing its name. During the ARAB-ISRAELI WAR OF 1948, securing Beersheba was crucial for Israeli control of southern Palestine, and the Palmach, (regular Zionist military force) captured the town on October 21, 1948. Most of the fifty-five hundred Palestinians living there at the time were expelled.

Beersheba became home to many Jewish immigrants after the 1948 war. Its population in the mid-1990s stood at over 115,000.

Michael R. Fischbach

Bernadotte, Folke

Swedish diplomat

1895–1948 Stockholm

Count Folke Bernadotte, a scion of the Swedish royal family, was the first of several "peace brokers" who have attempted to mediate between Israel and the Arabs. Before his appointment as U.N. mediator for Palestine on May 14, 1948, with a wide mandate to "promote a peaceful adjustment of the future situation of Palestine," Bernadotte had served as president of the Swedish Red Cross. The count took up the challenge of his U.N. task with an unusual persistence and a naïve humanitarianism. Before his assassination at the hands of Zionist terrorists in Jerusalem on September 17, 1948,

Bernadotte's efforts led to the successful conclusion of two truces in the ARAB-ISRAELI WAR OF 1948. Bernadotte has also been credited by some as being the first diplomat to warn the U.N. openly of the existence of a serious Palestinian refugee problem.

Working closely with his American assistant, Dr. Ralph S. Bunche, Count Bernadotte also put forth two sets of proposals for a political settlement in the Mideast. Both the tentative suggestions he offered to the parties in late June 1948 and the comprehensive proposals he submitted to the United Nations in mid-September proved utterly unacceptable to Arabs and Israelis alike. What became known as the Bernadotte Plan of September 1948 included provision for the reallocation of the Negev to Arab sovereignty while Galilee was confirmed as future Israeli territory. Another key proposal was that "the right of the Arab refugees to return to their homes in Jewish-controlled territory at the earliest possible date should be affirmed by the United Nations." Bernadotte's final proposal was for the establishment of a conciliation commission to continue working for "the peaceful adjustment of the situation in Palestine."

Although a number of political considerations prevented any U.N. action on Bernadotte's proposals for an Arab-Israeli settlement, parts of his final report were transformed into the landmark United Nations General Assembly Resolution 194(III) of December 11, 1948, which established the UNITED NATIONS CONCILIATION COMMISSION FOR PALESTINE and resolved that the Palestinian REFUGEES "wishing to return to their homes and live at peace with their neighbours should be permitted to do so at the earliest possible date, and that compensation should be paid for the property of those choosing not to return."

Neil Caplan

Bethlehem

Known in Arabic as Bayt Lahm, Bethlehem is a major center for Palestinian Christianity because it contains one of Palestine's most significant CHRISTIAN CHURCHES and because it has long constituted a major site of Christian pilgrimage.

Located eight kilometers south of JERUSALEM, Bethlehem has been inhabited since ancient times. Venerated as the reputed birthplace of the Hebrew king David, Bethlehem in the last one thousand years has been more significantly affected by the fact that it is considered the birthplace of Jesus. A church was first erected over the presumed birth site in approximately 330 C.E., although the edifice of the present church of the Nativity dates from a later period.

Capturing Bethlehem was a major objective of Crusader armies, which took the town in 1099. Even after its final return to Islamic control in 1244, its shrines engendered controversy. The theft of a relic in the Church of the Nativity, for example, was a factor leading the Ottoman Empire into the Crimean War in 1854, and various Christian sects have clashed over rights to the church.

Because Bethlehem is a major center for Christian pilgrimage, tourism has long constituted a vital aspect of the town's economy, in terms of both tourist accommodations and the manufacture of religious articles made of wood, brass, and mother-of-pearl. Bethlehem has also long been the WEST BANK's second most important manufacturing town after NABLUS, noted for its textiles. Moreover, the town is the home of BETHLEHEM UNIVERSITY, a private Roman Catholic institution that attained university status in 1973.

Recent history has affected Bethlehem considerably. The town grew during the PALESTINE MANDATE from some 6,600 inhabitants in 1922 to some 8,800 in 1944. Its population swelled to 14,000 in 1948 after it was controlled by Egyptian forces and settled by thousands of Palestinian refugees from the ARAB-ISRAELI WAR OF 1948. The town was then incorporated into the Jordanian-controlled West Bank until it was captured by Israel in June 1967. The Israeli occupation has adversely affected the town; from 1967 to 1996, 61 percent of its land was confiscated, declared a military area, or declared a nature reserve area by Israeli authorities.

After redeployment of Israeli forces, the PALESTINIAN AUTHORITY assumed control of Bethlehem on December 21, 1995. By the mid-1990s, its population stood at thirty-five thousand.

Michael R. Fischbach

Bethlehem University

A private, Roman Catholic coeducational university sponsored by the Vatican and located in the West Bank city of Bethlehem, Bethlehem University attained its present university status in 1973. Its origins extend back to 1893, however, as a secondary school established by the American La Salle family.

Bethlehem University now offers diplomas as well as A.A., B.A., and B.S. degrees. Arabic and English are the languages of instruction. During the 1994–95 academic year, 2,086 students attended the university, most of them Palestinians and many of them Christians.

Michael R. Fischbach

Bir Zeit University

The first school with university status in the Occupied Territories, Bir Zeit University was first established in 1924 by Nabiha Nasir as a school in Bir Zeit (or Birzeit), near RAMALLAH. It developed into Bir Zeit College, offering two-year programs, before becoming a private, secular university offering four-year degree programs in 1972. Over three thousand students were enrolled during the 1994–95 academic year at Bir Zeit. As of the early 1990s, the university employed some 225 professors and instructors.

Bir Zeit, a center for anti-Israeli activism, in its nationalist activities often proved to be a barometer by which wider political trends in the Occupied Territories could be measured. Student groups associated with FATAH, the POPULAR FRONT FOR THE LIBERATION OF PALESTINE (PFLP), and the DEMOCRATIC FRONT FOR THE LIBERATION OF PALESTINE (DFLP) made significant inroads into the student population by the 1980s as PALESTINE LIBERATION ORGANIZATION (PLO) groups began eroding the earlier influence of the Communists in the territories as a whole. In turn, Islamic student groups grew stronger at Bir Zeit during the 1980s and 1990s as the Islamic trend began challenging the influence of secular PLO groups throughout the territories. The school's strong secular tradition and relatively large numbers of Christian students initially limited the growth of Islamist student groups. However, an Islamic bloc secured the greatest number of votes in student council elections in the spring of 1996, slightly more than the Fatah-oriented bloc.

Students and faculty at Bir Zeit also involved themselves in significant ways in the wider WEST BANK society. In 1972, university students organized a work program through which volunteers from the university and community carried out economic development projects such as land reclamation. Students were eventually required to complete a community service requirement before graduation; many undertook activities such as planting olive seedlings on empty land, a tactic to forestall confiscation by Israeli authorities, who began wholesale expropriations of unregistered, uncultivated land in the early 1980s. In 1974, the Legal Aid Committee was established to assist students arrested by occupation authorities by hiring lawyers for them and paying their fines.

Bir Zeit's educational program often suffered from the rigors of the occupation. HANNA NASIR, the university's president since 1972, was deported by Israel in November 1974 and not allowed to return until May 1993. In the fall of 1982, nonresident faculty members were required to sign a loyalty oath stating that they would deny any assistance to the PLO or other such political organizations, and occupation authorities barred or deported nineteen foreign faculty members who refused to sign. Israeli censorship regulations prevented the importation of certain publications deemed subversive, including those that were available at Israeli universities. Troops often stormed the university or closed it. Bir Zeit was closed on eight different occasions from 1979 to 1984, for periods ranging from four days to three months. The most serious closure occurred during the INTIFADA, from January 1988 until July 1992. Moreover, hundreds of Bir Zeit students were arrested, imprisoned, or killed during the long years of the occupation.

Bir Zeit has long played an important role in the Palestinian nationalist movement by serving as a venue for contending political viewpoints and in training a rising generation of local leaders.

Michael R. Fischbach

Bishara, Azmi

academic, politician

1956– Nazareth

Born into a Christian family, Bishara was the founder of the National Committee of Arab Secondary School Students in 1974, as well as founder of the Arab Students Union in Israel. After obtaining a Ph.D. in philosophy at Humboldt University in East Berlin, he was the head of the philosophy department at BIR ZEIT UNIVERSITY in the WEST BANK and senior researcher at the Van Leer Jerusalem Institute.

The New Communist List (RAKAH) to which Bishara belonged was beset with dissension and defections in the 1990s. Bishara was among a younger generation of activists who left the Party and joined with Arab nationalists to establish the Democratic National Assembly—Brit Leumit Demokratit (BALAD). Bishara was elected to the Knesset in May 1996 as part of a coalition that joined Balad with the Rakah-dominated Democratic Front for Peace and Equality. In 1999, he ran for prime minister—the first Palestinian ever to do so—but eventually withdrew before the May elections.

Michael R. Fischbach

Black September

Black September was a terrorist organization formed after the Jordanian civil war, which began in September 1970 and flared again in July 1971. Because the fighting between Jordanian and Palestinian military forces ended in defeat for the Palestinians and resulted in their mass expulsion from Jordan, Palestinians came to call the period in which the civil war began Black September, and the organization was named accordingly. Black September is widely believed to have been formed by leaders within FATAH, although the decision may not have had majority sanction and Fatah always denied any association with the group.

Black September's mission was to restore the Palestinians' fighting image and the lost honor of the Palestinian cause in the wake of the setback in Jordan. Operations were intended to bring the Palestinian issue to the attention of a world that in the early 1970s seemed not to know or care about the Palestinian struggle or Palestinian grievances against Israel. The group's goal was also to restore the faith of the Palestinian people in their leaders' ability to wage a credible fight against the Palestinians' enemies, including Israel itself, those who supported Israel, and the Arab governments, who were increasingly seen to have betrayed the Palestinian cause.

Black September's first operation, in November 1971, was the assassination of Jordanian prime minister Wasfi al-Tall, whom Palestinians regarded as the official most responsible for the 1970 and 1971 bloodshed in Jordan. The assassination was followed by other anti-Jordanian operations, and in 1972 the organization began to target terrorist actions more broadly. The most sensational Black September operation was the seizure and killing of eleven Israeli athletes at the Munich Olympic Games in September 1972. Black September's most notable operation against the United States was the killing in March 1973 of the U.S. ambassador and deputy chief of mission in Sudan.

Black September conducted few operations after mid-1973, and, apparently in response to criticism from Fatah and the PALESTINE LIBERATION ORGANIZATION that TERRORISM harmed the Palestinian cause, it was disbanded in 1974.

Kathleen Christison

BIBLIOGRAPHY

Cobban, Helena. *The Palestinian Liberation Organisation: People, Power and Politics.* Cambridge, England: Cambridge University Press, 1984.

Bludan Conference
1937, 1946

Arab conferences called first to respond to the 1937 Partition Plan then to the Anglo-American Commission of Inquiry. When the PEEL COMMISSION recommended the partition of Palestine in July 1937, the ARAB HIGHER COMMITTEE immediately rejected their conclusions and began lobbying Arab governments for assistance in combating the decision. The committee petitioned the PALESTINE MANDATE for permission to convene a general Arab conference in Jerusalem but was refused. As a result, the conference was organized instead in Bludan, Syria, on September 8, 1937, with the Iraqi prime minister Naji al-Suwaydi presiding.

The Bludan Conference rejected the PARTITION PLAN and created a number of committees to research ways to fight it. It adopted several resolutions affirming Palestine's place as part of the Arab world and rejecting both partition and any attempt to establish a Jewish state in Palestine.

In the wake of the findings of the ANGLO-AMERICAN COMMISSION, 1945–46, and the angry Arab reaction to it, the ARAB LEAGUE convened a second and historically more important conference in Bludan on June 8, 1946, to formulate an Arab response.

Invitations were extended to prime ministers, foreign ministers, defense ministers, and other Arab state officials.

The conference denounced the findings of the Anglo-American Commission regarding Palestine and criticized Western policy as well, especially that of the United States. The delegates forwarded several significant recommendations to the Arab League detailing ways in which the Arab states could assist the Palestinians in opposing the commission's findings. Among these were a suggestion to reconstitute and finance the ARAB HIGHER COMMITTEE for Palestine and recognize it as the official representative of the Palestinian people, a suggestion that was subsequently carried out.

The Arab League accepted the conference's recommendations and began working publicly to negotiate an alternative to the Anglo-American Commission's recommendation with Britain. At the same time, it secretly began discussing three plans: to cut petroleum sales to the United States and Britain, to send military advisers to train Palestinian guerrillas, and to dispatch forces from various Arab armies into Palestine in the event of war. The last two plans—originally recommended by the Bludan Conference—were actually carried out by the league, forming the basis for Arab military intervention in the ARAB-ISRAELI WAR OF 1948.

Michael R. Fischbach

Boullata, Kamal

Bullata; artist, literary critic
1942– Jerusalem

Kamal Boullata attended the Accademia di Belle Arte in Rome and the Corcoran Academy for the Fine Arts in Washington. After settling in the United States in 1968, he taught at Georgetown University and became a prominent abstract artist. In the 1990s he lived in Morocco and France. Among other artistic motifs, Boullata is noted for his employment of Arabic calligraphy in ART that deals with Sufi poetry and expresses Palestinian nationalist statements.

A writer as well, Boullata is also a literary critic and has edited several works on poetry.

Michael R. Fischbach

British Mandate

See PALESTINE MANDATE.

Budayri Family

A Jerusalem family active in Palestinian political affairs during the Ottoman and Mandate periods.

Kamil (?–1923?; administrator, journalist) Head of the BEERSHEBA and RAMLA subdistricts during the LATE OTTOMAN PERIOD, Muhammad Kamil Budayri helped uncover the Jewish NILI (acronym for *netzah y israel lo yeshaker* [from 1 Sam. 15:29]) spy ring that worked against the Ottoman government during the First World War. Arrested as an Ottoman official by British troops in 1918, he returned to Jerusalem after nine months of exile in Egypt.

Kamil became involved in Arab nationalist causes, joining the ARAB CLUB and attending the 1919 General Syrian Congress in Damascus. He was jailed after the disturbances in Jerusalem in April 1920. In 1921, Kamil, a journalist, began publishing *al-Sabah,* which was associated with the ARAB EXECUTIVE.

Kamil maintained contacts with the powerful leader Abd al-Aziz Al Sa'ud of Najd. He mysteriously disappeared during one of his journeys to visit the Sa'udis in the Arabian peninsula.

Khalil (1906–1983; Jerusalem; physician, activist) Khalil studied in Germany in 1922–23, in Egypt in 1924–25, and in Geneva in 1925–29. He later specialized in ophthalmology in London. Khalil was also a communist activist, writing for the Swiss socialist publication *le Travail* while in Europe and joining the PALESTINE COMMUNIST PARTY.

Kamil coordinated a series of pamphlets issued by Palestinian intellectuals during the Palestinian general strike in May 1936. These pamphlets called upon Palestinians to expand the strike to include a policy of "noncooperation" with PALESTINE MANDATE authorities. He was arrested by British authorities that year and imprisoned for six months.

In March 1946, Khalil became a member of the reconstituted ARAB HIGHER COMMITTEE and was appointed to the Palestinian delegation to the United Nations (U.S. authorities refused him entry into the UNITED STATES, however). He was later briefly detained by Egyptian authorities in the GAZA STRIP in 1948.

Khalil published *Sitta wa Sittun Aman ma al-Haraka al-Wataniyya al-Filastiniyya* (Sixty-Six Years with the Palestinian National Movement) in 1982.

Musa (1946– ; Jerusalem; academician) Son of Khalil, Musa Budeiri (Budayri) pursued his studies in England at Oxford University, Durham University, London University, and the London School of Economics. He taught philosophy and cultural studies at BIR ZEIT UNIVERSITY from 1974 to 1996 and has directed the Centre for Area Studies at AL-QUDS UNIVERSITY in Jerusalem since 1996. He is author of *The Palestinian Communist Party, 1919–1948: Arab and Jew in the Struggle for Internationalism*.

Michael R. Fischbach

C

Camp David Accords

The Camp David accords of September 1978 defined the elements of a permanent peace agreement between Israel and Egypt and attempted to establish a framework for achieving peace between Israel and its other neighbors. Negotiated at Camp David, Maryland, between the Egyptian president, Anwar Sadat, and the Israeli prime minister, Menachem Begin, with the active mediation of the U.S. president, Jimmy Carter, the accords envisaged the establishment of Palestinian autonomy in the Israeli-occupied WEST BANK and GAZA STRIP. After several months of further negotiation, the accords were adopted as the Egyptian-Israeli Peace Treaty, signed in Washington, D.C., on March 26, 1979.

Under the accords, delegations from Israel, Egypt, and Jordan—the latter two including Palestinian delegates—were to meet to establish procedures for electing, and for defining the responsibilities of, a Palestinian self-governing authority for the West Bank and Gaza. As later defined in letters accompanying the Egyptian-Israeli Peace Treaty, negotiations on the establishment of the Palestinian self-governing authority were to begin one month after ratification of the treaty and to be completed within a year. At the end of that year (April 1980), the self-governing authority would be elected, and a five-year transition period of Palestinian autonomy would begin. Negotiations on the final status of the West Bank and Gaza among Israel, Egypt, Jordan, and the elected representatives of West Bank and Gaza Palestinians were to begin no later than the third year of the transition period and to be completed by the end of that period. Final-status negotiations would consist of two tracks: one dealing with the status of the West Bank and Gaza and the other dealing with peace between Israel and Jordan.

Although the Camp David accords spoke of guaranteeing the sovereignty and territorial integrity of states in the area and addressed the need to recognize the "legitimate rights of the Palestinian people," as well as the Palestinians' need to "participate in the determination of their own future," such questions as precise border locations, security arrangements, and the fate of Palestinian refugees were to be left for final-status negotiations. The key issue of Israeli withdrawal from the West Bank and Gaza during the transition period was left deliberately ambiguous. In order to accommodate Prime Minister Begin's view that UNITED NATIONS SECURITY COUNCIL RESOLUTION 242 and its call for Israeli withdrawal did not apply to the West Bank and Gaza, Presidents Carter and Sadat agreed to avoid linking any final-status arrangements to the resolution. The official version of the accords carries the meaningless formulation that future negotiations would be based on Resolution 242 but says nothing about basing an actual final agreement on the resolution.

The Israeli position prevailed on the issue of Israeli settlements in the West Bank and Gaza, an issue critical to the future disposition of those territories. President Carter has said that during the Camp David talks, he secured Prime Minister Begin's agreement to a freeze on settlement construction until the end of the transition period, an agreement that Begin would ratify through a letter to Carter to accompany, but not constitute an integral part of, the accords. Begin, on the other hand, has insisted that he agreed only to a three-month freeze; this limited freeze is what he stipulated in a letter to Carter.

The Egyptian-Israeli Peace Treaty, which grew out of the Camp David accords, is widely regarded—by Arabs and by most of the American, Egyptian, and Israeli officials who negotiated it—as a separate peace agreement that had the effect of taking Egypt, the strongest Arab party, out of the ARAB-ISRAELI CONFLICT, leaving the other Arab parties with significantly diminished diplomatic and military leverage against Israel. Most analysts have concluded that Prime Minister Begin no longer had an incentive to work for a resolution of the Palestinian issue because he had secured a peace agreement with the Arab state most capable of threatening Israel militarily; moreover, he had negotiated an autonomy arrangement for the West Bank and Gaza that lacked any provision for Israeli withdrawal, imposed no limit on Israel's land confiscation or settlement construction in the territories, and held out no credible promise to the Palestinians of an end to Israeli occupation.

For these reasons, Palestinians and other Arabs rejected the accords, and, in the belief that President Sadat had betrayed both the Palestinian cause and the cause of Arab unity, expelled Egypt from the ARAB LEAGUE and other Arab forums. Jordan and the Palestinians refused to participate in the Egyptian-Israeli autonomy talks, which ultimately broke down after three years of sporadic meetings. Hampered by Israel's restrictive concept of autonomy and Egypt's reluctance to negotiate without a Palestinian mandate, the talks never made substantial progress.

Kathleen Christison

BIBLIOGRAPHY

Carter, Jimmy. *Keeping Faith: Memoirs of a President.* New York: Bantam Books, 1982.

Dayan, Moshe. *Breakthrough: A Personal Account of the Egypt-Israel Peace Negotiations.* New York: Alfred A. Knopf, 1981.

Fahmy, Ismail. *Negotiating for Peace in the Middle East.* Baltimore: Johns Hopkins University Press, 1983.

Quandt, William B. *Camp David: Peacemaking and Politics.* Washington, D.C.: The Brookings Institution, 1986.

Cattan, Henry

jurist

1906– Jerusalem

Cattan is a *licencié-en-droit* from the University of Paris and holder of an LL.M. from the University of London. He later practiced law in Palestine during the PALESTINE MANDATE and taught at the Government Law School in JERUSALEM from 1932 to 1942. Cattan also worked on behalf of the Palestinian national cause, serving on the third ARAB HIGHER COMMITTEE (AHC) in 1946. He represented the AHC before the U.N. General Assembly in 1947–48 and was appointed by the ARAB LEAGUE to carry out discussions with the U.N. mediator Count FOLKE BERNADOTTE in 1948.

Over the years, Cattan has authored numerous books dealing with LAW and the international legal aspects of the Palestinian question, including *Palestine and International Law* and *Palestine, the Arabs, and Israel.*

Michael R. Fischbach

Center for Palestine Research and Studies

Established in NABLUS in March 1993, the Center for Palestine Research and Studies (CPRS) is an independent, nonpartisan scholarly institute that sponsors research and analysis on a wide range of issues relating to the Palestinian people. The center's interests focus on domestic Palestinian affairs, relations with Israel, relations with the Arab world, relations with the wider world, and the peace process.

In addition to publishing policy papers and organizing workshops, lectures, and conferences, the center publishes the quarterly journal *al-Siyasa al-Filastiniyya* (Palestine policy). It also conducts opinion polls and maintains a library.

The center's overall director from 1993 to 1996 was KHALIL SHIKAKI, who after 1996 served as director of research.

Michael R. Fischbach

Christian Churches

There are in the Holy Land thirty-five Christian Churches, which can be divided into four categories: Catholic, Orthodox, Monophysite, and Protestant. The oldest among the Christian Churches is the Greek Orthodox, which has about 44,000 followers. In the nineteenth century, other Christian groups—Catholic and Protestant—settled in Palestine. Until then, Catholic institutions in JERUSALEM and Palestine were protected by the Franciscans resident in the Holy Land since the fourteenth century. The Greek Catholic (Melkite) Church is the most important among the Uniate (linked to Rome) churches in Palestine, including the Armenian, Maronite, Syrian, and Coptic Churches.

These Christian communities have faced the same problems encountered by other minorities in the Middle East—that is, an identity issue and the interreligious rivalries and squabbles peculiar to the Holy Land and Jerusalem. The fundamental issue for the Christian minority in the Holy Land has been that of acceptance and equal footing. The same has applied to other non-Muslims under Islamic rule. In fact, throughout history, under Arab and Turkish domination, non-Muslims (Christians and Jews) were treated as *dhimmis*—tolerated minorities—by the Muslim majority. In the Ottoman Empire, Islamic tolerance of Christians was defined by the *millet* (community) system. Local communities of a particular religious confession were autonomous in the conduct of their spiritual and civil affairs such as administration, marriage, inheritance, property, and education.

The *millet* system estranged Christians from political life and deepened suspicions between them and Muslims. After the fall of the Ottoman Empire and in reaction to their plight, Middle Eastern Christians were at the forefront of Arab nationalism and the secular movement in the Arab world, and some among them founded socialist parties, such as the Ba'th [Resurrection] party, now in power in SYRIA and Iraq.

For Palestinian Christians, the dilemma relating to their identity was compounded by their status as a minority in Israel after the establishment of a Jewish state in 1948. In a sense, it was the second time in the history of Christianity that a Christian minority found itself living in the midst of a Jewish majority.

Unlike some groups in Lebanon that opted to follow a policy of total opposition to their Muslim counterparts, Christians in the Holy Land have found themselves on the same side as Muslims regarding the Arab-Israeli-Palestinian dispute.

In addition to the problems posed by the definition of their identity, the different Christian communities have had to overcome centuries of distrust and ill feeling among themselves. This situation is highlighted by rivalries—for example, between the Greek Orthodox church, which is the oldest in the Holy Land, and the other Christian denominations (Catholic, Protestant, and others). Moreover, the Orthodox community cannot accept the fact that sometimes the VATICAN talks about Jerusalem and the HOLY PLACES as if it had an exclusive mandate to speak on behalf of all Christians. In recent years, however, efforts were undertaken to discuss controversial issues and work together toward adopting common ground among Christian churches.

In 1974, Orthodox and Protestant churches created the Middle East Council of Churches (MECC), which is active through its offices in Cyprus and Lebanon. The MECC fosters several programs in emergency relief for Palestinian refugees in Lebanon. It also implements programs in the WEST BANK, GAZA STRIP, Jordan, and Galilee. These programs include education, health care, vocational training, and social service centers. In 1990, Catholic churches in the Middle East joined the MECC. In addition to its programs, MECC is involved in spreading awareness of issues arising from the Arab-Israeli-Palestinian conflict. For instance, MECC organizes seminars and study tours and acts as a platform for local Christian leaders to alert world public opinion to ongoing problems such as the unresolved issue of Jerusalem or illegal acts committed by Jewish settlers in the Palestinian OCCUPIED TERRITORIES.

Through the National Council of Churches (NCC), U.S. churches (Methodist, Presbyterian, Lutheran, Episcopalian, United Church of Christ, Orthodox Church in America, and others) provide technical, financial, and personnel support to sister communities in the Middle East. In addition, the NCC organizes for its members study tours and pilgrimages to the Holy Land and fosters interfaith relations with Muslim and Jewish committees in the United States, Europe, and the Middle East. The NCC is also involved in educating and helping Christians understand the Middle East from religious, social, cultural, and political perspectives. The same applies to Christian denominations outside the United States. The basic position adopted by these churches regarding the Arab-Israeli conflict has three main tenets: (1) all parties should refrain from the use of violence; (2) Arab states and the Palestinians should recognize Israel and Israel should acknowledge the right to self-determination of the Palestinians; and (3) the status of Jerusalem should be the subject of negotiation.

Some Christian churches have expressed discontent about unilateral Israeli actions in Jerusalem. In order to express their concern, some members of the NCC have established programs and initiatives. In 1987, the U.S. Interreligious Committee for Peace in the Middle East was created. It includes prominent members of the Jewish, Christian, and Muslim communities. Every year the committee convenes major consultations throughout the United States calling for negotiations and mutual recognition between Israelis and Palestinians. Another initiative created by some Christian churches is to use lobbying and public advocacy with the U.S. government to implement these churches' platform for the Middle East.

Some Christian churches, mostly those active in American Christianity, support Christian ZIONISM and are hostile to Palestinians. These are the evangelical, fundamentalist, and Pentecostal churches. Most of these churches believe that contemporary Israel will play a crucial role in the second coming of Christ, the appearance of the anti-Christ, and the End Time at Armageddon.

George E. Irani

BIBLIOGRAPHY

Horner, Norman A. *A Guide to Christian Churches in the Middle East.* Elkhart, Ind.: Mission Publications, 1989.

Kimball, Charles. "Protestant and Catholic Churches Support for Palestinians." *The Link* 23(3) (July–August 1990).

Nijim, Basheer K. *American Church Politics and the Middle East.* Belmont, Mass.: AAUG, 1982.

Ruether, Rosemary Radford, and Herman J. Ruether. *The Wrath of Jonah: The Crisis of Religious Nationalism in the Israeli–Palestinian Conflict.* San Francisco: Harper & Row, 1989.

Valognes, Joan Pierre. *Vie et mort des Chétiens d'Orient des origines à nos jours.* Paris: Fayard, 1974.

Churchill Memorandum
1922

In June 1922, the British HIGH COMMISSIONER FOR PALESTINE, Sir Herbert Samuel, issued a statement in the name of Secretary of State for Colonies Winston Churchill clarifying Britain's Palestine policy in light of the outbreak of Palestinian political violence in 1921. A commission of inquiry had determined that the violence directed at Jews stemmed from Arab hostility "connected with Jewish immigration and with their conception of Zionist policy." Samuel accordingly encouraged Churchill to explain Britain's conceptualization of the BALFOUR DECLARATION to Jew and Arab alike.

Also called the Churchill White Paper and the White Paper of 1922, the memorandum reasserted British support for the idea of a Jewish national home in Palestine. It noted that the Jewish presence in Palestine was based on "a right and not on sufferance." The statement defined the national home as

> the further development of the existing Jewish community *[yishuv]*, with the assistance of Jews in other parts of the world, in order that it may become a centre in which the Jewish people as a whole may take, on grounds of religion and race *[sic]*, an interest and a pride.

The memorandum noted that, to accomplish this, "it is necessary that the Jewish community in Palestine should be able to increase its numbers by immigration."

Yet the memorandum also tempered Zionist visions "to the effect that the purpose in view is to create a wholly Jewish Palestine" by rejecting the idea of transforming Palestine into a land "'as Jewish as England is English.' His Majesty's Government regard any such expectations as impracticable and have no such aim in view." Concerning the Palestinians, the memorandum affirmed Britain's commitment to prevent "the disappearance or the subordination of the Arabic *[sic]* population, language, or culture in Palestine" or "the imposition of Jewish nationality upon the inhabitants of Palestine as a whole." And, significantly, it stated that absorption of Jewish immigrants would be limited to the "economic capacity of the country."

Although Zionist leaders believed the statement represented Britain's backing off from the Balfour Declaration, they acquiesced to it because of the realization that the memorandum stopped short of ruling out the eventual establishment of a Jewish state. In fact, in 1936 Churchill confirmed to the PEEL COMMISSION that he had not intended to imply such a prohibition. Palestinian leaders, on the other hand, rejected the memorandum because it upheld the Balfour Declaration and because it still allowed Jewish immigration.

Philip Mattar

BIBLIOGRAPHY

Hurewitz, J. C. *The Middle East and North Africa in World Politics: A Documentary Record,* 2d rev. ed. Volume 2. *British-French Supremacy, 1914–1945.* New Haven, Conn.: Yale University Press, 1979.

——. *The Struggle for Palestine.* New York: Schocken Books, 1976.

Lesch, Ann Mosley. *Arab Politics in Palestine, 1917–1939: The Frustrations of a Nationalist Movement.* Ithaca, N.Y.: Cornell University Press, 1979.

Collège de Frères

The Collège de Frères was established in 1875 by the Franciscan Order just inside the New Gate in Jerusalem's Old City. It was part of a system of *frères* schools, which are Roman Catholic secondary schools, located in Jerusalem, Bethlehem, Jaffa, and Haifa.

Michael R. Fischbach

D

Dajani Family (Jaffa)

The Dajani family of JAFFA is not related to the more prominent family of the same name from Jerusalem.

Burhan (1921– ; Jaffa; economist, academician) Burhan received a B.A. from the American University of Beirut (AUB) in 1940 and taught there in 1944. He later received a law diploma from the Government Law School in Jerusalem in 1948.

In 1950, Burhan established *al-Hadaf* newspaper in Jerusalem. In 1951, he was appointed general-secretary to the Union of Arab Chambers of Commerce, Industry and Agriculture in Beirut. He was also a founder of the INSTITUTE FOR PALESTINE STUDIES. He taught economics at AUB and three other universities in Beirut. He is a leading intellectual living in Amman.

Kamil (politician) Kamil helped found the ISTIQLAL PARTY in 1932, and later assisted in forming the pro-HUSAYNI Palestine ARAB PARTY in 1935. Kamil was also a member of the reconstituted ARAB HIGHER COMMITTEE in 1945.

Michael R. Fischbach

Dajani Family (Jerusalem)

Leading figures in the Opposition (to the HUSAYNI FAMILY) led by the NASHASHIBI FAMILY, members of the Dajani family helped form the Palestinian Arab National Party in 1923 and were later associated with the NATIONAL DEFENSE PARTY.

Arif (?–1930; politician) Mayor of JERUSALEM during World War I, Arif was the dominant figure among the Jerusalem Dajanis at that time. A founder and later president of the MUSLIM-CHRISTIAN ASSOCIATION in Jerusalem, he headed a national gathering of Muslim-Christian associations from all over Palestine, the first major gathering of nationalist figures in Palestine, in February 1919. As such, he became one of the most important of these figures during the early days of the PALESTINE MANDATE. He was elected the first vice president of the ARAB EXECUTIVE in December 1920 and later became a pillar of the Nashashibi-led Opposition.

Hasan Sidqi (1898?–October 1938; lawyer, journalist) One of the founders of the LITERARY Club in 1918, he became a significant figure in the Opposition during the 1920s. In 1927, he was one of the founders of the LIBERAL PARTY. As head of the Arab Car Owners' and Drivers' Association during the 1930s, he helped organize a strike of transport workers in the spring of 1936, an act that directly contributed to the calling in May 1936 of a nationwide strike among Palestinians coordinated by the ARAB HIGHER COMMITTEE. Reported to have cooperated with the Jewish Agency, Hasan Sidqi was assassinated in 1938 in the internecine fighting among Palestinian factions during the Arab revolt.

Ahmad Sidqi (scholar) One-time director of the PALESTINE LIBERATION ORGANIZATION (PLO) research center and cofounder of its scholarly journal, *Shu'un Filastiniyya,* he served on the PLO executive committee from 1977 to 1985.

Michael R. Fischbach

Dakkak, Ibrahim

Ibrahim Daqqaq; engineer, architect, activist
1929– Jerusalem

Ibrahim Dakkak left the WEST BANK for Cairo to pursue his studies; there he received a B.S. in science and mathematics in 1952 from The American University in Cairo. Later he went to Istanbul, where he earned a second B.S. degree in civil engineering from Roberts College in 1961.

Dakkak was active in a number of professional and nationalist organizations in the West Bank beginning in the late 1960s. Within his profession, he chaired the Engineers Association of the West Bank from 1967 to 1986. From 1969 to 1977, he served as chief engineer for the major al-Aqsa Restoration Project at the HARAM AL-SHARIF in JERUSALEM, which repaired Islam's third holiest site. In 1967–1968, he served as founding director of Jerusalem's al-Maqasid Hospital, one of the territories' few Arab hospitals. He also served as a founding member of the Council for Higher Education from 1977 to 1987.

Dakkak was also politically active on the West Bank through his service as chair of the ARAB THOUGHT FORUM beginning in 1977. The forum was one of the first indigenous institutions in the West Bank to wrestle with questions of Palestinian national development and other issues relating to the future of the Occupied Territories and its next generation of leaders. Dakkak and the forum were also instrumental in establishing the NATIONAL GUIDANCE COMMITTEE in response to the 1978 CAMP DAVID ACCORDS, which the committee opposed. The committee, which Dakkak served as secretary from 1978 to 1982, proved to be a major bridge between local Palestinian activists in the territories and the PALESTINE LIBERATION ORGANIZATION (PLO) in exile.

Dakkak is author of *Back to Square One: A Study of the Re-Emergence of the Palestinian Identity in the West Bank, 1967–1980.*

Michael R. Fischbach

Darawisha, Abd al-Wahhab

Darawsheh; politician
1943– Iksal

A native of Galilee, Darawisha studied history and education at Haifa University. He thereafter worked as a secondary school teacher and principal. A member of the Labor Party, Darawisha was first elected to the Knesset in 1984. Darawisha left the party in January 1988 in protest over the harsh policies instituted by Defense Minister Yitzhak Rabin, a fellow member of the Labor Party, to combat the INTIFADA in the Occupied Territories.

Darawisha established the Democratic Arab Party (DAP) shortly thereafter and was elected to the Knesset in the November 1988 elections. The DAP was one of the first openly Arab political parties to contest Knesset elections, and Darawisha's action indicated a shift in the political attitudes of the PALESTINIAN CITIZENS OF ISRAEL toward support of more openly Arab political parties in the wake of the Intifada. He later worked with a faction of the Islamic movement in Israel to form a new party, the United Arab List, to contest the May 1996 Knesset elections and was elected.

Darawisha was one of several prominent Palestinians in Israel who tried to serve as bridges between Israel and its Palestinian citizens and the wider ARAB WORLD. In March 1994, he visited Syria with Egyptian travel documents and met with Syrian president Hafiz al-Asad—the first such public meeting between senior Palestinian political figures from Israel and the Syrian leadership. He later joined a delegation of Israeli Palestinians on a second trip to Syria in August 1997.

Michael R. Fischbach

Darwaza, Izzat

politician, writer
1889–1985 Nablus

An Ottoman bureaucrat in Palestine and Lebanon, Izzat Darwaza became involved in Arab nationalist politics during the LATE OTTOMAN PERIOD. A member of the al-Fatat, Arab nationalist organization, he helped coordinate the Arab Congress held in Paris in 1913.

After the Ottoman defeat, Darwaza moved to Damascus, where he was an advocate of pan-Syrian unity under the leadership of Faysal bin Husayn of the Hashemite family, as well as a foe of ZIONISM. He helped establish the Palestinian Society as well as the Society of Palestinian Youth, an armed organization formed to combat Zionism in Palestine.

Darwaza continued his nationalist activities after returning to Palestine. He helped establish the

ISTIQLAL PARTY in 1932, and during the Arab revolt of 1936–1939, he directed Palestinian guerrilla activity from Damascus. Darwaza also served on the fourth ARAB HIGHER COMMITTEE beginning in 1947.

Later in his life, Darwaza wrote numerous books on Arabo-Islamic and Palestinian history, including *Hawl al-Haraka al-Arabiyya al-Haditha* (On the modern Arab movement) and *al-Qadiyya al-Filastiniyya fi Mukhlalaf Marahiliha* (The Palestine problem in its various stages). His six-volume memoirs have also been published.

Michael R. Fischbach

Darwish, Ishaq

Politician

1896–1974 Jerusalem

Ishaq Darwish studied in Beirut before serving with the Ottoman military during the First World War. Thereafter, he was a member of the ARAB CLUB in JERUSALEM, which functioned from 1918 to 1920 and was headed by his uncle, AL-HAJJ AMIN AL-HUSAYNI. Darwish was also the first secretary of the MUSLIM-CHRISTIAN ASSOCIATION.

Darwish continued his nationalist activities during the PALESTINE MANDATE. For many years, Darwish was an aide to al-Husayni, the mufti of Jerusalem. He helped establish the pan-Arab ISTIQLAL PARTY in 1932. While living in exile in 1947, he was a member of the fourth ARAB HIGHER COMMITTEE.

After the ARAB-ISRAELI WAR OF 1948, Darwish lived in Beirut and London for most of the rest of his life.

Michael R. Fischbach

Darwish, Mahmud

Palestinian poet

1941– Birwa

During the ARAB-ISRAEL WAR OF 1948, Darwish's family fled the advancing Israeli army to Lebanon, where they lived as refugees for one year. When they "infiltrated" back into Israel, their village of Birwa, near Acre, no longer existed; it had been razed by the Israeli army, and a new Jewish settlement stood on its ruins. The family relocated to another Arab village, where Darwish grew up as an "internal" refugee. These traumatic childhood experiences of uprootedness and dislocation left an indelible mark on the poet's nascent consciousness.

By way of formal education, Darwish attended only elementary and secondary Arab schools in Galilee. After graduation from secondary school, he moved to Haifa to work in journalism. In 1961 he joined the Israeli Communist Party and remained active in its ranks until his permanent departure from Israel in 1971. Since then he has moved from one to another of the following capitals: Cairo, Beirut, London, Paris, and Tunis. In the late 1990s, he shuttles back and forth between Amman and Ramallah. He has been active in Palestinian national politics and has occupied several important positions in the cultural apparatus of the PALESTINE LIBERATION ORGANIZATION (PLO), including chief editor of the Palestinian literary and cultural periodical *al-Karmil,* formerly published in Nicosia, later in Ramallah. In 1969 Darwish was awarded the Lotus Prize by the Union of Afro-Asian Writers.

Darwish began writing poetry at an early age. His first collection, *Asafir Bila Ajniha* (Wingless birds, 1960) appeared when he was only nineteen. Mostly traditional in form and style, the love lyrics of this collection have a modest artistic value. For this reason the poet disregarded this collection when compiling his collected works, which began to appear in 1973. It was his second collection, *Awraq al-Zaytun* (Olive leaves, 1964), that established his reputation and gained him the epithet "poet of the Palestinian resistance," by which he is still widely known in much of the Arab world.

In general, it is possible to distinguish three distinct phases in Darwish's poetry. The first phase spans the period before his departure from Israel in 1971, the second from 1971 to 1982, and the third from 1982 to the present. Thematically, Darwish's poetry deals with the loss of Palestine. Although Darwish's preoccupation with Palestinian concerns has remained constant, his treatment of these concerns has evolved considerably through the years.

All the poems of the first phase deal with two general topics: love and politics. The political poems stand out for their powerful polemics and fiercely defiant tone. Against Zionist claims on Palestine, they affirm the indissoluble historical bond between Palestinians and their land. A primary objective of these poems is precisely to strengthen the resolve of the Palestinian peasants in resisting Israel attempts to dislodge them from their ancestral land. All artistic and aesthetic considerations are strictly subordinated here to this political imperative.

The love poems foreshadow the eventual transformation of the beloved female into the beloved homeland that is characteristic of Darwish's subsequent poetry. The transformation appears complete in *Ashiq Min Filastin* (A Lover from Palestine; 1966, 1970). This intimate love relationship between poet and land grows steadily more intense until it reaches the fervor of mystical union in Darwish's later poems.

Darwish's encounter with the reality of the Arab world proved disillusioning and occasioned a withdrawal from certainty and an inward turn in his poetry. The common images of daily life in the homeland, such as the faces of family and friends and the topography of the landscape, become the object of poetic meditation in exile. A gripping note of nostalgia for Galilee, Haifa, Mount Carmel, and the coast of Palestine reverberates through the poems of the second phase. Darwish's first collection in exile, *Uhibbuki aw la Uhibbuki* (I love you, I love you not, 1972), suggests the direction and scope of the change in his poetry. Away from the homeland, it becomes a constant struggle to retain intact the details of its identifying characteristics. The words, pictures, memory, and dreams join those of wounds and death as key terms in Darwish's poetic diction. In the working of dream and memory the body of the beloved female blends imperceptibly with that of the homeland until they become virtually indistinguishable.

Although the introspective turn imparts to Darwish's poetry a more personal, almost confessional quality, his progressively more frequent appeal to the prophetic tradition of the three great monotheistic religions imparts to it a universal dimension. The cross, crucifixion, and especially wounds and sacrificial death are permanent motifs. Darwish also makes extensive use of the Old Testament prophets, notably Isaiah and Jeremiah, on whom he frequently calls to condemn Israel's acts of injustice against the Palestinians. *Uhibbuki aw la Uhibbuki* begins with seventeen psalms to Palestine. In tone and style, Darwish's moving lamentations echo those of the Old Testament, which Darwish, bilingual in Arabic and Hebrew, is able to read in the original.

Darwish's poetic output has continued unabated during the third phase. Two important poems he wrote after the 1982 Israeli invasion of Lebanon, however, have left a strong mark on this phase. Both *Qasidat Bayrut* (Ode to Beirut, 1982) and *Madih al-Zill al-Ali* (A eulogy for the tall shadow, 1983) are narrative poems of substantial length. The subject of both is the heroic Palestinian resistance to the Israeli siege of Beirut during the summer of 1982. Following the tradition of the classical Arab poets, Darwish abandons the subjective voice of the lyricist and sings the collective heroics of his people in the plural voice. Stanzaic in form, both poems mark a return to a simpler, more direct, and clearer style than that of the poems of his second phase. Of the two poems, the second is considerably longer and more accomplished artistically. It introduces into modern Arabic poetry the city (Beirut) and the sea (Mediterranean) as objects of sustained poetic interest. It also continues Darwish's cultivation of the prophetic voice. Darwish assumes the voice of the Prophet of Islam, Muhammad, to chastise the Arab regimes for abandoning the Palestinians and the Lebanese to the Israeli onslaught. Darwish's harshest invectives are reserved for the oil-rich Arab monarchies. No other modern Arab poet has used the language, style, and motifs of the Qu'ran and the prophetic tradition as effectively as has Darwish.

Muhammad Siddiq

Dayr Yasin

Dayr Yasin lay five kilometers west of Jerusalem, and in the late 1940s it was inhabited by some 600 Palestinians. Although the village had signed a nonaggression pact with the Jewish Haganah to avoid the Zionist-Palestinian hostilities that had broken out in late 1947, it lay along the route from Tel Aviv to Jerusalem that the Haganah had decided to open through Operation Nachshon in April 1948. The two dissident Zionist military organizations, Irgun Zvai Leumi (Irgun) and Lohamei Herut Yisrael (or the Stern Gang) (LEHI) decided to attack Dayr Yasin and informed the Haganah of their intentions.

Some 100 Irgun and LEHI forces attacked Dayr Yasin on April 9, 1948. They sustained enough casualties from the defending villagers that a small contingent of the Haganah's Palmach troops was called in to assist them in capturing the village.

Thereafter, Irgun and LEHI fighters massacred many surviving villagers. The total number often cited as killed was 254 Palestinians, including some 100 women and children. However, a few Palestinian scholars put the figure closer to 100 killed. Some of the survivors were later paraded through the streets of Jewish West Jerusalem. Dayr Yasin's remaining inhabitants were expelled from the village.

Although the Haganah, Jewish Agency, and the Chief Rabbinate condemned the massacre, news of the slaughter spread quickly among Palestinians. It became a major factor in sparking the panicked flight of Palestinian refugees from the Zionist-Arab fighting in the late spring of 1948.

Michael R. Fischbach

Decentralization Party

Arabic, al-Lamarkaziyya

A society founded in Cairo in January 1913 by Syrians who embraced the cause of equal rights for the Arabs within the framework of a multinational Ottoman state.

Based in Cairo, a city whose sophisticated cultural atmosphere attracted Syrian intellectuals in Ottoman times, the Decentralization Party's executive committee, which consisted of eight Muslims, five Christians, and one Druze, tried to promote its reform program in the face of serious opposition from the Committee of Union and Progress (CUP) as well as from conservative Syrian elites who accused the party of being an agent of European powers. The party's program called for administrative decentralization in the Arab provinces, the recognition of Arabic as an official language in provincial business, the appointment of a greater number of local Arab officials, and the granting of wider powers to provincial councils. Through Palestinian activists, the Decentralization Party was able to establish branches in NABLUS, JENIN, TULKARM, and JAFFA. However, the party never gained widespread support either in Palestine or elsewhere, and its membership was to a great degree limited to disenchanted members of notable families.

Muhammad Muslih

Declaration of Principles

See OSLO AGREEMENTS.

Democratic Front for the Liberation of Palestine

Created on February 21, 1969, as a result of a split with the POPULAR FRONT FOR THE LIBERATION OF PALESTINE (PFLP), the Popular Democratic Front for the Liberation of Palestine (PDFLP) became, in August 1974, the Democratic Front for the Liberation of Palestine (DFLP). Its principal leaders were its secretary-general NAYIF HAWATIMA, YASIR ABD RABBO, Abu Layla (real name Qays al-Samarra'i), Salah Ra'fat, and Abu Adnan (Abd al-Karim Hamad).

The PDFLP situated itself, in 1969, on the extreme Left of the Palestinian scene, touting Marxism-Leninism, condemning the Arab regimes as reactionary or petit bourgeois (Egypt and Syria), and calling for a prolonged popular struggle against Israel, a strategy that was in keeping with that of the South Vietnamese National Liberation Front against the United States. It was also prone to calling for the creation of a proletarian revolutionary party. Its media outlet was *al-Shara'a* (The spark, a reference to Lenin's journal *L'Iskra*). It also created in Beirut a weekly publication, *al-Hurriyya* (Freedom), which became one of the most important organs of discussion on the Arab Left.

The PDFLP, in keeping with its strategy to overthrow the Arab regimes, demanded "all power to the resistance," contributing to the conflict with King Husayn and to the BLACK SEPTEMBER conflict in 1970. Relocated in Lebanon in 1971, the DFLP altered its strategy, supported FATAH, established alliances with "progressive" Arab nations (Algeria, Syria, South Yemen), and entered negotiations with socialist nations open to collaboration with progressive Jews. After the 1973 war, the PDFLP contributed to the idea of a "Palestinian national authority" in all liberated areas of Palestine, a concept that was approved at the twelfth PALESTINE NATIONAL COUNCIL (PNC) meeting in Cairo in June 1974.

During the Lebanese civil war (1975–1990), in which it actively participated on the side of the national movement, the DFLP distanced itself from Fatah. It condemned the CAMP DAVID ACCORDS of 1978 and 1979. It favored an alliance with Syria and condemned any rapprochement of the PALESTINE LIBERATION ORGANIZATION (PLO) with Egypt and Jordan. This position sidelined the DFLP after the 1982 war against the PLO in Lebanon. In November 1988, it approved the resolutions of the PNC that supported the partition of Palestine and proclaimed the independence of the Palestinian state.

The international decline of the Left; the breakup of the Soviet Union, with which it had been allied for many years; and its inability to define a strategy different from that of Fatah weakened the DFLP at the end of the 1980s. A split led by the deputy secretary-general of the organization, Yasir Abd Rabbo, occurred in 1991. Opposed to the OSLO AGREEMENTS, the DFLP is, with the PFLP, the principal antagonist of YASIR ARAFAT and has suspended its participation in the PLO Executive Committee.

Alain Gresh

Dome of the Rock

See AL-HARAM AL-SHARIF.

Dudin, Mustafa

politician

Dudin served in the Egyptian administration in the GAZA STRIP after the ARAB-ISRAELI WAR OF 1948 and, beginning in 1968, worked for the Jordanian government as a parliamentarian, ambassador, and cabinet minister. Dudin left Jordan for the WEST BANK in 1975.

In the wake of the 1978 CAMP DAVID ACCORDS, Israel sought to create an alternative to the political power exercised by the PALESTINE LIBERATION ORGANIZATION (PLO) among West Bank Palestinians. Israeli officials decided to sponsor such organizations in the form of the Village Leagues. Dudin established the first league, the Village League of the Hebron District, in Dura, near Hebron, in August 1978. He declared that its purpose was strictly local and that it would avoid national politics. But by 1982, Dudin, by then the head of a grouping of Village Leagues throughout the West Bank called the Movement of Palestinian Leagues, called for Palestinian-Israeli peace talks under the leadership of Jordan's King Husayn.

The Village Leagues were widely viewed as collaborationist and never seriously challenged the PLO among West Bank Palestinians. Dudin resigned from the movement in September 1983.

Michael R. Fischbach

Dusturiyya School

Established in Jerusalem in 1909 by the prominent writer and educator KHALIL AL-SAKAKINI, the Dusturiyya School became a model in structure and curriculum for private, secular secondary EDUCATION in Palestine. During the PALESTINE MANDATE, it was renamed the Wataniyya School.

Michael R. Fischbach

E

Economic History

Since its very beginning, the Zionist movement has frequently described Palestine before Jewish colonization in 1882 as a neglected, uninhabited, and barren land. The representation of Palestine is emphasized in the famous definition of Zionism as "the return of people without land to a land without people," which was articulated by British author and Zionist Israel Zangwill. The historical record, however, shows otherwise. Benjamin Beit-Hallahmi, an Israeli author writes, "There are stories of how early Zionist leaders were unaware of the existence of a native population in Palestine: they thought the land was uninhabited and were shocked to discover the Arab. It is hard to believe such stories. It does not seem plausible that this group of educated Europeans were unaware of such basic facts of life. Looking at the writings of Zionist leaders and intellectuals at the turn of the century, we discover that the presence of natives was not only known but recognized immediately as both a moral issue and a practical question." He then goes on to quote some writings from the 1880s and 1890s supporting his claim. (See Beit-Hallahmi, 1992, p. 72.) In fact, by the mid-nineteenth century, Palestine had a developed system of land ownership, with relatively high land prices, an export-oriented agriculture economy, and vital, growing urban centers. Indeed, Zionist colonization until World War I showed no appreciable success precisely because Palestine did not have the free land or the "frontier" characteristics that had been essential to the colonization of North and South America, Australia, and South Africa. (See Kimmerling, *Zionism and Territorial Dimension of Zionist Politics.*) The subsequent success of the Zionist project was the result of strategic, political, and military factors that enabled the colonizers to overcome these problems. On purely economic grounds, however, Palestine was not susceptible to European/Zionist colonization. (Beit-Hallahmi, 1992, p. 66)

The British PALESTINE MANDATE lasted almost a quarter of a century (1922–48), serving as the midwife for the Jewish homeland in Palestine. The Mandate began with the Jewish economy's accounting for less than one-fifth (19 percent) of the whole Palestinian economy and ended with its constituting more than half (58 percent). (See Metzer, 1992.)

The results of the ARAB-ISRAELI WAR OF 1948 were disastrous for the Palestinian economy. Seven hundred and fifty thousand Palestinians were expelled as REFUGEES to neighboring countries; only 150,000 others stayed inside what became the state of Israel. Those Palestinians who remained were mostly peasants, spread over many villages and small towns of the hinterland, and the Palestinian character of most of the urban centers remaining inside Israel was completely destroyed (Khalidi, 1989).

Since the establishment of the state of Israel, the Palestinian economy has been effectively confined to the WEST BANK and GAZA STRIP. The former was annexed by Jordan in 1950, and the Gaza Strip came under Egyptian military administration after 1948. Both areas were occupied by Israel in June 1967. In September 1993, the PALESTINE LIBERATION ORGANIZATION (PLO) and Israel signed an agreement to establish a limited "interim self-government agreement" in the Occupied Territories, part of which would be under the control of the Palestinian Authority (PA).

This article is divided into three parts. The first describes some important features of the Palestinian economy in the nineteenth and early twentieth centuries. The second focuses on the radical economic changes brought by the British Mandate, and on the Zionist colonization, which led to the breakup of Palestine. The final part is devoted to the economics of the West Bank and Gaza Strip under the Israeli occupation.

The Palestinian Economy in the Nineteenth Century and Early Twentieth Century In the nineteenth century, Palestine, together with the rest of the Arab world, was part of the Ottoman Empire. The economic relations among Arab countries were somewhere between those of a customs union and those of a common market. The Palestinian economy was fully integrated with the economy of Greater Syria along historical lines of trade, population movements, and political development.

At the beginning of the nineteenth century, most Palestinians were poor peasants (*fallahin*), earning a subsistence living by working the land. Power and wealth were in the hands of the village shaykhs, who operated as tax farmers for the Ottoman authority. By mid-century, great economic transformations had taken place, the result of two developments. The first was the tax reform (*tanzimat*) instituted in the Ottoman Empire in the 1850s, which resulted in the substantial weakening of the traditional power of the village shaykhs and their hold over the agricultural economy. The undermining of tax farming paved the way for consolidating the position of the wealthy landowning families of the large towns. This shift in the power structure brought an important change in agrarian ownership conditions, especially the birth of an embryonic bourgeoisie with enough capital to penetrate the agricultural hinterland. Thus, the mid-nineteenth century witnessed the beginning of commercialization in Palestinian agriculture and the beginning of an exportable surplus.

The second key economic development in Palestine was the European penetration that began in the 1830s. This laid the ground for the opening of European markets to Palestinian agricultural exports, and, more generally, for the gradual integration of the Palestinian economy into the world market. Each European power—Great Britain, France, Germany, and Russia—was interested in establishing a presence in the "Holy Land" as part of its strategic designs for expansion into the eastern Mediterranean.

As early as the 1850s, there were three Palestinian ports exporting agricultural goods to Europe, JAFFA in the south, and HAIFA and ACRE in the north. Exports included soap, olive oil, sesame, wheat, barley, corn, dura, vegetables, cotton, and oranges.

At the beginning of the 1870s, trade activities started to involve imports as well as exports. Imported goods included rice from Italy and Egypt; sugar from France; coffee from South America and Arabia; manufactured cotton goods from Britain; cloth from Switzerland and Germany; iron and dry goods from Germany, Britain, Austria, and France; and construction lumber from Asia Minor. Table 1 shows the development of Palestinian trade in Jaffa over the period 1857–1882.

TABLE 1

Exports and Imports of the Port of Jaffa

YEAR	EXPORTS	IMPORTS
1857	15,583,350	
1860	14,968,500	
1863	26,039,100	
1874	26,562,000	14,575,500
1876	56,283,900	29,776,575
1879	52,272,500	31,642,000
1882	37,802,744	36,964,663

Values of goods in piasters: the English sovereign was equivalent to 117.5 piasters in 1857, 126.5 in 1872, and 154 in 1882.

Source: Alexander Schölch, *Palestine in Transition: (1856–1882): Studies in Social, Economic and Political Development.* Washington, D.C.: Institute for Palestine Studies, 1993.

In addition to being Palestine's main port, Jaffa became the center for the production and trade of oranges. According to American estimates, there were 500 orange groves around Jaffa at the beginning of the 1880s, constituting more than 2,000 acres of land and 800,000 trees.

The expansion of agricultural production and trade stimulated other economic activities, such as construction, soap production, and the manufacture of devotional items. The most significant result of this economic upswing was the growth of Palestinian towns (see Table 2). JERUSALEM, BETHLEHEM, NAZARETH, and SAFAD arose as cultural and religious centers, becoming great attractions for European tourists. Jaffa and Haifa were centers of import-export activity and trade with Hawran and central Syria. NABLUS, HEBRON, and Gaza developed mainly on the basis of local and regional trade, and each specialized in certain activities. Weaving and pottery became important activities in Gaza. Grape production, manufacture of water bags, and glasswork were the specialty of Hebron. Nablus concentrated on soap manufacturing and cotton processing. This economic expansion was accompanied by an increase in population (see Table 3).

TABLE 2

Demographic Development of Major Cities in Palestine 1800–1922

	1800	1840	1860	1880	1922
Jerusalem	9,000	13,000	19,000	30,000	65,000
Haifa	1,000	2,000	3,000	6,000	24,000
Jaffa	2,750	4,750	6,250	10,000	47,000
Gaza	8,000	12,00	15,000	19,000	17,000
Hebron	5,000	6,500	7,500	10,000	16,600
Nablus	7,500	8,000	9,500	12,500	16,000
Safad	5,500	4,500	6,500	7,500	8,800
Total	54,000	70,000	90,000	120,750	228,600

Source: Alexander Schölch, *Palestine in Transition (1856–1882): Studies in Social, Economic and Political Development.* Washington, D.C.: Institute for Palestine Studies, 1993, p. 38.

TABLE 3

Economic Establishments in Three Palestinian Cities (1871–1872)

	JERUSALEM	JAFFA	GAZA
Shops	910	332	785
Warehouses	141	188	35
Khans	2	6	6
Mills	14	3	1
Ovens	22	10	9
Soap factories	20	11	10
Oil presses	9	7	16

Source: Alexander Schölch, *Palestine in Transition (1856–1882): Studies in Social, Economic and Political Development.* Washington, D.C.: Institute for Palestine Studies, 1993, p. 118.

For most of the nineteenth century, the contribution of Jews to the economy of Palestine was insignificant. Jews constituted a very small indigenous religious minority, living mainly in the four cities of Jerusalem, Safad, Hebron, and TIBERIAS and dependent largely on charitable assistance from Europe. As late as 1856, of a Jewish population in Jerusalem of approximately 6,000, not more than 47 persons were engaged full time in trade, and not more than 150 were craft workers. In 1864, the British Council in Jerusalem reached an agreement with the Ottoman authority to extend the privilege of the European Capitulatory Arrangement to the Jewish residents of the Holy Land. This preferential treatment, along with the increased presence of Europeans in Palestine, spurred an increase in the Jewish population in Palestine in the second half of the nineteenth century, from 5,000 to 6,000 in 1800 to 17,000 by mid-century and 25,000 in 1881. However, the rate of Jewish population increase was less than that of the general population, and it was not accompanied by an appreciable change in Jews' economic condition.

The active colonization of Palestine by Zionists started with the first wave of immigrants between 1882 and 1903. Unlike their predecessors, who had been immigrating to Palestine for centuries, members of this wave did not simply enter Palestine to live, worship, and die in the "Holy Land." Rather, they desired to colonize the country as a first step toward building a national home for the Jews. But their economic achievements from 1882 to 1919 were meager. During the great Jewish exodus from Eastern Europe and Russia (1905–14), 1 million Jews emigrated to North America, and just 30,000 emigrated to Palestine. Moreover, 80 percent of those who did go to Palestine returned to Europe after a few months. The campaign to build the national home in Palestine fared no better. The whole Zionist achievement over the entire period represented no more than the building of a few agricultural settlements, whose survival was dependent on financial assistance from Europe and on Arab labor.

The British Mandate and the Breakup of Palestine

The transformation in the economic conditions of the Jews started, however, immediately after the British army occupied Palestine in 1918. At that time, the British military authority recognized the right of Jews to immigrate to Palestine, as well as their right to buy land, both of which had been illegal during Ottoman rule.

Following the postwar breakup of the Ottoman Empire, the League of Nations awarded Great

TABLE 4
Expenses and Investments of the Keren ha-Yasod (Foundation Fund) of the Jewish Agency

	PALESTINIAN POUND	PERCENTAGE
Immigration and training	3,654	18.3
Agriculture settlements	5,892	29.5
Employment and housing	2,024	10.1
Urban settlements, commerce, and industry	1,363	6.8
Education and culture	2,269	11.4
Security, emergency measures	3,414	17.1
Health and welfare	423	2.1
Administration of the Jewish Agency	934	4.7
Total	19,972	100.0

Source: B. Kimmerling, *Zionism and Economy*. Cambridge, Mass.: Schenkman Publishing Co., 1983, p. 33.

Britain the Mandate over Palestine in 1922. In July 1920 a national Jewish assembly had been elected; it was recognized by the British government in 1927 as representing the Jewish community and was consequently granted some power to collect taxes.

During the 1920s, two very important Jewish organizations, which proved crucial in shaping later events, were created: the General Federation of Jewish Workers, known as the Histadrut, and the semimilitary defense organization, known as the Haganah. From its inception, the Histadrut was not intended to be an ordinary labor organization. It was designed by the Jewish labor parties as an organizational framework within which a new economic system could be built. Accordingly, the Histadrut established many agricultural communities (kibbutz, moshav), industrial establishments, banks, insurance services, and a complete health system involving hospitals, clinics, and pharmacies. These establishments served as the nucleus of a new economic system, a parallel economy, which, together with Zionism's socialist political subculture, proved to be very attractive to the new immigrants, helping to keep them in the country and reducing emigration to North America. In addition, the Histadrut was responsible for running the secret organization of the Haganah, including its military training and its illegal purchases and smuggling of weapons. As early as the beginning of the 1930s, secret factories producing light weapons and ammunition were run by the Histadrut.

Historians have recognized five waves of Jewish immigration (*aliya*) to Palestine over the period 1882–1947, two of which were particularly instrumental in the development of the Jewish economy. The second *aliya* (1919–23) consolidated the position of the socialist Jewish labor parties and gained eventual leadership of the Zionist organization. It comprised some 37,000 immigrants, most of whom were young and socialist. The ascendancy of labor to leadership gave the labor movement the upper hand in allocating the resources of the Zionist organization (the Jewish National Fund). Table 4 presents the distribution of expenditures of the Jewish Agency over the Mandate period: it shows clearly that the most resources were allocated to activities under the control of labor. It is worth noting that almost as many resources were allocated to military preparation (security and emergency measures) as to immigration.

The Fifth *aliya* (1931–36), by contrast, consolidated in Palestine the position of Jewish capital, which started to penetrate the economy from the earliest days of the Mandate. The British authority was quick to grant Jews the monopolistic rights to establish water and electricity companies serving both Jewish and Arab communities. At the same time, many Jewish industrial establishments were created with public capital imported from Jews in Europe and North America. The unique characteristic of the fifth *aliya,* however, was that most of the immigrants were of German origin, with relatively advanced levels of education and their own private capital: it is estimated that they brought with them the equivalent of 63 million Palestinian pounds. This flow of capital, together with the skills of its owners, proved very effective in developing the Jewish textile, chemical, and mineral industries. World War II, and the consequent disruption of industrial imports from Europe, gave a

TABLE 5

Arab Employment in the Jewish Economy (1936)

	TOTAL EMPLOYMENT IN JEWISH ECONOMY	PALESTINIAN EMPLOYMENT	PERCENTAGE OF PALESTINIANS
Agriculture	20,000	7,000	35.0
Construction	13,700	1,700	12.4
Industy and handicrafts	21,900	1,900	8.4
Transportation and ports	5,000	1,000	25.0
Commercial services	6,400	400	6.7
Other services	15,000		
Total	82,000	12,000	14.6

Source: B. Kimmerling, *Zionism and Economy*. Cambridge, Mass.: Schenkman Publishing Co. 1983, p. 50.

huge boost to Jewish industry and contributed to its fast growth in the first half of the 1940s in classic import-substitution mode.

The factors just described facilitated the very substantial growth of the Jewish economy in Palestine during the Mandate period. Through immigration, the Jewish population was growing at a rate of 8.5 percent a year, so that the population doubled every eight years, as the Jewish gross national product grew at the rate of 13.5 percent, so that it doubled every five years. Thus, the Jewish economy not only was able to absorb mass immigration, but also to raise living standards: per capita income was rising at the rate of 5.2 percent a year and doubling every thirteen years.

Statistics show that the income of Palestinians also grew during the 1930s and 1940s. Some estimates suggest that their per capita income was growing at 2.3 percent a year over the period 1936–1947. However, this growth was to some extent a growth of income and not a growth in the productive capacity of the Palestinian economy. Two important sources of this growth were the income generated by Palestinian employment in the Jewish economy (Table 5) and the income generated from Palestinians employed by the British authority in construction works, especially for the war effort.

Jewish capital penetration of economic activity created many distortions in incentives and prices for the Palestinian economy. The largest and most apparent price distortion involved the price of land. The Zionist drive to buy land markedly increased prices and made it expansion of Palestinian agriculture and industry uneconomical. Table 6 compares the average prices of Palestinian land during the mandate. The impact of Zionist colonization and land acquisition raised the price from levels similar to those in America in 1910 to a level more than twenty times as high by 1944.

TABLE 6

A Comparison of the Prices of Palestinian and US Lands*

YEAR	1910	1922	1936	1940	1944
Palestine	20	34	128	268	1,050
United States	10–30	(n.a.)	31	32	45

Prices are in US dollars for the average *dunum* [1,000 square meters]

Source: B. Kimmerling, *Zionism and Territory: The Socioterritorial Dimensions of Zionist Politics*. Berkeley: University of California Press, 1983, p. 11.

It should be emphasized, however, that the Zionist effort to buy Palestinian land had not resulted in any appreciable changes in the percent of Jewish land ownership of Palestine in 1948. The Jews owned only 7 percent of Mandatory Palestine. As a result of the 1948 war and the expulsion of 750,000 Palestinians from those parts of Palestine that became part of Israel, Jews gained control over 77 percent of the land. After the declaration of the state of Israel, new laws of ownership were issued that allowed confiscation of all public lands and of the lands belonging to Palestinians who were driven outside the country during the war—that is, the majority of all Palestinians.

After 1948, only 150,000 Palestinians remained in their villages (these PALESTINIAN CITIZENS OF ISRAEL became known as "Israeli Arabs"). the parts of Palestine not occupied by Israel consisted of two non-contiguous territories: the West Bank (annexed by Jordan) and the Gaza Strip (which came under the Egyptian military administration).

For eighteen years (1948–1966), the Palestinian areas in Israel remained under military rule. During that period, drastic demographic and economic changes took place. Great portions of Palestinian land were confiscated by the state to accommodate new Jewish settlements and towns. The fabric of society and economy in Arab Galilee was wholly transformed.

After 1968, the status of the Palestinian sector and its inhabitants vis-à-vis the state improved somewhat. And by the 1980s, a vocal Palestinian leadership had emerged to assert the right of a "national minority" that accounted for 17 percent of Israel's total population.

The Economics of the West Bank and Gaza Strip

Since the Israeli military occupation of the West Bank and Gaza Strip in June 1967, Israel has implemented plans to achieve the "Zionization" of these areas. The overall strategy has involved coordinating economic, political, and military efforts to bring about a drastic and irreversible change in demography and control over land ownership. In short, the intention has been to destroy the Palestinian character of the territories.

In a 1993 report on the economic condition of the Occupied Territories, the World Bank described the economic environment created by the occupation as having the following characteristics: a declining natural resource base, regulatory restrictions that held back the expansion of the private productive sector, asymmetric market relations with Israel and other countries that caused a bias toward export of labor and raised domestic wages, fiscal compression that held back the expansion of the private sector.

The declining natural resource base is the result of a systematic Israeli policy toward Palestinian land and water resources that has the aim of placing under Israeli control the largest possible area of land and the maximum amount of WATER. A 1993 U.N. report estimated that by the end of 1992, Israel had confiscated 68 percent of the total land of the West Bank and 49 percent of the Gaza Strip. Palestinians in the West Bank use only 15 to 20 percent of the available water originating in the area; the rest is used by Israeli settlers and Israel. Part of the confiscated land was declared a closed military area, and the rest has been used to build new Jewish settlements. By the end of 1991, the number of these settlements had reached at least 156 in the West Bank and 18 in the Gaza Strip, with a total Jewish population of 250,000. As a result of this policy, the irrigated cultivated area in the West Bank and Gaza has declined by 6 percent, and the prices of land and of water have been distorted, increasing to very high levels in comparison to both Israel and neighboring Arab countries.

The restrictions imposed on the Palestinian business sector included requiring permits for all undertakings involving the acquisition of land, the construction of buildings, the starting of new business, the transportation of goods, and all export and import activities. Outright denials as well as long delays in issuing these permits place a heavy burden on business activities. Israeli tax regulations impose another major cost on the Palestinian economy. Palestinian firms had to pay value-added tax (VAT) on all their imports of raw materials through Israel. They were subsequently reimbursed, but the long delays in receiving the refunds caused these firms severe cash flow problems and shortages of capital. This resulted in loss of around 10 percent of the value of their finished products.

Asymmetric trade relations have been created by precluding Palestinian products from entering the Israeli market except on selective and limited bases. However, the heavily subsidized Israeli products have free entry into the Palestinian market. At the same time, Palestinian trade with the rest of the world has to go through Israel. These regulations have made Palestinian trade completely dependent on Israel. Indeed, 90 percent of all Palestinian imports come from Israel, and 70 percent of the exports go to Israel. Moreover, Palestinian trade with Israel and the rest of the world suffers from a huge deficit. Palestinians used to be able to pay for this deficit by export of labor services to Israel, and from the remittances of foreign currencies sent home by Palestinians working in the Gulf states. Since 1991, however, the latter source has become increasingly marginal, while security developments since 1993 have rendered the former source increasingly unreliable.

One of the most harmful indirect economic effects of the Israeli occupation has been the complete neglect of Palestine's physical and social infrastructure. Urban roads are neither improved nor propery maintained. Rural roads are left without improvements and proper maintenance, relegated to local councils and to private and foreign volunteer organizations. The state of electrical and telecommunication services is underdeveloped: their level and quality are below those of Jordan and Egypt. Similarly, the occupation authorities have neglected social services. It is estimated that 80 percent of the annual health-services expenditures in the West Bank and Gaza Strip comes from external sources. Similarly, more than half of the territories' expenditures on education are provided by the United Nations Relief and Works Agency for Palestine Refugees in the Near East (UNRWA) and from private sources.

This neglect of the public sector and public services by the Israeli authority in the Occupied Territories is especially striking in light of the huge transfer of resources from the Palestinian economy to the Israeli treasury. This has been conducted through three channels: (1) the taxes paid by Palestinians to Israel, in the form of VAT levied on local production, and the custom duties on products imported through Israel; (2) income tax and social security contributions paid by Palestinians working but not residing in Israel; (3) the profit received because the Palestinians use Israeli currency as a legal tender. Estimates of the total of these three sources vary, but some calculate that, by the late 1980s, it was equal to one-fourth of the Palestinian gross national product (GNP).

The cumulative impact of these measures has made the Palestinian economy suffer from a chronic incapacity to generate enough employment for its steadily growing labor force. Table 7 shows that the number of Palestinians working in Israel over the previous two decades was never less than 28 percent of total Palestinian employment, actually reaching almost 40 percent in 1987. It also shows the increasing dependence of Palestine's economy on external sources of income. Income generated by workers in Israel (net factor income), plus remittances and external aid (net transfers), account for more than one-third of Palestine's GNP, paying for the trade deficit that constitutes more than one-third of gross domestic product (GDP).

TABLE 7

Macroeconomic Aggregates of the West Bank and Gaza Strip (1972–1990)

	1972	1975	1980	1987	1990
			(Thousands)		
Population	1,010.9	1,092.2	1,172.0	1,408.2	1,546
Labor force	191.2	206.6	218.5	283.9	314
Total domestic employment	136.4	138.4	140.6	168.9	175
Employed in Israel	52.4	66.3	75.1	108.9	105
	(Millions of Constant 1990 U.S. Dollars)				
Gross domestic product (GDP)	559.8	939.5	1,155.9	1,881.4	1,302
Net factor income	206.8	341.4	405.2	732.5	548
Gross national product (GNP)	766.6	1,280.9	1,565.1	2,613.9	1,850
Exports	196.1	355.4	415.0	475.5	149
Imports	423.2	855.8	775.2	1,073.6	794
Net transfers	111.3	68.0	126.0	137.9	149

Source: Calculated from UNCTAD, *Prospects for Sustained Development of the Palestinian Economy in the West Bank and Gaza Strip, 1900–2010: A Quantitative Framework* (Geneva: UNCTAD/ECOC/SEUIG, 1994) (Table 1/1, p. 17.)

This hostile economic environment is widely considered to be one of the underlying causes of the Palestinian uprising of December 1987 (the INTIFADA). A primary objective of the Intifada was to minimize the economic benefits that Israel gains from the occupation, and thus to achieve some degree of Palestinian economic self-sufficiency. The first two years of the uprising witnessed a range of experiments in "participatory development," efforts that involved families, communities, and professional associations. These initiatives, through popular boycotts of Israeli goods, had some initial success in reorienting consumption patterns away from Israeli products while stimulating local production. Activists also made some progress in reorientating trade via creative efforts in marketing and negotiations with European organizations.

The Israeli authority, however, adopted an "iron fist" policy to crush the uprising, including harsh economic measures. According to the United Nations, these included "sieges of villages and communities, bans on movement of goods or people, ploughing under crops, arbitrary confiscation of produce and unwarranted administrative delays which have left produce rotting in transport." In addition, tax authorities aided by military forces carried out hundreds of collective raids to enforce payments of income tax, value-added tax, and other taxes, fees, or fines.

After three years of daily bloody confrontations, strikes, curfews, and harsh economic measures, Palestine's level of economic activity had been greatly reduced, with declines in both agricultural and industrial production. This general disruption of economic activity was further aggravated by the GULF CRISIS, 1990–1991, which resulted in the loss of thousands of Palestinian jobs in the Gulf states, and hence the loss of a valuable external source of income for Palestine's weakened domestic economy. Return of workers from the Gulf to the West Bank and Gaza Strip greatly exacerbated the problem of Palestinian unemployment. Moreover, the Israeli closure of the territories in March 1993 and the loss of thousands of Palestinian jobs in Israel caused mass unemployment and put the very survival of the Palestinian economy at stake.

The Economics of Limited Self-Rule (1994–1999)

On September 13, 1993, the PLO and the State of Israel signed a Declaration of Principles (DoP) recognizing each other and designating a period of five years (May 1994–May 1999) as one of an interim limited self-rule for the Palestinians in the West Bank and Gaza Strip. It was envisaged that during this period three important tasks would be undertaken. First, a withdrawal of the Israeli Army from most of the Palestinian territories with the exception of East Jerusalem, and the establishment of a democratically elected Palestinian Legislative Council and duly appointed Palestinian Authority as a government. Second, negotiation to conclude an agreement resolving final status issues, which includes borders, Jerusalem, refugees, water, and security. Third, the creation of confidence building measures between the two sides that would replace the confrontation of the occupation and allow the PA to adopt economic policies conductive to reconstruction and development.

The establishment of Palestinian limited self-rule in parts of the West Bank and Gaza Strip, which has taken place in stages since May 1994, brought about two conflicting economic effects. The formation of a national authority with a commitment to reconstruction and development was a positive development that engendered expansion in both the public and the private sectors. While many harmful features of the occupation are still in existence, various positive changes have taken place and contributed to improvement in the economic policy environment. This change of environment has stimulated investments from domestic sources and from Palestinian expatriates, especially in communications, tourism, and services. But the sporadic eruption of violence, the intermittent closures of borders, the continuing Israeli confiscation of Palestinian land, and the building of Jewish settlements, have created a poisonous atmosphere that has reduced economic activities for prolonged periods of time, and deepened the feeling of mistrust and uncertainty that were harmful to investment and growth. Understandably, the negative events proved stronger than the positive constructive development and, as a result, the Palestinian economy continued to perform well below potential during the years of self-rule, as it did during the occupation. Indeed, in 1996–1997 it suffered a major contraction that was associated with very severe problems of unemployment and the spread of poverty.

Fadle Naqib

BIBLIOGRAPHY

Abed, George. *The Palestinian Economy.* London: Routledge, 1988.

Aharoni, Y. *The Israeli Economy: Dreams and Realities.* London: Routledge, 1991.

Beit-Hallahmi, B. *Original Sins: Reflections on the History of Zionism and Israel.* New York: Olive Branch Press, 1992.

Farsoun, Samih K. and Christina Zacharia. *Palestine and the Palestinians.* Boulder, Col.: Westview, 1996.

Issawi, Charles, ed. *The Economic History of the Middle East: A Book of Readings.* Chicago: University of Chicago Press, 1966.

Jiryis, S. *The Arabs in Israel.* New York: Monthly Review Press, 1976.

Khalidi, W. *From Haven to Conquest.* Beirut: Institute for Palestine Studies, 1971.

Kimmerling, B. *Zionism and Territory: The Socioterritorial Dimensions of Zionist Politics.* Berkeley: University of California Press, 1983.

——. *Zionism and Economy.* Cambridge, Mass.: Schenkman Publishing Company, Inc., 1983.

Laqueur, Walter. *A History of Zionism.* New York: Schocken Books, 1972.

Metzer, Jacob. "The Arab Economy in Mandatory Palestine and the Administrated Territories." In *Economic Development and Cultural Change,* pp. 844–865.

Owen, Roger. *The Middle East in World Economy, 1800–1914.* London: Methuen, 1981.

Sachar, H. *A History of Israel—from the Rise of Zionism to Our Time.* New York: Alfred A. Knopf, 1982.

Schölch, Alexander. *Palestine in Transition (1856–1882): Studies in Social, Economic and Political Development.* Washington, D.C.: Institute for Palestine, 1993.

Shakhashiro, K. *The Education System in the West Bank and Gaza Strip.* Bir Zeit: University Press, 1992.

Stanley, F., et al. *Securing Peace in the Middle East, Project on Economic Transition.* Cambridge, Mass.: The MIT Press, 1994.

Smith, Barbara J. *The Roots of Separation in Palestine: British Economic Policy, 1920–1929.* Syracuse, N.Y.: Syracuse University Press, 1993.

United Nations Conference on Trade and Development (UNCTAD) *Prospects for Sustained Development of the Palestinian Economy in the West Bank and Gaza Strip, 1900–2010: A Quantitative Framework.* Geneva: UNCTAD 1994.

——. *Assistance to the Palestinian People.* Geneva: UNCTAD, 1990.

——. *Assistance to the Palestinian People.* Geneva: UNCTAD, 1991.

——. *UNCTAD's Assistance to the Palestinian People.* Geneva: UNCTAD, 1993.

World Bank. *Developing the Occupied Territories: An Investment in Peace.* 6 vols. Washington, D.C.: World Bank 1993.

Zureik, E. *Palestinian in Israel: A Study in Internal Colonization.* London: Routledge, 1979.

Education

The history of formal education in Palestine over the last century has reflected the upheavals that have affected Palestinian society as a whole. At no time until the 1990s have Palestinians had the opportunity to determine the shape of their own educational system. Education at all levels has been decided by the dominant powers of the time, whether the Ottomans, the British, the Israelis, or the Arab states to which the majority of Palestinian refugees fled after 1948.

Nevertheless, dispossession and economic instability have made the achievement of educational qualifications an important goal for most Palestinians. Parents and older siblings often sacrifice a great deal to provide promising youngsters a higher education, which seems to offer a portable asset in an uncertain world. However, by the late 1970s, some Palestinian intellectuals, critical of the education offered both in the Arab world and under Israeli rule, were beginning to put more emphasis on the content of education and to assess what sort of educational system they wanted to see for the future.

Developments in the Ottoman Period The development of mass formal education in Palestine began during the nineteenth century. From the first, developments were piecemeal, creating a patchwork of schools reflecting different cultural perspectives and using different languages.

The Ottoman Empire created state schools in its provinces in the latter part of the century. There were some ninety-five state schools in Palestine by 1914. Only a few of these were high schools, and for further education, Palestinians had to go to Constantinople.

There were also a larger number of private schools established by Christian missionary and church organizations from a number of countries, including Britain, France, Germany, Russia, and the United States. These schools taught in a variety of languages and with different religious and cultural perspectives. Although Muslim as well as Christian families sent their children to these schools and some schools became widely respected, Palestinians often remained suspicious about the intention to proselytize.

Muslim private schools developed at the turn of the century in reaction to both the Turkish bias of state schools and the growing numbers of foreign missionary schools. By 1914, there were 379 such schools at various levels. This development reflected a growing Arab nationalist consciousness and a renewed emphasis throughout the Arab provinces of the Ottoman Empire on Arabic language and literature.

Although the numbers of pupils at school rose, formal education still only reached a small and privileged section of the Palestinian population. The opportunities for girls to go to school were likewise very limited.

The British Mandate Period During the British PALESTINE MANDATE (1920–48) the state-funded school system was expanded as private schools also increased in numbers and enrollment. Publicly funded school education for the Palestinian population was provided directly by the British authorities, in contrast to the rapidly growing Jewish sector, in which education was provided in Hebrew and financed largely by a Zionist organization, Vaad Leumi.

The limited finances made available by the British meant that by the end of the Mandate period, the demand for education, especially at primary level, far outstripped availability. Educational enrollments among Palestinians lagged far behind those in the Jewish population. By 1944, only 32.5 percent of Palestinians aged five to fourteen years were at school, compared with 97 percent of Jews in the same age group. Teacher training for Palestinians also remained inadequate, with many teachers lacking formal qualifications.

Throughout the Mandate period, political conflict affected the education system. Palestinians resented their lack of control over the content and growth of education. Political activism by teachers and students was seen as a threat by the Mandate authorities. The period of the 1936 general strike and the subsequent Palestinian rebellion of 1937–1939 disrupted education, especially in rural areas, drawing schools into the nationalist political struggle as well.

The Fragmentation of Palestinian Education: 1948–1967 After the ARAB-ISRAELI WAR OF 1948, the geographical division of Palestine and the dispersion of the Palestinian community—with some 726,000 people being uprooted and dispossessed between 1948 and 1950—were reflected in educational provision. Nonetheless, the demand for education greatly increased. The dispossession and extreme insecurity that Palestinians experienced made education appear all the more important. It represented a way to escape for those who were growing up in refugee camps and a portable asset for a population that had lost homes, land, and a secure future. By the 1980s, Palestinians had one of the highest proportions of university graduates in the Arab world.

Educational provision became further fragmented according to the authority under which the scattered Palestinian population lived. In the area controlled by Israel, the authorities set up a separate Arab education system. In the GAZA STRIP, under Egyptian control, education followed the Egyptian curriculum, in the WEST BANK and East Jerusalem, the Jordanian education system was in force. In the countries with the largest refugee populations—Jordan, Lebanon, and Syria—schooling was provided partly by the governments concerned and partly by the United Nations Relief and Works Agency (UNRWA) for Palestine Refugees in the Near East.

UNRWA established its own school system open to all refugee children, whether or not they lived in refugee camps. These schools were established in the West Bank, Gaza Strip, Lebanon, Jordan, and Syria. They generally provided the first nine years of education: the primary and preparatory levels. Beyond preparatory level, refugee children had to enter either government or private schools. UNRWA schools followed the curriculum of the controlling authorities but appointed their own teachers and set their own standards, supervised by the United Nations Educational, Scientific, and Cultural Organization (UNESCO). Graduates of UNRWA schools had to go on to state or private secondary schools, depending on availability and access.

During the 1950s and 1960s, Palestinians benefited from the general expansion of education in the Arab countries that hosted refugees, as well as from the provision of nine years' education by UNRWA. However, access to education depended on a variety of often difficult relationships: between host governments and UNRWA and between UNRWA and the Palestinians themselves.

Nowhere did these relationships fluctuate as violently as in Lebanon. During the 1950s and 1960s, UNRWA played the leading role in school education, providing ten years of schooling (as opposed to nine years elsewhere). Most Palestinian children attended these schools, and state schools accounted for only a tiny proportion of enrollment. At secondary level, access for Palestinians has always been difficult because of weak state services. Private schools for Palestinians have flourished in Lebanon, but they are generally expensive and concentrated in Beirut and other urban centers, accessible mostly to middle-class Palestinians.

After the 1948 war, Palestinians who remained in Israel became a minority in their own country. The Israelis created a separate Arabic-language schooling system whose main goal was to create a "loyal minority," although one that was neither trusted nor accepted by the majority society. PALES-

TINIAN CITIZENS OF ISRAEL were placed under military rule until 1966 and remained second-class citizens in many respects.

As part of these efforts to create a loyal minority, any signs of Palestinian identity were suppressed. This was reflected clearly in school curricula. The goals of the history curriculum, for example, differed sharply between the Jewish and Arab systems. In Jewish schools, the aim was not only to instruct students in the "culture of mankind" but also "to instill Jewish national consciousness" and "the feeling of a common Jewish destiny." Arab students were only asked "to value correctly the part played by Jews and Arabs in the culture of mankind." Their curriculum aimed to "instill an awareness . . . of the importance of the State of Israel for the Jewish people . . . and a sense of the common fate of the two peoples, Jewish and Arab."

Palestinian national identity was suppressed in other ways. The Arabic middle-school curriculum excluded contemporary Palestinian and Arab LITERATURE, much of which refers directly or indirectly to the Palestinians' struggle. The curriculum also imposed the standard Zionist view of the recent history of the region and of the creation of Israel. Political considerations also affected the presentation of geography. Hundreds of Palestinian villages within the borders of 1948 Israel had been destroyed or renamed by the Israelis, and these Arab place names vanished from history and geography textbooks.

Although the separate system did keep Arabic alive as a language, Palestinians were disadvantaged in their access to jobs and higher education in part because of their weak command of Hebrew, Israel's dominant language. Teachers in that system were Palestinians but were strictly investigated by the internal security services, and their classroom performance was scrutinized.

Before 1967, higher education was available to Palestinians in some Arab countries, particularly Egypt. However, few Palestinians inside Israel gained access to Israeli universities. In 1969–1970, only 1.6 percent of Israeli university students were "non-Jews," although Palestinians made up about 15 percent of the population.

Education in the Occupied Territories after 1967

After the 1967 war, the situation changed. Israel occupied and subsequently annexed East Jerusalem. Schools within the expanded Jerusalem city boundaries came under the control of the Arab Department in the Israel Ministry of Education. Jordanian textbooks were replaced by those used in the Arab school system in Israel.

Public education in the West Bank and Gaza Strip came under the jurisdiction of the Israeli military government, though the Jordanian and Egyptian curricula were retained. Thus the syllabus and curriculum continued to be set by these countries. The Israelis censored or withdrew textbooks that they regarded as hostile to Israel and excluded all references to Palestinian nationalism and to Arab place names relating to Palestine before 1948.

Education in the West Bank and Gaza Strip became ever more entwined with politics during the Israeli occupation. The Israelis sought to control what was taught in schools, by both control of written materials and surveillance of teachers. Those who challenged the occupation could face dismissal, relocation, or, at the very least, blocks to promotion. On the other hand, schools, colleges, and universities became places of resistance to the occupation. Students questioned what they were taught as well as the system of occupation under which they lived.

Israeli control of education was most intense in state schools—financed and under direct Israeli control—which in 1993 enrolled 62 percent of school pupils. These schools have suffered most from a combination of out-of-date curricula, financial and political restrictions by the Israelis, and poor teacher-training facilities. Students still are learning by rote material that was developed in the 1960s and 1970s. Funding per pupil in schools run by the Israeli Civil Administration in 1991 was U.S.$153 per head.

UNRWA schools have also been constrained by curriculum and "security" problems, though they do spend more per student—$334 per student in Gaza and $425 per student in the West Bank. Overall, UNRWA provides 31 percent of all schooling for Palestinians (though they offer primary and preparatory schools only) but more than 50 percent of such schooling in the Gaza Strip. This reflects the proportion of camp-dwelling refugees in the Gaza Strip compared with the West Bank.

Private schools account for only about 8 percent of total enrollment of Palestinians, predominantly in the West Bank. Many Palestinian private schools are sponsored by Christian and Muslim religious institutions. Private schools have been better funded and have had more freedom to experiment with new teaching methods and educational approaches than other schools. Although they are under the supervision of the Civil Administration, they suffer less interference.

Despite these difficulties, Palestinians enjoyed a considerable expansion of educational enrollment from the 1960s until the 1980s. Marked changes were higher female enrollment and larger numbers of girls remaining at school to secondary level. The uncertainties of the early years of the Israeli occupation encouraged more people beyond the urban middle and professional classes to seek education for their children. By 1980, girls made up about 45 percent of primary enrollment and 40 percent of secondary-school enrollment.

The problems in Palestinian education increased after 1978 as the conflict between Palestinians and the occupation forces intensified. Schools, universities, community colleges, and teacher-training colleges were regarded by the Israelis as hotbeds of nationalism, and consequently, they suffered persistent interventions that disrupted the educational process. A major form of punishment was closure of institutions. Students and staff were arrested and detained, often without being charged. Curfews and roadblocks prevented students and staff from reaching their places of work.

Even when the Israeli civil administration replaced the military government in 1981, the situation for education did not change. Finance for public schools was further restricted, causing teachers to go on strike over low wages, and the infrastructure of schools further deteriorated. In the 1980s, UNRWA also suffered increasing financial problems, which worsened education for Palestinians still more.

Higher education developed locally after 1967 because the Occupied Territories were then cut off from relatively easy access to Arab universities, which also imposed more restrictive quotas for Palestinian students. In all, six Palestinian universities were created by the early 1980s, all private institutions with external sources of funding. The oldest, BIR ZEIT UNIVERSITY, was already a junior college before 1967. The other universities were AL-NAJAH NATIONAL UNIVERSITY in NABLUS; BETHLEHEM UNIVERSITY, AL-QUDS UNIVERSITY, and Hebron University, all in the West Bank; and the Islamic University and al-Azhar University in the Gaza Strip. Later, the Jerusalem Open University began enrolling Palestinian students in 1990. By 1986 there were also nine community colleges offering two-year courses on the West Bank, and four UNRWA technical and vocational training centers, one of which was in the Gaza Strip. The Israeli authorities run three teacher-training schools (two in Gaza) and two agricultural schools on the West Bank.

The development of local higher education for Palestinians played an important role in widening access to university and college education, particularly for women. Families who could afford to do so sent their sons abroad to study, but it grew increasingly acceptable for women to attend local universities. By the early 1980s, women made up about 40 percent of the student body. Total enrollment in universities was estimated at 16,368 in 1991–92.

However, all the universities faced great difficulties with development and planning. They had perennial problems with the Israeli authorities over building permits for campus expansion, and they were forced to pay taxes and duties on educational materials from which Israeli universities were exempted. Many books banned from Palestinian university libraries *were* available in Israeli universities. Financial uncertainties also began to cause problems in the 1980s as the recession in the Gulf states dried up a sizable source of support.

A dramatic challenge to the status and independence of the Palestinian universities was Israeli Military Order 854 (MO 854) of 1980, which transferred to the Israeli occupying authority control over curriculum, administration of students, and hiring and firing of faculty in private institutions. In 1982, the Israeli authorities demanded that all "foreign" staff in West Bank higher education institutions, including Palestinians who did not have residence in the occupied territories, sign a loyalty oath rejecting affiliation with any organization deemed hostile to Israel and denying membership in the PALESTINE LIBERATION ORGANIZATION (PLO). Many lecturers refused to sign, and in 1982–83, twenty-eight staff members from al-Najah University, five from Bir Zeit University, and one from Bethlehem University were deported. Subsequently, the loyalty oath was dropped from the work permit form and MO 854 was said to be "frozen," though it remained in existence.

A similar attack on the independence of the Islamic University in Gaza took place between 1983 and 1985, using Egyptian administration orders—which Egypt had enforced when it ruled Gaza between 1948 and 1967—to demand that staff obtain work permits from the Israeli authorities, who also demanded to supervise the university's finances. The Israelis refused to recognize the university as an institution of higher education, treating it as a religious institute. This gave them grounds under military rule for confiscating the university's budget in 1982 and only releasing it in tranches every three months, although the funds were from independent donations. This process continued over the following two years, causing serious arrears in salary payments for the university's staff.

With the expansion of higher education for Palestinians in the early 1980s, questions were raised about the education being offered. The stunted and dependent state of the Occupied Territories' economy did not allow qualified people to find jobs, and those with professional qualifications were increasingly inclined to leave the country. Concerns also were expressed about the development of overlapping facilities in the various universities, in the absence of an overall authority to plan higher education. The Council for Higher Education, composed of representatives of universities, municipalities, trade unions, and community bodies, was established in 1978 to oversee universities and colleges, but it had only limited power.

The early 1980s also saw the development of new forms of Palestinian education outside the formal system. Some of the universities created extramural departments that offered literacy classes and health education to surrounding communities. Furthermore, voluntary committees emerged in the early 1980s focusing on primary health care, education and literacy, and women's needs. The women's committees, the product of a new generation of educated women, addressed the question of educated women's working outside the home. The women's committees also became involved in the development of preschool education and the promotion of literacy. Nevertheless, illiteracy among older women, especially in villages, remained high. According to Israeli figures, at the beginning of the 1990s, 28.5 percent of women aged thirty-five to forty-four were illiterate, compared with only 7.4 percent of men in that age group.

The INTIFADA began in late 1987. In response, the Israelis essentially shut down most formal educational institutions either totally or for long periods during the following three years. Even kindergartens were affected. Universities managed to sustain various levels of off-campus instruction, but without access to libraries and laboratories.

In the first years of the Intifada, community mobilization to maintain education at all levels was intense. Efforts were made by teachers, parents, and neighborhood committees to create alternative forms of education outside schools and universities, although the Israeli authorities attempted to prevent these initiatives, going so far as to block the distribution of self-learning packets. Although the impact of the self-education movement was patchy and sporadic, it did lead to experiments in the design of public-centered learning materials—a major innovation for teachers and pupils alike.

Thus, for many young people, learning became an activity of the streets, not of the classroom. Large numbers of them were injured or killed, and many were left with disabilities that required specialized educational help. The psychological scars caused by the experience of violence, death, and imprisonment have yet to be confronted fully.

The education system faces many problems. Most students from primary school to university level have lost several years of schooling. There has therefore been a marked decline in standards over the past few years while educational institutions face a backlog of students needing to catch up on the lost years. Young people are also less respectful and more questioning of authority, and that attitude has led to clashes with teachers as well as within families. Generally speaking, teaching methods have yet to adjust to these new realities.

The Palestinian economy remains in a depressed state. Jobs are scarcer than they were before the Intifada as the possibilities of working inside Israel have been greatly reduced. In addition, since the OSLO AGREEMENTS, closures of the Occupied Territories have been frequent, further reducing access to the Israeli labor market. The loss of income caused by these closures and by the loss of remittances from the Gulf since the 1991 war has reportedly reduced both school and university enrollments. If this situation continues, it may create a setback for women's education as the pressure on young women to marry rather than continue their college education increases when job prospects are poor.

The universities emerged from the Intifada period in a financially weakened state, having also lost funds that before 1991 had come from government and private donors in the Gulf. They now badly need more secure sources of funding. They began to reopen partially in 1990; Bir Zeit University only received permission to reopen in April 1992. They struggle with students whose basic education has been interrupted and deficient. At the same time, since the 1993 Declaration of Principles, restrictions on movement imposed by the Israeli authorities within the Occupied Territories—in particular, entry into Jerusalem—have continued to disrupt attendance by students and staff.

The provision of technical and vocational education remains inadequate for Palestinians in Israel. Many of the programs that do exist have not taken into account technological change, and most still adhere to rigid divisions between the types of work regarded as acceptable for men and women.

All these issues are a challenge to the new PALESTINIAN AUTHORITY. Education in the West Bank and Gaza Strip had been handed over to Palestinian Authority, along with other social services. Work has been carried out on a new curriculum, but this can only be effectively implemented if sufficient funds become available and the training of new teachers and in-service training of the existing teaching force can be upgraded.

Future improvements in both the fabric and the equipment of schools, better training of teachers, and improved prospects for students to use their skills depend on future financial support from the international community. In 1993, the World Bank estimated that £127 million was needed as an initial input for infrastructural development. So far, the confusion and difficulties facing the Palestinian Authority have meant that neither international funds nor local tax revenues have been secured.

Palestinians in the Israeli Education System After 1967 By the late 1970s some changes had been made in the Israeli education system's treatment of Palestinians. Despite Israeli apparent efforts in this regard, the Arab education system has not succeeded in destroying Palestinians' specific sense of national identity. In fact, Palestinians' anger over educational inequality and suppression of nationalist sentiments led to the creation of their own organizations dedicated to the preservation of their culture. By the end of the 1980s, they had come to play an important role both in compaigning for improvements in the education system and in lending support to teachers and students by providing workshops and supplementary classes.

Revisions in the curriculum in the 1980s allowed students greater access to modern Palestinian literature as part of the Arabic literature curriculum (1981), and changes were made in the curriculums for history, Hebrew, Arabic, and civics. However, these changes have mostly affected upper secondary schools rather than the primary or secondary lower cycle. Another contentious issue is the amount of time allocated in the Arabic and Hebrew curricula to subjects related to these respective cultures.

Despite some improvements in the Arabic middle-school curriculum, the Arab education system in Israel remains separate and unequal. Since 1948, the Arab system has been severely underfunded, as a result of the general poverty and therefore the low tax base of Palestinian towns and villages and their lack of access to special support funds available to underprivileged Jewish communities. This inequality is the main focus of campaigns by Israeli Palestinians to improve the education system. Although some promises of improvements were made by Israeli education ministers, serious inequalities remained.

Matriculation levels for Palestinians are low compared with even those of the least privileged Jewish students, and there is a high percentage of dropouts at both the elementary and secondary levels. Some of the reasons, particularly for female dropouts, are cultural, but they also reflect low achievement, an ambivalent attitude to education, and low self-esteem among many Palestinian students. Far fewer Arab than Jewish students reach the last year of secondary school, and of those who entered for the final matriculation examination (the Bagrut) in 1989–1990, only 45 percent passed in either the general or vocational stream, compared with 67 percent among Jewish students (Israel; Central Bureau of Statistics, *Statistical Abstract of Israel.* Jerusalem: 1993, Table 22.25).

There is a serious shortage of school buildings, classrooms, and textbooks for Palestinians in Israel. Nursery education (before the beginning of compulsory education) is widely available and subsidized for the Jewish community but receives no government assistance in the Arab section, where only voluntary and private care is available. Palestinian organizations have also identified a need for funds to provide school inspectors, teacher training, and special teaching for children with psychological and physical disabilities. Teachers in the Arab system remain overworked and do not spend enough time in training. According to a recent study, no school head, school inspector, or teacher is ever appointed without approval from the security services.

Education for Refugees in Arab Countries The PLO exercised control over Palestinian refugee camps in Lebanon from the early 1970s until 1982, when it was expelled from Lebanon. During this period, it was able to influence what was taught in UNRWA schools to reflect Palestinian nationalist ideas, something that previously had been impossible when the Lebanese government had controlled the camps.

However, during this period, the Lebanese education system was undermined by a number of factors. The civil war, lasting more than a decade, as well as the Israeli invasion of Lebanon in 1982 caused large-scale physical destruction in many of the camps and areas where Palestinians lived. Many people were displaced internally, often several times, losing homes and family members. Consequently, schools were damaged, staff lost, and children unable to attend classes. In some of the southern camps, physical destruction, mainly from Israeli bombing, had been going on since the early 1970s. Meanwhile, UNRWA faced frequent financial crises. The factional conflicts within the Palestinian movement further added to the disruption of education.

Lebanon is well provided with universities, and significant numbers of Palestinians managed to attend university there. Palestinian organizations offered scholarships and assistance to poorer students living in Lebanon. However, the disruptions of the civil war made sustained study difficult because access was often made impossible by the fighting. The more privileged sections of the Palestinian community either moved abroad or sent their children abroad to study in this period.

By contrast, access to vocational training has been limited, while unemployment rates among Palestinians in the camps has remained high. Palestinian and Lebanese nongovernmental organizations in Lebanon have provided small-scale training in the camps for both men and women and attempted to generate local employment.

Since the mid-1980s, the Palestinian community in Lebanon has lived in a kind of limbo, and the peace agreements have made no provisions to secure that community's future, either to return to Palestine or to remain settled in Lebanon. In the camps, rising school dropout rates are reported, at both primary and preparatory levels. UNRWA schools in the camps are dilapidated and often overcrowded as the distribution of pupils has changed since the 1970s and 1980s. School books and materials are no longer provided free of charge.

In Syria and Jordan, there always has been considerable emphasis on keeping control over the Palestinian refugee communities and their political activities, and that control has affected educational institutions. However, access to state as well as UNRWA schools has been easier and more consistent there than in Lebanon. Jordan also granted citizenship to Palestinian refugees resident there and to inhabitants of the West Bank.

Problems in finding employment in host countries and in the West Bank and Gaza Strip led many young Palestinians to emigrate to the oil-rich Gulf states from the 1950s until the end of the 1970s. The boom in the Gulf region provided both unskilled work and skilled jobs for well-educated professionals and administrators.

The largest Palestinian community developed in Kuwait, where it numbered some 400,000 in 1990. Many children were brought up and went to school there, although Palestinians for the most part could not obtain naturalization and were not permitted to own property. UNRWA did not function in the Gulf, and schooling was offered through the state systems and private schools. An arrangement between the PLO and the Kuwaiti government provided financial support for Palestinian pupils. Palestinians could attend local universities in the Gulf, though the wealthier members of the community usually sent at least their sons abroad to study.

After the Iraqi occupation of Kuwait (August 1990–February 1991), the Kuwaiti government forced most of the Palestinians to leave, reducing the community to about 30,000 by 1993. Over 300,000 Palestinians with Jordanian citizenship went to Jordan, although many never had lived there before. A smaller group went to the West Bank, Syria, or Lebanon. Those from the Gaza Strip who had no Israeli identity document but only an Egyptian travel document effectively became stateless. In Jordan, this influx increased the population by about 10 percent and caused serious strains on the state and UNRWA education systems through increased enrollments.

The Palestinian National Authority took over responsibility for education in the West Bank and the Gaza Strip from 1994, giving Palestinians an opportunity to determine, for the first time, their own education policies. The new Ministry of Education and Higher Education (MEHE) inherited a legacy of long-term problems from the years of the Israeli Occupation and from closures and disruption related to the Intifada. Teacher training was inadequate and the system was carrying a substantial number of untrained teachers. Morale in the profession was low, while school infrastructure and facilities were run down and in need of major refurbishment. Other matters of concern were large class size and the low levels of student attainment resulting from the disrupted schooling of the Intifada years. Technical and vocational educational education also remained poorly developed.

Some international aid has been directed to education, particularly secondary schools, but education has to compete for finance with other urgent needs for social services and infrastructural refurbishment. The loss of employment for Palestinians in the Israeli labor market combined with the difficulties in developing the local economies the West Bank and Gaza Strip have limited the financial resources available to the PNA. The prolonged security closures imposed on the West Bank and especially on the Gaza Strip by authorities between 1994 and 1999 that caused economic hardships that discouraged poorer children from completing school.

By the end of the 1990s, the MEHE had unified the matriculation exams (Tawjihi) previously divided between the Jordanian and Egyptian authorities, and ended all external control over the curriculum. It had embarked on revision of the school curriculum and the development of in-service teacher training, extracurricular activities, including reading schemes, libraries and training workshops, developed rapidly during the second half of the 1990s.

The university sector in the West Bank and Gaza Strip with 20,000 students enrolled by 1992, has continued to expand to a total of eight institutions: in 1991, al-Azhar University was established in Gaza on the same campus as the Islamic University, with links to al-Azhar University in Cairo, though the two are administratively separate. Al-Quds University, established in Amman in 1985, officially moved its base to Jerusalem in 1994. Nonetheless, throughout the 1990s, prolonged closures imposed by the Israelis between the West Bank and the Gaza Strip, and within the fragmented West Bank disrupted the work of both students and faculty who could not get to their institutions.

The universities also face new challenges: during the occupation their major achievements were to serve as centers of national resistance and to prevent a large scale brain drain of young people from the territories. By the end of the 1990s, their role was seen as developing a more skilled workforce, with the accompanying pressure to expand enrollments and raise standards. The return of Palestinians from abroad to work in the universities has provided a boost but funds for capital projects, previously provided mainly by private donors from the Arab world and beyond, are now scarce and concerns have been expressed about the long-term funding prospects for these universities.

In Israel, curriculum reforms initiated in the early 1990s confirmed the shift away from the total exclusion of Palestinian history, culture, and literature from the curriculum, which had characterized the earlier period. Many subjects previously taboo are more openly discussed. However, the basic subordination of the Arab education system to the goals of the Israeli State, and the use of education as a mechanism for controlling the Palestinian Arab minority, still persists. Furthermore, success rates at school is still the poorest among Palestinian Arab Israelis as a group. For example, in 1995, it was reported that only 44 percent of Arab youngsters reached the second sixth form grade (the matriculation year), compared with 83 percent of Jewish Israelis. At university level, student enrollment remains far below increasing proportion in the population while Arab representation in the ranks of tenured university teaching staff was 16 out of 4,700 tenured positions in 1995.

The impact of the "peace process" on the economic and educational progress in the West Bank and Gaza Strip during the late 1990s has by no means matched expectations, while for Palestinian refugees in surrounding states, especially in Lebanon, conditions have deteriorated. The UNRWA school system remains in place for refugee communities, but the future of the organization is unclear, and it has experienced severe pressure on budgets for schools in the Arab world. In Lebanon, particularly, the Palestinian community faces severe difficulties with the loss of PLO funding, and the diversion of attention toward the areas under PNA control.

Sarah Graham-Brown

BIBLIOGRAPHY

Developing the Occupied Territories: An Investment in Peace. Vol. 6. *Human Resources and Social Policy.* Washington, D.C.: World Bank, 1993.

Facts and Figures on the Education and Culture System in Israel. Jerusalem: Ministry of Education and Culture, 1990.

Graham-Brown, S. *Education, Repression and Liberation: Palestinians.* London: World University Service, 1984.

al-Haj, Majid. "Arab Education" in Yaacov, Iram and Mirjam Schmida, eds., *The Educational System of Israel.* Westport, Conn.: Greenwood Press, 1998.

al-Haj, Majd. *Education and Social Change Among the Arabs in Israel.* Tel Aviv: International Centre for Peace in the Middle East, 1991.

Learning the Hard Way: Palestinian Education in the West Bank, Gaza Strip, and Israel. London: World University Service, 1993.

Mari, S. K. *Arab Education in Israel.* Syracuse, N.Y.: Syracuse University Press, 1978.

Palestinians and Higher Education: The Doors of Learning Closed. London: World University Service/Association of University Teachers, 1990.

Tibawi, A. L. *Arab Education in Mandatory Palestine.* London: Luzc, 1956.

Egypt

Egyptians from all sectors of society and across the political spectrum have historically supported the cause of Palestinian self-determination. On the other hand, successive Egyptian regimes—from the monarchy through Jamal Abd al-Nasir, Anwar Sadat, and Husni Mubarak—have used, and occasionally manipulated, the Palestinian cause to further the perceived national interests of the Egyptian state.

From the 1930s to the 1970s, Palestine was practically the only issue around which all facets of Egyptian political opinion could coalesce. Egyptian political leaders, from Mustafa al-Nahhas of the Wafd to Hasan al-Banna of the Ikhwan al-Muslimin to Nasir supported the Palestinian cause. Similarly, the Egyptian public, overwhelmingly sympathetic to the Palestinians, frequently showed its support through strikes and public demonstrations. During the 1930s, university and secondary school students annually went out on strike to protest the BALFOUR DECLARATION and to declare their commitment to Palestinian independence.

Recognizing the popularity of the Palestinian cause among the general Egyptian population, Kings Fu'ad and Faruq both gave at least verbal support to the Palestinians. In rallying behind the Palestinian struggle against ZIONISM, the monarchy hoped to bolster its legitimacy at home while securing political support from Muslims, many of whom were antagonistic to Zionism for religious reasons.

During the interwar era, most Egyptians viewed the conflict in Palestine from a secular, Arab nationalist perspective. Abd al-Rahman Azzam, a leading Egyptian politician with close ties to the palace, expressed this viewpoint in his 1932 article, "The Arabs Are the Nation of the Future," published in the Palestinian journal *al-Arab.* In this essay Azzam expounded on the dream of one united Arab nation of which Palestine was an integral part. As first secretary-general of the ARAB LEAGUE (1945–1952), Azzam was a determined spokesperson for pan-Arabism and Palestinian rights to self-determination. However, when he spoke of "Egyptians first, Arabs second, and Muslims third," Azzam also reflected the contradictions of Egyptian commitment to Arabism.

Broad-Based Political Support The Wafd, the leading nationalist Egyptian political party, representing a cross section of the Egyptian population from 1919 to 1952, was also firmly committed to an independent Palestine with a Palestinian Arab majority. As early as 1931, Palestinian leader AMIN AL-HUSAYNI had met with Nahhas, the Wafdist leader, to secure his support for Palestinian demands against both the British and the Zionists. Other Egyptian political parties followed suit, although the small Egyptian Communist Party, with many Jewish members, while rejecting Zionism, initially failed to recognize the mounting popularity of the nationalist cause. Following Moscow's lead, Egyptian communists accepted the 1947 U.N. proposal for a two-state solution, but differences over policies regarding Palestine subsequently led to a split within the party.

In contrast, Islamic organizations, particularly the Society of Muslim Brothers (Ikhwan al-Muslimin), championed the Palestinian cause from the outset. The Ikhwan founder and leader, Hasan al-Banna, was deeply committed to Palestine, and this support was reflected in the organization's journals, pamphlets, and public statements. Viewing the conflict as both a political and religious one, al-Banna opposed the splitting of the Arab and Muslim worlds and described Zionism as another form of cultural and political imperialism. Al-Banna urged mass involvement in the struggle against Zionism, arguing that only committed Muslim volunteers, not governments, could defeat the Zionist endeavor. In 1935, Abd al-Rahman al-Banna, Hasan's brother, met with Amin al-Husayni, the mufti of JERUSALEM and pledged support for the cause. The following year, Hasan al-Banna raised money to assist the Arab strike in Palestine. The Ikhwan also sent volunteers to fight in the Arab revolt (1936–1939) and in the 1948 war.

Egyptian women also strongly supported the Palestinian cause. At the Arab Feminist Congress held in Cairo in 1944, Huda Sha'rawi, founder and leader of the Egyptian women's movement, gave an impassioned speech calling for equal rights of all Arab, but particularly Palestinian, women. The congress affirmed the right to self-determination of a largely Arab Palestine and called for an end to Jewish immigration. Telegrams were sent to U.S. president Franklin Delano Roosevelt and the British prime minister Winston Churchill to protest their pro-Zionist stands. The delegates also urged Arab leaders to buy land in Palestine to deter further Jewish purchases. The congress demonstrated the high level of political consciousness—particularly regarding the Palestine question—among Egyptian and other Arab women, especially those in the upper class.

Egyptians supported the Palestinians and opposed the Zionists for three main reasons: First, as a people engaged in their own struggle for national independence, they were deeply sympathetic to the Palestine national movement. Second, most Egyptians viewed Zionism as a form of Western imperialism that sought to divide and dominate the Arab world. Third, Egyptians recognized that they and the Palestinians were natural allies in their common fight against British imperialism. In addition, Egyptian politicians and the king believed that strong support for the Palestinians strengthened Egypt's position against the Hashemite monarchies in Jordan and Iraq in the ongoing rivalry for dominance within the Arab world.

Because of their animosity toward the British, many Egyptians were openly supportive when, in 1944, young members of the Stern gang assassinated Lord Moyne, British minister of state in the Middle East, as he returned to his Cairo residence. Although Egyptians were opposed to the creation of a Jewish state in Palestine, the assassins were seen as having struck a welcome blow against British imperialism.

Political parties in Egypt, particularly the Wafd, and King Faruq also viewed the creation of the Arab League in 1945 as a means of fostering Arab unity, Egyptian hegemony within the Arab world, and Palestinian independence. Egypt took a leading role in advocating both causes within the league. The United Nations decision in November 1947 to partition Palestine led to violence in Egypt. Anti-Jewish demonstrations broke out, and a number of Jewish businesses were burned. When the first Arab-Israeli war began in 1948, Egyptians enthusiastically supported the Palestinians. Although the army was clearly unprepared for battle, the war was, initially, a popular one. Nasir reflected general Egyptian opinion when he wrote in *The Philosophy of the Revolution,* "fighting in Palestine was not fighting on foreign territory. Nor was it inspired by sentiment. It was a duty imposed by self-defense."

The disastrous defeat in the ARAB-ISRAELI WAR OF 1948 led to disillusionment throughout Egypt.

Some Egyptians, particularly in the upper class, openly criticized the Palestinians for having sold land to the Jews and for not having fought hard enough in the war. Domestically, the king and the monarchy were thoroughly discredited and the Wafd, too, was viewed as incapable of rectifying the problems. As a result, many young army officers, including Nasir, resolved that revolution was the only viable alternative to the bankruptcy of the monarchy and the political parties on both the Left and the Right.

After the 1948 war, the GAZA STRIP was placed under an Egyptian military administration. With a huge population of some 240,000 Palestinians, many of them refugees, Gaza posed economic and political problems for the Egyptian government. While publicly supporting the Palestinian cause, King Faruq banned political activity by Palestinians in Gaza and disbanded the Palestinian national committees. Before and immediately after the 1948 war, a few Palestinians moved to Egypt, where, as in most of the rest of the Arab world, they were generally forbidden work permits and citizenship. Although a few wealthy Palestinians residing in Egypt prior to 1948 did secure citizenship, the majority had difficulty securing even limited travel papers or Egyptian identification documents. After 1948, approximately 15,000 Palestinians resided in Egypt; after the 1967 war and the resultant new wave of refugees from the Occupied Territories, the numbers swelled to over 33,000. However, Palestinians in Egypt remained scattered and poorly organized.

The Nasirist Era After the 1952 revolution, Palestinians placed high hopes in Nasir, believing that, under his leadership, Egypt and the Arab world in general would resolve their conflict with Israel and secure them their national rights. Nasir, however, hoped to defuse the potentially volatile situation by giving verbal support to Palestinians while avoiding full-scale military confrontations with Israel. He emphasized the need to raise the economic status of all Arabs so that they would be able to face Israel on an equal footing.

Domestically, Nasir eased the no-work restrictions and increased the social services available to Palestinians. Government scholarships for Palestinians led to the hope of upward mobility and EDUCATION for thousands of needy students. By the 1960s, over 5,000 Palestinian students, many from Gaza, were enrolled in Egyptian institutions, and the General Union of Palestinian Students (GUPS) became a major political force on campuses throughout the nation.

Nasir described Egypt as belonging to three circles: Arab, African, and Islamic. The majority in all three circles opposed Zionism as a form of Western imperialism and supported what they considered to be the legitimate demands of the Palestinians for self-determination. Although he was in fact personally sympathetic to the Palestinians, Nasir, as had earlier Egyptian leaders, also recognized that by championing the Palestine cause he could make Egypt the leading power within the Arab world.

Although Nasir was depicted in the West and in Israel as a hard-liner on the Palestinian issue, he actually attempted on a number of occasions to resolve the conflict by negotiating, through secret channels, for a settlement with Israel. In 1954 he went so far as to propose the resettlement of some refugees in the Sinai Peninsula. But after Palestinians in Gaza held massive demonstrations against the resettlement plan, it was quickly dropped. Likewise, behind-the-scene negotiations for a compromise were broken off after Israeli military attacks into Gaza in 1954 and 1955 and the so-called Lavon Affair in 1954, when Israeli agents bombed U.S. installations in Egypt, rigging them so as to place the blame on the Egyptians.

The attacks on Gaza impelled Nasir to seek additional armaments for the ill-equipped Egyptian army. At the same time, he increased Palestinian involvement in the local administration of Gaza and permitted the creation of a small Palestinian armed group, who launched some armed fedayeen ("self-sacrificer") raids into Israel. The increase of fedayeen raids into Israel led to mounting tension along the Israeli–Egyptian borders and was a contributing factor in the 1956 war. After Israel reluctantly returned Sinai and Gaza to Egypt in the aftermath of the 1956 war, Palestinian political activity in Gaza escalated. Partly as a means of controlling Palestinian unrest, but also to counter growing Syrian influence, Nasir sponsored the recognition of a "separate entity," the PALESTINE LIBERATION ORGANIZATION (PLO), under the leadership of AHMAD SHUQAYRI, at the Arab summit meeting in 1964. Although technically autonomous, the PLO was initially highly dependent upon Egypt.

However, the military debacle in the 1967 war seriously undermined Nasir's regional and domestic power. After the war, Arab leaders met in Khartoum; although they agreed not to recognize Israel or to negotiate until all the Occupied Territories (Gaza, Sinai, WEST BANK, Jerusalem, and Golan Heights) were returned, they did not call for the destruction of Israel or for military action. After 1967, the Palestinians, recognizing that Arab leaders, including Nasir, had failed to secure their national rights, moved toward more independent positions. As the PLO gained political and military autonomy, Egypt's influence diminished.

Even during his last years in office, Nasir continued to use so-called back-door or secret channels to reach a negotiated settlement with Israel. As late as spring 1970, he invited Nahum Goldmann, president of the World Jewish Congress, to Egypt for talks. But when Israeli leaders, particularly Golda Meir, publicly disavowed these contacts, the negotiations—as had all previous ones—failed. Nasir's last major political act before his death in 1970 was a negotiated cease-fire in the BLACK SEPTEMBER warfare between Jordanian and Palestinian forces.

Shifts under Sadat In spite of his public protestations to the contrary, Anwar Sadat, Nasir's successor, distanced himself from the Palestinian cause. Sadat stressed Egyptian, not Arab, nationalism and, from the outset, viewed the 1973 war primarily as a means to take the conflict off the back burner and to bring the United States in as a mediator between Egypt and Israel. The new regime also started to complain about the high economic and human costs Egypt had endured as a result of its support for the Palestinians. Although Sadat continued to render lip service to the cause of Palestinian self-determination, he clearly signaled his willingness to accept a separate settlement.

In 1977 Sadat became the first Arab leader to visit Israel openly, and in the following year he signed the CAMP DAVID ACCORDS, which provided a framework for the return of Egyptian territory in the Sinai and for a formal peace treaty with Israel. The U.S.-brokered Egyptian-Israeli peace treaty was signed in 1979. In his speech given at the White House ceremonies marking the occasion, Sadat did not even mention the Palestinians. The treaty provided for the establishment of full diplomatic ties between Israel and Egypt and the eventual return of the entire Sinai Peninsula to Egypt. Gaza was not included in the agreement and Israel continued its military occupation of the Palestinian territory. In addition, the United States agreed to provide a much-needed economic aid package (totaling over $2 billion per annum) to Egypt and an even greater amount to Israel. The continuation of U.S. aid to Egypt has been predicated on compliance with the peace treaty.

Recognizing that the treaty effectively neutralized Israel's most potent enemy without any written commitments regarding Palestinian autonomy, Israeli withdrawal from Gaza or the West Bank, or a resolution regarding the disputed status of Jerusalem, the Palestinians and other Arabs were outraged. After the separate peace settlement, Egypt and Sadat were ostracized by the rest of the Arab world. Sadat was viewed as a traitor, not only by Palestinians, but by many Egyptians as well. Leading Egyptian officials, including the highly respected foreign minister, Isma'il Fahmi, resigned. Sadat responded by repressing political dissent. Students were expelled for antigovernment and pro-Palestinian demonstrations, GUPS was forced to close, and Palestinians were refused work permits or jobs in government service.

In 1978 after Yusuf al-Siba'i, a noted Egyptian journalist and supporter of Sadat's policies, was assassinated by Palestinian gunmen in Cyprus, Sadat launched a major crackdown on the PLO and its supporters in Egypt, even though the PLO had publicly expressed regret for the killing. Palestinian organizations were banned, Palestinians were forbidden to hold government jobs, many social service institutions were forced to close, and political and religious leaders, along with many journalists and intellectuals, were imprisoned.

Muslim groups were particularly incensed by the separate treaty and vowed revenge. Sadat's recognition of Israel, coupled with mounting economic and political crises within Egypt, was a major factor behind his assassination at the hands of Egyptian Islamists in 1981.

Building on the earlier tenets of the Ikhwan al-Muslimin, Islamist groups such as al-Jama'a al-Islamiyya, from the 1970s to the present, based their opposition to Israel on religious grounds. Whereas the PLO was traditionally careful to differentiate between Judaism and Zionism, contemporary resurgent Islamic organizations in Egypt used the terms *Jews, Zionists,* and *Israelis* interchangeably. Believing that Palestinian nationhood could only be achieved by an armed force of devout Muslims living under an Islamic government, most Egyptian Islamists opposed any concessions to Israel. Members of the Gama'a al-Islamiyya and other Islamists depicted the conflict as a continuation of a historic struggle between Jews and Muslims and believed that Arab/Muslim losses to Israel resulted from a lack of devotion among Muslims and from the failures of Arab regimes to abide by Islamic law, the Shari'a. On this basis, these groups also criticized the PLO for its lack of religious fervor. Not without justification, Egyptian Islamists and others also pointed out that had Egypt not been neutralized by the Camp David Accords and the peace treaty, Israel would probably not have been able to besiege and bombard Beirut for seventy-seven days during the 1982 war.

Uneasy Alliances Under Mubarak On the other hand, the 1982 war in Lebanon provided the opportunity for Husni Mubarak, who succeeded Sadat, to bring Egypt back into the Arab fold. Although Egypt did not accept any PLO evacuees from Beirut, Mubarak mended fences with the Palestinians, subsequently had a much-publicized televised meeting with YASIR ARAFAT, and during the 1980s often acted, through private and public diplomatic channels, as an intermediary between the PLO and the United States. At the same time, he maintained what was often referred to as a "cold peace" with Israel. Mubarak characterized Egyptian relations with Israel as normal but not special.

When the INTIFADA began in 1987, many Egyptians, especially students, progressive political leaders, and urban workers, showed their ongoing commitment to the Palestinians by participating in massive demonstrations to support the uprising. Islamist groups, with thousands of student members, were particularly effective in mobilizing demonstrators in universities, but Egyptian armed forces crushed the more violent uprisings. And the bourgeois elite, many of whom had benefited financially from the influx of foreign trade and aid monies into Egypt after the peace with Israel, remained largely apethetic or even hostile to the Palestinian cause.

Although Mubarak was quick to condemn Israel's brutal treatment of Palestinians during the Intifada, he did not abrogate the peace treaty with Israel. After the declaration of independence and the creation of a provisional government by the PALESTINE NATIONAL COUNCIL (PNC) in 1988, Mubarak recognized the new state and praised the PNC's acceptance of UNITED NATIONS SECURITY COUNCIL RESOLUTIONS 242 AND 338. During this time, he pushed for a dialogue between the Palestinians and the Israelis and advocated convening an international peace conference. Egypt's fulsome cooperation with the United States and the international coalition in the GULF CRISIS, 1990–91, caused a temporary distancing in relations with the PLO.

Although Mubarak supported the international peace conference in Madrid and the OSLO AGREEMENTS, both the Declaration of Principles signed between the PLO and Israel in 1993 and the direct negotiations between the Palestinians and the Israelis marginalized Egypt's importance either as a mediator or as an effective force to resolve the conflict. Furthermore, Egyptian Islamists, particularly the now banned al-Jama'a al-Islamiyya, the leading activist Islamic party, condemned both the PLO and Mubarak for compromising with Israel. Many Egyptian Islamists, as well as others in the Muslim world, have been willing to risk confrontations with both Israel and the PLO to obtain full independence for the Palestinians. In Egypt, Islamists mounted a violent insurrection against the Mubarak regime which retaliated with equal or greater force. Although the ongoing insurrection during the 1990s weakened the Mubarak regime, the government, dominated by the army, continued in power.

The victory of the Likud Party under hard-liner Benjamin Netanyahu in the 1996 Israeli elections complicated Mubarak's attempts at diplomacy. Although Mubarak had publicly expressed a preference for the Labor leader, Shimon Peres, he initially reacted calmly to the Likud victory. However, after Netanyahu stalled on withdrawing from HEBRON and reneged on other peace agreements, Mubarak reacted angrily, threatening to withdraw from negotiations for further economic cooperation and demanding that Israel fulfill its agreements with the Palestinians.

In spite of his obvious misgivings about the Netanyahu government, Mubarak continued to push the peace process forward. In 1998, he joined Arafat in support of the Wye Plantation agreement, and in 1999 he encouraged the new Israeli government of Ehud Barak to be more forthcoming toward the Palestinians. Hence Mubarak's regime continued to weather the stormy political climate and uncertainty over the future of Palestinian demands for an independent nation.

The Future On one hand, Egypt must fulfill the terms of the separate peace with Israel in order to maintain amicable relations with the United States and to assure the continuation of economic aid, on which the regime has become dependent. On the other hand, to survive politically, Mubarak must be seen as responding, on regional and international fronts, to the demands of the general Egyptian public for the creation of an independent Palestinian state. The Mubarak regime has continued its struggle to maintain an equilibrium between these two forces.

Janice J. Terry

BIBLIOGRAPHY

Abdelnasser, Walid M. *The Islamic Movement in Egypt: Perceptions of International Relations, 1967–1981.* London: Kegan Paul International, 1994.

Beinin, Joel. *Was the Red Flag Flying There? Marxist Politics and the Arab-Israeli Conflict in Egypt and Israel, 1948–1965.* Berkeley, Calif.: University of California Press, 1990.

Butros-Ghali, Butros. "The Foreign Policy of Egypt in the Post-Sadat Era." *Foreign Affairs* 60 (Spring 1982).

Cantori, Louis J. "Egyptian Policy." In *The Middle East Since Camp David,* ed. by Robert O. Freedman. Boulder, Colo.: Westview Press, 1984.

Dawisha, A. I. *Egypt in the Arab World (1952–1970): The Elements of Foreign Policy.* New York: Halsted, 1977.

Gause, F. Gregory III. "The Arab World and the Intifada." In *The Intifada: Its Impact on Israel, the Arab World, and the Superpowers,* ed. by Robert O. Freedman. Miami: Florida International University Press, 1991.

Korany, Bahgat, and Ali E. Hillal Dessouki. *The Foreign Policies of Arab States.* Boulder, Colo.: Westview Press, 1984.

Talhami, Ghada. *Palestine and the Egyptian National Identity.* New York: Greenwood, 1992.

Taylor, Alan. *The Arab Balance of Power.* Syracuse, N.Y.: Syracuse University Press, 1982.

Vatikiotis, P. J. *The History of Modern Egypt: From Muhammad Ali to Mubarak.* 4th rev. ed. Baltimore: Johns Hopkins University Press, 1991.

Elmusa, Sharif

al-Musa; academician, poet, translator
1947– al-Abbasiyya

Elmusa fled his native village east of JAFFA during the ARAB-ISRAELI WAR OF 1948 and spent his youth in the al-Nuway'ima refugee camp near JERICHO. He studied at Cairo University, where he obtained a B.A. in civil engineering in 1970. Elmusa then traveled to the United States, where he earned an M.S. in civil engineering from Northeastern University and a Ph.D. in regional development and planning from the Massachusetts Institute of Technology in 1986. From 1988 to 1989 he taught at Georgetown University.

Elmusa is a leading expert on development and water resources in the Middle East. He has worked as a research fellow or consultant on projects with the Applied Research Institute of Jerusalem, Yarmuk University, and the INSTITUTE FOR PALESTINE STUDIES since the early 1990s. In 1997, he worked through the United Nations Development Programme and United Nations World Food Plan to help the PALESTINIAN AUTHORITY establish objectives for economic development in the WEST BANK and the GAZA STRIP.

Elmusa is also a poet and translator of Arabic literature into English. Some of his poetry has been translated into English and has appeared in a number of books and periodicals. Other poems of his were published in *Grape Leaves: A Century of Arab American Poetry,* which he coedited in 1988. Since 1982 he has also worked on the Project for Translation from Arabic, a program to translate Arabic poetry, fiction, and drama.

Elmusa's academic works include *Negotiating Water: Israel and the Palestinians* (1996) and *A Harvest of Technology: The Super-Green Revolution in the Jordan Valley* (1994). He also helped supervise the research and writing of *All That Remains: The Palestinian Villages Occupied and Depopulated by Israel in 1948* (1993).

Michael R. Fischbach

Embroidery

At some period prior to the early nineteenth century, the seeds of a beautiful costume art were sewn in rural Palestine; that art had a spectacular efflorescence during the first half of the twentieth century. Dresses, coats, and flowing head veils of hand-woven cotton and linen in natural shades or dyed indigo blue or rusty red were richly embellished with an extraordinary profusion of brilliantly colored silk embroidery and taffeta and satin patchwork.

This artistic tradition developed among the Arab farmers who formed the majority of the population of Palestine until the middle of this century. It was an exclusively female art form, created and sustained by peasant women in hundreds of small villages throughout the country. Each region and even each group of villages had its own distinctive styles and patterns, all subject to constant changes in fashion.

Nineteenth Century We do not know when these village artists began to adorn their costumes, nor can we document the earliest sources of their techniques and patterns. The oldest traditional garments that have been preserved are probably no older than the early nineteenth century, and travelers and historians of earlier periods do not describe women's costumes in informative detail. All we can assume is that the decorative panels of embroidery and patchwork that are the most striking feature of village women's festive garments evolved originally from functional stitching and protective patchwork on everyday working clothes and that costume styles and embroidery patterns, techniques, and color schemes were all affected by a multiplicity of local and foreign influences.

Historically many thousands of Christian and Muslim pilgrims have visited Palestine wearing or bearing as gifts or as goods for sale costumes and textiles from many different countries; some female visitors married and settled in Palestine and passed on their embroidery skills and ideas; cloth and clothing have long been imported from Europe and Asia as well as other parts of the Middle East; and Palestine has been conquered and administered by a succession of foreign powers, each of which left some mark on local fashions.

However, many peoples are exposed to similar influences without developing such a complex and lavish costume art, so the impetus and sustaining roots of the Palestinian embroidery tradition must be sought within the culture and society of the Palestinian villagers.

The beautiful, colorful, and ornate art of embroidery is in striking contrast to the otherwise humble material culture of the Palestinian peasantry and could only have developed in a culture in which women's skill and creativity were admired and encouraged by both sexes. Women maintained the form's rigorous aesthetic standards by appreciating and criticizing each other's work, and fathers and husbands generally provided the money to pay for the expensive materials—no small consideration for peasant farmers. Embroidery was also sustained by the desire to gain prestige from the display of wealth—the expenditure of not only surplus cash but also of women's precious time and labor.

The most admired embroidery was executed with small, neat stitches; had well-planned patterns; and conformed to local conventions in its choice and arrangement of colors and motifs. Embroidery was an important expression of village identity and pride, and women relished even small differences between their embroidery and that of other villages. It was important for young women that their embroidery be in the latest fashion, and for older women, for whom the flamboyant styles of youth were considered unsuitable, that their embroidery be subdued.

Richly embroidered garments were not of course worn for toiling in the fields or the home—embroidery was too precious to risk its being spoiled during everyday chores. It was reserved for embellishing garments worn for special social and ceremonial occasions such as formal visits, religious feast days, and above all, key family celebrations—circumcisions and weddings.

A girl prepared her first embroidered garments for her own wedding trousseau, and she wore the most richly decorated dress in her collection for the first time during her wedding ceremonies as a dramatic and colorful proclamation of her new marital status. Girls began to embroider around the age of six, learning from their mothers and other older women the techniques, the large vocabulary for embroidery stitches and motifs, and the combinations of colors and patterns peculiar to their village. At the same time, they absorbed the exacting standards of the art. Acknowledged experts, who were usually also innovators always on the lookout for new motifs to introduce to their villages, were admired and copied by other women.

In the late nineteenth century, there were two major styles or traditions of embroidery in Palestine corresponding to major differences in women's costume between the north and south of the country.

In the hills of Galilee in the north of the country women wore a short-sleeved calf-length coat most often made of blue or russet-colored cotton handwoven and dyed locally (with indigo and kermes [red dye]) over white or blue ankle-length pants of similar cotton and a long-sleeved tunic of fine white cotton or silk. A colorful checked or striped cotton or silk sash was wrapped round the waist over the coat. The head was covered with a bonnet bedecked with coins, and over it, a scarf or veil, usually of maroon or black silk, tied above the forehead with a headband.

The most beautifully ornamented garments were the coats of indigo-blue cotton, which the embroidery artists of Galilee treated like a painter's canvas, embellishing the fabric so heavily with appliqué patchwork and silk stitching that most of it was concealed. Rectangular and irregularly shaped patches of red, yellow, and green taffeta and striped or ikat-patterned satin were applied on the sleeves and on the front of the coat, or inside the front so they would be glimpsed when it flapped open. The silk fabrics and threads for decorating these outfits were imported from the great Syrian weaving centers of Damascus, Aleppo, and Hums.

Moreover, the lower back and sides of the coats were beautifully embroidered in lustrous floss silks, mainly in satin stitch combined with a variety of other stitches—running stitch, cross-stitch, satin stitch, hem stitch, and drawn-thread work, often all combined on the same garment. As in all Palestine, the predominant embroidery color was red, enlivened with touches of other colors. The patterns used were mainly geometric, with various combinations of diamonds, triangles, rectangles, and chevrons arranged in rows. On some coats, the embroidery was worked as an unbroken panel, concealing the background material. More commonly, the handwoven blue cloth was revealed between discrete motifs, contrasting with and accentuating the smooth, lustrous texture of the embroidery. The pant legs were embroidered in a similar manner.

We know from travelers' accounts that these costumes were being worn in the 1860s, but as with all Palestinian costume, we cannot now trace the origins or early development of styles of dress and ornamentation. We can be sure, however, that they will have been affected by the same (universal) principles that governed costume styles during the better-documented and researched period from the end of the nineteenth century—the desire to display wealth, good taste, and skill, and the ever-present drive to emulate the changing fashions of social superiors. Thus, by the early twentieth century, new styles of costume based on the fashions of the Turkish ruling class had been adopted by the Galilee village women, and embroidered coats and pants ceased to be worn.

Twentieth Century In southern Palestine (south of the NABLUS area), Turkish fashions had little influence on village costume. Until the 1940s the village women wore ankle-length dresses of locally woven natural (creamy-white) or indigo blue cotton or linen with tight-fitting or triangular sleeves, bound around the waist with a colorful silk, cotton, or woollen girdle. Various regional styles of coin-bedecked bonnet were worn by married women until recently, covered with flowing white cotton or linen head veils. Festive dresses were as lavishly and colorfully embellished with embroidery and appliqué as the ceremonial coats of Galilee, and often bonnets and veils were embroidered as well. In some areas women also embroidered cushion covers of red, green, and yellow taffeta to decorate their homes.

On dresses, the embroidery was arranged symmetrically in panels on the chest, sides, and lower back of the skirt, and sometimes on the sleeves. The shapes and sizes of the embroidered panels, as well as the motifs employed, varied from area to area. Head veils worn for festive occasions were embroidered in bands around the edge and were sometimes sprinkled all over with motifs.

The main embroidery stitch of southern Palestine is the cross-stitch, with a variety of other stitches playing a supporting role—satin stitch, herringbone stitch, running stitch, and specific stitches used for oversewing edges, joining seams, and attaching patchwork. Until the 1930s, as in Galilee, Syrian floss silk was used; it gave a thick stitch usually concealing the cross shape of the stitch, and yielding embroidery with a rich sheen and voluptuous texture, especially when it was executed in solid blocks as on the most magnificent dress in the bridal trousseau in certain regions. The patterns were executed from memory or copied from another garment and were sewn directly onto the material, the open weave of the handwoven fabrics enabling the embroideress to count the warp and weft threads and plan her motifs and overall design.

The oldest cross-stitch embroidery motifs are simple geometric shapes used alone or in rows, or combined with others to make more complex patters. Most are abstract, but some clearly represent trees, plants, and flowers. Many of these designs were inspired by the decorations and patterns village women saw on buildings, tiles, carpets, and textiles when they visited the towns and their markets. In the late nineteenth century, curvilinear and naturalistic motifs depicting natural figures such as flowers and birds were introduced by European missionaries who set up schools and embroidery classes in predominantly Christian villages such as Ramallah, and these new motifs eventually spread throughout southern Palestine.

Various shades of the dominant red embroidery color and different combinations of subsidiary colors were preferred in different areas, and like other features of costume and embroidery, were self-conscious expressions of local identity. Chemically dyed silks were not widely available in Palestine until the 1920s, when small touches of brilliant greens and pinks become common in the embroidery of certain areas.

From the 1930s, closely woven machine-made cottons and later human-made fibers imported from Europe and Asia replaced local materials, mercerized (perle) cotton threads replaced floss silk, and many new embroidery patterns were imported via the European pattern books sold with the embroidery threads. These new patterns, which had to be executed on waste canvas, became very popular during the 1950s, as did others imported in magazines later, and they predominate on the embroidered dresses worn today. There was also a shift from the dominant red of the older embroidery—yellow, orange, green, blue, and pink, alone or combined in the same dress, all became popular.

The other main southern Palestinian embroidery technique, strikingly different from cross-stitch, was couching in silk, silver, or gilt cord. This was twisted into elaborate floral and curvilinear patterns, and it was filled and framed with satin and herringbone stitches in brilliantly colored floss silk. This expensive and luxurious style of embroidery was initially a specialty of Bethlehem, Bayt Sahur, and Bayt Jala, mainly Christian villages south of Jerusalem, where women used it for decorating the best dresses in their trousseaus, for broadcloth or velvet jackets, and for their distinctive fez-shaped headdresses. The people of these villages were wealthier and more urbanized than those of other villages, who looked up to them and wanted to emulate them. So as village people became financially better off from the late 1920s, Bethlehem-style embroidery became more and more fashionable in southern Palestine, and wedding trousseaus often included one or more dresses ornamented with panels of couching. This embroidery was produced commercially by women in Bethlehem and its neighboring villages, and by professional embroideresses in other villages.

In many villages of the coastal plain of the Mediterranean and in the hills north and south of Hebron, the most important trousseau dress was also embellished with appliqué panels of red of orange taffeta sewn onto the front of the skirt between the panels of embroidery. These were shaped and slashed in a variety of ways revealing the indigo blue fabric of the dress beneath, and were sometimes lightly embroidered. The front edges of a short-sleeved coatdress worn in the villages of the Jaffa area until the 1920s were also edged with taffeta or satin patches and were sometimes tied with silk tassels and sprinkled with sequins. In many areas decorative satin or velvet patches were also sewn on the yokes of the finest dresses, and in the Bethlehem and Jerusalem areas striking chest panels in red, yellow, and green taffeta with zigzag appliqué borders were attached to dresses of luxurious fabrics of mixed silk and linen. Zigzag appliqué was also widely used to edge neck openings, cuffs, and hems.

Post 1948 Palestinian culture and society were severely disrupted by the establishment of the state of Israel in northern, western, and parts of southern Palestine in 1948. During the hostilities surrounding this event, nearly half the rural population fled in fear or were driven out of their villages and became refugees in eastern Palestine (now called the WEST BANK) or in neighboring countries. Many more became refugees as a result of the ARAB-ISRAELI WAR OF 1967.

Nevertheless, traditional costume and the art of embroidery were still flourishing in the 1990s, albeit greatly changed, in the villages and refugee camps of Gaza and the West Bank, and among southern Palestinians in the refugee camps of Jordan and Syria. Many new embroidery patterns (such as large flowers and birds) and colors (especially shaded threads) of foreign origin are popular across the whole spectrum of village and refugee camp society; at the same time, subtle features have been retained to indicate a woman's original village or region in Palestine. Other distinctive new embroidery patterns and color combinations (such as the white, black, green, and red of the Palestinian flag) have been created to express national identity and aspirations.

Shelagh Weir

BIBLIOGRAPHY

Amiry, Suad, and Vera Tamari. *The Palestinian Village Home*. London, British Museum Publications 1989.

Weir, Shelagh, and Serene Shahid. *Palestinian Embroidery*. London: British Museum Publications, 1988.

Weir, Shelagh. *Palestinian Costume*. Austin: University of Texas Press, 1989.

Erekat, Saeb

Sa'ib Urayqat; academic, politician

1955– Jericho

Saeb Erekat pursued his studies abroad, earning a B.A. and M.A. in international relations from San Francisco State University and later a Ph.D. in conflict resolution and peace studies from Bradford University in Britain in 1983.

Erekat began teaching in the political science department at AL-NAJAH NATIONAL UNIVERSITY in NABLUS in 1979 and was director of public and external relations at the university from 1982 to 1986. He has also served as secretary-general of the ARAB STUDIES SOCIETY since 1992 and on the editorial staff of *al-Quds* newspaper since 1982. In April 1988, he was one of four Palestinians participating with Israeli officials in an American television program on the INTIFADA.

Erekat was selected as vice-chair of the Palestinian delegation to the MADRID PEACE CONFERENCE, 1991, and he continued to serve as a negotiator through the subsequent rounds of peace talks. He and the other negotiators were surprised by the secret Israel–PALESTINE LIBERATION ORGANIZATION (PLO) agreement reached behind their backs in the summer of 1993. After a crisis in the PLO over whether Palestinians from inside or outside the Occupied Territories should take the lead in the negotiations, Erekat was appointed to the PLO's Higher Committee for the Peace Talks in Tunis.

Committed to the Israeli-PLO accords, Erekat was appointed minister for local government in the PALESTINIAN AUTHORITY in May 1994 and later made head of both the Official Elections Commission and the delegation negotiating elections with the Israelis for the new PALESTINIAN LEGISLATIVE COUNCIL. During the elections, held in January 1996, Erekat was himself elected to the council.

Michael R. Fischbach

Europe

The modern history of Europe and Palestine began a new chapter in May 1948, when a frustrated Britain relinquished its PALESTINE MANDATE to the United Nations (U.N.). Thereafter, the United States would gradually replace Britain as the dominant Western power in the region. Indeed, from the European perspective, the post-1948 era is best understood as a persistent, sometimes humiliating, and largely unsuccessful effort to recover its former status and influence. Nevertheless, Europe has had a defining influence in the Middle East, and without taking it into account, progress on the peace process cannot be fully understood. The period breaks down into two parts, before 1970 and after, when European Community (EC) members finally decided to adopt a common foreign policy toward the Middle East and Palestine.

The Americanization of the Middle East 1948–1970 During the post-1948 war years, Britain, France, and the United States worked closely together to seek a solution to the Palestine question. This included cooperating in the United Nations; appointing the Swedish count FOLKE BERNADOTTE as U.N. mediator and the U.S. diplomat Ralph Bunche, who succeeded Bernadotte after his assassination and negotiated the 1949 armistice agreements; and in 1950, establishing the United Nations Relief and Works Agency for Palestine Refugees in the Near East (UNRWA) to minister to three-quarters of a million Palestinian refugees. In the 1950 Tripartite Declaration, the three powers sought to stabilize the area (and keep out the Soviet Union) by restricting arms sales to states of the area and preventing armed aggression by any state. Despite some effort, Britain failed in 1951 to form a Middle East Defense Organization, which it had wanted to be composed of Britain, France, the United States, Turkey, and Egypt. In 1955, however, Britain did join with the United States, Turkey, Iran, and Afghanistan to form the anti-Soviet Central Treaty Organization (CENTO), a sort of Middle East North Atlantic Treaty Organization (NATO), which was never effective. In the summer of 1955, Britain and the United States collaborated on a peace plan code-named *Alpha,* aimed at coaxing Egyptian president Jamal Abd al-Nasir to make peace with Israel in return for Western economic aid and some Israeli concessions. However, all of these efforts failed, overwhelmed by the intensifying conflict, self-interest of nations, ambitions of national leaders, and above all, the Suez Crisis of October 1956. A furious U.S. president Dwight D. Eisenhower stopped France, Britain, and Israel's attack on Egypt at the moment of "victory" and drummed them out of the Middle East, disgraced and humiliated, while Nasir became a national and international hero.

During the decade between Suez and the ARAB-ISRAELI WAR OF 1967, Palestinians got short shrift from most of the European world. Neither Britain nor France played any future part in the Palestine question, except for continued arms sales to Israel. Nevertheless, these were portentous times for Europe. With the end of the Algerian War in 1962, French president Charles de Gaulle began quietly to mend France's fences with the Arab world, which he coldly calculated was more important to France than Israel was or would be. Thus, in May 1967, when Israeli foreign minister Abba Eban desperately called on de Gaulle to win his support in the coming war, de Gaulle dismissed him with a curt "Ne faites pas la guerre" (Don't make war). This was the beginning of a fourteen-year effort by de Gaulle and his Gaullist successors to orient EC policy toward the Arab world and to promote a European foreign policy independent of the United States.

After the 1967 war, which generated another 300,000 Palestinian refugees, Europe woke up to the magnitude of the Palestinian issue. In the U.N. the United States negotiated UNITED NATIONS SECURITY COUNCIL RESOLUTION (SCR) 242, designed to bring about a peaceful resolution to the ARAB-ISRAELI CONFLICT, with British ambassador Lord Caradon (Sir Hugh Foot), rejoicing in the sobriquet "Father of 242" for finessing the resolution through the diplomatic thickets. But even SCR 242 failed to mention the Palestinians, except as refugees.

Europe Strives to Recover Influence In 1970, as a result of the Davignon, or Luxembourg, Report on European political unity, EC members decided to adopt a common foreign policy concentrating on two issues, the Conference on Security and Cooperation in Europe (CSCE) and the Middle East peace process. The latter emerged in 1971, in the wake of the fruitless U.N. Jarring Mission and the U.S. Rogers Plan, as the "Schumann paper," calling for Israeli withdrawal from the Occupied Territories, the internationalization of JERUSALEM, the assignment of peacekeeping troops, and the choice of return or compensation for Palestinian refugees. British prime minister Edward Heath, eager for Britain to join the EC, aligned British policy with France. European politicians began to court PALESTINE LIBERATION ORGANIZATION (PLO) leader YASIR ARAFAT; to permit the PLO to set up offices in their capitals; and to emphasize the legitimacy of Palestinian demands for self-determination.

This shift to a more independent European foreign policy was forcefully confirmed during the 1973 October War, which was Suez in reverse, with the Europeans' condemning the United States for intervening on the side of the Israelis. America's NATO allies refused overflight rights to the U.S. airlift of arms to Israel, were shocked by President Richard Nixon's nuclear alert, and were panicked by the Arab oil embargo. On November 6, the EC produced the unambiguously pro-Arab Brussels Declaration, which recommended a strict interpretation of SCR 242 and recognized, for the first time, officially and publicly, the "legitimate rights of the Palestinians." But it was a pyrrhic victory. According to Eban, the Brussels Declaration meant not "peace in the Middle East" but "Oil for Europe," a move that only confirmed Israel's deep distrust of Europe. A furious Secretary of State Henry Kissinger criticized the Europeans for knuckling under to the Arabs. As a result, the United States (and Israel) totally excluded Europe from the American peace process, which led to the CAMP DAVID ACCORDS and the autonomy negotiations.

Excluded from the peace process, EC members turned to the U.N., where support for the Palestinian cause was already well advanced, and where they presented EC views and supported U.N. resolutions calling for Palestinian autonomy, self-determination, independence, and statehood. In 1974, the EC launched the Euro-Arab Dialogue, in which the political status of the Palestinians became a central element. It was also during these years that the EC earned the reputation for making toothless declarations, which led to Arab frustration and disappointment, Israeli contempt, and American indifference. In June 1980, the EC issued the Venice Declaration, the high-water mark of an independent EC policy calling for an international conference based on SCRs 242 and 338 leading to Palestinian independence. This move succeeded in further annoying the United States and Israel not so much because of the substance but because of the perception that it was a European attempt to launch a substitute for the autonomy negotiations, which, the Americans were at some pains to point out, were "the only game in town." However, within a year it all blew over. In May 1981, the newly elected French president, François Mitterrand, who brought with him a European socialist sense of solidarity with the Israeli Labor Party, denounced Venice as a mistake and pledged French (European) cooperation with Camp David. Further, by that time the Palestinian question had sailed in from the fringes to be finally and firmly anchored in mainstream. Thus, in spite of everything, European efforts had helped to change the world. It was a hopeful moment.

But it was not destined to last for long. The decade of the eighties was a decade of disaster for the peace process. President Reagan's "Fresh Start" (a 1982 proposal to launch a new Middle East peace plan to end the fighting after the June invasion) and other, European and Arab, peace efforts foundered in the turbulent tide of violence that swept the Middle East: the Soviet invasion of Afghanistan, the Iran-Iraq War, the Israeli invasion of Lebanon, and the INTIFADA, the most obvious. There was one exception. At a special session of the U.N. General Assembly session on Palestine held in Geneva in December 1988, Arafat declared that the PLO would renounce terrorism, accept SCRs 242 and 338 as the basis for negotiations, and recognize Israel's right to exist, the three conditions that had been required by the United States for it to deal with the PLO. The Europeans (French) took credit for nursing Arafat's change of heart and hoped to parlay it into a full-scale European-led peace initiative. However, Arafat went on to declare, "Now the ball is in America's court!" In any case, the Iraqi invasion of Kuwait in August 1990 brought that and a number of U.S., Arab, and European peace proposals to an abrupt halt.

Europe's Reemergence The GULF CRISIS, 1990–1991, which followed, turned out to be a watershed of sorts for Europe nonetheless. After languishing for decades in what Kissinger called a "wallflower" role, Europe suddenly asserted itself in its first material involvement since Suez. The British prime minister, Margaret Thatcher, meeting with President George Bush at Aspen, Colorado, encouraged President Bush to stand firm. François Mitterrand, who led the EC into taking an immediate, open, and vigorous response directly and through the U.N. joined the United States in the field. With regard to the peace process, France and Europe tried to get in on the ground floor as Mitterrand made a bid at the forty-fifth United Nations General Assembly for Western leadership. After the Gulf Crisis, having had an active role in the fighting, the Europeans felt sure they had as much right to leadership as the Americans.

However, the United States did not want its primary role as peacemaker eroded by the Europeans, Gulf war cooperation notwithstanding. The U.S. secretary of state, James Baker, revived the Geneva formula with U.S.-Soviet cosponsorship of the MADRID PEACE CONFERENCE, 1991, excluding the Europeans, who had hoped for more than "a fold-down seat and observer status." In the end it didn't matter. Madrid was entirely ceremonial, lasted a day, and served only to launch the real negotiations. What Europe did achieve at Madrid was a role as one of the principals in the "multilaterals," a separate set of five negotiations on the basic issues of water, economic development, refugees, arms controls, and the environment. Meetings of these groups continued over the months while the bilaterals were unproductive.

It was not the sterile bilaterals but secret Norwegian-sponsored negotiations in Oslo that broke the logjam and gave the bilaterals new life. The OSLO AGREEMENTS also spurred the European Union (EU) into action. It pledged over 600 million ecus in aid to the territories, to the police force of the PALESTINIAN AUTHORITY, and to the elections. Both Prime Minister Shimon Peres and Chairman Arafat held up Europe as the model for building a new regional political economy. At the November 1995 Barcelona conference, the EU adopted the ambitious EU-Mediterranean Partnership Agreement on trade and development. EU members led by France began to demand a political role commensurate with their economic contribution and recognition that it was Europe that brought Arafat and the PLO into the councils of nations and pushed Palestinian rights to the center of negotiations.

The assassination of Prime Minister Rabin, a wave of HAMAS bombings in Israel, and the May 1996 election of Prime Minister Benjamin Netanyahu brought the peace process, except for the Wye River agreement in October 1998, to an abrupt end, worsening materially the plight of the Palestinians. It was not until the election of a new prime minister Ehud Barak, in 1999 that the peace process was revived. Implementation of the Oslo and Wye accords is subject to the vagaries of politics and events. But the EU stands committed to its full economic and political support of the process. Historic affinities will then have a chance to reassert themselves and to restore the natural relationship shattered in 1956 at Suez.

Robert K. Olson

BIBLIOGRAPHY

Allen, David, and Alfred Pijpers, eds. *European Foreign Policy-Making and the Arab-Israeli Conflict.* The Hague: Nijhoff, 1984.

Carter, Jimmy. *The Blood of Abraham.* Boston: Houghton Mifflin, 1985.

Eban, Abba. *An Autobiography.* Jerusalem: Steinmatsky's Agency Ltd., 1977.

Eisenhower, Dwight D. *Waging Peace: The White House Years, 1958–1961.* New York: Doubleday and Co., Inc., 1964.

Federal Republic of Germany. *European Political Cooperation (EPC),* 4th ed. Wiesbaden, Germany: 1982.

Garfinkel, Adam M. *Western European Middle East Diplomacy and the U.S.* Philadelphia: Foreign Policy Research Institute, 1983.

Kissinger, Henry. *Years of Upheaval.* Boston: Little Brown, 1982.

Shultz, George P. *Turmoil and Triumph.* New York: Charles Scribner's Sons, 1993.

Exodus

1947–1949

Since 1949, two contradictory and simplistic explanations have dominated debate about the Palestinian exodus from the areas that became the State of Israel after the ARAB-ISRAELI WAR OF 1948. One explanation, usually given by the Palestinians and their supporters, is that the Zionists forcibly expelled Palestinians in a planned, systematic policy. The other, usually given by Israel and its supporters, is that the Palestinians fled voluntarily—that is, not under compulsion—and that both Palestinian leaders and Arab leaders from other nations ordered or requested that they leave, in order to clear the ground for the planned Arab invasion of May 15, 1948.

Documents declassified in the 1980s and early 1990s—principally Israeli, but also American, British, and United Nations (U.N.)—present a far more complex picture, in which the flight of approximately 700,000 Palestinians occurred for somewhat different reasons in different localities at different times. Much depended on local circumstances, particularly on local initiatives by Jewish commanders and officials as well as Arab commanders and notables.

The Zionist leadership in Palestine during the late 1930s and early 1940s had generally favored (and quietly espoused) a "transfer" solution to the problem posed by a large Palestinian minority in the prospective Jewish state. However, during the crisis of 1948, Israel's political leaders, headed by David Ben-Gurion—although certainly desirous of having the smallest Arab minority possible in ISRAEL and often "nudging" and, more rarely, ordering, their military commanders to clear various areas of Palestinians—never translated this transfer thinking into actual, comprehensive, systematic policy because of moral and internal as well as political and external constraints on the Israeli leadership. Although there was never any formal policy decision or central directive, however, there was something like a consensus, especially among the military, in favor of clearing the Palestinians out of Israeli territory, for both military and political reasons. In certain large campaigns, such as Operation Hiram in the Galilee in October 1948, commanding officers issued expulsion directives.

At the same time, there is no evidence that the governments of the Arab states or the Palestinian

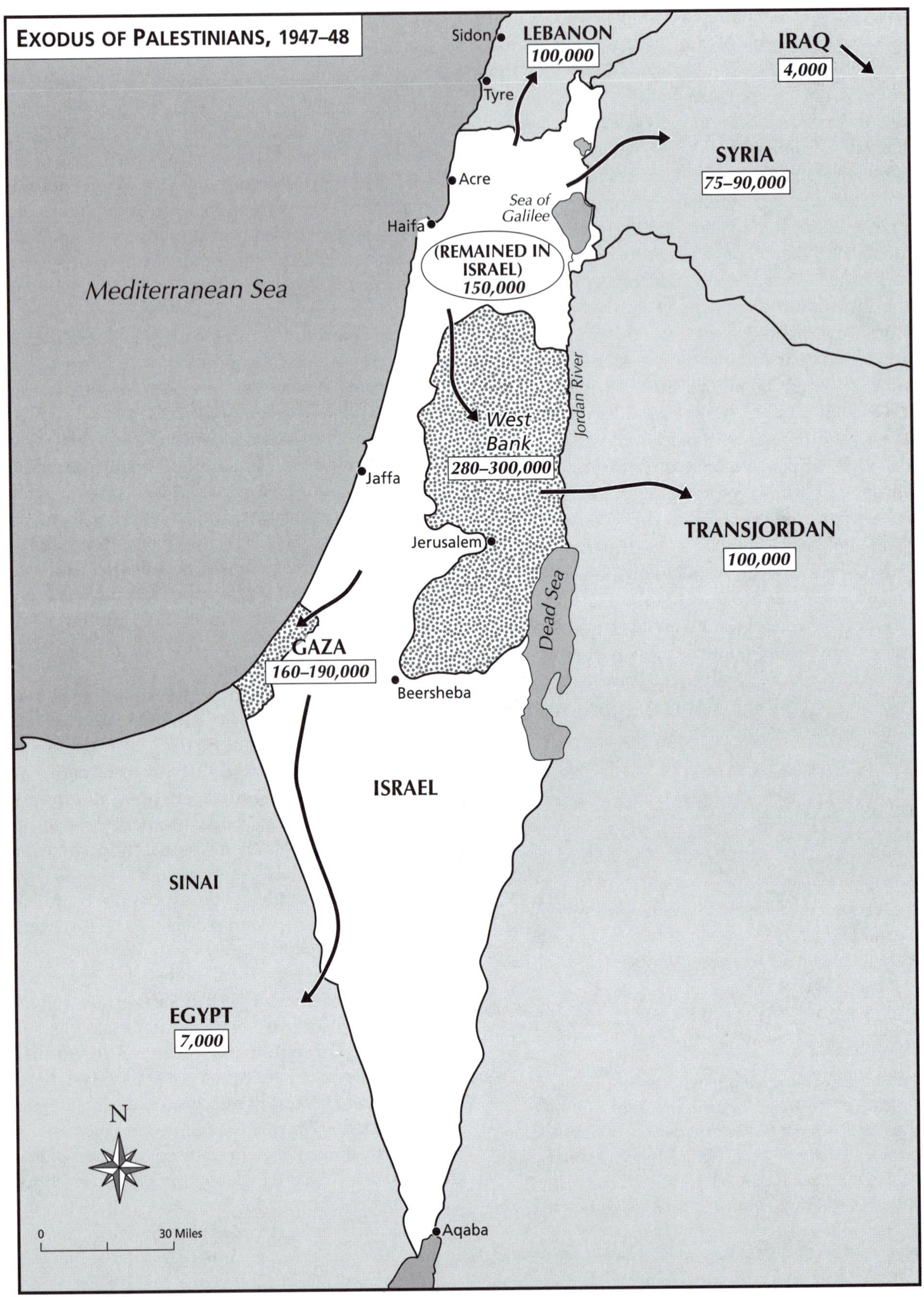
EXODUS OF PALESTINIANS, 1947–48
Sidon
LEBANON
100,000
IRAQ
4,000
Tyre
SYRIA
75–90,000
Acre
Sea of Galilee
Haifa
(REMAINED IN ISRAEL)
150,000
Mediterranean Sea
Jordan River
West Bank
280–300,000
Jaffa
TRANSJORDAN
100,000
Jerusalem
Dead Sea
GAZA
160–190,000
Beersheba
ISRAEL
SINAI
EGYPT
7,000
N
0
30 Miles
Aqaba

national leadership ever decided on a blanket policy of evacuation. Nor was such a policy ever espoused, ordered, or implemented in the course of the war. On the contrary, there is evidence, especially from early March and May 1948, that the external ARAB HIGHER COMMITTEE and external Arab leaders wanted the Palestinians to stay put in their villages and towns, and that they even made efforts to persuade them to stay or, if already in exile, to return. At the same time there is an abundance of evidence from a large number of localities that local leaders, the Jordanian Arab Legion, and the Arab Higher Committee did issue orders at specific times to specific villages and to vulnerable groups such as women and children to evacuate actual or potential war zones. However, in most areas at most times, the Palestinian population was left by its national leaders and by the Arab states to its own devices—and evidence that the leadership at all levels was confused about what course to follow.

Clearly, the major reason for flight in most areas at most times was Jewish attack—by the Haganah, Irgun Zvai Leumi, Lohamei Herut Yisrael (known as LEHI and the Stern Gang), or the Israel Defense Forces (IDF)—or else Palestinian fears of an impending Jewish attack. Most Palestinians left no region or large town prior to Jewish attack; most regions and towns were evacuated either during an attack or in an attack's immediate wake. Often, a preliminary mortar barrage, rather than infantry or mechanized assault, triggered flight, but many villages emptied even before mortar bombs began to fall. In many areas, a "psychosis of flight" (in the words of one Israeli intelligence document) took hold; the fear was infectious. Flight from one house prompted flight from neighboring houses; flight from one village or urban neighborhood inspired flight from surrounding villages and neighborhoods; flight from towns prompted flight from satellite villages; and flight from satellite villages triggered flight from towns.

The months of warfare, starting in December 1947, had a progressive demoralizing effect, principally in the cities. The constant sniping and bombing, the unemployment and rising food prices, a feeling of isolation and weakness in the face of a powerful enemy, the breakdown of services and of law and order, lack of support from and confidence in surrounding Arab states, and the presence of Arab volunteers or irregulars from outside, who occasionally intimidated, robbed, or otherwise harmed the local population, all contributed to Palestinian society's swift disintegration and collapse when the Haganah/IDF moved over to the offensive in April–May 1948.

Several dozen villages and a number of towns, principally LYDDA and RAMLA, were depopulated as a result of explicit Jewish expulsion orders. Other villages were intimidated into flight by threats and deliberate psychological warfare. Reports or rumors of Jewish atrocities—of which there were a fair number—in one place helped propel into flight the inhabitants at other sites.

As background—and preconditioning—to the exodus, it is worth pointing to a number of inherent weaknesses that made Palestinian society particularly vulnerable to war: a relative lack of education and widespread illiteracy, and general political and economic underdevelopment; a lack of effective and representative political and military institutions; a relative scarcity of weaponry and military infrastructure (bomb shelters, fortifications, arms production facilities); a political and social elite—fatally disunited since the 1920s—without a tradition of public or military service, who eventually proved, incompetent, uninspiring, and, at times, cowardly; important social divisions and alienation between the urban and rural masses and the elite, between Muslims and Christians, and between town and country; and deep-seated clan feuds inside particular villages, between neighboring villages, and between neighboring clusters of villages. In addition, one historical factor is relevant—the British suppression of the Arab rebellion of 1936–39, which contributed considerably to the general enfeeblement of Palestinian society (loss of cadres, loss of weaponry, apoliticization of much of the elite, and exile of leaders).

The exodus unfolded in four-and-a-half stages, mainly following the development of the war:

Stage I, December 1947–March 1948, saw many of the elite families leaving the country for havens in Beirut, Transjordan, Egypt, and Syria. The expansion of Arab-Jewish hostilities, especially in the mixed Arab-Jewish towns (Haifa, Tel Aviv–Jaffa, JERUSALEM), and the British preparations to withdraw unnerved the middle and upper classes, leading to a closure of businesses, offices, and schools. Most of the Palestinian population of the coastal plain departed from Palestinian centers in eastern Palestine, some people intimidated into flight by the Jewish dissident organizations (the Irgun Zvai Leumi and Lohamei Herut Yisrael), others by a feeling of isolation and vulnerability in a largely Jewish-populated area. It is estimated that as many as 75,000 left their homes during this stage.

Stage II, April–June 1948, saw the bulk of the Palestinian urban population evacuate TIBERIAS, Haifa, Jaffa, West Jerusalem, Beisan, SAFAD, and ACRE, along with the flight of most of the rural population from the Jerusalem Corridor, Jezreel valley, Jordan valley, Baysan, and Eastern and Western Galilee. In such places as Tiberias and Haifa, the flight of the local leadership and its persuasion of the rest of population that flight was the best available option were important in the mass exodus that followed. Moreover, the flight from main towns inevitably demoralized those in the satellite villages and precipitated flight from them. In all, some 250,000 to 300,000 Palestinians fled during this stage, in which the Haganah—in the early part of the war on the defensive—went over to the offensive, more or less in line with its "Plan D," which provided for Jewish seizure and defense of the country's border areas and the main routes between the major Jewish clusters of population in preparation for the expected pan-Arab invasion of Palestine. Plan D gave the regional Haganah commanders carte blanche to depopulate, destroy, or mine Palestinian villages considered hostile or potentially hostile, in effect allowing the brigade and battalion commanders to evict villagers at will. About two dozen Palestinian villages were depopulated by Jewish expulsion orders during this period, including al-Dumayra, Miska, Khirbat al-Sarkas, Arab al-Nufay'at, Khirbat Azzun, Zarnuqa, Huj, Yubna, Sumsum, and Najd. News (and rumors) of Jewish atrocities against Palestinian villagers, often broadcast by Arab media, served during April and May (and again in October and November) to unnerve the remaining Arab population and induce flight. The massacre at DAYR YASIN by Irgun Zvai Leumi and Lohamei Herut Yisrael troops in April—and the subsequent broadcasts about it in the Arab media—were crucial in this respect.

Stage III, July 8–18, 1948, the "Ten Days," in traditional Israeli historiography, saw the IDF, newly equipped and organized after the First Truce, take the offensive in the Lower Galilee and NAZARETH ("Operation Dekel"), the Lydda-Ramla area ("Operation Dani"), and the northern Negev approaches. The IDF captured dozens of Palestinian towns and villages, and, in consequence, another 100,000 inhabitants took to their heels. Most of them—perhaps some 60,000—were expelled by the IDF from Lydda and Ramla, the largest expulsion of the war and the one for which there is persuasive evidence tracing the orders to Ben-Gurion. This expulsion was indicative of the greater readiness among IDF commanders by this time to expel Palestinian communities.

Stage IV, October–November 1948, saw the flight of about 200,000 Palestinians, mostly from the southern coastal plain and the northern Negev to the GAZA STRIP and from the northern Galilee to Lebanon during the two major IDF offensives, Operations Yoav and Hiram. The swift and very visible collapse of Arab armies certainly contributed to the demoralization of the civilian population, previously "protected" by those armies. IDF atrocities (especially in Operation Hiram), expulsion orders (especially by General Yigal Allon, commanding officer Southern Command, during Operation Yoav), and intimidation contributed to the flight, though many of Galilee's Palestinian inhabitants were not expelled and remained to live in Israel.

During the immediate postwar period, until October 1950, Israel's policy of clearing its border areas of Palestinian communities resulted in the evacuation of perhaps another 20,000 Palestinians, including thousands of Bedouins expelled to Sinai and the Hebron Hills and more than 2,000 Palestinians transferred—partly with their agreement—from Majdal and Ashkelon to the Gaza Strip. Periodic expulsion of Bedouin communities from the Negev continued during the 1950s.

During April–June 1948, a major policy decision to bar the return of the REFUGEES, both during the war and after it, crystallized in the Israeli cabinet. Both political leaders and the public viewed the possible return of the refugees as potentially calamitous, both politically and militarily, and understood that the absorption of masses of new Jewish immigrants was dependent upon the availability of the newly abandoned land, villages, and urban neighborhoods. At the same time, the Arab states, burdened with the refugee problem, made repatriation of all or most of the refugees a sine qua non of any movement toward peace. By and large, Western governments supported the repatriation of the refugees, embodying this provision in United Nations General Assembly Resolution 194 of December 1948, but they proved unable or unwilling to apply sufficient pressure on Israel to force implementation. Both the Palestinians and the Arab states resisted the resettlement of the refugees in the Arab countries, viewing repatriation both as just and as a potential tool for destabilizing Israel. Taken together, these policies resulted in the perpetuation of the refugee problem.

Benny Morris

BIBLIOGRAPHY

Gabbay, Rony. *A Political Study of the Arab-Jewish Conflict: The Arab Refugee Problem (a Case Study).* Geneva: Librarie E. Droz, 1959.

Khalaf, Issa. *Politics in Palestine: Arab Factionalism and Social Disintegration, 1939–1948.* Albany, N.Y.: SUNY Press, 1991.

Khalidi, Walid, ed., *All That Remains: The Palestinian Villages Occupied and Depopulated by Israel in 1948.* Washington, D.C.: Institute for Palestine Studies, 1992.

Masalha, Nur. *Expulsion of the Palestinians: The Concept of "Transfer" in Zionist Political Thought: 1882–1948.* Washington, D.C.: Institute for Palestine Studies, 1992.

Morris, Benny. *The Birth of the Palestinian Refugee Problem, 1947–1949.* Cambridge: Cambridge: University Press, 1988.

——. *1948 and After: Israel and the Palestinians.* Oxford, England: Clarendon Press, 1990.

Nazzal, Nafez. *The Arab Exodus from Galilee, 1948.* Beirut: Institute for Palestine Studies, 1978.

Palumbo, Michael. *The Palestinian Catastrophe.* London: Faber & Faber, 1987.

F

Farsoun, Samih

Farsun scholar and activist
1937– Haifa

Having fled Palestine with his family in 1948 and grown up in Beirut, Samih Farsoun immigrated to the United States in the 1950s to attend college and has lived there since. Farsoun received master's and doctor's degrees in sociology in 1962 and 1971 from the University of Connecticut. He has written and lectured extensively on the Palestinian situation, as well as on social change in the Arab world. He has been chairman of the Department of Sociology, American University, and later became dean of the Faculty of Arts of the American University of Sharjah in the United Arab Emirates.

Farsoun has been particularly active among PALESTINIAN AMERICANS and in Arab-American organizations. He is a founding member and past president of the Association of Arab-American University Graduates (AAUG), and from 1987 to 1990, he edited the *Arab Studies Quarterly,* published by AAUG. He also helped found and was the chairperson of the Palestine Congress of North America, an association of Palestinian organizations and individuals that formed in 1979 and disbanded in 1983. He has served on the boards, and was a founding member, of the Palestinian charitable organization the Jerusalem Fund, as well as the Center for Policy Analysis on Palestine, a Washington, D.C.–based study center.

Farsoun has been highly critical of the Declaration of Principles signed in September 1993 by Israel and the PALESTINE LIBERATION ORGANIZATION (PLO). He believes that, because of the PLO's loss of stature, especially since its support of Iraq during the GULF CRISIS, 1990–91, the PLO leader, YASIR ARAFAT, has leapt at anything Israel offered and conceded far more than was necessary. Farsoun is particularly disturbed that such major Palestinian concerns as the right to return to Palestine and the need to end Israeli confiscation of Palestinian land are now being treated simply as matters for negotiation rather than as inalienable rights.

Kathleen Christison

BIBLIOGRAPHY

Farsoun, Samih, ed. *Arab Society: Continuity and Change.* London: Croom Helm, 1985.

——, ed. *Iran: Political Culture in the Islamic Republic.* London: Routledge, 1992.

Farsoun, Smith, ed., and Christina Zacharia. *Palestine and the Palestinians.* Boulder, Colo.: Westview Press, 1997.

Fatah

Fath; Fateh

The word *fath* means "conquest" or "victory" in Arabic; it is also the reverse acronym of *Harakat al-Tahrir al-Watani al-Filastini,* the Arabic name of the oldest and most important PALESTINE LIBERATION ORGANIZATION (PLO) organization, the Palestinian National Liberation Movement.

Fatah founders, who include YASIR ARAFAT, SALAH KHALAF, KHALIL AL-WAZIR, and KHALID AL-HASAN, cannot agree on the exact date of the group's formation. Although most leaders locate the movement's origins in 1959, Khalil al-Wazir, also known as Abu Jihad, has maintained that Fatah was founded in 1957. Leaders do agree that the movement was born at an informal gathering of disaffected Palestinians who had been influenced by the experiences of fighting Israeli occupation in the GAZA STRIP in 1956: young people from middle-class backgrounds who lacked a coherent ideological outlook, though most of them harbored sympathy for the Egyptian branch of the Muslim Brotherhood. The movement did not establish an organizational structure but focused instead on disseminating its message to large segments of the Palestinian population in Lebanon, Syria, Jordan, Kuwait, Egypt, and Gaza. The only evidence of the movement's early existence was the publication of its irregular magazine *Filastinuna,* "Our Palestine."

Program The movement always insisted on "armed struggle" as the only path for Palestine's liberation. This commitment to political violence was the product of Israeli military superiority, as well as the universally popular notion of "people's liberation war" among third world nations seeking independence in the late 1950s and early 1960s, especially after the success of the Algerian revolution. Many Palestinians were also aware of the attempts by some Arab regimes to settle the ARAB-ISRAELI CONFLICT through diplomatic means—at the expense of Palestinian national rights. However, the movement was explicitly opposed to choosing any political ideology for fear of alienating any element of the Palestinian population: Fatah believed that the liberation of Palestine required the unification of Palestinians from all classes. This advocacy of national unity appeased wealthy Palestinians who were uncomfortable with the radicalism of the Arab nationalist movement and the Ba'th Party. Some of Fatah's founders, such as Khalid al-Hasan and Yasir Arafat himself, were even tied to ruling oil interests. They appreciated that wealthy Palestinians could provide the movement with the financial resources necessary for achieving political independence from Arab regimes.

This principle of avoiding ideology remained at once the major weakness and major strength of Fatah. The movement succeeded in attracting more members than any other Palestinian independence group but failed to create a meaningful organization that could in fact speak for the diverse elements within its ranks. Yet, if the movement did not present a program, it offered a new ideology of "Palestinianism." Fatah was committed to independent Palestinian decision making. The very title of its magazine, *Filastinuna,* sent a twofold message: to ISRAEL, that the Palestinians would not abandon their attachment to their homeland, and to Arab regimes, that the Palestinians would no longer allow them to dominate Palestinian decision making in the name of Arab unity and brotherhood.

The growth of Fatah was gradual, more spontaneous reaction to events than a calculated effort to fulfill a vision of Palestine's political future. Through its postal address, *Filastinuna* attracted thousands of enthusiastic members; HANI AL-HASAN (himself an influential student leader at the time) admitted that the sheer number of applicants made it impossible for the leadership to guard itself against hostile infiltration. In fact, the movement suffered throughout its history from manipulation by both Israel and Arab governments.

Organization Fatah came into official existence on the night of December 31, 1964, when AL-ASIFA ("The Storm"), founded as the military arm of the movement, claimed responsibility for a failed attack inside Israel. The announcement was intended to signal the beginning of a new phase in the struggle in which Palestinian fighters would no longer take orders from Arab governments. The name *fatah* was not used to prevent embarrassment if matters went contrary to plans. The date still is celebrated as the birth of the Palestinian revolution by Fatah enthusiasts. The dramatic announcement of "armed struggle" was also a reaction to the creation of the PLO, which many Palestinians perceived as a tool of Jamal Abd al-Nasir who had hand-picked AHMAD SHUQAYRI as its head. Fatah gained further support after the 1967 war, when the loss of the WEST BANK and Gaza dashed the faith of most Arabs in the ability of Arab regimes to achieve full—or even partial—liberation for Palestine. The movement benefited greatly from the ouster of Shuqayri as chair of the PLO in the wake of the 1967 defeat; at that point, Arafat and his supporters were able to gain control of the PLO, giving Fatah a political and material advantage that no other PLO organization was able to challenge.

Fatah did not follow any organizational model. It remained a loose association of factions, each with its own head. Even its intelligence apparatus was not centralized, as each leader formed his own military/intelligence branch. Nevertheless, the movement created a fighting force and, despite its inability to pose a serious military threat to Israel, was able to confront Israel face-to-face in the al-Karama battle in March 1968.

Fatah had established its headquarters in Jordan, but in 1970 the Jordanian army evicted all PLO forces, which were relocated to Lebanon. The BLACK SEPTEMBER showdown reinforced the rift between the left and right wings of Fatah, although the effectiveness of both wings was undermined by the divisiveness within their ranks. The right-wing factions, headed by Khalid al-Hasan, were impatient with the existence of the Palestinian Left and urged its expulsion from Fatah. The Left, represented at the time by Salah Khalaf, refused to blame the September 1970 massacres on two leftish factions of the PLO, the POPULAR FRONT FOR THE LIBERATION OF PALESTINE (PFLP) and the DEMOCRATIC FRONT FOR THE LIBERATION OF PALESTINE (DFLP).

Fatah's greatest challenge was avoiding what the political literature called *secondary contradictions*—all conflicts that did not specifically involve Israel. Despite its best efforts, the movement could not keep out of Jordanian or Lebanese internal affairs, especially when Lebanese leftist factions insisted on dragging the PLO into domestic Lebanese problems. Fatah simply could not live up to its slogan calling for the aiming of *all* rifles in the direction of the "Zionist enemy." In Jordan, Lebanon, and elsewhere, the movement discovered that many of its enemies did in fact reside outside Israel.

The more that Fatah became embroiled in Lebanese affairs, the more ineffective it became. Fatah was further weakened as many Arab governments obtained influence within the movement. Many of Fatah's Lebanese and Palestinian critics saw this influence as *dakakin* (Arabic, "shops"), implying that one could buy any ideological products one wished within the movement.

Arafat did very little to bring about organizational reform because, historically, his ascendance had been tied to his ability to play off factions and leaders against one another. The flow of Arab oil money into Fatah increased the degree of corruption among its leaders and irreparably damaged its reputation among the masses, especially when the movement did not fare well in battle during the Lebanese sojourn of the 1980s. The movement suffered further after the success of Israel and its agents in assassinating the movement's top elite, including such founders as Abu Jihad (Khalil al-Wazir) and Abu Yusuf (Muhammad Yusif al-Najjar).

Fatah never enjoyed a permanent base; it had to build a dispersed structure in the Occupied Territories and in the Arab countries where Palestinian refugees resided. Before 1970, the movement set up its headquarters in Jordan, where Fatah's relations with the Jordanian government were strained as a result of the attempts of King Husayn to control the movement and represent it in international forums. During this period, the movement was committed to what it called "a secular and democratic Palestine" as a solution to the Palestinian problem. It advocated the elimination of ZIONISM "in Palestine" and the creation of an alternative government that would allow Jews, Christians, and Muslims to live side by side in the former territory of Palestine. In the West and Israel, this solution was considered tantamount to advocating the destruction of Israel.

Some Fatah leaders began considering what was known as "the two-state solution" (advocating accepting Israel's existence in return for Israeli acceptance of a Palestinian state in the West Bank and Gaza, including East JERUSALEM) as early as 1968, despite the vehement rejection of that idea by most rank-and-file members.

Fatah was hesitant to publicize its internal debates; it feared the criticisms of both leftist PLO organizations and those Arab regimes that on principle did not accept the existence of Israel. The movement was also opposed to UNITED NATIONS SECURITY COUNCIL RESOLUTION 242 because it did not address the national dimension of the Palestinian question; nor did the PLO leadership want to endorse any international resolution that would grant legitimacy to Israel. Furthermore, many Palestinians were convinced that armed struggle was the main path of liberation.

The DFLP supported early on the "two-state solution" and was the first PLO organization to call for an understanding of the Jewish question. Opinion within the movement was not uniform, and the leadership was secretive about its diplomatic plans and internal deliberations.

Moderation The Lebanon phase of the history of Fatah began in 1970, when the PLO was expelled from Jordan, and ended in 1982, when the Israeli invasion of Lebanon led to the PLO's eviction from Lebanon. The Lebanese civil war exhausted and distracted Fatah, although it did expose Fatah's members to the rich ideological spectrum of Lebanese politics.

Arafat expanded Fatah once he established his base of operations in Lebanon but kept a tight grip over its organizational structure. He tolerated internal dissent as long as it did not lead to a diminution of his authority or a democratization of decision making. Fatah's dominance within the PLO remained intact over the years thanks partly to Arafat's popularity and control over the PLO's vast financial and military resources. The CAMP DAVID ACCORDS took the movement by surprise and led Arafat to consider more seriously the possibility of diplomatic solutions. Over the years, Fatah accepted the two-state solution and concluded that military struggle was not in fact achieving victories for the Palestinian national movement. The U.S. election of the Reagan administration, with its efforts to make King Husayn responsible for Palestinian political representation, increased Palestinian popular frustration and dashed Arafat's hope for a military victory. Arafat's support for Iraq during the GULF CRISIS further angered Fatah's veterans in Arab Gulf states. This, along with the collapse of the SOVIET UNION, increased pressure on Arafat to seek a political solution to the Palestinian problem, even if it entailed accepting a limited version of Palestinian national goals. Nevertheless, hard-liners within Fatah continued to preach armed struggle and "full liberation of Palestine," although they were vastly outnumbered by the moderate camp headed by Arafat and his supporters.

The PLO-Israel agreement of 1993, embodied in the OSLO AGREEMENTS, did not resolve the several financial crises within Fatah. Dissension within the movement is by no means new—ABU NIDAL had led a group away in 1973, as had, SA'ID MURAGHA (Abu Musa) in 1983, to name the two most notable cases—but the murder of key Fatah leaders such as Salah Khalaf and Khalil al-Wazir encouraged Arafat to operate with complete disregard for the movement's internal rules. Within the central committee and the revolutionary council, Fatah's two highest ruling bodies, strong opposition to Arafat's rule exists. FARUQ AL-QADDUMI, also known as Abu al-Lutf, seems to represent the loyal opposition to Arafat, although some elements of the opposition distrust Arafat too much to accept his continued leadership. The relocation of PLO leadership to Gaza and the WEST BANK in 1994 shifted the political center of gravity of the movement back from the diaspora to within Palestine.

As'ad AbuKhalil

BIBLIOGRAPHY

Amos, John. *Palestinian Resistance.* New York: Pergamon Press, 1980.

Cobban, Helena. *The PLO.* New York: Cambridge University Press, 1984.

Gresh, Alan. *The PLO: The Struggle Within.* London: Zed Press, 1985.

Hart, Alan. *Arafat.* Bloomington: Indiana University Press, 1989.

Khalil Husayn, Hasan. *Abu Iyad.* Amman: Matba'at al-Dustur, 1991.

al-Rayyis, Riyad Najib, and Dunya Habin Nahhas. *Al-Masar al-Sa'b: al-Muqawama al-Filastiniyya* (The difficult path: The Palestinian resistance). Beirut: Dar al-Nahar, 1976.

Yusuf, Samir. *Abu Jihad.* Cairo: al-Markaz al-Misri al-Arabi, 1989.

Folklore

Although townsfolk crowded the cities and Bedouins wandered over the southern desert, for the most part Palestine has been an agricultural society. The preponderance of Palestinian tradition is made up of the customs, arts, and values of the *fallah,* the hardworking "tiller of the soil." Governed by the rhythm of crops and looking for support only from God and the extended family, the *fallah* has imbued Palestinian folklore with the presence of nature, the importance of family and clan, and a devoutness that includes the veneration of the prophets and saints who were once believed to walk about this "holy land."

The Wedding Since family is central and children are prayed for, the wedding is a major event incorporating the full range of folk arts. It is celebrated with singing and dancing and gifts of clothes and money, and it is consecrated with a *dabiha,* the butchering of a lamb or a goat to be distributed among the poor and shared with well-wishers in a lavish meal. Fall used to be the time for marriage, after the harvest earnings were in. Nowadays summer is the wedding season, when workers in the Gulf countries and students abroad come home on vacation.

Marriage Conditions in a Palestinian Village (Helsinki, 1931, 1935), a two-volume study by the Finnish anthropologist Hilma Granqvist, written after a three-year stay in Artas, remains the most detailed reference on the subject.

Almost as elaborate as weddings were the ceremonies surrounding the circumcision of young boys. Other events calling for a *dabiha* are the return of a son from prison or military service and the completion of a house. In the past, the whole village would take part in raising the characteristic domed roof and in eating the festive meal that followed.

Traditional Costume A considerable expenditure for a bridegroom was the *kiswat al-arus,* the bridal finery: several dresses for the bride and new outfits for members of the wedding. Shopping for the trousseau was attended by song and ritual. The finest dress was saved for the newlywed's first appearance in public as a married woman. Wearing all her jewelry and accompanied by singing women she proceeded to the well, *tal'at al-bi'r.*

The woman's *thawb* is a modest ankle-length gown with long sleeves traditionally sewn from handwoven strips of cotton, linen, or silk in natural white or dyed indigo or black. However, panels of EMBROIDERY that decorate the chest, sides, and back hem with dazzling combinations of colored thread transform these dresses, each a unique creation of its wearer, into works of art. They are included in the collections of museums worldwide. Among the designs, executed mainly in cross-stitch, are symbolic patterns like a triangular "cypress" denoting longevity or an S-shaped "leech" for good health. Regional variants in the use of color or design identify the provenance of a dress. Wedding garments of rich velvet and striped silk were showpieces heavily encrusted with embroidery, sometimes even with gold or silver cord. These could be ordered from professional embroiderers, notably from Bethlehem, which was known for the use of intricate couching and satin stitch. A short jacket, the *takisira,* or a long coat went over the *thawb.* Everywhere a flowing head cloth covered the hair. Under this, married women wore a snug cap and displayed their wealth by sewing rows of gold or silver coins along its front edge.

Women in villages and refugee camps still wear embroidered dresses but use machine-made cloth, synthetic thread, and lurex. The flag of Palestine and the Dome of the Rock are among the newer embroidery motifs. Younger women wear Western dress or, if they are Islamist, full-length tailored garments in sober colors with a severe head scarf.

The men's garb consisted of a long striped gown, *qumbaz,* over roomy, narrow-cuffed trousers, *sirwals,* and a cloak, *abaya,* of natural beige, brown, or black wool. The white head cloth is held in place with a double ring of black cording, *iqal.* Supporters of FATAH favor black-and-white checked *kufiyya* head cloths.

Folk Song, Dance, Music Chanting and singing punctuated every phase of Palestinian life. Weddings, which are preceded by several days of celebration involving the whole community, invite happy trilling from the WOMEN, *zagharid,* and much singing. There were songs to mark the arrival of the wedding clothes; the decoration of the bride with patterns of red henna; the mournful farewell to the departing daughter, *tarwida;* the salute to the uncles who will always protect her; the welcome to the bride by the groom's family ("Our bride will always be as precious as sifted wheat"); the praising of the bountiful feast and the generous feast giver; and so on. Traditional refrains are interspersed with words improvised for the occasion.

The women express their joy by singing and clapping their henna-stained hands, trilling and dancing with arms raised, finger snapping and shoulders and hips shaking to the rhythm of *tabla* or *durbakka* drums. This takes place indoors or in the shelter of the courtyard.

In contrast, the men assemble outside the groom's house on the nights preceding the procession of the bride from her father's home to her new home, *zaffat al-arus.*

Under a full moon or around a bonfire the young men dance the *dabka* to the sound of the shepherd's flute, the *shabbaba* or the *yarghul,* also known as *mijwiz,* a double-piped instrument with a sound like that of a bagpipe. Holding onto each other's belts or shoulders, the men form an open circle and move in unison while drumming the ground with their feet in complex steps. Their leader, the *lawwih,* twirls a scarf or short stick above his head. Aware of the women, who are watching from the rooftops, individual dancers break off one by one to show their skill and grace in brief solos.

Folk Poetry Much sought-after for any celebrations are the folk poets. Now heard on the radio, seen on television, and recorded on cassette, they used to travel from wedding to wedding, receiving gifts of food or cash. A good voice and a quick mind are essential, since the poet sings his poems, often to a one-stringed *rababa,* and he is expected to compose verses tailored to his audience using their names and characteristics to praise or tease them.

A popular form is the *zajal,* or "challenging song." In this two poets compete in an impromptu debate in verse, thinking up their rhymed responses as the listeners chant a refrain. Witty puns and humor are especially appreciated. A common rhyme scheme is for three half lines in a couplet to end on the same sound while the fourth rhymes with the fourth half line of all other couplets in a poem or song. Dr. Abdullatif M. Barghouti of BIR ZEIT UNIVERSITY has published collections of oral poetry and folk songs in the spoken Arabic of Palestine. He identifies some two dozen types of folk poetry, from laments to lullabies; he notes that love songs, including love of family, friends, and country, predominate. Politics has also been a subject for Palestinian folk and formal poets. In his *Encyclopedia of Palestinian Folklore* (Amman, 1977–1981, in Arabic), Nimr Sirhan discusses a folk poet jailed by the British for a poem berating the Zionists. Contemporary poets sing of the heroes and martyrs of the INTIFADA, of Israeli prisons and identity cards.

Storytelling Whereas folk poets' words are original, the professional storyteller, the itinerant *rawi,* is a reciter of epics and romances whose protagonists predate Islam. His performance might stretch over several evenings, attracting listeners to the coffeehouse that engages him. Household tales are women's work told in the intimacy of the family circle as they are in other cultures. Furnished with magic carpets and mirrors, and peopled with supernatural ghouls and jinn, these stories belong to the Arabic narrative tradition, as do epics and romances. The distinguished features are the Palestinian setting and the detail from *fallahi* rural life. Heroines' teeth are "white as hailstones," they have arms "smooth like peeled cucumbers," and even princes know how to yoke an ox and when to press the olives. The Palestinian "Good Apprentice and the Bad" are baker's boys from NABLUS on their way to earn extra cash helping with the Gaza harvest. In addition, there are a number of stories set in Palestine's countryside about local saints and biblical figures like Moses and the Virgin Mary, who once lived there.

Superstitions The majority of Palestinians are practicing Muslims and Christians and the name of God is constantly on people's lips. No task or journey is begun without first invoking God's protection, *bismillah;* no child is admired or success mentioned without adding the expression *mashallah,* "such is God's will." But beyond religious faith, there are numerous superstitious measures to ward off harm and attract good fortune.

Great danger is believed to result from the "evil eye," the eye of envy, which can precipitate calamity, especially in times of great joy or well-being. During wedding and circumcision processions, a pitchfork dressed up in flashy clothes used to be held aloft to attract "the eye" away from the bride or young boy. The custom seems to survive in modern wedding motorcades. The decoration of the bride's car is a minor folk art in itself, and one of the salient features is a plastic doll on the roof, presumably to draw attention away from the passenger.

Elaborate precautions used to be taken to protect newborn babies, especially males. Names like *Saqr* and *Nimr* ("hawk" and "leopard") were given to frighten off hostile demons. Nowadays, in addition to jewelry spelling the name of God, amulets, lumps of alum, blue beads, and miniature eyes and hands of Fatima are still attached to children's clothes to stave off evil.

In a dry land fertility is a blessing so the farmer's calendar is dotted with auspicious and ill-omened days guiding seasonal activities. Water, precious and also magical, was sometimes thrown on the ground as a bride entered her new home for fruitfulness, or she carried a jar of water.

Though not officially recognized in Islam, saints and holymen were believed to intercede and fulfill prayers. Childless women would visit a saint's tomb and make a vow, tying a strip of cloth to the sanctuary window bars or a nearby tree to mark the visit. Saints were honored with a festival called *mawsim,* of which that of Nabi Musa (Moses) was the most important. During the British PALESTINE MANDATE, the mufti of Jerusalem AL-HAJJ AMIN AL-HUSAYNI, led tens of thousands from the al-Aqsa Mosque down to the shrine near JERICHO. In poetry, song, and speeches, popular and nationalist feeling would be aired at such a gathering.

Folklore and Identity The linking of folklore to national identity was a feature of nineteenth-century European nationalism. In Palestine, "land of the Bible," the earliest systematic studies of Palestinian folk customs and beliefs were undertaken by Western Orientalists and biblical scholars. In 1865, the Palestine Oriental Fund was created in London "to investigate the Holy Land." The French established the École Biblique in Jerusalem in 1890, looking to Palestinian ethnography for the remains of customs described in the Bible. Gustaf Dalman, who headed the German Evangelical Institute in Jerusalem from its inception in 1902, wrote seven volumes about the customs and work lives of Palestinian peasants; the books were part of the institute's *Studies for Furthering Christian Theology*. In America, Elihu Grant at Haverford College published his book, *The People of Palestine,* in 1921, "to fill the places and figures of the biblical past with life."

By the 1920s, Dr. Tawfik Canaan, one of the first Palestinians to take a scholarly interest in folklore, wrote that "the uncontaminated patriarchal Palestinian atmosphere is fading away." He attributed the erosion of his country's heritage to "the introduction of European methods of education, the migration of Europeans to Palestine . . . and above all the Mandatory power." A physician by profession, Dr. Canaan was a passionate researcher, visiting 235 shrines while preparing his book *Mohammedan Saints and Sanctuaries*. Claiming to be no more than a collector of folklore for experts to use and interpret, he wrote for the *Journal of the Palestine Oriental Society,* as did Omar al-Bargouthi and Stephan H. Stephan. Writing in English, French, and German, these early folklorists, who were also interested in ARCHAEOLOGY, often were graduates of mission schools; though proud of their culture, they could not escape the Orientalist temper of their time.

Folklore and Resistance In 1948, nearly half the population was displaced, over 400 villages were destroyed, and hundreds of thousands of self-sufficient *fallahin* became refugees crowded into camps. Village women no longer needed to build the traditional clay storage bins with molded "tree of life" designs: their United Nations (U.N.) rations came ready-packed. Those who had no access to the wheat stalks wove baskets and mats out of plastic. But large numbers clung to their embroidered costumes to keep alive the identity of their villages within the refugee camps. In time, embroidery was developed into a source of income. Cross-stitch cushions and hangings now decorate Palestinian homes from San Francisco to Melbourne, Australia, reminders of the lost past.

In the diaspora, Widad Kawar of Amman has assembled a representative collection of authentic embroidered costumes, which has traveled on exhibition across the world, demonstrating the reality of a Palestinian culture even as politicians debate the existence of Palestine. Similarly, Hanan Munayyer and Farah Munayyer exhibit their growing collection of Palestine costumes in libraries, museums, and colleges in the UNITED STATES. After 1967, when Israel occupied what remained of Palestine, a conscious embrace of things Palestinian permeated the community. A new generation of Palestinian scholars writing in Arabic for Arabs began to collect and research their folklore. The Palestine Research Center in Beirut founded by the PALESTINE LIBERATION ORGANIZATION included published works on Palestinian folklore. BIR ZEIT UNIVERSITY offers folklore and oral history courses and its press publishes texts of folk narratives. Founded to provide services to families in need, In'ash al-Usra Society added a folk museum, crafts revival, and the publication of folklore to its activities. Inside Israel, a Research Center for Arab Heritage was created in al-Tayyiba—*Palestinian* is an unacceptable adjective in Israel. The center organized a four-day conference on Palestinian folklore in 1987.

The work of formal artists is infused with folklore. Embroidery patterns and even the earth and stubble of the threshing floor find their way into the paintings of Sliman Mansur and Nabil Canani, and folktale motifs are found in the stories of EMILE HABIBI; GHASSAN KANAFANI, and ANTON SHAMMAS drew on folk motifs, as do the scripts of the West Bank al-Hakawati theater troupe.

While the West had been fascinated by Palestinian customs as living illustrations of the Bible, the Palestinians looked to their tradition for an identity within the Arab world. The hardships of the INTIFADA further validated the traditional premodern ways of survival. *Sumud,* steadfastness, which inspired the Intifada, is a *fallahi* quality: the patient endurance of the agriculturalist in the fact of nature's punishments. The struggle against Israeli occupation also generated new heroes and new habits. Conspicuous was the severe curtailment of the wedding celebration, often reduced to a shared cup of coffee. When Israel made it a punishable offense to display the colors of the Palestinian flag or even to hang red, white, black, green, and white on the same clothesline, youths would defiantly munch watermelon where Israeli soldiers could see them: Red fruit, black seeds, green skin, white pulp—here is material for future folklorists.

Inea Bushnaq

BIBLIOGRAPHY

Arnitah, Yusra. *Al-Funun al-Sha'biyya fi Filastin* (Folk arts in Palestine). Beirut: Palestine Research Center, 1968.

Bauer, Leonhard. *Das Palästinische Arabisch.* Leipzig: J. C. Hinrichs, 1926.

al-Barghuthi, Abdullatif. *Hikayat Jan min Bani Zeyd* (Djinn stories from the Bani Zeyd). Jerusalem: Bir Zeit University Press, 1979.

——. *Al-Aghani al-Arabiyay al-Sha'biya fi Filastin wa al-Urdun* (Arab folksongs from Palestine and Jordan). Birzeit: Bir Zeit University Press, 1979.

——. *Diwan al-Ataba al-Filastini* (Ataba songs of Palestine). Birzeit: Bir Zeit University Press, 1986.

al-Barghouthi, Omar. "Judicial Courts among the Bedouins of Palestine." *Journal of the Palestine Oriental Society II* (1922).

Canaan, Tawfik. "Aberglaube und Volksmedizin im Lande der Bibel." *Abhandlungen des Hamburgischen Kolonialinstitute* XX (1914).

——. "Haunted Springs and Water Demons in Palestine." *Journal of the Palestine Oriental Society* (1920–1921).

——. "Folklore of the Seasons of Palestine." *Journal of the Palestine Oriental Society* 3 (1923).

——. *Mohammedan Saints and Sanctuaries in Palestine.* London, 1927.

——. "Plant-Lore in Palestine Superstition." *Journal of the Palestine Oriental Society* 3 (1928).

——. "The Child in Palestinian Arab Superstition." *Journal of the Palestine Oriental Society* 7 (1927).

——. "The Palestinian Arab House: Its Architecture and Folklore." *Journal of the Palestine Oriental Society* 12 (1932), 13 (1933).

——. "The Curse in Palestinian Folklore." *Journal of the Palestine Oriental Society* 15 (1935).

Crowfoot, Grace M. "Folktales of Artas." *Palestine Exploration Quarterly* 83 (1951), 84 (1952).

——. Arabiyya al-Sha'biyya and Louise Baldensperger. *Arab Folk Stories from Artas.* A new edition with transliteration and colloquial Arabic text prepared and edited by Abdullatif al-Barghouthi and illustrated by Sliman Mansur. Birzeit: Bir Zeit University Press, 1987.

——. and Louise Baldensperger. *From Cedar to Hyssop: A Study in the Folklore of Plants in Palestine.* London: 1932.

Dalman, Gustaf. *Arbeit und Sitte in Palästina,* 7 vols. Gütersloh: Bertelsmann, 1928–1942.

——. *Palästinischer Diwan.* Leipzig: J. C. Hinrichs, 1901.

Granqvist, Hilma. *Marriage Conditions in a Palestinian Village,* 2 vols. Helsinki: Akademische Buchhandlung, 1931 & 1935.

——. *Birth and Childhood Among the Arab: Studies in a Muhammedan Village in Palestine.* Helsinki: Soderström, 1947.

——. *Child Problems Among the Arabs: Studies in a Muhammedan Village in Palestine.* Helsinki: Soderström, 1950.

Haddad, E. N. "The Guesthouse in Palestine." *Journal of the Palestine Oriental Society* 2 (1922).

——. "Political Parties in Syria and Palestine (Qaisi and Yemeni)." *Journal of the Palestine Oriental Society* 1 (1921).

Hanauer, J. E. *Tales Told in Palestine.* Cincinnati, Ohio: Jennings & Graham, 1904.

——. *Folklore of the Holy Land: Moslem, Christian and Jewish.* London: Sheldon, 1935.

Jaussen, Antonin. *Coutumes Palestiniennes I: Naplouse et son District.* Paris: Paul Geuthner, 1927.

Kawar, Widad. *Costumes Dyed by the Sun.* Tokyo: Bunk Publishing Bureau, 1982.

al-Khalili, Ali. *Al-Turath al-Filastini wa al-Tabaqat* (Social class in Palestinian folklore). Beirut: Dar al-Adab, 1979.

——. *Al-Batal al-Filastini fi al-Hikaya al-Sha'biyya* (The Hero in Palestinian folktales). Jerusalem: Mu'assasat Ibn Rushd, 1979.

——. *Aghani al-Amal wa al-Ummal* (Work songs and workers). Jerusalem: Manshurat Salah al-Din, 1979.

Muhawi, Ibrahim, and Sharif Kanaana. *Speak Bird Speak Again: Palestinian Arab Folktales.* Berkeley: University of California Press, 1989.

Rajab, Jehan. *Palestinian Costume.* New York: Kegan Paul International, 1989.

al-Sarisi, Umar. *Al-Hikaya al-Sha'biyya fi al-Mujtama al-Filastini: Dirasah wa Nusus* (The folktale in Palestinian society: Study with texts). Beirut: Al-Mu'assasa al-Arabiyya li al-Dirasat wa'al-Nashr, 1980.

Schmidt, Hans and Paul Kahle. *Volkserzahlungen aus Palästina,* 2 vols. Göttingen: Vandenhoeck & Ruprecht, 1918 & 1930.

Serhan, Nimr. *Al-Hikaya al-Sha'biya al-Filistiniyya* (Palestinian folktales) Beirut: Al-Mu'assasa al-Arabiyya li al-Dirasat wa'al-Nashr, 1974.

——. *Aghanina al-Aba'biyah fi al-Daffa al-Gharbiyya* (Our folksongs in the West Bank). Amman: Manshurat Wizart al-I'lam al-Urduniyah, 1968.

——. *Mawsu'at al-Fulklur al-Filastini* (Encyclopedia of Palestinian folklore). Amman: published by the author, 1977–1981.

Stephan, Stephan Hananiyah. "Palestinian Animal Stories and Fables." *Journal of the Palestine Oriental Society* III (1923).

——. "Animals in Palestinian Folklore." *Journal of the Palestine Oriental Society* V (1926), VIII (1928).
Stillman, Y. K. *Palestinian Costume and Jewelry*. Albuquerque: University of New Mexico Press, 1979.
Weir, Shelagh. *Palestinian Costume*. London: British Museum Publications, 1989.

Freij, Elias

Ilyas Frayj; mayor of Bethlehem
1920–1998 Bethlehem

Born into a Christian family, Elias Freij was one of the longest-serving mayors of the WEST BANK, having been first elected as mayor of BETHLEHEM in 1972. He was long a leading figure in the town, serving as president of the Bethlehem Chamber of Commerce and Industry beginning in 1970 and chair of the board of trustees of BETHLEHEM UNIVERSITY beginning in 1973.

Freij was a leading figure within the traditionalist establishment in the West Bank, which maintained good relations with Jordan. He differed in this regard from many of the mayors elected during the 1976 municipal elections in the West Bank, who were more militantly supportive of the PALESTINE LIBERATION ORGANIZATION (PLO). Freij, on the other hand, was a moderate; he was the only mayor in the Occupied Territories to meet with Egyptian president Anwar Sadat during his November 1977 visit to Jerusalem. Freij was also never deposed by Israeli authorities.

Freij's tenure as mayor included the difficult years of the INTIFADA, during which the town of Bethlehem, the birthplace of Jesus Christ, halted its annual Christmas celebration. Closing the event, while depriving the town of badly needed tourist revenues, helped publicize the Intifada to an international audience.

Even though his positions had sometimes run contrary to those of the PLO, Freij was selected to serve on the Palestinian negotiating delegation at the MADRID PEACE CONFERENCE, 1991. After the Israeli-PLO accords were signed and while still mayor, he was appointed minister of tourism and monuments in the PALESTINIAN AUTHORITY in May 1994.

In 1997, Freij resigned his posts as mayor and minister for health reasons. After a long illness, he died in Amman, Jordan; he was buried in Bethlehem.

Michael R. Fischbach

French Reports, 1931–1932

After the WESTERN (WAILING) WALL DISTURBANCES, 1929, the British government ordered Lewis French, the new director of development for the Mandatory government, to draft reports on Palestinian agriculture and the problem of growing landlessness among Palestinian farmers.

French's reports were submitted in December 1931 and April 1932. In both, French determined that Zionist LAND purchases and settlement of immigrants had a deleterious effect on Palestinian farmers because they led to landlessness. French believed that the solution lay not with a proposed scheme to increase agricultural production but with a limit on Zionist land purchases.

Both Zionists and Palestinians reacted strongly against the French Reports for reasons of their own, and British authorities did not implement their recommendations.

Michael R. Fischbach

Futuwwa

Futuwwa was a paramilitary youth movement founded in 1935 and associated with the HUSAYNI FAMILY of JERUSALEM. Some Futuwwa members fought as guerrillas during the 1936–1939 revolt. The group was reorganized in 1946 and headed by Kamal Urayqat.

Michael R. Fischbach

G

Gaza Strip

General Characteristics The Gaza Strip is a territory that was under direct Israeli military occupation and subject to military government rule between 1967 and 1993. In September 1993, with the signing of the OSLO AGREEMENTS by ISRAEL and the PALESTINE LIBERATION ORGANIZATION (PLO), the Gaza Strip came under limited Palestinian autonomy for the first time, although Israel retains ultimate control over the area.

Palestinians in the Gaza Strip are stateless. In 1997, the population was estimated to be 1 million people, with nearly half below the age of fourteen years. Approximately 70 percent of Gazans are REFUGEES of the ARAB-ISRAELI WAR OF 1948 and their descendants, now in their fifth generation. The Gaza Strip is a rectangular piece of land, 28 miles long, 4.3 miles wide at its northern end, 7.8 miles wide at its southern end, and 3.4 miles wide at its most narrow point. It encompasses an area that is approximately 140 square miles or one-fifteenth the size of the WEST BANK, with one of the highest population densities in the world. Bordered by Israel on the north and east, Egypt on the south, and the Mediterranean Sea on the west, the Gaza Strip lies in the southwestern corner of Mandatory Palestine, and its geographical boundaries have not changed since its inception in 1948. As a result of its political status since 1967, the Strip has no official capital; its chief cities are Gaza City, Khan Yunis, and Rafah. The Gaza Strip also contains eight refugee camps, home to more than 300,000 people.

The population of the Gaza Strip is almost entirely Palestinian, and Arabic is the primary language spoken. There is a small community of 5,000 Jewish settlers who also inhabit the region. Ninety-nine percent of the Arab populace are Sunni Muslims, with a tiny minority of Christians, most of whom belong to the Greek Orthodox Church. Broadly speaking, Palestinians in the Gaza Strip fall into three historic social groups: urban, peasant, and Bedouin. In 1948, the distinction between the indigenous Gazan and the refugee was introduced; after 1967, with the beginning of Israeli occupation and the rise of the PLO, distinctions based on political affiliation were incorporated as well.

Considerable geographical variation characterizes the territory that begins in the northern third of the Strip, an area belonging to the red sands of the Philistian Plain, and ends in the southern two-thirds, an area (south of Gaza's main watercourse, the Wadi Gaza) considered a part of the more fertile sandy loess of the northern Negev coast. Three narrow but distinctive bands of land define Gaza's physiographic structure: a wide belt of loose sands in the west, running from the shoreline to a sand dune ridge 120 feet above sea level; a central depression with highly fertile alluvial soils; and a sandstone ridge in the east extending into the northern Negev. The Strip belongs to the coastal plain, one of four climatological regions in the area. Stretching from Gaza to ACRE along the coast, and southeast to the Plain of Esdraelon, the coastal plain is distinguished by its proximity to the sea and produces a climate of considerable heat and humidity in the summer (mean summer temperatures of 24°–27° Celsius) and cool, equally humid days with limited rainfall in the winter (mean winter temperatures of 13° to 18° Celsius).

The ECONOMY of the Gaza Strip is small, underdeveloped, and weak, generating almost half of its national product from external sources. During

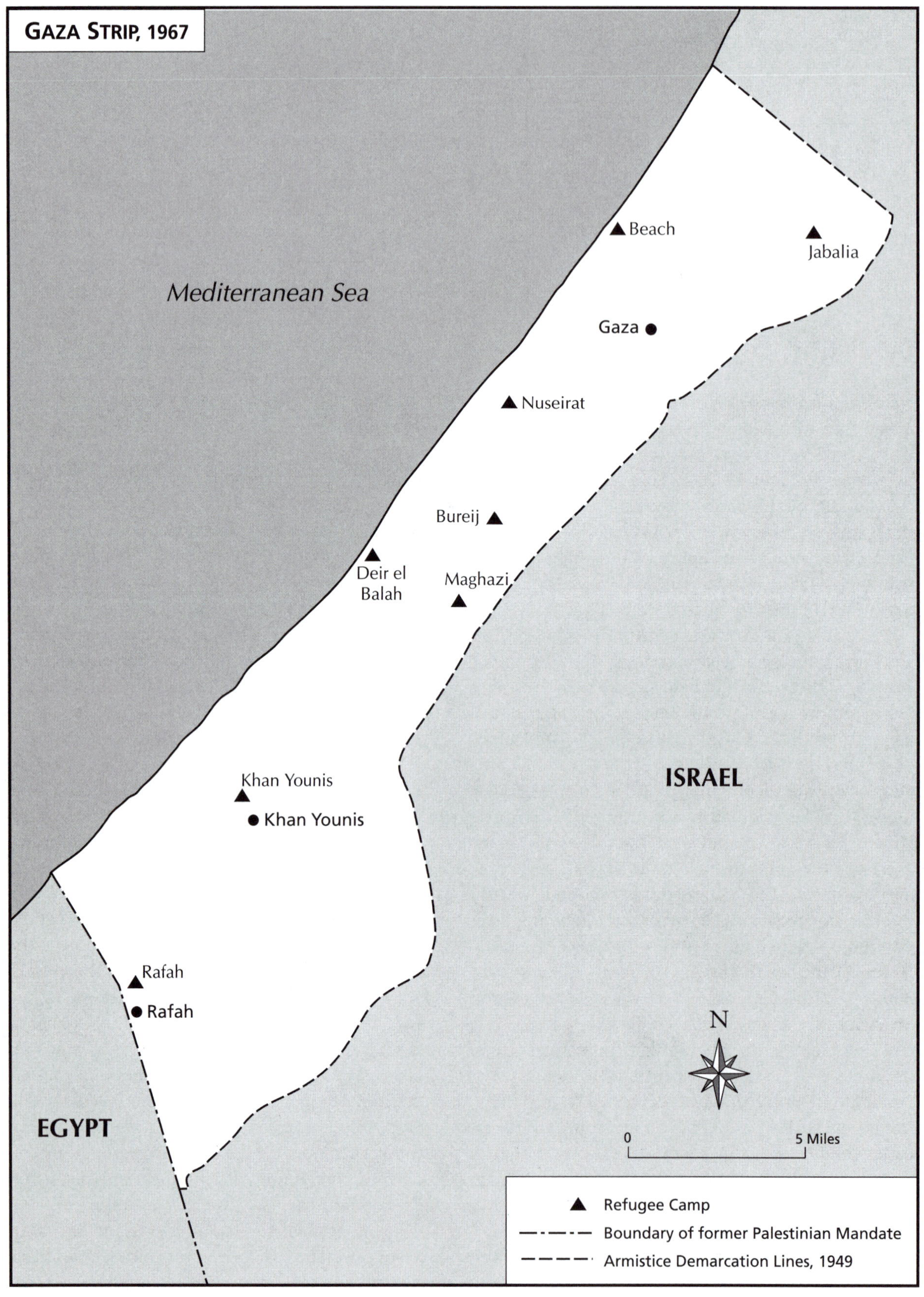
GAZA STRIP, 1967
Mediterranean Sea
Beach
Jabalia
Gaza
Nuseirat
Bureij
Deir el
Balah
Maghazi
ISRAEL
Khan Younis
Khan Younis
Rafah
Rafah
N
EGYPT
0
5 Miles
Refugee Camp
Boundary of former Palestinian Mandate
Armistice Demarcation Lines, 1949

direct Israeli rule, the local economy was integrated with and became dependent upon the Israeli market for both employment and trade. By 1988, Israel employed close to 70 percent of Gaza's labor force and had become the territory's primary export and import market. The Gaza Strip and West Bank, furthermore, had also become Israel's second largest export market after the United States. Natural resources are extremely limited and diminishing. Between 1967 and 1988, for example, the Israeli government confiscated 51 percent of the land in the Gaza Strip, much of it agricultural. The steady depletion of local water resources by both Palestinians and Israelis was not seriously addressed by the Israeli government, and at present rates of consumption, the Gaza Strip will be devoid of fresh water in about fifteen years. The territory contains no mineral resources of any known significance.

Traditionally, the Gaza economy was largely agricultural, and its primary export has been citrus, but because of the problems of land and water, agriculture fell below services as the main contributor to national output by the late 1980s. The industrial sector was always small and weak, and, despite some growth since 1967, still accounted for the smallest share of the national product. Given its weak productive base, the Gaza economy has always been heavily dependent on imports, primarily from Israel. Imports from the Arab world have been prohibited and those from Europe are extremely limited through Israeli tariff regulations. Export markets other than Israel and the Arab world have also been few because of official trade policies that prohibited Palestinians from entering markets used by Israel. This fact alone has had a negative impact on local economic development. In 1988, however, under pressure from the European Economic Community (EEC), the Israeli government allowed direct trade between the Gaza Strip and Europe, although this trade was very small.

Through 1994, the Israeli military government, the United Nations Relief and Works Agency (UNRWA), and private institutions administered education in the Gaza Strip. The government school system was inherited from Egypt, and the entire educational structure, which runs through high school, had been left intact. In 1994, the newly established PALESTINIAN AUTHORITY (PA) assumed control of the government school system. UNRWA still operates schools in the refugee camps through the eighth grade and uses the same curriculum as the government schools. Because of official Israeli restrictions, private schooling remained minimal despite the fact that the Gaza Strip is considered the flagship of Palestinian education. Throughout nearly thirty years of Israeli occupation, there were only three private institutions in the Gaza Strip offering classes from kindergarten through secondary school. The Islamic University and al-Azhar University are the only institutions providing college level instruction. The former has a total capacity of 5,000 students, and the latter 3,000. During direct Israeli occupation, cultural institutions were quite rare because military laws restricted their development. In the Strip, they included the YMCA, the Gaza Artists Association, the French Cultural Center, and the Gaza Cultural Center.

Prior to 1996, when a PALESTINIAN LEGISLATIVE COUNCIL was elected, government in the Gaza Strip was restricted to the local level; it included four municipal councils, nine village councils, and three local committees. Between 1982 and 1994, the Gaza municipality, the largest in the territory, had no mayor or municipal council and remained under the direct control of the Israeli Ministry of the Interior. The municipal councils in Dayr al-Balah and Rafah were also disbanded and their mayors Israeli-appointed. The only functioning council with an elected mayor existed in Khan Yunis.

History The earliest knowledge of Gaza dates to the third millennium B.C.E. The Old Testament names Gaza (City) as one of five cities belonging to the Philistines, and it is the burial place of Hashim ibn Abd Manaf, the great-grandfather of the Prophet Muhammad, as well as the site of Samson's death. Prior to the formation of the Gaza Strip in 1948, the Gaza region was an important administrative unit of Palestine. Under Ottoman rule (1516–1917), the district of Gaza, which stretched from south of Jaffa to Khan Yunis, was part of the province of Jerusalem, and was controlled directly from Constantinople, indicating its importance to the regime. The Gaza district included the towns of Khan Yunis, Majdal, Faluja, and Ramla. By the mid-seventeenth century, the town of Gaza, known for its tolerance of religious minorities, counted among its 26,000 inhabitants Jews and

Christians, in addition to Muslims. The town enjoyed a period of particular prosperity under the benign rule of Husayn Pasha. Economic activity was predominantly agricultural and focused on the production of cereal grains. Industry was primitive and noted for the manufacture of soap and wine. During the early to mid-eighteenth century, however, Gaza fell victim to Bedouin raids. The resulting insecurity caused farmers to flee, and over two-thirds of the cultivable area of the Gaza district remained deserted.

In 1799, Napoleon had taken the strategically situated town of Gaza in order to defend against the invasion of Egypt, which he had wrested from Ottoman control as part of his eastern campaign. Peace and prosperity only returned to Gaza in the latter part of the eighteenth century. Between 1750 and 1882, its population increased from 6,000 to 16,000, reaching 40,000 by 1906. The nineteenth century saw a steady diminution of Ottoman power and a concomitant rise in the influence of the West, which culminated in the establishment of British rule in 1917.

The Mandate Period During PALESTINE MANDATE (1922–1948), the Gaza region was made one of six administrative districts, and with Gaza City as its capital, spanned the entire southern half of Palestine. The importance assigned to Gaza was in large part due to its proximity to Egypt. The area's strategic economic significance was obvious to Mandate officials, whose desire to promote trade and commerce across the border with Egypt encouraged renewed prosperity for the town of Gaza and for the region as a whole. During the Mandate period, Gaza had evolved into a prosperous marketing center with good connections to the outside world. Each year, close to 20 percent of Palestine's entire citrus crop and 150,000 tons of grains were collected in Gaza town for domestic trade and export. (Before 1948, the area that became the Gaza Strip did not constitute an independent economic unit. Rather it was integrated into the economy of southern Palestine and existed primarily as an export and marketing center for its hinterland.) Although the British successfully promoted commerce and trade, the local economy remained traditional in structure, tied to precapitalist agriculture. Economic growth brought improved living standards as seen by Gaza's growing population and declining infant mortality rates.

Despite growing political tensions between Palestine's Arab and Jewish communities, the Gaza district remained relatively unaffected since Jews were officially prohibited from purchasing land there. The chaotic last months of the Mandate, however, resulted in the call for the partition of Palestine into a Jewish and an Arab state; the Gaza district was to be a central part of the latter. The residents of Gaza opposed partition and the division of their agricultural lands that partition would have imposed.

The 1948 Arab-Israeli War and the Imposition of Egyptian Occupation As a result of the Arab-Israeli War of 1948, two-thirds of the Gaza district was lost to the new state of Israel. The town of Gaza and thirteen other localities were incorporated into an artificially created entity known as the Gaza Strip, which was less than one- third of the area intended under the partition plan, and just over 1 percent of Mandatory Palestine. The Gaza Strip, whose prewar population numbered 80,000, was flooded by 250,000 refugees fleeing the war and placed under Egyptian military rule from 1948 to 1967. During Egypt's tenure, the Egyptian army assumed control over Gaza's civil and security affairs. Political activity of all kinds was prohibited. Egyptians held all high-level administrative positions. Refugees were excluded from mainstream social and economic affairs, and indigenous Gazans were carefully monitored. Everyone in the Gaza Strip was officially classified as stateless and ineligible for any passport. A nightly curfew was imposed.

Economically, the immediate postwar situation was urgent. Separated from the agricultural area it once served and from the rest of the Palestinian hinterland, the Strip lost much of its prime agricultural and grazing land to Israel and its port was closed. As a result, the indigenous economy virtually collapsed. The massive influx of refugees further strained an already weakened economic base. Politically, the refugees also presented an urgent problem. Refugee repatriation and compensation became the focus of Arab-Israeli tensions. Israel made it clear that it would never allow a full repatriation of Palestinian refugees living in Gaza, and the Arab states indicated that they would not absorb displaced Palestinians. In 1950, UNRWA began relief operations for Gazan refugees and by 1952 had established eight refugee camps throughout the Gaza Strip. UNRWA assumed full responsibility for the refugee community, providing food, housing, health care, and education.

During the early to mid-1950s, infiltrations by Palestinians and Israelis across the Gaza–Israel border assumed increasingly violent dimensions. The Egyptian government, fearing continued Israeli attacks, imposed harsh security measures on Gaza residents. On February 28, 1955, Israel attacked an Egyptian military installation in Gaza and thirty-nine people were killed. This event was an important factor in Egyptian–Israeli relations. It convinced President Jamal Abd al-Nasir to shift his foreign policy priorities from inter-Arab matters to the ARAB–ISRAELI CONFLICT. As a result, Nasir's attempt to prevent Palestinian border raids into Israel gave way to a policy that actively sponsored such raids. Israeli policy similarly became more offensive, and, in 1956, it culminated in the Suez crisis. As a result of the Suez war, Israel gained control of the Gaza Strip in November 1956. Under pressure from the United States, however, Israel was forced to withdraw from Gaza in March 1957 when Egypt reassumed control.

The ten years between 1957 and 1967 focused greater Egyptian attention on the economic and political needs of the Gaza Strip. After Suez, Nasir emerged as a major proponent of the Palestinian cause. In order to secure a base of support in Gaza, he expanded the boundaries of economic and political expression.

At the economic level, the government opened the Gaza port and declared Gaza a free-trade zone for consumer and industrial goods, many of which were banned in Egypt. The government extended new markets to Gaza's citrus producers and sold lands registered for public use to local residents. The Egyptians also expanded the local educational system and improved health care services. However, the refugee population and Gaza's indigenous poor remained impoverished, dependent upon UNRWA and other external sources of assistance.

The Egyptian government did lessen the constraints on organized political activity in Gaza but did not eliminate them. In 1957, the government allowed the establishment of a legislative council in Gaza. In 1959, the government similarly encouraged the establishment of the Palestine National Union and in later years approved the formation of the General Federation of Trade Unions and the Palestine Women's Society. In 1962, the Egyptians gave the chairmanship of Gaza's legislative council, formerly in the hands of an Egyptian official, to a local Palestinian. In the same year, the Egyptian government also provided Gaza with a constitution. Perhaps the most significant political change was the formation of the PLO in Gaza in January 1964. Three Gazans served on the PLO's executive committee. Egypt further allowed the PALESTINE LIBERATION ARMY, the military wing of the PLO, to set up a base in Gaza and supplied it with light arms. Although little violence broke out across Gaza-Israeli lines between the birth of the PLO and the June 1967 war, tensions between Israel and the Arab states escalated.

Israeli Occupation The June 1967 war ended with an Israeli victory and the imposition of Israeli military rule in the Gaza Strip. Israel immediately embarked on a normalization program that sought to restore services in a variety of areas. The government also secretly deliberated the Allon Plan, which provided for the formal annexation of the Gaza Strip and the resettlement of 350,000 Gazan refugees in northern Sinai and the West Bank. Although the Allon Plan was never officially adopted, the government did evict some 40,000 people from the Gaza Strip by December 1967.

From the beginning, Gazans actively resisted the occupation. Within less than a year of Israel's occupation of the Gaza Strip, a protracted period of armed struggle (1967–1971) broke out between the Palestine Liberation Army and the Israeli military. Civil disobedience also was widespread. In 1970, the Israeli army, under the command of Ariel Sharon, embarked on a campaign to rid the Gaza Strip of all resistance. By early 1972, Sharon's efforts proved successful: Large numbers of guerrillas had been killed, and control over the refugee camps, the guerrilla's base of support, had been secured. In September 1971, at the request of the Israeli government, a leading Palestinian citrus merchant, Rashad Shawwa, agreed to become mayor of Gaza. Shawwa formed a municipal council, but he and his council received intense criticism, since many nationalists viewed their appointments as a political compromise with the occupier. In October 1972, Shawwa resigned; Israel's reinstatement of direct military rule in the Gaza Strip followed. In October 1975, Shawwa agreed to be reappointed as mayor of Gaza City.

The 1978 CAMP DAVID ACCORDS calling for autonomy in the Gaza Strip and West Bank touched off an explosive phase in Gaza's political history. Most Gazans interpreted the accords as a renunciation by Egypt of all claims on the Gaza Strip, and so they opposed them. One month after Camp David in September 1978, a rally was held in Gaza to denounce the agreement and to propose comprehensive negotiations for Palestinian self-determination that were to include the PLO. After the rally, Israel imposed restrictions on political activity in Gaza and tensions increased. Furthermore, President Sadat, angered over Gaza's rejection of the Camp David accords, froze salary payments to officials employed in Gaza by the Egyptian government before 1967 and prohibited the admission of Gaza students to Egyptian universities.

On December 1, 1981, the Israeli government instituted a civil administration in the Gaza Strip and West Bank. An integral part of the military structure, the civil administration was given responsibility over all nonmilitary sectors such as health, education, and social services. Interpreted as the first step toward the implementation of Menachem Begin's autonomy plan and the annexation of the territories, the imposition of the civil administration generated considerable opposition from Palestinians. In protest, Mayor Shawwa immediately announced a general strike. The Israeli authorities dismissed Shawwa and Gaza's municipal council was disbanded. In August 1982, amid heightened tensions emanating from the Lebanon war, the Israeli Interior Ministry assumed full control over the Gaza municipality and resumed direct rule to the Strip. At this time, the government also increased Jewish civilian settlement inside the Gaza Strip.

By the outbreak of the Palestinian uprising on December 8, 1987, Gaza had no elected mayor, no election process, and no right to public assembly. Channels for political or legal expression did not exist. Heightened civilian settlement brought with it contestations over vastly limited natural resources, especially land and water. In November 1988, the PALESTINE NATIONAL COUNCIL called for the establishment of a Palestinian state in the Gaza Strip and West Bank alongside Israel. The MADRID PEACE CONFERENCE, 1991, began in October. The Palestinian delegation was headed by a Gazan, Dr. HAYDAR ABD AL-SHAFI. Almost two years later in September 1993, Israel and the PLO signed an agreement in Oslo, Norway, to implement partial autonomy in the Gaza Strip and the West Bank town of JERICHO.

The Post-Oslo Period In May 1994, the Israeli army withdrew from Gaza's most populated areas and redeployed to other parts of the Strip. One month later, YASIR ARAFAT returned to Gaza and the PALESTINIAN AUTHORITY (PA) was officially established. The impact of the army's redeployment and the PA's arrival was immediate and positive. Gaza's nightly curfew ended, allowing people to walk the streets at any hour without fear of arrest or harassment. Personal security was much improved as the PA assumed control over many internal functions. New stores and restaurants appeared and remained open into the evening hours, giving the territory a sense of normalcy it had not known for decades.

Despite these positive changes, however, economic conditions in the Gaza Strip continued to deteriorate in the postagreement period. The primary reason for Gaza's economic decline was Israel's closure of the territory (and the West Bank and East Jerusalem), imposed in March 1993 as a security measure and never once lifted. Closure either bars or significantly reduces the number of Palestinians allowed to work in Israel and severely restricts trade levels, a critical source of income for Gaza's domestic economy. By early 1996, unemployment in the Gaza Strip averaged 30 percent, reaching 50 percent during periods of total closure. The resulting income loss cost the local economy nearly $3 million daily, roughly equivalent to total donor pledges in 1995. By 1999, economic conditions had declined even more.

Closure and unemployment directly contributed to growing levels of poverty, especially in Gaza. By early 1996, at least 20 percent of Gaza's population and 10 percent of the West Bank's lived at or below an absolute poverty level of $500–$650 per capita annually. The average Gazan family spent almost 60 percent of its monthly income on food, 1 percent on health care, and 3 percent on education. By 1998 close to 40 percent of Gazans were impoverished.

The political downturn of the Oslo peace process stands in marked contrast to the expectations that first accompanied it. Nowhere is this more apparent than in the Gaza Strip, where political and economic tensions remained high by 1999.

Sara Roy

BIBLIOGRAPHY
Abed, George T. *The Palestinian Economy: Studies in Development Under Prolonged Occupation*. London: Routledge, 1988.
Aruri, Naseer, ed. *Occupation: Israel over Palestine*, 2d ed. Belmont, Mass.: Association of Arab-American University Graduates Press, 1989.
Benvenisti, Meron. *The West Bank and Gaza Atlas*. Jerusalem: The Jerusalem Post Press, 1988.
Roy, Sara. "From Hardship to Hunger: The Economic Impact of the Intifada on the Gaza Strip." *American-Arab Affairs* (Fall 1990).
——. "Gaza: New Dynamics of Civic Disintegration." *Journal of Palestine Studies* (summer 1993).
——. *The Gaza Strip: The Political Economy of De-Development*. Washington, D.C.: Institute for Palestine Studies, 1995.
——. *The Gaza Strip Survey*. Boulder, Colo.: Westview Press, 1986.
——. "Separation or Integration: Closure and the Economic Future of the Gaza Strip Revisited." *Middle East Journal* (Winter 1994).
The World Bank and the Palestinian Economic Policy Research Institute (MAS): *Developed Under Adversity? The Palestinian Economy in Transition*. Jerusalem: 1997.

Geneva Conferences

1950, 1973

There were two notable conferences held in Geneva, Switzerland, for the purpose of working toward Arab-Israeli peace. The first was convened by the UNITED NATIONS CONCILIATION COMMISSION FOR PALESTINE (UNCCP) between January 30 and July 15, 1950, attended by delegations of Israel, Egypt, Lebanon, and Syria. The UNCCP's original goals for the conference were to achieve progress on such minor issues as the reunion of families, unblocking of frozen Palestinian bank accounts in Israel, and readjustment of armistice lines to restore divided farmlands. Following the pattern established at the LAUSANNE CONFERENCE (1949), the UNCCP met separately with Arab and Israeli delegations but also attempted to establish several joint Arab-Israeli technical committees.

Much of the activity at Geneva in 1950 was sidetracked—and ultimately deadlocked—by disputes over procedure rather than debates over substance. Israel repeatedly asked the UNCCP to convene direct talks with Arab delegates. The Arabs tried to induce the commission to submit its own comprehensive proposals for mediation and would agree to meet with Israelis only on condition that Israel accepted the United Nations General Assembly Resolution 194 (of December 1948) regarding the right of Palestinian REFUGEES to return to their homes. Simultaneous separate and secret Israeli-Jordanian negotiations in the Middle East also distracted attention from the 1950 peace efforts at Geneva.

The next Geneva Conference was a much shorter affair, but one with longer-term consequences. The conference was convened in pursuance of UNITED NATIONS SECURITY COUNCIL RESOLUTION 338 (October 22, 1973), which called for an end to the fighting between Egypt and Syria and Israel and opened on December 21, 1973, at the Palais des Nations. It was cochaired by the U.S. secretary of state, Henry Kissinger, and the Soviet foreign minister, Andrei Gromyko, and was attended by the U.N. secretary-general and by the foreign ministers of Israel, Egypt, and Jordan. Syria was invited but refused to attend.

The opening session of that conference consisted of formal ceremonies and speeches by each of the invited participants, followed by a few brief rebuttals. On the second day, the conference adjourned, having agreed to set up a military working group, which never became operative. Behind the façade of the Geneva Conference, Dr. Kissinger went on to negotiate several disengagement agreements through "shuttle diplomacy" between Cairo and Tel Aviv and between Damascus and Tel Aviv during 1974 and 1975.

In a procedural sense, the 1973 Geneva Conference was unique in two ways: its joint sponsorship by the two superpowers and the agreement of representatives of Israel, Egypt, and Jordan to meet around the same table, acknowledging each other's presence and statements. The Geneva Conference never formally reconvened after December 1973, but its American and Soviet cochairs occasionally considered the wisdom of inviting the Middle Eastern governments concerned to "resume" the Geneva Conference, especially after the installation of the Carter administration in January 1977. On October 1, 1977, the superpowers actually did issue a joint call to the parties to consider reconvening the Geneva Conference. With both Egypt and Israel reluctant to see the SOVIET UNION become actively involved in the diplomatic process, the joint U.S.-U.S.S.R. statement helped precipitate

President Anwar Sadat's offer to visit JERUSALEM and the subsequent bilateral Egyptian-Israeli peace process, which led to the 1978 CAMP DAVID ACCORDS and the 1979 peace treaty between the two states.

No Palestinian delegation was present at either of the two Geneva Conferences. In 1973, Israel objected to attending any meeting to which the PALESTINE LIBERATION ORGANIZATION, which it branded as a "terrorist organization," was invited.

Neil Caplan

BIBLIOGRAPHY

Mallison, W. Thomas, and Sally V. Mallison. *The Palestine Problem in International Law and World Order.* New York: Longman, 1983.

Playfair, Emma. "Legal Aspects of Israel's Occupation of the West Bank and Gaza: Theory and Practice." *Occupation: Israel over Palestine,* ed. by Aruri and H. Naseer Belmont, Mass.: Association of Arab-American University Graduates Press, 1989.

Geneva Convention

The Fourth Geneva Convention Relative to the Protection of Civilian Persons in Time of War was adopted in 1949—after ratification by United Nations members, including Israel and neighboring Arab states—to prevent the kinds of atrocities committed by Nazi Germany against civilians during World War II. According to Article 4 of the convention, its protections extend to those who "find themselves, in case of a conflict or occupation, in the hands of a Party to the conflict or Occupying Power of which they are not nationals." The convention proscribes individual and mass transfers of a native population out of its own territory, collective punishments administered by an occupying power, detention outside the occupied territory, and settlement of the occupier's own population into an occupied territory.

Palestinians living in the WEST BANK and GAZA STRIP, both of which came under Israeli occupation as a result of the ARAB-ISRAELI WAR OF 1967, believe they should be protected by the convention, and several United Nations Security Council resolutions have affirmed that the convention does indeed apply to these territories. Israel, however, does not agree that the convention applies; arguing that it concerns areas that are the de jure territory of another nation, Israel maintains that because Jordan's annexation of the West Bank was never recognized by most states, and because Egypt never asserted sovereignty over Gaza, these areas were not under any nation's de jure control. The convention, however, does not in fact specify that previous control of an occupied territory must have been de jure. The dispute over the convention's interpretation has never been adjudicated by an international court.

Kathleen Christison

Geography

Palestine lies on the southeastern shore of the Mediterranean basin. As delineated in 1922 under the British PALESTINE MANDATE, Palestine comprised 26,320 square kilometers of land (not including lakes), or 10,162 square miles. Using the unit of surface area employed in the Levant, the *dunum* (standardized at 1,000 square meters by the British), this area comprised 26,320,000 *dunums*.

Approximately 160 miles long and some 70 miles wide, Palestine during the Mandate was bounded by the Mediterranean Sea and the 1907 border with Egypt on the west; Wadi Araba, the Jordan River, and the border with Syria on the east; and the border with Lebanon on the north.

Topography Palestine possesses a varied topography characterized by five main features: the mountainous regions of Galilee and the central massif of the West Bank; four low-lying plains regions (the coastal plain, the Plain of Acre, the Huleh Plain, and the contiguous Plain of Esdraelon and Jezreel Valley); the Jordan valley; the Beersheba region; and the arid southern Naqab (Negev) desert.

Palestine's highest point is Jabal Jarmaq (Hebrew, Mount Meron) in the Galilee, which climbs to 1,208 meters (3,963 feet). Its lowest point, and the lowest point on earth, is the Dead Sea at 392 meters (1,286 feet) below mean sea level.

In 1922, three main bodies of water were found in Palestine, all in eastern Palestine: Lake Huleh (which Israeli authorities had drained by 1958), Lake Tiberias (the Sea of Galilee), and the Dead Sea. Palestine's main river is the Jordan River, running some 250 kilometers north to south in eastern Palestine until it empties into the Dead Sea. Other rivers are the Yarmuk, which empties into the Jordan River near Lake Tiberias; the Muqatta (Kishon), which empties into the Bay of

Acre near HAIFA; and the Awja (Yarkon), which empties into the Mediterranean near JAFFA.

Climate Palestine's climate varies by region. The plains regions are hot and humid in the summer and moderate in the winter. The mountainous regions are somewhat cooler and drier in the summer and cold in the winter. The Jordan valley is very hot and dry in the summer and moderate in the winter. The Beersheba region and southern desert are very hot and dry in the summer and cold in the winter.

The rainy season in Palestine is from October to April, with occasional snowfalls in the mountainous areas. Winds come generally from the west.

Administrative Boundaries Palestine did not comprise a single administrative unit during the period of Ottoman rule. By the mid-nineteenth century, the area that would constitute Palestine in 1922 was included within three administrative subprovinces (alternatively called *sanjaq*s, *mutasarrifliq*s, or *liwa*s): Acre, Nablus, and Jerusalem. These were subordinated to the province (*eyalet* or *vilayet*) of Sidon, or Beirut. In 1864, they were subordinated to the province of Syria, or Damascus, but only until 1887, when they returned to the province of Beirut. Jerusalem, however, was an independent subprovince governed directly from Istanbul at various times since the 1840s and permanently from 1867. Within each subprovince were smaller units, such as *qada*s (*kaza*s) and *nahiya*s.

After the Ottoman defeat in World War I, Palestine was occupied by British troops. Separated from the other regions that were former Arab provinces of the Ottoman Empire, Palestine was administered by the British under a mandate granted by the League of Nations. By 1922, Palestine's borders had been delineated. The British divided the country into seven "districts," each in turn divided into "subdistricts": Galilee, Haifa, Samaria, Lydda, Gaza, Jerusalem, Bethlehem, and Jericho. In the 1940s, the latter two were subsumed within the district of Jerusalem.

The ARAB-ISRAELI WAR OF 1948 and the subsequent armistice agreements of 1949 saw 77 percent of Palestine pass into Israeli hands. The new state of Israel controlled the plains, the Galilee, the "Little Triangle" region of the central massif, the northern Jordan valley, the Beersheba region, and the vast Naqab (Negev) Desert. Most of the mountainous central massif was held by Jordanian and Iraqi troops and annexed by Jordan in 1950. This was known as the WEST BANK, in reference to the west bank of the Jordan River (Jordan proper was referred to as the East Bank). Jordan divided the West Bank into three provinces, Nablus, Jerusalem, and Hebron, each subdivided into smaller units. Part of the Mandate era Gaza district was occupied by Egyptian troops and administered by Egypt thereafter. It came to be known as Gaza, or the GAZA STRIP.

After the ARAB-ISRAELI WAR OF 1967, Israel occupied the West Bank and Gaza. The only part of these territories actually annexed by Israel was East Jerusalem; the rest remained under Israeli occupation. Israel did not use the term *West Bank* but *Judea and Samaria* instead.

The agreements signed between Israel and the PALESTINE LIBERATION ORGANIZATION in 1994 and 1995 granted various levels of authority over the West Bank and Gaza to the PALESTINIAN AUTHORITY (PA). The PA exercises authority over civil and security matters relating to Palestinian inhabitants in Gaza and the so-called Area A of the West Bank and civil matters only in Area B of the West Bank as delineated in the 1995 Israel-PLO Interim Agreement.

Michael R. Fischbach

BIBLIOGRAPHY

Geography: Israel Pocket Library. Jerusalem: Keter Publishing House, 1972.

Great Britain: Naval Intelligence Division. *Palestine and Transjordan.* Oxford, England: Oxford University Press, 1943.

A Survey of Palestine: Prepared in December 1945 and January 1946 for the Information of the Anglo-American Committee of Inquiry. London: His Majesty's Stationery Office, 1946. Reprint. Washington, D.C., Institute for Palestine Studies, 1991.

al-Ghuri, Emile

politician, author, journalist
1907– Jerusalem

Al-Ghuri was born in Jerusalem. A graduate of the University of Cincinnati (Ohio) with an M.A. degree in political science, he published a bilingual weekly in Jerusalem in 1933 under the title *Arab Federation/al-Wahda al-Arabiyya,* in addition to the Arabic twice weekly *al-Shabab* (The Youth) in 1934.

A strong supporter of AL-HAJJ AMIN AL-HUSAYNI and a prominent representative of the Greek Orthodox community, he held several political positions. He was elected to the ARAB EXECUTIVE in 1933 and became in 1935 the secretary-general of the Palestine ARAB PARTY, a member in delegations that the ARAB HIGHER COMMITTEE (AHC) dispatched abroad to raise funds and to represent the Palestinian cause. He joined al-Husayni in Iraq but was soon captured in 1941 in Iran by the British. Although the British allowed him to return to Palestine in 1944, he was prohibited from engaging in politics. He also was manager of the Arab Office, which the AHC established to promote the Palestinian cause. He participated in the LONDON CONFERENCE (1946–47).

After the ARAB-ISRAELI WAR OF 1948, Emile continued to serve in the AHC as publicist and representative in various forums, including the United Nations and the 1955 Bandung Conference on economic and cultural cooperation among nonaligned nations. In 1966, Emile held positions in the Jordanian government, first as member in the lower house of parliament (1966), then as minister for work and social affairs (1969), and later as minister of state for cabinet affairs. Emile published several books on Palestine and the Arab nationalist movement; the best known is *Filastin Ibra Sittin Aman* (Palestine through sixty years), 2 vols., Beirut: Dar al-Nahar, 1972.

Muhammad Muslih

Glock, Albert

archaeologist, academic
1925–1992 Gifford, Idaho

Albert Glock studied theology at Concordia Seminary in St. Louis, Missouri, and worked as a Lutheran minister from 1951 to 1957. From 1957 to 1975, he taught Old Testament history and theology at Concordia. He later received a Ph.D. in biblical studies and archaeology from the University of Michigan.

Glock began focusing his attention on archaeology in Palestine in the late 1970s. His first archaeological experience in the region was at Shechem in 1962. Beginning in 1971, he worked at the American School of Oriental Research's Albright Institute and headed it from 1978 to 1981. Believing that Western archaeologists had exhibited little interest in the Palestinian people on whose land they worked, and had shown even less interest in sharing their findings with them, Glock began teaching at BIR ZEIT UNIVERSITY in the WEST BANK in 1976. He eventually established the Institute of Archaeology at the university—the first of its kind in the Occupied Territories—and directed it until his death in 1992. He also continued excavating sites like Tall Ta'annik, Tall Janin, and Tall Salata, while training Palestinian archaeologists in the territories. Throughout his life, he believed that archaeology was an important tool for strengthening Palestinian nationalism and that Western archaeologists should appreciate Palestine's present-day Arab inhabitants as much as its ancient ruins.

Glock was shot and killed by unknown assassins at Bir Zeit University on January 19, 1992. Israeli authorities never investigated the case, and the results of a PALESTINE LIBERATION ORGANIZATION study of the killing were never made public. The PALESTINIAN AUTHORITY initiated an investigation into Glock's death in 1995.

Michael R. Fischbach

Gulf Crisis

1990–1991

The Gulf crisis, which began August 2, 1990, when Iraq invaded KUWAIT, resulted in one of the worst setbacks for the Palestinians in modern times. Only the Arab revolt of 1936–1939 and the ARAB-ISRAELI WARS OF 1948 and 1967 were more costly. By the time the seven-month crisis ended in late February 1991, the thriving Palestinian community in Kuwait had been destroyed, and Gulf oil states' financial and diplomatic backing that had sustained the PALESTINE LIBERATION ORGANIZATION (PLO) for two decades had been withdrawn. The PLO was forced to close many of its offices around the world and cut off funds to thousands of needy Palestinians and scores of vital institutions in the WEST BANK, GAZA STRIP, and Arab countries. Indeed, the organization was in rapid decline when the Israel-PLO accord of September 13, 1993, rescued it. The agreement, however, did not immediately mitigate the damage to the PLO and Palestinians caused by the Gulf crisis. The magnitude of the Palestinians' setback is attributed to the PLO's policy during the crisis.

PLO Reaction to the Iraqi Invasion PLO policy during the Gulf crisis should be examined first and foremost in light of the resolutions of the two ARAB LEAGUE meetings in Cairo in August 1990, and in relation to regional and international reactions during the first few days after the Iraqi invasion of Kuwait. It was then that the PLO policy was first perceived, or misperceived. The first set of Arab League resolutions, voted on by foreign ministers on August 3, condemned "Iraqi aggression" and demanded "the immediate and unconditional withdrawal" of Iraqi forces from Kuwait, but it also called for an Arab summit to facilitate a negotiated settlement and, significantly, "categorically reject any foreign intervention." Fourteen of the twenty-one representatives present voted for the resolution; the PLO, Jordan, Mauritania, Sudan, and Yemen abstained; Iraq voted against the resolution, and Libya absented itself.

During the seven days between the first Arab League meeting and the second meeting on August 10, world reaction was swift. On August 4, the Organization of the Islamic Conference (OIC) voted to condemn Iraq's actions, but, at the vote, the PLO "refrained" from approving the resolution. By the eve of the Arab summit on August 10, most of the international community, together with fourteen Arab countries, whether willingly or under pressure from the United States, had condemned the Iraqi invasion. The Arab summit only reinforced the growing United States–led international effort against Saddam Husayn, the Iraqi dictator. The summit condemned the "Iraqi aggression," rejected Iraq's annexation of Kuwait, and called for immediate Iraqi withdrawal and restoration of the legal government of Kuwait. Most significantly, it denounced an Iraqi threat against the Gulf states and supported Saudi Arabia's and the other Gulf states' "right to self-defense": In other words, it supported their requests for foreign troops and for Arab troops assigned to fight alongside the Saudi armed forces.

This time, the PLO—along with Iraq and Libya—voted against the resolutions. Jordan, Mauritania, and Sudan approved the resolutions with reservation, and Algeria and Yemen abstained; Tunisia did not attend. Twelve of twenty-one members voted for the resolutions and for sending of troops to Saudi Arabia. Saddam retaliated the same day by declaring *jihad,* or holy war, to free Mecca and Medina. Despite this threat, the PLO did not criticize the Iraqi statement nor distance itself from it.

There were a number of unofficial PLO statements during the first few days of the invasion. GEORGE HABASH, leader of the POPULAR FRONT FOR THE LIBERATION OF PALESTINE (PFLP), said on August 4 that oil was an Arab weapon that must be used against the Zionists. Two days later, the Voice of Palestine in Algiers, the PLO's radio station, declared that the Iraqi invasion was a challenge to the United States, which refused to accept that Arab oil should become the strategic weapon of the Arabs; at the same time, it characterized the PLO stance as noncommital. Baghdad-based MUHAMMAD ABBAS (Abu al-Abbas), leader of the PALESTINE LIBERATION FRONT (PLF), praised Saddam for "destroy[ing] the bases of retrogression on the road to a . . . pan-Arab unity and awakening."

Thus, during this critical period between August 2 and August 10, the PLO's "position" consisted of the following: an abstention vote on an Arab League resolution condemning the invasion, calling for withdrawal, but rejecting foreign intervention; a "refrain[ment]" on the OIC resolution condemning the invasion; a vote against an Arab League resolution calling for condemnation, withdrawal, and foreign intervention; a Voice of Palestine radio broadcast expressing neither support nor condemnation of Iraq; and unofficial statements that implicitly or explicitly condoned the invasion. The cumulative effect of these actions was a perception throughout most of the world—including Palestinians in the West Bank, Gaza Strip, and Jordan—that the PLO supported Saddam and opposed the international consensus.

In response, a few moderates attempted to explain the PLO position. BASSAM ABU SHARIF, an adviser to the PLO chairman, YASIR ARAFAT, said that the PLO "cannot be [for] any forceful taking of any country." More forthcoming was SALAH KHALAF (Abu Iyad), second in command to Arafat, who said, "It is unacceptable to occupy others' territory by force." In the West Bank, the leading Palestinian activist, FAYSAL AL-HUSAYNI, said that the Palestinians opposed any occupation, and leading (unnamed) Palestinians who were associated with the four factions in the territories declared that it is "not permissible to occupy land by force." Such statements were cautious and lacked the PLO's official imprint, perhaps because of a veiled threat from

Saddam against the PLO. After all, Iraq gave the PLO $48 million annually and had become its second base after Tunis.

It was not until the PLO's first official statement on August 19, and Arafat's first policy speech on August 29, that the PLO official position was announced. Both contained four "principles" that guided PLO policy until the end of the crisis:

The PLO declared that it was not a party to the conflict and would not take sides. It cited the role that the Arab League had played successfully in 1973, when a similar dispute erupted between Iraq and Kuwait. At the August 10 summit, it proposed that a delegation go to Baghdad to negotiate with Saddam but accused the Egyptian president, Husni Mubarak, of preempting Arafat by not allowing a vote on his proposal.

It sought an Arab-negotiated settlement in which "higher pan-Arab interests," including those of Kuwait and Iraq, would be achieved. It is not clear what the PLO's "Arab solution" entailed, although the Libyan–PLO peace plan of August 6 may serve as an example: Kuwait would pay compensation to Iraq (presumably for the oil that Kuwait "illegally" pumped from the disputed Rumayla oil field), Kuwait would lease Warba and Bubiyan islands to Iraq, Iraq would delineate its borders with Kuwait, and Libyan and Palestinian troops would replace Iraqi forces in Kuwait.

The PLO rejected foreign intervention, believing it would cause a destructive war harmful to the economic, human, and military interests of the Arab states and "open the door to Israeli expansion and imperial forces which seek to control the area's wealth and its destinies, eradicate the Palestinian issue, and Balkanize the area." Consequently, it called for the withdrawal of U.S. troops and their replacement with United Nations (U.N.) forces.

The PLO supported the Iraq "initiative" of August 12, which linked Iraq's withdrawal from Kuwait with Israel's withdrawal from the Occupied Territories, including Jerusalem; from the Golan; and from southern Lebanon; as well as Syria's withdrawal from Lebanon. All sanctions against Iraq would be suspended, to be implemented instead "against any country that refuses to withdraw from territories it is occupying."

The equivocal PLO statements, with their refusal to condemn the invasion and call for withdrawal, did little to mend the public relations damage. There were, in fact, elements within the PLO and the Palestinian diaspora who advocated such measures. Abu Iyad understood the dangerous implications of the crisis to the Palestinians, and he repeatedly but carefully spoke out against the occupation. HANI AL-HASAN and KHALID AL-HASAN, members of the Central Committee of FATAH with close ties to the Saudi monarchy, were vocal dissenters from the PLO policy. So was Jawwad al-Ghusayn, head of the PALESTINIAN NATIONAL FUND, who bluntly spoke against the "illegal" occupation and for Kuwaiti legitimacy. A few prominent Palestinians also criticized the PLO position. One of them, the philanthropist ABD AL-MUHSIN QATTAN, resigned from the PNC. WALID KHALIDI and EDWARD SAID, the most prominent Palestinian intellectuals in the West, denounced Saddam Husayn and the invasion of Kuwait, and Khalidi criticized the PLO position. These voices, however, represented minority views in the diaspora.

The majority within the PLO, led by Arafat and FARUQ AL-QADDUMI, the PLO's "foreign minister," were not critical of the invasion and repeatedly expressed solidarity with and support for Saddam. Qaddumi bluntly said on August 24, "We stand alongside Iraq to defeat all these colonialist armies trying to harm it; their destiny will be nothing but failure and defeat, God willing." The same day Arafat himself sent a message affirming the support and solidarity of the PLO with Iraq in its confrontation with outside aggression.

The PLO officially adopted a neutral stance, but its actions and statements served to indicate otherwise. The PLO's voting record, the symbolic significance of Arafat's embracing and kissing Saddam on Iraqi television, the perceptions of most Palestinians as to where the PLO stood, and messages of solidarity with Saddam—in contrast to the absence of a clear and categorical official rejection and condemnation of the occupation of Kuwait and support for withdrawal—all indicate that the media and public perception about PLO support for Saddam were generally accurate.

Why did the PLO adopt such a policy? There is no doubt that Arafat genuinely and tirelessly attempted to mediate a settlement to the deteriorating crisis. This crisis, however, was not merely a border dispute, as in 1973. Indeed, the day Saddam invaded Kuwait the crisis became a regional problem of such magnitude that the Arab League was unable to resolve it. With each passing day, the crisis slipped through Arab hands so that on August 6, 1991, when Saudi Arabia accepted U.S. troops on its soil, it became an international problem—a conflict between Iraq and the United States, well beyond Arafat's ability to mediate.

Arafat is known to be a master of ambiguity, which allows him to appear to be all things to all people. His "yes/no" approach to politics and diplomacy had served him well in keeping disparate Palestinian groups together and in surviving the mine fields of Arab politics. The PLO's position during the Gulf crisis seems to be consistent with this approach. Unfortunately for the PLO, ambiguity in times of major crisis is virtually impossible to sustain, especially for an organization without a territorial base. In any case, after the early days, most people knew the PLO position, especially those in the Gulf, where Arafat was seen as the appeaser and ally of Saddam and where his peace plans were seen as nothing more than parroting of Iraqi demands for Kuwaiti capitulation.

On August 7 Arafat was warned about his policy by King Fahd of Saudi Arabia, and he became persona non grata in the Gulf shortly thereafter. The PLO position quickly earned the hostility of the Gulf state rulers and alienation from the international community. Arafat surely understood the significance and the consequences of his actions, so why did he not shift gears on August 10, or August 25 at the next Arab League meeting (which he boycotted), or on November 8 when the United States announced the doubling of its troop deployment from 200,000 to 400,000 soldiers, guaranteeing an offensive military option? Three overriding factors informed PLO policy in this regard:

Strategic Assessments Arafat had established with Iraq a temporary strategic alignment, both diplomatic and military, prior to the invasion. Mass Soviet Jewish immigration to Israel and Prime Minister Yitzhak Shamir's talk of a "big Israel," U.S. inability to influence Israel, and the failure of PLO diplomacy from 1988 until the suspension of the U.S.-PLO dialogue in June 1990 convinced the PLO that it needed the diplomatic leverage and military might of the most powerful Arab country, Iraq, to induce Israel to give up the WEST BANK and GAZA STRIP. Saddam offered assistance and rhetorically championed the Palestinian cause.

When the crisis began, Arafat apparently made a number of assumptions. He reportedly told private audiences that the United States would not fight battle-tested Iraq, and that if there were a war either Iraq would win or the United States would get bogged down in the desert. In either case, Iraq would insist on a diplomatic solution to the Palestinian problem. That is why, days before Operation Desert Storm started, Arafat told a rally in Baghdad that, if the United States and its allies wanted to fight, "then we say welcome, welcome, welcome to war. . . . Iraq and Palestine [will be] together, side by side."

Behind these and other statements are a number of miscalculations: that the United States, which considered oil a vital interest, would not go to war for it; that the Arab oil states would not call on foreign troops to protect them; that the United States was not resolved to drive Saddam out of Kuwait and deny him the fruits of the invasion, including enhanced influence over other oil states; that linkage to the Palestinian issue would be acceptable to the United States, Israel, Syria, and the Gulf countries; and, most significantly, that the high-tech military machine of the superpower United States and its twenty-eight allies would either get bogged down or be defeated by the developing country of Iraq.

These miscalculations highlight a number of flaws regarding the PLO's decision-making process, aside from the generally endemic problems of the inefficiency, inertia, nepotism, corruption, and factionalism of its institutions. These flaws include the lack of separation between the legislative and the executive; Arafat's manipulation and circumvention of such key institutions as the PNC; the absence of modern institutions such as policy planning apparatus; the paucity of knowledge of U.S. policy; and Arafat's autocractic decision-making powers. Such flaws, however, do not fully explain why a pragmatist such as Arafat would flirt with the radical solutions offered by Saddam.

PLO statements justifying its policies were replete with pan-Arab ideological rhetoric—such as oil as a strategic Arab weapon and the need to confront Western imperialism and conspiracies. These pan-Arab notions were current in the 1950s and 1960s when the founders of the PLO were emerging as leaders. Whereas the pan-Arab ideal survived among the masses—for whom Arabic,

Islamic heritage, and cultural and psychological bonds transcended frontiers—the Arab regimes drifted apart. For example, Egypt, the Arab captain, abandoned ship in 1978 when it agreed to the CAMP DAVID ACCORDS, and Syria supported Iran during its war against a fellow Arab country, Iraq, between 1980 and 1988. The reality was that the Arab world was in disarray. In other words, Palestinian leaders were predisposed to Saddam's radical notions of Arab nationalism and, frustrated by the failure of diplomacy, alarmed by the influx of Jews from the Soviet Union into Israel and the fast pace of Israeli land expropriation and settlements in the last remaining portions of Palestine, they returned to the revolutionary passions of their past, confident that there was an Arab power that could stand up to Israel and its ally, the United States.

Popular Support for Saddam Even if the PLO had modern institutions to inform its policies, it still would have had to cope with a ground swell of Palestinian public support for Saddam, primarily in Jordan, the West Bank, and the Gaza Strip. Palestinians were frustrated and desperate over the harsh twenty-three year Israeli occupation. More than 800 civilians had been killed in the INTIFADA since 1987. About 200,000 Jewish immigrants had poured into Israel and 1 million were predicted over the next few years. Israel had already absorbed more than 60 percent of the West Bank, where 90,000 Israelis, together with 120,000 in East Jerusalem and 4,000 in the Gaza Strip, settled among, respectively, almost 1 million, 150,000, and 750,000 Palestinians. In June 1990 Shamir formed the most radical right-wing government in Israeli history, one that included Tzomet, a party that advocated the expulsion of Palestinians from the Occupied Territories, and whose leader, Rafael Eitan, along with Shamir, had described Palestinians in subhuman terms. Neither the thirty-three month Intifada nor twenty-one months of PLO diplomacy—based on PLO recognition of Israel, acceptance of UNITED NATIONS SECURITY COUNCIL RESOLUTION 242, and renunciation of terrorism—had seemed to produce results or relief for the Palestinians; Saddam offered them hope by challenging Israel and proposing linkage.

Both the speed with which the United States and its allies moved against Iraq and the United States's unwillingness to link the two occupations angered and further galvanized the Palestinians behind Iraq. Most saw a hypocritical double standard in American behavior: Whereas the United States had moved quickly and forcefully to end one occupation, basing its mandate on a U.N. resolution, it allowed Israel to continue to occupy Arab territories and annex Jerusalem and the Golan, despite dozens of U.N. resolutions. The United States condemned the Iraqi aggression of Kuwait, yet had acquiesced when the Israeli military, led by Ariel Sharon, had invaded Lebanon in 1982.

A telephone poll conducted by the weekly newspaper *al-Nadwa* the day after Saddam offered his August 12 linkage proposal found that 84 percent of West Bankers considered him a national hero, 58 percent supported his invasion of Kuwait, and 83 percent approved of Arafat's support of Saddam. Although the poll was not scientific, it is useful as a rough barometer of the public mood. Arafat found it hard to ignore such public support. Neither did he ignore the mood of the radicals within FATAH and the PLO, among the Palestinian rejectionists in Damascus, and among Islamists in the Occupied Territories.

Arafat had monitored these groups constantly and had expended much energy and time outmaneuvering them. Indeed, he had sacrificed diplomatic advantages—such as the U.S.-PLO dialogue, as a result of his refusal to condemn the failed PLF raid on a Tel Aviv beach in May 1990—to maintain national unity and his leadership. Thus, he decided to heed not only his grass-roots constituency, as he repeatedly and defensively explained, but also the sentiments of the radicals and the mood of those swayed by the passions of the radicals. In effect, Arafat flirted with radicalism and lost at an enormous cost to his people.

The Costs The Gulf crisis had disastrous consequences for the region, disrupting the lives of millions of expatriates and costing the area an estimated $620 billion. Iraq's infrastructure was severely damaged and tens of thousands of people were killed and injured. According to Middle East Watch, the United States and its Coalition allies may have deliberately targeted Iraq's infrastructure and bombed civilian residences, destroying thousands of homes, to encourage Iraqis to overthrow Saddam's regime, even though such actions were in violation of international law. Kuwaitis suffered the ravages of both the war and the occupation—including the use of torture, summary executions, and rape. About 600 Kuwaitis were killed, Kuwaiti institutions were looted of their equipment and banks of their deposits and bullion worth $2 to $3 billion, and hundreds of oil wells were set on fire by the fleeing Iraqis. The looting, destruction, sabotage, and liberation cost Kuwait an estimated $65 billion, not including the cost of reconstruction. Kuwaitis were emotionally scarred and bitter, feeling that the Palestinians had betrayed them. No sooner had Kuwait been freed than Kuwaitis sought revenge against the Palestinian community in their midst.

Palestinians had started immigrating to Kuwait in 1948–49, after they fled or were expelled from Palestine. Their arrival coincided with the country's development of its oil industry. Palestinians played significant roles in building Kuwait's infrastructure, working as teachers, civil servants, and industrialists. Despite their contributions to Kuwaiti society, the Kuwaiti government placed restrictions on Palestinians' residency, for example, forbidding an adult son of a Palestinian worker to stay in the country unless he found a Kuwaiti sponsor. When a worker's job ended, so did residency. A Palestinian could not retire in Kuwait even after lifelong employment there. These restrictions created hardships for Palestinians, who, unlike other foreign workers, had neither a homeland in which to retire nor a country to which their sons could go.

Yet, since Kuwait was the richest country per capita in the Arab world, the Palestinian community there thrived, and a few became very wealthy. The government allowed the PLO to collect a 5 percent "tax" from Palestinian employees for the Palestinian National Fund. In addition, Kuwait supported the PLO diplomatically and financially, although the organization complained that in early 1990 Kuwait did not pay its subsidy to the PLO and, instead, increased its support for the Islamic Resistance Movement (HAMAS), its rival in the Occupied Territories. Before the invasion, about 350,000 Palestinians resided in Kuwait.

Some Palestinians in Kuwait were emotionally predisposed toward Saddam because of his pledge to challenge Israel and in response to the massive U.S. buildup against Iraq. Most, however, were disturbed by the unprovoked invasion and the repression and looting that followed. The Fatah and PLO offices in Kuwait organized a demonstration supporting the emir, sponsored leaflets criticizing the occupation, and discouraged Palestinian youth from joining the Iraqi-organized neighborhood guard force during the occupation. Some Palestinians joined Kuwaiti resistance cells, contributing to the imprisonment of 5,000 Palestinians by the Iraqi security forces. Palestinian support for the Kuwaitis led to Iraqi threats against Palestinian leaders, and perhaps to the assassination of the Fatah leader Rafiq Qiblawi.

On the other hand, some Palestinians supported the Iraqi forces. Abu al-Abbas sent 400 PLF members while the Iraqi Ba'th-sponsored ARAB LIBERATION FRONT sent 300 Palestinians to Kuwait. These Palestinians manned roadblocks, placing them in visible confrontations with the local population, and some assisted Iraqis in interrogation and torture centers. Kuwaitis did not distinguish between these outsiders and local Palestinians, of whom a few, especially those belonging to George Habash's PFLP, assisted the Iraqis.

The majority of Palestinians remained neutral, although not in Kuwaiti eyes. The occupation was as harsh for the Palestinians as it was economically devastating. More than half of the Palestinians in Kuwait left during the fall of 1990, in addition to about 30,000 who were on vacation when Iraq invaded the country in August, leaving about 150,000 by December. Lacking the resources that sustained Kuwaitis, some Palestinians did not heed Kuwaiti calls to boycott government offices and commercial trading, arguing that maintaining water, health, and electric services helped the entire population. In addition, some 2,000 to 3,000 Palestinian teachers went to work and about 5,000 children attended school. Although the majority of Palestinians—perhaps 70 percent—boycotted their jobs, those who did not were visible reminders to Kuwaitis of Palestinian "collaboration."

During the weeks after liberation, Kuwaiti resistance members, civilians, and some military and security men turned on the Palestinian community. Hundreds were arbitrarily arrested, denied due process, beaten, and tortured, leading to many deaths. Kuwaiti "trials" of Palestinians were arbitrary, prompting criticism in the international press. In one case, a Palestinian received a fifteen-year sentence for wearing a T-shirt bearing Saddam Husayn's picture. Kuwaiti officials and human rights groups spoke out but were largely ineffective until Crown Prince Sa'ad al-Abdullah al-Sabah, who was also martial-law governor, threatened to arrest and hang from lampposts six members of the royal family who had participated in the kidnaping and torture. By then, the Palestinian community had dwindled even further. With more official restrictions and refusal to renew work permits, it was reduced to some 30,000 residents, or less than 10 percent of its original size. During the first year after the invasion, the community lost at least $8 billion in income and assets.

A number of factors explain the persecution of the Palestinians. First, prior to the invasion, there existed in Kuwait a predisposition to reduce the number of non-Kuwaiti residents, particularly Palestinians, because of the size of the Palestinian community; after the invasion, it was a timely opportunity to do so. Second, after liberation many Kuwaitis believed that the Palestinian community had been a fifth column, and some groups used the Palestinian minority as scapegoats to divert attention from local problems and promote national unity. Third, and most significantly, the Palestinians were easy targets of Kuwaiti revenge: Kuwaitis sought to punish the PLO by destroying the Palestinian community in Kuwait.

The economic ripple effect of this development was felt intensely in Jordan. Most of the Palestinian refugees from Kuwait fled to Jordan, many of them with no money, shelter, or jobs. The Gulf crisis, especially the embargo on trade with Iraq and the end of trade with Saudi Arabia, hurt the Jordanian economy severely. The cost to the 1.6 million Jordanian Palestinians in 1990 and 1991 amounted to $2.5 billion.

Hardship also occurred in the West Bank and Gaza Strip, to which tens of thousands of Palestinians returned from Kuwait. Per capita income had already declined by 35 percent as a result of the Intifada. The Gulf crisis resulted in the loss of remittances, subsidies, and trade, all amounting to a loss of hundreds of millions of dollars that annually came from external sources. This further reduced per capita income by another 15 to 20 percent, down to $800 annually, or half what it was in 1987. In Gaza, economic deterioration resulted in a dramatic decline in the standard of living, a doubling of child labor, the need for supplementary feeding programs of the United Nations Relief and Works Agency, and a substantial increase—100,000 families—in Palestinians needing emergency food relief. Some of this loss was due to a six-week curfew Israel imposed on the Occupied Territories during the crisis.

The international human rights organization Human Rights Watch called the curfew "the most severe act of collective punishment" of the occupation, an act inflicting "lasting harm to the economy and welfare of Palestinians." Israel imposed a blanket curfew on Gaza on January 16, 1991, at the start of the air war, and a similar one on the West Bank a day later (although Jewish settlers were excluded), because it feared an explosion of violence. Farmers were unable to water, harvest, or sell their products, and business activity virtually ceased. Most of the 120,000 Palestinians who worked in Israel were prevented from doing so, and even when the curfew was substantially lifted in early March, less than half of the laborers were allowed into Israel to work. In addition, fewer than 5 percent of the Palestinians were issued gas masks for protection against threatened Iraqi chemical attacks, even after Israel's High Court condemned the practice as "patent discrimination."

The Arab states' support for the PLO and for the Palestinian cause depended on friendly relations and on the PLO's avoidance of involvement in inter-Arab disputes. PLO support for Saddam antagonized many Arab governments, especially in the Gulf states, that had sustained the PLO. Financial and political support to the PLO was an early casualty of the crisis. According to the PLO, its annual support had consisted of $72 million from Saudi Arabia, $48 million from Iraq, and $24 million from Kuwait. These amounts do not include the PLO "tax" on Palestinians in Kuwait, which was estimated at $50 million annually, nor Gulf grants to the Occupied Territories, nor Palestinian remittances.

Another setback to the Palestinians was the loss of Arab consensus on the Palestine question—established by the Alexandria Protocol in 1944 (see ARAB LEAGUE)—which allowed Arab regimes to champion the Palestinian cause in international forums. This helped the Palestinians to achieve almost unanimous support, particularly at the United Nations.

One of the chief architects of this accomplishment had been Abu Iyad, whose assassination on January 15, 1991, was a blow to the PLO. He was the most capable Palestinian political strategist and had helped steer the organization from attacks on Israelis in the 1970s to recognition of Israel and the opening of U.S.–PLO talks in the 1980s. During the Gulf crisis, he was opposed to linking the Palestinian cause with Iraqi withdrawal from Kuwait, because he did not want the Palestinian "cause associated with the destruction of the Arab region." He told Saddam that he was destroying the Palestinian movement. Saddam was outraged and threw Abu Iyad out of his office. The PLO accused Israel of Abu Iyad's assassination, although the assassins belonged to the Fatah Revolutionary Council of ABU NIDAL, which had broken away from the PLO in the mid-1970s. It is unlikely that Abu Nidal, who had recently returned to Baghdad after a ten-year absence, acted without Saddam's consent or even instigation, perhaps as a warning to the PLO not to abandon him on the eve of the war.

Abu Iyad's outspokenness was rare, however. As the PLO was committing its worst political blunder, most of the Palestinian political elite failed to alert their people of the impending consequences. Of the dozens of Palestinian intellectuals around the world, only a few spoke out clearly and unequivocally; the rest were silent, defended the PLO position, or were swept away by the ideological passions of the moment.

Philip Mattar

BIBLIOGRAPHY

Daily Report, Foreign Broadcasts. Washington, D.C.: Foreign Broadcast Information Service, 1990, 1991.

Freedman, Lawrence, and Efraim Karsh. *The Gulf Conflict, 1990–1991 Diplomacy and War in the New World Order.* Princeton, N.J.: Princeton University Press, 1993.

Ibrahim, Ibrahim, ed. *The Gulf Crisis: Background and Consequences.* Washington, D.C.: Center for Contemporary Arab Studies, 1992.

Khalidi, Walid. *The Gulf Crisis: Origins and Consequences.* Washington, D.C.: Institute for Palestine Studies, 1991.

Mattar, Philip. "The PLO and the Gulf Crisis." *Middle East Journal* 48(1) (winter 1994): 31–44.

Salinger, Pierre, and Eric Laurent. *Secret Dossier: The Hidden Agenda Behind the Gulf War.* New York: Penguin Books, 1991.

Sifry, Micah L., and Christopher Cerf, eds. *The Gulf War Reader: History, Documents, Opinions.* New York: Random House, 1991.

Habash, George

intellectual, resistance leader
August 2, 1926– Lydda

Born into a family of Greek Orthodox merchants, George Habash and his family were forced in July 1948 to leave their native town, LYDDA, in what became one of the most infamous cases of deliberate mass expulsions of Palestinians by the Israeli army. Having fled to Beirut, Habash pursued his studies in pediatric medicine at the American University of Beirut and graduated first in his class in 1951. The same year he was arrested after a demonstration. In 1952, he founded the Arab Nationalist Movement (ANM) with WADI HADDAD (a Palestinian), Ahmad al-Khatib (a Kuwaiti), and Hani al-Hindi (a Syrian).

Determined to spread the movement abroad, Habash opened a Clinic of the People and a school for Palestinian REFUGEES in Amman at the end of 1952. He remained there until 1957. Active during the events of 1956–57 in Jordan, he went underground in April 1957 after the proclamation of martial law by King Husayn. Convicted in absentia, he fled to Syria after it had joined with Egypt to form the United Arab Republic (UAR). Attracted like many Arab nationalists to the ideas of Jamal Abd al-Nasir, he looked to extend the influence of the ANM to different Arab countries. For him, contrary to the cadres who formed FATAH, Arab unity was the engine of the liberation of Palestine. The Syrian secession from the UAR in 1961 and the subsequent return of the Ba'th to power in that country forced Habash to take refuge in Beirut. In April 1964, he created, within the ANM, a regional command for Palestine that regrouped the Palestinian members of the organization.

The ARAB-ISRAELI WAR OF 1967 dealt a hard blow to Nasir's prestige and gave affirmation to the Palestinian fedayeen movement. On December 11, 1967, Habash played a key role in the creation of the POPULAR FRONT FOR THE LIBERATION OF PALESTINE (PFLP) and became its secretary-general. The PFLP was a radical leftist and nationalist group opposed to any Arab concession to Israel because Israel was not ready to reciprocate. It was equally uncompromising toward the West and conservative Arab regimes, both of whom, together with Israel, were the enemies of the Palestinian people and their struggle for liberation.

Habash was detained by the Syrian authorities in March 1968, fell out of grace with Wadi Haddad in November 1968, and returned to Amman at the beginning of 1969. During this period a break occurred with the ANM leftists led by NAYIF HAWATIMA. Defending radical positions and rejecting UNITED NATIONS SECURITY COUNCIL RESOLUTION 242 and all attempts at political settlement—notably the ROGERS PLAN—his group pushed toward a confrontation with King Husayn. The hijacking of three planes at the Zarqa airport in September 1970 unleashed the events known as BLACK SEPTEMBER and the expulsion of the fedayeen organizations from Jordan.

When Habash's group took refuge in Lebanon, as did other groups of the PALESTINE LIBERATION ORGANIZATION (PLO), Habash played an active role during the Lebanese civil war (1975–76) on the side of the ANM. After the signing of the CAMP DAVID ACCORDS, he worked to reinforce the unity of the resistance, but, in 1980, he had a grave stroke that left him unable to be involved in political affairs for many months.

Violently opposed to the OSLO AGREEMENTS, Habash contributed to the organization of the

Damascus-based opposition, included for the first time Islamist organizations outside the PLO—HAMAS and ISLAMIC JIHAD. Remaining intransigent, affectionately called *al-Hakim* ("the Doctor" or "the Sage"), George Habash has maintained a great amount of respect among Palestianians, notably for his consistent refusal to align his organization with any Arab regime and for his revolutionary zeal in pursuing his goal of liberating Palestine.

Alain Gresh

Habibi, Emile

politician, writer
1922–1996 Haifa

Emile Habibi was born in HAIFA, although his family were Protestant Christians originally from nearby Shafa Amr. After working in Haifa's oil refinery, Habibi worked as a radio announcer from 1941 to 1943. He joined the PALESTINE COMMUNIST PARTY (PCP) in 1940 and was later involved in the National Liberation League, which grew out of the PCP in September 1943.

After the formation of Israel of 1948, Habibi helped form the Israeli Communist Party (ICP) and became a senior Palestinian Communist figure. He represented the ICP in the Knesset from 1952 to 1965 and was a leading figure in the New Communist List (RAKAH), which emerged from the ICP in 1965. Habibi represented Rakah in the Knesset from 1965 to 1972 and edited its weekly newspaper, *al-Ittihad,* which he turned into a daily in 1983. Habibi later challenged the positions that Rakah adopted toward the SOVIET UNION in the late 1980s, when the staunchly orthodox Communist Party criticized the reforms initiated by the Soviet leader Mikhail Gorbachev. He left the party in 1991 after Rakah supported the failed hard-line coup against Gorbachev.

Habibi was also a major Arab writer, and his novels, plays, and short stories were widely acclaimed throughout the Arab world. In 1974, he published a classic of modern Arabic fiction that was translated into English (and fourteen other languages) as *The Secret Life of Saeed, the Ill-Fated Pessoptimist: A Palestinian Who Became a Citizen of Israel.* In 1991, he established the Arabesque House Publishing Co. in Haifa, and in 1995 he founded the monthly literary journal *Masharif.*

Habibi's writings were recognized by numerous awards, including the Jerusalem Medal of the PALESTINE LIBERATION ORGANIZATION in 1990 and the Israel Prize—Israel's top cultural prize—in 1992. His acceptance of the latter was criticized by some Palestinians, who claimed it legitimized the domination of the PALESTINIAN CITIZENS OF ISRAEL. Habibi countered that, on the contrary, it represented an acknowledgment of their achievement.

A pillar of the Palestinian community who had remained in what became Israel in 1948 only to face decades of adversity, Habibi died in May 1996. He requested that his tombstone simply read, "Emile Habibi—Remained in Haifa."

Michael R. Fischbach

Hadawi, Sami

administrator, author
1904– Jerusalem

Sami Hadawi was born to a JERUSALEM Christian family, but his mother moved the family to Amman, in 1915, when his father, an Ottoman soldier, was killed in World War I. Although Hadawi never again resumed formal studies, he retained the knowledge of English and German he had acquired while a youth in Jerusalem and became an unofficial translator for British troops who entered Amman in 1918.

Hadawi returned to Palestine in 1919 and was employed by the British Palestine Authorities the following year. He served as a clerk in the district administration of Jerusalem and worked with Sir Ronald Storrs, Sir Harry Luke, and others. In 1927, he began a long involvement in LAND matters when he assumed duties in the land settlement department. From 1938 to 1948, he worked as a land valuer assessing taxation in urban and rural areas. Hadawi's expertise contributed to the Mandatory government's exhaustive work, *Village Statistics 1945: A Classification of Land and Area Ownership in Palestine.*

The ARAB-ISRAELI WAR OF 1948 drove Hadawi into exile. In 1949, he was employed by the Jordanian government. From 1952 to 1956, he worked as a land specialist for the UNITED NATIONS CONCILIATION COMMISSION FOR PALESTINE (UNCCP) in New York determining the extent of the property left behind by Palestinian REFUGEES in 1948.

After leaving the UNCCP, Hadawi helped open a Palestinian information office in the UNITED STATES in 1959 and later worked in the ARAB LEAGUE offices in New York and Dallas. He served as director of the INSTITUTE FOR PALESTINE STUDIES in Beirut from 1965 to 1968. Hadawi retired thereafter and moved to Toronto. He has authored scores of books and pamphlets, including *Bitter Harvest, Palestine: Loss of a Heritage,* and *Palestinian Rights and Losses in 1948.*

Michael R. Fischbach

Haddad, Wadi

resistance leader
1927–1978 Safad

Born to a Greek Orthodox family, Wadi Haddad finished his medical studies at the American University of Beirut in 1952. Along with fellow Palestinian GEORGE HABASH, he established a clinic in Amman, Jordan, for poor Palestinians. In 1956, he worked in clinics in Palestinian refugee camps administered by the United Nations Relief and Works Agency for Palestine Refugees in the Near East (UNRWA) in the Jordan valley.

An activist as well as a physician, Haddad helped to establish—again with Habash—the influential pan-Arab nationalist organization, the Movement of Arab Nationalists. Imprisoned by Jordanian authorities in 1957, Haddad escaped to Syria in 1961. After the Arab defeat of June 1967, Haddad and Habash became founding members of the POPULAR FRONT FOR THE LIBERATION OF PALESTINE (PFLP).

Haddad was the main PFLP strategist behind the hijackings, TERRORISM, and spectacular acts of violence for which the PFLP, and the Palestinian liberation movement in general, became notorious in the late 1960s and early 1970s. He reportedly planned the hijacking of an Israeli El Al jet, which was forced to land in Algeria in July 1968—the first instance in which Palestinians hijacked an aircraft. He was also involved in the famous September 1970 hijacking of four aircraft, which were forced to land in Jordan, an event that precipitated the violent clash between Palestinian guerrillas and the Jordanian army later that month known as BLACK SEPTEMBER.

In 1971, the PFLP decided to halt some of these activities. Haddad and others objected and left in 1972 to form a new group to continue such exploits, POPULAR FRONT FOR THE LIBERATION OF PALESTINE—EXTERNAL OPERATIONS. He was formally expelled from the PFLP in 1976.

Haddad died in East Germany on March 28, 1978, reportedly of leukemia, and was buried in Baghdad.

Michael R. Fischbach

Haifa

Arabic, Hayfa; Hebrew, Hefa

Haifa lies along the Mediterranean Sea on the Gulf of Acre at the foot of Mount Carmel. A small fishing village in the nineteenth century, Haifa developed gradually into a major seaport in northern Palestine. The dramatic changes in its size, economy, and demography ensued as the city was transformed by a variety of forces, including the modern global economy and ZIONISM.

Haifa's origins are ancient, although the site of the present-day city dates to the late eighteenth century, when it was established by Zahir al-Umar, the "strongman" of northern Palestine. Haifa was ruled thereafter by Ahmad Jazzar Pasha, who governed from ACRE; was briefly conquered by Napoleon's army in 1799 before being occupied by Ibrahim Pasha's Egyptian forces, and finally came under direct Ottoman rule after 1840.

Haifa contains several important religious shrines. Jews venerate the Cave of Elijah. The city also contains the tombs of two major figures in the Baha'i faith: the Bab (Mirza Ali Muhammad), buried on Mount Carmel, and Abbas Efendi, the son and successor of the faith's founder, Baha'ullah.

It was during the LATE OTTOMAN PERIOD that the port began its transformation into a modern city. Aspects of this change were the growth in Haifa's population and the change in its demographic character. Haifa's population stood at some 4,000 Palestinians at the beginning of the nineteenth century. Its population began growing during the second half of that century, when its largely Muslim and Christian Palestinian demographic character likewise began to change. In 1869, German farmers from the religious Templar Society movement settled in Haifa. In the 1880s, Jews began arriving from Europe—even before the onset of political Zionism.

At the same time, Haifa began to be transformed by the period's global economy and global transportation. Increasing numbers of European steamships began calling on Haifa's ports as Europe's trade with the eastern Mediterranean increased. In 1859, the Russians built a quay to facilitate such trade, and the Ottomans built the first port facilities in 1908. The Ottoman government had earlier linked Haifa with TIBERIAS by road, and by 1905, they linked it to Damascus via a spur of the Hijaz railroad. By 1919, the city was also connected to Egypt via railroad. By World War I, Haifa had replaced Beirut as the main port serving northern Palestine, southern Syria, and the Transjordanian hinterland. Grain and other commodities flowed in its direction.

The period of the British PALESTINE MANDATE witnessed the acceleration of these processes. The new deep-water harbor that opened in 1933 was the largest public-works project carried out by the British in Palestine during the Mandate, and it heightened Haifa's economic importance. Haifa was also the terminus of an oil pipeline extending from Iraq; it housed an oil refinery as well. The city was home to one of Palestine's two civil airports. Haifa's population grew during the Mandate from 24,634 in 1922 to some 128,000 in 1944, of whom 66,000 were Jews.

During the 1948 Arab-Israeli fighting, the city fell to Zionist forces on April 23 of that year. After Haifa's capture by the Haganah, all but some 3,000 Palestinians fled the city and became refugees. The city became a mostly Jewish city thereafter and is now one of Israel's largest cities, home to some 223,600 inhabitants by 1992.

Michael R. Fischbach

Hallaj, Muhammad

scholar

1932– Qalqiliya

Muhammad Hallaj is a scholar of Palestinian affairs. He went to the United States in the 1950s to attend college and obtained a doctorate in political science from the University of Florida in 1966. After teaching there for four years, he returned to the Middle East to teach first at the University of Jordan in Amman from 1970 to 1975 and then at BIR ZEIT UNIVERSITY on the WEST BANK from 1975 to 1981. Hallaj took a year's sabbatical at Harvard University in 1981, intending to return to Bir Zeit, but when Israeli occupation authorities denied him a work permit for the West Bank, he settled permanently in the United States.

Hallaj published the magazine *Palestine Perspectives* from 1983 to 1991. He has written extensively on Palestinian affairs and has contributed chapters to several edited collections on the Palestinian situation and the Israeli occupation. From 1991 to 1994, he served as director of the Center for Policy Analysis on Palestine, a Washington, D.C.-based study center. He was appointed to the PALESTINE NATIONAL COUNCIL in 1991 and from 1991 until the spring of 1993 served as head of the Palestinian delegation to the multilateral talks on REFUGEES that grew out of the MADRID PEACE CONFERENCE, 1991. He is a member of the board of commissioners of the Palestinian Independent Commission for Citizens' Rights, a Palestinian human rights monitoring organization based in the West Bank.

Hallaj believes that the Declaration of Principles signed in September 1993 by ISRAEL and the PALESTINE LIBERATION ORGANIZATION (PLO) might have led to a meaningful peace but have been implemented so poorly that it cannot resolve the conflict. Israel, he feels, is using the agreement as a vehicle to reorganize its occupation of the West Bank and Gaza, not to end it. He also criticizes the PLO leadership for a lack of competence, particularly for failure to mobilize the Palestinian people to work toward nation building.

Kathleen Christison

BIBLIOGRAPHY

Hallaj, Muhammad. *Palestine Is, But Not in Jordan.* Belmont, Mass.: Association of Arab-American University Graduates Press, 1983.

Hamami, Sa'id

diplomat

1941–1978 Jaffa

Sa'id Hamami was born in the Palestinian coastal town of JAFFA during the final decade of the British PALESTINE MANDATE. In 1948, his family was forced into exile as a result of the ARAB-ISRAELI WAR OF 1948 and settled in Amman, JORDAN, where Hamami completed his primary and secondary education.

Hamami subsequently enrolled at the University of Damascus, where he graduated with a B.A. in

English literature in the early 1960s. He thereafter worked as a journalist and teacher.

Hamami joined the Palestine National Liberation Movement (FATAH) in 1967 and was for some time active in its military wing, AL-ASIFA ("The Storm"). In February 1969 he was appointed a Fatah delegate to the PALESTINE NATIONAL COUNCIL (PNC), the parliament-in-exile of the PALESTINE LIBERATION ORGANIZATION (PLO), indicating that he rather quickly became one of the movement's senior cadres.

In 1972, Hamami was appointed the PLO's first representative to the United Kingdom. Because the United Kingdom did not recognize the PLO and would not allow the organization to open an office on British territory, Hamami's official position was that of director of the Palestine Information Office of the Office of the ARAB LEAGUE in London. He was nevertheless considered an effective diplomat and articulate spokesperson and in addition to numerous political contacts developed extensive relations with the British press and intelligentsia.

Particularly after the October 1973 Arab-Israeli war, Hamami's presence in London coincided with increasing European support for Palestinian rights and growing Palestinian acceptance of a negotiated settlement to the ARAB-ISRAELI CONFLICT. Hamami not only benefited from these trends but also actively encouraged them. In important articles published in the November 16 and December 17, 1973, editions of *The Times* of London, Hamami emerged as the first Palestinian official to call openly for "mutual recognition" between ISRAEL and the Palestinians. It is inconceivable that he could have done so without the personal approval of the PLO chairman, YASIR ARAFAT, the more so because he was not disciplined for his statements. Contrary to Israeli claims that Hamami's conciliatory proclamations were designed to camouflage the PLO's "real" objective of destroying Israel and thus deceive his Western audience, there is no doubt that they were genuine trial balloons floated on behalf of the PLO leadership.

Hamami argued with increasing vigor for a negotiated two-state settlement to the Israeli-Palestinian conflict, which he believed would lay the foundation for the peaceful evolution of a secular democratic state throughout historic Palestine. In addition, he was also one of the earliest Palestinian advocates of direct contacts with Israelis, and in 1974 was the first PLO official to meet an Israeli when he met clandestinely with the Israeli journalist and parliamentarian Uri Avnery. Subsequent meetings with Avnery and other Israelis followed. Through Avnery an informal channel was established to the Israeli prime minister, Yitzhak Rabin, but the latter categorically rejected all messages communicated to him.

During his lifetime, Hamami emerged as the most visible Palestinian proponent of a two-state solution and dialogue with Israelis to achieve this objective. This position earned him extreme hostility in Israel, which sought to portray the PLO as terrorists unfit for recognition. Ultimately, however, he fell victim to a violent feud between the PLO and Iraq when he was assassinated in London on January 4, 1978, by the Fatah Revolutionary Council, led by Sabri al-Banna (also known as ABU NIDAL).

Hamami was buried in Amman, Jordan, and remains a symbol of hope for Israeli-Palestinian reconciliation.

Muin Rabbani

BIBLIOGRAPHY

Avnery, Uri. *My Friend, the Enemy.* Westport, Conn.: Lawrence Hill and Co., 1987.

Gresh, Alain. *The PLO: The Struggle Within: Towards an Independent Palestinian State,* Rev. ed., trans. by A. M. Berrett. London: Zed Books, 1988.

Hamas

Acronym of *Harakat al-Muqawama al-Islamiyya,* "Islamic Resistance Movement," Hamas was born of the INTIFADA in 1987 as a wing of the Muslim Brotherhood Society in Palestine. The creation of Hamas and its wide participation in the Intifada marked the true beginning of Muslim Brotherhood resistance to the post-1967 Israeli occupation, as well as the rise of political Islam in the WEST BANK and the GAZA STRIP. A few years after the Intifada, the Muslim Brotherhood, and particularly Hamas, began to pose a serious challenge to the dominant nationalist trend led by the PALESTINE LIBERATION ORGANIZATION (PLO) competing with the PLO over the identity, direction, and leadership of the Palestinian society.

Ever since its foundation, Hamas has continued to grow in strength and popularity. The group was initially formed by Shaykh AHMAD YASIN, founder and leader of the Islamic Center, a leading Muslim Brotherhood organization in Gaza. A number of Islamic figures aided Yasin and continued to lead the movement after his imprisonment by the Israeli authorities in 1989. Hamas went on to expand during the years of Intifada, and the movement began to be led by a *majlis shura,* an advisory council, whose members reside both inside and outside Palestine.

Hamas's aims and strategies are spelled out in the charter it issued in August 1989. Its position is also defined by the Muslim Brotherhood Societies in Jordan and Egypt. Hamas considers Palestine an Islamic trust that no one has the right to surrender and believes that the solution to the Palestine problem rests in abolishing the state of Israel and establishing an Islamic state in historic Palestine.

After the signing of the OSLO AGREEMENTS and other related agreements between Israel and the PLO in September 1993 and the subsequent establishment of the PALESTINIAN AUTHORITY in areas of the West Bank and Gaza, Hamas's capabilities, influence, and popularity began to recede. Hamas, which opposed the Oslo agreements, had to deal with the Palestinian Authority in these areas as the only political and legislative frame of reference and the only authority that possessed the legal means of coercion. In light of the changing circumstances, the uncertain future of the peace process, and the influence of ISLAMIC FUNDAMENTALISM, the future of Hamas remains equally uncertain in terms of the rise, demise, or evolution of the movement.

Ziad Abu-Amr

al-Haq

Established in 1979 at the initiative of WEST BANK lawyers Raja SHEHADEH and Jonathan Kuttab, al-Haq has long been a major Palestinian human rights and legal services organization in the Occupied Territories. Al-Haq has researched the legal situation surrounding international law and the Israeli occupation of the West Bank and has issued many publications documenting Israeli practices that violate international standards of law and human rights.

Al-Haq also serves as a legal services resource for the Palestinian community and is affiliated with the International Commission of Jurists in Geneva, Switzerland. It maintains a library in RAMALLAH, where it provides information and legal assistance to the public.

Michael R. Fischbach

al-Haram al-Sharif

On the eastern side of the Old City of JERUSALEM lies a raised rectangular platform that contains several important religious shrines venerated by millions worldwide. The site, also known as the Temple Mount, was occupied by the first and second Jewish temples (the Temples of Solomon and Herod, respectively), both built over the place where Jewish tradition says the patriarch Abraham prepared to sacrifice his son, Isaac, to God. The platform is surrounded by the remnants of the last temple's retaining wall, the exterior of which is the Western, or Wailing, Wall (Hebrew, ha-Kotel ha-Ma'aravi). The Wall is the holiest site in Judaism, a site of prayer and pilgrimage. In Arabic the platform is called al-Haram al-Sharif, "the Noble Sanctuary," because it contains two important Islamic shrines: The first is the Dome of the Rock (Arabic, Qubbat al-Sakhra), incorrectly called the Mosque of Omar. It was built as a sanctuary (Arabic, *mashhad*) for pilgrims by the tenth caliph, Abd al-Malik ibn Marwan, between 685 and 691 C.E. Measuring fifty-six by forty-two feet, the rock over which the structure was erected is the place from which Muslims believe the Prophet Muhammad ascended to heaven on a nocturnal journey (known as the Mi'raj). While doing so, he tethered his "fabulous steed" (al-Buraq) in an area located in the interior portion of the Western Wall at Temple Mount, which later took the name al-Buraq. The other Islamic shrine at Temple Mount is the early eighth-century edifice al-Masjid al-Aqsa (al-Aqsa Mosque).

Al-Haram al-Sharif is the third holiest place in Islam after the mosques of Mecca and Medina, as it was the original direction of prayer for Muslims and remains an important site for pilgrimage. Both mosques on the site underwent extensive renovations in the 1920s (and the Dome of Rock in the early 1990s as well).

Philip Mattar

al-Hasan, Hani

resistance leader
1937– Haifa

Brother of KHALID AL-HASAN, one of the founding members of FATAH, Hani al-Hasan himself became involved in resistance politics when he led the General Union of Palestinian Students while studying construction engineering at the University of Darmstadt in West Germany. He joined Fatah in 1963 and soon became a leading figure in the movement. He became a member of Fatah's central council and served as deputy to SALAH KHALAF (Abu Iyad) in the group's intelligence service. By 1967, he had become Fatah's senior figure in EUROPE and in 1974 was appointed chair of its Palestinian political affairs department. He also was a member of the PALESTINE NATIONAL COUNCIL. Internationally, al-Hasan became Fatah's main contact with China.

Despite the fact that al-Hasan eventually became a senior adviser to the PALESTINE LIBERATION ORGANIZATION (PLO) chairman, YASIR ARAFAT, he was critical of Arafat's embrace of the Iraqi president, Saddam Husayn, during the GULF CRISIS, 1990–1991, and the resulting war. He was also one of several senior Fatah figures who voiced criticism of the 1993 Israeli-PLO accords, criticism that led to serious dissention within the movement. Al-Hasan maintained his position of dissent even after the establishment of the PALESTINIAN AUTHORITY, although he returned to the GAZA STRIP from exile in November 1995.

Michael R. Fischbach

al-Hasan, Khalid

Abu Sa'id; founder and leading member of Fatah
1928–1994

Khalid Muhammad al-Hasan was born the eldest of six children to a prominent Sunni Muslim family in HAIFA during the British PALESTINE MANDATE.

Employed by the British military at the end of the Mandate, he was evacuated to the Sinai Peninsula in May 1948. The following year, he rejoined his family in Sidon, Lebanon, where they had been forced into exile. In 1950 he moved to Damascus, where he worked as a private tutor until his arrest for involvement in Islamist politics.

Al-Hasan left Syria in 1952 for KUWAIT, where he would continue to reside until the GULF CRISIS, 1990–1991. The following year, he joined the civil service as a typist at the Kuwait Development Board. He was in rapid succession promoted to the position of assistant general-secretary, then to that of assistant general-secretary of the Planning Board, and finally to the key position of general secretary of the Municipal Council Board. Because of his major role in the development of Kuwait, he was one of the few Palestinians to acquire Kuwaiti citizenship.

It was in Kuwait that al-Hasan first met YASIR ARAFAT and KHALIL AL-WAZIR (also known as Abu Jihad) and formed part of the core that later in that decade founded FATAH. A member of its Central Committee (and ex officio of its subsequently established Revolutionary Council) from the outset until his death, al-Hasan was during its formative years frequently at odds with Arafat; he led the faction that insisted on a collective rather than individualistic leadership and opposed a "premature" initiation of military operations. Arafat and al-Wazir, crucially supported by al-Hasan's brother, HANI AL-HASAN, emerged victorious when they persuaded Fatah to launch military operations on January 1, 1965. Largely as a result of the prestige he derived from his decision, Arafat ultimately settled the question of leadership style in his favor as well.

After Fatah assumed control of the PALESTINE LIBERATION ORGANIZATION (PLO) in 1968–69, al-Hasan served on its Executive Committee from 1969 to 1973, when he was also the director of the PLO's Political Department. He thereafter filled the post of chairman of the Foreign Relations Committee of the PALESTINE NATIONAL COUNCIL (PNC) until his death. No less importantly, al-Hasan in 1969 forged Fatah's first official links with Saudi Arabia, and within Fatah thereafter consistently advocated coordination with Saudi policy and a crucial link between the movement and the Gulf monarchies.

A senior adviser to Arafat throughout the 1970s and 1980s despite their differences, and additionally an early convert to the concept of a negotiated settlement of the Israeli-Palestinian conflict, al-Hasan during this period often served as a roving ambassador and troubleshooter for the PLO and used his considerable diplomatic and public relations skills to spearhead its diplomatic offensive in the West.

Al-Hasan early emerged as the leading conservative within Fatah (and therefore the PLO). His opposition to a 1973 PNC resolution to overthrow the Jordanian monarchy led him to resign from the PLO Executive Committee, and in 1990 he definitively broke with Arafat because of the PLO chair's costly embrace of the Iraqi leader, Saddam Husayn. Stripped of his Kuwaiti citizenship after the GULF CRISIS, 1990–1991, nevertheless, al-Hasan moved to Morocco, from where he launched an unsuccessful challenge against Arafat.

Although al-Hasan rose to international prominence as a "voice of Palestinian moderation," he condemned the September 13, 1993, Israeli-Palestinian Declaration of Principles on Interim Self-Government Arrangements as a violation of internationally recognized Palestinian national rights that could not serve as a basis for a just peace, and that had furthermore not been submitted to the PNC for debate and ratification. He died of cancer on October 8, 1994.

In addition to numerous interviews and press statements, al-Hasan published several booklets in Arabic as well as one in English setting out his views on a resolution of the Israeli-Palestinian conflict.

Muin Rabbani

BIBLIOGRAPHY

Cobban, Helena. *The Palestinian [sic] Liberation Organization: People, Power and Politics.* Cambridge, England: Cambridge University Press, 1984.

Hart, Alan. *Arafat: Terrorist or Peacemaker?* London: Sidgwick & Jackson, 1984.

al-Hassan, Khaled. *Grasping the Nettle of Peace: A Senior Palestinian Figure Speaks Out.* London: Saqi Books, 1992.

al-Hasi, Aqila Agha

rebel and the de facto ruler of northern Palestine for more than a quarter of a century

?–1870 Gaza

Al-Hasi joined the 1834 revolt against the Egyptians; after Ibrahim Pasha's success in quelling the rebellion, al-Hasi and his men retreated to Jordan, where he strengthened his ties with the tribes of the area. When Ottoman rule was restored in Syria, Bilad al-Sham, in 1841, al-Hasi returned to northern Palestine to serve the *walis* (governors) of ACRE, helping to maintain security and protect the local trade routes. His influence later reached NAZARETH, al-Marj, TIBERIAS, and SAFAD, where people paid him a yearly tax as a kind of protection. In 1848, the American explorer W. F. Lynch visited Palestine and credited al-Hasi's success in defending Lynch and his team against one huge attack. Lynch's writing and photograph of al-Hasi published in European publications gave al-Hasi some fame, especially among European travelers and explorers who visited the area. The Ottomans objected to his influence and attempted to get rid of him. He was arrested by the Ottoman authorities in 1853 and exiled to Serbia but fled after one year and returned to Galilee. In 1857 the Turks encouraged some nonofficial Kurdish forces to fight al-Hasi, but he defeated them in a famous battle in Hittin.

Al-Hasi's relations with the Europeans were good, especially because of his treatment of Christians and Jews, whom he helped maintain their security in Galilee. This won him the friendship of consuls, especially the French consul. His most famous action was protecting the Christians during the events of 1860 in Lebanon and Syria. Although the level of violence in Acre and Nazareth was nowhere near that of Syria and Lebanon, Napoleon III sent al-Hasi a medal and a gun as a gesture of appreciation. When Edward, the prince of Wales (later King Edward VII), visited Palestine in 1862, he visited al-Hasi's tent and presented him with a gift, also in gratitude for that protection.

In 1863 the Ottomans decided to abolish the nonofficial forces in the region and suggested that al-Hasi and his men wear official military uniforms and work within the Ottoman army. Al-Hasi refused, resigned from his post, and went to Transjordan. After failing to maintain security in the area, the Ottomans returned al-Hasi to Galilee in 1864. That year he was visited by the English traveler H. B. Tristram, who sought his protection. With the Tanzimat period of reforms, the Ottomans were determined to abolish local leadership in order to strengthen central rule. They sent in large numbers of soldiers and heavy weapons to quell local opposition.

Al-Hasi returned from Transjordan to the area in 1866, when he was its de facto ruler, but because of his advanced age he was less combative in his last days. The situation had changed markedly during the Tanzimat policy of centralization and modernization. Shortly before his death in 1870 he received a medal from the emperor of Austria, who had visited Palestine in 1869. His name was famous for a long time, especially among local Christians and foreigners grateful for his protection.

Adel Manna

Hawatima, Nayif

guerrilla

1935– Salt, Jordan

Born into a family of Greek Catholic Jordanian peasants, Nayif Hawatima began his higher education in Cairo in 1954 and joined the Movement of Arab Nationalist (MAN) of GEORGE HABASH in the same year. On his return to Jordan in 1956, he participated in revolutionary activity for which he was condemned in absentia to death. In 1958, he participated in the Lebanese civil war and then sought refuge in Iraq, where General Abd al-Karim Qasim had overthrown the pro-British monarch. There he led a local section of the MAN before going to South Yemen, where he contributed to the Yemeni struggle against British colonialism.

The June 1967 war marked a turning point in Hawatima's activity. Notably, he pulled away from the Nasirism that characterized the MAN during the preceding years. He benefited from Jordanian amnesty and returned to the kingdom, where, at the beginning of 1968, he rejoined the POPULAR FRONT FOR THE LIBERATION OF PALESTINE (PFLP), which had been created from the ANM. As leader of the leftist wing of the movement, he violently criticized "the Arab petit bourgeoisie" responsible, according to him, for the ARAB-ISRAELI WAR OF 1967 defeat and incapable of leading the struggle for the liberation of Palestine. He broke with the PFLP in February 1969 and created the Popular Democratic Front for the Liberation of Palestine (PDFLP), which became the DEMOCRATIC FRONT FOR THE LIBERATION OF PALESTINE (DFLP) in August 1974.

In 1970, he opened a dialogue with the extreme leftist, anti-Zionist Israeli organization Matzpen. At the end of 1973, Hawatima became one of the most ardent supporters of the idea of transitional stages before creating a revolutionary government in all liberated areas of Palestine or founding a "Palestinian ministate." He contributed, therefore, to the majority—composed of FATAH, AL-SA'IQA, and the Palestine National Front in the Occupied Territories—which, within the PALESTINE NATIONAL COUNCIL in 1974 and 1977, would adopt these issues.

During the 1980s, Hawatima drew away from Fatah and YASIR ARAFAT. He especially condemned the 1993 OSLO AGREEMENTS and denounced Arafat as a "new Pétain."

Alain Gresh

Haycraft Commission

1921

In 1921, British authorities established a commission, officially called the Commission of Inquiry, headed by the chief justice of Palestine, Sir Thomas Haycraft, to investigate the outbreak of Palestinian violence against Jews in JAFFA and surrounding areas. The disturbances took place in May 1921, after a Zionist Labor Day march in Jaffa, and resulted in the deaths of forty-seven Jews and forty-eight Palestinians, the latter largely through the actions of British security forces.

In October 1921 the commission issued its report, which stated that the Palestinian violence stemmed from a fear of the political and economic impact of Zionist immigration into Palestine, which Palestinians feared would lead not only to unemployment but to their subjugation at the hands of ZIONISM.

Michael R. Fischbach

Hebron

Hebron is a major WEST BANK town lying on the southern end of the central mountain ridge of Palestine. The city is holy to both Jews and Muslims because it is the location of the Cave of Machpelah, which contains tombs of the biblical and Qur'anic figures Abraham, Isaac, and Jacob, along with their respective wives, Sarah, Rebekah, and Leah. The tomb is enclosed by a sacred compound known as *al-Haram al-Ibrahimi,* which houses a mosque built over the tombs. Hebron is called *al-Khalil* (The Friend) in Arabic in reference to Abraham, who in sacred literature was called the "Friend of God." It is called *Hevron* in Hebrew.

Hebron's origins extend back to ancient days. Conquered by the Arabs in the seventh century and the Crusaders in 1168 C.E., the city experienced a period of growth under the Mamluks, when it was a stop on the pigeon post route from

Egypt eastward toward al-Karak in Transjordan. The city was sacked by the Egyptians in 1834. Under the Ottomans, Hebron began a renewed process of growth and development. Its population began expanding beyond the city's walls in the late nineteenth century and had reached some 16,500 by the onset of the British PALESTINE MANDATE in 1922.

Agriculture has been a mainstay of Hebron's economy. The region is particularly noted for its fruits and olives. However, the city was a noted manufacturing center for centuries, most famous for its glassware.

Hebron is a trading town for the villagers and Bedouins living in the region, as well as a link between Palestine and Transjordan. The city is also the home of HEBRON UNIVERSITY, which opened in 1971 and attained university status in 1980.

Hebron's history in the twentieth century has been tremendously affected by the ARAB-ISRAELI CONFLICT. An overwhelmingly Palestinian city, Hebron was traditionally one of the four holy cities for Jews in Palestine. Nationalist tensions between Palestinians and Zionist Jews over the Western Wall in JERUSALEM led to violence in August 1929, violence that spread to Hebron when Palestinians attacked and killed sixty-four Jewish inhabitants. Thereafter, the remnant of the Jewish community left the city. Hebron was defended by Egyptian and Jordanian troops in the ARAB–ISRAELI WAR OF 1948 and became part of the Jordanian-controlled West Bank.

The Israeli occupation of the West Bank in June 1967 also affected Hebron in significant ways. In the wake of the occupation, Jews were allowed to worship in the mosque in the Haram al-Ibrahimi and descend into the Cave of Machpelah. A civilian Jewish settlement called Kiryat Arba'a was established near the city in 1968, and Jewish settlers, especially militant religious nationalists under Rabbi Moshe Levinger, were allowed to move into Hebron itself to reestablish the historic Jewish presence there.

The presence of the settlers has led to violence between Jews and Palestinians. In 1980, six settlers from Kiryat Arba'a were ambushed and killed in the city. In 1983, armed settlers entered the Islamic College and fired indiscriminantly at Palestinian students, killing three. Yet the worst violence occurred in February 1994, when an American-born settler shot and killed twenty-nine Palestinians worshiping in the Haram al-Ibrahimi mosque.

The presence of the Jewish settlers in Hebron also constituted a problem during negotiations between the PALESTINE LIBERATION ORGANIZATION and Israel over the Israeli redeployment from the West Bank. Because the city contained settlers, Hebron was the last West Bank city from which Israeli troops redeployed. Even then, the "Protocol Concerning the Redeployment in Hebron" signed by Israel and the Palestine Liberation Organization in January 1997, after lengthy negotiations allowed the PALESTINIAN AUTHORITY control over only some 80 percent of the city. Al-Haram al-Ibrahimi and the downtown Palestinian market remained under Israeli control.

Michael R. Fischbach

Hebron University

Hebron University is a private, coeducational Islamic institution first established as a college in the WEST BANK city of HEBRON in 1971. It attained its current university status in 1980. The university offers diplomas, as well as B.A. and B.S. degrees. Arabic and English are the languages of instruction. Some 1,446 students studied there during the 1995–96 academic year.

Michael R. Fischbach

High Commissioner for Palestine

In June 1920, Britain replaced the military government it had established in Palestine in December 1917 with a civilian administration headed by a high commissioner. The legal basis for Britain's rule in Palestine was the PALESTINE MANDATE to rule the country and assist it in the "development of self-governing institutions" granted by the League of Nations, although the commissioner in fact ruled the country as a Crown colony on behalf of the British government in London.

The high commissioner exercised full governing power, including powers of censorship, deportation, detention without trial, demolition of the homes of suspects, and collective punishment. These powers were wielded against both the Jewish and Arab populations. The high commissioner relied on an executive council comprising the chief secretary, attorney general, and treasurer of the Palestine government, as well as on an advisory council. From 1920 to 1923, the advisory council consisted of British officials from the government as well as Palestinians and Jews appointed by the commissioner. Thereafter, all the advisory council's members were officials.

The high commissioner also proposed creating a legislative council as part of the British commitment to establish self-governing institutions. The mutually exclusive political goals of the Jewish and Arab communities and Britain's commitment to the BALFOUR DECLARATION frustrated this goal, however, and the high commissioner exercised sole authority in Palestine until the end of the Mandate in May 1948.

Names and dates of appointments of the high commissioners are as follows:

Sir Herbert Samuel:	July 1, 1920
Lord Plumer:	August 14, 1925
Sir John Chancellor:	November 1, 1928
Sir Arthur Wauchope:	November 20, 1931
Sir Harold MacMichael:	March 3, 1938
Viscount Gort:	October 31, 1944
Sir Alan Gordan Cunningham:	November 21, 1945

Philip Mattar

BIBLIOGRAPHY

Palestine Government. *A Survey of Palestine for the Information of the Anglo-American Committee of Inquiry,* 2 vols. Jerusalem: Government Printer, 1946: Reprint. Washington, D.C.: Institute for Palestine Studies, 1991.

Holy Places

The religious importance of JERUSALEM and the surrounding region arises from the presence of holy shrines highly revered by adherents of Judaism, Christianity, and Islam.

Jewish Holy Places The major Jewish holy places in Palestine include the Cave of the Machpelah in HEBRON, believed to be the tomb of Abraham, Isaac, and Jacob (this is also a holy place for Muslims, who also revere these figures); the Jewish cemetery on the Mount of Olives; the Tomb of David and the Western (Wailing) Wall in Jerusalem; Rachel's Tomb in BETHLEHEM; and a number of ancient and modern synagogues. Twice destroyed during its history, the Temple of Solomon survives only in a remnant of the Western Wall. Some Orthodox Jews believe that the Temple will be rebuilt when the Messiah comes.

Throughout its troubled history, Jerusalem has been a sacred place for the followers of Judaism. According to Jewish law, when Jews pray, they must face in the direction of the "City of Eternity," as it is specified in the Bible. After the destruction of the first Temple of Solomon (587 B.C.E.) and the dispersal of the Jewish people, the Jews took a sacred oath that stated, in the words of Psalm 137: "If I forget Thee, O Jerusalem, Let my right hand forget her cunning. Let my tongue cleave to the roof of my mouth, If I remember Thee not, If I set not Jerusalem above my chiefest joy."

There is a certain amount of overlap between Jewish holy places and highly revered Muslim shrines. For example, the HARAM AL-SHARIF compound, which includes the Dome of the Rock and the Aqsa mosque, is built on the site of the second Jewish Temple, located near the Western Wall.

Christian Holy Places For Christians, Jerusalem is the place where Jesus preached his message and where he was crucified and died. Moreover, in the New Testament, Jerusalem symbolized the new covenant between God and his people redeemed by the Messiah. This Christian expectation is explicated in the New Testament, according to the Apostle John:

> Then I saw a new heaven and the first earth had passed away, and the sea was no more. And I saw the holy city, the new Jerusalem coming down out of heaven from God, repaired as a bride adorned for her husband . . . and death shall be no more, neither shall there be mourning nor crying nor pain anymore, for the former things have passed away. (Revelation 21:1–4)

In Jerusalem, the holy places of Christendom include the Basilica of the Holy Sepulchre, the Cenacle, the Church of Saint Anne, the Tomb of the Virgin, the Garden of Gethsemane, the Sanctuary of the Ascension, and the Mount of Olives.

One of the major holy shrines of Christianity, the Basilica of the Holy Sepulchre, was built between 325 and 335 under the rule of Roman emperor Constantine. Legend has it that Constantine's mother, Saint Helena, discovered the Tomb of Christ and the three crosses under the rubble of a pagan temple. The basilica was supposedly built to honor her discovery. In 1099, the basilica was destroyed under the rule of the Fatimid caliph al-Hakim. In 1149, Crusaders built a new basilica that encompassed the hill of Calvary, where Jesus was crucified, and the Holy Sepulchre. Ownership of the Holy Sepulchre is still a source of conflict among various Christian communities: Greek Orthodox, Greek Catholics (Melkites), Roman Catholics, Armenians, Copts, Syrians, and Ethiopians. Since Ottoman domination, the keys to the basilica have been in the hands of Palestinian Muslims, the NUSEIBEH FAMILY. In recent years a modus vivendi was reached regarding the restoration of the edifice.

Major Christian holy places outside Jerusalem include the Church of the Nativity in Bethlehem, the Basilica of the Transfiguration on Mount Tabor, the Basilica of the Visitation in Ayn Karim, the Sanctuary of the Beatitudes on Lake Tiberias, the Garden Tomb, and the Basilica of the Annunciation in NAZARETH. Most of these Christian holy places are under the care of the Franciscan Custody of the Holy Land, established by the Vatican to oversee Catholic property and presence in Palestine.

Muslim Holy Places For Muslims, Jerusalem (al-Quds) is sacred because of its association first with Abraham and his descendants and later with the Prophet Muhammad and his followers. Although Jerusalem is never mentioned in the Qur'an, Muslims believe that the Prophet made a miraculous journey by night to Jerusalem. He rode on a winged steed (al-Buraq) from Mecca to the Aqsa Mosque (*al-masjid al-aqsa,* "the distant shrine") in Jerusalem. There the Prophet supposedly ascended into heaven until he reached the seventh heaven. This night journey is described in the Qur'an:

> Glory be to Him, who carried His servant by night from the Holy Mosque [Mecca] to the Farthest Mosque [Jerusalem] the precincts of which We [God] have blessed, that We might show him [Muhammad] some of our signs. (Surah 17:1)

From then on, the site of the Jerusalem temple, referred to in the Qur'an as the Farthest Mosque, has been a sacred place of worship for Muslims, second only to Mecca and Medina in Saudi Arabia.

The Haram al-Sharif, which includes the Dome of the Rock, built between 685 and 691 C.E. by Caliph Abd al-Malik, constitutes a bone of contention regarding control among four Arab–Islamic actors: Jordan, Morocco, Palestine, and Saudi Arabia. Jordan, which controls the *waqf* (endowment) of property for religious purposes, such as mosques, schools, and hospitals, in 1992 disbursed $8 million for the restoration of the Dome. Moreover, the PALESTINIAN AUTHORITY expressed its discontent with the Israel–Jordan peace accord because it bestows on the Hashemite Kingdom of Jordan the right to supervise the holy places of Islam in Jerusalem. King Husayn stated, and his son King Abdullah reiterated, that Jordan had no intention of maintaining the control of the Muslim *waqf* in Jerusalem. For the Palestinians, the holy places of Islam in Jerusalem must be placed under the authority of the fledgling Palestinian government.

Controversy over Israeli Control The present and future status of the holy places is also a point of contention between the Catholic Church and the state of Israel. For the Vatican, the holy places, especially those located inside the Old City of Jerusalem, should be placed under international supervision, the United Nations Educational, Scientific and Cultural Organization (UNESCO), for instance. Since its unilateral annexation of Jerusalem in 1980, the Israeli government, facing international protests and condemnation, stated that it was willing to guarantee each of the communities right of access to the holy places.

George E. Irani

BIBLIOGRAPHY

Cattan, Henry. *Jerusalem.* London: Croom Helm, 1981.

Collin, Bernardin. *Les Lieux-Saints.* Paris: Presses Universitaires de France, 1968.

Ingram, O. Kelly, ed. *Jerusalem: Key to Peace in the Middle East.* Durham, N.C.: Triangle Friends of the Middle East, 1978.

Lauterpacht, Elihu. *Jerusalem and the Holy Places.* Anglo-Israel Association, pamphlet no. 19, 1980.

Le Morzellec, Joelle. *La question de Jerusalem devant l'Organisation des Nations-Unies.* Brussels: Établissements Emile Bruylant, 1979.

Wilson, Evan M. *Jerusalem, Key to Peace.* Washington, D.C.: Middle East Institute, 1970.

Hope-Simpson Commission
1930

After the 1929 WESTERN (WAILING) WALL DISTURBANCES, Britain dispatched the SHAW COMMISSION, 1930, to investigate their origins. In March 1930, the commission determined that the Palestinian violence had stemmed from the community's anxiety over the adverse effects of Zionist immigration and land purchases. It recommended that British authorities limit both practices. In October, British prime minister Ramsay MacDonald of the Labour Party appointed Sir John Hope-Simpson head of a second commission formed to investigate the questions of Zionist immigration, settlement, and development.

The Hope-Simpson Commission subsequently issued a report stating that nearly 30 percent of Palestinians were landless and linked this condition with Zionist land purchases. It also noted that unemployment among Palestinians was worsened by the Zionist policy of only hiring Jewish workers in the Jewish sector.

British authorities used the commission's findings and recommendations to formulate a 1930 policy paper known as the Passfield White Paper. The White Paper revived the idea of forming a legislative council for Palestine and recommended limiting Jewish immigration and land acquisitions by linking them with the absorptive capacity of Palestine's economy.

Publication of the Passfield White Paper created a sensation in Britain. Chaim Weizmann resigned as head of the World Zionist Organization and the Jewish Agency, stating that the White Paper violated the BALFOUR DECLARATION and the PALESTINE MANDATE. The opposition Conservative Party joined the fray by decrying both the language and recommendations contained in the White Paper. Faced with pressure from both the Zionists and the Conservatives, Prime Minister MacDonald addressed the furor in the February 1931 MacDonald Letter. In the letter, denounced by the Arabs as the "Black Letter," MacDonald backed away from the White Paper, with the result that the Hope-Simpson Commission's findings did not alter British policy in Palestine.

Philip Mattar

Human Rights

The history of the Palestinians has been linked historically with the emergence of human rights as an issue in world politics. It was in 1948—the year that roughly half of all the world's Palestinians became refugees from their homes—that the United Nations General Assembly adopted the Universal Declaration of Human Rights, the most authoritative statement of international human rights standards. This achievement was a landmark in advancing the human rights principle that the way a government treated people subject to its authority was a matter of international, and not just domestic, concern.

Two decades later, Israel's occupation of the WEST BANK and the GAZA STRIP coincided with the early days of the international independent human rights movement. During the next quarter-century, and especially during the INTIFADA, Israel's treatment of Palestinians became one of the best-documented human rights issues anywhere in the world thanks to the monitoring efforts of Palestinian, Israeli, and international human rights organizations; journalists (especially the outspoken Israeli press); Western governments; and various U.N. agencies (including the Special Committee to Investigate Israeli Practices Affecting the Human Rights of the Population of the Occupied Territories, created by the General Assembly in 1968). The account contained in this entry reflects the relative abundance of information about human rights in the Israeli Occupied Territories compared to other phases of Palestinian history.

Internationally recognized human rights are set forth in a variety of treaties and legal instruments. They can be classified into sometimes overlapping categories, among them civil and political rights (for example, the right to free expression and to fair trial), economic and social rights (such as the right to the highest attainable standards of health and the right to education), and collective rights (such as the right to political self-determination). The parallel legal regime of humanitarian law addresses the obligations of belligerent parties in their treatment of noncombatants during war and military occupations. Humanitarian law, notably the Fourth GENEVA CONVENTION of August 12, 1949, addresses the treatment of civilians under military occupation. In the view of virtually the entire international community, the Fourth Geneva Convention has been applicable to Israeli military rule over the Gaza Strip and the West Bank since 1967, despite Israel's refusal to accept its de jure applicability.

The violation of two universally recognized rights lies at the root of the plight of the Palestinian people: (1) the right to self-determination, including the right enshrined in Article 1 of the International Covenant on Civil and Political Rights, to "freely determine their political status and freely pursue their economic, social and cultural development," and (2) the right to return to one's country.

International law provides no exact formula specifying how two basic rights should be implemented in the case of the Palestinians: whether, for example, self-determination requires statehood (although the U.N. General Assembly has passed resolutions affirming that it does); as for the right to return, jurists disagree on whether international law grants refugees a right to return to specific homes and land and on whether the right to "return" is inherited by the children of refugees who were born in another country. Actualization of this right is complicated further by the fact that the "country" from which the 1948 refugees fled is today a different country, namely, Israel. What is clear is that the nonsatisfaction of the basic rights of return and self-determination continues to define the plight of the Palestinian people.

Most Palestinian refugees fall into one of three categories: (1) those who fled or were forced out of what became Israel as a result of the 1948 war, (2) those who fled or were forced out of the West Bank and Gaza Strip during the 1967 war, and (3) those who, since 1967, lost their right to reside in the West Bank or the Gaza Strip as a result of Israel's refusal to renew their residency permits. Together, the Palestinian population consisting of these groups and their descendants—not counting those who emigrated for economic reasons—exceeds that of Palestinians who reside in what was Mandatory Palestine (Israel, the West Bank, and the Gaza Strip).

Since 1948, Palestinians have suffered massive violations of civil, political, social, and economic rights, both in the land of the former PALESTINE MANDATE (1922–48) and in the countries of the diaspora. Only a minority of Palestinians today reside in places where their right to engage in peaceful political expression and association is not in some way circumscribed.

1948–1967 After the ARAB-ISRAELI WAR OF 1948, Palestinians residing in the state of Israel were subject to military rule and the provisions of the 1945 British Defense (emergency) regulations. The Israeli military authorities who were responsible for Palestinian towns and villages imposed regular curfews, restricted travel, placed individuals in administrative detention, and banned certain nationalist newspapers and associations, notably the political party al-Ard.

The lifting of military rule over Israel's Palestinian population in 1966 helped to strengthen legal protection of the rights of Israeli Palestinians. However, they continued to face discrimination in the allocation of state funds for education, housing, employment, and social services. In addition, the expropriation of land for public use continued to affect the Palestinian community disproportionately.

Jordan's King Abdullah, and later his grandson, King Husayn, exercised control over the Palestinians living in the West Bank, which Jordan annexed in 1950. Restrictions on political activity on both the East Bank and the West Bank fell heavily on Palestinians, who tended to be more politically engaged than Jordan's non-Palestinian population. The Amman-based authorities invoked emergency and martial laws to crack down on unrest and opposition activity in the West Bank. The Communist Party and certain other parties were outlawed and their members jailed. Jerusalem-based Palestinian newspapers were pressured to restrain their nationalist line. Tight restrictions on foreign travel were employed as a means of applying political pressure on individuals. Demonstrations were often put down by force, with resulting casualties.

The Israeli Occupation Israel's occupation of the West Bank and the Gaza Strip ushered in a new era for Palestinians. On the West Bank and Gaza Strip, the Israeli military government employed harsh measures to suppress political activity that it saw as endangering Israeli security. No political parties were permitted; meetings and demonstrations could not take place without prior approval of the military authorities. Books and publications could not be sold or imported without prior authorization, and many books with a nationalist theme were censored. Newspapers were occasionally suspended for violating the requirement to submit articles to prior censorship; other publications were permanently closed on the grounds that they were affiliated with illegal movements. The Palestinian flag was banned. Youths risked jail terms for wearing T-shirts with the flag's red, green, white, and black colors.

Human rights abuses soared during the INTIFADA, when Israeli authorities employed harsh measures to suppress mass demonstrations, rock throwing, and other forms of resistance. These included severe beatings by soldiers of suspected rock throwers and demonstrators, and sometimes of innocent bystanders, especially during the first year of the Intifada. For a time, beatings appeared to be administered as a matter of official policy: Minister of Defense Yitzhak Rabin announced in the second month of the Intifada, January 1988, that riots would be quelled by the use of "force, might and beatings." Despite subsequent denials and clarifications by Israeli officials, soldiers continued to beat Palestinians in formal or de facto custody with little risk of facing punishment by their superiors.

Israeli security forces killed over 1,200 Palestinians between December 1987 and the end of 1995. Of those killed, more than 260 were younger than sixteen years of age. The persistent and inappropriate use of live ammunition by soldiers against unarmed demonstrators was a main cause of these deaths and of the more than 100,000 Palestinian injuries that occurred during the same period. The use of excessive force was reinforced by Israel's lack of political will to investigate and punish soldiers suspected of using their weapons in violation of their standing orders. Soldiers also engaged in numerous acts of wanton property damage when carrying out arrests and searches. Israel Defense Force undercover units assigned to tracking down suspected activists shot dead well over 100 Palestinians, often making no effort to arrest them before using deadly force.

At the peak of the Intifada, the number of West Bank and Gaza Palestinians held in Israeli jails on charges or accusations of politically motivated activity reached approximately 14,000, or nearly 1 per 100 residents. This figure exceeded that recorded at the time for any country in the world that released such data. In response to the explosion of the prison population, Israel rapidly built tent detention camps. By far the largest was Ketziot, located in the Negev desert inside Israel, known for its harsh and decidedly substandard conditions. In 1991, Ketziot's population exceeded 7,000.

From 1988 until 1993, over 100,000 Palestinians were detained and jailed, and roughly 4,000 to 6,000 men and women were placed under interrogation each year, the majority of them subjected to some form of ill treatment or torture. Several men died while under Israeli interrogation during this period, as a result of either torture or medical neglect.

During the 1990s, Israeli interrogation methods came under increasing international and domestic scrutiny. The United Nations Committee against Torture in 1997 and again in 1998 rejected Israel's contentions that its practices did not amount to torture. In 1998, Israel's Supreme Court agreed for the first time to hear arguments regarding the legality of interrogation methods under Israeli law.

Israeli settlers harassed and opened fire on Palestinians on many occasions during the Intifada. Israeli settlers killed over 100 Palestinians between 1988 and 1995, including 29 worshipers machine-gunned by a settler in a mosque in HEBRON in February 1994. Provocations and vandalism by settlers and their use of disproportionate force in response to Palestinian stone and bottle throwing were encouraged by the lax response of Israel's law-enforcement authorities and courts to such attacks.

The deportation of Palestinians, a clear-cut violation of the Fourth Geneva Convention, has been one of the most contested weapons used by Israel against suspected political activists. Deportations have prompted the adoption of more critical U.N. Security Council resolutions than any other Israeli abuse. Between 1967 and 1987, Israel deported over 1,000 Palestinians. In the first five years of the Intifada, another 66 suspected activists were deported. In December 1992, Israeli authorities carried out the largest single deportation, rounding up and expelling 415 suspected Islamist activists in Lebanon in response to the killing of 6 members of the Israeli security forces. After strong international protests, Israel agreed to allow the phased return of the deportees within one year, instead of the two years announced by the government at the start of the operation.

Collective punishments, prohibited by the Fourth Geneva Convention, were imposed on Palestinians in various forms: for example, Palestinian family homes were demolished or sealed if one family member was suspected of having carried out fatal attacks on Israelis. Over 400 Palestinian homes were razed as a punitive measure between December 1987 and March 1996; a somewhat greater number were partially demolished or sealed shut, either partially or entirely. The Israeli authorities claimed that such demolitions were effective in deterring attacks. Hundreds of additional Palestinian homes were demolished not because they were threats to Israeli security but rather because they had allegedly been built without the required permits, which are notoriously difficult for Palestinian homeowners to obtain from Israeli authorities.

Collective punishments were often imposed not only on families but on entire villages or sometimes on the entire population under occupation. Villages were banned from travel as punishment for the political activism of some of their residents, and schools and universities were shut by military order for extended periods. In 1988, all six Palestinian universities were shut on the grounds that they were centers of Intifada activities; they did not begin to reopen until 1990. All West Bank primary and secondary schools were closed by military order during much of the first eighteen months of the Intifada, and shut sporadically thereafter.

Curfews, often ordered in response to violent demonstrations, were maintained for prolonged periods, with little regard for the food and healthcare needs of the confined population. For a full month during the GULF CRISIS, 1990–1991, Israeli authorities confined 1.7 million Palestinians to their homes, completely shutting down the Palestinian economy and education system and turning day-to-day life into an ordeal.

In 1989, Israeli authorities began to implement a permit system to control Palestinian entry from the West Bank and Gaza Strip into Israel and annexed east Jerusalem. This policy was tightened progressively over the next several years, largely in response to attacks inside Israel committed by Palestinians. The system developed into a highly restrictive policy preventing large numbers of Palestinians from traveling not only into Israel but also between the Gaza Strip and the West Bank, into annexed East Jerusalem, and even between sections of the West Bank, since north-south trips required traversing Jerusalem. Entry permits were denied by Israeli military officials without providing applicants with either a justification or an opportunity for a court hearing. Many of those denied permits had no security record.

On many occasions, Israel imposed "closures," invalidating permits and preventing the entire population of the Gaza Strip and/or West Bank from entering or traveling across Israel. These closures were imposed in response not only to attacks on Israelis but also on certain Jewish holidays and, notably, during the Gulf war. The Closure Policy was tightened further in 1996, with adverse impact on health care, employment, higher education, and family life.

The permit system is only the most salient of a range of permissions that Palestinians are required to obtain from Israeli authorities in order to conduct their day-to-day lives. Their requests are routinely reviewed by the General Security Service (the Israeli secret police) and are handled in an arbitrary and inefficient manner that the Israeli human rights group B'Tselem has characterized as "bureaucratic harassment." Although less flagrant than a beating or a detention, this form of abuse affects nearly all Palestinians living under occupation.

The Intifada saw the flourishing of human rights monitoring in the Occupied Territories. During this period, independent Palestinian associations and lawyers emerged as the most sophisticated, professional, and active human rights community in the Arab world. Leading organizations included AL-HAQ (Ramallah), the Palestine Human Rights Information Center (Jerusalem), the Mandela Institute (Ramallah), and the Gaza Center for Rights and Law. Israeli and international organizations also contributed to documenting the nature and extent of abuses committed under the occupation. With the establishment of Palestinian partial self-rule in the West Bank and Gaza Strip in 1994, a human rights ombudsman body was created with the consent of PALESTINE LIBERATION ORGANIZATION (PLO) chairman YASIR ARAFAT. Called the Palestinian Independent Commission for the Rights of the Citizen, the agency received complaints from Palestinians against the PALESTINIAN

AUTHORITY, visited Palestinian-run prisons, and investigated deaths in detention and other possible abuses. Its first high commissioner was HANAN MIKHA'IL ASHRAWI, who was replaced in 1995 by a Gaza psychiatrist, EYAD EL SARRAJ.

The Diaspora The governments of Arab countries generally treated Palestinian refugees no better than they treated their own citizens, and often worse. For example, Palestinians living in Syria enjoyed no more freedom to join political groups of their choosing or to speak out against the policies of President Hafiz al-Asad than did his Syrian subjects. Scores of Palestinians, from both Syria and Lebanon, were being held in Syrian jails in 1990, most of them—like their fellow Syrian political prisoners—without charge or trial. Many were subjected to torture during interrogation. On the other hand, Syria, unlike Lebanon and Egypt, granted equal rights for Palestinians to health care, free education, employment, and property ownership.

The more than 350,000 Palestinians residing in Lebanon, especially those residing in refugee camps, have suffered grievous abuses at the hands of various parties. Christian Phalangist militia massacred hundreds of Palestinian civilians at Tall Za'tar refugee camp in 1976 and in the SABRA AND SHATILA MASSACRE in 1982, to name just two such incidents. The Israeli army, ostensibly responding to armed attacks and shelling by groups based in Lebanon, launched air, land, and sea assaults and bombardments notable for their disproportionate scale and their disregard of civilian life. Noncombatants accounted for most of the tens of thousands of Lebanese and Palestinians killed over the course of major Israeli operations in Lebanon in 1978 (code-named "Operation Litani"), 1982 ("Operation Peace for Galilee"), 1993 ("Operation Accountability"), and 1996 ("Operation Grapes of Wrath"). Palestinian civilians were also caught in the cross fire between Syrian troops and their allies who did battle with Palestinian factions. With the intervention in 1976 of Syrian troops on the side of some Christian forces, Syria became complicit in the abuses committed against Palestinian civilians by certain militias. It also committed some of its own, including the detention without charge of scores of Palestinians and their transfer to Syrian prisons.

In no Middle Eastern country except Jordan have Palestinian refugees as a group, or their descendants, been granted some form of citizenship. Whatever the political origins of this policy, it has made Palestinians particularly vulnerable to deprivation of their rights. In Lebanon, Palestinians do not have the right to travel or to work; they must obtain special permits to go abroad and return and to hold a job, and they are barred from numerous professions.

In Kuwait, hundreds of thousands of Palestinians are permitted to work. However, their lack of citizenship puts them at the mercy of Kuwait's Foreign Residents Act, which gives the government wide discretion to deport non-Kuwaiti nationals, even those who hold valid residence permits. After Kuwait's liberation from Iraqi occupation in 1991, the Palestinian community shrank to a tiny fraction of its preinvasion size of 350,000 to 400,000 when the government refused to allow most Palestinians who had fled during the Iraqi occupation to return, and then expelled most of those who had remained.

In 1995, the government of Libya summarily expelled several hundred Palestinian residents, in a self-described effort by the Libyan leader, Mu'ammar Qadhdhafi, to expose the hollowness of the Palestinian self-rule agreement. Some were later permitted to return.

Abuses by Palestinians Palestinians have been associated with human rights not only as victims but as victimizers. Beginning in the 1960s, the Palestine Liberation Organization and some of its constituent groups launched "military operations" aimed at civilian rather than military targets, thereby violating a fundamental principle of humanitarian law. Victims included hundreds of Israeli and non-Israeli civilians, killed mostly on Israeli soil but elsewhere as well. Militant Islamist movements, such as HAMAS, continued to target Israeli civilians as well as soldiers in the 1990s after this tactic had been repudiated by the PLO.

In south Lebanon during the 1970s, with the emergence of a de facto Palestinian state within a state, PLO fighters participated in the factional conflicts that escalated into the Lebanese civil war. Like the other factions, PLO fighters often engaged in lawless behavior toward civilians, particularly Christian and Shi'ite villagers.

Between 1988 and 1995, Palestinian activists assassinated over 800 Palestinians in the West Bank and Gaza Strip who were purportedly suspected of collaboration with the Israeli authorities. These assassinations amounted to summary punishment, often carried out after the torture of the suspect and without a fair trial. Many observers stated that at least some suspects were either targeted in error or for reasons other than suspected collaboration. The Israeli Ministry of Defense stated that of those killed, only 35 to 40 percent were employed by the government or were in some other way connected to a branch of the Israeli administration.

In 1994, the Palestinian Authority began to govern portions of the West Bank and Gaza Strip. The early years of Palestinian self-rule proved to be troubling in human rights terms. The patterns of Israeli abuse described here continued in those areas where Israel's defense forces continued to exercise direct rule over Palestinians. In addition, Israel continued to restrict the rights of Palestinians no longer under its direct rule through its tight controls over the movement of persons and goods.

Despite pledges by Chairman Yasir Arafat and other officials of the Palestinian Authority to respect international human rights standards, patterns of arbitrary arrests, torture, unfair trials in state security courts, press censorship, and other abuses emerged. Attacks carried out by Palestinians on Israeli targets were routinely followed by roundups by Palestinian security forces of hundreds of suspected opponents of the peace process, who were held for weeks and often months without charge. The first five years of self-rule witnessed at least twenty-one known deaths of Palestinians while in custody. The multiplication of internal security agencies and their often intimidating conduct created an atmosphere in which many Palestinians feared reprisals for speaking critically of Arafat's rule. The continuing refusal by Arafat to ratify the Basic Law, passed by the PALESTINIAN LEGISLATIVE COUNCIL in 1997, left Palestinians living under self-rule without any clear statement of their rights.

Eric Goldstein, with research assistance from Steven Rothman

BIBLIOGRAPHY

Electronic Sources:

Amnesty International (www.amnesty.org)

B'Tselem/The Israeli Center for Information on Human Rights in the Occupied Territories (www.btselem.org)

Human Rights Watch (www.hrw.org)

Palestinian Center for Human Rights (pchrgaza.com)

United States Department of State (www.gov/www/global/human_rights)

Printed Sources:

Cohen, Ester Rosalind. *Human Rights in the Israeli-Occupied Territories: 1969–1982.* Manchester, England: Manchester University Press, 1985.

Kretzmer, David. *The Legal Status of the Arabs in Israel.* Tel Aviv: International Center for Peace in the Middle East, 1987.

Peleg, Ilan. *Human Rights in the West Bank and Gaza: Legacy and Politics.* Syracuse, N.Y.: Syracuse University Press, 1995.

Shehadeh, Raja. *Occupiers' Law: Israel and the West Bank.* Rev. ed. Washington, D.C.: Institute for Palestine Studies, 1998.

Husayn-McMahon Correspondence
1915–1916

Between July 14, 1915, and March 30, 1916, British High Commissioner in Egypt Sir Henry McMahon carried on a correspondence with al-Sharif Husayn bin Ali of Mecca outlining the terms under which the latter would support Britain by leading an Arab revolt against the Ottoman Empire during World War I. In the letters, not published until 1939, the Sharif sought independence for the Arabian regions of the empire. The regions he outlined included the Arab Peninsula (excluding Aden), Iraq, Palestine, Transjordan, and Syria up to Turkey in the north and Persia in the east. Husayn bin Ali also sought to restore the Islamic caliphate.

McMahon accepted the sharif's terms on October 24, 1915, but with several important exceptions. Britain wanted coastal areas along the Gulf region of the Arabian Peninsula, "where Britain is free to act without detriment to the interests of her ally France" placed under British supervision. McMahon also excluded "the districts of Mersina and Alexandretta and portions of Syria lying to the west of the districts of Damascus, Homs, Hama and Aleppo" in Syria.

The Arabs concluded that Britain thus accepted Arabia, northern Iraq, central Syria, and Palestine (considered southern and not western Syria) as the Arab regions that would become independent. Accordingly, they launched the Arab revolt against the Ottomans in 1916. But Syria was given to the French after the war, and Britain promised to assist the Zionist movement in building a national home for the Jewish people in Palestine. British claims that McMahon's letters intended to exclude Palestine from the areas to be granted Arab independence did little to assuage the Arabs' feelings of betrayal.

Just which areas were promised independence has long been a source of controversy in large part because McMahon's pledges were deliberately vague and were part of a series of contradictory promises made to secure French, Arab, and Jewish support for Britain's war effort.

Philip Mattar

BIBLIOGRAPHY

Kedourie, Elie. *In the Anglo-Arab Labyrinth: The McMahon-Husayn Correspondence and Its Interpretations, 1914–1939.* Cambridge: Cambridge University Press, 1976.

Monroe, Elizabeth. *Britain's Moment in the Middle East 1915–1956.* Baltimore: Johns Hopkins University Press, 1963.

Smith, Charles D. "The Invention of a Tradition: The Question of Arab Acceptance of the Zionist Right to Palestine during World War I." *Journal of Palestine Studies* 22 (Winter 1993): 48–63.

al-Husayni, al-Hajj Amin

preeminent Palestinian leader during most of the Palestine Mandate
1895–1974 Jerusalem

Born in JERUSALEM, Amin al-Husayni (*hajj* is an honorific title) was a scion of one of the most prominent Palestinian Muslim families, who were landed notables and holders of religious office, such as mufti (Islamic legal expert). He studied in Cairo briefly at al-Azhar University and at the Dar al-Da'wa wa al-Irshad of Rashid Rida, the Muslim reformer and precursor of Arab nationalism, and at the Military Academy in Istanbul. He served in the Ottoman army in 1916, but his loyalty to the Ottoman Empire was shaken by the Turks' attempts to impose their language and culture on their Arab subjects. On returning to Palestine in 1916, he participated in the British-supported Arab revolt of 1916 against the Turks and worked for the establishment of an independent Arab nation. In 1918 he was elected president of al-Nadi al-Arabi (the ARAB CLUB), a literary and nationalist organization opposed to Zionist claims on Palestine. After participating in a violent anti-Zionist demonstration in 1920, he escaped to Damascus, where he worked for the short-lived Arab nationalist government of Emir (later King) Faysal. The first British HIGH COMMISSIONER FOR PALESTINE, Sir Herbert Samuel, pardoned him and appointed him in 1921 to succeed his brother as mufti of Jerusalem and, in January 1922, president of the SUPREME MUSLIM COUNCIL, set up to manage Muslim affairs. This gave him control over Muslim courts, schools, religious endowments (*awqaf*), and mosques, and an annual revenue of P£50,000. An avid nationalist, Amin in August 1922 joined in opposing the formation of the LEGISLATIVE COUNCIL proposed by Samuel. Palestinian leaders feared that acceptance of the council was tantamount to acceptance of the British PALESTINE MANDATE, incorporating Britain's support for the establishment of the Jewish "national home," which had been approved in July by the League of Nations. In addition, they did not find the council's composition or its powers fair. The council allotted 43 percent (ten of twenty-three) of the membership to the Palestinians even though they constituted 89 percent of the population, and it was not allowed to discuss political matters. When the council was rejected by the Palestinian leaders, Samuel proposed the ADVISORY COUNCIL, with a similar composition and mandate. It too was rejected.

The mufti's opposition was not significant in 1922 and 1923 because the political affairs of the Palestinian community were managed by the Palestine ARAB EXECUTIVE under the leadership of the former mayor of Jerusalem (1918–20), MUSA KAZIM AL-HUSAYNI. Al-Hajj Amin was too new to his jobs and too busy with religious matters during the early 1920s to become involved in political issues.

Rise to Leadership It was not until 1929 that the mufti became the preeminent political leader of the Palestinians. His rise coincided with the decline of the Arab Executive and with the perception that he had stood up to the Zionists during the WESTERN (WAILING) WALL DISTURBANCES, although there is no evidence to indicate that the mufti was involved in organizing and leading the outbreaks. The morning of August 23, 1929, he delivered a pacifying speech at the Haram al-Sharif (Islam's third holiest shrine) to a crowd that had heard a rumor that Jews were going to attack the Haram. After the sermon, he urged people to return to their villages and, in an effort to forestall trouble, sent word to the British police to increase quickly the number of units at the Haram. When the crowds came out of the Damascus gate, he tried to disperse them, and when the violence spread that afternoon, he issued an appeal for Arabs to be patient.

From 1929 to 1936, the mufti cooperated with the British while attempting to change British policy. He reassured Sir John Chancellor, the third high commissioner, in October 1929 that he considered himself as "one who was, in a sense, an officer of the State." Chancellor reported that the mufti promised to maintain order and to cooperate because he considered it his duty to do so. The mufti told Chancellor that the Arabs were amicably disposed toward Great Britain, both because of self-interest and because of their belief in Britain's tradition of justice. When a militant approached the mufti with an offer "to organize bands for a guerrilla campaign," Amin rejected the offer, stating that he was seeking a political solution instead.

The mufti's policies during this period were shaped by his willingness to negotiate and accept compromise solutions. He was involved in indirect negotiations with the British in September and October 1929, from which emerged a draft settlement providing for the establishment of a parliament in which Jews and Arabs would be proportionally represented; Palestine would remain under the authority of a British high commissioner, who would safeguard Zionist interests, including immigration. Whereas the mufti accepted the draft proposal, Zionist leaders rejected the plan because it would have confined Jews to a minority in Palestine.

It was the mufti, too, who dispatched the secretary of the SUPREME MUSLIM COUNCIL and the Palestine Arab Executive, JAMAL AL-HUSAYNI, to London in December 1929 to meet with the colonial secretary.

In the Passfield White Paper in October 1930, the British met Palestinian demands on immigration and land purchase, but this was the result of recommendations of the SHAW COMMISSION, (1930) and the HOPE-SIMPSON COMMISSION (1930) rather than the mufti's efforts. However, Zionist pressure on the minority government of Ramsay MacDonald forced the government to withdraw these concessions in the MacDonald letter of January 13, 1931. Partly in response to the letter, the mufti convened a General Islamic Congress in December 1931 to unite the Arabs and Muslims against the Zionists, and to make the British aware that their interests lay in the Muslim and Arab worlds rather than with the Zionists. The effect of the congress on the British was negligible.

Indeed, efforts by the mufti and his colleagues were largely unsuccessful. A general strike and demonstration against Jewish immigration, held by the executive in October 1933 while the mufti was out of the country, resulted in twenty-five deaths. Political parties were formed and private and public protests were held, but they were ineffective in halting immigration. In fact, Jewish immigration increased from 4,075 in 1931 to 61,854 in 1935, and the influx contributed to the worsening of the political situation.

In light of the deteriorating situation, why did the mufti maintain his dual policy of cooperation with the British and nonviolent opposition to the Zionists during two decades when the threat to Palestinian national existence was becoming more ominous? A number of fundamental reasons can be suggested.

First, the HUSAYNI FAMILY belonged to that patrician class of notables in whom defense of the political status quo and cooperation with the imperial power to guarantee stability were deeply ingrained. Al-Hajj Amin al-Husayni's statements to British officials and his actions indicate a constant awareness of his status as an official appointed by the Palestine government. Should he challenge British discretionary power, he would lose the posts of mufti of Jerusalem and president of the Supreme Muslim Council.

Second, like others of his generation and despite his nationalist fervor, the mufti admired what he perceived as British fairness and sense of justice—personal qualities of British officials such as Herbert Samuel and Arthur Wauchope, with whom he met frequently. He repeatedly affirmed his allegiance to the British rulers on the basis of these personal qualities, even while he was aware that British officials, regardless of their personal preferences, were the instruments of what he considered an unjust policy.

Third, he believed that the British were too strong for the Palestinians to oppose successfully and that, in any case, their presence in Palestine would be transitory, as it appeared to be in EGYPT, Iraq, and Transjordan. Finally, he thought that

Britain's pro-Zionist policy would change when the British realized that their interests lay with the Muslim and Arab countries and not with the Zionists. He further believed that the Palestinians, with the help of fellow Muslims and Arabs, might influence the British through petitions, delegations to London, protests, and demonstrations. He opposed political violence or preparation for revolutionary resistance. On the contrary, he surreptitiously assisted the British authorities in defusing violent outbreaks. In short, he affirmed, by word and deed, a preference for nonviolent methods.

Exile Years Although the mufti since 1922 had managed to pacify his two masters, the British with loyalty pledges and cooperation and the Palestinians with religious and political rhetoric, in April 1936 he was forced by the militant anti-British public mood to choose between them. When violence flared on April 15–19, 1936, and a general strike began to spread, the public urged him to assume the leadership of the strike against Jewish immigration and land purchase and for the establishment of a national government. Although he resisted for ten crucial days, the mufti, who had a propensity for inertia and timidity, gave way to political action. Had he remained on the sidelines with nothing to show but a record of failure, he would have been overtaken by events and by more militant leaders. By accepting the leadership of the newly organized ARAB HIGHER COMMITTEE, which comprised all five political parties, he became the leader of the general strike. This decision was the beginning of the end of his policy of cooperation, and of British confidence in him.

Several events over the next few years served to radicalize him further. In 1937 the British submitted a plan to partition Palestine. The mufti, as did most Palestinians, rejected partition and continued to lead the revolt. The British decided to strip him of his offices and arrest him for his part in the violence. He escaped to Lebanon and continued to lead what was becoming a general revolt from Beirut and Damascus.

By the summer of 1938, many cities, including Jerusalem, had been taken by the rebels, but it was only a matter of time before Britain, whose forces outnumbered the Palestinians' ten to one, crushed the revolt. The Palestinians paid a high price for the 1936–1939 revolt in terms of their economy, social fabric, and military and political structure. Of a population of 960,000, 3,074 Palestinians were killed, according to conservative British estimate. In addition, 110 were hanged, and 6,000 were incarcerated in 1939 alone.

The mufti grew bitter and uncompromising in matters vital to the future of his people. He rejected the 1939 White Paper, even though its terms—restricting Jewish immigration to 75,000 during five years, limiting land sales, and planning for an independent Palestine with an Arab two-to-one majority in ten years—were obviously favorable to the Palestinians. In the final months of 1939, al-Hajj Amin left Lebanon for Iraq, where he sought to encourage a pan-Arab challenge to British control over Iraq and, ultimately, over Palestine. The prospect of a revolt in Iraq alarmed three parties with vital interests in Palestine: the Zionists, the Hashemites, and the British. Pinhas Rutenberg, a Zionist representative who a year earlier had been counseled by Emir Abdullah of Transjordan to eliminate the mufti, traveled to London to urge the British to assassinate the Palestinian leader. The Foreign Office found the proposal impractical. Yet, five months later the mufti became such a grave threat to British interests that Winston Churchill, the new British prime minister, approved his assassination. Members of the Irgun, a revisionist Zionist underground movement, were flown to Iraq to carry out the assassination with the help of the British army but failed to kill the mufti, who escaped to Iran.

The mufti then fled to the Axis countries, first to Italy, then to Germany. He claimed that he had nowhere else to go because the British had put a price on his head. He cooperated with the Germans and conducted propaganda for them, believing that they would help the Arabs expel the British once Germany defeated Britain in the Middle East. His association with the Germans tainted his career and limited his freedom of action during the critical period between 1946 and 1948.

He returned to the Arab world in 1946 with the aim of continuing the struggle against the Zionists and establishing a Palestine state. However, he totally misjudged the balance of forces between the Arabs and the Zionists. When the United Nations General Assembly passed the partition resolution on November 29, 1947, the mufti organized a general strike and political violence.

Assessment Though astute, charismatic, incorruptible, and ascetic in his dedication to his people, the mufti pursued policies that were a failure and unwittingly contributed to the dispossession of the Palestinians. During the first period, even though he understood the ominous threat of ZIONISM to Palestinian national existence, the mufti cooperated with the British Mandatory government of Palestine and rejected methods of national self-defense at a time when such methods might have helped his cause. He opposed the Balfour policy, but through such ineffective methods as petitions, delegations, and strikes. He succeeded in uniting Muslim and Christian Palestinians and helped awaken the national spirit but did not mobilize the Palestinian masses for action. Notwithstanding Palestinian and Zionist claims to the contrary, he did not lead a single act of political violence between 1920 and 1936.

The four instances of political violence in 1920, 1921, 1929, and 1933 were not revolts. They were localized, spontaneous riots that resulted in no sustained policy changes by the British. On the other side, the Zionists had organized a quasi-government, together with a labor union, an educational system, a national press, and, most importantly, a military force. The Zionists increased their land holdings from 650,000 *dunums* (162,500 acres) in 1919 to 1,410,000 *dunums* (352,500 acres) in 1936, while their population grew from about 50,000 in 1917 to 384,000 in 1936. They sought to become the majority and to establish a state, and wrote and said so repeatedly. Most Zionist leaders, including Chaim Weizmann and later David Ben-Gurion, considered the Palestinians treacherous, inclined to blackmail, fanatic, and inferior. They planned, in numerous secret meetings, to expel the "natives" or otherwise dominate them. Although these plans were not known at the time, the mufti and a number of Palestinians anticipated some form of expulsion and domination. Nevertheless, he was mostly passive or used only ineffectual methods of resistance. In short, despite the growth of the *yishuv*, the Jewish community in Palestine, he did not galvanize his people to defend themselves against what appeared to be inevitable domination. A massive revolt in 1929 combined with Palestinian compromise proposals concerning the LEGISLATIVE COUNCIL (that is, self-government under British rule) might possibly have resulted in a change in British policy that would have constrained the growth of the *yishuv*. It was perhaps the last opportunity for the Palestinians to alter dramatically their political future in Palestine.

It was not until 1936 that the mufti participated in a revolt, and only after he was forced to choose between his British employers and his people. By then it was too late. The Jewish community was far too powerful. Conversely, the British had lost their discretionary power in Palestine and had become umpires adjudicating between the two communities. Moreover, they could not easily retreat from their promises to the Jews. The most they could offer the Palestinians was partition plan of the PEEL COMMISSION, 1937, which was rejected by the mufti.

The Peel proposal provided no viable opportunity for Palestinians. Under this proposal, the Jews, who owned 5.6 percent of the land, were to receive 40 percent of the most fertile region, from which most Palestinians would be transferred; the British would keep the third holiest city of Islam, Jerusalem; and Transjordan's Emir Abdullah would receive the rest. In other words, the Palestinians were being asked to give their blessing to the dismemberment of Palestine among three outside parties: the Zionists from Eastern Europe, the British, and Abdullah, who was from the Hijaz (Arabian Peninsula).

The first real opportunity came in 1939, in the form of the 1939 White Paper proposal, which severely restricted Jewish immigration and land transfer and promised an independent Palestine in ten years on the basis of a Palestinian majority of two to one. It came close to what the mufti and other leaders had been asking for. To have rejected such a policy was shortsighted at a time when the Palestinian community was, as a result of British suppression of the Arab revolt, depleted of leadership, institutional structures, arms, and even the will to fight on, and when the Zionist side was growing in strength.

The mufti returned to the Middle East in 1946 to find that the struggle for Palestine was jeopardized by Abdullah's ambition, supported by the British, and by rivalry and disunity within the ARAB LEAGUE, which now took responsibility for Palestine. Zionist military, diplomatic, and financial strength had been considerably increased. Yet the mufti, who was consulted by the Arab League, rejected almost every offer to send Palestinians to testify to commissions or to meet with the British and the Zionists. He rejected all proposals—those calling for trusteeship, cantonization, and partition—that did not offer Palestinians an Arab Palestine. The Palestinians' legal and moral case was a strong one: they had occupied Palestine for at least 1,300 years, and Palestinians were in the majority and owned or had customary rights over most of the land. But the mufti misjudged the balance of forces and was unrealistic in not adjusting his demands to the realities on the ground. The demands he made between 1946 and 1948 were almost identical to the position he maintained a quarter of a century before.

The 1947 partition resolution was the last opportunity for the mufti. The resolution was less attractive than the Peel partition in terms of territory. The Zionists were to get 55 percent of Palestine, when they owned only 7 percent. Most Palestinians and Arabs viewed it as a great injustice and hardly a fair compromise. Yet, because the resolution held out the prospect of an independent Palestinian state in part of Palestine, it represented the only hope of preventing Abdullah and the Zionists from taking over the whole of the country between them, as they had agreed to do prior to the 1948 war.

In short, the mufti's cooperation during the first two decades of British rule and his rejectionism during the last decade unwittingly contributed to the ultimate defeat of the Palestinians. Some other leader, armed with a modern education, knowledge of world affairs, a sense of strategy and timing, and, above all, realism might have taken better advantage of opportunities.

Yet the overriding factors that frustrated Palestinian nationalism have less to do with the policies and actions of a single leader than with the balance of forces. It was British policy, backed by British military might and by international (that is, European) support for the British Mandate and for Zionist colonization, that was primarily responsible for providing the yishuv time to grow, through immigration and land purchases, and time to establish quasi-governmental and military institutions. The Palestinians were a weak, underdeveloped agrarian society and never a match for the British army nor, after 1939, for the Zionist forces. Their power to influence the destiny of Palestine was secondary to that of the three other parties with strategic and territorial interests in Palestine: the British, the Zionists, and, to a lesser extent, the Hashemites.

Philip Mattar

BIBLIOGRAPHY

Elpeleg, Zvi. *The Grand Mufti: Haj Amin al-Hussaini, Founder of the Palestinian National Movement.* London: Frank Cass, 1973.

Al-Husayni, Muhammad Amin. *Haqa'iq an Qadiyyat Filastin,* 2d ed. Cairo: Dar al-Kitab al-Arabi bi-Misr 1957.

Khadduri, Majid. "The Traditional (Idealist) School—the Extremist: Al-Hajj Amin al-Husayni." In *Arab Contemporaries: The Role of Personalities in Politics.* Baltimore: Johns Hopkins University Press, 1973.

Mattar, Philip. *The Mufti of Jerusalem: Al-Hajj Amin Al-Husayni and the Palestinian National Movement.* Rev. ed. New York: Columbia University Press, 1992.

——. "Response to Rafael Medoff." *The Journal of Israeli History* 18(1) (1997): 105–112.

Medoff, Rafael. "The Mufti's Nazi Years Reexamined." *The Journal of Israeli History* 17(3) (1996): 317–333.

Porath, Yehoshua. "Al-Haj Amin al-Husayni, Mufti of Jerusalem: His Rise to Power and Consolidation of His Position." *Asian and African Studies* 7 (1971): 212–256.

Schechtman, Joseph B. *The Mufti and the Führer: The Rise and Fall of Haj Amin el-Husseini.* New York: Thomas Yoseloff, 1965.

al-Husayni Family

Descendants of the Prophet Muhammad, the Husayni family occupied numerous positions in the Islamic establishment of JERUSALEM from Ottoman times, including the posts of mufti (expert on Islamic law), and *naqib al-ashraf* (denoting lineage from the Prophet), as well as owning extensive landholdings and holding many secular positions in the Ottoman and Mandate civil administration. During the PALESTINE MANDATE, leading figures of the Husayni family exerted tremendous influence over the Palestinian national movement and generally dominated it, particularly Musa Kazim, al-Hajj Muhammad Amin, and Jamal.

Abd al-Qadir (1908–1948; Jerusalem; guerrilla leader) Son of MUSA KAZIM AL-HUSAYNI, Abd al-Qadir studied at the American University in Cairo and was awarded a B.A. in 1932. During 1936–1938, he was a charismatic guerrilla leader in the Jerusalem area during the Arab Revolt. Exiled from Palestine, he fought with the Iraqi army against the British in 1941.

As violence escalated in Palestine during the late 1940s, he organized Palestinian guerrillas from his home in Cairo. He himself entered Palestine in late 1947 to lead the Army of the Holy Struggle (Jaysh al-Jihad al-Muqaddis) of AL-HAJJ AMIN AL-HUSAYNI against Zionist forces. He was killed fighting with Palmach forces during the Battle of al-Qastal, near Jerusalem.

Ishaq Musa (1903–1990; academic, writer) Ishaq Musa received a Ph.D. at the University of London and later taught at The American University of Beirut, the American University in Cairo, and the Institute for Arab Studies of the ARAB LEAGUE. Ishaq Musa also worked as an education officer in the Mandatory government in Palestine beginning in 1934.

Ishaq Musa was also a member of the Islamic Studies Committee at al-Azhar University in Cairo and the Baghdad Academy. In 1945, he helped establish the Arab Cultural Committee in Palestine. One of Palestine's most prominent writers, he produced *The Moslem Brethren: The Greatest of Modern Islamic Movements* and *Mudhakkarat Dajaja* (The Memoirs of a chicken).

Munif (1899–1983; newspaper editor) Munif edited the newspaper *al-Jami'a al-Arabiyya,* which supported the Husayni faction in Palestinian politics in the 1930s.

Sa'id (1878–1945; Politician) Sa'id studied at the Alliance Israelite Universelle school in Jerusalem, where he learned Hebrew and became acquainted with the aims of ZIONISM. Subsequently, he served with the Ottoman government as a censor of Hebrew-language newspapers in Palestine.

Sa'id served as mayor of Jerusalem from 1902 to 1906. Sympathetic to the Ottoman decentralists, he was elected in 1908 and 1914 as a representative of the Jerusalem district to the Ottoman Parliament, where he argued against Zionism. In the spring of 1920, he briefly served as foreign minister for the Arab government of Faysal bin Husayn in Damascus. After his return to Palestine, he effectively avoided politics.

Hind (social service leader) Hind has been actively involved with the Arab Children's House in East Jerusalem, a children's charitable organization established in 1948 to care for and educate young people whose parents died in the first Arab–Israeli war.

Michael R. Fischbach

al-Husayni, Faysal

political leader
1940– Baghdad

Son of Abd al-Qadir al-Husayni and grandnephew of AL-HAJJ AMIN AL-HUSAYNI, Faysal al-Husayni took an early interest in Palestinian politics, opening offices for the PALESTINE LIBERATION ORGANIZATION (PLO) in East Jerusalem shortly after its establishment in 1964. He received military training in Syria in 1966–1967 and organized PALESTINE LIBERATION ARMY fighters in Lebanon in June 1967 at the behest of the Syrians.

Back in Jerusalem in the summer of 1967, Husayni met with YASIR ARAFAT, then in hiding in the WEST BANK, and became associated with FATAH. He was arrested by the Israelis in October 1967 for arms possession and served one year in prison. Beginning in 1979, he founded and chaired the ARAB STUDIES SOCIETY. Husayni also became a member of the Supreme Muslim Council in the West Bank, in 1982. He was jailed on several occasions by Israeli occupation authorities.

By the mid-1980s, Husayni had risen to become the senior representative of Fatah in the West Bank. However, he also stood at the pinnacle of an emerging cadre of leaders in the Occupied Territories who, although loyal to PLO groups in exile, nonetheless represented local interests and were attuned to local needs. These figures directly faced the harsh realities of Israeli occupation on a daily basis, leading some of them to begin exploring the possibilities of a negotiated settlement that could ameliorate the population's suffering while securing important national objectives. Husayni emerged as one such "moderate," acknowledging Israel's presence as a fact and viewing negotiations as the only solution to Palestinians' problems.

The PLO recognized the inherent threat to its leadership represented by indigenous activists like Husayni. The Likud government was also aware of Husayni's potential for undermining the role of the PLO, a group with whom Israel long had refused to negotiate directly, and consequently initiated a series of secret meetings with Husayni during the summer of 1987. The subject of the talks were plans for Palestinian autonomy in the Occupied Territories. Eventually, each side was prepared to discuss arrangements with its respective leadership—in Husayni's case, with the PLO in Tunisia. However, these talks collapsed when Israeli prime minister Shamir backed away from them and ordered Husayni arrested.

Released in June 1988, Husayni began working on a document that would establish the basis for Palestinian independence within the territories. His stature as the leading PLO activist in the West Bank was confirmed in April 1991, when he headed a team of Palestinians who met for talks with U.S. secretary of state James Baker as part of an American peace initiative. The United States, like Israel, refused to negotiate directly with the PLO but was well aware that Husayni was in contact with the PLO and was speaking for it.

As holder of a Jerusalem identity card and a person openly identified with the PLO, Husayni was not permitted by Israel to sit on the joint Jordanian–Palestinian delegation at the MADRID PEACE CONFERENCE, 1991. However, he headed the seven-member steering committee that directed the delegation during the conference and the subsequent 1991–1993 Israeli–Palestinian negotiations in consultation with the PLO.

Husayni was unaware of the secret Israel–PLO talks in Oslo until their revelation in August 1993. Initially, a political crisis emerged, centering on the question of who should be the guiding force in negotiations: the PLO in exile or the indigenous leadership of the Occupied Territories who had been participating in official talks since 1991.

Subsequently, Husayni was appointed to the PLO's Higher Committee for the Peace Talks in Tunis in August 1993. He later returned to the Occupied Territories to mobilize support for the agreement. In April 1996, he was appointed to the PLO's executive committee.

Husayni continued to work on behalf of the agreement and the new PALESTINIAN AUTHORITY (PA) that emerged from it. In 1995, he was involved in secret preparatory talks between the PA and Israel regarding the future of Jerusalem. In May 1996, he was appointed PA minister for Jerusalem affairs.

Michael R. Fischbach

al-Husayni, Jamal
politician, diplomat
1892–1982

Jamal al-Husayni attended ST. GEORGE'S SCHOOL and the American University of Beirut. He played an important role in the Palestine national movement during the British PALESTINE MANDATE. He was secretary of the ARAB EXECUTIVE, a committee of politicians who led the Palestinian national struggle in the 1920s and early 1930s, and secretary of the SUPREME MUSLIM COUNCIL, a body formed in January 1922 to handle Muslim community affairs in Palestine. In 1935 al-Husayni was elected president of the newly formed Palestine ARAB PARTY (PAP), a HUSAYNI FAMILY–led political body whose leaders fought for Palestinian independence primarily through nonviolent pressure tactics against the British government; he became the editor of the new party's organ, *al-Liwa'.* One year later al-Husayni became a member of the ARAB HIGHER COMMITTEE (AHC). Initially formed to coordinate the local committees of the 1936 strike, the committee sought to act as a united front against the British-supported Jewish National Home policy. A seasoned politician, and a relative and close aide to the mufti (expert on Islamic law) of Jerusalem, AL-HAJJ AMIN AL-HUSAYNI, al-Husayni participated as member (1930) and as president (1939) of the Palestinian delegations dispatched to the LONDON CONFERENCE to discuss Palestinian national demands with the British government. He also served on the AHC's delegations to the ARAB LEAGUE and the United Nations. The mufti escaped to Lebanon in the fall of 1937 after the British crackdown on Palestinian political leaders and activists; there al-Husayni later joined him, and from there he fled to Iraq, then to Iran, where he was arrested by the British in 1942 and detained in Southern Rhodesia, now Zimbabwe. While in exile, al-Husayni tried to revive the AHC within Palestine, but his efforts bore no fruit, partly because the British imposed a ban on political organizing and partly also because the leaders of other political organizations, including the ISTIQLAL PARTY and the NASHASHIBI FAMILY faction, found no interest in supporting the AHC. After the disaster of 1948, al-Husayni served as foreign minister for the short-lived ALL-PALESTINE GOVERNMENT, formed by the AHC in Gaza in September 1948. He later settled in Saudi Arabia, where he was an adviser to King Sa'ud between 1953 and 1964. Al-Husayni died in Beirut and was buried there.

Muhammad Muslih

al-Husayni, Musa Kazim

politician

b. 1850? 1853?–1934 Jerusalem

The son of Salim al-Husayni, Ottoman mayor of JERUSALEM toward the end of the nineteenth century, Musa Kazim al-Husayni pursued his studies in Istanbul and later served in numerous government positions throughout the Ottoman Empire from 1892 and 1913 in such countries as Syria, Transjordan, and Yemen.

Musa Kazim was appointed mayor of Jerusalem by British military authorities in March 1918 on the death of his brother, Husayn, who had been mayor from 1909 to 1918. The British later removed him in April 1920 in the wake of the *al-Nabi* Musa political disturbances because of a speech he had given during the unrest in support of the independent government of Faysal bin Husayn in Damascus.

Musa Kazim was a major figure in the Muslim–Christian Associations that began to emerge in 1918. He was later elected president of the ARAB EXECUTIVE, formed by the third of the ARAB CONGRESSES, which had been held in HAIFA in December 1920. As head of the Arab Executive, Musa Kazim thus became the most significant Palestinian nationalist figure during the early 1920s.

One of the main ways in which Musa Kazim articulated Palestinian demands was through meetings with British officials, including in London. In August 1921, he headed the first of four delegations that traveled to London between 1921 and 1930 for talks with colonial authorities. At the first conference, the delegation argued for abolition of the BALFOUR DECLARATION, suspension of Zionist immigration, and establishment of a unitary, independent, and representative government in Palestine that would eventually become federated with surrounding Arab states. In keeping with this final demand, he later led the struggle against a British proposal to convene a legislative council in Palestine that would include Zionist representatives.

Musa Kazim represented an older generation of Palestinian leaders who came of age during the Ottoman Empire and were therefore accustomed to such genteel political methods as petitions, conferences, and delegations. By the time of the fourth delegation Musa Kazim led to London in March 1930, his influence and that of the Arab Executive were already waning as younger and more radical Palestinians grew weary of his lack of success in pressuring Britain to respond to Palestinian nationalist demands. Among these impatient compatriots was his relative, AL-HAJJ AMIN AL-HUSAYNI, head of the SUPREME MUSLIM COUNCIL beginning in 1922. Growing factionalism also weakened the position of Musa Kazim and the Arab Executive, especially that between al-Hajj Amin's councilists and the opposition led by the NASHASHIBI FAMILY.

Musa Kazim was beaten during an October 1933 demonstration in JAFFA protesting Zionist immigration that was broken up by British police. He never fully recovered and died five months later.

By the time of his death, Musa Kazim's influence had faded. The Arab Executive, representing his generation's style of leadership and political tactics, fell apart at that time.

Michael R. Fischbach

al-Hut, Shafiq

politician, writer

1932– Jaffa

After secondary studies in JAFFA, Shafiq al-Hut fled Palestine for Beirut along with his family in April 1948 during the ARAB-ISRAELI WAR OF 1948. He obtained a B.A. in biology from the American University of Beirut in 1953 and later worked as an educator, and, from 1958 as a journalist for several Lebanese periodicals.

Al-Hut was a senior figure in the Palestinian resistance movement. He established the Palestine Liberation Front in 1961. In 1964 he attended the first meeting of the PALESTINE NATIONAL COUNCIL, which gave rise to the PALESTINE LIBERATION ORGANIZATION (PLO), and in 1965 he was appointed the PLO's representative to Lebanon in Beirut—an important PLO post that he would hold until 1993. He and others came into increasing conflict with PLO chairman AHMAD SHUQAYRI, a conflict that ended with Shuqayri's resignation in

December 1967. In the mid-1960s, al-Hut was a leading figure in a short-lived Palestinian resistance group associated with the pan-Arab Movement of Arab Nationalists called the Heroes of the Return. He was later friendly with FATAH although never a member of it. He eventually rose to hold positions on the PLO central committee and executive committee.

In August 1993, al-Hut resigned from his PLO positions to protest the OSLO AGREEMENTS reached between the PLO and Israel.

Michael R. Fischbach

I

Inshas Conference
1946

In May 1946, Egypt's King Faruq called for the world's first summit meeting of Arab heads of state to consider the report of the ANGLO-AMERICAN COMMISSION, 1945–1948, and other issues of importance to Egypt and the Arab world. The meeting convened on May 29, 1946, at Faruq's estate in Inshas, Egypt, though not all Arab rulers attended personally. The summit eventually rejected the commission's report, calling instead for creation of an independent state in Palestine, a halt to Jewish immigration, and retention of regulations limiting Jewish land purchases.

In early June 1946, the council of the ARAB LEAGUE met at the BLUDAN CONFERENCE in Syria to forge a more detailed proposal regarding Palestine.

Michael R. Fischbach

Institute for Palestine Studies

Established in Beirut in December 1963, the Institute for Palestine Studies became the first and only research and publishing center of its kind and one of the most important research centers of any kind throughout the Arab world. The institute was created as an endowed, nonprofit institution that would maintain no party, government, or other political affiliation. In addition to its main offices in Beirut, it has branches in Paris and Washington. In September 1994, the institute opened the Institute for Jerusalem Studies branch in East Jerusalem.

One of the institute's main activities has been collecting books, documents, and manuscripts for its libraries and archives. The institute's library in Beirut houses the Arab world's largest collection dealing with the Palestinians, ZIONISM, and the ARAB-ISRAELI CONFLICT. In addition to over 40,000 volumes, the library contains journals, newspapers, documents, maps, and photographs.

A second goal of the institute has been to promote a scholarly interest in modern Hebrew. The first Arab organization to show such an interest, the institute opened a school for teaching of Hebrew and the translation and publication of Hebrew-language documents, including reports of the World Zionist Congress and Israeli Knesset debates.

A third goal of the institute over the years has been the production of scholarly material, some of it copublished, such as the series with Columbia University Press. One of the main ways the institute has produced quality scholarship on topics relating to the Palestine problem has been through its journals: three quarterlies, *Journal of Palestine Studies* (published by the University of California Press), *Revue d'études palestiniennes,* and *Majallat al-Dirasat al-Filastiniyya.* The institute has also published over 450 books in English, French, and Arabic, including studies of political and socioeconomic life in pre-1948 Palestine. It also took the lead in the mid-1960s in making available documents relating to the Palestinians. This annual series was eventually issued in both Arabic and English. The institute also publishes U.N. documents relating to the Arab-Israeli question.

A more recent activity of the institute has been the study of the peaceful resolution of the Arab–Israeli conflict. With the help of a grant received from the Ford Foundation in the wake of the OSLO agreements, the institute began holding seminars and publishing policy papers on "final status" issues to be negotiated by Israel and the PALESTINE LIBERATION ORGANIZATION. Such issues include Palestinian REFUGEES, JERUSALEM, Jewish settlements, security and borders, WATER rights, and sovereignty.

Michael R. Fischbach

Intifada
1987–1992

The Road to Rebellion Despite predictions during 1986 and the first part of 1987 that Palestinians in the WEST BANK and the GAZA STRIP were exhausted and would soon lose the will to resist Israel's continuing drive into these territories, spontaneous and widespread protest demonstrations erupted in December 1987, showing that Palestinians under occupation had in fact lost neither the political will nor the capacity to challenge Israeli government policies. In the months that followed, protests and acts of civil disobedience coalesced into a coordinated uprising embracing virtually all sectors of Palestinian society, a rebellion that some compared to the revolt of 1936–1939, which soon became known as the *intifada,* literally translated as the "shaking off."

The spark that ignited the Intifada was an accident at the Israeli military checkpoint at the north end of the Gaza Strip. On December 8, 1987, an Israel Defense Force (IDF) tank transport vehicle crashed into a line of cars and vans filled with men from Gaza who were returning home after a day of work in Israel, killing four and seriously injuring seven others. The funerals that night for three of the deceased quickly turned into a massive demonstration. Fueled by rumors that the crash had been deliberate, allegedly in retaliation for the stabbing of an Israeli businessman in Gaza the day before, thousands of Gaza residents went into the streets to express their grief and demonstrate their anger.

Protests continued the next day and produced direct confrontations with the Israeli military, with IDF forces killing one young Palestinian and wounding many others as they fired tear gas and live ammunition into the crowds in an attempt to restore order. There were additional demonstrations in the days that followed, and protests soon spread to the West Bank as well, expanding in both scope and intensity to a degree that caught most Israelis and even many Palestinians by surprise.

Two different sets of pressures were impinging on the Occupied Territories at this time, producing a determination among Palestinians to sustain the Intifada. The first and more important was the result of conditions in the Occupied Territories, including those specifically related to the Israeli occupation. The second resulted from events on the international scene that deepened the sense of isolation among Palestinians in the territories.

Conditions in the territories were shaped by the harsh Israeli occupation, whose practices were routinely described as an "Iron Fist" during the years leading up to the Intifada. One major objective of the Israeli government was the suppression of Palestinian nationalism. Thus, for example, occupation authorities frequently closed Palestinian universities on the grounds that students were engaging in political activities and organizing opposition to the occupation, rather than pursuing their studies. Other Israeli actions included deportations, press and school text censorship, and such forms of collective punishment as curfews and the demolition of homes.

The government in Jerusalem also sought to lay a foundation for Israel's permanent retention of the West Bank and Gaza. This effort included the confiscation of Palestinian LAND; the control of WATER resources, to which Palestinian agriculturists were given only limited access; and a variety of other policies linking the economic and administrative infrastructure of the territories to Israel. This collection of policies, often referred to as "creating facts on the ground," was designed not only to prevent movement toward Palestinian self-determination but also to create a network of Jewish interests in the West Bank and Gaza that would make it difficult for any future Israeli government to consider relinquishing these territories, even in exchange for peace.

The most important aspect of Israel's effort to create facts in the Occupied Territories, and thereby to ensure that the West Bank and Gaza would remain under Israeli control, was the expanding presence of Jewish settlers in these areas. Whereas there had been 2,000 to 3,000 Jews living in the territories a decade earlier, on the eve of the Intifada there were roughly 63,000 Jews living in some 130 Israeli settlements in the West Bank and another 2,500 or so residing in seventeen communities in Gaza. This was in addition to developments in East Jerusalem, where Jewish neighborhoods and satellite communities ringing the city to the north, east, and south continued to expand. Further, beyond the long-term implications of the growing settler presence, some Jewish settlers engaged in provocative actions that intensified the day-to-day abuses associated with occupation. Settlers frequently sought to harass and intimidate Palestinians, apparently believing that at least grudging acceptance of the occupation could be produced by displays of determination and power.

The result of these occupation policies is described in the following terms by the Palestinian-American scholar Emile Nakhleh, who visited the area in mid-1987, several months before the beginning of the Intifada. Writing of the situation in Gaza in particular, he reported in the Spring of 1988 in the *Middle East Journal* that the area "resembles a pressure-cooker ready to explode. In this 'forgotten corner of Palestine,' one witnesses overcrowding, poverty, hatred, violence, oppression, poor sanitation, anger, frustration, drugs and crime. The Palestinian population is daily becoming more resentful and rebellious. The military occupation responds by becoming more insecure and oppressive."

Although less important than conditions inside the West Bank and Gaza, developments on the international scene also contributed to Palestinian anger during the period preceding the Intifada. One such development was a move by the United States to close the PALESTINE LIBERATION ORGANIZATION (PLO) information office in Washington, D.C. This effort was challenged by Arab-American and other organizations on constitutional grounds, but the challenge was turned down by a U.S. federal judge early in December 1987.

Perhaps the most disturbing development on the international scene from the Palestinian point of view was the failure of an emergency summit meeting of Arab states, convened in Amman, Jordan, in mid-November 1987, to devote any serious attention to the situation in the Occupied Territories or to the Palestinian struggle more generally. The meeting gave priority to the seven-year-old Iran-Iraq war, as Jordan's king, Husayn, and a number of other Arab leaders indicated that they now considered Iran, rather than ISRAEL, to be the most serious threat to the Arab world. In addition, YASIR ARAFAT was treated with disdain by Husayn and other Arab leaders at the Amman summit, reinforcing the feeling of many in the West Bank and Gaza that they had been betrayed and abandoned.

These developments in the territories and on the international scene help to explain why the accident at the Gaza checkpoint produced disturbances of such intensity, and why these disturbances soon coalesced into a general uprising. On the one hand, Palestinians in the territories embraced the idea of *sumud,* or steadfastness, reflecting a determination to remain on their land and resist occupation despite Israel's superior power. On the other, especially after the emergency Arab summit in Amman, these Palestinians concluded that only their own efforts offered any hope for a change in the status quo. As expressed in the *UFSI Staff Reports, 1988–89* by a knowledgeable American scholar, Ann Mosley Lesch, who visited the Occupied Territories at this time, "Palestinians felt they had reached a dead end . . . [there was a] sense of total blockage internally combined with the sense that no help could be expected from the outside."

The Profile of the Intifada Palestinians displayed a new assertiveness as protest activities expanded in both scope and intensity during the weeks that followed. As one analyst, Daoud Kuttab, concluded, in *al-Fajr* on May 31, 1988, with respect to the continuing unrest in Gaza, expressions of anger and grief "seemed more determined and fierce" than in the past.

In the West Bank, demonstrations began in the refugee camps but soon spread to major towns and thereafter to the roughly 500 villages of the region. Demonstrators chanted slogans, raised Palestinian flags, and threw stones at the Israeli soldiers who sought to disperse them. Young Palestinians also frequently threw stones at Israeli vehicles, including those of Israeli civilians traveling in the Occupied Territories. Makeshift roadblocks constructed of rocks, or occasionally of burning tires, were erected in a further attempt to disrupt normal circulation, especially at the entrances to villages or in urban neighborhoods that the Palestinians sought to prevent Israelis from entering.

The uprising was also clearly visible in East Jerusalem, a development that further differentiated the Intifada from earlier protests of Israeli occupation. Palestinian residents of the city declared a general strike that suspended commercial life on an unprecedented scale, and they maintained their refusal to resume business as usual as the uprising continued, reopening shops only for the conduct of essential business and only for short periods prescribed by the emerging leadership of the Intifada.

Equally significant, in contrast to earlier efforts at resistance, East Jerusalem became the scene of numerous clashes between Israeli police and Palestinian demonstrators, some of which were violent. As acknowledged by the Middle East correspondent Yehuda Litani of the *Jerusalem Post,* "The latest Palestinian achievement is the redivision of United Jerusalem." Writing when the Intifada was barely two months old, in February 1988, he noted that "both Jews and Arabs living here know that for the last few weeks the city has been practically redivided. Many ask themselves if it was ever united."

Although their actions met with only limited success, Israeli leaders undertook a series of measures in an effort to suppress the Intifada. In addition to detaining and deporting suspected activists, Israeli authorities attempted to suppress protest demonstrations, when necessary dispersing demonstrators by firing live ammunition. They also pursued a policy that the government described as "force, might, and beatings," under which IDF troops used clubs to subdue protesters. Moreover, Israeli soldiers were encouraged to break the bones of young Palestinians, to break either their legs, so they would be unable to run, or their hands, so they would be prevented from throwing stones.

These and other acts of violence by the IDF resulted in a steadily mounting number of Palestinian fatalities. Although figures vary from one source to another, at least 284 Palestinians were killed during the first year of the Intifada, and by the end of the fourth year, in December 1991, the number of Palestinian deaths had reached 802. This does not include Palestinians killed by settlers and other Israeli civilians, the number of whom was approximately 40 by December 1991. Almost all of these deaths were the result of shootings, although a small number were caused by beatings and other violent acts. Most of the Palestinians killed were young: 22 percent below the age of seventeen and fully 78 percent below the age of twenty-five, according to B'Tselem, an Israeli human rights organization.

This violence was in addition to the severe administrative measures that Israel employed in its effort to contain the Intifada. Measures of collective punishment, including those used previously, were particularly important. For example, universities were closed until further notice by occupation authorities, although several institutions managed to hold some classes in secret. Many primary and secondary schools were also shut for prolonged periods. At least 423 Palestinian homes in the West Bank and Gaza were blown up by Israeli troops during the first four years of the Intifada, usually because it was believed that a young man who lived there had thrown stones at Israeli soldiers, and another 277 homes were sealed to prevent use by their owners. In addition, entire communities were placed under curfew, sometimes for a week or more, preventing people from leaving their homes at any time, even to obtain food. As with other forms of collective punishment, these actions fell heavily not only on protesters but also on men and women who had not taken part in protest-related activities.

Finally, thousands of Palestinians were arrested and detained, some for prolonged periods and the overwhelming majority without trial. In February 1989, the Israeli defense minister, Yitzhak Rabin, announced that 22,000 Palestinians had been detained since the beginning of the Intifada and that 6,200 were being held in administrative detention at that time. By December 1991, at least 90,000 Palestinians had been arrested, many for offenses as minor or poorly defined as "acts likely to disturb the peace" or "failure to prevent another individual from committing an offense." In addition to these arrests, 15,000 Palestinians had been placed in administrative detention, not for any offense but as a precaution because they *might* be a security threat in the future. Under military regulations in force in the Occupied Territories, an individual suspected of illegal activities, such as membership in an organization supporting the uprising, could be held without trial for a period up to six months, and administrative detention was also renewable without trial at the end of this period.

Despite these efforts to suppress the Intifada, or at least to contain it, the uprising retained its vigor throughout 1988, 1989, and most of 1990. There were scores of strikes, which severely disrupted the routines of work, commerce, transportation, and other public activities in the Occupied Territories. There were also hundreds of demonstrations and other protest activities, some, as noted, leading to violent confrontations between Israelis and Palestinians. Virtually no sector of Palestinian society was untouched by the Intifada, which to a large extent succeeded in sweeping away whatever degree of normalcy had characterized life under occupation.

Organization and Leadership Emerging patterns of organization and leadership are among the factors that differentiate the Intifada from prior Palestinian efforts to arrest Israel's drive into the West Bank and Gaza. The political institutions that crystallized to give direction to the Intifada and to deal with the problems and opportunities it created included both popular neighborhood committees and a unified national leadership structure. Furthermore, at both the local level and beyond, the new institutions were to a large extent led by the members of a new political generation.

Local committees established themselves in neighborhoods and villages throughout the West Bank and Gaza, their purpose not only to carry forward the Intifada but also to assume responsibility for a wide range of social services. Initially, these committees were formed in response to the hardships caused by the uprising. For example, it was necessary to organize the delivery of food to refugee camps and villages placed under curfew and to arrange for the care of Palestinians wounded in clashes with Israeli security forces. The local committees soon expanded their work, however, assuming responsibility for a wide range of basic needs, such as the provision of health and hygiene-related services and the establishment of educational programs after schools were closed by Israeli authorities.

Although these local committees to an important extent emerged spontaneously during the first weeks of the Intifada, Palestinian scholars point out that they also built on the mass-based organizations that had developed during the 1980s. These included trade UNIONS, women's societies, youth groups, labor committees, and other groups that had expanded their activities in response to Israel's crackdown on nationalist institutions. Further, the Intifada committees carried forward the populist ideology of these organizations. They emphasized mobilization of the more marginal and disadvantaged sectors of Palestinian society and also, in the judgment of some analysts, often explicitly rejected what they saw as the more "elitist and nepotistic" aspects of the traditional nationalist movement in the West Bank and Gaza. This populist orientation was also reflected in an emphasis on self-reliance and self-sufficiency, with disengagement from Israel an important associated goal. For example, there were calls for Palestinians to boycott Israeli products, to refuse to pay taxes, and to avoid working in Israel.

The work of the local committees soon fostered the emergence of a broader leadership structure. Known as the Unified National Leadership of the Uprising (UNLU), this structure remained underground; its members were unknown and it communicated through leaflets, *bayanat,* that were printed in secret and distributed at night throughout the Occupied Territories. At the time the first leaflet appeared, on January 4, 1988, the UNLU was composed only of individuals from the West Bank, although within a few weeks the command structure had been expanded to include representatives from the Gaza Strip as well. As its name implied, the UNLU was broadly representative and inclusive of the diverse political tendencies found among Palestinians in the Occupied Territories. It incorporated individuals identified with FATAH, the POPULAR FRONT FOR THE LIBERATION OF PALESTINE, the DEMOCRATIC FRONT FOR THE LIBERATION OF PALESTINE, the PALESTINE COMMUNIST PARTY, and ISLAMIC JIHAD.

In addition, the most important members of the UNLU were not professionals, academics, journalists, or other well-known veterans of Palestinian political life, but individuals who did not belong to the traditional elite and who, in at least some cases, were young enough to remember only vaguely, if at all, the period before Israel's occupation of the West Bank and Gaza. As in the case of popular committees, the emergence of the Unified National Leadership thus reflected the changing patterns of political recruitment that had taken shape in recent years and contributed to the ascendancy of a new political generation.

As noted, the UNLU shunned any visible political role; it operated covertly, concealed the identity of its members, and issued instructions through leaflets printed and distributed in secret. Leaving interviews and press conferences to others, the UNLU addressed itself to Palestinians under occupation rather than to the international community. Its goal was not to generate sympathy and support for the Palestinian cause but to give direction and organization to the uprising in the territories.

The leaflets through which the UNLU communicated were initially printed at a single location, but Israeli interference soon required that the process be decentralized. Thus, beginning sometime early in 1988, it became the practice to transmit the centrally composed text of each new directive by telephone, fax, or other means to many different locations for retyping, duplication, and distribution by local committees operating independently of one another. Leaflets were numbered and dated, and during the first half of 1988 they appeared at a rate of about one every week and a half, so that twenty-four had been issued by the end of August 1988. After this period, they continued to appear with regularity but at somewhat greater intervals.

The directives issued by the UNLU produced a shift from spontaneous to organized resistance as the Intifada progressed. The leaflets, usually two pages in length and giving instructions for the coming week or two weeks, announced commercial strikes, transportation strikes, mass demonstrations, and other protest activities. Most of the directives issued by the UNLU advocated civil disobedience and called for action of a nonviolent character. According to an analysis prepared by the Palestine Center for the Study of Non-Violence in Jerusalem, dated May 31, 1988, "In the seventeen leaflets to date, 163 actions were called, the overwhelming majority of which were specifically nonviolent in nature. Of the twenty-seven methods of demonstrating resistance to the occupation, twenty-six of these are non-violent" (Assaily 1988).

Although support from the UNLU appears to have been broad and compliance with its directives largely voluntary, youthful activists sometimes played a role in ensuring that instructions transmitted through the leaflets were fully implemented. For example, Palestinian teenagers in the larger towns and in many other communities organized themselves into small "strike forces," patrolling their neighborhoods in order to ensure that businesses closed when so directed and that other instructions were obeyed.

The outbreak of the Intifada and the emergence of a local leadership structure provided both challenges and opportunities for the PLO. The Palestinian organization, which commanded the allegiance of people in the territories but whose leaders and tactics had become the focus of considerable criticism, was taken by surprise by the events of December 1987. The PLO thus sat on the sidelines during the initial phase of the uprising. A productive partnership between "inside" and "outside" Palestinians soon developed, however. Although the UNLU continued to have wide discretion with respect to decisions about the day-to-day course of the Intifada, the PLO retained responsibility for broad political themes. The UNLU also issued its directives in the name of the PLO.

Islamic groups played a role in mobilizing participation in the Intifada, giving the uprising yet another of its distinctive features. ISLAMIC JIHAD, a clandestine society that seems to have come into existence in 1985 or 1986, helped to organize the first protest demonstrations of the Intifada, especially in Gaza. Appealing to the population in the name of Islam, activists employed mosques for organizational purposes and broadcast appeals and instructions from loudspeakers that normally call the faithful to prayer. Although represented on the UNLU, Islamic Jihad also published a number of its own leaflets.

A new Islamic organization, Harakat al-Muqawama al-Islamiyya, the Islamic Resistance Movement, was established in January 1988 and quickly became the most important Islamic group working to sustain and amplify the Intifada. Known by its acronym, HAMAS, the Arabic word for "zeal" or "ardor," the organization officially described itself as a wing of the Muslim Brotherhood in Palestine. Hamas's ability to seize the mantle of Islamic activism was due, in part, to its ties to the Muslim Brotherhood, which had always been the largest and most influential Islamic organization in the Occupied Territories. Hamas also assumed a more important role in the Intifada after an Israeli crackdown in the spring of 1988 that brought about the arrest or deportation of key Islamic Jihad leaders. By the second half of 1988, leaflets distributed by

Hamas were appearing with approximately the same frequency as those of the UNLU.

At least three sets of factors help to explain the emergence of this ISLAMIC FUNDAMENTALISM in the Intifada. First, developments in Palestine were influenced by the growth of Islamic movements in other Middle Eastern countries. This includes Iran, where Islamic activists had mounted a successful revolution and taken power; Lebanon, where Muslim political groups had for several years been fighting Israeli forces occupying the southern part of the country; and Egypt and Jordan, where local chapters of the Muslim Brotherhood had long been important political parties. Second, Islamic movements in Palestine gained popularity and influence by delivering services to the local population and by building a strong grassroots organization. Muslim groups operated schools and clinics in many towns, villages, and refugee camps, for example. These groups were also active on university campuses and in many high schools. Finally, the Islamic influence was abetted by the Israeli government's opposition to an exchange of land for peace. The PLO had for several years shown an interest in such a solution to the conflict, only to appear impotent in the face of Israel's continuing intransigence. With declining confidence in the diplomatic option toward which the PLO had been moving, many in the Occupied Territories concluded that the rejectionism advocated by militant Islam offered the best chance of securing Palestinian rights.

Propelled forward by popular determination, with organization and direction provided by both the Unified National Leadership of the Uprising and by Islamic movements, most notably Hamas, the Intifada emerged as a full-blown rebellion early in 1988 and increased in scope and intensity throughout the remainder of the year and during 1989 and 1990 as well.

The Impact in Israel Palestinians under occupation were seeking by the rebellion that began in December 1987 to send a message to both Israel and the world. The content of this message was made explicit in conversations between Palestinian intellectuals and the large number of foreign journalists who flocked to the region to report on the spreading disturbances: "We exist and have political rights, and there will be no peace until these rights are recognized." The message also proclaimed that occupation was unacceptable and that continued Israeli rule over the West Bank and Gaza, even with provisions for Palestinian autonomy, would be met with continuing resistance.

The Israeli public was the most important audience to which the Palestinians' message was addressed. In the debates and discussions inside Israel, then–Prime Minister Yitzhak Shamir and others on the Right of the political spectrum had frequently argued that most Palestinians in the Occupied Territories were actually content to live under Israeli rule. Asserting that the material conditions of most inhabitants of the West Bank and Gaza had improved significantly since 1967, these leaders told the Israeli public that only a few radicals affiliated with the PLO were calling for Israeli withdrawal. The vast majority of the Palestinian population, by contrast, was said to recognize and appreciate the improvement in their standard of living that had accompanied occupation, and accordingly to seek no more than local or regional autonomy under continuing Israeli rule.

A related Israeli government claim was that continuing occupation of the West Bank and Gaza was without significant costs from the Israeli point of view. Shamir and like-minded Israelis insisted that the Palestinian inhabitants of these territories did not constitute a serious obstacle to development in accordance with the design of Israelis committed to permanent retention of the West Bank and Gaza. Palestinian acquiescence, they asserted, meant there would be few burdens associated with the maintenance of order and little to prevent ordinary Israeli citizens from conducting themselves in the West Bank and Gaza as if they were in their own country.

The Intifada was intended to show these assertions to be myths in a way that could not be explained away by apologists for occupation. Palestinians sought to leave no room for doubt about their implacable opposition to occupation, and also to foster in Israel a recognition that the course charted by the country's leaders was a costly one, which was not in the interest of the Jewish state.

Moreover, evidence that the Palestinians' message was having an impact in Israel was offered by a significant change in the way that most Israelis looked at the West Bank and Gaza after December 1987, a change often described as the resurrection in Israeli political consciousness of the "Green

Line," the pre-1967 border separating Israel from its Arab neighbors. In the twenty years between the June war and the outbreak of the Intifada, those parts of the Green Line running between the West Bank and Gaza on the one hand and Israel on the other had become nearly invisible to many Israelis. The Intifada transformed that perception, however, leading most Israelis to regard the West Bank and Gaza as zones of insecurity that should be avoided as much as possible.

Although Israelis increasingly recognized that what they had been told about Palestinian political sentiments and the cost-free character of occupation was not correct, they did not necessarily conclude that their country should withdraw from the West Bank and Gaza and accommodate Palestinian nationalism. For example, some right-wing Israelis committed to the permanent exercise of Jewish sovereignty over the West Bank and Gaza began to think about removal of the Palestinians from these territories. Described as a policy of "transfer," this was a disturbing but nonetheless logical response to the Palestinian uprising from the perspective of those committed to territorial maximalism.

However, the Intifada also reinforced the views of those committed to territorial compromise. It gave new vigor to their arguments that it was not in Israel's interest to retain the West Bank and Gaza. Moreover, the Intifada led some Israelis to reexamine commonly held assumptions about the strategic importance of the Occupied Territories. For example, many IDF officers asserted that withdrawal from the West Bank and Gaza was acceptable from a military point of view, and some even argued that the territories had become a security burden. According to this analysis, the Intifada had transformed the IDF into a police force charged with keeping order in the Occupied Territories, undermining Israel's military preparedness as a result. More specifically, military operations in the West Bank and Gaza were said to have lowered morale, disrupted training, and undermined the IDF's organizational coherence, thereby making Israel weaker vis-à-vis Syria and other external challenges.

Yet another indication of the Intifada's impact on Israeli political and strategic thinking was a significant increase in support for negotiations with the PLO. In part, this was the result of a peace initiative launched by the PLO in 1988, and particularly the endorsement of a two-state solution to the Israeli-Palestinian conflict adopted at an emergency meeting of the PALESTINE NATIONAL COUNCIL in November 1988. More generally, however, as both Israeli and Palestinian analysts have pointed out, this diplomatic initiative had an impact on Israeli attitudes largely because it reinforced and amplified the challenge to the status quo put forward by the Intifada. In any event, in a significant departure from their pre-Intifada thinking, many in Israel began moving toward the conclusion that the Palestinian problem is the core of the ARAB-ISRAELI CONFLICT, and that in order to deal with this problem it would be necessary for Israel to negotiate with the PALESTINE LIBERATION ORGANIZATION.

Evidence of this movement is provided by opinion polls carried out in late 1988 and throughout 1989 and 1990 by the Leonard Davis Institute, which reported that more than half of the Israeli public was "in favor," or "definitely in favor," of talks with the PLO. Changing Israeli attitudes were also reflected in the statements of many politicians and intellectuals, including a few affiliated with parties of the Right, and in a number of public encounters between Israelis and PLO officials.

Loss of Coherence and Momentum The year between summer 1990 and summer 1991 saw attention in the Middle East shift from the Israeli-Palestinian conflict to the crisis in the Persian Gulf, beginning with Iraq's invasion of Kuwait on August 2, 1990, and followed, first, by diplomatic efforts to restore Kuwaiti sovereignty and then, early in 1991, by a massive United States–led military campaign to oust Iraq from Kuwait. Palestinians, as well as others, were affected by these developments. The PLO emerged from the GULF CRISIS, 1990–1991, in a weakened position, with elements of its leadership bitterly condemned by Gulf Arab governments for their alleged support of the Iraqi invasion of Kuwait. The loss of financial assistance from these governments also intensified the economic hardships of Palestinians living in the West Bank and Gaza.

Perhaps the most important aspect of the grim situation that prevailed in the Occupied Territories after the Gulf Crisis is the loss of direction that had come to characterize the Intifada. In the spring and summer of 1991, and throughout the remainder of the year, inhabitants of the West Bank and Gaza frequently complained about increasing disorganization and mounting pressures within their own community. Among the most important of their complaints: competition and in-fighting among rival political factions, rather than cooperation in the pursuit of common objectives; behavioral constraints enforced by one segment of the population on another, such as the harassment by Muslim activists of women who did not wear Islamic dress; and rising crime and delinquency, reflecting a breakdown of the social order and diminished respect for authority inside the Palestinian community.

Most Palestinians insisted that the origins of these problems were to be found in the conditions of occupation and in Israeli efforts to suppress the uprising. Nevertheless, many also acknowledged that elements within their own community had contributed to the Intifada's loss of direction, and to the fact that the uprising in the territories was in danger of becoming, or indeed had already become, more injurious to Palestinians themselves than to the Israelis who occupied their homeland.

The Intifada's loss of direction was also reflected in Palestinian-against-Palestinian violence—an especially troubling development. Much of this violence involved action taken against collaborators, especially those who had allegedly helped Israel to infiltrate Palestinian organizations or to identify and locate wanted activists. On April 1, 1991, for example, suspected collaborators were shot and killed by unknown assailants in Qalqilya and Gaza, and the next day another suspected collaborator was found dead in RAMALLAH. Killings of this sort began during the second year of the uprising and had resulted in approximately 450 Palestinian deaths by the end of the Intifada's fourth year.

Against this background, the Intifada not only lost its direction and coherence but for the most part came to an end in 1992. There continued to be sporadic acts of resistance to Israeli occupation, including strikes called by the UNLU and Hamas, which enabled some Palestinians to assert that the uprising was going forward. More accurate, however, is the analysis of the Palestinian sociologist Salim Tamari, who wrote in spring 1991 that the crisis in the Gulf had been associated with a turning point in the uprising, including "a fundamental break with its initial strategy and tactics." The vast majority of Palestinians remained committed to the Intifada and its political objectives, but many had nonetheless come to believe that the efficacy of its tactics had been depleted. Thus, Tamari concluded, "What people need today is a reprieve, a breathing space that allows them to rebuild their economy while waging a protracted political struggle of disengagement with Israel."

Despite this loss of coherence and momentum, the Intifada stands as a milestone in the history of the Palestinian resistance. Indeed, seen in historical perspective, the uprising emerges as a watershed event, contributing directly to a change of government in Israel and to the decision of the new Israeli government to seek a negotiated settlement with the Palestinians.

Coupled with the peace proposals put forward by the PLO in November 1988, the Intifada provided the stimulus for a series of Israeli, American, and Egyptian peace initiatives. None bore immediate fruit, principally because the Israeli government in power at the time remained firmly opposed to negotiations with the PLO and to any accommodation involving territorial compromise. This changed with the Israeli elections of June 1992, however, in which parties committed to an exchange of land for peace were given a mandate by the electorate. The 1992 balloting is sometimes described as the "Intifada election," and it is in the wake of this election that Israel entered into secret negotiations with the PLO. These negotiations and the September 1993 agreement to which they led almost certainly would not have come to pass had the uprising not forced a large number of Israelis to recognize the contradictions inherent in their country's occupation of the West Bank and Gaza, and to conclude, therefore, that it is in Israel's interest to seek peace on the basis of territorial compromise and an accomodation with Palestinian nationalism.

Mark Tessler

BIBLIOGRAPHY

Assaily, Nafez. "Intifada: Palestinian Nonviolent Protest—An Affirmation of Dignity and Freedom." report published by the Palestine Center for the Study of Non-Violence, May 31, 1988.

Brynan, Rex, ed. *Echoes of the Intifada: Regional Repercussions of the Palestinian Israeli Conflict.* Boulder, Colo. Westview Press, 1991.

Hunter, Robert F. *The Palestinian Uprising: A War by Other Means,* 2d ed. Berkeley: University of California Press, 1993.

Daoud Kuttab, in *Al-Fajr* (English-language edition), May 31, 1987.

Lesch, Ann Mosley. "The Palestinian Uprising: Causes and Consequences." *Universities Field Staff International Reports, Asia* 1 (1988–89).

Litani, Yehuda. *Jerusalem Post,* February 8, 1988.

Lochman, Zachary, and Joel Beinin, eds. *Intifada: The Palestinian Uprising Against Israeli Occupation.* Boston: South End Press, 1989.

Melman, Yossi and Dan Raviv. *Behind the Uprising: Israelis, Jordanians, and Palestinians.* New York: Greenwood Press, 1989.

Nakhleh Emile. "The West Bank and Gaza: Twenty Years Later." *The Middle East Journal* 42 (Spring 1988): 210.

Nasser, Jamal, and Roger Heacock, eds. *Intifada: Palestine at the Crossroads.* New York: Praeger Publishing, 1990.

Peretz, Don. *Intifada: The Palestinian Uprising.* Boulder, Colo.: Westview Press, 1990.

Schiff, Ze'ev, and Ehud Ya'ari. *Intifada: The Palestinian Uprising—Israel's Third Front.* New York: Simon & Schuster, 1990.

Tamari, Salim. "The Next Phase: Problems of Transition." In *Palestinian Assessments of the Gulf War and Its Aftermath.* Jerusalem: Palestinian Academic Society for the Study of International Affairs, 1991, p. 15.

al-Isa, Isa

journalist
1878–1950 Jaffa

After studies at the Syrian Protestant College (later called The American University of Beirut), Isa al-Isa and his cousin, Yusuf Da'ud al-Isa, established the newspaper *Filastin* in JAFFA in 1911. During the PALESTINE MANDATE, al-Isa and *Filastin* supported the "opposition" faction headed by the NASHASHIBI FAMILY.

Michael R. Fischbach

Islamic Fundamentalism

The emergence of Islamic fundamentalism among Palestinians, in both Palestine and the diaspora, and the rise of Islamic political groups in the Occupied Territories started in the late 1970s and coincided with an Islamic revival throughout the Arab world.

The rise of Islamic fundamentalism among Palestinians may be attributed to a number of factors. The first is the loss of Palestine in 1948. The establishment of a Jewish state in its place is perceived by Islamic fundamentalists as an encroachment on Muslim land. Israel is considered an alien body in the heart of the Arab and Muslim worlds, and a spearhead of Western hegemony.

The second factor is the 1967 defeat of the Arab states by Israel. This defeat and the subsequent Israeli occupation of the remainder of Palestine and other Arab land have forced Palestinians and other Arabs to acknowledge their weakness. Fundamentalists usually attribute this weakness to secularism and the failure to embrace Islam and apply its teachings.

Third is the Islamic revolution of 1979 in Iran. This is perhaps the most important factor in the rise of Islamic fundamentalism in general, and in Palestine in particular. The revolution restored confidence in Islam as a viable alternative to secularism and provided Muslims in other countries with a model to emulate.

The fourth factor is the decline of the PALESTINE LIBERATION ORGANIZATION (PLO) since the late 1970s. This decline has been a function of several setbacks suffered by the PLO, which prevented the organization from winning the independence for Palestine to which it had committed itself and that had inspired its widespread acceptance. The PLO's consequent evolution from ideological purity to political pragmatism created an ideological vacuum that was soon filled by Islam, the only available alternative.

Fifth is the Palestinian popular uprising of 1987, the INTIFADA. This, clearly, was the most important factor in the growth of Palestinian Islamic fundamentalism. The Intifada defined the content of Palestinian Islamic fundamentalism as nationalist and political, projecting it as a movement whose primary objectives, as illustrated by the charter of the Islamic Resistance Movement (HAMAS), were resistance to Israeli occupation and liberation of Palestine. The prominent and effective participation of the Islamic movement in the Intifada created significant popular support, and it emerged as a serious rival to the PLO, challenging its political program and contending with it for the leadership of the Palestinian society.

In both the Occupied Territories and the diaspora, there are three major Palestinian Muslim fundamentalist groups: Hamas, ISLAMIC JIHAD, and the Islamic Liberation Party. Hamas, which was formed in 1987, is a wing of the Muslim Brotherhood Society in Palestine; Islamic Jihad is a splinter group of the society. The Islamic Liberation Party, established in 1953, had suspended all activities from 1967 until after the Intifada, when the party resumed its activities, especially on university campuses, though only on a limited scale. Nevertheless, the Islamic Liberation Party has an insignificant impact on Palestinian politics.

Hamas is considered the most influential of the Palestinian fundamentalist groups. It is known for its extensive following, particularly compared to that of the other two groups, and for its military wing, Kata'ib Izz al-Din al-Qassam ("Izz al-Din al-Qassam Brigades"). The Islamic Jihad is narrowly based and more action-oriented than the other two groups, focusing on violent acts of resistance to Israeli occupation.

Both Hamas and the Islamic Jihad are led by a *majlis shura* (advisory council). The leaderships of both groups, in and out of Palestine, have been subjected to repeated imprisonment, deportation, and exile by the Israelis.

Since 1987, the fundamentalists have extended their control to numerous Palestinian social and educational institutions, as well as professional associations, student councils, welfare organizations, and charity associations in both Palestine and the diaspora. Their influence is also manifest in their increased political presence in society at large, especially at the campuses of Palestinian universities. The fundamentalists, especially the followers of Hamas, have developed a parallel social infrastructure of their own, including nursery schools, kindergartens, neighborhood libraries, and sports clubs. They also compete for the control of Palestinian civil organizations. Moreover, they enjoy significant influence in the *waqf* (Islamic endowment) institutions, although these are subject to official PALESTINIAN AUTHORITY control.

Whatever their differences, Palestinian Islamic groups are all labeled fundamentalist because they share certain objectives and tactics: primarily, the establishment of an Islamic state in Palestine, which would require the dismantling of Israel. However, fundamentalist groups differ in their approaches to realize this common objective.

Hamas, for example, is considered less militant than the revolutionary Islamic Jihad: whereas Shaykh AHMAD YASIN, the leader of Hamas, occasionally resorts to ambiguous statements for tactical reasons, his counterparts in the Islamic Jihad are categorical in their rejection of Israel's right to exist. The Islamic Jihad is also committed to changing the existing order in the Arab and Muslim worlds; the Islamic Liberation Party believes that the liberation of Palestine can be achieved only after the establishment of an Islamic state elsewhere, which will then proceed to liberate Palestine.

Until recently, Hamas and the Islamic Jihad were competitive and hostile groups. Their dispute was not doctrinal; rather, it sprang from different interpretations of religious doctrine as well as different readings of political reality. After the Intifada in 1987, however, differences between the two groups have narrowed and they have developed a similar political line regarding Palestine while embracing the same tactics for resisting Israeli occupation.

The relationship between the Palestinian Muslim fundamentalists and the PLO was characterized by a struggle for the leadership of the Palestinian people. As the PLO's influence declined, the fundamentalists became more vocal in their challenge to the PLO.

Palestinian Muslim fundamentalist groups maintain relations with other Islamic groups or countries, relations on which they rely for financial support in addition to local sources of funding. Hamas enjoys intimate links with the Muslim Brotherhood societies in Jordan and Egypt. Hamas and the Islamic Jihad are also supported by Islamic groups in other Arab countries, the United States, and Europe, and both organizations maintain good relations with Iran and Sudan.

The Palestinian Muslim fundamentalists have opposed the Palestinian–Israeli peace process, the Oslo Declaration of Principles of September 13, 1993, and subsequent Palestinian–Israeli agreements; they have also refused to participate in the Palestinian Authority, which was established in Gaza and Jericho.

In the aftermath of several suicide bombings carried out by members of Hamas and the Islamic Jihad inside Israel in 1996, which resulted in the deaths of scores of Israelis, the Palestinian Authority subjected the two movements to harsh measures, including a ban on their military wings, imprisonment of their leaders and members, and closure of several institutions belonging to them. If the peace process is stalemated, the influence and popularity of the Palestinian Muslim fundamentalists are likely to increase.

Ziad Abu-Amr

BIBLIOGRAPHY

Abu-Amr, Ziad. *Islamic Fundamentalism in the West Bank and Gaza: The Muslim Brotherhood and the Islamic Jihad.* Bloomington: Indiana University Press, 1994.

——. "Hamas: A Historical and Political Background." *Journal of Palestine Studies* (Summer) 1993.

al-Shaqaqi, Fathi. *Al-Khomeini: al-Hall al-Islami wa al-Badil* (Khomeini: The Islamic solution and alternative). Cairo: al-Mukhtar al-Islami, 1979.

Jarbawi, Ali. *Al-Intifada wa al-Qiyada al-Siyasiyya fi al-Diffa al-Gharbiyya wa Qita' Ghazza* (The Intifada and the political leadership in the West Bank and Gaza Strip). Beirut: Dar Abu Tali'a, 1989.

——. "Palestinian Elites in the Occupied Territories: Stability and Change Through the Intifada." In *Intifada: Palestine at the Crossroads,* ed. by Jamal R. Nassar and Roger Heacock. New York: Praeger Publishing, 1998.

Legrain, Jean-François. "A Defining Moment: Palestinian Islamic Fundamentalism." In *Islamic Fundamentalism and the Gulf Crisis,* ed. by James Piscatori. Chicago: The American Academy of Arts and Sciences, 1991.

——. "The Islamic Movement and the Intifada." In *Intifada: Palestine at the Crossroads,* ed. by Jamal R. Nassar and Roger Heacock. New York: Praeger Publishing, 1990.

Mithaq Harakat al-Muqawama al-Islamiyya—Hamas (The charter of the Islamic resistance movement—Hamas), August 18, 1988.

Rashad, Ahmad J. "Hamas: The History of the Islamic Opposition Movement in Palestine." In *The Middle East: Politics and Development Occasional Paper,* Series no. 2. Washington, D.C.: United Association for Studies and Research, 1993.

Schiff, Ze'ev, and Ehud Ya'ari. *Intifada.* New York: Simon & Schuster, 1989.

Islamic Jihad

A small Islamic fundamentalist group, the Islamic Jihad movement started in the early 1980s as a splinter group of the Muslim Brotherhood Society in Palestine. The group was founded by Fathi al-Shaqaqi, who was assassinated in 1995 in Malta by Israeli agents, and a number of young, well-educated Islamists who represented a new breed of Palestinian leadership (see also ISLAMIC FUNDAMENTALISM).

The Islamic Jihad was initially inspired by the Islamic revolution in Iran. Although sharing the views of the Muslim Brotherhood toward Palestine and Israel, the Islamic Jihad distinguished itself by making the struggle for Palestine its primary concern. Despite its small size, the secretive Islamic Jihad became known for its violent attacks against Israeli targets and for its early role in the INTIFADA.

The Islamic Jihad is known for its following among the young and the poor in Palestinian society. After the Muslim Brotherhood's participation in the Intifada and the formation of HAMAS, which also undertook violent resistance to the Israeli occupation, the Islamic Jihad lost its distinct character and appeal. Fifteen years after its establishment, it remained a small organization with limited popularity and influence.

Ziad Abu-Amr

Israel

In 1949, armistice agreements between Israel and EGYPT, JORDAN, and SYRIA divided Palestine into Israel, the GAZA STRIP, and the WEST BANK. At that point, there remained in the area that became Israel only about 150,000 of the 700,000 to 800,000 Palestinians who had formerly lived there. (Until May 1948 both the Jewish and Arab population of Palestine were called *Palestinians;* after the establishment of the state of Israel Jews who were formerly "Palestinian" were called *Israeli.*) The Palestinians had actually begun fleeing as early as November 1947, when the United Nations passed its resolution to partition the British-ruled PALESTINE MANDATE into Arab and Jewish states and an international enclave including the JERUSALEM and BETHLEHEM regions. Most Palestinians became REFUGEES in the Jordan-occupied West Bank and the Egyptian-occupied Gaza Strip—two territories whose combined indigenous population before 1947 had totaled approximately 500,000—and in the neighboring states of Jordan, LEBANON, and Syria.

Repatriation Those who remained were permitted to become PALESTINIAN CITIZENS OF ISRAEL. However, with few exceptions, those who had fled or were expelled from territory under Israeli control after November 1947 were not permitted to return, and their LAND and property were seized by the Israel Custodian of Absentee Property. Israel maintained that it was not responsible for the flight of the Palestinian refugees and had no obligation to repatriate them. It claimed that, because Palestinian leaders and the leaders of the surrounding Arab states had encouraged the refugees to leave their homes, responsibility for their flight and for care of the refugees lay with those leaders. When the United Nations initially raised the issue of Palestinian repatriation in 1948–49, Israeli officials protested that the immediate return of the refugees would be militarily advantageous to the Arab states, still at war with Israel. Israeli military authorities argued that the rehabilitation and care required for a mass return of Palestinian refugees would engage the services of many personnel then serving in the armed forces. In addition, since many refugees had lost identification documents, it would be easy for a large "fifth column" to penetrate the country.

Instead of repatriation, Israeli officials called for resettlement of the refugees in Arab countries. They advanced a recurring argument for resettlement: that Israel, with only one-hundredth of the land in the Middle East, was burdened with one-sixtieth of the population. Despite this disproportion, Israeli officials said, Israel was willing to resettle hundreds of thousands of displaced persons from Europe, whereas the Arab states, with their vast territories, had done little if anything for the Palestinian refugees.

Nevertheless, to show goodwill in their response to the plight of the refugees, Israel in 1949 offered to repatriate approximately 200,000 refugees and to accept the 70,000 indigenous inhabitants of Gaza as citizens on two conditions: that Egypt would agree to relinquish control of the Gaza Strip to Israel, and that international aid would be provided for refugee resettlement. When this offer was rejected by the Arab countries, Israel, under pressure from the United States, offered to permit the return of 100,000 refugees as part of an overall resettlement plan to be implemented under the auspices of a special U.N. body. However, the Arab states also considered this proposal to be unsatisfactory.

Israeli political leaders were divided over proposals of the Labor government to repatriate a limited number of refugees. The Mapam Party supported the proposals. The Herut Party, led by Menachem Begin (who later would become prime minister and leader of the nationalist Likud bloc), considered any repatriation of Palestinians a threat to the country's security and demanded a national referendum on the issue. The leader of the conservative General Zionists (which later amalgamated with Herut) believed that only an agreement based on the transfer of the Palestinian refugees to the Arab countries and of Jews from Arab countries to Israel would solve the refugee problem. Leaders of the orthodox United Religious Front insisted that, if Palestinians were to be repatriated, the proportion of Jews to Arabs had to be maintained at the then-existing ratio of 950,000 Jews to 150,000 Arabs. Only the Palestinian members of the Knesset supported the concept of repatriation.

After 1949–50, Israel did not renew its offer to repatriate any large numbers of Palestinians. All the country's Zionist political parties rejected any large-scale return of Palestinian refugees. They feared that a large number of Palestinians would constitute a security risk and, because of their higher birth rate, would jeopardize the Jewish character of the state. Also, Palestinian property had been absorbed by Jews and now constituted an important part of the Israeli economy. Thus, large-scale repatriation of Palestinians was considered by virtually all Zionists to be tantamount to destruction of the Jewish state.

As a result of negotiations with the United States and the UNITED NATIONS CONCILIATION COMMISSION FOR PALESTINE, as well as of requests from Palestinian citizens of Israel, an agreement was reached in 1949 to reunite several thousand Palestinian families by permitting repatriation of a limited number of refugees who had close relatives in Israel. Those repatriated generally included wives and minor children of "Arab bread-winners lawfully resident in Israel." Family reunion was permitted on an individual, case-by-case basis and proceeded slowly. By the early 1960s, the number of Palestinians repatriated totaled about 50,000. After the 1967 Six-Day War, Israel authorized a separate repatriation scheme for the West Bank and East Jerusalem. About 60,000 Palestinians were permitted to return to the West Bank and 10,000 others to East Jerusalem. Israel perceived the repatriation of refugees under the family reunion schemes as a humanitarian gesture, not as a refugee right.

Policies Toward Refugees Economic factors were a major consideration in Israel's policies toward

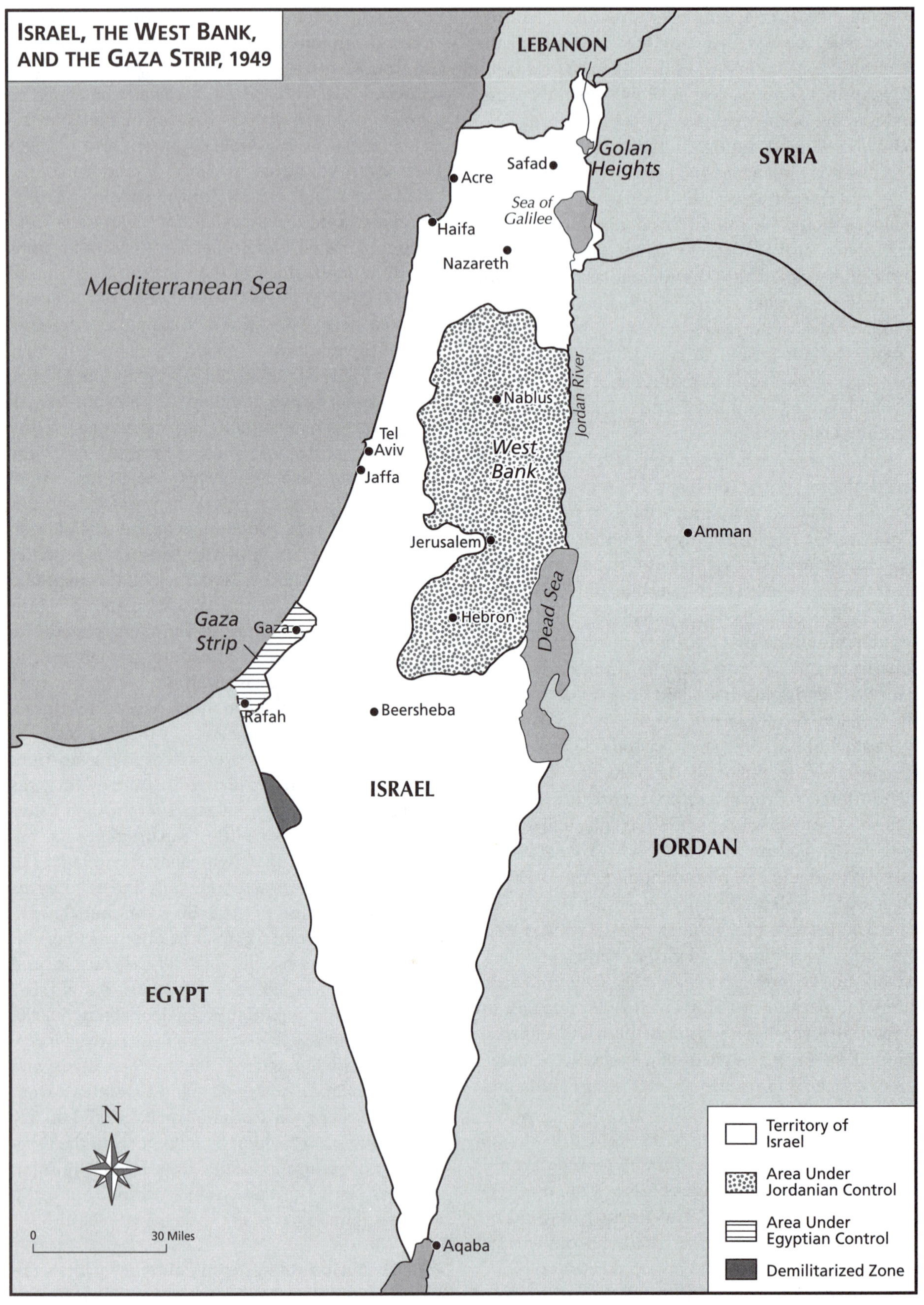
ISRAEL, THE WEST BANK, AND THE GAZA STRIP, 1949
LEBANON
SYRIA
Golan Heights
Safad
Acre
Sea of Galilee
Haifa
Nazareth
Mediterranean Sea
Jordan River
Nablus
Tel Aviv
Jaffa
West Bank
Jerusalem
Amman
Dead Sea
Gaza Strip
Gaza
Hebron
Rafah
Beersheba
ISRAEL
JORDAN
EGYPT
N
0
30 Miles
Aqaba
Territory of Israel
Area Under Jordanian Control
Area Under Egyptian Control
Demilitarized Zone

the Palestinian refugees. Palestinian fields, orchards, vineyards, homes, shops, factories, and businesses absorbed by Israel provided shelter, economic sustenance, and employment for the nearly 700,000 new Jewish immigrants who arrived between 1948 and 1951. In addition, as a result of the 1949 armistice agreements, Israel had extended its frontiers from the approximately 6,000 square miles allocated to it in the 1947 PARTITION PLANS to 8,000 square miles by taking over 2,000 square miles of territory that the plans had allocated to the Arab state. Israeli authorities also assumed control of Palestinian property in this area and made it available for use by the new Jewish immigrants.

Most belongings of Palestinian refugees, including land, immovables, and movables—household effects, vehicles, farm animals, and the like—were initially seized by the Custodian of Absentee Property and later distributed through a variety of other agencies to Israeli Jewish citizens. In effect, the Absentee Property Law merely legalized the de facto seizure of property that had occurred during the 1948 war. Under the law, absentees were defined as Palestinian citizens who had left their places of habitual residence on or after November 29, 1947, the date of the partition resolution. Thus, the definition included not only Palestinian refugees who had fled the territory controlled by Israel but also thousands of Palestinians who had moved from one part of Israeli-held territory to another during the war. The Custodian was granted arbitrary power to make decisions defining absentees and their property. Much information concerning the use, amounts, and distribution of abandoned Palestinian property and the government's policy toward it remained secret. For that reason, many responsible Israeli Jews criticized the law and the actions of the Custodian. In several instances, Israel's Supreme Court questioned the Absentee Property Law and the actions of the Custodian, calling them arbitrary, excessive, and an abuse of civil law.

Between 1948 and 1953, a total of 350 of the 370 new Jewish settlements established in Israel were on former Palestinian property. According to reports of the Custodian of Absentee Property, by 1954 more than one-third of the country's Jewish population lived on former Palestinian land, and an additional 250,000 Israeli Jews, including one-third of the new immigrants, lived in abandoned Palestinian urban property. Entire cities, such as Jaffa, Acre, Lydda, Ramla, Baysan, and al-Mijdal Gad, plus some 400 towns and villages and large parts of 94 others, had been abandoned by Palestinian refugees who had fled or been expelled and taken over by Jewish settlers. These areas contained nearly a quarter of all buildings in Israel at the time. Most of the 120,000 *dunums* of Palestinian orange groves—about half the citrus land in Palestine at the end of the Mandate—were seized by the Israeli government. In addition, some 40,000 *dunums* of vineyards, at least 10,000 *dunums* of other orchards, and nearly 95 percent of Israel's olive groves had formerly belonged to refugees. Abandoned Palestinian land was about two-and-one-half times the total area of Jewish-owned property at the end of the Mandate.

The Jewish Agency (which preceded the government of Israel) had accepted the 1947 U.N. partition resolution that divided Palestine into a Jewish and an Arab state with an international enclave consisting of the Jerusalem region. Although this acceptance implied recognition of a Palestinian state, soon after Israel was established, government policy rejected provisions of the partition resolution. Israel claimed that Palestinian opposition to the plan and Arab "aggression" in the 1948 war invalidated full implementation of the plan. Thus, approximately 2,000 square miles of the Palestinian state envisaged in the partition plans came under Israeli control during the spring and summer of 1948 and was made subject to Israeli law. For all practical purposes, this territory became part of the Jewish state. In 1950, Israel moved its capital from Tel-Aviv to West Jerusalem, effectively nullifying the provision of the partition plans that had provided for an international regime in Jerusalem. After the ARAB–ISRAELI WAR OF 1967, Israel declared that the western Jewish sectors of the city, Arab East Jerusalem, and several of the surrounding West Bank villages had been incorporated into an expanded Jerusalem municipality subject to Israeli LAW.

The Occupied Territories The occupation of the West Bank and Gaza Strip in 1967 placed approximately 900,000 additional Palestinians under Israeli jurisdiction. With the exception of East Jerusalem, Israel governed these territories as occupied areas. Thus, Palestinians in the occupied areas were not granted Israeli citizenship as were those who lived within the 1949 armistice frontiers. The exception was in East Jerusalem, where the Palestinian residents were offered the option of retaining Jordanian citizenship or becoming Israeli citizens. Few Palestinians accepted the Israeli offer of citizenship, because it would imply their recognition of Israeli sovereignty over Jerusalem.

From 1967 until 1995, the Israeli army operated a military government in the West Bank and Gaza. Under the military regime, Palestinians could be arrested and imprisoned without the right of habeas corpus, could be expelled from the country, and could have their property confiscated or destroyed by the army without a civil trial. Military governors, who were Israeli army officers, had total executive and legislative powers that enabled them to make new laws, cancel old ones, and suspend or annul existing laws. Israeli control of the Palestinian economy, including LAND and WATER, resulted in subordination of Palestinian economic life to Israel's needs. No Palestinian political organizations were permitted to function, and manifestations of Palestinian nationalism were banned.

Until the CAMP DAVID ACCORDS in 1978, the Israeli government refused to consider the Palestinians as a distinct nation. Rather than Palestinians, they were called "Arabs of the Land of Israel" (*Arevi Eretz Yisrael*). This formed the basis of the official argument that the Arabs of Mandatory Palestine were not entitled to independence; the government argued that, as a part of the Arab world, they already had more than twenty other states in which they could be resettled. Golda Meir, who became prime minister after the 1967 war, articulated this view by publicly denying the existence of a Palestinian people.

The nationalist Likud government of Prime Minister Menachem Begin, which came to power in 1977, maintained the revisionist Zionist goal of incorporating all of mandatory Palestine within the borders of Israel. The West Bank and Gaza, according to Begin, were integral parts of Eretz Yisrael and could not be separated from the Jewish state, although the Palestinian inhabitants could be given limited autonomy with control over education, health, social welfare, and similar functions.

Nevertheless, the international environment changed by the late 1970s. Even the United States, Israel's most important international ally, recognized the critical status that Palestinians had assumed in terms of resolving the Arab–Israeli conflict. Under pressure from the United States, Israel for the first time recognized the Palestinians as a distinct people in the Camp David accords of 1978–79, which included reference to the "legitimate rights of the Palestinians." In the Camp David accords, Israel agreed to an autonomy plan for the West Bank and Gaza that proposed limited self-government but with Israel in control of security, foreign affairs, and other significant functions. The Begin government described the plan as autonomy for the Palestinian population, but not for the Occupied Territories in which they resided.

The Begin government made no serious efforts to implement those provisions of the Camp David accords pertaining to Palestinian autonomy. On the contrary, Ariel Sharon, as minister of defense, attempted to outmaneuver the Palestinian national movement in the early 1980s through the establishment of a civil administration and local village leagues run by Palestinians *not* affiliated with the PALESTINE LIBERATION ORGANIZATION (PLO). However, after the establishment in 1984 of an Israeli National Unity Government with the Labor Party's Shimon Peres as minister of defense, Sharon's "civil administration" scheme to control Palestinian political life was abandoned.

Intifada Israel's efforts to control the Palestinians in the 1980s sparked a major wave of opposition among Palestinians that became known as the INTIFADA. Although there had been numerous Palestinian demonstrations against Israeli rule during the first twenty years of occupation, the Intifada, which erupted in December 1987, was on a more massive scale than any previous resistance. The military government severely repressed the Intifada by arresting thousands of Palestinians; nevertheless, it continued at a sustained level for several years. During this period, both Israeli and Western human rights organizations documented frequent instances of Israeli use of torture and maltreatment of Palestinian prisoners. Government policies in the Occupied Territories and tactics for dealing with Palestinian resistance caused a serious rift within Israeli society. Many young men opposed to the occupation refused to perform military service, whereas, on the other hand, right-wing critics charged that the government was not using sufficient force to suppress Palestinian opposition to the occupation.

A major consequence of the Intifada was a change in Israeli attitudes vis-à-vis Palestinian self-determination and toward the PLO. Nevertheless, this change was gradual, and until 1993 neither Likud nor Labor was willing to recognize Palestinian demands for independence or the PLO, which was the organization internationally accepted as representing the Palestinians. Although a small but increasing number of Israelis recognized the possibility of Palestinian self-determination in a separate Palestinian state after 1987, this view was not acceptable to the major political parties. The Labor and Likud blocs held different interpretations of the "Palestinian legitimate rights" mentioned in the Camp David accords. Likud interpreted legitimate rights as autonomy under Israeli control. In contrast, the Labor Party was willing to accept the right of self-determination within a Jordanian–Palestinian context—a sort of Palestinian–Jordanian federation—"no third state between the Jordan and the Mediterranean." Labor's policy toward Palestinian legitimate rights was further complicated by adherence to the Allon Plan, which provided for continued Israeli control over strategic parts of the West Bank with Jordanian civil authority restored only in heavily populated areas. However, after Jordan's King Husayn relinquished responsibility for the West Bank in July 1988, Labor was forced to abandon its "Jordanian option." Within the party, there was increasing recognition that a peaceful solution of the Arab–Israeli conflict had to be found through recognition of Palestinian self-determination and negotiations with the PLO.

Israeli attitudes toward Palestinian rights were affected by the common perception of the PLO as a terrorist organization, which was due to the numerous attacks on civilians undertaken by PLO-affiliated organizations. Labor declared that it would not recognize the PLO until it amended its charter to accept UNITED NATIONS SECURITY COUNCIL RESOLUTIONS 242 AND 338, renounce TERRORISM, and publicly recognize the state of Israel. Since the early 1970s, Israel's various intelligence agencies had waged a secret war against PLO officials in the Middle East and in Europe. Furthermore, the Prevention of Terror Law, passed by the Knesset in 1986, prohibited all contact with the PLO by Israeli citizens.

Peace Process Although Likud seemed unaffected by the attitudinal changes that Labor was undergoing, the United States in 1991 persuaded Prime Minister Yitzhak Shamir's government (1986–1992) to enter direct negotiations with Palestinians who would be part of a joint Jordan-Palestinian delegation at the MADRID PEACE CONFERENCE, 1991. However, Shamir placed so many restrictions on Palestinian representation that the negotiations achieved no substantive progress until a new Labor government, headed by Yitzhak Rabin, was elected in 1992. One of the first acts of the Rabin government was to propose legislation repealing the 1986 law barring contacts with the PLO. After the Knesset repealed the law in January 1993, Labor Party leaders made statements calling for direct negotiations with the PLO and for Israeli withdrawal from the Gaza Strip.

The Rabin government initiated secret negotiations with the PLO in Oslo, Norway, that led to a radical change in Israel's policy vis-à-vis the Palestinians and the PLO. The secret talks in Oslo resulted in an agreement between Israel and the PLO that was signed on September 13, 1993, at a public ceremony in Washington, D.C., presided over by the U.S. president, Bill Clinton. The agreement was sealed by a historic handshake between Rabin and the PLO chairman, YASIR ARAFAT. The agreement, the Declaration of Principles (DOP), initiated a new phase in relationships between Israel and the Palestinians.

Also known as the "Gaza-Jericho First" agreement, the DOP called for the transfer of authority from Israel to an elected PALESTINIAN LEGISLATIVE COUNCIL in Gaza and in Jericho. With certain exceptions, police functions were to be transferred from the Israeli military to a Palestinian force. The agreement included protocols calling for the establishment of the joint Israeli-Palestinian Committee for Economic Cooperation and for joint programs to administer electricity, water, transport, and other similar services. The DOP created a five-year transition period that was to precede a final settlement, although final status arrangements could be started two years after implementation of the transition period.

The agreement was followed by months of difficult negotiations over issues such as the size of the Jericho self-government area, the status of Israeli settlements in the Occupied Territories, and the duties and functions of Israeli forces and of the new Palestinian police force. Growing impatience among Palestinians and Israeli Jews resulted in increased violent opposition to the DOP and numerous incidents led to acts of terrorism against both Jewish and Palestinian civilians. Within both political camps were militant opponents of the DOP. Many Israeli settlers threatened to resist with force any attempt to implement the DOP. In the West Bank and Gaza, HAMAS also threatened to topple the agreement. In Israel, the political opposition parties, including Likud, Tzomet, Moledet, and the National Religious Party, vehemently opposed any agreement with the PLO or any agreement based on Israeli withdrawal from the West Bank and Gaza.

During 1994, Israel and the PLO signed three agreements for implementation of the DOP. They included pacts providing for an open economic relationship between Israel and the newly established PALESTINIAN AUTHORITY (PA); provisions for Palestinian self-rule in the Gaza Strip and the Jericho enclave; and transfer to Palestinian control of tourism, education, health, culture, and taxation in the West Bank and Gaza. The self-rule agreement signed by the PLO president, Arafat, and the Israeli prime minister called for withdrawal or redeployment of Israeli forces from Jericho and Gaza and establishment of the PA. This agreement was to initiate a five-year interim period for negotiating a permanent solution for the future of relationships between Israeli and the PA. The agreement opened the way for Arafat's return to Palestine and his establishment as *ra'is* (see PALESTINIAN AUTHORITY) of the PA.

After several months of arduous and at times acrimonious negotiations, a further agreement was signed in September 1995 by Israel and the PA, extending self-rule from Gaza and Jericho to Palestinian cities and villages in the West Bank. Called Oslo II or the Taba agreement, this pact provided for Israeli withdrawal or redeployment in three regions of the West Bank.

Relations between the government of Israel and the PA began to detoriorate after the assassination of Prime Minister Rabin in 1995 and the election of Benjamin Netanyahu, leader of the Nationalist Likud Party (bloc), in May 1996. Although Netanyahu had opposed the OSLO AGREEMENTS and the policies of his Labor government predecessors, he stated that his government would implement the Oslo provisions. When first elected Netanyahu shunned contact with PA president Arafat, but by September 1996 they met and stated their commitment to the peace process. In January 1997 Israel and the PA initialed the Hebron protocol, providing for Israel's withdrawal from 80 percent of HEBRON. Occupied by some 500 mostly Orthodox Jewish settlers, Hebron is the home of more than 150,000 Palestinians. The focus of the conflict between Jews and Muslims is the disputed tomb of the patriarchs, which, according to the agreement, is to remain under Israeli control, although Muslims would be given access. Israeli troops would remain in areas occupied by Jewish settlers. The agreement also called for three further pullbacks during 1997–98 from West Bank areas designated by Israel as Palestinian. According to the agreement about 9 percent of the West Bank would be controlled by the PA, with 27 percent under joint administration. The rest of the West Bank would be controlled by the Israeli army.

Relations between Israel and the PA worsened soon after the Hebron agreement when Netanyahu announced that Israel would withdraw from only a small sector of the West Bank. The crisis intensified further after bombings in Israel by Islamic militants and Israel's retaliation with severe travel restrictions on Palestinians and cutting off of payment of funds due the PA under the Oslo accords.

The peace process was brought to a halt when Netanyahu ordered construction of a new Jerusalem housing development at Jabal Abu Ghunaym Har Homa in Arab East Jerusalem, which the PA charged violated the Oslo accords. For more than a year further implementation of the Oslo accords was frozen as a result of the acrimonious relations between the Netanyahu government and the PA. Plans for implementing the final status peace agreement were also halted as Israel refused to withdraw from the areas designated in the Hebron and other accords. Netanyahu charged that the PA had failed to carry out provisions providing for security.

After more than a year of stalemate, the United States urged Israel and the PA to renew negotiations at the Wye River Plantation in Maryland; the result was the Memorandum of October 23, 1998. The Wye River agreement supposedly set the stage for conclusion of the much delayed final status arrangements by May 1999. Wye provided for further redeployment of Israeli forces from the West Bank, gave high priority to Israel's security concerns, and nullified the PALESTINE NATIONAL CHARTER terms calling for Israel's destruction. Other interim issues to be concluded were the establishment of a Palestinian airport, seaport, and industrial park in Gaza and the West Bank, and the release of several hundred Palestinian political prisoners.

Although the Palestinians amended the charter shortly after the Wye meeting and Israel withdrew from a small additional sector of the West Bank, further implementation of the accord was brought to a halt by disagreements within the Israeli cabinet over withdrawal. As a result of these developments, the Netanyahu government fell, new elections in Israel were called, and the peace process was again brought to a halt until the election of Ehud Barak in 1999.

Don Peretz

BIBLIOGRAPHY

Abu-Lughod, Ibrahim. *The Transformation of Palestine: Essays on the Origin and Development of the Arab-Israeli Conflict.* 2d ed. Evanston, Ill.: Northwestern University Press, 1987.

Benvenisti, Meron. *Conflicts and Contradictions.* New York: Villard Books, 1986.

——. *The West Bank Data Project: A Study of Israel's Policies.* Washington, D.C.: American Enterprise Institute, 1984.

Binur, Yoram. *My Enemy, My Self.* New York: Penguin, 1989.

Cohen, Abner. *Arab Border Villages in Israel: A Study of Continuity and Change in Social Organization.* Manchester, England: University on Manchester Press, 1965.

Elazar, Daniel J., ed. *Judea, Samaria, and Gaza: Views of the Present and the Future.* Washington, D.C.: American Enterprise Institute, 1982.

Flapan, Simha. *The Birth of Israel: Myths and Realities* New York: Pantheon, 1988.

Halabi, Rafik. *The West Bank Story.* Rev. ed. San Diego, Calif.: Harcourt Brace, 1985.

Harkabi, Yehoshafat. *Israel's Fateful Hour.* New York: Harper & Row, 1988.

Heller, Mark A., and Sari Nusseibeh. *No Trumpets, No Drums: A Two-State Settlement of the Israeli-Palestinian Conflict.* New York: Hill & Wang, 1991.

Khaori, Fred. *The Arab Israel Dilemma,* 3d ed. Syracuse, N.Y.: Syracuse University Press, 1985.

Lesch, Ann Mosely. *Political Perceptions of the Palestinians in the West Bank and the Gaza Strip.* Washington, D.C.: Middle East Institute, 1980.

Lukacs, Yehuda, ed. *The Israeli-Palestinian Conflict: A Documentary Record 1967–1990.* Cambridge, England: Cambridge University Press, 1992.

Lustick, Ian. *Arabs in the Jewish State: Israel's Control of a National Minority.* Austin: University of Texas Press, 1980.

Morris, Benny. *The Birth of the Palestinian Refugee Problem.* New York: Cambridge University Press, 1987.

Peretz, Don. *Israel and the Palestine Arabs.* Washington, D.C.: Middle East Institute, 1958.

——. *Intifada: The Palestinian Uprising.* Boulder, Colo.: Westview Press, 1990.

Roman, Michael, and Alex Weingrod. *Living Together Separately: Arabs and Jews in Contemporary Jerusalem.* Princeton, N.J.: Princeton University Press, 1991.

Sahliyeh, Emile. *In Search of Leadership: West Bank Politics since 1867.* Washington, D.C.: Brookings Institution, 1987.

Segev, Tom. *The First Israelis.* New York: Free Press, 1986.

Shalev, Aryeh. *The West Bank: Line of Defense.* New York: Praeger, 1985.

Shipler, David K. *Arab and Jew: Wounded Spirits in a Promised Land.* New York: Times Books, 1986.

Tessler, Mark. *A History of the Israeli-Palestinian Conflict.* Bloomington: Indiana University Press, 1994.

Israeli Arabs

See PALESTINIAN CITIZENS OF ISRAEL.

Israeli Invasion of Lebanon

See ARAB-ISRAELI WAR OF 1982.

Israeli Settlements

Jewish settlement in the land of ISRAEL was and remains an expression of the enduring vitality of ZIONISM and its vision. For Israelis generally, there has traditionally been no vital distinction between the settlement policies practiced in the prestate era and those that evolved in the wake of Israel's occupation of the WEST BANK, GAZA STRIP, Golan Heights, and Sinai in June 1967. All are a product of the still unfinished consolidation of Jewish sovereignty in Palestine.

Rationale The Zionist experience of state building in Palestine taught Israeli leaders that civilian settlements were the building blocks with which sovereignty was created and that defined Israeli's territorial limits.

JEWISH SETTLEMENTS IN THE WEST BANK, 1982
Mediterranean Sea
Ginat
Jenin
Reihan
Mevo Dotan
Sanur
Irit
Mehola
Jordan River
Tulkarm
Shomron
Elon Moreh
Qedumim
Nablus
Brakha
Hamra
Qalqilya
Alfei Menashe
Qarnei Shomron
Mekhora
Argaman
Ma'aleh Shomron
Yaqir
Emmanuel
Netafim
Tapuah
Massu'a
Elqana
Beit Abba
Ariel
Gittit
Tel Aviv
Ma'leh Adumin
Shlomtzion
Shiloh
Tomer
Gilgal
Aleret
JORDAN
Netiv Hagdud
Ofra
Ramallah
Beit El
Rimonium
Givat Ze'ev
Jericho
Beit Ha'rava
Mitzpeh Jericho
Almog
Jerusalem
Ma'aleh Adumim
Har Gilo
Bethlehem
ISRAEL
Efrat
Kfar Etzion
Migdal Oz
Ma'aleh Amos
Mitzpeh Shalem
Telem
Qiryat Arba
Dead Sea
Hebron
Adora
Yaqin
Negohot
Karmel
N
Zohar
Eskolot
0
10 miles
Settlements Established Before 1977
Settlements Established After 1977
Major Palestinian Towns

Security, sovereignty, and settlement are inextricably linked. For as then-minister of defense, Moshe Dayan, explained, Israeli settlements in the Occupied Territories are essential, "not because they can ensure security better than the army, but because without them we cannot keep the army in those territories. Without them the IDF [Israel Defense Forces] would be a foreign army ruling a foreign population."

Settlements established by Labor Party governments during the 1967–77 period of its rule were located according to what was in an Israeli context a minimalist but ever expanding conception of its territorial and ideological requirements. The Allon Plan, as Labor's settlement plan came to be known, called for a territorial division of land in the Occupied Territories according to the following essential principles.

In the West Bank, Israel would annex and settle, in both urban and rural communities, the following areas:

- JERUSALEM and its immediate environs
- "security belt" 20 kilometers wide running the length of the Jordan valley
- The entire Judean desert, possibly including HEBRON

Allon and Dayan Plans According to the Allon Plan, named after Labor Party minister Yigal Allon, about one-quarter (later expanding to about 40 percent) of the West Bank's territory and population was to be annexed by Israel. The southern Gaza Strip would also be annexed, as would the Golan Heights and a strip of Sinai linking Eilat to Sharm al-Shaykh.

The Allon Plan was succeeded by the Dayan Plan in 1973. Dayan, then minister of defense, believed in a functional rather than a territorial solution to the disposition of the Occupied Territories. Israel, according to this concept, would settle everywhere throughout the territories and award Palestinians a measure of autonomy consistent with Israeli interests. But Israel would remain permanently in the occupied areas.

Dayan's "Five No's," announced in September 1973—"Gaza will not be Egyptian. The Golan will not be Syrian. Jerusalem will not be Arab. A Palestinian state will not be established. We will not abandon the settlements we have established"—signaled the adoption of Labor's maximalist program of settlement. Under this banner, the populated West Bank heartland in the area between NABLUS and RAMALLAH and the Green Line border separating Israel from the West Bank would be opened to Jewish settlement.

During the first decade of occupation, Labor established both the physical infrastructure and political institutions for the creation and expansion of a permanent Israeli civilian presence in the territories. But what Labor had adopted incrementally over the course of a decade, the Likud Party, spurred by popular movements led by Gush Emmunim (Bloc of the Faithful)—for whom the 1967 victory was understood as a divine signal to settle the Occupied Territories—embraced as its raison d'être and the key to its political renaissance.

Expansion under Likud When the Likud Party, led by Menachem Begin, formed its first government in 1977, there were 50,000 Israelis living in annexed Jerusalem, but only 7,000 settlers in forty-five civilian outposts in the remaining territories.

In September 1977 Begin's minister of agriculture, Ariel Sharon, unveiled "A Vision of Israel at Century's End," which called for the settlement of 2 million Jews in the Occupied Territories. The Likud plan viewed settlement as an instrument to disrupt the territorial continuity of Palestinian habitation and thus preempt the political possibility of Palestinian self-determination. It stressed the establishment of numerous settlement points as well as larger urban concentrations in three principal areas:

- A north-south axis running from the Golan through the Jordan Valley and down the east coast of Sinai
- A widened corridor around Jerusalem
- The populated western slopes of the Samarian heartland, which Labor had only just begun to colonize

This last wedge of Israeli settlement was of prime concern to Likud strategists, particularly Sharon, who was intent on establishing Israeli settlements in this area in order to separate the large blocs of Palestinian population on each side of the Green Line north of Tel Aviv.

During the 1980s, Likud governments allocated approximately $300 million annually for the development and expansion of Jewish settlement in the West Bank. Annual construction fluctuated between 1,000 and 2,000 housing units each year. This investment in infrastructure and housing created the conditions for a takeoff in settler population. By the end of 1985, the population stood at 42,000, a 100 percent increase from that in 1982. By 1990, West Bank settlers numbered 76,000. In addition, 120,000 Israelis were living across the Green Line in annexed East Jerusalem, 10,000 more were in the Golan Heights, and 3,000 lived in Gaza.

In 1990 there were approximately 240,000 Israelis living in occupied territory—140,000 in annexed Jerusalem, 3,000 in the Gaza Strip, 12,000 in the Golan Heights, and 85,000 in the West Bank. By 1995 these numbers had increased to 170,000 in Jerusalem, 6,000 in the Gaza Strip, 13,000 in the Golan, and 140,000 in the West Bank—an increase of 90,000 over the 1990 total and a testament to the tremendous increase in settlement construction that accompanied the influx of immigrants from the Soviet Union during 1989–92.

The Israeli settler population in the West Bank need only grow by an average of 10 percent annually until 2005 for the number of settlers in the West Bank to total 500,000.

Policies of the Rabin Government The "Fundamental Policy Guidelines of the Government," adopted by the Labor-led coalition of Yitzhak Rabin after Labor's victory over Likud in mid-1992, contained no mention of a settlement or construction freeze but committed Rabin to "refrain from moves and actions that will disrupt the orderly conduct of negotiations (with the PLO, Jordan, and Syria)." The new government also pledged to maintain the security of settlers and to "consolidate and strengthen settlements along the confrontation lines [the Jordan Valley and Golan Heights]." Rabin also pledged to accommodate the settlements' "natural growth."

On July 28, 1992, the government announced that it would not sign contracts for 3,136 settlement housing units approved in the 1992 (Likud) budget and would void the contracts on an additional 3,545 units where construction had not yet begun. In addition, plans were canceled for 2,000 units in the Gaza Strip and another 1,100 in the Golan Heights—part of a nationwide cutback of 12,000 units planned by the previous government. No cutbacks were made in the area of "Greater Jerusalem"—defined by Minister of Construction and Housing Benjamin Ben Eliezer to include Ma'ale Ephraim, Givat Ze'ev, Ma'ale Adumim, Betar, and Gush Etzion.

Most of the units canceled existed only on paper. These cutbacks were accompanied by the announcement of a decision to complete construction of 9,850 units in settlements throughout the West Bank, 1,200 in the Gaza Strip, and 1,200 in the Golan Heights.

The completion and occupancy of these units allowed the increase of the settler population in the West Bank to 150,000.

The Rabin government's National Master Plan for construction, development, and immigrant absorption correctly envisaged a settler population of 140,000 in the West Bank and Gaza Strip by 1995. The percentage of Israelis living in the West Bank and Gaza Strip under a Rabin government would increase, according to the plan, from 1.7 percent in 1990 to 2.3 percent of the country's total population.

The settlement policies of the government of Yitzhak Rabin focused on consolidating the successful urban/suburban core of West Bank settlement communities developed by Likud governments since 1977 rather than on expanding politically divisive, marginal, and demographically questionable outposts.

Rabin's policy was particularly apparent in the area of annexed East Jerusalem and its West Bank hinterland of metropolitan or "Greater" Jerusalem—a region whose permanent annexation by Israel Rabin declared beyond political debate.

"Jerusalem and outlying areas cannot be defined by us as a political issue or as a security issue," explained Rabin soon after his election. "United Jerusalem under Israeli sovereignty will remain our capital forever. For us it is the heart and the soul of the Jewish people."

The Rabin government's construction plans for West Bank and Jerusalem settlements rivaled and in some respects surpassed the settlement construction efforts of the Shamir government during 1989–92. The government planned to build in the 1995–98 period about 30,000 apartments beyond the Green Line.

The program represented a marked increase in the pace of construction initiated by the Rabin government in the Occupied Territories during its first two years. During this period Rabin completed more than 11,000 units inherited when the Labor Party defeated the Likud Party in 1992. The completion and sale of most of these units, particularly in the region around Jerusalem and along the 1967 border, had by 1995 created a market for additional housing.

The principal points of the government plan for 1995–98 included the following:

- Construction of 15,000 apartments in East Jerusalem settlement neighborhoods beyond the 1967 borders (Pisgat Ze'ev, Neve Ya'akov, Gilo, and Har Homa)
- Building of 13,000 apartments in the nearby urban region (Ma'ale Adumim [6,000], Givat Ze'ev [1,000], Betar [5,000], Givon, Har Adar, and Efrat)
- Creation of 3,000 apartments in other West Bank locations

A shorter term plan for the construction of 4,100 dwelling units in the West Bank settlements of Greater Jerusalem was approved in January 1995. At the time, a cabinet committee on settlement construction reaffirmed the "top priority" it attached to "the strengthened construction of united Jerusalem," and promised the allocation of "special resources" to this end.

Commenting on the government's intentions, Minister of Foreign Affairs Shimon Peres remarked, "There will be building, but without declarations."

Policies of the Netanyahu Government Soon after the election of Benjamin Netanyahu and the defeat of Shimon Peres in May 1996, the new Likud minister of finance Dan Meridor offered an important insight into the settlement issue in the context of relations both domestic and foreign. He explained in a July 19, 1996, interview in the newspaper *Yediot Aharanot:*

> we have to praise Yitzhak Rabin may he rest in peace and Shimon Peres who during the last four years raised the number of Jews in Judea and Samaria by 40 percent. During their tenure, thousands of homes were built in Judea and Samaria and the number of Jews increased from 100,000 to 140,000.
>
> But we need not be thankful only to them. But we should also praise the Israeli left which didn't utter a word about this for four years; and to the American government which knew but didn't care. And also we should give thanks to the Palestinian Authority which saw that we were building but did not permit this to disrupt the peace process.
>
> It is clear as can be that we will not do less in this regard [settlement construction] than the Labor Party. I already told the American ambassador that he can rest easy about one thing—that Labor's policy of massive settlement will not change. Maybe we will do it a little differently. And perhaps in places a little different. But it is clear that if we are serious in our intention not to return to the 1967 lines, words alone will not suffice. Settlement is one of the things that determines the map of the country. Therefore if we stop settlement in one place or another it means that we have surrendered that place. I don't think that we have to behave provocatively, but it is necessary to continue the settlement enterprise in Judea and Samaria in a sober and controlled manner, and within our economic limitations. There are communities which for sure were dried out in recent years, and that will certainly be rectified.

The policies announced by the Netanyahu government would increase the Israeli population in the West Bank and Gaza Strip by approximately 50,000 people to 200,000 during the four-year period 1996–2000.

After Netanyahu's 1996 victory, settlement expansion entered a new phase only in the second half of 1997. At that time, new construction was observed at 93 of the 130 settlements in the West Bank, in settlements close to Jerusalem as well as isolated posts in the West Bank heartland—a graphic illustration of the breadth of the effort under way by the Netanyahu government and settlement groups. Because of their distance from existing facilities, at least thirteen of these construction sites could be characterized as new settlements, although they were considered by Israel to be part of existing settlements. Press reports in Israel placed the number of new units under construction at 5,000 during 1997. Other sources confirmed the approval and initial construction of 4,000 units in West Bank settlements, enough to increase the settler population in the West Bank and Gaza Strip by more than 10 percent.

Since mid-1997, settlement expansion in the West Bank occurred not only in those settlements within easy commuting distance from the cities of Jerusalem and the Tel Aviv metropolis, but in the rural, isolated outports throughout the West Bank as well. The increasing dependence upon market forces in the housing market appears not to have stopped the expansion of settlements in these latter areas.

Oslo II provided the opportunity for the redeployment of the Israeli army, allowing the Palestinian Authority to assume its civil and security responsibilities according to the schedule provided for in the agreement. The Israeli army began its withdrawal from Jenin on November 13, 1995, followed by Tulkarm on December 10, 1995, Nablus and other villages in the Tulkarm area on December 11, 1995, Qalkiliya on December 17, 1995, Bethlehem on December 21, 1995, and finally Ramallah on December 28, 1995. Hebron was left as the last of the West Bank towns from which Israeli soldiers were to redeploy under Oslo II in order to allow time to work out the security issues arising from the presence of 450 Israeli settlers in the city center. The Hebron Protocol, which does not constitute a new agreement, was concluded on January 15, 1997. Under the provisions of the protocol, the city is divided into two parts: Israel retains full security control over the settlement enclaves in downtown Hebron [H2], the Kiryat Arba' settlement just outside the city, and the surrounding area necessary for the movement of the settlers and the army; while the Palestinian Authority is responsible for security for the rest of Hebron [H1], although this responsibility remains closely monitored by Israeli Authorities.

On October 23, 1998, Israel and the Palestinian Authority agreed in the Wye memorandum to a revised timetable for the phased implementation of the first and second "further redeployments" (FRD) of Israeli military forces outlined in the Oslo II accords signed in September 1995.

The first of three redeployments was initially scheduled to begin in October 1996. The third redeployment was to have been completed, according to the Oslo II timetable, by October 1997. The Wye memorandum makes no mention of a date for this third redeployment, called for in Oslo II.

Timetable for First and Second "Further Redeployments" according to the Wye Memorandum

	AREA A	AREA B	AREA C
IDF redeployments in 1995–1996	2%	26%	72%
Stage I (November 16, 1998)	9.1	20.9	70.0
Stage II (November 16–December 21, 1998)	9.1	26.9	65.0
Stage III (December 14–January 31, 1999)	17.2	23.8	59.0 (incl. 3% nature reserve)

Stage I of the Wye redeployments—initially offered to the Palestinians, and rejected in March 1997—was completed in November 1998. The Israeli cabinet decided in December 1998 to postpone indefinitely additional redeployments.

According to former Israeli prime minister Benjamin Netanyahu, at the end of the redeployments agreed to at Wye, Israel will still be in full security control of 82 percent of the West Bank and Gaza, of which 59 to 60 percent will be also under full Israeli civil control.

The Wye memorandum, like previous agreements since 1993, contains no meaningful restriction on settlement expansion.

The land under exclusive Israeli control amounts to around 71.8 percent of the West Bank (Area C) and 20 percent of the Gaza Strip. In addition, 30 percent of the area of East Jerusalem is under effective Israeli ownership. No similar estimates are available for the Golan Heights, although it is known that more than 17,000 inhabitants of Syrian nationality are living in a few villages close to the borders of Syria and Lebanon and that a similar number of Israelis have settled there.

By 1999 Israel had established approximately 150 settlements in the West Bank with a civilian population of 175,000; in East Jerusalem approximately 180,000 Israelis were resident; in the Gaza Strip, 6,000 settlers lived in 16 settlements; and in the Golan Heights, 16,500 settlers resided in 33 settlements. By the end of 1999, more than 375,000 Israelis are living in over 200 communities established since 1967 in the West Bank, East Jerusalem, the Gaza Strip, and the Golan Heights.

Benjamin Netanyahu's settlement record during his almost three-year tenure has not been inconsiderable. He has presided over the increase of the settler population from 150,000 to more than 180,000 in the West Bank and Gaza Strip, a rise of 20 percent. Israeli government sources claim that 20,000 dwelling units have been constructed, if not necessarily completed and occupied, in the West Bank and Gaza Strip under Netanyahu. Almost 14,000 units have been sold during the same period.

During 1998, existing West Bank settlements were expanded by 8,219 *dunums*, and those in East Jerusalem by 8,400 *dunums*. Netanyahu has inaugurated six new industrial parks—in the south Hebron area, near Ma'ale Mikmash, at Keddumim, Shaked, Ma'ale Ephriam, and Ariel. During his tenure twenty new neighborhoods in existing settlements and more than 100 new "footholds"—some of which are destined to evolve into new and distinct settlements, have been established. Five paramilitary settlements, known as *nahals,* have been transformed into permanent civilian settlements—at Giva'ot near the Etzion Bloc, Rachelim, near Shilo, and Hemdat, Avnat, and Baroush in the Jordan valley.

In the aftermath of the Wye accords, the Israeli cabinet approved the construction of 20 "bypass roads" at a cost of $70 million throughout the West Bank. The purpose of the roads is to strengthen the Israeli presence in the West Bank—by forging modern communication, security, and transport links between settlements and Israel. By early January 1999, 14 of the 20 were in advanced stages of construction.

Geoffrey Aronson

BIBLIOGRAPHY

Chua, Dale. "Fiscal Policy and Its Impact on Private Sector Activity." In *The Economy of the West Bank and Gaza Strip.* Washington, D.C.: International Monetary Fund, 1998.

Foundation for Middle East Peace. *Report on Israeli Settlement in the Occupied Territories.* Washington, D.C.: Foundation for Middle East Peace, July–August, 1999.

Qumsieh, Violet. "The Environmental Impact of Jewish Settlements in the West Bank". *Palestine-Israel Review* 5, no. 6 (1998): 33.

United Nations, Economic and Social Commission for Western Asia. "Survey of Economic and Social Developments in the ESCWA Region," 1997–1998 (E/ESCWA/ED/1998/5).

Istiqlal Party

Reconstituted in August 1932 by activists associated with an earlier pan-Arab party of the same name, the new Istiqlal Party represented the rise of a more militant trend in nationalist politics led by educated men frustrated by the failure of the leading nationalist figures to check British support for ZIONISM in the 1920s and early 1930s. Unwilling to work within the context of the British PALESTINE MANDATE to confront Zionism, Istiqlal leaders like AWNI ABD AL-HADI, AKRAM ZU'AYTIR, and IZZAT DARWAZA contended that the only way to combat Zionism was to work for the end of the Mandate, to be replaced by a Palestinian government.

The Istiqlal not only opposed what it perceived as the failed moderation of the ARAB EXECUTIVE and the SUPREME MUSLIM COUNCIL, it also criticized the division in Palestinian nationalist ranks stemming from the bitter HUSAYNI FAMILY–NASHASHIBI FAMILY rivalry. The fact that both of these families were from JERUSALEM whereas many Istiqlal figures were from NABLUS lent a regional flavor to the Istiqlal's challenge for leadership of the nationalist movement.

The Istiqlal incurred the wrath of the Supreme Muslim Council president, AL-HAJJ AMIN AL-HUSAYNI, the leading nationalist figure by the early 1930s, by criticizing what it perceived as his moderation. Without adequate institutional and financial support, the Istiqlal was unable to combat al-Husayni's attempts to check the party's challenge to his leadership of the nationalist movement and declined after 1933. The leading party figure, Awni Abd al-Hadi, was appointed to the ARAB HIGHER COMMITTEE in 1936.

Michael R. Fischbach

J

Jabari, Muhammad Ali

mayor of Hebron
1900? 1901?–1980 Hebron

Muhammad Ali Jabari studied at al-Azhar University in Cairo, earning degrees in 1918, 1921, and 1922 before returning to Palestine. He later earned a degree in Islamic law in 1931 and adopted the religious title *al-shaykh.*

Jabari became mayor of HEBRON in 1940. A supporter of Jordan's King Abdullah, he chaired the December 1949 Jericho Conference that called for unity with Jordan. A pillar of the pro-Jordanian WEST BANK establishment, Jabari continued to serve as mayor as well as senator and minister of education in the Jordanian government.

Immediately after Israel's occupation of the West Bank in 1967, Jabari argued for creating an autonomous Palestinian entity rather than returning to Jordanian control in the event of an Israeli withdrawal. He attracted few followers, and by 1972 he was advocating a confederal arrangement with Jordan instead. A traditional-style leader, Jabari lost the 1976 mayoral elections in a race that symbolized the rise of a new generation of pro–PALESTINE LIBERATION ORGANIZATION nationalist leaders in the West Bank.

Michael R. Fischbach

Jabra, Jabra Ibrahim

writer
1919? 1920?–1994 Bethlehem

After studies at the ARAB COLLEGE in Jerusalem, Jabra Ibrahim Jabra studied at Exeter University and received an M.A. in English literature at Cambridge University. He returned to Jerusalem and taught at al-RASHIDIYYA SCHOOL from 1944 to 1948, before moving to Iraq after the ARAB–ISRAELI WAR OF 1948.

Jabra was a major figure in Palestinian LITERATURE. He wrote numerous works of poetry, fiction, and literary criticism in both Arabic and English. His books include a collection of prose poetry, *Lamat al-Shams* (Agony of the Sun), published in 1981, and *Hunters in a Narrow Street,* written in English and published in 1955. His autobiography, *Al-Bir al-Ula* (The first well), was published in 1987.

Jabra received several Iraqi and Palestinian literary awards, including the Jerusalem Medal for literary achievement of the PALESTINE LIBERATION ORGANIZATION.

Michael R. Fischbach

BIBLIOGRAPHY

Jayyusi, Salma Khadra ed. *Anthology of Modern Palestinian Literature.* New York: Columbia University Press, 1992.

Jaffa

Known in Arabic as *Yafa,* in Hebrew as *Yafo,* and in ancient biblical writings as *Joppa,* Jaffa has been occupied for millennia and conquered by numerous invaders and empires, including Romans, Crusaders, Ottomans, Napoleon, the Egyptian campaign of Ibrahim Pasha, the British, and finally, Israel. Along with ACRE, Jaffa was one of Palestine's main two seaports until the twentieth century. It was a trade city of major importance, as well as the traditional point of arrival for first pilgrims and later Jewish immigrants.

Given the city's fertile and irrigated farmland and central location, agriculture and trade were the mainstays of Jaffa's economy. Jaffa was also noted for its large fruit groves, particularly its famous orange groves, home of the renowned Jaffa orange, which was exported throughout the world.

Jaffa's position as Palestine's gateway to the world made it one of the country's most important centers of trade. Trade grew during the Egyptian period, and Jaffa's size and importance grew further as Palestine became increasingly linked with the industrial European economy in the nineteenth century. Importing and exporting were facilitated by the opening of a railroad line to Jerusalem in 1892. After World War I, the railroad line starting in Qantara was extended through Jaffa to Haifa. Jaffa was also a center for fishing and the manufacture of soap and olive oil, as well as benefiting from tourism and pilgrimage.

Jaffa's population began to grow in the nineteenth century, just as its demography began to change. Population increased from 23,000 in 1892 to 70,000 just prior to World War I. Not all of the new inhabitants were Arabs, however. Settlers from the German religious Temple Society movement arrived in 1869. The Roman Catholic Franciscan Order built a monastery on the site of the citadel, and French and Italian merchants began arriving as trade with Europe expanded. Beginning around 1841, Sephardic Jews from North Africa began settling in Jaffa as well. They were joined by European Jews from the 1880s. Despite the establishment of the all-Jewish city of Tel Aviv in 1909 just to the north of Jaffa, Jaffa's Jewish population continued to grow.

Jaffa was also one of the main cultural centers for Palestinians. Its writers made important contributions to the Palestinian literary movement, and most of the country's Arabic newspapers were published there.

The PALESTINE MANDATE and the Palestinian-Zionist conflict affected Jaffa's fortunes considerably. The city's population grew from 47,000 in 1922 to some 94,000 in 1944 (of whom 28,000 were Jews). But because of the 1936 general strike in the Palestinian sector, Haifa and Tel Aviv quickly eclipsed Jaffa in its role as the main port in Palestine, despite the opening of Jaffa's harbor that year. The city was also affected by the rising nationalist tensions between Jews and Palestinians, especially given the fact that Jaffa was the main port of entry for Jewish immigrants. Intercommunal violence escalated into general violence in April 1921. In June 1936, large parts of the old city were demolished by the British in the midst of the general strike.

In April 1948, during the ARAB-ISRAELI WAR OF 1948, Jaffa was attacked by Irgun and Haganah forces; it surrendered on May 13. After a mass exodus, only some 3,600 of its Palestinian inhabitants remained in the city by the end of 1948. The decline of Jaffa thereafter was signified by its merger with Tel Aviv and the establishment of a joint municipality.

Michael R. Fischbach

Jarallah Family

A large landowning family from Jerusalem, the Jarallahs claim descent from the Prophet Muhammad. As *ashraf* (plural of the Arabic word *sharif*, denoting lineage from the Prophet), several members held a variety of religious posts in Jerusalem.

Husam al-Din (religious scholar) A religious scholar who studied at al-Azhar University in Cairo, he was elected mufti (Islamic law expert) of Jerusalem in April 1920. British authorities convinced him to step down the following month, however, after a pressure campaign orchestrated by the HUSAYNI FAMILY. He was replaced by AL-HAJJ AMIN AL-HUSAYNI.

Michael R. Fischbach

Jenin

The northernmost of the three towns delimiting the triangle region of north-central Palestine, Jenin (Arabic, *Janin*) lies at the northern end of the central mountains of the WEST BANK region.

Jenin was an administrative center for several governments during the twentieth century. The Ottomans made Jenin the center of an administrative district bearing its name and linked it with NABLUS and Baysan via railroad. During the PALESTINE MANDATE, the British again made it the center of a subprovince bearing its name. Jenin's population doubled from some 2,000 to 3,990 between 1918 and 1945.

Agriculture was always a mainstay of Jenin's economy. Its 18,769 *dunums* of LAND produced bountiful harvests, and the town was particularly noted for its fruits and vegetables.

Jenin was the scene of fighting during the ARAB-ISRAELI WAR OF 1948. Jewish Haganah forces captured the town briefly in June 1948 but withdrew after a battle with Palestinian and Iraqi forces. Occupied thereafter by first the Iraqi and later the Jordanian armies, Jenin was eventually incorporated into the Jordanian-controlled West Bank. The armistice line, which cut Jenin off from most of its traditional markets in the areas controlled by Israel to the north and west, had a dramatic effect on trade. The town's population also swelled to some 10,000 with the influx of Palestinian REFUGEES. Meanwhile, the subsequent expansion of the built-up areas of the town reduced the area devoted to agriculture. The result was a decline in the dominance of agriculture in the city's ECONOMY.

Jenin was captured by Israel forces in June 1967 and remained occupied until the Oslo peace process (see OSLO AGREEMENTS) led to an Israeli withdrawal. The second West Bank town evacuated by Israeli forces, Jenin was under the full control of the PALESTINIAN AUTHORITY by November 13, 1995.

Michael R. Fischbach

Jericho

Lying in an oasis in the Jordan valley, Jericho (Arabic, *Ariha*) is one of the oldest continuously inhabited cities on Earth. It is a city rich in archaeological and historical significance, and one that has featured prominently in recent Palestinian history. For thousands of years, Jericho's oasis waters and rich farmland have been the basis for its irrigation and agriculture, including the planting of citrus fruits and bananas. Trade was also important to Jericho, as the city has lain on centuries-old trade and communication routes linking the Jordan valley to other parts of Palestine and the wider Middle East. Jericho is also a major center for tourism, drawing visitors to its archaeological sites, pilgrims to nearby religious complexes, and tourists fleeing colder locales during the winter months.

As the largest inhabited area in the lower Jordan valley, Jericho was the center for an administrative district during the Ottoman era beginning in 1908. During the British PALESTINE MANDATE, Jericho was the seat of a subprovince bearing its name until its abolition in 1944; the Jordanians reinstituted the subprovince during their rule in the WEST BANK.

Jericho has witnessed many important events associated with the ARAB-ISRAELI CONFLICT. Jordanian troops controlled Jericho during the ARAB-ISRAELI WAR OF 1948. The town was the site of the December 1948 Jericho Congress, which called for Jordanian rule in the West Bank. Three refugee camps were established outside the town as well. In June 1967, Israel occupied Jericho, and almost all of the REFUGEES living in the three camps near the city fled to Jordan.

After nearly three decades of Israeli occupation, beginning in June 1967, Jericho was the first West Bank town from which Israeli forces withdrew as a result of the 1993 OSLO AGREEMENTS signed by Israel and the PALESTINE LIBERATION ORGANIZATION (PLO). Palestinian and Israeli negotiators had considered an Israeli withdrawal from the GAZA STRIP and Jericho as a preliminary step to a final settlement. The subsequent Cairo accords of May 1994 led to the withdrawal of Israeli troops from Jericho and Gaza and the transfer of power in those areas to a new PALESTINIAN AUTHORITY (PA). Troops of the PLO's PALESTINE LIBERATION ARMY entered the town on May 13, 1994, and the PA assumed control thereafter.

Michael R. Fischbach

Jerusalem

Bayt al-Maqdis; al-Quds al-Sharif; al-Quds

Jerusalem's Significance for Palestinians The importance of Jerusalem to Christianity and Islam, the religions practiced by the overwhelming majority of Palestinians, lies at the heart of the city's significance to them. Moreover, vital political, cultural, and geographical factors underscore the centrality of the city for the Palestinians.

For Palestinian Christians, Jerusalem contains numerous HOLY PLACES associated with the Bible generally and with the life, death, and resurrection of Jesus in particular. According to the Bible, the Arabic translation of which refers to the city as *Urshalim,* Jesus worshiped in the Hebrew second Temple that stood on Mount Moriah (also called Temple Mount) in the Old City of Jerusalem, now known in Arabic as al-Haram al-Sharif ("the Noble Sanctuary"). The city also witnessed the events of Passion Week, including the Last Supper on Mount Zion, Jesus' arrest in the Garden of Gethsamane at the foot of the Mount of Olives, and his trial, crucifixion, and burial. The Via Dolorosa ("The Way of sorrows") through the Old City marks the path trodden by Jesus on his way to execution. The ancient Church of the Holy Sepulchre in the Old City's Christian Quarter, the present edifice of which dates from Crusader times, was built in 335 C.E. over the site reputed to be that of Jesus' execution and burial. Additionally, Christian tradition points to the summit of the Mount of Olives as the site of the ascension of Christ into heaven after his resurrection.

With the advent of Islam in the seventh century C.E., Jerusalem assumed a great importance to Muslims both in Palestine and throughout the Islamic world. Outside Mecca and Medina, Jerusalem is the holiest place on earth for Muslims. The city is associated with the life of the Prophet Muhammad, who, according to Islamic tradition, tethered Buraq, his "fabulous steed," to a spot near Temple Mount during his nocturnal journey to heaven. This event is commemorated in the Islamic holiday al-Israwa al-Mi'raj. The centrality of the city to Islam is also seen in the fact that it was the first *qibla,* or direction of prayer, although Mecca soon replaced it.

The Muslim Arabs' conquest of Jerusalem in 638 C.E. soon saw the erection of some of Islam's holiest shrines in the Old City. The Dome of the Rock shrine, known in Arabic as Qubbat al-Sakhra and sometimes erroneously in English as the Mosque of Omar, was completed by the Umayyad dynasty in 691. It is built over a stone where Islamic tradition maintains that Abraham prepared to sacrifice his son, Isma'il (Ishmael) in obedience of God's command, and whence Muhammad made his nocturnal journey to heaven as well. The Dome of the Rock is considered one of the first great Islamic public buildings ever built and one of the earliest examples of Islamic architecture; inscriptions from the Qur'an on the Dome of the Rock's tiles represent some of the oldest written forms of the Qur'an in existence. Near the Dome of the Rock stands the al-Aqsa Mosque, originally constructed in the first decade of the eighth century. The present structure dates from 1033. The city's most important mosque and the third holiest mosque in the world, it has stood as the focal point for Muslim worship in Palestine since its construction. The walled compound containing al-Aqsa and the Dome of the Rock is known as al-Haram al-Sharif.

Jerusalem is also home to numerous Islamic pious endowments (*waqfs*), tombs, libraries, cemeteries, schools, and other institutions. *Waqfs* were established throughout the Islamic period, especially during Ottoman times (1517–1918). The Tekiyye Hospice, built in 1551 and endowed through *waqf* funds, contained a school, mosque, *sufi* (Islamic mystical) lodge, *khan* (travelers' hospice), and soup kitchen. The Mamilla cemetery in West Jerusalem contains the remains of numerous figures from the early Islamic period.

Jews also venerate Jerusalem (Hebrew, Yerushalayim) as the ancient capital of the Hebrew kingdom and the site of their first Temple, constructed on Temple Mount during the reign of King Solomon in the tenth century B.C.E. Jerusalem was also the site of the second Temple, which was enlarged during the reign of King Herod (ruled 37–4 B.C.E.). A remnant of the exterior wall of this temple still stands, and is known as the Western Wall (Hebrew, *ha-Kotel ha-Ma'aravi*), or the Wailing Wall. The wall comprises the southwest corner of al-Haram al-Sharif today. Jews also venerate the Mount of Olives and its ancient cemetery, revering such tombs as the one reputed to be that of King David on Mount Zion and that of Simon the Just. The city also houses numerous yeshivas (academies devoted to the study of rabbinic literature).

Jerusalem is also the political and cultural center for Palestinians. Its political importance was reflected in the fact that the Ottomans made it the administrative center of the independent subprovince (*sanjaq*) of Jerusalem, which was governed directly from Istanbul after 1867. Control of Islam's third holiest city was an important source of legitimacy for such Islamic rulers as the Ottoman sultans.

More recently, the city has represented a key aspect of Palestinian political aspirations during

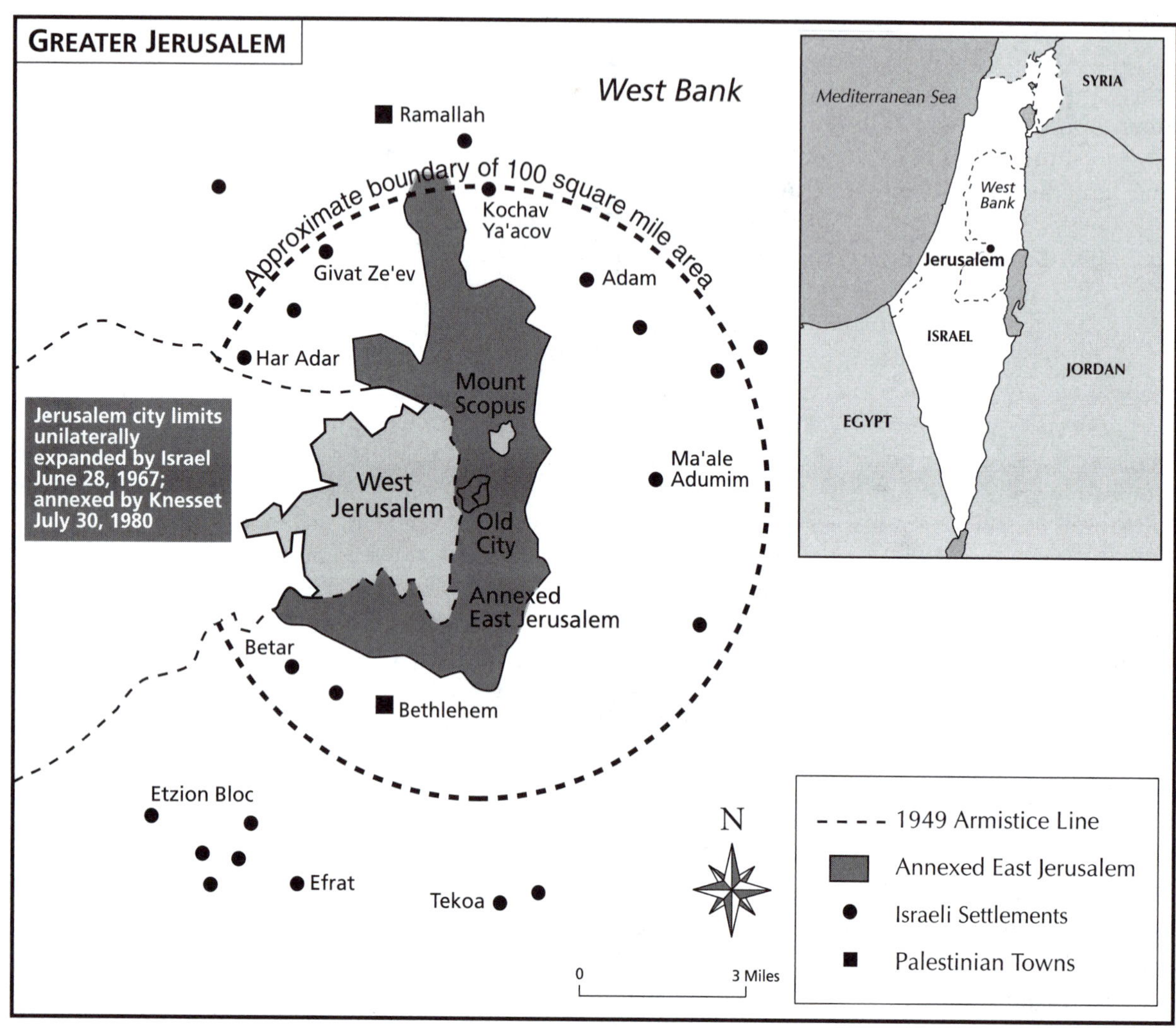
GREATER JERUSALEM
West Bank
Ramallah
Approximate boundary of 100 square mile area
Kochav Ya'acov
Givat Ze'ev
Adam
Har Adar
Mount Scopus
Jerusalem city limits unilaterally expanded by Israel June 28, 1967; annexed by Knesset July 30, 1980
West Jerusalem
Old City
Ma'ale Adumim
Annexed East Jerusalem
Betar
Bethlehem
Etzion Bloc
Efrat
Tekoa
N
0
3 Miles
1949 Armistice Line
Annexed East Jerusalem
Israeli Settlements
Palestinian Towns
Mediterranean Sea
SYRIA
West Bank
Jerusalem
ISRAEL
JORDAN
EGYPT

SOURCE: Foundation for Middle East Peace, January, 1995

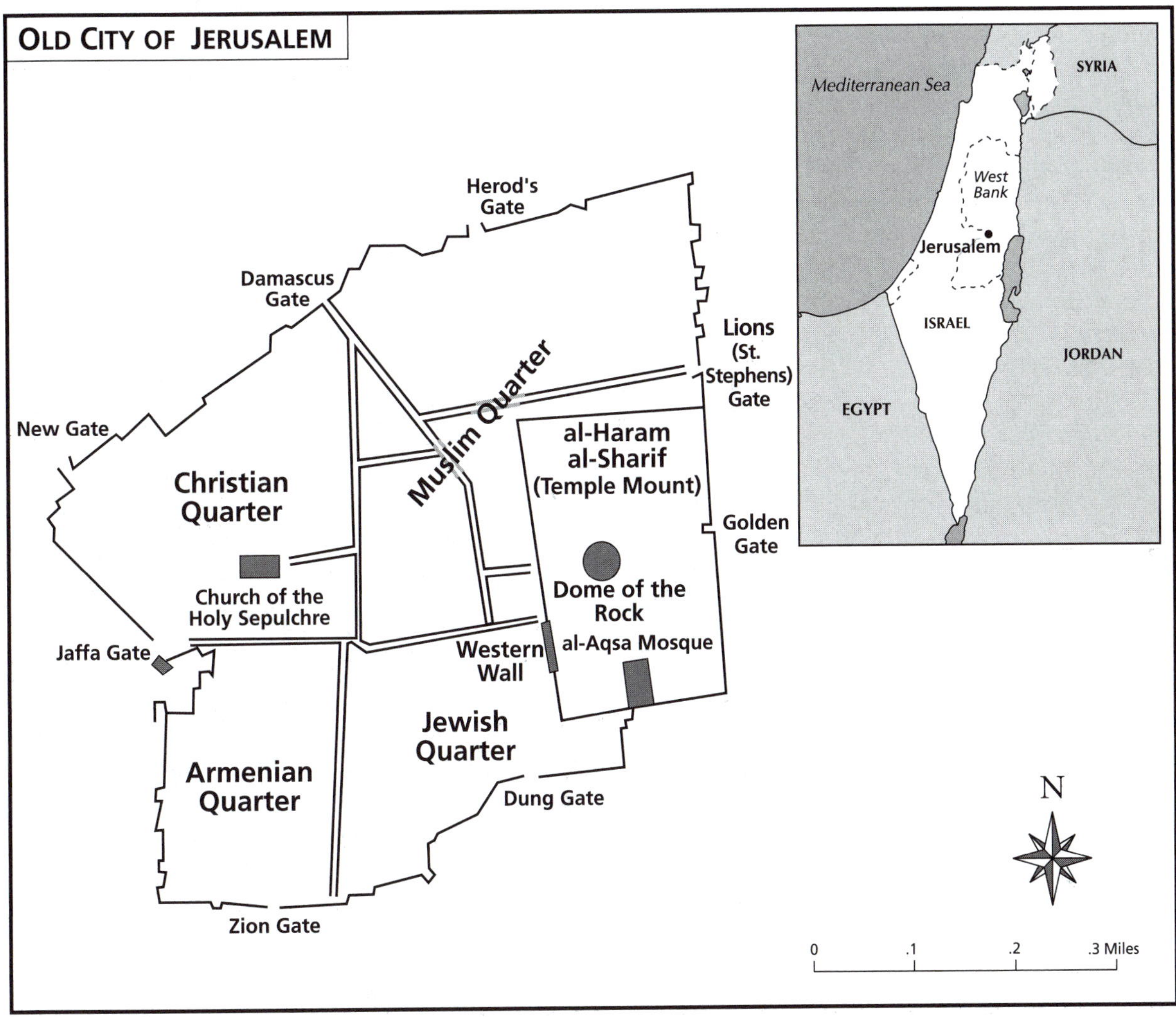
OLD CITY OF JERUSALEM
Herod's Gate
Damascus Gate
Lions (St. Stephens) Gate
New Gate
Muslim Quarter
Christian Quarter
al-Haram al-Sharif (Temple Mount)
Golden Gate
Church of the Holy Sepulchre
Dome of the Rock
Jaffa Gate
Western Wall
al-Aqsa Mosque
Jewish Quarter
Armenian Quarter
Dung Gate
Zion Gate
Mediterranean Sea
SYRIA
West Bank
Jerusalem
ISRAEL
JORDAN
EGYPT
N
0
.1
.2
.3 Miles

the twentieth century even though Palestinians never exercised national control over it. The city's vital geographical location in the heart of Palestine has made its control central for any Palestinian political entity. Additionally, many of the leaders of the Palestinian national movement in the early and mid-twentieth century hailed from the city's leading families, some of whom trace their ancestry to the Islamic conquest of the city in the seventh century. They include the HUSAYNI FAMILY, the KHALIDI FAMILY, the NASHASHIBI FAMILY, the DAJANI FAMILY (JERUSALEM), the ALAMI FAMILY, and the JARALLAH FAMILY. The PALESTINE LIBERATION ORGANIZATION (PLO), the most significant organization in Palestinian political history, was established at a conference in the city in 1964. Finally, the PLO's 1988 Declaration of Palestinian Independence named Jerusalem as the capital of a Palestinian state.

Culturally, the city has exercised a central role in modern Palestinian life thanks to the numerous schools, charitable and religious institutions, libraries, newspapers, theater groups, and literary societies established during the twentieth century. Palestine's best two secondary schools during the PALESTINE MANDATE, the ARAB COLLEGE and RASHIDIYYA SCHOOL, were located in the city. The person holding the leading Islamic office in the city, that of mufti (Islamic law expert), was elevated under the Mandate to become essentially the mufti of all Palestine. The KHALIDI LIBRARY, established in 1900, houses hundreds of medieval Arabic manuscripts and remains the largest private library of its kind in Palestine. And the first two newspapers published in Palestine, *al-Quds al-Sharif* and *al-Ghazal,* appeared in Jerusalem in 1876.

Jerusalem in Palestinian History

Ottoman Period

The Ottoman Turks conquered the city in 1517 and built the walls that still surround the Old City from 1537 to 1541. By the end of the Ottoman era, there were seven gates leading into the Old City: Damascus Gate (Arabic, Bab al-Amud), New Gate (al-Bab al-Jadid), Jaffa Gate (Bab al-Khalil), Zion Gate (Bab al-Nabi Da'ud), Dung Gate (Bab al-Maghariba), St. Stephen's, or Lion's, Gate (Bab Sittna Maryam), and Herod's Gate (Bab al-Zahira). Four more gates are blocked, the most famous is the Golden, or Mercy Gate (Bab al-Dahriya or Bab al-Rahma). The Old City was also characterized by its residential districts or quarters: the Muslim Quarter, the Christian Quarter, the Armenian Quarter, and the Jewish Quarter. Until the third quarter of the nineteenth century, almost no city dwellers lived outside the city walls.

Yet during the Ottoman period, Jerusalem became subject to political and demographic changes from Europe that the city's walls could not keep out. As European powers renewed their interest in Christian holy sites in the city, Ottoman authorities took measures to ensure the special status of Jerusalem. Beginning in the 1840s and permanently after 1867, Jerusalem was made the administrative center of an independent subprovince (*sanjaq*) directly controlled by Ottoman authorities in Istanbul. Jerusalem's importance to both the empire and Europe alike was demonstrated by the visit of Kaiser Wilhelm II of Germany to the city in 1898.

The Ottomans also oversaw the gradual movement of European Jews to Jerusalem over several centuries, a process that would lead to a demographic shift away from Palestinians and in favor of Jews by the end of the nineteenth century. Jewish immigration accelerated, beginning in the second half of that century. The Jewish quarter of Mishkenot Sha'ananim, completed by 1860, was the first settlement constructed outside the Old City's walls in modern times and represented the establishment of what became known as the New City or West Jerusalem. Most Jews who immigrated over the Ottoman centuries did so for religious reasons, although the onset of political Zionist immigration in the fourth quarter of the nineteenth century spread the seeds of an eventual political conflict with Palestinians for control of the city.

During World War I, the Ottomans fought Allied troops in Palestine. With the British advancing from Egypt under the command of General Sir Edmund Allenby, the Ottoman army decided in December 1917 to withdraw from the city to spare it the ravages of combat. Jerusalem's Palestinian mayor, Husayn Salim al-Husayni, surrendered the city, whereupon it was occupied on December 9, 1917, by British forces.

The Mandate

Beginning in 1917, Jerusalem was subject to British military rule in Palestine until June 1920 and the creation of a civil administration headquartered in the city under a high commissioner.

The first HIGH COMMISSIONER FOR PALESTINE was Sir Herbert Samuel, a Zionist Jew. Jerusalem would remain the administrative center of the district of Jerusalem and Palestine's capital throughout the Mandate. According to the first British census in Palestine, the city's population stood at 33,971 Jews and 28,112 Palestinians in 1922.

Unlike the Ottomans, the British facilitated the Zionist transformation of Palestine generally and of Jerusalem specifically by allowing Jewish immigration and land purchases. Mounting Palestinian-Zionist nationalist tensions were often focused on Jerusalem, given the city's importance to Jews and Arabs alike. Palestinian fears of political as well as demographic displacement at the hands of Zionists led to outbreaks of violence in Jerusalem as early as April 1920.

In August 1929, far more serious political violence, known as the WESTERN (WAILING) WALL DISTURBANCES, stemming from Palestinian-Zionist tensions over Jewish worship at the Western Wall (part of an Islamic *waqf* [religious endowment]), broke out in Jerusalem and quickly spread to other cities. The disturbances led to the formation of several British commissions of inquiry and were among the first major incidents to prompt the British to reassess their role in fostering the Zionist venture in Palestine.

Throughout the Mandate, Jerusalem became the center of the Palestinian political struggle against the British and against ZIONISM. The major religious and nationalist organizations that exerted leadership in the Palestinian community—the ARAB EXECUTIVE, the SUPREME MUSLIM COUNCIL, the ARAB HIGHER COMMITTEE, and several of the major political parties—were headed by politicians from Jerusalem. The city assumed an important position in the 1936–39 Arab revolt waged by Palestinians against the British and Zionists. Stamps issued by Palestinian guerrillas depicted the Dome of the Rock, and guerrillas briefly took control of the Old City in October 1936.

The demographic effects of Zionist immigration by the twilight of British rule in Palestine were reflected in the city's population statistics. Jerusalem's population in the late 1940s consisted of some 60,600 Palestinians, evenly divided between Christians and Muslims, and 97,000 Jews. Jews resided in the Jewish Quarter in the Old City and in various neighborhoods in West Jerusalem.

1948–1967

After Britain's 1947 decision to end its rule in Palestine, effective May 15, 1948, Jerusalem became a major strategic objective as Palestinians, Zionists, and the surrounding Arab states prepared for war. This came despite the fact that the United Nations proposed including Jerusalem within an international zone controlled by neither side. Localized Palestinian-Zionist fighting of late 1947 to May 1948 and the full-scale Arab-Israeli war that broke out in May 1948 eventually left Jerusalem a divided city, neither side of which lay under the control of Palestinians. Zionist forces not only held the Jewish areas in West Jerusalem but captured Palestinian areas in the western part of the city as well on April 30, 1948. However, they controlled only the Jewish Quarter of the Old City. The rest of the Old City, the eastern districts, and the eastern suburbs were entered by Jordanian forces on May 18. The ensuing Zionist-Jordanian fighting for the Jewish Quarter was among the most bitter of the entire war, and Zionist forces in the quarter surrendered ten days later. The July 1948 cease-fire left the city divided into East and West Jerusalem, controlled by Jordan and Israel, respectively.

Jerusalem and its centrality to the Palestinian national cause were thereafter significantly transformed by both Jordan and Israel, most noticeably by the latter. Perhaps the most significant early result of Israel's capture of West Jerusalem was the depopulation of its Palestinian inhabitants. Zionist forces captured not only the predominantly Jewish portions of West Jerusalem, but the Palestinian and mixed districts as well. These included Qatamon, Talbiyya, Mamilla, Sham'a, Musrara, Upper Baq'a, Lower Baq'a, al-Shaykh Badr, the Greek Colony, the German Colony, and Abu Tawr. In the process, over 60,000 Palestinians fled or were driven out from the city and four surrounding villages that Israel included within the expanded boundaries of West Jerusalem: Lifta, DAYR YASIN, al-Maliha, and Ayn Karim. Through this expansion, the surface area of West Jerusalem, which Israel began considering its de facto capital as early as December 1948, stood at some 37,000 *dunums* (1 *dunum* = 1,000 square meters) by 1967. Land belonging to Palestinian refugees from the city, estimated at 40 percent of West Jerusalem prior to 1948, was placed under the Israeli Custodian of Absentee

Property office and eventually sold to the Development Authority in 1950, whereupon it was subject to exclusive Jewish use. Israel's parliament, the Knesset—the building itself was built on Palestinian land—declared that Jerusalem was the capital of Israel in January 1950.

Although Jordan's control of East Jerusalem did not change the Arab character of the city, it nonetheless affected the city's fortunes. No Jew remained in any part of the city after 1948, and the 60,000 Palestinian residents were made Jordanian citizens after Jordan's annexation of the West Bank in April 1950. The city's political importance was likewise diminished in comparison to that of Jordan's capital, Amman. Simmering Palestinian political resentments against Jordan's annexation and its monarch, King ABDULLAH, led to Abdullah's assassination at the hands of a Palestinian in the Haram al-Sharif in July 1951.

After 1967

The fighting for Jerusalem during the June 1967 Arab-Israeli war proved the heaviest and costliest to Israel of any front during the war. Capturing the Old City was a major goal of the Israeli army; it was accomplished by paratrooper units entering from the Mount of Olives on June 7.

Almost immediately after the end of hostilities, Israel began to alter the Arab character of East Jerusalem as it had that of West Jerusalem. Israel formally annexed East Jerusalem and united it with West Jerusalem on June 28, 1967. In addition, a large area of some 72,000 *dunums* to the north, east, and south of the Old City were incorporated into the boundaries of the new, unified city. On July 30, 1980, the Knesset enacted the "Basic Law on Jerusalem," which declared that a unified Jerusalem was the "eternal" capital of Israel.

Israeli policy since 1967 has seriously eroded the Palestinian demography of East Jerusalem just as it did in West Jerusalem after 1948. This was immediately seen in the Old City. In the Maghribi Quarter, adjacent to the Western Wall and al-Haram al-Sharif, Israeli forces demolished 135 homes and at least 2 historic mosques built on *waqf* land and displaced over 600 Palestinians on June 8, 1967, in order to build a square for Jewish worshipers in front of the Wall. In April 1968, the government initiated a plan to repopulate the Jewish Quarter with Jewish residents by expropriating 116 *dunums* of Palestinian-owned land in the Old City. This process eventually affected some 6,000 Palestinians. Religious Jews began an aggressive campaign in the 1970s to take up residence in the Christian and Muslim quarters, where few Jews had lived historically, as well.

It is not only in the Old City that the full weight of the Israeli's policy of Judaizing East Jerusalem has been felt. As early as February 1971, Israel announced its intention to construct Jewish settlements outside the Old City to surround the Arab areas of East Jerusalem from the north, east, and south. Since 1967, Israeli authorities have confiscated about one third of the 72,000 *dunums* of Palestinian land annexed in 1967 in order to construct settlements such as Neve Ya'akov, Ramot Eshkol, and Gilo.

When Israel and the PLO signed the Declaration of Principles in September 1993, the success of Israel's demographic policy of Judaizing Jerusalem was reflected in the city's population statistics: the population of the expanded city stood at 564,300: 260,900 in Jewish West Jerusalem, and 303,400 in East Jerusalem (of whom 150,600 were Palestinians and 152,800 Jewish settlers). Jews comprised 73.3 percent of the total population.

In addition to cadastral and demographic changes, the Israeli occupation of East Jerusalem has affected the city's cultural and political importance to Palestinians. A particularly volatile trend has been the threat to religious shrines and worshipers. Muslims have feared that Israeli archaeological digs near the Haram al-Sharif since 1967 might compromise the structural integrity of the area. In August 1969, an Australian Christian set a fire in al-Aqsa Mosque and destroyed a pulpit placed there in the twelfth century by the Islamic ruler Nur al-Din. Several attempts by Jewish militants to blow up the Islamic shrines on al-Haram al-Sharif were foiled in the early 1980s. In April 1982, an American-born Israeli shot his way into the Dome of the Rock, killing two Palestinians and injuring many others. And in October 1990, Israeli border police opened fire on Palestinian demonstrators in the Haram al-Sharif, killing seventeen. The explosion of Palestinian anger that led to confrontations between Israelis and Palestinians throughout the WEST BANK and the GAZA STRIP in September 1996 after the opening of a tunnel near al-Haram al-Sharif by Israeli authorities must be understood in light of these events.

On the political level, Israel undercut Palestinian institutions in Jerusalem and detached the city from the rest of the occupied West Bank after unification in 1967. East Jerusalem's municipal council was dismissed in June 1967. Its mayor, Ruhi al-Khatib, who was also chair of the Higher Committee for National Guidance that was formed to coordinate anti-Israel protests, was deported in March 1968. Palestinians living in East Jerusalem were also separated administratively from other Palestinians in the Occupied Territories and granted Israeli residency status. Most recently, Israeli authorities prevented Palestinians from Jerusalem from participating in the Arab-Israeli peace talks that commenced in 1991, refused to allow the PALESTINIAN AUTHORITY, established in 1994, to conduct official business in the city, and steadfastly maintained that Jerusalem was the undivided, "eternal" capital of Israel, over which it would not relinquish sovereignty.

Jerusalem and the Peace Process Because of Jerusalem's significance, it has remained central to the ARAB-ISRAELI CONFLICT and the peace process. Its future has also been discussed in special terms that differ from those proposed for other areas of Palestine. By the mid-1990s, Jerusalem's status became one of the central questions awaiting resolution by the Israeli-PLO peace process begun in 1993.

Jerusalem's special position and centrality to a territorial resolution to the Zionist-Palestinian conflict was recognized as early as 1937, when the British PEEL COMMISSION first proposed partitioning Palestine between Jews and Palestinians but maintaining British rule over Jerusalem given its special status. In November 1947, the United Nations (U.N.) General Assembly voted in favor of PARTITION PLANS that proposed making an area including Jerusalem an international zone—a *corpus separatum*—to be governed by a U.N. trusteeship council. The 1948 fighting and the division of the city into Israeli and Jordanian hands rendered this concept inoperable. A 1949 proposal by the UNITED NATIONS CONCILIATION COMMISSION FOR PALESTINE for a joint administration of holy sites similarly never came to fruition. As a result of the unsettled situation, the international community refused to recognize the 1950 declaration of Jerusalem as Israel's capital, Israel's 1967 annexation of East Jerusalem, and its expansion of the city's boundaries. Most countries therefore demurred at situating their diplomatic missions in the city, particularly after 1967.

Jerusalem retained its significance for the Palestinians despite the division of the city between 1948 and 1967 and Israel's complete control over it after 1967. In 1964, the Palestine Liberation Organization (PLO) was created at a conference held in East Jerusalem. The rise of the PLO in the late 1960s and its preeminent position as the leading Palestinian nationalist institution led to a variety of strategic visions of Palestine after its liberation from Israel. Jerusalem always featured large in these visions. By the 1970s, the PLO had pledged itself to a two-state solution in which a Palestinian state would be established in the West Bank and Gaza with Jerusalem as its capital. This vision was enshrined in the November 15, 1988, Declaration of Palestinian Independence, in which the PLO declared Jerusalem as capital of the Palestinian state.

The wider Arab and Islamic world has also maintained interests in Jerusalem. Jordan administered East Jerusalem and its shrines in 1948–67 and retained its interest in the holy sites and *waqf* land even after King Husayn's 1988 decision to disengage from the West Bank. Jordan undertook major restorations on al-Haram al-Sharif in 1958 and again in the early 1990s. Additionally, the Israeli-Jordanian peace treaty of October 1994 makes reference to Jordan's historic role vis-à-vis Jerusalem's Islamic shrines. Saudi Arabia has also demonstrated an interest in the city's Islamic shrines. And in 1975, the Islamic Conference Organization established a Jerusalem Committee headed by Morocco's King Hasan II.

The future of Jerusalem became one of the most important issues facing the Israeli-Palestinian peace process begun in Oslo in 1993. The two sides agreed to postpone formal talks on the city until final status discussions. However, Israeli officials have long stated their opposition to any cessation of sovereignty over any part of the city and have forbidden the Palestinian Authority (PA) to conduct official business from the city. In particular, Israeli authorities took measures to prevent PA officials from using ORIENT HOUSE in East Jerusalem for such purposes as meeting with foreign dignitaries.

Mounting Palestinian frustration with the lack of progress in the final status talks, continued restrictions on Palestinians' entering Israel, and other issues exploded into violence in Jerusalem and other areas in the West Bank and Gaza in September 1996. The event that triggered the violence was Israel's opening of a tunnel running adjacent to al-Haram al-Sharif. During the disturbances, Israeli security forces fired on demonstrators on the Haram, killing several.

✦ ✦ ✦

The situation facing Palestinians in Jerusalem continued to worsen in the late 1990s. Israel's controversial decision to construct a largely Jewish settlement on the hilltop known as Jabal Abu Ghunaym (Hebrew, Har Homa) in the southern portion of East Jerusalem provoked widespread international outcry and brought the peace process to a virtual standstill. Israeli authorities also began a campaign to confiscate the identification cards of Palestinian Jerusalemites who resided outside the city limits and maintained their "closure" of the city to residents of the West Bank and Gaza for long periods. The lack of government-approved town planning schemes also meant the expansion of Palestinian residential areas to ease crowding was virtually impossible.

Both Palestinian and Israeli officials maintained maximalist positions regarding the city's political status and their respective intentions to declare Jerusalem their capital. But reports surfaced in the mid-1990s of a secret Palestinian willingness to consider making the nearby locality of Abu Dis, east of the Old City, the capital of a future Palestinian state. Similarly, polls indicated that although most Israelis considered the city their eternal capital, they cared much less about retaining control over heavily Palestinian districts outside the Old City in East Jerusalem.

The future of Jerusalem continued to be one of the most important aspects of the peace process for Palestinians. It will also be one of the most difficult issues to resolve in the final status negotiations between Chairman Arafat and the government of Ehud Barak.

Michael R. Fischbach

BIBLIOGRAPHY

Asali, K. J., ed. *Jerusalem in History.* New York: Olive Branch Press, 1990.

Bovis, Eugene H. *The Jerusalem Question, 1917–1968.* Stanford, Calif.: The Hoover Institution Press, 1971.

Cohen, Amnon. *Economic Life in Ottoman Jerusalem.* Cambridge, England: Cambridge University Press, 1989.

Peters, F. E. *The Distant Shrine: The Islamic Centuries in Jerusalem.* New York: AMS Press, 1993.

Talhami, Ghada. "Between Development and Preservation: Jerusalem under Three Regimes." *America-Arab Affairs* 16 (1986): 93–107.

Tamari, Salim, ed. *Jerusalem 1948: The Arab Neighbourhoods and Their Fate in the War.* Jerusalem: Institute of Jerusalem Studies and Badil Resource Center, 1999.

Tibawi, A. L. *Jerusalem: Its Place in Islamic and Arab History.* Beirut: Institute for Palestine Studies, 1969.

Wilson, Evan M. *Jerusalem: Key to Peace.* Washington, D.C.: The Middle East Institute, 1970.

Jewish Settlements

See ISRAELI SETTLEMENTS.

Jibril, Ahmad

guerrilla leader
b. 1935 Ramla

A graduate of Britain's royal military academy at Sandhurst, Ahmad Jibril reached the rank of captain in the Syrian army before being expelled during the first days of the 1958 Syrian-Egyptian union. He was in contact briefly with FATAH in 1965 before creating his own organization of commandos—the PALESTINE LIBERATION FRONT, which, from the end of 1966 to the beginning of the 1967 war, conducted a number of military operations against Israel. In December 1967, he joined the POPULAR FRONT FOR THE LIBERATION OF PALESTINE (PFLP), but he quit in November 1968, criticizing the organization for adopting extreme positions, losing itself in political debates, and not according enough importance to armed struggle. He created the POPULAR FRONT FOR THE LIBERATION OF PALESTINE GENERAL COMMAND, which became famous for its sensational military operations.

Alain Gresh

Jiryis, Sabri

lawyer, activist, scholar
1938– Fassuta, Galilee

Sabri Jiryis studied law at the Hebrew University of JERUSALEM in 1957–1962 before practicing law in Israel. He later became a leading figure in the pan-

Arab nationalist al-Ard movement, which emerged in 1959 as a vehicle for noncommunist activism of PALESTINIAN CITIZENS OF ISRAEL. He helped edit its newspaper, *al-Ard,* which appeared in 1959. Israeli authorities viewed al-Ard with considerable suspicion and eventually banned the movement in 1964. Jiryis himself was placed under house arrest or had his movements limited to the city of HAIFA several times. In 1966, he published in Hebrew the classic work *The Arabs in Israel,* a rigorous examination of the various methods by which Israel systematically discriminated against its Palestinian citizens. It was later translated into several languages.

Israeli authorities arrested Jiryis during the ARAB-ISRAELI WAR OF 1967. After his release, Jiryis joined FATAH and was responsible for its operations in northern Israel. Arrested again in February 1970, he was released three months later after the intervention of his French publishers. He left Israel for LEBANON and became active with the PALESTINE LIBERATION ORGANIZATION (PLO). In 1973, he began working for the Palestine Research Center in Beirut, serving as head of its Israel section. In 1978, he rose to become the center's director-general; Jiryis continued to head the center after it moved to Nicosia, Cyprus, in the wake of the 1982 Israeli invasion of Lebanon.

In 1976–77, Jiryis was involved in a series of contacts with Israeli leftists associated with the Israel-Palestine Peace Council along with the Fatah figure ISAM SARTAWI. The meetings discussed Palestinian willingness to recognize Israeli national rights and were important early Palestinian-Israeli peace contacts.

After the Israeli-PLO peace agreements of 1993 and 1994, the PLO Research Center was transferred to areas under the control of the new PALESTINIAN AUTHORITY (PA). The PA then reappointed Jiryis, whom Israel allowed to return to live in the Galilee, as director-general of the new center.

Michael R. Fischbach

Jordan

Annexation of the West Bank In December 1948, with Arab Legion troops holding the rump of eastern Palestine (the WEST BANK), King ABDULLAH of Jordan initiated a series of steps intended to incorporate that territory into his realm. First, conferences in JERICHO, NABLUS, and RAMALLAH brought together pro-Hashemite Palestinian notables to pledge their loyalty and call for the unity of the East and West Banks under Abdullah. Next, the Jordanian government dissolved all Palestinian bodies that had been active during the PALESTINE MANDATE period. Then, in March 1949, Jordan appointed governors for the JERUSALEM, Nablus, and Ramallah districts. Finally, West Bank governmental departments were gradually integrated into their respective Jordanian ministries. The use of the word *Palestine* in official Jordanian documents was subsequently forbidden, as were separate Palestinian institutions. After elections in 1950, Abdullah officially annexed the West Bank, and the legal systems of the two banks were integrated.

Close commercial and familial ties had long connected the East and West Banks. The Transjordanian bureaucracy under the British included Palestinians, just as the merchant class on the East Bank had prominent Palestinian members. In addition, the proximity of Nablus to al-Salt and of al-Karak to HEBRON had led to considerable familial and commercial relations over the years. Hence, even from the beginning, the definition of who was Jordanian as opposed to Palestinian was by no means clear. However, the identity issue did not assume real salience until Jordan extended citizenship to all Palestinians resident in the newly enlarged kingdom: some 70,000 who had taken refuge on the East Bank, the 400,000–450,000 original West Bank residents, the 280,000 refugees on the West Bank, and the tens of thousands of other Palestinians who had taken refuge in the area controlled by the Arab Legion but who were not listed on official refugee rosters. In this way, more than 800,000 Palestinians were added to a Transjordanian population of about 450,000. Although many Palestinians were undoubtedly grateful for the passport citizenship conferred, many others were resentful of the Hashemites because of their close relationship with the British, the administrators of the Mandate who had lain the groundwork for a Jewish national home in Palestine. In addition, however, Palestine had been more urbanized, had been more economically diverse, and had had a more developed infrastructure than Transjordan. Hence, despite the long-standing family and business ties, the union of the two banks was an uneasy merger.

Although some members of Palestinian notable families were soon appointed to Jordanian government posts and began to develop a stake in the new unified entity, most Palestinians had a different experience. In the early years, many were destitute and simply struggled to survive. Some Palestinians sought work in the nascent Gulf oil states to escape the poverty of the refugee camps. Economic opportunities in the West Bank were limited because central government policy between 1948 and 1967 gave preference to investment in the East Bank as part of a deliberate effort to prevent the reemergence of a West Bank political leadership capable of challenging the Hashemites.

During the 1950s, anti-Hashemite or antiregime sentiments were not limited to Jordan's Palestinian community. The most notable expression of cross-bank antiregime solidarity occurred in the 1955 demonstrations against the Baghdad Pact. This nationalist surge in Jordan was short-lived, however. Martial law was imposed after a coup attempt in April 1957. Thereafter, political parties were outlawed, and organizing of all forms was heavily restricted among Palestinians and Transjordanians alike.

Although Palestinians were well aware of their historical experience, a broad-based sense of Palestinian nationalism did not emerge in Jordan until the 1960s. An important turning point occurred in 1964 with the founding of the PALESTINE LIBERATION ORGANIZATION (PLO), which constituted the opening chapter in what became an ongoing competition between the PLO and the monarchy for the loyalty of Jordan's Palestinians. Because Jordan was the only Arab state to have annexed a part of Palestine and to have enfranchised its residents, it was also the only Arab state threatened territorially and in terms of constituency by the establishment of the PLO. Although the PLO promised not to recruit among Jordan's Palestinians, relations between the PLO and Jordan quickly deteriorated.

The 1967 War The 1967 war was a major turning point, for it discredited both the leaders and the militaries of the Arab frontline states. Moreover, during the hostilities, the Israelis drove out or triggered the departure to the East Bank of another 265,000 Palestinians, most of them from the 1948 refugee camps in the West Bank. The subsequent Israeli occupation then deprived Jordan of the West Bank's agricultural and tourism revenues and triggered an economic recession in the kingdom. As a result of this combination of factors, King Husayn was either unable or unwilling to prevent the expansion of the nascent Palestinian guerrilla organizations on Jordanian soil, and a range of Palestinian military, economic, sociopolitical, and health-care institutions developed in Jordan in the 1968–70 period. However, as the Jordanian army and economy began to recover from the 1967 defeat, the state soon began to move against the guerrillas, among whom were many Jordanians, largely from the north, who opposed the Hashemites. The first major battles in 1970, known as BLACK SEPTEMBER, resulted in the expulsion of the Palestinian resistance from the capital into the northwest of the country. Subsequent fighting in July 1971 drove those who remained to Syria and Lebanon. The institutions that had developed after the 1967 war were destroyed or closed, and any attempts at reviving them were suppressed by the Hashemite regime.

Although most Palestinians had no role in the 1970–71 confrontations and Palestinian members of the armed forces did not mutiny, the battles left deep scars on both Palestinians and Jordanians. Transjordanians came to view Palestinians as potential traitors, as Palestinians viewed Transjordanians as extensions of a repressive security apparatus. Despite the regime's subsequent focus on East Bank affairs, the private sector, which was overwhelmingly Palestinian and increasingly wealthy because of its business interests in the Gulf, appeared to have implicitly agreed that as long as Jordan provided an atmosphere conducive to economic stability, the Palestinian business community would not mount a political challenge. The 1970s witnessed an economic boom in Jordan, and, as a result, the regime enjoyed two solid bases of support: the (largely Transjordanian) upper echelons of the army and security services and the (largely Palestinian) bourgeoisie. Despite shifts in regional relations, including with the PLO, this was a formula that lasted until the political and economic crisis of 1989.

PLO-Jordanian ties continued to be a central element in shaping Jordan's relations with its Palestinian citizens. In 1974, when the Rabat Arab League Summit designated the PLO the sole legitimate representative of the Palestinians, a move that Husayn opposed, the monarch dissolved the

Jordanian parliament, half of whose members held seats representing West Bank districts. In 1976, when municipal elections on the West Bank put pro-PLO mayors in office, Jordan instituted a policy of mandatory military service for all Jordanians, intended to reinforce Hashemite claims to Palestinian allegiance. Previously, Palestinians had generally not served in the military.

Regional events such as Egypt's 1979 peace with Israel and the 1982 Israeli invasion of Lebanon drew Jordan and the Palestinians together, at least on an official level. After the PLO's defeat in 1982, both Jordan and the PLO became involved in renewed peace initiatives, and the two began serious discussions of political coordination. In this context, in order to reassert Jordan's ties to the West Bank, Husayn recalled the long-dormant parliament in January 1984. Later in the year, the seventeenth meeting of the PALESTINE NATIONAL COUNCIL was held in Amman, and in February 1985, the PLO and Jordan announced an accord on a joint approach to peace negotiations.

Disengagement Jordan also courted its (largely Palestinian) expatriates, especially those in the Gulf, to interest them in investing in the kingdom through an annual series of conferences begun in July 1985. However, by 1986, PLO–Jordanian political coordination had unraveled, and it became clear that these conferences were also intended to reinforce the loyalty of these Palestinians to Jordan. Jordan then announced an ambitious $5 billion development plan for the Occupied Territories. The expressed aim was to support the steadfastness of the population under occupation, but the underlying intent was to reinforce Hashemite–West Bank patronage lines. Amman's failure to attract external funding forced it to abandon the development plan in 1987. Jordan's political disengagement from the West Bank began in 1988. The following year, Arab oil producers refused to renew aid commitments to Jordan. They then took the further step of resolving to channel all future aid to the West Bank through the PLO. This decision coincided with the Palestinian uprising, which had begun in December 1987. Fearing a possible spillover of unrest onto the East Bank, the regime responded by stepping up internal repression. The mounting domestic and regional problems prompted King Husayn on July 31, 1988, to announce the kingdom's legal and administrative disengagement from the West Bank. Jordan thereby stripped West Bankers of their citizenship (although they continued to carry passports that did not imply citizenship) and, in effect, challenged the PLO to assume what had been Jordanian responsibilities in the territory.

Although the disengagement shocked the Palestinian communities on both banks, it eventually became clear that the king's move had opened the way for the future establishment of a Palestinian state on the West Bank. The disengagement, Husayn's subsequent liberalization of the political system beginning in 1989, and his refusal to join the anti-Iraq coalition during the GULF CRISIS, 1990–1991, led to a gradual change in the Palestinian community's perceptions of the king. By 1990, a growing number of Palestinians were expressing loyalty to him if not necessarily to the Jordanian state.

However, tensions between Palestinians and Transjordanians grew, as was demonstrated in September 1993 when some East Bankers demanded that Palestinians who might be returning to a Palestinian state not be permitted to participate in Jordanian elections, a demand that the authorities rejected. Jordan's signing of its own peace accord with Israel in October 1994 did nothing to reduce tensions. Indeed, various strands of an emerging Transjordanian nationalism that share an exclusivist, anti-Palestinian component have taken shape.

Intermarriage as well as other forms of association between Palestinians and Transjordanian have increased over the years, further blurring the distinction between the two communities and complicating the question of identity. Nevertheless, there is no question that the concerns of the nascent Transjordanian nationalist group strike a chord with many Transjordanians whose own positions are less extreme. Until the final details of the Palestinian-Israeli negotiations are agreed upon, and the broader question of the political status of Palestinian communities elsewhere in the Arab world is decided, uncertainties and fears regarding the future will continue to complicate the relationship between Palestinians and Transjordanians. The fate and identities of the two communities appear likely to become even more closely, if not easily, intertwined.

Laurie A. Brand

BIBLIOGRAPHY

Brand, Laurie A. *Palestinians in the Arab World: Institution Building and the Search for State.* New York: Columbia University Press, 1988.

——. "Liberalization and Changing Political Coalitions: The Bases of Jordan's 1990–91 Gulf Crisis Policy." *Jerusalem Journal of International Relations* 13(4): 1–46.

——. "In the Beginning Was the State: The Quest for Civil Society in Jordan." In *Civil Society in the Middle East,* ed. by August Richard Norton. Leiden: Brill, 1994.

——. *Jordan's Inter-Arab Relations: The Political Economy of Alliance Making.* New York: Columbia University Press, 1995.

Cohen, Amnon. *Political Parties in the West Bank under the Jordanian Regime, 1949–1967.* Ithaca, N.Y.: Cornell University Press, 1982.

Day, Arthur. *East Bank/West Bank: Jordan and the Prospects for Peace.* New York: Council on Foreign Relations, 1986.

Gabren, Peter. *Jordan: Crossroads of Middle Eastern Events.* Boulder, Colo.: Westview Press, 1985.

Mazur, Michael. *Economic Growth and Development in Jordan.* London: Croom Helm, 1979.

Mishal, Shaul. *West Bank/East Bank: The Palestinians in Jordan, 1949–1967.* New Haven, Conn.: Yale University Press, 1978.

Plascov, Avi. *The Palestinian Refugees in Jordan, 1948–1967.* London: Frank Cass, 1981.

Satloff, Robert. *Troubles on the East Bank: Challenges to the Domestic Stability of Jordan.* The Washington Papers, 123. Westport, Conn.: Greenwood Press, 1986.

Kanafani, Ghassan
revolutionary journalist and writer
1936–1972 Acre

Ghassan Fayiz Kanafani was born in Mandatory Palestine (see PALESTINE MANDATE). The son of a Sunni Muslim middle-class lawyer, he attended French missionary schools until forced into exile during the 1948 Palestine war.

After a brief stay in Lebanon, his family eventually settled in Damascus, where Kanafani completed his secondary education and received a United Nations Relief and Works Agency for Palestine Refugees in the Near East (UNRWA) teaching certificate in 1952. That same year he enrolled in the Department of Arabic Literature at the University of Damascus but was expelled in 1955 as a result of his involvement in the pan-Arabist Movement of Arab Nationalists (MAN), to which he had been recruited by Dr. GEORGE HABASH when the two met in 1953. His thesis, "Race and Religion in Zionist Literature," formed the basis for his 1967 study *On Zionist Literature.*

In 1955 Kanafani left Syria for a teaching position in Kuwait, and the following year he became editor of the MAN newspaper *al-Ra'i* (Opinion), until Habash persuaded him to move to Beirut and join the staff of MAN's official mouthpiece *al-Huriyya* (Freedom) in 1960. While in Kuwait, Kanafani also wrote the first of numerous short stories and began to take a serious interest in Marxism.

Forced underground in 1962 because he lacked official papers, Kanafani reemerged the following year as editor in chief of the new progressive Nasirite newspaper *al-Muharrir* (The Liberator) and editor of its weekly supplement, *Filastin* (Palestine). In 1963 he also published his first and best-known novel, *Men in the Sun,* which has since been translated into numerous languages and made into several screenplays.

Kanafani's prolific literary output, highly acclaimed for its innovative techniques, social consciousness, and fluent understanding of the Palestinian condition, won him the Lebanese Literature Prize (awarded for the novella *All That's Left to You*) in 1966 and, posthumously, the Afro-Asian Writers' Conference Lotus Prize in 1975. An important figure in modern Arab fiction, he also introduced the concept of "resistance literature" in two studies in Palestinian LITERATURE under Israeli occupation published in 1966 and 1968.

In 1967, Kanafani joined the editorial board of the Nasirite newspaper *al-Anwar* (Illumination); he served as editor-in-chief of its weekly magazine and wrote widely read opinion pieces for the magazine as well. That year he also participated in the founding of the POPULAR FRONT FOR THE LIBERATION OF PALESTINE (PFLP), which emerged as the radical Marxist Palestinian branch of the defunct MAN. Elected to its politburo and appointed its official spokesman, Kanafani in July 1969 resigned from *al-Anwar* to establish and edit the PFLP's weekly organ, *al-Hadaf* (The target). Before the year was out, he published two more novellas, *Return to Haifa* and *Sa'd's Mother.* He also began work on a third novella and completed a short story.

Along with Habash, with whom he was on close terms, Kanafani had made the transition from Nasirite pan-Arabism to revolutionary Palestinian nationalism. As the PFLP spokesperson and an author of its 1969 August Programme, he continuously demonstrated his deep commitment to the Palestinian struggle. On July 9, 1972, several weeks after the PFLP claimed responsibility for an attack by three Japanese Red army gunmen at Lod

Airport that left twenty-six dead, Kanafani, age thirty-six, and a young niece were killed by a bomb planted in his car by the Israeli Mossad. Shortly after his death his only historical study, *The 1936–1939 Revolution in Palestine,* examining the popular rebellion that began the month he was born, appeared. Several novels, one begun in 1966, were never finished.

In death, Kanafani was immortalized by his people. His birthday, April 9, has inspired a national event during which Palestinians celebrate his life and work (in the Occupied Territories with strikes and demonstrations), and his face has adorned every issue of *al-Hadaf* since his assassination. His Danish wife, Anni Hoover, has remained with their two children in Beirut, where she is involved with the Ghassan Kanafani Cultural Foundation.

Ghassan Kanafani was above all a product of his times. His journalism and fiction skillfully narrate the tribulations and aspiration of his people and generation.

Muin Rabbani

BIBLIOGRAPHY

Kanafani, Ghassan. *Al-Athar al-Kamila* (Collected works). 7 vols. Beirut: Dar al-Tali'a, 1972– .

Siddiq, Muhammad. *Man Is a Cause: Political Consciousness and the Fiction of Ghassan Kanafani.* Seattle: University of Washington Press, 1984.

Kassim, Anis

al-Qasim; legal expert
1925– Haris

Kassim was born in the NABLUS subdistrict and pursued secondary studies at RASHIDIYYA SCHOOL and the ARAB COLLEGE in Jerusalem. On his graduation in 1945, the mandatory government selected him to study law at the University of London. He completed his studies there in 1948 and earned an M.A. in law and became a barrister in law in 1950. Kassim later studied oil and natural gas law in the United States. In 1952, he began working as a legal adviser for the Libyan ministry of justice, from which he resigned in 1960. Kassim thereafter returned to the University of London and obtained a Ph.D. in law from the University of London in 1969.

After the signing of the OSLO AGREEMENTS in 1993, the PALESTINE LIBERATION ORGANIZATION asked him to prepare a study of basic constitutional documents for the PALESTINIAN AUTHORITY (PA). In February 1996, PA president YASIR ARAFAT appointed him to a committee created to draft a basic law for the PA.

Michael R. Fischbach

Kassim, Anis Fowzi

Anis Fawzi al-Qasim; legal expert

Kassim received an LL.M. from George Washington University in Washington, D.C., in 1970. An expert on international law, he has edited the *Palestine Yearbook of International Law* since 1984 and chaired the legal committee of the PALESTINE NATIONAL COUNCIL. Kassim also served on the steering committee that guided the activities of the Palestinian negotiating team during the Arab-Israeli talks of the MADRID PEACE CONFERENCE, 1991.

Michael R. Fischbach

Kassis, Nabeel

Nabil Qassis; academic
1947–

Nabeel Kassis holds a Ph.D. in physics and has taught theoretical physics at BIR ZEIT UNIVERSITY. He has also played a role in Arab-Israeli peace talks and in the consolidation of the PALESTINIAN AUTHORITY. He was deputy head of the Palestinian delegation to the MADRID PEACE CONFERENCE, 1991, and served on the board of directors of the Palestinian Economic Council for Development and Reconstruction (PECDAR), which emerged from those talks in 1993. Kassis is also the director of the Palestinian Economic Policy Research Institute.

Michael R. Fischbach

Khalaf, Salah

Abu Iyad; PLO leader
1933–1991 Jaffa

Abu Iyad was born to a middle-class family in JAFFA, where he attended the Marwaniyya School and joined a paramilitary youth organization. Then, in 1948, his family was displaced when ISRAEL was created; they settled in Gaza, where he completed his secondary education. In 1951, he enrolled in a teachers' college in Cairo, where he met YASIR ARAFAT. When Arafat was elected president of the Palestinian Student Union in 1952, Abu

Iyad served as his deputy, in 1956 he succeeded Arafat as president. In 1957, he earned a degree in philosophy and returned to Gaza to pursue a career in teaching. In 1959, he joined Arafat in Kuwait, where he obtained a teaching position.

Abu Iyad became one of a select group of Palestinian activists who founded the Fatah movement. As a result, he left Kuwait to join other Fatah members in Damascus, which was hospitable to the Palestinian movement at the time. There he emerged as one of the architects of PALESTINE LIBERATION ORGANIZATION (PLO) policy toward Arab governments and helped the PLO establish ties with Jamal Abd al-Nasir, who had initially been suspicious of Fatah's intentions.

Abu Iyad was considered a major leader of the leftist camp within Fatah. He was critical of conservative Arab regimes, particularly of their influence over Arafat. Like other founders of Fatah, he harbored some sympathy for the ideology of the Muslim Brotherhood. His leftism was, however, devoid of any marxist tendencies. His ideology, like that of Fatah as a whole, was ill defined, although he did prefer to work with the "progressive" Arab regimes. For him, the aim of the liberation of Palestine was a "clear thought" and ideology, although he did not (unlike other Palestinian leaders) feel the need for the elaboration of a political vision. Abu Iyad was put in charge of security and intelligence, including counterintelligence, and in that capacity he succeeded in sending infiltrators to rival Palestinian organizations, including the Fatah Revolutionary Council, led by ABU NIDAL. His intelligence work displeased some military cadres within Fatah, who thought he was intruding on their territory. Abu Iyad enjoyed strong support within the movement, however, especially among students, from whom he promoted such key leaders as Abu al-Hawl and HANI AL-HASAN.

Abu Iyad's role in Palestinian activism extended far beyond Fatah: he protected Palestinian leftist groups in the late 1960s and early 1970s, a time when more conservative Fatah leaders recommended the suppression of rival Left organizations. He maintained close ties with the POPULAR FRONT FOR THE LIBERATION OF PALESTINE (PFLP) and the DEMOCRATIC FRONT FOR THE LIBERATION OF PALESTINE (DFLP) over the years and was often assigned to promote Fatah's views to other PLO organizations. Abu Iyad was probably the first PLO leader to declare officially that the movement's goal was the establishment of a "secular democratic state in Palestine" comprising both Palestinians and Jews—an idea favored by the PLO's left wing, which fiercely opposed the two-state solution until the late 1970s.

Khalaf's role within the Palestinian national movement became more important in 1970 in Jordan, where he advocated nonconfrontation with the Jordanian regime, although—in contrast with the PLO's right wing—he later refused to blame the PFLP and the DFLP for the massacres that resulted from the Jordanian war against the Palestinians. (Both organizations became easy targets for Fatah leaders, who avoided self-criticism.) Nevertheless, he was arrested by the Jordanian government and forced to issue declarations that did not conform to his own views; his comrade, Muhammad Yusuf al-Najjar, had to disavow his statements. Abu Iyad was later accused by Israel and the UNITED STATES of creating the BLACK SEPTEMBER organization and masterminding its violent operations. Western publications also reported that Abu Iyad had hired Ali Hasan Salama as its operational chief. The Fatah leadership, however, never admitted any role in the creation of that organization.

Abu Iyad's role in Lebanon made him one of the most famous Palestinian leaders. He used the relative safety of Lebanon to solidify his security and intelligence apparatus and to establish contacts with regional and international intelligence services. He often cooperated with European intelligence agencies to thwart attacks by rival Palestinian organizations, providing them with crucial information about Abu Nidal and his followers in return for diplomatic and financial support.

Abu Iyad was bitterly criticized by some Lebanese for getting too personally involved in the Lebanese civil war. He was not reluctant to take sides among the numerous warring factions and is best remembered for asserting, "The road to Palestine passes through Junya [a Christian town in Lebanon]." He favored a policy of active military and political support of the Lebanese National Movement, which championed the Palestinian cause in Lebanon. (Other Fatah leaders, including Arafat, were reluctant to commit PLO forces in Lebanon to the Lebanese National Movement's total victory.) As a result, Abu Iyad's relations with the Syrian regime deteriorated in 1976, when Syrian forces intervened in Lebanon against the PLO and its Lebanese allies.

In 1982, Abu Iyad opposed the withdrawal of PLO forces from Beirut. He assured Lebanese and Palestinian leaders that Israel would not dare send its troops into West Beirut, but his words did not calm the fears of those who had been exhausted by the Lebanese civil war. After the evacuation of PLO forces from Lebanon in the summer of 1982, Abu Iyad settled in Tunisia with other PLO leaders. He refused to join the dissident movement within Fatah in 1983, despite the appeals of the leftist leaders SA'ID MURAGHA (Abu Musa) and Abu Salih.

Abu Iyad remained personally loyal to Arafat despite their many political differences. Like Arafat, he moderated his views in his later years and came to advocate face-to-face negotiations with Israel. He also made direct appeals to the Israeli public, and in 1988 he even endorsed peaceful existence with Israel. In 1990, Abu Iyad took another dissident position: he publicly disagreed with the PLO's support for the Iraqi occupation of Kuwait in 1990.

Abu Iyad was assassinated in January 1991 by what PLO sources identified as a bodyguard of the PLO leader Abu al-Hawl, who was also assassinated that night. Reports suggested that the gunman belonged to Abu Nidal's organization, although the PLO has never investigated the assassination.

As'ad AbuKhalil

BIBLIOGRAPHY

Abu Iyad, with Eric Rouleau. *My Home, My Land: A Narrative of the Palestinian Struggle.* New York: Times Book, 1981.

Amos, John. *Palestinian Resistance.* New York: Pergamon Press, 1980.

Cobban, Helena. *The Palestinian Liberation Organization: People, Power and Policies.* New York: Cambridge University Press, 1984.

Husayn, Hasan Khalil. *Abu Iyad.* Amman: Matba'at al-Dustur, 1991.

Khalid, Layla

hijacker, political activist
1944– Haifa

Born to a relatively well-to-do family of eight children, Layla Khalid found herself in Lebanon after her hometown fell into the hands of armed Zionists. She entered the American University of Beirut in 1962 and joined the Movement of Arab Nationalists. She left the next year to teach in Kuwait, where, in 1968, she joined the POPULAR FRONT FOR THE LIBERATION OF PALESTINE (PFLP). She returned to Amman, where she attended paramilitary training courses. On August 29, 1969, she participated in the hijacking of a Trans World Airlines plane en route to Damascus. On September 6, 1970, she participated in an unsuccessful hijacking attempt of an El Al plane, for which she was sentenced to prison in London. She was released in a matter of weeks and became a member of the Central Committee of the PFLP.

Alain Gresh

Khalidi Family

Despite the Khalidi family's long tradition of religious scholarship and leadership in Jerusalem, its influence began to wane by the nineteenth century.

Ruhi (1861? 1864?–1913; Jerusalem; administrator, legislator, author) After completing his studies at the Sultanic School in Istanbul in 1893, he frequented the circles of Jamal al-Din al-Afghani, the Islamic reformer. Rubi studied the philosophy of Islamic sciences and Oriental literature at the Sorbonne, after which he taught there.

From 1898 to 1908, Ruhi served as Ottoman consul in Bordeaux, France. Associated with the Ottoman decentralist movement, and a supporter of the constitution with liberal views, he was elected to the Ottoman parliament representing the Jerusalem district both in 1908 and in 1912 (the second time as deputy president of the parliament). He used his post to warn of the danger of ZIONISM, which he predicted would result in the eviction of the Palestinians.

Ruhi wrote about history, politics, and literature in the Arab press, under the name al-Magdini because of his fear of the wrath of the Ottoman authorities. He also authored books on Palestinian and Arab history, as well as on comparative literature, including a work on the French writer Victor Hugo.

Ahmad Samih (1896–1951; Jerusalem; educator, writer, social reformer) Ahmad Samih completed his studies at the pharmacy school at The American University of Beirut in 1917. After service in the Ottoman military during World War I, he worked for the education department of the PALESTINE MANDATE government from 1919 to 1925. From 1925 to 1948, Ahmad Samih headed a teacher training school in Jerusalem, which was renamed the ARAB COLLEGE, the best secondary school in the country. In 1941, he was appointed assistant director of education for the Mandate.

Ahmad Samih was a writer as well, producing works on psychology, history, and education. Many of his writings were incorporated into standard textbooks in a number of Arab countries, including *Anzimat Al-ta'lim* (Systems of education). He also translated a number of foreign works into Arabic, including the works of Wilhelm Stekel and Robert Sessions Woodworth, such as Woodworth's *Psychology: A Study of Mental Life.*

Ahmad Samih was also keenly interested in Palestinian orphans. In the early 1940s, he founded the General Arab Committee for Orphans and opened a school in Dayr Amr, Jerusalem, for the sons of Palestinians killed in the Arab revolt of 1936–39. He later added a girls' school nearby. After the Palestinian refugee exodus in 1948, Ahmad Samih established another school for orphaned refugees in Hinniyya, southern LEBANON.

Husayn Fakhri (1894–1962; Jerusalem; Politician) After medical studies at The American University of Beirut and Istanbul University, he served in the Ottoman army and later the Arab Army of Emir Faysal bin Husayn in Syria. After brief service in Faysal's government in 1920, he returned to Palestine to work in the Mandatory government's department of health from 1921 to 1934.

Husayn Fakhri was the last mayor of Jerusalem elected by the city's entire population, from 1934 to 1937. In 1935, he established the REFORM PARTY to maintain a balance between the warring Palestine ARAB PARTY and the NATIONAL DEFENSE PARTY, although the Reform Party mainly advocated positions closer to those of the latter. He was a member of the ARAB HIGHER COMMITTEE, established in April 1936, and was exiled by the British from 1937 to 1942. Husayn Fakhri attended the 1939 LONDON CONFERENCE and joined the reconstituted Arab Higher Committee in 1946.

Husayn Fakhri occupied several cabinet positions in the Jordanian government after Jordan's annexation of the WEST BANK, including foreign minister in 1953 and 1955 and prime minister for several days in April 1957 after King Husayn's dismissal of Prime Minister Sulayman al-Nabulsi.

Ahmad Samih (1948– ; Beirut; scholar, diplomat) Son of Walid Khalidi and grandson of his namesake (1896–1951), Ahmad Samih studied at Oxford University and the University of London. He was an associate at the Royal Institute of International Affairs in London and a senior member of Saint Antony's College of Oxford University. He is editor of *Majallat al-Dirasat al-Filastiniyya* for the INSTITUTE FOR PALESTINE STUDIES in Beirut.

From 1991 to 1993, Ahmad Samih was a member of the Palestinian delegation at the Palestinian-Israeli negotiations held in Washington, D.C., and a senior adviser on security issues at the talks held between Israel and the PALESTINE LIBERATION ORGANIZATION that produced the Interim Agreement in 1995.

Michael R. Fischbach

Khalidi, Rashid

intellectual

1948– New York

Rashid Khalidi, though born in the United States, is a member of the prominent KHALIDI FAMILY of Jerusalem noted for centuries for its scholarship. He was born in New York while his father was attending graduate school and was raised there when the family could not return to Jerusalem after the 1948 war. Khalidi received a B.A. from Yale University in 1970 and a Ph.D. from Oxford University in 1974. He has taught in Lebanon at the American University of Beirut and at several universities in the United States, including Georgetown, Columbia, and the University of Chicago, where he was the director of Middle East studies.

Khalidi has written and edited numerous works of Palestinian history, the most recent of which is on Palestinian identity. He served as an adviser to the joint Jordanian-Palestinian delegation to the MADRID PEACE CONFERENCE, 1991. Until June 1993, he also advised the Jordanian-Palestinian delegation to the subsequent bilateral negotiations held in Washington, D.C. He served as president of the Middle East Studies Association in 1994 and is president and a founding member of the American Committee on Jerusalem, an organization formed in 1996 to publicize both Palestinian history in Jerusalem and Palestinian claims to that city.

Khalidi has been critical of the Declaration of Principles signed by Israel and the PALESTINE LIBERATION ORGANIZATION in September 1993 because he is skeptical that the agreement will meet what he regards as minimal Palestinian demands: the withdrawal of Israeli forces from the WEST BANK and the GAZA STRIP, the evacuation of Israeli settlements, and the formation of a Palestinian state.

Kathleen Christison

BIBLIOGRAPHY

Khalidi, Rashid. *British Policy Towards Syria and Palestine, 1906–1914*. London: Ithaca Press for the Middle East Centre, St. Antony's College, Oxford, 1980.

——, ed. *The Origins of Arab Nationalism*. New York: Columbia University Press, 1991.

——, ed. *Palestine and the Gulf, 1982*. Beirut: Institute for Palestine Studies, 1982.

——. *Palestinian Identity: The Construction of Modern National Identity*. New York: Columbia University Press, 1997.

——. *Under Siege: P.L.O. Decisionmaking During the 1982 War*. New York: Columbia University Press, 1986.

Khalidi, Walid

influential twentieth-century Palestinian intellectual

1925– Jerusalem

Walid Khalidi's impact has been felt in three main areas of endeavor: scholarship, institution building, and politics and diplomacy. In each Walid Khalidi has been a pioneer, an innovator, and an important Palestinian voice within an Arab context.

Khalidi's extensive writings have played an important part in defining and explaining key elements of the Palestinian national narrative for Westerners, Arabs, and Palestinians alike. His 1978 article "Thinking the Unthinkable," published in *Foreign Affairs*, powerfully crystallized a trend that had been growing in strength in Palestinian political thinking since the 1973 war but was little known in the West. It probably constitutes the most important single contribution to the public debate whereby Westerners and Israelis finally came to accept the validity of the idea of a Palestinian state in the WEST BANK and GAZA STRIP.

The scholarly institutions Khalidi has helped to found and serve, notably the INSTITUTE FOR PALESTINE STUDIES (IPS), as well as the Royal Scientific Society in Amman and the Center for Arab Studies in Beirut, have been instrumental in imparting rigor to writing and research in the Arab world, in training young scholars, and in supporting publishing and research on a wide range of subjects. Finally, Khalidi has played an important role in defining post–World War II Arab nationalism as being centered on the Palestine question. His often intensive involvement in inter-Arab politics, in the politics of a number of Arab countries, and in Palestinian politics has generally been little known. He has been influential at different times within the inner councils of Harakat al Qawmiyyin al-Arab (the Movement of Arab Nationalists), of which he was long an important theorist; the POPULAR FRONT FOR THE LIBERATION OF PALESTINE (PFLP); FATAH; and the PALESTINE LIBERATION ORGANIZATION (PLO).

Walid Khalidi was born in Jerusalem in 1925, one of five children of Ahmad Samih al-Khalidi, principal of the government ARAB COLLEGE, the leading Arab educational institution in Mandatory Palestine. He came from the KHALIDI FAMILY of Jerusalem that had produced legists, educators, scholars, and political leaders since before the Crusades and through the Mamluk, Ottoman, and PALESTINE MANDATE eras. His background gave him family connections that were useful to him in later life; it also helps to explain his conservative, indeed almost patrician, outlook and his strong sense of duty and public responsibility.

Khalidi grew up in a home that was a cultural and intellectual meeting place for Palestinians, Jews, and Westerners during the Mandate period. His father was an authority on Islamic and Palestinian history, and his Lebanese stepmother, Anbara Salam al-Khalidi, was a leading author, translator, and feminist of the period. In addition to the rich intellectual sustenance provided by this environment, Khalidi benefited from tutoring by G. B. Farrell, the director of education in Mandatory Palestine. He completed his education at London and Oxford universities in 1945 and 1951, respectively, where he took degrees in philosophy and Islamic studies. Thereafter he took up an appointment at Oxford as a university lecturer.

Before doing so, however, Khalidi worked for several years in the ARAB LEAGUE office in Jerusalem, headed by MUSA AL-ALAMI. Founded by the Arab League in order to put the Palestinian case before the world, the Arab office, which was staffed mainly by young Palestinians, served as the unofficial Palestinian foreign and information ministry, albeit with the most modest of resources. In these years in Jerusalem, Khalidi learned firsthand about the complexities and Palestinian politics and the treacherous currents of inter-Arab relations and experienced the disastrous defeats of 1947–48. These traumatic experiences were fundamental in shaping his vision of the Palestinian predicament, of the Arab world, and of the international system.

Having meanwhile married Rasha Salam, with whom he had two children, Ahmad Samih and Karma, Walid Khalidi settled into the routine life of an Oxford don after 1951, teaching in the Faculty of Oriental Studies and researching and writing on Islamic philosophy. This quiet period in his life was not to last. Outraged by British involvement in the tripartite British-French-Israeli attack on Egypt in October 1956, Khalidi resigned his position at Oxford and returned to Beirut to join the Political Studies and Public Administration Department of the American University of Beirut (AUB), where he rapidly reached the rank of professor, and continued to teach—with interruptions during which he served as a visiting professor at Princeton and Harvard Universities—until 1982. In his decades of teaching at the AUB and elsewhere, Khalidi influenced several generations of students, many of whom went on to be scholars, political leaders, diplomats, and professionals throughout the Arab world.

Soon after returning to Beirut in 1956, Khalidi once again began to play a role in Arab politics. Deeply impressed by the growing Arabist inclinations of the regime of Jamal Abd al-Nasir in Egypt and by the possibilities it appeared to offer for changing the regional balance of power, Khalidi met in Cairo with Nasir as an emissary of his brother-in-law, the Nasirist Lebanese politician and later prime minister Sa'ib Salam. When Salam became embroiled in the Lebanese Civil War of 1958 as one of the leaders of the Arab nationalist opposition to President Camille Chamoun, Khalidi was one of his closest advisers. At the same time, he was a member of the inner circle of the Movement of Arab Nationalists, as a friend and confidant of many of its leaders, including Dr. GEORGE HABASH, Hani al-Hindi, and Dr. WADI HADDAD. In addition to helping to shape the movement's Arabist and Palestine-oriented ideology and programs, Khalidi had a profound influence on generations of young Arabs in Beirut, which in these years was a center of Arab intellectual ferment. Those affected included cadres of the movement and members of the Union of Palestinian Students at the AUB and elsewhere who heard his lectures on Arabism, the Palestine question, inter-Arab and international politics, and other subjects.

The Arab defeat of June 1967, in the wake of which he served as an adviser to the Iraqi delegation to the U.N., represented a watershed for Khalidi as for many other Palestinians. Earlier, in 1963, he had been instrumental in founding the INSTITUTE FOR PALESTINE STUDIES, with the help of Professor Constantine Zurayq of the AUB; Burhan DAJANI, secretary-general of the Union of Arab Chambers of Commerce; and later Nabih Faris, professor of Arab history, and several other colleagues, among others, Isam Ashur and Sami Alami, and the financial support of a number of leading Palestinian and Arab businessmen, including HASIB SABBAGH, UMAR AQQAD, and ABD AL-MUHSIN QATTAN. This independent, private institution based in Beirut played a major role in helping to crystallize the sense that the Palestinians had to help themselves. For some, although not for Walid Khalidi and many of his cofounders of IPS, this realization was tied to the belief that the Palestinians should not depend unduly on the Arab regimes to solve their problems for them. This widespread belief was reflected on the political level in the founding of the PLO and the rise of the Fatah movement in these same years.

The debacle of 1967 was decisive in turning this trend into the dominant force in Palestinian politics. Thereafter, Walid Khalidi, who had earlier been one of the most ardent exponents of an Arabist approach to the Palestine questions, adopted and supported this new tendency while always considering that the Arab states had a vital role to play in the resolution of the problem of Palestine. While maintaining contacts with the leaders of the Arabist Movement of Arab Nationalists who founded the PFLP after the 1967 war, he also developed ties with YASIR ARAFAT, SALAH KHALAF (Abu Iyad), and other leaders of Fatah, which rose to prominence in the mid-1960s.

In succeeding years, Khalidi maintained good relations with the leaders of the main Palestinian factions, a number of prominent Lebanese politicians, the Egyptian leadership, the Jordanian monarchy, and key figures in a number of Arab regimes. This enabled him to mediate conflicts, propose solutions, and influence outcomes in a number of situations, including the Jordanian and Lebanese civil wars, internal Palestinian dissension, and Palestinian-Egyptian and Palestinian-Syrian disputes. Khalidi was not always successful in his endeavors (some of which are known only to the participants to this day), but he continued to play the role of behind-the-scenes mediator and facilitator even after he had moved to Cambridge, Massachusetts, where he took up a position as a senior research associate at the Center for Middle East Studies at Harvard University in 1982.

Khalidi's efforts in the realms of mediation, diplomacy, and advocacy were not always appreciated: for example, some in the Palestinian resistance movement were critical of his attempts to defuse the Lebanese conflict by what they saw as unwarranted concessions to their foes. For this and other reasons, these efforts increasingly took place behind the scenes and quite frequently left both him and his Palestinian and Lebanese interlocutors frustrated. His articles calling for a Palestinian state and a negotiated resolution of the Arab-Israeli conflict, although quite influential in the United States and Europe, were highly unpopular with the more radical trends in Palestinian politics, including the PFLP and many within Fatah (although they gradually won mainstream support). Never a populist or an advocate of "people's war" or guerrilla tactics, even when these ideas were highly fashionable among Palestinians and other Arabs in the 1960s and early 1970s, Khalidi was a firm believer in the importance of power in politics. His study of the U.S.-Soviet nuclear balance convinced him that the United States was the stronger of the two superpowers, and that it was imperative for the Palestinians and the Arabs to recognize this fact and act accordingly. Such ideas were not popular in many Arab quarters at the time.

Khalidi's most recent public role in Arab and international diplomacy was his service as a member of the Jordanian-Palestinian joint delegation to the MADRID PEACE CONFERENCE, 1991, and the first two subsequent rounds of bilateral negotiations with ISRAEL in Washington, D.C. Palestinian representation at Madrid was subject to stringent and humiliating Israeli conditions that the United States, as cosponsor of the conference, acquiesced to and imposed on the PLO. On the basis of these conditions, Khalidi would have been excluded from participation in the Palestinian section of this joint delegation because he was a Palestinian from Jerusalem, lived outside the Occupied Territories, and had close links to the PLO. To compensate for allowing Israel this veto power over which Palestinians it would negotiate with, U.S. secretary of state James Baker and his assistants negotiated the inclusion of a Palestinian from Jerusalem in the Jordanian part of the delegation, over which Israel could not exercise a veto. In filling this role, Walid Khalidi was thus the thin edge of a wedge that ultimately led to Israel's negotiating directly with the PLO.

The range and extent of Walid Khalidi's writings explain part of his great political and intellectual influence over more than five decades. They include a series of seminal articles on the ARAB-ISRAELI WAR OF 1948 and its antecedents, which established key points regarding the exodus of about three quarters of a million Palestinians from their homes in 1947–49; the role of Zionist military offensives in precipitating this exodus; and the course of the 1948 war. These articles include "Plan Dalet: Zionist Blueprint for the Conquest of Palestine," "The Fall of Haifa," "Why Did the Palestinians Leave?" and *"Suqut Filastin,"* published from 1957 to 1961, mainly in *Middle East Forum,* as well as an article published in 1986 in *The End of the Palestine Mandate* (edited by W. R. Lewis and R. W. Stookey, Austin: University of Texas Press). They constitute the results of an extensive research project on the 1948 war on which Khalidi spent many years, learning to read Hebrew in the process. These efforts never resulted in the major book he had originally planned to write, although shorter works on the partition of Palestine, the Zionist movement, and the DAYR YASIN massacre were published in Arabic in 1998. However, his pioneering insights into this period have since been borne out by a new generation of historians, Israeli, Arab, and Western, who have utilized newly opened archives to substantiate points Khalidi made as long as forty years ago on the basis of the evidence available at the time.

Another major project that has been a continuing focus of Khalidi's scholarly efforts has been chronicling the evolution of the Zionist movement, and examining the political, social, cultural, and economic fabric of Arab Palestine, which was torn asunder in 1948. This has resulted in the publication of three substantial volumes edited or compiled by Khalidi, *From Haven to Conquest: Readings in Zionism and the Palestine Problem until 1948* (Washington, D.C.: Institute for Palestine Studies, 1972), *Before Their Diaspora: A Photographic History of the Palestinians* (Washington, D.C.: Institute for Palestine Studies, 1984), and *All That Remains: The Palestinian Villages Occupied and Destroyed by Israel in 1948* (Washington, D.C.: Institute for Palestine Studies, 1992), the latter two books extensively illustrated. Representing collective research that drew on the resources of the Institute for Palestine Studies and of dozens of researchers, these three volumes are tied together by Khalidi's organizing vision of the clash between ZIONISM and the Palestinians, and by his lengthy and tightly argued introductions, which constitute the backbone of each work. He has in addition published a book on the Lebanese conflict based on his own involvement, *Conflict and Violence in Lebanon: Confrontation in the Middle East* (Cambridge, Mass: Harvard University Press, 1979), and scores of articles in English and Arabic, and many of his writings have been translated into other languages.

At the same time, some have argued that Khalidi's intense involvement in institution building, politics, public advocacy, and diplomacy during many phases of his long career, sometimes with inconclusive or negative results, has hindered him from completing a task which he could do better than anyone of his generation: writing a comprehensive history of the 1948 conflict and the loss of Palestine. In this he resembles a number of members of his own and perhaps other generations of Palestinians: torn between the abiding urge to chronicle, analyze, and explain the tragedy of their people and the impatient desire to do something in the present to alleviate this ongoing tragedy.

In his concerns, and in his successes and failures, Walid Khalidi is exemplary of the generation of Palestinian intellectuals and scholars who were shaped by the events of the era between the loss of part of Palestine in 1948 and the occupation of the rest of it in 1967. Like that of others of this generation, his life's work has been defined by the need to fill the voids in Palestinian national life created by these traumatic events. More than many of them, he has been successful in helping to create lasting structures, notably the IPS, which have helped to take the place of those that were destroyed, or could not be established, in Palestine as a result of the catastrophes that befell its people. The Palestinians have suffered greatly since 1948 from the absence of such institutions as a unified education system, national research institutes, museums, and other cultural frameworks to help formulate and propagate a unified national narrative. As a result, they have been heavily dependent on structures such as those that Khalidi and others of his generation managed to build in the diaspora and inside Palestine, some created independently, like the IPS, and some within the context of the PLO.

Although Khalidi was largely successful in institution building, and was often deeply involved in urgent day-to-day political issues, his writings, his lectures, his advocacy, and his public diplomacy have played a major role over the long term in shaping the Palestinian and Arab response to the loss of Palestine, and in charting out a course that would enable the Palestinians to reestablish themselves on the map of the Middle East. It is a measure of his success at these difficult tasks that ideas that he has advocated through much of his career, such as adoption of the establishment of an independent Palestinian state in the West Bank and Gaza Strip as the Palestinian national objective, are now broadly accepted.

Rashid Khalidi

al-Khalidi, Yusuf Diya

scholar, diplomat, administrator
1842–1906

Yusif al-Khalidi studied at al-Aqsa mosque in Jerusalem and then at the Protestant College in Malta for two years. Later he studied medicine in Istanbul for one year, then switched to study engineering at Robert College. After his father's death, he returned to Jerusalem, where, in 1867, he established a school. Al-Khalidi was mayor of Jerusalem for six years, during which many streets were established, others were repaired, and a sewage system was created. He also arranged for paving a road between Jerusalem and JAFFA.

In 1874, when Rashid Pasha (a friend of al-Khalidi's) was the Ottoman foreign minister, al-Khalidi went to Istanbul to work as a translator at the sultan's office. After six months, he was appointed vice-consul in Buti, a Russian port on the Black Sea. When Rashid Pasha lost his post, al-Khalidi was dismissed, too, and spent time visiting Odessa, Kiev, Moscow, and Saint Petersburg. In 1875, he went to Vienna, where Rashid Pasha was ambassador, and worked as a teacher of Arabic at the School of Oriental Languages. At that point, he showed interest in politics and non-Muslim minorities in Jerusalem. He published two letters on the situation of Jews in Jerusalem in the London-based journal *The Jewish Chronicle.*

In 1875, al-Khalidi returned to Jerusalem and became mayor again. In 1877 he was elected to the Ottoman parliament, where he became the only member representing Palestine. He was very active in supporting reform policies and the constitution declared in 1876, and he criticized Sultan Abdülhamit's authoritarian policies. In February 1878, Abdülhamit disbanded the parliament and sent ten active opposition members, including al-Khalidi, into exile.

In 1879, al-Khalidi lectured at the University of Vienna, and the next year he published a collection of the works of the pre-Islamic poet Labid, which was later translated into German by the German Orientalist Hober. In 1881, al-Khalidi returned to Palestine and was appointed governor of Jaffa, then Marj'iyun in Lebanon. Later he became governor of Motki in northeast Turkey, where he mastered Kurdish and compiled an Arabic-Kurdish dictionary that was published in Istanbul in 1893. Alarmed at the dangers of the Zionist movement's aspirations in Palestine, in 1899 he wrote a letter to Theodor Herzl, founder of political ZIONISM, via Zadok Kahn, the chief rabbi of France. In the letter, al-Khalidi stated that since Palestine was already populated, the Zionists should find another area. He wrote, "In the name of God let Palestine be left in peace." Kahn passed the letter to Herzl, who answered Khalidi on March 19, 1899, assuring him that, if the Zionists were unwanted, "We will search and, believe me, we will find elsewhere what we need." To our knowledge the correspondence did not continue after March 1899. Al-Khalidi spent his last days under the close scrutiny of Abdülhamit's spies and died in Istanbul in 1906.

Adel Manna

Khalidi Library

The Khalidi Library is an important private center for Islamic manuscripts and the largest private library in Palestine. Opened in 1900 in a thirteenth-century Mamluk building in the Old City of JERUSALEM, and supported by a Khalidi family *waqf* (endowment), the library houses more than 1,200 manuscripts (mostly Arabic, with some in Persian and Ottoman Turkish), numerous other documents, and over 5,000 books. Many of the library's manuscripts date from medieval times, including a thirteenth-century work once presented to the famous Islamic leader Salah al-Din (Saladin).

Michael R. Fischbach

Khatib Family

landowning family of Jerusalem, several of whose members served in various positions in the Jordanian government

Anwar (politician) Anwar was mayor of JERUSALEM shortly after Jordan's annexation of the WEST BANK and later served in several cabinet positions. Viewed as a liberal member of the opposition, he served as minister of economics and construction in the early 1950s and later became minister of public works in the cabinet formed by the leftist Sulayman al-Nabulsi in 1956. He remained a significant figure in the pro-Jordanian West Bank establishment. Khatib was governor of the Jerusalem province at the time of Israel's June 1967 occupation of the West Bank. In 1991, he was appointed to the Jordanian delegation to the Arab–Israeli peace negotiations.

Ruhi (1912? 1913?–1994; politician) Ruhi was mayor of Jordanian East Jerusalem from 1957 to 1967. He was deposed by Israeli occupation authorities in June 1967 because he refused to work with Israeli municipal officials after Israel's annexation of East Jerusalem. In September 1967, he assumed the position of chair of the Higher Committee for National Guidance, an organization that tried to coordinate anti-Israeli protests. In March 1968, occupation authorities deported him to LEBANON. Israel allowed him to return in May 1993 along with twenty-four other deportees. He died on July 6, 1994.

Michael R. Fischbach

Khatib, Ghassan

economist, activist
1954– Nablus

A leading figure in the Palestine People's Party (formerly the PALESTINE COMMUNIST PARTY) in the WEST BANK, Khatib was arrested as a result of his anti-Israeli activism in 1974 after a crackdown on the Palestine National Front; he was released in 1977.

Since his graduate studies in economic development at Manchester University in Britain, Khatib lectured at BIR ZEIT UNIVERSITY and has directed the Jerusalem Media and Communication Center, which brings the foreign media directly into contact with Palestinian viewpoints. Since 1988, he has also headed the United Agricultural Company, a nonprofit organization that channels European development aid to help West Bank farmers.

Khatib was chosen as a member of the Palestinian delegation to the MADRID PEACE CONFERENCE, 1991, although he later resigned, citing lack of progress in the negotiations. He became a vocal critic of the 1993 OSLO AGREEMENTS, particularly because they failed to restrict the continued building of Israeli settlements.

Michael R. Fischbach

al-Kidwa, Nasser

Nasir al-Qudwa; physician, diplomat
1953– Gaza

Muhammad Nasser al-Kidwa became active in Palestinian nationalist circles while a student. He joined FATAH in 1969 and in 1974 was elected to the executive committee of the General Union of Palestinian Students (GUPS). He later served as the GUPS president. Al-Kidwa completed his studies at the Faculty of Dentistry at Cairo University in 1979, the same year that he joined the Palestine RED CRESCENT. He became an observer member of its executive committee the following year.

Al-Kidwa later rose to occupy several senior positions in Fatah and the PALESTINE LIBERATION ORGANIZATION (PLO). He was elected to the PALESTINE NATIONAL COUNCIL in 1975 and has remained there since. Al-Kidwa became a member of the PLO's Central Council in 1981 and an observer member of Fatah's Revolutionary Council; he was elected as a full member in 1989. Since 1986, al-Kidwa has served as a senior PLO diplomat at the United Nations (U.N.) in New York. He was appointed the alternate permanent observer of the PLO to the U.N. in 1986; he assumed the position of permanent observer of Palestine to the U.N. in 1991.

Michael R. Fischbach

King Abdullah and the Zionists

The triangular relationship among Emir Abdullah ibn Husayn of Transjordan (later king of Jordan), the Zionists, and the Palestinians is only one thread in the complex web that makes up the ARAB–ISRAELI CONFLICT, but its importance cannot be overestimated. Of all Arab rulers, Abdullah was most directly and deeply involved in the struggle between Palestinians and Zionists over Palestine. This involvement began when the British appointed him emir of Transjordan in 1921, and it did not end until his assassination by a Palestinian nationalist in 1951. Throughout this period, Abdullah maintained close relations with the British, the Palestinians, and the Zionists. In all three circles, his method was the same—personal diplomacy.

Special Relationship The irreconcilable conflict between the Arab and Jewish national movements in Palestine provided the setting for the emergence of the special relationship between the Hashemite emir and the Jewish Agency. The two sides had a common protector, Britain, and a common enemy, AL-HAJJ AMIN AL-HUSAYNI, the mufti (Islamic law expert) of Jerusalem and the leader of the Palestinians. Al-Hajj Amin had not only opposed the Zionist movement, but was also Abdullah's principal rival for the loyalty of the Palestinians and for the control of Palestine. Consequently, the triangular relationship that developed in Palestine under the British PALESTINE MANDATE was characterized by growing cooperation between Abdullah and the Zionists against the mufti.

Abdullah was ambitious, and he pursued his plans for territorial expansion in all directions. His ultimate ambition was Greater Syria. Initially, Palestine did not feature prominently in his plans. In the first decade and a half of his reign, the emphasis in his relations with the Zionists was on cultivating good neighborly relations and economic cooperation. In 1933, despite British and Arab opposition, Abdullah granted the Jewish Agency an option to lease his private land in Ghawr al-Kibd, on the east bank of the Jordan River. Although the Jewish Agency did not exercise the option, it paid the impecunious emir what amounted to a political subsidy. It was not until 1937, when the PEEL COMMISSION suggested that Palestine might be partitioned and that Abdullah might rule the Arab part, that Palestine became the main focus of Abdullah's territorial ambition.

During World War II, Al-Hajj Amin al-Husayni threw in his lot with Nazi Germany; Abdullah and the Zionists remained loyal to Britain. Britain rewarded Abdullah for his loyalty by conferring formal independence on the Mandated territory of Transjordan in March 1946. The Zionists, in the aftermath of the Holocaust, intensified the struggle for a state of their own. However, they needed an Arab leader willing to accept a partition of Palestine and to live in peace with a Jewish state; King Abdullah appeared to be the only ruler prepared to accept the partition of Palestine.

Secret Agreement After the end of World War II, contacts between Abdullah and the Zionists began to assume political and strategic dimensions. Britain's decision to give up its Mandate over Palestine spurred the two sides to coordinate their strategies. Contacts evolved into a series of talks that culminated in a meeting between Abdullah and Golda Meir on November 17, 1947. At this meeting, an agreement in principle was reached to divide Palestine after the termination of the British Mandate. Meir rejected Abdullah's suggestion of a Jewish republic within a Greater Transjordan. She made it clear, however, that the Zionists would look favorably on Abdullah's plan to annex "the Arab part of Palestine" to his kingdom in return for recognition of the Jewish state. This agreement laid the foundation for mutual restraint during the first Arab-Israeli war and for continuing collaboration in the aftermath of that war.

With the passage of the U.N. resolution of November 29, 1947, which called for replacing the British Mandate with a Jewish and an Arab state, the struggle for Palestine entered a decisive phase. Neither Abdullah nor the Zionists allowed the U.N. partition plan to affect their own secret partition plan, which excluded an Arab state. Abdullah opposed the proposed Arab state because he believed it would be ruled by his political rival, the mufti of Jerusalem. The Zionists, although they accepted the U.N. plan, also had deep misgivings about the prospect of a state headed by the mufti.

Al-Hajj Amin, for his part, rejected the U.N. partition plan and launched a guerrilla war in Palestine to frustrate it. The unofficial phase of the Palestine conflict lasted from December 1, 1947, until the expiration of the British Mandate on May 15, 1948. During this phase, the British prepared the ground for Abdullah's annexation of the parts of Palestine that the United Nations had assigned to the Arab state. Meanwhile, the Jewish forces mounted a counteroffensive that devastated Palestinian society and set in motion the first waves of Palestinian REFUGEES.

Abdullah, who had hoped for a peaceful partition of Palestine between him and the Zionists, came under mounting Arab pressure to go to the rescue of the embattled Palestinians. Against the advice of the mufti, the Arab League decided to commit the regular armies of its member states to do battle against the Zionists. Golda Meir was dispatched to Amman on May 10, 1948, to dissuade Abdullah from throwing in his lot with the other Arab states. However, her mission ended in failure. Abdullah did not feel that he could stand alone against the tide in favor of intervention in Palestine that was sweeping through the Arab countries.

After the expiration of the British Mandate at midnight on May 14, 1948, the Jews proclaimed the establishment of their own state, ISRAEL. The following day, the armies of the neighboring Arab states, including Transjordan's Arab Legion, invaded Palestine. The official phase of the war lasted until January 7, 1949.

Implementation On the battlefield, the Arab Legion proved itself to be the most effective Arab army, but it was under strict instructions not to encroach on the territory of the Jewish state. All the members of the Arab coalition were nominally committed to saving Palestine for the Palestinians, but, in fact, they each pursued their own separate national interests. As a result of these inter-Arab divisions, the Palestine war developed into a general land grab. The winners were the Israelis, who expanded the borders of their state considerably beyond the U.N. lines, and Abdullah, who captured the WEST BANK and later annexed it to his kingdom. The losers were the Palestinians, who suffered the trauma of defeat, dispossession, and dispersal.

The signing of the armistice agreement between Israel and Transjordan on April 3, 1949, marked the official demise of Arab Palestine. The agreement was signed in the name of the Hashemite Kingdom of Jordan. It was the first time that this title was used officially: *Palestine* and *Transjordan* gave way to *Israel* and the *Hashemite Kingdom of Jordan*. The name *Palestine* disappeared from the map of the Middle East.

Union between the two banks of the Jordan was formally proclaimed in April 1950. The Palestinians for the most part resigned themselves to annexation by Jordan, if only to avert the threat of being overrun by the Israeli army. They were so demoralized and divided that the idea of an independent Palestinian state seemed to be no more than a pipe dream and the union of the West Bank with the East Bank of the Jordan appeared to be the most sensible course of action.

Abdullah wanted to secure his enlarged kingdom by concluding a peace agreement with Israel. A draft agreement between Jordan and Israel had been initialed in February 1950, but strong opposition from rival Arab states forced him to suspend the negotiations. After the Act of Union was passed, negotiations were renewed, but their momentum had been broken. Although Abdullah continued his direct talks with the Israelis literally until his dying day, a formal peace settlement with Israel was beyond his reach. He was assassinated by a Palestinian in 1951.

In broad historical perspective, it can be seen that the early contacts between Abdullah and the Zionists gave birth to a unique bilateral relationship revolving around the problem of Palestine. This complex relationship was punctuated by endless crises and misunderstandings, by discord and disagreements. Yet, it was founded on a solid bedrock of common interests, above all in containment of Palestinian nationalism; that perception of common interests was the secret of the relationship's resilience and durability.

The special relationship between Abdullah and the Zionists not only is interesting in itself but also is of critical importance to an understanding of the nature and dynamics of the Arab-Israeli conflict. This conflict is usually portrayed as a simple bipolar affair in which a monolithic and implacably hostile Arab world is pitted against the Jews. By focusing on Abdullah's role, one gets a rather different picture of the forces at play in the making of the Arab-Israeli conflict. In particular, one can appreciate better the underlying divisions within the Arab world, divisions that the Zionists exploited to the full in the struggle for Palestine. In short, the real line-up in the struggle for Palestine was not between Arabs and Palestinians against the Zionists, but, in a very real sense, between Abdullah and the Zionists against the Palestinians.

Avi Shlaim

BIBLIOGRAPHY

Abdullah of Jordan, King. *My Memoirs Completed: Al-Takmilah.* London: 1978.

Glubb, Sir John Bagot. *A Soldier with the Arabs.* 1957. Reprint. New York: Harper, 1967.

Graves, Philip R., ed. *Memoirs of King Abdullah.* London: 1950.

Kirkbride, Sir Alec. *From the Wings: Amman Memoirs, 1947–1951: Amman Memoirs, 1947–1951.* London: Frank Cass, 1976.

Shlaim, Avi. *Collusion across the Jordan: King Abdullah, the Zionist Movement, and the Partition of Palestine.* New York: Columbia University Press, 1988.

Wilson, Mary C. *King Abdullah, Britain and the Making of Jordan.* New York: Cambridge University Press, 1987.

King-Crane Commission
1919

Disagreement prevailed among the Allies about the future of certain Arab regions of the Ottoman Empire after the Ottomans' defeat in the World War I. U.S. president Woodrow Wilson, who advocated self-determination, opposed British and French plans to annex the regions of Syria, Palestine, and Iraq. The proposed League of Nations advocated that instead the areas be placed under the temporary control of one of the victorious powers, which would be granted a "mandate" to rule while guiding the areas toward eventual self-government. The League's Covenant stated, "The wishes of these communities must be a principal consideration in the selection of a mandatory power."

The United States proposed at the Council of Four (Britain, France, Italy, and the United States) that a commission made up of the members travel to Syria, Palestine, and Iraq to determine the inhabitants' feelings. Only the United States agreed to participate, in no small part because of Anglo-French disagreements and because of the desire of both England and France to occupy the region according to their own plans. The commission thus consisted only of two Americans appointed by President Wilson: Henry C. King and Charles R. Crane.

The King-Crane Commission toured Syria and Palestine (but not Iraq) in June and July 1919. They interviewed Arab leaders in Syria and Lebanon regarding the future of these areas and both Arab and Jewish figures in Palestine regarding its future. The commission determined that the Arab population in these areas rejected the mandate concept, which they understood as another form of colonialism. Arabs apparently sought instead an independent Arab kingdom in Syria under Emir Faysal as king that included Lebanon and Palestine. If forced to accept a mandate, they indicated preference for an American mandate, given that the United States had no colonial legacy. Britain was their second choice; they were opposed to French control.

The commission also investigated the question of ZIONISM. Although initially supportive, they determined that Zionist actions would precipitate the "complete dispossession of the present non-Jewish inhabitants of Palestine, by various forms of purchase." King and Crane therefore recommended limiting Jewish immigration to Palestine, reducing the scope of the Zionist endeavor, and dropping plans for establishing a Jewish commonwealth in Palestine.

The report had no impact on the postwar settlement. Wilson suffered a paralytic stroke before he could read it, and Britain and France ignored the recommendations and divided the areas between them; France took control of Syria, and Britain ruled Iraq and Palestine.

Philip Mattar

BIBLIOGRAPHY

Hurewitz, J. C. *The Middle East and North Africa in World Politics: A Documentary Record*, 2d rev. ed. Vol. 2: *British-French Supremacy, 1914–1945*. New Haven, Conn.: Yale University Press, 1979.

Monroe, Elizabeth. *Britain's Moment in the Middle East 1915–1956*. Baltimore: Johns Hopkins University Press, 1963.

Palestine Government. *A Survey of Palestine for the Information of the Anglo-American Committee of Inquiry*, 2 vols. Jerusalem: Government Printer, 1946. Reprint. Washington, D.C.: Institute for Palestine Studies, 1991.

Smith, Charles D. *Palestine and the Arab-Israeli Conflict*. New York: St. Martin's Press, 1988.

Kuttab, Da'ud

journalist

April 1, 1955– Jerusalem

Kuttab was managing editor of the English edition of the Jerusalem newspaper *al-Fajr* from 1982 to 1986. He since has worked as a free-lance journalist and columnist for a variety of media organizations, including those based in Europe and the United States. Since 1990, he has been the producer for Al Quds Television Productions.

Kuttab is also active in the arts. Since 1991, he has served as secretary and member of the board of trustees for Al-Hakawati, the Palestinian National Theater, and he has presided over the Jerusalem Film Institute.

Long recognized as a leading English-language journalist in the Occupied Territories during the Israeli occupation, Kuttab soon found himself embroiled in controversy after the establishment of the PALESTINIAN AUTHORITY (PA). When the PA closed the pro-Jordanian Jerusalem daily newspaper *al-Nahar* in July 1994, Kuttab organized a petition in protest of the PA's press policies. The PA subsequently barred Kuttab from writing for the newspaper *al-Quds* under his own name. In May 1997, PA authorities arrested Kuttab, but they released him without charges one week later.

Michael R. Fischbach

Kuwait

Prior to the Iraqi invasion on August 2, 1990, nearly 400,000 Palestinians lived in Kuwait; as of the late 1990s that number had shrunk to 31,000. The long-established community had had a major impact on the economic life of Kuwait. Palestinians held important technical positions in the bureaucracy and professions, as well as in banking, commerce, and petty trade. Palestinians tended to live in distinct residential neighborhoods with their own community institutions and social life. Until the GULF CRISIS, they maintained a cooperative relationship with the Kuwaiti government and focused their political efforts on assisting Palestinians in Lebanon and the Israeli-occupied territories. However, even before the Gulf crisis, Kuwaiti leaders expressed concern that the fast-growing Palestinian community might, before long, outnumber the 600,000 Kuwaiti citizens; that transformation of the demographic balance would have potentially complex political ramifications.

1948 War The Palestinian experience in Kuwait underwent three distinct phases, marked by the years 1948, 1967, and 1975. Kuwait's discovery of oil coincided with the Palestinian dispersion in 1948–49: laborers, teachers, and civil servants sought jobs in underdeveloped Kuwait and helped to create the bureaucratic infrastructure of the new state. Palestinian-Jordanians constituted 16 percent of the expatriates and 7.3 percent of the entire 1957 population, which more than doubled to 31.4 percent of expatriates and 16.6 percent of the population by 1965.

After Israel occupied the WEST BANK and GAZA STRIP in June 1967, the number of Palestinians resident in Kuwait escalated. Most of them entered as families since the men did not want to leave their wives and children under Israeli military rule. Another wave of immigrants entered during the Lebanese civil war, which began in 1975. Palestinian-Jordanians numbered 77,712 in 1965, but 147,696 in 1970, and 204,178 in 1975.

Kuwaiti Restrictions The Kuwait government introduced restrictions in response to the increase in size of the foreign community, of which Palestinians represented the largest single group. From 1965 the government required that industrial firms have 51 percent Kuwaiti ownership and that only Kuwaitis own banks and financial institutions. After 1968, residency permits could be obtained only through the Kuwaiti employer; foreigners had to leave the country as soon as their employment ended, and only 10 percent of public school children and university students could be non-Kuwaiti nationals. However, the government allowed the PALESTINE LIBERATION ORGANIZATION (PLO) to operate its own schools from 1968 to 1976; they enrolled 16,000 children in elementary and junior high schools by the final year.

In the late 1970s and early 1980s, official policies tightened further in response to the Lebanese civil war, the Islamic revolution in Iran, and the Iran–Iraq war. The government feared that regional tensions would reverberate inside Kuwait and was concerned that foreigners outnumbered Kuwaiti citizens. The local PLO office worked closely with the government to prevent the infiltration of radical groups, which, it was feared, might jeopardize the community's status. In return, the government deducted 5 percent from the salaries of Palestinian employees as a "tax" to the PLO's PALESTINIAN NATIONAL FUND. However, the closure of the PLO schools in 1976 and ban on foreign children's attending public schools if their parents immigrated after 1962 caused hardships for many Palestinians since most families had arrived after 1967. The government's 50 percent tuition subsidy for Palestinian children enrolled in private schools partially alleviated that hardship.

More fundamentally, the pressure for Kuwaitization of the bureaucracy gained force in the early 1970s, as young Kuwaiti nationals began to graduate from teachers' training institutes and return from foreign universities. Since Kuwaiti citizens had preferential access to government jobs, the relative share of Palestinians in professional and civil service positions dropped substantially. For example, whereas 49 percent of the teachers were Palestinian in 1965, 25 percent were by 1975. Children born to Palestinian residents had few opportunities to enter government service and their parents risked being replaced by Kuwaiti nationals. Nonetheless, the Palestinian community continued to grow and to be involved in all sectors of the economy. By 1990, government planners were discussing ways to reduce the absolute number of foreigners in Kuwait; such policies would have had a particularly severe impact on Palestinians.

Gulf Crisis The Palestinian community in Kuwait was divided by the Iraqi occupation. Some were caught up in the preinvasion enthusiasm that many Palestinians felt for Saddam Husayn as a leader who could stand up to Israel. They hoped that negotiations to end Iraqi rule over Kuwait would be linked to Israeli-Arab negotiations to end Israel's far-longer occupation of the Golan Heights, West Bank, and Gaza Strip. Most Palestinians, however, were shocked at the invasion, the looting by Iraqi soldiers, and the arrests and torture by Iraqi security forces. The PLO office organized a demonstration on August 5, 1990, that supported the

Kuwaiti emir and also issued several leaflets that criticized the occupation. Palestinian officials restrained youths from displaying support for Iraq and withstood Iraqi pressure to mount demonstrations favoring their rule. Some Palestinians joined resistance cells, and an estimated 5,000 Palestinians were jailed by Iraqi security forces. Nonetheless, the Palestinian image was damaged when Iraq sent some 700 members of radical Palestinian groups headquartered in Baghdad to man roadblocks and work with Iraqi security inside Kuwait.

The occupation disrupted all aspects of Kuwait's economic and social life. In that context, more than half of the Palestinians fled the country. By the end of 1990, only 150,000 remained in Kuwait, where they lived in apartment blocks, exposed to Iraqi raids, and pressured to change their identity cards and the license plates on their cars. Seventy percent of Palestinians boycotted work, even though their bank accounts were frozen and they lacked a network for financial support comparable to the Kuwaiti resistance movement.

However, many Palestinians employed in government offices in the water, electricity, education, and public health sectors remained in their jobs. Maintaining those services enabled the population as a whole to survive the occupation, but many Kuwaitis viewed working as an act of treason. They particularly criticized Palestinians for sending their children to school, since Kuwaitis boycotted the educational system. Iraq began to fire and harass Palestinian teachers by late November 1990, but that was not observed by Kuwaitis, who instead felt that Palestinians were maintaining life as normal.

Kuwaiti Reaction The Palestinian community welcomed the end of Iraqi rule, but they became the scapegoat for PLO policies that tilted toward Iraq. They were immediately attacked by Kuwaiti private citizens and returning soldiers. In the first three days after liberation, 400 young Palestinian men were kidnapped from their homes or off the streets; those who were killed were buried in mass graves in Riqqa cemetery. Most were arrested randomly, although a few were specifically targeted as alleged collaborators. By June 1991, Palestinian sources claimed that 6,000 had been detained for varying periods in security offices, the military prison, police stations, schools, and even private homes. By October 1991, the government had forcibly deported 2,000 of those detained Palestinians across the border to Iraq.

In addition to creating pervasive fear of arrest, the government instituted sweeping restrictions. Virtually no Palestinians were reinstated in their government positions; the government recruited Egyptians, instead, as teachers and doctors. Children were not allowed to attend the government schools or to receive tuition vouchers, as punishment for continuing to study during the Iraqi occupation. The 300 Palestinian students at the university were not allowed to resume their academic program in September 1991, and no Palestinians were admitted to the university. Security offices confiscated identity cards or refused to issue new ones to most Palestinians as a way to pressure them to leave. The PLO office was forced to close, as well as the Palestine RED CRESCENT society, Women's Union, and other Palestinian welfare organizations.

Restrictions on bank withdrawals were lifted on August 3, 1991, giving Palestinians access to their savings. But pensions, severance pay, and unpaid salaries are only made available on presentation of a stamped exit visa. This policy resulted in a mass exodus to JORDAN, since Palestinians who carried Jordanian passports were eager to enroll their children in school by September. Moreover, Palestinians who lacked residency permits were ordered to leave by November 15, 1991—a deadline that was later extended to May 31, 1992—or else face detention, a substantial fine, and deportation.

By the end of August 1991, 70,000 Palestinians remained in Kuwait. (Jordan alone had absorbed over 250,000 and ISRAEL had admitted another 30,000 to the West Bank and 7,000 to Gaza.) Only 31,000 remained in Kuwait in 1999. That figure included 7,000 who carried Egyptian travel documents. Those persons (or their parents) came from the Gaza Strip prior to 1967, carrying Egyptian transit documents that they renewed periodically. Since they were absent from Gaza in 1967, they were not counted in the Israeli census; subsequently, they could only visit Gaza as tourists. Israel would not admit them or their Kuwait-born children since they lacked Israeli-issued identity cards. Egypt and Jordan would only accord them transit rights. The Egyptian government argued that Kuwait should let them stay and return to their jobs. Although the Kuwait government issued temporary residence permits to 5,000 in 1999, the remaining 2,000 stayed on in limbo in Kuwait, lacking access to work, schooling, and social welfare.

Even those Palestinians who managed to gain residency permits generally had to work for the private sector rather than the government, and their permits were renewed annually. Sections of Kuwait City that had been heavily populated by Palestinians were deserted. Only 10 percent of the pre–Gulf crisis Palestinian community continued to reside, precariously in Kuwait. The perceived threat that Palestinians might outnumber Kuwaitis had been forcibly ended and the once-vibrant community had been scattered.

Ann M. Lesch

BIBLIOGRAPHY

Brand, Laurie A. *Palestinians in the Arab World: Institution Building and the Search for State.* New York: Columbia University Press, 1988.

Dumper, Michael. "Letter from Kuwait City: End of an Era." *Journal of Palestine Studies* 21, 1 (Autumn 1991): 120–123.

Ghabra, Shafeeq. "Palestinians in Kuwait: Victims of Conflict." *Middle East International* 197 (April 5, 1991): 21–22.

Lesch, Ann M. "Palestinians in Kuwait." *Journal of Palestine Studies* 20, 4 (Summer 1991): 42–54.

Middle East Watch. *A Victory Turned Sour: Human Rights in Kuwait Since Liberation.* New York: Human Rights Watch, September 1991.

——. *Nowhere to Go: The Tragedy of the Remaining Palestinian Families in Kuwait.* New York: Human Rights Watch, October 1991.

L

Land

One of the most important aspects of the Palestinian-Israeli conflict has been the struggle to control land. The success of ZIONISM in establishing a Jewish state in Palestine was a direct result of its ability to create facts on the ground through the movement's control of land and through the settlement of land by immigrants. In both the Ottoman and British Mandatory periods, Zionist land acquisition policies occurred through legal channels. The largest amount of land that Zionists came to control, however, was gained through military conquest and expropriation after the ARAB–ISRAELI WARS OF 1948 and 1967.

Land in Palestine Under the Ottomans Land has always been important to the economy of Palestine. Though Palestine was not a single administrative unit under Ottoman rule, many of the country's cultivable regions lay within the *sanjak*s of JERUSALEM, NABLUS, and ACRE. The land area of Palestine, as later delineated during the period of the British PALESTINE MANDATE, was 26,320 square kilometers (10,162 square miles). Rain-fed agriculture dominated the economy, especially the cultivation of cereals, olives, fruits, and cotton. Although there are no trustworthy Ottoman era figures, a 1931 British study determined that only 33 percent of the land area was cultivable. The remainder was too rocky, mountainous, or arid for farming. Agriculture generally was pursued by Palestinian Arab cultivators living in village communities, some of whom owned and farmed collectively in a system known as *musha*.

As part of the Tanzimat reorganizations of the mid-nineteenth century, the Ottoman government provided greater structure to state land policy by promulgating the 1858 Land Code. This established the basis for land law in Palestine throughout the nineteenth and twentieth centuries. The code classified land into legal categories. *Mulk* land, for instance, was privately owned. Title to *miri* land technically lay with the state, which sold inheritable usufructuary rights (legal rights to fruits or profits derived from land owned by another) to cultivate the land; most cultivable land in Palestine was classified as *miri*. Other categories included land within villages set aside for community purposes (*matruka*), religious endowment land (*waqf*), unclaimed and uncultivated land lying outside villages (*mawat*), and various types of state land, the title and control of which were under direct state control.

Subsequent legislation provided for wide-scale registration of land rights. Registration began in Palestine in the late 1860s, with usufructuary rights registered to the villagers working the land. In other instances, large stretches were registered to influential persons who were not residents of the villages, especially along the coast and in swampy inland valleys like Marj ibn Amir (Plain of Esdraelon). Where they encountered *musha* land, the Ottomans sometimes forced partitioning into individual plots.

The registration of land rights in the name of private owners made possible their sale. Palestine's growing incorporation into the world market, with its demand for agricultural commodities, worked together with the new land laws to stimulate entrepreneurial investment in land (as in the case of Marj ibn Amir) and therefore a market for land. Beginning in the early 1880s, such transactions in land also facilitated the Zionist aim of buying land to build a Jewish state in Palestine, a

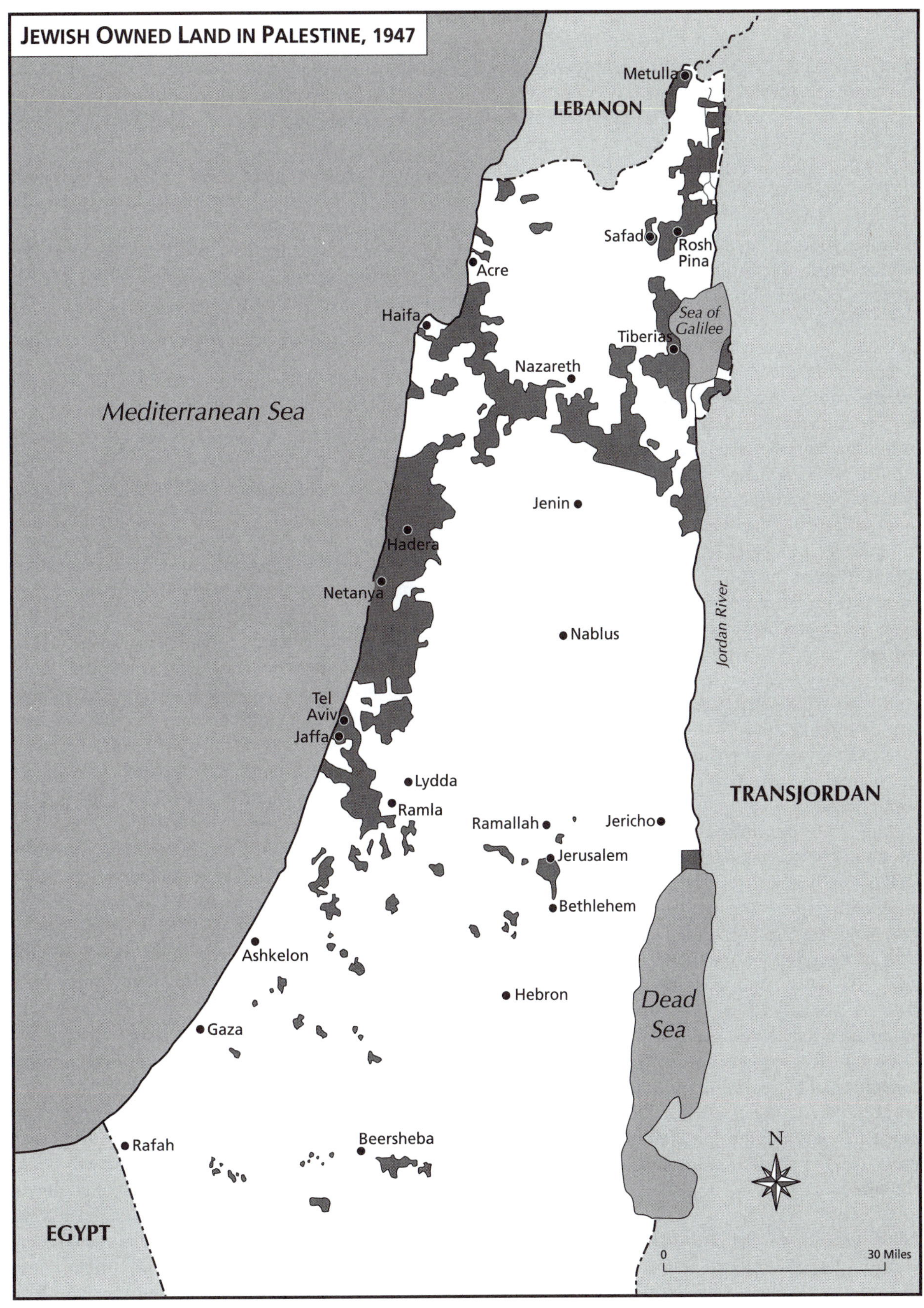
JEWISH OWNED LAND IN PALESTINE, 1947
LEBANON
Metulla
Safad
Rosh Pina
Acre
Haifa
Sea of Galilee
Tiberias
Nazareth
Mediterranean Sea
Jenin
Hadera
Netanya
Nablus
Jordan River
Tel Aviv
Jaffa
Lydda
Ramla
Ramallah
Jericho
TRANSJORDAN
Jerusalem
Bethlehem
Ashkelon
Hebron
Dead Sea
Gaza
Rafah
Beersheba
N
EGYPT
0
30 Miles

process that resulted eventually in transforming the nature of the land in Palestine. The scope of land owned by Jews in Palestine prior to the onset of significant Jewish immigration was negligible—only 22,530 *dunums* (1 Ottoman *dunum* was approximately 919 square meters), or 0.09 percent of the total land and 0.26 percent of the cultivable land by 1882. As groups of Jews began moving to Palestine, bodies like the Palestine Jewish Colonization Association (established in 1891) began buying land for settlements. Estimates of the amount of land purchased by such groups vary, but it appears to have been some 400,000 *dunums* by 1920.

Starting in the early twentieth century, however, the World Zionist Organization (WZO) also began acquiring land as part of a coordinated effort to build a Jewish homeland. The Jewish National Fund (JNF, established in 1901) and the Palestine Land Development Company (established in 1909) were created by the WZO for acquiring and holding land for this end. Land purchased by the JNF was held in perpetuity for the Jewish people and leased to Jewish immigrants only. Unlike the earlier settlements, which employed Palestinian farm workers, the JNF required lessees to use Jewish labor only. To ensure this, the fund required as a condition of sale that sellers remove any Palestinian tenant farmers who were working on the land. In these ways, Zionist land purchases spelled the permanent alienation of the land from Palestinian residence and usage.

The JNF purchased little land during the Ottoman period, as its activities were limited by a lack of funds and Ottoman laws restricting foreign landholdings in Palestine. In some instances, the group resorted to subterfuge, such as registering land in the name of Jews who were Ottoman citizens. By 1919, the JNF owned some 16,400 *dunums*, a small figure in relation to total Jewish holdings in Palestine.

Certain Palestinians began warning of the consequences of increased Zionist land purchases and immigration by the eve of World War I. Calls were made in the Ottoman Parliament and the Arabic press to take measures to check further Zionist activities.

Land in Mandatory Palestine Britain, at war with the Ottomans during World War I, occupied Palestine in 1917–18 and subsequently was granted a Mandate over the region. Mandatory authorities retained the Ottoman Land Code but devoted more attention to land questions than the Ottomans, particularly technical matters like surveying and settlement of claims to land rights. Official surveying began in 1922, and the British standardized the *dunum* at 1,000 square meters. The Land (Settlement of Title) Ordinance of 1928 empowered land officials to investigate and settle claims to land rights throughout the country. From 1928 to 1948, settlement of rights was completed to 5,240,000 *dunums*, largely along the coastal plain and in the northern Jordan valley. Although contributing to rising land prices, the greater security of rights and ease of transfer stemming from the process facilitated Zionist land purchases.

Britain's policy affected land politically through its official support for Zionism. As a result of the 1917 BALFOUR DECLARATION, Britain pledged to facilitate development of a Jewish "national home" in Palestine. Unlike the Ottomans, the British allowed open Zionist land acquisitions and immigration; Zionist land purchases accelerated correspondingly. In the 1920s, transactions generally were carried out between Zionist purchasing agencies and major landowners possessing large holdings along the fertile coastal plain and the inland valleys. Other transactions involved persons owning smaller estates. From 1921 to 1925, for instance, several large landowning families in Lebanon, including the Sursuq family, sold 240,000 *dunums* in Marj ibn Amir. Such acquisitions reduced the time and effort required in purchasing contiguous plots from a large number of small peasant landowners. However, most Zionist purchases tended to be smaller in scale, although still conducted with Palestinian owners of large estates, who often were absentee landowners. By the end of the Mandate, some 70 percent of land purchased by the JNF and other Zionist bodies had been sold by large owners, the Mandate government, or corporate bodies; the rest was obtained from small peasant cultivators.

In the 1920s, Zionist land acquisitions were accomplished with an eye toward expanding holdings in established areas of Jewish settlement through contiguous purchases from large landowners. Jews bought 513,500 *dunums* in this way from 1920 to 1929. Beginning in 1929, however, political factors led to a shift in strategy. Palestinian political violence in that year prompted the British to conclude that the rising Palestinian landlessness triggered as a consequence of Zionist land purchases was a significant factor in Jewish-Arab tensions. Legislation was enacted in 1929 and 1933 to protect the rights of tenant farmers who might be evicted as a result of sales, although this did not address the question of owner-cultivators rendered landless by selling their own land. Eventually, in 1940, the British curtailed Jewish purchases from Palestinian owners altogether in certain regions. Second, the wide-scale Palestinian uprising of 1936–39 led to British proposals for an eventual partitioning of Palestine into Jewish and Arab zones. Finally, the 1939 White Paper diminished Britain's commitment to Zionism.

To prepare for an uncertain future, Zionist land officials changed their acquisition strategies in the 1930s and 1940s. In order to buy as much land as possible, transactions were cultivated with any Palestinian wishing to sell, not just large owners. Thus 331,600 *dunums* was acquired during the 1930s, as was 238,000 *dunums* from 1940 to 1948 despite restrictions on Palestine sales to Jews. Second, land was bought in the largely Palestinian regions in mountainous northern and central Palestine for political and military purposes: to expand the scope of Jewish settlement and establish defensive positions.

By the end of the Mandate in 1948, Jews owned 1,734,000 *dunums* in Palestine, 54 percent of which belonged to the Jewish National Fund. Although this land represented only 6.59 percent of the total, it did constitute some 20 percent of Palestine's cultivable land.

Land in Israel During the 1948 fighting in Palestine, Zionist forces gained control of ten times as much land as they had held prior to the 1947 decision by the United Nations to partition Palestine into Arab and Jewish states. As a consequence, the Jewish state, Israel, was established on 20,255 square kilometers, or 77 percent, of Palestine. The vast majority of this had not been owned by Jews before the 1948 war. Israel quickly consolidated its hold over Palestinian-owned land in the country, and more than 400 Palestinian villages ceased to exist in the process. A Custodian of Absentee Property was created in 1948 to control the land left behind by more than 726,000 Palestinian REFUGEES (whom Israel called "absentees"). In 1951, the UNITED NATIONS CONCILIATION COMMISSION FOR PALESTINE estimated that 16,324,000 *dunums* had been abandoned by the refugees. After years of studying the issue, the same body later reported in 1964 that the land amounted to 7,069,091 individually owned *dunums*, although this figure excluded a large amount of land that, while Arab, was not individually owned by Palestinians. Israel claimed that the Custodian of Absentee Property absorbed only 3,250,000 *dunums*. Beyond land owned by individual refugees, Israel's state property office controlled somewhere over 12,500,000 *dunums* in other lands not owned by Jews prior to 1948, most in the arid southern region.

Israel never let the refugees return, and their land was soon disposed of to various Israeli and Zionist agencies. The Jewish National Fund (JNF) bought 1,102,000 *dunums* in 1949. The Absentee Property Law of March 1950 and the Development of Property (Transfer of Property) Law of July 1950 allowed a new Israeli development authority the right to purchase more of the Custodian's land. Before this could occur, the JNF bought another 1,272,000 *dunums* in October 1950. All the remaining land in the Custodian's possession was then transferred to the development authority in 1953.

Legislation enacted in 1960 created a new Israel Lands Administration (ILA), which was given control over the lands of the JNF, the development authority, and the state property office. Other legislation passed that year forbade the ILA to alienate land under its control, known thereafter as "Israel lands." The lands could only be leased. But since the council administering the ILA was made up almost equally of representatives of the state and the JNF, the JNF's "Jewish only" policies regarding leases were regularly voiced in reaching decisions. However, former JNF land under the ILA's control still could not be leased to non-Jews under any circumstances, a long-standing JNF policy that continued after the ILA's creation.

Many Palestinians who remained in Israel lost land over the years as the state and quasi-state Zionist organizations like the JNF and the Jewish Agency (responsible for Jewish immigration into Israel) sought to expand the scale of Jewish land ownership. Approximately 51 percent of the 160,000 PALESTINIAN CITIZENS OF ISRAEL were declared "absentees" and had their property, estimates of which range from 300,000 to 1,000,000 *dunums*, confiscated. Certain villages, such as

Ghabasiya and eleven others in Galilee, were declared "closed" and depopulated. The authorities forced out the inhabitants of still others, like Iqrit and Kufr Bir'im in Galilee, by claiming they lay within "security zones." In other cases, land belonging to Palestinian villages was placed within the administration boundaries of Jewish municipalities or local governing councils; some of this property has been expropriated, and usage of the rest restricted.

By 1962, some 93 percent of the land in Israel had become "Israel lands": 15,205,000 *dunums* (90 percent) controlled by the state, including the Development Authority; and 3,570,000 (10 percent) by the JNF. Palestinians in Israel owned only 810,200 *dunums*—4 percent of the land in Israel.

Continued Israeli confiscation of Palesinian land in Israel's Galilee region prompted massive protests on March 30, 1976. Security forces crushed the protests, killing six Palestinians. Therfore, Palestinians worldwide have celebrated March 30 as "Land Day."

Land in the West Bank and Gaza from 1948 to 1967 Arab forces managed to hold a relatively small portion of Palestine during the 1947–48 fighting. Jordanian and Iraqi forces occupied 5,672 square kilometers of central and eastern Palestine, which became known as the WEST BANK. Egyptian forces held 370 square kilometers in the southwest corner of Palestine, which became known as the GAZA STRIP.

Jordanian and Egyptian authorities did not significantly transform land tenure patterns or the Palestinian character of the land. The most significant land policies were carried out by Jordan in the West Bank. The Jordanians tried to finish the campaign to settle and register land rights initiated by the British. Although this process was started in 150 villages from 1952 to 1967, much West Bank village land remained unregistered by the time of Israel's 1967 occupation.

Land in the Israeli-Occupied West Bank and Gaza Israel occupied the West Bank and Gaza in the June 1967 Arab-Israeli War, bringing all of the former Palestine Mandate under its control. Although Israel did not annex the areas, except East Jerusalem, and maintained preexisting Ottoman, British, and Jordanian land laws, the occupation soon transformed the character of the land in fundamental ways. Overall Israeli land policy was guided by narrow security concerns devised by the Labor Party. Land was requisitioned for military bases and, according to the 1967 Allon Plan, for raising several civilian settlements as Israeli defensive outposts in the Jordan valley. Israel confiscated Jordanian state land (eventually determined to comprise 680,000 *dunums*) and 430,000 *dunums* of land declared "abandoned" by Palestinians who had taken refuge in Jordan and elsewhere. When it expropriated privately owned land, Israel based its confiscation policy on Article 52 of the 1907 Hague Convention, which allows occupying armies to requisition private land for the duration of the occupation.

The Likud bloc's victory in 1977 fundamentally changed Israel's attitudes toward land in the territories. The Likud was fiercely committed to allowing Jews to live in the territories, not only for security purposes but also for ideological reasons: it considered the territories a part of the historical Jewish patrimony and a legitimate site for permanent Zionist settlement. Likud openly allowed the Jewish nationalist-religious Gush Emmunim ("Bloc of the Faithful") movement to erect civilian settlements outside the Jordan valley in areas near Palestinian villages. Secular settlements for Jewish commuters into Tel Aviv and Jerusalem were also constructed according to the World Zionist Organization's Drobles Plan. The plan, announced in September 1980, was a modification of an earlier five-year plan for building settlements in such a way as to surround Palestinian communities and isolate them from one another. By 1981, the number of settlements in the West Bank had increased from 36 to over 100 under Likud; the number of settlers increased from 3,200 to 67,700 by 1987. Additionally, over 21,700 *dunums* of land had been expropriated by 1980 to expand Jewish residential and industrial sites around East Jerusalem.

The change in policy required new methods for seizing land because in 1979 the Israel High Court of Justice had ruled that establishing permanent civilian settlements on private land temporarily requisitioned for military purposes contravened the Hague Convention. Israeli officials therefore adopted new measures by which they quickly controlled much more land than before. Because the convention allows an occupier latitude to control state lands (as opposed to private land) belonging to the former power, the government reinterpreted Ottoman law (the basis for the Jordanian land law still in effect) to declare unregistered, uncultivated land in the West Bank as "state land" and then seize it for settlements. The fact that a significant proportion of land in the West Bank had not been registered during the Jordanian campaign to settle land rights facilitated Israel's task. Some 1,470,000 *dunums* thus was identified and mapped by the Israelis as "state land" in addition to the Jordanian state land already confiscated; 800,000 *dunums* of this new land actually had been taken over by 1984.

Land was seized by other means as well, including expropriations for "public use," declarations of "nature reserves," and over one million *dunums* (including some state lands already seized) declared "closed" for security purposes. Furthermore, Palestinians were hampered severely in their ability to utilize what land remained under their control. Israel required permits for activities like digging wells, planting trees, and building homes, in addition to restricting urban expansion.

By the mid-1980s, nearly 50 percent of land in the West Bank was under Israeli control—more than 2,300,000 *dunums*—as was 30 percent of the land of Gaza. Most of this area has not yet been used; only some 20 percent of confiscated West Bank land has been utilized for settlements. An additional 570,000 *dunums* left in Palestinian hands faced severe restrictions on usage. The effect on Palestinian agriculture has been significant in certain areas. In the fertile Jordan valley, for instance, some 50 percent of the cultivable land had been taken over by the early 1980s. By 1995, 147,000 Israeli civilians were living in 156 settlements in the West Bank and Gaza, with an additional 200,000 in East Jerusalem and the nine settlements in its vicinity.

Land and the Oslo Peace Accords Israel continued to confiscate land in the West Bank and Gaza even after signing the OSLO AGREEMENTS with the PALESTINE LIBERATION ORGANIZATION starting in September 1993. The subsequent September 1995 Israeli-Palestinian Interim Agreement led to a redeployment of Israeli troops from parts of the Occupied Territories but left 73 percent of the West Bank under Israeli control pending final status negotiations with the PALESTINIAN AUTHORITY. Following up on decisions taken before 1993, Israeli authorities took over an estimated 250,000 *dunums* between September 1993 and the spring of 1996. Additionally, over 15,000 *dunums* was confiscated to build roads enabling Jewish settlers to bypass Palestinian localities and some 23,000 *dunums* has been taken over by settlers.

✦ ✦ ✦

Control of land proved the ultimate arbiter of power in the Israeli-Palestinian conflict and constituted the ultimate political quest of the Palestinians in the twentieth century. The vast amounts of land in Palestine obtained by Israel through conquest in the 1948 and 1967 Arab-Israeli wars, Israel's stubborn refusal to return it to the Palestinians, and its transformation of the conquered land's demography through Jewish settlements have shattered Palestinian society and frustrated Palestinian goals of creating some kind of state on a portion of historic Palestine.

The peace process has not challenged this assessment. Despite the general commitments to redeploy its military from parts of the West Bank and Gaza made during the Oslo peace process, Israel still controlled all of its own territory plus most of the Occupied Territories by mid-1999. Although the Palestinian Authority exercised full civil and security authority over most of Gaza, it had full control of only 10 percent of the West Bank after various Israeli redeployments from 1994 to 1998. The Palestinian Authority maintained civil authority over a further 19 percent of the West Bank but was forced to share security authority there with Israel. Israel continued to exert full control over the remaining 70 percent of the West Bank. Nor were the areas handed over to the Palestinians geographically contiguous. Rather, Israel redeployed from patches of territory divided from one another by Israeli settlements, bypass roads, and military checkpoints. Israeli forces have still been able to impose travel restrictions, which isolated the various patches of Palestinian territory from one another and turned a viable Palestinian political entity into a geographic fiction.

For these reasons, the loss of their land is perhaps the most important reason one can cite to explain the long national trauma of the Palestinian people in the twentieth century.

Michael R. Fischbach

BIBLIOGRAPHY

Benvenisti, Meron. *The West Bank Data Project: A Survey of Israel's Policies.* Washington, D.C.: American Enterprise Institute for Public Policy Research, 1984.

Fischbach, Michael R. "Time Implications of Jordanian Land Policy for the West Bank." *Middle East Journal* 48 (Summer 1994).

——. "Settling Historical Land Claims in the Wake of Arab-Israeli Peace." *Journal of Palestine Studies* 27, 1 (Autumn 1997): 38–50.

Gerber, Haim. *The Social Origins of the Modern Middle East.* Boulder, Colo.: Lynne Rienner Publishers, 1987.

Granott, A. *The Land System in Palestine: History and Structure.* Trans. by M. Simon. London: Eyre & Spottiswoode, 1952.

Hadawi, Sami. *Palestinian Rights and Losses in 1948: A Comprehensive Study.* London: Saqi Books, 1988.

Jiryis, Sabri. *The Arabs in Israel.* Trans. by Inea Bushnaq. New York: Monthly Review Press, 1976.

Lehn, Walter, with Uri Davis. *The Jewish National Fund.* London and New York: Kegan Paul International, 1988.

Peretz, Don. *Israel and the Palestine Arabs.* Foreword by Roger Baldwin. Washington, D.C.: The Middle East Institute, 1958.

Ruedy, John. "Dynamics of Land Alienation." In *The Transformation of Palestine,* ed. by I. Abu-Lughod. Evanston, Ill.: Northwestern University Press, 1971.

Shafir, Gershon. *Land, Labor and the Origins of the Israeli–Palestinian Conflict 1882–1914.* Cambridge, England: Cambridge University Press, 1989.

Stein, Kenneth W. *The Land Question in Palestine, 1917–1939.* Chapel Hill: University of North Carolina Press, 1984.

A Survey of Palestine, Prepared in December 1945 and January 1946 for the Information of the Anglo-American Committee of Inquiry. Government of Palestine, 1946–1947. Reprint, Washington, D.C.: Institute for Palestine Studies, 1991.

Late Ottoman Period
(1700–1917)

Palestine became a part of the Ottoman Empire in 1516 after the defeat of the Mamluks (a military caste of non-Arab slaves) in Syria (Bilad al-Sham) and in Egypt the following year. The four centuries (1517–1917) of Ottoman rule in this region were the longest among the different Islamic regimes. Nonetheless, very little is known about the history of the country and its people during that period.

Understanding the history of Palestine in the late Ottoman period (1700–1917) is particularly important for an understanding of Palestinian SOCIETY and politics. During the eighteenth and nineteenth centuries, the Palestinian sociopolitical elite was formed and transformed. Palestine was integrated into the world capitalist market, and its ECONOMY was shaped, like that of other Middle Eastern countries, according to its dependent position in the world economy. Then, after Europe rediscovered the Holy Land, Zionist settlement in Palestine became possible in the last decades of the nineteenth century. The roots of these transformations can be traced back to the eighteenth century.

The First Popular Uprising in Palestine The years 1703–1705 were eventful in the history of southern Palestine (the *sanjak*s of Gaza, JERUSALEM, and NABLUS). Mehmet Pasha Kurd Bayram, the governor of Damascus (1701–1703), made an attempt to implement a new policy of centralization and reorganization of his province. His actions were part of the reform policies conducted by the Ottoman government under the auspices of the Köprülü dynasty, prime ministers (grand viziers) since 1656. However, the pasha's attempts to collect heavy taxes from the *sanjak*s of Gaza, Nablus, and Jerusalem faced serious opposition from the population.

The bloody clashes between the governor and his army on the one hand and the Bedouin and the fellahin (peasants) on the other hand turned into the first popular rebellion in Jerusalem, led by the Naqib al-Ashraf of the City (head, or *naqib,* of the descendants of the Prophet Muhammad). The young *naqib,* Muhammad ibn Mustafa al-Wafa'i al-Husayni, and his supporters expelled the subgovernor and took control of Jerusalem. Several attempts by the Ottomans to put an end to this rebellion failed. Eventually, factionalism inside the city and an Ottoman army sent from Damascus in 1705 liquidated the uprising. The *naqib* and dozens of his followers fled the city. The Ottomans searched for him until he was arrested and escorted to Istanbul, where he was executed in 1707.

The demise of the *naqib* and his followers made possible the rise of another notable family in Jerusalem. The Ghudayyas were appointed *naqib*s and muftis (experts in Islamic law) of Jerusalem. In the late eighteenth century, one branch of the Ghudayyas, the sons of Abd ul-Latif, adopted *al-Husayni* as their family name. This branch of the Husaynis (see HUSAYNI FAMILY) consolidated its posi-

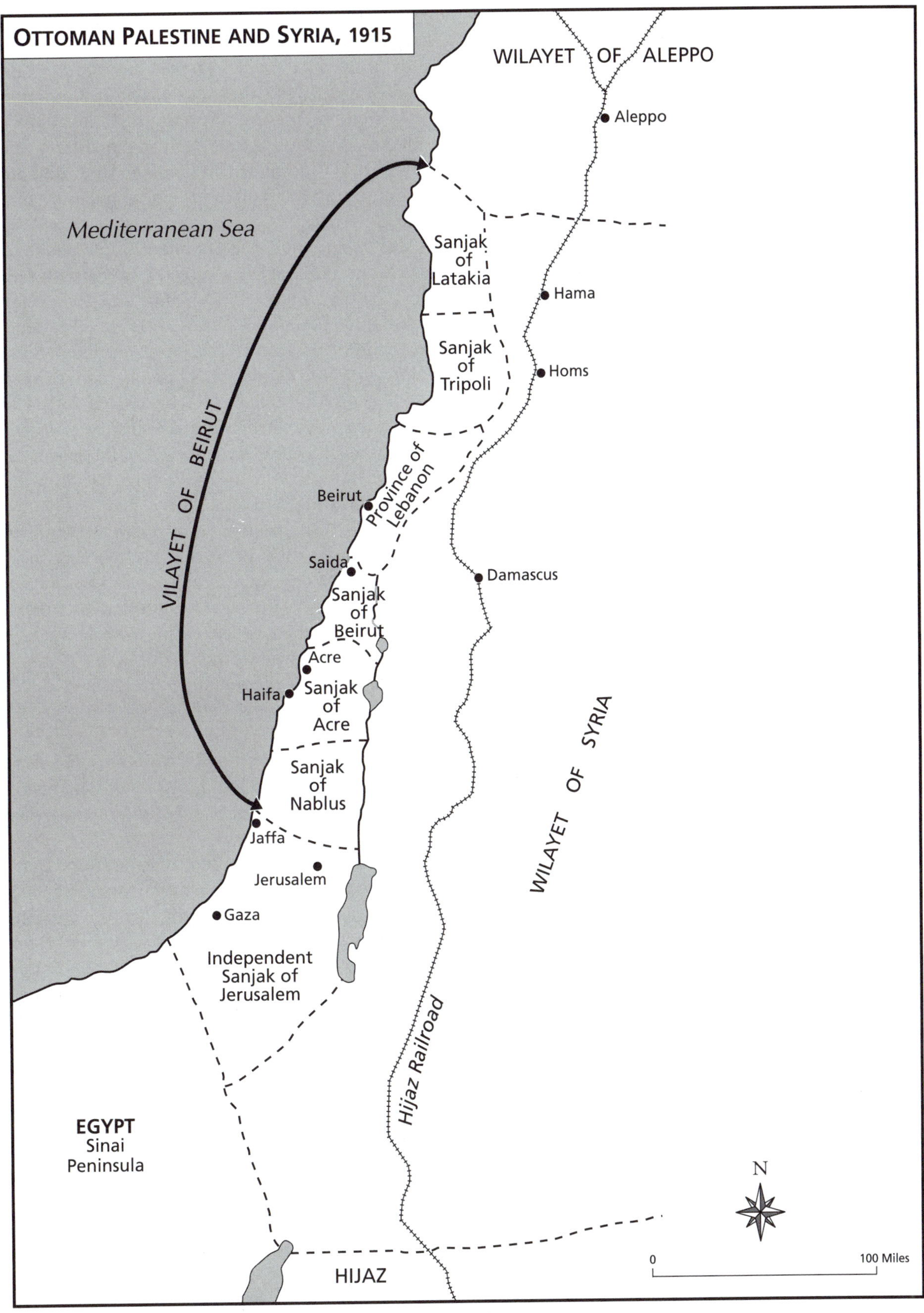

OTTOMAN PALESTINE AND SYRIA, 1915
WILAYET OF ALEPPO
Aleppo
Mediterranean Sea
Sanjak of Latakia
Hama
Sanjak of Tripoli
Homs
VILAYET OF BEIRUT
Province of Lebanon
Beirut
Saida
Damascus
Sanjak of Beirut
Acre
Haifa
Sanjak of Acre
Sanjak of Nablus
Jaffa
Jerusalem
Gaza
Independent Sanjak of Jerusalem
WILAYET OF SYRIA
Hijaz Railroad
EGYPT
Sinai Peninsula
HIJAZ
N
0
100 Miles

tion among Jerusalem notables during the late Ottoman period and led the Palestinian national movement after World War I.

Zahir al-Umar al-Zaydani The northern part of Palestine—the Galilee—also witnessed fundamental changes in the early eighteenth century. The Zaydani family, who immigrated into the eastern Galilee from the Hijaz in the late seventeenth century, served the Shihabis of Mount Lebanon as tax collectors (*multazims*) of the region. Umar Zaydani became a famous shaykh and *multazim* in various regions (*nahiyas*) of upper and eastern Galilee in the early eighteenth century. However, it was under the second generation of the Zaydanis, led by Zahir, Umar's son, that the family came to dominate the Galilee.

Several towns and villages were built and fortified as strongholds and capitals of the Zaydanis. Most famous among these were TIBERIAS, SAFAD, Dayr Hanna, and Shafa Amr. The Zaydanis finally reached their zenith after Zahir al-Umar made ACRE his capital (1746–1775). During that period, sons and relatives of Zahir were governors of subdistricts in the Galilee and sustained their own rule, in the centers of government mentioned, as administrative assistants of "Zahir's little kingdom."

The extensive planting of cotton in the western Galilee and its export to Europe from Acre's harbor were a solid economic basis of the Zaydani rule. The villages of the Galilee flourished, and Acre became one of the most important coastal cities of Syria and Palestine. French and other European merchants moved into Zahir's capital. Many people from Lebanon and the Galilee immigrated to Acre, and its population witnessed a rapid growth in a short period.

The ambition of Zahir al-Umar to expand his domain in southern Palestine faced fierce resistance from the notable families of JENIN, Nablus, and Gaza. Furthermore, the governors of Damascus to whom these *sanjak*s belonged, as well as the government in Istanbul, tried to curb Zahir's attempts at expansionism. Therefore, they supported the rivals of the Zaydanis, such as the Madis, the Jarrars, and the TUQAN FAMILY. This coalition blocked the expansion of Zahir south of HAIFA and into the Esdraelon valley (Marj ibn Amir) in the 1750s and 1760s.

At that time, Ali Bey al-Kabir succeeded in seizing power in Egypt and became the real governor of that country. Under his rule, the Mamluks reawakened their interests in Syria and Palestine. Zahir al-Umar, who shared the same ambitions, allied himself with Ali Bey al-Kabar and together they tried to capture Damascus. This alliance with Ali Bey, their revolt against the sultan, and their attempt to annex Damascus to their domain by military force constituted the beginning of Zahir's demise.

Also at this time, the Ottoman Empire was facing a serious military challenge in its war with Russia (1770–74). At the end of that war, the sultan decided to liquidate Zahir's rule in Palestine. Meanwhile, Ali Bey al-Kabir was beaten by the ambitious Mamluk and army commander Muhammad Bey Abu al-Dhahab, who became governor of Egypt. Abu al-Dhahab invaded Palestine with the blessing of the sultan in early 1775. Zahir was an old man by this time and, believing that he could face the invading Egyptian army, fled Acre. However, Abu al-Dhahab's sudden death in June, in front of Acre's walls, drew Zahir back to his capital for a while. At this stage, the Ottomans were keen on terminating the Zaydani ambitions to rule in the Galilee. Ahmad Jazzar Pasha, who was nominated to lead the war against Zahir, was appointed governor of Sidon immediately after Zahir's death in August 1775.

Jazzar and the Mamluk Dynasty in Acre (1775–1831) Ahmad Pasha al-Jazzar, who was a Mamluk of Bosnian origin, governed the province of Sidon for three successive decades (1775–1804). In addition he was appointed as governor of Damascus several times for almost nine years. In 1803, one year before his death at the age of eighty, he was appointed to head Sidon, Tripoli, and the Damascus provinces. Furthermore, a few months before al-Jazzar's death in May 1804, the sultan nominated him as governor of Egypt. Though he did not in fact perform his governorship in Cairo, this nomination illustrated Jazzar's might and capabilities.

From the point of view of the people of Palestine, al-Jazzar (known as "the butcher") is remembered mainly as a tyrant and merciless governor. He embezzled the people's money and punished his rivals and opponents severely. However, some contemporary *ulama* of Palestine and many Muslims appreciate his building projects in Acre, his capital. His mosque and the walls and fortifications of the city are evidence of his strength and might. Jazzar consolidated his fame when he succeeded in blocking Napoleon's invasion in 1799.

Many Orientalists highlight the French invasion as the beginning of the modern era in the history of the Middle East. However, a serious study of Napoleon's attempt to conquer Syria and Palestine yields no evidence to support this conclusion. Neither Napoleon's failed invasion nor Jazzar's death in 1804 produced any fundamental transformation in the history of Palestine. Whereas French rule in Egypt (1798–1801) generated long-standing change in Egypt's political and social history, Napoleon's short appearance in Palestine had very little impact in this region. The Mamluk dynasty in Acre—under Sulayman Pasha (1804–19) and Abdullah Pasha (1819–31)—sustained the economic and political regime of the late eighteenth century. Under the successors of Jazzar, Acre enjoyed stability and superiority over the neighboring administrative capitals of the Syrian provinces (Sidon, Tripoli, and Damascus).

In the early nineteenth century, the *sanjak* of Gaza and JAFFA, which belonged to the province of Damascus, was transferred to the domain of Sulayman Pasha, governor of Acre. Muhammad Abu Maraq, a Gazan who challenged Jazzar in 1801–1803 and eventually fled Jaffa, returned to the region in 1805. He promised the sultan that he would invade the Hijaz in order to liberate the Islamic Holy Cities from the Wahhabis. The sultan accepted his offer and granted him 7,500 burses (a burse contained 500 piasters) to help meet the expenses of the campaign. However, instead of fighting the Wahhabis, Abu Maraq embezzled more money from the population and refrained from invading the Hijaz from Gaza. In 1807, Sulayman Pasha was ordered to terminate his rule in Jaffa and Gaza and to return the 7,500 burses to the Ottoman treasury. Abu Maraq succeeded in defending himself in Jaffa for several months. Eventually, however, the governor of Acre sent Muhammad Abu Nabbut, one of his high-ranking Mamluk officers, who captured Jaffa from Abu Maraq. The latter fled Jaffa again, and Abu Nabbut was appointed governor of the *sanjak* of Gaza and Jaffa by Sulayman Pasha.

Abu Nabbut's rule in Jaffa (1807–18) was a turning point in the lot of this city, which had suffered from successive invasions and wars since 1770. Abu Nabbut's stable rule and his policy of building the city and fortifying its walls were the first steps in Jaffa's rise. Abu Nabbut built his grand mosque, public water fountains, a market, and developed the port of the city. His projects of renovation and construction made possible the city's demographic and economic rise. It is not an exaggeration to say that, under Abu Nabbut, Jaffa joined Acre and Haifa as modern coastal cities.

During Sulayman Pasha's rule (1804–19), Palestine benefited from a peaceful and prosperous era. Contrary to Jazzar's practices, most of Sulayman's investments were designed to promote peace and security in the region. His lenient attitude toward the local governors and elites gained him his title *al-Adil,* "The Just." The *sanjak*s of Lajjun, Nablus, and Jerusalem continued to be part of the province of Damascus. Nonetheless, Sulayman involved himself in keeping order and making peace between local rivals in these regions rather than suppressing rebels and uprisings, as Jazzar Pasha, his predecessor, had. Furthermore, Sulayman invested his money in several projects for renovations and building in Jerusalem and its surroundings.

Abdullah Pasha, who succeeded Sulayman in 1819, was a son of a senior Mamluk of Jazzar. Unlike his predecessor, he antagonized the Ottoman government, which made an attempt to remove him from his rule in Acre in the early 1820s. Paradoxically, it was Muhammad Ali, governor of Egypt, who supported Abdullah and mediated a compromise with the sultan in Istanbul. However, Abdullah's rule was characterized by bloody clashes with local governors in Lebanon and Palestine. Unlike Jazzar and Sulayman Pasha, he was not appointed to govern the province of Damascus. Nonetheless, Acre maintained its stability and political superiority over the neighboring administrative centers in Lebanon and Syria.

The governor of Acre also maintained his predecessor's involvement in the local politics of Nablus and Jerusalem. In 1825–26, a rebellion broke out in Jerusalem and its surroundings. The local subgovernor (*mutasallim*) of the city was expelled and the rebels controlled the city. The governor of Damascus was not able to suppress the uprising. Eventually, the sultan asked Abdullah Pasha to do the job, and his army completed the mission without shedding much blood. However, a few years later the governor of Acre faced a rebellion in the Mount of Nablus. The rebels, led by the Jarrars, a local elite family, sustained their resistance for several months. Eventually, Abdullah Pasha decided to compromise with the Nablusites in 1831. He decided to gather all his troops and energy to face a more serious challenge from the Egyptian front. It was this invasion of the Egyptian troops in 1831 that terminated the role of Acre's governors in Palestine.

Muhammad Ali, the governor of Egypt (1805–48), succeeded in building a centralized and modern regime. Unlike the Ottomans, he created a modern and efficient army within a short period in the early nineteenth century. After his success in fighting the Wahhabis in the Hijaz and the Greek rebels in Greece, he asked the sultan to give him Syria and Palestine in return for his military services in Greece. When he realized that the sultan did not intend to fulfill his wishes, he made no secret of his preparations to invade the region. The sultan responded by strengthening the position of Abdullah Pasha. The province of Tripoli and the *sanjak*s of Nablus, Jerusalem, and Lajjun were given to the governor of Acre. Thus the five *sanjak*s of Palestine and Lebanon came under the rule of Abdullah Pasha in 1831.

In October 1831, Muhammad Ali sent his troops, led by his son, Ibrahim Pasha, to invade Palestine. Unlike Napoleon's troops, the Egyptian army faced no serious challenge in the Mediterranean. Ibrahim Pasha also faced no resistance from the Palestinian population. His army captured Gaza and Jaffa easily and marched quickly toward Acre. In December 1831, Ibrahim Pasha laid siege to the city and captured it six months later.

Egyptian Rule (1832–1840) The predominant school of thought among scholars who study the history of Syria and Palestine holds that the decade of Egyptian rule in this region was the beginning of its modern history. These scholars believe that Muhammad Ali affected the history of Palestine in the same manner that the French invasion affected Egypt. To support this thesis, historians highlight the fundamental reforms or modernization policies implemented by the Egyptian administration of Muhammad Ali during the 1830s. Primary among these reforms were the equalizing of rights among the *dhimmis* (Christians and Jews) and the abolishing of several restrictions and taxes imposed on them. During the Egyptian era, European political, cultural, and religious infiltration in Palestine increased tremendously through missionary and consular activities. The centralizing policies of the Egyptian administration undermined the autonomous position of the local elites. *Ulama,* city notables, and rural shaykhs lost many of the positions they had seized since the eighteenth century.

The reforms of the Egyptian administration alienated the local elites. The decision to recruit young people of Palestine into the Egyptian army and collect arms from them generated a widespread rebellion in 1834. Unlike previous uprisings against Ottoman governors, this rebellion aimed at undermining the legitimacy of Muhammad Ali's rule in Palestine. Furthermore, whereas the previous rebellions were restricted to one region or *sanjak,* the 1834 uprising was supported by a large segment of the population from the Galilee in the north to Gaza and Hebron in the south. These and other particularities of this rebellion make it representative of a new model of uprising very similar to the national rebellions in the modern history of the Middle East.

The rebellion broke out first in the northern part of the country: the Safad and Nablus mountains. *Ulama* and notables of Safad were among those who initiated the rebellion in their region. They even sent a letter to Khalil al-Shihabi (son of Bashir) in an attempt to get his support for the uprising. The Shihabis who allied themselves with the Egyptian administration responded negatively. Furthermore, Bashir rebuked the notables of Safad and threatened to punish them personally. Safad was one of the strongholds of the uprising, during which the Jewish Quarter in the city was attacked and looted. This act represented a new era of communal strife in greater Syria against the background of Westernization and colonial penetration in the region.

The main stronghold of the rebellion was Nablus and its surroundings. Qasim al-Ahmad, Jarrar, and other families who allied themselves with the Egyptians felt betrayed by the new rulers. An attempt to conscript their young men into the army and to seize their arms antagonized the population, who feared losing autonomy. The shaykhs of the *nahiya*s (subdistricts), were the natural leaders of this peasant rebellion in spring 1834. The Madis in Mount Carmel and the Galilee, the Jarrars, and Qasim al-Ahmad in the Nablus district led the rebellion in northern Palestine.

In the Mount of Jerusalem, Abu Ghawsh, head of the Yaman faction, and Ibn Samhan, head of the Qays, led the uprising in the region. The Amru family of Dura in the Mount Hebron were prominent among the Hebronite rebels. The Wahidi, Ta'amri, and other Bedouin tribes joined the widespread rebellion. *Ulama* and notables of the Palestinian cities (Safad, Nablus, Jerusalem, and Hebron) gave their support and legitimacy to the uprising. Thus, the rebellion encompassed the majority of the population in Palestine, particularly in the hilly regions. Except for the Abd al-Hadis, who remained faithful to the Egyptians, the sociopolitical elite in Palestine was united in the rebellion.

The suppression of the uprising in 1834 was not an easy mission, even for a strong modern army. Ibrahim Pasha asked his father to send more troops from Egypt. In addition to the ABD AL-HADIS FAMILY of Nablus, the Shihabis of Mount Lebanon played an active role in the campaign against the rebels. In May 1834, Ibrahim Pasha was able to start his offensive march against the rebels in the Nablus and Jerusalem regions. His troops faced fierce resistance from the rebellious peasants. However, the uprising was brutally liquidated in one region after the other. A few leaders of the rebellion, such as Ibrahim and Jabr Abu Ghawsh, changed sides after realizing the military superiority of the Egyptian troops. Within three months, Ibrahim Pasha was able to recapture the Nablus and Jerusalem mountains. Many rebels withdrew to the Hebron region and then to al-Karak in Transjordan.

At least a few hundred soldiers were killed on the Egyptian side and many more injured. However, the people of Palestine paid a higher price in this short but intense and bloody uprising. More than one thousand people were killed or executed. Village strongholds of the rebels were pillaged and destroyed. Not a few of the prominent leaders of the uprising were executed, such as Madis, Qasim al-Ahmad, Jarrars, and Samhans. Other leaders fled the country and found refuge among the Bedouin in Transjordan. Ibrahim Pasha also arrested dozens of the *ulama* and notables and sent them into exile in Egypt and elsewhere. The backbone of the sociopolitical elite in Palestine was broken and the Egyptian administration was free to implement its reforms in Palestine. However, Ibrahim Pasha lost the support of the population, who preferred to see the Ottomans back in the country, after their experience with the centralized Egyptian administration.

In 1839, Sultan Mahmut II was keen on recapturing Syria and Palestine from Muhammad Ali. Unlike in the early 1830s, the European powers were ready to support the sultan's troops. Notwithstanding the Nezib defeat, the fleeing of the Ottoman fleet to Alexandria, and the death of Mahmut II, the Egyptians were eventually pushed out of Bilad al-Sham (Greater Syria).

European support was essential in expelling Muhammad Ali from this region. However, the population in Lebanon, Palestine, and elsewhere played an important role in the fighting against the Egyptians. Ibrahim Pasha recognized the new balance of power and withdrew his troops. Muhammad Ali accepted the London Accord in 1840, and the Ottomans were back in Syria and Palestine less than a decade after they lost their control. These were the only years Palestine was out of Ottoman control between 1516 and World War I.

Palestine During the Tanzimat Period (1839–76)

The Ottoman administration realized the importance of the Holy Land for the Europeans and decided to please them by continuing the policies implemented by the Egyptians during the 1830s. It is possible to differentiate between two periods of the Ottoman reforms, or *Tanzimat*. The earlier period lasted until the end of the Crimean War (1853–56). The second one began with Hatt-i Sherif in 1856 and ended with the Sultan Abdülhamit II's ascendance to the throne in 1876.

During the earlier period of the Tanzimat (1840–56), the Ottoman government made an effort to continue a policy of centralization and reforms. One of the first administrative measures taken by the Ottomans in Palestine was the choice of Beirut to replace Acre as the capital of the Sidon province.

Beirut emerged in the early nineteenth century as a flourishing financial and cultural port city. It superseded Acre, and Jerusalem became the most important administrative center in Palestine from the 1840s on. Gaza and Jaffa were annexed to the *sanjak* of Jerusalem immediately after the restoration of Ottoman rule in Palestine. In 1842, the *sanjak* of Nablus was included. Thus, Jerusalem became the capital of Palestine from Rafah in the south to the Esdraelon valley in the north. The Galilee was the only region left as part of the province of Beirut.

From the mid-nineteenth century, Jerusalem witnessed an increase in missionary activities and flourished as a cultural and religious center. During Egyptian rule, Muhammad Ali opened the city for consular and missionary work. In 1838, Britain established the first European consulate in Jerusalem. Prussia, France, and other countries followed the British precedent in the 1840s. Churches, schools, hospitals, and other public buildings were constructed by missionary societies. The European involvement in the Holy Land during the second half of the nineteenth century was fundamental in transforming the old Jerusalem into a modern and growing city.

The withdrawal of the Egyptian troops from Palestine enabled the shaykhs of *nahiya*s and villages to regain their old positions. Meanwhile, the Ottomans attempted to consolidate a central administration. The conflict of interests between the two sides generated a series of confrontations. Palestine witnessed a transitional period of instability until the late 1850s, when the Ottomans reestablished their control. In Mount Nablus, the strife was particularly intensive and continuous, so much so that one historian even labeled it a civil war. Nevertheless, the repercussions of political instability in Palestine were far less dreadful than in the neighboring regions of Syria and Lebanon, where hundreds of people were killed in communal civil war.

The Ottomans were not able to put an end to the autonomous role of rural shaykhs until the end of the Crimean War (1853–56). Mustafa Suraya, who arrived in Jerusalem in 1857, waged a war against the Lahham, Amru, and Abu Ghawsh shaykhs. Similar attacks were launched against the Abd al-Hadis and other shaykhs of the Nablus *nahiyas*. By 1859 the strongholds of these rural leaders were captured and partially destroyed. The center of power was transferred from the countryside to the city notables and state functionaries. In the Vilayet Law of 1864, the office of *nahiya* shaykh was abolished. Instead, the rural areas came under the control of *mudir*s (subdistrict governors) and *mukhtars*, who replaced the autonomous shaykhs.

Aqila Agha al-Hasi played a distinctive role in the history of Lower Galilee during the first phase of the Tanzimat. Born in Gaza, he followed his father, Musa Agha al-Hasi, in serving Abdullah Pasha as a commander of the Hawwara Bedouin military unit. In 1834 he took part in the rebellion and later found refuge among the Bedouin tribes of Transjordan. After the restoration of Ottoman rule in the region, Aqila moved back to the Esdraelon valley and became responsible for peace and security in Lower Galilee. He sustained his position until the late 1850s, notwithstanding several attempts by the government to get rid of him. However, during the next decade the Ottomans succeeded in expanding direct control of Aqila's region. Thus, the Ottomans set the stage for implementing their policy of centralization and Westernization.

Fundamental Transformation (1858–1878) The second phase of the Tanzimat brought radical change to the people of Palestine. Unlike the earlier reforms of the Ottomans, the later Tanzimat generated structural transformation, which directly affected the destiny of the population. Deserted villages were repopulated, and new ones emerged in the valleys and coastal areas. Haifa and Jaffa flourished as port cities and superseded Safad, Nablus, and Hebron. As a result of its improving security, communication, and standard of living, Palestine witnessed impressive demographic growth; within two decades, the population increased from 350,000 in the early 1850s to 470,000 toward the end of the 1870s.

In addition to the Hatt-i Humayun of 1856, two administrative laws were fundamental in the transformation of Palestine during the second half of the nineteenth century: the Land Law of 1858 and the Vilayet Law of 1864. The 1858 law was central to the process of privatizing the primary source of production, the land. The opportunity to purchase state and public land generated a process of class stratification in Palestine as elsewhere in the Middle East. Old, established notables as well as merchants, bankers, and state functionaries became big landowners, while some peasants became landless serfs. Privatization of land and the new opportunities for trade with Europe widened the class gaps in the Palestinian society.

The Vilayet Law of 1864 was key to establishing new administrative and municipal councils in the big cities. Bureaucratic departments replaced religious and other semiautonomous bodies. Secular state laws superseded the Islamic *shari'a,* and new consular, merchant, and civil courts were established. *Ulama,* the only intellectuals of the premodern Islamic society, lost much of their role to the emerging Westernized elite. The graduates of the new state and missionary schools were better qualified for serving the government and its policy. The most prominent example of this group in Jerusalem is YUSUF AL-KHALIDI (1842–1906), mayor of the city and the only representative from Palestine in the first Ottoman Parliament, 1877–78.

Jerusalem emerged as the capital of Palestine and eventually became an independent subprovince, or *mutasarifiyya,* directly connected to the Ottoman capital, Istanbul, in 1872. The Old City inside the walls gradually lost its supremacy to the new quarters, built by Jews, Palestinians, and Europeans. From the 1850s, Jerusalem witnessed a demographic, political, and cultural transformation in addition to the rise of its distinctive administrative role. The old established families of the Holy City were able to strengthen their sociopolitical and economic bases. Thus the Husaynis, who had suffered a temporary setback during the Tanzimat period, were able to restore their leading role among the local elite in Sultan Abdülhamit II's reign. They emerged as the natural leaders of the Palestinian people in the early twentieth century. The KHALIDI FAMILY, who supported the reform policies, lost ground in the last phase of the Ottoman rule. A new ascending family appeared in Jerusalem, the NASHASHIBI FAMILY, who became the main competitors of the Husaynis, particularly in the aftermath of World War I.

During the second half of the nineteenth century, Palestine was transformed demographically, politically, and socially. The population of the country increased from about 350,000 in the 1850s to more than 600,000 at the turn of the century. However, the ratio of town dwellers to rural residents did not change dramatically and continued to constitute about 20 percent of the population. This stability—the absence of urbanization at that time—is due to the expanding export of agricultural products to Europe, the absence of industrialization in the cities, and the growing sociocultural gap between the peasants and the townspeople in Palestine.

The Ottoman reforms, the integration of the economy into the world capitalist market, and the centralized administration of the country brought progress and prosperity to the people of Palestine. However, the distribution of wealth was not equal and the socioeconomic gap between the city merchants and notables on the one hand and the peasants on the other hand widened dramatically. The old bonds and social institutions that had given some protection to the peasants and the poor during many generations of autonomy in hilly districts of Palestine disintegrated. Thus, the Palestinian society became more dependent politically and economically on the Europeans and Ottomans and more fragmented internally. The notables of the city benefited most from the policy of modernization and coaptation with the Ottoman authorities. The new challenges of colonialism and ZIONISM were dealt with tribally by this elite, who clung to their class and family orientation while facing the new challenges of modernity and nationalism.

The Beginning of the Palestinian-Zionist Conflict

After the dissolution of the first Ottoman Parliament in 1878, Sultan Abdülhamit II seized absolute power and ruled the empire for another three decades without a constitution. Abdülhamit's authoritarian regime faced growing national sentiment in the Balkan and Middle Eastern countries and responded with more repressive measures. In Palestine, as elsewhere in the Ottoman domain, the government encouraged pan-Islamic, conservative ideologies and waged war against nationalism and Westernization. Nonetheless, projects of developing communication, housing, EDUCATION, and the like, continued to be supported by the government. In the international arena, Sultan Abdülhamit allied himself with rising Germany and made an attempt to hinder the growing British and French colonial infiltration in the empire.

In Palestine, British influence increased steadily from the 1830s. However, in the aftermath of the opening of the Suez Canal, this region became much more important for the colonial powers. In 1882, Britain occupied Egypt and intensified its involvement in the Middle East. In Palestine, the first Zionist settlers began their project of colonizing the country in the early 1880s. Eventually both sides realized their common interest as European outsiders. Thus the BALFOUR DECLARATION in 1917 was the culmination of a long political and cultural alliance.

Zionist ideology was born and nurtured in Europe against the background of anti-Semitism and the Western rediscovery of the Holy Land in the nineteenth century. Zionist activists started to immigrate into Palestine in spite of Sultan Abdülhamit's negative attitude toward Zionism and the West. Nevertheless, Jewish settlers were able to purchase land and establish forty new settlements during the last phase of Ottoman rule. Furthermore, in 1908 they began the project of building the first Jewish city in Palestine, Tel Aviv. Abdülhamit's negative response to several offers from Theodor Herzl, leader of the Zionist movement, did not coincide with fundamental steps to block the growing Zionist enterprise. The Ottoman attitude did not change much under the Young Turks (1909–14), who seized power in 1908 and terminated the sultan's absolutist regime by restoring Parliament and the constitution.

During the early phase of the Zionist enterprise, the Palestinians did not perceive Zionism as a serious threat to their community. The new immigrants and settlers faced only sporadic, ineffective resistance of two kinds. One type was local clashes between the colonizers and neighboring Arab Bedouin and fellahin. There were, for example, casual skirmishes between the Jewish settlers of Petah Tikva and Metula on the one side and their Arab neighbors on the other, characterized by conflicts among their different customs concerning cultivation of land, grazing, and the like. However, the local conflicts over customary rights were only the upper layer of an encounter between two cultures and perceptions of land ownership and the meanings of neighbors' relations. Until 1908, the clashes between neighboring Palestinian peasants and Zionist settlers were sporadic and stemmed from local conflicts between neighbors rather than orchestrated national resistance to Zionist settlers.

A different kind of resistance arose from the city notables and middle-class patriots, who expressed their opposition to Zionism in several ways. For example, they sent a petition from Jerusalem in 1891, signed by its mufti and other notables. In this petition the Ottoman government was asked to stop mass immigration and settlement of Jews in Jerusalem and its surroundings. Another clear voice of opposition to the Zionist venture in Palestine was expressed in a private letter sent by Yusuf Diya al-Khalidi to Herzl in March 1899. Al-Khalidi, former mayor of Jerusalem and one of the most prominent Arab intellectuals of his generation, expressed sympathy toward persecuted Jews in Europe while maintaining an ardent opposition to the Zionist plan of establishing a Jewish state in Palestine.

In the wake of the Young Turks' rise to power in 1908 and the restoration of the constitution, more and more Arab opposition to Zionism was expressed publicly. Members of Parliament such as Ruhi al-Khalidi, Sa'id al-Husayni, and Hafiz al-Sa'id demanded restrictive measures against Jewish immigration into Palestine. The journalist Najib Nassar, in HAIFA, attacked the Zionist endeavor and exposed its dangers on the pages of his paper, *al-Karmil.* Other journalists and politicians expressed their fear that the government was not doing enough to stop Zionist colonization of Palestine. Muslim and Christian Arabs were united in their rejection of the Zionist enterprise.

Young national activists from Palestine participated in open and secret political clubs and societies. The Young Turks' relatively free press and publication policy after 1908 made it possible for still more Palestinians to express their opposition to Zionism. During the election campaigns for the Ottoman Parliament, the candidates competed in criticizing Jewish immigration and colonization in Palestine. However, as long as the region was a part of the Ottoman Empire, Arab nationalists relied on the Ottoman government and engaged very little in actual active resistance.

On the eve of World War I, the Arabs in Palestine were still the vast majority of the population, even though the Jews had increased their numbers dramatically during the nineteenth century. In spite of more than three decades of Zionist immigration, in the early twentieth century, Jews represented little more than a tenth of the population. Most of the Palestinians, particularly the fellahin of the hilly regions, were not severely affected by Zionist colonization. National feelings, whether Arabist and national or local and patriotic, were limited to a small number of townspeople. These realities explain the mild resistance to the Zionist enterprise by the people of Palestine until World War I.

The repercussions of the war years (1914–18) were catastrophic for the Palestinians. The country was transformed into a military camp. Young people were conscripted into the Ottoman armies and sent to fight far away from their country. Animals and food products were confiscated by the government. Natural disasters, such as locust hordes and epidemics, added to the suffering of the population. Most of the people in the country supported the Ottomans. However, after the beginning of the Arab revolt of Sharif Husayn in 1916, Jamal Pasha and his comrades increased their repressive measures. The harsh policy of this Turkish commander of the Fourth Army antagonized more Arabs, who transferred their support to the national cause. Many came to remember the World War I years, wrongly, as representative of Ottoman centuries of repression and injustice. This perception continued to nourish much of the national literature that deals with the long Ottoman rule in the Middle East.

Meanwhile, the British army succeeded in rebuffing two Ottoman attacks on the Suez Canal. In the counterattack launched in 1917 British soldiers entered Palestine. They occupied Gaza in early November and marched toward Jerusalem the next month. Political decisions that affected the destiny of the country and its people were being made in London. The British government concluded its negotiations with Zionist leaders and issued the Balfour Declaration on November 2, 1917. The collapse of the Ottoman Empire, which ended four centuries of Ottoman rule in Palestine, and the Balfour Declaration promising a Jewish state in Palestine represented another major turning point in the history of the country.

Adel Manna

BIBLIOGRAPHY

Abu-Manneh, Butrus. "The Hussayni's: The Rise of a Notable Family in 18th Century Palestine." In *Palestine in the Late Ottoman Period,* ed. by David Kushner. Jerusalem: Yad Izhak Ben-Zvi Press, 1986.

——. "Jerusalem in the Tanzimat Period." *Die Welt der Islams,* 30 (1990): 1–44.

Ben-Arieh, Y. *A City Reflected in the Times: Jerusalem in the 19th Century,* 2 vols. Jerusalem: Yad Izhak Ben-Zvi Press, 1977–1979.

Cohen, Amnon. *Palestine in the 18th Century.* Jerusalem: Magnes Press, 1973.

Crecelius, Daniel. "Egypt's Reawakening Interest in Palestine During the Regimes of 'Ali Bey al-Kabir and Muhammad Bey Abu al-Dhahab, 1760–1775." In *Palestine in the Late Ottoman Period,* ed. by D. Kushner. Jerusalem: Yad Izhak Ben-Zvi Press, 1986.

Doumani, Beshara. *Rediscovering Palestine: Merchants and Peasants in Jabal Nablus, 1700–1900.* Berkeley, Calif.: University of California Press, 1995.

Kark, Ruth. *Jaffa: A City in Evolution 1799–1917* (in Hebrew). Jerusalem: Yad Izhak Ben-Zvi Press, 1984.

Kimmerling, Baruch, and J. Migdal. *Palestinians: The Making of a People.* New York: The Free Press, 1993.

Mandel, J. Neville. *The Arabs and Zionism Before World War I.* Berkeley, Calif.: University of California Press, 1976.

Manna, Adel. *A'lam Filastin fi Awakhir al-'Ahd al-'Uthmani (1800–1918)* (The notables of Palestine at the end of the Ottoman period: 1800–1918). Beirut: Institute for Palestine Studies, 1995.

——. "The Rebellion of Naqib al-Ashraf in Jerusalem, 1703–1705." *Cathedra* 53 (Sept. 1989): 49–74.

——. "Continuity and Change in the Socio-Political Elite in Palestine During the Late Ottoman Period." In *The Syrian Land in the 18th and 19th Century,* ed. by Thomas Philipp. Stuttgart: 1992.

Ma'oz, Moshe. *Ottoman Reforms in Syria and Palestine 1840–1861.* Oxford, England: Oxford University Press, 1968.

——, ed. *Studies on Palestine During the Ottoman Period.* Jerusalem: Magnes Press, 1975.

Muslih, Muhammad. *The Origins of Palestinian Nationalism.* New York: Columbia University Press, 1988.

Rosen, Minna. "The Naqib al-Ashraf Rebellion in Jerusalem and Its Repercussions on the City's Dhimmis." *Asian and African Studies* 18, no. 3 (November 1984): 249–270.

Schölch, Alexander. *Palestine in Transformation, 1856–1882: Studies in Social, Economic, and Political Development.* Washington D.C.: Institute for Palestine Studies, 1993.

Shafir, Gershon. *Land, Labor, and the Origins of the Israeli Palestinian Conflict 1882–1914.* Cambridge: Cambridge University Press, 1989.

Shamir, Shimon. "Egyptian Rule (1832–1840) and the Beginning of the Modern Period in the History of Palestine." In *Egypt and Palestine: A Millennium of Association (1868–1948),* ed. by Amnon Cohen and Gabriel Baer. Jerusalem: Magnes Press, 1984.

Tibawi, Abdul-Latif. *British Interests in Palestine 1800–1901.* London: Luzac, 1961.

Lausanne Conference
1949

Organized by the UNITED NATIONS CONCILIATION COMMISSION FOR PALESTINE (or Palestine Conciliation Commission [UNCCP]) at the Hotel Beau Rivage in Lausanne, Switzerland, between April 27 and September 12, 1949, the conference was attended by authorized delegations of Israel, Lebanon, Egypt, Jordan, and Syria; Iraq was invited but declined. Several delegations representing Palestinian REFUGEES—notably one led by Muhammad Nimr al-Hawwari and Aziz Shehadeh—attempted, without success, to be recognized officially and received by the UNCCP.

The format of the conference consisted of a long series of parallel UNCCP-Arab and UNCCP-Israeli meetings, with no official direct Arab-Israeli talks. After the opening sessions, the four delegations of the Arab states appeared before the UNCCP only en bloc. Outside the official sessions, many informal discussions took place between commissioners and members of the various delegations, and a number of formal memoranda and position papers were circulated. Secret unofficial Arab-Israeli contacts also took place outside the formal framework of the conference in various European locations, but these—like the conference itself—produced no political agreements.

An early accomplishment—and one of the only achievements—of the conference was the signing of a document known as the Lausanne Protocol. The first of its two paragraphs stated that, in the interest of achieving the objectives of the December 11, 1948, United Nations General Assembly resolution regarding refugees as well as territorial questions, the UNCCP had submitted a "working document" (the November 1947 partition map adopted by the United Nations General Assembly) "as a basis for discussions." The second paragraph announced the agreement of the delegations to cooperate with the UNCCP "with the understanding that the exchanges of views . . . will bear upon the territorial adjustments necessary to implement the above-indicated objectives." This formulation served the very practical purpose of enabling the stalled Lausanne talks to proceed by responding to Arab insistence on making the refugee question the first priority while acceding to Israeli wishes by unblocking the way to discussions on territorial issues. Israeli representatives immediately took to ignoring and undermining the protocol, characterizing the document as merely a "procedural device" and attributing no political significance to their country's signature. Arab representatives soon began presenting their case based on the Protocol to the UNCCP, the United States, and the world, accusing Israel of bad faith by failing to honor its signature; their signing the protocol, they claimed, had amounted to official acceptance of the 1947 partition boundaries by Israel.

During the course of the conference, Israel made two consecutive proposals: (1) it offered (with U.S. State Department support) to annex the GAZA STRIP, held by the Egyptian army since 1948, and to resettle its refugee population; and (2) it offered to repatriate a maximum of 100,000 Palestinian refugees as part of an overall settlement. Both were unacceptable to the Arab side, which insisted on complete and unconditional implementation of paragraph 11 (return of refugees) of the United Nations General Assembly resolution of December 1948. Though producing no agreement on the main issues of refugee repatriation/resettlement and of recognized boundaries, the conference did finalize some Israeli arrangements for the reunification of refugee families. It also created a mixed technical committee to study the implementation of an accord on the unblocking of frozen bank accounts.

Neil Caplan

Law

At no stage in their history did Palestinians enjoy the unfettered freedom to make their own laws. They have always lived under the authority of others. After the establishment of the PALESTINIAN AUTHORITY by virtue of the Declaration of Principles of September 13, 1993, signed by Israel and the PALESTINE LIBERATION ORGANIZATION, they acquired a partial right to legislate (described later). In the Palestinian territories of the WEST BANK and the GAZA STRIP, where the largest concentration of Palestinians lives, law emanates from five different historical periods: (1) the Ottoman period, 1517–1917; (2) British rule, 1917–1948; (3) the Jordanian (West Bank) or Egyptian (Gaza) period, 1948–67; (4) Israeli occupation, 1967 on; (5) the Palestinian Authority, 1994 on.

The Ottoman Period 1517–1917 The three areas of Ottoman law that remain relevant are in civil matters, LAND, and personal status. The Ottoman Civil Code, or *Mejelle,* first published in 1869, which comprised sixteen books, continues to serve as a partial basis for several areas of law in the Palestinian territories, including contract, property, and sale law.

The main objective of the Land Code of 1858 was to bring the state into direct relations with the cultivators of the land. The main structure of land law in the code remains applicable, even though the laws governing interests in land have been supplemented and modified by much later legislation.

During the Ottoman period, citizens of states granted special privileges in Palestine (capitulations) were under the jurisdiction of their own consular courts in matters of personal status. Muslim courts were competent in matters of personal status regarding local Muslims. Local Christian and Jewish authorities exercised a limited jurisdiction in matters of child custody and marriage. The practice of leaving only residual jurisdiction for the civil courts in matters of personal status still applied in the Palestinian territories by the 1990s.

Except for these three areas, little of the Ottoman legislation remains applicable in the Palestinian territories.

British Rule 1917–1948 The British military occupation of Palestine, which began with the entry of the Egyptian Expeditionary Force into Palestine in 1917, ended in 1920, when the civil administration was established. In 1922 the League of Nations placed Palestine under a British Mandate. The preamble of the terms of the Mandate stated: "[T]he Mandatory should be responsible for putting into effect the declaration originally made on November 2nd, 1917, by the government of His Britannic Majesty, and adopted by the said powers, in favor of the establishment in Palestine of a national home for the Jewish people." Article One of the Mandate vested Britain with "full powers of legislation and of administration, save as they may be limited by the terms of this mandate."

During the Mandatory period, all legislation was issued by the Mandatory government. However, most aspects of civil law continued to be enforced. For example, according to Article 46 of the Palestine Order-in-Council, 1922, "[T]he jurisdiction of the Civil Courts shall be exercised in conformity with the Ottoman Law in force in Palestine on November 1st, 1914." The Mandatory government was active in issuing laws, or ordinances, that came to govern most aspects of the life of Palestine's inhabitants. These include the different versions of the Defense (Emergency) Regulations, the last of which was dated 1945. These regulations gave the British HIGH COMMISSIONER FOR PALESTINE a range of administrative powers to deport Palestinians, place them under administrative detection, demolish their homes, and restrict their political activity. All ordinances, government regulations, and notices were published in an official gazette in the three official languages, Arabic, English, and Hebrew. The revised edition of the laws and ordinances of 1934 was published in three bound volumes. This text constitutes the majority of the law in force in the Gaza Strip and part of the law in force in the West Bank. In Gaza, for example, the laws relating to companies, banking, criminal justice and procedure (including evidence), town planning, local government, and taxation are those promulgated during the British PALESTINE MANDATE.

The Jordanian Period: The West Bank 1948–1967 In November 1947, the United Nations voted to terminate the League of Nations Mandate and to partition Palestine into separate Jewish and Arab states. Much of the area allotted to the Arab state was seized by the Jewish state, which became the independent country of Israel in 1948. Two noncontiguous areas remained under the occupation of Egypt and Jordan. The territory occupied by Jordan became known as the West Bank.

Between 1948 and 1950 the West Bank came first under military, and later under civilian, administration of the Hashemite Kingdom of Jordan. Military Proclamation Number 2 of 1948 provided for the application in the West Bank of laws that were applicable in Palestine on the eve of the termination of the Mandate. On November 2, 1949, military rule was replaced by a civilian authority by virtue of the Law Amending Public Administration Law in Palestine, Number 17, of 1949. Article 2 of the law vested the king of Jordan with all the powers that had been granted to the king of England, his ministers, and the High Commissioner of Palestine by the Palestine Order-in-Council of 1922. Article 5 confirmed that all laws, regulations, and orders that were applicable in Palestine until the termination of the Mandate should remain in force until repealed or amended. After the first general elections in 1950, the Joint Jordanian Parliament, with twenty members from the East Bank and twenty from the West Bank, met with a Jordanian senate and unanimously declared the unification of both banks of the Jordan in one state called the Hashemite Kingdom of Jordan.

On January 8, 1952, a new Jordanian constitution came into force. Article 25 provided that "the legislative power shall be vested in the National Assembly and the King." By 1967 the National Assembly had passed laws applicable to a great variety of matters, including commerce, labor, criminal law and procedure (including evidence), arbitration, companies, taxation, private and public land, banking, public and local administration, social welfare, health, and EDUCATION. Certain laws, such as the 1947 Civil Wrong (torts) Ordinance, remained applicable in the West Bank only and were not subject to any amendment. The Ottoman Land Code as well as the Civil Code (Mejelle) remained in force in both the east and west banks of Jordan. However, many of their provisions were amended or replaced by subsequent Jordanian legislation. All the laws, regulations, and public notices during the Jordanian period were published in an official gazette. Matters of personal status continued to be within the exclusive jurisdiction of religious courts. The regular courts assumed jurisdiction over such matters only in exceptional instances.

The Egyptian Period: The Gaza Strip 1948–1967 The Gaza Strip came under Egyptian control in 1948 but was never annexed to Egypt. Egyptian Ministerial Order Number 274, issued on August 8, 1948, vested an Egyptian administrator general with all the powers of the high commissioner. According to Order Number 6 issued on June 1, 1948, the administrator general declared that all the laws in force during the Mandate should continue to be applicable in Gaza. From November 1956 to March 1957 the area came under Israeli military rule. During this period, the Israeli area commander issued several orders, which were annulled by the Egyptian administrator general on reassuming control.

On November 25, 1955, the Basic Law of Gaza was issued by the prime minister of Egypt. According to Article 23 of this law a Legislative Council was established to pass laws, which then had to be approved by the administrator general of the Gaza Strip. On March 5, 1962, a new constitution for the Gaza Strip, issued by the president of the United Arab Republic, confirmed the Legislative Council. In its brief existence (1955–67) the council made many regulations and passed a few laws relating to labor, the professions, matters of personal status, and the Muslim religious courts, but the majority of the pre-1948 law remained intact.

The Israeli Occupation, 1967 and After The Israeli military assumed authority over the West Bank and the Gaza Strip on June 7, 1967. In Proclamation Number 2, the commander of the West Bank declared that "the laws that were in force in the territory on 7 June 1967 shall remain in force to the extent that it does not contradict this proclamation or any proclamation or order issued by me and the changes arising out of the establishment of the authority of the Israeli Defense Force in the territory." By virtue of Article 3, the area commander assumed all executive, legislative, and judicial powers. A similar proclamation was issued in the Gaza Strip on the same date. The Israeli government refused to consider the Palestinian territories as occupied areas to which the provisions of the Fourth Geneva Convention Relative to the Protection of Civilian Persons in Time of War should be applied.

Between 1967 and 1994, Israel issued 1,407 military orders in the West Bank and 1,100 in the Gaza Strip. Military orders reinstated the British Defense (Emergency) Regulations of 1945 and introduced Israeli law into the Palestinian territories. Orders dealing with insurance, traffic, and the value-added tax were almost identical to Israeli laws on the same subject. Otherwise, pre-1967 laws were retained, although in many instances amended by military orders.

A number of the military orders issued by the area commanders enabled and encouraged Israeli Jews to settle in the Palestinian territories. These orders involved amendments to the land law, local administration, land use planning, and relationship between the settlers and the Palestinian community. In most aspects of their life, Israeli Jewish citizens living in these settlements were subject to Israeli legislation. This was achieved through extraterritorial legislation passed by the Knesset (Israeli parliament) or military orders that adopted the Israeli legislation and declared its exclusive application to the Jewish settlers living in the Palestinian territories.

In November 1981, the area commanders of the West Bank and the Gaza Strip issued orders establishing a civilian administration (Order 947 in the West Bank and 725 in the Gaza Strip) "to administer the civilian affairs (of the Palestinian inhabitants) in the area." Thereafter, civilian affairs have been administered by the head of the civilian administration, an Israeli military officer appointed by the area commander. Matters defined as military, as well as all residual powers, remained under the direct administration of the area commander.

In June 1967, Israel annexed East Jerusalem and applied Israeli law to its inhabitants. They thus fell under the same legal status as the Palestinians living in Israel since 1948. Israel defines itself as "a Jewish state in Eretz Israel." Although formal commitment to equality between Jew and non-Jew can be found in the Declaration of the Establishment of Israel, the laws in force in Israel discriminate in overt and covert ways against non-Jewish citizens in several areas, including access to and use of natural resources, the right to be reunited with family members living outside the country, and various aspects of political, social, and economic life.

The Palestinian Authority Areas, 1994 and After The Declaration of Principle signed by Israel and the Palestine Liberation Organization on September 13, 1993, set the terms for interim arrangements. In Article One, the two parties agreed that "the aim of the Israeli-Palestinian negotiations within the current Middle East peace process is, among other things, to establish a Palestinian Interim Self-Government Authority, the elected Council (the 'Council') for the Palestinian people in the West Bank and the Gaza Strip, for a transitional period not exceeding five years, leading to a permanent settlement based on [United Nations] Security Council Resolutions 242 and 338." From the Declaration of Principles and subsequent agreements negotiated on the basis of it, it was clear that the jurisdiction of the Palestinian Authority will not include the Jewish settlements in the Gaza Strip and the West Bank. The legislative power of the new Palestinian council is circumscribed by the necessity of obtaining Israeli approval for all new laws adding to or amending existing legislation, including the military orders and other mandatory and Jordanian laws, which remain in force.

On May 15 and 17, 1994, the area commanders of the West Bank and the Gaza Strip issued proclamations, both designated as Number 4, confirming the withdrawal of the Israeli army from the Gaza Strip and the Jericho area and the transfer of the Palestinian Authority according to the Agreement on the Gaza Strip and the Jericho Area signed on May 4, 1994, of those civilian and military powers previously held by the Israeli military and civilian administrations. In the Gaza Strip, the civilian administration was abolished. However, the Israeli military government continued to hold ultimate responsibility over Israeli settlers and over all other matters, including external security and foreign affairs, not transferred to the Palestinian Authority.

A Dual System of Law For the duration of the Interim Period, a dual system of law will continue to be administered. The Palestinian Authority will administer the Palestinian inhabitants according to the agreements signed with Israel, and the Israeli settlers will continue to live under Israeli laws. The power of the Palestinian Authority to amend the law is specified in Article 7.9 of the May 4, 1994, agreement: "[L]aws and military orders in effect in the Gaza Strip or the Jericho area prior to the signing of this Agreement shall remain in force, unless amended or abrogated in accordance with this Agreement." The exclusion of the settlers from the jurisdiction of the Palestinian Authority is confirmed by the Declaration of Principles and the Agreed Minutes signed on September 13, 1993, as well as by all subsequent agreements signed by the two sides. It is also confirmed unilaterally by Israel in Proclamations Number 4 promulgated by the area commanders of the West Bank and the Gaza Strip.

The PALESTINIAN LEGISLATIVE COUNCIL was empowered by the Declaration of Principles "to legislate, in accordance with the Interim Agreement, within all authorities transferred to it." The Agreed Minutes to Article 4 stipulate that its jurisdiction shall not extend to Jerusalem, the settlements, Israeli military locations, and Israeli citizens. The Palestinian Authority in the Gaza Strip administers the laws that were in force when it assumed power on May 4, 1994. Most of the laws follow the English common law tradition. When the power of the Palestinian Authority is extended to the rest of the West Bank, the laws administered there, many of which follow the French civil law tradition, will be mainly Jordanian. According to Article 4 of the Declaration of Principles, however, the West Bank and the Gaza Strip constitute "a single territorial unit, whose integrity will be preserved during the interim period."

The elected Palestinian Legislative Council held its first session in Gaza City on March 7, 1996. Three years later it had still not passed a basic law and had done very little to unify the laws of the Gaza Strip and the West Bank. The laws it did pass included the following: Publications Law (1995), Law for the Establishment of Palestinian Energy Authority (1995), Law for the Establishment of the Palestinian Water Authority (1996), Law Regarding Communications and Telecommunications (1996), Palestinian Monetary Law (1997), Local Councils Law (1997), Encouragement of Investment Law (1998), and Industrial Estates and Free Zones Law (1998).

The Declaration of Principles provides for the final status negotiations, which "will commence as soon as possible, but not later than the beginning of the third year of the interim period" and "will lead to the implementation of Security Council Resolutions 242 and 338." If as a result of these negotiations Palestinians achieve statehood, they will finally have the right to live under law of their own making.

Raja Shehadeh

BIBLIOGRAPHY

Benvenisti, Meron. *The West Bank Data Project: A Survey of Israel's Policies.* Washington, D.C.: American Enterprise Institute for Public Policy Research, 1984.

Cattan, Henry. *Palestine and International Law,* 2d ed. London: 1976.

Coon, Anthony. *Town Planning Under Military Occupation: An Examination of the Law and Practice of Town Planning in the Occupied West Bank.* Dartmouth, N.H.: Dartmouth Press, 1992.

Developing the Occupied Territories: An Investment in Peace. Vol. 3. Washington, D.C.: The World Bank, 1993.

Hooper, C. A. *The Civil Law of Palestine and Trans-Jordan.* Vol. 1. London: Sweet & Maxwell Limited, 1934.

Index of Israeli Military Orders, 1967–1992 with Brief Summary of Each. Jerusalem: Jerusalem Media and Communication Center, 1993.

Kretzmer, David. *The Legal Status of the Arabs in Israel.* Boulder, Colo.: Westview Press, 1990.

Lustick, Ian. "Israel and the West Bank after Elon Moreh." *Middle East Journal* 35 (Autumn 1981): 557–577.

Mallison, Thomas W., and Sally V. Mallison. *The Palestine Problem in International Law and World Order.* London: Longman Group, 1986.

Playfair, Emma. *International Law and the Administration of Occupied Territories.* New York: Oxford University Press, 1992.

Quigley, John. *Palestine and Israel: A Challenge to Justice.* Durham, N.C.: Duke University Press, 1990.

Shehadeh, Raja. *From Occupation to Interim Accords: Israel and the Palestinian Territories.* The Hague: Kluwer Law International, 1997.

——. *Occupier's Law: Israel and the West Bank.* Rev. ed. Washington, D.C.: Institute of Palestine Studies, 1988.

League of Arab States

See ARAB LEAGUE.

Lebanon

The story of the Palestinian diaspora in the Arab world is an account of displacement and exile compounded by the exclusionary and discriminatory policies of the host Arab countries. Nowhere is this truer than in the case of the Palestinian refugees in Lebanon, who have faced institutionalized discrimination in education, employment, housing, and association. This entry traces the Palestinian experience in Lebanon from 1948, when the first wave of Palestinian refugees arrived in the south, and covers both the subject of Palestinians in Lebanon—their numbers, their social and political status, the role of the PALESTINE LIBERATION ORGANIZATION (PLO), and its infrastructure—as well as Lebanon's policy toward Palestinians and the Palestinian issue.

The Palestinian experience in Lebanon can be divided into four phases. The period 1948–67 covers the first wave of Palestinian refugees after the ARAB-ISRAELI WAR OF 1948, ending with the ARAB-ISRAELI WAR OF 1967. The focus of the second phase, 1967–70, is on the second wave of refugees after the June war which ended with the bloody events of BLACK SEPTEMBER, Jordan's crackdown against the Palestinian resistance movement in 1970. The third period, 1970–82, begins with the third wave of refugees from Jordan after Black September and ends with the 1982 Israeli invasion of Lebanon. The final phase, 1982 to the present, includes the expulsion of the PLO from Lebanon after the Israeli invasion, the end of the Lebanese civil war, and the consequent implications for the Palestinian refugees.

A considerable difficulty exists in compiling an accurate account of the numbers of Palestinians in Lebanon because of their residence in both the camps and urban areas, their lack of official status (since they are not technically classified as "refugees"), and the differing criteria for estimating a population that is growing through births and new waves of migration from outside Lebanon. Estimates of the number of Palestinians are also influenced by politics. Whereas the PLO inflates the number of Palestinians residing in Lebanon, the Lebanese government underestimates the figures. The PLO estimates the number of refugees to be 600,000; a more reliable figure is that of the United Nations Relief and Works Agency for Palestine Refugees in the Near East (UNRWA), which estimated a total of 342,000 in 1995.

The First Phase, 1948–1967 The Palestinian presence in Lebanon began with the first 1948 Arab–Israeli war, in which hundreds of thousands of Palestinian citizens either were expelled or fled into the various surrounding Arab countries. Of those, some 100,000 Palestinian refugees fled into Lebanon, where they awaited the end of hostilities to return to their historic homes in Galilee and the coastal cities. The fact that the first wave of Palestinian refugees clustered mainly in southern Lebanon indicated that neither the refugees nor their hosts had expected their stay to last long, let alone be permanent. Partly as a result, international relief organizations took some time to cope with the new situation and set up emergency services. Hence, it was not until the 1950s that the United Nations Relief and Works Agency was established to care for the Palestinian refugees.

By contrast, the initial response of both the Lebanese government and the society was prompt and sympathetic. Palestinians were offered shelter, aid, accommodation, and other forms of assistance. President Bishara al-Khuri and Premier Rashid al-Sulh visited the refugee encampments in the south, assuring them, "Our house is your house," according to Rosemary Sayigh, who has written extensively about the predicament of the Palestinian refugees in Lebanon. This warm support, she argues, was the product of a mood of Arab fraternalism generated by the spirit of anticolonialism. Furthermore, the historian WALID KHALIDI suggests that Khuri's decision to admit large numbers of refugees was designed to appeal to Muslim opinion within Lebanon. Thus, from the onset, the Palestinian presence was deeply entangled in domestic Lebanese politics, thereby overburdening a delicate sectarian balance.

Class differences played an important role in the reception of the various Palestinian strata. Whereas upper- and middle-class Palestinians were welcomed with open arms, the rural and urban masses were treated as "vagrants" and "strangers." As the political scientist Cheryl Rubenberg put it: "During the first twenty years of their stay in Lebanon, the (lower-class) Palestinians lived a wretched existence, subsisting solely on the services provided by UNRWA, and experiencing repression from both the Lebanese army and Lebanese secret police." The main cause of difference, notes Sayigh, lay in the socioeconomic ties formed between Lebanese and Palestinians of urban middle- and upper-class backgrounds before 1948; such ties served as a form of social capital that helped the well-off refugees adapt to their new life in Lebanon.

Although initially the Lebanese government and public responded to the Palestinian refugees with short-term relief, they did not envision the need for long-term support. Far from having a strategic blueprint of how to deal with the Palestinian refugees, the Lebanese government acted purely on an ad hoc basis. In fact, after the initial euphoria, the Lebanese state—relying on an indifferent public sentiment—began the slow process of establishing a system of control, directed mainly at the camps' population.

Consequently, in the mid-1960s a new political consciousness emerged among Palestinian refugees. Initially, resistance to Israeli occupation was not the main target of the refugees' political activities because they assumed that they would return home soon. Once the refugees realized that they would not be allowed back, however, many joined the Palestinian Resistance Movement (PRM). The Movement for the National Liberation of Palestine (FATAH) and the PLO were formed by the mid-1960s. Palestinian political activists were bound to clash with Lebanese authorities, who opposed all attempts at organization, either political or social. Little wonder that the second part of the 1960s witnessed an escalation of the confrontation between the Palestinians and their Lebanese hosts.

The Second Phase, 1967–1970 The politicization of the camp population intensified after the 1967 Arab–Israeli war and subsequent pressure by Israel. Although the 1967 war did not result in a large flight of Palestinians into Lebanon (a few thousand refugees), it was a decisive factor in motivating Palestinians to take charge of their destiny by building up armed cadres and cells. The PRM became the major organizing political and military force dedicated to the liberation of Palestine, meaning the return of the Palestinians to their occupied homes in Israel. Between 1967 and 1969, the resistance movement made major political inroads in the refugee camps, establishing a military presence in south Lebanon. This new development triggered bloody clashes between the resistance movement and the Lebanese army, leading to PRM's takeover and control of the refugee camps by September 1969.

In the late 1960s, Arab support for the Palestinian resistance movement was at a high point. The Palestinians, using their political and military assets inside and outside Lebanon, forced the Lebanese government to redefine its relations with the refugees and the various resistance organizations. The result was the 1969 Cairo Agreement, which began a new phase in Palestinian–Lebanese relations. The agreement's most important clauses included four political concessions to Palestinians: (1) their right to work, residence, and movement within Lebanon; (2) the establishment of Palestinian committees to manage the refugee camps; (3) the creation of an armed Palestinian military police to patrol the camps; and (4) the recognition of the right of Palestinians not only to have a military presence in Lebanon but also to join the struggle for the liberation of Palestine.

The Cairo Agreement had serious implications for Palestinian–Lebanese relations and for intra-Lebanese politics as well. After 1969, the resistance movement was empowered to challenge the Lebanese state by building up parallel Palestinian institutions. Palestinian autonomy further expanded after the 1971 expulsion of the PLO from Jordan. A sharp polarization of the Lebanese into pro- and anti-Palestinian segments took place. A coalition of nationalists, Christians, and conservatives resented the Palestinians' perceived encroachment on Lebanese sovereignty, blaming some of their compatriots—leftists and Islamic and Arab nationalists—for what they saw as sacrifice on the altar of the Palestinian–Israeli conflict. Thus Palestinian activism exacerbated not only Lebanese–Palestinian tensions but also stresses within Lebanon itself. Given the weakness of the Lebanese state, the die was cast for a bloody confrontation in which the Palestinians would be deeply involved.

The Third Phase, 1970–1982 Before 1971, the PLO had operated mainly out of Jordan, using Lebanon only as a supporting front. But the 1970–71 defeat and expulsion of the Palestinian resistance movement from Jordan made Lebanon the movement's major theater of military operations against Israel. After 1971, the armed presence of the Palestinians in Lebanon increased significantly. Lebanese society became further polarized: one segment supported the Palestinian military resistance; the other was adamantly opposed to Palestinian presence in Lebanon, objecting especially to the armed struggle against Israel. The PLO's misconduct in south Lebanon, coupled with its violation of Lebanese sovereignty and human rights, played an important role in the breakdown of the Lebanese state in the mid-1970s.

The apparent militarization of Palestinian interaction with their Lebanese hosts was intensified during the 1975 Lebanese war, in which Palestinians fought alongside Lebanon's leftist/Islamist alliance against the country's Christian/right-wing elements. Although many Lebanese like to blame the Palestinians for the 1975–90 civil war, it is more accurate to note, as does Hani Faris, that "conflicts arising out of the armed presence of the Palestinians were being superimposed on socioeconomic and political conflicts between Lebanon's religious sects."

Not surprisingly, the civil war alliance between the Palestinians and Lebanese Islamists/leftists helped ease the social and political tensions between the refugees and some of their Muslim hosts. Urban Palestinians mixed freely with their Lebanese counterparts on a variety of levels—traditional neighborly behavior and other significant interactions such as intermarriage. According to Sayigh, although different types of parochialism existed within both the PLO and the Islamic/leftist alliance, "The slogan of *sha'b wahid* (one people) was given reality at the mass level, especially in the areas of greatest residential mixing, the popular quarters of Beirut and Sidon."

A sense of community also developed within the refugee camps, where the tightly knit social relations of the Palestinian hometown were re-created, serving as a basis for group solidarity and identity. The Lebanese state and bureaucracy continued to discriminate, however, against both urban and camp Palestinians by limiting their socioeconomic mobility and education, and by preventing them from improving conditions in the squalid refugee camps. Little wonder that the general level of education of Palestinians significantly decreased, so that in 1979, 25 percent of the camp work force was illiterate, 35.9 percent semiliterate, only 23.8 percent had finished primary school, and only 0.4 percent had a vocational training diploma.

As a result Palestinians continued to depend on external forces for livelihood and a functional economy. The economic problems of the refugees worsened when several thousand Palestinians fled from Jordan after bloody BLACK SEPTEMBER in 1970, which added a big burden on the strained Palestinian economy and left fewer jobs to the growing number of refugees. The bureaucratic economy developed by the PLO within the refugee camps supplemented the desperate economic situation by employing more than 50 percent of the camps' population.

Ultimately, however, the Lebanese civil war had a devastating impact on Palestinian politics. The war distracted the Palestinians from their focal struggle against Israel as well as allowing Israel and its ultranationalist Lebanese allies to portray the Palestinians as a larger-than-life threat. This, coupled with Israel's concern over the growing political and military strength of the PLO, prepared the ground for the 1982 Israeli invasion of Lebanon.

The Fourth Phase, 1982–Present Israel's 1982 invasion of Lebanon brought further misery to Palestinian refugees, who endured heavy, indiscriminate bombardment; a siege; and massacres, two of which—the SABRA AND SHATILA MASSACRE—shocked the conscience of the world. Thousands of Palestinian civilians were killed and injured, and most of Palestinian infrastructure—hospitals, small factories, and schools—was destroyed. Losing their traditional protector and employer, the PLO, which was forced to move its headquarters from Lebanon to Tunisia, Palestinian refugees were left at the mercy of the Lebanese state and militia, particularly the Shi'ite Amal militia. During the "war of camps," which raged between 1985 and 1987, Amal vented its hostility against PLO loyalists and Palestinian civilians alike, killing many refugees and destroying many dwellings in the process.

Discrimination against Palestinians continues, as the Lebanese bureaucracy has been both unable and unwilling to cope effectively with the refugees. Palestinians are still considered ordinary refugees, thus ignoring their legitimate long-term residence rights and needs. They lack legal protection, social security, and medical treatment in government hospitals; bureaucratic obstacles also restrict their freedom of travel and occupation. The refugees' predicament is compounded by the general contempt, even hostility, that most Lebanese feel toward them. As Jihad Zeine of the Lebanese daily, *al-Safir,* cited by Sayigh, indicated, the Lebanese reaction to the Palestinians ranges between two poles: "indifference at one end and negativism at the other, with negativism varying between active hostility and passive dislike." For example, the tourism minister, Nicolas Fattush, responded to reports that some Palestinians from Libya would be coming to Lebanon by retorting that his country would not be a "dump" for "human garbage."

Since the end of the Lebanese civil war in 1990, the government has actively encouraged Palestinians to emigrate to other countries, or at least to leave Lebanon. The pressures on Palestinians to emigrate include constraints on space and shelter, denial of civic rights, reduction of the numbers of Palestinians with residence permits, and restrictions on travel. For example, in 1995, Lebanon decided that all Palestinians carrying Lebanese travel documents would henceforth be required to obtain visas to enter the country. The implication of this new ruling is that these laissez-passer holders no longer have the legal right to reside in Lebanon.

The visa ruling fits a pattern of Lebanese policies concerning the Palestinians, as stipulated by the 1989 Ta'if agreement ending the Lebanese war: reestablishment of the government's control over the refugee camps and refusal of *tawtin,* the permanent settlement of Palestinians in Lebanon. In an interview with *al-Safir* in 1994, the Lebanese foreign minister, Faris Buwayz, made it clear that his country's eventual aim was to be rid of all Palestinians currently residing there. Therefore, the government has refused to rebuild destroyed homes or provide more shelter for Palestinians, who suffer a severe housing crisis due to the destruction wrought by years of conflict and civil war. The result is a critical deterioration in the condition of Palestinians in Lebanon.

✦ ✦ ✦

At the onset of the Palestinian exodus in 1948, the refugees were viewed sympathetically by both state and society in Lebanon. However, as Lebanese politics polarized along sectarian and class lines, Palestinian refugees were blamed for the instability and decay of political life in Lebanon. The situation was further compounded by the 1975 Lebanese civil war, in which the Palestinians became entangled. The treatment of the refugees worsened after the end of hostilities in Lebanon in 1990.

The refugees' conditions deteriorated in the late 1990s, given the general anti-Palestinian mood in Lebanon and the neglect of their plight by the ongoing PLO-Israeli peace talks. Indeed, Palestinians in Lebanon feel that the peace process is passing them by. They increasingly voice their anger and their frustration at both the outside world and their traditional leaders. A Palestinian refugee, quoted by the scholar Muhammad Ali Khalidi, expresses it this way: "Our own leaders have sacrificed our right of return for autonomy. We feel forgotten and abandoned."

Fawaz A. Gerges

BIBLIOGRAPHY

Barakat, Halim. *Lebanon in Strife: Student Preludes to the Civil War.* Austin, Tex.: University of Texas Press, 1977.

Cooley, John. "The Palestinians." In *Lebanon in Crisis: Participants and Issues,* ed. by P. Edward Haley and Lewis Snider. Syracuse, N.Y.: Syracuse University Press, 1979.

Faris, Hani. "Lebanon and the Palestinians: Brotherhood or Fratricide?" *Arab Studies Quarterly* 3, no. 4 (1981).

Khalidi, Muhammad Ali. "Palestinian Refugee in Lebanon." *The Washington Report on Middle East Affairs* (November/December 1995).

Khalidi, Rashid. *Under Siege: P.L.O. Decision Making During the 1982 War.* New York: Columbia University Press, 1986.

——. "The Palestinians in Lebanon." In *Toward a Viable Lebanon,* ed. by Halim Barakat. London and Sydney: Croom Helm and Center for Contemporary Arab Studies, Georgetown University, 1988.

——."The Palestinians in Lebanon: Social Repercussions of Israel's Invasion." *The Middle East Journal* 38, no. 2 (spring 1984).

Khalidi, Walid. *Conflict and Violence in Lebanon: Confrontation in the Middle East.* Cambridge: Center for International Affairs, Harvard University, 1979.

Palestinian Red Crescent Society (PRCS). *Medical Services, Past, Present and Future in Lebanon.* Beirut: PRCS, 1992.

Rubenberg, Cheryl. "Palestinians in Lebanon: A Question of Human and Civil Rights." *Arab Studies Quarterly* 6, no. 3 (1984).

Salam, Nawaf. "Between Repatriation and Resettlement: Palestinian Refugees in Lebanon." *Journal of Palestinian Studies* 24, no. 1 (Autumn 1994).

Salibi, Kamal. *Crossroads to Civil War: Lebanon 1958–1976.* Caravan: New York, 1976.

Sayigh, Rosemary. *Palestinians: From Peasants to Revolutionaries.* London: Zed Books, 1979.

——. *Too Many Enemies: The Palestinian Experience in Lebanon.* London and New Jersey: Zed Books, 1994.

——. "Palestinians in Lebanon: Status Ambiguity, Insecurity and Flux." *Race and Class* 30, no. 1 (July–September 1988).

——."Palestinians in Lebanon: Harsh Present, Uncertain Future." *Journal of Palestine Studies* 25, no. 1 (Autumn 1995).

Sosebee, Stephen J. "Progress toward Statehood Tightens Noose Around Palestinians in Lebanon." *The Washington Report on Middle East Affairs* (February/March 1996).

United Nations. "Report of the High Commissioner General of UNRWA." A/48/13 (1992).

Legislative Council

The League of Nations granted Britain, which had occupied Palestine in December 1917, a mandate to rule the country and foster the "development of self-governing institutions." Accordingly, HIGH COMMISSIONER FOR PALESTINE Sir Herbert Samuel proposed creation of a legislative council in August 1922. The council would include twenty-three members: eleven British officials (including the high commissioner) and twelve elected members, of whom ten would be Palestinians (eight Muslims and two Christians) and two Jews.

The scope of the council's powers was to be limited. It would have no authority over the important question of Jewish immigration and LAND purchases, since Britain had pledged to support such Zionist activities through the BALFOUR DECLARATION. However, Samuel addressed Palestinian concerns over such matters by proposing that the elected members form a committee to advise the Palestine government on immigration.

Palestinian leaders rejected Samuel's proposal because they considered it an acceptance of the PALESTINE MANDATE and the Balfour Declaration. They also objected to the council's limited powers and to the formula granting Palestinians only 43 percent of the council's seats, whereas they constituted 88 percent of the population. The objections voiced by the Palestine ARAB EXECUTIVE and the SUPREME MUSLIM COUNCIL led to a Palestinian boycott of the February 1923 council elections. The Jews accepted the proposal, although they objected to receiving only two seats. Samuel held the proposal in abeyance after low voter turnout in the elections.

The idea of a legislative council resurfaced under High Commissioner Sir John Chancellor. The WESTERN (WAILING) WALL DISTURBANCES of 1929 led to suspension of the proposal once again, although it was revived as one of the proposals contained in the 1930 Passfield White Paper. This time Palestinian leaders accepted it even though it was an identical proposal to that of 1922. Jewish leaders rejected their relegation to minority status in the council, however, and sought a parity formula by which the numbers and economic impact of world Jewry would be considered.

Discussions lasted until 1935, when the proposed composition had changed to include fourteen Palestinians (five nominated), eight Jews (five nominated), five officials of the Palestine government, and one nominee representing commercial interests. Palestinians were divided over the proposals, and the Jews opposed it strongly. In the end, the British suspended the idea and it was never revived.

Philip Mattar

BIBLIOGRAPHY

Great Britain and Palestine, 1915–1945. Information Papers No. 20. London: Royal Institute of International Affairs, 1946.

Lesch, Ann Mosely. *Arab Politics in Palestine, 1917–1939: The Frustrations of a Nationalist Movement.* Ithaca, N.Y.: Cornell University Press, 1979.

Porath, Y. *The Emergence of the Palestinian-Arab Nationalist Movement, 1918–1929.* London: Frank Cass, 1974.

Liberal Party

The Liberal Party was established in late 1927 in JAFFA and Gaza to operate outside the bitter rivalry between the HUSAYNI FAMILY and NASHASHIBI FAMILY of Jerusalem that had rent the nationalist movement in the early and mid-1920s. Among its founders was the editor of the newspaper *Filastin,* ISA AL-ISA. As such, the party represented a wider feeling of frustration among Palestinian businessmen and professionals residing outside Jerusalem who were not aligned with either faction and who believed the Palestinians' ability to push for Palestinian independence was being compromised by disunity. The party also advocated a program of social reforms.

The party's main contribution to the nationalist movement was its impact on the seventh of the ARAB CONGRESSES, convened in June 1928. The congress created an expanded ARAB EXECUTIVE as one step toward unifying nationalist ranks and reducing the crippling effects of the Husayni-Nashashibi rivalry.

Michael R. Fischbach

Literary Society

With roots in an Arab association in Istanbul founded in 1909, the Literary Society (al-Muntada al-Adabi) in Palestine was established in November 1918 as an anti-Zionist association. Of the several chapters throughout the country, the Jerusalem branch, led by the NASHASHIBI FAMILY, was the most significant.

Michael R. Fischbach

Literature

A distinct Palestinian literature did not develop until the twentieth century. However, its origins can be traced to the nineteenth century, although that period in Palestine was a continuation of the long era of literary and intellectual stagnation also experienced by the other Arab provinces of the Ottoman Empire. Early in the nineteenth century, Egypt and Lebanon became the first Arab provinces to establish cultural relations with Western countries: Egypt as a result of Muhammad Ali Pasha's modernizing reforms after Napoleon's Egyptian campaign; Lebanon because of its large Christian minorities' affinities with Europe. Literary activities in Palestine leading to a similar cultural renaissance did not begin until the 1880s.

Conditions in Late Nineteenth Century Turn-of-the-century Palestinian literature was mostly expressed in verse with hackneyed styles and sometimes in rhymed prose with heavy verbal embellishments. Limited to the few steeped in classical Muslim learning, its main concerns were religious. The few exceptions were panegyrics praising some Ottoman functionaries and funeral elegies. For example, the verse of Yusuf Isma'il al-Nabhani (1849–1932), a prolific prose writer on Islamic topics, was devoted almost totally to praising the Prophet Muhammad, defending Islam and the Ottomans, and eulogizing Ottoman officials. Likewise, Salim al-Ya'qubi (1880–1946), known as Abu al-Iqbal, wrote poems praising the Ottoman sultan, provincial governors, and other notables. However, Abu al-Iqbal was more politically oriented than al-Nabhani, and his poems advocated the unification of the Muslim world, criticized Sharif Husayn's Arab revolt against the Ottomans, and attacked the Zionist project of a national home for the Jews in Palestine.

By the end of the nineteenth century, several factors had helped to change the cultural conditions of Palestine. Perhaps the most important was the growth of schools. Traditional Muslim and Christian education based on memorizing religious scriptures had gradually been replaced by the establishment of modern institutions of learning, most at the elementary level but a few at the secondary level. Most of these schools were run by the Ottoman education authorities, a few operated by private Muslim associations, and others sponsored by the local churches of Palestine: Greek Orthodox, Greek Catholic, and the Roman Catholic Franciscan monks. In the twentieth century, more and more schools were established by British, German, and American Protestant missionaries; by French and Italian Roman Catholic orders; and by Russian Orthodox emissaries. The learning of languages other than Arabic and Turkish opened new horizons to both the Christian and Muslim graduates of these schools. Instead of being limited to Beirut, Cairo, and Istanbul for higher studies, some graduates went to Europe and, on their return to Palestine, contributed to the cultural development of the country. The introduction of printing presses into Palestine furthered this cultural development by multiplying the number of books and by increasing their availability in schools, replacing the limited and slow dissemination of knowledge by oral instruction, memorization, and copying of manuscripts and eventually encouraging a rise in the level of literacy.

The social and economic conditions of Palestine were also gradually improving by the end of the nineteenth century, and the country began to experience a sense of national identity as its intellectuals, now with wider horizons and with relations outside Palestine, established contacts with cultural movements in other Arab provinces of the Ottoman Empire, with particular interest in those seeking autonomy or even independence. At the same time, concern over Zionist designs on Palestine increased after the First Zionist Congress in Basel, Switzerland, in 1897. As Palestinians began to learn more about ZIONISM, Palestinian literature grew to reflect this concern, which became the dominant Palestinian literary theme in the twentieth century, particularly after the BALFOUR DECLARATION of 1917 and the approval of the British PALESTINE MANDATE by the League of Nations in 1922—without Palestinian consent. Palestinians felt that their very existence in their own land was being threatened.

Palestine Mandate The foremost Palestinian poet in the first half of the twentieth century was Ibrahim Tuqan (1905–41), of the TUQAN FAMILY of Nablus, whose innovative poetry during the British Mandate was put to the service of the national cause, when not dealing with the love themes with which he was equally adept. His patriotic poems alerted Palestinians to the dangers of Zionism, celebrated Palestinian heroes resisting British and Zionist policies, sarcastically criticized inept Palestinian leaders, and mercilessly lambasted the Palestinian traitors and brokers who had facilitated Zionist land purchases. Tuqan's poems were published posthumously in the book *Diwan Ibrahim* (Ibrahim's collected poems, 1955). His friend Abd al-Rahim Mahmud (1913–48) proclaimed Tuqan's nationalist message in similar fiery and committed poems until he was killed fighting Zionists in the battle of al-Shajara during the war that led to the establishment of Israel in 1948. Mahmud's *Diwan* (Collected poems) was published in 1958.

Other key poets of the British Mandatory period included Abd al-Karim al-Karmi (1907–80), known as Abu Salma, who treated national topics in his poetry to great effect. Abu Salma lived to witness the loss of Palestine and as an exile wrote powerful poems lamenting the injustice of this loss, remembering the ancestral homeland with anguished love, and affirming the will of Palestinians to regain it in the name of their everlasting attachment to it. His collection, *Min Filistin Rishati* (From Palestine is my pen, 1971), like his *Diwan* (Collected poems, 1978), abounds with these feelings, which are given further expression in his posthumous collection, *Lahab al-Qasid* (Flames of poetry, 1984).

Prose writing grew with the increase in Palestinian printed MEDIA in the twentieth century. In 1908, the Ottoman constitution had been promulgated, permitting civil liberties theretofore stringently restricted. After this political development, newspapers were established in Palestine. Among the most influential were Najib Nassar's *al-Karmil* (Carmel), established in HAIFA in 1908; the *Filistin* (Palestine) of ISA AL-ISA, established in Jaffa in 1911; and Jamil al-Khalidi's *al-Dustur* (The constitution), established in Jerusalem in 1912. During the British Mandate, more newspapers were founded in Jaffa: Shaykh Abdullah al-Qalqili's *al-Sirat al-Mustaqim* (The straight path, 1925), Ibrahim al-Shanti's *al-Difa* (The defense, 1934), Shaykh Sulayman al-Taji al-Faruqi's *al-Jami'a al-Islamiyya* (The Islamic league, 1936), as well as several other newspapers founded in Palestinian towns.

With the advent of journalism, literary prose gradually gained flexibility, discarding its burdensome verbal embellishment as writers treated urgent social, political, and cultural issues. Palestinian writers often contributed to the periodicals of neighboring Arab countries that kept them abreast of literary developments in the Arab world. The essay gained ground as a new literary genre. Among the foremost Palestinian essayists were two scholars enamored of the Arabic language, KHALIL AL-SAKAKINI (1878–1953) and Muhammad Is'af al-NASHASHIBI (1882–1948). Both their poetry and their prose were a breath of fresh air for Palestinian literature. Al-Sakakini emphasized intellectual originality and authentic personal feeling; al-Nashashibi recreated a classical style while treating modern ideas. Al-Sakakini authored more than a dozen books, including his collection of essays, *Mutala'at fi al-Lugha wa al-Adab* (Readings in language and literature, 1925), and the two-volume work *Ma Tayassar* (What's available, 1943–46). His most endearing writings, however, are his letters to his son, Sari, when the latter was in college, and collected in *Sari* (1935); his book on the death of his wife, *Li-Dhikraki* (In memory of you, 1940); and his memoirs *Kadha Ana Ya Dunya* (Such am I, O world, 1955), published posthumously by his two daughters, Hala and Dunya. Equally prolific and influential but more difficult to emulate, al-Nashashibi wrote such books as *Qalb Arabi wa Aql Urubbi* (An Arab heart and a European mind, 1924) and *al-Islam al-Sahih* (True Islam, 1936); called for modernization; and used a literary style that approached that of the best Arabic classics.

Taking their lead from such masters, younger Palestinian essayists filled the pages of the burgeoning journals with articles written in a sprightly modern style that dealt with pressing matters of daily life. Among these essayists were Bulus Shihada (of the SHEHADEH FAMILY), Arif al-Azzuni, Abdullah Mukhlis, Khalil al-Budayri, IZZAT DARWAZA, Mustafa Darwish al-Dabbagh, Asma Tubi, Najati Sidqi, and Mahmud Sayf al-Din al-Irani. Some of these writers also began to express themselves in the developing genres of short stories and novels. The ground for this development was prepared by the well-known essayist Khalil Baydas (1875–1949), whose translations from Russian fiction in the late nineteenth and early twentieth centuries helped make the genre of fiction popular and respectable. In 1908, Baydas founded *al-Nafa'is al-Asriyya* (Modern treasures), a literary journal devoted to short stories as well as serialized novels that he translated, mostly from Russian, and later published separately. His collection of short stories, *Masarih al-Adh'han* (Pastures of the minds, 1924), demonstrates Baydas's style of writing fiction that aimed at the moral edification of the reader.

By 1948, the growing number of Palestinian fiction writers and translators included Najati Sidqi (b. 1905), Mahmud Sayf al-Din al-Irani (1914–78), and Abd al-Hamid Yasin (1908–75). Their short stories concentrated on the portrayal of social conditions, focusing particularly on the poor and lowly and depicting the inner feelings of their characters, as in Sidqi's collection *al-Akhawat al-Hazinat* (The sad sisters, 1953), al-Irani's *Ma al-Nas* (With people, 1955), and Yasin's *Aqasis* (Short stories, 1946). Dr Ishaq Musa al-Husayni (1904–90), a well-known literary scholar and critic from the HUSAYNI FAMILY and a noted essayist, published an allegorical novella in 1943 entitled *Mudhakkirat Dajaja* (Memoirs of a hen), which received wide acclaim in the Arab world as much for its imaginative style as for its sharp but veiled criticism of society and its ethics. The pioneering women who wrote fiction include Samira Azzam (1927–67) and Najwa Qa'war Farah (b. 1923), who wrote short stories of extreme delicacy and poignancy, including some dealing with women's issues. In her five collections, for example, Samira Azzam demonstrated skillful control of her narrative art and compassionate treatment of her subject; Najwa Qa'war Farah, who also wrote prose poems, demonstrated great sensitivity and deep insight into the human condition in her six collections.

Exodus The war that led to the establishment of Israel in 1948 catastrophically disrupted Palestinian society: some Palestinians found themselves under Israeli control; others dispersed as stateless REFUGEES in camps scattered over the Middle East; still others went into exile in the Arab world and elsewhere. Palestinians continued to denounce the injustice done to them, retaining their attachment to their homeland, their will to reconstruct its social fabric, and their commitment to create in Palestine an independent state of their own. These thoughts and feelings became the mainstay of Palestinian literature. For example, MAHMUD DARWISH (b. 1942), who lived in Israel until 1971, wrote poems expressing love for Palestine and celebrating human dignity; he is arguably the foremost Palestinian poet of the second half of the twentieth century. His popularity in the Arab world is so extensive that his *diwan,* which includes eight collections published between 1964 and 1977, had been printed thirteen times by 1989. Selections of Darwish's poetry translated into English include *Selected Poems* (1973), *The Music of Human Flesh* (1980), and *Sand and Other Poems* (1986). His friends Samih al-Qasim (b. 1939), TAWFIQ ZAYYAD (1917–64), and Salim Jubran (b. 1941), who have remained in Israel, continue to celebrate their distinct Palestinian identity and their love for their homeland, while calling for human rights. FADWA TUQAN (b. 1917), sister of Ibrahim Tuqan, abandoned her earlier romantic poems after the West Bank, where she lived, was occupied by Israel in 1967. Her poems now call for justice for the Palestinians and their cause. The personal emotion that animated her early collections, *Wahdi ma al-Ayyam* (Alone with the days, 1955) and *Wajadtuha* (I found it, 1957), has been transformed into a nationalist feeling of solidarity with her people's resistance to occupation, as in her *al-Fursan wa al-Layl* (Horsemen and the night, 1969).

Tawfiq Sayigh (1923–71) and JABRA IBRAHIM JABRA (1920–94), who have lived in exile outside occupied Palestine since 1948, remember their youth spent in the homeland and deplore the world's indifference to the Palestinians' plight. They both express themselves in prose poems of rare beauty. Sayigh merges his spiritual anguish in search of God with his political anguish in search of a homeland and his personal anguish in search of romantic fulfillment, as in his *Thalathun Qasida* (Thirty poems, 1954), *al-Qasida K* (The poem K, 1960), and *Mu'allaqat Tawfiq Sayigh* (The ode of Tawfiq Sayigh, 1963). Jabra expresses his political and personal alienation in poems marked by deep pain as well as ongoing hope for national rebirth, as in his *Tammuz fi al-Madina* (Tammuz in the city, 1959), *al-Madar al-Mughlaq* (The closed circuit, 1964), and *Lam'at al-Shams* (The agony of the sun, 1978).

Kamal Nasir (1925–73), another committed poet in exile, evinced immense lyrical appeal and deep political passion. He expressed his deep pain and ebullient nationalist spirit in *Jirah Tughanni* (Singing wounds, 1960) and in hundreds of prose articles before being killed by Israelis at his apartment in Beirut. Nasir's posthumously published works include *al-Athar al-Shi'riyya* (Poetic works, 1974) and *al-Athar al-Nathriyya* (Prose works, 1974).

Mu'in Busaysu (1927–84), an activist poet who was often in prison, was also a playwright. His autobiographical *Dafatir Filistiniyya* (Palestinian notebooks) was published in English as *Descent into the Water: Palestinian Notes from Arab Exile* (1980). He wrote more than ten books of poetry, including *Filistin fi al-Qalb* (Palestine in the heart, 1965) and *al-An Khudhi Jasadi Kisan min al-Raml* (Now take my body as a sandbag, 1976). They were collected in his *al-A'mal al-Shi'riyya al-Kamila* (Complete poetic works, 1981). Most of his later poetry reflected the Palestinian struggle in Lebanon's civil war. He joined the PLO exodus from Lebanon after Israel's 1982 invasion and published in Tunis his long poem *Kam min Dulu'ika wa al-Hisaru Yadiqu Qad Waqafat Ma'ak* (How many of your ribs stood up with you as the siege narrowed, 1983), which castigated the Arab regimes that failed the Palestinians while describing his own experiences.

Younger poets continue to express the Palestinian vision of a free homeland. They include Murid Barghuthi (b. 1944), Izz al-Din al-Manasra (b. 1946), Ahmad Dahbur (b. 1946), and Ibrahim Nasrullah (b. 1954). Some of these poets began their literary careers writing poetry that followed the established rules of classical Arabic prosody. Soon after 1948, when Arabic poetry in Egypt, Iraq, Lebanon, and Syria burst out into free verse, Palestinian poets joined this rebellious impulse, which, they felt, expressed their own vision of a fractured world in need of innovation, reconstruction, and new values liberated from tradition. Clearly, Palestinians, although looking inward to fathom their own predicament, were at the same time alert to literary trends in the Arab world and responsive to European and U.S. movements.

Palestinian fiction writers were under similar cultural influences in the second half of the twentieth century as their maturing narrative art was increasingly appreciated by Arab readers. Jabra Ibrahim Jabra's earlier fiction, written before 1948, prepared him to write such masterful later novels as *Hunters in a Narrow Street* (London, 1960), translated into Arabic an *Sayyadun fi Shari' Dayyiq* in 1974; *al-Safina* (The ship, 1970); al-Bahth an Walid Mas'ud (Search for Walid Mas'ud, 1978); and *al-Ghuraf al-Ukhra* (The other rooms, 1986). His fictional universe teems with Palestinians wanting to break out of life under siege.

If Jabra's characters are drawn mostly from the bourgeois world, those of another fiction writer, GHASSAN KANAFANI (1936–72), are taken mainly from the misery of the Palestinian refugee camps he experienced. His *Rijal fi al-Shams* (Men in the sun, 1963) tells the story of three Palestinian refugees who die concealed in the empty water tank of a truck, silently waiting in the sun of the border to be smuggled into Kuwait to work. Kanafani's novel *A'id ila Haifa* (Return to Haifa, 1968) shows a Palestinian protagonist who realizes the necessity of armed struggle; his modernist novel *Ma Tabaqqa Lakum* (What's left for you, 1966) portrays a Palestinian struggling for a dignified life, finally wrestling with and defeating an Israeli soldier. A politically committed Palestinian, Kanafani was killed in 1972 in Beirut when his booby-trapped car exploded.

In Israel, EMILE HABIBI (1921–93) writes Palestinian fiction that is innovative but deeply rooted in Arabic classics. Habibi's novels are characterized by black humor that is highly critical of the Israeli treatment of Palestinians. His *Sudasiyyat al-Ayyam al-Sitta* (Sextet of the six days, 1969) blends memory with hope in portraying Palestinians on both sides of the Green Line dividing Israel from the West Bank as they meet each other after twenty years of separation when all Palestine came under Israeli control after the 1967 war. Habibi's masterpiece, *al-Waqa'i' al-Ghariba fi Ikhtifa Sa'id Abi al-Nahs al-Mutasha'il* (The strange events of the disappearance of Sa'id Abu al-Nahs, the pessi-optimist, 1974), is a unique novel in Arabic literature problematizing in a tragic-comic manner the insecure and mixed feelings of Palestinians as precarious citizens of Israel. Another Palestinian writer from Israel, ANTON SHAMMAS (b. 1950), who now lives in the United States, writes in both Arabic and Hebrew. His novel in Hebrew, *Arabescot* (Arabesques, 1986), has been translated into other languages, including English (1988), winning him international acclaim. *Arabescot* deals with the attachment of generations of Palestinians to their ancestral soil and with their anguished need for reunion and a free expression of their national identity. Other Palestinian fiction writers in Israel include Tawfiq Fayyad (b. 1939), Muhammad Naffa (b. 1940), Muhammad Ali Taha (b. 1941), Zaki Darwish (b. 1944), and Riyad Baydas (b. 1960). Their short stories and novels depict the unfavorable conditions of life for Palestinians under Israeli control and assert the need for human dignity.

Among the contemporary women fiction writers of Palestine, Sahar Khalifa (b. 1941) is the most accomplished. She has written five novels, some of which have been translated into several languages. Of those, *al-Subbar* (1976), translated into English as *Wild Thorns* (1985), portrays life in the Occupied Territories of Palestine and the resistance movement against Israeli occupation. A very articulate feminist, she successfully shows that women's struggle for emancipation is an integral part of the struggle for national liberation. In another novel, *Mudhakkirat Imra'a Ghayr Waqi'iyya* (Memoirs of an unrealistic woman, 1986), she carries this theme further to include women's struggle against constraining cultural traditions as part of the national struggle. A younger woman, Liyana Badr (b. 1950) has published a novel in English, *The Sundial* (1989), in addition to collections of short stories and novellas in Arabic. Her fiction reflects Palestinian life, particularly in refugee camps in Lebanon, in a touching and compelling way.

A new generation of Palestinian male fiction writers includes Rashad Abu Shawar (b. 1942), whose novel *al-Ushshaq* (Lovers, 1977) and whose collections of short stories depict Palestinian experiences similar to his own in refugee camps, and Yahya Yakhlif (b. 1944), one-time secretary-general of the Union of Palestinian Writers and Journalists. Yakhlif has written three novels and several collections of short stories. His novels *Najran Taht al-Sifr* (Najran under zero, 1975) and *Tuffah al-Majanin* (Fools' apples, 1982) are strong indictments of Arab society. His novel *Buhayra Wara al-Rih* (A lake behind the wind, 1991) chronicles the Palestinian experiences of the 1948 war.

Other key Palestinian fiction writers include Khalil al-Sawahiri (b. 1940), Mahmud Shuqayr (b. 1941), Mahmud Shahin (b. 1947), Gharib Asqalani (b. 1948), Faruq Wadi (b. 1949), and Akram Haniyya (b. 1953). Like that of their predecessors, their fiction is deeply committed to the liberation of Palestine and its people.

Issa J. Boullata

BIBLIOGRAPHY

Abu Ghazaleh, A. *Arab Cultural Nationalism in Palestine.* Beirut: Institute for Palestine Studies, 1973.

Aruri, N., and E. Ghareeb, eds., trans. *Enemy of the Sun: Poetry of Palestinian Resistance.* Washington, D.C.: Drum and Spear Press, 1970.

Ashrawi, H. M. "The Contemporary Palestinian Poetry of Occupation." *Journal of Palestine Studies* 7, no. 3 (1978): 77–101.

——. *Contemporary Palestinian Literature under Occupation.* Bir Zeit: Bir Zeit University, 1976.

Elmessiri, A. M., ed., trans. *The Palestinian Wedding: A Bilingual Anthology of Contemporary Palestinian Resistance Poetry.* Washington, D.C., Three Continents Press, 1982.

Jayyusi, S. K., ed. *Anthology of Modern Palestinian Literature.* New York: Columbia University Press, 1992.

——. "Introduction: Palestinian Literature in Modern Times." In *Anthology of Modern Palestinian Literature,* ed. by S. K. Jayyusi. New York: Columbia University Press, 1992.

Peled, M. "Annals of Doom: Palestinian Literature, 1917–1948." *Arabica,* 29, 2 (1982): 143–183.

Sulaiman, K. A. *Palestine and Modern Arab Poetry.* London: Zed Press, 1984.

al-Udhari, A. ed., trans. *Victims of a Map: Samih al-Qasim, Adonis, Mahmud Darwish.* London: Zed Press, 1984.

London Conference

1939, 1946–1947

In November 1938, after the recommendations of the PEEL COMMISSION and the WOODHEAD COMMISSION were published, the British government issued a White Paper calling for a conference of Zionist and Arab leaders to discuss the future of Palestine. Under the leadership of Prime Minister Sir Neville Chamberlain, this first conference opened in Saint James Palace in February 1939 and lasted until March.

The British met separately with Zionist and Arab leaders, the latter including delegations from Palestine, Egypt, Iraq, Transjordan, Yemen, and Saudi Arabia. However, they barred the paramount Palestinian political figure, AL-HAJJ AMIN AL-HUSAYNI, from attending. Other leading Palestinian figures did attend, including al-Husayni's cousin, JAMAL HUSAYNI; MUSA AL-ALAMI; and GEORGE ANTONIUS. After the conference ended inconclusively, the British government issued the MACDONALD WHITE PAPER, 1939.

After the issuance of the MORRISON-GRADY PLAN IN JULY 1946, British authorities again invited Jewish and Arab representatives to London to discuss the plan's recommendation for creating a unitary, federal trusteeship in Palestine. The second London conference opened in September 1946, although neither Palestinians nor Zionists attended: Palestinians refused to participate unless al-Hajj Amin al-Husayni was allowed to attend as head of the ARAB HIGHER COMMITTEE, and the Zionist movement objected to the concept of a unitary state instead of partition. The conference reopened in February 1947, and the British government eventually proposed an independent Palestinian state, with a Jewish minority, after a five-year transitional period under British trusteeship. Both the Arab Higher Committee and the Zionist movement rejected the proposal.

Faced with such rejection, the British government announced within weeks of the conference's close that it would turn over the question of Palestine to the United Nations.

Michael R. Fischbach

Lydda

Arabic, al-Lidd; Hebrew, Lod

Lydda's historical importance has stemmed from its position along communications and trade routes. It lies sixteen kilometers southeast of JAFFA and constitutes the western gateway between the coast and JERUSALEM.

Lydda's origins are ancient. It was the object of strategic campaigns of numerous empires. The Romans called it Diospolis. Its importance was eclipsed after 716 C.E. by that of the neighboring town of RAMLA, which was established by the Arabs. Captured by the Crusaders, Lydda later became a stop on the Mamluk dynasty's mail route between Gaza and Damascus.

Lydda's importance to the communications network grew tremendously during the PALESTINE MANDATE. In 1919, it was made a stop on the Qantara-Haifa railroad line and became the country's main railroad junction. North of Lydda, Mandate authorities later constructed Palestine's largest and only international airport. Lydda's population growth reflected the town's mounting importance: an urban area of some 7,000 in 1912, it grew to 11,250 in 1931 and 18,250 in 1946.

Lydda's land in the coastal plain was fertile, producing a variety of agricultural products, including citrus fruits. Given its strategic location, trade was also a key dimension of Lydda's economy. In addition to its shops, Lydda was home to a weekly market that drew thousands of people from neighboring villages. The town was also a center for traditional manufacturing.

Along with that of neighboring Ramla, the fate of Lydda and its inhabitants during the ARAB-ISRAELI WAR OF 1948 was a microcosm of the wider Palestinian experience. It was defended by Palestinian forces, irregular volunteers from Jordan, and units of the Jordanian Arab Legion. Lieutenant General John Glubb, the Briton commanding the legion, refused to divert legion units from the important position of Latrun to reinforce Arab forces in the town. Lydda subsequently fell to the Palmach on July 11, 1948, whereupon all but some 1,000 of its inhabitants were expelled.

As of 1992 Lydda (Hebrew, Lod) had some 41,600 inhabitants.

Michael R. Fischbach

M

MacDonald White Paper
1939

Named after British secretary of state for colonies Malcolm MacDonald, the White Paper of 1939 was issued on May 17, 1939, after the failure of the LONDON CONFERENCE of February–March 1939. (Saint James Conference). The White Paper set a new British policy for the future of Palestine in which Britain officially abandoned partition as a workable solution to the Palestine question. The White Paper stated, "His Majesty's Government now declares unequivocally that it is not part of their policy that Palestine should become a Jewish state," and declared its intention to allow the establishment of an independent Palestinian state after a ten-year transitional period in which Jewish immigration was limited. It also called for restrictions of Jewish LAND purchases in Palestine.

The ARAB HIGHER COMMITTEE and the paramount Palestinian political figure, AL-HAJJ AMIN AL-HUSAYNI, skeptical that the British would honor their pledge, especially after ten years, rejected the White Paper despite its seeming intention to meet several key Palestinian political demands. Other Palestinian and Arab leaders accepted it, however. Zionist leaders uniformly denounced it because it would limit Jewish immigration and Zionist ability to establish a Jewish state.

Michael R. Fischbach

Madrid Peace Conference
1991

After the defeat of Iraq in the Gulf War of January–February 1991, the UNITED STATES and the SOVIET UNION co-convened an international conference in Madrid, Spain, to discuss a diplomatic end to the ARAB–ISRAELI CONFLICT. They called for the conference to initiate two parallel negotiating tracks: a bilateral track that involved specific talks between Israel and the Arab parties, and a multilateral track that involved many delegations discussing region-wide issues. The conference opened on October 30, 1991, and included delegations from Israel, Syria, Lebanon, and Egypt and a joint Jordanian-Palestinian delegation.

Israel and the United States refused to allow a separate Palestinian delegation to attend the conference, nor would they allow the PALESTINE LIBERATION ORGANIZATION (PLO) to participate openly. The Palestinian representatives in the joint Jordanian–Palestinian delegation were counseled by an advisory committee that maintained contact with the PLO.

The conference lasted until November 1 and was immediately followed by bilateral talks in Madrid between Israel and each of the Syrian, Lebanese, and Jordanian–Palestinian delegations. Israel agreed to meet with the Palestinians separately from the Jordanians. The multilateral talks commenced in January 1992 in Moscow.

Michael R. Fischbach

Mandate See PALESTINE MANDATE.

Mansour, Camille
Mansur; academic
1945– Haifa

Mansour carried out undergraduate studies at The American University of Beirut, after which he obtained Ph.D.'s in political science and Islamic studies from Paris University-Sorbonne. From 1974 to 1979, he was editor in chief of *The Yearbook of Palestine and the Arab-Israeli Conflict* for the INSTITUTE FOR PALESTINE STUDIES (IPS) in Beirut. After one year as a visiting scholar at Harvard University in 1979–80, Mansour returned to Beirut, where he chaired the IPS research department from 1980 to 1984.

Since 1984, Mansour has been a professor of international relations and Middle Eastern politics at the Sorbonne. In September 1994, he moved to the PALESTINIAN AUTHORITY (PA) to help establish the Law Center at BIR ZEIT UNIVERSITY, which he heads.

Mansour was also involved in the Middle East peace process and the consolidation of the PA. One of the Palestinians' most capable strategists, he served on the steering committee that guided the activities of the Palestinian negotiating team from October 1991 until February 1994. In February 1996, PA president Yasir Arafat appointed him to a committee created to draft a constitution for the PA.

Mansour is author of several works, including *Les Palestiniens de l'intérieur, Beyond Alliance: Israel in U.S. Foreign Policy,* and *The Palestinian-Israeli Negotiations: An Overview and Assessment, October 1991–January 1993.*

Michael R. Fischbach

Martyrs' Works Society

The Palestinian Martyrs' Works Society (SAMED), is a highly innovative PALESTINE LIBERATION ORGANIZATION (PLO) institution. Its major objectives are to train and employ, or to find employment for, Palestinians; to supply the material necessities of life to the Palestinian community at affordable prices; and to increase solidarity between the Palestinian nation and other peoples in developing countries. The group has two main sectors, industrial and agricultural, as well as a number of smaller divisions, such as the Cinema Production Center. SAMED functions in most major Middle Eastern Palestinian communities except in the Occupied Territories, where, prior to the OSLO AGREEMENTS, it was prohibited.

In the industrial sector, SAMED's labor-intensive, worker-managed factories produce clothes, plastics, furniture, kitchenwares, dishes, shoes, toys, textiles, processed food products, and other manufactured items. These commodities are sold at a fraction of the cost of comparable goods in the markets of host countries. Moreover, all workers are Palestinian. Thus SAMED not only provides individuals employment opportunities but also renders economic sustenance to whole families.

At the height of its operations in 1982, SAMED had forty-three factories employing approximately 5,000 individuals; it has trained 30,000 persons who have gone on to work elsewhere. In one example of its productive capacity, in 1981, SAMED factories in Lebanon produced half a million pieces of ready-to-wear clothing—more than the Palestinian community could consume—which it was exporting to the SOVIET UNION, Gulf countries, and Eastern European states.

In Lebanon, where a majority of SAMED's factories existed, the ARAB-ISRAELI WAR OF 1982, was quite destructive; however, in the ensuing years, there have been significant reconstruction and development efforts. SAMED also produces a prominent monthly scholarly journal on economics, *Samed al-Iqtisadi.*

Agriculture constitutes the second major sector in SAMED and reflects the PLO's strong focus on international relations. The most important initiatives in this area are its substantial agricultural cooperatives in Sudan, Somalia, Uganda, Guinea-Bissau, Guinea, and Iraq. There are smaller farms in Yemen, Syria, Egypt, Uganda, and Mali. Some of the larger cooperatives occupy as much as 4,500 acres; SAMED holdings total some 12,500 acres. Production includes lemons, mangoes, pineapples, sesame, bananas, poultry, cattle, and sheep.

These projects provide some products for Palestinian consumption, but their primary aim is political. Palestinians use their technical expertise and volunteer activity to develop ties with other nations and to increase support for the Palestinian cause. In each of the projects, skilled Palestinian workers train unskilled Africans and Arabs, helping them develop their agricultural resources, pursue agrarian reform projects, and construct dams and canals.

Cheryl Rubenberg

Masri Family

The Masri family rose to influence in NABLUS during the twentieth century through their commercial activities. A number of its members are in business or have served in government positions in the Jordanian government.

Hikmat (1907– ; Nablus; businessman, politician) Hikmat obtained a B.A. at the American University of Beirut. A member of the NASHASHIBI FAMILY–led opposition during the PALESTINE MANDATE, he was later elected to the Jordanian parliament several times in the 1950s and served as speaker of parliament in 1952–53 and 1956–57. After service as a cabinet minister, he was appointed senator in 1963. Considered a major pro-Jordanian figure in the WEST BANK, he served as mayor of Nablus and as chair of the board of trustees of AL-NAJAH NATIONAL UNIVERSITY in that city.

Tahir (1942– ; Nablus; politician) Tahir studied at North Texas State University, al-Najah University in Nablus, and Aleppo College in Syria. After working for the Central Bank of Jordan, he held several positions in the Jordanian government, including serving as a member of parliament in 1973–74 and as minister of state for the Occupied Territories in that period. Because Tahir had good relations with the PALESTINE LIBERATION ORGANIZATION, King Husayn appointed him prime minister in June 1991 at a time of increased activity directed at negotiating an end to the ARAB-ISRAELI CONFLICT. Tahir resigned the following November after a vote of no confidence in the Jordanian Parliament. He himself was elected to parliament in November 1993.

Zafir (1942–1986; Nablus; politician) Zafir was deputy mayor of Nablus in the late 1970s but resigned after a dispute with Israeli occupation authorities. When Israel deposed the pro-PLO mayor, Bassam Shak'a, in March 1982, Nablus remained without a Palestinian mayor until December 1985. In that month, occupation authorities appointed Masri mayor as part of a plan to appoint new mayors to major West Bank towns in coordination with Jordan. Despite securing PLO approval to accept the position, Masri was assassinated on March 2, 1986, by a Palestinian faction opposed to any cooperation with Israeli authorities.

Munib (1936– ; Nablus; businessman) Holding an M.S. in geology, Munib worked with the Phillips Petroleum Company in several Middle Eastern countries in the early 1960s. In 1970–71, he served as minister of public works in the Jordanian government. He formed the Engineering & Development Group in 1971 in Beirut and continues to head it out of its London offices.

A member of the board of directors of the PALESTINIAN NATIONAL FUND and the Arab Bank, Ltd., Munib has also served on the Palestine Liberation Organization's central council. He was the first treasurer of the Geneva-based Palestinian Welfare Association, and in 1995 he was one of the several prominent Palestinian businessmen who established a committee to promote dialogue with the PALESTINIAN AUTHORITY. A billionaire, Masri runs the Palestinian Development and Investment Company (PADICO), which by 1999 had became the largest and most influential company in the West Bank and Gaza, with major interests in telecommunications, finance, tourism, real estate, and manufacturing.

Sabih (businessman) Based in Amman, Sabih heads Astra Farms Company, an agribusiness firm, and is also involved with the Palestine Development and Investment Company (PADICO) in the WEST BANK and the GAZA STRIP. A large landowner in Jordan, he also was a major food contractor for Allied armies during the GULF CRISIS, 1990–1991. Sabih is a member of the Geneva-based Palestinian Welfare Association.

Michael R. Fischbach

Matar, Ibrahim

economist

1941– Jerusalem

After receiving a B.A. in business economics at the American University of Beirut in 1963 and an M.A. in economic development at Indiana University at Bloomington in 1966, Matar served as founding chair of the department of business and economics at BETHLEHEM UNIVERSITY from 1973 to 1976. From 1976 to 1985, he worked as director of rural development for the Mennonite Central Committee in Jerusalem, where he was among the first to carry out detailed research into and publicize Israeli settlement activity in the Occupied Territories. He served as the WEST BANK representative of American Near East Refugee Air (ANERA) from 1985 to 1997 and is the founding chair of the Arab Development and Credit Company, the first nonprofit financial institution in the West Bank.

Michael R. Fischbach

Media

The media have played a vital role in Palestinian history, especially in the realm of politics. Daily and weekly newspapers, magazines, and radio broadcasts have proved to be important avenues for mobilizing support for various political trends over the course of modern Palestinian history. This has especially been true given that membership in political parties and organizations has never extended beyond a relatively few individuals. And in the absence of any other nationwide forums for discussing political and social issues, the media have served as the primary means by which Palestinians have pursued political dialogue in the twentieth century.

Arabic language journalism in Palestine apparently began in 1876, when the Ottoman Empire underwent a short-lived experiment in constitutional reform. Two official Ottoman government publications, *al-Quds al-Sharif* and *al-Ghazal,* appeared in JERUSALEM in that year. A number of publications were established later in 1908, the year of the Young Turk coup d'état against Sultan Abdülhamit II and the return to constitutional rule. Some journals dealt with literary and cultural subjects. Others, like *al-Karmil* (established in 1908) and *Filastin* (1911), were important media for disseminating early Palestinian political aspirations vis-à-vis ZIONISM. Literary journals like *al-Nafa'is al-Asiriyya* also played an important role in stimulating Palestinian literary and intellectual consciousness.

The period of the British PALESTINE MANDATE witnessed a tremendous growth in the number and variety of Palestinian publications as increased education swelled the number of literate Palestinians and as the growing Zionist-Palestinian conflict stirred political passions. Over two hundred Arabic language newspapers and journals were established in Palestine, and several of the Ottoman era continued to be published.

The major newspapers generally supported a particular political party or trend. The leading papers sided either with the faction associated with the HUSAYNI FAMILY of Jerusalem (and particularly AL-HAJJ AMIN AL-HUSAYNI, head of the SUPREME MUSLIM COUNCIL), known as the "Councilists," or with the faction associated with the NASHASHIBI FAMILY of Jerusalem, known as the "Opposition." Major pro-Husayni papers included *al-Sabah, al-Aqsa,* and *al-Jami'a al-Islamiyya, Filastin, Mir'at al-Sharq,* and *al-Nafir.* These and other political papers all called for an end to Britain's support for Zionism. Numerous literary and scholarly publications also emerged.

Palestinian radio broadcasting took place under government auspices. In 1936, the Mandatory government began a domestic Palestinian service in English, Hebrew, and Arabic. The Arabic section broadcast news, plays, and musical selections. Its first director was Ibrahim Tuqan, Palestine's poet laureate, who resigned in 1940 after government accusations that his choice of broadcasting material was inciting Palestinian nationalist feelings.

Palestinian journalism was devastated as a result of the ARAB-ISRAELI WAR OF 1948, and the Palestinian exodus. Only one paper continued publication in the new state of Israel, the Communist *al-Ittihad.* In the Jordanian-occupied WEST BANK, *al-Difa* and *Filastin* resumed publication in Jerusalem, and several other journals began publication during the 1950s and 1960s.

The rise of Palestinian resistance organizations in exile in the 1960s and 1970s led to a number of Palestinian political and cultural publications. The FATAH movement's clandestine *Filastinuna* was among the first of these. Many groups associated with the PALESTINE LIBERATION ORGANIZATION (PLO) issued publications, including *Filastin al-Thawra* (PLO), *al-Hurriya* (DEMOCRATIC FRONT FOR THE LIBERATION OF PALESTINE [DFLP]), and *al-Hadaf* (POPULAR FRONT FOR THE LIBERATION OF PALESTINE [PFLP]). Scholarly journals also emerged, including *al-Dirasat al-Filastiniyya* and *Shu'un Filastiniyya.* Although a number of Arab governments offered Palestinian-oriented radio broadcasts, the Palestine Liberation Organization's *Sawt Filastin* and Fatah's *Sawt Fatah* in the mid-1960s were the first major Palestinian programs to emerge. The PLO also established its own news agency, *Wikalat al-Anba al-Filastiniyya* (WAFA).

After Israel's occupation of the West Bank and the GAZA STRIP in 1967, one Jerusalem newspaper (*al-Quds*) resumed publication; others emerged later. Occupation law in the West Bank and Gaza has repeatedly led to censorship and the closing of publications even though by publishing in Jerusalem, Palestinian newspapers and journals were technically subject to Israeli law rather than occupation law: by annexing East Jerusalem, Israel in effect extended its own law to the city.

The 1993 Israeli–PLO accords created a PALESTINIAN AUTHORITY (PA) in part of Gaza and the West Bank. The end of Israeli occupation and the emergence of Palestinian resistance organizations into the open led to the establishment of several new publications, including both official PA and opposition papers like *al-Watan* and *al-Umma.* Opposition papers and even the Jerusalem dailies from earlier times, such as *al-Nahar,* found themselves facing censorship now not from Israel but from the new Palestinian Authority, which was quite hostile to criticism. *Sawt Filastin* radio began broadcasting in Jericho under PA authority, and an official Palestinian television station began broadcasting in February 1996.

Selected List of Palestinian Media

Ottoman Period

Filastin	(Jaffa biweekly; est. 1911)
al-Ghazal	(Jerusalem monthly; official Ottoman paper est. 1876)
al-Karmil	(Haifa biweekly; est. 1908)
al-Nafa'is al-Asiriyya	(Haifa; literary; est. 1909)
al-Quds al-Sharif	(Jerusalem monthly; official Ottoman paper; Turkish and Arabic; est. 1876)
Suriyya al-Janubiyya	

Mandate

al-Aqsa	(Jerusalem weekly; associated with Councilists; est. 1920)
al-Arab	
Bayt al-Maqdis	
al-Difa	(Jaffa daily; associated with ISTIQLAL PARTY in 1930s; supported Councilists in late 1940s; est. 1934)
Filastin	(Jaffa daily; associated with Opposition in 1930s; in 1940s, supported Istiqlal Party; est. 1911)
al-Haya	
al-Ittihad	(Jaffa; Communist; 1944)
al-Jami'a al-Arabiyya	(Jerusalem daily; Councilist; est. 1927)
al-Jami'a al-Islamiyya	(Jaffa daily; Opposition; est. 1933)
al-Karmil	(Haifa biweekly; est. 1908)
Lisan al-Arab	
al-Liwa	
Mir'at al-Sharq	(Jerusalem biweekly; est. 1919)
al-Nafir	(Haifa weekly; Opposition; est. 1933)
al-Sabah	(Jerusalem weekly; Councilist; est. 1921)
Sawt al-Sha'b	
Yarmuk	

Post-1948 Exile

al-Dirasat al-Filastiniyya	(quarterly; scholarly, issued by INSTITUTE FOR PALESTINE STUDIES; est. 1990)
al-Fikr al-Dimuqrati	(Cyprus; oriented toward Popular Front for the Liberation of Palestine)
Filastin	(monthly; ed. by ARAB HIGHER COMMITTEE)
Filastin al-Thawra	(weekly; PLO; est. 1972)
Filastinuna	(monthly; Fatah; 1959–64)
al-Hadaf	(Popular Front for the Liberation of Palestine)
al-Karmil	(Beirut, then Cyprus; quarterly; literary)
Shu'un Filastiniyya	(research journal; issued by the PALESTINIAN RESEARCH CENTER; est. 1971)

West Bank, 1948–1967

al-Difa	(Jerusalem daily; est. 1934; ceased publication in 1968)
Filastin	(Jerusalem daily; est. 1911; ceased publication in 1967)
al-Hadaf	(Jerusalem weekly; est. 1950)
al-Jihad	(Jerusalem; est. 1955; ceased publication in 1968)
al-Manar	(Jerusalem daily; est. 1960)
al-Quds	(Jerusalem daily; reest. 1967)

Israel

al-Ard	(ACRE weekly; pan-Arab nationalist; 1959–60)
al-Ittihad	(Haifa daily; Israeli Communist Party; est. 1944)
al-Jadid	(Haifa; literary journal; associated with New Communist List [RAKAH]; est. 1953)
al-Sinara	(NAZARETH; popular press)

West Bank, 1967–1993

al-Ahd	(Jerusalem weekly; linked to PFLP; closed in 1986)
al-Awda	(Jerusalem weekly; issued by Palestine Press Service; closed 1986)
al-Bayadir	(Jerusalem monthly; literary; est. 1976)
al-Bayadir al-Siyasi	(Jerusalem; political, pro-PLO; est. 1982)
al-Fajr	(Jerusalem daily; pro-PLO; 1972–93)
al Fajr Palestinian Weekly	(Jerusalem English-language weekly; 1980–93)
al Mithaq	(Jerusalem weekly; linked to PFLP; 1980–86)
al-Nahar	(Jerusalem daily; pro-Jordanian; est. 1987)
al-Quds	(Jerusalem daily; pro-Jordanian, later pro-PLO; est. 1968)
al-Sha'b	(Jerusalem daily; pro-PLO; est. 1972)
al-Tali	(Jerusalem weekly; pro-Communist; est. 1978)
al-Usbu al-Jadid	(Jerusalem weekly; est. 1979)

Areas Controlled by Palestinian Authority Since 1994

al-Aqsa	(Palestinian Authority)
al-Awda	(reemerged in 1994)
al-Istiqlal	(ISLAMIC JIHAD)
al-Nahar	(Jerusalem daily; pro-Jordanian; est. 1987)
al-Quds	(Jerusalem daily; originally pro-Jordanian, later pro-PLO; est. 1968)
al-Sha'b	(Jerusalem daily; pro-PLO; est. 1972)
al-Umma	(PFLP)
al-Watan	(HAMAS)

Radio and Television

Palestinian Broadcasting Service	(government of Palestine; est. 1936)
Sawt al-Asifa	[later, Sawt Fatah] (Fatah radio; est. 1968)
Sawt Filastin	(PLO radio; Palestinian Authority radio from 1994; est. 1965)
al-Quds	Palestinian Arab Radio (POPULAR FRONT FOR THE LIBERATION OF PALESTINE GENERAL COMMAND; est. 1988)
Palestine Broadcasting Corporation	(areas under Palestinian Authority; began operating 1996)

Michael R. Fischbach

Morrison-Grady Plan
1946

Several weeks after the report of the ANGLO-AMERICAN COMMISSION, 1945–46, was issued in May 1946, American and British authorities formed a second commission to determine the future of Palestine. Headed by the American Henry Grady and the Briton Herbert Morrison, this commission issued the Morrison-Grady Plan in July 1946.

This plan called for a unitary federal trusteeship in Palestine. A Jewish province comprising some 17 percent of the country and a Palestinian province comprising some 40 percent would be created. JERUSALEM and the southern Negev (Naqab) Desert would remain under British control. Britain would also maintain overall control of the entire trusteeship even while each province exercised self-rule.

The Morrison-Grady Plan also proposed immediate admittance into the Jewish province of the 100,000 Jewish refugees discussed in the Anglo-American Commission's report but called for further immigration to be limited by the country's economic absorption capacity.

Michael R. Fischbach

Moughrabi, Fouad
leading Palestinian scholar in the United States
1942– Ayn Karm

Fouad Moughrabi was born in the section of West JERUSALEM now known as Ein Kerem. He fled to BETHLEHEM with his family when Ayn Karm was captured by Israeli forces in the 1948 war. He grew up in Bethlehem and, although a Muslim, attended French-run Roman Catholic schools. He moved to the United States in 1960 to attend Duke University and has lived in America since then, except for a period in the 1960s when he studied for a doctorate at the University of Grenoble in France.

Moughrabi specializes in public opinion polling. He coedited, with Elia Zureik, *Public Opinion and the Palestine Question* (New York: St. Martin's Press, 1987). He has written numerous articles on the Palestinian situation and on American attitudes toward Israel and the Palestinians. He is professor of political science and Middle East affairs, University of Tennessee at Chattanooga.

Kathleen Christison

Muhsin, Zuhayr

teacher, political activist
1936–1979 Tulkarm

After finishing his studies in Amman, Zuhayr Muhsin joined the Ba'th Party in 1953, was detained in 1957 by Jordanian authorities, lost his job, and was expelled. After going to Qatar and then to Kuwait, he moved in 1967 to Syria, where he aided in the creation of Sa'iqa, of which he became the secretary-general in June 1971 after the organization fell under the control of Hafiz al-Asad, who had seized power in November 1970. From July 1968 to July 1971 he was vice chairman of the PALESTINE NATIONAL COUNCIL (PNC), and an ex officio member of the Executive Committee of the PALESTINE LIBERATION ORGANIZATION.

He was a member of a committee that drew up the program adopted by the PNC in June 1974 that advocated the creation of a Palestinian entity in any occupied territory liberated from Israel and stated publicly his support for the partition of Palestine. He advocated the line imposed by Syria, including during the Lebanese civil war of 1975–76, when the Syrian troops fought against the Lebanese National Movement and the Palestinian resistance. He was injured in an attack in Cannes, France, on July 25, 1979, and died the next day. His assailants were never apprehended.

Alain Gresh

Muntada al-Adabi al-

See LITERARY SOCIETY.

Muragha, Sa'id Musa

Abu Musa; resistance commander
1927?–

Muragha served in the Jordanian army and studied at the Sandhurst military academy in Britain before defecting to Palestinian resistance forces in 1970. After joining FATAH, he rose to the rank of colonel and became deputy military chief of the PALESTINE LIBERATION ORGANIZATION (PLO) operations room in Lebanon. As a high-level commander in southern Lebanon, he tried to stop the Syrian advance into the area during Syria's intervention against the PLO in 1976. He survived a Syrian-inspired assassination attempt in 1978. Muragha later played an important role in the PLO's defense of Beirut during the 1982 Israeli invasion of Lebanon.

In May 1983, Muragha and other Fatah military commanders in eastern Lebanon were angered when the PLO chairman, YASIR ARAFAT, promoted several officers accused of corruption and cowardice during the Israeli invasion merely on the basis of their political loyalty to him. An intra-Fatah crisis develop in mid-1983 as Muragha added more political demands dealing with the direction and leadership style of Fatah and the PLO.

The standoff between the rebels and pro-Arafat loyalists descended into open fighting in October 1983. With Syria's help, rebel forces gained the upper hand and besieged Arafat and his loyalists in refugee camps in northern Lebanon until they were evacuated from Tripoli in December 1983 in a United Nations–sponsored evacuation.

Muragha's movement was popularly known as Fatah-Uprising, although it formally used the name Fatah. It joined several Syrian-oriented anti-Arafat coalition over the years, including the National Alliance (1984), the PALESTINIAN NATIONAL SALVATION FRONT (1985), and the National Democratic and Islamic Front, or "Damascus Ten" (1993).

Michael R. Fischbach

Muslim-Christian Associations

The first Muslim-Christian Associations (MCAs) were founded in JERUSALEM and JAFFA in late 1918 in response to the Zionist Commission's parade commemorating the BALFOUR DECLARATION. MCA boards comprised leading notables, Muslim and Christian religious functionaries, prominent journalists and lawyers, and sometimes village *shaykhs.* They galvanized opposition to ZIONISM in the early years of British rule.

The Jerusalem and Jaffa MCAs convened the First Congress of the Muslim-Christian Societies, later known as the First Palestinian Arab Congress,

in Jerusalem (late January 1919), presided over by Arif al-Dajani, president of the Jerusalem MCA. Its thirty participants framed a national charter to present to the Paris peace conference that demanded Palestinian unity with Syria, denounced the Balfour Declaration, and rejected British rule. The resolutions reflected the radicalism of the Nablus MCA and of participants active in the pro-Syrian al-Nadi al-Arabi (ARAB CLUB) and the then pro-French al-Muntada al-Adabi (LITERARY SOCIETY). The resolutions were later moderated to call for an autonomous Palestine within independent Syria since senior MCA officers—notably the congress's president, the head of the Greek Orthodox community; those who sought ranking positions in the PALESTINE MANDATE administration; and citrus growers in the Jaffa MCA who exported fruit to England—did not want to antagonize Britain.

MCAs petitioned the KING-CRANE COMMISSION, 1919, sent by the Paris peace conference, and expressed their opposition to the creation of a Jewish national home in Palestine while upholding equality for Jewish residents. In February–March 1920, after the first public reading of the Balfour Declaration and Faysal's coronation in Damascus, MCAs cooperated with al-Nadi al-Arabi and al-Muntada al-Adabi to protest Zionism and call for Arab independence.

When Faysal's government fell in July 1920, the pan-Arabism of al-Nadi al-Arabi was undermined and the pro-French views of al-Muntada al-Adabi were discredited. MUSA KAZIM AL-HUSAYNI, removed as mayor of Jerusalem in spring 1920, joined Dajani to head the Jerusalem MCA and convene in Haifa (December 1920) the third of the ARAB CONGRESSES, which formed the ARAB EXECUTIVE. The Arab Executive relied on the local MCAs for grassroots mobilization. Local societies financed their own activities, sent reports to the secretariat, and organized petitions and other campaigns on instructions from Jerusalem. Local MCAs pressed the Arab Executive to act; in June 1923 MCAs insisted it convene the Sixth Congress to prevent Sharif Husayn of Mecca from signing a treaty with Britain that would ignore Palestinian rights. MCAs deplored communal violence, as demonstrated by their efforts in Jaffa to dispel rumors and calm residents during riots in May 1921. They stressed political action, notably a campaign to boycott LEGISLATIVE COUNCIL elections in 1922–23.

MCAs weakened in the mid-1920s when Palestinians were divided by factional tension. AL-HAJJ AMIN AL-HUSAYNI, president of the SUPREME MUSLIM COUNCIL, was charged by his opponents with diverting funds to subsidize MCAs. Competitive associations were formed by opponents of the HUSAYNI FAMILY. Nonetheless, MCAs revived after the WESTERN (WAILING) WALL DISTURBANCES, 1929, which radicalized the national movement. The Jaffa MCA was taken over by activists and led demonstrations in October 1933 against Jewish immigration and LAND purchases. The Nablus MCA changed its name to the Patriotic Arab Association in July 1931 to emphasize its enhanced militancy, but by then, MCAs were no longer the main local-level organizations supporting the Arab Executive. The Arab Executive itself, increasingly bypassed by radical groups, folded in 1934.

Ann M. Lesch

BIBLIOGRAPHY

Lesch, Ann Mosely. *Arab Politics in Palestine, 1917–1939: The Frustration of a Nationalist Movement.* Ithaca, N.Y.: Cornell University Press, 1979.

McTague, John J. *British Policy in Palestine, 1917–1922.* Lanham, Md.: University Press of America, 1983.

Muslih, Muhammad Y. *The Origins of the Palestinian Nationalism.* New York: Columbia University Press, 1988.

Porath, Yehoshua. *The Emergence of the Palestinian-Arab National Movement 1918–1929.* London: Frank Cass, 1974.

——. *The Palestinian Arab National Movement, 1929–1939: From Riots to Rebellion.* London: Frank Cass, 1977.

N

al-Nabhani, Taqi al-Din

Islamic militant
1909–1979 Izjim

Born in Ijzim, a village south of HAIFA, Taqi al-Din al-Nabhani studied at al-Azhar University and Dar al-Ulum in Egypt, after which he returned to Palestine and held administrative positions in the Islamic court system in Haifa, Hebron, Jaffa, and Jerusalem. Called by the title *al-shaykh,* a religious scholar, he was later appointed as a judge in the Islamic courts of Baysan, Hebron, Ramla, and Lydda before fleeing Palestine for Beirut in 1948. Nabhani soon returned to the WEST BANK, where he served as an Islamic court judge in Jerusalem and a teacher in the Islamic College in Amman.

Nabhani was also an Islamic militant concerned with the Palestine problem. He had joined the Muslim Brotherhood while in Egypt and was active in the movement on returning to Palestine. He also maintained ties with the Palestinian leader AL-HAJJ AMIN AL-HUSAYNI during the PALESTINE MANDATE. During the period of Jordanian rule in the West Bank, however, Nabhani grew critical of the Brotherhood's close links with the Jordanian regime because of its pro-Western leanings. He also thought the Brotherhood's understanding of Islam was "inauthentic."

In November 1952, Nabhani broke with the Brotherhood and established the Liberation Party in Jerusalem. The party advocated Nabhani's vision of a militant, pan-Islamic, and anti-Western struggle for liberating Palestine. Because the party advocated replacing the Hashemite regime with an Islamic government, it was unable to operate legally and Nabhani was arrested. Nabhani left Palestine for Syria in 1953 and moved to Lebanon in 1959. He died and was buried in Beirut in 1979.

Michael. R. Fischbach

Nablus

The easternmost of the three towns delimiting the Triangle region of Palestine, Nablus is the biblical city of Shechem and historically one of Palestine's most important towns. The site of Nablus has been inhabited since ancient times. The city takes its name from the Roman city of Neapolis that was built west of Shechem in the year 70 C.E. The town and its vicinity contain such biblical shrines as Jacob's Well and the Tomb of Joseph. In addition, Nablus was the center of the Samaritan presence in Palestine until this century.

Nablus has played an important role in modern Palestinian history. It featured strongly in the political turmoil of the nineteenth century, when the Ottoman state moved against the powerful village-based families who had long controlled the region. A number of prominent Arab nationalists were from Nablus during the Ottoman era, and the city continued to produce important nationalist figures during the PALESTINE MANDATE and the Israeli occupation as well. Families from Nablus have contributed many politicians and bureaucrats who have served many administrations both in Palestine and abroad.

Nablus has always occupied an important place in the economy of Palestine and neighboring countries. The city has been the most important manufacturing center in Palestine, known particularly for goods processed from agricultural products such as olive oil soap, food products, and textiles. In recent times, capital inflows from expatriate workers have allowed the expansion of Nablus's trade and industry. The city has key trade ties with neighboring areas, both within Palestine and abroad (for instance, with al-Salt in JORDAN).

Alongside Nablus's political and economic importance lies its cultural importance in Palestinian history. Nablus was an important administrative center under Ottoman, British, and Jordanian rule as central Palestine's largest town. Its population rose from some 8,000 in 1882 to 17,400 in 1931 to 23,250 in 1945. Its wealthy families possessed enough capital to lead lives of opulence. Nablus is also the home of AL-NAJAH NATIONAL UNIVERSITY, which opened in 1918 as a private secondary school and attained university status in 1977. Many of Palestine's most famous writers, poets, and academicians have hailed from Nablus.

Nablus was controlled by Iraqi forces during the 1948 Arab-Israeli War. It then became part of the Jordanian-controlled WEST BANK and was eventually designated the administrative center of a province bearing its name. Its population grew significantly as a result of the influx of refugees and reached 53,000 in 1966. Possessing strong nationalist credentials, Nablus became a center for anti-Israeli resistance during Israel's occupation of the West Bank. In particular, it was a stronghold of secular nationalist organizations like FATAH during the INTIFADA, when Islamic groups grew in importance.

After the redeployment of Israeli forces from the town in the wake of the OSLO AGREEMENTS, the PALESTINIAN AUTHORITY assumed control of Nablus on December 12, 1995.

Michael R. Fischbach

al-Najah National University

Al-Najah College was founded as a private secondary school in NABLUS in 1918. Its curriculum stressed Arab cultural nationalism more than did most Palestinian schools. From 1930 to 1946 the school was noted for holding an annual festival that included the presentation of nationalist plays.

Al-Najah became a teacher training college in 1965 and attained university status in 1977. A coeducational institution, al-Najah grants bachelor's and master's degrees; Arabic and English are the languages of instruction. Some 5,551 Palestinian students attended al-Najah during the 1994–95 academic year. Along with BIR ZEIT UNIVERSITY, al-Najah is one of the two most important universities on the WEST BANK.

Michael R. Fischbach

Najjada

The Najjada was a youth movement formed by Muhammad Nimr al-Hawari in October 1945. It was less political than the FUTUWWA movement backed by the HUSAYNI FAMILY.

Michael R. Fischbach

al-Nashashibi, Fakhri

politician

1899–1941 Baghdad

An important member of the NASHASHIBI FAMILY of JERUSALEM and nephew of its leading member, RAGHIB AL-NASHASHIBI, Fakhri worked in the PALESTINE MANDATE government in the early 1920s. He was a pillar of the Nashashibi-led "Opposition" to the HUSAYNI FAMILY during the Mandate and was an official in a number of Opposition organizations, such as the LITERARY SOCIETY, the Palestinian Arab National Party, and the NATIONAL DEFENSE PARTY. Nashashibi also led fierce propaganda campaigns against the Husaynis and their leader, AL-HAJJ AMIN AL-HUSAYNI.

Although he joined in the Arab revolt of 1936, Nashashibi later supported Britain's 1937 partition plan and became a leading organizer of the anti-Husayni "Peace Gangs" in 1938. During World War II, Nashashibi helped recruit Palestinians into the British army. Hated by followers of Husayni and accused of collaborating with the Zionists, Nashashibi was assassinated in Baghdad in 1941.

Michael R. Fischbach

al-Nashashibi, Raghib

politician

1883–1951 Jerusalem

Hailing from one of Jerusalem's most prominent families, al-Nashashibi studied engineering and worked as an engineer for the Jerusalem district for the Ottoman government. He later represented the Jerusalem province for the Ottoman Parliament in 1914 and served in the Ottoman military during World War I.

Al-Nashashibi was appointed mayor of JERUSALEM by British military authorities in 1920 after their dismissal of MUSA KAZIM AL-HUSAYNI. He served as major until he lost the 1934 mayoral elections.

Nashashibi was a senior Palestinian politician during the PALESTINE MANDATE and, as the pillar of the "Opposition" (Arabic, al-Mu'arida) faction, he was the rival of the "Councilist" faction led by the AL-HUSAYNI FAMILY. Al-Nashashibi helped form such "Opposition" associations as the LITERARY SOCIETY in 1918 and the Palestinian Arab National Party in 1923. He later formed the NATIONAL DEFENSE PARTY (NDP) in December 1934. As leader of the NDP, he served on the first ARAB HIGHER COMMITTEE from its inception in April 1936 until he withdrew in July 1937, when he fled to Egypt to avoid the internecine violence between "Councilists" and the "Opposition."

Although not always articulating such beliefs publicly, al-Nashashibi believed in trying to forge the best possible political settlement with the British through negotiations marked by flexibility. Consequently, he attended the LONDON CONFERENCE, 1939, and accepted the 1939 MACDONALD WHITE PAPER.

Long an ally of Transjordan's Emir Abdullah, al-Nashashibi supported Abdullah's ambitions in Palestine and served as the first governor of the WEST BANK after its annexation by Jordan in 1950. That same year, he served as Jordanian minister of agriculture and of transportation, and from 1951, minister without portfolio with authority over AL-HARAM AL-SHARIF in Jerusalem.

Michael R. Fischbach

Nashashibi Family

The Nashashibis established themselves in JERUSALEM in the fifteenth century. In late Ottoman times, the family owed its status to Uthman al-Nashashibi, a landowner who was elected to the Ottoman Parliament in 1912, and RAGHIB AL-NASHASHIBI (1883–1951), who was chief engineer of the Jerusalem district, and a member of the Ottoman Parliament in 1914. Raghib, who later became the head of the family, led the Opposition (al-Mu'arida) that sought in Mandatory times to challenge the leadership and policies of the HUSAYNI FAMILY–dominated Councilist camp (al-Majlisiyyun). Another politically active member of the family was FAKHRI AL-NASHASHIBI (1899–1941), a controversial figure whose excessive ambition, questionable tactics, and advocacy of compromise with the British and the Zionists created many enemies for him and ultimately led to his assassination in Iraq. A third distinguished member of the family was Is'af (1882–1948), a pan-Arab writer whose literary talent won him recognition in the Arab world.

Muhammad Muslih

Nasir, Hanna

academic

1936– Jaffa

Hanna Nasir studied at the American University of Beirut before receiving a Ph.D. in nuclear physics at Purdue University in the United States. Beginning in 1972, he served as the founding president of BIR ZEIT UNIVERSITY. Cousin of the PALESTINE LIBERATION ORGANIZATION (PLO) spokesman Kamal Nasir, who was assassinated in Beirut by Israeli agents in 1973, Nasir was perceived as a moderate pro-PLO figure in the WEST BANK.

When pro-PLO demonstrations broke out at Bir Zeit after the November 1974 appearance of the PLO chairman, YASIR ARAFAT, at the United Nations, Israeli authorities arrested Nasir and four others whom they accused of inciting the protests and of associating with "illegal organizations," a reference to the underground Palestine National Front. Deported to Lebanon, Nasir made his way to Amman, Jordan, where he retained his position as president of Bir Zeit University and worked out of its liaison office. From 1981 to 1984, Nasir also served on the PLO executive committee and, for a time, as head of the PALESTINIAN NATIONAL FUND.

Israel allowed Nasir to return along with twenty-four other deportees in May 1993, whereupon he resumed his duties at Bir Zeit University.

Michael R. Fischbach

National Bloc Party

The National Bloc Party was founded in October 1935 by Abd al-Latif Salah, head of a wealthy Muslim family possessing large estates in the vicinity of TULKARM and a former supporter of the HUSAYNI FAMILY camp when he served on the SUPREME MUSLIM COUNCIL in the early 1920s. The party had limited success even in Tulkarm and NABLUS, partly because the NATIONAL DEFENSE PARTY of the NASHASHIBI FAMILY dominated these areas and partly because its founder was not always consistent in his political position. At one time he advocated the idea of cooperation with the British; at other times he favored noncooperation with the British authorities in the hope of gaining support among activist young politicians who supported indefinite noncooperation and civil disobedience, believing that the British should be the primary target of the Palestinian national struggle.

During the war years, the National Bloc was almost defunct. It was reconstituted in February 1944. It remained, however, a party of old-guard political bosses who represented the interests of an upper economic stratum of Palestinian Arab society.

Muhammad Muslih

National Defense Party

The National Defense party was formally founded in December 1934 under the presidency of RAGHIB AL-NASHASHIBI, a scion of the prosperous Muslim NASHASHIBI FAMILY of JERUSALEM. The party, previously known as the Opposition (al-Mu'arida), continued to act as an anti-HUSAYNI FAMILY camp, maintaining in the process close relations with Amir Abdullah of Transjordan, and though it opposed sale of LAND to Jews and advocated limiting of Jewish immigration, advocating the tactic of conciliation and compromise with the British and Zionists. The party's slogan was *khudh wa talib* ("Take what you can now and ask for more later"). In terms of popular support, the party trailed the more influential Husayni bloc (Councilists, or al-Majlisiyyun), originally represented by the SUPREME MUSLIM COUNCIL and later by the Palestine ARAB PARTY, founded in March 1935 under the presidency of JAMAL AL-HUSAYNI. The party's main supporters were Arab mayors and anti-Husayni urban and rural elites, including Al-Hajj Nimr al-Nabulsi, Hasan Sidqi al-Dajani, FAKHRI AL-NASHASHIBI, and middle-class Christians such as Ya'qub al-Farraj and Mughannam Mughannam. Except a handful of opposition elements in Palestine, the National Defense Party was the only political grouping formally to accept partition with the Arab state linked to Transjordan, and the 1939 MACDONALD WHITE PAPER. Lack of resources, inter-Palestinian disputes, and British heavy-handedness sapped the energies of the party and prevented the emergence of a unified leadership for the national movement. Accused of collaboration, Fakhri al-Nashashibi was assassinated in Baghdad in 1941. By the mid-1940s, the party was defunct as a political group.

Muhammad Muslih

BIBLIOGRAPHY

Lesch, Ann Mosely. *Arab Politics in Palestine, 1917–1939.* Ithaca, N.Y.: Cornell University Press, 1979.

Porath, Yehoshua. *The Palestinian Arab National Movement, 1929–1939.* London: Frank Cass, 1977.

National Guidance Committee

One of the first major expressions of indigenous Palestinian leadership in the Occupied Territories during the 1970s was the National Guidance Committee. The committee was established in November 1978 to mobilize opposition to the CAMP DAVID ACCORDS signed by Egypt and Israel and to deal with the threat to the future of the territories posed by Israel's new Likud government. The committee was formed in part by the ARAB THOUGHT FORUM, another expression of a rising political and professional leadership cadre in the territories.

The committee proved to be a major bridge between local Palestinian activists in the territories and the PALESTINE LIBERATION ORGANIZATION (PLO) in exile. The committee's main work was to organize anti-Israeli activism in the WEST BANK. It consisted of representatives of local corporate, regional, and political interests; its members included mayors, journalists, and representatives of unions, student groups, welfare agencies, and the Supreme Islamic Council. Therefore, the committee was able to articulate indigenous West Bank concerns rather than merely reflecting the positions of PLO groups in exile. The establishment of the committee was an indication of the growing importance of the Occupied Territories in wider PLO strategic thinking, as well as of its new generation of leaders.

The committee was weakened by Israeli repression and by factionalism among the various groups represented in it; it dissolved after it was banned in March 1982 during a period of significant unrest in the territories that was finally suppressed by Israeli forces.

Michael R. Fischbach

Nazareth
al-Nasira

Nazareth lies at the convergence of the Plain of Esdraelon and the Galilean hills along trade and communications routes. It is the capital and most important town in Lower Galilee.

As the hometown of Jesus Christ, Nazareth has always had a strong Christian presence, attracting European Christian powers through the centuries. Thus, Nazareth was the site of considerable fighting during the Crusades, when it was actually destroyed by the Mamluk al-Zahir Baybars in 1263. In 1606, the Ottoman sultan Ahmet I struck an agreement with King Henry IV of France allowing the stationing of consuls in Ottoman cities. This and the tolerance exhibited by local rulers like Fakhr al-Din II and Zahir al-Umar led to the strengthening of the Christian presence in the town. The Cave of the Annunciation was granted to the Roman Catholic Franciscan Order. In 1730, the Roman Catholics built a church there; the present-day Roman Catholic Church of the Annunciation is the largest Christian church in the Middle East.

An unusual town in that it lacked city walls, Nazareth grew during the late Ottoman period. Its population rose from some 3,000 in 1852 to 8,500 by World War I. Nazareth was an important center for textile production and agriculture, and a great market was held outside the town. It was also an important center for Ottoman and German forces in Palestine during World War I.

The British PALESTINE MANDATE witnessed several important developments in Nazareth. It became the seat of the province of Galilee, had its first hospital constructed in 1944, and benefited from the presence of numerous schools. The Zionist purchase of the Plain of Esdraelon (Marj ibn Amir) and the subsequent loss of its Palestinian population and settlements hurt trade in Nazareth, however. Nevertheless, the town's population rose to 14,200 by 1944: 8,600 Christians and 5,600 Muslims.

Nazareth surrendered to the Haganah on July 16, 1948, after the ARAB LIBERATION ARMY withdrew, but most of its inhabitants remained. The demographic effects were tremendous in the long run, however: Israeli authorities constructed a nearby Jewish settlement, Natzeret Illit (Upper Nazareth), in 1957, and the influx of Muslim refugees eventually led to a Muslim majority in the town. Nazareth today is the capital of Arab Galilee and is a stronghold of the Democratic Front for Peace and Equality, dominated by the New Communist List (RAKAH). By 1992, its population stood at some 52,000.

Michael R. Fischbach

Nuseibeh Family
Nusayba

An old JERUSALEM family who formerly owned much LAND, the Nuseibeh had declined significantly in political influence by the twentieth century. By long-standing tradition, this Muslim family has possession of the keys to the Church of the Holy Sepulchre in Jerusalem.

Anwar (1913–1986; lawyer, politician) Anwar received an M.A. from Queen's College, Cambridge University. He was appointed to the reconstituted ARAB HIGHER COMMITTEE in 1946 and later served as secretary-general of the short-lived ALL-PALESTINE GOVERNMENT formed in the GAZA STRIP in 1948. Afterward, he held several ministerial posts in the Jordanian government, including serving as Jordan's representative to the Jordan–Israel Mixed Armistice Commission (1951), minister of defense (1953), minister of education (1954–55), governor of the JERUSALEM province (1961–63), and ambassador to Britain (1965–67).

Hazem (1922– ; Hazim; politician) After studies at the American University in Beirut, Hazem received a Ph.D. from Princeton University in 1945. Thereafter, he served in a variety of roles for the Jordanian government, including appointments as foreign minister (1962–63, 1965), a number of ambassadorships, and the post of permanent representative to the United Nations (1976–85).

Michael R. Fischbach

Nuseibeh, Sari
academic, activist
1949– Jerusalem

Member of a prominent JERUSALEM family, Nuseibeh trained at Oxford University (B.A., 1971) and Harvard University (Ph.D., 1978) and taught at BIR ZEIT UNIVERSITY from 1978 to 1988. A moderate FATAH supporter who advocated dealing with Israel and Israelis, he helped convene secret talks between Fatah's leading figure in the WEST BANK, FAYSAL AL-HUSAYNI, and high-ranking figures from the Likud government during the summer of 1987. He also suggested that Palestinians request that Israel annex the Occupied Territories and thus be forced to grant them the civil and political rights associated with full citizenship.

A leading figure promoting the new generation of indigenous leaders from the Occupied Territories, Nuseibeh took the initiative to organize Fatah "political committees" to generate support for the MADRID PEACE CONFERENCE, 1991, even before the Palestinian delegation or the PALESTINE LIBERATION ORGANIZATION (PLO) could approve such a move. In 1991, he served on the seven-member steering committee to the Palestinian delegation at the MADRID PEACE CONFERENCE. Nuseibeh heads Maqdis, the Jerusalem Center for Strategic Studies, which deals with issues that Palestinians will face in the future. He is also president of AL-QUDS UNIVERSITY in Jerusalem. He is author, with Mark Heller, of *No Trumpets, No Drums: A Two-State Settlement of the Israeli–Palestinian Conflict* (1991).

Michael R. Fischbach

Orient House

Located in the Wadi al-Jawz area of East Jerusalem, Orient House (Bayt al-Sharq) has been owned by the al-HUSAYNI FAMILY for over a century. It served as a hotel during the LATE OTTOMAN PERIOD, when it housed such famous guests as Kaiser Wilhelm II of Germany.

Orient House was selected as the home of the ARAB STUDIES SOCIETY, established in 1979 by FAYSAL AL-HUSAYNI. Because of al-Husayni's role as the chief FATAH representative in the WEST BANK, Orient House served as an intellectual center for Palestinians in East Jerusalem. It assumed a political status as well when Palestinian negotiators met there during the Palestinian-Israeli negotiations that began in 1991. Al-Husayni also began entertaining foreign diplomats and officials there, including the Turkish prime minister, Tansu Ciller, in November 1994.

Israeli officials, angry at what they perceived as violations of agreements reached during peace talks that forbade the Palestinians from conducting political business from Jerusalem, tried to prevent Orient House's use as a political center and made it a central issue in ongoing talks with the PALESTINIAN AUTHORITY. However, tensions over the Orient House eased when Ehud Barak was elected prime minister in 1999.

Michael R. Fischbach

Oslo Agreements

As the public Israeli-Palestinian negotiation set in motion by the 1991 MADRID PEACE CONFERENCE dragged on inconclusively in Washington, D.C., in 1992 and 1993, Norwegian foreign minister Johan Jorgen Holst arranged for secret talks in Oslo between two Israeli academics, Yair Hirschfeld and Ron Pundik, and the PALESTINE LIBERATION ORGANIZATION (PLO) official AHMAD QURAY, who maintained contact with PLO chairman YASIR ARAFAT. Eventually, Israeli foreign minister Shimon Peres, on behalf of Prime Minister Yitzhak Rabin, entered the talks, which were kept secret from the world and from the Israeli and Palestinian negotiators in Washington, D.C.

By August 1993, the two sides had agreed on a Declaration of Principles outlining an Israeli redeployment from parts of the occupied WEST BANK and the GAZA STRIP and the establishment of a provisional Palestinian self-rule government. Israel and the PLO would publicly recognize one another and negotiate a series of agreements to finalize these arrangements. Final status issues, such as the borders between the Palestinian entity and Israel; the return of Palestinian REFUGEES; Jewish settlements in the Occupied Territories; the future of JERUSALEM; and the question of eventual statehood for the Palestinian entity, were to be negotiated at a later date.

Peres and Quray initialed an agreement in Oslo in August 1993. This was followed by a September 9 letter from Arafat to Rabin pledging that the PLO recognized both Israel and UNITED NATIONS SECURITY COUNCIL RESOLUTION 242, stating that the PLO renounced TERRORISM and violence, and declaring that it would amend the portions of the PALESTINE NATIONAL CHARTER that called for the destruction of Israel. Rabin in turn wrote to Arafat on September 12 that Israel recognized the PLO and would commence further negotiations with it.

Once news of the secret talks was made public in late August 1993, the United States offered to host a ceremony at which the Declaration of Principles, also called the Oslo accords, would be signed. Israeli, American, Russian, and Palestinian officials, including Arafat, hitherto persona non grata in the United States, gathered at the White House on September 13, 1993, for the signing ceremony.

The Oslo peace process produced several subsequent Israeli-PLO agreements:

- The Gaza-Jericho Agreement (also called the Cairo accords), signed May 4, 1994
- The Transfer of Powers, signed August 29, 1994
- The Interim Agreement and Elections (also called the Taba accords or Oslo II accords), signed September 28, 1995
- The Protocol Concerning the Redeployment in Hebron, signed January 15, 1997
- The Wye River agreements, signed October 23, 1998
- The Sharm al-Shaykh Memorandum, signed September 9, 1999

Michael R. Fischbach

Ottoman Palestine See LATE OTTOMAN PERIOD.

P

Palestine Communist Party

Jews and Palestinians founded the Palestine Communist Party (PCP) in 1922, but tensions between the two communities resulted in a breakup in 1943, when most of the Palestinian members organized the National Liberation League (NLL). After the ARAB-ISRAELI WAR OF 1948, when Jordan annexed the WEST BANK, some members of the NLL formed the Jordan Communist Party in 1951. Communists in the GAZA STRIP maintained a true Palestinian identity with the creation of the Communist Party of Gaza; Palestinians in Israel joined the Israeli Communist Party. It was not until after the 1967 war that the question of forming a separate Palestinian communist party was raised as a result of Arab communist support for UNITED NATIONS SECURITY COUNCIL RESOLUTION 242. The armed Palestinian resistance was suspicious of this resolution because it upheld in principle support of the partition plan adopted by the United Nations General Assembly in November 1947.

The communists of Jordan played an important role in the struggle against the Israeli occupation, notably in the creation of the Palestine National Front in August 1973. During the summer of 1975, the Jordanian Communist Party transformed its branch in the West Bank into the Palestine Communist Organization. However, struggles within the Jordanian Communist Party led in February 1982 to the establishment of the revived PCP, which would include the communists from Gaza. The new PCP affirmed its total support for the PALESTINE LIBERATION ORGANIZATION (PLO) claim to be the "sole legitimate representative of the Palestinian people." Its members favored recognition of Israel. Its leadership inside the territories exercised real influence, and on several occasions the PCP came into conflict—notably for control of the unions—with FATAH, which feared the emergence of alternative political leadership to the PLO in the Occupied Territories.

A representative of the PCP, Sulayman Najjab, was elected to the PLO Executive Committee for the first time in April 1987. After the breakup of the Soviet Union, the PCP was renamed the Palestine Peoples Party (PPP). Its secretary-general is Bashir Barghuthi, a journalist from RAMALLAH. The PPP supports but is critical of the OSLO AGREEMENTS.

Alain Gresh

Palestine Liberation Army

The Palestine Liberation Army (PLA) was established in 1964 as the regular armed forces of the newly created PALESTINE LIBERATION ORGANIZATION (PLO). It consisted of three groups of forces, often called "brigades," trained and deployed by host Arab states: the Qadisiyya Forces in Iraq, the Hittin Forces in Syria, and the Ayn Jalut Forces in Egypt.

By the June ARAB-ISRAELI WAR OF 1967, there were some 7,000 troops in the PLA. Forces from Ayn Jalut fought in the GAZA STRIP during that war, and afterward units from Qadisiyya were moved to Jordan to bolster Jordanian defenses. The PLA's numbers were reduced to some 4,000 after the fighting.

The PLA later saw action during the PLO Jordanian fighting in September 1970 and July 1971. Egypt airlifted Ayn Jalut to Syria to assist the PLO, but it never saw action. Units from Qadisiyya in Jordan and Hittin entering from Syria fought with the PLO. After Syria's decision to withhold air cover, Hittin's thrust was blunted by Jordanian forces. It and Qadisiyya withdrew to Syria along with other Palestinian forces and remained stationed there after the Palestinian defeat, while Ayn Jalut returned to Egypt. Jordan regrouped former PLA forces remaining in the country into the Zayd bin Haritha Forces in 1971; however, the PLO did not immediately recognize them. By the late 1970s, however, all PLA forces in Jordan were recognized by the PLO and referred to as the Badr Forces.

The PLO established its new headquarters in Beirut after 1971. Although few PLA troops loyal to the PLO were stationed in Lebanon, the PLO did establish a small PLA unit in the "Fatah-land" region of southern Lebanon (the Mus'ab bin Umayr unit). Total PLA strength in 1971 stood at approximately 5,000 troops. During the October 1973 Arab-Israeli war, PLA units stationed in Egypt and Syria fought on the Sinai and Golan fronts, respectively.

The most significant issues facing the PLA into the mid-1970s continued to be political. Political problems had emerged even earlier: when guerrilla organizations like FATAH took over the PLO after the 1967 war, tensions arose between the PLA and the new PLO leadership. These tensions lasted until the Jordanian-Palestinian crisis of 1970–71.

Even more serious was the degree of control exercised over the PLA by the Arab states. Although the PLO theoretically controlled PLA forces, those located outside Lebanon were in fact subject to orders from the host states. Hittin and Qadisiyya forces in Syria were under complete Syrian control by 1971. When the PLO supported the leftist coalition during the 1975–76 Lebanese civil war, Egypt and Iraq sent PLA forces to fight with the PLO. Syria sent units from Hittin and Qadisiyya as well, although it eventually ordered them to end the civil war in 1976 by fighting against the PLO to stem a Palestinian leftist victory. The spectacle of inter-Palestinian fighting prompted many in Qadisiyya and Hittin to desert the Syrians and join the PLO.

These problems resurfaced during the 1980s: during the Syrian-supported mutiny within the Fatah movement in Lebanon in late 1983, some Hittin troops in Lebanon refused to follow Syrian orders and fight alongside the mutineers, deserting to forces loyal to the Fatah/PLO head, YASIR ARAFAT, instead.

PLA forces under PLO control in Lebanon underwent considerable change after 1976. The PLO reorganized the Syrian-controlled PLA troops that had defected into the Shaqif Forces and the Armored Regiment. By the late 1970s, Arafat had ordered Fatah to merge its logistical and administrative units with the PLA as part of a general regularization of Palestinian guerrilla forces. PLA strength reached some 7,000 by 1979. This process continued after the 1982 Israeli invasion of Lebanon.

After seeing action in Beirut during the invasion, several thousand PLA troops withdrew from the city along with all other Palestinian forces and were redeployed in several Arab countries. Some formations were given new names, like the Aqsa Forces in Iraq; others were assigned old names. The Fatah-PLA merger was completed soon after Fatah integrated its fighting units into the PLA. At its 1983 meeting in Algiers, the PALESTINE NATIONAL COUNCIL changed the PLA's name to the Palestinian National Liberation Army (PNLA) to reflect the merger (Fatah's official name is the Palestinian National Liberation Movement). PNLA forces stood at some 8,500 in 1983, and by 1993 were stationed in eight Arab countries.

The 1993 Israel-PLO accords allowed the newly created PALESTINIAN AUTHORITY in Gaza and Jericho to deploy PNLA troops as part of its security forces. In May 1994, troops from Aqsa in Iraq moved into Jericho, and troops from Ayn Jalut and Hittin in Egypt, and Badr in Jordan, moved into Gaza. By the mid-1990s, total PNLA strength stood at close to 7,000. This includes the several thousand PLA troops remaining in Syria, including those in a new formation called the Ajnadayn Forces that was formed after 1982.

Michael R. Fischbach

BIBLIOGRAPHY

Sayigh, Yezid. *Armed Struggle and the Search for State: The Palestinian National Movement, 1949–1993.* Institute for Palestine Studies series. Oxford: Oxford University Press, 1997.

Palestine Liberation Front

The Palestine Liberation Front (Jabhat al-tahrir al-filastiniyya) was formed in April 1977 as the result of a schism within the POPULAR FRONT FOR THE LIBERATION OF PALESTINE–GENERAL COMMAND (PFLP-GC).

The PLF was founded in the context of intense Syrian–Iraqi rivalry for influence within the Palestinian national movement and, more precisely, Baghdad's success in enticing a leading PFLP-GC cadre, MUHAMMAD ABBAS (also known as Abu al-Abbas) to defect from the pro-Syrian PFLP-GC and accept Iraqi patronage. In addition, the mainstream FATAH faction of the PALESTINE LIBERATION ORGANIZATION (PLO), which was experiencing serious tensions with Damascus and improving relations with Iraq, also assisted the formation of the PLF.

The PLF's initial period was characterized by intense rivalry between Abbas and the PFLP-GC leader, AHMAD JIBRIL, for the loyalties of the PFLP-GC rank and file, a conflict made all the more bitter by Abbas's decision to give his organization the same name Jibril had employed when he first engaged in guerrilla activities in 1965. These tensions reached a climax in August 1978 when a bomb, generally believed to have been placed by the PFLP-GC, destroyed the PLF headquarters in Beirut, killing over 200 people.

The PLF has from the outset been a small group of at most several hundred active members. Although not ideologically committed to Ba'thism, it takes its cue from Baghdad on all issues of relevance. Within the PLO, it has generally been supportive of—and supported by—Fatah, although it was not allotted a seat on the PLO's Executive Committee until 1984. Its headquarters have been located in Tunis since 1982.

The PLF achieved international notoriety in October 1985, when several of its guerrillas seized control of the Italian cruise ship *Achille Lauro* on the open seas after their intent to infiltrate the Israeli port of Ashdod as tourists was uncovered. In the ensuing crisis, an elderly American Jewish invalid was shot dead and thrown overboard, and an Egyptian civilian airliner transporting the hijackers, who had surrendered to Abbas in Egypt and were accompanied by him, was diverted to Italy by the U.S. Air Force while en route to Tunis (where the PLO had pledged to "discipline" the hijackers). Although Egypt described the American action as "air piracy" and Italy refused to extradite Abbas to the United States, the entire affair did incalculable damage to the PLO.

In May 1990, on the eve of the Baghdad ARAB LEAGUE Summit, PLF guerrillas attempted a seaborne raid on a Tel Aviv beach, but all were killed before reaching shore. The incident prompted the United States to suspend its short-lived dialogue with the PLO, and to insist on Abbas's removal from the PLO Executive Committee as one precondition for the resumption of talks. Abbas eventually vacated his seat after the 1991 session of the PALESTINE NATIONAL COUNCIL (PNC), reflecting both the acute embarrassment he was causing his colleagues and Iraq's diminished regional power in the aftermath of the GULF CRISIS, 1990–91.

The PLF has refrained from open opposition to the September 13, 1993, Israeli–Palestinian Declaration of Principles on Interim Self-Government Arrangements, the only choice open to it in view of Iraq's own ambivalent position and its need to maintain its relationship with Fatah. With the emergence of the PALESTINIAN AUTHORITY, in which the PLF has no role, the PLF's longer-term prospects are questionable.

Muin Rabbani

BIBLIOGRAPHY

Cobban, Helena. *The Palestinian Liberation Organisation: People, Power and Politics.* Cambridge: Cambridge University Press, 1984.

Gowers, Andrew, and Tony Walker. *Behind the Myth: Yasser Arafat and the Palestinian Revolution.* London: W.H. Allen, 1990.

Palestine Liberation Organization

Arab governments formed the Palestine Liberation Organization (PLO) at a summit conference in January 1964 in order to channel revitalized nationalism among Palestinian exiles. The governments were aware of the growing disillusionment among Palestinians and hoped to contain their frustration by forming the PLO. Indeed, by the early 1960s, Palestinians had begun to lose confidence in the notion that Arab states would fight to regain their lost territory. The prospects for Arab unity appeared distant, particularly as a result of the 1961 failure of the Egyptian-Syrian union and the rivalry among radical military regimes. ISRAEL was rapidly consolidating its economic, demographic, and military presence. In response, some Palestinians formed small underground guerrilla cells to attack Israel. The most important of the guerrilla groups was FATAH, founded in Kuwait in 1958 by YASIR ARAFAT and several colleagues.

Establishment The 422-member PALESTINE NATIONAL COUNCIL (PNC), the PLO's policymaking parliament, first convened in JERUSALEM in May 1964. The PNC elected a fifteen-member Executive Committee, which elected as chair the veteran diplomat AHMAD al-SHUQAYRI. The PNC endorsed the uncompromising PALESTINE NATIONAL CHARTER, which sought to restore Palestine to Arab rule and refused to accept Israel's right to exist. The PNC also formed the PALESTINE LIBERATION ARMY (PLA), whose units were attached to the armed forces of EGYPT, Iraq, SYRIA, and later JORDAN. Middle- and upper-class in composition and closely circumscribed by Arab governments, the PLO nevertheless represented a critical step in the process of reestablishing a Palestinian political center.

Initially, the guerrilla groups remained aloof from the PLO. Believing that the new organization was too closely allied to Arab governments, the fedayeen (guerrillas) preferred to maintain independent—and secretive—policies. For example, Fatah launched its first raid into Israel in 1965. The fedayeen had a twofold strategy: to assert that self-reliance was the route to liberation and to catalyze popular mobilization that would shame Arab rulers into fighting Israel.

The June 1967 war transformed the situation, since the WEST BANK and GAZA STRIP fell under Israeli control and Arab armies were discredited. PLO officials were also discredited, since their rhetoric was not matched by deeds. The lawyer Yahya Hammuda replaced Shuqayri as chair in December 1967, promising to reform the PLO. During 1968–69, guerrilla organizations became dominant in the PLO because the public viewed the fedayeen as braver than the Arab armed forces in confronting Israel. Volunteers swelled guerrilla ranks after they withstood Israel's attack on al-Karama, Jordan, in March 1968.

The PLO charter, amended at the fourth PNC in July 1968, reflected the guerrillas' emphasis on popularly based armed struggle. The amended charter rejected Zionism and the partition of Palestine, termed Judaism "a religion . . . not an independent nationality" (Article 20), and called for "the total liberation of Palestine" (Article 21). The charter upheld Arab unity but emphasized that just as the PLO would "not interfere in the internal affairs of any Arab state" (Article 27), it would also "reject all forms of intervention, trusteeship and subordination" by Arab governments (Article 28). The charter could only be amended by a two-thirds vote of the entire membership of the PNC at a special session.

At the fifth PNC, in February 1969, the guerrilla groups held more than half the seats and used their new power to oust the old-guard politicians. They selected Arafat to chair the PLO Executive Committee. His views were reflected in the Fatah call for the establishment in Palestine of a democratic, nonsectarian state in which all groups would have equal rights and obligations regardless of race, color, or creed.

As chair, Arafat also commanded the PLA. PLA units in Egypt, Iraq, and Syria were adjuncts to the government's armies, but the units stationed in Jordan gained substantial autonomy of operations between 1968 and 1970. In 1969, Arafat also formed the Palestinian Armed Struggle Command (PASC) as a police force to maintain order in refugee camps in Jordan and Lebanon.

Umbrella of Diverse Groups By June 1970 the Unified Command of the guerrilla groups included not only Fatah, the largest organization, but also a dozen other groups. The most important of these included the POPULAR FRONT FOR THE LIBERATION OF PALESTINE (PFLP), founded by the Greek Orthodox physician GEORGE HABASH, who previously had been active in the radical Movement of Arab Nationalists that sought to overthrow monarchies and establish socialist regimes; the Popular Front for the Liberation of Palestine–General Command (PFLP-GC), led by AHMAD JABRIL, an army officer who had broken away from the PFLP in 1968 and focused on military and terrorist operations against Israel; the DEMOCRATIC FRONT FOR THE LIBERATION OF PALESTINE (DFLP), headed by a Jordanian, NAYIF HAWATIMA, who left the PFLP in February 1969 although he shared its radicalism; Sa'iqa, formed in Syria in 1968 in order to guarantee Syrian influence within the PLO; the ARAB LIBERATION FRONT (ALF), formed in January 1969 under Iraqi sponsorship. The only significant political force excluded from the PLO was the PALESTINE COMMUNIST PARTY, which had a strong presence in the West Bank and Gaza Strip but lacked guerrilla forces and adhered to a diplomatic stand that accepted the partition of Palestine into two states.

The PLO provided an umbrella for diverse groups, whose views varied widely. The guerrillas often worked at cross-purposes, agreeing only on the ultimate goal of liberating Palestine. Fatah focused on freeing Palestine from Israeli rule and sought amicable relations with Arab governments, whereas the PFLP and DFLP worked to overthrow conservative Arab regimes prior to liberating Palestine. Sa'iqa and the ALF were controlled by rival branches of the Ba'th Party, which emphasized Arab unity rather than Palestinian nationalism. Sa'iqa and the ALF often fought each other more bitterly than they did the other groups. The organizations also differed on tactics: Fatah, Sa'iqa, and the DFLP denounced the PFLP and PFLP-General Command for involving innocent third parties by hijacking foreign airplanes in 1969–70.

Immediately after the 1967 war, Arab regimes felt compelled to support the rapidly growing Palestinian guerrilla movement. The Palestinian cause retained such moral authority that criticism was unthinkable. Nonetheless, Egypt and Jordan accepted the November 1967 UNITED NATIONS SECURITY COUNCIL RESOLUTION 242, which accorded Israel the right to live in peace and security within its prewar borders. Resolution 242 merely mentioned the Palestinians as REFUGEES, not as people with political rights. The contradiction between PLO aims and Arab governments' policies became apparent in 1970. Washington proposed a negotiated settlement in which Jordan and Egypt would regain land but would ignore the Palestinian interests. When the PLO denounced this policy, the Rogers Plan, it collided with the two Arab regimes on which Palestinians relied most heavily.

The PLO in Jordan and Lebanon The PLO had become a state within a state in Jordan, using Jordan's territory as the base from which to attack Israel. Its presence challenged the authority of King Husayn, particularly when radical Palestinian movements called for the overthrow of the monarchy. When the PLO denounced the Rogers Plan and then the PFLP hijacked airplanes to Jordanian airfields, the king turned against the Palestinian movement. The Jordanian army defeated the PLO in a bloody showdown in September 1970. The army seized control over the refugee camps in a series of battles that lasted until late 1971 and eventually forced the guerrillas to flee to Lebanon.

The civil war in Jordan revealed the fragility of the PLO's military structure and the incoherence of its political strategy. The PLO could not find a secure base from which to strike Israel. It could not stand up to the Arab regimes when their interests clashed. Maximalist goals could not be sustained by its actual power.

Nonetheless, the fedayeen reemerged in neighboring Lebanon in the 1970s. The Cairo agreement of November 1969 regulated their presence in the refugee camps and along the border with Israel. The PLO developed a sophisticated organizational structure in Lebanon, which included eleven hospitals and sixty clinics run by the Palestinian RED CRESCENT society in the refugee camps. SAMED, the Palestine MARTYRS' WORKS SOCIETY, established and operated handicrafts and light industries that provided employment for refugees; products included ready-to-wear clothes, blankets, shoes, leather bags, toys, and furniture. Planning and research centers conducted and published studies on economic, social, and political issues; issued the academic journal *Shu'un Filastiniyya* (Palestinian affairs); and documented Palestinian history. Affiliated organizations included unions of workers, engineers, writers, journalists, teachers, students, and women. These organizations initiated activities in Palestinian communities throughout the Middle East, serving to link the widely scattered people and provide them with tangible ways in which they could express their nationalism and cultural identity. The PALESTINIAN NATIONAL FUND handled fund-raising in the Arab states among individuals and governments.

Institutional Structure The institutional structure of the PLO solidified during the early 1970s. According to the PLO's Fundamental Law, the PNC was the supreme legislative authority and met every two years. In practice, its meetings were irregular and its membership fluctuated from about 300 to over 400. About 30 percent of PNC members were from guerrilla organizations, 20 percent from affiliated mass movements and trade unions, 20 percent from the Palestinian diaspora in the West, and 30 percent from nonaffiliated individuals, distinguished intellectuals, and persons deported by Israel.

As a result of its unwieldy size, the PNC created a Central Council in 1975. Composed of members of the PNC, the approximately fifty-member council was intended to implement PNC resolutions. In practice, it also met irregularly and served as an informal intermediary level legislative body.

The Executive Committee, elected by the PNC, wielded the most power since it met continuously and its members served on a full-time basis. Each of its fifteen members had a portfolio and supervised part of the bureaucracy. The head of the Political Department served as the de facto foreign minister and oversaw PLO offices abroad. The Information Department operated a news agency, published a newspaper in Arabic, and issued publications in English and French.

Moderation Palestinian despair after the defeat in Jordan in the early 1970s was signaled by TERRORISM launched by BLACK SEPTEMBER commandos. Operations included the assassination of Jordan's prime minister in Cairo and the kidnapping and murder of eleven Israeli athletes at the Olympic Games in Munich, Germany, in September 1972. Guerrillas raided northern Israel from strongholds in south Lebanon, prompting Israeli retaliation with aerial and artillery bombardments against refugee camps and Lebanese villages.

Despite the escalating violence, PLO leaders began to revise their objectives. The eleventh PNC (January 1973) resolved in secret to form an umbrella structure in the Occupied Territories that would work politically rather than militarily to end Israeli rule. The Palestine National Front (PNF) would help residents overcome their demoralization and build a nationalist political structure on the West Bank and Gaza Strip. The PNF, inaugurated on August 15, 1973, called for "independence and self-determination" and an end to Israeli occupation. The PNF encompassed all political groups that opposed a return to Jordanian rule and accepted the concept of a state alongside Israel. Its principal components came from Fatah and the Communist Party (CP), even though the CP was not included in the PLO institutional framework.

The Arab-Israeli war in October 1973 caused further shifts in the PLO position. The twelfth PNC, in June 1974, advocated the establishment of an independent national authority over every part of Palestinian territory that was liberated but rejected the idea of a permanent peace with Israel. Nonetheless, hard-line groups such as the PFLP withdrew from the Executive Committee, accusing Arafat of recognizing Israel. Moreover, in the 1976 elections for municipal councils on the West Bank Palestinian nationals campaigned successfully on platforms that called for an end to Israel's occupation and implicitly supported the PNF.

The internal shift crystallized at the thirteenth PNC (March 1977), which stressed the Palestinians' right to establish their independent national state on their own land. Fatah had achieved paramount influence within the PLO because the PFLP had failed to mobilize other groups behind its REJECTION FRONT after 1974 and Sa'iqa had virtually collapsed in the wake of Syrian-supported attacks on Palestinians during the initial phase of the Lebanese civil war.

The PLO also consolidated its standing in the Arab world beginning in October 1974 when the ARAB LEAGUE summit conference at Rabat affirmed the right of the Palestinian people to establish an independent national authority under the command of the PLO, defined as the sole legitimate representative of the Palestinian people. The PLO's international role was enhanced in November 1974 when, after Arafat's address to the U.N. General Assembly, the PLO secured observer status at the U.N.

Setbacks The PLO's strategic shift from the goal of reclaiming all Palestine to that of forming a state alongside Israel did not have the intended diplomatic impact. It was sidetracked by the civil war in Lebanon, the Israeli invasions of Lebanon in March 1978 and June 1982, and Egyptian president Anwar Sadat's bilateral negotiations with Israel, which culminated in the March 1979 peace treaty. The civil war in Lebanon, which erupted in 1975, threatened the PLO's territorial base and forced them to take sides in an internal conflict. Palestinian guerrillas had to devote resources and energies defending refugee camps and fighting powerful Lebanese militias. The 1978 Israel invasion of southern Lebanon underscored the vulnerability of Palestinian refugees and triggered local Lebanese antagonism toward them. The Egyptian-Israeli peace accord provided for a transitional period of self-rule on the West Bank and Gaza Strip that excluded the PLO and downplayed the prospects of Palestinian statehood. Indeed, after 1979, Israel dismantled the municipalities in the West Bank and Gaza Strip and accelerated the establishment of ISRAELI SETTLEMENTS in order to destroy the prospect of Palestinian self-rule and consolidate its own control.

The Israeli invasion of Lebanon in 1982 forced the PLO to withdraw its headquarters to distant Tunis and to scatter its troops in several Arab countries. With the withdrawal of the PLO from Beirut, Palestinians living in nearby refugee camps no longer were safeguarded. In September 1982, they suffered vengeful attacks by Israeli-protected Lebanese militias that massacred several hundred civilians in the SABRA AND SHATILA MASSACRE.

The PLO was divided and weakened by the Israeli invasion. The Fatah officer SA'ID MURAGHA (Abu Musa) denounced Arafat for evacuating Beirut and south Lebanon and called for renewed combat against Israel. The Syrian government had long sought to control the PLO and replace Arafat as its head. Syria unleashed Abu Musa's forces against Arafat loyalists in bitter battles within refugee camps in northern Lebanon during 1983. Damascus also hosted the leaders of the PFLP, DFLP, and PFLP-GC, who criticized Arafat's efforts to negotiate an end to the conflict.

Diplomatic Efforts Nonetheless, Arafat reinvigorated his diplomatic efforts and formed a counterweight with his erstwhile antagonists Egypt and Jordan. He made a dramatic visit to Egypt in December 1983 after fleeing the internecine fighting in north Lebanon. Arafat also worked out a negotiating formula with King Husayn in February 1985, after the seventeenth PNC, held in Amman (November 1984). The two leaders called for a joint Jordanian-Palestinian delegation to an international peace conference, accepted the land-for-peace concept associated with U.N. Resolution 242, and called for a confederation of Jordan and a Palestinian state on the West Bank and Gaza Strip.

The joint accord was intended to appeal to the United States, which insisted on a major role for Jordan in negotiations and rejected full independence for the Palestinians. Washington, however, did not respond and Arafat was left exposed politically after making major concessions without tangible gains. Hard-liners in the PLO derided him for believing he could achieve results through diplomacy. Moreover, tensions escalated after the Israeli air raid on the PLO headquarters in Tunis on October 1, 1985, and the hijacking of the *Achille Lauro* cruise ship by the PALESTINE LIBERATION FRONT (PLF) of MUHAMMAD ABBAS (Abu al-Abbas). Although the PLF was a member of the PLO Executive Committee, the operation appeared designed to undermine any negotiations and damage Arafat's credibility. The multiple pressures forced Arafat to backtrack; King Husayn then renounced the joint accord in February 1986.

Despite these tensions, Arafat reconsolidated the movement at the eighteenth PNC, held in Algiers in April 1987. Despite Syrian opposition, the PFLP and DFLP resumed their seats on the Executive Committee. For the first time, the dovish Palestine Communist Party joined the PLO and gained a seat on the Executive Committee. Only the numerically insignificant Abu Musa dissidents and PFLP-GC remained outside the PLO's fold. The PFLP-GC continued to hijack planes and bomb European airports. The reassembling of most groups under Arafat's leadership, however, strengthened the PLO's hand in the Arab world and in the Occupied Territories.

The Intifada The PLO was thus well positioned to respond to the popular INTIFADA ("shaking off") that swept the West Bank and Gaza Strip in December 1987. Initiated spontaneously, the Intifada gained some coherence through the Unified National Leadership of the Uprising (UNLU), which included activists from Fatah, PCP, PFLP, and DFLP. The PLO leadership sensed the shift in morale and strategy produced by the Intifada and responded to its initiatives at the nineteenth PNC, held in Algiers on November 1988. The nineteenth PNC endorsed the establishment of an independent state on the West Bank and Gaza Strip, with its capital in East Jerusalem. U.N. Resolutions 181 and 242 would be the state's legal underpinning—the first time that the PLO endorsed the U.N. General Assembly's partition plan of 1947 and U.N. Security Council Resolution 242 of November 1967. The PNC resolution also called for security and peace for every state in the region and renounced the use of terror. In a December 1988 press conference, Arafat explicitly affirmed the right of Israel to exist as a Jewish state. He underlined the PNC's renunciation of terrorism. The PLO Central Council subsequently elected Arafat president of Palestine in April 1989. The United States responded by opening direct political discussions with the PLO through its ambassador in Tunis.

The combined force of the Intifada and PNC resolutions proved insufficient to change official Israeli attitudes. The Israeli government placed onerous conditions on negotiations and accelerated the construction of settlements; some cabinet members even suggested that Palestinians be deported en masse. The PLO suffered a diplomatic setback when the United States suspended its dialogue in June 1990, in the wake of an aborted seaborne attack on Israel by Abu-al-Abbas's PLF. In frustration, the PLO turned to the Iraqi president, Saddam Husayn, for strategic support. Husayn had hinted in April 1990 he would attack Israel with long-range chemical weapons if Israel attacked Jordan or deported Palestinians. Palestinians hoped that his threatened balance of terror would prevent their expulsion.

From the Gulf Crisis to Oslo Iraq's invasion and occupation of KUWAIT in August 1990 posed a dilemma for the PLO. Arafat could not condone that occupation without seeming to justify Israel's occupation of the West Bank and Gaza. Although Arafat stressed the need for Iraq and Kuwait to negotiate a settlement, he strongly opposed the presence of United States military forces in Saudi Arabia. The PLO's apparent tilt toward Iraq was accompanied by popular-level enthusiasm that reached fever pitch among Palestinians when Iraq hit Israel with Scud missiles during the air war in January 1991.

In the aftermath of Iraq's defeat, Palestinians were traumatized and the PLO was isolated. Saudi Arabia and Kuwait cut all financial aid to the PLO, Syria continued to disarm Palestinian enclaves in Lebanon, and the disintegration of the Soviet Union removed an important diplomatic counterweight to the United States. The PLO accepted the U.S. terms for the multilateral talks at the MADRID PEACE CONFERENCE, 1991, and bilateral negotiations began in Washington, D.C., in December 1991. The Palestinian negotiating team were from the West Bank and Gaza but referred to the PLO in Tunis for instructions. Negotiations focused on establishing a five-year period of self-rule, with the final status left for later negotiations. The election of a Labor Party government in Israel in summer 1992 gave hope for renewed vigor in the negotiations. However, the talks remained stalemated, as a result of the lack of direct participation by the PLO and of Israel's deportation of more than 400 Islamist activists in December 1992, which caused the Palestinian negotiators to withdraw from the negotiations until May 1993.

Just as the public negotiations foundered, a secret track of PLO-Israeli talks reached a dramatic conclusion. Meeting under the auspices of the Norwegian foreign minister, the two sides hammered out a Declaration of Principles that was signed in a formal ceremony in Washington, D.C., on September 13, 1993. Both parties realized that failure to conclude an accord undermined their own internal power and legitimacy. If Arafat could not gain self-rule and recognition of the PLO, then the uncompromising Islamists could overwhelm his movement. Moreover, Israel had finally comprehended that excluding the PLO from negotiations guaranteed their failure: only the PLO could deliver. At the White House, Arafat stated the Palestinians' hope "that this agreement . . . marks the beginning of the end of a chapter of pain and suffering . . . [and ushers] in an age of peace, coexistence and equal rights."

The agreement provided for Palestinian self-rule in the entire Gaza Strip and in Jericho within a few months, followed by Palestinian civil administration over the rest of the West Bank for a five-year interim period. Negotiations over Gaza and Jericho were not completed until May 1994, when Israeli troops withdrew and Palestinian police assumed their duties. Arafat entered Jericho in June. The transition to Palestinian self-rule promised to be complex, given Arafat's personalized style of rule and unwillingness to delegate authority, as well as the substantial institutional reforms required in order to operate a government after twenty-seven years of Israeli rule. Friction occurred between the PLO officials who moved from Gaza to Tunis and the local leaders in the West Bank and Gaza Strip, who had their own priorities and ambitions.

Prospects for the PLO The PLO has been transformed organizationally and politically since its formation in 1964. Originally the instrument of governments and then the umbrella for guerrilla movements, the PLO is now being displaced by protostate institutions. PLO aims, articulated by the authoritative PNC, have shifted from liberating all Palestine to establishing a state alongside Israel. The means for achieving that goal have altered from armed struggle to active diplomacy. With the establishment of self-government in the Occupied Territories, the PLO's raison d'être has eroded. Arafat convened the PNC in April 1996 and December 1998 to rescind articles in the National Charter that called for the destruction of Israel. Otherwise, the PLO is virtually moribund. This leaves Palestinians in Lebanon and other countries without effective representation as a means to articulate their urgent concerns.

Ann M. Lesch

BIBLIOGRAPHY

Cobban, Helena. *The Palestinian Liberation Organization.* New York: Cambridge University Press, 1984.

Franji, Abdallah. *The PLO and Palestine.* London: Zed Press, 1982.

Gresh, Alain. *The PLO: The Struggle Within.* London: Zed Press, 1985.

Khalidi, Rashid. *Under Siege: PLO Decisionmaking During the 1982 War.* New York: Columbia University Press, 1986.

Lesch, Ann Mosely. "The Palestinians." In *The Government and Politics of the Middle East and North Africa,* ed. by David E. Long and Bernard Reich. Boulder, Colo.: Westview Press, 1995.

Mishal, Shaul. *The PLO Under Arafat.* New Haven, Conn: Yale University Press, 1986.

O'Neill, Bard E. *Armed Struggle in Palestine.* Boulder, Colo.: Westview Press, 1978.

Quandt, William, Fuad Jabber, and Ann Mosely Lesch. *The Politics of Palestinian Nationalism.* Berkeley: University of California Press, 1973.

Rubenberg, Cheryl. *The Palestine Liberation Organization: Its Institutional Infrastructure.* Belmont, Mass.: Institute of Arab Studies, 1983.

Sahliyeh, Emile. *The PLO After the Lebanon War.* Boulder, Colo.: Westview Press, 1986.

Sayigh, Yazid. *Armed Struggle and the Search for State: The Palestinian National Movement, 1949–1993.* Institute for Palestine Studies series. Oxford: Clarendon Press, 1997.

Sela, Abraham, and Moshe Ma'oz, eds. *The PLO and Israel: From Armed Conflict to Political Solution, 1964–1994.* New York: St. Martin's Press, 1997.

Palestine Liberation Organization Institutions

A most remarkable aspect of the PALESTINE LIBERATION ORGANIZATION (PLO) has been its extensive building of institutions—political, cultural, economic, and social. Two of the most important political institutions are the PALESTINE NATIONAL COUNCIL (PNC) and the Executive Committee (EC). Important cultural institutions include the Association for Theater and Palestinian Popular Art, Graphic Arts, the Palestine Cinema Institute, the Folklore Dance Troupe, the PALESTINIAN RESEARCH CENTER, and the Exhibition Branch. In the economic sphere, the PALESTINIAN NATIONAL FUND (PNF) and the Palestine MARTYRS' WORKS SOCIETY (SAMED) are highly significant. Major social institutions include the Palestinian RED CRESCENT society, the Department of Education, the Institute for Social Affairs and Welfare, and the multiple unions in which Palestinians have organized themselves. All these institutions, with the exception of many of the unions, have been initiated by and remain under the jurisdiction of FATAH.

They are highly complex organizations performing a variety of roles that include meeting the functional needs of the Palestinian people, nation building, instilling the value of education, enhancing the PLO's international support, and catalyzing the psychological transformation of the Palestinians from having a "refugee" outlook to seeing themselves as self-reliant, productive, independent individuals. Organizations that meet functional needs provide health care, employment, education, and welfare.

The PLO's main political objectives—nation building—is a part of all the PLO's institutions. The PLO sees this task as the solidifying and deepening of the identification of the Palestinian people with the Palestinian nation.

Cheryl Rubenberg

Palestine Mandate
(1922–1948)

Palestine was ruled by Great Britain from 1917 to 1948, initially as occupied enemy territory and later as a mandate from the League of Nations. The Mandate was assigned to Britain at the SAN REMO CONFERENCE, 1920 after World War I, which ratified the division of the Ottoman Empire's Arab provinces between France and Britain. France gained control over Syria and Lebanon; Britain acquired Iraq as well as Palestine. Although all these territories were designated Class A mandates, which meant that they would soon gain self-rule, Palestine was placed under unique provisions, because Britain had promised the Zionist movement in the BALFOUR DECLARATION (November 2, 1917) that Jews could establish a national home in the territory.

The Palestine Mandate (approved by the Council of the League of Nations on July 24, 1922 and came into force officially on September 29, 1923)

MANDATE PALESTINE'S SUBDISTRICTS, 1937
SYRIA
Lake Hula
SAFAD
ACRE
SYRIA
Sea of Galilee
TIBERIAS
NAZARETH
HAIFA
BEISAN
Mediterranean Sea
JENIN
TULKARM
NABLUS
TRANSJORDAN
JAFFA
RAMALLAH
JERICHO
RAMLA
JERUSALEM
BETHLEHEM
GAZA
Subdistrict Boundaries
Cities with Same Name
Dead Sea
HEBRON
N
BEERSHEBA
EGYPT
0
10 Miles

emphasized the creation of a Jewish National Home. It referred to the Palestinians as "non-Jewish communities," although they constituted 90 percent of the population. The preamble emphasized "the historical connection of the Jewish people" with Palestine as "the grounds for reconstituting their national home in that country." The Mandate enjoined Britain to place "the country under such political, administrative, and economic conditions as will secure the establishment of the Jewish national home . . . and the development of self-governing institutions" (Article 2). Britain was also required to "facilitate Jewish immigration under suitable conditions" and "encourage . . . close settlement by Jews on the land" (Article 6). Article 4 provided for a Jewish agency, as a public body that would cooperate with the Palestine government "in such economic, social and other matters as may affect the establishment of the Jewish national home and the interests of the Jewish population in Palestine." No comparable public body was provided for the Palestinian community.

Although the Mandate stated that Britain must safeguard "the civil and religious rights of all the inhabitants of Palestine, irrespective of race and religion," and other articles indicated that the civil and religious rights of the non-Jewish communities must not be prejudiced, the Palestinians' political and national rights were ignored in the Mandate provisions. The right to self-determination integral to the Syrian, Lebanese, and Iraqi mandates was absent in the Palestinian case.

Demographic changes over the ensuing thirty years chart the transformation of Palestine under the Mandate: the share of the Palestinian population dropped from 89 percent, according to the British census of 1922, to 72 percent in 1931 and an estimated 69 percent in 1946. The shift in landholdings was less dramatic, since Jewish-owned land was still only 7 percent of the total land surface in 1947. Nevertheless, Zionist policies that banned the resale of land to non-Jews and required owners to hire only Jewish labor multiplied the negative impact of those land purchases on the Palestinians.

British Rule Britain ruled Palestine as a colony, under the jurisdiction of the Colonial Office and headed by the HIGH COMMISSIONER FOR PALESTINE, who had unfettered executive and legislative powers. The first high commissioner was appointed on July 1, 1920, more than three years before the Mandate was ratified by the League of Nations. The advisory Executive Council and district commissioners were exclusively British, although they had Palestinian and Jewish assistants. Palestinians and Jews worked in the administrative departments, under British heads. The only elected bodies were the municipalities and the organs of the Jewish community. Although some prominent Palestinians participated in an ADVISORY COUNCIL established by the high commissioner in the fall of 1920, they did so as individuals, not as representatives of the public. Moreover, they understood that the council was temporary, to be superseded by constitutional representative organs.

Britain controlled communication between the Palestinian residents and the Permanent Mandates Commission (PMC) of the League of Nations, which oversaw the mandatory system. The memoranda sent by the Palestinians each year to the PMC were first submitted to the Palestine government, which attached its comments before sending the documents to the British Colonial Office and the PMC. Although the Palestinians occasionally sent delegations to the league headquarters in Geneva, they could not address the PMC directly. In any event, the PMC was composed largely of colonial powers who were not inclined to question Britain or to support the political claims of indigenous peoples.

Palestinian Petitions Until the mid-1920s, Palestinian leaders believed they could persuade Britain to relinquish its pro-Zionist policy and grant the Palestinians self-government. Organized through the ARAB EXECUTIVE, they used various methods of persuasion and obstruction to make their position clear. They sent petitions and delegations to London and the League of Nations. They argued on legal grounds that the Mandate violated Article 22 of the Covenant of the League of Nations, which stated that former Ottoman territories "can be provisionally recognized" as independent nations. They also insisted that British promises of Arab independence in the HUSAYN-MCMAHON CORRESPONDENCE, 1915–16, predated and outweighed the Balfour Declaration. These arguments were rejected, however, by the British government.

The CHURCHILL MEMORANDUM, 1922, published after a Palestinian delegation spent nearly a year in London lobbying for independence, did modify British policy slightly. First, the colonial secretary, Winston Churchill, promised that the Jewish community would not dominate or impose Jewish nationality on the indigenous Palestinian population. Second, he introduced regulations to control Jewish immigration, based on "the economic capacity of the country at the time to absorb new arrivals," so that the population as a whole would not be deprived of employment. Nonetheless, those modifications did not satisfy the Palestinian leaders. Prior to the ratification of the Mandate in September 1923, they hoped to overturn rather than merely revise its provisions. Similarly, the Palestinians rejected proposals for a legislative council, an advisory council, and an ARAB AGENCY; since these bodies would be based on the Mandate, their participation would mean that they accepted the Balfour Declaration as the basis of Palestinian political life.

The constitution proposed in the fall of 1922 included the Balfour Declaration. Furthermore, the Palestinian members of the legislative council would be outnumbered by the combined vote of the Jewish representatives and the British ex officio members. The high commissioner could veto legislation, and the legislative council could not discuss immigration. That sensitive subject would be considered by a special advisory commission composed of the three religious communities, Muslim, Christian, and Jewish, which would propose policies to the high commissioner; he would not be obliged to follow its advice. The structure and powers of the legislative council did not reassure the Palestinian politicians, since they would not gain the means to limit Jewish immigration and the political influence of the Zionists. Therefore, all the political groups except the Zionist-funded National Muslim Societies boycotted the 1923 elections. Rather than form a clearly unrepresentative legislative council, the high commissioner canceled the elections. The Palestinians won a victory in principle.

The Arab Executive also boycotted the new Advisory Council that the high commissioner appointed, since it appeared to replace the Legislative Council. Moreover, Palestinians rejected forming an Arab Agency, which the British claimed would parallel the Jewish Agency established by the Mandate. The Arab agency, however, unlike the Jewish Agency, would be appointed by the high commissioner and would not be incorporated into the Mandate instrument. Agreeing to the Arab Agency would mean that the Palestinians accepted the Arab and Jewish communities as having equal standing in Palestine, whereas their fundamental premise was that Palestine was and should remain an Arab country. When they rejected these proposals, the Palestinians believed that Britain would recognize that the only just solution was a national representative government that would accord the Arabs self-determination. However, Britain concluded that the Palestinians were stubborn and intractable and decided not to make more political offers, hoping that, in time, the Palestinians would accept the status quo.

Violent Protests Palestinians also protested through demonstrations and violence. The earliest demonstrations were held in February 1920 to protest the first official public reading in Palestine of the Balfour Declaration. Demonstrations were held in March 1920 to support the proclamation of independence by the second of the ARAB CONGRESSES in Damascus. The religious celebration of al-Nabi Musa (the Prophet Moses) in April 1920 degenerated into violent attacks of the Jewish quarter of the Old City of Jerusalem. Violence also flared up in Jerusalem on November 2, 1920, the third anniversary of the Balfour Declaration. In May 1921, violent clashes took place in Jaffa and neighboring rural areas. The Palestinian community also boycotted certain visiting dignitaries and stayed away from the September 1922 ceremony at which the high commissioner took the constitutional oath. A complete boycott was maintained against Lord Balfour when he went to Jerusalem in 1925 to dedicate The Hebrew University.

The Palestinians' attempts to influence British policy through delegations, political strikes, and election boycott appeared to have failed by the mid-1920s. Although British officials in Palestine took seriously this evidence of discontent, the actions had minimal impact in London, where policy was made. Consequently, Palestinians began to disagree over an appropriate political strategy. Some leaders believed they must grasp any available levers of power in order to influence policy; others held that only total opposition would force the British to rethink their policy. In the mid-1920s the former viewpoint prevailed, partly because fears of Jewish immigration had diminished. In 1927, for example, Jewish emigration actually exceeded immigration, and the danger of Jewish statehood appeared to recede.

Given their increased confidence, Palestinian politicians contested elections for the SUPREME MUSLIM COUNCIL in 1926 and for the municipal councils in 1927. The different factions joined together to discuss with a British official in 1926 a new constitutional proposal. The talks foundered because Britain refused to grant the Palestinians the degree of autonomy they sought.

Palestinians' fears revived in 1928 when Jewish immigration and economic life took an upward turn. Moreover, the British confirmed a Zionist concession to extract salts from the Dead Sea and the Jewish National Fund expanded its land purchases. The World Zionist Organization was enlarged to include wealthy non-Zionists in the United States in an umbrella organization, the Jewish Agency. Those developments led Palestinians to overlook their political differences and convene a congress in July 1928 that elected the forty-eight-member Arab Executive incorporating all the factions. The Palestinians also tried to accelerate constitutional discussions with British officials in Palestine, but the communal violence that erupted in August 1929 caused the British to cancel those discussions.

The Western Wall Discussions The outbreak of violence was rooted in the long-festering difficulties between Muslim and Jewish communities over the Western (Wailing) Wall, which was legally Muslim property and sacred to Muslims as part of al-HARAM AL-SHARIF compound. Jews also venerated it as the site of the Temple destroyed by the Romans. Jews traveled to pray and lament at the Western Wall, as the only remaining part of the Temple. Their customary right of access under the Ottoman regime (1517–1917) had not included the right to bring the full accoutrements for a religious service. As part of their growing political militancy, Jews sought to expand their rights and even to purchase the wall area. An incident at the wall on the Day of Atonement, Yom Kippur, in September 1928 escalated into a political campaign to secure additional rights. Muslims asserted counterrights and the British could not find an acceptable compromise. The final catalyst occurred in August 1929, when Jewish youths staged a political demonstration at the wall, singing the Zionist national anthem and raising the Zionist flag. Muslim counterdemonstrators the next day destroyed Jewish prayer petitions inserted into crevices in the wall, and unrelated violent incidents escalated into rapidly spreading attacks on Jewish communities in Hebron, Jerusalem, and Safad during the next weeks, causing 133 Jewish and over 116 Palestinian deaths.

The bloody outbreak of the WESTERN (WAILING) WALL DISTURBANCES, 1929, demonstrated Muslim anger but hurt Palestinians politically. The British and Zionists cited the violence as proof that the Palestinians were backward and unprepared for independence. Some British officials, however, realized that the Palestinians required a constitutional means to express their grievances if another outbreak were not to occur.

The violence also heightened political mobilization among the Palestinians. A women's congress, an all-Palestine congress, farmers' congresses, and youth congresses were held in 1929–30. The Arab Executive sent a blue-ribbon delegation to London in the spring of 1930 to demand that Britain stop immigration, make land inalienable, and establish a democratic government in which Palestinians and Jews would have proportionate representation. When Britain rejected these demands, offering only to study the land and immigration issues and to introduce certain constitutional changes, the Palestinian delegation abruptly departed.

The 1929 violence caused the British to re-examine their policy in Palestine. A British commission, the SHAW COMMISSION, 1930, led by Sir Walter Shaw, inquired into the causes of the violence. An international commission on the Wailing Wall, appointed by Britain and the League of Nations, examined systematically the conflicting Muslim and Jewish claims. A British report by Sir Hope-Simpson, who headed the HOPE-SIMPSON COMMISSION, 1930, detailed the shortage of available land for settlement; it endorsed the Passfield White Paper in October 1930, which called for limitations on Jewish immigration and land purchases. Moreover, the Passfield White Paper stated for the first time that Britain's obligations to the Jewish and Arab communities were "of equal weight." For a brief period it appeared that the government would adopt an even-handed approach to Palestine. However, secret negotiations between the Jewish Agency and a special cabinet committee resulted in

Britain's repudiating much of the substance of the Passfield White Paper. A letter from Prime Minister J. Ramsay MacDonald to Chaim Weizmann in February 1931 accorded Jewish institutions the right to hire only Jews and to lease land only to Jews; it emphasized that the economic absorptive capacity of only the Jewish sector of the economy was the criterion for immigration quotas. Even though MacDonald's letter maintained the concept of dual obligations, its provisions shocked the Palestinians. It underlined the degree of influence that Weizmann wielded in the British capital.

Rising Militancy The MacDonald letter marked a turning point in Palestinians' attitude toward Britain. The younger generation lost faith in the Arab Executive's moderate tactics. A conference of 300 young politicians in August 1931 pressured the Arab Executive to act more militantly against the British. Palestinians also resigned in 1932 from Mandate advisory committees that the British had established in Jerusalem.

The Arab Executive convened a Grand National Meeting, which called for the gradual introduction of a policy of noncooperation with all aspects of the Mandatory government, in Jaffa in March 1933. Palestinians boycotted the visiting colonial secretary, although some politicians were eager to discuss Legislative Council proposals with him. Radical groups persuaded the Arab Executive in October 1933 to sponsor demonstrations in Jerusalem and Jaffa, which violated a government ban and led to clashes with the police. When the Histadrut (Jewish Labor Federation) picketed Jewish orange groves, building sites, and businesses that hired Arabs in order to pressure them to hire only Jews, Palestinian politicians organized counterpickets and called for the boycott of Jewish produce.

A few Palestinians formed paramilitary groups to counter the Zionists, distract the British, and call attention to the seriousness of their grievances. An early example was a small band from Safad called the Green Hand Gang who hid in remote mountains in 1929–30 until they were routed by the British military. More importantly, Shaykh IZZ AL-DIN AL-QASSAM formed secret cells in HAIFA. As president of the Haifa Muslim Society and a preacher among dispossessed *fallahin* (peasants) in shantytowns nearby, he attracted dedicated followers when he called them to prepare for a revolt. In November 1935 Shaykh al-Qassam and a few followers took to the hills to launch that revolt. He was killed a week later in a gun battle with British police, but he became a martyr, eulogized throughout Palestine. His call to militant action gained wider currency.

The political and military radicalization of Palestinians increased in direct proportion to the rapidly mounting Jewish immigration that followed Adolf Hitler's rise to power in Germany in 1933. Nonetheless, the established Palestinian leaders held to a moderate course. They continued to press for a Legislative Council and for legislation to restrict land purchases. However, a temporary leadership vacuum developed when the Arab Executive dissolved after its elderly president, MUSA KAZIM AL-HUSAYNI, died in 1934. Subsequently, several political parties were formed, of which the most important were the NATIONAL DEFENSE PARTY, sponsored by RAGHIB AL-NASHASHIBI (former mayor of Jerusalem), and the ARAB PARTY, the vehicle of the HUSAYNI FAMILY.

Despite their factionalism and personal animosity, the leaders of all the parties except the pan-Arab ISTIQLAL PARTY (Independence Party) joined to present their set of national demands to the high commissioner in November 1935. That meeting took place in the wake of the death of Shaykh al-Qassam. Palestinians discussed with the British a new proposal for a Legislative Council that the high commissioner had outlined. Even though Zionist pressure caused the House of Commons to oppose election of a Legislative Council as "premature," the Palestinian leaders hoped to send a delegation to London to persuade Britain to implement that proposal. Those discussions ended after a general strike engulfed Palestine in April 1936.

The General Strike The general strike was precipitated by a chain of events: an attack on Jewish travelers by followers of Shaykh al-Qassam on April 15, 1936, followed by an inflammatory funeral demonstration by Jews in Tel Aviv and the retaliatory killing of two Arabs near Petah Tikvah. Palestinian groups in Jaffa and Nablus called for a strike. They demanded that Britain suspend Jewish immigration and begin negotiations to form a national government before they would end the strike. Residents of virtually all towns formed "national committees" to coordinate the strike effort. Responding to this grass-roots pressure the senior politicians abandoned their plan to send a delegation to London on April 21 and formed an ARAB HIGHER COMMITTEE on April 25. AL-HAJJ AMIN AL-HUSAYNI, president of the SUPREME MUSLIM COUNCIL, became its president. Local national committees, "national guard" units, labor societies, Muslim and Christian sports clubs, boy scouts, the Jaffa boatmen's association, women's committees, and various other local groups directed different aspects of the strike under the loose coordination of the Arab Higher Committee. The national committees held a congress on May 7 that called for civil disobedience, nonpayment of taxes, and stoppage of municipal government. The British authorities responded by banning further congresses.

Virtually all Arab business and transportation ceased operation. Distribution centers for grains, fruits, and vegetables were established. Government officials contributed 10 percent of their salaries to the strike fund, rather than join the strike, since they feared their positions would be taken by Jews. Frustration built up among the officials to such an extent that the high commissioner permitted them to sign a petition that endorsed the national demands. Many municipalities closed, and the Supreme Muslim Council continued only its religious functions.

Sporadic violence began in May, after the British announced a new immigration quota instead of responding to the strikers' demand to halt immigration. Violence built up during the summer despite heavy British punitive measures, which included demolishing sections of Jaffa, imposing collective punishment on villages, and detaining suspects without trial. Individual acts of sabotage expanded into engagements by small guerrilla bands with the British military. The Lebanese guerrilla leader FAWZI AL-QAWUQJI went to Palestine in August 1936, heading a band of Syrians, Iraqis, and Palestinians.

The strike lasted nearly six months, longer than any other general strike in the Middle East or Europe. Because Syrian nationalists had just wrung significant concessions from the French after a fifty-day strike, Palestinians were optimistic about the efficacy of this pressure tactic. British high commissioners had suspended Jewish immigration in the wake of the 1921 and 1929 riots, and, thus, Palestinians viewed as feasible the precondition that immigration be suspended during negotiations to form a national government. However, the British government not only refused to suspend immigration but announced new quotas. The British offer of a royal commission to investigate the political situation once the strike ended seemed an insufficient basis for ending the strike in view of the Palestinians' disappointing experience with the 1930 commission.

The strike persisted until October, punctuated by mediation attempts by the emir of Transjordan and the foreign minister of Iraq. Over time, the Palestinians realized that the Jewish community actually benefited economically from the strike. Moreover, Palestinian citrus growers faced financial losses if they could not export their oranges to Europe in the autumn. Fearing that the strike had become counterproductive, the Arab Higher Committee suggested to the Arab kings that they appeal for an end to the strike on the grounds that the Palestinians could present their demands to the royal commission. As soon as the kings issued the appeal, it was accepted formally by the Arab Higher Committee. The strike ended without any of the preconditions met but with the hope that the Arab rulers would have the weight to persuade Britain to alter its policies.

The Peel Commission The PEEL COMMISSION, 1937, entered Palestine in November 1936; its final report, issued in July 1937, recommended territorial partition. The Jewish state would comprise a third of Palestine and include all of Galilee, even though the Jewish population of Galilee was negligible. The Arab areas would merge with Transjordan and be ruled by its emir, Abdullah. Palestinians were stunned by the idea of partitioning Palestine and denying them statehood. Both the Arab Higher Committee and NASHASHIBI FAMILY party, which had just broken ranks, publicly rejected the Peel Commission Report. However, Raghib al-Nashashibi privately hinted that the might accept partition if he could become prime minister under Emir Abdullah.

The Peel Commission Report reignited Palestinian anger. By September 1937, anomic violence and political murders spread throughout Palestine. The British then used the assassination of the Galilee district commissioner, Lewis Anderson, as the pretext for a wholesale roundup of nationalist leaders. The Arab Higher Committee and local committees were proscribed and al-

Hajj Amin al-Husayni was removed from the presidency of the Supreme Muslim Council. The members of the Arab Higher Committee were deported or forbidden to return to Palestine; Al-Hajj Amin escaped to Lebanon.

Rather than destroying the nationalist movement, the arrests catalyzed the local people. Violence intensified in the towns and countryside. The arrests had eliminated the responsible local leaders on whom the British relied to control mobs, cool passions, and articulate grievances. In their place, local guerrilla bands sprang up and coalesced into regional groups. There were little coordination and considerable rivalry among regional commanders. The commanders also vied for support from Damascus, where the rump Arab Higher Committee established itself and attempted to supply military equipment and funds for the *mujahidin* (fighters). Although al-Hajj Amin was living in exile, he remained the leader of the national movement.

The rebellion peaked in the summer and early fall of 1938, encompassing most of the countryside. Rebels infiltrated into towns and forced government offices, post offices, banks, and police stations to close. The Old City of Jerusalem was placed under a five-day siege in October 1938 before the rebels were rooted out.

To contain the popular insurrection, the British increased troop numbers and built a wire fence along the border with Syria. They searched villages, demolished houses whose owners were suspected of harboring rebels or weapons, and held hundreds of suspects in detention camps without trial. However, the main reason that the revolt lost momentum was the report of the WOODHEAD COMMISSION, 1938, which found partition unfeasible on technical grounds. Britain then announced that it would reassess the whole political situation at a Round Table Conference in London. Palestinians felt the revolt, which had cost the lives of over 3,000 Palestinians, had achieved a political victory.

The 1939 White Paper The LONDON CONFERENCE was attended by delegates from the Zionist movement, Palestinians, and Arab officials from Egypt, Iraq, Saudi Arabia, Transjordan, and Yemen. The Zionist leaders and Arabs met separately with the British negotiators. Both sides rejected the MACDONALD WHITE PAPER that the British issued in May 1939, after the conference had disbanded. Under its terms, Palestine would become independent in ten years if conditions permitted. Moreover, the Palestinians would have to approve Jewish immigration after a five-year quota was filled, and the British would restrict Jewish land purchases. The Zionist leaders denounced the British for withdrawing the promise of partition and statehood; they refused to let their future depend on the goodwill of the Palestinians. Many Palestinians felt privately they should accept the White Paper, but Al-Hajj Amin argued that it did not contain a guaranteed time limit. Moreover, he remained persona non grata to Britain, which had refused to invite him to the conference.

The White Paper proved a pyrrhic victory for the Palestinians. By 1939 the Jewish community in Palestine was too strong and too well mobilized to be contained. Jewish activists responded to the White Paper with strikes, bombs in Palestinian markets, terrorist attacks on some Palestinian villages, increased clandestine military training, and massive propaganda efforts in Europe and the United States. The Palestinian community was weakened, politically and economically, by the two years of the revolt. Exhausted, and lacking effective leadership inside the country, Palestinians could not act to benefit politically from the White Paper. The outbreak of World War II in the fall of 1939 would affect the future of Palestine dramatically.

Disarray During World War II During the war years, serious divisions among the Husaynis, the Nashashibis, and Istiqlal Party members prevented Palestinian leaders from forming a common front. Husayni supporters were in disarray because al-Hajj Amin fled to Germany, where he collaborated with the Axis powers, and the British detained JAMAL AL-HUSAYNI in Southern Rhodesia. Moreover the British banned political activity during most of the war years.

Toward the end of the war, Arab rulers intervened to impose a semblance of unity. In 1944, a Syrian leader induced Istiqlal leaders and Husayni supporters to accept the appointment of MUSA AL-ALAMI as the Palestinian delegate to the Alexandria conference that established the ARAB LEAGUE. Alami then took charge of league efforts to establish information offices abroad and buy land in Palestine: he earned the enmity of both the Husaynis and the Istiqlal for his refusal to place his activities under their control. Despite Alami's efforts to chart an independent course, his projects came under the supervision of the Arab Higher Committee, which the Arab League reconstituted and funded in 1946. Although the Husaynis soon dominated the revived Arab Higher Committee, the British did not allow al-Hajj Amin al-Husayni to return to Palestine.

The Palestinian politicians did not lay out a systematic plan to counter the recommendations of the ANGLO-AMERICAN COMMISSION, 1945–1946, which called for establishing a unitary state, ending restrictions on Jewish land purchase, and admitting 100,000 Jewish refugees from Europe immediately. The Palestinians also did not organize any coherent opposition to the United Nations (U.N.) Special Committee's recommendation of partition in September 1947, which was endorsed by the General Assembly in November. That plan called for the Jewish state to cover 55 percent of Palestine, although Jews were only a third of the total population and owned 7 percent of the land. Moreover, the area allotted to the Jewish state included as many Palestinian residents as Jews. The Palestinian state would cover 40 percent of the land, and the final 5 percent would compose a U.N.-administered zone centered on Jerusalem.

The Arab states sketched general plans to support the Palestinians diplomatically but lacked a clear-cut and coordinated strategy. Local committees, which had led the 1936 strike, were not revived until December 1947. Not until April 1948 did the Arab Higher Committee propose that Arab civil servants assume control of their departments once Britain evacuated Palestine in May. Efforts were made to renew guerrilla warfare in the countryside under Abd al-Qadir al-Husayni, son of Musa Kazim, and Fawzi al-Qawuqji, the commander of 1936. Qawuqji headed the Arab League–sponsored ARAB LIBERATION ARMY; however, the major Haganah offensive in April 1948 killed Abd al-Qadir and overran Palestinian urban centers such as ACRE, HAIFA, TIBERIAS, SAFAD, and JAFFA, before the British officially withdrew on May 14 and the state of Israel was proclaimed.

In the ensuing fighting between Israel and the Arab armies, only the seacoast around Gaza and the central hill region were held by the Arabs, effectively reducing the Palestinian areas to 23 percent of the land. In addition, at least 726,000 of the 1.3 million Palestinians were expelled or fled into exile. The British Mandate thus ended with the Palestinians' worst fears realized. The concept of "dual obligation," briefly articulated by the British in 1930, had never been pursued seriously. Moreover, the Zionists' drive for statehood, increasingly urgent after the rise to power of the Nazis and then propelled by the horror of the Holocaust, could not be contained.

Palestinians were caught in an impossible situation throughout the Mandate period. Unable to persuade the British to grant them independence when they tried petitions, reasoned memoranda, and delegations, they also could not exercise effective pressure through obstructive tactics or violence. The other Arab mandated territories gained independence after World War II, but the aspirations of the Zionist movement blocked self-determination for the Arabs of Palestine. Over time the two communities grew increasingly estranged. By the mid-1930s the British lost control over the situation. When their imperial power waned and Palestine lost its strategic significance, the British turned over the problem to the newly formed United Nations, which deemed partition the only feasible means to apportion the land between the two peoples. The Palestinians lost the most from that plan. They could not acquiesce to losing more than half of their territory, but they lacked the means to block the partition. In the end, they lost most of the land and their community was torn apart in the 1948 war. Decades passed before they could reestablish their political community on part of their homeland.

Ann M. Lesch

BIBLIOGRAPHY

Abu Lughod, Janet L. "The Demographic Transformation of Palestine." In *The Transformation of Palestine,* ed. by Ibrahim Abu-Lughod. Evanston, Ill.: Northwestern University Press, 1971.

Government of Palestine. *A Survey of Palestine.* Vols. 1 and 2. Jerusalem: Government Printer, 1946. Reprint, Washington, D.C.: Institute for Palestine Studies, 1991.

Hurewitz, J. C. *The Struggle for Palestine.* 1950. Reprint, New York: Schocken Books, 1976.

John, Robert, and Sami Hadawi. *The Palestine Diary. Vol. 1, 1914–1945.* Beirut: The Palestine Research Center, 1970.

Lesch, Ann Mosely. *Arab Politics in Palestine, 1917–1939: The Frustration of a Nationalist Movement.* Ithaca, N.Y.: Cornell University Press, 1979.

——. "Palestine: Land and People." In *Occupation: Israel over Palestine,* ed. by Naseer Aruri. Belmont, Mass.: Association of Arab-American University Graduates, 1989.

——. "The Palestine Arab Nationalist Movement Under the Mandate." In *The Politics of Palestinian Nationalism,* ed. by William B. Quandt, Fuad Jabber, and Ann Mosely Lesch. Berkeley, Calif.: University of California Press, 1973.

Marlowe, John. *The Seat of Pilate: An Account of the Palestine Mandate.* London: The Cresset Press, 1959.

Porath, Yehoshua. *The Emergence of the Palestinian Arab National Movement 1918–1929.* London: Frank Cass, 1974.

——. *The Palestinian Arab National Movement, 1929–1939: From Riots to Rebellion.* London: Frank Cass, 1977.

Palestine National Charter

The Palestine National Charter, *al-Mithaq al-Qawmi al-Filastini,* is a 1964 PALESTINE LIBERATION ORGANIZATION (PLO) document outlining Palestinian national demands after the 1948 disaster. It was adopted by the PALESTINE NATIONAL COUNCIL in its first meeting, May–June 1964. A special committee (*lajnat al-mithaq,* "charter committee") drafted the charter, which reflected the Arab political mood of the time as well as ideology of its framers, most of whom were notables serving as public officials, professionals, and business people in various parts of the Arab world.

The charter outlined five principles. First, it called for the total liberation of Palestine, which in effect meant the dismantling of Israel. Commitment to this goal was expressed sixteen times in the twenty-nine articles of the charter; all other goals were subordinated to this vision of total liberation.

Second, the charter emphasized the principle of self-determination. This principle, however, was not clearly articulated. The charter did not spell out whether the Palestinians would exercise self-determination within the context of an independent Palestinian state, or within the context of a liberated Palestine that would be united with one or more Arab states (Articles 4 and 10). Since the word *state* was totally absent from the charter, one can surmise on the basis of the tone of the articles and the political persuasion of most of the charter committee that preference was given to a liberated Palestine that would be an integral part of one united Arab nation.

Third, the charter offered a definition of who was a Palestinian, and whether or not this definition applied to Israeli Jews. In an attempt to emphasize the indissoluble link between the Palestinians and their homeland, the charter defined the Palestinians as the "Arab nationals" *(al-muwatinun al-Arab)* who "resided normally in Palestine until 1947," in other words, until the dispossession of the Palestinians after the U.N. partition resolution of November 1947. The charter also stipulated that "Jews who are of Palestinian origin will be considered Palestinians if they are willing to live loyally and peacefully in Palestine" (Article 7).

Fourth, the charter endorsed the status quo that had existed in the WEST BANK and the GAZA STRIP by stipulating that the Palestine Liberation Organization would not exercise any sovereignty over those areas (Article 24). The framers of the charter adopted this position because the PLO leadership was too subservient to the Arab governments, whose political prescriptions rested more on perpetuating the status quo than on disrupting it. Moreover, the principle of territorial sovereignty was overshadowed by the dream of Arab unity, which gripped the imagination of the Palestinian and Arab masses. This explains why Article 16 vaguely linked "national sovereignty" *(al-siyada al-wataniyya)* to the abstract idea of "national freedom" *(al-hurriyya al-qawmiyya).*

Fifth, the charter did not specify the means that should be adopted to achieve "total liberation" of Palestine. Armed struggle and revolution, two principles that occupied a central position in the ideologies of most national liberation movements of the time, were not mentioned. Rather, the notion of Arab unity was implicitly viewed as the principal instrument of Palestinian liberation.

The 1964 charter was amended in July 1968. The amended version was later superseded by subsequent Palestine National Council decisions based on the principle of the existence of a Palestinian state living in peace alongside an Israel confined to its pre-1967 borders.

Muhammad Muslih

BIBLIOGRAPHY

Harkabi, Y. *Palestinians and Israel.* Jerusalem: Keter Publishing House, 1974.

Muslih, Muhammad. *Toward Coexistence: An Analysis of the Resolutions of the Palestine National Council.* Washington, D.C.: The Institute for Palestine Studies, 1990.

Palestine National Council

The Palestine National Council is the highest body of the PALESTINE LIBERATION ORGANIZATION (PLO). As the PLO's quasi parliament, it defines the organization's policies and programs; indeed, it was the PNC that in effect created the PLO when it adopted at its first meeting in May–June 1964 the Fundamental Law that set out the distribution of powers among the various bodies of the PLO. The original aim of creating the PNC was to secure a seating of Palestinian political forces and individuals that would be as representative as possible.

The PNC formulated the political programs of the PLO. It elected a presidential office composed of the chair of the PLO, two vice-chairs, and a secretary. It considered the report of the PLO Executive Committee on the status of PLO institutions and their achievements, the report of the PALESTINIAN NATIONAL FUND, the budget, and all other matters submitted for consideration. Two-thirds of the PNC membership was required for a quorum. Decisions are taken by a simple majority, except decisions about changes in the PLO charter, which can take place only with the support of two-thirds of the entire PLO membership. According to the PLO's Fundamental Law, the council should meet once a year, though this schedule has not been strictly observed; it may also hold emergency sessions when it deems necessary. Because of the geographical dispersal of the Palestinians and the restrictive political environments in which they operate, elections to the PNC have never been held, but the membership does represent a broad cross section of the Palestinian people living in the diaspora as well as in the WEST BANK and the GAZA STRIP.

PNC membership has ranged from 150 to 410; at present, it includes about 410 members. Since 1969, when political power in the PLO became concentrated in the hands of the political-commando organizations, the PNC membership has represented the proportional strength of these organizations as well as of the various mass movements and associations (trade UNIONS; women's, teachers', and students' associations; various professional unions; and so on). It also reflects the relative size of the Palestinian communities in the diaspora, including large numbers of "independents," or Palestinians not affiliated with any of the political-commando organizations.

FATAH always has had more delegates to the PNC than any other group except the independents, as a result of its political and military preponderance. Because many independents favored Fatah's more centrist and nonideological approach, they tended to shift the balance of forces even more decisively in favor of Fatah—and of YASIR ARAFAT. It is for this reason that the smaller leftist/Marxist organizations such as the POPULAR FRONT FOR THE LIBERATION OF PALESTINE (PFLP), the DEMOCRATIC FRONT FOR THE LIBERATION OF PALESTINE (DFLP), and the pro-Syrian Sa'iqa, have been unable to constitute an effective counterweight to the Fatah/independent coalition. Not only are their constituencies much smaller than Fatah's, but the political differences among them tend to keep them at odds with one another and even to force some of them to side with Fatah in return for political protection or for positions in the PLO or the PALESTINIAN AUTHORITY (PA).

On January 20, 1996, Palestinian elections were held in Gaza and the West Bank under the supervision of more than 1,500 international observers, including official and nongovernment organizations. In these elections, 676 Palestinian candidates ran for a PALESTINIAN LEGISLATIVE COUNCIL and two for president. The elections produced the first Palestine council ever elected. This council represents only Palestinians living in Gaza and the West Bank, as diaspora Palestinians could not vote in the elections. Practically speaking, the new Palestinian Legislative Council replaced the original PNC. However, the new council has no real policymaking powers. It is overwhelmingly dominated by Fatah and its supporters. Of eighty-eight representatives, seventy-one are affiliated with Fatah in one way or another. Unlike the original PNC, the new council is not the forum in which official Palestinian policies are debated and formulated. For most of the 1990s, responsibility for formulating such policies was concentrated in the hands of Yasir Arafat.

During the years in which it was a policymaking body (1964–91), the PNC held twenty-one sessions. The more important have included those in 1964 (held in JERUSALEM, May 28–June 2, 1964), which established the PLO and adopted the PALESTINE NATIONAL CHARTER; in 1968, which witnessed the ascendance of the guerrilla movement and the focus on Palestinian nationalism and armed struggle, as was made clear in the session's amendment of the 1964 charter in 1969, at which the concept of a secular democratic state was introduced in a collective official Palestinian document; in 1974, which took the first step to endorsing a two-state solution and adopting a policy focused on diplomatic efforts to resolve the Israel-Palestinian conflict; in 1988, which embodied with unprecedented clarity the PLO's acceptance of a Palestinian state living in peace alongside an ISRAEL contained within its pre-1967 borders; and in 1991, which authorized the PLO to participate in peace talks with Israel on the eve of the launching of the MADRID PEACE CONFERENCE.

The programs adopted at these PNC sessions have been superseded by the Oslo agreements as well as by subsequent agreements and understandings between Israel and the Palestinian Authority. As part of the Oslo agreements, the Palestinian Legislative Council elected in 1996 was to remove in 1997 from the 1968 Palestine National Charter all references to the destruction of the state of Israel.

Muhammad Muslih

Palestine Red Crescent Society

See RED CRESCENT.

Palestine Research Center

The Palestine Research Center is an important institution that serves as a repository of Palestine's historical, political, and cultural heritage, documenting and studying the Palestine question. It was established in Beirut in 1965; however, during the ARAB-ISRAELI WAR OF 1982 in Lebanon, Israel confiscated the entire archive. In December 1983 the collection was returned to the Palestinians and was subsequently reconstituted in Cyprus.

The Research Center comprises some 25,000 volumes in Arabic, Hebrew, English, and French, in addition to microfilms, manuscripts, and documents. Its work is divided into three general areas: documentation, research, and information. The center has its own printing press and produces books, pamphlets, and an intellectual journal, *Shu'un Filastiniyya* (Palestinian affairs). Since its inception, it has published some 400 books and pamphlets in six categories: Palestine Studies Series; Palestine Book Series; Palestine Research Series; Facts and Figures Series; Palestine Diary; and Map and Pictures Series. The center translates many of its publications into foreign languages including English, French, German, Dutch, Spanish, Italian, and Japanese.

Cheryl Rubenberg

Palestinian Americans

Palestinians in the UNITED STATES probably number between 150,000 and 200,000, although available statistics are very imprecise. Except for a period of several years at midcentury, official United States immigration figures throughout most of the twentieth century have counted Palestinians together with immigrants from Arab countries. Many Palestinians immigrated since 1967, when Israel occupied the WEST BANK and the GAZA STRIP, but the United States dropped "Palestinian" as a separate immigration category in that year. Good census figures are also lacking. In any case, Palestinian Americans constitute both a small minority of the worldwide Palestinian population and a minuscule proportion of the United States population.

The first Palestinians are believed to have immigrated to the United States late in the nineteenth century. Most of the Arab traders at the Philadelphia Centennial Exposition of 1876 were from JERUSALEM, and traders from both Jerusalem and the West Bank town of RAMALLAH attended the Chicago Exposition of 1893 to sell olive wood carvings and other crafts. Soon thereafter, apparently enticed by these traders' tales of America, inhabitants of Ramallah began to immigrate. Because Ramallah was a largely Christian Palestinian town, Ramallites tended to adapt more readily than Muslim Arabs to America's predominantly Christian society. The Ramallah immigrants also shared a common religious heritage with the Eastern rite Christian immigrants from LEBANON and SYRIA, who had been established in the United States since the 1880s.

Many immigrants from the BETHLEHEM area followed the Ramallites. Within twenty years after the first immigration from Ramallah, villagers from neighboring Muslim towns, undoubtedly attracted by the success of the Ramallites, also began immigrating, initiating a "chain migration" that has sent generations of people from the same towns to the United States. These towns include Dayr Dibwan, Bayt Haninay, and Baytuniyya, which now all have sizable American communities.

Many of these early-twentieth-century Palestinian immigrants worked for several years in the United States—in the retail trades, in auto assembly plants, in textile factories, in mines, in restaurants, as peddlers, occasionally in the U.S. armed forces—then returned home for a brief time, and continued alternating periods at home with periods working in the United States until retirement. Many of these immigrants immigrated initially as young unattached men and either sent money home to parents or saved to be able to afford to get married. The wives usually were natives of the same Palestinian village and very often remained at home when the husband returned to the United States. Although many of these early immigrants ultimately brought wives and families to America, and though almost all became American citizens, most retained strong ties to Palestine. They often retired in Palestine rather than in America.

Political turmoil in Palestine in the 1940s and the creation of Israel changed many of these immigration patterns. Many who had continued the overseas commute before 1948 settled permanently in the United States thereafter. Although West Bank inhabitants were not displaced by the 1948 war, the economic dislocation and unsettled political situation caused by the war induced many who already had ties with the United States to relocate there. Palestinians who were displaced by Israel's creation did not enter the United States in large numbers, but the influx was great enough to create a noticeable change in the type of Palestinian immigrant. Whereas immigrants to this point had been overwhelmingly Christian, were generally uneducated, and were part of a chain of migration, those who arrived after 1948 tended more often to be Muslim, to be better educated, to have immigrated alone rather than as part of a chain of migration, and very often to have immigrated because, unable to live in Palestine, they had found nowhere preferable. Presumably, more displaced Palestinians would have immigrated to the United States after 1948 had it not been for restrictive U.S. immigration laws in effect from 1924 to 1965.

Post-1967 Immigration The 1967 war and the Israeli occupation of the West Bank and Gaza produced another change in the pattern of Palestinian immigration. By this time, restrictive immigration laws had been eased, and as a result, substantial numbers of Palestinians began migrating to the United States. As many as half of all Palestinians in the United States are believed to have immigrated since 1967. Many West Bankers and Gazans caught outside the Occupied Territories without the Israeli-issued identity cards that Israel made a requirement for residency were forced to make the United States their permanent home. Large numbers of others emigrated voluntarily rather than live under Israeli occupation. Still others left because of political upheaval or economic dislocation in the Arab countries where large numbers of Palestinians live.

With the post-1967 immigrants has come a markedly increased political consciousness among Palestinian Americans. These immigrants have conveyed to their compatriots a sense that Palestinians under occupation are enduring hardship and that the need for resolution of the Palestinian problem is urgent. The outpouring of American support for Israel during the 1967 war, the strong U.S. ties to Israel since then, and the unfavorable image that the PALESTINE LIBERATION ORGANIZATION (PLO) has had in the United States have also raised the political consciousness of Palestinian Americans, in many ways opening a gulf between them and their adopted home. Many Palestinians feel that Americans and the U.S. government not only do not support the Palestinian cause but actively oppose it. Although most Palestinians have become well integrated in American society, many feel that no matter how much they wish to become integrated, they will never truly be welcome. This perception of being on the outside of a tight American-Israeli relationship has tended to bring Palestinian Americans closer together and has given them the sense of being challenged to maintain their national identity. In the late 1980s and early 1990s, the INTIFADA in the West Bank and Gaza reinforced this solidarity, giving Palestinian Americans an increased sense of pride in their Palestinian heritage.

Political and Social Organizations Since 1967, and particularly in the 1980s and 1990s, Palestinian Americans have been increasingly active politically in the United States. In numbers disproportionate to their size, they have been involved in Arab-American organizations formed to fight anti-Arab discrimination, to lobby for Arab causes, and to promote greater Arab participation in the American political system: groups like the

American-Arab Anti-Discrimination Committee, National Association of Arab Americans, Arab-American University Graduates, and Arab American Institute. In addition, Palestinian Americans have formed institutes to study and disseminate information on Palestinian issues: the Center for Policy Analysis on Palestine and the American Committee on Jerusalem. Palestinians also run several charitable groups, including the United Palestinian Appeal, the Jerusalem Fund, and the United Holyland Fund.

Some half-dozen West Bank villages that have sent large numbers of immigrants to the United States sponsor social and fraternal organizations. Chief among these is the American Federation of Ramallah Palestine, which represents the approximately 25,000 Ramallites now estimated to live in the United States. Ramallites, who constitute by far the largest group of Palestinian Americans, are a close-knit community, often living together in neighborhood clusters, socializing together, and intermarrying with other Ramallites. Originally, the federation was formed in 1958 with the intent of bringing young Ramallites to a setting where they could meet and eventually marry others from the community. Over the years, the federation has become more politicized. Its annual convention still is considered a major social event for the Ramallah community—a kind of extended family reunion—but it now has a political function as well and is seen as a means not only of maintaining the Ramallites' cultural heritage but also of asserting their political identity as Palestinians. The word *Palestine* was added to the federation's name in the 1970s—a clear political statement—and two of its members usually serve on the PALESTINE NATIONAL COUNCIL, the legislative arm of the PLO.

Despite the tendency of the Ramallites and some other village groups to cluster in neighborhood enclaves wherever they live, most other U.S. Palestinians tend not to do this. Palestinian communities are dispersed throughout the country, chiefly in large cities but also in smaller towns. The most sizable communities are in Detroit, Chicago, San Francisco, and Brooklyn.

Many of the Palestinian community's leading scholars and intellectuals live and work in the United States. WALID KHALIDI, scion of a prominent JERUSALEM family and the dean of Palestinian intellectuals, is a Middle East scholar at Harvard University. EDWARD SAID, a prominent author and literary critic, has lived in the United States since 1950, teaching for most of his adult life at Columbia University. Several other Palestinian American intellectuals are well known as commentators on Middle East affairs. Palestinian Americans also have been active in medicine, in sports, and in all areas of the arts; the artist KAMAL BOULATTA, the poet Samuel Hazo, and the popular singer Tiffany are all Palestinians.

Kathleen Christison

BIBLIOGRAPHY

Abu-Laban, Baha, and Suleiman, Michael W., eds. "Arab Americans: Continuity and Change." *Arab Studies Quarterly* 11 (spring/summer 1989): 1–314.

Cainkar, Louise. "Palestinian Women in the United States: Coping with Tradition, Change, and Alienation." Ph.D. dissertation, Evanston, Ill., Northwestern University, 1988.

Christison, Kathleen. "Pulled Between Home and Homeland." *Christian Science Monitor,* 7, 14, 21, and 28 October 1988.

Hitti, Philip K. *The Syrians in America.* New York: George Doran, 1924.

Hooglund, Eric, ed. *Taking Root: Arab-American Community Studies,* Volume II. Washington, D.C.: American-Arab Anti-Discrimination Committee, 1985.

Naff, Alixa. *Becoming American: The Early Arab Immigrant Experience.* Carbondale: Southern Illinois University Press, 1985.

Orfalea, Gregory. *Before the Flames: A Quest for the History of Arab Americans.* Austin: University of Texas Press, 1988.

Zogby, James, ed. *Taking Root, Bearing Fruit.* Vol. 1. Washington, D.C.: Arab-American Anti-Discrimination Committee, 1984.

Palestinian Authority

The 1993 and 1994 accords signed between Israel and the PALESTINE LIBERATION ORGANIZATION (PLO) as a result of the OSLO AGREEMENTS called for creation of a Palestinian Interim Self-Governing Authority (PISGA) to administer those parts of the Occupied Territories evacuated by Israel pending the negotiation of final arrangements. In practice it was referred to as the Palestinian Authority (PA). It began functioning after the Israeli redeployment from the GAZA STRIP and JERICHO in May 1994.

The PA was provisionally led by the PLO chairman YASIR ARAFAT, who appointed a twenty-four-member council of ministers. It first met in Gaza in July 1994. As agreed upon by Israel and the PLO, elections were held among Palestinians in the West Bank and Gaza, including East Jerusalem, in January 1996 for a president and an eighty-eight-seat PALESTINIAN LEGISLATIVE COUNCIL to replace the provisional PA government. Arafat was overwhelmingly elected president. In May 1996, Arafat then constituted a twenty-two-member executive authority (cabinet), with slightly more than one-half of its members from the Palestinian Legislative Council.

The PA was granted civil authority over Palestinians in the West Bank and Gaza in stages, beginning with those in Gaza and Jericho. By early 1997, PA governmental ministries and departments were completely responsible for civil and security matters in most of Gaza and several West Bank towns (the so-called Area A of the Occupied Territories), and civil and some security matters in Palestinian villages in the West Bank (the so-called Area B). Among its duties, the PA issued passports and postage stamps. Security was carried out by a host of PA security forces that included former PALESTINE LIBERATION ARMY troops, exiled PLO figures, and local Palestinian recruits. By late 1990s, these forces included the National Security Forces, Civil Defense, Civil Police, Coastal Police, Border Police, Force 17/Presidential Guard, and University Police. There were also several intelligence agencies, including the Preventative Security Service, General Security Service, Special Security Force, and Military Intelligence.

Since the question of the transition of the PA into an eventual Palestinian state has been a contentious issue for the two sides, each has taken pains to define the PA's status in its own way. Palestinians refer to the PA as the Palestinian *National* Authority (PNA), the word *national* added to emphasize the Palestinians' political aspirations. Similarly, Palestinians refer to Arafat as *president,* one translation of the Arabic word *(ra'is)* used as his title in the various PLO Israeli agreements. Israelis, on the other hand, refer to him as *chairman,* because that title does not imply statehood.

Michael R. Fischbach

Palestinian Citizens of Israel

As a result of the fighting in 1948, 87 percent of the Palestinian population of what became ISRAEL were displaced. Of those who filtered back into Israel, all but 20,000 or 30,000 were again expelled. Another 8,000 were legally admitted into Israel under family reunification programs. Nonetheless, the overwhelming majority of refugees were forced to remain outside the country. In 1950, the number of Palestinians living inside the state of Israel was approximately 160,000. By the end of 1999, this population had grown to more than 1 million (excluding the Palestinians of East Jerusalem and the Golan Heights), representing nearly 15.5 percent of Israel's citizenry.

The geographical distribution of Palestinian localities concentrated within central and western Galilee, a strip of land along Israel's "narrow waist" known as "the Little Triangle," and the northern Negev is a direct reflection of the course of fighting in 1948 and of Jewish efforts that intensified over the course of the war to reduce the number of Palestinians who would be left within the new state's boundaries. Except for NAZARETH, and small Palestinian populations remaining in "mixed cities" such as HAIFA, JAFFA, ACRE, RAMLA, and Lod (LYDDA), the overwhelming majority of Palestinian Israelis live in rural areas. After four decades, however, the population of some villages and towns, such as Umm al-Fahm and Shafa Amr, have grown so much that they rank, in terms of population, as small cities.

Approximately 78 percent of Israeli Palestinians are Muslim, 12 percent Christian, and 10 percent Druze. The Muslim majority includes a small number of non-Arab Circassians. Aside from a shared identity as Palestinians, the Arabs in Israel have a great deal in common with Palestinians who came under Israeli rule in the WEST BANK and GAZA STRIP as a result of the ARAB-ISRAELI WAR OF 1967. The two communities are linked by marriages and friendship that go back before 1948, and economic networks within which Palestinians living within Israel have served as middlemen, merchants, or subcontractors for West Bank and Gaza laborers or products. Muslim seminaries in both Gaza and the West Bank have trained many young religious leaders in Israel. The "Islamic movement" inside Israel also has had very close ties to the various Muslim movements within the Occupied Territories, especially the Muslim Brotherhood and HAMAS. During the INTIFADA, Palestinians inside Israel were a significant source of moral, econom-

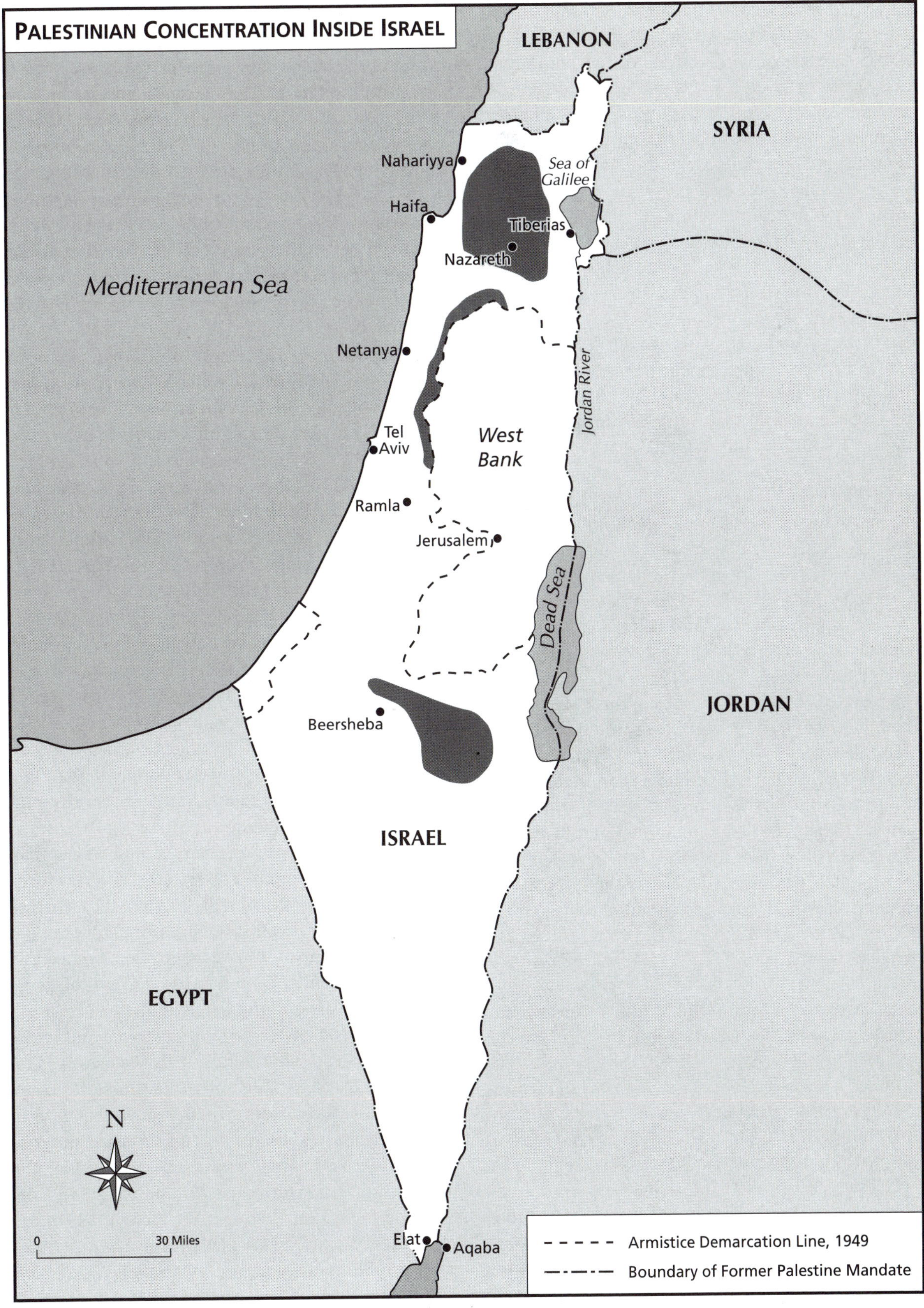
PALESTINIAN CONCENTRATION INSIDE ISRAEL
LEBANON
SYRIA
Nahariyya
Sea of Galilee
Haifa
Tiberias
Nazareth
Mediterranean Sea
Netanya
Jordan River
Tel Aviv
West Bank
Ramla
Jerusalem
Dead Sea
JORDAN
Beersheba
ISRAEL
EGYPT
N
0
30 Miles
Elat
Aqaba
Armistice Demarcation Line, 1949
Boundary of Former Palestine Mandate

ic, and logistical support for their compatriots within the territories. Leaders of the Intifada are known to have used Israeli Palestinian telephone lines, printing facilities, and financial resources to produce leaflets, sustain clandestine activities, and coordinate efforts with Palestinian leaders outside the country. Especially since the late 1970s, Palestinian Israelis also have lent what political influence they have to the Palestinian cause by voting for parties and movements opposed to permanent Israeli rule of the West Bank and Gaza Strip. Members of the Israeli parliament elected by Palestinian votes also played a crucial role in the negotiations that led to the Labor Party–Meretz government formed after the 1992 elections. That government recognized the PALESTINE LIBERATION ORGANIZATION (PLO) and initiated the negotiations that led to the OSLO AGREEMENTS.

Just as every Palestinian community has been shaped by the vicissitudes of life within its host environment, so too has the Palestinian community within Israel developed along a distinctive trajectory, reflecting in part the changes that have occurred within Israel's dominant Jewish population. Thus, the experience of Palestinians living in Israel has been shaped at least as much by their being citizens of the state of Israel as by their being Palestinians. As a consequence of the 1948 war the Palestinians of those parts of Palestine that became the state of Israel were transformed from members of the majority population into a shattered and disorganized minority within a largely hostile state avowed to be both "Jewish/Zionist" and "democratic." It was the fate of this Arab minority, bereft of the energizing influence, economic resources, and political weight of its exiled urban elites, to reveal the practical contradictions between these two images of Israel.

From 1948 to the End of the Military Government

The history of Palestinians living in Israel can be divided into three periods. From this community's point of view, the first period, from 1948 until 1966, was dominated by attempts to recover from the shock of the 1948 war and by preoccupation with economic survival and the struggle over LAND expropriation. Those living in border areas suffered greatly from the results of the border wars conducted to block infiltration from the West Bank, Gaza, and Lebanon, and from clashes between Israeli and Syrian forces. Since almost half the Arabs in Israel were legally classifiable as "absentees" under the deliberately exclusionary Absentee Property Law, tens of thousands had to adjust to the fact that, although residents and citizens of the country, they were barred from returning to their villages or taking possession of their lands. Until after the 1956 war (including the Kufr Qasim massacre of forty-three Palestinian citizens by border guard units enforcing an unannounced curfew), the general anxiety that afflicted the community was intensified by concerns that another mass expulsion at some point would be attempted.

Although formally citizens of the state, Palestinian citizens of Israel have lived, and to an important extent still live, under a far-reaching system of control. This system has reflected the view of most Israeli Jews that Palestinian citizens of Israel have been, above all, an extension of the Zionist land acquisition and settlement objectives. Until its abolition in 1966, the key institutional expression of this system was the military government. Established on the basis of the "Emergency Regulations" used by the British during the PALESTINE MANDATE period, the military government enforced a harsh array of travel restrictions on Palestinians living in the Galilee, the "Little Triangle," and the Negev. Military governors had wide powers to grant or withhold all manner of permits, licenses, and permits. These powers were used not only to maintain close surveillance of Palestinians for security purposes, but also to regulate the flow of Palestinian labor to Jewish cities and farms, siphon Palestinian votes for the dominant Labor Party, thwart efforts at independent political activity, prevent Palestinians displaced from their villages but still resident in the country from returning to their homes and lands, and facilitate the expropriation of large amounts of Palestinian-owned land.

Confiscation of Palestinian land was and is the single heaviest blow suffered by Palestinians in Israel since the establishment of the state. Large amounts of Palestinian-owned land were seized in the 1950s and 1960s via a complex assortment of laws and administrative practices, including the Cultivation of Waste Lands Ordinance (1948), the Emergency Land Requisition Law (1949), the Absentee Property Law (1950), the Land Acquisition (Validation Acts and Compensation) Law (1953), the Law of Prescription (1958), and Article

125 of the Emergency Regulations, allowing the closure of areas to cultivators.

Despite their economic weakness and political insecurity, the Palestinian community survived and managed to make their voice heard. Palestinian parliamentarians elected on the Israeli Communist Party list (after 1965, Palestinian communists formed a separate party, RAKAH) and in Mapam (a left-wing Zionist party), along with small groups of intellectuals, made vigorous protests against land seizures and demanded abolition of the military government. With the help of other tiny but vocal and sympathetic Jewish groups, Palestinian religious and local leaders also gained attention and some limited redress of their grievances via petitions, letters to the editor in Israeli newspapers, and court cases. Palestinians thereby bolstered their rights as citizens, helping to soften and then bring an end to the military government and its suffocating system of travel restrictions. They gained rights to membership in the Histadrut, established a number of important legal precedents, and constructed, under close supervision by the authorities, an array of local councils, schools, and religious courts, which helped establish an institutional and officially sanctioned basis for the communal life and individual rights of non-Jews in the Jewish state.

From the End of the Military Government to the Likud Victory The second period of Palestinian life in Israel began in 1966 with the abolition of the military government. Although the system of control remained in force, it operated more discreetly to maintain the subordination of the Palestinian community and put its resources at the disposal of the government and the country's Jewish majority. This was accomplished by drawing on the resources of the police, the security services, the army, the Arab departments of relevant ministries and of the Histadrut, and the "National Institutions" (Jewish National Fund, Jewish Agency, and World Zionist Organization). Efforts were made to expand the base of the government's influence in the Palestinian sector from traditional clan leaders and notables to educated, reform-oriented younger men who could be kept within the sphere of officially sanctioned activity as second-echelon officials in various Arab departments, in the Arab school system, and in Labor Party–dominated local councils.

Overseeing this system was the Office of the Adviser to the Prime Minister on Arab Affairs. Until its abolition in 1985, this office was always headed by a veteran of the security services. It used blacklisting, de facto discrimination, manipulation of local politics, and an elaborate patron-client system for rewarding those who were termed "positive" elements while punishing those described as "negative," "nationalist," or "extremist." Additional Palestinian land was expropriated. Discrimination in the allocation of government grants, loans, WATER rights, and access to "public" agricultural land continued.

By the early 1970s, however, a new, more assertive Palestinian leadership began to emerge. Although local elections still revolved mainly around *hamula* (clan) affiliation, younger, better educated leaders embarrassed the government by drawing attention to the drastic levels of discrimination suffered by Palestinian communities in terms of social services, grants to local councils, approved master plans for construction, employment opportunities, water allocations, and so on. Palestinian student organizations at Israel's leading universities, a countrywide organization of Palestinian mayors, and a disciplined communist party (Rakah), of hundreds of dedicated young Palestinian activists, were able to bring the political demands of Palestinian citizens of Israel into public view and, in general, give credence to the idea that Palestinians in Israel had the right, as citizens, to organize and to demand equality before the law and access to public goods. Contact with Palestinians from the West Bank and the Gaza Strip under Israeli occupation after June 1967, heightened the political sensibilities of Palestinians in Israel while strengthening the Palestinian dimension of their identity.

During this period, Palestinian citizens of Israel were not often successful in defying the government and the Labor Party establishment. However, they did force the authorities, on occasion, to admit to unfair treatment of Palestinian citizens and communities and to resort, at times, to publicly exercised force, thereby exposing the gap between Israel's claims of having an Arab minority who were prospering within the "only democracy in the Middle East" and the reality of a semisecret apparatus of control, suppression, and exploitation operating against Palestinians on behalf of the Jewish majority. The most dramatic such instance occurred in March 1976. In response to government threats of a new round of land expropriations in the central Galilee, the Palestinian mayors, in cooperation with Rakah, organized a one-day general strike. Army forces sent into Palestinian localities provoked clashes that led to six Palestinian deaths. March 30 thereafter became a day of commemoration and celebration of the land for all Palestinians.

After the strike, Yisra'el Koenig, an Interior Ministry official in charge of Arab affairs in the Galilee, wrote a confidential memorandum advising an intensified program of intimidation and discrimination against Palestinian citizens of Israel. Publication of the Koenig Memorandum marked the first time that the privately held attitudes of government officials responsible for the affairs of the Arabs in Israel gained wide recognition in a context that held them to be unworthy of Israeli democracy. Subsequently, an Israeli prime minister met for the first time with elected representatives of Israeli Palestinians to discuss fundamental issues. Although then prime minister Yitzhak Rabin, categorically rejected their proposal to view the country as a binational state, he did renounce the approach to Arab affairs outlined by Koenig and acknowledged the need for high-profile efforts to integrate the Palestinian citizens into the life of the country.

Ironically, during this second period of Palestinian life in Israel both the Palestinian and the Israeli dimensions of their political identities were stimulated. In the late 1950s and 1960s, Palestinians in Israel shared the excitement of Arabs throughout the region with the slogans of pan-Arab nationalism and the charismatic leadership of Jamal Abd al-Nasir. Israel's victory in the June 1967 war, however, damaged Nasir's prestige, dashed any real hopes that Arab military power could change the status of the Palestinian minority in Israel, and led to a weakening of Israeli Palestinian identification with pan-Arabism. On the other hand, contact with Palestinians in the occupied West Bank and Gaza Strip strengthened the community's identification with Palestinian nationalist aspirations. Many Palestinians in the diaspora had tended to view Palestinians in Israel as less committed to their cause than Palestinians elsewhere; by the late 1970s the Palestine Liberation Organization began to call upon these Palestinians to use their rights as Israeli citizens, including their right to vote, to support the cause of an independent Palestinian state. Simultaneously, the demonstrated permanence of the Jewish state and a gradual expansion of economic opportunities for Palestinian citizens enhanced their willingness to identify as Israeli citizens. This tendency toward "Israelization" was reflected in attitudinal surveys and in a public discourse by Palestinian representatives who framed demands and criticisms of government policies on the basis of their rights as equal Israeli citizens.

The Likud Victory The third period of Palestinian life in Israel began with the Likud Party election victory over the Labor Party in May 1977. It was marked by continuing inequality but also by real progress in the socioeconomic realm and by increasingly independent and influential experiments in political mobilization. Although half of Israeli Palestinian workers still must leave their communities for Jewish cities and farms to find employment, and although large-scale industry is virtually nonexistent in the Palestinian sector, retail services, workshops, newspapers, publishing houses, and other small enterprises had become more prevalent by 1990 than they were previously.

Change also is reflected in Palestinian employment patterns. Between 1977 and 1997, the percentage of Palestinians (and other non-Jews) employed as "agricultural workers" or as unskilled and semiskilled laborers dropped from 30.5 percent to 11.8 percent. By contrast, the percentage employed as skilled workers rose from 39.9 percent to 51.1 percent. The proportion employed in white-collar jobs, including administrators and managers, scientific and academic workers, and clerical workers, rose from 5.3 percent to 23.7 percent.

Politically, the right-wing victory in 1977 was both frightening and promising for Palestinian citizens of Israel. Although they worried about potentially more repressive policies in the short run, they also benefited from the seesaw battle for control of the government that ensued between Israel's right-wing and left-wing blocs. In a context of generational changes within their own elite, a sharpened sense of themselves as Palestinians, the entrenched position of Rakah and the Democratic Front for Peace and Equality (Hadash) it organized in 1977, the Committee for the Defense of Arab

Lands that Rakah sponsored, and the politically independent Association of Arab Mayors, Palestinians in Israel have sought to turn polarized political competition among Jews, between Right and Left, hawk and dove, religious and secular, to their advantage. Independent Arabic newspapers and journals appeared, Palestinian political parties became part of the Israeli political landscape, Palestinian politicians regularly were given "realistic" places on non-Arab party lists for the Knesset (Israeli Parliament), and Palestinians headed Arab departments of various ministries. Funds for Palestinian education increased substantially; demolition orders against thousands of Palestinian houses were lifted; and public pronouncements by Israeli leaders, including Prime Minister Yitzhak Rabin, drew attention to injustices committed against the Palestinian community in Israel.

Change was neither sudden nor complete. In 1980, the political mobilization of Palestinians had reached the point that Rakah activists judged it possible to move toward creation of a mass-based, countrywide Palestinian movement in support of equality for Palestinians as citizens; avowal by Palestinians in Israel of their identity as an integral part of the Palestinian people; recognition of the PLO as the official representative of the Palestinian people; and establishment of a Palestinian state alongside the state of Israel. At a meeting in Shafa Amr bringing together Israeli Palestinian leaders from across the political spectrum, a charter expressing these views was adopted. However, a representative "congress of the Arab masses," to be held in Nazareth in December 1980, which was to form the basis of a countrywide Palestinian political movement, was prevented by then–Prime Minister and Defense Minister Menachem Begin. With the support of the Labor Party opposition Begin invoked the sweeping powers of the emergency regulations to ban the congress and all meetings that might be called to discuss or protest the ban.

This was the first time since the al-Ard movement was outlawed in 1965 that the government had used the full force of the law to prevent creation of a Palestinian political party in Israel, but it also may have been the last time. Al-Ard was an Arab nationalist group in Israel in the early and mid-1960s that fought against land expropriation and the Military Government and sought to run as a list for the Knesset. The 1980 crackdown on Rakah attempts to organize Palestinians in Israel as a full part of the Palestinian national struggle and the government's refusal to accept the binational formula advanced by the Palestinian mayors spurred the growth of more radical elements, such as the "Sons of the Village" movement (Abna al-Balad) and the Progressive National Movement, which advocated boycotts of Israeli parliamentary elections.

Although since 1980 the emergency regulations have occasionally been used to impose restrictions on individual Palestinian activists in Israel, in general, intensified competition for Palestinian votes between Labor and Likud created a vested interest, among the Labor Party and its allies, in vigorous and free Palestinian political activity. This interest has protected many forms of Palestinian political mobilization from the kind of Draconian prohibitions imposed in 1980 and earlier on al-Ard. Political space thereby has been created for Israeli Palestinians to stage numerous municipal, general, and commercial strikes in support of demands for equal services and in sympathy with Palestinian struggles in the Occupied Territories. Opportunities also have been opened for politicians such as ABD AL-WAHHAB DARAWISHA, a former Labor Party parliamantarian; Muhammad Mi'ari, a veteran of the al-Ard movement; AZMI BISHARA, an influential intellectual; and Muslim religious leaders such as Abdullah Nimr Darwish of Kufr Qasim and Shaykh Ra'id Salah of Umm al-Fahm to build political parties and movements able to vie successfully for power at both the local and national levels. In 1984, Mi'ari headed the Arab-Jewish Progressive List for Peace (PLP), which won two seats in the parliament. In 1988 the PLP slipped to one seat, and in 1992 it failed to pass the threshold for representation. Darawisha's Arab Democratic Party (ADP) was the first independent all-Arab political party to win representation in the parliament. It won two seats in both the 1988 and 1992 elections.

It is widely understood that the Labor-Meretz government led by Yitzak Rabin, which came to power in 1992, owed its existence to a blocking majority that included, as a decisive element, Palestinian parliamentarians. It is now also clear that no Labor Party–led government can be formed, and no Labor candidate for prime minister can emerge victorious, without strong support and high turnout among the Palestinian voters. Accordingly, the Rabin government made unprecedentedly strong symbolic and public commitments to Arab-Jewish equality, and although some important steps were taken in closing the gap in education and municipal services, the government's performance disappointed most Israeli Palestinians. No independent Palestinian party was permitted to join the governing coalition, and many promises made in the social and economic spheres were not fulfilled. Nor were the former inhabitants of Bir'im and Iqrit permitted to return to the village from which they were removed in 1948.

Indeed one of the most popular explanations for Benjamin Netanyahu's razor thin defeat of Shimon Peres in the election of the prime minister of 1996 was that a sizable minority of Palestinian voters reacted to the government's disappointing policies and the bloody consequences of an artillery barrage directed at a Lebanese village by staying home or by casting blank ballots. Although 89 percent of the Palestinian vote in Israel went to Shimon Peres over Benjamin Netanyahu, their contribution did not quite outweigh the similarly lopsided vote garnered by Netanyahu among ultra-Orthodox Jews. In parliament, though, the Palestinian parties were more successful. Darawisha's ADP joined forces with others, including Islamist figures, to form the United Arab List, which won four seats. Rakah's Democratic Front for Peace and Equality, which has been losing support among Israeli Palestinians, formed an alliance with Azmi Bishara and his supporters along with the Abna al-Balad movement; together they won five seats. But with a right-wing government in power that owed little to Palestinian constituents, and without enough seats to tip the balance in parliament toward the Labor Party, they could score few successes.

The 1999 Elections In the 1999 election for the fifteenth Knesset, more than 90 percent of the Israeli Palestinian voters chose Ehud Barak for prime minister; however, their ballots were not as critical as in the previous election because Barak won a Jewish majority. The Palestinian parties increased their Knesset representation from nine to ten (one Hadash member is Jewish), but divisions and the failure of a strong leadership to emerge led to fragmentation of Arab political representation. The election marked the first time a Palestinian woman, Husniyya Jabarra of Meretz, was elected to the Knesset. It was also the first time that a Palestinian, Balad Party's Azmi Bishara, ran for the office of prime minister, even though it was symbolic and he withdrew just before the elections (so as not to contribute to Netanyahu's reelection). While the Palestinian political community was disappointed by Barak's failure to designate one of them in his cabinet, they were partially compensated by the appointment of the United Arab List Hashem Mahameed to the prestigious Knesset Foreign Affairs and Defense Committee.

The Future In general, although most Palestinians in Israel support the efforts of those Zionist parties working for implementation of the Oslo agreements, they fear that once their political services no longer are needed they will be returned to the sidelines of public life and will suffer disproportionately from the state's efforts to absorb the huge wave of Russian and Ethiopian immigration. Nor do all Palestinians in Israel share a commitment to full integration, including service in the armed forces. Some of them have raised the slogan of Palestinian cultural or other forms of autonomy within the Green Line. Others consider this a dangerous position, likely to be used by extremist Jewish groups to deny equal citizenship rights to Palestinians. Whether or not this view of Arab-Jewish relations prevails, the fact that it is raised and discussed freely indicates just how much wider the effective boundaries of Palestinian life within Israel became in the 1990s compared to those in previous decades.

The future of the Palestinians in Israel will be determined in large measure by the role they are allowed to play in the achievement of peace. To the extent their participation in this process helps to establish them as a legitimate part of the Israeli public, they will be better able to protect and improve their economic and political position in the postpeace environment. If they are excluded from the process, the Israel that emerges is more likely to be a society less tolerant of a non-Jewish presence within its smaller borders. As always, a crucial element will be the extent of political unity displayed by the community. As the appeal of Rakah fades, Palestinians in Israel are confronted with the same struggle between Islamist populism and secularly oriented nationalism that is arising in almost every Middle Eastern country. Managing this division, in addition to the kinship, communal, and local attachments that always have hindered efforts at united political action, largely will determine whether Palestinian electoral clout can be translated into an effective struggle for equal rights as Israeli citizens and Palestinian nationals.

Ian S. Lustick

BIBLIOGRAPHY

el-Asmal, Fouzi. *To Be an Arab in Israel.* Beirut: Institute for Palestine Studies, 1978.

Grossman, David. *Sleeping on a Wire: Conversation with Palestinians in Israel.* New York: Farrar, Straus & Giroux, 1993.

Haidar, Aziz. *Social Welfare Services for Israel's Arab Population.* Boulder, Colo.: Westview Press, 1989.

al-Haj, Majid. *Social Change and Family Processes: Arab Communities in Shefar-Am.* Boulder, Colo.: Westview Press, 1987.

al-Haj, Majid, and Henry Rosenfeld. *Arab Local Government in Israel.* Boulder, Colo.: Westview Press, 1990.

Jiryis, Sabri. *The Arabs in Israel.* New York: Monthly Review, 1976.

Khalidi, Raja. *The Arab Economy in Israel: The Dynamics of a Regional Development.* New York: Croom Helm, 1988.

Kretzmer, David. *The Legal Status of the Arabs in Israel.* Boulder, Colo.: Westview Press, 1990.

Landau, Jacob M. *The Arabs in Israel: A Political Study.* Oxford: Oxford University Press, 1969.

Lustick, Ian. *Arabs in the Jewish State: Israel's Control of a National Minority.* Austin: University of Texas Press, 1980.

Mari'i, Sami K. *Arab Education in Israel.* Syracuse N.Y.: Syracuse University Press, 1978.

Nabhleh, Khalil, and Elia Zureik. *The Sociology of the Palestinians.* New York: St. Martin's Press, 1980.

Rekhes, Elie, ed. "The Arab Minority in Israel: Dilemmas of Political Orientation and Social Change." *Asian and African Studies* 27, 1 and 2 (March/July 1993).

——. *Arabs and Jews in Israel.* Vol. 1. *Conflicting and Shared Attitudes in a Divided Society.* Boulder, Colo.: Westview Press, 1989.

——. *Arabs and Jews in Israel.* Vol. 2. *Change and Continuity in Mutual Intolerance.* Boulder, Colo.: Westview Press, 1989.

Smooha, Sammy. *Social Research on Arabs in Israel, 1977–1982: A Bibliography.* Vol. 2. Haifa: The Jewish Arab Center, University of Haifa, 1984.

Zureik, Elia T. *The Palestinians in Israel: Study in Internal Colonialism.* London: Routledge & Kegan Paul, 1979.

Palestinian Legislative Council

The Israeli-Palestinian Interim Agreement on the WEST BANK and the GAZA STRIP of September 1995 (known as the Oslo II accord) declared that, on the redeployment of Israeli occupation forces, a Palestinian council would assume power over Palestinian life in the Occupied Territories of the West Bank and Gaza. The council would possess both legislative and executive authority. To prepare for the election of the council, the PALESTINIAN AUTHORITY (PA) that had functioned as a temporary government in the territories since May 1994 organized elections, which took place on January 20, 1996.

The elections were greeted with considerable enthusiasm by the population of Gaza and the West Bank, including East Jerusalem. Voters chose among 672 candidates vying for eighty-eight seats from sixteen electoral districts. The balloting was considered free and fair, with international observers present at voting stations. Voter participation was high: some 88 percent of eligible voters in Gaza and 70 percent in the West Bank and East Jerusalem participated. Official FATAH candidates won fifty two of the seats, and Fatah dissidents and independents took another sixteen; the remainder of the seats were captured by Islamists and independents.

The Palestinian Legislative Council (PLC) inaugurated its first session on March 7, 1996, in Gaza. AHMAD QURAY was chosen as the PLC's first speaker. The PLC later confirmed the executive authority (cabinet) chosen by PA president YASIR ARAFAT. The PLC has held its two annual sessions both in Ramallah and in Gaza, although its actual meetings have taken place in cities throughout the West Bank and Gaza to keep it and its representatives in close contact with the populace.

A major challenge faced early by the PLC was its uneasy relationship with Arafat, the executive authority, and the PA's security apparati. The PLC was frustrated in the struggle waged by some of its members to provide significant input into the decision-making process in the West Bank and Gaza. Few major pieces of legislation enacted by the PLC had been ratified by Arafat by late 1999. The PLC adopted numerous drafts of the Basic Law, only to face delays in its ratification. The PLC was also active in passing recommendations and conducting investigations into corruption and abuses by PA security forces, the most notable of which was its July 1997 call for Arafat to dismiss his entire cabinet and bring charges against one member for corruption. Arafat, however, rebuffed the PLC's call.

Michael R. Fischbach

Palestinian National Fund

The Palestinian National Fund (PNF) was established in 1964 by the first meeting of the PALESTINE NATIONAL COUNCIL in order to finance the activities of the PALESTINE LIBERATION ORGANIZATION (PLO). First headed by the Palestinian banker Abd al-Majid SHOMAN, the PNF has been directed by Jawad Ghusayn since 1984. Its main office was in Damascus until 1983, but it has since dispersed its offices throughout Europe and the Middle East.

The PNF's income has been derived from four main sources over the years: contributions pledged by Arab states, donations from wealthy Palestinians, a "liberation tax" assessed on expatriate Palestinians working in certain Arab countries that is then channeled to the PNF, and profits from PNF investments. With the funds at its disposal, the PNF finances a number of PLO activities and institutions, including the PALESTINE LIBERATION ARMY, the Palestine RED CRESCENT society, the PALESTINIAN RESEARCH CENTER, schools, and hospitals. It also provided funds to assist Palestinians living in the Occupied Territories during the Israeli occupation. The PNF has represented the PLO in Arab and international financial organizations.

Michael R. Fischbach

Palestinian National Salvation Front

The Palestinian National Salvation Front (PNSF) was established in Damascus in March 1985 to oppose the February 1985 accords reached by the PALESTINE LIBERATION ORGANIZATION (PLO) chair, YASIR ARAFAT, and Jordan's King Husayn, accords that called for a confederated Jordanian-Palestinian state in the Occupied Territories. Backed by SYRIA, whose relations with the PLO were frosty, the PNSF comprised the POPULAR FRONT FOR THE LIBERATION OF PALESTINE (PFLP) and the organizations formerly grouped in the National Alliance: the POPULAR FRONT FOR THE LIBERATION OF PALESTINE-GENERAL COMMAND, the PALESTINIAN POPULAR STRUGGLE FRONT, SAI'QA, and Fatah Uprising (Abu Musa group). The PALESTINE LIBERATION FRONT joined as well.

The PFLP left the PNSF in 1987. Although the PNSF and its leader, Khalid al-Fahum, continued to issue statements into the early 1990s, its role as the main challenger to the PLO's position was eclipsed by the formation of the National Democratic and Islamic Front (the "Damascus Ten") in 1993.

Michael R. Fischbach

Palestinian Popular Struggle Front

Established in early 1968 by Bahjat Abu Gharbiyya and Fayiz Hamdan, the Palestinian Popular Struggle Front (PPSF) (sometimes referred to as Popular Struggle Front) was long associated with hard-line Palestinian and Arab positions vis-à-vis the ARAB-ISRAELI CONFLICT. Backed by SYRIA, the PPSF was often a member of groupings critical of the PALESTINE LIBERATION ORGANIZATION (PLO) chair, YASIR ARAFAT, including the REJECTION FRONT (created in 1974) and the PALESTINIAN NATIONAL SALVATION FRONT (formed in 1985).

The PPSF was rent by dissension in the early 1990s. Samir Ghawsha, the group's leader since 1974, was ousted and replaced by Khalid Abd al-Majid in April 1992. The main faction continued to be headed by Ghawsha, returned to the PLO mainstream, and supported the OSLO AGREEMENTS. The other faction retained the traditional hard-line stance and joined the National Democratic and Islamic Front, which had formed in 1993 to oppose the Oslo accords.

Michael R. Fischbach

Palin Commission

1920

Anti-Zionist violence broke out in April 1920 among Palestinians celebrating the Muslim festival of al-Nabi Musa near Jerusalem. Five Jews and four Palestinians died in the disturbances, after which British authorities cracked down on several prominent Palestinian nationalist figures.

In May 1920, the British Foreign Office established a commission headed by Major General P. C. Palin to investigate the origins of the violence. The

Palin Commission issued a report, never made public, on July 1, 1920. In it, the commission stated that the source of Palestinian nationalist frustration was Palestinians' belief that the promises of Arab independence made by Britain to Arab leaders during World War I had not been kept. Additionally, the commission noted the Palestinians' fear of ZIONISM, while criticizing the "arrogance" of the Zionist Commission.

Michael R. Fischbach

Partition Plans

Various proposals have been made, mainly inspired and supported by British and Zionist elements, to divide the territory of Palestine between its rival Palestinian and Zionist claimants. Until August 1937, the World Zionist Organization (WZO) was officially committed to the creation of "a national home in Palestine," but without ever formally clarifying whether this meant "all" or only "part" of Palestine. Taking as its reference point the extensive area covered by the original PALESTINE MANDATE granted to Great Britain, Zionist revisionists would retroactively consider Britain's creation of a separate Emirate of Transjordan (between the Jordan River and the Iraqi frontier) in 1921 as the "first partition" of Mandatory Palestine. The "Jewish national home" provisions of the BALFOUR DECLARATION were thereafter interpreted as applying only to Palestine west of the Jordan.

The first concrete proposal for partition occurred in 1932 in a secret internal memorandum written by Dr. Victor Jacobson (1869–1934), who was serving as the WZO's representative in Geneva, seat of the League of Nations. Jacobson's "Territorial Solution" contained a proposal to create two separate "sovereign, autonomous" entities or cantons in Palestine in order to remove mutual Palestinian and Jewish fears of domination by the other. Most Zionist leaders who learned of the plan in 1932 and 1933 rejected what they felt was its defeatist mentality.

Peel Commission The partition of Palestine first became practical politics in 1937 when the PEEL (Royal) COMMISSION, sent to investigate the causes of the Arab revolt of April 1936, issued its recommendations (Cmd. 5479, London, July 1937). The penetrating historical study of the problems of Arab-Jewish relations was pessimistic about a workable solution but recommended that the best chance for peace might lie in the partition of Palestine into a small Jewish state and an Arab area to be joined with Transjordan to form an Arab state (see map 11). A transfer of Palestinian population from the proposed Jewish area (especially the Galilee) was an integral part of the radical "surgery" being proposed for the country.

The official Zionist attitude was reserved, and in many ways negative, but privately many key decision makers welcomed partition. The twentieth Zionist Congress, which met in Zurich in August 1937, mandated the Executive by a two-to-one vote to continue to negotiate with the British "with a view to ascertaining the precise terms . . . for the proposed establishment of a Jewish state." Despite a few tentative flickers of possible acceptance by individuals (notably RAGHIB AL-NASHASHIBI and the Emir Abdullah of Transjordan), Arab rejection of the Royal Commission report was widespread and categorical. In a letter to the Permanent Mandates Commission of the League of Nations, the ARAB HIGHER COMMITTEE for Palestine (AHC) declared on July 23, 1937, that "peace in the land" could only be achieved on the basis of the following principles:

- The recognition of the right of the Arabs to complete independence in their own land.
- The cessation of the experiment of the Jewish National Home.
- The cessation of the British Mandate and its replacement by a treaty similar to treaties existing between Britain and Iraq, Britain and Egypt, and France and Syria, creating in Palestine a sovereign state.
- The immediate cessation of all Jewish immigration and of LAND sales to Jews pending the negotiation and conclusion of the treaty.

Like the WZO, the AHC declared itself prepared to engage in further discussions with the British, proposing to negotiate "in a reasonable spirit" for provisions to protect British interests, for safeguards to the holy places, and "for the protection of all legitimate rights of the Jewish population or other minorities in Palestine."

Palestinian nationalist leaders were quite successful in rallying support from the neighboring Arab governments, who joined in a pan-Arab campaign against partition both in the Middle East and

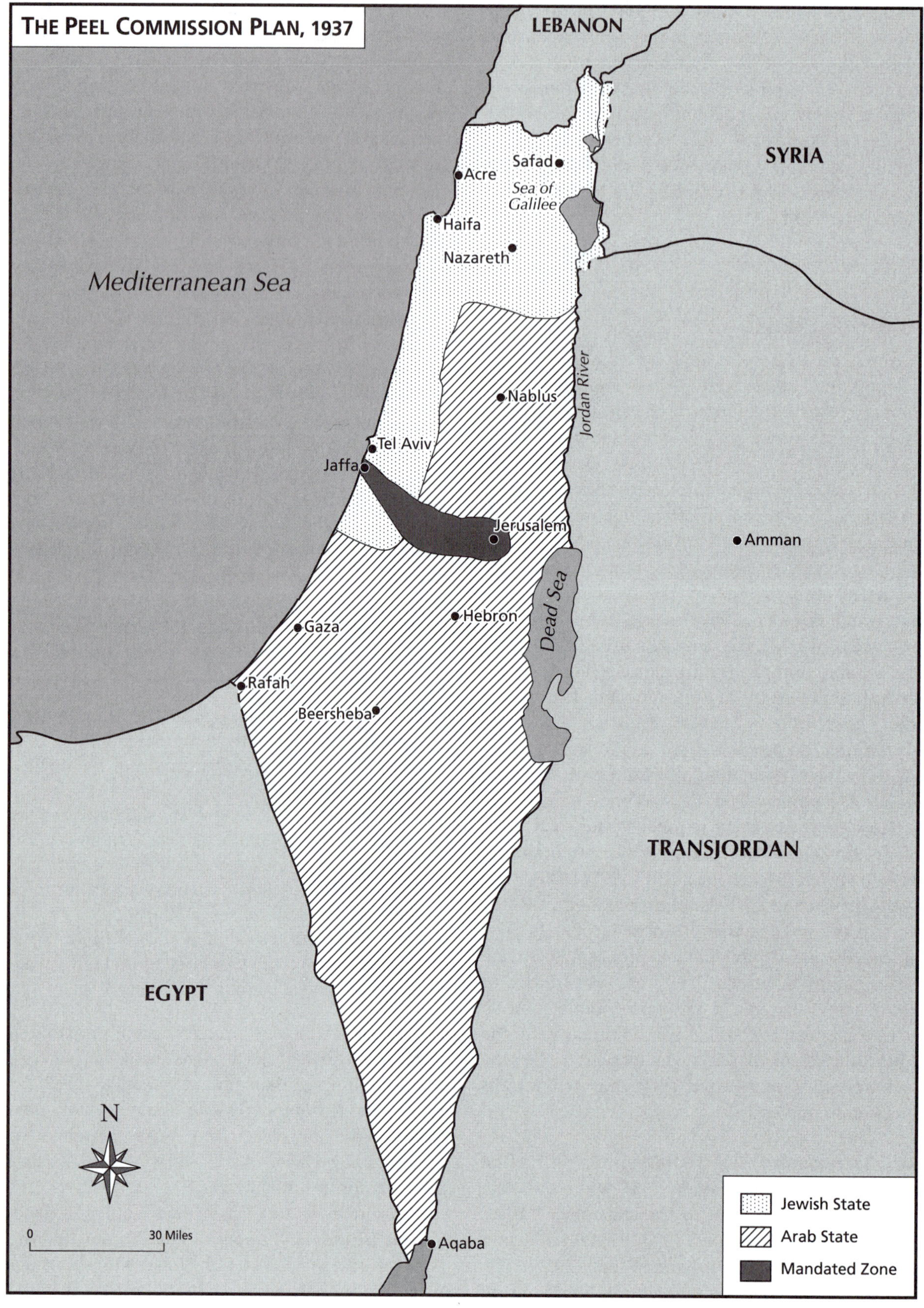
THE PEEL COMMISSION PLAN, 1937
LEBANON
SYRIA
Safad
Acre
Sea of Galilee
Haifa
Nazareth
Mediterranean Sea
Jordan River
Nablus
Tel Aviv
Jaffa
Jerusalem
Amman
Dead Sea
Hebron
Gaza
Rafah
Beersheba
TRANSJORDAN
EGYPT
N
0
30 Miles
Aqaba
Jewish State
Arab State
Mandated Zone

at the League of Nations headquarters in Geneva. The colonial secretary in London was particularly outraged by what he considered the provocative and vehement Iraqi tirades against partition. In September 1937, Palestinians officially coordinated their antipartition stand with the backing of the neighboring states at the BLUDAN CONFERENCE in Syria, where a Palestinian National Covenant was also promulgated.

Woodhead Commission Arab objections to partition, along with indications of divisions among Jews and Zionists (most prominent among the dissenters was the former HIGH COMMISSIONER FOR PALESTINE Sir Herbert Samuel) had their cumulative effect on British policymakers, who also feared the impact of German and Italian propaganda directed at exploiting Arab dissatisfaction with their Palestine policies. On January 5, 1938, London published a White Paper (Cmd. 5634) announcing the appointment and terms of reference of a commission that was to visit Palestine to gather evidence regarding the technical feasibility of partitioning the country. Despite the appearance of being a natural follow-up to the Peel report, this move was widely—and correctly—interpreted as an indication that partition was neither as imminent nor as certain as had once been supposed. The WOODHEAD COMMISSION gathered evidence and deliberated for most of a year, 1938, during which a Palestinian rebellion had resumed and intensified. In early November, the Woodhead Report (Cmd. 5854) concluded that the Peel partition plan was unworkable but was unable to recommend an alternative. Except for a 1943 secret recommendation of a cabinet committee that was never acted on, there were no further indications that the British might favor partition as a solution to the Arab-Zionist conflict over Palestine. Subsequent British plans leaned rather toward cantonal or federal arrangements.

U.N. Partition Resolution Although the World Zionist Organization was officially committed by the Biltmore Program of 1942 to the demand for transforming all of Palestine into a Jewish commonwealth, in early 1946 members of the Jewish Agency Executive began lobbying behind closed doors for a solution based on partition. It was the September 1947 majority report of the United Nations Special Committee on Palestine (UNSCOP) that brought the partition proposal back into the public debate. Seven of the UNSCOP members believed that only through partition could the "conflicting national aspirations" of Arabs and Jews "find substantial expression." They felt their proposal was "based on a realistic appraisal of the actual Arab-Jewish relations in Palestine." Attempting to follow the demographic distribution on the ground, the proposed partition map (see map 12) was an awkward patchwork of intersecting triangles. Apart from an international enclave comprising the area of Jerusalem and Bethlehem, the remainder of Mandatory Palestine was to be divided between a proposed Arab state and a proposed Jewish state. The Arab state would have occupied less than half of the remaining territory and incorporated a population of 715,000 Arabs and 8,000 Jews. The Jewish state would have occupied over half the remaining territory, including the largely uninhabited Negev, and it would have incorporated a population of 500,000 Jews and 416,000 Arabs. A minority of UNSCOP's members dissented from this recommendation, preferring instead a federated state with an Arab majority and Jewish communal autonomy.

The UNSCOP majority report set the battle lines for the diplomatic and military maneuvering that marked the final months of the Mandate period. During the three months leading up to the U.N. General Assembly vote on partition of November 29, 1947, Zionist efforts were mobilized toward ensuring the endorsement of the majority plan by the United Nations. Arab and Muslim diplomatic representatives worked for the plan's defeat, denouncing the injustice and the unacceptability of partition as a solution and predicting that, if partition were sanctioned by the world body, it would lead to war.

On November 29, the UNGA adopted the UNSCOP proposals (Resolution 181) with minor amendments by a vote of 33 to 13 with 10 abstaining. Among the countries voting in favor were the United States, the Soviet Union and the other communist countries, France, Belgium, the Netherlands, Nordic Europe, British Commonwealth countries, and most Latin American states. All six Arab member states voted against the proposals, as did Afghanistan, Cuba, Greece, India, Iran, Pakistan, and Turkey. Great Britain, China, Ethiopia, Yugoslavia, Mexico, and five Latin American states abstained. For a short while after the

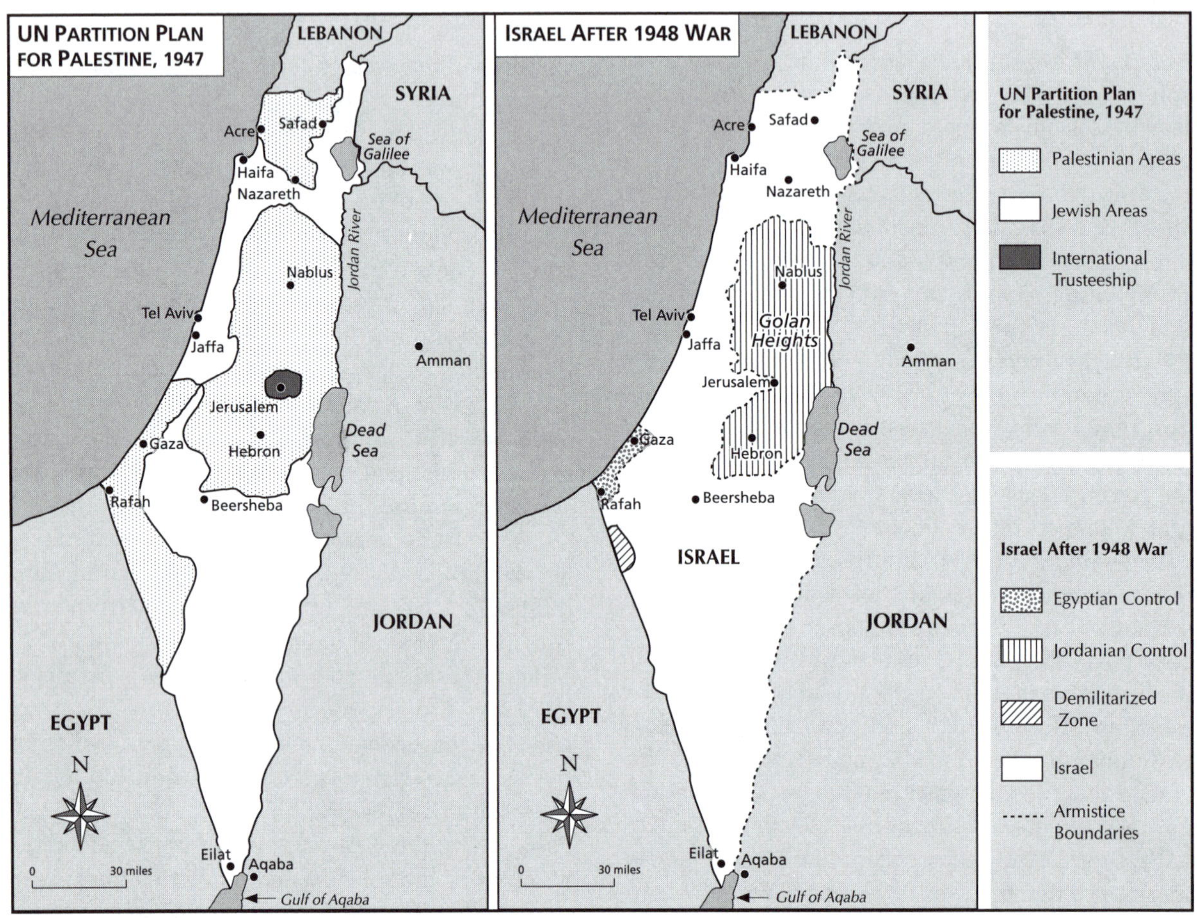
UN PARTITION PLAN FOR PALESTINE, 1947
LEBANON
SYRIA
Acre
Safad
Sea of Galilee
Haifa
Nazareth
Mediterranean Sea
Jordan River
Nablus
Tel Aviv
Jaffa
Amman
Jerusalem
Dead Sea
Gaza
Hebron
Rafah
Beersheba
JORDAN
EGYPT
N
0
30 miles
Eilat
Aqaba
Gulf of Aqaba
ISRAEL AFTER 1948 WAR
LEBANON
SYRIA
Acre
Safad
Sea of Galilee
Haifa
Nazareth
Mediterranean Sea
Jordan River
Nablus
Tel Aviv
Golan Heights
Jaffa
Amman
Jerusalem
Gaza
Dead Sea
Hebron
Rafah
Beersheba
ISRAEL
JORDAN
EGYPT
N
0
30 miles
Eilat
Aqaba
Gulf of Aqaba
UN Partition Plan for Palestine, 1947
Palestinian Areas
Jewish Areas
International Trusteeship
Israel After 1948 War
Egyptian Control
Jordanian Control
Demilitarized Zone
Israel
Armistice Boundaries

historic vote, Arab representatives warned of the impossibility of implementing partition without violence and sought to reopen discussions on possible alternative solutions, such as communal autonomy or federal arrangements. But there were no real negotiating opportunities at the eleventh hour that could avert the implementation of the proposed partition. Zionists and Arabs prepared to fight the first ARAB-ISRAELI WAR of 1948 over the U.N. partition resolution and the question of the legitimacy of creating a Jewish state out of Mandatory Palestine.

Neil Caplan

Peel Commission
1937

In May 1936, the British government decided to dispatch an investigatory commission to study the situation in Palestine in light of the outbreak of the Arab revolt. The six-man body, officially called the Royal Commission of Inquiry and headed by Lord Robert Peel, arrived in Palestine in November 1936 after the first phase of violence had subsided.

The Palestinian leadership initially decided to boycott the hearings arranged by the Peel Commission, leaving the commission to interview Zionist leaders and British officials. The leadership later changed its mind, and AL-HAJJ AMIN AL-HUSAYNI testified before the commission in January 1937.

The Peel Commission issued the Royal Commission Report in July 1937. It offered the first official British suggestion that the only way to resolve the conflicting national aspirations of both Zionists and Palestinians was to end the PALESTINE MANDATE and partition Palestine between the two communities. The report recommended creation of three entities: a Jewish state in Galilee and the coast, an even smaller British Mandate zone in the central part of Palestine and the city of NAZARETH, and a Palestinian state that included the remainder of Palestine joined with Transjordan. The report also suggested restricting Jewish immigration to 12,000 annually for five years. Later, the commission added proposals that called for resettling the Palestinian and Jewish populations into the new Jewish and Palestinian states, respectively.

Few on either side were satisfied by the proposals. The ARAB HIGHER COMMITTEE and other Palestinian figures rejected it. The Zionist movement was troubled by the small size of the proposed Jewish state, though leaders did cautiously advocate discussing the proposal. The League of Nations's Permanent Mandates Commission was also concerned about the recommendations, but it too chose not to reject the principle of partition.

Michael R. Fischbach

Performing Arts

Palestinian theater has served a number of important functions over the course of the twentieth century. One of these was political: as a vehicle by which Palestinian political aspirations could be articulated. By utilizing the Arabic language and familiar Arab cultural themes, theater became a method of asserting the Arab, Palestinian nature of the Palestinian people in the face of foreign rule and Zionist control.

Palestinian theater can be traced to the waning years of Ottoman rule. Schools and literary association performed both Western and Arab plays. In 1915, for instance, the LITERARY SOCIETY produced a play about Salah al-Din in JERUSALEM, as did the ARAB CLUB in 1920. The 1920s witnessed the rise of theater groups, perhaps the most important of which were those of Khalil Baydas in NAZARETH and the troupe belonging to Shaykh Muhammad al-Salih's Rawdat al-Ma'arif al-Wataniyya school in Jerusalem. Other troupes were established thanks to the inspiration of several Egyptian theater companies that toured Palestine between 1925 and 1932. Such Palestinian groups included the one directed by the pioneering playwright Nasri al-Jawzi.

Palestinians were active in writing plays as well as producing them. A leading playwright was Jamil al-Bahri, who wrote a number of plays between 1923 and 1930. One of the earliest figures to write nationalist plays was Najib Nassar, an important writer and newspaper editor, and of Lebanese origin an early opponent of ZIONISM.

An important dimension of the Palestinian performing arts during the PALESTINE MANDATE were plays broadcast on the government's radio station. Nasri al-Jawzi and other members of the Jawzi family were instrumental in presenting such works from 1936 to 1948 as a form of Arab cultural resistance to Zionism.

Poetry became a major vehicle for expressing nationalist sentiment after the 1948 Arab-Israeli war; Palestinian theater staged a comeback beginning in the 1960s. The writer GHASSAN KANAFANI played an important role in this regard through plays like *The Door* (1964). Palestinian resistance movements also established theatrical groups, including the FATAH Palestinian Theatrical Group.

Palestinian theater also reemerged in the Occupied Territories. Unlike in traditional Arabic-language theater, many plays performed in the Occupied Territories utilized colloquial Palestinian dialect to express everyday Palestinian popular resistance to Israeli rule. In late 1970, the theater company A'ilat al-Masrah (Family of the Theater) tried to perform a play by the noted Palestinian writer and playwright Samih al-Qasim but were prohibited by occupation authorities. Of more lasting import was al-Balalin (The Balloons), a company established in the late 1960s by Mustafa al-Kurd and François Abu Salim. Al-Balalin managed to perform such political shows as *Darkness,* although the group ceased functioning in 1976 when al-Kurd was deported by Israeli authorities. The importance of a growing number of theater troupes led to the First Palestinian Theatre Festival in RAMALLAH in 1973.

The most famous theatrical group in the WEST BANK was also its first professional troupe, al-Hakawati (The Storyteller). A resurrection of al-Balalin, al-Hakawati utilized a modern, Western style that drew on traditional Palestinian folklore and literary themes. Its first performance took place in 1978. In 1983, al-Hakawati leased al-Nuzha theater in East Jerusalem and created the West Bank's first theater-cultural center. By the 1990s, it was calling itself the Palestinian National Theatre—al-Hakawati.

Michael R. Fischbach

Popular Front for the Liberation of Palestine

The Popular Front for the Liberation of Palestine (PFLP) is the second only to FATAH in importance within the PALESTINE LIBERATION ORGANIZATION (PLO). Created in December 1968 by GEORGE HABASH, the PFLP is known for its activism in Jordan in the late 1960s and early 1970s. Very influenced by the theories of the Movement of Arab Nationalists, the PFLP envisioned its actions within the pan-Arabist framework, affirming that "the road to Jerusalem goes through Amman." The group acquired international notoriety by plane hijacking, the first of which was against an Israeli El Al plane on July 23, 1968. The PFLP played a decisive role in pushing the Palestinian resistance into confrontation with Jordan's King Husayn, which led to the BLACK SEPTEMBER setback in September 1970. It was also during 1968–71 that the PFLP actively participated in armed resistance against Israel in the GAZA STRIP (where it had strong support), a resistance that Israel's General Ariel Sharon broke in 1971.

Taking refuge in Lebanon like the other Palestinian organizations, the PFLP altered its positions. On the one hand, it became more radical in its social plan, abandoned its anticommunism, adopted Marxism, and drew nearer to the socialist countries. On the other, starting in 1972, it renounced "external operations," preferring to concentrate its attacks on Israel itself.

After the October 1973 war, the PFLP was the catalyst forming the opposition to the new tendencies within the PLO that favored the creation of a revolutionary power in all liberated Palestinian territories. It rejected the ideas of the GENEVA CONFERENCE, OF 1973, and condemned the November 1974 participation of YASIR ARAFAT in the United Nations General Assembly. At the time, the PFLP's only ally on the regional or international scene was Iraq. The REJECTION FRONT organized by the PFLP included the ARAB LIBERATION FRONT (ALF), the POPULAR FRONT FOR THE LIBERATION OF PALESTINE–GENERAL COMMAND, and several other small groups within the PLO. In 1974, the PFLP quit the PLO Executive Committee.

During the Lebanese civil war (1975–76), the PFLP again sided with Fatah to combat Syrian intervention. In 1981, it regained its place in the PLO Executive Committee, although unity was short-lived. The 1982 Israeli war in Lebanon and Yasir Arafat's rapprochement with EGYPT and Jordan resulted in the creation of a new PFLP-backed rejectionist front: the PALESTINIAN NATIONAL SALVATION FRONT. The outbreak of the INTIFADA in December 1987 permitted the resistance to regain its unity. The PFLP did not oppose, in November 1988, the proclamation of an independent Palestinian state, even if it did not agree with certain decisions of the PALESTINE NATIONAL COUNCIL, notably the acceptance of UNITED NATIONS SECURITY COUNCIL RESOLUTIONS 242 AND 338.

The PFLP condemned the OSLO AGREEMENTS between Israel and the PLO. Along with the DEMOCRATIC FRONT FOR THE LIBERATION OF PALESTINE, HAMAS, and ISLAMIC JIHAD, it organized opposition to Yasir Arafat, denouncing him once again as a traitor.

Alain Gresh

Popular Front for the Liberation of Palestine—External Operations

In 1971, the POPULAR FRONT FOR THE LIBERATION OF PALESTINE (PFLP) decided to halt some of the spectacular acts of political violence and terrorism, such as airplane hijackings, that had drawn attention to the Palestinian cause but at considerable public relations expense. WADI HADDAD, the mastermind behind these operations, disagreed with this policy and continued such activities. Criticized by other PFLP leaders, by the mid-1970s Haddad had formed his own organization to continue these exploits, Popular Front for the Liberation of Palestine—External Operations, although he maintained his connections with the mainstream PFLP.

The most famous attack carried out by the External Operations group was the June 1976 hijacking of a French aircraft carrying Israeli passengers. The jet landed in Entebbe, Uganda. Israeli commandos freed the hostages in a dramatic airborne rescue several days later.

The group splintered within a few years of Haddad's death in 1978. Among the groups formed out of it was the Arab Organization of 15 May.

Michael R. Fischbach

Popular Front for the Liberation of Palestine-General Command

Born of a split in the POPULAR FRONT FOR THE LIBERATION OF PALESTINE (PFLP) in November 1968, the Popular Front for the Liberation of Palestine-General Command (PFLP-GC) has been led since its inception by AHMAD JIBRIL. It is characterized above all by its military actions and by its persistent refusal, over many years, to adopt a political solution that would imply recognition of the state of Israel.

On February 2, 1970, the PFLP-GC exploded a bomb on a Swissair jet en route to Tel Aviv, killing its forty-seven passengers and crew members, of whom six were Israeli. In April 1974, the organization took hostages at the kibbutz of Kiryat Shimona, killing about twenty.

In June 1974, for the first time, the PFLP-GC was elected to the PALESTINE LIBERATION ORGANIZATION (PLO) Executive Committee. It suspended its participation several months later, in protest over the change in the PLO stance. During 1975–76, Jibril's second-in-command, Abu al-Abbas, charged that the PFLP-GC was too pro-Syrian. He broke away and created the PALESTINE LIBERATION FRONT. A notorious operation in 1987—a member of the PFLP-GC landed an ultralight aircraft in Israel and killed six Israeli soldiers—had important repercussions in the West Bank and Gaza and contributed to the outbreak of the INTIFADA.

Sponsored at different times by the Syrian, Libyan, and Iraqi regimes, the PFLP-GC has perceived itself as the vanguard of the Palestinian forces rejecting compromise with Israel. It has participated in different coalitions, which, in 1974, 1982–83, and after the OSLO AGREEMENTS, have opposed the orientation of the PLO majority.

Alain Gresh

Population

Total Population

The Problem of Identity

The evaluation of Palestinian population presents unique difficulties. Foremost of these is a lack of data. However, a more fundamental problem is one of defining the Palestinians. The ultimate definition of nationality is personal. Those who consider themselves to be Palestinians are Palestinians. The only real measure of "national identity" is self-identification, not legal citizenship. Unfortunately, self-identification seldom is reflected in population statistics. Instead, demographers have information on categories such as place of birth, citizenship, and mother tongue. No population registrar in the Ottoman Empire, the Palestine Mandate, Jordan, or Israel ever asked a census question on national self-identification. The Ottomans did not even consider the possibility of such a question; the others did not want to know.

For the Ottoman period, the answer to the question of Palestinian identity is, statistically at least,

TABLE 1.
Palestinian Population, 1860–2000 (thousands)

YEAR	WITHIN PALESTINE		ISRAEL	WEST BANK*	GAZA	OUTSIDE PALESTINE	TOTAL
1860	411						411
1890	553						533
1914	738						738
1918	689						689
1931	860						860
1940	1,086						1,086
1946	1,308						1,308
1950	1,170	*of which*	165	765	240	304	1,474
1960	1,340		239	799	302	647	1,987
1970	1,412		367	677	368	1,289	2,701
1980	1,992		531	964	497	2,100	4,092
1990	2,731		687	1,373	671	3,302	6,033
2000	3,787		919	1,836	1,032	4,667	8,454

*including East Jerusalem

fairly simple. The Ottomans kept records only by religious affiliation. Although they did not use "national" distinctions such as Syrian, Iraqi, or Palestinian, one can consider as Palestinians those Ottoman subject Muslims and Christians who lived in Palestine (defined as the area that would become the Palestine Mandate) between 1517 and 1917. This includes very few whose descendants would not consider themselves Palestinians. The same criteria can be applied to the British Mandate Palestinian citizen Christians and Muslims (including Druzes, who were registered as Muslims by the Ottomans and thus must be included as Muslims in any comparisons to Ottoman data).

After the Palestinian expulsion and flight in 1948, identification becomes particularly difficult. In the absence of detailed surveys, demographers cannot know certainly whether the children of intermarriages of Palestinians and non-Palestinians are Palestinians. Also, what proportion of the children of Palestinians who came to the Americas or western Europe consider themselves to be Palestinians? Anecdotal evidence and what is known from political activity indicate that Palestinians have kept their national identification in whichever country they live. Therefore, Muslims and Christians who either live in Palestine or whose ancestors did so until 1948 are considered here to be Palestinians. This surely includes some who do not consider themselves to be Palestinians and excludes some who do, but there is no statistical option. It also should be noted that when Palestinians married non-Palestinians, demographic statistics in effect count one-half of the children as Palestinians.

The Quality of the Data

Population data on the Ottoman Palestinians are limited, but they are sufficient to provide reasonable approximations of total population. There are scant Ottoman data on important statistics, such as age of marriage, fertility, and mortality, although mortality and fertility rates have been estimated through the use of demographic techniques. Mandate figures, although often imprecise, are much better, because they are much more detailed. They allow accurate estimations of mortality, fertility, migration, and other demographic variables. The most valuable data on population in the Mandate period come from the census taken by the British in 1931. Not only does it provide the sort of data needed for accurate demographic calculation (such as, population by single ages), but the statistics are more reliable than any others taken in Ottoman or Mandate times. The breadth of statistics in the 1931 census approaches that of censuses taken in Western Europe or the United States during the same period, even if it is not quite as accurate. Another Mandate census, that of 1922, is both less accurate and less detailed, and thus is of less value.

The quality of Mandate statistics declined after the 1931 census. Civil unrest, followed by World War II, made it impossible for the British to take another census. They were forced to adopt unreliable statistical procedures, such as estimating the total population by adding registered births and subtracting registered deaths. Because neither births nor deaths were properly recorded, the results were unsatisfactory. After 1948, the statistical situation deteriorated even further in the WEST BANK and the GAZA STRIP. The Jordanians took censuses of the West Bank in 1952 and 1961. The second was more complete than the first, but neither was complete. Gaza's citizens were not enumerated between 1931 and 1967, when the Israelis made a census of both Gaza and the West Bank. The Israeli census provided the most valuable data yet collected. No census was taken after 1967. However, Israeli demographers have made valuable surveys and studies of demography and fertility in Palestine. Israeli counts of Palestinians within the 1948 borders are accurate, given the usual limitation of any census taking.

Enumerating Palestinian numbers after 1948 is a difficult proposition. In order to know the numbers of any population accurately, the population must be counted, and the Palestinians outside Israel's borders were counted poorly and sporadically. Often, Palestinians arrived in countries, including most of those in the Middle East immediately after 1948, which did not take accurate censuses. Political situations made the picture all the more obscure. Some countries that did count their population fairly accurately did not wish to distinguish between native and Palestinian populations. Some who estimated the Palestinian population greatly over- or underestimated numbers in accordance with the estimators' political intentions.

All of these points must be kept in mind when any statistics on Palestinians are presented, including those presented here. All figures on Palestinian population are estimations. By making different assumptions on fertility and mortality rates, demographers may arrive at slightly different conclusions. It is nevertheless possible to arrive at reasonable estimates of the Palestinian population. Table 1 presents the population of the Palestinians in the world from 1860 to 2000.

Figures for 1860 to 1914 in Table 1 include Muslim and Christian legal residents of Ottoman Palestine. Aliens and Ottoman subjects legally resident elsewhere, such as soldiers, government officials, and merchants, are excluded. The figures for the Mandate Period (1918, 1931, 1940, and 1946) include the Muslim, Christian, and Druze citizens of Palestine; noncitizens are excluded. After 1931, British statistics did not list the Druze separately, but included them in the "other" category with Samaritans, Baha'is, and others. For post-1931 data the Druze have been assumed to be the same proportion of the "other" category as they were in 1931. Bedouin are included in all the figures. All the data for the Ottoman and Mandate periods have been adjusted for undercounting of women and children, using the calculations in *The Population of Palestine* (McCarthy, 1990).

Statistics for the period 1950 to 2000 have been drawn from a number of sources, including censuses, when available, and estimations of Palestinian population in the Arab countries in 1990 made by the U.S. Census Bureau (U.S. Census Bureau, 1991). The Census Bureau calculations, which consider available data from censuses and population surveys, are the best available estimation of the Palestinian population in the Arab countries and Israel in 1990. Information on known fertility and mortality rates has been combined to create model projections of the Palestinian population at ten-year intervals. Insufficient data make it impossible to provide much information on subpopulations of the Palestinians. Ethnically and linguistically they are Arabs. Levels of linguistic assimilation among migrants to Europe and America are unknown. The major statistical division among Palestinians is religious. In Ottoman times, 11 to 12 percent of the Palestinians were Christians, the rest Muslims (a category in which the Ottomans included Sunnis, Shi'ites, and Druze). As a result of a lower birth rate, emigration, and a higher mortality rate in World War I, the Christian population steadily dropped from 1914 to 1967 (11 percent in 1914, 9 percent in 1931, 8 percent in 1967) within the borders of Palestine. The religious breakdown of the Palestinians after 1967 is unknown.

The Palestinian population has experienced sustained growth since the latter half of the nineteenth century. The one exception to this pattern occurred during World War I. As a result of the conditions of war, and particularly the fact that Palestine was a major battlefield of the war, 6 percent of the Muslims, and 13 percent of the Christians, of Palestine emigrated or died during the war. Growth during the nineteenth- and twentieth-century Ottoman period was similar to that experienced in most of the Ottoman Empire and remained at a moderate level before World War II. During the period before 1945, a relatively high mortality rate slowed growth. After the war, high fertility and decrease in mortality made the Palestinian population one of the fastest growing in history.

Fertility Since the middle of the nineteenth century, and probably long before, the proportion of children born to the Palestinian Arabs—their fertility—has been among the highest recorded for any population. The average number of children born to a Palestinian woman who lived through her childbearing years (the total fertility rate [TFR]) was slightly more than 7. The high fertility of Palestinians living in Palestine remained constant from Ottoman times until the late 1970s, when it began to diverge by regions. In the late 1970s, fertility among residents of the Gaza Strip actually began to rise, reaching more than an average of 7.6 children (TFR of 7.62) in 1979 before it decreased slightly. On the West Bank, fertility declined more rapidly. The Palestine Demographic Survey of 1995, found that the Gaza TFR was 7.41, that of the West Bank, 5.44. In Israel, Palestinian fertility remained high until the 1970s, when it began to drop quickly, reaching a TFR of 4.9 in 1983 and 4.6 in 1989. The fertility of Palestinians in Israel remained at approximately that level in 2000.

There was considerable difference in the fertility of Muslim and Christian Palestinians during the British Mandate and particularly after 1948. During the Mandate period, the average Christian woman had two-thirds as many children as the average Muslim woman. In Israel, that figure was even lower. In the 1960s and 1970s, Christian Palestinian women in Israel had on average less than half as many children as Muslim Palestinian women. This differential was most likely due to cultural and economic variation. Christian women tended to marry later, thus leaving less time for childbearing. In 1931, for example, Mandate statistics show that 75 percent of the Muslim women aged fifteen to forty-four were married, but only 65 percent of the Christians. Whereas one-third of the Muslim women aged fifteen to nineteen were married, one-fifth of the Christians were. Christians were better educated and more urban: in 1931, 76 percent of Christians were urban, 25 percent of Muslims; 70 percent of Christian males over age twenty-one were literate, 18 percent of Muslim males). Both these factors traditionally reduce fertility. Christians, at least from the 1960s on, were also more likely to use methods of artificial birth control. Conversely, Muslim women married and began to have children early. In the 1970s, the average Palestinian Muslim woman had already had two or more children by age twenty-four, and an average of nearly six children by age thirty-four. Very few Muslim women used contraceptive techniques.

Muslims were a large majority of the Palestinians, so their fertility set the pattern. Fertility decline, never great, was affected by a change in Muslim marriage practices. In 1931, three-fourths of Muslim women twenty to forty-four were married, slightly more than half in 1967. Change in patterns of early marriage was particularly marked: 45 percent of the females fifteen to nineteen (Muslims and Christians) were married in 1931; by 1967 the number of married females in this age group had fallen to 19 percent on the West Bank and 14 percent in Gaza. By 1990, the number of married fifteen- to nineteen-year-old females had dropped to approximately 10 percent (Ennab, 1994). The 1995 Palestine Demographic Survey found a median age of marriage of twenty-three for males and eighteen for females.

Outside Palestine, Palestinian fertility generally remained high. Palestinian women in Syria, for example, had on average two to three more children than native Syrian women. Palestinians in Jordan experienced even higher fertility than Palestinians in the West Bank or Gaza, a TFR of 7.6 in 1979 and 7.4 in 1989. In other regions, however, Palestinian fertility declined. The reasons for this varied by country. To a large extent, the fertility of Palestinians has declined when their economic status has risen, a phenomenon seen worldwide in most cultures. Palestinian fertility in Egypt was two-thirds of that in the West Bank and Gaza. Palestinian fertility in Kuwait initially was high (6.4 TFR in 1970), but was below 4.5 by the mid-1970s. Little is known of the demographic picture of Palestinians outside the Middle East. If they follow the pattern of other Arab migrants to Europe and the United States, their fertility probably slowly adjusted to that of their countries of residence. By 1990, their fertility would have been more similar to that of those countries than that of the West Bank or Gaza, though still higher than the European standard.

Despite changes in factors such as age of marriage, the Palestinian population will increase

TABLE 2
Palestinian Mortality, 1860–2000

	MALE LIFE EXPECTANCY AT BIRTH (YEARS)	FEMALE LIFE EXPECTANCY AT BIRTH (YEARS)	INFANT MORTALITY RATE* (/1,000)	CRUDE DEATH RATE (/1,000)
PALESTINE				
1860	22	24	380	42
1914	30	32	290	32
1931	35	37	240	30
1940	37	39	220	28
ISRAEL				
1950	42	45	200	21
1960	58	62	50	9
1970	63	67	45	6
1980	65	70	40	5
1990	68	72	36	4
2000	76	78	10	3
WEST BANK AND GAZA				
1950	42	45	200	21
1960	43	46	190	20
1970	44	46	170	19
1980	56	60	100	10
1990	63	67	60	6
2000	70	74	27	4

*in one year, deaths of children under age one divided by births

rapidly for generations. Even if Palestinians immediately and precipitously lowered their fertility, the population would still greatly increase. This is due to the effect of past years of high fertility on the age structure. So many children were born in the past thirty years that the population necessarily will increase as these children have children themselves. In fact, there is little to indicate that the fertility of these children will drop precipitously. Even if Palestinian fertility in Gaza and on the West Bank were to fall very rapidly, the population would still double in less than thirty years.

Mortality As indicated in Table 2, the mortality rate (defined as the proportion of deaths to the total population) among the Palestinians diminished greatly from 1860 to 2000, with the greatest decrease in modern times. The table displays a standard measure of mortality, expectancy of life at birth: the average number of years a Palestinian male or female could expect to live from birth. The statistic is heavily affected by deaths among children. For example, 29 percent of the children born in 1914 could be expected to die before reaching age one and 43 percent would die between birth and age five. Those who reached age five could expect to live quite a bit longer—on average to slightly past age fifty.

In the Ottoman period, Palestinians experienced the same general increase in life expectancy as inhabitants of the other Ottoman Mediterranean coastal regions. Mortality decline in the latter half of the nineteenth century was similar to that seen in other parts of the Ottoman Empire. The decline was not due to medicine or doctors. The cause was an improvement in public security, trade, and production—changes resulting from the increased power of the central government. There were enough to eat, a bit more money, and relative peace from internal conflicts and Bedouin raids. The end of major epidemic diseases was statistically less significant, but still important. By 1870, the great cholera epidemics were over. Plague, traditionally the worst epidemic killer, effectively disappeared in the 1840s.

Despite the troubles of 1929 and 1936–39, the situation of civic calm and increased trade and industry generally continued and improved during the Mandate years. In addition, the Mandate period saw the advent of modern medicine. However, the effect of medical science on population growth in Palestine was slight until after World War II, when antibiotics diminished mortality. More important were improvements in sanitation, water supplies, and government-sponsored public health works. Consequently, dysentery and malaria both began to decrease markedly as causes of death.

The spread of modern medicine in Israel, prenatal and postnatal care, and the continuation of Mandate policies such as vaccination and draining of malarial swamps gradually lowered the Palestinian mortality rate in Israel. In 1950, the life expectancy at birth of Palestinian Arabs in Israel was more than twenty years lower than that of Jews, but in 1980, it had improved to six years lower than Jewish life expectancy. Greatly decreased infant mortality obviously had great effect. In Gaza and the West Bank, mortality rate decline was much slower. This is not surprising, given the miserable health conditions of REFUGEES, who began their refugee status living in tents with limited food and little clean water. The wonder is that the mortality rate was not much worse. The credit for this and much of the subsequent improvement in mortality goes to the United Nations Relief and Works Agency for Palestine Refugees in the Near East (UNRWA)—which drained swamps, vaccinated children, and provided pure water and health clinics—and to the cooperation of the Palestinians themselves.

Table 2 presents only data from Palestine proper. However, there seems to have been considerable variation in mortality rate among the Palestinians outside Palestine. Countries to which Palestinians emigrated seldom kept mortality statistics that separated Palestinian deaths from others. Demographers agree that after the 1960s Palestinian mortality generally followed the mortality level of the country in which they resided. In some countries, such as Kuwait, it may have been slightly worse; in others, such as Egypt, slightly better. This reflected the fact that the Palestinians generally had a lower standard of living than the Kuwaitis and a better standard than the average Egyptian. Palestinian mortality rate followed the general pattern seen among populations in the same geographic region. The mortality rate in Saudi Arabia, Jordan, and Syria in the 1980s was virtually the same as that in the West Bank and Gaza.

Table 2 combines mortality rates for the West Bank and Gaza into one set of data. There is some evidence from Israeli statistics that mortality rate in Gaza may have been slightly lower than that of the West Bank. This is disputed by some demographers. Were it true, the life expectancy as shown in the table would change by only approximately one year.

Infant mortality rate among the Palestinians in Gaza and the West Bank remained relatively high until 1990. The pattern there resembled that of surrounding Arab countries, what might be called Middle Eastern standard mortality decline, in which adult mortality rate decreases much more quickly than infant mortality rate. The infant mortality rate of Palestinians in Israel resembles that of Kuwait or some European countries. It may be noted that infant deaths in Gaza and the West Bank always have been poorly reported, so the infant mortality rates given here are drawn from standard demographic tables.

Migration In the Ottoman and Mandate periods, migration was a minor factor in the demographic makeup of the Muslim and Christian (though obviously not the Jewish) population of Palestine. Although there was a certain amount of seasonal labor migration to and from Palestine, analysis of Ottoman statistics (McCarthy, 1990) yields evidence of little permanent migration of Arabs into or out of Palestine from 1860 to 1914. The number of Arabs who left Palestine on the Ottoman defeat in World War I was negligible.

Mandate authorities did not record migration properly before 1932; non-Jewish immigration was recorded fairly well, but not emigration. Statistics indicate that only 838 more Muslims entered Palestine than left from 1932 to 1946. Numbers of both Muslim immigrants and Muslim emigrants were relatively small. For example, from 1937 to 1939, a yearly average of only 305 Arab residents of Palestine was registered as leaving Palestine permanently. Christian immigration was much greater than emigration, a net surplus of 20,051, but the statistics do not discriminate between Arab and other

Christians, and many of the Christian migrants were not Arabs. Arab immigrants emigrated primarily from Lebanon and Syria. A large majority of Arab emigrants from Mandatory Palestine went to the United Kingdom, the next largest group to other Arab countries, and some to Latin America.

The 1948 Expulsion and Flight

The 1948 expulsion and flight of Palestinians were, by proportion of the population affected, among the largest forced migrations in modern Middle Eastern history. It affected approximately 53 percent of the Arab population of Palestine, 82 percent of the Arabs who resided in the portion of Palestine that became Israel.

Because no count of the refugees could have been taken during their exodus, analysts necessarily must look at the populations before and after the events to arrive at the numbers of refugees. Subtracting the numbers who remained within the armistice borders of Israel from the number who were in the same area before the war would yield approximately the number who emigrated or died in the war. The numbers of Arabs in Palestine at the end of the Mandate and inside and out of Israel after the war are known (Table 1), but ascertaining the numbers who lived within and without the 1948 armistice borders is difficult. It has proved impossible to trace exactly the population of Palestine by district in 1947–48, which would be essential to a complete accurate analysis. Therefore, this study has taken the best analysis of the division of population numbers inside and out of the 1948 borders before the war, that of Janet Abu-Lughod (Abu-Lughod, 1971), as a base. (It is not possible to accept all of the Abu-Lughod thesis, because she assumes that the official Mandate statistics were accurate, when in fact they were undercounts of population and erroneous on fertility and mortality [see McCarthy, 1990]. She also counts all those not listed as Jews as Palestinian Arabs, whereas all noncitizens, as well as non-Druze listed along with the Druze under the category "Other" in the British data, should be excluded. For example, a Syrian Arab in Palestine in 1948 may have been forced to flee, but he was a Syrian expelled from Palestine, not a Palestinian.)

Of the 1,358,000 Palestinian Arab citizens of Palestine in 1948, approximately 873,000 resided within what would become the Israeli borders, 485,000 without. The Israelis recorded 156,000 non-Jews in 1948, a number that included perhaps 1,000 non-Arabs, leaving 155,000 Palestinians in Israel. This means that 718,000 Palestinians either were refugees or died during the war. Note that this number depends on the somewhat imprecise estimation of the numbers who lived on both sides of the border before the war, and so should be taken as a mean estimate. However, statistically it cannot be wrong by more than 5 to 10 percent (for other analyses, see Khalidi, 1992; Bachi, 1977).

Of the Palestinian religious groups, Muslims had the highest proportion of their numbers as refugees, Christians somewhat less. Relatively few of the Druze became refugees.

UNRWA Statistics

Statistics compiled by UNRWA are often applied to estimates of Palestinian population, particularly for the 1948 period. However, demographic use of the figures of the UNRWA presents insurmountable problems.

The UNRWA figures are in essence not records of population but records of distributed rations. In the chaotic time immediately after the Palestinian exodus, families naturally maximized their benefits whenever possible by claiming extra members and not registering deaths so that extra rations could be claimed. Hungry refugees cannot be faulted for this, but it does confuse statistical data. In addition, as the UNRWA recognized, large numbers in Gaza and on the West Bank who were not refugees, but whose livelihoods had been disrupted or were simply malnourished, managed to claim UNRWA rations. Thus the number of those whom the UNRWA called "alleged relief recipients" in 1949 when added to the nonrefugee population was considerably more than the actual population (Peretz, 1958), although the numbers the UNRWA estimated for actual refugees, 726,000 in 1949, are very close to the 718,000 figure given above.

Ironically, as the social situation calmed and the UNRWA was able to take better statistics, the data became less valuable for estimation of total Palestinian numbers because it *excluded* so many Palestinians—those who were not recipients. Nevertheless, the record of those supported by UNRWA has value in itself, and a representative set of statistics is given in Table 3. Note what may be a progressively larger overcount of actual refugees. The 1997 Palestine Census listed 393,375 in the

TABLE 3

Refugees Registered with UNRWA.

	REGISTERED REFUGEES 1950	REGISTERED REFUGEES 1959	REGISTERED REFUGEES 1979	REGISTERED REFUGEES 1992	REGISTERED REFUGEES 1999	IN CAMPS 1979	IN CAMPS 1992	IN CAMPS 1999
Jordan*	506,200	586,706	699,553	1,042,123	1,512,742	182,000	237,677	274,816
West Bank		321,722	472,573	569,741	82,299	124,307		153,380
Gaza	198,227	245,343	358,898	582,863	798,444	201,672	320,467	437,650
Lebanon	127,600	129,228	219,561	324,219	370,144	103,661	169,321	204,999
Syria	82,194	109,506	203,830	306,042	374,521	57,924	88,924	109,315
Israel†	45,800							
Total	960,021	1,070,783	1,803,564	2,727,820	3,625,592	627,956	904,696	1,180,160

* including West Bank in 1950 and 1959

† Jewish refugees

Sources: UNRWA, 1959; UNRWA, 1979; UNRWA, 1999; Peretz, 1958; Peretz, 1993.

West Bank and 640,140 in Gaza who identified themselves as "registered refugees," considerably fewer than the UNRWA figures.

Migration After 1948

After 1948, Palestinian high fertility and the limited economic potential of the land led to out-migration. The West Bank, in particular, had sizable out-migration from 1948 to 1967. The population of the West Bank from 1950 to 1960 (Table 1) demonstrates this phenomenon: If all the 765,000 residents in 1950 had remained in the West Bank, their high fertility would have meant a population of 1 million in 1960, but the population was actually 799,000. The "missing" Palestinians were out-migrants.

The nature of Palestinian migration changed radically after 1948. No longer a small-scale migration to Europe and the Americas, emigration was now large-scale and directed mainly to the Arab world. Emigration usually involved two steps: First refugees went to the West Bank or Gaza, then on to other regions for economic reasons. Most migrants from the West Bank went to the East Bank. Improving economic conditions on the East Bank and Jordanian citizenship made the East Bank an attractive target area for the migration of unskilled labor. While the West Bank had a higher standard of living than the East Bank until 1948, Jordanian development policies, which overwhelmingly favored the East Bank, ensured that the West Bank became relatively impoverished. High levels of population growth could only be supported by industrialization, and what industrialization existed was directed to the East Bank. The unemployed from the West Bank naturally went East. Palestinian skilled labor went all over the Arab world and on to Europe and the Americas, taking advantage of opportunities that were unavailable to the unskilled. Kuwait is the most well-known example of post-1948 migration. Approximately 40,000 Palestinians resided in Kuwait in 1960, more than 300,000 in 1990. Figures from Saudi Arabia are imprecise, but they indicate an even faster growth of Palestinian population, from very few in the early 1960s to more than 200,000 in 1990. The nature of this out-migration, the quest for work, is demonstrated by the sex ratio of the populations both in Palestine and in the target countries. Women outnumbered men by approximately 2 percent in the West Bank and Gaza, Palestinian males outnumbered Palestinian females by 10–15 percent in Arabian Peninsula countries.

Migration rates from Gaza were much lower than from the West Bank. Until the 1960s the Egyptian government restricted immigration. During the 1948 war, Egypt initially had accepted Palestinian refugees in Egypt proper, but soon changed its policy. Palestinians in Egypt were encouraged to go to the West Bank and emigration from Gaza was restricted. In effect, only those Gazans who possessed marketable skills, a very limited number, were allowed to work in Egypt. Gazans who wished to emigrate to other Arab countries had to both pay an exit tax and obtain a residence visa from the Arab country to which they wished to emigrate, neither of which was often possible. The situation eased considerably in the 1960s, but emigration remained under West Bank levels. Neither the Gaza Palestinians nor the Egyptians wished Egypt to formally annex the Gaza Strip, as Jordan had annexed the West Bank. Therefore, unskilled workers did not possess an open market for their labor, one of the few benefits afforded the West Bank Palestinians by Jordan.

The Israeli government has published statistics on emigration from the West Bank and Gaza. However, there is confusion over questions such as who was an emigrant and whether the emigration was "permanent." The Israeli authorities registered a yearly average of 12,934 more emigrants than immigrants from the West Bank and Gaza from 1967 to 1986. The excess of emigrants was much larger in some years; the highest figures were 25,200 in 1967, 48,200 in 1968, 23,880 in 1980, and 23,376 in 1981. These figures obviously have omitted many migrants, in particular large numbers of refugees in 1967, and their reliability must be questioned.

The extent of Palestinian emigration is perhaps best understood from the numbers of Palestinians inside and outside Palestine in Tables 1 and 4. Until the 1948 war, almost 100 percent of the Palestinians lived in Palestine. Only 67 percent lived in Palestine in 1960, 52 percent in 1970, and 45 percent in 1990.

The second major Palestinian migration came as a result of Israeli conquest of the West Bank and Gaza in 1967. From the Israeli occupation to 1970, nearly 50,000 Palestinians left Gaza. Judged on the basis of the emigration rates from 1960 to 1967, 35,000 would normally have emigrated for economic reasons from June 1967 to 1970. This leaves 15,000 who can be considered to be "extra migrants" or forced refugees. (Larger numbers are often given for forced migration from Gaza, but these usually include both the economic migrants who would normally have left in any case and many who had already migrated from Gaza before the 1967 war and were unable to return because of the Israeli presence.)

The West Bank suffered much worse from the Israeli occupation. Approximately 825,000 Palestinians lived in the West Bank in June 1967. When the Israeli government took a census of the West Bank in September 1967, it recorded 664,000 (including East Jerusalem); 161,000 Palestinians, 20 percent of the population, had gone. Perhaps 20,000 more migrated between September 1967 and 1970. As was the case with the 1948 refugees, these figures are approximate. The actual number of refugees may have been slightly higher or lower. As a result of events surrounding the Gulf crisis and war, the major part of the Palestinian population of Lebanon migrated, mainly to Jordan. Only approximately 30,000 Palestinians remained in Kuwait in 2000.

Palestinians in the World

Because of their high fertility and emigration, Palestinians have become a more sizable population outside of Palestine than within. The proportion of Palestinians outside of the borders of Mandate Palestine has been increasing since 1948. After the mid-1970s, most Palestinians lived outside of Palestine. By 1990, almost 60 percent resided elsewhere.

Many of the figures in Table 4 are necessarily estimates. For the year 2000, figures for Lebanon, the Gulf States, and "other" are less reliable than others, because of lack of accurate census counts and high migration. For the Arab world outside of Palestine in 1990 and 2000, the figures are primarily drawn from the detailed analysis made by the U.S. Census Center for International Research in 1991. Figures for the West Bank and Gaza for 1990 and 2000 are projected from the 1997 Palestinian census (see Table 5).

"Economic" migration continued at a high level through the 1970s, then declined in the 1980s. The decrease was primarily due to worsened economic conditions in the Gulf countries and Jordanian laws restricting immigration. Emigration thus no longer functioned as a safety valve for high fertility. Low emigration conditions continued into the 1990s. There is debate over Israeli statistics that showed greatly lessened emigration, but there is no doubt that emigration is much lower than at earlier times. Indeed, after the Gulf War, an unknown amount of reverse migration to Palestine has occurred. Palestinian numbers outside of Palestine will continue to increase rapidly due to the effects of high fertility, but the relative proportion of Palestinians outside of Palestine probably will not continue to increase. Beset by their own problems with overpopulation, the countries surrounding Palestine are unlikely to accept renewed immigration. Unless political and economic conditions change drastically, it is also

TABLE 4

Palestinians in 1970, 1990, and 2000 by Country of Residence (De Facto Population)

COUNTRY	PALESTINIANS IN 1970	PERCENTAGE OF TOTAL PALESTINIANS	PALESTINIANS IN 1990	PERCENTAGE OF TOTAL PALESTINIANS	PALESTINIANS IN 2000	PERCENTAGE OF TOTAL PALESTINIANS
Gaza	368,000	13.6	671,000	11.1	1,032,000	12.2
W.Bank	677,000	25.1	1,373,000	22.7	1,836,000	21.7
Israel	367,000	13.6	687,000	11.3	919,000	10.9
Jordan	592,000	21.9	1,524,000	25.3	2,626,000	31.1
Lebanon	247,000	9.1	332,000	5.5	463,000	5.5
Syria	156,000	5.8	302,000	5.0	411,000	4.9
Egypt	33,000	1.2	40,000	0.7	48,000	.6
Libya	10,000	.4	28,000	0.5	37,000	.4
Iraq	15,000	.5	30,000	0.5	42,000	.5
Kuwait	140,000	5.2	312,000	5.2	30,000	.4
S.Arabia	31,000	1.1	206,000	3.4	299,000	3.5
Other Gulf	25,000	.9	87,000	1.4	105,000	1.2
Other	40,000	1.5	441,000	7.3	606,000	7.2
TOTAL	2,701,000	100.0	6,033,000	100.0	8,454,000	100.0

*includes East Jerusalem

some rounding error

Sources: Author's calculations, based on national censuses, PLO, 1983; Kossaifi, 1980; U.S. Census, 1991; PCBS, 1997.

TABLE 5

The Palestine Census of 1997

GOVERNORATE	POPULATION			
	MALE	FEMALE	BOTH SEXES	SEX RATIO
Jenin	103407	99619	203026	103.8
Tubas	18583	18026	36609	103.1
Tulkarm	67781	66329	134110	102.2
Qalqilya	37002	35005	72007	105.7
Salfit	24695	23843	48538	103.6
Nablus	132818	128522	261340	103.3
Ramallah & al-Bira	106988	106594	213582	100.4
Jerusalem	166001	162600	328601	102.1
Jericho	16491	16222	32713	101.7
Bethlehem	70238	67048	137286	104.8
Hebron	207689	197975	405664	104.9
West Bank	**951693**	**921783**	**1873476**	**103.2**
North Gaza	93365	90008	183373	103.7
Gaza	186970	180418	367388	103.6
Dayr Al-Balah	74819	73058	147877	102.4
KhanYunis	101607	99097	200704	102.5
Rafah	62052	60813	122865	102.0
Gaza Strip	**518813**	**503394**	**1022207**	**103.1**
Palestinian Territories	**1470506**	**1425177**	**2895683**	**103.2**

*includes population counted during the period of 10–24/12/1997, uncounted population estimates according to post enumeration survey and population estimates for those parts of Jerusalem annexed by Israel in 1967

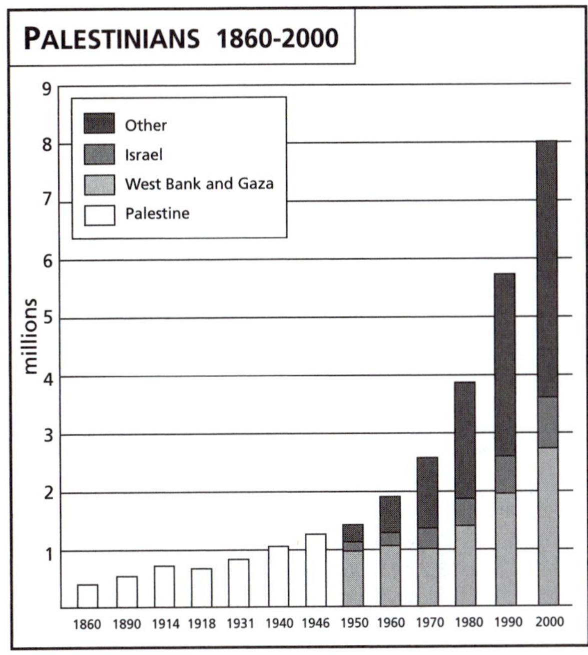

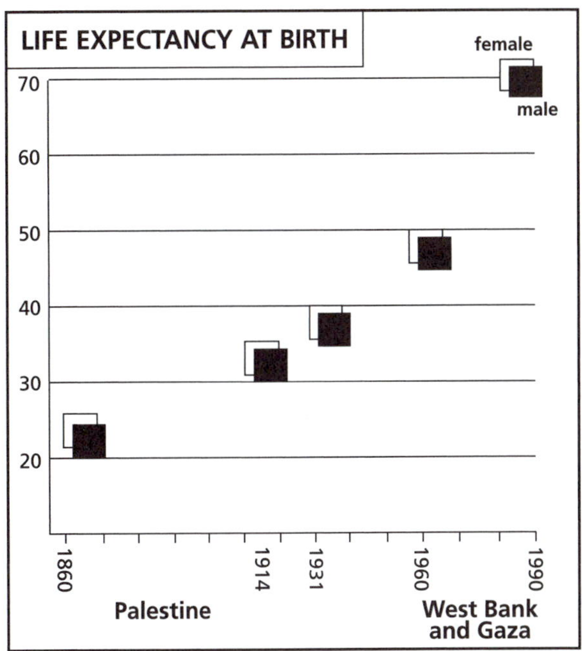

unlikely that the Gulf States will much increase their draw of skilled Palestinian labor.

Within the West Bank and particularly in Gaza diminished migration has exacerbated an already bad demographic situation. It is difficult to see how the agricultural or industrial base of Palestine can cope with the increased numbers that will result from high Palestinian fertility. Population density in the West Bank went from 52 per square mile (135 per square kilometer) in 1950 to 73 per square mile (190 per square kilometer) in 1990. The population density of Gaza, already great at 255 per square mile (660 per square kilometer) in 1950, was 660 per square mile (1,710 per square kilometer) in 1990. By comparison, the population densities of the Netherlands and England in 1990 were approximately 139 persons per square mile (360 per square kilometer). Possessing neither the agricultural potential nor the economic base of either the Netherlands or England, Palestine can expect a demographic crisis.

The census taken by the Palestinian Central Bureau of Statistics was partially a de jure enumeration. It included students and others who had been away from Palestine for a year or less, as reported by other members of their households. About 325,253 nonresident Palestinians were included. It is thus not strictly comparable with the other data in the article, which are de jure—counts of only those actually in residence on the date of the census or estimate.

Justin McCarthy

BIBLIOGRAPHY

Abu-Lughod, Janet L. "Demographic Characteristics of the Palestinian Population: Relevance for Planning Palestine Open University." Annex 1 of *Palestine Open University Feasibility Study, Part II.* Paris: UNESCO, 1980.

——. "The Demographic Transformation of Palestine." In Ibrahim Abu-Lughod, ed., *The Transformation of Palestine: Essays on the Origin and Development of the Arab-Israeli Conflict,* Evanston, Ill.: Northwestern University, 1971.

Bachi, Roberto. *The Population of Israel.* Jerusalem: Institute of Contemporary Jewry, Hebrew University, 1974.

Benvenisti, Meron. *The West Bank Data Project.* New York and London: American Enterprise Institute for Public Policy Research, 1984, and later reports of the project.

POPULATION

Brand, Laurie A. *Palestinians in the Arab World: Institution Building and the Search for State.* New York: Columbia University Press, 1988.

Courbage, Youssef, "Reshuffling the Demographic Cards in Israel/Palestine." *Journal of Palestine Studies* 28, no. 4 (1999): 21–39.

Ennab, Wael R. *Population and Demographic Developments in the West Bank and Gaza Strip until 1990.* New York: United Nations Conference on Trade and Development, United Nations, 1994.

Friedlander, D., Z. Eisenbach, and C. Goldscheider. "Modernization Patterns and Fertility Change: The Arab Population of Israel and the Israel-Administered Territories." *Population Studies (London)* 33, no. 2 (July 1979): 239–254.

Gabriel, Stuart A., and Eitan F. Sabatello. "Palestinian Migration from the West Bank and Gaza: Economic and Demographic Analysis." *Economic Development and Cultural Change* 34, no. 2 (January, 1986): 245–262.

Hagopian, Edward, and A.B. Zahlan. "Palestine's Arab Population: The Demography of the Palestinians." *Journal of Palestine Studies* 3, no. 4, (1974): 33–73.

Hill, Allan G. "The Palestinian Population of the Middle East." *Population and Development Review* 9, no. 2 (June, 1983): 293–316.

Khalidi, Walid, ed. *All That Remains: The Palestinian Villages Occupied and Depopulated by Israel in 1948.* Washington, D.C.: Institute for Palestine Studies, 1992.

Kossaifi, George. "Demographic Characteristics of the Arab Palestinian People." In Khalil Nakhleh and Elia Zureik, eds. *The Sociology of the Palestinians.* New York: St. Martin's Press, 1980.

McCarthy, Justin. *The Population of Palestine: Population History and Statistics of the Late Ottoman Period and the Mandate.* New York: Columbia University Press, 1990.

Palestine Liberation Organization, Economic Department, Central Bureau of Statistics. *Palestinian Statistical Abstract.* Number 5, Damascus, 1983 and earlier years.

Palestinian Central Bureau of Statistics. *Population, Housing, and Establishment Census, 1997.* Ramallah: Palestinian Authority, 1998.

Palestinian Projections for 16 Countries/Areas of the World, 1990 to 2010. Washington, D.C.: Center for International Research, Bureau of the Census, 1991.

Peretz, Don. *Israel and the Palestine Arabs.* Washington, D.C.: Middle East Institute, 1958.

——. *Palestinians, Refugees, and the Middle East Peace Process,* Washington, D.C.: United States Institute of Peace Press, 1993.

Projections of Population in Judea, Samaria and the Gaza Area up to 2002: Based on the Population in 1982. Jerusalem: Israel Central Bureau of Statistics, 1987.

Roof, Michael K., and Kevin G. Kinsella. *Palestinian Arab Population, 1950 to 1984.* Washington, D.C.: U.S. Bureau of the Census, 1985.

Roy, Sara. *The Gaza Strip: A Demographic, Economic, Social and Legal Survey.* The West Bank Data Base Project. Boulder, Colo.: Westview Press, 1996.

Schmelz, U. O., G. Nathan, and J. Kenvin. *Multiplicity Study of Births and Deaths in Judea-Samaria and Gaza Strip-North Sinai.* Jerusalem: Israel Central Bureau of Statistics, 1977.

United Nations Relief and Works Agency for Palestine Refugees in the Near East. "Palestine Refugees and Other Displaced Persons." Mimeograph. New York: UNRWA, 1979.

Zureik, Elia, *Palestinian Refugees and the Peace Process.* Washington, D.C.: Institute for Palestine Studies, 1996.

Q

al-Qaddumi, Faruq

Abu al-Lutf, head of the PLO's political department

1931– Jinsafut

Faruq al-Qaddumi was born near NABLUS to a wealthy family and grew up in HAIFA. He was uprooted in 1948 when Israel was established and he returned to Nablus. Al-Qaddumi joined the Ba'th Party soon after and has preserved his Ba'thist sympathies over the years. He obtained a degree in economics in 1958 and worked in Libya, Saudi Arabia, and KUWAIT, where he was employed by the Ministry of Health. With YASIR ARAFAT, whom he had met in Cairo in the 1950s, and others, he helped found FATAH and became one of its leaders. After his expulsion from Kuwait in 1966, he settled in Damascus and devoted himself full-time to revolutionary activities. He was put in charge of building ties between the new Palestinian movement and Arab countries, especially Egypt.

Al-Qaddumi was elected to the Executive Committee of the PALESTINE LIBERATION ORGANIZATION (PLO) in 1969. In 1973 he replaced Muhammad Yusuf al-Najjar, who was assassinated by Israeli gunmen in Beirut, as head of the Political Department of the PLO. Al-Qaddumi transformed the post to that of the foreign minister of the Palestinian national movement. He cultivated strong ties with "progressive" Arab regimes and with socialist countries. His Ba'thist ties allowed him to remain close to the Syrian and Iraqi regimes over the years. He remained a vocal advocate of the Syrian regime within the PLO even when Arafat's relationship with Damascus deteriorated in the wake of the 1982 Israeli invasion of Lebanon. The Syrian government has always considered al-Qaddumi an acceptable alternative to Arafat's leadership, and Qaddumi briefly considered joining the SA'ID MURAGHA (Abu Musa) defection from the PLO in 1983. Like other PLO leaders, al-Qaddumi initially shunned publicity and favored secretive work even when dealing with diplomatic issues. The entrenchment of the PLO in Lebanon, however, pushed him into the limelight. His role in Beirut, which began after the expulsion of the PLO from Jordan in 1970, was that of a chief diplomat of a state: receiving ambassadors and directing the PLO's missions around the world, a role that enabled him to secure diplomatic recognition of the PLO in more than ninety countries. He was also able to improve the PLO's relationships with Arab governments, especially the ones that opposed diplomatic solutions of the Palestinian problem. However, al-Qaddumi is not credited with any important political initiative in his long career, and his power base within Fatah and the PLO remains weak.

The role of al-Qaddumi's Political Department was transformed by the influx of oil money into the PLO in the 1970s. The PLO was gaining international recognition, and al-Qaddumi concentrated on guiding the international diplomatic presence of the organization. He is sometimes criticized for allowing Arafat and other Fatah leaders to appoint unqualified individuals as diplomats in key foreign capitals. Positions in the PLO diplomatic corps were rarely allocated on the basis of merit; rather, posts were regularly granted to those who had proved their personal loyalty to Arafat.

Al-Qaddumi was unprepared for the post–SOVIET UNION era. The PLO's missions in Russia and Eastern Europe were quickly rendered obsolete, because they had failed to establish ties with the dissident movements there. Furthermore, the missions were held to very little accountability in their expenditures, adding to the PLO's reputation for corruption. Al-Qaddumi, however, was not known as one of the notoriously corrupt figures of the PLO. He uniquely safeguarded his private life and that of his children.

The PLO-Israeli agreement of 1993, as well as the subsequent Oslo II accord, proved how marginal al-Qaddumi's role was. Arafat needed al-Qaddumi's support because of his credibility within the Palestinian national movement and the Arab world at large, but he did not seek al-Qaddumi's advice on the critical issue of Israeli-Palestinian diplomacy. In fact, al-Qaddumi, the so-called foreign minister of the PLO, was kept in the dark during the secret PLO-Israel talks in Oslo, perhaps because al-Qaddumi did not want to associate himself with a deal that he did not favor in the first place. MAHMUD ABBAS (also known as Abu Mazin) had assumed many of al-Qaddumi's responsibilities in the last several years, and during the PLO-Israel negotiations, Arafat brought him closer to the center of decision making. The PLO-Israel agreement left al-Qaddumi embarrassed: he did not want to break with Arafat completely, probably because he needed the financial resources that Arafat alone controlled, yet he publicly criticized Oslo concessions. In the mid-1990s, al-Qaddumi developed ties with Palestinian opposition groups in Damascus. But his need for Arafat's financial support (which is crucial for the preservation of Qaddumi's own mini bureaucracy) led Qaddumi to improve his relations with the PALESTINIAN AUTHORITY. He remains a likely successor to Arafat.

As'ad AbuKhalil

BIBLIOGRAPHY

"Abu Lutf." *Fichier du Monde Arabe* (Arab world file) 469 (March 31, 1976).

Reich, Bernard, et al. *An Historical Encyclopedia of the Arab-Israeli Conflict*. Westport, Conn.: Greenwood Press, 1996.

al-Qassam, Izz al-Din

Muslim preacher and revolutionary
1880?–1935 Ladhaqiyya, Syria

Born in a village near Ladhaqiyya, Syria, al-Qassam studied at the famous Muslim college in Cairo, al-Azhar University. He thereafter was known as a shaykh, and is reported to have come into contact with the Rashid Rida, a Syrian Muslim reformer.

After his return to Syria, al-Qassam joined guerrillas fighting against occupying French forces in the Alawi region of Jabal Sahyun in 1919–20. French authorities sentenced him in absentia to death for his activities, and al-Qassam fled to HAIFA, Palestine, following France's suppression of Syrian resistance.

Al-Qassam became an increasingly well-known figure in the Palestinian Islamic establishment in the 1920s. In 1921, he became a teacher at a Muslim school and was appointed preacher at Haifa's new Istiqlal mosque by the SUPREME MUSLIM COUNCIL in 1922. In 1929, he was appointed marriage registrar at the city's Islamic court. While serving in his various capacities, al-Qassam espoused a puritanical religious lifestyle that particularly appealed to some Palestinian youth. His travels throughout Palestine brought him into contact with many people, particularly among the poorer classes, who admired him. Others feared his views, leading to calls for his dismissal from his position as preacher.

In addition to his religious views, al-Qassam began developing revolutionary political ideas. He advocated an armed uprising against British authorities in Palestine as a result of his conviction that it was they who were ultimately responsible for the successes of ZIONISM in the country. Believing that Palestinians needed to be organized properly before challenging the British, al-Qassam cofounded the Young Men's Muslim Association in 1928 to work with the Boy Scout movement in preparing Palestinian youth for revolution. The groups began collecting weapons, training young men, and attacking Jewish settlements from 1931 to 1933. Reportedly al-Qassam even approached AL-HAJJ AMIN AL-HUSAYNI, mufti (expert in Islamic law) of Jerusalem and president of the Supreme Muslim Council, with the idea of leading a revolt in the northern part of Palestine while al-Husayni led one in the south. Al-Husayni reportedly declined, noting that he advocated political, not military, action.

By the mid-1930s, al-Qassam believed that Palestinian nationalist leaders' political methods were ineffective and argued for revolution instead. However, with only some two hundred followers, who still needed arms and training, al-Qassam believed that the time for revolution was not yet at hand.

Nevertheless, two factors proved important in changing his mind. First was the record number of Jewish immigrants (62,000) arriving in Palestine in 1935. The second was the British authorities' October 1935 interception of a shipment of arms destined for underground Zionist forces. Al-Qassam decided to take action and departed Haifa with his forces to steal arms from a police post. Discovered, al-Qassam's men killed a policeman before fleeing. Hundreds of policemen gave chase. Al-Qassam and two of his followers died in a shootout on November 21, 1935, rather than surrender.

Al-Qassam was hailed as a martyr throughout Palestine. His memory lived on in groups like the Ikhwan al-Qassam (Qassam Brotherhood), which tried to carry out his goal of armed insurrection. In fact, an Ikhwan al-Qassam attack that killed two Jews in April 1936 helped trigger the Arab revolt of 1936–39, the most significant armed Palestinian uprising against British rule during the PALESTINE MANDATE. Al-Qassam's legacy also was commemorated during the INTIFADA, when the Islamic fundamentalist organization HAMAS was established in 1988. Its military wing, Izz al-Din al-Qassam Kata'ib (regiments), violently confronted Israeli occupation forces in the WEST BANK and the GAZA STRIP. Hamas opposed the OSLO AGREEMENTS and continued its violent attacks on Israeli military and civilians thereafter.

Philip Mattar

Qattan, Abd al-Muhsin

businessman, philanthropist
1929– Jaffa

Qattan's family took up residence in KUWAIT after the ARAB-ISRAELI WAR OF 1948; there they developed close ties to the ruling family. Qattan himself established the al-Hani Contracting Company in 1959 and worked for the Kuwaiti ministry of electricity.

In addition to his business and philanthropic activities, Qattan has also been active in Palestinian politics. He was a longtime member of the PALESTINE NATIONAL COUNCIL and was elected its president in 1968. He resigned from the council in 1990. In 1983, he was one of the founding members of the Geneva-based Palestinian Welfare Association.

Michael R. Fischbach

al-Qawuq ji, Fawzi

guerrilla leader
1890–1977 Tripoli

Al-Qawuqji left Lebanon for studies in Istanbul as a youth and graduated from the Ottoman military academy in 1912. During World War I, he fought against British troops in Iraq and Palestine, although he later deserted and joined the Arab revolt. Qawuqji later served the Syrian kingdom established by Emir Faysal bin Husayn in Damascus until its downfall at the hands of the French in 1920. Thereafter, he participated in anti-French guerrilla activities during the 1925 Syrian uprising. Qawuqji served as a military adviser for other Arab regimes in the 1920s, first for the Saudis in 1928 and later for Iraq, beginning in 1932.

Qawuqji's Arab nationalist feelings also fed into the growing Zionist-Palestinian conflict. On the outbreak of the 1936 Palestinian revolt, Qawuqji began organizing Arab volunteers in Transjordan, SYRIA, LEBANON, and Iraq to assist Palestinian guerrilla fighters. In August 1936, he entered Palestine with several hundred troops and took up positions in the area of NABLUS and JENIN as commander-in-chief of the revolutionaries, although he refused to cooperate with other guerrilla forces in the HEBRON area associated with the HUSAYNI FAMILY faction (led by Abd al-Qadir al-Husayni) and harshly attacked the leading Councilist figure, AL-HAJJ AMIN AL-HUSAYNI. Qawuqji's forces left Palestine in October 1936 when the fighting temporarily subsided. His military service and nationalist feeling later led to his participation in the Kaylani revolt in Iraq in 1941.

Qawuqji's most significant intervention in Arab and Palestinian affairs was to occur in 1947 and 1948. The ARAB LEAGUE, meeting in December 1947 at Alayh, Lebanon, decided to raise and dispatch troops to assist the Palestinian people in stemming the foreseen creation of a Jewish state in Palestine. In December 1947, Qawuqji was appointed commander-in-chief of this force, the ARAB LIBERATION ARMY (ALA). Never very effective on the battlefields of northern and central Palestine, Qawuqji and the 4,600 ALA troops who entered Palestine were ordered withdrawn by the Arab leadership in May 1948 as regular Arab armies entered the fray. Qawuqji briefly returned that same month to assist the Palestinians of Jerusalem to defend themselves against Zionist attacks. He and his forces later were involved with fighting in northern Palestine along with Syrian and Lebanese forces.

After the 1948 war, Qawuqji never again returned to the battlefield but lived out the remainder of his life in Beirut, where he died in 1977.

Michael R. Fischbach

al-Quds University

Al-Quds University was established in 1984 through a merger of four other institutions, and it is the only Palestinian university in JERUSALEM. Students can obtain degrees and certificates in six faculties: arts, sciences, medicine, law, Islamic studies and jurisprudence, and allied health professions. Additionally, they can obtain an M.A. through the Institute of Islamic Archaeology. Some 11,000 students were enrolled at the university as of 1997.

Michael R. Fischbach

Quray, Ahmad

Abu Ala; Qurai; Korei; economist, politician

October 12, 1937– Abu Dis

Born in a suburb of JERUSALEM Quray moved from the WEST BANK in 1968 to work in banks in JORDAN and Saudi Arabia. He joined FATAH and directed the MARTYRS WORKS SOCIETY (SAMED) organization of the PALESTINE LIBERATION ORGANIZATION (PLO) in Beirut beginning in the 1970s. In 1982, he became the deputy director of the PLO's department of economic affairs and a member of Fatah's central committee beginning in 1989.

Quray also played a major role in the Palestinian–Israeli negotiations that led to the Israeli redeployment from the Occupied Territories and the establishment of the PALESTINIAN AUTHORITY (PA). He was the main Palestinian figure carrying out the secret talks with Israeli officials in Oslo, Norway, behind the backs of the official Palestinian delegation negotiating with the Israelis in Washington, D.C., in 1993. In 1994, Quray was appointed the PA's minister of economy and trade and head of the Palestinian Economic Council for Development and Reconstruction (PECDAR). He later was a lead negotiator during the talks held in Taba, Egypt, that led to the Israeli–PLO Interim Agreement of September 1995.

Quray was elected to the PA's PALESTINIAN LEGISLATIVE COUNCIL in January 1996 and became its speaker. He is seen as a senior figure within the PA and a potential successor to the PA leader, YASIR ARAFAT.

Michael R. Fischbach

R

Rajub, Jibril

activist, security official
1953– Dura

Rajub joined the FATAH movement as a teenager and worked to organize Fatah cells near his village in the HEBRON hills of the Israeli-occupied WEST BANK. He later spent seventeen years in Israeli jails, beginning in 1968, to become one of the senior Fatah officials in Israeli custody.

Released as part of a prisoner exchange between Israel and a Palestinian faction in 1985, Rajub emerged as a major Fatah figure in the West Bank. Israeli authorities deported him in 1988, whereupon he made his way to PALESTINE LIBERATION ORGANIZATION (PLO) headquarters in Tunis to become a top-level adviser to the PLO chairman, YASIR ARAFAT. Rajub helped organize the INTIFADA uprising as a deputy to the Fatah security chief, KHALIL AL-WAZIR (Abu Jihad).

After the establishment of the PALESTINIAN AUTHORITY (PA) in 1994, Rajub moved to JERICHO to assume his new duties as head of the PA's Preventative Security Force (PSF) in the West Bank with the rank of colonel. The PSF remains one of the most important of the PA's intelligence agencies.

Michael R. Fischbach

Rakah

Rakah is the Hebrew acronym for *Reshima Komunistit Hadasha* (New Communist List); it was formed in 1965 out of a split in the Israeli Communist Party (ICP). By the 1960s, Israeli and Palestinian members of the ICP had become increasingly polarized over the ARAB-ISRAELI CONFLICT. Although both sides were Marxists dedicated to internationalism and antiimperialism, Jewish and Arab Communists differed over the proper stance vis-à-vis Arab nationalist leaders like Egyptian president Jamal Abd al-Nasir. Unlike Jewish activists, many Palestinians in the ICP supported Nasir as a symbol of the antiimperialist struggle in the Arab world. The support of the SOVIET UNION for such figures heightened tensions within the pro-Soviet ICP.

In August 1965, leading Palestinian Communists such as TAWFIQ TUBI, EMILE TUMA, and EMILE HABIBI left the ICP and established Rakah. Despite the fact that the Jewish Communist Meir Vilner became Rakah's chair, the new party was overwhelmingly Palestinian. It has consistently returned representatives to the Knesset over the years and constituted the main voice of dissent among the PALESTINIAN CITIZENS OF ISRAEL over the decades.

In 1977, Rakah formed the Democratic Front for Peace and Equality (known by the Hebrew acronym Hadash) in order to garner votes from non-Communist Palestinian voters. Hadash initially inherited Rakah's position as the non-Zionist party securing the largest number of Palestinian votes in Knesset elections, although inroads made by other Arab parties such as the Arab Democratic Party and the Progressive List for Peace and by Islamic movements cut into Hadash's support in the late 1980s. In the 1999 elections, Hadash lost two of its five Knesset seats as a result of AZMI BISHARA'S decision to run independently.

Michael R. Fischbach

Ramallah

Ramallah lies sixteen kilometers north of Jerusalem in the hills of the central WEST BANK. It was the center of the administrative subdistrict carrying its name during both the PALESTINE MANDATE and Jordanian rule.

Ramallah is a noteworthy Palestinian town for several reasons. It has long possessed a strong Christian presence; by the mid-1940s, Christians constituted 4,440 of Ramallah's 5,080 inhabitants. The town is also famous for its strong professional and educational heritage. Many of Ramallah's inhabitants emigrated to the United States in the twentieth century; some returned with educational degrees and investment funds. American Quakers established a girls' school in Ramallah in 1889. BIR ZEIT UNIVERSITY, one of the leading Palestinian institutions of higher learning, is located in nearby Bir Zayt.

Ramallah's population remained relatively stable during the Mandate. It was approximately 5,000 from the late Ottoman period through the 1940s. Economically, some of its population worked the town's 14,706 *dunums* of land; others were involved in artisanal and modern manufacturing, trade, and summer tourism. At 860 meters above sea level, Ramallah was also the site of Palestine's only radio transmission station during the Mandate and is currently also the site of the PALESTINIAN AUTHORITY radio and television facilities.

The town was occupied by Jordanian forces during the 1948 fighting and was incorporated into the Jordanian-controlled West Bank. The 1967 Israeli occupation of the West Bank affected Ramallah significantly. As an intellectual center in the West Bank, it had many inhabitants who participated in the INTIFADA; Israeli authorities closed Bir Zeit University from 1988 to 1992 as a result.

After redeployment of Israeli forces from the town as a result of the peace accords signed between Israel and the PALESTINE LIBERATION ORGANIZATION, the Palestinian Authority assumed control of Ramallah on December 26, 1995, and later located some of its administrative offices there.

Michael R. Fischbach

Ramla

Located in Palestine's coastal plain, Ramla differs from many Palestinian towns in its relatively recent origins. It was established by the Arabs in 716 C.E. and contains the tomb venerated by Muslims as that of the Qur'anic figure Salih.

Ramla constituted a very important point along communications and transportation lines (including railroad) in Palestine. This fact has long placed it at the center of campaigns by various invaders throughout history, many of which—including those of the Crusaders and Napoleon Bonaparte—have seized it from its Muslim defenders. Ramla was also a longtime administrative center in Palestine. It was the capital of the *jund filastin* during the early Islamic period, and the center of the subdistrict bearing its name during the PALESTINE MANDATE. The Mandate era witnessed a phenomenal growth in the town's population as well: from some 6,500 before the World War I to 16,380 by 1946.

Given its location along important caravan routes from Syria to Egypt and later the railroad between JERUSALEM and JAFFA, trade long constituted an important part of Ramla's economy. Agriculture was also important; among the most important crops grown in the town's 38,983 *dunums* of land were olives and fruit, especially oranges. Ramla was long an important center for artisanal production. Among its well-known products were textiles and carpets, dairy products, olive oil, and olive oil soap.

Along with that of neighboring LYDDA, the fate of Ramla and its inhabitants during the ARAB-ISRAELI WAR OF 1948 was a microcosm of the wider Palestinian tragedy. It was defended by Palestinian forces, irregular volunteers from JORDAN, and units of the Jordanian Arab Legion that had entered Palestine on the British withdrawal in May 1948. Hard pressed to defend the legion's position at Latrun, the Briton commanding the legion, Lieutenant General John Glubb, refused to reinforce the legion detachment despite the Zionist threat to the town. Ramla was captured by Palmach forces on July 12, 1948, whereupon all but 400 of its 15,000 residents were immediately expelled.

Michael R. Fischbach

Rantisi, Abd al-Aziz

physician, Islamic activist
1947– Yibna

From a village southwest of Ramla, Rantisi's family fled to the GAZA STRIP during the ARAB-ISRAELI WAR OF 1948. He completed medical studies at the University of Alexandria in Egypt in 1971, after which he returned to practice medicine in Gaza. He served as head of pediatrics at Khan Yunis Hospital until he was dismissed by Israeli authorities in 1983; thereafter, he worked in clinics and was a lecturer at the Islamic University in Gaza.

Rantisi became a leading Islamic activist in Gaza. In 1973, he helped found the Islamic Center in Gaza, which was associated with the Muslim Brotherhood. He was a leading figure within HAMAS after its creation in 1988 and was its effective leader in Gaza after Israel arrested the Hamas spiritual leader, AHMAD YASIN, in May 1989. Rantisi himself served time in Israeli prisons during the INTIFADA and was eventually deported to southern Lebanon along with over 400 other Palestinians in December 1992. He attained international exposure as spokesperson for the deportees. Allowed to return the following year, Rantisi was again imprisoned in December 1993 until his release in April 1997.

Michael R. Fischbach

Rashidiyya School

The Rashidiyya School was originally a public elementary school established by Ottoman authorities. During the PALESTINE MANDATE, it became one of the few Ottoman schools to be maintained by the new government of Palestine.

The Rashidiyya School developed into one of the two best public secondary schools for boys in Palestine during the Mandate, along with the ARAB COLLEGE. It expanded during the 1940s to fill the need for educating promising boys who were not admitted into the Arab College's teacher preparation program. The Rashidiyya School eventually offered a four-year curriculum with two tracks (literary and scientific), as well as two-year postgraduation programs (premedical and preengineering). In addition to its own examinations, the Rashidiyya School prepared students for the University of London's intermediary exams.

By the 1945–46 school year, 310 students were enrolled in the school, including 26 in the postgraduation program.

Michael R. Fischbach

Reagan Plan

The Reagan Plan was announced by President Ronald Reagan in September 1982. Crafted by Secretary of State George Shultz after Israel's invasion of Lebanon in June of that year, the plan proposed giving the Palestinians autonomy in the WEST BANK and the GAZA STRIP during a five-year transition period leading to negotiations on final disposition of these territories.

Under the plan, Palestinians, including those in East Jerusalem, would elect a self-governing authority and enjoy autonomy, as well as control of the land and its resources, subject only to a guarantee of water to Israel. Reagan urged that Israel freeze construction of new Israeli settlements in the West Bank and the Gaza Strip during the transition period but assured Israel that the United States would not support the dismantling of existing settlements. The final status of the territories would be negotiated after the transition period, but Reagan made it clear that the United States would not support either an independent Palestinian state or permanent Israeli control over the area. The United States's preference was for Palestinian self-government in association with Jordan. Jerusalem would remain united, its final status to be determined in negotiations.

The Reagan Plan was based on the CAMP DAVID ACCORDS of September 1978 but went further in its inclusion of East Jerusalem Palestinians in the group allowed to vote for a self-governing authority and in its conception of autonomy as including land and resources as well as people. In affirming U.S. support for UNITED NATIONS SECURITY COUNCIL RESOLUTIONS 242 AND 238 as the basis for a peace agreement, Reagan reiterated that peace should be predicated on the principle of exchanging land for peace. He specifically noted that the United States believed that the withdrawal provision of the resolution applied to all fronts, including the West Bank and Gaza. Israel, on the other hand, maintained that it had already fulfilled its obligations under the resolution by withdrawing from the Sinai Peninsula in accordance with the 1979 Egyptian-Israeli Peace Treaty.

The Reagan Plan was rejected immediately by Israel, which objected to Reagan's call for its eventual relinquishment of control over the Occupied Territories, to the inclusion of East Jerusalem Palestinians in elections, and to the proposed freeze on settlement construction. After an Arab summit held shortly after the Reagan Plan was announced, the Arabs put forth the Fez Plan, which was similar in many respects. The United

States never encouraged this plan, however, and the Reagan Plan was finally rejected by Jordan and the PALESTINE LIBERATION ORGANIZATION (PLO). After the Israeli rejection, even the United States never seriously pursued Reagan's initiative.

Kathleen Christison

BIBLIOGRPPHY

Quandt, William B. *Peace Process: American Diplomacy and the Arab-Israeli Conflict Since 1967.* Washington, D.C.: The Brookings Institution; Berkeley: University of California Press, 1993.

Red Crescent

The Palestine Red Crescent Society (PRCS), the Palestinian equivalent of the Red Cross or Red Crescent of other nations, provides medical and health care, both preventive and curative, to the Palestinian people. It operates fifteen major hospitals and forty-four principal clinics in Lebanon, Syria, Egypt, Sudan, Tunisia, Yemen, and Qatar. This geographical diversity reflects the demographics of the Palestinian diaspora. Until very recently, the PRCS was prohibited from offering services in the Occupied Territories. In both the hospitals and the clinics, services are provided either free or for a nominal fee to both Palestinians and nationals of the host countries.

All PRCS hospitals have specialized departments, such as maternity, pathology, pediatrics, radiology, orthopedics, dentistry, obstetrics, oncology, urology, and dermatology, as well as the full range of surgical subspecialties. In addition to such medical and surgical care, each hospital is distinguished by units of particular importance to the Palestinian people. For instance, the Nazareth Pediatric Hospital and the Ramla Physiotherapy and Rehabilitation Center, both part of the Akka Hospital complex in Beirut, reflect the PRCS's concern for the youngest members of society and for those who seek to end the occupation.

At Ramla, for example, strikingly modern therapy includes hydrotherapy, electrotherapy, physiotherapy, diathermy, massage, and vocational rehabilitation. There is also a facility for the manufacture of prostheses that fits some 400 devices yearly. In addition to artificial limbs, the center produces therapeutic shoes, braces, splints, and corsets. Most of the individuals who work in this unit are themselves wearers of artificial limbs and draw psychological succor as well as financial remuneration from their productive work.

The PRCS provides preventative medicine on a large scale in nearly all the Palestinian communities throughout the Middle East. In addition to the forty-four clinics, virtually every Palestinian locale—especially the most impoverished—has a clinic that deals with the prevention, detection, and, to a lesser extent, treatment of contagious diseases such as tuberculosis, dysentery, and viral and bacterial infections. The most important function of these centers is community public health education, including, for example, instruction for families in boiling and purifying water, antirodent campaigns, and programs to encourage families to have their children vaccinated.

Cheryl Rubenberg

Reform Party

Established in June 1935 by Husayn Fakhri al-KHALIDI, a member of one of the notable Muslim families of Jerusalem, the Reform Party had followers in Jerusalem, Ramallah, Jaffa, Gaza, and their suburbs. Among its supporters were mayors and retired civil servants who respected al-Khalidi's independence and determination to prevent domination by the HUSAYNI FAMILY. The party had a collegial leadership with al-Khalidi, who was mayor of Jerusalem at the time, sharing the post of secretary with Mahmud Abu Khadra, a former mayor of Gaza, and Shibli Jamal, a Christian active in Palestinian politics since the early years of British rule. Aware of the importance of augmenting Arab influence vis-à-vis the Zionists and their British sponsors, the Reform Party found merit in accepting the proposed LEGISLATIVE COUNCIL as an intermediate step that it hoped would lead to full-fledged independence.

Muhammad Muslih

Refugees

The term *Palestinian refugees* refers to those Palestinians and their descendants who fled or were expelled from their homes in Mandatory Palestine during the year that followed the November 1947 passage of the United Nations partition resolution and those Palestinians who fled or were driven out

TABLE 1
Distribution of registered population as of 30 June 1999

FIELD	REGISTERED POPULATION	NUMBER OF CAMPS	TOTAL CAMP POPULATION	REGISTERED PERSONS NOT IN CAMPS	PERCENTAGE OF POPULATION NOT IN CAMPS
Jordan	1,512,742	10	274,816	1,237,926	81.83
Lebanon	370,144	12	204,999	165,145	44.62
Syrian Arab Republic	374,521	10	109,315	265,206	70.81
West Bank	569,741	19	153,380	416,361	73.08
Gaza	798,444	8	437,650	360,794	45.19
Total	3,625,592	59	1,180,160	2,445,432	67.45

during and immediately after the June 1967 war. Since 1948, the Palestine refugee problem has been one of the most intractable and controversial in the ARAB-ISRAELI CONFLICT, with bitter disputes over the causes of the flight, the total number of refugees, and possible solutions to the problem.

Because of ambiguities about the definition of refugees and the fact that there were only estimates of the original number who were in Palestine, there are no precise figures of the total number of Palestinian refugees. The figures provided by the United Nations Relief and Works Agency for Palestine Refugees in the Near East (UNRWA), which was established in 1949, are usually considered the most credible. The following is the UNRWA definition of Palestinian refugees:

> A Palestine refugee is a person whose normal residence was Palestine for a minimum of two years preceding the conflict in 1948, and who, as a result of this conflict, lost both his [sic] home and his means of livelihood and took refuge in one of the countries where UNRWA provides relief. Refugees within this definition and the direct descendants of such refugees are eligible for Agency [UNRWA] assistance if they are: registered with UNRWA; living in the area of UNRWA operations and in need.

UNRWA refugee camps were established in the GAZA STRIP, LEBANON, SYRIA, JORDAN, and the WEST BANK. The number initially provided for by UNRWA in 1950 was 914,000.

By 1999, there were fifty-nine UNRWA camps located in five UNRWA field areas: the West Bank (nineteen camps), the Gaza Strip (eight camps), Jordan (ten), Lebanon (twelve), and Syria (ten). A total of 3,625,000 Palestinians—approximately 50 percent of all Palestinians worldwide—were registered with UNRWA as refugees by 1999 (Table 1). However, only about a third of the refugees actually lived in camps; in Jordan, about 19 percent of the total refugee population lived in UNRWA camps, and in Lebanon more than 54 percent were camp residents. The largest refugee camps were in Gaza, four of which housed more than 60,000 inhabitants each.

The refugees who fled during 1947–48 left those parts of Palestine that became the state of Israel within boundaries defined by the 1949 armistice agreements with Egypt, Syria, Lebanon, and Jordan. They constituted about half the estimated 1,380,000 Arab population of Mandatory Palestine in May 1948. Palestinians, the Arab states, and their supporters maintained that the refugees were forced from their homes by Zionist (prior to May 1948) or Israeli military and paramilitary units. The government of Israel denied responsibility for the refugee flight. It blamed Palestinian leaders and the leaders of surrounding Arab countries, which Israel claimed had urged the refugees to flee. However, since 1985, Israeli scholars have documented many instances in which the Israeli military forced Palestinians to leave. Undisputed—and major—causes of the refugee flight were the collapse and near-total disruption of Palestinian society due to the chaos of the first Arab-Israeli war.

A second major refugee exodus followed the June 1967 war, when more than 300,000 Palestinians fled or were forced out of the Jordanian West Bank and the Egyptian-administered Gaza Strip, which were occupied by the Israeli army. Some 120,000 of these Palestinians were second-time refugees who had spent the previous twenty years in camps under Jordanian or Egyptian jurisdic-

MAJOR PALESTINIAN REFUGEE CAMPS AFTER 1948
Homs
Nahar al Bard
Khan Askar
LEBANON
Debayeh
Gourad
Dekwaneh
Wawel
Mar Elias
Jisr al Pasha
Shatila
Burj al Barajneh
Ain al Hilwa
Anjar
Mieh Mieh
al Bass
Rashdiya
Khan Danum
Khan esh Shih
SYRIA
Mediterranean Sea
ISRAEL
Derra
Irbid
Jenin
Nur Shams
Tulkarm
Askar
No.1
Balata
al Sufo
Jarash
al Husan
al Bikah
Zarka
Dayr Ammar
Jalazone
Karamah
Hussein
Amari
Nuweimeh
Marka
Kalandya
Ein es Sult
Aida
Mulaskar
Dheishe
Aqabat Jabr
Talbiya
Arrub
Gaza Beach
Jabalya
Nusseirat
al Burejj
Beit Djibrin
Dayr al Balah
al Muazi
Fawwar
Dead Sea
al Rafah
Khan Yunis
JORDAN
N
0
30 Miles
EGYPT
Established After the 1948 War
Abandoned in 1967
Palestinian Refugee Camp

tion. In addition to the second-time refugees who had been displaced from their homes, thousands of indigenous West Bankers and Gazans fled. The latter were classified as "displaced persons" although they did receive UNRWA identification cards. In addition to those formally classified as refugees or displaced persons, there are tens of thousands of Palestinians unable to return to their homes in Israel or in the Occupied Territories as a result of restrictions placed on their return by the Israel government.

Since 1949–50 those classified as refugees by UNRWA have received assistance from the international organization, the amount determined by the economic situation of the individual refugee family. Initially, most refugees lived in camps established by U.N. agencies. However, by the 1990s, over 1,700,000 lived in cities, towns, or villages outside the camps, where they received from UNRWA education, health care, food rations, and other social services according to need. Annual expenditures for these services increased from $33.6 million a year in 1950 to over $351.5 million by 1997. As increasing numbers of refugees found employment or became partially self-sufficient, UNRWA's emphasis shifted from relief to EDUCATION and technical training, so that more than half the organization's budget went for educational services by the 1990s and more than half its more than 20,000 employees served in the UNRWA school system.

The refugees initially lived in tents, but as it became apparent that they would not return to their homes soon, more permanent living quarters were constructed; by the 1990s, many camps were adjunctive to, or suburbs of, large urban centers such as Amman, Beirut, Damascus, and JERUSALEM. Although the number of refugees has more than doubled, most camps have been unable to expand in area, resulting in extremely crowded and uncomfortable living conditions.

In most areas, the internal affairs of camps are run by the Palestinians themselves. The PALESTINE LIBERATION ORGANIZATION (PLO) has played an important role in the political organization of the refugees and in establishment of services to supplement those of UNRWA. Refugee frustration with low wages, poor living conditions, and inability to return to Palestine has caused social and political unrest. Life for the refugees in Lebanon is difficult. They have problems in obtaining work permits and in finding employment in other than temporary unskilled jobs. The PLO initiated several projects to enable refugees to sustain themselves; these included handicraft workshops under the MARTYRS' WORKS SOCIETY (SAMED), a PLO organization for refugee economic rehabilitation. Some refugee camps became bases for Palestinian guerrilla activity, a condition that led to armed conflict between the Palestinians and various Lebanese militias as well as periodic clashes with Israel's armed forces. The refugees were active in the anti-establishment militias during the civil war from 1974 to 1995.

The GULF CRISIS, 1990–91, affected Palestinians in two ways. First, more than 300,000 Palestinians, most of them with Jordanian passports, were forced to return to Jordan from KUWAIT, Iraq, Saudi Arabia, and other Gulf states. Although they were not technically refugees, the haste of their relocation and their situation in Jordan were essentially those of refugees. The second, and potentially positive, consequence of the Gulf Crisis occurred after the MADRID PEACE CONFERENCE, 1991, when a refugee working group was established as one of five multilateral groups organized to deal with functional problems related to an overall peace settlement. For the first time since the Palestinian refugee problem emerged in 1947–48, this multinational group is studying ways to resolve aspects of the refugee question, including the right of return, payment of compensation for Palestinian LAND left in Israel, refugee economic and social rehabilitation, and political status of refugees unable to return to their homeland. In the OLSO AGREEMENTS between Israel and the Palestinian authorities, the refugee issue was deferred to the final status negotiations, which by 1999 still had not taken place.

Don Peretz

BIBLIOGRAPHY

Artz, Donna. *Refugees into Citizens: Palestinians and the End of the Arab-Israeli Conflict.* New York: Council on Foreign Relations, 1997.

Morris, Benny. *The Birth of the Palestinian Refugee Problem.* Cambridge, England: Cambridge University Press, 1987.

Peretz, Don. *Israel and the Palestine Arabs.* Washington, D.C.: Middle East Institute, 1958.

——. *Palestinians, Refugees, and the Middle East Peace Process.* Washington, D.C.: United States Institute of Peace, 1993.

United Nations. *Report of the Commissioner-General of the United Nations Relief and Works Agency for Palestine Refugees in the Near East.* Annual reports 1950–94. New York, 1950–1994.

Viorst, Milton. *Reaching for the Olive Branch: UNRWA and Peace in the Middle East.* Bloomington, Indiana University Press, 1989.

Rejection Front

The Rejection Front was established in Baghdad in October 1974 by Palestinian groups opposed to the strategy being discussed within the PALESTINE LIBERATION ORGANIZATION (PLO) of seeking a negotiated settlement to the ARAB-ISRAELI CONFLICT based on recognition of Israel and creation of a Palestinian state in the Occupied Territories. Spearheaded by the POPULAR FRONT FOR THE LIBERATION OF PALESTINE, the Rejection Front argued for continuing armed struggle with the goal of liberating all of Palestine.

Other groups in the Rejection Front included the ARAB LIBERATION FRONT, the POPULAR FRONT FOR THE LIBERATION OF PALESTINE-GENERAL COMMAND, the PALESTINIAN POPULAR STRUGGLE FRONT, and, later, the PALESTINE LIBERATION FRONT. It was backed by Iraq and the Iraqi Ba'th Party.

Changing PLO strategy in the wake of the 1978 CAMP DAVID ACCORDS led the front's members to resume activity within the PLO, with the result that the front ceased activity by 1980.

Michael R. Fischbach

Religious and Ethnic Communities

Most Palestinians consider themselves descendants of the Cananites and successive invaders, including the Arabs, who conquered Palestine in 638 C.E. The population became Arabized and most, except for the small Christian and Jewish communities, became Muslim. In 1922, a British census showed that Muslims made up 78.3 percent of the population, Jews 11.1 percent, and Christians 9.5 percent. By the 1990s the overwhelming majority of over 6 million Palestinians (93.4 percent) were Sunni Arab Muslims. The sacredness of Palestine to Muslims stems from its association with the development of monotheism, starting with Judaism and ending with Islam. Jerusalem, the first *qibla* toward which Muslims were asked to turn in prayer, is the third holiest city, after Mecca and Medina. The sacred nature of Jerusalem was enhanced for Muslims with the Night Journey of the Prophet, al-Isra wa al-Mi'raj, celebrated each year on the twenty-seventh day of the lunar month Rajab. In the Night Journey, the Prophet was taken by the Angel Gabriel from Mecca to the Dome of the Rock in Jerusalem, al-Isra, and together they ascended into heaven, al-Mi'raj.

Mosques are found in cities, towns, villages, and refugee camps. Although they are frequented daily by more pious believers, it is the Friday noon prayers that attract the largest numbers of believers. During the month of Ramadan, thousands of Muslims from all over Palestine journey to Jerusalem's AL-HARAM AL-SHARIF, the Noble Sanctuary, which encloses both the Dome of the Rock and the Aqsa Mosque. In addition to al-Haram al-Sharif, Muslims also venerate the Ibrahimi Mosque in HEBRON, where the tombs of the Prophets are found, including that of Ibrahim (Abraham), considered to be the first Muslim. Hebron's Arabic name, *al-Khalil,* is derived from an adjective denoting Abraham as God's friend. Palestinian culture, given the long history of Islam in the country, is imbued in all of its spheres with influences of Islamic civilization. This can be observed not simply in the architecture of mosques, houses, and public buildings, but also in the ordering of life along religious principles, events, and ceremonies. Islam is thus a strong element in the self- and group identification of Palestinian Muslims.

Although the overwhelming majority of Muslims are Sunni Arabs, there are both religious and ethnic minorities among them. Historically, the most important minority has been the Druze, who live in eighteen villages in the Galilee and Mount Carmel regions, which are part of ISRAEL. The Druze are an offshoot of a Shi'ite Ismai'li sect that originated with the Fatimid caliph al-Hakim (985–1021). There are 77,000 Druze in the Galilee (many of whom identify with Israel) 10,000 Druze in four villages in the occupied Syrian Golan Heights, and more than 200,000 in Lebanon and Syria. Druze speak Arabic, celebrate the al-Adha feast like Sunni Muslims, and make a pilgrimage to the tomb of Nabi Shu'ayb (Jethro, the father-in-law of Moses) at Hittin near TIBERIAS. Druze sociocultural and religious affinity revolves around their community with links with other Druze communities.

The Circassians, who number 3,000, inhabit two villages in the Galilee: Kufr Kanna and Rihaniyya. They migrated from the Caucasus mountains in the 1860s after Russian control expanded over their territories. As a result, Muslim Circassians, joined by a small number of Chechens, dispersed over Syria, Jordan, Iraq, and Palestine. Circassians are Sunni Muslims, a fact that has eased their assimilation into Arabic culture in Palestine and elsewhere. Circassians retain their distinctive linguistic, cultural, and national character, and they strive to celebrate weddings and other events in line with their traditions. There are a number of Circassian families in the West Bank and Gaza, but, because of their low numbers and geographical dispersal, they do not constitute an independently viable community such as that which exists in the Galilee. Israel conscripts both Circassian and Druze men into the army.

The al-Maghariba live in a quarter of Jerusalem carrying their name. Al-Maghariba are North Africans, mostly from Morocco, who, en route to Mecca, opted to remain in Jerusalem. Over the years, the Maghrabi community has grown to an estimated three thousand. In political matters, they identify fully with other Palestinians but retain customs from their countries of origin. Similar to the Maghariba are families of Afghani origin and others of sub-Saharan African origin. All these have been assimilated almost completely into Arab culture and Palestinian society.

A small group of supposed Gypsy origin, perhaps from central Europe, reside in Bab Hutta in the eastern walled part of the Old City of Jerusalem. The origin of these families probably traces to earlier events that attracted bands of gypsies to perform and entertain the population of the city. Although they profess Sunni Islam, it is rare that intermarriage with their Muslim neighbors takes place. The men traditionally work in occupations deemed unacceptable to the larger population, such as sewage maintenance and garbage disposal. In the past, women begged or engaged in selling drinks and trinkets to passersby in their neighborhood, which is in proximity to the northeastern entrance to al-Haram al-Sharif compound. Face and body tattoos mark both men and women. Since the 1970s the Gypsies have experienced improvements in their economic situation due to the opening up of new occupational opportunities, including white-collar jobs for educated younger members. The small size of their community makes most Palestinians oblivious to the presence of Gypsies as a distinct ethnic group.

The Samaritans are a small and special Jewish community numbering 300 persons. They live in the city of NABLUS. The Samaritans do not accept the whole Torah and claim descent from the tribes of Joseph and his sons Manasseh and Ephraim. They consider Mount Gerizim in Nablus, and not Jerusalem, as the location of the true Temple and thus their most holy site. In addition to the Nablus community, there is a Samaritan community in Holon, Israel, with similarly small numbers. The Samaritans marry only within their own group, speak Arabic in their daily life, and use an archaic form of Hebrew in their liturgy.

Palestinian Christians worldwide number about 400,000 and make up 6.6 percent of the Palestinian people. In the 1990s, 180,000 Christians resided within the boundaries of British Mandatory Palestine (the WEST BANK, the GAZA STRIP and Israel). An estimated 95 percent of Palestinian Christians are Arabs, and they share a similar culture with Palestinian Muslims. Palestinian Christians are concentrated in certain towns. In the West Bank they live predominantly in East Jerusalem, Bayt Sahur, RAMALLAH, BETHLEHEM, Bayt Jala, Zababida, and Bir Zayt. In Israel, Palestinian Christians live in the city of NAZARETH and a number of villages in the Galilee. There also is a small community of Palestinian Christians in Gaza. Approximately 52 percent of all Palestinian Christians are Greek Orthodox, and 30 percent are Roman Catholics. There are small numbers of Greek Catholics (5.7 percent)—Catholics who use Greek rather than Latin in their liturgy—and Protestants (4.9 percent).

Among the Christian ethnic minorities are the Ethiopians, Armenians, Russians, Copts, and Syrian Orthodox. The Ethiopian number between fifteen and twenty black families. Ethiopia became Christian in 322 C.E. and Ethiopian monks have lived in the country since the end of the fourth century. In the Middle Ages, there was a prosperous Ethiopian community in Jerusalem, which by the fifteenth century had accrued much influence and property. Until 1951, the Ethiopian church was subordinate to the Coptic patriarch of Alexandria, but since 1959 it has had its own patriarch and maintains its independence as the Church of

Ethiopia. Ethiopians still own property and a number of churches in the country. They also claim rights in the HOLY PLACES, especially Dayr al-Sultan, the monastery situated on the roof of the Chapel of Saint Helena, which is part of the church of the Holy Sepulchre. The community is headed by a bishop who leads the Easter week ceremonies in which hundreds of Ethiopian pilgrims participate. Among the celebrations is the colorful procession on Easter Saturday on the roof of the Holy Sepulchre, which symbolizes the search for the body of Christ. Hundreds of Palestinians participate in this procession as onlookers and some as active participants. Relations between Ethiopians and the larger society have always been good, and some Ethiopians have learned Arabic and in fact have partly assimilated into the society.

The Armenians, numbering around 1,500, mostly in Jerusalem, have had a long presence in Palestine dating back to the fifth century. The relationship between Armenia and Jerusalem goes back to 301 C.E., when Armenia became Christian. As a result, Armenian pilgrims made their way to the Holy Land, where they built monasteries and churches. The Armenian quarter in southwest Jerusalem makes up one-sixth of the old walled city and comprises part of the landed properties, residential buildings, and schools of the church. The Armenian community is headed by a patriarch who is one of the three guardians of the Christian holy places; the other two are the Greek Orthodox and Roman Catholic patriarchs. Many of the Armenians descend from families who fled the 1915–16 massacres in Turkey.

The Russian Orthodox in Palestine are religious functionaries and administrators who take care of Russian Orthodox property in Jerusalem and elsewhere. In the eleventh century, Byzantine Orthodox Christianity became the state religion of Russia and a tradition of pilgrimage to the Holy Land ensued and lasted until the 1917 revolution. In the nineteenth century the church started to establish its educational, social, and religious institutions, but after the revolution, the church was divided into two: one loyal to Moscow and the second loyal to a branch of the church headquartered in New York. Both have property and churches in Jerusalem, each with its own head, the archimandrite, assisted by monks and nuns. Magnificent and imposing buildings of Russian architecture point to the influence that the Russian Orthodox once had in Jerusalem and in the rest of Palestine. The church, at present, is inactive except for the hospitality provided for occasional Russian visitors and sporadic contact with the local population.

The Copts bear a name whose linguistic root is that of the word EGYPT. It is in Alexandria that Saint Mark started the first Christian congregation among the Egyptians. Many of the first monks in Palestine were Egyptians who were introduced to the Christian monastic tradition in the Egyptian desert. There is a small Coptic community in Palestine of sixty to eighty families. Since the mid-thirteenth century, a bishop representing the Coptic church of Egypt sits in Jerusalem. The church is active in secondary education and has completed an imposing building in Bayt Hanina, a northern suburb of Jerusalem, which serves as a high school and a community college. The church also has aided its parishioners in completing a housing project in which Coptic families from Jerusalem and its environs live.

The Syrian Orthodox originally converted to Christianity in historical SYRIA. The church experienced good fortune with the Arab conquest of the seventh century but declined after the Mongol invasion of the late fourteenth century. The Syrian Orthodox do not number more than 1,500 in Palestine, although some in the community estimate their numbers at more than 3,500. Their liturgy is distinguished by its West Aramaic dialect, which resembles the language that Jesus Christ spoke. The Syrian Orthodox identify strongly with Palestinians, and some of their members are prominent in the media, scouting, and private business. Like the Armenians, they tend to be artisans.

Bernard Sabella

BIBLIOGRAPHY

Glass, Cyril. *The Concise Encyclopedia of Islam.* San Francisco: Harper & Row Publishers Inc., 1989.

Hinnells, John R., ed. *The Fact On File Dictionary of Religions.* New York: Facts On File, 1984.

Johansson, Agneta, and Donald Bostrom. *Faces of Jerusalem.* Sodertälje, Sweden Forlag, Bokforlaget Libris, 1993.

Minority Rights Group. *World Directory of Minorities.* London: Longman International Reference, 1994.

Pacini, Andrea, ed. *Christian Communities in Arab Islam. The Challenge of the Future.* Turin, Italy: Edizioni Fondazione Giovanni Agnelli, 1966.

Prior, Michael, and William Taylor, eds. *Christians in the Holy Land, The World of Islam Festival Trust.* London: 1994.
Shimoni, Yaacov. *Political Dictionary of the Middle East.* Jerusalem: Weidenfeld & Nicholson, Steimatzky, 1972.
Tapper, Richard, ed. *Some Minorities in the Middle East.* Occasional Paper 9. London: Centre of Near and Middle Eastern Studies, School of Oriental and African Studies, University of London, 1992.
Ziring, Lawrence. *The Middle East: A Political Dictionary.* Santa Barbara, Calif.: ABC-CLIO, 1992.

Royal Commission See PEEL COMMISSION, 1937.

Rock, Alfred Butros
politician, citrus merchant
1885–1956 Jaffa

Alfred Butros Rock, a politically active Palestinian nationalist, opposed Jewish immigration at an early age and fled to Greece around 1905 after an Arab-Jewish brawl in which a Jewish immigrant was killed. His support for the revolt of Sharif Husayn against the Ottoman Turks in 1916 led to his deportation to Anatolia and the confiscation of some of his possessions. Rock served as a member of Palestinian delegations who traveled abroad on various diplomatic missions, including the fourth delegation that the ARAB EXECUTIVE dispatched to London in 1930 after the WESTERN (WAILING) WALL DISTURBANCES, 1929, and the delegation that participated in the 1939 LONDON CONFERENCE, 1939, 1946–47, convened by the British government to resolve the issue of the future of Palestine. He was a member of the ARAB HIGHER COMMITTEE, the ARAB PARTY, and the municipal council of JAFFA.

Muhammad Muslih

Rogers Plan

The Rogers Plan was a series of proposals put forward by U.S. Secretary of State William Rogers in late 1969 as a framework for resolving the Egyptian-Israeli and Jordanian-Israeli conflicts. Based on UNITED NATIONS SECURITY COUNCIL RESOLUTIONS 242 AND 338, the plan envisaged Israeli withdrawal from the Sinai Peninsula and from the WEST BANK and the GAZA STRIP, all territories occupied in 1967, with only "insubstantial alterations" in border demarcations. In return, the Arab nations would recognize Israel's territorial integrity and sovereignty within pre-1967 borders.

The first part of the Rogers Plan drew the outlines of a peace settlement between Egypt and Israel. It was presented to the SOVIET UNION in October 1969 as part of superpower talks under way throughout 1969 to resolve the Middle East conflict. Rogers presented a parallel plan for a Jordanian-Israeli settlement in December 1969, and he gave a public speech in that month outlining the proposals for both the Egyptian and the Jordanian front. Consistent with Resolution 242, the Rogers Plan did not mention the Palestinians specifically, but only called for a just settlement of the "refugee problem."

The Rogers Plan was rejected by Israel, Egypt, and the Soviet Union and was never pursued as established U.S. policy. Henry Kissinger, then national security adviser, actively opposed the plan in the belief that no peace settlement was possible at the time and that the proposal would antagonize both sides while giving the Soviet Union a diplomatic advantage.

Kathleen Christison

BIBLIOGRAPHY

Kissinger, Henry. *White House Years.* Boston: Little, Brown and Company, 1979.
Quandt, William B. *Peace Process: American Diplomacy and the Arab-Israeli Conflict since 1967.* Washington, D.C.: The Brookings Institution; Berkeley: University of California Press, 1993.
Rogers, William. "A Lasting Peace in the Middle East: An American View." *Department of State Bulletin* 62, 5 (January 1970).

S

Sabbagh, Hasib

businessman, philanthropist
1920– Tiberias

Sabbagh graduated from the ARAB COLLEGE in Jerusalem in 1938 and received a B.A. in civil engineering from the American University of Beirut in 1941. That same year, he helped establish the Consolidated Contractors Company in HAIFA. The company relocated to Beirut in 1950 after the ARAB-ISRAELI WAR OF 1948 and became one of the largest contracting firms in the Middle East.

Sabbagh has also devoted himself to Palestinian nationalist causes and philanthropy. He has served on the PALESTINE NATIONAL COUNCIL, including on its central council. In 1978, he established the Diana Tamari Sabbagh Foundation in memory of his late wife. The foundation has donated millions of dollars over the years to a variety of causes, particularly educational groups. In 1982, Sabbagh also helped found the Welfare Association in Geneva. In the 1990s he was assisted in his philanthropic endeavor by his daughter Sara. He was the founder of the Center for Muslim-Christian Understanding at Washington, D.C.'s, Georgetown University in 1993 and created an endowed chair for Middle Eastern affairs at the Council on Foreign Relations in New York in 1995.

Michael R. Fischbach

Sabra and Shatila Massacre

The Israel Defense Forces (IDF) besieged West Beirut shortly after invading Lebanon on June 6, 1982. Intent on destroying the military and civilian infrastructure of the PALESTINE LIBERATION ORGANIZATION (PLO) trapped in Beirut, the IDF bombarded the city for seven weeks until a U.S.-brokered cease-fire went into effect in August. After American assurances that Palestinian civilians left behind would be protected, the PLO withdrew from the city under the supervision of a multinational force that included American troops. The force itself withdrew shortly thereafter.

Israeli troops entered West Beirut in violation of the cease-fire agreement on September 15, after the assassination of the Lebanese president, Bashir Jumayyil, on the previous day. The Israeli defense minister, Ariel Sharon, and the IDF chief of staff, Rafael Eitan, allowed the Israeli-supported and anti-Palestinian Phalange militia, under the leadership of Elie Hubayqa, to enter the two Palestinian refugee camps of Sabra and Shatila to deal with what Sharon described to the American journalist Morris Draper as "2,000–3,000 terrorists who remained behind. We even have their names." On September 16–18, the Phalange massacred hundreds of Palestinian civilians in the camps. Most of the victims were women, children, and old men. Israeli authorities estimated the dead at 800; others placed the figure at 1,500.

The massacre and Israel's role in it prompted international condemnation. Some 400,000 Israelis (8 percent of the population) demonstrated against the government of Prime Minister Menachem Begin and called on the government to launch an investigation. The three-member Kahan Commission, headed by the Israeli supreme court president, Yitzhak Kahan, determined that Sharon, Eitan, and other Israeli officials were "indirectly responsible" for the massacre because they had allowed the Phalange into the camps. The commission also noted that officials like Eitan and Foreign Minister Yitzhak Shamir had received information about the killings yet ignored it and permitted the Phalange to remain longer in the camps.

An international commission was also established under former United Nations assistant secretary-general Sean MacBride. This commission held Israel directly responsible under international law because, as an occupying power, it maintained jurisdiction over the camps. The MacBride Commission also criticized Israel for planning and allowing the Phalange's entry into Sabra and Shatila, facilitating its actions once there, preventing survivors from fleeing, and failing to halt the killings once it heard reports about them. Despite the two commissions' findings, no one in Lebanon or Israel was prosecuted for the massacres.

Philip Mattar

BIBLIOGRAPHY

The Beirut Massacre: Press Profile, 2d ed. New York: Claremont Research and Publications, 1984.

Government of Israel. *The Kahan Commission Report.* Jerusalem, 1982.

Smith, Charles D. *Palestine and the Arab-Israeli Conflict.* New York: St. Martin's Press, 1988.

Tessler, Mark. *A History of the Israeli–Palestinian Conflict.* Bloomington: Indiana University Press, 1994.

Safad

Safad lies in the hills of eastern Galilee and was long the most important town in northern Galilee. Its strategic and economic value stemmed from the fact that it lay along historic trade and communications lines between Syria and Egypt. Safad's importance thus made it a prize for various armies over the centuries, including those of Crusaders, Napoleon Bonaparte, and various Islamic dynasties. War was not the only disaster to befall Safad; like other towns in Palestine, it sustained damage during earthquakes, particularly the severe earthquake of 1837. It was also the administrative center of the subdistrict carrying its name, beginning in the Ottoman era in 1886 and during the period of the British PALESTINE MANDATE. Governmental presence led to the establishment of schools, beginning in 1880.

Safad was a relatively large Palestinian town during the first half of the twentieth century. Its population stood at some 12,000 during World War I, although this number had dropped to 8,761 in 1922 as a result of wartime exigencies. The population had returned to some 13,300, 20 percent of whom were Jews, by 1948. Historically, economic activity centered around trade, artisanal production (especially wool and cotton textiles), and, given its location in the hills, summer tourism. Safad's 1,429 *dunums* of land was largely hilly, restricting agriculture predominantly to horticulture.

Safad was also long a center of Jewish life in Palestine. Along with JERUSALEM, HEBRON, and TIBERIAS, it was one of the cities considered holy by Jews in Palestine. Beginning in the early sixteenth century, Safad was the center of the Kabbala movement of Jewish mysticism. Jews lived in the western district of the town, which was sacked by Palestinians during the WESTERN (WAILING) WALL DISTURBANCES, 1929, and twenty-six of its inhabitants killed.

Safad's strategic location made it a site of conflict during the Arab–Israeli fighting of 1948. Zionist forces made the capture of Safad their main objective in the days prior to Britain's evacuation of Palestine in May 1948. On May 11, 1948, Safad was secured by Zionist forces of the Palmach. Its Palestinian population fled thereafter, and Jews thus subsequently constituted the majority of the 2,300 persons who remained in the town.

Noted today as an Israeli arts center, Safad (Hebrew, *Tzfat*) had a population of 16,600 by 1992.

Michael R. Fischbach

Safieh, Afif

Afif Safiyya; academician, diplomat
1950– Jerusalem

Safieh pursued his secondary studies at the COLLÈGE DE FRÈRES school in Jerusalem. He finished his university studies in political science and international relations at the Catholic University of Louvain (CUL) in Belgium, where he was active in the General Union of Palestinian Students. Safieh later was a researcher at CUL and at Harvard University's Center for International Affairs in 1981–87.

Safieh has long served as a diplomat for the PALESTINE LIBERATION ORGANIZATION (PLO) in Europe. He was deputy director of the PLO Observer Mission to the United Nations in Geneva from 1976 to 1978 and head of the PLO's office on European and U.N. Affairs in Beirut from 1978 to 1981. In 1980, Safieh was dispatched as special envoy to the Vatican. He was the PLO's representative in the Netherlands from 1987 to 1990 and in London since 1990.

Safieh's diplomatic skills proved useful in PLO negotiations with the United States and Israel. He was involved in the talks that led to the first direct talks between the United States and the PLO in 1988–90. Safieh later was instrumental in arranging a 1992 meeting in London between PLO officials and Israeli academics that later led to the secret Oslo talks between the PLO and the Israeli government.

Michael R. Fischbach

Said, Edward

internationally prominent intellectual
1935– Jerusalem

Edward Said's career has combined distinguished academic achievement with passionate political interventions on behalf of the Palestinian and Arab peoples. In recent years, his work has received increasing attention in the Arab world (as a result of translations of his key books and a series of new publications in Arabic journals and newspapers), but his early reputation was earned in the American academy and public sphere. There he is recognized not only as the leading spokesperson for the Palestinian cause in the United States, but also as one of the figures responsible for the redirection of literary and cultural studies away from narrow academic seclusion and toward an investigation of the *worldliness* of literary and cultural production. This kind of worldliness—a notion most readily identifiable with Said himself—is related to the ways in which authors and texts are actively involved in, rather than insulated from, the making and transformation of the world. For Said, such acts of active involvement are a matter not only of theoretical discussion but of actual practice.

Said was born in 1935 in Jerusalem, the eldest of the five children of Hilda Musa and Wadie Said, who owned a stationery firm in Jerusalem with branches in Cairo and Beirut. With his sisters, the young Edward was raised first in Jerusalem and later in Cairo, where he attended the well-known Victoria College. He completed his secondary education at a boarding school in the United States and then went on to Princeton University for his undergraduate education and to Harvard University for graduate training and a Ph.D. He was appointed as an assistant professor of English and comparative literature at Columbia University in New York, where (apart from guest professorships and fellowships at other major universities) he has remained ever since; he became university professor in 1990. After spending a year of leave in Beirut, he married in 1970; the Saids have two children and live in New York City. In addition to his academic achievements, Said is also an accomplished pianist; he is a music editor at *The Nation* and has written music reviews for a number of other magazines, as well as essays on opera and a study of musical aesthetics.

Said has produced well over a dozen books, but there can be no question that *Orientalism* (1978) marks the most important turning point in his academic and intellectual career. It also marks the point of departure for his political engagement, which takes on new meaning if it is retrospectively framed between *Orientalism* and one of Said's later books, *Representations of the Intellectual* (1994). This is not to understate the importance of his earlier writing, including essays on a variety of literary and political topics as well as his books *Joseph Conrad and the Fiction of Autobiography* (1966) and *Beginnings* (1975). The latter presents a thoughtful redirection of the familiar literary emphasis on endings to the more complicated and often more interesting question of beginnings and intentionality.

These are issues that Said also addressed in a number of essays on literary and theoretical topics, many of which are compiled in *The World, the Text and the Critic* (1982), and which are among the earliest American engagements with the "new wave" of French critical theory, long before the latter had become fashionable in academic circles and had been transformed into a guild of specialized expertise inaccessible and even incomprehensible to outsiders. Much of Said's work can be seen as an attempt to make this kind of theory comprehensible in a worldly dimension, and, moreover, as an attempt to put it to use for the understanding and contestation of worldly situations, rather than merely practicing it for its own sake only in the rarefied atmosphere of the classroom or the pages of the academic journal. For Said, this is above all a question of accessibility and *audience*, which is to say, a question of the "irrelevance" of the closeted academic specialist versus the wordly "relevance" of the engaged intellectual fighting for the truth in a public sphere dominated by the paid "experts" of corporate and state power.

In all his work, Said's political and intellectual independence is unquestionable. Unlike some of his radical colleagues, he is not willing to dismiss the Western literary and cultural canon, and yet, unlike his conservative colleagues, he is not willing to go on celebrating it in an uncritical sense either. What Edward Said is best known for, however, is not his scholarly accomplishment and often contradictory—but always productive—intellectual mobility and freedom, but his willingness to put his theoretical convictions to practice, no matter what the potential cost to him, and to do so with great moral conviction and unquestionable courage.

Said and Intellectual Practice One of the characteristics that Edward Said is best known for is his fierce and uncompromising independence, both within the Palestinian struggle and in terms of his intellectual formation, in the direction of his thought and intellectual career as well as his political activism. His approaches to scholarship and even to reading itself have always been idiosyncratic, drawing on various traditions but ultimately taking on their own unique consistency and identity. The kind of "contrapuntal" approach to texts for which he has become famous—emphasizing contextual circumstances rather than textual details—draws on varied intellectual traditions, from culturalist marxism (most readily identifiable with Raymond Williams and Antonio Gramsci) to the conservative high-cultural "Great Tradition" scholarship of critics such as Eric Auerbach, R. P. Blackmur, and Matthew Arnold; and from the archaeological "discourse analysis" of Michel Foucault and his followers to the intellectual giants of the third world, including C. L. R. James, Aimé Césaire, and above all Frantz Fanon. And yet, although Said's approach to culture is indebted to each, it is not easily identifiable with—and certainly not assimilable into—any of these approaches.

By its very nature, Said's oppositional approach to culture, best exemplified in *Culture and Imperialism* (1993), is one that also defies any easy encapsulation or containment within a specific academic discipline or area of "expertise." Said's method is always that of the outsider, the amateur, the intellectual in exile—free precisely to make connections and to highlight issues that would otherwise be unmentioned or even unnoticed by the certified experts of academic knowlege who are trapped by their own institutional commitments as well as the narrow standards to which they are forced to conform. Just as his approach cannot be defined by association with a particular school of thought, it cannot be restricted to a particular discipline or field: it takes the world as the primary "text" for the critic to understand. It resists specialization and professionalization and the narrow confines of academic careerism. The product of someone who prefers the role of the free-thinking amateur to that of the licensed expert, Said's work realizes and short-circuits disciplinary rigidity and conformity in the service of intellectual as well as political freedom.

This is not to say that Said sees no value in specialized knowledge. He has, for example, repeatedly criticized the almost total ignorance of American society and culture and politics in the Arab world (where there are few, if any, institutes of American studies, and no institutes of Israeli studies: in other words, no Arab counterparts to the various American or Israeli institutes dedicated to the study of the Arab world, or to the army of paid Orientalist pseudoexperts who dominate the American media). Said has also expressed astonishment at the way in which the PALESTINE LIBERATION ORGANIZATION (PLO) could negotiate at Oslo without any specialized legal consultants, without an adequate knowledge of English, without even "a decent map, without any real command of the facts and figures, and without any serious attention to what Israel was all about and what the Palestinian people's interest dictated."

In fact, Said's lack of narrow disciplinary affiliation not only allows him a genuine kind of intellectual as well as political freedom to roam, it also lets him address audiences of various kinds of different contexts, and in fact to *create* audiences and contexts when necessary. Indeed one of the most important and enduring lessons Said has taught is related to the relationship that all of his work ultimately returns to, namely, that between an intellectual and his or her audience, whether it is that of the paid media "expert" and the general public, or that of the restricted traditional scholar and other scholars, or that of the constant oppositional amateur and the world.

It is of course with the latter, the oppositional intellectual, that Said most ardently defines himself. Combining the approaches of Julien Benda and Antonio Gramsci, Said insists that the true intellectual—unlike the paid professional scribe, the member of a career guild, Gramsci's "traditional" intellectual—is always an oppositional intellectual like him. "The intellectual," he argues,

> is an individual endowed with a faculty for representing, embodying, articulating a message, a view, an attitude, philosophy or opinion to, as well as for, a public. And this role has an edge to it, and cannot be played without a sense of being someone whose place it is publicly to raise embarrassing questions, to confront orthodoxy and dogma (rather than producing them), to be someone who cannot easily be coopted by governments or corporations, and whose *raison d'être* is to represent all those people and issues that are routinely forgotten or swept under the rug. The intellectual does so on the basis of universal principles: that all human beings are entitled to expect decent standards of behavior concerning freedom and justice from worldly powers or nations, and that deliberate or inadvertent violations of these standards need to be testified and fought against courageously.

Said and Orientalism It was his 1977 *Orientalism* that marked Said's dramatic departure from a narrowly circumscribed academic audience to an audience with much greater dimensions, spanning not only various academic disciplines but also the world of policymakers and media "experts," as well as the general public in Europe, the United States, and the Arab world. Now available in about thirty languages, *Orientalism* is one of those rare books that inaugurate or signal a new moment in the history of ideas, so much so, in fact, that its main arguments now seem obvious and are more often than not taken for granted in contemporary literary and cultural studies, as well as in other fields of inquiry (anthropology, history, sociology). However, the cult of "expertise" in the service of state power that is the book's primary object of critique persists, and the names of some of the contemporary practitioners of that cult (e.g., Thomas Friedman, Fouad Ajami, Bernard Lewis) are familiar to readers of Said's work as recurring exemplary instances of what he identifies as the degenerate media-celebrity version of such learned Orientalist scholars as Sir William Jones and Silvestre de Sacy, who, though still committed to imperialist projects, were also devoted to learning and knowledge.

The main argument of *Orientalism* seems (in retrospect) to be not only obvious but actually quite simple: the Orient does not exist as such. Rather, it is brought into being through the representations of scholars, artists, musicians, poets, experts, policymakers—Orientalists—who generate ways of seeing this imagined reality, largely through producing a corresponding set of pictures, categories, histories, documentations, essences, truths, facts, by and through and with reference to which this space and its peoples could be understood, managed, and controlled. Thus the Orient takes on a reality through these textual representations and indeed *becomes* a reality, albeit only insofar as these representations are believed in and are allowed to persist.

It is at this level that Said's argument has often been criticized (by, among others, Sadiq al-Azm), or perhaps misread, as an inevitable story of intercultural distortion, and indeed there are elements of this in the book, particularly in its occasional reliance on language opposing "truth" and "untruth" or "reality" and "fiction." However, Said's main thesis is not that *Orientalism* misrepresents a preexisting reality, but rather that it generates a reality of its own; not that it distorts the truth, but rather that it creates its own truths. It is at this level, too, that Said has been criticized for not providing "alternatives" to the discourse of Orientalism as a way to understand the Orient, though this critique seems to be misplaced given that Said's argument is precisely that the Orient does not exist in the first place—and hence it simply *cannot* be more "adequately" or "truthfully" represented, for the representation and the distortion are coextensive, one and the same thing.

A more compelling criticism (produced by, among others, Benita Parry and Homi Bhabha) is that Said, in pursuit of his argument, overgeneralizes and even exaggerates the representing power of Orientalism, as well as its historical scope, in the process not allowing enough room for changes in the discourse of Orientalism; or, for that matter, for counterrepresentations; or for the extent to which these representations are either accepted, contested, or subverted by "Orientals" themselves. And yet such criticisms need to be seen as continuations of the critical elaboration of Orientalism that Said inaugurated in his ground-breaking study, albeit in directions that he left unmapped and unexplored, though he would return to them in later texts, including *Culture and Imperialism*.

Said and the Question of Palestine Said has extended his interest in Orientalism and imperialism to other areas of scholarship and activism. It is no coincidence that most of his work returns to the question of representation, and to the power of representation (as opposed to the powerlessness of nonrepresentation). Said's emphasis has been the capacity or incapacity to represent selves and others. Here of course his involvement with the Palestinian struggle for self-determination (that is, self-representation) has special relevance. His *The Question of Palestine* (1979) begins as a critical examination of the representations of Palestine and Palestinians in both European colonialist and Zionist discourse. Indeed, it is important for Said to situate ZIONISM in the context of European colonialism, from which it emerged and from which it received both material and moral support (money, weapons, but also, as Said demonstrates, a certain political-epistemological indebtedness to the power knowledge of colonial Orientalism).

According to Said, the Palestinian people's resistance to Zionism and Israeli occupation takes the form not only of a guerrilla struggle and mass solidarity with that struggle, and not only of the formation of a national organization (at a certain historical moment, the PLO), but also of the telling of the story of Palestine—asserting a vision and a story of peace and justice that contests the violent and oppressive stories of colonialism, Orientalism, and Zionism. Thus, the struggle is for the Palestinians' capacity to represent themselves not just institutionally but also discursively: "We must stand in the international theater created out of our struggle against Zionism, and there we must diffuse our message dramatically."

Said has certainly played an important role in this self-representation of the Palestinian people in numerous newspaper and magazine articles and countless television appearances, as well as in such works as *The Question of Palestine* (1979) and *After the Last Sky* (1985). Elsewhere, too, he has often emphasized the degree to which his work and his Palestinian identity are inseparable, even to the extent of "speaking for" the Palestinians by offering his own experience as representative—that is, speaking *as* a Palestinian: "My sense of belonging to the Palestinian people, my pride in their heroism, and my pain at their sufferings and defeats are not things people can take away from me: they are certainly more lasting and deeper than crude and opportunistic and the ephemeral desires of leaders. I am a Palestinian who was born in Jerusalem and was forced as a result of the 1948 Catastrophe to live in exile, in the same way as many hundreds of thousands of Palestinians were." Thus, Said's role as Palestinian spokesperson in the United States has been a dual one: explicitly speaking on behalf of the Palestinians, but also simply speaking *as* a Palestinian, and thus constantly bringing the question of Palestine to consciousness in all kinds of audiences (aesthetic, political, scholarly, musical) that are as often as not unconnected with—and might have remained unaware or unconcerned with—the Palestinian experience.

In this sense, Said's engagement with the Palestinian cause has always transcended his direct involvement with national organizations such as the PALESTINE NATIONAL COUNCIL (PNC), of which he was a member from 1977 until 1991. Even within the PNC, Said always insisted on playing the independent role of an exilic intellectual, not attached to any particular faction of the national movement and hence preserving his capacity for critique. Until quite recently, Said's role within the PNC and his relationship to the power structure of the PLO have been understated. Now it is known, for example, that in 1978 he served as an unofficial intermediary between Cyrus Vance, President Carter's secretary of state, and the PLO leadership in Beirut, transmitting an offer for negotiations based on UNITED NATIONS SECURITY COUNCIL RESOLUTIONS 242 AND 338—an offer from the United States that was far more favorable than what the PLO received in the 1993 Oslo agreements. All of Said's efforts notwithstanding, the offer was rejected out of hand by an uninterested YASIR ARAFAT in the spring of 1979.

Said's most visible presence in the PNC was in 1988, during what may be retrospectively regarded as one of the high points of the national struggle, namely, that year's exuberant INTIFADA-inspired PNC meeting in Algiers. Said played an important role in the drafting and translation into English of the Palestinian Declaration of Independence, based on a two-state solution to the struggle for self-determination. After 1988, however, when it became increasingly clear that the inner leadership of the PLO was proceeding without regard to the PNC and its resolutions and declarations (or, according to Said, to the needs and desires of the great majority of the Palestinian people), and in the buildup to the MADRID PEACE CONFERENCE, 1991, which he felt was taking place on unacceptable terms, Said resigned from the PNC.

Since then, and especially since the "capitulation" represented by the 1993 Oslo agreements, Said has become an increasingly outspoken critic of the so-called peace process and particularly of Arafat and his PALESTINIAN AUTHORITY. In works such as *The Politics of Dispossession* (1994) and *Peace and Its Discontents* (1995), which are both for the most part made up of previously published English- and Arabic-language newspaper and magazine articles, Said has denounced the Oslo-based peace process as total surrender. He argues that "for the first time in the twentieth century an anti-colonial national liberation movement had not only discarded its own considerable achievements but had made an agreement to cooperate with a military occupation before that occupation had ended." Moreover, he insists that it is impossible to argue or act on the flawed premise that these peace agreements with Israel represent a "beginning on which we can build for the future." Although his explicit criticisms of Arafat and the PLO/PA leadership, as well as the changing nature of the Israeli military occupation, are new, Said's position remains as it has been from the beginning, namely, an assertion of a different view of the question of Palestine, one based on seeing the Palestinian struggle as one for true justice and true peace. And Said, as always, argues for this vision from a truly independent standpoint. His memoir, *Out of Place*, was published in 1999.

Saree Makdisi

BIBLIOGRAPHY

Said, Edward. *After the Last Sky: Palestinian Lives.* Photographs by Jean Mohr. New York: Pantheon; London: Faber, 1986.

——. *Beginnings: Intention and Method.* Baltimore: Johns Hopkins University Press, 1978. Reprint of the edition published by Basic Books in 1975.

——. *Culture and Imperialism.* New York: Knopf/Random House, 1983.

——. *Joseph Conrad and the Fiction of Autobiography.* Cambridge, Mass.: Harvard University Press; London: Oxford University Press, 1966.

——. *Orientalism.* New York: Pantheon Books; London: Routledge & Kegan Paul; Toronto: Random House, 1978. Runner-up in the criticism category of the National Book Critics Circle Award.

——. *Out of Place.* New York: Knopf, 1999.

——. *Peace and Its Discontents: Essays on Palestine in the Middle East Peace Process.* Preface by Christopher Hitchens. New York: Vintage, 1995. Published in Britain as *Peace and Its Discontents: Gaza-Jericho, 1993–1995.* London: Vintage, 1995.

——. *The Question of Palestine.* New York: Times Books, 1979.

——. *Representations of the Intellectual: The 1993 Reith Lectures.* New York: Pantheon Books, 1994.

"The Text, the World, the Critic." *Bulletin of the Midwestern Modern Language Association* 8, 2 (fall 1975): 1–23.

Saint George's School

Madrasat al-Mutran

Opened just north of the Old City in JERUSALEM in 1898, Saint George's was a prominent private Anglican boys school run along the lines of a British public school. Many of Palestine's most prominent families sent their sons to study at Saint George's, which educated such noted figures as JAMAL HUSAYNI, IZZAT TANNOUS, and WALID KHALIDI.

Michael R. Fischbach

al-Sa'iqa

Al-Sa'iqa (Arabic, "thunderbolt") was established by the Syrian wing of the pan-Arab nationalist Ba'th Party in 1968 and was the main pro-Syrian Palestinian organization in the late 1960s and 1970s. Its early leaders included Dafi Jumani, ZUHAYR MUHSIN, Yusuf Zu'ayyin, and Mahmud al-Mu'ayita, most of whom were not Palestinians. Later leaders included Isam al-Qadi and Sami al-Attari.

Sa'iqa's influence within Palestinian politics has waned considerably over the years. It commanded a relatively large number of men under arms in the early days of the Palestinian resistance movement, although over the years its recruits have largely been Palestinians from refugee camps in Syria and soldiers seconded from the Syrian army.

However, it joined its Syrian patrons in fighting PALESTINE LIBERATION ORGANIZATION (PLO) forces in Lebanon in 1976 and lost considerable support among Palestinians as a result. Its credibility was further undermined in 1983, when it supported FATAH rebels against forces loyal to the Fatah and PLO leader, YASIR ARAFAT, in Lebanon.

Saiqa ceased operating within the PLO in 1983, and its membership in the PALESTINE NATIONAL COUNCIL was suspended the following year, when it joined the anti-Arafat National Alliance. In 1985, it joined the Syrian-based PALESTINIAN NATIONAL SALVATION FRONT and in 1993, the National Democratic and Islamic Front, which opposed the OSLO AGREEMENTS signed by Israel and the PLO.

Michael R. Fischbach

al-Sakakini, Khalil

educator, writer

1878–August 13, 1953 Jerusalem

Khalil al-Sakakini's career began during the LATE OTTOMAN PERIOD, when he taught school in JERUSALEM. In the wake of the Young Turk coup in 1908, he broke new educational ground by establishing the DUSTURIYYA [Constitutional] SCHOOL in Jerusalem as a private, secular alternative to both foreign mission schools and Ottoman government schools. Offering a secular curriculum, it served as a model for other such private schools in Palestine. It was one of the first schools in Palestine to publish its own newspaper, *al-Dustur,* which al-Sakakini edited from its appearance in 1910 until 1913. (The school was later renamed the Wataniyya School during the period of the British PALESTINE MANDATE.) He was also active in the Orthodox revival among Orthodox Christian Arabs during the late Ottoman period.

After running afoul of Ottoman authorities and serving time in prison away from Jerusalem, al-Sakakini joined the Arab Revolt in 1917. Back in Jerusalem, he remained interested in politics through election to the ARAB EXECUTIVE at the third of the ARAB CONGRESSES in June 1923.

Al-Sakakini remained interested in EDUCATION and LITERATURE. He served as an educational inspector for government schools under the Mandate and headed one of Palestine's best secondary schools, al-Nahda College. An essayist, al-Sakakini developed a keen interest in the Arabic language. He wrote *al-Jadid fi al-Qira'a al-Arabiyya* (The new method of reading Arabic) for use in Palestinian schools. In January 1948, he was elected to the Arabic Language Academy in Cairo on the recommendation of the famous Egyptian writer Taha Husayn. Al-Sakakini also wrote books on Palestinian history. His diaries were published in 1955 as *Kadha Ana, Ya Duniya* (Such am I, o world).

Michael R. Fischbach

SAMED See MARTYRS' WORKS SOCIETY.

San Remo Conference

1920

The San Remo Conference was a meeting of the Supreme Council of the Paris Peace Conference, April 18–26, 1920, in San Remo, Italy, which considered the disposal of former Ottoman territories, including Palestine

Supporters of ZIONISM directed an extensive campaign at San Remo for Britain to be granted trusteeship over Palestine so as to be able to implement the promises incorporated in the BALFOUR DECLARATION of November 1917. British diplomats also had to contend with French objections to their claim to a mandate over Palestine.

On April 24, the council decided to assign the PALESTINE MANDATE to Great Britain according to the terms of the Balfour Declaration; a separate Mandate for Syria was awarded to France. In Jerusalem, General Sir Louis Bols, head of the British Military Administration, addressed the "Heads of All Sects" on the subject on April 28, proclaiming the dawning of a new era of stability and prosperity. On this occasion, the text of the controversial Balfour Declaration was read officially for the first time in Palestine. Arab nationalists attempted to organize a Palestinian congress in NABLUS, but the British authorities refused permission for such a meeting. News of the European powers' decision marked the end of a period of intense protest against Britain's support for Zionism and in favor of Palestinian union with Syria, striking, in the words of one scholar, "a heavy blow to the young Palestinian national movement."

Neil Caplan

El Sarraj, Eyad

Iyad al-Sarraj; physician, human rights activist

April 27, 1944– Beersheba

After attending secondary school in Gaza after the ARAB-ISRAELI WAR OF 1948, from 1963 to 1971, El Sarraj studied medicine at Alexandria University, where he received M.B. and B.Ch. degrees. After work in pediatrics in the GAZA STRIP and in psychiatry at the Bethlehem Mental Hospital from 1971 to 1973, he studied psychology at the University of London's Institute of Psychiatry from 1974 to 1977 and was awarded the D.P.M.

After his return to Gaza in 1977, El Sarraj worked in the department of health from 1977 to 1981 and was director of Mental Health Services from 1981 to 1988. He spent nine months as a visiting research fellow at Oxford University's Refugee Studies Programme in 1989–1990 then returned to Gaza and in 1991 founded the Gaza Community Mental Health Programme, which he still heads.

El Sarraj is also known for his many activities on behalf of Palestinian human rights. He has been commissioner general of the Independent Palestinian Commission for Citizens' Rights since August 1995. His criticism of the human rights situation in the PALESTINIAN AUTHORITY (PA) has angered PA authorities, who arrested him three times: December 1995, May 1996, and June 1996 (the last time for seventeen days).

Internationally recognized for his human rights work, El Sarraj received a prize from the Physicians for Human Rights. He is a member of the International Federation of Physicians for Human Rights and the International Federation for Health and Human Rights and was a founding member of the Campaign Against Torture in the Middle East. He also serves on the board of directors of the ARAB STUDIES SOCIETY. El Sarraj has been a member of the PALESTINE NATIONAL COUNCIL and was a negotiator during the Israeli-Palestinian bilateral peace talks.

Michael R. Fischbach

Sartawi, Isam

resistance figure, early peace activist

1935–1983 Acre

Sartawi earned a B.A. in Baghdad and later studied medicine there before specializing in cardiology and obtaining an M.D. in the United States.

Sartawi turned his interests toward politics in 1967 when he left the United States to fight with FATAH. He also helped establish the Palestine RED CRESCENT Society. In 1968, he left Fatah and established a short-lived Nasirist commando movement, the Action Organization for the Liberation of Palestine (AOLP). The AOLP was soon absorbed back into Fatah in 1971.

Sartawi thereafter rose to become an adviser on Europe and North America to YASIR ARAFAT, head of both Fatah and the PALESTINE LIBERATION ORGANIZATION (PLO), as well as a member of Fatah's revolutionary committee. He became an articulate PLO moderate who made contact with leftist, peace-oriented Israelis beginning with his meetings with Arie Eliav and other members of the Israel-Palestine Peace Council in 1976–77. In 1979, Sartawi received the Austrian Kreisky Prize along with Eliav for his efforts in exploring a peaceful end to the ARAB-ISRAELI CONFLICT, including the recognition of Israel by the PLO.

Faced with criticism by Palestinian hard-liners, Sartawi tried to resign from the PALESTINE NATIONAL COUNCIL on several occasions. Arafat refused to accept his resignation each time and defended him. Sartawi was eventually shot and killed in Portugal at a meeting of the Socialist International, allegedly by the hard-line Fatah Revolutionary Council organization (the ABU NIDAL group).

Michael R. Fischbach

Saunders Document

In November 1975, in testimony before the U.S. House of Representatives, Deputy Assistant Secretary of State for Near East Affairs Harold Saunders outlined a position on the Palestinian question that for the first time recognized the issue as a political question critical to the resolution of the ARAB-ISRAELI CONFLICT. This testimony came to be known as the *Saunders Document.* Noting that "in many ways" the Palestinian issue was the "heart" of the conflict, Saunders stated that no Arab-Israeli peace would be possible unless Palestinian "legitimate interests" were taken into account. Although the UNITED STATES had always regarded the Palestinian issue as a humanitarian concern, Saunders observed that because the Palestinians expressed a political identity, they were a political factor that must be considered.

Saunders's statement constituted the first U.S. recognition of the political origins of the Palestinian condition and of the Palestinians' national aspirations. The statement had the prior approval of Secretary of State Henry Kissinger and was timed to follow the second Egyptian-Israeli disengagement agreement of September 1975 in order to demonstrate that the United States anticipated taking further steps in the peace process. Kissinger disavowed the statement, however, when ISRAEL reacted with strong disapproval. The testimony nonetheless had a long-term impact because it raised awareness among U.S. policymakers and citizens that Palestinians were a distinct people with a national identity.

Kathleen Christison

BIBLIOGRAPHY

Quandt, William B. *Peace Process: American Diplomacy and the Arab-Israeli Conflict since 1967.* Washington, D.C.: The Brookings Institution; Berkeley: University of California Press, 1993.

Saunders, Harold H. "Department Gives Position on Palestinian Issue." *Department of State Bulletin* 73 (December 1, 1975): 797–800.

Sayigh Family

prominent family of scholars

The Sayigh family were Protestant Christians who moved to TIBERIAS from southern Syria during the PALESTINE MANDATE and produced a number of prominent scholars.

Anis (1931– ; Tiberias; scholar) After studies at the American University of Beirut, Anis received a Ph.D. in history from Pembroke College, Cambridge University. From 1966 to 1974, he directed the PALESTINIAN RESEARCH CENTER of the PALESTINE LIBERATION ORGANIZATION, which his brother, Fayez, had established in Beirut. He was injured in an Israeli letter bomb attack in July 1972. He was editor in chief of the massive Arabic-language *Palestinian Encyclopedia.*

Fayez (1922–1980; Kharba, Syria; Fayiz; scholar, diplomat) Fayez obtained a B.A. at the American University of Beirut in 1941 and an M.A. in 1945. He then taught there for several years. While in LEBANON, he was active in the Syrian Social Nationalist Party (Parti Populaire Syrien) from 1943 to 1947.

After obtaining a Ph.D. from Georgetown University in 1949, he taught at a number of prestigious universities, including Stanford University and Oxford University. From 1950 to 1955, Fayez worked for the United Nations (U.N.) and later for the Yemeni delegation to the U.N. from 1955 to 1959. In 1964, he was chosen as a member of the executive committee of the PALESTINE LIBERATION ORGANIZATION (PLO). He also served on the PALESTINE NATIONAL COUNCIL and established the PLO's PALESTINIAN RESEARCH CENTER in Beirut in 1965. He later worked as observer for the ARAB LEAGUE at the U.N. and, beginning in 1972, with the Kuwaiti delegation to the U.N.

Fayez was buried in Beirut after his death in New York.

Yusif (1916– ; Syria; Yusuf; economist, politician, diplomat) Yusif studied at The American University of Beirut (AUB) and Johns Hopkins University. During the PALESTINE MANDATE he headed the Palestinian branch of the Syrian Social Nationalist Party and was an official in the Bayt al-Mal, the national fund of the ARAB HIGHER COMMITTEE. Imprisoned by the Israelis in 1948 and exiled in 1949, he later taught at AUB, Harvard, Princeton, and Oxford from 1953 to 1974.

A noted Arab economic analyst, he also worked as an adviser to the Kuwaiti government (1964–65), the Organization of Arab Petroleum Exporting Countries (1973–77), and the Arab Fund for Economic and Social Development in Kuwait (1976–present).

Yusif has also maintained his involvement in the Palestinian national movement over the years. He established the Planning Center of the PALESTINE LIBERATION ORGANIZATION (PLO) in 1968 and directed it until 1971. He thereafter chaired the PALESTINIAN NATIONAL FUND (1971–74). He has been a member of the PALESTINE NATIONAL COUNCIL since the 1960s and was a member of the PLO executive committee from 1968 to 1974. From 1992 to 1993, he led the Palestinian delegation to the Multilateral Working Group for Economic Development as part of the Arab-Israeli peace talks. After the OSLO AGREEMENTS he supervised production of a seven-year economic plan for development in the PALESTINIAN AUTHORITY (PA) and subsequently negotiated an international assistance program for the PA.

Yezid (1955– ; United States; Yazid scholar, diplomat) The son of Yusif Sayigh, Yezid obtained a B.Sc. in chemistry at the American University of Beirut in 1979, then a Ph.D. in war studies at King's College, London University, in 1987. He was a research fellow at St Antony's College, Oxford University, and the International Institute for Strategic Studies in London before serving as assistant director of the Centre for International Studies at Cambridge.

As an expert on Middle Eastern military capabilities, Yezid was an adviser to the Palestinian delegation during bilateral Israeli-Palestinian peace talks from 1991 to 1993. He also headed the Palestinian delegation to the Multilateral Working Group for Arms Control and Regional Security from 1992 to 1994, and helped negotiate the Gaza-Jericho implementation agreements signed by Israel and the PALESTINE LIBERATION ORGANIZATION in 1993 and 1994. He is the author of *Armed Struggle and the Search for State: The Palestine National Movement, 1949–1993.* Institute for Palestine Studies series Oxford: Oxford University Press, 1997.

Michael R. Fischbach

Shaath, Nabil

businessman, activist
1938– Safad

After fleeing Palestine for Cairo in 1948, Shaath eventually received a Ph.D. in public administration at the University of Pennsylvania's Wharton School, where he later taught. After his return to Egypt, Shaath headed the National Institute of Management Development in Cairo from 1963 to 1969 and eventually headed TEAM International, one of the largest management consulting firms in the Arab world. Shaath was a professor of business administration at the American University of Beirut from 1969 to 1976.

Shaath has held senior positions in the Palestinian national liberation movement. A longtime member of the central council of FATAH and head of the political committee of the PALESTINE NATIONAL COUNCIL from 1971 Shaath rose to become one of the most senior advisers on economic and diplomatic matters of the PALESTINE LIBERATION ORGANIZATION (PLO) chairman, YASIR ARAFAT. This role became particularly important in the early 1990s as the PLO became involved in the Arab-Israeli peace process. Because Israel and the United States refused to allow the PLO to participate directly in the talks, the group dispatched Shaath, considered a moderate, to head a team of PLO officials who coordinated the stands articulated publicly by the Palestinian component of the joint Palestinian-Jordanian negotiating team. Shaath continued to head PLO's behind-the-scenes involvement in the multilateral Israeli-PLO negotiations, which continued throughout 1992 and 1993.

Shaath was also involved in direct secret talks with the Israeli government behind the backs of the Palestinian negotiators. In July 1993, he met with the Israeli cabinet minister Yossi Sarid in Cairo, the first formal meeting ever held between a top PLO official and an Israeli cabinet member acting with the knowledge of Israel's prime minister. The two discussed the so-called Gaza-Jericho First option, a diplomatic plan calling for phased Palestinian autonomy in certain areas of the occupied WEST BANK and the GAZA STRIP beginning with Gaza and the West Bank town of JERICHO. He was also involved in secret direct Israeli-PLO negotiations in Norway during 1993 that led to the September 1993 Israel-PLO Declaration of Principles and attended its signing in Washington, D.C. He was appointed the PLO's chief negotiator in talks that opened in October 1993 in Taba, Egypt, designed to facilitate implementation of the details of the first stages of Palestinian autonomy. As opposition to the negotiations mounted among Palestinians, Shaath's role in the process was criticized by some.

After establishment of the PALESTINIAN AUTHORITY (PA) in Gaza and Jericho in the spring of 1994, and despite charges of corruption, Shaath, who had headed the Palestinian Economic Council for Development and Reconstruction (PECDAR) since late 1993, was appointed minister of planning and economic cooperation. In this capacity, he exerted tremendous influence over the PA's economic and financial matters. Later, in January 1996, he was elected to the PA's PALESTINIAN LEGISLATIVE COUNCIL. The PA president, Yasir Arafat, also appointed him to a committee created to draft a constitution for the PA in February 1996.

Michael R. Fischbach

Shahid, Leila
diplomat

Leila Shahid worked for the INSTITUTE FOR PALESTINE STUDIES in Beirut and was a member of FATAH. She has served the PALESTINE LIBERATION ORGANIZATION (PLO) as a diplomat, heading its offices in The Hague and later Paris. In 1989, she became one of the first two women in the PLO ever to hold the rank of ambassador.

Michael R. Fischbach

Shammas, Anton
writer, translator
1950– Fassuta, Galilee

Shammas pursued his studies in art history and English and Arabic literature at the Hebrew University of Jerusalem from 1968 to 1972. He was an editor of the Jerusalem literary journal *al-Sharq* from 1970 to 1975 and later was a producer of Arabic-language programs for Israeli television from 1976 to 1986. Shammas was a free-lance journalist in the early 1980s, writing for Hebrew-language Israeli newspapers. Shammas moved to the United States in 1987; he has been teaching at the University of Michigan at Ann Arbor since 1988.

Shammas emerged as a major Palestinian writer, especially among the PALESTINIAN CITIZENS OF ISRAEL. His writing deals with aspects of his identity as a Palestinian living within ISRAEL and includes poetry, fiction, and nonfiction. Most of his work has appeared in Hebrew, including his most significant work, the 1986 novel *Arabesqot* (Arabesques). His only Arabic-language book is a collection of poems published in 1974, *Asir Yaqazati wa Nawmi* (Prisoner of my wakefulness and sleep).

Michael R. Fischbach

Sharabi, Hisham
intellectual
1927– Jaffa

Born into a well-to-do family, Hisham Sharabi spent his childhood in JAFFA and ACRE. He studied at the Friends School in RAMALLAH and at the American University in Beirut, where he graduated in 1947 with a B.A. in philosophy. He earned an M.A. in philosophy in 1949 and a Ph.D. in the history of culture from the University of Chicago in 1953.

Sharabi's political activism started at an early age, when he joined the Syrian Social Nationalist Party (SSNP) in 1947. He was deeply influenced by its leader, Antun Sa'ada, whose charisma and stern, uncompromising determination, especially on the issue of Palestine, appealed to the young Sharabi. Sa'ada confided in Sharabi, showing great interest in the promising young intellectual.

While Sharabi was studying in the United States, Palestine fell to the Israeli forces in 1948. At Sa'ada's behest, Sharabi returned in 1949 to resume his activities with the SSNP and became the editor of SSNP's monthly magazine, *al-Jil al-Jadid* (The new generation). In June of that year the Lebanese regime cracked down on the SSNP, putting most of its members in prison and executing Sa'ada. After fleeing to Jordan, Sharabi went back to the United States to resume his studies. In 1953 he started teaching history at Georgetown University. He attained full professorship in only eleven years. In 1955 he officially ended his affiliation with the SSNP.

Until 1967, Sharabi was in what he himself calls "silence in exile," writing and publishing in English only to fulfill academic requirements. The 1967 defeat and the 1968 student movement transformed Sharabi both intellectually and politically. He abandoned his liberal views and became a leftist, rereading Marx and Freud with a fresh eye and incorporating them into his ground-breaking analysis of Arab SOCIETY. He became very active in Palestinian and Arab affairs. After giving numerous talks across campuses, Sharabi moved to Beirut in 1970 to work in the Palestine Planning Center and was visiting professor at the American University in Beirut in 1970–71. At around the same time, translations of his English work *Arab Intellectuals and the West* began to appear in Arabic, *al-Muthaqqafun al-Arab wa al-Gharb.* The eruption of the Lebanese civil war in 1975 thwarted his plans to settle in Lebanon. Instead he stayed at Georgetown, where he was professor of European intellectual history and holder of the Omar al-Mukhtar chair of Arab culture.

Sharabi has had an important role in building institutions to promote awareness and understanding of the Palestine issue and the Arab world. In 1971, Sharabi was chosen to be editor of the *Journal of Palestine Studies,* published by the INSTITUTE FOR PALESTINE STUDIES. He cofounded the Center for

Contemporary Arab Studies at Georgetown University, the only academic center solely devoted to the study of the Arab world in the United States, in 1975. In 1979, he founded the Arab-American Cultural Foundation and Alif Gallery in Washington, D.C. In 1990, he founded the Center for Policy Analysis on Palestine, a Washington, D.C.-based institution that provides information, publishes papers, and sponsors talks and symposia pertaining to the Arab-Israeli conflict. Sharabi is also the founder and chair of the Jerusalem Fund, a Palestinian charitable organization that provides scholarships for students from Palestine. Sharabi retired from his post at Georgetown University in 1998.

Sharabi is best known as a committed, influential writer and scholar who remains a unique phenomenon as an Arab intellectual living in the West. Despite half a century of exile, he has maintained a lively dialogue with the Arab world through his substantial contributions in Arabic and English. He has been one of the few intellectuals who dared to critique and propose a break with the leftist and nationalist establishments in order to chart a new epistemological horizon for Arab intellectuals. His *Muqaddimat li Dirasat al-Mujtama al-Arabi* (Introduction to the study of Arab society), published in 1975, was a trail-blazing work and has had, and still has, a great impact on Arab intellectuals and educators, especially Palestinians. His two-volume autobiography, *al-Jamr wa al-Ramad: Dhikrayat Muthaqqa Arabi* (Embers and ashes: Memoirs of an Arab intellectual), published in 1978, and *Suwar al-Madi: Sira Dhatiyya* (Images of the past: An autobiography), published in 1993, are already classics. Unparalleled in their candor, the two volumes eloquently depict and critique the experience of a whole generation of Arab intellectuals, most of which has ended in compulsory or self-imposed exile, replete with dreams, disillusionment, and defeat. *Neopatriarchy: Theory of Distorted Change in Arab Society* appeared in 1988 and was published in Arabic as *al-Nizam al-Abawi* (1989) and in French as *Le Patriarcat* (1996). It provided an alternative way to understand Arab society and has had a great impact on scholarly and intellectual circles in the Arab world. Sharabi's other work in Arabic, which is organically linked to the works discussed, is *al-Naqd al-Hadari li al-Mujtama al-Arabi* (Cultural critique of Arab society (1990).

For Sharabi, social change cannot be achieved merely by a revolution or a coup. In a postrevolutionary world, change is a very complicated and dangerous process that entails a complete transfer from neopatriarchy to modernism on all levels. Arab intellectuals must carefully walk an independent route through which they are capable of choosing what is suitable from the tools and concepts of both modernism and postmodernism in order to achieve modernism. Aware that a new critical discourse by itself cannot effect sociopolitical change directly and must go hand in hand with praxis, Sharabi stresses that such a discourse is the first step to serious change. Intellectuals can influence the battles for sociopolitical change. Prerequisites for this new critical discourse are putting an end to the hegemony of metaphysics and philosophers and engaging in horizontal dialogues in society, not between ideological theorists. Another prerequisite is a new understanding and attitude toward language, reading, and writing (texts). Patriarchal language is ceremonial and ritualistic, leaving no space for dialogue and discussion. Sharabi confesses that even he himself writes under its hegemony. Reading equals writing in its critical role and importance. In order to liberate themselves and break with patriarchal structures, Arab intellectuals must master a foreign language in order to be able to translate the new intellectual concepts and categories and lay the grounds for a new language and new consciousness. The new critical discourse must overthrow the hegemony of any one discourse, even the secularist or revolutionary-nationalist. It must provide more than a description of the alternative to existing structures, but rather a social and intellectual preparation for the terrain required for establishing alternative structures. If read correctly, the critical-secularist text can challenge, and pose a serious threat to, the dominant powers and their ideologies. As for the fundamentalist movements, they should be confronted only as political forces. Engaging in theological debates or appeasing such movements is a lost battle.

The issue of women is the most crucial for Sharabi. He was deeply affected and transformed by his readings of feminist writings and realized how this issue was never addressed seriously and was given only lip service, even by secularist and leftist intellectuals. The oppression of women is the cornerstone of the (neo)patriarchal system. Therefore, women's liberation is an essential condition for overthrowing the (neo)patriarchal hegemony. Women are the time bomb at the heart of (neo)patriarchal societies.

Sharabi's other works include *Government and Politics in the Middle East in the Twentieth Century* (1962), *Nationalism and Revolution in the Arab World* (1966), *Arab Intellectuals and the West* (1970), and *al-Rihla al-Akhira* (The last journey), a novel in Arabic (1987). He has also edited *The Next Arab Decade: Alternative Futures* (1988) and *Theory, Politics and the Arab World: Critical Approaches* (1991).

Sinan Antoon

Shaw Commission
1930

The British dispatched a commission of inquiry to investigate the WESTERN (WAILING) WALL DISTURBANCES, 1929, which had led to the deaths of 133 Jews and more than 116 Palestinians. The commission, headed by Sir Walter Shaw, issued a report in March 1930 linking the violence with "the Arab feeling of animosity and hostility towards the Jews consequent upon the disappointment of their political and national aspirations and fear for their economic future." Furthermore, the report noted that Palestinians feared that through "Jewish immigration and land purchases they may be deprived of their livelihood and placed under the economic domination of the Jews."

On the basis of these findings, the Shaw Commission report recommended a policy toward Jewish immigration and land acquisition that would have effectively curtailed the Zionist endeavor in Palestine. The British government delayed acting upon the recommendation until the HOPE-SIMPSON COMMISSION, appointed in May 1930, studied the questions of Jewish immigration, development, and land purchases.

Philip Mattar

Shehadeh Family
Shihada

Bulus (1882–1943; Ramallah; journalist, poet, politician) After studies in JERUSALEM, Bulus became the director of the Orthodox School in HAIFA in 1907. A member of the Committee of Union and Progress, he was sentenced to death after he delivered a speech in Haifa condemning Sultan Abdülhamit II but escaped to Egypt. He returned to Palestine in 1908 to direct Orthodox schools in Haifa and BETHLEHEM and served in the Ottoman military during World War I. He later taught at the famous RASHDIYYA SCHOOL in Jerusalem from 1919 to 1922.

While in exile in Egypt, Bulus began writing articles in the Egyptian media. In 1919, he established the newspaper *Mir'at al-Sharq* in Jerusalem—the first Arabic-language newspaper published in the city after World War I. Bulus and *Mir'at al-Sharq* supported the NASHASHIBI FAMILY–led "Opposition" during the PALESTINE MANDATE.

Bulus was also active in Palestinian nationalist activities, serving as a member of the ARAB EXECUTIVE from 1926 to 1938 and attending the ARAB CONGRESSES in Jerusalem, Haifa, and NABLUS. He was also one of the founders of the pro-Opposition Palestinian Arab National Party in 1923.

Aziz (1921–1985; Bethlehem; lawyer) The son of Bulus Shehadeh, Aziz was born in Bethlehem and studied law at the Government Law School in Jerusalem. He worked as a journalist from 1933 to 1936 before being admitted to the Palestine Bar in 1936 and practicing law in JAFFA.

Aziz moved to RAMALLAH in 1948 because of the first Arab-Israeli war. He became one of the leading lawyers of the WEST BANK, successfully defending two defendants on trial for complicity in the 1951 assassination of Jordan's King Abdullah. Along with his brother Fuad, he served as defense counsel at the 1974 trial of Greek Catholic archbishop Hilarion Cappuci (charged by Israel with smuggling arms into the West Bank). The Shehadeh brothers' law firm was the largest in the West Bank during the period of the Israeli occupation.

Politically, Shehadeh was an advocate of self-determination for Palestinians even when it meant clashing with the policies articulated by Palestinian and Arab leaders. He was an official elected at the General Refugee Congress in Ramallah in March 1949, part of a trend in which Palestinian refugees sought to represent their own interests at the time of the LAUSANNE CONFERENCE in 1949 rather than adopt the line of the ARAB HIGHER COMMITTEE or the Arab states. After the Israeli occupation of the West Bank in 1967, Aziz circulated a proposal for creating a Palestinian political entity in the

West Bank through negotiations with Israel. His proposal led to a meeting with the Israeli defense minister, Moshe Dayan, in March 1968 but was condemned by most West Bank leaders and the PALESTINE LIBERATION ORGANIZATION (PLO).

Shehadeh was stabbed and killed on December 2, 1985, under circumstances that remain unclear.

Fuad (1925– ; son of Bulus Shehadeh; lawyer) Fuad completed his secondary studies at SAINT GEORGE'S SCHOOL in Jerusalem. After studies at the American University of Beirut, he received a law degree from the Government Law School in Jerusalem and entered private practice.

He and his brother, Aziz, practiced law in Ramallah after the ARAB-ISRAELI WAR OF 1948; he was vice-chair of the Jordanian Bar Association from 1964 to 1969. The two brothers worked together on such famous cases as the 1974 trial of the Greek Catholic archbishop, Hilarion Cappuci, and the 1979–81 case involving Israel's request to extradite Ziyad Abu Ayn from the United States to stand trial for TERRORISM. Assisted in the 1990s by his two sons, Nadeem and Karim, Fuad remains one of the most prominent lawyers in the West Bank, specializing in such fields as personal status law and land law. He has written on legal and political matters widely.

Raja (1951– ; Ramallah; lawyer) Son of Aziz Shehadeh, Raja studied literature and philosophy at The American University of Beirut. After receiving legal training in Britain, he returned to the West Bank and established a private legal practice in 1978.

In 1979, Shehadeh cofounded AL-HAQ (Law in the Service of Man), the West Bank affiliate of the International Commission of Jurists, and codirected it until 1991. Al-Haq has played a major role in documenting the legal aspects of Israeli HUMAN RIGHTS abuses in the Occupied Territories. Therefore, Shehadeh has become a major figure dealing with the international legal dimensions of the Israeli occupation, whose careful work has influenced others systematically to record and publicize Israeli violations of Palestinian rights in the territories.

Shehadeh has also served as a member of the International Advisory Council of the Netherlands Institute of Human Rights and the Human Rights Advisory Group of the World Council of Churches. He is author of several books, including *Occupiers' Law, Israel and the West Bank, Samed: A Journal of Life in the West Bank,* and *The Third Way.*

Michael R. Fischbach

Shikaki, Khalil

Shiqaqi; leading political scientist
1953– Rafah, Gaza

Shikaki studied political science at The American University of Beirut, receiving a B.A. in 1975 and an M.A. in 1977. He obtained a Ph.D. in political science from Columbia University in 1985. Shikaki has taught at AL-NAJAH NATIONAL UNIVERSITY since 1986. A capable administrator and scholar, he directed the CENTER FOR PALESTINE RESEARCH AND STUDIES in NABLUS from its establishment in March 1993. He is editor of the quarterly *al-Siyasa al-Filastiniyya* (Journal of Palestine policy).

Shikaki also served as a member of the Independent Palestinian Election Group formed to prepare for the January 1996 elections of the PALESTINIAN AUTHORITY.

Shikaki's brother, Fathi, was deported from the Occupied Territories in 1988 and headed the ISLAMIC JIHAD organization until his assassination in Malta in October 1995.

Michael R. Fischbach

Shoman Family

Shawman

The Shoman family hails from Bayt Hanina, north of JERUSALEM, and is noted for its banking activities.

Abd al-Hamid (1890–1974; Bayt Hanina; banker) Born on the outskirts of Jerusalem and lacking formal education, Abd al-Hamid emigrated to the United States in 1911 and established successful business operations in New York and Baltimore. He was also active in Arab circles in America, becoming a member of such organizations as the Palestinian Revival Association (established in 1921).

Abd al-Hamid returned to Palestine in 1929 and tried to establish a Palestinian-Egyptian bank in cooperation with the Egyptian banker and economist Tal'at Harb. The 1929 political disturbances in Palestine led Harb to back away from the project, but Abd al-Hamid proceeded with the project anyway. In 1930, he established the Arab Bank, Ltd., in

Jerusalem. The bank grew to become one of the two largest Arab banks in Palestine during the PALESTINE MANDATE. After its move to Amman, which followed the ARAB-ISRAELI WAR OF 1948, it became one of the most important banks in the Arab world.

Abd al-Hamid also used his financial position to assist Palestinian nationalist causes, including helping establish the PALESTINIAN NATIONAL FUND and financing a committee made up of Palestinian political parties in 1945 that ultimately led to the reconstitution of the ARAB HIGHER COMMITTEE. He was also noted as a philanthropist.

Abd al-Hamid was buried in Jerusalem after his death in Czechoslovakia.

Abd al-Majid (1912– ; Bayt Hanina; banker) Son of Abd al-Hamid Shoman, Abd al-Majid received an M.A. in economics at New York University. He has worked with the Arab Bank, Ltd., since 1946, as deputy chairman from 1949 to 1974 and as chairman and general manager since 1974. From 1964 to 1969, Abd al-Majid was the first chair of the Palestinian National Fund and of the Welfare Association starting in 1983. He retired from the Jordanian senate in 1988. In 1995, Abd al-Majid headed a group of prominent Palestinian businessmen who established a committee to promote dialogue with the PALESTINIAN AUTHORITY.

Abd al-Hamid (1947– ; Jerusalem; banker) The son of Abd al-Majid Shoman and grandson of his namesake (1890–1974), Abd al-Hamid received a B.B.A. from the American University of Beirut. He has worked at the Arab Bank, Ltd., since 1972 and serves on the board of trustees of the Abd al-Hamid Shoman Foundation.

Michael R. Fischbach

Shultz Initiative

In March 1988, in response to the INTIFADA in the WEST BANK and Gaza, U.S. secretary of state George Shultz proposed a complex negotiating schedule for resolving the Israeli–Palestinian conflict. In Shultz's proposal, negotiations on arrangements for a transition period in the Occupied Territories would take place between Israel and a joint Jordanian–Palestinian delegation over what was expected to be a six-month period. The transition period itself would last for three years, during which time further negotiations on a permanent agreement would take place. Simultaneously, other bilateral peace talks would be conducted between Israel and any Arab state ready to negotiate. An international conference under United Nations auspices but without any real power would serve as an umbrella for the separate bilateral talks. Neither Israel nor any Arab party accepted the initiative, and the plan collapsed when Jordan severed all administrative ties to the West Bank in July 1988.

Kathleen Christison

Shuqayri, Ahmad

diplomat

1908–1980 Tibnin, Lebanon

Born in Lebanon during the exile of his father, al-Shaykh AS'AD SHUQAYRI, Ahmad pursued his studies in the family's hometown of ACRE and in JERUSALEM after his return to Palestine in 1916. He studied at The American University of Beirut in 1926–27 until his expulsion by French authorities for participation in Arab nationalist activities.

Shuqayri continued his involvement in nationalist activities after returning to Palestine and studying law. He became active in the ISTIQLAL PARTY and was employed by the prominent Palestinian lawyer and nationalist AWNI ABD AL-HADI. Shuqayri defended Palestinians arrested by the British on security charges during the 1930s, until he fled into exile in Cairo on the defeat of the Arab revolt in 1939. During the 1940s, he worked in the Arab Information Office in Washington, D.C., which was maintained by the ARAB HIGHER COMMITTEE; he later headed its central Arab Information Office in Jerusalem.

After leaving Palestine for Lebanon during the ARAB-ISRAELI WAR OF 1948, Shuqayri worked for more than fifteen years as a diplomat for a number of Arab governments. In 1949–50, he was a member of the Syrian delegation to the United Nations. The ARAB LEAGUE appointed him its assistant general-secretary from 1950 to 1957. He worked as the representative of Saudi Arabia to the U.N. and its minister of state for U.N. affairs. The Saudis dismissed Shuqayri in 1963 as a result of disagreement about Egypt's role in the Yemeni civil war.

Shuqayri returned to his focus on Palestinian affairs in September 1963, when he accepted the position of Palestine's representative to the Arab League. The summit of Arab leaders that met in January 1964 charged him with determining the feasibility of establishing an organization for harnessing the nationalist energies of the Palestinian people. After Shuqayri's call for a conference, the first meeting of the PALESTINE NATIONAL COUNCIL was held in East Jerusalem in late May and early June 1964. The meeting gave rise to the PALESTINE LIBERATION ORGANIZATION (PLO), which Shuqayri was appointed to head.

Shuqayri's tenure as the PLO's first chair occurred at a time when the PLO carried out its mission of promoting Palestinian participation in the liberation of Palestine in close cooperation with the wider Arab world's struggle with Israel under the leadership of Egyptian president Jamal Abd al-Nasir. Although Shuqayri offered grand and bellicose oratory about the liberation of Palestine, the PLO's PALESTINE LIBERATION ARMY forces were safely stationed with the armies of host Arab states.

The humiliating defeat inflicted on the Arab regimes by Israel in June 1967 led to Shuqayri's political demise. Like Abd al-Nasir, he was tarnished by the disaster. This and the growing criticism of his leadership led Shuqayri to resign as PLO chair on December 24, 1967. He lived in Cairo and Tunisia for the remainder of his life, until his death in Jordan while seeking medical treatment. Shuqayri was buried in the Jordan valley within sight of Palestine, in the cemetery adjacent to the tomb of one of the heroes of the seventh-century Islamic conquests, Amir bin Abdullah bin Jarrah (known as Abu Ubayda).

He wrote several books, including, in 1969, Arba'un *Aman fi al-Haya al-Arabiyya wa al-Dawliyya* (Forty years in Arab and international life).

Michael R. Fischbach

Shuqayri, As'ad

religious figure, politician

1860–1940 Acre

After studying with Jamal al-Din al-Afghani and Muhammad Abduh at al-Azhar University in Cairo in the late 1870s, Shuqayri served as civil and religious judge in the Ottoman judiciary in Shafa Amr, Galilee, and al-Ladhaqiyya in Syria. He bore the title al-Shaykh as a result. As'ad moved to Istanbul in 1905 and served in Sultan Abdülhamit II's library. He also was a judge in Adana, in Anatolia.

As'ad was elected to the Ottoman Parliament representing ACRE in 1908 as a high-ranking member of the Committee of Union and Progress (CUP), for which he opened a branch in Jerusalem. He was elected to the parliament again in 1912. During this time, he was an opponent of independence and separation from the Ottoman empire. During World War I, he was appointed mufti for the Ottoman Fourth Army under the command of the CUP leader Jemal Pasha, who used harsh measures to suppress Arab nationalists. The Palestinian press accused him of encouraging Jemal's actions. He settled briefly in Adana after the war. After returning to Haifa, he was arrested as a former Ottoman official by British authorities and imprisoned in Alexandria, Egypt, for fourteen months. He returned to Acre in 1921 after his release.

Although basically an Ottoman traditionalist opposed to Arab nationalism, he became involved in Palestinian politics during the PALESTINE MANDATE. Particularly hostile to the leadership of AL-HAJJ AMIN AL-HUSAYNI in the SUPREME MUSLIM COUNCIL after 1922, he became a pillar of the NASHASHIBI FAMILY–led Opposition faction in northern Palestine.

Michael R. Fischbach

Siniora, Hanna

journalist

1937– Jerusalem

Hanna Siniora studied pharmacy in India and received a B.S. in 1969. He headed the pro–PALESTINE LIBERATION ORGANIZATION (PLO) Jerusalem daily newspaper *Al-Fajr* after the kidnapping of the paper's editor in 1974 and was its editor in chief from 1983 until its demise in 1993. He founded the English-language weekly *Al-Fajr Jerusalem* in 1980.

Michael R. Fischbach

Society

Whereas the twentieth century saw the reemergence of Palestine as a separate administrative entity, nineteenth-century Palestine was, in terms of cultural and social patterns, an extension of the Syrian provinces of Ottoman Western Asia. These affinities included ecological patterns, land tenure and cropping arrangements, contrast in habitat between coastal regions and highland townships, urban-rural dichotomies, and a relatively autarchic village economy.

Like Anatolia, Syria, and Mount Lebanon, Palestine was dominated numerically by an autonomous peasantry, a tax-farming system (which replaced the earlier mode of military fiefs), a distinct differentiation between an urban mercantile culture, and a rural communal organization of agricultural production (Firestone, 1975). Social organization and social consciousness, judging from the few narratives that survived from that period, were distinctly localized and kinship-bound (Rafiq and Bahjat, 1916). Cities and villages were joined by ties of patronage and fictional kinships.

The entry of Palestine into modernity, in the sense of its integration to the global economy and its intensive exposure to European technological innovation, has been variously periodized by the Napoleonic invasion at the turn of the century, by the Egyptian military campaign (1831–40) of Ibrahim Pasha, and more particularly by the introduction of the Ottoman administrative reforms of 1839 and the commoditization of land under the Code of 1858 (Schölch, 1993).

Toward the end of Ottoman rule, the Palestinian village, seemingly immobile, had gone through important transformation that affected its physical characteristics as well as its relations with the holders of power in the cities. The turn of the century heralded the harnessing of nomadic incursions on the peasantry, substantial demographic growth in the countryside, and establishment of an effective—though rudimentary—network of transportation that linked the village to regional centers and to demands of the external markets. Structurally, the period saw a radical reorganization in the land tenure system and the modes of agricultural production: from communal ownership of the land to absentee private property; from subsistence farming to monetization, commodity production, and export of agricultural yield (Owen, 1982).

The village remained the source of revenue and power, but not the seat of authority. Its big landlords, tax farmers, government functionaries, artisans, merchants, and notables were all located in the four or five major urban centers, constituting the privileged elite that had established its hegemony over Palestine (Doumani, 1995; Seikally, 1995). Yet despite those hierarchical cleavages and disparities in wealth, Palestinian society was divided by lineage units and other forms of kinship and quasi-kinship identifications in which class formations were hardly visible. And although the city-village dichotomy permeated the consciousness of Palestinians when they reflected on groups outside their local community (as evidenced in the folkloric literature), it was nevertheless a consciousness mediated through other identification that they believed to be primary (Nimr, 1974; Owen, 1982). These were mainly regional loyalties, religious affiliations, and clan affiliations. Throughout the first half of the nineteenth century, with minor exceptions, the peasantry of Palestine were divided by factions based on clan alliances and relations of patronage with urban landlords and notables.

New Land Tenure System The role of the state during this period was largely confined to the management of the taxation system in order to increase its revenues, and the installation of a proper infrastructure for that purpose. In addition to the passage of legislation regulating the commercial code and laws abolishing the guilds and encouraging industrial development, a chief instrument for breaking with the "policy of provision" was the promulgation of the land code aimed at establishing private property in agriculture.

One of the main features of the administrative reforms (*tanzimat*) in the late Ottoman period was that it marked the transition from a tribute-exacting mode of extraction (based on tax farming—a system of decentralized collection of taxes) to a more complex system of surplus appropriation in agriculture (Schölch, 1993). This change was dictated by the pressure exercised by the European powers on the Ottoman state to repay its debts and interests on massive loans after the incorporation of the Ottoman social formation into the world capitalist economy. The Ottoman state sought to increase its revenues from land by a process of eliminating the *multazimun* (tax farmers), although not always successfully, and allowing for more direct access to the immediate producers (Owen, 1982). It also encouraged the formation of large landed estates with the hope of developing agricultural capitalism. The significance of land registration under these reforms is that it established a market for farm land and allowed for the transfer of this land to the hands of urban merchants.

Decline in Rural Autonomy An immediate result of the reform in Palestine was the decline in rural autonomy. This was a consequence of a series of administrative decrees (beginning with the Land Code of 1858) aimed at the regulation of land ownership, which facilitated the dissolution of the communal *musha* ownership of village lands by the peasants and the rise of absentee landlordism (Tamari, 1990). But since the reform aimed at increasing agricultural productivity, it had other stabilizing results. Those included the establishment of security from external pillage in the countryside, substantial growth in the urban population, and integration of the region in a network of transportation routes and a railroad system.

Ottoman administrative reforms also contributed to the separation of the Jerusalem *sanjak* (which included, at that period, a majority of the population of the boundaries of Palestine after World War I) from the northern *sanjak*s (districts) of Acre and NABLUS (which included the best agricultural lands). Jerusalem differed from the main urban centers of Palestine in that it was detached from its rural hinterland (Gerber, 1985). Its elite, in the main, were not absentee landlords, and were predominantly a class of urban patricians made up of administrative functionaries, religious notables (*ashraf*), and merchants.

Two consequences of the administrative separation of Jerusalem for local politics in the second half of the nineteenth century can be cited here: one was the relative independence of, and possibly privilege accorded to, the Jerusalemite notables by virtue of their direct relationship to the sultanate in Istanbul. This autonomy was also influenced by the interest in the Holy City (with undisguised imperialist ambitions) of the European powers, reflected by the large number of missions, legations, and other European representative offices in the city. This relative autonomy, however, had a marked negative consequence on general political life in southern Palestine, namely, the weakness of local voluntary associations for the advancement of education and social welfare—in contrast with conditions in the northern districts and Damascus, where such associations were vigorous. This weakness flowed from the strong dependence of Jerusalem on the central government (Schölch, 1993). In terms of its social economy Jerusalem's could be characterized as having then a "parasitic" social structure: its dependence on religious endowments and international charities and its weak organic links with its surrounding village.

The other consequence of administrative separatism was the intensification of factional rivalry between Jerusalem-based clans and Nablus-based clans. The roots of these conflicts extend beyond the administrative reform. Northern notables traditionally complained of the way their fate was tied to "the whims of the Jerusalem effendis" (notables)—as expressed by the Nablus historian Ihsan al-Nimr. This hostility persisted even after the unification of Palestine under the British PALESTINE MANDATE (Nimr, 1974). Several decades later, when al-Istiqlal, the ISTIQLAL PARTY, the only mass-based pan-Arabist party, began to mobilize Palestinian Arabs around an anti-Zionist and antiimperialist program, it invariably encountered factional opposition from the Jerusalem clan-based parties of the HUSAYNI FAMILY and the NASHASHIBI FAMILY. Those difficulties were due in no small degree to the fact that the leader of al-Istiqlal, AWNI ABD AL-HADI, belonged to a family of big landowners in the Jenin (Nablus) area, but primarily to the platform of al-Istiqlal, which was critical of clan-based parties.

The social basis of clan power seems to have been associated with two interrelated features. One was the number of people that clan notables could mobilize on their side in factional struggles—a factor that was dependent, as far as peasants were concerned, on the amount of land under control of the clan head and the intricate system of patronage he concluded with his sharecroppers and semiautonomous peasants, including his ability to act as their creditor in an increasingly monetized economy. The second feature was the accessibility of the clan head and the relatives/aides to public office—hence his ability to extend services to his clients in return for their support in factional conflicts (including votes for municipal elections, which became a major arena of rivalry under British rule).

Power over the peasantry, expressed in this system of patronage, and the support of that power by the holding of public office were mutually reinforcing. Influential village patriarchs who succeeded in consolidating large estates for themselves after the dissolution of the *musha* system would soon send a few of their capable sons or relatives to establish themselves in the regional center or alternatively acquire a public post themselves (Doumani, 1995). It has been suggested that the power of those potentates can be measured by the degree of transition in residence from their rural base to the district center.

Land ownership under semifeudal conditions (leasing the land to sharecroppers through the *wakil,* the landlord's agent) was not always necessary as a basis for factional power. There were cases in Palestine in which a clan's power was rooted almost exclusively in the holding of public administrative office—that is, in its ability to organize its members' skills in the service of the state, with land ownership and mercantile activities playing a marginal role (Ashour, 1948). This seems to have been the case with the Nashashibi clan, who—after the Husaynis—became central contenders for the leadership of the nationalist movement.

The challenges posed by the Zionist movement and its success in creating modern and independent Jewish institutions, as well as the inability of the colonial government to accommodate Palestinian nationalist aspirations, all compelled the machinery of factional politics to perform a role to which it was thoroughly unsuited. Although the Arab leadership was capable of effective mobilization of the masses against the British colonial presence, and for independence, dislodging the Jewish colonies would have required a radically different strategy (Shafir, 1989). That strategy would have involved the nationalist movement in a protracted struggle and class alignments that in all likelihood would erode the system of patronage on which their very power was based.

It would be a mistake, however, to think of Palestinian national politics during the Mandate as based entirely on factionalism. Both al-Istiqlal and the Communists had social bases (especially among urban professionals and sections of the working class) that were secular and devoid of patronage. But both were unsuccessful in challenging the factional leadership of AL-HAJJ AMIN AL-HUSAYNI and the ARAB HIGHER COMMITTEE and remained marginal movements.

On the other hand, factional alliances in Palestine were remarkable in that, after the intensification of Jewish settlement, they transcended both regional divisions (especially the endemic rivalries referred to previously between the Jerusalem and Nablus clans) and religious-ethic divisions. It is suggested, furthermore, that the urban-rural dichotomy has little explanatory value in Palestinian factional politics since faction leaders were mainly urban-based "representatives" of the hierarchical system of rural "clients" and kinsmen reaching all the way to the small peasant debtor and landless laborer.

The extended role of the colonial state apparatus after World War I paradoxically strengthened the role of the leading families of Palestine since alternative institutional mechanisms of intermediate power were absent. They became the mediators of the state to the rural population and urban poor as well as their representatives to the central authorities. Both the limitations and strengths of the factional system were demonstrated in the response of the traditional leadership to the 1936 revolt.

The spontaneous peasant uprisings that marked the initial period of the revolt compelled the two main nationalist parties—the ARAB PARTY, representing the Husayni faction, and the NATIONAL DEFENSE PARTY, representing the Nashashibis—to merge in the framework of the Arab Higher Committee. However, the Husaynis' stronger links to the land, Al-Hajj Amin's role as the mufti (Islamic law expert) of Jerusalem, and the National Defense Party's past record of collaboration with the British authorities, all ensured that the Nashashibis would play a secondary role on the committee.

Class and Kinship Among the peasantry, factional alignments were expressed during the nineteenth century and for a good part of the twentieth, within the framework of putative, or fictitious, affiliations that cut across regions, religious sets, and classes. The most important of those peasant divisions were the Qaysi and Yamani factions.

Although common to many regions of greater Syria under the Ottoman Empire, in Palestine these divisions were unique in that they persisted as forms of political affiliation a long time after they lost their (seeming) function. In Syria and Lebanon Qaysi and Yamani factions seem always to have been expressed through clan alignments (Granqvist, 1935). In the majority of cases extended families, and certainly individuals, could not belong to different factions within the same clan, but there were exceptions. Nominally these factions trace the origin of the clan to its fictitious roots in northern or southern (Yamani) Arabia during the Arab migrations to greater Syria after the Islamic conquest. In practice, however, they had the primary function of establishing the basis for loose alliances in the event of interclan conflicts. Such alliances cut across the village-city dichotomies and often united Christian and Muslim families.

Fictive affiliations, however, do not seem to have taken the same form throughout Palestine. In a comprehensive study of Qaysi-Yamani divisions in nineteenth-century Palestine, Miriam Hoexter distinguishes two main regional patterns of clan alliances: those prevailing in the Nablus mountains and those in the central highlands. In Nablus, indigenous notables and landlords ruled the countryside, whereas in Jerusalem, the local *majlis* was governed by an Ottoman pasha (Hoexter, 1973).

The use of the term *party* (*hizb* or *saff*) in most references to Qaysi and Yamani factions should not obscure the tribal character of these affiliations. The divisions acted as symbols of permanent identification around which members of a clan can be mobilized to secure various (and variable) objectives of their clan heads and tribal leaders. Some social historians of Palestine have dismissed the picture of a perennial "tribal" conflict in which this factionalism has traditionally been portrayed, suggesting a framework on which Qaysi-Yamani divisions can be seen as having the objective of mobilizing the resources of a particular clan leader against the claims of rival families to gain public offices and tax farming contracts.

The decreasing isolation of the Palestinian village (cash crops, Jerusalem-Jaffa railroad, centralization of government) and the decline of the patronage system associated with the rise of share tenancy during the Mandate period affected these alignments negatively. Qaysi-Yamani affiliations lost their effectiveness as foci of clan identification when a new, more complex system of alliances was needed to meet the transformed relations between the peasantry and the urban sector, on the one hand, and the Jewish social structure, on the other. Nevertheless, they continued to surface throughout the Mandate period, and villages took account of them in public festivities lest the amassed crowds in one place should trigger latent conflicts to explode along Qaysi-Yamani lines (Schölch, 1993; Owen, 1982).

Class Formation While the old regional divisions in Palestine—based on administrative zones under Ottoman and British rule—began to lose their original significance, new divisions began to emerge, reflecting the integration of the region's economy into the European capitalist market. Colonial penetration also contributed to the development of a modern infrastructure, to a large extent for reasons of military strategy. By World War I, Palestine had the greatest ratio of railroad track per capita in the Middle East, although the economic impact of modern transportation was not as dramatic as in Egypt.

The building of the Jaffa-Jerusalem railroad line (later Jerusalem-Haifa, and linked to the Hijaz railway), the growth of citriculture with a European market, and the proliferation of wage labor related to the British war efforts and the employment of Palestinians in the government bureaucracy, all led to the decline of the subsistence character of agriculture and the semifeudal relations hinging on it.

Many absentee landlords who resided in the main cities, and a few state functionaries, whose wealth did not rest on land, began to reinvest their agricultural surplus in export-import trade and in light industries. A Royal Commission Report prepared during the revolt year of 1936 challenged the predominant picture of a vigorous modern Jewish industrial economy dwarfing an Arab sector based presumably on craft production. "Arab industry," the report states, "is also diversified (as Jewish Industry) and consists of some large undertakings and numerous small ones which, in the aggregate, form an appreciable contribution to the industry of Palestine" (Himadeh, 1938). The main urban industries in the Arab sector included soap manufacturing, flour milling, and production of textiles and construction material. Agrarian capitalism also flourished during the Mandate and was based on citrus plantations in Jaffa, Gaza, and the Ramla and LYDDA regions. Olive oil extraction was the main form of manufacture in the rural sector in which wealthy peasants and landlords invested their capital—although it tended to remain primitive in its technology.

Thus, a new class of merchants and manufacturers was growing in the coastal cities of Gaza,

Jaffa, and Haifa—all constituting the Mediterranean outlets of Palestine to Europe. This growth of a coastal bourgeoisie was accompanied by important demographic changes: the town population in general, and the coastal cities in particular, increased substantially.

The city of Jaffa had the fastest rate of growth, even before the Mandate. It quadrupled its size between 1880 and 1922 alone, becoming the economic and cultural nerve center of Arab Palestine.

The thirties also saw the beginning of large-scale rural-urban migration, which reflected both the increase in the employment potential of the cities and a rise in the agricultural labor surplus. A new regional dichotomy was emerging between the main coastal cities—centers of trade, newspapers and literary magazines, and urban Jewish migration—and the inner mountain cities (Nablus, SAFAD, and HEBRON)—seats of conservatism and the traditional leadership. But this was not a dichotomy between the abode of the bourgeoisie and the abode of the landed classes. For unlike the landed elites, the Palestinian bourgeoisie did not *behave* as an integrated class during this period. This was related to the composition of the mercantile and manufacturing entrepreneurs in Palestine. As in the neighboring Arab countries, the bourgeoisie was a stratum with strong kinship and social bonds linking it to the landed classes. Those entrepreneurs who were not landlords either had patronage relationships with them or were related to them by marriage. Furthermore, most landlords found it convenient to invest their agricultural surplus in real estate transactions, construction, or posts "bought" for their sons (for instance, through marriage bonds)—in all cases, nonproductive activities.

However, this process of differentiation did not generate the growth of a significant manufacturing class. The urban elites, the class of landlords and urban notables, did not have control over the colonial state apparatus, and because of the heavy competition from the autonomous Jewish sector (which, except in the period of the boycott, had unhindered access over the Arab consumer market) the *external* condition for the growth of the Arab bourgeoisie did not develop. A very small portion of the agricultural surplus was invested in manufacturing enterprises. Those "landed businessmen" who did invest in manufacture (such as the MASRI FAMILY, of the Nablus soap industries) were few and together were not capable of generating enough employment for the masses of dispossessed peasants, peasant-workers, and urban laborers who were looking for jobs (Owen, 1982). Those entrepreneurs were also too closely linked to the landed elite to develop their own distinct consciousness and separate ideology. Nevertheless, recent research about Palestinian investments in coastal enterprises indicate that a vigorous urban entrepreneurial class was growing in the 1940s and was having significant links with Lebanese, Syrian, Egyptian, as well as European establishments (al-Jundi, 1986).

Flight and Dismemberment The consequences of factionalism became evident when the main confrontation finally came about between the Zionist and Arab forces in 1948. The vertical segmentation of the Palestinian society, on which the edifice of its primordial political fabric prevailing in the thirties and forties operated, was shattered from without—with the resulting physical dislocation of both the agrarian and urban communities (the Arab population of the city of Haifa, for example, was reduced by the outflow of Palestinian refugees from 80,000 to a few thousand in one week).

During the initial period of communal clashes between Jews and Arabs, which extended over the latter part of 1947 and early 1948, a substantial section of the Palestinian elite (landlords, businessmen, and professionals) constituted the majority of the tens of thousands of Palestinians who fled the country. Given the absence of an extragovernmental body in Palestinian society (equivalent, for example, to the Jewish Agency) that could coordinate the Palestinian resistance and provide basic services to a community steadily being deserted by its elites, the impending breakup of its political will was unavoidable. Coupled with the intensive bombardment faced by cities like Jaffa, Lydda, and Ramla, this exodus was a decisive factor in the collapse of the social fabric of Palestinian society and the mass desertion of towns and villages by their inhabitants.

The major dislocation that affected Palestinian society from 1948 and the disappearance of the relation of patronage on which factional politics rested compel us to look to different categories of analysis to understand these changes. Although most Palestinians remaining in Palestine still dwelt in rural districts (in the Galilee, the Triangle area of north-central Palestine, and the West Bank—but not Gaza), their collectivity can no longer be characterized as a peasant society: that is, a society that derives its main livelihood from agriculture and in which the family farm constitutes the basic unit of social organization. This is especially true of the rural sector of PALESTINIAN CITIZENS OF ISRAEL: as it was progressively incorporated into the Jewish economy, its former peasants began to relate to it mainly as wage workers. To the extent that factional politics persisted in the Arab village, it was due to the external manipulation by Israeli political parties of a traditional clan structure that was losing its viability and inner dynamic. In the nineties, however, clan politics reemerged in parties that were ostensibly nationalist and socialist (Arab Democratic Party, the Democratic Front for Peace and Equality).

As a consequence of the war the peasantry of Palestine was dismembered and relocated in three different social formations: (1) those who remained in the state of Israel, constituting a submerged underclass of peasant-workers (approximately 25 percent of the total); (2) those who became REFUGEES in the neighboring Arab states and the remaining regions of Palestine, constituting a reserve army of labor in the periphery of the major urban centers of the host countries (Amman, Nablus, Gaza, Beirut, Damascus, JERICHO, and RAMALLAH)—together amounting to 40 percent of the total; (3) those who remained in their villages in those parts of Palestine that were appropriated by JORDAN and Egypt in 1948, the West Bank and Gaza, whose social fabric was altered as a result of being incorporated, albeit in a different manner, from the refugees, into the new social formation—the latter constituting approximately 30 percent of the peasantry (Hilal, 1975; Heiberg, 1993).

The urban refugees, composed predominantly of the artisans, professionals, landowners, and traditional working class of colonial Palestine, were successfully integrated, at least at the economic-occupational level, into the Arab host countries—most notably in Jordan, Kuwait, the Gulf states, and to a lesser extent, Lebanon. It was from their ranks that the Palestinian intelligentsia, unable to assimilate itself politically into these new formations, became an archproponent of pan-Arab nationalism, and later of Palestinian nationalism. Above this intelligentsia lurks an eminently successful Palestinian bourgeoisie whose members were reconstituted from the sons of the defrocked landed elite of old Palestine and whose fortunes were accumulated in the new diaspora of Middle East oil. In every state in the Gulf they are found today among the most prominent bankers, export-import merchants, ministers, government advisers, managers of companies, and planners. Their less fortunate kinsmen swell the ranks of the professional and semiprofessional groups in these states.

The process of dislocation of Palestinians affected the different segments of the dispersed population in a variety of ways, depending on their former location in the class structure and on the social formation in which they were relocated. The term *declassment* itself cannot be used as an all-explanatory category for the fate of the Palestinians, especially since large groupings among the Palestinians, including a substantial segment of the landed elite, improved their standing. Others, like the peasants of the West Bank, retained their land and social fabric intact after the wars of 1948 and 1967.

Declassment of Palestinians in Israel Whether substantial class differentiation has occurred among the Palestinians of Israel or not remains the subject of some controversy. There seems to be a consensus, however, that the quantitative integration of the Palestinian "underclass"—mainly rural laborers and peasants commuting daily to Jewish urban centers from their villages—has led to a qualitative impact on the relationship between Palestinian and Jewish society. In formal terms this change can be described as the transformation of Palestinian and Jewish societies from two *parallel* social structures into a single social structure *hierarchically integrated* in a relationship of dominance. Still in need of elaborate empirical substantiation are the amount and character of social differentiation that took place within Palestinian society corresponding to its progressive subordination to Jewish society.

Several ethnographic studies of the fate of Palestinian villages in Israel (such as those conducted by Khalil Nakhleh, Henry Rosenfeld, Sharif Kana'ana, and Amnon Cohen) illuminate the changing social and political trends among the Palestinian population inside Israel.

In one such relationship the Israeli state, through limiting the options of political affiliation open to Palestinian villagers and tying voting behavior to the Zionist parties with material inducements for voters (jobs, and so on), reinforces faction-based conflicts in the village, especially those with a strong confessional (religious) base. Thus, factionalism here persists but in a clearly different context than the one prevailing prior to 1948: patronage today is related to access to privileges spared by the Israeli state to the Palestinian population through the Zionist parties. It has become a means for Zionist legitimization in the Palestinian sector.

An indicator of the qualitative changes in the social composition of Palestinian citizens of Israel can be observed in the shifting employment structure. The most notable shift has been the absolute decline in farm employment, from 58.2 percent in 1954 to less than 10 percent in the 1990s. But the alternative avenues of employment have been in those sectors that display a high degree of instability in work tenure (such as construction and catering), and hence in the formation of a cohesive working class. In three decades Palestinian employment in construction and public works increased considerably but also was supplanted by the emergence of a new professional and business class among Palestinian citizens of Israel.

Since the early eighties we witness a richer diversification in the occupational structure of Palestinian citizens of Israel, who, while maintaining their village-based dwellings and (sometimes) plots, succeeded in promoting themselves, in considerable numbers, into the ranks of the self-employed (construction subcontracting, retail, and other occupations), into professional employment (Rosenfeld, 1978: 396), and into a militant intelligentsia (trained, in part, in Hebrew educational centers) that openly identifies itself with Palestinian nationalism. Rosenfeld describes a policy of "deterritorialization," based on land confiscation and aimed at maintaining the submerged underclass character of the Palestinian population, as having backfired as a result of changes emanating from the work process itself. This process has objectively diminished the class-ethnic cleavages that previously separated Jewish and Palestinian social structures within the Israeli state, and now has to be reinforced at the political level by the state.

Reviving interfamilial rivalries was not the only means of maintaining the diminishing social cleavage between the Palestinian and Jewish population. It was also a consequence of the prolonged physical backwardness of the Palestinian village, where a majority of Palestinians continue to live. While the restrictions on village development channeled attempts at self-improvement in the direction of migrations to Jewish urban areas, village backwardness continued to create a peasant-worker underclass.

This process by which structural (socioeconomic) and institutional (political-administrative) mechanisms reinforce each other in ensuring Israeli-Jewish hegemony over the Palestinian minority is not self-perpetuating, however. Lustick has suggested such a system of control composed of three leverages: (1) segmentation, the internal fragmentation of the Palestinian community that prevents them from exercising united political action; (2) dependence, the reliance of Palestinians on the Jewish economy for sources of livelihood; (3) co-optation, the selective manipulation of Palestinian factionalism, especially at the village level, by Zionist parties and institutions. Although these three components of control operate simultaneously to ensure Palestinian quiescence at the political level, they are not foolproof, as evidenced by the increasing assertions for national and local representation in the country's political system (Lustick, 1980). Subsequently, the normalization of relations between Israel and the Arab countries after the peace agreements of the 1990s led to the emergence of demands for equality that were atomized and based on individual self-enhancement by the new professional class, rather than collective equality in citizenship for the Palestinian minority.

This process of declassment characterized the status of Palestinians in Israel for most of the first three decades after the state was established. However, almost all Palestinian citizens of Israel are landless, and an increasingly significant proportion of those who are landed have used their village base to challenge their submerged class structure. Yet the fact remains that a considerable section of the Palestinian wage-earning population in Israel was, and to a large extent still is, dependent on employment in relatively unskilled and unstable occupations (construction, the services, and seasonal agriculture) and suffers from the institutional obstruction by the Israeli economy of the emergence of viable Arab enterprises and a professional stratum (for example, through unofficial quotas on the number of available seats for Palestinian students in the scientific departments in Israeli universities that prevailed until quite recently). But such dependence and obstruction are not defined by the rigidity of the occupational structure, or other strictly economic factors. Rather they are limited and constantly being modified by political considerations, such as the Israeli conception of "security," and the maintenance of a Jewish majority in "sensitive" fields of employment—that is, by ideologically defined factors. During the sixties and seventies the need of the Israeli state for a "positive" Palestinian intelligentsia (as local Palestinians who accommodate the general policies of the state were referred to) invited its opposite: the emergence of an oppositional intelligentsia that has contributed effectively since the early sixties to the opening of the universities and other previously closed avenues of employment and mobility to a new generation of Palestinian youth. The privatization of the corporate economy during the 1980s and 1990s opened further opportunities for mobility to Palestinian professionals and entrepreneurs.

The Palestinian Exile The refugee camp populations in the Arab exile constitute the core of Palestinians dispersed in 1948, and again in 1967. Unlike the camp refugees in Gaza and the West Bank, those living in Jordan, Syria, and Lebanon do not reside in the periphery of a relatively dynamic and expanding economy in need of constant sources of cheap labor as the case was in Israel. The construction boom in Jordan (mid-seventies), enhanced with the influx of (rich) refugees from the Lebanese civil war, changed this situation there, but only temporarily. Until the mid-1980s it may be said that the camp refugees (a majority of Palestinians in Lebanon and Syria—and almost a third of the Palestinians in Jordan) acted as a reserve army of the unemployed for the host economies. With the recession of the Gulf economy, and particularly after the GULF CRISIS, 1990–1991, Palestinians had extremely restricted access to these economies.

The position of those refugees has been described succinctly by Elias Sanbar as "expulsion for the means of production." Until 1982, when the Israeli invasion of Lebanon shattered the social fabric of the Palestinian community, wage labor in the refugee camps supplemented United Nations Relief and Works Agency for Palestine Refugees in the Near East (UNRWA) and other stipends from migrant relatives. Together with Kurdish and illegal Syrian migrants, as well as Lebanese Shi'ite farmers from the south, the Palestinians constituted a competing source of cheap and expendable labor for local Beirut industries. A comprehensive survey conducted in a Beirut camp on the eve of the civil war confirms this position. Tall al-Za'tar, which was destroyed and many of its inhabitants massacred by Phalangist forces in 1976, was not untypical of urban refugee camps such as those situated in Amman, Damascus, Zarqa, and Irbid (it had certain features, however, that set it apart from those camps: for example, it contained a substantial proportion [23 percent] of non-Palestinian refugees, and it had a considerable number of Palestinian refugees of pastoral nomadic background, mainly from the Hula region). The camp, located in East Beirut in a district containing 29 percent of all Lebanese manufacturing industries, employed 22 percent of the total labor force and absorbed 23 percent of the industrial capital investments in Lebanon (Sanbar, 1984).

Even in a labor force dominated by "lumpen" elements, a considerable degree of social differentiation prevailed. Besides the substantial number of peddlers and itinerant laborers, the camp population includes a large number of shopkeepers, drivers, teachers, artisans, vegetable peddlers, and other semiprofessionals (such as nurses). The camps in addition had a number of contractors and medium-sized merchants who lived in their periphery, some of whom had become Lebanese citizens. A limited degree of occupational mobility was enhanced by the availability of free university education to refugee students.

Unemployment figures, though high, were surprisingly lower than those for the Lebanese labor force, even when seasonal fluctuations are taken into account. But there is an important difference: Palestinian refugees constitute in their majority former peasants who have lost their lands and whose residence in Lebanon, by virtue of their insecure legal status, is far more vulnerable than that of indigenous migrant peasant-workers. The latter, a considerable number of whom have access to land or to relatives with land, can cushion the impact of recession, or individual unemployment, by periodic return to their villages. But the situation after the eviction of the PALESTINE LIBERATION ORGANIZATION (PLO) from Lebanon after 1982 has changed much of this picture, and the situation of the camp refugees has become much more tenuous since then, with significant trends of individual household migration to the Scandinavian countries and Canada recorded.

It was this situation of social and economic marginality that established the camp refugees as the bearers of the "cult of return" (*al-awda*) to Palestine as the core of their political ideology, and it was from their ranks that the fighting cadres of the various contingents of the Palestine liberation movement were recruited. The "cult of return" and the organizational independence of Palestinian movements that it entailed, however, were not always forms of self-imposed political restrictions. Both in Jordan and in Lebanon the Palestinians entered into various forms of alliances with the local forces in order to face the repression of the national authorities—but the conditions under which the Palestinian refugees lived and worked rendered these alliances much weaker than if they were fully integrated in the host countries.

But although the effective social base of the PLO existed in Jordan (1967–71) and Lebanon (1971–82) among its refugee camps and rootless intelligentsia, its political constituency was dispersed in several social formations, throughout the Arab world and the state of Israel. As the quest for nationhood altered the movement's ideological direction, from the cult of return to the quest for sovereignty, and from total liberation to limited statehood, so did the PLO's political center of gravity begin to gravitate from its diaspora to those segments of Palestine that remained "intact": in the West Bank and Gaza.

The West Bank and Gaza: The Logic of Old Hierarchies The conditions of declassment described for dispersed refugees in urban Lebanon, Syria, and Jordan do not take into account the fact that close to half the Palestinian people still live in (historic) Palestine—integrated since 1967 through common Israeli rule—most of them residing in relatively stable communities, in or near the place of their birth. Only in Gaza do refugee camps constitute a slight majority (around 55 percent) of the population. In the West Bank they are less than 20 percent, and in the Galilee and the Triangle refugees (though not living in camps) constitute less than 15 percent of the total Palestinian population. Furthermore, most of the remaining Palestinians living in other parts of the state of Israel (villages around West Jerusalem, the Negev (Naqab), the Lydda-Ramla area, and Jaffa) have retained their places of residence (Zureik, 1979).

What are crucial to the Occupied Territories are the manner in which the Palestinian labor force was incorporated into the Israeli economy and—since 1994—the emergence of the Palestinian national economy under the aegis of the PALESTINIAN AUTHORITY. In the three decades of Israeli rule over the territories Israel has engineered the integration of the West Bank into the Israeli economy. Until the Gulf Crisis this process involved the employment of nearly half the Palestinian labor force in Israeli enterprises on a daily basis and the opening up of Gaza and the West Bank as markets for Israeli commodities. Of those workers involved the overwhelming majority were of peasant origin (73.2 percent were rural-based, as opposed to 26 percent evenly divided between urban and refugee residents), but few of them today are agriculturalists (Hilal, 1975; Taraki, 1990; Kimmerling and Migdal, 1993).

Israeli rule did give rise to a stratum of war profiteers—connected mostly with labor contracting, construction, and real estate transactions. But it did not change qualitatively the character of the local middle classes. Any growth effects it may have had were probably canceled by the desertion of sectors of the commercial bourgeoisie to Jordan after 1967. Israeli-Palestinian joint enterprises emerged in the form of subcontracting firms (in textiles and construction), but their growth rates soon declined after the late seventies, probably as a result of the impact of political uncertainty on business transactions. Employment in Israel, the most crucial variable in this connection, did create a new stratum of workers from urban refugees and surplus rural labor.

The diversity between Gaza and the West Bank is rooted partly in the different forms of agricultural production (the predominance of capitalist citrus plantations in Gazan agriculture as opposed to small and medium-sized farms in the West Bank), and partly in the massive weight of the refugee population in Gaza. But it is also related to the nature of Jordanian and Egyptian rule between

1948 and 1967 in those two regions (Nakhleh and Zureik, 1981).

The West Bank escaped the destruction of its landed-commercial elite and underwent a pattern of limited structural mobility in its occupational and class composition. The Jordanian army and bureaucracy, the expansion of the educational system, and a high rate of out-migration (the latter supplementing a sizable portion of household income), all combined to modify the direction of social change in a different way from that experienced by Palestinians who remained in Israel and by Gazans under Egyptian rule.

Mediation of Israeli Rule On the surface the difference between the West Bank and the Galilee would seem to be the degree of integration within Jewish society, which obtains as a result of—among other factors—the civic enfranchisement of the Israeli Palestinian population (tenuous as it is) into the state of Israel, and conversely, the colonial relationship between the state and the Palestinians of the West Bank and Gaza. This is admittedly a controversial position, for there are those who argue that the difference is one in the degree of colonial domination between the two communities, rather than one of qualitative dichotomy. What this problem amounts to is how one interprets the nature of mediation in Israeli rule in the two Palestinian communities before the establishment of autonomous rule in 1994.

In the Galilee, where 60 percent of Israel's Palestinians are concentrated, this mediation is articulated through a relatively vigorous civil society: that is, through the system of political parties, local councils, clan alliances, and a personal nepotistic network of favoritism that permeates these agencies. The structural foundation of this mediation is the occupational integration of the Palestinian labor force in the Jewish economy. A considerable degree of coercion and intimidation is nevertheless used to supplement those institutions in order to guarantee the acquiescence of Palestinians to Israeli Jewish society whose raison d'être excludes them (as Arabs) from its policy. But coercion, since the abolition of the military government in 1961, has been a secondary mechanism of political control. In the West Bank and Gaza, by contrast, mediation of Israeli rule until 1994 has proceeded primarily through the machinery of the military government. The use of systematic physical coercion to maintain Israeli hegemony has far exceeded that used among Palestinian citizens of Israel during the formative years of the Jewish state, when the military government ruled supreme in the Galilee (1948–66). Despite the presence of similar structural trends of integration at the economic level between the two regions of Israeli control, the difference cannot be attributed simply to the missing constitutional factor, that is, the enfranchisement of Palestinian citizens of Israel and its absence among Palestinians in the West Bank and Gaza. This situation continues today despite the granting of Palestinian identity papers to residents of the West Bank and Gaza (1994).

One important factor that may explain the different responses to Israeli rule in the two regions is their social composition. Whereas the West Bank has maintained its rural and urban hierarchies, albeit in a modified form, Galilean rural society had lost its original landed elites and intelligentsia and had, therefore, to deal on its own with overwhelming odds (Nakhleh and Zureik, 1981). The continued links between West Bank Palestinians and the Arab world, through Jordan, provided that society with a network of commercial, political, and cultural ties that were denied to Palestinian citizens of Israel and drastically curtailed their political options.

We have traced the consequences of dislocation of traditional agrarian Palestine and the emergence of three distinct social formations in which the remnants of that society are embedded today. The centrality of the West Bank (and Gaza) in those formations lies in two aspects of this configuration: it is the only segment of historic Palestine in which agriculture constitutes a critical component of the region's political economy, and it is the arena in which Palestinian sovereignty is being contested today. In contrast to the predicament of the Palestinians in the Israeli and neighboring Arab formations, West Bankers were the least subject to the convulsions in social structure that Palestinians underwent elsewhere. They alone have retained a semblance of a social order that bears continuity with the nation's historic past. Only there is a Palestinian peasantry, divorced from its coastal landlords and urban elite, still entrenched in the highlands of the West Bank mountains and in the valleys of the Jordan. But since the "divorce" was accompanied by a massive population transfer, reimposed on its traditional order by changes in the nature of its hegemonic elites and by its reintegration into the framework of three considerably different societies (the Jordanian, Egyptian, and Israeli), one cannot treat the remaining society and peasantry as a reduced segment of the original whole.

The Intifada: Social Consequences The INTIFADA (1987–93) was a sustained grass-roots movement of civil insurrection against Israeli rule. The nationalism of the Intifada, and its broadly (and unclearly) defined objectives of national independence, succeeded initially in mobilizing hundreds and thousands of people in acts of civil disobedience against Israeli control. As the years progressed, however, and with increased Israeli repression against the rebellion, the movement began to lose its mass base and was confined to street action against the army by bands of activists.

Of all the social consequences of the rebellion, the most visible was the massive involvement of youth and children in spontaneous acts of resistance to the colonial forces. Tens of thousands of young people, including students, children below age fifteen, and lumpen elements in refugee camps and urban areas, were mobilized. Many of those youths were outside the arena of organized political groups and were eventually mobilized by political groups as well as in the form of enraged street bands that had a rather tenuous political relationship to the national or Islamic movements (Nassar and Heacock, 1991). Although their main target was the Israeli army, border police, and settlers, the main consequence of their activity—as far as social structure is concerned—was to challenge traditional parental authority prevalent in Palestinian society.

This social dynamic was already observable from the early sixties with the economic independence of young people, including young women, set in motion through the breakup of the economy of the traditional house as a result of work demands outside the family farm and the family business, and the massive expansion of educational institutions—at the primary, secondary, and university levels.

This challenge to the traditional authority of the Palestinian family took several forms during the Intifada. Young people, including women, found legitimate justification for spending prolonged periods outside their homes, and therefore away from the controlling authority of the parents (escape from arrest, organizing activities, and so on). Parental authority was challenged directly by youth claims for a higher authority consecrated by political commitments to their political groups and therefore to the "national cause." These claims were furthermore deemed acceptable and legitimate by society at large; quite often public pressure overrode narrow family concerns for the safety and (in the case of women) honor of the family. Even in mourning quite often the political group took over the tasks of the family in organizing and receiving ritual condolences.

One of the most intimate domains of family control was the choosing of marriage partners for their children. Increasingly this task was invaded by considerations of political unions dictated by political expediencies, security, and even love born in the "heat of struggle." Although the rate of such marriages should not be exaggerated, they should not be discounted as a *social*—as opposed to an individual—phenomenon.

Against this challenge to the authority of the Palestinian patriarchy an opposite trend emerged during the Intifada: in many villages and refugee camps women are married off earlier and quicker, in order to preempt their involvement in political activity. Many young men took advantage of the regime of social austerity ushered in by the social uprising, including the lowering of the *mahr* (bride price) and the cancellation of expensive wedding ceremonies, to marry cheaply and early. The result, as can be gleaned from religions court records, was an approximate drop of two years in the average age of young women at marriage as compared with that in pre-Intifada days. These early marriages mean two things: higher fertility rate (now incorporated into a national cult of procreation) and tighter control over the social life of young women, who had little chance of a public life before marriage.

The generalized proclamation of independence of youth should be seen in this context as primarily a male phenomenon, and one that often exercises itself as an agency of control over the mobility of women: either in the context of early marriages, or, as in refugee camps, in dictating the dress codes and free movements of female relatives. But this independence is not expressed only in the negative act of control over women. It has a twin emancipatory and anomic function: emancipatory in the sense that parents no longer control the activities of their (mostly) male children—either at home or in the street.

One consequence of this malaise is that the self-discipline inculcated by the school systems has all but disintegrated at the primary level and has been weakened considerably at the secondary and university levels. Another consequence is that the mass political parties (including the religious movements) have lost their organizational control over enraged youth, who often claim titular affiliation to their leadership.

The Reassertion of Family Control Despite these features of social anomie associated with the Intifada, the Palestinian family has displayed substantial resilience. As in the aftermath of the 1948 war (and probably during the 1936 revolt) Palestinians fell back on family resources to protect themselves from the loss of control of the world surrounding them. Among peasants this meant rejuvenation of neglected lands. In the urban context it meant the strengthening of the family firm and domestication of resources. In both cases an internal division of labor was reasserted in which the weakened extended family regained many of its eroding functions. During the Intifada we witnessed an enhanced role for the family shop (in the cities) and the attempt to revive the marginalized family plot in highland dry farming—which was in an advanced state of neglect as a result of the movement of labor from the village to urban construction sites.

But it would be premature to regard these trends as constituting a social counterrevolution, since the involvement of young people in the labor market outside their homes produced a lifestyle and individual predispositions that were very hard to roll back. It would be more accurate to see this trend as acting as a cushion against the uncertainties of economic upheavals generated by the critical combination of Israeli repression, the Gulf Crisis, and the restrictions of movement that accompanied the Intifada. It is in the realm of these attitudes that we should try to locate the persistence of traditionalism or its decline.

Cultural Resistance and Disengagement The Intifada witnessed a series of organizational efforts leading to the emergence of a new civil society in Palestine. We can distinguish two periods of cultural resistance (in the 1970s, and during the Intifada) that generated forms of self-identity that distinguished Palestinian social life from that experienced by the exile communities. In both cases the implicit objective (made explicit during the Intifada) was to *disengage* from the network of control established by the Israelis over their subject population.

During the seventies cultural resistance took several forms, among them the revival of traditions of music and theater that was localized and independent of currents in the Arab world—inspired to a large extent by motifs drawn from Palestinian folklore and the emergence of several voluntary youth movements in community work, mostly linked to university student unions. Much of these movements were inspired by a radical perspective of uniting intellectual labor with manual labor and were in fact so successful that they were incorporated in the official university curriculum of three universities. A third form was the movement for adult education, whose objective was to wipe out illiteracy among working adults and introduce rural women to functional literacy. The movement succeeded in mobilizing hundreds of university students to roam outlying districts and set up makeshift classes. It also introduced innovative techniques of adult education through learning by doing and use of specialized adult texts.

Eventually this movement was stifled by institutionalization: it became part of the regular routinized university curriculum and "higher committees" of adult education, losing its voluntarist character. The loss of momentum and dispersal of the cultural movement of resistance to a large extent, however, resulted from the decline of the political movement after the withdrawal of Palestinians from Lebanon.

The parallel movement during the Intifada was similarly based on a strategy of disengagement from Israel, in the form of a boycott of Israeli commodities and its civil administration, and the building of alternative organs of power in anticipation of statehood. The movement was given critical momentum when the Israeli army closed all schools; even kindergartens were closed by military order.

Popular committees were organized by clandestine groups in urban neighborhoods throughout the West Bank and Gaza to fulfill the educational needs of locked out pupils. Since the number of university-trained Palestinians was monumental (on a per capita basis it compares with that of Israel—fully one-third of high school graduates were enrolled in universities and polytechnics), there was an abundance of available teaching staff. At the university level classes were convened in hotels, mosques, churches, and homes. Education acquired the status of a subversive activity.

This secret ritual allowed by interventions in the range and character of traditional curriculum, as well as innovations in the style of instruction and learning process, to a degree that was unimagined in supervised teaching. Students began to rely on a higher proportion of home study. Teachers allowed, by necessity, for a wider range of initiative and participation by their pupils.

In a few cases independent educational committees, primarily in the private sector, undertook to write and disseminate alternative textbooks. Calls were made to revamp the standard general examination, which determines the fate of all high school graduates, but those were soon terminated by popular hostility to the idea and the sheer administrative complexity of the scheme.

This experiment at reconstructing the educational system was short-lived. The popular committees, the semiclandestine units that directed neighborhood activities during the years 1988 and 1989, were crushed by brute force through a series of house-to-house searches, arrests, imprisonments, and deportations. Mass organizations that survived the police hunt directed their main activities at noncultural activities, such as peasant cooperatives, women's associations, trade union activities, and straightforward political action. Since the popular committees were seen by the Israelis (and particularly by the then-minister of defense, Yitzhak Rabin) as the backbone of the insurrection, no distinction was made between cultural forms of resistance and other types of street action. The movement had to be crushed as a whole, beginning with its "soft" infrastructure—the neighborhood committees.

Within the movement itself there were internal factors that mitigated against the success of educational reform. Traditional school curricula and established procedures of examination were the gateway for career advancement in society. Any attempt to tamper with this system was fiercely resisted not only by the educational establishment but from the ranks of the national movement itself. The excessive factionalism of the youth movement meant that any attempt to address substantive issues in the educational system were seen as divisive and premature (that is, that such issues should be handled by an independent state institution). Underneath this resistance to radical reform was the unwillingness of any wing within the movement to tackle the thorny problem of introducing changes in curriculum, methods of teaching, or examination that would require self-discipline of the student population; this was seen as diversionary within the resistance movement. Parents' committees were hardly sympathetic to an experiment that they saw as disrupting their children's chance for social advancement by tampering with the "rules of the game."

The movement for cultural renewal espoused by the popular committees in the first part of the Intifada, like its predecessor in the 1970s, was aborted by a combination of official repression and the internal reticence and conservatism of the nationalist movement.

The Intifada succeeded in planting the seeds of future emancipatory cultural politics. In contrast to the experience of the Algerian revolution, it had an implicitly Gramscian conception of power that is forged before independence and *toward* independence. But this conception—as we have seen—is contentious within the movement as a whole, and there is no guarantee that it would be implemented. At the core of the crisis is a system that has ceased to deliver on its earlier promises, both at the level of being a vehicle of class mobility (because of the archaicness of its curriculum) and at the level of improving the status of its practitioner (because it is no longer relevant to the needs of society).

Achieving statehood was seen as a precondition for generating much-needed educational reform. But as the experience of other colonial countries clearly attests, it was a necessary but not sufficient condition.

State Formation: New Social Dynamics Israeli withdrawal from the West Bank urban and rural areas, which commenced with the signing of the

Interim Palestinian-Israeli Agreement in the winter of 1995, created a new dynamic between the Palestinian social formation and its diaspora. The return to Palestine of PALESTINE LIBERATION ORGANIZATION cadres with YASIR ARAFAT, the creation of a huge bureaucracy and a public sector, and the partial return of Palestinian investors from abroad, all contributed to the consolidation of a new regime that has shifted the political, social, and ideological (but not the cultural) weight of Palestinian society to the country.

The election in 1996 of the eighty-eight member PALESTINIAN LEGISLATIVE COUNCIL (PLC) created new possibilities for a diversified political system in which the arbitrary tendencies of the executive would be tempered by the elected council. The new nascent state-to-be, however, displayed several authoritarian features: a multiplicity of security organs unfettered by due process, extralegal security courts, state monopolies not subject to legislative accountability, and a draft basic law that remained unratified by the executive.

A new social dynamic is now emerging in Palestine, one in which the strain will no longer be between the "external" and the "internal" elements, but within society. The contours of this tension are already taking form in the manner in which civil society is reformulating itself: the assertion of community-based groups to defend their autonomy against the encroachment of the state, the struggle for a free press, the degree of autonomy afforded to the judiciary, the independence of the academic establishment, the nature of legislation in the Palestinian state, and so on. Behind it lies the protracted struggle of Palestinian society to wrest control over its remaining territories from the remnants of Israeli occupation and the settlements that were established throughout the West Bank and Gaza.

Salim Tamari

BIBLIOGRAPHY

Abu Lughod, Ibrahim, ed. *The Transformation of Palestine.* Evanston, Ill.: Northwestern Press, 1971.

Ashour, Issam. "Nizam al-Muraba'a fi Suriyya wa Lubnan wa Filistin." *al-Abhath* (Beirut) 1, 3 (1948–1949): 32–48; 1, 4 (1948–1949): 47–69; 2, 1 (1948–1949): 61–72.

Carmi, Shulamit, and H. Rosenfeld. "The Origins of the Process of Proletarianization and Urbanization of Arab Peasants in Palestine." *Annals of the American Academy of Arts and Science* 220 (1975): 470–485.

Doumani, Beshara. *Rediscovering Palestine: Merchants and Peasants in Jabal Nablus, 1700–1900.* Berkeley: University of California Press, 1995.

Farsoun, Samih, and Christine Zacharia. *Palestine and the Palestinians.* Boulder, Colo.: Westview Press, 1997.

Firestone, Yaakov. "Crop-Sharing Economics in Mandatory Palestine." *Middle East Studies* 11, 2–23 (1975): 175–194.

Gerber, Haim. *Ottoman Rule in Jerusalem 1890–1914.* Berlin: Klaus Schwarz Verlag, 1985.

Granqvist, Hilma. *Marriage Conditions in a Palestinian Village*, 2 vols. Helsingford; 1935.

Heiberg, Marianne, et al. *Palestinian Society in Gaza, the West Bank and Arab Jerusalem.* Oslo: The Norwegian Institute of Social Science Research (FAFO-Oslo), 1993.

Hilal, Jamil. *Al-Diffa al-Gharbiyya, al-Buniyya al-Iqtisadiyya wa al-Ijtima'iyya 1948–1974.* Beirut: Markaz al-Abhath al-Filastini, 1975.

———. *Al-Nizam al-Siyasi al-Filistini.* Beirut: Institute for Palestine Studies, 1998.

Himadeh, Said, ed. *Economic Organization of Palestine.* Beirut: American University Press, 1938.

Hoexter, M. *The Role of the Qais and Yemen Factions in Local Political Divisions: Jabal Nablus Compared with the Judean Hills in the First Half of the Nineteenth Century.* Jerusalem: Jerusalem Academic Press, 1973.

al-Jundi, Ibrahim. *al-Sina'a fi Filastin Ibban al-Intidab al-Baritani* (Industry in Palestine during the British Mandate). Amman: Samid Publications, 1986.

Khalidi, Rashid. *Palestinian Identity: The Construction of Modern National Consciousness.* New York: Columbia University Press, 1997.

Khalidi, Walid, ed. *All That Remains: The Palestinian Villages Occupied and Depopulated by Israel in 1948.* Washington, D.C.: Institute for Palestine Studies, 1992.

Kimmerling, B., and J. Migdal. *Palestinians, The Making of a People.* New York: Macmillan, 1993.

Lustick, Ian. *Arabs in the Jewish State: Israel's Control of a National Minority.* Austin: Texas University Press, 1980.

Lutfiyyeh, Abdallah. *Baytin: A Jordanian Village.* The Hague: Mouton, 1966.

McCarthy, Justin. *The Population of Palestine: Population History and Statistics of the Late Ottoman Period and the Mandate.* New York: Columbia University Press, 1988.

Mansour, Camille, ed. *Les Palestiniennes de l'intérieur.* Paris: Les Livres de la Revue d'étude Palestininnes, 1989.

Moors, Annalies. *Women, Property and Islam: Palestinian Experiences, 1920–1990.* Cambridge, England: Cambridge University Press, 1995.

Nakhleh, Khalil, and Elia Zureik, eds. *The Sociology of the Palestinians.* London: Croom Helm, 1981.

Nassar, Jamal, and Roger Heacock, eds. *Intifada: Palestine at the Crossroads.* New York: Praeger, 1991.

Nimr, Ihsan. *Ta'rikh Jabal Nablus wa al-Balqa,* 3 vols. Nablus: al-Tahir Library, 1974.
Owen, Roger, ed. *Studies in the Economic and Social History of Palestine in the Nineteenth and Twentieth Centuries.* London: Macmillan, 1982.
Palestinian Central Bureau of Statistics. *The Demographic Survey in the West Bank and Gaza Strip: Preliminary Report.* Ramallah, 1996.
Rafiq, Muhammad, and Muhammad Bahjat. *Wilayat Bayrut: Wilayat Bayrut, Akka wa Nablus.* Vol. I. Beirut: Iqbal Press, 1916.
Sakakini, Khalil. *Kadha ana ya Dunya: al-Yawmiyyat.* Jerusalem: al-Matba'a al-Tijariyya, 1955.
Sanbar, Elias. *Palestine 1948, l'expulsion.* Paris: Livre de la Revue d'étude Palestiniennes, 1984.
Schölch, Alexander. *Palestine in Transformation 1856–1882.* Washington, D.C.: Institute for Palestine Studies, 1993.
Seikally, May. *Haifa: Transformation of an Arab Society 1918–1939.* London: I. B. Tauris, 1995.
Shafir, Gershon. *Land, Labor and the Origins of the Israeli-Palestinian Conflict 1882–1914.* Cambridge, England: Cambridge University Press, 1989.
Tamari, Salim. "Revolt of the Petite Bourgeoisie: Urban Merchants and the Palestinian Uprising." *Palestine at the Crossroads,* ed. by Heacock and Nassar. New York: Praeger, 1990.
———. "Historical Reversals and the Uprising." *Echoes of the Intifada: Regional Repercussions of the Israeli-Palestinian Conflict,* ed. by Rex Brynen. Boulder, Colo.: Westview Press, 1991.
———. "The Persistence of Sharetenancy in the Palestinian Agrarian Economy." In *The Rural Middle East: Peasant Lives and Modes of Production,* ed by K. Glavanis and P. Glavanis. London: Zed Press, 1990.
Taraki, Lisa, ed. *Al-Mujtama Al-Filastini fi al-Diffa al-Gharbiyya wa Qita Ghazza.* Acre: Dar al-Aswar, 1990.
Zureik, Elia. *The Palestinians in Israel: A Study in Internal Colonialism.* London: Routledge & Kegan Paul, 1979.

Sourani, Raji

Surani; lawyer, human rights activist
1953– Gaza

Raji Sourani (pursued secondary studies in Gaza and BETHLEHEM before studying law for a time at Beirut Arab University. He received an LL.B. From Alexandria University in Egypt in 1977, whereupon he returned to the GAZA STRIP to practice LAW.

Sourani repeatedly fell afoul of Israeli occupation authorities in Gaza. He was imprisoned on several occasions, including from 1979 to 1982, and worked to defend Palestinians arrested for alleged security violations.

A human rights activist, Sourani has served with the Palestine Human Rights Information Center and the Committee for the Defense of the Child. Sourani headed the Gaza Center for Rights and Law from 1991 to 1995. Briefly arrested in February 1995 after his call for an investigation of PALESTINIAN AUTHORITY (PA) state security courts, Sourani was dismissed from the center by the PA in April 1995. Since then he has headed the Palestinian Center for Human Rights in Gaza.

Michael R. Fischbach

Soviet Union

Until World War II the Union of Soviet Socialist Republics (U.S.S.R.) gave almost no attention to the subject of Palestine, opposing ZIONISM as a bourgeois-nationalist movement and generally disdaining the Arabs as pro-British. Moscow's objective after the war was to eject the British from the region, for which purpose the Soviets suspended their opposition to Zionism. While giving some support to the idea of a federal state of Jews and Arabs in Palestine, Moscow opted for the idea of partition in 1947. The U.S.S.R. indirectly provided arms and aid to the Jews in the war of 1948, blaming Arab opposition to Israel on British influence. Soviet support for Israel gradually disappeared after the departure of the British in 1948, and, after the death of Stalin in 1953, Moscow began actively supporting the Arab states against Israel. At first, however, the Soviets viewed the ARAB-ISRAELI CONFLICT as one between existing nations (and a convenient vehicle for their competition with the West), failing to recognize the Palestinians as a people and, therefore, refusing formal contact with the PALESTINE LIBERATION ORGANIZATION (PLO) when it was founded in 1964.

Indirect relations with the Palestinians were begun only after a secret trip to Moscow by the PLO chair YASIR ARAFAT, as a member of Egyptian president Jamal Abd al-Nasir's delegation in July 1968. The U.S.S.R.'s recognition of the Palestinians as a people and the PLO as a national liberation movement followed. This change in attitude and the ensuing but gradual development of the Soviet-Palestinian relationship were responses to Arab states' focus on the Palestinian issue and, increasingly, a counter to expanded U.S. involvement in the Arab-Israeli conflict. During BLACK SEPTEMBER (1970), for example, the Soviet Union failed to provide even propaganda support for the Palestinians. Yet by 1972, it was supplying arms to the PLO. In July–August 1974, Arafat was for the first time an official guest of the Soviet government, and the Soviets publicly advocated a Palestinian state in a September 8 speech by President Nikolai Podgorny. In 1976 a PLO office was opened in Moscow, and in 1978, after the CAMP DAVID ACCORDS between Israel and Egypt, the Soviets officially recognized the PLO as the sole representative of the Palestinian people. Accordingly, the PLO office was accorded embassy status in 1981. These developments occurred primarily in response to increasing U.S. involvement in negotiations of the Arab-Israeli conflict, for the Palestinian issue was perceived as the Achilles heel of the Americans' position. Thus, American inroads were generally countered by some kind of augmentation of Soviet political or material support for the PLO. The Soviets were, however, unwilling to provide support that might jeopardize their own efforts to become part of the negotiating process or to escalate the conflict to the point of risking a U.S.-Soviet military confrontation. Out of this concern, for example, Moscow refused to assist the Palestinians against the 1982 Israeli invasion of Lebanon. In virtually all decisions, Moscow placed its global considerations above those of its relations with a national liberation movement, limiting its aid to political support, training, and supplies.

Concern over global politics continued to shape Soviet policy. Moscow opposed a formal split in the PLO after the war in Lebanon, fearing that such a split would both weaken the organization and strengthen Syrian control. The Soviets then suspended aid and training to FATAH when Arafat held a PALESTINE NATIONAL COUNCIL (PNC) meeting in Amman, Jordan, November 22–28, 1984, and entered into an agreement with Washington's ally, Jordan's King Husayn, in February 1985, apparently with the intention of dealing with the United States. Subsequently, Moscow mediated a reunification of the PLO, resuming relations and aid to Fatah only after an Arafat-Husayn agreement was abandoned in 1986 and abrogated at the PNC meeting in Algiers on April 20, 1987. By this time, the leadership in Moscow had changed and Mikhail Gorbachev was revamping Soviet foreign policy, including policy toward the Arab-Israeli conflict. Advocating international relations based on a balance of interests and seeking genuine cooperation with the United States, Gorbachev urged Arafat in 1987 to seek an accord with Israel based on the security interests of Israel as well as the national interests of the Palestinians. At the same time, Gorbachev began a gradual resumption of Soviet relations with Israel, eventually reducing aid and support to the PLO while cooperating with the United States to bring about a negotiated settlement of the conflict.

Throughout the Soviet-PLO relationship there were significant differences in objective and policies of the two entities. Soviet support was a function of its competition with the United States and was thus affected by both the strategic and the tactical aspects of this competition. PLO interest in Moscow was presumably no less guided by self-interest, but Palestinian objectives were limited to the struggle with Israel. Conflicts arose, therefore, over a number of issues of concern to the PLO that did not serve Soviet interests. For example, Moscow sought early PLO acceptance of UNITED NATIONS SECURITY COUNCIL RESOLUTIONS 242 AND 338 so that the organization could participate in an international conference. Such a conference was sought by Moscow primarily to prevent an American monopoly on peacemaking in the region, so much so that in the 1970s the U.S.S.R. was even willing to hold such a conference (Geneva in December 1973 and a planned conference in 1977) without the PLO, so long as Moscow shared in the convening. At the same time, the Soviets urged the PLO to accept Israel's existence and to strive for a Palestinian state limited to the West Bank and Gaza. They viewed the goal of destruction of Israel and the creation of a democratic, secular state in all of Palestine as unrealistic and likely to precipitate a third world war. Similar Soviet concerns over escalation, war, and direct U.S.-Soviet confrontation generally led Moscow to advocate political settlement over armed struggle. Although it provided the PLO with arms and training for armed struggle, it sought to direct the PLO away from terrorism and guerrilla warfare.

While the Soviets sought influence over the PLO, the PLO jealously guarded its independence, refusing to admit communists to the PLO executive, for example, until the 1987 PNC in Algiers after the Soviet-mediated reunification of the organization. Eventually, Moscow developed a close relationship with NAYIF HAWATIMA and his Marxist DEMOCRATIC FRONT FOR THE LIBERATION OF PALESTINE (DFLP), though the U.S.S.R. had a number of rifts with the more radical though still Marxist POPULAR FRONT FOR THE LIBERATION OF PALESTINE (PFLP), mainly related to the opposition of the PFLP leader, GEORGE HABASH, to a two-state solution and the PFLP's support of terrorism. However, both the DFLP and the PFLP were too small to give Moscow the influence it sought within the PLO. By contrast, Fatah, though considered bourgeois, nationalist, or, at best, nonideological, was viewed by Soviet strategists as the most powerful PLO faction. Thus, even as they occasionally criticized Fatah on ideological grounds, even as they aided and trained other factions, the Soviets dealt primarily with Fatah until the 1985 Arafat-Husayn accord.

After that accord, under Gorbachev's new foreign policy, the Arab-Israeli conflict and with it the Palestinian issue became a hindrance rather than a vehicle for the pursuit of Soviet interests. Although Moscow continued to support Palestinian rights to self-determination and to advocate an international conference on the issue, it also increasingly tended to support measures as a security system that would meet Israeli needs while accepting much of Washington's approach as a way of reducing if not eliminating the conflict. In the GULF CRISIS, 1990–91, for example, the Soviet regime supported the United States (despite opposition from certain quarters in Moscow) and condemned the PLO's support for Saddam Husayn.

In the last days of the Soviet Union, and increasingly since Russia has existed as an independent state, domestic pressures for an independent foreign policy and restoration of Russia as a superpower have led to some Russian interest in reviving support for the Palestinians. The Middle East has not, however, become a significant issue in the new Russia, particularly as the country faces serious domestic problems and far more pressing foreign policy issues.

Galia Golan

BIBLIOGRAPHY

Cobban, Helena. *The Palestinian Liberation Organization.* Cambridge, England: Cambridge University Press, 1984.

Dannreuther, Roland. *The Soviet Union and the PLO.* New York: St. Martin's Press, 1998.

Freedman, Robert. "Soviet Policy toward International Terrorism." In *International Terrorism,* ed. by Y. Alexander. New York: Praeger, 1976.

Golan, Galia. *The Soviet Union and the Palestine Liberation Organization: An Uneasy Alliance.* New York: Praeger, 1980.

——. *Soviet Policies in the Middle East from World War II to Gorbachev.* Cambridge, England: Cambridge University Press, 1990.

——. *Moscow and the Middle East: "New Thinking" on Regional Conflict.* London: Royal Institute for International Relations, Pinter Press, 1992.

Supreme Muslim Council

The end of Ottoman rule in Palestine (1516–1917) and the onset of the British PALESTINE MANDATE meant that Islamic *waqf* and *shari'a* courts no longer were headed by the Ottoman Shaykh al-Islam and administered by the Ministry of Awqaf but by British officials. Palestinian Muslims were disturbed by the prospect of a Christian power governing their religious institutions and by two Zionist officials, the British HIGH COMMISSIONER FOR PALESTINE, Sir Herbert Samuel, and the legal secretary in charge of these institutions, Norman Bentwich.

In the wake of anti-Zionist Palestinian rioting in 1921, and wishing to provide Palestinians with autonomous institutions, as had been provided to the Zionist movement, Samuel proposed creation of a Supreme Muslim Council. In December 1921, he issued an order creating the council for "the control and management of Moslem Awqaf and Sharia affairs in Palestine." The council would include a president and four member (two of whom would represent the Jerusalem district, and one member each for the Nablus and Acre districts). Samuel suggested that the Palestinian secondary electors to the last Ottoman parliament elect the members, who would be paid salaries from government and *waqf* funds. During the first election of January 9, 1922, AL-HAJJ AMIN AL-HUSAYNI, the mufti of Jerusalem, was elected president with a budget of £50,000.

The Supreme Muslim Council became al-Husayni's vehicle for creation of both an Islamic cultural revival in Palestine and for his own rise to political power. The council established a Muslim orphanage, restored religious buildings, supported schools, and expanded health clinics. One of the council's most significant achievements was a major restoration of the mosque and shrine complex within the HARAM AL-SHARIF in Jerusalem, the third holiest shrine in Islam. The renovation project focused international Islamic attention on Palestine and Jerusalem's importance for both Palestinians and Muslims throughout the world.

By the early 1930s, al-Husayni had become the leading nationalist figure throughout Palestine. After his leadership of the Arab revolt that began in 1936, British authorities dismissed him and dissolved the council in 1937. Thereafter, its members were appointed until the end of the Mandate in 1948.

Philip Mattar

Syria

Syrian-Palestinian relations are rooted in a long common sociocultural and geopolitical history. Before the breakup of its territorial unity after the final defeat of the Ottoman state in 1917, Syria embraced the area along the eastern Mediterranean between Turkey and EGYPT, including Palestine. The evolution of Syrian-Palestinian relations can be traced by examining political developments both inside and outside Syria since late Ottoman times through four phases. In these phases, certain factors remain constant, in particular Syria's historical ties with Palestine and the influence that the convergence of Syrian nationalism and pan-Arabism had on Syrian foreign policy related to the Palestine question. Other factors, however, changed with changing circumstances, most notably the relationship between the Syrian government and the nationalist leadership of the Palestinians.

Phase One: Unity and Crisis, 1864–1920 In the first phase, Syria and Palestine constituted one geographic unit linked to the larger framework of the Ottoman state despite the provincial reorganization of Syria that the Ottoman government had instituted in the 1860s in order to centralize its authority throughout the empire. People and goods moved freely between Syria and Palestine unhindered by borders or administrative processes. There were strong political ties among active members of the class of urban notables. This class exercised effective political control in both Syria and Palestine. Although members of this class competed with each other for positions of local dominance during the nineteenth century, many of those who failed to acquire senior positions in the Ottoman imperial bureaucracy found themselves acting together in a loosely organized political front in the early part of the twentieth century.

A combination of factors, primarily the Young Turk revolt of 1908, brought about this development. By following a policy of centralization and Turkification in the Arab provinces of the empire, the Young Turks threatened the interests of the Syrian political elite, thus forcing them to fashion the new ideology of Arab nationalism. This ideology was destined to replace Ottomanism, or political loyalty to the Ottoman state and its family-based leadership.

At the core of the new ideology of Arab nationalism lay an emphasis on the primacy of the Arabs and their great cultural heritage. Disaffected members of the local Syrian leadership who lost their offices in the Ottoman imperial bureaucracy under the impact of Turkification policies seized the nascent idea of Arab nationalism and used it as a weapon with which to advance their Palestinian and Lebanese intellectuals and activists, who joined nationalist literary societies and clandestine organizations. Members of these societies aimed at redressing the balance of power between Arabs and Turks in the empire through political decentralization and reintroduction of Arabic. Some pressed for Arab independence, encouraged on the one hand by Ottoman repression, and on the other by British promises of support.

During this time of great tension between Arabs and Turks, disaffected Syrians and Palestinians discovered how much they had in common and began to collaborate in the cause of Arab nationalism. During the brief existence of Faysal's Kingdom of Syria (1918–20), the Arab nationalists from Syria, Palestine, and other Arab provinces were brought together in Damascus by a desire to foster pan-Syrian unity as a first stage in the development of Arab unity. The framework of their collaboration, however, collapsed under the impact of internal political factionalism and, to a greater extent, the pressures of the British and French, who were determined to gain imperial control of the Arab nations.

The interaction between Syrians and Palestinians during this phase extended beyond the sphere of politics. Their contact took place in a cultural and social environment that was largely homogeneous, despite some ethnic and class variations. Palestinian merchants had strong trading links with merchants of such Syrian inland trade centers as Aleppo and Damascus and with merchants in seaports such as Alexandretta, Beirut, Latakia, and Sidon. Similarly, the merchants of these trade centers had close links with Palestinian cities, especially Nablus, and with the Palestinian seaports of Acre and Jaffa.

Moreover, by virtue of being the starting point of the annual Muslim pilgrimage to Mecca, Damascus acted as a meeting place for Muslim pilgrims from all parts of the Ottoman Empire. There were also cultural links between Palestine and Syria. Educated Palestinians read books and articles published in Damascus and Beirut, and some wealthy Palestinian families sent their sons to study abroad, especially to The American University of Beirut. In addition, the circulation of newspapers (such as *al-Muqtabas* of Damascus, *al-Mufid* of Beirut, and *al-Karmil* of Haifa) and magazines as well as books on various subjects encouraged a cultural give-and-take among such important cities as Beirut, Damascus, Tripoli, Jerusalem, Haifa, and Nablus.

In addition, intermarriage brought the two people together. It occurred mainly between upper-class Palestinian families and upper-class Syrian and Lebanese families, such as the KHALIDI FAMILY in Jerusalem and the Salaam family in Beirut, or the NASHASHIBI FAMILY and the Sulhs, and the AL-ALAMI FAMILY and the Jabiris.

Finally, Palestinians and Syrians developed local political bonds among themselves, primarily through the Ottoman Parliament in Istanbul, where Syrian delegates joined the strong Palestinian campaign against Zionist immigration and the transfer of LAND to Zionists in Palestine. Links were also forged in the Arab political societies that emerged in the last years of the Ottoman Empire.

Phase Two: Separation and Cooperation, 1920–1948 After 1920, three main developments in Syria and Palestine affected their interaction: (1) the official partition of geographical Syria into separately administered mandates under France (Syria and Lebanon) and Britain (Palestine); (2) the creation of new frontiers and customs barriers that obstructed the free passage of goods and people; (3) the British-supported Jewish National Homeland policy and its formal incorporation into the PALESTINE MANDATE, which was formulated to satisfy Zionist interests.

As a result of these changes, the bonds between Syrians and Palestinians loosened perceptibly. The free movement of Syrians and Palestinians between Damascus and Jerusalem, Beirut and Jaffa, was interrupted. Intermarriage and joint economic ventures became less frequent. The focus of Syrian and Palestine politics also changed. The Ottoman provincial administration and the Ottoman Parliament that had brought Syrians and Palestinians together were gone. Instead, Syrian and Palestinian nationalists formed their separate independence movements. Although these movements maintained their ideological commitment to the goals of Arab unity and independence, their character and organization developed according to the logic of territorial nationalism.

Interaction between Syrians and Palestinians did continue throughout this phase, but it was neither as active nor as intensive as it had been in earlier times. This interaction manifested itself most conspicuously in Syria's transit trade with Palestine as well as Syrian support for the Palestinian national cause. From an economic standpoint, Palestine was Syria's most lucrative export market, generating large profits for Syrian businesspeople, particularly those involved in the cloth weaving and confectionery industries. This explains why the vast majority of this industrial class supported Syrian and Palestinian boycotts of Jewish products. Apart from political considerations, Syrian businesspeople believed that Zionist economic enterprises in Palestine posed a potential threat to Syria's economic interests.

Syrian support for the Palestinian national cause took several forms. On the popular level, support emanated not only from the fact that Syria and Palestine were historically a single geographic region, but also from the belief that the creation of a Jewish state in Palestine, with powerful Western support, would become yet another obstacle to Arab unity and would threaten the integrity of neighboring Arab territories. Demonstrations, strikes, and donations collected in solidarity with the Palestinians were concrete manifestations of Syrian public sympathy.

One of the most prominent Syrians who devoted his life to the Palestinian cause was Shaykh IZZ AL-DIN AL-QASSAM. Born in Jabla near al-Ladhaqiyya about 1880, al-Qassam fled to Haifa after the fall of Faysal's government in 1920. A pan-Arabist with a fundamentalist Muslim attitude bearing the imprint of the Hanbali school of Islamic jurisprudence, al-Qassam preached strict adherence to Islam and encouraged clandestine military activities against the Mandatory government and the Zionist settlements in Palestine. In 1928, he helped organize the Young Men's Muslim Association in Haifa, an organization that acted as the center of underground military resistance. His group of activists, also known as *Ikhwan al-Qassam* tried to launch a revolt against the British in the hills near Jenin in November 1935, but their attempt was aborted when a large force of British policemen raided the hideout, killing the Shaykh and two others. Al-Qassam was eulogized as a national martyr and the clandestine military activities of his organization served as an important catalyst to the General Strike of 1936 and the revolt that ensued.

The Syrian press also paid close attention to the Palestine question, taking every opportunity to criticize the Zionists and their British sponsors. When Syria was in a deep economic depression between 1930 and 1933, 25,000 to 30,000 Syrians from the Hawran region fled to Palestine for a brief period in the spring of 1933. Prominent activists in the Syrian national movement, such as Shukri al-Quwwatli, frequently traveled between Syria and Palestine in an effort to secure pan-Arab support for the cause of Syrian independence. Palestinian aid to this cause took several forms, including media support, fund-raising drives, and the offer of refuge to Syrian activists, especially during the Great Syrian Revolt of 1925–27.

As to dominant members of the Syrian nationalist leadership, their interaction with the Palestinians was an exercise in balancing support for pan-Arab demands with support for realpolitik considerations. Their support tipped sometimes in favor of the pan-Arab cause, at other times in favor of protecting Syria's own interests.

In their years of exile during much of the 1920s, Syrian nationalist leaders like Shaykh Rashid Rida, Riyad al-Sulh, and Shaykh Kamil al-Qassab worked within the framework of the Syrian-Palestinian Congress, a body created by Syrian and Palestinian exiles in early 1921 to promote a Greater Syria union. They tried to convince the leadership of the nationalist movement in Palestine to work with them toward the goal of pan-Syrian unity, but the Palestinian leaders resisted, not only because they believed that the political circumstances of Palestine were different from those of Syria and therefore required separate efforts, but also because they were apprehensive over the moderate approach to Zionism shown by important Syrian figures, including Emir Shakib Arslan and the leaders of the Party of Syrian Unity—Rida, al-Sulh, and al-Qassab.

While in exile in Egypt in 1922, the Party of Syrian Unity leaders had conducted talks with several Zionist leaders, including Dr. D. Eder, chairman of the Zionist Commission in Jerusalem, and Felix Menashe, an Egyptian Jewish leader. These talks resulted in a tentative draft agreement based on two points: Jews would support Arab demands for independence, while Syrians would recognize Jewish rights, although not on the basis of the BALFOUR DECLARATION or the instrument of the Palestine Mandate. Through this understanding, the Syrian leaders hoped to win Zionist, and therefore British, support for their struggle against the French Mandate authority in Syria. The Syrian hopes, however, were misplaced because the British adamantly opposed any arrangement that would undermine their relations with France. In addition, the World Zionist Organization lacked the ability to persuade the British to reorder their strategic priorities in the Arab East. Cooperation with the French was a sine qua non for fulfilling those priorities.

There were also differences between Syrians and Palestinians who were active in the Syrian-Palestinian Congress. These differences stemmed from personal and ideological rivalries that originated in the 1916 Arab revolt; they were also a function of the composition of the congress itself. Having a stronger Syrian and Lebanese component, the Executive Committee of the congress seemed to the Palestinians to be preoccupied with Syria. The congress eventually split along personal and ideological lines, and, by 1927, two separate and antagonistic factions had emerged. The pan-Arabist faction was led by Shukri al-Quwwatli; the advocates of a Syria-first program were led by Dr. Abd al-Rahman Shahbandar.

In the years 1936–39, when Palestine was in the throes of a popular revolt, the National Bloc government in Syria adopted a very cautious position toward Palestine. This position assumed two conflicting dimensions that revealed the dynamic between the emotional push of pan-Arabism and the powerful pull of personal ambition and local Syrian interests. Thus the National Bloc, cognizant of the overwhelming popular sympathy for the Palestine cause in Syria, granted political asylum to numerous Palestinian activists who escaped the heavy-handedness of the British authorities and even tolerated the smuggling of arms and guerrillas from Syria into Palestine. However, the National Bloc leadership was reluctant to mobilize fully and openly behind the Palestine revolt for two reasons. First was the fear that open support for the revolt might alienate the British, and thus jeopardize Syria's negotiations with France at a time when Syrian independence seemed to be within reach. Second was the consideration that the upheaval in Palestine might render Palestinian markets inaccessible to their goods. Hailing from landowning and mercantile families, the National Bloc leaders sympathized with the concerns of the Syrian mercantile class, whose leading members recommended restraint in dealing with the Palestine revolt.

Only a few National Bloc leaders, most notably Shukri al-Quwwatli, were fully active in solidarity work with the Palestinian rebels. Quwwatli and his group of pan-Arabists were in Palestine in 1936 seeking support for Syria's independence struggle. Within Syria, activities on behalf of the Palestine revolt undertaken by ordinary Syrians as well as by former army officers and organized political groups, particularly the League of National Action, continued unabated until the collapse of the revolt in Palestine in 1939. Best known among the Syrians who commanded rebel groups in Palestine was FAWZI AL-QAWUQJI, a Lebanese-born former Syrian Legion captain and a hero of the Great Syrian Revolt. Al-Qawuqji arrived in Palestine with other Syrian volunteers in August 1936 and declared himself the commander in chief of "the Arab Revolution in Southern Palestine." His intervention, which came to an end in late November 1936, helped Palestinian rebels improve their fighting tactics and their organizational skills.

The collapse of the Palestine revolt in 1939 coincided with the demise of the National Bloc government in Syria. The National Bloc's lukewarm commitment to the Palestine revolt put it on the defensive vis-à-vis the Syrian public and ultimately contributed to its resignation in February 1939. Of course, domestic Syrian factors were also at play, most notably divisions within the National Bloc itself, its controversial policy of "honorable cooperation" with the French, local separatist movements, a sagging economy, and Turkey's annexation with Western connivance of Alexandretta. However, the dilemmas and complications associated with supporting the Palestinian cause continued to haunt Syrian politicians until the end of this phase and beyond. Support of Palestinian goals became the single most important source of legitimacy for Syrian leaders, who had to balance between support for Palestine and support for Syrian self-interest.

The 1948 Palestine war revealed again the awkward situation that this balancing act tended to create for the Syrian leadership. Now in its second year of independence, Syria's army was no match for the superior Israeli forces. Yet, Syrian leaders had to bow to public pressure, ignoring in the process their own military officers, including the Syrian chief of staff, General Abdullah Atfi, and Colonel Husayn Hakim, the commander of the Syrian detachment that participated in the Palestine war, both of whom counseled against intervention in Palestine without adequate military preparation.

When the ARAB LEAGUE decided in April 1948 to send its ARAB LIBERATION ARMY into Palestine under the leadership of Fawzi al-Qawuqji, Syria did send one brigade of 1,876 men. The Syrian brigade, although lacking in experience and equipment, seized three small Palestinian areas stretching from Lake Hula to Lake Tiberias. Yet, on all other fronts, Israeli forces seized sizable chunks of Palestinian territory after decisively undermining the half-hearted and improvised Arab military efforts to save Palestine. In Syria, government leaders paid a price for the Palestine disaster: the loss of political positions under the impact of military coups, the first of which was the March 1949 coup of Colonel Husni al-Za'im.

Phase Three: Precarious Rule, Conflicting Orientations, 1948–1970 During much of the third phase, Syria was a relatively weak and unstable state, alternately conspired against and courted by regional and global powers. Thus, internal power struggles, exploited by external rivalries and challenged by the policies of a powerful and dynamic Israel, provided the dominant pattern of Syrian politics, especially with respect to the Palestine question. Within this context, two orientations emerged in Syria. The first favored a policy of living with the status quo that had emerged after the Palestine war, even though that status quo was seen as having inflicted injustice on the Palestinians. In contrast, the second orientation called for the overthrow of the status quo, primarily through a war of national liberation or revolution.

The policy of living with the status quo was favored by the elements of the political elites who had ruled Syria before its union with Egypt in 1958. They viewed Israel as powerful and well protected by the West, whereas they saw Syria as weak and lacking any real external protectors. Army dissensions and the deep cleavages of civilian politics distracted Syrian leaders from giving sustained effort to the Palestine question and even encouraged some of them to seek accommodation with Israel, partly to win Western support for themselves. Many of the ruling elite were conservative-minded notables concerned primarily with securing Syria's independence and maintaining their own positions of local dominance, even if this meant striking deals with foreign powers.

Husni al-Za'im, for example, sought an end to Syria's active conflict with Israel in return for an Israeli territorial concession in the Lake Tiberias and Jordan River area. In his thinking, this would neutralize the Israeli military threat and help Syria get Western support for social and economic development. Al-Za'im also proposed to settle 250,000 or 300,000 Palestinian refugees in northeastern Syria, even though Syria at that time hosted only 70,000 Palestinian refugees. However, Israel showed no interest in al-Za'im's proposal and within a brief four and a half months al-Za'im was overthrown in a military coup in August 1949, staged by Sami Hinnawi, a pro-Hashemite who drew close to Iraq before his downfall in December 1949.

Hinnawi's successor, the anti-Hashemite Adib al-Shishakli, who held power in Syria directly and indirectly until February 1954, was a self-styled reformer who favored a policy of neutralism but at the same time was not opposed to an Arab-Western rapprochement on a basis of equality. Al-Shishakli's orientation amounted to a policy of living with the status quo as far as Palestine was concerned. Subsequently, when Syria merged with Egypt in February 1958, the Palestine question, as well as almost everything else, was left to Jamal Abd al-Nasir, the charismatic Egyptian leader who sought and was given the role of uniting the Arabs and liberating Palestine.

After Syria's secession from its union with Egypt in 1961, Syrian involvement in Arab unity efforts slackened. However, the Ba'th coup of March 8, 1963, opened the road to a radical change in Syria's posture toward the Palestine question. The Ba'th revealed a growing interest in a revolutionary social program based on socialism and class struggle. After three years of internal power struggles, Salah Jadid emerged as head of a Ba'th government. With respect to the Palestine question, the regime of Salah Jadid was the most extreme that Syria had seen. Although the root causes of this extremism were the 1948 dispossession of the Palestinians and the rivalry with Nasirism, two major developments provided the immediate political dynamic of the new Syrian orientation. One was Israel's diversion of the waters of the Jordan, and the other was the emergence in 1965 of a dynamic Palestinian resistance movement committed to the liberation of Palestine through revolutionary armed struggle.

Israel's Jordan diversion project, which was nearing completion almost three years before Jadid came to power in February 1966, went hand in hand with a deliberate Israeli policy of escalation along the Israeli-Syrian frontiers. The overriding priority of the new Ba'thist leaders was to take up the Israeli challenge, not only because they were determined to check what they believed to be an Israeli policy of expansionism, but also because they believed that Syria's vital interests as a riparian state were at stake. Previous Syrian governments took the same position but used a new weapon in the struggle with Israel: Palestinian guerrillas. In an atmosphere charged with powerful emotion for the Palestine cause, Syria called for a "popular liberation war" to free Palestine and defeat the forces of imperialism and reaction.

Jadid's embrace of the Palestinian guerrillas, together with the escalating tension on the Israeli-Syrian border, played a critical role in precipitating the crisis that led to the 1967 war. After the June 1967 debacle, Syria's leaders continued to support the developing Palestinian resistance movement and established the Ba'th party's own resistance organization SA'IQA ("Thunderbolt"). They assisted FATAH and other Palestinian groups and hosted units of the PALESTINE LIBERATION ARMY (PLA). When the Jordanian civil war erupted in September 1970, Syria was the only country that came to the aid of the Palestinian resistance.

Yet Syria's backing for the Palestinian resistance movement was not unconditional. The Syrian leadership assessed the effects of its policy on regime security and on its rivalry with Iraq and Egypt. For example, unhappy with the independent streak exhibited by GEORGE HABASH, leader of the POPULAR FRONT FOR THE LIBERATION OF PALESTINE and recipient of Iraqi support, Syria detained him in jail for several months in 1968. YASIR ARAFAT also spent time in Syrian prisons before he became PALESTINE LIBERATION ORGANIZATION (PLO) chairman. The Syrian government even hindered the free movement of Palestinian guerrillas across the border with JORDAN. Moreover, as the struggle for power intensified in the course of 1968 between Salah Jadid, leader of the ruling civilian wing of the Ba'th, and Hafiz al-Asad, leader of the military wing, Jadid expanded the size of Sa'iqa in order to counterbalance the Asad faction. Thus, in supporting the resistance, the Ba'thists tried, in their own way, to strike a balance between their commitment to the Palestinian cause and their stubborn desire to preserve their hold on power.

Phase Four: The Supremacy of Geopolitics, 1970–1996 During the final phase, Syria's policy toward the Palestine question was first and foremost a product of one man and one factor: The man was Hafiz al-Asad. The factor was geopolitics. Unlike many of his predecessors, Asad sought to contain Israel without giving it a pretext to attack Syria. In pursuit of this goal, he embarked concurrently on establishing stable state institutions under his command and building balances of power between Syria and Israel and between Syria and its Arab rivals. With respect to Israel, Asad sought a near-equality of power; with regard to his Arab rivals, he aimed at preponderance. Asad's determination to cut an impressive figure for his country led to a Syrian-Israeli contest that has shaped to a great degree Syria's posture toward the Palestine question in general and the Palestinian resistance in particular.

The balance that Asad sought required not only the assured flow of arms from the Soviet Union but also a multifront strategy with Egypt and Syria as the principal partners (1970–75) and with Lebanon and the Palestinians acting as satellites in Syria's orbit. At the time, the PLO was the organizational expression of the Palestinians and its backbone was Fatah, an organization led by Yasir Arafat. In the 1970s, the PLO, which also comprised other Palestinian resistance groups, was based in Lebanon, where it had its institutional infrastructure including militia forces. The PLO's insistence on maintaining its independence and on formulating its own strategies vis-à-vis Israel and other regional and international players clashed with Asad's wish for dominance. The dynamic of this clash, which was inserted into a context of personal animosity between Asad and Arafat, provided the dominant pattern of Syrian-Palestinian relations. During this phase, these relations have undergone a cycle of three distinct changes.

A Friendship of Expediency, 1970–1975.

The first period was characterized by Syrian support for the PLO when it was an independent factor to be reckoned with in Lebanon. Such a policy served Asad's Lebanon strategy of maintaining a balance between the PLO-supported Lebanese Left (National Movement) and the Lebanese Right, which was led by the Maronite political establishment. The PLO, in its turn, welcomed Syrian backing because, after the Jordanian catastrophe of 1970–71, it was determined never to face again a regular army on its own, and also because Syria's help was important for the Palestinian armed presence and activity in Lebanon. Part of this period witnessed close Syrian-Palestinian cooperation in the political and military spheres. This cooperation was the product of a mutual desire to redress the Arab balance with Israel in the aftermath of the second Egyptian-Israeli disengagement agreement of September 1975. The agreement signaled Egypt's retreat from its commitments to the Arab struggle against Israel, thus undermining a major pillar on which Asad's strategy of balance had rested. Doubts existed between Asad and the PLO nevertheless, as the PLO tried to chart an independent strategy for itself, and as Syria tried to influence PLO policies by manipulating the Palestine Liberation Army, Sa'iqa, and smaller Palestinian groups.

Confrontation and Conciliation, 1975–1982.

The most dominant aspect of the second period was the Lebanese civil war. This was also a time when Lebanon evolved as the main arena of the Syrian-Israeli struggle. A mix of conflictual and conciliatory practices was present throughout these years. The tendency toward conflict between Syrians and Palestinians was evident when Asad realized in 1975–76 that, by virtue of being the dominant power in Lebanon, the PLO had the key to peace or war. Although Arafat was inclined to continue the war against the Lebanese Right in hopes of exercising real influence over a Lebanon controlled by the Lebanese Left, Asad cautioned restraint, arguing that, if unchecked, Arafat's behavior would give Israel a pretext to intervene. Encouraged by Egypt and Iraq, Asad's principal Arab rivals, Arafat resisted Asad's counsel, thus preparing the ground for the Palestinian encounter with the Syrian army in the summer of 1976. Asad's unpopular war on the Palestinians and his defense of the Lebanese Right were aimed at achieving two strategic objectives. One was to discourage the Maronites from opting for partition and creating in the process a pro-Israeli Maronite state on Syria's border. The second was to prevent the Lebanese Left from creating a radical regime friendly to Iraq, Syria's main Arab rival. This conflictual aspect of Syrian-Palestinian relations ended with the Riyadh summit of October 1976, which created the Arab Deterrent Force responsible for the enforcement of the cease-fire in Lebanon. The Syrian contingents formed the bulk of this 30,000 strong force.

The cease-fire did not divert Asad from his overriding objective of containing the PLO and its leftist Lebanese allies. Asad may even have wanted to remove Arafat from the PLO and put in his place Khalid al-Fahum, a pro-Asad PLO Palestinian based in Damascus. However, three events made detente with the PLO Asad's preferred course of action by the fall of 1976. First was Israel's expanding involvement in Lebanon's affairs, especially its intimate relationship with the Maronites and its hegemony over southern Lebanon. Second, the Arab outcry against Syria's war in Lebanon put Asad on the defensive in the court of Arab public opinion, thus contributing to Asad's decision to paper over his differences with the PLO. Third was the Soviet disapproval of Syria's intervention in Lebanon. Interested in helping its Palestinian and leftist friends in Lebanon, but at the same time anxious not to cause a breach with Syria, Moscow urged all parties to close ranks. When Asad continued his intervention against the Palestinian-leftist alliance, the Kremlin postponed new arms contracts with Syria. The fact that the Soviets resorted to this measure at a time when Israel appeared to be on the offensive in Lebanon clearly influenced Asad's thinking.

Later developments had an even greater influence on the Syrian president. These included the Likud's advent to power in Israel in May 1977, as well as the CAMP DAVID ACCORDS of September 1978 and the subsequent Egyptian-Israeli peace treaty of March 1979. Egypt's defection from the Arab fold shaped to a great degree Asad's posture toward the PLO and toward other Arab actors. Determined to stop Anwar al-Sadat from drawing the rest of the Arab world after him, Asad embarked on a strategy of joining forces not only with the PLO but also with his archenemy, the Iraqi president, Saddam Husayn, and later with Iran after the fall of the shah in February 1979. Although Asad's entente with Iraq was short-lived, his alliance with revolutionary Iran proved to be durable. By contrast, the Syrian-PLO alliance, which was temporarily solidified by a common opposition to Camp David and fear of Israel, barely survived the Israeli invasion of Lebanon in 1982.

Asad supported PLO efforts to restore a presence in southern Lebanon in the belief that controlled conflict with Israel would demonstrate the futility of a peace process that excluded Syria. Nevertheless, his post–Camp David strategy of deterring Israel through a Syrian-led Arab East clashed with a PLO that was determined to formulate its own strategies and make its own decisions to pursue a diplomatic settlement with Israel.

Separate Paths, 1982–1999.

The final phase of Syrian-Palestinian relations opened with the Israeli invasion of Lebanon in June 1982. Syrian-Palestinian relations during this phase were influenced by four factors: (1) Arafat's meeting with the Egyptian president, Husni Mubarak, on December 22, 1983, two days after Arafat's forced departure from Tripoli, Lebanon, and almost sixteen months after the PLO's expulsion from Lebanon (August 21, 1982) under the military pressure of the Israeli invading force; (2)

the fostering of closer Jordanian-PLO ties as manifested in the Amman Agreement of February 1985, which called for the formation of a joint Jordanian-Palestinian delegation in peace talks on the basis of UNITED NATIONS SECURITY COUNCIL RESOLUTIONS 242 AND 338 and the establishment of an independent Palestinian state in confederation with Jordan; (3) the Palestinian uprising (INTIFADA), which began on a mass scale in the West Bank and Gaza on December 9, 1987, and which forced the PLO to act more decisively in its search for a peaceful settlement with Israel, as was illustrated in the Palestinian Declaration of Independence issued at the nineteenth PALESTINE NATIONAL COUNCIL meeting of November 12–15, 1988; and (4) the political fallout from the 1993 Oslo agreement.

The PLO's policy toward Egypt, Jordan, and Israel influenced Syrian-Palestinian relations in two ways. First, it strengthened Asad's resolve to delegitimize Arafat by supporting the Fatah dissidents who rebelled against him in Lebanon in May 1983. The manipulation of the dissidents as well as of other anti-Arafat Palestinian groups based in Damascus such as Sa'iqa and the POPULAR FRONT FOR THE LIBERATION OF PALESTINE constituted the backbone of Asad's retaliatory strategy against Arafat and the rest of the mainstream leadership of the PLO.

Moreover, Arafat's new interest in a peaceful settlement reinforced Asad's fears of another Camp David–style deal involving the Palestinians and Jordanians. Such a deal threatened to strike at the very roots of Asad's strategy of comprehensive peace on all fronts, thus weakening his bargaining position vis-à-vis Israel. To a great degree, the fears of Asad explain his support for the Amal militia's drive against the Palestinians in Lebanon in 1985 and 1986 in what was known as the "war of the camps."

The OSLO AGREEMENTS had many consequences. It created yet another source of suspicion between Asad and the PLO. This in turn further reinforced Asad's interest in maintaining his tactical alliance with the anti-Arafat Palestinian opposition based in Damascus. It also caused Asad to add HAMAS and ISLAMIC JIHAD, two Islamic Palestinian organizations opposed to the Oslo agreements, to the repertory of manipulative instruments with which he tried to influence Palestinian politics.

Objectively, however, Asad did not try to sabotage the Israeli-PLO agreement, partly because he did not have the wherewithal to do so, but more importantly, because he was unwilling to do anything that would antagonize the UNITED STATES. Other realpolitik considerations were also at play. Asad recognized the divergent interests of Syria and the PLO, indeed, of each Arab entity involved in the peace process. He also recognized that each of the problems between the Arabs and Israel had its own peculiarities. Thus, he expected the negotiating tracks of the various Arab parties to proceed at different speeds.

Despite the dominance of realpolitik calculations in Asad's dealings with the Palestinians, and despite the wounds inflicted on both sides by the push and pull of events, the Syrian leader retained part of the ideological baggage from the era of pan-Arabism. Asad's own experience as a lifelong Ba'th party activist, as well as the fact that Palestine was once part of Syria, induced him to extend Syria's sway over the Palestinians. This partly explains why Syria serves as a basis for the anti-Arafat Palestinian opposition. At the same time, it also sheds light on a theme often raised in Asad's statements: "Palestine is southern Syria, and Syria is northern Palestine." On the practical level, this does not guide Asad's policy toward the Palestinians or toward Israel, but it does indicate the emotional difficulty involved in overcoming the past and coming to grips with the reality of the present, including the reality of Palestinian independence.

Muhammad Muslih

BIBLIOGRAPHY

Drysdale, Alasdair, and Raymond A. Hinnebusch. *Syria and the Middle East Process.* New York: Council on Foreign Relations Press, 1991.

Hinnebusch, Raymond A. "Syrian Policy in Lebanon and the Palestinians." *Arab Studies Quarterly* 8, no. 1 (1986): 1–20.

Hopwood, Derek. *Syria, 1945–1986: Politics and Society.* London: Unwin Hyman, 1988.

Khoury, Philip. *Syria and the French Mandate: The Politics of Arab Nationalism, 1920–1945.* Princeton, N.J.: Princeton University Press, 1987.

Kissinger, Henry. *Years of Upheaval.* Boston: Little, Brown and Company, 1982.

Ma'oz, Moshe, and Avner Yaniv, eds. *Syria under Asad: Domestic Constraints and Regional Risks.* New York: St. Martin's Press, 1986.

Mattar, Philip. *The Mufti of Jerusalem, Al-Hajj Amin al-Husayni and the Palestinian National Movement.* Rev. ed. New York: Columbia University Press, 1992.

Muslih, Muhammad. *The Origins of Palestinian Nationalism.* New York: Columbia University Press, 1988.

Petran, Tabitha. *Syria.* London: Ernest Benn, 1972.

Porath, Y. *The Emergence of the Palestinian-Arab National Movement 1918–1929.* London: Frank Cass, 1974.

——. *The Palestinian Arab National Movement 1929–1939, from Riots to Rebellion.* London: Frank Cass, 1977.

Quandt, William. *Decade of Decisions: American Policy toward the Arab-Israeli Conflict, 1967–1976.* Berkeley: University of California Press, 1977.

Seale, Patrick. *The Struggle for Syria: A Study of Post-War Arab Politics.* London: Oxford University Press, 1965.

——. *Asad: The Struggle for the Middle East.* Berkeley: University of California Press, 1988.

Sheehan, Edward. "How Kissinger Did It: Step by Step in the Middle East." *Foreign Policy* 22 (spring 1976).

Tibawi, A. L. *A Modern History of Syria.* London: McMillan, 1969.

Vance, Cyrus. *Hard Choices: Critical Years in America's Foreign Policy.* New York: Simon & Schuster, 1983.

Viorst, Milton. "The Shadow of Saladdin." *New Yorker,* January 8, 1990.

T

Tamari, Salim

academic

1945– Jaffa

After studying at Bir Zeit College in the WEST BANK, Tamari received a B.A. in politics from Drew University, New Jersey, United States and an M.A. in sociology from the University of New Hampshire. He completed a Ph.D. in sociology from the University of Manchester in 1983. A sociologist at BIR ZEIT UNIVERSITY since 1971, Tamari has also codirected Bir Zeit's Mediterranean Studies Unit since 1994. In September 1994, he was appointed director of the Institute for Jerusalem Studies, a branch of the Beirut-based INSTITUTE FOR PALESTINE STUDIES that publishes the *Jerusalem Quarterly File.* He has also served on the refugee committee in the multilateral peace talks that began in the wake of the 1991 MADRID PEACE CONFERENCE.

A noted Palestinian scholar and leading sociologist, Tamari has produced numerous sophisticated studies dealing with sociology, development, urban studies, and other issues relating to Palestinian society in the Occupied Territories. His works include *Palestinian Refugee Negotiation: From Madrid to Oslo II* (1996) and *Jerusalem 1948* (1999).

Michael R. Fischbach

Tannous, Izzat

Tannus; physician, politician

1896– Nablus

Tannous attended SAINT GEORGE'S SCHOOL in Jerusalem during the LATE OTTOMAN PERIOD. He later obtained an M.D. in 1918 from the Syrian Arab College in Beirut (now the American University of Beirut) before returning to Palestine to pursue a medical career in Jerusalem.

Tannous was active politically during and after the PALESTINE MANDATE, particularly in a role of spokesman for Palestinian causes in the West. In the 1930s, he became a member of the ARAB PARTY and headed the Arab Information Office in London. In 1945, he established a London office for the ARAB LEAGUE as well. Tannous joined the third ARAB HIGHER COMMITTEE (AHC) in 1946 and later headed the treasury department of the fourth AHC.

After the first Arab-Israeli war, Tannous established the Arab Palestine Office in Beirut in 1949 and the Palestine Arab Refugee Office in New York in 1954. He was a founding member of the PALESTINE LIBERATION ORGANIZATION (PLO) in 1964 and headed its office in New York until 1968.

Tannous's book *The Palestinians: Detailed Documented Eyewitness History of Palestine under British Mandate* was published in 1988.

Michael R. Fischbach

Temple Mount

See HARAM AL-SHARIF, AL-.

Terrorism

The use of terrorism as a political weapon has been a persistent aspect of the conflict over Palestine since at least the 1920s. Prior to 1948, both Palestinian and Jewish groups perpetrated terrorist acts as part of strategies intended to frighten civilians or to force changes in British policy. After the establishment of ISRAEL, some organized Palestinian groups resorted to terrorism as a means both to publicize their grievances and to exert political pressure. Some Israeli government agencies employed state-sanctioned terrorism both to repress Palestinian resistance activities and to avenge acts of Palestinian violence against Israeli civilians. After 1967, underground groups of Israeli settlers on the WEST BANK resorted to terrorist tactics to intimidate Palestinians.

In trying to present an overview of how Palestinians and Israelis have used terrorism and simultaneously have been its victims, one encounters the problem of definition. In fact, there is no uniformly accepted definition of terrorism. Because a primary motive of most terrorist acts is political, definitions of terrorism tend to be politicized. For example, with specific reference to Israel and the Palestinians, Western and pro-Israeli writers have tended to dismiss the notion of state terrorism as being applicable to any Israeli actions directed against Palestinians, whereas pro-Palestinian writers have tended to refer to Palestinian acts of violence against Israeli civilians as legitimate tactics in a national liberation struggle.

Despite the lack of a clear definition, it is possible to describe the commonly agreed upon characteristics of terrorism. *Terrorism* is a term generally used to describe organized but unpredictable acts or threats of violence against governments, people, or property. The purpose of actual or threatened violence is to achieve a specific political objective. The political goals of terrorism include intimidating or punishing civilians, governments, or opponents; forcing changes in group behavior or government policy, or possibly overthrowing a government; obtaining recognition for a political group or cause; raising the morale of sympathizers while demoralizing opponents; gaining support from reluctant allies; and getting publicity for goals or grievances. Terrorist practices include—but are not limited to—airplane hijacking, arbitrary arrest and detention, assassination, bombing, hostage taking, kidnapping, sabotage, and torture. During the course of the Israeli–Palestinian conflict, beginning with the 1920 anti-Jewish riots in Jerusalem and continuing into the 1990s, all variety of terrorist acts, as well as the aforementioned objectives, have been associated with its political violence.

Palestine Mandate After the establishment of the British PALESTINE MANDATE, individuals and small groups of Palestinians carried out isolated terrorist acts during the 1920s to protest both British domination of their country and the immigration to it of European Jews. The most serious incident was the WESTERN (WAILING) WALL DISTURBANCES, OF 1929, a week of Palestinian-Zionist violence that left 116 Arabs and 133 Jews dead. In the wake of these riots, the Palestinian religious leader Shaykh IZZ AL-DIN AL-QASSAM organized a clandestine group that carried out several terrorist operations against Jews in the HAIFA region during the early 1930s.

Al-Qassam was killed in 1935 in a shoot-out with British security. His violent death transformed him into a national folk hero and inspired the creation of several Palestinian groups that during the Palestine revolt of 1936–39 carried out terrorist attacks on Jewish settlements, sabotage against infrastructure installations, and assaults on British forces. Fearing domination by the rapidly growing Jewish immigrant population or even expulsion by them from their homeland, these Palestinian groups sought through the use of violence to discourage further Jewish immigration and to force Great Britain to grant independence to Palestine.

During the 1930s Zionists organized secret groups to retaliate for the killing of Jews and to intimidate Palestinian civilians. The most violent of the covert Zionist groups was Irgun Zvai Leumi ("National Military Organization"), organized by David Raziel and Avraham Stern in 1937. After the announcement of the MACDONALD WHITE PAPER that restricted Jewish immigration to Palestine, the Irgun began attacking British personnel to induce Britain to change its policy. Although by the outbreak of World War II, the British largely had suppressed Palestinian groups that engaged in terrorism, the Jewish Irgun remained active until 1940, when its leaders agreed to observe a truce—only on attacks against the British but continuing attacks against Palestinians—while Britain fought Germany. This decision prompted Avraham Stern to break away and form a separate organization, Lohamei Herut Yisrael ("Fighters for the Freedom of Israel"), popularly known as the Stern Gang, which carried out several sensational terrorist actions against Britain between 1940 and 1948, including the 1944 assassination of the British colonial secretary, Lord Moyne, in Cairo.

Meanwhile, Menachem Begin—an immigrant from Poland who eventually would become prime minister of Israel (1977–83)—had taken over as leader of Irgun. In 1944 he decided that the organization would resume attacks on the British. Begin believed that both the British and the Palestinians wanted to prevent the establishment of a Jewish state in Palestine; thus, he viewed Irgun's actions as constituting justified defense of the Jewish right to statehood. The Irgun's more sensational terrorist acts included the blowing up of Jerusalem's King David Hotel in July 1946, resulting in the death of over 90 men and women, and the May 1948 massacre of more than 100 Palestinian civilians in the village of DAYR YASIN near JERUSALEM. In his subsequent memoirs, *The Revolt,* Begin credited events at Dayr Yasin with causing panic that induced thousands of Palestinians to flee. After the establishment of Israel and the subsequent involvement of the Stern Gang in the September 1948 assassination of United Nations mediator Count FOLKE BERNADOTTE, the new government ordered the dissolution of both Irgun and the Stern Gang.

Fedayeen The next phase of terrorism in Israel began in the early 1950s when individual Palestinian REFUGEES in the West Bank (which had been annexed by JORDAN) and the GAZA STRIP (then controlled by EGYPT) clandestinely crossed into Israel to attack people or property. By 1955, organized groups calling themselves fedayeen (Arabic, *fida'iyyin,* or "self-sacrificers") had begun to carry out activities inside Israel. The fedayeen perceived themselves as guerrilla fighters engaged in a war of national liberation of their homeland, which was occupied by an enemy—Israel. The fedayeen drew inspiration from the Algerians' struggle for independence (1954–62) from French rule.

After the 1956 Suez crisis—the war of Britain, France, and Israel against Egypt—YASIR ARAFAT and several of his associates founded FATAH, the Palestinian national liberation movement, which eventually would become the largest and most influential of the fedayeen groups. Fatah initiated actions inside Israel beginning in 1965 and claimed responsibility for some four dozen attacks prior to the June 1967 war. The operations carried out by the various fedayeen groups, as well as the emergence of a distinct Palestinian nationalism, prompted the Arab governments to sponsor in 1964 the formation of an umbrella group, the PALESTINE LIBERATION ORGANIZATION (PLO), which they intended to use as a vehicle to control all the fedayeen. However, Israel's humiliating 1967 defeat of Egypt, Jordan, and Syria, along with its capture of the Palestinian territories of the Gaza Strip and the West Bank, served to enhance the credibility of the fedayeen, whom many average Arabs came to perceive as heroic groups daring to challenge Israel.

The increasing prestige of the fedayeen helped Fatah win a majority control of the PLO, thus enabling Arafat to become its chairman in 1969. Under Arafat's leadership, the PLO quickly evolved into a significant political organization that operated autonomously of any Arab government.

Israel's occupation of Gaza and the West Bank also served as a major catalyst in the strategic thinking of some Palestinian guerrilla leaders. GEORGE HABASH, who founded the POPULAR FRONT FOR THE LIBERATION OF PALESTINE (PFLP) in December 1967, argued that fedayeen raids had demonstrated that Palestinians could be only minimally successful in guerrilla warfare against Israel's military strength. The new situation called for a strategy of "revolutionary violence" against Israel and the initiation of "foreign operations" against Israel's international supporters. The use of "revolutionary violence," according to David Hirst, in *The Gun and the Olive Branch,* would shock the world into recognition of the Palestinians' plight and force the leaders of Arab countries to become involved more actively in the struggle against Israel.

The PFLP's first venture into international terrorism occurred in July 1968 with the hijacking of an Israeli passenger jet, which was forced to fly from Rome to Algeria. A rash of hijackings and attacks on Israeli planes at European airports followed. In September 1969 the PFLP hijacked its first non-Israeli plane, an American passenger jet, which was forced to fly from Athens to Syria. The PFLP's most sensational hijacking was the September 1970 commandeering of four international civilian aircraft in as many days. All four planes, including three that had been diverted to Jordan, subsequently were blown up after the passengers had been released. Although the spate of airplane-related terrorism garnered for the Palestinians the international publicity of their cause sought by Habash, it failed to win international sympathy for their tactics and, more importantly, brought the entire fedayeen movement into direct confrontation with several Arab governments.

The September 1970 hijacking precipitated the civil war in Jordan between the fedayeen organizations and the Jordanian army. During nine days of battles in the Palestinian refugee camps of Jordan, more than 3,000 Palestinians, mostly civilians, were killed and at least 10,000 were wounded. Although the Jordanian army was victorious, agreement negotiated by Arab heads of state who were anxious to contain the crisis permitted the fedayeen to maintain an organizational presence in Jordan.

In subsequent months, however, continuing clashes between the fedayeen and the army resulted in all Palestinian guerrillas' being expelled from Jordan in July 1971. This major defeat in Jordan led to a further rethinking of fedayeen strategy. Habash and other leaders, including AHMAD JIBRIL, who had broken with Habash in 1968 to establish the POPULAR FRONT FOR THE LIBERATION OF PALESTINE–GENERAL COMMAND, and NAYIF HAWATIMA, who had left the PFLP in 1969 to create the Popular Democratic Front for the Liberation of Palestine (renamed the DEMOCRATIC FRONT FOR THE LIBERATION OF PALESTINE [DFLP] in mid-1974), now argued that Arab leaders who had betrayed Arab nationalism had to be replaced before Palestine could be liberated. In the wake of the debacle in Jordan, this argument received a sympathetic hearing even from some Fatah members, who, prior to September 1970, had rejected Habash's ideas about the value of international terrorism and had disapproved of Palestinians' becoming entangled in the politics of Arab states. Consequently, a special revenge team, BLACK SEPTEMBER, was created in 1971 with at least tacit Fatah support. The covert Black September movement was believed to be under the direction of SALAH KHALAF (Abu Iyad), who assigned its cadres the dual mission of continuing acts of international terrorism against Israel—for publicity value—and avenging the deaths of fedayeen killed during the fighting in Jordan.

Black September's first act of international terrorism was the November 1971 assassination in Cairo of the Jordanian prime minister, Wasfi al-Tall, the man Palestinians held most responsible for the events in Jordan during September 1970. The group's most sensational terrorist action was the September 1972 attack on Israeli athletes at the Munich Olympic Games. The unsuccessful effort by eight Black September terrorists to take the Israelis as hostages ended after twenty hours with eleven athletes and five Palestinians dead.

The Munich incident prompted Israel's secret service, Mossad, to launch its own retaliatory campaign of assassinating fedayeen leaders. Mossad's most successful operation was the 1973 helicopter landing in Beirut of hit squads that murdered three PLO officials in their own apartments. (Lebanon had become the new center for the PLO and fedayeen after they were driven out of Jordan in 1970–71.) Other Palestinians were killed by car and letter bombs attributed to Mossad agents. Years later, Zvi Zamir, who headed Mossad from 1968 to 1974, as quoted in *Foreign Report,* May 25, 1995, acknowledged: "It was terrorism what we did in those days. . . . [But] one should understand that we had no other way."

Black September's violence distressed some Arab governments as much as it did Israel. From the perspective of Arab leaders, a nadir was reached in March 1973 when Black September terrorists seized the Saudi Arabian embassy in Sudan. Several diplomats attending a reception were held hostage, including the U.S. ambassador, who was subsequently shot to death.

For the more radical fedayeen, this incident served two important goals. First, the United States, which they regarded as the principal supporter of Israel and thus the number one imperialist enemy, had been dealt a blow. Second, the government of Saudi Arabia, which they believed had betrayed Arab nationalism and the Palestinian cause, was also punished.

However, more moderate fedayeen leaders recognized that the Sudan incident represented a potential diplomatic disaster since it risked the loss of critical financial and political support from Arab states like Saudi Arabia and Kuwait. Within Fatah, influential voices counseled that Black September's spree of international terrorism had become a major liability for the Palestinian movement. Thus, Fatah used its clout within the PLO to have Black September dissolved.

After Sudan, no more terrorist incidents were claimed in the name of Black September, although several shadowy groups with names such as the Sons of the Occupied Lands, the Seventh Suicide Squad, the Punishment Organization, the Organization of Arab Nationalist Youth, and the Martyr Abu Mahmud Group carried out several sensational acts of international terrorism during 1973 and 1974. However, the major fedayeen groups like the

PFLP, the PFLP–General Command, and the DFLP actually had shifted their strategy away from the use of international terrorism back to an emphasis on operations within Israel. For example, the PFLP had debated the value of airplane hijacking at its 1972 conference and had decided that this type of operation no longer served the Palestinian cause.

The PFLP–General Command was the first organization to demonstrate the new tactic of focusing on Israel. In April 1974, three of its cadres entered Israel from Lebanon and seized an apartment building in the northern town of Kiryat Shmona; eighteen civilians, including eight children, died in the incident. One month later, DFLP guerrillas, also from Lebanon, took ninety Israeli high school students hostage in the northern town of Maalot. When Israeli soldiers stormed the school after several hours of negotiations, the three guerrillas and twenty students were killed; all of the seventy other students were wounded.

To retaliate for the use of Lebanon as a base for attacks into Israel, the Israeli air force bombed Palestinian refugee camps in Lebanon after any incident. Although Israel argued that the camps were legitimate targets because terrorists had their bases within them, their real objective was to terrorize Palestinian and Lebanese civilians into ceasing support for the fedayeen groups. While the Israeli retaliatory raids contributed to polarizing the Lebanese into factions that opposed and supported the presence of the PLO in Lebanon, they did not intimidate the fedayeen, who continued to fire rockets into northern Israel and covertly cross the border to carry out operations. In March 1978 Fatah sent into Israel a seaborne guerrilla unit that hijacked a bus on a coastal highway; thirty-one Israelis and six Palestinians were killed in this incident. Israel retaliated by launching a major invasion of southern Lebanon and establishing there a six-mile-wide defense corridor over which it retained de facto control even after withdrawing. In addition, Israel continued its campaign of trying to decapitate the guerrilla movement by dispatching elite hit squads around Europe and the Middle East to assassinate Palestinian leaders. Israel was able to deflect international criticism of its actions through a successful propaganda campaign that virtually made the word *Palestinian* synonymous with *terrorist* during the 1970s.

From Terrorism to Diplomacy In the period from mid-1978 until early 1985, there was actually a marked decline in terrorist operations undertaken by Palestinian groups against Israel. One reason was that Fatah actively campaigned against the use of terrorism as part of its deliberate strategy to win international diplomatic recognition for the PLO as the legitimate representative of the Palestinians under Israeli occupation in Gaza and the West Bank. Perhaps of equal importance was the progressive involvement of all fedayeen groups in Lebanon's escalating civil war, which had begun in 1975. Nevertheless, occasional sensational terrorist acts were carried out, most notably those undertaken by anti-PLO cadres loyal to ABU NIDAL, a former member of Fatah who broke with Arafat in 1974 because he rejected the moderate approach adopted by Fatah and the PLO. It was the unsuccessful effort by an Abu Nidal cadre to assassinate the Israeli ambassador to Britain that precipitated Israel's 1982 invasion of Lebanon.

Despite efforts by the PLO to become involved in the peace process, Israel considered the PLO a terrorist organization and a major threat to its permanent control of the West Bank and Gaza. Thus, one of the primary reasons for Israel's 1982 invasion of Lebanon was to destroy the PLO infrastructure and leadership that had become established in that country. With the PLO eliminated, the government of Menachem Begin believed that the Palestinians of the West Bank and Gaza would settle for its version of "autonomy." Israel also hoped to establish a Maronite Christian–dominated government in Lebanon, convinced that such a regime would share the Israeli objective of preventing the reemergence of a Palestinian nationalist movement. However, in spite of a summer-long siege of Beirut, Israel was unable to deal the PLO a mortal blow and finally had to accept an internationally protected withdrawal of the fedayeen from Lebanon. From its new base in Tunis, the PLO gradually reconstituted itself as an effective political force, much to the irritation of Israel.

The September 1985 murder of three Israelis in Cyprus, an incident that Israel accused Fatah of undertaking, initiated a renewed spiral of terrorist operations by Israel and the Palestinians. Israel dispatched its air force to Tunisia in October 1985 to bomb the PLO headquarters in an apparent attempt to assassinate Arafat. Although Arafat was not injured, the incident left more than sixty Palestinians and Tunisians dead and sparked calls for retaliation. Less than one week later, MUHAMMAD ABBAS's small PALESTINE LIBERATION FRONT responded to this incident by hijacking in the Mediterranean an Italian cruise ship, the *Achille Lauro,* which was en route to Israel, and killing one passenger, an elderly, disabled American Jew. The incident eventually involved several countries, including the United States. After mediation by the Egyptian government, which had secured the release of the ship in return for the hijackers' safe passage back to Tunis, U.S. air force planes intercepted the civilian jet carrying the hijackers, forcibly removed them, and detained them at a U.S. air base in Italy.

The *Achille Lauro* and several less sensational terrorist incidents that were undertaken by Palestinian groups opposed to the PLO's moderation delayed but did not derail the movement toward mainstream Palestinian acceptance of Israel's existence within most of historic Palestine. The PLO gradually moved toward a formal renunciation of terrorism, which it finally announced in December 1988. This public declaration, combined with the inability of Israeli security forces to suppress the INTIFADA ("Uprising") that had erupted in Gaza and the West Bank at the end of 1987, paved the way for an eventual reconciliation between the PLO and Israel, symbolized by the September 1993 Declaration of Principles agreement. That accord provided for mutual recognition of Israel and the PLO and established procedures for the gradual transfer of Israeli authority in the Occupied Territories to the PLO, beginning with the GAZA STRIP and the West Bank town of JERICHO. The PLO also committed itself to cooperating with Israel in suppressing Palestinian groups and individuals who engaged in terrorism.

The PLO's recognition of, and cooperation with, Israel galvanized those Palestinian groups who still espoused the creation of a Palestinian state in all of historic Palestine. In addition to established organizations like the PFLP–General Command, new groups had emerged in the Occupied Territories during the course of the Intifada. The most prominent of these new groups was the Islamic Resistance Movement (Harakat al-Muqawama al-Islamiyya, popularly known by its Arabic acronym, HAMAS) and ISLAMIC JIHAD. Hamas and the other groups opposed to the Declaration of Principles formed a "Steadfastness Front" to challenge the agreement, which they perceived as a betrayal of the Palestinian dream of liberating the homeland.

The 1993 Declaration of Principles and subsequent PLO-Israeli government negotiations on transferring political authority in the Occupied Territories to Palestinians also alarmed those Jewish groups that opposed any Israeli withdrawal from territory they considered to be the "Land of Israel." These latter sentiments were particularly strong among those Israeli settlers who moved to the West Bank after 1967. During the late 1970s and early 1980s, some settlers had been active in a clandestine group known as Terror-Neged-Terror (TNT), which carried out terrorist operations against West Bank Palestinians. TNT's most sensational act was the planting of car bombs that seriously injured the mayors of NABLUS and RAMALLAH in June 1980. Other Israeli settlers joined Rabbi Meir Kahane's Kach organization, which advocated the expulsion of all Palestinians from the West Bank. Extremists among the Israeli settlers denounced the 1993 accord and the subsequent 1995 agreement between Israel and the PLO regulating the withdrawal of Israeli security forces from West Bank towns and villages. The most sensational terrorist actions intended to prevent Israeli withdrawal from the West Bank included the February 1994 massacre of thirty-seven Muslim worshipers in the Ibrahimi Mosque at the Cave of the Patriarchs in HEBRON and the November 1995 assassination of Prime Minister Yitzhak Rabin by a Jewish religious student. In the former incident, at least twenty-nine Palestinians were shot to death by Baruch Goldstein, a settler and member of the Jewish terrorist group Kach, who entered the Hebron mosque brandishing a rifle; eight others were killed in the subsequent panic stampede and random shooting by police trying to control the situation.

The Hebron massacre provided Hamas, as well as other Palestinians affiliated with Islamic Jihad, the PFLP–General Command, and the DFLP, with what they believed was justification to undertake revenge actions against Israelis. Since 1994 these groups have claimed responsibility for a number of terrorist incidents that have taken place within Israel, including shootings, stabbings, and planting of bombs on public transport. Many operations inside Israel have involved suicide bombs carried by members of special Hamas-affiliated groups known as the Izz al-Din al-Qassam Brigade and the Yahya Ayyash Units. The most sensational terrorist incidents included the October 1994 bombing of a bus in Tel Aviv that killed 22 and wounded 48; the February 1996 bus bomb in Jerusalem that killed 23 and injured 49; the March 3, 1996, bus bomb in Jerusalem that killed 19 and wounded 10; the March 4, 1996, suicide bomb in Tel Aviv that killed 15 and injured 126; and the July 2, 1997, suicide bombs in Jewish West Jerusalem that killed 16 Israelis and injured more than 170 others. In addition, since 1994 Hamas members assassinated, in Gaza and the West Bank, fellow Palestinians whom they accused of "collaborating" with Israel.

The bombings were cited by the Israelis as evidence that the new PALESTINIAN AUTHORITY (PA) was unable or unwilling to control extremists in Gaza, Jericho, and the twelve West Bank towns that came under its control during the winter of 1995–96. Accordingly, the government of Israel used the continuance of violent acts to justify repeated delays in negotiating agreements for implementing provisions of the OSLO AGREEMENTS and imposed closures on West Bank towns and villages.

For many Palestinians, the May 1996 election of the Likud Party leader, Benjamin Netanyahu, who had campaigned on a promise to revise the agreements with the PLO, to the post of Israeli prime minister tended to confirm Hamas arguments that Israel never would permit the creation of an independent Palestinian state. Thus, even though Hamas cadres after 1993 no longer had the positive image of fedayeen leading resistance to occupation but had acquired a generally negative image as opponents of the peace process, the political wing of the movement benefited from disillusionment with the peace process that had became prevalent among Palestinians especially during the tenure of prime minister Netanyahu (1996–99). Similarly in Israel, extremist Jews who espoused the use of violence to reverse the peace process had succeeded at least in sowing widespread doubts about security if implementation of the Oslo accords were to be undertaken too hastily and without safeguards to assure the permanence and growth of Israeli settlements in the West Bank.

Eric Hooglund

BIBLIOGRAPHY

Abu Iyad, with Rouleau, Eric. *My Home, My Land: A Narrative of the Palestinian Struggle.* New York: Times Books, 1981.

Begin, Menachem. *The Revolt.* Rev. ed. New York: Dell, 1978.

Cobban, Helena. *The Palestinian Liberation Organization: People, Power and Politics.* Cambridge, England: Cambridge University Press, 1984.

Gresh, Alain. *The PLO, The Struggle Within: Towards an Independent Palestinian State.* Atlantic Highlands, N.J.: Zed Books, 1988.

Hart, Alan. *Arafat: A Political Biography.* Bloomington: Indiana University Press, 1984.

Hirst, David. *The Gun and the Olive Branch: The Roots of Violence in the Middle East.* Reprint. London: Macdonald, 1983.

Katz, Samuel. *Guards Without Frontiers: Israel's War Against Terrorism.* London: Arms and Armour, 1990.

Laqueur, Walter. *The Age of Terrorism.* Boston: Little Brown and Company, 1987.

Long, David E. *The Anatomy of Terrorism.* New York: The Free Press, 1990.

Sayigh, Rosemary. *Palestinians: From Peasants to Revolutionaries.* London: Zed Books, 1979.

Schiff, Zeev, and Raphael Rothstein. *Fedayeen: Guerrillas Against Israel.* New York: David McKay, 1972.

Schmid, Alex P., and Albert Jongman et al. *Political Terrorism.* Amsterdam, Oxford, and New York: North-Holland Publishing Co., 1983.

Schoenberg, Harris O. *A Mandate for Terror: The United Nations and the PLO.* New York: Shapolsky Publishers, 1989.

Sterling, Claire. *The Terror Network: The Secret War of International Terrorism.* New York: Rinehart & Winston, 1981.

Zadka, Saul. *Blood in Zion: How the Jewish Guerrillas Drove the British Out of Palestine.* London: Brassey's, 1995.

Tibawi, A. L.

Abd al-Latif Tibawi; academic
1910–

After graduation from the ARAB COLLEGE in JERUSALEM, Abdul Latif Tibawi received a B.A. from The American University of Beirut and an M.A. from London University. On his return to Palestine, he taught in RAMLA before working as the personal assistant to the director of education in the Mandatory government from 1931 to 1935. He later rose to become assistant district inspector of education in JAFFA from 1935 to 1941 and district inspector in the LYDDA and Gaza districts after 1941.

Tibawi eventually left Palestine to live and teach in the West. After obtaining a Ph.D., he held positions in both Harvard University and London University and retired from teaching in 1976. He also wrote a number of works that were translated into several languages, including *Arabic and Islamic Themes: Historical, Educational and Literary Studies; A Modern History of Syria, Including Lebanon and Palestine;* and *Anglo-Arab Relations and the Question of Palestine, 1914–1921,* as well as several books and articles on "Orientalist" historiography.

Michael R. Fischbach

Tiberias

Tabariya

Tiberias lies along the western shore of Lake Tiberias (Sea of Galilee) in the Galilee region. Founded in the first quarter century C.E., it was named after the Roman emperor bearing the same name despite its far more ancient origins. The city was long an important part of the administrative apparatus in Palestine for various governments. It was the headquarters of the Jund al-Urdunn province during the early Islamic period, as well as of the subdistrict of Tiberias, itself subsumed within the district of Acre, during both Ottoman and Mandate times. Its lands comprised some 15,000 *dunums* as of 1945.

Historically, the walled town lay along caravan routes connecting Syria and Egypt and therefore possessed important strategic importance. It was an important prize in the Muslim-Crusader fighting of the twelfth and thirteenth centuries, passing back into Muslim hands for the last time in 1247. Napoleon Bonaparte captured the town in 1799 during the French campaign in the Middle East. Tiberias suffered greatly during a severe earthquake in 1837, however, and its walls were never rebuilt.

Tiberias was noted for its warm climate and mineral water baths south of the town, which drew tourists seeking relief from ailments. Although agriculture was a mainstay of the economy, as elsewhere, fishing was also an important dimension of the Arab economy through the Mandate period. And as a center for government, it possessed schools, hospitals, and other such institutions.

Tiberias was greatly affected by the onset of ZIONISM and the Israeli-Palestinian conflict. Because it is a site of previous Jewish populations, Jews began to resettle in Tiberias after an edict issued by the Ottoman sultan Süleiman the Lawgiver (the Magnificent) in 1562. The town, site of the tomb of the Jewish religious scholar Maimonides, became one of the four holy towns for Jews in Palestine, along with JERUSALEM, HEBRON, and SAFAD. Jews comprised over half of the town's population of 6,950 in 1922 at the onset of the British PALESTINE MANDATE. The influx of Jews due to Zionist settlement saw the town's population increase to 11,310 in 1944.

During the 1948 fighting between Palestinian residents and the Haganah in the city, the latter managed to capture the Palestinian districts by April 18, 1948. Tiberias's Palestinian population fled, evacuated to NAZARETH by British forces in one of the first large-scale Palestinian refugee exoduses of the war. The town thereafter became an exclusively Jewish town of some 6,000 in the new state of Israel. The largely Jewish population of Tiberias (Hebrew, Teverya) totaled 35,000 in the late 1990s.

Michael R. Fischbach

Tibi, Ahmad

physician, politician

1957– al-Tayyiba

Tibi studied at The Hebrew University of JERUSALEM and completed medical studies there in 1983. A gynecologist, he later practiced at Hadassah Hospital in Jerusalem.

In the 1980s, Tibi was a major connection for Israelis seeking to meet with officials of the PALESTINE LIBERATION ORGANIZATION (PLO) when such contacts were still forbidden under Israeli law. Tibi himself first met the PLO chairman, YASIR ARAFAT, in 1984 and later arranged visits for Israelis seeking to meet Arafat in Tunis or PLO officials elsewhere. In this way, Tibi was instrumental in establishing contacts between Israeli groups such as Peace Now and the Citizens Rights Movement and the PLO. His relationship with the PLO at times created problems for him in ISRAEL, where officials at times barred him from traveling to the Occupied Territories or even traveling abroad.

By 1991, Tibi had become a vital emissary and mediator for the PLO. He brought PLO officials together with not only leftist Israelis but government officials as well. His importance to the PLO was symbolized by his service as an adviser to the

Palestinian delegation at the MADRID PEACE CONFERENCE, 1991, despite the fact that he was an Israeli citizen. Tibi later became a "back channel" link by which Arafat and the Israeli prime minister, Yitzhak Rabin, could communicate directly, not through their respective negotiators, during the secret Israeli-PLO talks in the summer of 1993 that led to the Oslo accords of August 1993. He also helped mediate between the PLO and HAMAS during a period of tension in late 1994 and continued to function as a senior adviser for Arafat thereafter.

Tibi emerged as an important actor within Palestinian political circles in Israel by the mid-1990s. He allied himself with the Islamic movement and later formed a new political organization, the Arab Movement for Change, in December 1995 but ultimately withdrew from the Knesset elections prior to the balloting of May 1996.

Michael R. Fischbach

Transfer

The first United States ambassador to Israel, James McDonald, in *My Mission in Israel,* tells of a conversation he had with the first president of Israel, Chaim Weizmann, in the course of which Weizmann referred to the 1948 Palestinian exodus as a "miraculous simplification of Israel's tasks." McDonald added that not one of the "big three"—Weizmann, David Ben-Gurion, and Moshe Sharett (Shertok)—and no responsible Zionist leader had anticipated such a "miraculous clearing of the land."

Zionist Support and Plans for Transfer In fact the Palestinian exodus of 1948 was less of a "miracle" than the culmination of over half a century of efforts, plans, and, in the end, brute force. From the beginning of the Zionist enterprise to found a Jewish National Home—or state—in Palestine the Zionists have been confronted with what they termed the "Arab Problem": the fact that the "Land of Israel" was already populated. One of the proposed solutions to that problem was the notion of transfer. The transfer concept was embraced by the highest level of Zionist leadership, including virtually all the founding fathers of the Israeli state and almost the entire Zionist political spectrum. Nearly all the founders advocated transfer in one form or another, including Theodor Herzl, Leon Motzkin, Nahman Syrkin, Menahem Ussishkin, Chaim Weizmann, David Ben-Gurion, Yitzhak Tabenkin, Avraham Granovsky, Israel Zangwill, Yitzhak Ben-Tzvi, Pinhas Rutenberg, Aaron Aaronson, Zeev Jabotinsky, and Berl Katznelson. The latter, one of the most influential leaders of the Mapai Party and often described as the conscience of Labor Zionism, had this to say in a debate at the World Convention of *Ihud Poalei Tzion* (the highest forum of the Zionist world labor movement) in August 1937:

> The matter of population transfer has provoked a debate among us: Is it permitted or forbidden? My conscience is absolutely clear in this respect. A remote neighbour is better than a close enemy. They [the Palestinians] will not lose from being transferred and we most certainly will not lose from it. In the final analysis, this is a political and settlement reform for the benefit of both parties. I have long been of the opinion that this is the best of all solutions. . . . I have always believed and still believe that they were destined to be transferred to Syria or Iraq. (Masalha, 1992).

Supporters of transfer included Arthur Ruppin, a cofounder of Brit Shalom, a movement advocating binationalism and equal rights for Arabs and Jews; moderate Mapai leaders such as Moshe Sharett and Eliezer Kaplan; and Histadrut leaders such as Golda Meir and David Remez. But perhaps the most consistent advocate of transfer was Yosef Weitz, the director of the Jewish National Fund's Settlement Department, who was at the center of the Zionist LAND purchasing activities. His intimate involvement in land purchase made him sharply aware of the project's limitations. As late as 1947, after almost half a century of tireless efforts, the collective ownership of the Jewish National Fund which constituted over one half of the *yishuv* total, amounted to a mere 3.5 percent of the land area of Palestine. Clearly, land purchase was not the only way for Zionists to acquire control of Palestine. A good summary of Weitz's political beliefs is provided by his diary entry dated December 20, 1940:

> Amongst ourselves it must be clear that there is no room for both peoples in this country. No "development" will bring us closer to our aim to be an independent people in this small country. After the Arabs are transferred, the country will be wide open for us; with the Arabs staying the country will remain narrow and restricted. . . . There is no room for compromise on this point . . . land

> purchasing . . . will not bring about the state; . . . The only way is to transfer the Arabs from here to neighbouring countries, all of them, except perhaps Bethlehem, Nazareth, and Old Jerusalem. Not a single village or a single tribe must be left. And the transfer must be done through their absorption in Iraq and Syria and even in Transjordan. For that goal, money will be found—even a lot of money. And only then will the country be able to absorb millions of Jews . . . there is no other solution. (Masalha, 1992)

In 1930, against the background of the WESTERN (WAILING) WALL DISTURBANCES, 1929, Weizmann, then president of both the World Zionist Organization and the newly established Jewish Agency Executive, actively began promoting ideas of Arab transfer in private discussion with British officials and ministers. In the same year, Weizmann and Pinhas Rutenberg, who was both chair of *yishuv*'s National Council and a member of the Jewish Agency Executive, presented the British colonial secretary, Lord Passfield, with an official, albeit secret, proposal for the transfer of Palestinians to Transjordan. This scheme proposed that a loan of 1 million Palestinian pounds be raised from Jewish financial sources for the resettlement of Palestinian peasants in Transjordan. This proposal was rejected by Lord Passfield. However, the justifications Weizmann used in its defense formed the cornerstone of subsequent Zionist arguments for transfer. Weizmann asserted that there was nothing "immoral" about the concept; that the "transfer" of Greek and Turkish populations in the early 1920s provided a precedent for a similar measure for the Palestinians; and that the uprooting and transfer of Palestinians to Transjordan, Iraq, Syria, or any other part of the Arab world would merely constitute a relocation from one Arab district to another.

For Weizmann and other leaders of the Jewish Agency, the transfer was a systematic procedure, requiring preparation and a great deal of organization, to be planned by strategic thinkers and technical experts. Although the desire among the Zionist leadership to be rid of the native population remained constant until the "miraculous clearing of the land" in 1948, the methods of transfer envisaged changed according to circumstances over the years. Thus the wishful belief in the early years of ZIONISM that the Palestinians could be "spirited across the border," in the words of Theodor Herzl, or that they would simply "fold their tents and slip away," to use the formulation of Zangwill, soon gave way to more realistic assessments. From the mid-1930s onward, the Jewish Agency produced a series of specific plans, generally involving Transjordan, SYRIA, or Iraq. Some of these plans were produced by three "Transfer Committees": the first two committees, set up by Moshe Shertok (Sharett), the head of the Jewish Agency's Political Department, operated between 1937 and 1944, and the third was appointed by the Israeli cabinet in August 1948. As of the late 1930s, some of these plans included proposals for agrarian legislation and citizenship restriction and various taxes designed to encourage the Palestinians to transfer "voluntarily."

Because of the Zionist leadership's concern with not provoking unfavorable British public opinion, Weizmann's 1930 proposal of transfer to Transjordan remained confined to private talks with British officials. In fact, until 1937, the leadership had largely refrained from airing this sensitive issue and was careful not to support the principle of transfer publicly, despite its importance to the achievement of Zionist goals. More importantly, for reasons of political expediency, the Zionists calculated that transfer plans could not be carried out without Britain's support, and perhaps only if Britain itself implemented the transfer.

However, as the Zionist leaders grew more confident about the eventuality of Jewish statehood, their approach became more daring. Indeed, despite increasing Palestinian opposition and resistance to Zionist policies (culminating in the outbreak in April 1936 of the Arab rebellion), Zionism's prospects had continued to improve. Meanwhile, immigration continued to rise with growing persecution of Jews in Europe. Between 1931 and 1936 the Jewish population rose from 17.8 to 29.5 percent.

British Plans The Zionists were tireless in trying to shape the proposals of the PEEL COMMISSION, 1937. The most significant proposal of transfer submitted to the Commission—the one destined to shape the outcome of its findings—was put forward by the Jewish Agency in a 1937 memorandum containing a specific paragraph on Arab transfer to Transjordan. The Peel Commission's principal recommendation was the partition of Palestine into two sovereign states, one Arab and one Jewish. The Peel report added a specific recommendation for what it delicately called an "exchange" of populations—some of the 225,000 Arabs residing in the territory allotted to the Jewish state against the 1,250 Jews living in the territory envisaged for the Arab state.

Not surprisingly, the Peel Commission's recommendations were vehemently rejected by all shades of Palestinian opinion. They also triggered an unprecedented explosion of violence among the Palestinian peasantry in the countryside. The ongoing Arab rebellion, which had been witnessing a lull, intensified. For the Zionists, on the other hand, the Peel Commission represented the first official British recognition of ultimate Jewish sovereignty and legitimized two basic Zionist concepts. First, it endorsed the Zionist interpretation of the BALFOUR DECLARATION (that the "Jewish National Home" meant a Jewish state), and second, it sanctioned the long-sought-after Zionist dream of Arab transfer from such a state.

The "big three," Weizmann, Shertok, and especially Ben-Gurion, enthusiastically endorsed the transfer proposal. The importance Ben-Gurion, then chairman of the Jewish Agency (practically the government of the *yishuv*), attached not merely to transfer but to forced transfer is seen in his diary entry of July 12, 1937: "The compulsory transfer of the Arabs from the valleys of the proposed Jewish state could give us something which we never had, even when we stood on our own feet during the days of the First and Second Temple"—a Galilee free of Arab population.

Ben-Gurion believed that if the Zionists were determined in their effort to put pressure on the Mandatory authorities to carry out forced removal, the plan could be implemented:

> We have to stick to this conclusion in the same way we grabbed the Balfour Declaration, more than that, in the same way we grabbed Zionism itself. We have to insist upon this conclusion [and push it] with our full determination, power and conviction. . . . We must uproot from our hearts the assumption that the thing is not possible. It can be done. (Masalha, 1992)

Ben-Gurion went so far as to write, "We must prepare ourselves to carry out" the transfer.

Ben-Gurion was convinced that few, if any, Palestinians would "voluntarily" transfer themselves to Transjordan. A letter to his son, Amos, dated October 5, 1937, shows the extent to which transfer had become associated in his mind with expulsion: "We must expel Arabs and take their places . . . and, if we have to use force—not to dispossess the Arabs of the Negev and Transjordan, but to guarantee our own right to settle in those places—then we have force at our disposal."

From 1937, extensive discussions on Arab transfer were held in the Zionist movement's highest bodies, the Zionist Agency Executive and the World Convention of *Ihud Poalei Tzion,* as well as extensive discussions in the various official and nonofficial "Transfer Committees." Many leading delegates justified Arab removal politically, morally, and ethically as the natural and logical continuation of Zionist colonization in Palestine. Although these debates revealed a general endorsement of the "moral" justification of the concept, the differences centered on the question of "compulsory transfer" and on whether such a course would be practical in the late 1930s–early 1940s without Britain's support or even actual participation in implementation. Various transfer plans were put forward or supported by mainstream *yishuv* leaders, generally involving Transjordan, Syria, or Iraq. The few critics of these schemes in the *yishuv,* notably leaders of the Hashomer Hatzair movement and the Ihud group (mainly Moshe Smilansky), both of which advocated an Arab-Jewish binational state in Palestine, dismissed the concept of transfer as "dangerous" and "anti-socialist." However, the general support these schemes received and the attempt to promote them by mainstream and official labor leaders—Weizmann, Ben-Gurion, Katznelson (died in 1944), Shertok, Kaplan, Granovsky, Ussishkin, Weitz, and Golda Meir, some of whom played a decisive role in the 1948 war—highlight the ideological intent that made the Palestinian refugee expulsion in 1948 possible.

Transfer during the 1948 War With the ARAB-ISRAELI WAR OF 1948, the Zionists succeeded in many of their objectives; if they did not have a completely homogeneous Jewish state, at least they had one in which the Palestinians were reduced to a small and manageable minority. The notion of transfer or expulsion was heatedly denied by Zionist leaders, and the evacuation of some three quarters of a million Palestinians was officially ascribed not to Zionist policy but to orders issued by the Arab armies. The long debates about transfer within the Jewish Agency and other top Zionist leadership bodies, in which for the most part the issue was not morality but feasibility, and "liberals" were distinguished from "hardliners" by whether they favored "voluntary" or "compulsory" transfer, were seemingly forgotten. Pushed to the background, too, were the tireless preparations such as those of Yosef Weitz and the "Transfer Committee" within the Jewish Agency aimed at bringing about the "miraculous clearing of the land" that took place in 1948.

The evacuation of the great majority of the Palestinians in 1948 occurred against a background of war and military campaigns. From the territory occupied by the Israelis in 1948, about 85 percent of the Palestinians were driven out. It was a time when opportunities were not to be missed, as Weitz, then the head of the official Israel government "Transfer Committee," had exhorted his countrymen.

The fact that no written blanket orders unambiguously calling for the wholesale expulsion of the Arab population have been found has been cited by the Israeli historian Benny Morris as indicating the absence of premeditated design or transfer policy in 1948. Morris concluded that the exodus was born of the exigencies of war.

However, the following points should be kept in mind. First, Plan Dalet, which is a straightforward document, constituted a master plan for expulsion. More importantly, the 1948 exodus was the result of painstaking effort and unswerving vision stated and restated with tedious and almost obsessive repetitiveness for over fifty years.

Nur Masalha

BIBLIOGRAPHY

Buseilah, Raja'i. "The Fall of Lydda 1948: Impressions and Reminiscences." *Arab Studies Quarterly* 3, no. 2 (Spring 1981): 123–151.

Flapan, Simha. *The Birth of Israel: Myths and Realities.* New York: Pantheon, 1988.

Khalidi, Walid. *All That Remains: The Palestinian Villages Occupied and Depopulated by Israel in 1948.* Washington, D.C.: Institute for Palestine Studies, 1992.

——. "The Fall of Haifa." *Middle East Forum* (December 1959): 22–32.

——. "Why Did the Palestinians Leave?" *Middle East Forum* (July 1959): 21–24, 35.

Masalha, Nur. *Expulsion of the Palestinians: The Concept of "Transfer" in Zionist Political Thought, 1882–1948.* Washington, D.C.: Institute for Palestine Studies, 1992.

——. *A Land Without a People: Israel, Transfer, and the Palestinians, 1949–1996.* London, Faber & Faber, 1997.

——. "On Recent Hebrew and Israeli Sources for the Palestinian Exodus, 1948–49." *Journal of Palestine Studies* 18, no. 1 (Autumn 1988): 121–137.

Masalha, Nureldeen, and F. Vivekananda. "Israeli Revisionist Historiography of the Birth of Israel and Its Palestinian Exodus of 1948." *Scandinavian Journal of Development Alternatives* 9, no. 1 (March 1990): 71–79.

McDonald, James G. *My Mission in Israel, 1948–1951.* New York: Simon & Schuster, 1951.

Morris, Benny. *1948 and After.* New York: Oxford University Press, 1990.

Nazzal, Nafez. *The Palestinian Exodus from Galilee, 1948.* Beirut: Institute for Palestine Studies, 1978.

Palumbo, Michael. *The Palestinian Catastrophe.* London: Faber & Faber, 1987.

Sanbar, Elias. *Palestine 1948: L'expulsion.* Paris: Institute for Palestine Studies, 1984.

Shoufani, Elias. "The Fall of a Village." *Journal of Palestine Studies* 1, no. 4 (Summer 1972): 108–121.

Simons, Chaim. *International Proposals to Transfer Arabs from Palestine 1985–1947.* Hoboken, N.J.: Ktav Publishing Co., 1988.

Tubi, Tawfiq
politician
1922– Haifa

Tubi has been one of the leading Palestinian communists during the past half century. From a Greek Orthodox family, he studied at The American University of Beirut after completion of his secondary school studies at the Bishop Gobat School (Zion School) in Jerusalem in 1939. After his return to Palestine, he worked for the PALESTINE MANDATE department of public works from 1943 to 1948.

Tubi joined the PALESTINE COMMUNIST PARTY (PCP) in 1940. Active in the labor movement, he worked with the Palestine Arab Workers' Society and helped organize the Rays of Hope Club in Haifa to unify Palestinian labor groups. In September 1943, he was a major figure in the establishment of the National Liberation League out of the PCP.

Tubi remained in the Galilee after the establishment of Israel and participated in the conference that led to formation of the Israeli Communist Party (ICP) in 1948. He was elected to the Knesset from the ICP that same year—the youngest member of the body—and rose to the party's central committee. In 1965, Tubi was one of the main figures who established RAKAH, the New Communist List, from the ICP. From 1990 to 1993, he served as the party's secretary-general. Tubi continued to represent the ICP and later Rakah in the Knesset from 1949 to 1977 and represented the Rakah-led Democratic Front for Peace and Equality in the Knesset from 1977 to 1990. Tubi also edited and published the Communist newspaper *al-Ittihad.* Throughout his long tenure, he pushed for greater equality for PALESTINIAN CITIZENS OF ISRAEL.

Tubi's membership in organizations like the Israel Committee for Peace, the International Peace Council, and the Movement for Friendship with the Soviet Union led him to travel extensively and to serve as a conduit between the Palestinian community in Israel and the wider Arab world. He met with various Arab leaders in this capacity as early as 1951 and eventually met YASIR ARAFAT, chair of the PALESTINE LIBERATION ORGANIZATION, in September 1982.

Michael R. Fischbach

Tulkarm

Lying some fifteen kilometers from the coast, Tulkarm forms the western hub of the historic "Triangle" region of Palestine and has been inhabited since Canaanite times. Its location between the coastal plain and the mountains of central Palestine made it an important stop along both trade and conquest routes over the course of history. Its resulting political importance was reflected in the fact that Ottoman authorities designated Tulkarm the administrative center of the Bani Sa'b subdistrict in the late nineteenth century. The mainstay of the town's economy was agriculture, and Tulkarm's fertile land produced grain as well as fruit and olives. The Tulkarm region was particularly famous for its watermelons.

During the PALESTINE MANDATE, Tulkarm retained its importance as an administrative center. It was designated the center of the subdistrict that took its name. The town's growing importance was also demonstrated in 1931 when it was chosen as the site for the Kedourie Agricultural School.

The end of the Mandate and the ARAB-ISRAELI WAR OF 1948 affected Tulkarm dramatically. Iraqi forces controlled the area during the fighting, and the town became part of the Jordanian-controlled WEST BANK. However, the Israeli-Jordanian armistice agreement of 1949 left some 30,000 of Tulkarm's 32,610 *dunums* of land in Israeli hands. The loss of agricultural land and jobs prompted some residents to seek employment outside the town and even abroad thereafter.

After nearly three decades of Israeli occupation of the West Bank, beginning in June 1967, Tulkarm was the third West Bank town from which Israeli occupation forces redeployed. The PALESTINIAN AUTHORITY assumed control of the town on December 10, 1995.

Tulkarm's population has grown considerably over the past 100 years. Its population during late Ottoman times was between 2,000 and 3,000 inhabitants, growing to some 8,000 in 1944 and 20,500 in 1961, to over 30,000 by 1981.

Michael R. Fischbach

Tuma, Emile

politician, historian
1919–1985 Haifa

Tuma completed his secondary school studies at the Bishop Gobat School (Zion School) in Jerusalem in 1937 and then enrolled in Cambridge University's law school. When World War II broke out in 1939, he was in Palestine, unable to return to England and complete his studies. That year, Tuma joined the PALESTINE COMMUNIST PARTY (PCP). He also helped organize the Rays of Hope Club in HAIFA to unify Palestinian labor organizations. He quickly rose to prominence in the PCP and in September 1943 helped form and headed the National Liberation League, which emerged from it. Tuma also owned and edited the communist weekly newspaper *al-Ittihad,* which appeared from May 1944.

After the first Arab-Israeli war, Tuma was active among Palestinian refugees in Lebanon and was imprisoned by Lebanese authorities for several months in Ba'labakk in 1948. After his return to Haifa in April 1949, he became one of the leaders and main ideologues in the Israeli Communist Party (ICP); the New Communist List, RAKAH, which emerged from the ICP in 1965; and the Democratic Front for Peace and Equality, established in 1977.

Like other communist leaders in Israel, Tuma met with figures from the PALESTINE LIBERATION

ORGANIZATION while on trips outside Israel. Thus, he served as an important bridge between the Palestinian community in Israel and the wider Palestinian world.

A historian as well as a politician, Tuma received a Ph.D. in history from the Academy of Soviet Studies in the SOVIET UNION in the mid-1960s and wrote numerous historical works, including *The Roots of the Palestine Problem* and *al-Haraka al-Ijtima'iyya fi al-Islam* (The social movement in Islam).

Tuma died while undergoing medical treatment in Hungary in 1985 and was buried in Haifa. The Emile Tuma Institute for Political and Social Studies was later established in Haifa in his memory.

Michael R. Fischbach

Tuqan, Fadwa

poet

1917– Nablus

Sister of the famous poet Ibrahim Tuqan and a member of the TUQAN FAMILY of NABLUS, Fadwa Tuqan has exerted an important influence on modern Palestinian poetry. In addition to introducing sensual themes into modern Arab verse, Tuqan broke with traditional poetic forms and became a pioneer in the use of free verse. Tuqan is also important for her frank discussions of Palestinian social life and especially of women's issues in LITERATURE. She discusses women's lives in pre-1948 Palestinian society forcefully in her 1985 autobiography, *Rihla Jabaliyya, Rihla Sa'ba* (A mountainous journey, a difficult journey). Her first collection of poetry, *Wahdi ma al-Ayyam* (Alone with the days), was published in 1952.

After the Israeli occupation of the WEST BANK in 1967, Tuqan began writing nationalist poetry. She soon became famous for poems like "The Freedom Fighter and the Land." Some of her poems were reproduced in *Filastin,* the underground newspaper issued in the Occupied Territories in the mid-1970s by the Palestinian National Front. Israeli general Moshe Dayan once equated the power of one of her poems to that of several Palestinian guerrilla fighters.

Despite her strongly nationalist poetry, Tuqan in fact met Dayan, then minister of defense, twice in late 1968, as part of Dayan's behind-the-scenes efforts to contact Arab leaders. Tuqan passed on a message from Dayan to Egyptian president Jamal Abd al-Nasir, and later offered to contact the FATAH leader, YASIR ARAFAT, although nothing came of the contacts.

Michael R. Fischbach

Tuqan Family

The Tuqan family was one of the traditional leading families in NABLUS during the Ottoman and PALESTINE MANDATE periods. Several members of the family distinguished themselves in the realms of EDUCATION and LITERATURE; others joined the NASHASHIBI FAMILY–led Opposition during the Mandate.

Ahmad (1903–1981; educator, politician) Ahmad studied at Cambridge University then taught at the ARAB COLLEGE in JERUSALEM. After the incorporation of the WEST BANK into JORDAN, he was director of education in the West Bank from 1950 to 1954. He later entered politics and served in several cabinet positions, including as foreign minister from 1967 to 1969, defense minister in 1969, and, briefly, prime minister in 1970.

During the early 1970s, Ahmad became chief of the Jordanian royal court, was appointed a senator in 1973, and was appointed chair of the board of trustees of the Univesity of Jordan.

Baha al-Din (1910– ; politician, historian) After studies at the American University of Beirut, al-Din served the Jordanian government in a number of capacities from 1932, including as ambassador to Britain from 1956 to 1958. He also wrote and translated several standard histories of Transjordan. His daughter, Aliya, was the third wife of King Husayn of Jordan from 1972 until her death in February 1977.

Ibrahim (1905–1941; Nablus, poet) Described as "Palestine's poet laureate," Ibrahim was the leading Palestinian poet during the Mandate. He first began publishing poetry in 1924 while studying at the American University in Beirut. After his return to Palestine in 1929, he began composing nationalist poems such as *al-Thulatha al-Hamra* (Red Tuesday), in commemoration of three Palestinian nationalists executed by the British in June 1930. He worked for the Arabic section of the Mandate government's radio broadcasting service from 1936 until 1940, when he resigned after official protests that his choice of material to broadcast was inciting Palestinian nationalist feelings.

Qadri (1911–1971; educator, writer) After receiving a B.A. in mathematics from the American University of Beirut, he served as a teacher and principal of al-Najah National College (later AL-NAJAH NATIONAL UNIVERSITY) in Nablus. From 1951 to 1955, he sat in the Jordanian national assembly and was Jordan's foreign minister in 1964. He was a respected writer throughout the Arab world, especially on the history of science but on culture and economics as well, and was a participant in the Palestinian cultural nationalist movement.

Sulayman (1893–1958; Nablus; politician) Sulayman was educated at Beirut Turkish College. He was a member of the Mandatory government's ADVISORY COUNCIL in the early 1920s before serving as mayor of Nablus from 1925 to 1948. Sulayman was also a member of the Nashashibi-led Opposition during the Mandate and a founder of the NATIONAL DEFENSE PARTY, which emerged in 1934. In April 1936, he lent early and crucial support to a call for a general Arab strike, which soon led to a nationwide strike and boycott. He was later supportive of the guerrilla bands who took part in the Arab revolt, although he helped form self-defense groups when pro-Councilist guerrillas began attacking Opposition figures before fleeing into exile in December 1937 to avoid the internecine violence.

After Jordan's annexation of the West Bank, Sulayman was appointed to the Jordanian senate, served in the royal court, and was minister of defense in 1951–52. After the political crisis of April 1957, he was appointed minister of defense and military governor until July 1957. As minister of defense of the ephemeral Iraqi-Jordanian federation of 1958, during the Iraqi coup of July 1958 he was in Baghdad, where he was killed along with other senior Jordanian and Iraqi officials.

Michael R. Fischbach

Turki, Fawaz

poet, writer
1940– Haifa

Fawaz Turki fled his native HAIFA with his family during the ARAB-ISRAELI WAR OF 1948 and grew up in the Burj al-Barajina refugee camp in Beirut. He left Lebanon and spent the majority of his adulthood in Australia, India, France, and the United States.

Turki has authored several personalized accounts of Palestinian life in exile that poignantly and sometimes bitterly describe the Palestinian problem and his own struggle with his Palestinian identity, including *The Disinherited: Journal of a Palestinian Exile* (1972), *Soul in Exile: Lives of a Palestinian Revolutionary* (1988), and *Exile's Return: The Making of a Palestinian American* (1994), a self-critical and controversial book. His English-language poetry appeared in *Poems from Exile* (1975) and *Tel Zaatar Was the Hill of Thyme, Poems from Palestine* (1978).

Michael R. Fischbach

U

Unions

The Palestinian people are among the most organized—and the most politicized—in the world. There are unions of workers, women, teachers, students, writers and journalists, lawyers, engineers, artists, youth, medical professionals, and others. There are Palestinian unions in virtually every country in which Palestinians have resided since 1948, including Syria, Brazil, the United States, Germany, Costa Rica, Australia, France, Canada, Greece, and the former SOVIET UNION. But what makes this PALESTINE LIBERATION ORGANIZATION (PLO) institution particularly striking is that unlike all the other PLO organizations, which have been able to operate only *outside* the Occupied Territories, the unions are as well organized—indeed, often better organized and with a broader base—*inside* the territories. Indeed, these mass organizations provided the backbone and the cadres of the nationalist struggle in the Occupied Territories during the INTIFADA.

Politically, each of the four main factions within the PLO—FATAH, the POPULAR FRONT FOR THE LIBERATION OF PALESTINE (PFLP), the DEMOCRATIC FRONT FOR THE LIBERATION OF PALESTINE (DFLP), and the Palestine Peoples Party (PP), formerly the PALESTINE COMMUNIST PARTY (PCP)—has its own union in each social-political category. Thus, for example, the second largest group of unionized individuals, women, are arrayed in four distinct associations: the Union of Women's Committees for Social Work (Fatah), the Union of Palestinian Women's Committees (PFLP), the Federation of Palestinian Women's Action Committees (DFLP), and the Union of Palestinian Working Women's Committees (PPP/PCP). All four women's union factions exist in practically all Palestinian communities in Palestine and throughout the diaspora. In addition, the PLO has its own women's organization, the General Union of Palestinian Women (Fatah/Independent). In 1988, at the height of the Intifada, women activists in the Occupied Territories established a Higher Women's Council, which functioned as a coordinating committee and incorporated the four primary political strands of the women's movement in cooperative endeavors. The same four-part structure exists in every other union—students, lawyers, youth, for example—and in nearly every Palestinian community.

Palestinian unions have enjoyed widespread appeal, particularly in the Occupied Territories, where many unions emerged in the 1970s and 1980s (some date their inception from the 1920s and 1930s). Unions were organized by trade, geographical locale, and political faction, with a dual emphasis on social and national rights. The labor movement, through its trade unions and workers organizations, is the largest and most important mass actor on the Palestinian scene. It has been enormously consequential both in providing concrete benefits and services to workers and in mobilizing the Palestinian people against the Israel occupation. During the Intifada, the labor unions made immense contributions in the creation and functioning of the popular committees, and in provision of both leaders and activists for the national struggle. The unions' preexisting organizational network proved a highly effective "underground" wherein political activists frequently escaped the Israeli dragnet.

Within the labor unions, there has been an impressive amount of internal democracy but at the same time, intense factional competition, which has decreased their potential effectiveness on both national and social issues. In the Occupied Territories, the four main labor unions are the Workers Unity Bloc (WUB), affiliated with the DFLP; the Progressive Workers Bloc (PWB), affiliated with the PPP; the Workers Youth Movement (WYM), affiliated with Fatah; and the Progressive Unionist Action Front (PUAF), affiliated with the PFLP. Each of these four federations includes smaller unions representing construction workers, restaurant and cafe workers, textile workers, carpentry workers, electricity workers, blacksmiths, woodworkers, and others.

Cheryl Rubenberg

BIBLIOGRAPHY

Hiltermann, Joost R. *Behind the Intifada: Labor and Women's Movements in the Occupied Territories.* Princeton, N.J.: Princeton University Press, 1991.

Mussalam, Sami. *The PLO: The Palestine Liberation Organization.* Brattleboro, Vt.: Amana Books, 1988.

Nassar, Jamal R. *The Palestine Liberation: From Armed Struggle to the Declaration of Independence.* Westport, Conn.: Praeger, 1991.

Rubenberg, Cheryl A. *The Palestine Liberation Organization: Its Institutional Infrastructure.* Belmont, Mass., Institute for Arab Studies: 1983.

United Nations

The United Nations (U.N.) has devoted more time and attention to the Arab-Jewish conflict over Palestine, called the question of Palestine and after 1948, the ARAB-ISRAELI CONFLICT, than to any other international issue. By its peacekeeping operations, it has contained several wars between Israel and the Arabs and prevented them from assuming wider and more dangerous proportions, and it has provided extensive relief assistance to large numbers of Palestinian REFUGEES who lost their homes and their livelihood as a result of those wars. Although the United Nations has not played a leading role in the peace process, which began with the MADRID PEACE CONFERENCE, 1991, and has opened the way to a negotiated peace settlement of the Palestine question, the 1947 U.N. partition plan and the "land for peace resolution" unanimously adopted by the Security Council in November 1967 contributed in no small measure to make that peace process possible.

United Nations Partition Plan The question of Palestine was brought before the United Nations in April 1947 by the United Kingdom as the Mandatory Power for the territory. The General Assembly quickly set up the United Nations Special Committee on Palestine (UNSCOP) to investigate the matter and recommend a solution. After visiting Palestine as well as several Jewish refugee camps in Europe, UNSCOP recommended, in a majority report, a plan of partition under which Palestine would be divided into two independent states, one Arab and one Jewish, the city of Jerusalem was to be placed under a special international regime. The Arab state would be allotted about 43 percent of Palestine, including the WEST BANK, the GAZA STRIP, Western Galilee, and a swath of the Negev Desert, and the Jewish state would get about 56 percent of the territory, including the central coastal area, Eastern Galilee, and most of the Negev. On November 29, 1947, the General Assembly approved the partition plan; it also established the United Nations Palestine Commission to implement the partition plan and decided that the British PALESTINE MANDATE should be terminated as soon as possible, but in any case no later than August 1, 1948 (General Assembly resolution 181 [II]).

The Jewish Agency for Palestine accepted the partition plan, but the Palestine ARAB HIGHER COMMITTEE and all Arab states rejected it. During the first months of 1948, the Palestine Commission informed the General Assembly of the steady deterioration of the situation in Palestine and its inability to fulfill its mission. Meanwhile, the United Kingdom announced that it would relinquish the Mandate over Palestine on May 14, 1948.

United Nations Mediator for Palestine On May 14, 1948, the General Assembly relieved the Palestine Commission of its duties and decided to appoint a United Nations mediator for Palestine (Count FOLKE BERNADOTTE of Sweden) to promote a peaceful adjustment of the situation in Palestine (General Assembly Resolution 184 [S2]). On the same day, on the termination of the British Mandate, the Jewish Agency proclaimed the state of Israel on the territory allotted to the Jewish community under the U.N. partition plan. War broke out immediately between the two communities of Palestine, and during the following days, the armies of the neighboring Arab states invaded the territory to support the Palestinians in the ARAB–ISRAELI WAR OF 1948.

The hostilities ceased in June 1948 under the terms of a truce called for by the Security Council and supervised by the U.N. mediator for Palestine with the assistance of a group of military observers, which became the United Nations Truce Supervision Organization in Palestine (UNTSO), the first peacekeeping operation in U.N. history.

After the cessation of hostilities, Count Bernadotte began his mediation effort. In a report to the General Assembly completed on September 16, 1948, he suggested that the original U.N. partition plans be amended in the light of intervening events. In this connection, he recommended that all of the Galilee should be allotted to Israel, that in return the Arabs should get all of the Negev, and that Jerusalem should be demilitarized and placed under effective U.N. control. He also recommended that the Palestinian refugees who had been displaced from their homes in Palestine as a result of war be allowed to return or be compensated and that the General Assembly establish a conciliation commission to promote a peaceful settlement of the Palestine question. But the next day, before his report reached the General Assembly, Count Bernadotte was assassinated in Jerusalem by Jewish terrorists of the Stern Gang. His deputy, Ralph Bunche, an American official of the U.N. Secretariat, was immediately appointed as acting mediator.

United Nations Conciliation Commission for Palestine In November 1948, after considering the report of Count Bernadotte, the General Assembly set up the UNITED NATIONS CONCILIATION COMMISSION FOR PALESTINE (composed of France, Turkey, and the United States) to assume "insofar as it considers it necessary" the functions assigned to the mediator and to assist the parties concerned in achieving a final settlement of the Palestine question. The General Assembly also decided that the Palestine refugees willing to return to their homes and live at peace with their neighbors should be permitted to do so and that compensation should be paid to those choosing not to return, and it instructed the Conciliation Commission to facilitate the repatriation, resettlement, and economic and social rehabilitation of the refugees and the payment of compensation to them (General Assembly Resolution 194 [III]).

In May 1949, the General Assembly decided, despite the opposition of the Arab states, to admit Israel to membership in the United Nations (General Assembly Resolution 273 [III]).

1949 General Armistice Agreements On his appointment as acting mediator, Bunche concentrated his efforts on consolidating the truce by a negotiated armistice regime, and he brought about the first agreements between Israel and the Arabs.

From February to July 1949, under his auspices, general armistice agreements were successively concluded between Israel and each of its four Arab neighbors, Egypt, Jordan, Lebanon, and Syria. Pending a political settlement of the Palestine question, these agreements gave temporary control of the Gaza Strip to Egypt, the West Bank including East Jerusalem to Jordan, and the remaining parts of Palestine including West Jerusalem (an area noticeably larger than the territory allotted to the Jewish community under the U.N. Partition Plan) to Israel. The application and observance of the terms of the agreements were supervised by mixed armistice commissions with the assistance of military observers of UNTSO.

On August 11, 1949, the Security Council noted with satisfaction the conclusion of the General Armistice agreements and decided that the acting mediator, having discharged all functions assigned to him, was relieved from further responsibility; it expressed the hope that the governments and authorities concerned would achieve agreement on the final settlement of all questions outstanding between them, bilaterally or with the assistance of the United Nations Conciliation Commission for Palestine (Security Council Resolution 73).

The 1949 General Armistice agreements, which were based on the military situation on the ground at the time of their conclusion, did not involve the Palestinian leadership and did not address the Palestine question. They were clearly intended as an interim measure that would lead to permanent peace in the region, for which a political settlement of the Palestine question was central. But that did not happen. The Conciliation Commission repeatedly reported that no progress could be achieved because of the unwillingness of the parties to implement the relevant General Assembly resolutions. In December 1949, as the problem of refugees remained unresolved, the General Assembly established the United Nations Relief and Works Agency for Palestine Refugees in the

Near East (UNRWA) to provide assistance to the refugees without prejudice to its previous decision regarding their return and resettlement (General Assembly Resolution 302 [IV]). UNRWA has remained active to this day.

Thus, instead of permanent peace, the General Armistice agreements were followed by a long period of instability, highlighted by an unending cycle of Palestinian commando raids against Israel and Israeli reprisals, by five more full-fledged wars between Israel and neighboring Arab states (the Suez crisis of 1956; the ARAB-ISRAELI WAR OF 1967; the ARAB-ISRAEL WAR OF 1973; the Israeli invasion of Lebanon of 1978; and the ARAB-ISRAELI WAR OF 1982 (Israeli invasion of Lebanon), and by many frustrating mediation efforts within and outside the United Nations.

In 1964, Palestinian leaders, with the support of the Arab states, set up the PALESTINE LIBERATION ORGANIZATION (PLO) with the destruction of Israel and the establishment of an Arab state in Palestine as its main objectives. Israel denounced the four general armistice agreements; the agreement with Egypt in 1956, during the Suez crisis, which was brought about by the decision of the Egyptian government to nationalize the Company of the Suez Canal and to close the canal to Israeli shipping; and the other three at the start of the Six-Day War in June 1967.

Security Council Resolutions 242 (1967) and 338 (1973) The issues dividing Israel and the Arabs became even more intractable after the June 1967 war, during which Israel seized large portions of territory from its Arab opponents: the Sinai Peninsula and the Gaza Strip from Egypt, the West Bank including East Jerusalem from Jordan, and the Golan Heights from Syria. On November 22, 1967, the Security Council unanimously adopted Resolution 242, known as the "land for peace resolution," which called on the parties to seek a comprehensive settlement in the Middle East and stipulated that the establishment of a just and lasting peace should be based on the application of two principles: withdrawal of Israeli armed forces from territories occupied in June 1967 and respect for the right of all the states in the region to live in peace within secure and recognized boundaries. The Security Council also affirmed the necessity of achieving a just settlement of the Palestine refugee problem, and it requested the secretary-general to appoint a special representative to promote a peaceful settlement. The resolution was accepted by Egypt, Israel, Jordan, and Lebanon, but it was rejected by Syria and by the PLO, who complained that it reduced the Palestine issue to a mere refugee problem.

Ambassador Gunnar Jarring of Sweden, who was appointed as special representative of the secretary-general in the Middle East, began his mediation mission in December 1967. But despite his strenuous efforts, the parties concerned did not alter their basic positions. In February 1971, in an attempt to advance his mediation effort, Jarring decided to seek first an agreement between Egypt and Israel and requested that they make simultaneous and reciprocal commitments: Israel to withdraw its forces from the occupied Egyptian territory (Sinai) and Egypt to enter into a peace agreement with Israel. Egypt accepted, but Israel refused. Several attempts at reviving this initiative failed, and the Jarring mission ceased to be active in early 1973.

In October of the same year, a new war broke out in the Middle East, between Israel on one side and Egypt and Syria on the other. In its effort to contain that war, the Security Council adopted, on October 22, 1973, resolution 338, in which it called on the parties to cease all fighting and to begin negotiations, under appropriate auspices, aimed at establishing a just and lasting peace in the Middle East in accordance with the principles laid out in Resolution 242. UNITED NATIONS SECURITY COUNCIL RESOLUTIONS 242 AND 338 served as a basis for all subsequent peace negotiations.

Israeli Invasions of Lebanon The Arab-Israeli conflict was further complicated in early 1978 by a new crisis, involving Israel, Lebanon, and the PLO. In March 1978, after a terrorist raid against Israel by PLO fighters based in Lebanon, the Israeli forces invaded that country and occupied most of the region south of the Litani River. On March 19, the Security Council called on Israel to withdraw its forces from Lebanese territory and established the United Nations Interim Force in Lebanon (UNIFIL) to confirm the withdrawal process and to restore international peace and security in southern Lebanon (Security Council Resolution 425).

UNIFIL's main task was in effect to contain an armed conflict between Israel and the PLO. But without the full cooperation of either, UNIFIL has not been able to fulfill its mandate. Israel refused to withdraw its forces from a border area, which it called "the security zone," and PLO armed elements continued to try to infiltrate the U.N. buffer zone. There were frequent incidents involving Israeli and PLO forces until July 1981, when a de facto cease-fire was established thanks to a joint mediation effort by the United Nations and the United States. But in June 1982 Israel invaded Lebanon for a second time, despite the cease-fire and the presence of UNIFIL, and forced the PLO to remove its headquarters and its armed forces from Lebanon. In 1985, under the pressure of continued harassment by Lebanese resistance groups, the Israeli forces withdrew from most of the occupied Lebanese territory but continued to hold the so-called security zone. Since then, the situation in southern Lebanon has remained tense, and PLO armed elements have returned to the region.

Peace Process The Jarring mission was the last mediation effort sponsored by the United Nations in the Middle East. Since then, the General Assembly has repeatedly called for a comprehensive, just, and lasting settlement of the Arab-Israeli conflict, which should include a solution of the Palestine question based on due recognition of the inalienable rights of the Palestinian people, including the right to self-determination. It has also called for the convening of an international peace conference on the Middle East with the participation of all parties concerned, including the PLO. But the General Assembly resolutions on these subjects, though adopted by overwhelming majorities, were usually opposed by Israel and the United States and had little practical effect.

The isolation of the United States within the U.N. on issues concerning Israel was a relatively recent development. During the initial phase of the Palestine conflict, the U.S. policy was to avoid direct involvement and to act through the United Nations. The decisions taken by the U.N. at the time were generally supported and often inspired by the United States. But after the June 1967 war, while the Arab side gradually agreed to negotiate with Israel on the basis of the "land for peace" principle, Israel remained reluctant to withdraw from occupied Arab land. In this changing situation, the continued U.S. support for Israel was no longer consonant with the views of an increasing majority of the U.N. General Assembly.

After the October 1973 war, which nearly drew the two superpowers into direct military confrontation, the United States became more actively involved in the Middle East and took over from the United Nations as the prime mover in the promotion of a peaceful settlement of the Arab-Israeli conflict, including the question of Palestine. The increasing urgency of finding such a settlement and Israel's refusal to accept a new U.N. mediation effort were no doubt major reasons for this shift in U.S. policy. It was evident that no settlement could be achieved without the help of a meditor, and with the exclusion of the U.N., the United States had become the only third party who could assume that responsibility with any hope of success.

After the GULF CRISIS, 1990–91, the United States played a key role in the convening of the MADRID PEACE CONFERENCE, 1991, which led to the first negotiations between Israel and the Palestinians (as members of a joint Jordanian-Palestinian delegation). And the first agreement between Israel and the PLO, known as the Declaration of Principles on Interim Self-Government Arrangements, which was negotiated in secret meetings held in Oslo under the auspices of the Norwegian government and launched the Oslo peace process, was formally signed at the White House in Washington, D.C., on September 13, 1993. The United States has followed closely the Oslo peace process from its very start. On several occasions, when direct negotiations between Israel and the PLO stalled, it intervened to jump-start them.

The United Nations played only a marginal role in the Madrid Conference, although the latter's objective was to achieve a comprehensive settlement of the Middle East conflict on the basis of Security Council Resolutions 242, 338, and 425. A representative of the secretary-general attended the conference as an observer, and the United Nations has been participating as an extraregional participant in the work of the multinational working groups that have been established by the conference to discuss regional issues, including the problem of refugees.

The U.N. has not been involved in the Oslo peace process, but since the signing of the Declaration of Principles, it has offered expertise and technical assistance to the newly established PALESTINIAN AUTHORITY, particularly with respect to institution building, and has enhanced its traditional economic and social programs in the West Bank and Gaza, the majority of which are carried out by UNRWA and the United Nations Development Programme. In addition to providing relief assistance and essential services to the Palestine refugees, whose number had increased to over 3.5 million by 1999 (about 1.3 million in the Gaza Strip and the West Bank and the remainder in Jordan, Lebanon, and Syria), UNRWA served until 1995 as a channel for international financial contributions to meet the payroll of salaries of the Palestinian police force. Other programs and agencies of the United Nations system are also becoming more active on the ground. Under the guidance of the U.N. special coordinator in the Occupied Territories, a post created by the secretary-general in June 1994, they are helping the Palestinian Authority to generate employment and cope with problems in health, education, environment, and sanitation, especially in Gaza.

The General Assembly has continued to consider the question of Palestine at each of its annual sessions. In the resolutions it has adopted since the OSLO AGREEMENTS, it has reaffirmed that the United Nations has a permanent responsibility with respect to the question of Palestine until the question is resolved in all its aspects in a satisfactory manner in accordance with international legitimacy, has asked the parties concerned to exert all the necessary efforts to ensure the continuity and success of the peace process, has stressed the need for the realization of the inalienable rights of the Palestinian people, and has called for increased international assistance to them.

F. T. Liu

BIBLIOGRAPHY

Gazit, Schlomo. *Palestinian Refugee Problem.* Tel Aviv: The Tel Aviv University, 1995.

Khouri, Fred J. "United Nations Peace Efforts." In *The Elusive Peace in the Middle East,* ed. by Malcolm H. Kerr. Albany: State University of New York Press, 1975.

Programme of Cooperation for the West Bank and Gaza Strip 1998–1999. United Nations Office of the Special Coordinator in the Occupied Territories. Gaza, 1998.

Progress Report of the UN Mediator on Palestine. General Assembly Official Records, third session, September 18, 1948, supplement no. 11 (A/648).

Report of the Commissioner-General of the United Nations Relief and Works Agency for Palestine Refugees in the Near-East, 1 July 1995–30 June 1996. General Assembly Official Records, fifty-first session, supplement no. 13 (A/51/13).

Report of the Commissioner-General of the United Nations Relief and Works Agency for Palestine Refugees in the Near-East, 1 July 1997–30 June 1998. General Assembly Official Records, fifty-third session, supplement no. 13 (A/53/13).

Report of the Committee on the Exercise of the Inalienable Rights of the Palestinian People, 1998. General Assembly Official Records, fifty-third session, supplement no. 35 (A/53/35).

Report of the Secretary-General Under Security Council Resolution 331 (1973) of 20 April 1973. Security Council Official Records, twenty-fourth Year, May 19, 1973, supplement for April, May, and June 1973 (S/10929).

Touval, Sadia. *The Peace Brokers: Mediators in the Arab-Israeli Conflict, 1948–1979.* Princeton, N.J.: Princeton University Press, 1982.

United Nations Resolutions on Palestine and the Arab-Israeli Conflict (1947–1992), 4 vols. Washington, D.C.: Institute for Palestine Studies, 1988.

Urquhart, Brian. *Ralph Bunche, an American Life.* New York: W.W. Norton, 1993.

Yearbook of the United Nations for the Years 1947–1996. New York: United Nations.

United Nations Conciliation Commission for Palestine

The United Nations Conciliation Commission for Palestine (UNCCP) was established as a three-member body by United Nations General Assembly Resolution 194 (III) of December 11, 1948. The governments of the United States, France, and Turkey designated representatives to sit on the UNCCP, whose chair initially rotated among the three on a monthly basis. The United Nations General Assembly resolution called upon the UNCCP to "take steps to assist the Governments and authorities concerned to achieve a final settlement of all questions outstanding between them." In accordance with other clauses in this historic resolution, the commission was to seek agreement among Arabs and Israelis regarding three issues:

- The Palestinian REFUGEES who had fled or had been expelled from their homes during the 1947–48 fighting, who should "be permitted to return to their homes at the earliest possible date"
- The final delimitation of the boundaries of the new Israeli state
- The establishment of an international regime for Jerusalem

From the start, the UNCCP had two parallel channels of communication with Arabs and Israelis: formal meetings with Arab *or* Israeli representatives, and informal, off-the-record talks, usually involving a single commissioner or staff member. Most of the real attempts at persuasion and conciliation were made during the latter type of meeting. As a result of the Arab states' firm position opposing direct dealings with the newly created Jewish state, the UNCCP, while paying lip service to the desirability of direct Arab-Israeli talks, assumed the role of go-between or courier between parties in conflict who would never actually meet around the same table.

The UNCCP's major activities and accomplishments took place during its first year of existence. The commissioners began a round of "shuttle diplomacy" of Middle Eastern capitals in February 1949, invited Arab foreign ministers to a conference in Beirut in March, and then organized the ambitious LAUSANNE CONFERENCE, 1949, where the commissioners met extensively with Arab and Israeli delegations between April and September, seeking without success a breakthrough on the territorial and refugee questions. The question of Jerusalem was relegated to a subcommittee operating separately from the Lausanne Conference; a proposed statute for the internationalization of Jerusalem was presented to the United Nations General Assembly in fall 1950.

From late January to mid-July 1950, the UNCCP convened another series of meetings with Israeli and Arab delegations, this time in Geneva, again with no progress to report on any major issue. The commission's final attempt at resolving political issues was the Paris Conference of September–November 1951. Unlike in its earlier peace efforts, the UNCCP prepared its own "comprehensive pattern of proposals" to submit to the parties, but the Paris Conference was bogged down in procedural wrangling, including Israel's challenge to the commission's right to submit its own proposals.

During its first three years of operation, the UNCCP was torn between two basic approaches to its task: whether it was to undertake "conciliation" in the narrow sense, dealing only with proposals put forth by the parties themselves; or whether, as successor to the late count, FOLKE BERNADOTTE, its functions should properly include "mediation" in a broader sense—the ability to propose its own peace plan for the consideration of Arabs and Israelis. The Arabs pressed for the latter; the Israelis insisted on the former approach.

After its failure at Paris in 1951, the UNCCP abandoned any further attempts to break the political deadlock and directed its attention to practical matters, especially the questions of reunification of families and inventorying of abandoned Arab LAND and other property in ISRAEL to be used when agreement would finally be reached over compensation of Palestinian refugees.

Neil Caplan

United Nations Security Council Resolutions 242 and 338

The June 1967 Arab-Israeli war led the United Nations (U.N.) Security Council to adopt the British-sponsored Resolution 242 on November 22, 1967, calling for an end to the conflict based on the concept of "land for peace": Israel would withdraw from Arab territory occupied in 1967 in return for peace treaties with Arab states. The preamble of Resolution 242 noted the "inadmissibility of the acquisition of territory by war and the need for a just and lasting peace in which every state in the area can live in security." Resolution 242's basic premises were "withdrawal of Israeli armed forces from territories of the recent conflict" and "the termination of all claims of states of belligerency and respect for the acknowledgment of the sovereignty, territorial integrity and political independence of every state in the area."

The parties to the conflict and the international community have understood Resolution 242 differently over the years. The Arabs argued that the provisions for Israel withdrawal "from territories of the recent conflict" applied to all of the territories Israel occupied in 1967, emphasizing the French text of the resolution, which spoke of *des territoires* (which can mean "*the* territories"). The PALESTINE LIBERATION ORGANIZATION rejected the resolution altogether until 1988 because it ignored Palestinian national rights and only spoke of a solution to the "refugee problem." Israeli opinion varied by party affiliation: the Labor Party maintained that any withdrawal must consider Israeli security needs, whereas the Likud Party argued that Israel's withdrawal from Sinai, completed in 1982, satisfied the call for withdrawal. Finally, the UNITED STATES noted that the word *the* was deliberately omitted in the English text (to read *territories occupied*, not *the territories occupied*) to secure Israeli support. According to U.S. officials at the time a withdrawal should occur with only minor boundary adjustments.

The ARAB-ISRAELI WAR OF 1973 prompted the second important security resolution dealing with Arab-Israeli peace, Resolution 338. Adopted on October 22, 1973, Resolution 338 called for a cease-fire, implementation of Resolution 242, and negotiations. It laid the basis for disengagement agreements between Israel and Syria in 1974 and Israel and Egypt in 1974 and 1975.

The United States has based all of its subsequent Middle East peace initiatives, including the ROGERS PLAN, the CAMP DAVID ACCORDS, the REAGAN PLAN, and the MADRID PEACE CONFERENCE, 1991, on the two resolutions.

Philip Mattar

BIBLIOGRAPHY

Quandt, William B. *Decade of Decisions: American Foreign Policy Toward the Arab-Israeli Conflict, 1967–1976.* Berkeley: University of California Press, 1977.

Smith, Charles D. *Palestine and the Arab-Israeli Conflict,* 2d ed. New York: St. Martin's Press, 1992.

United States

Official American attitudes toward the Palestinians have always been influenced by the U.S. relationship with Israel—or, before Israel's creation, by its relations with the Zionist movement—as well as by the U.S.-Soviet cold war rivalry, in which Palestinians never played a significant part. Only during the 1990s did the Palestinians begin to figure prominently in U.S. political and strategic considerations.

There has been a clear evolution in U.S. views, from the World War I years, when policymakers ignored the Palestinians altogether; through the quarter-century after the 1948 partition of Palestine, when Palestinians were regarded only as REFUGEES; to the Nixon-Kissinger and Carter eras in the 1970s, when U.S. policy began tentatively to take account of Palestinian "interests" and eventually of the Palestinians's "legitimate rights." Still, these changes have been gradual and halting. No American administration until that of George Bush in the early 1990s acted to include the Palestinians as legitimate partners in peace negotiations with Israel, and no administration has ever recognized the Palestinians's national aspirations.

President Woodrow Wilson (in office 1913–21) was not a strong supporter of ZIONISM, but he did openly endorse Britain's BALFOUR DECLARATION of 1917, which supported the establishment of a national home for the Jews in Palestine. Thus, Wilson established a Middle East policy from which the United States has never swerved. The declaration spoke of the Palestinians, who then constituted over 90 percent of Palestine's population, not as Palestinians or as Arabs, but as "non-Jews." Thereafter, American formulations on the issue continued to adopt this negative identification.

The KING-CRANE COMMISSION, 1919, a delegation sent by Wilson in 1919 to canvass Palestine's inhabitants, reported that the Zionist program anticipated "a practically complete dispossession of the present non-Jewish inhabitants," although these "non-Jewish" inhabitants, who constituted nine-tenths of the population, were "emphatically against" the Zionist program. The commission's observations were the only instance for the next two decades or more in which an official or semi-official United States body informed itself of the concerns of the Palestinians, but the commission's report appears to have had no impact on U.S. policy.

Throughout this period and into the 1940s, the United States accepted the Balfour Declaration without question as a legal instrument granting all or part of Palestine to the Jews. Democratic and Republican politicians, the media, and the small segment of the public who followed the issue generally sympathized with the Zionist cause and supported unlimited Jewish immigration to Palestine. President Franklin Roosevelt (in office 1933–45) came under criticism for his lack of concern about the fate of Jews during World War II, but as the war progressed, he was increasingly impressed by the Zionist notion that Jews needed Palestine as a haven from the Holocaust. American Zionist activists such as the Supreme Court justice Felix Frankfurter and Rabbi Steven Wise had ready access to Roosevelt and were able to keep the issue of Zionism before him.

After the King-Crane Commission, the United States took no note of Palestinians's increasing concern that Zionist plans and the growing Jewish immigration to Palestine would ultimately displace Palestinians from their homeland. In fact, President Roosevelt's idea of how to deal with conflicting Arab and Jewish claims in Palestine, never officially proposed but mentioned frequently to his friends and to the British, was to transfer tens of thousands of Palestinians out of Palestine to make room for Jewish immigration.

Harry Truman President Harry Truman (in office 1945–53) was ambivalent on the Palestine issue from the beginning. For some time, Truman resisted Zionist efforts to win his support for the establishment of a Jewish state in Palestine. He opposed the notion of any state based on a single race or religion, and he repeatedly expressed concern that a Jewish state would require U.S. military protection against militant Arab efforts to destroy it. Initially, Truman's principal interest in the issue was humanitarian. Although he did not support Jewish statehood, he did support large-scale Jewish immigration to Palestine as a means of relieving the plight of Jewish refugees displaced by the Second World War.

Truman was aware of Arab opposition to Jewish immigration, but he regarded it as unreasonable, tending not to understand that Palestinians viewed the Jewish influx as inevitably leading to their own reduction to minority status in Palestine. In an era in which the massive relocation of peoples, as in India, was seen as an appropriate means of resolving international conflicts, concepts like the Palestinians' attachment to the land or the relative justice of Arab versus Jewish land claims carried little weight in U.S. considerations. In any case, Palestinian objections were outweighed in U.S. considerations by the urgent needs of Jewish refugees, and by the domestic political pressures on Truman.

As it became increasingly clear that Britain, unable to resolve the Palestine issue, wished to disengage from the area, Truman experienced intense conflicting pressures—on the one hand, from Zionists in the United States and in his own entourage who sought his support for Jewish statehood, and, on the other hand, from diplomats in the U.S. government, particularly the State Department, who argued that the establishment of a Jewish state could lead to war, endanger U.S. oil supplies from Arabs and other U.S. commercial interests, and enhance influence of the SOVIET UNION in the area. Truman attempted for a time to ignore the importunings of both sides, but Zionist pressures ultimately prevailed. One of his closest friends, his former business associate Eddie Jacobson, was Jewish, and his closest White House aides—Clark Clifford, David Niles, and Max Lowenthal—were all strong Zionist supporters. He continued to listen to their quiet, pro-Zionist views even when he was most angry with more militant Zionist campaigners.

Truman's policy was governed throughout the Palestine debate by an element of bowing to the inevitable. Truman had no desire to involve the United States in the Palestine issue, but Britain's abdication forced his hand. Fearing that a failure to step in risked a serious loss of international prestige for the United States and would open the door to the Soviets in the Middle East, he committed the United States to playing a role. The choices facing him were not easy. He seemed to recognize the problems, both local and international, involved in establishing a Jewish state in an Arab region, but by the time the United Nations met in the fall of 1947 to vote on a proposal to partition Palestine into a Jewish and an Arab state, no viable alternatives to partition offered themselves. By this point, political opinion and a growing body of public opinion in the United States heavily favored Jewish statehood. Truman himself was undecided until days before the United Nations vote on November 29. In the end, he committed the United States to partition.

Israel's establishment as an independent state and its survival were inevitable by the time it declared independence on May 14, 1948. The credibility of the United Nations stood behind the establishment of a Jewish state, and by April 1948, Jewish forces in Palestine were confident of their ability to defeat the Arabs and assure the survival of their state. The United States could probably not have stopped creation of the new state even if it had wanted to, and Truman was accepting a fait accompli when he immediately recognized Israel. The perception that Israel was a creature of the United States had already been created by the time Truman extended recognition.

Thereafter, even those State Department officials who had opposed partition and Jewish statehood operated on the presumption that the situation existing on the ground at the end of the 1948 war was what should and would prevail. Israel was a sovereign state whose existence would continue, Jordan would control those parts of Arab Palestine not in Israeli hands, and U.S. policy toward the Palestinians would proceed from those basic realities. Official policy favored the resettlement of Palestinian refugees in the Arab states, which American officials believed would satisfy Palestinian grievances and resolve the Palestinian problem.

For the next few decades after 1948, until the Palestinians's own policies began to change, the United States treated the Palestinians only as refugees. Until the mid-1970s, all U.S. proposals regarding them involved humanitarian aid, limited repatriation to Israel in accordance with United Nations (U.N.) Resolution 194 of December 1948, and resettlement in the Arab countries. The United States did not pursue these proposals with any vigor, and it never supported the establishment of a Palestinian state. Nor did it ever support Israeli relinquishment to the Palestinians of territories captured during the 1948 war.

In fact, the United States supported Jordan's absorption of those areas of Palestine originally allocated to the Palestinian state. This remained the U.S. policy throughout the 1950s and 1960s, both because the division of Palestine between Israel and Jordan had become a fait accompli and because the Palestinians themselves never offered an option that the United States considered workable. Because the Palestinians demanded the dissolution of Israel and the return of all Palestine to Palestinian control, the United States felt free to ignore the Palestinians's political position.

The Palestinians were consistently left out of U.S. and international considerations because they did not constitute a state. U.N. Security Council Resolution 242, adopted after Israel's 1967 capture of territory from Jordan, EGYPT, and SYRIA, spoke of peace and territorial integrity for the *states* in the Middle East but addressed the Palestinians only as a "refugee problem." As late as 1969, when the Nixon administration put forth the ROGERS PLAN to resolve the ARAB-ISRAELI CONFLICT, the Palestinians were still spoken of only as refugees. Not until the 1970s, after the Palestinians had forced themselves on world attention with a series of spectacular acts of international terrorism and had begun to moderate their maximalist position, did the United State begin to regard them as a political factor. But even then, changes in the U.S. attitude continued to be limited by the fact that the Palestinians were not a sovereign nation and did not have to be treated as one.

The Palestinians were also a factor of little significance to the United States in its cold war struggle to limit Soviet influence in the Middle East. From the 1950s well into the 1980s, Israel's strategic importance and the Arab states' stability and political alignment were of far greater interest to American policymakers than any Palestinian concern. To the extent that the United States considered the Palestinians in political terms at all, it was as a radical, destabilizing element in the Middle East political picture.

During the cold war era, there arose two distinct schools of thought among U.S. officials with respect to Middle East policy. One school, often called the *globalists,* tended to view all developments in the Middle East in terms of U.S.-Soviet rivalry. The other school, known as *regionalists,* tended to focus on the significance of regional developments in a local context. Thus, the regionalist school looked on Arab hostility to Israel as arising from the events of 1948, particularly the dispossession of the Palestinians, whereas the globalist school was inclined to relate this hostility to Soviet aims in the area, often attributing it to Soviet inspiration and seeing a Soviet hand in virtually all local events. In an area of high cold war tensions, the globalist school was almost always ascendant in policymaking circles, with the result that policymakers virtually never took Palestinian grievances, the regional source of the conflict, into account and tended to view any disruption of the status quo as benefiting the Soviets.

The Nixon-Ford-Kissinger Era The Palestinians thus came to be viewed as agents of the Soviet Union, particularly during the tenure of Henry Kissinger, who served as national security adviser under President Richard Nixon (in office 1969–74) and as secretary of state in the administrations of both Nixon and Gerald Ford (in office 1974–77). Kissinger was a consummate globalist, guided in his Middle East policymaking almost solely by his view of U.S.–Soviet relations. Operating on the premise that Soviet influence in any region of the world could best be curbed by strengthening

America's allies and thwarting, or at least not assisting, Soviet friends, Kissinger defined U.S. goals in the Middle East as assuring Israeli military superiority while ignoring Arab concerns or making minimal efforts to wean the Arabs from Soviet influence. With respect to the Palestinians, this meant either ignoring their concerns or, when they appeared to threaten U.S. interests, as during the Jordan civil war in 1970–71, or when they conducted acts of international terrorism, actively attempting to thwart them.

After the 1973 war, in which an Egyptian-Iraqi-Syrian alliance attacked Israel, Kissinger increasingly saw the need to address the Palestinian issue in political terms, but because he perceived the Palestinians, specifically the PALESTINE LIBERATION ORGANIZATION (PLO), as terrorists and Soviet allies bent on the destruction of both Israel and Jordan, he did not view them as proper negotiating partners. Although he authorized secret contacts with the PLO in 1973 and 1974, his declared purpose was not to deal with the Palestinian issue but to buy time, mollifying the Palestinians in the hope of keeping them quiet while the peace process went forward on other fronts.

Throughout his involvement with the Middle East, Kissinger's efforts on the Palestinian issue were concentrated—largely in response to anti-Palestinian pressures from Israel—on finding ways to avoid addressing the matter. Israel had always studiously denied not only the centrality of the Palestinian issue to the Arab-Israeli conflict but the very existence of a separate Palestinian people. For example, Prime Minister Golda Meir had issued a well-publicized statement in 1969 denying that Palestinians had an identity distinct from that of the Arabs in general. Despite increased international and United Nations recognition of Palestinian identity and rights, including many U.N. resolutions supporting the Palestinian position, the United States continued throughout most of the Nixon-Kissinger era to follow the Israeli policy of denying that Palestinians existed as a separate people.

In the wake of the 1973 war, Kissinger initially envisioned negotiating a partial "disengagement" agreement between Israel and Jordan similar to those he mediated with Israel, Egypt, and Syria in 1974. However, when the Arab states attempted to block any return of occupied territory to Jordanian control and declared the PLO to be the sole legitimate representative of the Palestinian people, Kissinger dropped any thought of disengagement on the Jordan front. In 1975, as part of the second Sinai disengagement agreement with Egypt, Israel won a U.S. commitment not to "recognize or negotiate with" the PLO unless it first recognized Israel's right to exist and accepted U.N. Resolution 242. (This restriction was codified into U.S. law in 1985, with the added stipulation that the PLO must also renounce terrorism before the United States would negotiate with them.) Unwilling to fight Israel on this issue or to handle the growing domestic pressure against any dealings with the PLO, and not itself eager to face the Palestinian issue because of its cold war ramifications, the United States readily acceded to the Israeli-imposed constraints, although it interpreted these constraints as allowing it enough latitude to hold informal contacts with the PLO if ever necessary.

Despite Kissinger's attempts to avoid the Palestinian issue, in this period the United States arrived at a new awareness of the political dimensions of the issue. In late 1975, Deputy Assistant Secretary of State Harold Saunders, in congressional testimony that has come to be called the SAUNDERS DOCUMENT, characterized the Palestinian issue as the "heart" of the Arab-Israeli conflict and therefore as a political issue that had to be considered. Kissinger disavowed the testimony under Israeli pressure, but the Saunders Document did open the door to a new U.S. perception of the significance of the Palestinian issue. Although not recognizing the Palestinians's national aspirations, succeeding American administrations from the mid-1970s until Israel itself recognized the PLO in 1993 focused on attempts to reconcile the need to involve the Palestinians in the search for a political settlement with Israel's insistence that no such Palestinian role be permitted.

Jimmy Carter President Jimmy Carter (in office 1977–81) devoted much of his term to reconciling these contradictory factors. Carter set the tone for his Middle East policy with the appointment to the National Security Council staff of several officials—including National Security Adviser Zbigniew Brzezinski and Middle East director William Quandt—who had been involved in writing the Brookings Report, a proposal prepared before the 1976 presidential election urging the United States to pursue a comprehensive, as opposed to a step-by-step, solution to the Arab-Israeli conflict. The Brookings Report also endorsed the idea of a Palestinian state in the WEST BANK and the GAZA STRIP. Carter himself never supported independent Palestinian statehood, but he did support the notion of a Palestinian "homeland" of some sort, and he began his administration determined to involve the Palestinians, represented by the PLO if necessary, in the peace process. Unlike either his predecessors or his successor, Carter and his foreign policy aides, including Secretary of State Cyrus Vance, were willing to treat the PLO as the Palestinians' political representative, and in 1977 Vance spent considerable time negotiating with Israel and the Arab states a formula that would permit the PLO's attendance at a peace conference as part of a unified Arab delegation.

Carter's efforts to achieve real progress on the Palestinian issue were thwarted by Israel's vehement opposition, as well as by the PLO's inability to adopt a flexible formula for acceptance of Resolution 242. The final obstacle was the November 1977 trip to JERUSALEM of Egyptian president Anwar Sadat, which diverted all attention from organizing a comprehensive peace conference and led ultimately to the 1978 CAMP DAVID ACCORDS and a separate Egyptian-Israeli peace treaty in 1979. Despite the call in the accords for establishment of a Palestinian "self-governing authority" in the West Bank and Gaza, it was clear throughout the negotiations that the Israeli prime minister, Menachem Begin, would never relinquish Israeli control over any part of these territories or permit true Palestinian self-government.

There is an irony in the fact that the U.S. president most determined to seek some political solution to the Palestinian problem was faced by the Israeli leader most determined to thwart Palestinian aspirations. Carter added new concepts and new phrases to the American lexicon—for example, "Palestinian rights" and "Palestinian homeland"—but he was ultimately defeated by Begin's greater perseverance and by the pressures of Begin's American supporters. In the end, Carter was able to change the vocabulary of the Palestinian issue but not the reality.

Ronald Reagan The trend toward greater United States acceptance of the Palestinians as legitimate political contestants in the Arab-Israeli conflict suffered a setback with the advent in the 1980s of the Reagan-Shultz team, who were far more ready to support the hard-line policies of Begin and his successor, Prime Minister Yitzhak Shamir. President Ronald Reagan (in office 1981–89) and Secretary of State George Shultz both had an emotional connection to Israel that influenced their attitude toward all aspects of the Arab-Israeli conflict. Although in September 1982, early in Shultz's term as secretary of state, the United States launched a peace initiative known as the REAGAN PLAN, Reagan and Shultz never pursued either this initiative, or any of several proposals offered by the Arabs, or even a plan for an international peace conference pressed by moderate Israelis.

Shultz himself spoke often of the need to include Palestinians in the peace process, but he was firmly opposed to dealing with the PLO. Because he was unwilling to accept the West Bank Palestinians' loyalty to the PLO and was reluctant to challenge Israel's opposition to *any* Palestinian role in peace talks, he never seriously pursued the issue of Palestinian participation. Unlike Jimmy Carter, who had tried to find ways of including the Palestinians and the PLO, Reagan and Shultz never seriously faced the Palestinian issue and always actively sought to exclude the PLO from negotiations. Apparently taking his cue from the Israeli leadership, which believed it had destroyed Palestinian nationalism in the 1982 Lebanon war, Shultz conducted his Middle East policy, including the SHULTZ INITIATIVE, as though the PLO were a defunct organization and Palestinian nationalism a dead issue.

It is another irony, then, that it was George Shultz who finally authorized an official U.S. dialogue with the PLO. In late 1988, buoyed by the success of the West Bank-Gaza INTIFADA in turning world attention to the Palestinians' situation under the Israeli occupation, the PLO declared its acceptance of the two-state formula—that is, of an independent Palestinian state in the West Bank and Gaza, alongside Israel—recognized Israel's right to exist, accepted the validity of U.N. Resolution 242, and renounced terrorism. The PLO's concessions, and specifically its acceptance of the precise formula that the United States had demanded since 1975 as a condition for dialogue, forced Shultz's hand.

George Bush and James Baker The U.S.-PLO dialogue begun in December 1988 was established with considerable reluctance on the American side and was conducted at a low level, but the formal end of the taboo on contact with the PLO freed the Bush administration to maneuver through the peace process more efficiently. President George Bush (in office 1989–93) and his secretary of state, James Baker, had neither the previous administration's emotional feeling for Israel nor the Carter administration's conviction that the Palestinians deserved some sort of homeland. They approached the conflict as pure pragmatists, with little or no emotion or bias toward either side. Although they both eventually developed an intense personal dislike for the Israeli prime minister, Shamir, this was never translated into a political advantage for the Palestinians.

Although Bush and Baker believed that a successful American diplomatic intervention would enhance U.S. international prestige, they were not willing to risk failure. Their initial approach was thus extremely cautious, concentrated on procedural rather than substantive matters and deliberately geared toward achieving slow progress rather than dramatic breakthroughs. Their strategy, based on the assumption that Prime Minister Shamir wanted a peace settlement but would be difficult to move, was to let Shamir take the lead, cajoling him incrementally through the process. This cautious approach, however, yielded no progress. Shamir was interested only in continued Israeli control of the West Bank and Gaza and was impervious to Baker's threats to terminate the peace-seeking process.

The Iraqi invasion of Kuwait in August 1990 and the GULF CRISIS, 1990–1991, set peacemaking efforts on a new track. The cold war was ending, and the United States had emerged as the world's only superpower. This gave the United States the controlling hand in arranging a peace conference. In addition, President Bush's popularity in the United States was at an all-time high, and the American public was increasingly impatient with continued conflict between the Arabs and Israel—both factors that enabled Bush and Baker to maneuver around Israeli objections to the peace process. Finally, both the Palestinians and Israel were more vulnerable to U.S. pressure to make concessions, the Palestinians because they were severely weakened politically as a result of their support for Iraq during the war, the Israelis because they owed the United States a political debt for having defeated their strongest military enemy in the Arab world.

The most strikingly new aspect of the 1991 Bush-Baker peace initiative leading to the MADRID PEACE CONFERENCE, 1991, was that, in arranging for the conference, Secretary Baker dealt directly with West Bank and Gaza Palestinians known to have ties to the PLO. Thus he forced Israel, reluctantly and with heavy caveats, to acknowledge the Palestinians' central role in the peace process. Baker, in his extensive discussions with the Palestinians, was the first U.S. official to negotiate with Palestinians known to be speaking for the PLO.

The new U.S. willingness to deal seriously with Palestinian political concerns ultimately set the stage for the Israeli-Palestinian peace agreement of September 1993, the first of the OSLO AGREEMENTS. Because the Bush administration listened to the Palestinian perspective on ISRAELI SETTLEMENTS IN THE WEST BANK AND THE GAZA STRIP—particularly their fear that the settlements would lead to Israel's total absorption of the Occupied Territories and eventually foreclose the possibility of a peace agreement—Bush and Baker exerted strong pressure on Israel to freeze settlement construction. This pressure undoubtedly contributed to the defeat of Prime Minister Shamir and his hard-line Likud Party in Israel's 1992 general election, opening the way to an Israeli government more willing to deal with the Palestinians and to negotiate over the Occupied Territories.

Bill Clinton The record of President Bill Clinton on Palestinian-Israeli issues has been a mixed one, showing both unprecedented solidarity with Israel and, particularly in his later years in office, considerable understanding for the Palestinian perspective.

Clinton began his term with a focus on domestic issues and a disinterest in foreign affairs that discouraged U.S. intervention in the stagnating peace process. It is largely for this reason, in fact, that Israel's Labor government and the PLO leadership pursued the separate negotiations in Norway that ultimately led to the Oslo agreements. The United States remained aloof throughout the Oslo process. Moreover, although Clinton was active in organizing international aid donations to the Palestinian Authority and U.S. negotiators mediated later interim accords, including the Oslo II agreement of September 1995 and the Hebron agreement of January 1997, the administration essentially took a hands-off approach to the peace process until 1998.

Much of the reason for this aloofness lay in Clinton's difficult relationship with Israeli prime minister Benjamin Netanyahu during his term from 1996 to 1999; Netanyahu fundamentally opposed the peace process and delayed implementing the Oslo agreements. But the administration's basic approach to the process was rooted in the attitude that the United States should strive to remain apart from negotiations, not taking a position on any negotiating issue and remaining neutral between the parties. In the end, this approach promoted stagnation.

Clinton himself began to play a more active role in late 1998, when he intervened directly to negotiate the October Wye agreement calling for Israeli withdrawal from an additional 13 percent of West Bank territory. In December 1998, he addressed the Gaza conference at which Palestinian delegates formally rescinded provisions of the Palestinian National Charter advocating the destruction of Israel. During his speech to the conference, Clinton expressed understanding for the Palestinian plight under Israeli occupation and hinted at possible support for Palestinian aspirations to statehood. He later made other statements indicating an interest in Palestinian concerns and aspirations.

These statements, along with the close U.S.–Palestinian coordination that evolved after the Wye agreement and Clinton's confrontational relationship with Netanyahu, have been regarded by many Palestinians as highly significant symbolically and as signaling a new U.S. openness to the Palestinian perspective. At the same time, Clinton was widely regarded among Israelis and U.S. supporters of Israel during his first term as the most pro-Israeli president in history, and in concrete terms his administration has remained strongly pro-Israeli. This has been evident in the administration's failure to take real steps to halt Israeli settlement construction in the Occupied Territories; in its failure to prevent Israeli delays in implementing redeployments called for in the Wye agreement; in its apparent lack of concern about other Israeli occupation practices; and in its early decision to withdraw support for several U.N. resolutions that had provided the Palestinians with an aura of international legal support. For the most part, the position that further steps in the peace process should be left to the parties without U.S. intervention has put the Palestinians at a disadvantage by permitting Israel to maintain the status quo and, with no U.S. counterpressure, to consolidate and expand its control of the Occupied Territories.

Slow Evolution in U.S. Policy Each recent American president has clearly put his own mark on U.S. policy toward the Palestinians. This individual impact was most evident in the swings from Carter's interest in the Palestinian issue, to Reagan's total disinterest, to Bush's pragmatic recognition that a peace agreement could be achieved only if the Palestinians were included in the process. Despite the individual imprint of each president, however, U.S. policy has gradually moved from near-total ignorance of the Palestinian issue toward slow recognition, first that the question was more than a humanitarian issue of REFUGEES and finally that Palestinian concerns were central to achieving peace.

The evolution in American policy has been in large part a function of an evolution in Palestinian policy. The United States began to take heed of the Palestinian issue only in the early 1970s, after the Palestinians had attracted the world's attention with a series of international terrorist acts, and after they had hinted at a readiness to establish some sort of entity in the West Bank and Gaza, showing themselves capable of moderating their maximalist position and living alongside Israel. Only after the Palestinians put themselves forward as something other than refugees and began to press their national aspirations did the United States finally begin to treat the issue as a political one. Similarly, although the Reagan administration strove for eight years to ignore the PLO and avoid dealing with the Palestinian issue, the Palestinians once again brought their case to United States and world attention through the INTIFADA. With this uprising, as well as the acceptance of Israel's right to exist, they forced the United States to recognize the PLO and include the Palestinians in the peace process.

Kathleen Christison

BIBLIOGRAPHY

Christison, Kathleen. *Perceptions of Palestine: Their Influence on U.S. Middle East Policy.* Berkeley: University of California Press, 1999.

Lenczowski, George. *American Presidents and the Middle East.* Durham: University of North Carolina Press, 1990.

Neff, Donald. *Fallen Pillars: U.S. Policy Towards Palestine and Israel Since 1945.* Washington, D.C.: Institute for Palestine Studies, 1995.

Quandt, William B. *Peace Process: American Diplomacy and the Arab-Israeli Conflict Since 1967.* Washington, D.C.: The Brookings Institution; Berkeley: University of California Press, 1993.

———, ed. *The Middle East: Ten Years After Camp David.* Washington, D.C.: The Brookings Institution, 1988.

Spiegel, Steven L. *The Other Arab-Israeli Conflict: Making America's Middle East Policy, from Truman to Reagan.* Chicago: University of Chicago Press, 1985.

Suleiman, Michael W., ed. *U.S. Policy on Palestine from Wilson to Clinton.* Normal, Ill. Association of Arab-American University Graduates, 1995.

Tessler, Mark. *A History of the Israeli-Palestinian Conflict.* Bloomington: University of Indiana Press, 1994.

Tschirgi, Dan. *The Politics of Indecision: Origins and Implications of American Involvement with the Palestine Problem.* New York: Praeger, 1983.

V

Vatican

The welfare of more than 10 million Arab Christians living in the Middle East and North Africa has always been a source for concern for the Vatican. The presence of the Catholic Church in the Middle East goes far back in history. The Vatican's approach to the Middle East was largely guided by the geopolitical and cultural interests that Protestant and Catholic secular rulers deemed of high priority in the area. After World War I and the defeat of the Ottoman Empire, the League of Nations approved the British PALESTINE MANDATE on terms embodied in the BALFOUR DECLARATION (November 2, 1917), with its promise of the establishment of a Jewish homeland in Palestine. The status of JERUSALEM and the so-called HOLY PLACES then became the focus of a power struggle between France and Italy—the two Catholic powers most interested in Jerusalem—and, later on, between Palestinians and Israelis. The Vatican was caught in this power struggle, wanting to ensure that Catholic interests would be protected in Palestine now that a Protestant power, Britain, had become the arbiter among the conflicting Christian communities living there.

Since the establishment of the state of Israel in 1948, the Holy See has adopted a sympathetic stand toward the Palestinian people, regardless of their creed. This attitude was motivated principally by the Vatican's concern for the fate of Catholics in Palestine and the humanitarian needs of Palestinian refugees after the various wars between Arab and Israeli armies. After the ARAB-ISRAELI WAR OF 1948, the Vatican maintained close relations with local Catholic communities living in the Holy Land. These communities include the Greek Catholic (Melkite) Church, which is the largest of the communities (Uniates such as the Maronite, the Armenian, Syrian, and Coptic Churches) linked to Rome. The Melkite community was then headed by the archbishop of Saint John of Acre (Akka), Monsignor George Hakim. Hakim played an important role in the defense of his church's interests by acting as the go-between for the Vatican and the Israeli government. Catholic interests were also protected by the Latin Patriarchate and the Custody of the Holy Land, supervised by the Franciscans.

In the Israeli-Palestinian dispute, the Vatican has elected to choose the role of mediator and conciliator between Arabs and Israelis, Muslims and Jews, Muslims and Christians, and Jews and Christians. Since the mid-1960s, popes have condemned acts of TERRORISM by all sides and have called for a just and equitable solution to the ARAB-ISRAELI CONFLICT according to the resolutions adopted by the United Nations.

By the end of the 1960s, the Palestinians had resorted to guerrilla warfare. After the October 1973 war between Israel and the Egypt-Iraq-Syria alliance, however, moderate Palestinian leaders, inspired by the PALESTINE LIBERATION ORGANIZATION (PLO) chair, YASIR ARAFAT, toned down their call for armed struggle and expressed their readiness to accept a smaller Palestinian entity living side by side with Israel. These developments made it easier for the Vatican publicly to acknowledge Palestinian rights and to establish contacts with PLO leaders. In 1964, Pope Paul VI became the first pontiff to visit the Holy Land, and by the end of 1975 he had declared that both Palestinians and Israelis had to recognize each other's right to self-determination and nationhood. The same stand was adopted by Pope John Paul II, who welcomed

Arafat twice in Vatican City. After the INTIFADA in December 1987, John Paul II took the historic decision to appoint a Palestinian, Monsignor Michel Sabbah, as Latin patriarch of Jerusalem. The appointment of Sabbah was a clear indication of the Vatican's recognition that the Palestinians were enough of a nation to have one of their own take care of their spiritual and humanitarian needs.

In December 1993, the Vatican established formal diplomatic relations with the state of Israel. These relations are governed by a "Fundamental Accord" delimiting each party's rights and obligations. The Vatican's aim was to guarantee the rights—civil, religious, and political—of the Arab Catholic community living in Jerusalem and in Israel. Palestinian reactions were supportive, and only a few groups came out against the treaty. In other countries, such as Egypt and Lebanon, reactions to the Vatican's decision to establish official diplomatic relations with the Jewish state were in general negative. Arab religious and political leaders were surprised by the Vatican's decision; they had hoped that the Catholic Church would wait until the conclusion of an overall peace treaty in the Middle East to recognize the state of Israel. In 1994, the Holy See established a joint commission with the Palestinians to discuss the possibility of establishing diplomatic relations with the newly created autonomous Palestinian entity. In preparation for the second millennium since the birth of Christianity, the Vatican coordinated a series of celebrations (in Bethlehem and Nazareth) with both the Israeli government and the PALESTINIAN AUTHORITY.

George E. Irani

BIBLIOGRAPHY

Ferrari, Silvio. *Vaticano e Israele.* Turin, Italy: Sansoni Editore, 1991.

Irani, George Emile. *The Papacy and the Middle East: The Role of the Holy See in the Arab-Israeli Conflict.* Notre Dame, Ind.: Notre Dame Press, 1989.

Kreutz, Andrej. *Vatican Policy on the Palestinian-Israeli Conflict.* Westport, Conn.: Greenwood Press, 1990.

Water

Because humans divide the world into political units, water stored in rivers or aquifers passes from one unit to another. Such water resources are referred to as *common* or *shared international water resources.* The commonality of the resources and their scarcity, especially in the Middle East, have rendered them a source of conflict among the countries that share them.

Historic Palestine has a largely arid and semi-arid Mediterranean climate: wet and cold in winter, dry and hot in summer. Its main natural sources of water are aquifers, the Jordan River system, and numerous streams that carry runoff or floodwater. Although it is possible to study the natural water resources in the country without reference to its current political units (Israel, the WEST BANK, and the GAZA STRIP), these resources have long been a source of conflict between the Zionist movement and later Israel, on the one hand, and, on the other hand, the Palestinians and Arab state riparians in the Jordan River basin: JORDAN, LEBANON, and SYRIA. The use patterns of the Palestinians and Israelis have been profoundly impacted by political conflict, particularly since the ARAB-ISRAELI WAR OF 1967. In this conflict, Israel has held the advantage by a wide margin.

Topography The total area of Palestine under British rule (1917–48) was 27,024 square kilometers (1 square kilometer = 0.386 square mile): 26,320 square kilometers of landmass and 704 square kilometers of inland water. The region currently known as the West Bank has a landmass area of 5,540 square kilometers, and Gaza has 365 square kilometers, for a total of 5,910 square kilometers—about 23 percent of Palestine's landmass area—for the two regions. Israel's landmass area resulting from the 1949 armistice agreements, which do not exactly match the borders of the PALESTINE MANDATE, is 20,255 square kilometers.

Topographically, Palestine may be broadly divided into the following regions: the maritime or coastal plain, inland plains, central West Bank range, Galilee mountains, Jordan Rift valley, and Negev Desert. The coastal plain runs parallel to the Mediterranean from the border with Egypt in the south to the border with Lebanon in the north, interrupted in the north by Cape Carmel and Haifa Bay. It is about 270 kilometers long: 40 kilometers wide in the south in Gaza, decreasing to about 5 kilometers at the border with Lebanon; most of it is irrigable. The coastal plain overlies one of the main aquifers in the country. The interior plains include Marj ibn Amir (Esdraelon), traditionally viewed as the most fertile zone by Palestinians; Jezreel Plain; and Baysan (Bet She'an) Plain, all of which are wedged between, on the one hand, the Jordan Rift and the coastal plain and, on the other hand, the central range and the Galilee mountains.

The central range stretches between the maritime plain in the west and the Jordan Rift in the east. It is the topographical backbone of the country as well as the dominant hydrological region, for it is the principal water source of the chief renewable aquifer in Palestine, the Mountain aquifer, as well as the source of numerous wadis (beds or valleys of streams) and minor rivers flowing west toward the Mediterranean and east toward the Jordan River. The width of the mountains in this range varies from 24 to 40 kilometers, and the highest peaks exceed 1,000 meters above mean sea level. Good rainfall and moderate climate in the central range provide hospitable grounds for dry

WATER
Groundwater flow
Groundwater divide
Israel National Water Carrier
Armistice Demarcation Line, 1949
East Ghor Canal
Palestinian Territory Occupied by Israel (June 1967)
Syria/Israel Cease-Fire Line, 1967
Beaufort
Litani River
LEBANON
Quneitra
SYRIA
Jordan River
Golan Heights
Sea of Galilee
Haifa
Tiberias
Nazareth
Mukhaiba Dam
Yarmuk River
Mediterranean Sea
Jenin
Northern Aquifer
Tulkarm
Nablus
Jordan River
East Ghor Canal
Western Aquifer
West Bank
Tel Aviv
Mountain Aquifer
Amman
Ramallah
Jericho
JORDAN
Coastal Aquifer
Jerusalem
ISRAEL
Eastern Aquifer
Dead Sea
Gaza
Hebron
Gaza Strip
Rafah
N
Beersheba
EGYPT
0
20 Miles

SOURCE: The Jerusalem Fund

farming, especially for olive trees and, traditionally, wheat. The foothills of the range slope mildly to the west and sharply to the east, because the distance to the Mediterranean is greater than that to the Jordan River and because there is a precipitous fall in altitude in the Jordan valley.

The Galilee mountains make up all of northern Palestine, with the exception of the coastal plain between Acre and the Lebanese border and the Jordan Rift. Their, and Palestine's, highest peak is Mount al-Jarmaq (Meron), near the town of Safad, 1,208 meters above mean sea level. Dry farming, as in the central range, is the main form of agriculture in this region.

The Jordan Rift comprises but a small segment of the great Syrian-African Rift, extending from the Horn of Africa to Mount Amanos in Turkey. The Jordan Rift lies 210 meters below mean sea level at Lake Tiberias (Kinneret), or the Sea of Galilee, and about 400 meters below mean sea level at the Dead Sea, the lowest point on earth. The hydrological significance of the Jordan Rift stems from its cradling of the Jordan River system, the principal surface water source in Palestine, which it shares with Jordan, Lebanon, and Syria. The Jordan Rift is also fertile ground for irrigated agriculture thanks to the natural greenhouse effect created by its low elevation and to its warm winter temperature.

The Negev is a vast desert, nearly triangular, in the south of the country, claiming an area close to 12,500 square kilometers, or slightly less than half of Palestine's total area. It overlies a tremendous nonrenewable (or fossil) aquifer. Some of the land in the Negev is irrigable, though crops require large quantities of water because of very high daytime temperature.

Rainfall and Evapotranspiration The climate of Palestine is Mediterranean: winter is the season of precipitation and summer is dry, leaving the soil with a moisture deficit for most of the year and making irrigation mandatory for successful farming. The main form of precipitation and the origin of all water resources, apart from the Jordan River system, is rain. Massive snow, as occurred in 1991–92, for example, is rare, and dewfall is minimal. The chief characteristic of rainfall in Palestine is its pronounced variability, both in space and in time.

Commonly, the rainy season runs from October through the end of April, with January the rainiest month. Perhaps more than two-thirds of the annual rainfall occurs between November and February. The winter rain can be advantageous to crops because of lower evaporation. A 400- to 500-millimeter/year winter rainfall in Palestine might be the equivalent of 600–700 millimeters/year in a place like Arizona with summer rain. This advantage, however, is often compromised by the intensity of the rainfall, which is sometimes concentrated within a very few days, causing floods and soil erosion. This concentration of rainfall also reduces the amount of water infiltration into the soil, as well as the amount percolating to aquifers.

In addition to seasonal variation, rainfall fluctuates from year to year, with droughts that sometimes last for several years. Droughts greatly reduce replenishment of aquifers and surface watercourses and have deleterious effects on rain-fed or rain-watered agriculture.

Finally, Palestinian rainfall varies spatially. Generally, it tends to decrease from north to south, making Palestine a transitional zone between the Middle East's humid north and arid south. It also tends to decrease from higher to lower altitudes, and from areas with greater exposure to rain-bearing winds—like the western slopes of the central range—to areas exposed to down wind or rain shadows—like the eastern slopes of this range. Rainfall (south to north) averages between 300 and 600 millimeters/year in the coastal plain, 600–900 millimeters/year in the central mountains, 100–400 millimeters/year in the Jordan valley, and less than 100 millimeters/year in the Negev.

Much of the rainfall evapotranspires. Some also percolates deep underground, replenishing the aquifers. The remainder simply runs off. The available data on potential evapotranspiration are scant; it can amount to two-thirds of the rainfall in the central mounts to three-quarters in the coastal plain, and much greater than that in the Jordan valley and the Negev.

Natural Water Resources The natural water sources in what is now the West Bank and Gaza are summarized in Table 1. The data lack spatial and temporal long-term continuity and have been contested by both Israeli and Palestinian sources, so they ought to be considered tentative. Also, they are averages, and so do not reflect the sharp fluctuations common from year to year. Further, the volume of the Jordan River system in the table represents the total flow of the system, not just the contribution of Palestine.

Groundwater As indicated in Table 1, the West Bank and Gaza's chief water source is groundwater, for after evapotranspiration, most of the water percolates underground and little runs off, as a result of the highly absorbent rock formations in the area. The principal groundwater basin is the Mountain aquifer, which comprises three subbasins—eastern, northeastern, and western, according to the direction of the flow.

The water in the western aquifer, the most bountiful of the three, flows toward the Mediterranean; its natural drains are two main groups of springs: Ras al-Ayan (Rosh Haayan), which feeds the al-Awja (Yarkon) River, and al-Timsah (Tanninim). It has a replenishment area of 1,600–1,800 square kilometers. The northeastern aquifer flows toward the Baysan and Jezreel plains. Its natural drains are springs in the West Bank and Israel, and it has a replenishment area of 500–590 square kilometers. Both the northeastern and western aquifers are recharged from the West Bank. Both can be—and are—tapped from both Israel and the West Bank. Israel, however, essentially "replaced" the springs, draining both aquifers on its side of the border by hundreds of wells.

TABLE 1

Water Resources in Israel and the West Bank and Gaza (In million cubic meters per year)

Source	Potential
Renewable aquifers:	
Mountain:	
Eastern	100
Northeastern	140
Western	360
Gaza	50
Coastal	300
Galilee:	
Eastern	45(?)[a]
Western	145
Carmel	70
Araba (Arava)	25[b]
Surface:	
Jordan River basin	1,500
Floodwater	90
Fossil aquifer:	
Negev	70 bcm[c]

Sources: American Friends of the Middle East, *The Jordan Water Problem,* Washington, D.C., 1964; Ben Gurion University of the Negev with Tahal Consulting Engineering Ltd., "Israel Water Study for the World Bank," Washington, D.C.: World Bank 1994; and Arie Issar, et al., "On the Ancient Water of the Upper Nubian Sandstone Aquifer in Central Sinai and Southern Israel," *Journal of Hydrology,* 17 (1972): 353–74.

Notes: [a]This figure consists of the potential of one aquifer and the currently exploited volume, not the potential, of another aquifer. Thus the figure is an underestimate.

[b]Could be overexploited at 60 mcmy for an interim period.

[c]bcm = billion cubic meters.

The eastern aquifer flows toward the Jordan River and is naturally drained by several groups of springs in the West Bank. A small fraction of its flow discharges into the Jordan River and another leaks into Israel. That aquifer's replenishment area amounts to 2,000–2,200 square kilometers.

The second major renewable groundwater basin in Palestine is the coastal aquifer, which underlies the coastal plain in both Gaza and Israel and has been referred to in Gaza as the *Gaza aquifer.* It is tapped in both Israel and Gaza. It has a recharge area of 1,800 square kilometers.

In addition to the renewable aquifers, a tremendous nonrenewable (fossil) aquifer underlies the Negev desert, in Israel. The aquifer may contain a total of 70 billion cubic meters (bcm). Its water is brackish but suitable for irrigation.

Surface Water Surface water in Palestine is supplied by two sources, chiefly by the Jordan River, but also by runoff water inside the country.

Runoff water gathers in numerous streams. The vast majority of these streams originate at the watershed of the central mountains, with one group flowing east toward the Jordan River and the other west toward the Mediterranean. The western wadis can be tapped from Israel and the West Bank and Gaza; the eastern are tapped from Israel and the West Bank. The total volume of floodwater referred to in Table 1, 90 million cubic meters/year (mcm/y), is the mean annual exploitable volume, not the total runoff, which is estimated at 140 mcm/y. How much of this runoff can be tapped from Israel and how much from the West Bank and Gaza is unclear, especially since the volume of floodwater in the West Bank has been poorly monitored in the past. Harnessing floodwater is costly because it is distributed

TABLE 2
Riparians' Contribution to the Flow of the Jordan Basin (In million cubic meters per year)

SUBBASIN	AVERAGE	SYRIA	JORDAN	LEBANON	ISRAEL	W. BANK
Upper Jordan:						
Headwaters:						
Banyas	125	125				
Dan	250	125		125		
Al-Hasibani	125			125		
Al-Hula:						
Burayghith	10			10		
Springs	60				60	
Direct rainfall	90				90	
Eastern rim	35	35				
Western rim	15				15	
Evaporation	-60				-60	
Lake Tiberias:						
Local catchment[a]	210	75			135	
Direct rainfall	65				65	
Evaporation	-290				-290	
Yarmuk	435	320	115			
Lower Jordan:						
Eastern rim	210	210				
Western rim	65				30	35
Evaporation	-20	-10		-5		-5
Total	1325	680	315	260	40	30
(%)	100	51	24	20	3	2

Note: [a]Including saline springs.

among many streams and because its volume varies considerably from year to year.

The Jordan River originates at the slopes of Mount Hermon (Arabic, *Jabal al-Shaykh,* or "the old man's mountain," because its highest peaks are covered with snow all year) in Syria and Lebanon and empties into the Dead Sea. Mount Hermon, with a highest elevation of 2,800 meters above mean sea level and an annual precipitation of 1,200–1,500 millimeters, provides most of the water to the three tributaries—the Banyas, Dan, and al-Hasibani rivers—that constitute the Jordan River's headwaters. The Jordan River, which acquired its name from the point of confluence of these three tributaries, descends southward through Lake al-Hula (70 meters above sea level) and its contiguous marshlands, both drained by Israel between 1951 and 1958 against Syria's objections that parts of the irrigation canals are actually in the demilitarized zone. Ten kilometers away from its former exit from Lake al-Hula, the Jordan River tumbles down to become a deep gorge, until it finally reaches Lake Tiberias (Sea of Galilee or Lake Kinneret) at 212 meters below mean sea level. From its origins to its entry into Lake Tiberias, the Jordan River system is known as the *upper Jordan.* The pear-shaped Lake Tiberias is actually the river's largest freshwater reservoir, with a volume of 4,000 mcm, an area of 165 square kilometers, and a depth of 44 meters. The lake also drains areas in the Golan Heights to the east and in the Galilee mountains to the west, in addition to possessing saline springs on its shore and at its bottom.

A short distance from its debouchure at Lake Tiberias, the Jordan River receives its largest single feeder, the Yarmuk River, which drains large areas in Syria's Hawran Plain and the Golan Heights as well as in Jordan's northeast. Between its meeting with the Yarmuk River and its discharge into the Dead Sea, the Jordan River is fed by numerous small streams and minor rivers from Jordan in the east, and from Israel and the West Bank in the west. The stretch between Lake Tiberias and the Dead Sea is referred to as the *lower Jordan.* For hydrogeological reasons, the lower Jordan meanders significantly to the point where its river length (200 kilometers) becomes nearly double the distance between Lake Tiberias and the Dead Sea.

The Dead Sea itself is an elongated (north-south) inland lake that resembles a blue pendant at the end of the Jordan River. It drains an area of 40,000–47,000 square kilometers that includes—in addition to its main feeder, the Jordan River system—numerous streams from the west and east. The Dead Sea's dimensions vary according to the weather. Its maximum depth is 400 meters, its maximum length is 74–80 kilometers, and its maximum width is 16–18 kilometers. The water volume in the lake exceeds 140 cubic kilometers. Because of the diversion of water from the Jordan River system, the water level in the Dead Sea has dropped in recent years to 401 meters below mean sea level. The Dead Sea's water has a salinity of 250,000 milligrams/liter chlorides, or nine times greater than that of ocean water, and a density 20–30 percent more than the density of fresh water. Besides salt, Dead Sea water is rich in minerals, notably potash and bromide, and both Israel and Jordan exploit its mineral wealth. Before 1967, Israel controlled the southwestern quadrant of the sea, and Jordan the three other quadrants; however, the June 1967 war brought the northwestern quadrant under Israeli control.

Overall, the Jordan River system drains an area of 17,600–19,800 square kilometers and carries a flow of about 1,500 mcm/y, with wide variations from year to year. By far, Syria is the largest contributor of drainage area and of water flow to the Jordan River system, followed by Jordan and Lebanon; Israel and the West Bank are relatively minor contributors (Table 2).

From the point of view of water exploitation, the Jordan basin has some favorable characteristics. More than one half of its major tributaries is base flow, which reduces its susceptibility to rain fluctuations. Further, the steep slope of the Jordan Rift makes possible the utilization of gravity in the transportation of water within the parts of the rift. The steep gradients also create conditions suitable for hydroelectric power generation. Although the small volume of water in the basin severely limits the amount of electricity that can be tapped from the river system, especially when compared to today's consumption, the Jordan valley and the Dead Sea have inspired schemes that could generate significant amounts of hydropower by channeling water from the Mediterranean Sea or Red Sea and harnessing the elevation difference.

On the other hand, the low elevation of the Jordan Rift makes transporting water to higher elevations energy-intensive, hence costly. Also, because the extreme temperatures of the summer months caused high levels of evaporation, notably in Lake Tiberias and the al-Hula valley, before the lake and the marshlands were drained, they were drained. But even in the channel itself, the heat and the dense vegetation cover in the river's floodplain result in high rates of water loss, albeit partly productive loss, to evapotranspiration. Moreover, although the steep gradients may be advantageous for hydropower generation and diversion, the high velocity they impart to the water is responsible, particularly during winter floods, for extensive soil erosion, and in some years for damage to crops as well.

Control of Water Resources The water problem in Palestine can be attributed to the imbalance between the resources and population, stemming from the influx of Israeli immigrants, who also sought to take control of the scarce resources. Although the conflict between Israelis and Palestinians has centered on land, water has also been a primary object of contention. From the start, leaders of the Zionist movement saw water as key to the development of large-scale irrigation, itself a prerequisite for the absorption of large numbers of immigrants and for hydropower generation that could compensate for the country's lack of coal. But, coming as they did from Europe, where water is plentiful, the Zionist immigrants must also have been struck by the dryness of the country; had they come from the Arabian Peninsula, for example, water schemes would have been less of a preoccupation to them.

Water first became a major political issue in Palestine during the process of splitting up the territory of the Fertile Crescent between Britain and France after the defeat of the Ottoman Empire in World War I. Zionist leaders then lobbied the two

European powers to incorporate within the boundaries of Palestine the headwaters of the Jordan River as well as segments of the Yarmuk River and the Litani River (in today's Lebanon) after it bends west toward the Mediterranean. When, after prolonged negotiations, Britain and France finally drew the boundaries of their mandated territories in 1923, the Palestine that was assigned to the British PALESTINE MANDATE bounded some of these water sources, such as the lakes of al-Hula and Tiberias and the Dan River. Nonetheless, Palestine's boundaries did not include the Litani nor all of the Banyas, the Hasibani, or the Yarmuk, as the Zionist leaders had originally proposed. However, most of these aims were finally realized after the June 1967 war.

Britain and France sought to divide and regulate the use of the Jordan River basin, which had suddenly become a basin shared among Lebanon, Palestine, Syria, and Transjordan, as present-day Jordan was known until 1950. The most significant agreement between the two powers was the 1920 Anglo-French Convention, which accorded priority of access to the waters of the upper Jordan (from its origin to its exit from Lake Tiberias) and Yarmuk Rivers to Syria and Lebanon; Palestine was to use the residual or "surplus" water.

Another noteworthy development during those years was Britain's granting in 1921 of a seventy-year concession to Pinhas Rutenberg, a Zionist engineer and activist, for electric hydropower generation on the Jordan. Rutenberg created the Palestine Electric Corporation, Ltd., in 1923 and built a power plant just south of the place where the Yarmuk and the Jordan rivers met, a plant that was destroyed during the 1948 war. The terms of Rutenberg's concession allowed Transjordan to develop the Yarmuk water in excess of the station's requirement, but his corporation always claimed that there was no "excess water."

The conflict over the Jordan basin intensified after the creation of Israel in 1948. In 1953, the United States dispatched a special ambassador, Eric Johnston, to mediate the conflict. After two years of shuttle diplomacy, Johnston formulated what has become known as the Johnston Plan for dividing the basin waters among the Arab riparians and Israel. Johnston's division reaffirmed the Anglo-French Convention's assignment of priority of use to Syria and Lebanon, and extended it to Jordan as well. The plan, however, contained a political portion calling for Arab-Israeli cooperation in the development of the basin. The Arabs made their acceptance of that portion conditional on the resolution of the Palestinian problem, so the plan was never ratified. Nevertheless, both Jordan and Israel withdrew water in line with the plan until 1967, and the United States made its aid to Israel and Jordan for projects in the basin conditional on their adherence to the plan.

In 1959, Israel began plans for its "National Water Carrier," which from 1964 pumped water from the northwestern corner of Lake Tiberias at al-Tabigha and transported it through a system of canals, tunnels, and pipes to the coastal plain and the Negev and two areas where most of the irrigable land in Israel is located. In defense of the project it referred to the Johnston plan, urging the United States and the world community to stand by it. The Arab states objected to Israel's diversion scheme, arguing, among other things, that customary law did not allow out-of-basin transfer before the satisfaction of needs within the basin itself. To stop Israel from implementing its project, they attempted in 1964, after much hesitation and bickering, to divert the Hasibani and Banyas rivers' water. Israel responded by shelling the diversion sites, and the diversion scheme was aborted.

As a result of its occupation of the Golan Heights in the June 1967 war, Israel came to control all the headwaters of the Jordan River system and an even larger stretch of the Yarmuk River than it had before the war. It began to draw greater amounts of water from the basin than its Johnston plan quota, meanwhile censoring Jordanian and Palestinian water withdrawals. As a result of Israel's invasion of Lebanon in 1982 and its retention of a "security zone" in the south, Lebanon also has been unable to tap water from the basin.

As for groundwater, both the Palestinian and Jewish communities in Mandate Palestine pumped or diverted small quantities, some for household use but mainly for irrigation of crops, notably citrus and vegetables. By the mid-1940s, the irrigated land in the country was roughly 500,000 *dunums,* about half of it planted with citrus. The area of citrus cultivation by both sides was nearly equal, but the Palestinian vegetable area was nearly three times as large as the corresponding Jewish area, a disproportion that suggests greater use of irrigation water by the Palestinians than by the Jews.

As a consequence of the establishment of Israel, many of the groundwater resources, notably the coastal aquifer, fell beyond the reach of the Palestinian refugees who were expelled or fled to Gaza and the West Bank. The Israelis, on the other hand, maintained their access to the sources they had previously used. Both sides continued to develop the water resources on their side of the border, but the Palestinians, still reeling from the *al-nakba* (disaster), could not drill as many wells or draw as much water from the Mountain aquifer. Though it is unclear how Israel would have responded had Palestinians tried to extract more water from the northeastern and western basins of the Mountain aquifer than they did, the stringent controls Israel imposed on Palestinian withdrawals after 1967 may suggest that Israel was prepared to share only a limited amount of water.

The situation worsened further for the Palestinians after Israel seized the West Bank in 1967, thus gaining control of all the water resources west of the Jordan River, including basins that Jews had not had access to before, such as the eastern basin of the Mountain aquifer.

Israel effectively acted as a sovereign over the water resources in the West Bank and Gaza and over the areas of the Jordan River basin under its control. It declared the area adjacent to the Jordan River in the West Bank a closed military area, denying the Palestinians access to both land and water. Concerning the rest of the West Bank and Gaza, Israel issued a series of military orders—the main form of legislation in the two Palestinian regions under Israeli occupation—arrogating for itself the power to license well drilling and to set pumping quotas for those already drilled, enforced through metering and inspection. Israel also "leased" for forty-nine years—the standard period of stand-land lease in Israel—the management of the water sector in the West Bank and Gaza to Mekorot, the quasi-state-run Israeli water company. At the same time, the Palestinian water management bodies that had been in existence before 1967 were marginalized and relegated to administrative functions. Policy and technical matters were all put in the hands of the Israeli state's representatives.

The water issue has been taken up in the negotiations between Israelis and Palestinians begun at the MADRID PEACE CONFERENCE, 1991. The Declaration of Principles that the two sides negotiated in Oslo and signed in Washington, D.C., on September 13, 1993, contained two basic principles for resolving the water conflict: equitable allocation of water rights in, and joint management of, the common resources. Subsequent agreements have made transitional arrangements that gave the Palestinians a limited role in the management of their water sector, but a full-scale resolution of the water issues has been deferred to the final-status negotiations.

Water Use Water use in Palestine is characterized by a wide gap between the Israelis and Palestinians as well as between Jewish Israelis and Palestinian Israelis. The gap is manifested in the quantity and quality of the water used, level of service, and irrigation of agricultural land. Overall, Israel extracts more than 90 percent of the groundwater for its own and its settlers' use, compared to less than 10 percent used by the Palestinians in the West Bank and Gaza. Furthermore, Israel extracts water from all the aquifers, whereas the Palestinians are limited to the Mountain aquifer and the segment of the coastal aquifer that underlies Gaza.

In the Jordan basin, since 1967 Israel has diverted between 600 and 700 mcm/y. This quantity exceeds by 200–300 mcm/y Israel's quota of 400 mcm/y under the Johnston plan. The Palestinians, on the other hand, get none of the basin's water, even though the West Bank had been allotted 215 mcm/y under the plan. Even the small amounts that Palestinian farmers had pumped directly from the river to water crops along its western bank has been denied them since 1967, when Israel turned the river in the West Bank into a closed military area.

The Israeli-Palestinian Water Gap The water gap between Palestinians and Israelis is summarized in Table 3. The table tells us that the Palestinian per capita household use of water is one-fourth to one-third that of the Israelis. The water-use gap extends to Israel itself, where the centralized, ethnically based water allocation discriminates against the Palestinian Israeli population—those who are PALESTINIAN CITIZENS OF ISRAEL. The water quotas of the Palestinian citizens of Israel, who constituted about 16 percent of Israel's population in the early 1990s, were similar to those of the Palestinians in the West Bank and Gaza. Consequently, we can speak of a "Jewish–Palestinian" water gap in Palestine.

The low level of Palestinian household use is basically a function of the stringent conditions of supply, the lack of sewage systems, and the lack of piped water for one-third of the population in the West Bank, as well as of the high price of water—far higher than in Israel when compared to the relative per capita income of both sides.

TABLE 3

Summary Israeli-Palestinian Water Use

ITEM	PALESTINIAN	ISRAELI
Use per capita (cmy):		
Aggregate	104	371
Household	30	100
Use Growth (1967–90) (mcm)	20	334
Irrigated agriculture:		
Total area (1000 *dunums*)	200	2,057
Area per capita (*dunums*)	0.1	0.43
Irrigated/cultivated (%)	5	50
Irrigated/irrigable (%)	33–53	95

The water-use gap is even more striking in irrigation, which is the main water-consuming activity for both sides. For example, the irrigated area is four to five times greater per Israeli than per Palestinian, so that 95 percent of the irrigable land in Israel is irrigated, compared to only 25–33 percent in the West Bank. A similar gap can also be seen in Israel itself among Jews and Palestinians.

Above and beyond the irrigated area within its own borders, Israel has allowed the settlers in the West Bank and Gaza to irrigate tens of thousands of *dunums* (1 *dunum* = 0.10 hectare = 0.25 acre) of confiscated land, which consequently use most of the 40 mcm/y that the settlements take from the eastern aquifer.

The irrigation water gap is also evident in the types of crops grown by the two sides. The Palestinians irrigate virtually no crops other than vegetables and fruits, whereas the Israelis irrigate, in addition to horticultural crops, large areas of such field crops as wheat and cotton. Further, large amounts of irrigation water in Israel are devoted to export crops, chiefly vegetables, citrus, and cotton.

Water Pollution Quantities apart, Palestine's water resources have become increasingly polluted. Even where they are presently not polluted, pollution may be latent. Pollution makes water hazardous to public health, and salinity in particular may render it unfit for irrigation. Numerous contaminants can find their way into the water system, whether surface or underground, whether during transportation or usage or in situ. They may be biological (such as bacteria, viruses, parasites), organic chemical (such as benzene and vinyl chloride), or nonorganic chemical, whether toxic (lead, mercury) or nontoxic (nitrates and salt). The contaminants are diffused into the water through the release of untreated wastewater, dumping of municipal and industrial waste, storage (underground gasoline, for example), abandoned wells, urban storm runoff, landfills and dumps, agricultural inputs, and livestock. In Palestine, overpumping (pumping beyond an aquifer's safe yield) from the coastal and Mountain aquifers lowered the water table, thereby leading to a rise in salinity, in the coastal aquifer by the inland advance of the heavier seawater and in the Mountain aquifer by brine intrusion from adjacent rock formations. (Salinity makes water unfit for drinking and irrigation.) Salinity is most serious in Gaza, where more than 60 percent of the water has salinity concentration of 500 milligrams/liter (mg/l) chlorides, or double the safe drinking-water guidelines identified by the World Health Organization. In the Mountain aquifer, Israel has evaded salinity problems by shifting the locations of wells, but the problem may have only been postponed. Salinity has also been rising in the upper layers of the eastern basin of the Mountain aquifer; more specifically, in the upper layers from which the Palestinians pump their water.

Nitrate concentration from wastewater and organic fertilizers has also been on the rise. In Israel, nitrate concentration in the coastal aquifer doubled over the 1970s and 1980s. In Gaza, nitrate concentration in the aquifer underlying the refugee camps, which lack a sewage system, may have reached 90 mg/l, or double the allowable maximum concentration by European standards. Indeed, significant portions of the aquifer underlying Gaza may have become moribund as a result of pollution.

On the other hand, water quality is still excellent in the northeastern and western basins of the

Mountain aquifer and in most springs in the eastern aquifer. But this apparently good quality does not necessarily mean that there are no pollution hazards: usually, as a result of the slowness of groundwater movement, a good deal of time lapses between the release of a contaminant and its diffusion into an aquifer. In general, observers on both sides are concerned pollution could one day pose a serious threat to the water supply of both Israelis and Palestinians.

Pollution also plagues the Jordan River, notably its lower segment. Both Israel and Jordan dump their municipal waste into the lower channel and into the Yarmuk River as well. In 1964, Israel also diverted to this channel the largest saline springs on the shore of Lake Tiberias. As a result, the lower Jordan has become a "chemical soup" unfit for either human or agricultural use, with salinity reaching 2,000 mg/l chlorides. Fortunately, the two countries signed a water agreement as part of their 1994 peace treaty in which they pledged to take measures protecting the water of both the Jordan and the Yarmuk rivers, including desalination of most of the water of the saline springs that now empty into the river and treatment of wastewater to irrigation standards before its release into the Yarmuk River.

Sharif S. Elmusa

BIBLIOGRAPHY

American Friends of the Middle East. *The Jordan Water Problem.* Washington, D.C., 1964.

Atlas of Israel. New York: Macmillan Publishing, 1985.

Ben Gurion University of the Negev with Tahal Consulting Engineering, Ltd. "Israel Water Study for the World Bank." Washington, D.C., 1994.

Blake, G. S. *Geology and Water Resources of Palestine.* Jerusalem: Government of Palestine, 1947.

Conservation Foundation. *Groundwater Protection: The Final Report of the National Groundwater Policy Forum.* Washington, D.C., 1987.

Elmusa, Sharif S. "The Jordan-Israel Water Agreement: A Model or an Exception?" *Journal of Palestine Studies* 24, no. 95 (spring 1995): 63–73.

Encyclopaedia Judaica. West Jerusalem: Keter Publishing House, Ltd., 1971.

Falah, Ghazi. "Arabs versus Jews in Galilee: Competition for Regional Resources." *GeoJournal* 21, no. 4 (1990): 325–336.

Garfinkle, Adam. *War, Water and Negotiation in the Middle East: The Case of the Palestine-Syria Border, 1916–1923,* (occasional papers 115). Tel Aviv, 1994.

Government of Palestine. *A Survey of Palestine,* 2 vols. Reprint. Washington, D.C.: Institute for Palestine Studies, 1946.

Ionides, M. G. "The Perspective of Water Development in Palestine and Transjordan." *Journal of the Royal Central Asian Society* 33, part 3–4 (1946): 271–280.

Israel Central Bureau of Statistics. *Statistical Abstract.* West Jerusalem, various years.

Issar, Arie, et al. "On the Ancient Water of the Upper Nubian Sandstone Aquifer in Central Sinai and Southern Israel." *Journal of Hydrology* 17 (1972): 353–374.

Kahan, David. *Agriculture and Water Resources in the West Bank and Gaza (1967–1987).* West Jerusalem: West Bank Data Project, 1987.

Kahhaleh, Subhi. *The Water Problem in Israel and Its Repercussions on the Arab-Israeli Conflict.* Washington, D.C.: Institute for Palestine Studies, 1981.

Lonergan, C. Stephen, and David B. Brooks. *Watersheds: The Role of Fresh Water in the Israeli-Palestinian Conflict.* Ottawa: International Development Research Center (IDRC), 1994.

Lowi, Miriam L. *Water and Power: The Politics of a Scarce Resource in the Jordan River Basin.* London: Cambridge University Press, 1993.

Naff, Thomas, and R. C. Matson. *Water in the Middle East: Conflict or Cooperation.* Boulder, Colo.: Westview Press, 1984.

Nijim, B. K. "Water Resources in the History of the Palestine-Israel Conflict." *GeoJournal* 21, no. 4 (1990): 317–324.

Orni, Efraim, and Elisha Efrat. *Geography of Israel.* 3d ed. Philadelphia: The Jewish Publications Society of America, 1973.

Rofe and Raffety Consulting Engineers. *West Bank Hydrology, 1963–1965.* London: Central Water Authority, Jordan, 1965.

Stevens, Georgiana. *Jordan River Partition,* Stanford, Calif.: Stanford University Press and the Hoover Institution on War, Revolution and Peace, 1965.

Tahal Consulting Engineers, Ltd. "Israel Water Sector Review: Past Achievements, Current Problems and Future Options," (a report to the World Bank). Tel Aviv and Washington, D.C., 1990.

Toye, Patricia, ed. *Palestine Boundaries,* 4 vols. London: Archive Editions, 1989.

United Nations. *Water Resources of the Occupied Territory.* New York: United Nations, 1992.

al-Wazir, Khalil

Abu Jihad; PLO leader

1935–1988 Ramla

Khalil al-Wazir was born to a middle-class family in Ramla. He was displaced in 1948 when Zionist forces evicted Palestinians from that region. He settled in the Burayj refugee camp in the GAZA STRIP, where he completed his secondary education. He planned and executed military acts against Israeli targets and in 1954 was punished by the Egyptian authorities for such activities. Al-Wazir met YASIR ARAFAT in Cairo during his military training and remained close to him over the years. He attended classes at the University of Alexandria in 1956 but never completed college education.

Al-Wazir found work in Kuwait in 1959 and remained there, working as a teacher, until 1963. His stay in Kuwait put him in touch with his old friend Yasir Arafat, with whom he founded the FATAH movement. His wife, Umm Jihad (Intisar al-Wazir), was also involved in Fatah's political activities. Al-Wazir was one of the early full-time (*mutafarrigh*) members of Fatah after the Fatah Central Committee instructed him to open an office for the movement in Algeria. He was also one of the founding editors of *Filastinuna,* the official organ of Fatah. He was in charge of the recruitment and training of Fatah fighters, creating the nucleus of the fighting force of Fatah, later known as AL-ASIFA, "The Storm."

Al-Wazir settled in Algeria in 1963 and cultivated ties with military leaders in socialist countries. He opened the first office for Fatah in an Arab country and started the first military training camp for his movement. He visited China in 1964 and later preached "a people's liberation war," although he never supported communism as an ideology. In fact, his political sympathies lay with the conservative Muslim Brotherhood, which he had encountered in Gaza. Nevertheless, he also visited North Vietnam and North Korea, although, despite the false claims of PALESTINE LIBERATION ORGANIZATION (PLO) information brochures, he never received advanced military education there.

In 1965, Abu Jihad settled in Damascus, taking advantage of the Syrian Ba'thist regime's support of the doctrine of people's liberation war. He became the major link between underground activist cells inside ISRAEL and the Palestinian national movement. The 1967 defeat propelled him into a key leadership position with the PLO, made possible by his reputation as an expert on people's liberation war, considered the only solution at the time. He assumed major responsibilities in the Central Committee of Fatah, in the command of the forces of *al-Asifa,* on the PALESTINE NATIONAL COUNCIL, and on the Supreme Military Council of the PLO. He was also put in charge of commando operations in the Occupied Territories and inside Israel.

Abu Jihad played an important military role in JORDAN in 1970–71 during the BLACK SEPTEMBER clashes. He also supplied the encircled Palestinian forces in Jarash and Ajlun. Then, like other PLO leaders, he relocated to Beirut, where he kept a low profile until the eruption of the Lebanese civil war. He advocated a policy of full support for the Lebanese national movement and helped build up the forces of the PLO's Lebanese allies. Meanwhile, his main interest remained with the Occupied Territories; more than any other person inside the PLO and Fatah, Abu Jihad is credited with the development of underground cells in the WEST BANK and Gaza despite Israeli attempts to eradicate all vestiges of opposition to the occupation. Abu Jihad used his contacts with communist countries to augment the military power of the PLO. The resulting arms acquisition changed the PLO's fighting forces into a conventional army, rather than the "people's liberation forces" on which he had earlier insisted. Nevertheless, Abu Jihad remained close to his fighters; avoiding the lure of Beirut, he established his headquarters in Kayfun, near Alayh in Mount Lebanon.

Unlike other PLO leaders, Abu Jihad did not allow the Lebanese environment to discredit his role within the movement; he was never tainted by the massive corruption and thuggery that swept the ranks of PLO officials. Although he was less visible than most of his comrades, he commanded the respect and loyalty of most Palestinians, including members of rival organizations. His close relationship with Yasir Arafat was greatly to Arafat's benefit, since Arafat was being constantly challenged from within over his search for a diplomatic solution to the Palestinian problem: Abu Jihad provided the "revolutionary" cover that Arafat needed to continue his diplomatic pursuits.

Unfortunately for Arafat, Abu Jihad did not distinguish himself in the 1982 invasion of Lebanon, in which top PLO leaders retreated in the face of massive Israeli force. The subsequent defeat of the PLO in Lebanon forced Abu Jihad, along with other PLO leaders, to relocate farther away from Palestine, this time in Tunisia. There he lived with his family in a villa, a life-style more suited to his closely knit family than his former secretive and austere way of life.

The 1982 invasion of Lebanon seemed to have changed Abu Jihad's political and military philosophy; apparently, he lost faith in the PLO's ability to deliver a solution to the Palestinians from outside the Occupied Territories. Instead, he believed in the power of the masses in the West Bank and Gaza. In 1982, he began to sponsor youth committees in the Occupied Territories, committees that became the embryonic organization that later ignited the INTIFADA. However, Abu Jihad did not live long enough to see that uprising; he was assassinated by what is now believed to have been Israeli commandos in April 1988. His wife was with him when he died, and she quickly emerged as one of the top women within the PLO leadership. In 1996, she was appointed to a cabinet seat in Arafat's government in Gaza.

As'ad AbuKhalil

BIBLIOGRAPHY

Amos, John. *Palestinian Resistance.* New York: Pergamon Press, 1980.

Cobban, Helena. *The Palestinian Liberation Organization.* New York: Cambridge University Press, 1984.

Hart, Alan. *Arafat.* Bloomington: Indiana University Press, 1992.

Yusuf, Samir. *Abu Jihad.* Cairo: al-Markaz al-Misri al-Arabi, 1989.

West Bank

The term *West Bank* refers to the eastern part of the PALESTINE MANDATE, was created as a distinct territorial entity as a result of the first Arab–Israeli war in 1948–49. The region was to have comprised the major part of the Arab state envisaged in the 1947 U.N. partition plans. The area was occupied by military forces from the Hashemite Kingdom of Jordan in 1948 and annexed by that country in 1950. Subsequently, the term *East Bank* was generally used to refer to the territory east of the Jordan River (called Transjordan from 1922 to 1946); the *West Bank* was the territory to the west of the river. After Israeli occupation of the West Bank in the ARAB-ISRAEL WAR OF 1967, Israeli officials often called the West Bank by its biblical names, Judea and Samaria.

Geography and Population The West Bank is surrounded on three sides by Israel and bounded by the Jordan River and the Dead Sea on the east. It covers an area of 2,270 square miles (5,879 square kilometers). About 995,000 Palestinians lived there in 1967, but in the immediate aftermath of the Israeli occupation, about 350,000 left for the East Bank. The population has grown slowly but steadily since the end of 1967: an estimated 1.4 million Palestinians lived in the West Bank in 1997. In addition to the Palestinians, by 1999 about 180,000 Jewish settlers lived in the West Bank exclusive of greater East Jerusalem, which Israel also annexed in 1967. The first Jewish settlements were established soon after the inception of occupation; between 1977 and 1992, Israel followed an official policy of encouraging Jewish settlement throughout the West Bank even though this policy violated the GENEVA CONVENTION pertaining to territory occupied in time of war; Israel maintained that the West Bank was not subject to provisions of the Geneva Convention.

The West Bank contains the rural highlands of central Palestine, where rain-fed agriculture has traditionally been the mainstay of economic life. The principle Palestinian city is East Jerusalem, the center of Palestinian commercial, cultural, and political life. Other major cities include BETHLEHEM and HEBRON in the south, JERICHO in the east, and the northern cities of Jenin, NABLUS, Qalqiliya, RAMALLAH-al-Bira, and TULKARM. In 1994, 62 percent of the Palestinian population still was rural, living in 430 villages. Over 30 percent of the Palestinians were REFUGEES, many living in the nineteen refugee camps that the United Nations Relief and Works Agency for Palestine Refugees in the Near East (UNRWA) maintained in various parts of the West Bank.

The West Bank acquired its distinctive political character as a result of the 1948 war that severed it from the rest of Palestine, which was divided into the GAZA STRIP, occupied by Egypt, and the new state of Israel. The Arab Legion of Jordanian king Abdullah had initially taken control of the region in May 1948, when British forces left Palestine. As Palestinians fled areas under the control of the new state of Israel, the indigenous population of the West Bank, estimated at 450,000 in early 1948, was swollen by the influx of 350,000 refugees from the Mediterranean coastal plain, the

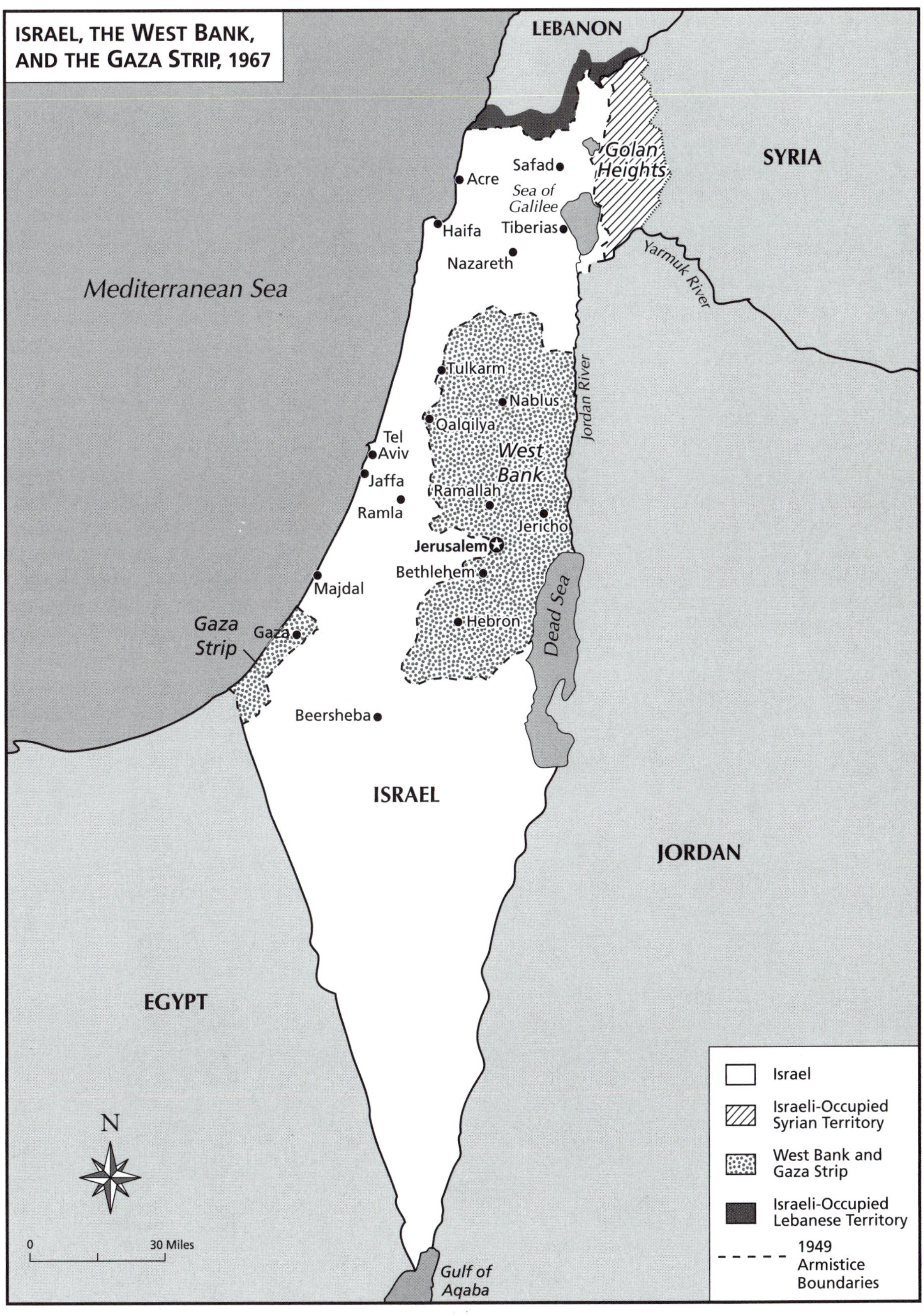
ISRAEL, THE WEST BANK, AND THE GAZA STRIP, 1967
LEBANON
SYRIA
Golan Heights
Safad
Acre
Sea of Galilee
Haifa
Tiberias
Nazareth
Yarmuk River
Mediterranean Sea
Tulkarm
Nablus
Jordan River
Qalqilya
Tel Aviv
West Bank
Jaffa
Ramallah
Ramla
Jericho
Jerusalem
Bethlehem
Majdal
Dead Sea
Hebron
Gaza Strip
Gaza
Beersheba
ISRAEL
JORDAN
EGYPT
N
0
30 Miles
Gulf of Aqaba
Israel
Israeli-Occupied Syrian Territory
West Bank and Gaza Strip
Israeli-Occupied Lebanese Territory
1949 Armistice Boundaries

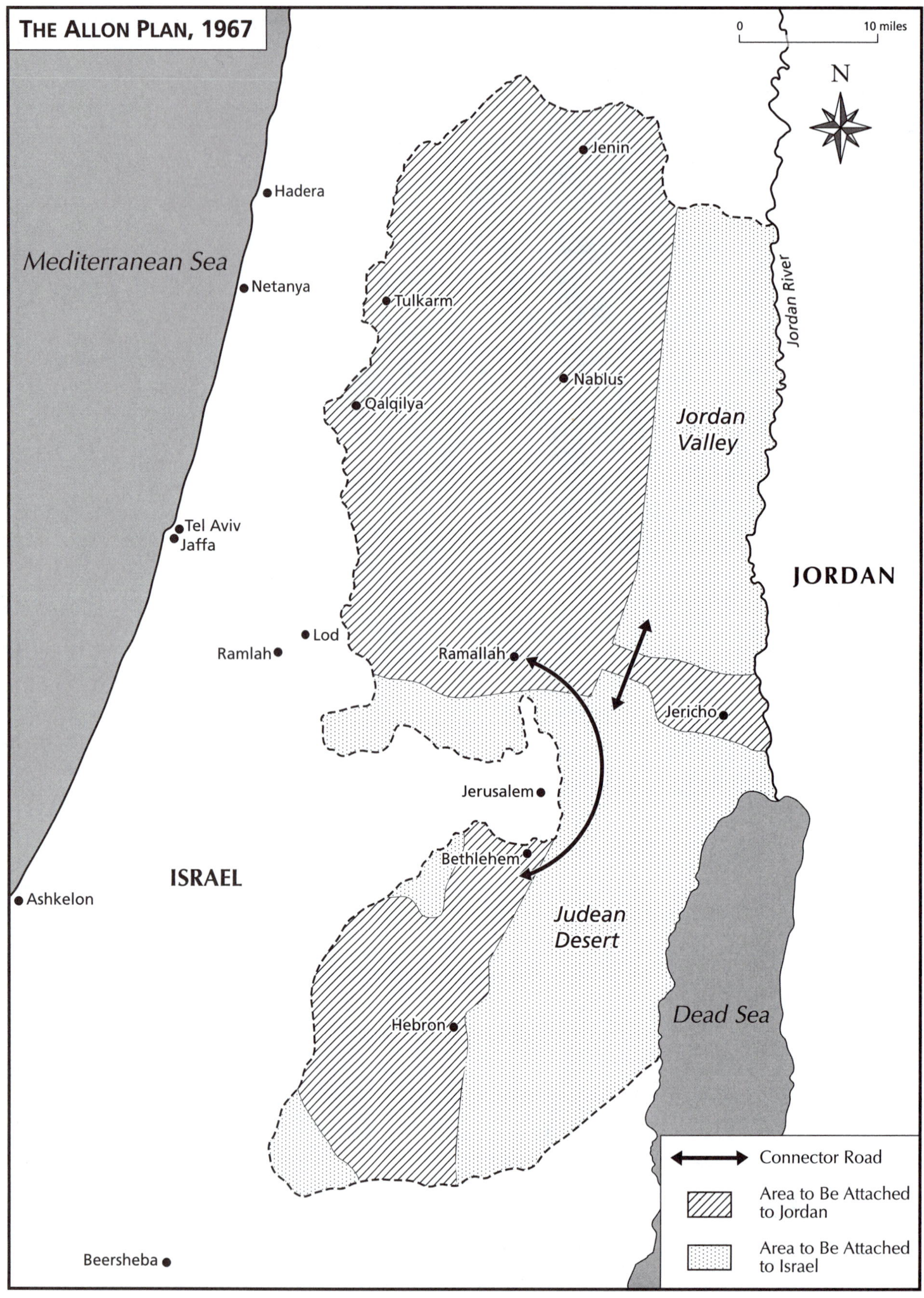
THE ALLON PLAN, 1967
0
10 miles
N
Mediterranean Sea
Hadera
Netanya
Tel Aviv
Jaffa
Lod
Ramlah
Ashkelon
Beersheba
ISRAEL
Jenin
Tulkarm
Nablus
Qalqilya
Ramallah
Jericho
Jerusalem
Bethlehem
Hebron
Jordan Valley
Judean Desert
Jordan River
JORDAN
Dead Sea
Connector Road
Area to Be Attached to Jordan
Area to Be Attached to Israel

Galilee, and the Negev. Beginning in 1950, refugees steadily moved to camps that UNRWA established in the East Bank, particularly in the Amman region. Nevertheless, the first Jordanian census, taken in 1952, enumerated a total West Bank population of 742,299.

As the West Bank was transformed from an integral part of Palestine into the western province of Jordan, it was isolated from much of the cultivatable land and the major urban markets of HAIFA, Tel Aviv and JAFFA, and West Jerusalem. Not only were close economic, political, and social ties with the rest of Arab Palestine severed, but scores of towns and villages along the new Jordan-Israel armistice frontier were cut off from traditional farmland that had been the basis of their economic life. In many instances, the 1949 armistice line sliced through villages, dividing families, farms, and even houses, with part in Israel and part in Jordan. However, cross-border contacts were forbidden because of the de jure state of war between Israel and Jordan.

As West Bank economic conditions deteriorated throughout the 1950s, Palestinian frustration increased; resentment of Jordanian authorities grew, and there was an escalation of frontier incidents caused by infiltration of Palestinians across the border to their former property, now in Israel. During the 1960s, infiltrators were often organized in guerrilla bands, and their raids inside Israel led to a policy of massive retaliation against West Bank border villages by the Israeli military. In November 1966, the Israeli army conducted one of its largest retaliatory raids when its armored forces invaded the West Bank with a major attack on the towns of Sammu, Jimba, and Khirbat Karkay in the vicinity of Hebron, producing dozens of casualties among Palestinian villagers and Jordanian troops. Shortly after the attack, inhabitants of the region staged protest demonstrations to denounce the Hashemite regime's inaction; they called for reprisals against Israel and demanded distribution of arms to residents of the border villages.

Jordanian Policy Jordanian attempts to integrate the West Bank into the Hashemite Kingdom shifted the region's orientation from the Palestinian cities in the West to the capital in Amman. All Palestinians living in the West Bank were granted Jordanian citizenship, although their passports identified them as West Bankers. In 1949, Jordan replaced the military government with a civil administration. During the 1950s, several Palestinians were appointed by King Husayn to the cabinet, and West Bank residents were allowed to vote in Jordan's national elections. The king also appointed seven Palestinians to a new twenty-member House of Notables; half the deputies elected to the new forty-member Chamber of Deputies were Palestinians. When both chambers adopted a resolution in 1950 supporting "complete unity between the two sides of the Jordan and their union into one state," the ARAB LEAGUE opposed the move. In fact, during the entire period of Jordan's sovereignty over the West Bank, only Great Britain and Pakistan officially recognized its annexation.

Palestinian disaffection with Hashemite rule grew steadily, beginning in the mid-1950s. One cause of the dissatisfaction was the perception that development of the kingdom was concentrated on the East Bank. By 1965, three-quarters of all industrial output was located in the East Bank; industry in the West Bank was small-scale, with 90 percent of factories employing fewer than ten workers, most of them processing primary goods such as food, beverages, tobacco, and textiles. Major industrial and infrastructural development such as electricity and transport also was in the east. Investors were encouraged to open new factories on the East Bank and even to transfer businesses there from the West Bank. The only major development projects that benefited the West Bank were the Yarmuk River Dam and the East Ghawr (Ghor) Canal, both of which increased arable areas owned by West Bank landowners; however, these projects were aborted by the 1967 war.

West Bank economic conditions and the preferential treatment shown to the east were major causes of high immigration to the East Bank. In fact, between 1949 and 1967, the Palestinian population of Amman and the rest of the East Bank became larger than the indigenous Jordanian population as a result of the influx from the West Bank. Despite Jordan's relatively high growth rate overall, unemployment remained high in West Bank towns and considerable underemployment characterized West Bank agriculture. The disparities between the two banks were demonstrated statistically by 1961, when West Bank per capita income was only half that in the East Bank.

The economic stagnation of the West Bank was a significant factor that stimulated labor migration to the oil-producing states of the Arabian Peninsula, beginning in the mid-1950s. Initially, Palestinian migrants to the Persian Gulf were professional, skilled, and semi-skilled workers. As labor shortages developed at the bottom of the Gulf wage scale, less skilled workers from the West Bank followed. By the mid-1960s, remittances sent home by these migrant workers provided a significant proportion of total income for many Palestinian families.

Regional differences within the West Bank were reflected in patterns of development, migration, and reactions to the Jordanian authorities. For example, in Hebron, the population tended to have fewer years of total education and fewer skills than in East Jerusalem, Nablus, or Ramallah. In 1961, less than 25 percent of Hebron's population was literate, compared to over 30 percent in other West Bank cities. In the surrounding area, almost 90 percent of the population lacked a primary education. The Hebron region was almost totally dependent on agriculture and lacked the variety of other economic activities that existed in the Jerusalem and Nablus regions. Consequently, migration from the Hebron region was higher than elsewhere on the West Bank.

The Jerusalem district, including the city and surrounding villages, was the most developed area. It had the highest rates of school attendance and literacy, and its rural population received more formal education than villagers elsewhere. The percentage employed in agriculture was less than in the other districts, and more than 50 percent of West Bank industry was located in the Jerusalem-Ramallah area, compared to less than 10 percent in the Hebron district. The city of Jerusalem received favored treatment because the Hashemite rulers considered it their "second capital."

In addition to the economic causes of tension between the West Bank and Amman, there was political competition between pro- and anti-Hashemite factions. King Abdullah and his successors attempted to gain the loyalty of Palestinian leaders with whom alliances had been formed during the Palestine Mandate by co-opting members of municipal councils and influencing local elections. Several pro-Hashemites, usually notables of high social standing, were appointed as provincial governors and to important posts in Amman. The most influential were members of the NASHASHIBI FAMILY or those who had worked closely with the Hashemites during the Mandate. Many Nashashibis had backed Abdullah's aspiration to become king of Palestine and had supported his annexation of the West Bank.

Some Palestinians granted the Hashemites "conditional legitimacy" while maintaining their ultimate objective of independence. Others accepted annexation for practical reasons: to obtain citizenship, passports, commercial licenses, employment, education, and social services. Consequently, many areas of Jordanian life came to be dominated by Palestinians. Nevertheless, Hashemite reservations about Palestinian loyalty were evidenced in the favoritism shown in appointing only East Bank residents to the most sensitive posts, such as high-ranking army, police, and security positions.

Palestinian Politics Among the most significant opponents of annexation were followers of the former mufti (Islamic law expert) of Jerusalem, AL-HAJJ AMIN AL-HUSAYNI. Competition between them and pro-Hashemites was reflected in the tension between the Egyptian-backed ALL-PALESTINE GOVERNMENT established in Gaza during 1948 and the Palestine Congresses organized under Abdullah's tutelage in Amman and Jericho during 1948–49. Although each faction claimed to be the true representative of Palestinian nationalism, both were controlled by non-Palestinian governments. The Gaza All-Palestine Government withered away with few, if any, accomplishments; the congresses, in effect, voted themselves out of existence when they backed annexation and recognized Abdullah as king of the new Hashemite Kingdom in 1950.

The Palestinian refugee population were the mufti's principal supporters, whereas the pro-Jordanian trend tended to be backed by nonrefugee Palestinians, including independent farmers, landowners, businesspeople, and professionals eager to maintain political stability as a foundation for secure economic development. The indigenous landowners and farmers often exploited refugee labor, a situation that both aggravated and reinforced political differences.

Friction between the West Bank's refugees and nonrefugees was also exacerbated by the situation along the cease-fire lines with Israel, where thousands of the refugees were located. The unstable situation led to bitter complaints by frontier villagers, not only against Israel and the refugees, but against the Jordanian government because of its failure to protect them from Israeli retaliatory raids. The Palestine National Guard, a security force that the government organized from among villagers in response to their demands, proved to be ineffective. The guard was inadequately armed and poorly trained; eventually (in 1965), it was amalgamated into the Jordanian army.

Events in the larger Arab world had a huge impact on political developments in the West Bank during the late 1950s and 1960s. Palestinians became increasingly disenchanted with their own leaders because of their failure during the 1948 war and their subsequent inaction. Instead, they turned to others such as Egypt's Jamal Abd al-Nasir, the Communists, and the Muslim Brotherhood or to pan-Arab movements such as the Ba'th. After a period of countrywide unrest in 1956, the National Socialists, a pro-Nasir party led by Sulayman al-Nabulsi, won enough votes to dominate the parliament and the government. Nabulsi's attempt to pursue an anti-Western policy led to his dismissal as prime minister by King Husayn in April 1957. Subsequently, the army was ordered to arrest some 500 of Nabulsi's sympathizers, and several parties that the government perceived as radical were outlawed.

Even after the crackdown on leftist and nationalist factions, the West Bank continued to be the center of anti-Hashemite establishment activity. It provided support for the banned parties, several of which continued to operate secretly. The growing political assertiveness of West Bank Palestinians probably was one of the reasons why the Arab League decided to revive a distinctive Palestinian political identity with creation of the PALESTINE LIBERATION ORGANIZATION (PLO) in 1964. Jordan reluctantly authorized the PLO to operate in the West Bank and permitted it to hold its founding congress in Jerusalem during May 1964.

By 1967, Nasir had become the dominant figure in inter-Arab politics, with a wide following in the West Bank. In most Arab countries, his colorful rhetoric and his anti-Western policies appealed to the disadvantaged and disaffected. He generated enthusiasm for a new round of battles with Israel, leading during May 1967 to mass demonstrations in the West Bank that urged King Husayn to participate in an anticipated war with Israel. The war began with Israel's preemptive attack on Egypt on June 5; King Husayn was subjected to great public pressure to join the battle. Ignoring warnings from Israel against any precipitous military action, Jordan initiated fire from Jerusalem but quickly was defeated, losing the West Bank, including East Jerusalem, after only three days. The loss of the West Bank led to another mass refugee flight and total transformation of the territory's demographic, political, and economic conditions.

Over 300,000 Palestinians crossed the Jordan River, reducing the population of the West Bank by nearly one-third in two months. Many fled because of fear; others, such as those in the Latrun region and in the large refugee camps near Jericho, were forced to leave by the Israeli military.

Israeli Occupation After 1967, Israel governed the West Bank under a military regime that imposed martial LAW on the indigenous Palestinian population. Shortly after the Israeli occupation, the old city of East Jerusalem and its hinterland were separated from the rest of the West Bank and for all practical purposes annexed to Israel. In 1981, the Israeli parliament (Knesset) underscored the annexation of East Jerusalem by voting that the unified city was the eternal capital of Israel. Although the Palestinian residents of East Jerusalem were offered Israeli citizenship, which implied recognition of Israeli sovereignty, only a few accepted. Those who accepted Israeli citizenship could vote in national elections; others, though not Israeli, could vote in municipal elections. Palestinians in the rest of the West Bank and those in Jerusalem who refused Israeli citizenship remained Jordanian citizens.

The Israeli military governor of the West Bank, an army general, was vested with the authority held by the former ruler, King Husayn, and was responsible to the minister of defense. The military governor had total executive and legislative power, enabling him to make new laws, cancel old ones, and suspend or annul existing ones. Under military rule, Palestinians could be arrested and imprisoned without habeas corpus rights, they could be deported from the country, and their property could be confiscated or destroyed by the army without civil trial. Israel ruled the West Bank as an occupied territory under the general terms of the Geneva Convention, but selectively interpreted the treaty; for example, Israel deported hundreds of indigenous West Bank Palestinians and established scores of new Jewish settlements in the West Bank contrary to provisions of the Geneva Convention. Israel maintained that the convention did not apply to the West Bank and Gaza because neither was an area that had belonged to the previous administrator, Jordan for the West Bank or Egypt for Gaza.

Palestinian resistance to the occupation began in June 1967 with opposition to Israeli plans to annex Jerusalem and to extend its borders into the West Bank. These early opponents were among the first of some 2,000 West Bank Palestinians forcibly deported between 1967 and 1994; those deported because of political activism included the mayors of several cities and towns and educators such as HANNA NASIR, the president of BIR ZEIT UNIVERSITY. Even though Israel banned Palestinian political organizations and all manifestations of Palestinian nationalism, a pattern of civic resistance to the occupation developed during the next twenty years consisting of strikes by merchants, businesses, and schools; demonstrations by marchers; display of Palestinian flags or national colors; and chanting of slogans calling for national independence.

Initial political opposition to occupation was managed by a vaguely defined national front or national union believed to be an offspring of Sulayman Nabulsi's National Socialist Party, the group that had been in the vanguard of opposition to the Hashemite regime during the 1950s, but after 1968 its organizations were inactive. By 1973 the PALESTINE NATIONAL COUNCIL had established a secret Palestinian National Front in the West Bank and Gaza as a political base for a future Palestine state. Formally established in August 1973, the Palestinian National Front (PNF) included supporters of FATAH, the DEMOCRATIC FRONT FOR THE LIBERATION OF PALESTINE, the POPULAR FRONT FOR THE LIBERATION OF PALESTINE, the Communists, and the Ba'th. After the PALESTINE LIBERATION ORGANIZATION (PLO) gained increasing credibility as the representative of all Palestinians, the PNF extended its influence in the West Bank. The outcome of the 1976 municipal elections, authorized by the Israeli authorities, provided evidence of shifting political trends. In 1972, the PLO opposed participation in municipal elections conducted under occupation with the result that those who won were traditional notables. In 1976, PNF supporters or sympathizers won overwhelmingly or obtained strong majorities in the principal towns. Only in Bethlehem did the incumbent non-PNF mayor, ELIAS FREIJ, keep his post.

Israeli economic policy was directed at the integration of the West Bank into Israel's economy through the creation of "new facts," extending the road network, linking it with highways in Israel; setting up military bases; organizing Israeli business and commercial operations in the region; and unifying the electricity grid with Israel's. Although agricultural productivity increased and living standards rose for many, there was a significant loss of land by Palestinian farmers. Approximately half the land in the West Bank was expropriated by Israel for establishment of new Jewish settlements, for "security" purposes, or for infrastructure facilitating Israeli development. Most peasants displaced from agriculture found employment in unskilled work at the bottom of the wage scale in Israel, and several tens of thousands left the West Bank to seek employment in neighboring Arab countries. Prior to the closures of the West Bank during 1993 and 1994, more than a third of West Bank Palestinian workers were employed in Israel in construction, agriculture, and services.

A major constraint on further development of Palestinian agriculture in the West Bank was the limited water supply. During the occupation, water sources were placed under control of Israeli authorities, who gave priority for water use to Jewish settlements. Under the "new facts" policy enunciated in 1967–69 by the Labor Party's minister of defense, Moshe Dayan, Israel was in the Occupied Territories by "right and not on sufferance, to visit, live and to settle." Under this policy, the first Jewish settlements were established in the Jordan valley and in other sites not heavily populated by Palestinians. To further economic integration, Jewish investment was encouraged through cheaper prices for raw materials, low interest rates, and other economic incentives. By 1977, some 4,200 Jews were established in thirty-six West Bank settlements.

Likud Policy Jewish settlement in the West Bank greatly increased after the Likud government took control of the Occupied Territories in 1977. Restrictions on areas where Jews could establish settlements were removed and the government increased its assistance to the settlers. Likud also adopted tougher policies toward Palestinian dissidents. Its program called for eventual incorporation of the West Bank and Gaza under Israeli hegemony. In December 1977, the Likud government proposed an autonomy plan that would have given Palestinians limited jurisdiction, under overall Israeli control, in matters such as education, social welfare, and health. When the Palestinian population rejected the plan, the Likud government attempted to impose it unilaterally by establishing a new civil administration run by the Israeli army and a system of Village Leagues made up of non-PLO Palestinian local authorities.

Likud attempts to subvert the PNF and the influence of the PLO in the West Bank through establishment of the Village Leagues and a new civil administration only intensified opposition to the occupation. Demonstrations against Likud policies erupted in violence and led the Israeli authorities to discharge the PNF mayors in 1982. The unrest in the West Bank was a principal factor leading to the June 1982 decision by Defense Minister Ariel Sharon to invade Lebanon, where Israel unsuccessfully attempted to destroy the PLO.

Tensions between Israeli authorities and West Bank Palestinians abated somewhat after establishment of a national unity government in Israel during 1984. However, by 1987 deteriorating economic conditions, continued seizure of Palestinian lands, growing uncertainty about Israel's future plans for the Occupied Territories, and disenchantment with twenty years of occupation erupted in a new uprising, the INTIFADA, which began in December 1987. The Intifada continued until the September 1993 Declaration of Principles (DOP) between the government of Israel and the PLO was signed.

In 1994 there were three major agreements between Israel and the PLO for implementation of the DOP. They included a pact dealing with economic relations between Israel and the PALESTINE AUTHORITY (PA) established by the DOP; an agreement on limited Palestinian self-rule in Gaza and the West Bank town of Jericho; and the transfer of authority over tourism, education, health, culture, and taxation from Israel to the PA in Gaza and Jericho.

Palestinian self-rule was further extended from Gaza and Jericho in an agreement signed by Israel and the PA in September 1995. This agreement called for withdrawal or redeployment of Israeli troops and establishment of PA jurisdiction in three regions of the West Bank. In Area A, with about a third of the Palestinian population in the six largest towns, constituting between 3 and 5 percent of the West Bank, full administrative control was turned over to the PA. In Area B, with about 450 Palestinian villages and other rural areas constituting about 25 percent of the West Bank, the PA assumed administrative and police authority but Israel retained responsibility for security until elections for the eighty-eight member PALESTINIAN LEGISLATIVE COUNCIL, which took place in January 1996. Area C, constituting over two-thirds of the West Bank, was sparsely settled except for Israeli settlements and military areas; it was to remain under Israeli control until establishment of the elected Palestinian Council. Israel was to "redeploy" its forces in Area C in 1997. However, implementation of these agreements, which for all practical purposes was to end twenty-eight years of Israeli rule over nearly all West Bank Palestinians except those in East Jerusalem and the villages annexed to it by Israel after 1967, was suspended by the right-wing Likud government, which opposed the OSLO AGREEMENTS.

Ending Israel's occupation of the West Bank was to be an initial step toward establishment of a Palestinian state. However, election of Benjamin Netanyahu, leader of the right-wing nationalist Likud Party, as prime minister in the 1996 Israeli election resulted in temporary suspension of agreements between the Palestinians and the previous Labor government. Likud opposed withdrawal from most of the area that was to be turned over to the new Palestinian Authority in 1996–97 and the redeployment of Israeli troops from many Palestinian villages to which the previous Labor government had agreed. However, by September 1996 Netanyahu and Arafat met and negotiations were renewed. In January 1997 Israel and Palestine authorities signed an agreement providing for Israeli withdrawal from 80 percent of Hebron, leaving Israeli forces in control of the 20 percent of the city inhabited at the time by some 250 Orthodox Jewish settlers. The agreement provided for further Israeli withdrawals, but these were suspended when relations with the Palestinians deteriorated.

The United States attempted to renew the negotiations after more than a year when it brokered a meeting between Israelis and Palestinians at the Wye River Plantation in Maryland in October 1998. The agreement provided for further Israeli withdrawal; however, the Netanyahu government suspended implementation. The defeat of Netanyahu in the 1999 Israeli election by Labor party leader Ehud Barak renewed possibilities of continued implementation of the Wye and final status agreements.

Ending Israel's occupation of the West Bank was to be an initial step to establishment of a Palestinian state. Major problems confronting the prospective Palestinian state in the West Bank included limited natural resources, especially water; a large number of refugees, constituting nearly a third of the population; massive unemployment; dependence on Israel's economy for employment; Israeli control of much of the communications and public utilities infrastructure; and a shortage of technically skilled personnel. The West Bank is also plagued by political divisiveness within the Palestinian community, with rivalries between Islamist groups such as HAMAS and ISLAMIC JIHAD and the PLO, and within the PLO among Fatah, the (PFLP), (DPFP), and the PALESTINE COMMUNIST PARTY.

Don Peretz

BIBLIOGRAPHY

Benvenisti, Meron. *The West Bank Data Project: A Study of Israel's Policies.* Washington, D.C.: American Enterprise Institute, 1984.

——, with Ziad Abu-Zayed and Danny Rubinstein. *The West Bank Handbook: A Political Lexicon.* Boulder, Colo.: Westview Press, 1986.

——, and Shlomo Khayat. *The West Bank and Gaza Atlas.* Jerusalem: West Bank Data Base Project, Jerusalem Post Distributor, 1988.

Bull, Vivian. *The West Bank: Is It Viable?* Lexington, Mass.: Lexington Books, 1975.

Cohen, Amnon. *Political Parties in the West Bank under the Jordanian Regime.* Ithaca, N.Y.: Cornell University Press, 1982.

Gharaibeh, Fawzi A. *The Economies of the West Bank and the Gaza Strip.* Boulder, Colo.: Westview, 1985.

Halabi, Rafik. *The West Bank Story.* Rev. ed. New York: San Diego, Calif.: Harcourt, Jovanovich, 1985.

Heiberg, Marianne, and Geir Ovensen. *Palestinian Society in Gaza, the West Bank and Arab Jerusalem.* Oslo: FAFO, 1993.

Lesch, Ann M. *Political Perceptions of the Palestinians on the West Bank and the Gaza Strip.* Washington, D.C.: Middle East Institute, 1980.

Nahleh, Emile, ed. *A Palestinian Agenda for the West Bank and Gaza.* Washington, D.C.: American Enterprise Institute, 1980.

Peretz, Don. *The West Bank: History, Politics, Society, and Economy.* Boulder, Colo.: Westview Press, 1986.

——. *Intifada: The Palestinian Uprising.* Boulder, Colo.: Westview Press, 1990.

Plascov, Avi. *The Palestinian Refugees in Jordan 1948–57.* London: Frank Cass, 1981.

West Bank Data Project

The West Bank Data Project was a research organization established in Jerusalem in 1982 to provide detailed analyses of conditions in the Occupied Territories.

Directed by Meron Benvenisti, former Israeli deputy mayor of Jerusalem, the West Bank Data Project received funding from American foundations such as the Rockefeller Foundation and the Ford Foundation and was administered by the Brookings Institution in Washington, D.C.

In the 1980s the project issued a number of detailed studies analyzing socioeconomic, demographic, spatial, political, and legal issues in the Occupied Territories in general and the WEST BANK in particular. The project's publications included analyses of settlement activity, industrialization, agriculture, and the Palestinian press; handbooks; atlases; and annual reports on the territories. Through such publications, the project played a major role in documenting the changes wrought by Israel in the Occupied Territories.

The project closed in the late 1980s after the onset of the INTIFADA.

Michael R. Fischbach

Western (Wailing) Wall Disturbances

1929

The Western Wall in the Old City of JERUSALEM is a holy site for both Muslims and Jews and became entwined in the rising political tensions between Arabs and Jews in Palestine. For Muslims, the wall constituted the western part of the HARAM AL-SHARIF ("the Noble Sanctuary") and was the site where they believed the Prophet Muhammad tethered his "fabulous steed," al-Buraq, during the Prophet's nocturnal journey to heaven. The wall was also the holiest site in Judaism as it was the remnant of the Jewish Second Temple.

On September 23, 1928, the eve of the holiest day in the Jewish calendar, Yom Kippur, the Day of Atonement, Jews placed a screen next to the wall in order to separate male and female worshipers who had gathered there. Palestinian Muslims complained to British authorities that this was an "innovation" that violated the status quo ante in force since Ottoman times. The British agreed and forcibly removed the screen. The incident transcended its religious nature when Jews and Palestinians alike politicized it over the following months. On August 15, 1929, a group of young Jews from the Revisionist movement staged a nationalist demonstration at the wall that sparked a Palestinian counterdemonstration the following day.

Intercommunal tensions led to violence on August 23, 1929, when Palestinians attacked Jews in the religious Mea She'arim section of Jerusalem. Rioters attacked similar religious and largely anti-Zionist Jewish groups in HEBRON, killing 64, and SAFAD, killing 26. In return, Jews killed Palestinians in a number of cities, although most Palestinian deaths were the result of British police and troops, who sometimes fired into crowds indiscriminately. More than 116 Palestinians died in the disturbances, as did 133 Jews.

British authorities dispatched the SHAW COMMISSION, 1930, to investigate the violence. It determined that the Jewish and Palestinian demonstration of August 15 and 16, respectively, was the immediate spark, but that Palestinian fear of Jewish immigration and land acquisitions was the ultimate cause.

Philip Mattar

BIBLIOGRAPHY

Mattar, Philip. "The Role of the Mufti of Jerusalem in the Political Struggle over the Western Wall, 1928–29." *Middle Eastern Studies* 19, no. 1 (January 1983): 104–118.

Palestine Government. *A Survey of Palestine for the Information of the Anglo-American Committee of Inquiry.* 2 Vols. Washington, D.C.: Institute for Palestine Studies, 1991.

Women

The mid-twentieth century ushered in an era of profound and far-reaching change for Palestinian women propelled by the war and uprooting of 1948 and subsequent life in exile or under Israeli rule, and later, under occupation. Dispersal, fragmentation, and occupation have had exceedingly contradictory effects on Palestinian women. These developments provided spaces in which women made significant social progress, particularly in the realms of education and public activism. However, life in exile or under occupation also put up obstacles in the way of emancipation. For example, the absence of an independent Palestinian state and legal system has precluded women activists from pursuing a vigorous campaign for reforms in personal status laws.

Media images of Palestinian women often appear contradictory. Articulate women holding prominent public positions are juxtaposed with women wearing traditional Islamic dress. These images capture, however briefly, the immense variety in Palestinian women's lives. One would be hard-pressed to identify an "essential" Palestinian woman. A monolithic frame of analysis that takes as a point of departure "patriarchy," "Islam," or "nationalism" glosses over the richness of Palestinian women's actual lives and activities and blurs the differences of region, religion, class, generation, and education, as well as the varying ways individual women have experienced their lives. Women belong to a multiplicity of social categories, and their identities are embedded in the complex set of positions they occupy. National location—in historic Palestine, under Israeli occupation, or in exile—is another salient category in Palestinian women's daily experiences and sense of self.

Family and Society The family is the primary unit of SOCIETY around which the lives of most Palestinian women are organized. The family stands as a framework, one that both constrains and strengthens. For example, the family can limit women's marital, educational, and employment options and yet simultaneously can offer an arena in which women can find protection, material security, and emotional support. Equally, the family can enable women to pursue education and employment and choose their marital partner and support their choices.

Although this entry may highlight certain general features of family life, it is important not to ignore variation through time and across social categories. A general feature of the Palestinian family is the role it plays in controlling women's mobility and sexuality. However, this control has a temporal dimension. Older, postmenopausal women enjoy a great deal more mobility, as stricter controls are exercised over unmarried women and adolescent girls.

Marriage and reproduction are the most significant events in the life of most young women. They are socialized from a very early age toward domesticity, child rearing, and a future defined in terms of their roles of wife and mother. As in the rest of the Arab world, marriages are family affairs. Such a crucial event, which creates economic and political ties between families, is not left to the whims of inexperienced youngsters. Carefully arranged marriages are understood to ensure a girl's security and to protect her honor. Although women are supposed to be obedient wives, room for negotiating their daily domestic lives is not insignificant. In spite of an ideology of patrilineality, women's ties to their natal families remain strong after marriage and provide a support network, both emotional and financial, diminishing men's potential for excessive control. The family's role in arranging marriage also means that in the event of a failed marriage they bear some responsibility and are morally compelled to take in divorced daughters.

Control of women is also vested in a public who are often ready to observe and criticize their comportment. Among Palestinians, a central idiom framing women's behavior is the notions of honor. Illicit sexuality and immodest behavior can damage seriously a women's potential for marriage as well as cast aspersions on her family's community standing and the masculinity of its male members. This is the cultural context in which the control over women's behavior is embedded. Infractions of the modesty code can be met with reprisals ranging from verbal chastising to various degrees of physical violence.

Most of what is known of Palestinian marriage practices pertains to the twentieth century. However, through an astute reading of legal documents, historians have been providing data on marriage, divorce, and inheritance in the eighteenth and nineteenth centuries. Differences have been discerned in marriage practices according to class. Wealthier, politically prominent families tended to exert more control over the arrangement of marriages and, as a result, were more likely to engage in early marriage and cousin marriage. Marriage was an intimate part of a complex strategy of families' extending and consolidating their economic and political alliances. For the rural and the urban poor, marriages carried a slightly different meaning. The couple was more clearly the central relationship established by marriage. The transfer of property by the groom to the bride on signing of the marriage contract constituted for these women a significant amount of property or capital.

Another class distinction in marriage was the apparently greater stability of upper-class marriages. Marriage among the rural and urban poor, among whom less compelling economic and political issues were at stake, was more likely to end in divorce and remarriage was easier. Brides tended to be older in these marriages and endogamy was less frequent.

Now and in the past, within the family, women's position and power undergo a series of transformations as she grows older. As a daughter under the control of parents and brothers, she is at her most subordinate and powerless. In extended families, the young bride, often a stranger in her husband's home, is also in a very subordinate position vis-à-vis her parents-in-law. Her mother-in-law commands both obedience and labor. For lower-class women, whose households do not usually include the servants available to upper-class women, domestic labor can be onerous. However, as a woman of any class bears children, especially sons, her status and power are enhanced. Eventually, as she progresses through the life cycle and herself becomes a mother-in-law, a woman wields more power in the domestic realm, for she directs the labor of more junior women. Thus, women's status is not a result simply of gender but of a complex intersection of age, class, and gender.

To speak of Palestinian women's legal status in the post-1948 period, when large numbers are in exile, it is fruitful to distinguish between religious laws governing matters of personal status (marriage, divorce, inheritance, and custody) and state laws governing women as citizens. In nearly all Arab states in which Palestinians reside, whether as citizens or as REFUGEES, personal status affairs are handled by the religious courts, either Muslim or Christian. Many of the Arab states where Palestinians reside have initiated reforms in Muslim personal-status laws. Yet women's right to divorce continues to be more limited than men's. Men have unilateral rights of divorce; women must show cause. Although Muslim women may initiate divorce on the grounds of desertion, disappearance, severe illness, impotence, or absence of support, the negative social implications of a divorced status tend to dissuade women from pursuing even these limited divorce rights. Custody laws that favor paternal ties and rights over maternal ones constitute another serious obstacle to women's pursuit of divorce.

According to Muslim inheritance laws, women inherit half of what men inherit (the exact amount varies, depending on whether it is LAND or monetary). Thus, in general, a daughter's inheritance is half that of her brother. In practice, many women do not receive even this allotted share. It is not uncommon for a woman willingly to cede her inheritance to her brothers in a publicly unacknowledged but very clear strategy to ensure moral and financial support from her brothers in the event of divorce or widowhood.

Education In the nineteenth century, schools for girls were established by European missionaries in urban areas. By the end of the nineteenth century, Ottoman government schools were available for girls as well. The effects of the 1948 disaster on women's education have been profound. The availability of United Nations–sponsored free elementary school (and sometimes middle and high school) in the refugee camps drew the vast majority of refugee girls, giving rise to a new generation of literate women. However, patterns of educational development are uneven. Although Palestinian girls and boys in Jordan and Kuwait attend elementary schools (in Kuwait males, 161,188; females, 155,360; in Jordan males, 139,509; females, 145,889) and secondary schools (in Kuwait males, 8,788; females, 8,014; in Jordan males, 34,262; females, 34,071) in nearly equal numbers, in the GAZA STRIP, boys are registered to attend at far greater rates than girls (all pupils from kindergarten to teacher training programs: males, 176,686; females, 93,051). In Lebanon during the 1980s, boys and girls attended school at similar rates at the elementary level (males, 28,072; females, 28,236); however, in secondary schools, boys outnumbered girls by more than two to one (males, 10,030; females, 4,217).

Access to host country universities opened higher education to larger numbers of women. Although women graduate from universities in lesser numbers than do men, they still constitute from 35 to 50 percent of university enrollments in the West Bank and Gaza Strip. The relatively greater ease of access to schools and the easing of familial obstacles to women's pursuit of education distinguish young women's lives from those of their often illiterate or minimally schooled mothers. Palestinians are reputed to have the highest per capita number of female university graduates in the Arab Middle East, a clear indication of the importance placed on education by a people who have few other resources, many of whom are stateless.

Economic Roles For the majority of Palestinian women, dispersal signaled economic upheaval as lands and livelihoods were lost. As wages replaced land, many women lost their traditional roles in agriculture and some entered the wage-labor force. The rapid and jolting decline of the once central role of agriculture in Palestinian society hastened the process of girls' acquiring education, and, by the 1970s, a small core of women professionals could be identified. What stands out sharply, however, is women's entrance into the realm of nationalist political life. As women's economic and political participation increased, social constraints eased. Both economic need and a political crisis that generated mass mobilization of all sectors of the population have contributed to an easing of the sociocultural constraints that once operated to limit women's extradomestic activities.

In Israel and in many areas of the West Bank, significant numbers of Palestinian rural women are still active in agriculture. They tend animals, work on the land, and engage in household labor. Yet, since 1948, Palestinian women's labor has undergone a process of proletarianization. Following on the heels of occupation, economic restructuring gave rise to a steep decline in the number of Palestinians working in agriculture. As men migrated to the oil-producing countries or went to work in Israel, women, particularly older unskilled women, became more active in agriculture. Their agricultural labor facilitated their families' subsistence on the low wages paid by Israeli employers to Palestinian labor. Some poorer, rural, landless women work for wages in Israel or in the commercial farming sector in the West Bank. Their labor, as Palestinians and as women, is the lowest paid.

As education has endowed women with skills and the status associated with agricultural labor has declined, women have entered the nonagricultural work force. Women account for 10 to 20 percent of the nonagricultural wage-labor force in the West Bank and Gaza Strip. The need for money and the availability of jobs in both Israeli and Palestinian industry have tempered traditional notions that women's working outside the home threatens family honor. Although work in Israel is still spoken of as shameful, nearly 10 percent of employed women travel to Israel to work in agriculture, industry, and domestic service. Within the West Bank and Gaza Strip, small industrial concerns, more in the nature of workshops, are frequent employers of women. Women's conditions of work are poor. Channeled into jobs classified as women's work, particularly textiles and food processing, they are paid less than men. If married, they may face the double burden of work and domestic labor.

In exiled Palestinian communities, women's labor is a function of the location of their residence (rural or urban), their educational level, and host-country regulations governing a Palestinian's right to work. Lebanon has imposed the strictest controls on Palestinians' right to work. Women in camps located in rural areas in the south can find seasonal agricultural work; women in urban camps have much more difficulty finding employment. When the PALESTINE LIBERATION ORGANIZATION (PLO) was headquartered in Lebanon, Palestinian women found employment in its national institutions, which encompassed industry and services. With the evacuation of the PLO from Beirut in 1982, and the enforcement of Lebanese laws that severely restrict where Palestinians may be legally employed, Palestinian women in Lebanon have faced exceedingly high rates of unemployment in all sectors except agriculture.

There exists a small but quite visible core of Palestinian professional women employed largely in the educational, medical, and social-service fields. Individuals such as HANAN MIKHAIL ASHRAWI, professor of English literature at BIR ZEIT UNIVERSITY and the Palestinian spokesperson during the early stages of the peace negotiations, and Rita Giacaman, professor of public health and health activist, exemplify the emerging cadre of women.

In both the Occupied Territories and Lebanon, the GULF CRISIS, 1990–91, and the diminishment of PLO funds and employment opportunities have had serious impact on the financial status of Palestinian families. In Lebanon, for example, war widows depended on a small monthly pension from the PLO's Office of Social Affairs. In the early 1990s, their payments stopped, leading to a deteriorating economic outlook and further impoverishment. Nationalist institutions that employed refugee women have ceased operations, and official restrictions on Palestinians' right to work in Lebanon have meant that this community is facing a severe economic crisis.

Political Activism Palestinian women's involvement in nationalist and feminist politics dates to the early part of the twentieth century. Since its inception in the 1920s, the Palestinian women's movement has been enmeshed in a tension between its nationalist and feminist goals. Women struggled on two fronts as they organized simultaneously for national rights and women's rights. Thus although the women's movement flourished in the context of nationalist politics, it was always more than a response to the national question. As Palestinian women entered the public political realm, their sense of their own capabilities grew. In general, in the seventy years since Palestinian women began to organize, nationalism has been the public framework in which they have done so. Nationalism has mobilized women and accorded their activism legitimacy. Within the confines of nationalism, women have unsettled cultural notions of their role in society, particularly in the workplace and in public life.

The Palestinian women's movement emerged in the 1920s in the larger context of Palestinian nationalism and growing opposition to ZIONISM and the British PALESTINE MANDATE. Women participated in public demonstrations—by and large, urban elite women who had formed associations for charitable work and educational endeavors for young women. The social and the political arenas were not separate spheres of activism for women: the links between national and social conditions and women's status were fairly clear to activists.

In Jerusalem in 1921, a group of upper-class, urban, educated women formed the Palestine Women's Union (PWU), the first Palestinian's women's political organization, considered the precursor of the General Union of Palestinian Women (GUPW). The agenda of the PWU, formed in the mid-1960s as a component of the PLO, was to organize women to participate in nationalist activities and provide charitable assistance to the poor. In 1929, between 200 and 300 representatives of various women's societies and members of the PWU met in Jerusalem to join forces, struggling against colonization and working for the national cause. From this meeting was born the Arab Women's Congress of Palestine.

In 1936–39, women increased their militancy and gained experience that would inform their activities in the battles of 1947–48. Peasant women were also becoming involved in nationalist politics as the 1936 revolt spread through the countryside. While urban women organized demonstrations, strikes, and boycotts of Zionist products, their rural compatriots took part in the defense of their villages, carrying weapons and messages, hiding men wanted by the British authorities, and on occasion participating in armed actions. During both the 1936–39 revolt and the war of 1947–48, women organized relief and medical care for the wounded and for the stream of refugees moving between Palestinian cities and towns in 1948. Yet, the rural-urban schisms retained their strength during this period, and women did not coordinate their activities across regions in any discernible way.

Until 1948, the Palestinian women's movement was the preserve of upper-class, educated urban women, and its leadership was in the hands of women from notable families (the HUSAYNI FAMILY, NASHASHIBI FAMILY, ABDAL-HADI FAMILY, ALAMI FAMILY, and KHALIDI FAMILY), whose husbands frequently were well known on the political scene, often holding positions on the ARAB EXECUTIVE. Yet, these women were not mere appendages of the male nationalist movement. Indeed, they were financially independent of the national movement and worked together in spite of their families' rivalries.

Palestinian women did not explicitly confront the cultural conventions governing gender, yet in practice, their public presence was serving notice that nationalist activities eventually would unsettle cultural notions of gender. Although Palestinian activists were aware of other Arab women's movements that directly addressed women's issues, they felt that their first priority was to work for national independence.

From 1948 to 1965, the Palestinian women's movement was fragmented and tightly controlled by various host Arab states. With the emergence of the Palestine Liberation Organization (PLO) in the mid-1960s, a centralized women's movement also emerged; its organizational expression was the General Union of Palestinian Women (GUPW). What were different about the emergent movement were the middle-class origin of its leadership, its attempts to engage in mass mobilization of women, and the closer, more dependent nature of its linkage with the larger national movement. With headquarters in Jerusalem, then Amman, and later Beirut and Tunis, the GUPW is the overarching organization in which women have worked to mobilize Palestinian women for national struggle. Composed of women's sections from the major Palestinian political organizations such as FATAH, the POPULAR FRONT FOR THE LIBERATION OF PALESTINE (PFLP), the DEMOCRATIC FRONT FOR THE LIBERATION OF PALESTINE (DFLP), and a series of smaller organizations and independents, the movement's publicly stated main goal is to mobilize women for national struggle. Women's emancipation is believed to follow on the heels of national liberation. Yet within the women's movement, there always have been subtle differences of opinion about the relationship between nationalism and feminism. Since the late 1970s, and more so with the advent of the 1987 INTIFADA (uprising) in the Occupied Territories, the peace process, and the formation of the PALESTINIAN AUTHORITY, an increasingly substantial and vocal minority has posited that women's issues must be an integral component of state formation.

During the era of the Palestinian resistance movement's presence and organization in Lebanon (1968–82), women made notable strides in employment, political activism, participation in military operations, and community-based social work. Nationalist organizing and struggle provided a context within which women were able to press their claims for more personal autonomy and mobility. Prolonged conflict and militancy opened spaces in which attitudes toward women underwent remarkable transformations. Although few women were in the military, the sensational operations of women such as LAYLA KHALID in the airplane hijackings of the early 1970s placed Palestinian women's militancy in the forefront of the international and local media. The national framework endowed legitimacy on both women's expanded political and economic participation and the social changes that ensued.

Since the 1960s, the family as an arena of social control over women has faced a number of challenges. Family control over marriages has shifted toward women's active participation in the decision-making process and points to the strengthening of the nuclear family and the conjugal couple. Women are also spending more time away from the home and family: they are working, studying, and engaging in political activities. It is important to point out that politically active women rarely broke ties with their families or engaged in protracted conflict with them. The kinds of strategies encouraged by the women's movement were gradual means of gaining a family's support for a daughter's activism. An attack on cultural notions of gender was not on the agenda of either the national movement or the Palestinian women's movement. Activists believed that any open assault on gender roles and family structure would only provoke a backlash that neither women nor the national movement would be able to confront. Thus, neither movement promoted an ideology of radical social change.

In the late 1970s, women in the Occupied Territories organized a series of grass-roots women's committees that, although nationally motivated, focused their energies on socioeconomic mobilization and initiation of change in both rural and urban sectors. They offered services, particularly in health, education, and child care; training and development of a number of income-generating projects. This enhanced their ability to set their agenda according to their own perception of women's needs rather than those imposed on them by the national movement. These committees were instrumental in organizing and sustaining neighborhood and local committees during the Intifada.

There has been a widespread recognition of the vitally important role played by women in sustaining the Intifada through the work of their grass-roots organizations, which are now critical social units in an emerging state.

Women were also often in the forefront of demonstrations and actively participated in confrontations with the occupying forces. Women were present on the diplomatic stage as well. The Palestinian negotiating team in the peace talks included two highly articulate and experienced activists from the Occupied Territories—Hanan Mikhail Ashrawi and SUAD AMIRY.

Participation in nationalist politics has had at times a profound impact on women's larger political consciousness. Restrictions on their participation in nationalist politics gave rise to a questioning of the gender order as young women fought with their families and the larger society for permission to engage in political activity. This emerging feminist consciousness existed in a state of seemingly muted tension with a political struggle framed in decidedly nationalist terms. A definitely feminist trend emerged in the wake of the Intifada as a growing Islamist movement, and the concessions of the nationalist movement to it convinced women that it was time to organize around a specifically feminist-nationalist framework, since they also saw the gains they had made during the Intifada being threatened by the increasingly conservative social climate promoted by the Islamists.

With the formation of the Palestinian Authority in the West Bank and Gaza Strip, the agenda of the Palestinian women's movement underwent a shift in direction and strategy. Women are now focusing on issues of policy. New women's centers envision their role as advocates for women's rights and services in the new Palestinian entity as well as in arenas where women can learn the skills they need to pursue their rights. Activist women see in the discourse of democracy a potential means of bridging the gap between feminist and nationalist discourses and agendas. The GUPW's Declaration of Principles on Palestinian Women's Rights, presented to YASIR ARAFAT in July 1994, made clear their agenda. This declaration demands complete equality of civil, political, educational, and work rights as well as the right to citizenship and its transmission to their children. Equally significant, they are asking for equality in personal rights, which is governed by Islamic laws on personal status. These demands are framed in terms of the discourse of democracy and individual rights.

The growing influence of Islamic groups such as HAMAS, particularly in the West Bank and Gaza

Strip, but also in the Palestinian exile communities, has reintroduced some of the restrictions on women that had been easing since the 1970s, propelled by women's political activism and growing participation in the work force. A conservative ideology of gender relations is evident in the reveiling of large numbers of women, often a barometer of social trends, and increasing pressures for gender segregation in public life.

Art and Cultural Production Although women are involved in nearly all forms of artistic production, there is an exclusively female artistic tradition of Palestinian EMBROIDERY. In pre-1948 Palestine, village women embroidered their dresses, head scarves, and cushions in bright, highly elaborate designs using the cross-stitch. Regional variations determined embroidery designs. Since the later 1960s, in the Occupied Territories and in the diaspora, Palestinian embroidery has been revived and suffused with new meaning. Palestinian women's charitable associations and social and cultural organizations affiliated with the PLO began to promote the production of embroidered items as a way to preserve Palestinian cultural heritage and as a source of income for women. Women in the refugee camps embroider items that are sold both locally and internationally through associations such as *Najda* (Palestine Aid Society) and *In'ash al-Usra* (Family Rehabilitation).

Elderly women are often repositories of Palestinian FOLKLORE and songs. In the Occupied Territories and among REFUGEES in Lebanon, projects to record these women's knowledge of oral culture are under way. Palestinian women have played a significant role in LITERATURE as well. The novelist Sahar Khalifeh (*Wild Thorns*) and the poetess FADWA TUQAN (*A Mountainous Journey*) are among the well-known and respected literary figures whose works have been translated into English.

Julie Peteet

BIBLIOGRAPHY

Antonious, Soraya. "Fighting on Two Fronts: Conversations with Palestinian Women." *Journal of Palestine Studies* 8, no. 3. (spring): 26–45.

Giacaman, Rita, and Penny Johnson. "Palestinian Women: Building Barricades and Breaking Barriers." In *Intifada: The Palestinian Uprising Against Israeli Occupation,* ed. by Zachary Lockman and Joel Beinin. Boston: South End Press, 1989.

Hammami, Rema. "Women, the Hijab and the Intifada." *Middle East Report* 20 (May–August 1991): 24–28.

Hilterman, Joost. *Behind the Intifada: Labor and Women's Movements in the Occupied Territories.* Princeton; N.J.: Princeton University Press, 1991.

Khalifeh, Sahar. *Wild Thorns.* Trans. by Trevor LeGassick and Elizabeth Fernea. London: al-Saqi, 1985.

Mogannam, Matiel. *The Arab Woman and the Palestine Problem.* London: Herbert Joseph, 1937. Reprint, Westport, Conn.: Hyperion Press, 1976.

Najjar, Orayb, with Kitty Warnock. *Portraits of Palestinian Women.* Salt Lake City: University of Utah Press, 1992.

Peteet, Julie. *Gender in Crisis: Women and the Palestinian Resistance Movement.* New York: Columbia University Press, 1991.

Sayigh, Rosemary. "Encounters with Palestinian Women under Occupation." *Journal of Palestine Studies* 10, no. 4 (summer 1981): 3–26.

———. "Femmes palestiniennes: Une histoire en quête d'historiens." *Revue d'études palestiniennes* 23 (spring 1987).

Tucker, Judith. "Ties That Bound: Women and Family in Eighteenth- and Nineteenth-Century Nablus." In *Women in Middle Eastern History: Shifting Boundaries in Sex and Gender,* ed. by Nikki Keddie and Beth Baron. New Haven, Conn, and London: Yale University Press, 1991.

Tuqan, Fadwa. *A Mountainous Journey.* St. Paul, Minn.: Graywolf Press, 1990.

Warnock, Kitty. *Land before Honour.* New York: Monthly Review Press, 1990.

Young, Elise. *Keepers of the History: Women and the Israeli-Palestinian Conflict.* New York: Teachers College Press, 1992.

Woodhead Commission
1938

In the face of Zionist and Palestinian opposition to the recommendation of the PEEL COMMISSION, 1937, that Palestine be partitioned between Jews and Palestinians, the British Foreign Office created the Woodhead Commission in January 1938 to reexamine the question of partition. The office was particularly concerned about continued hostility to British programs in Palestine throughout the ARAB WORLD at a time when war clouds loomed on the horizons of Europe and Italian troops were ensconced in Libya and Ethiopia.

The commission, chaired by Sir John Woodhead and officially called the Palestine Partition Commission, arrived in Palestine in April 1938 and carried out its investigations despite a boycott of its hearings by Palestinian leaders. The commission issued its findings in November 1938. The four members of the commission could not agree on a single proposal, but they did agree that Palestine could not be partitioned between the two communities as proposed by the Peel Commission. Nonetheless, they issued three proposals, known as Plans A, B, and C. The Zionist movement rejected the commission report because of the limited scope of the proposed Jewish state in all three plans.

Faced with such hostility and with the growing feeling that partition was unworkable, the British government issued a White Paper in November 1938 calling for a conference in London at which Zionists and Arabs could discuss the future of Palestine.

Michael R. Fischbach

Yasin, Ahmad

Islamic militant

1936– al-Jura

Born near Asqalan (Hebrew *Ashkelon*), Yasin and his family fled to the GAZA STRIP as a result of the ARAB-ISRAELI WAR OF 1948. After teacher training, Yasin worked as a teacher in Gaza from 1957 to 1964. He later studied at Ayn Shams University in Egypt in 1964–65 but was returned to Gaza by Egyptian authorities because of his involvement with the Society of the Muslim Brotherhood. He continued working as a teacher after the Israeli occupation of Gaza in 1967 until his retirement in 1984. He is addressed by the title al-Shaykh as a sign of religious respect.

Yasin had become the leading Islamic militant in the Occupied Territories by the 1980s. He was a key figure in the establishment of the Islamic Center in Gaza, the open expression of the underground Muslim Brotherhood, in 1973. He eventually ran afoul of Israeli occupation authorities and was imprisoned in April 1984. Released as part of a prisoner exchange in May 1985, he went on to establish the influential Islamic resistance group HAMAS during the INTIFADA in August 1988.

Yasin was imprisoned once again by the Israelis in May 1989. The ailing shaykh was released on October 1, 1997, and flown to Jordan for medical treatment as part of a deal whereby Jordan released two captured Israeli intelligence operatives who had tried to assassinate a Hamas leader in Jordan several days earlier. Yasin returned five days later to a hero's welcome.

Michael R. Fischbach

Z

Zayyad, Tawfiq

politician, poet
1929–1994 Nazareth

Zayyad rose to head the Israeli Communist Party (ICP) branch in NAZARETH after the creation of Israel. When (RAKAH) the New Communist List, split from the ICP in August 1965, Zayyad followed it and rose to prominence in the party. In 1974, he was elected to the Knesset from Rakah. The following year, Zayyad was elected mayor of Nazareth, Israel's largest Palestinian city, as part of the Rakah-backed Nazareth Democratic Front. He was also a key figure in the Rakah-dominated Democratic Front for Peace and Equality (DFPE), established in 1977. Zayyad resigned his Knesset seat in 1991 but remained active in the DFPE and was elected its head in 1992. Like Rakah, Zayyad supported the PALESTINE LIBERATION ORGANIZATION (PLO) and met with PLO figures in the United States in October 1981.

Zayyad was also a noted poet. His writings, especially his 1966 collection of poetry *Ashiddu ala Yadaykum* (Warmly I shake your hands), are considered classic works of Palestinian resistance LITERATURE. He also studied political economy and Russian literature in the SOVIET UNION from 1962 to 1964 and translated Russian literature into Arabic.

Zayyad was killed in an automobile accident on July 5, 1994, while returning to Nazareth from JERICHO after a meeting with the PLO chairman, YASIR ARAFAT.

Michael R. Fischbach

Zionism: Attitudes and Policies

Zionism emerged in European Jewish thinking in the midnineteenth century as an ideology that preached the unity of world Jewry, not merely as a religion but also as a nationality. Zionists believed that Jews constituted a national group who ought to end their centuries-old dispersion ("diaspora"; Hebrew, *galut*), return to "Zion" (Hebrew *Tziyon*), and rebuild their ancient homeland in *Eretz Yisrael,* the biblical Land of Israel. Zionists believed that such a return (often capitalized, as in "the central Jewish myth of Exile and Return") would lead to the redemption, both spiritual and physical, of the Jewish people.

Given its nineteenth-century European origins, classical Zionist thinking paid little or no heed to the indigenous population of the region to which Zionists would be migrating, which they would be claiming as their national home. Not for several decades would Zionist leaders begin to grapple with the obstacles, contradictions, and injustices inherent in the pursuit of their solution to the Jewish problem—a solution that was not achievable, in the end, without exacting a terrible price from the Palestinians.

Before the advent of Zionism, the core communities of Jews in Ottoman Palestine resided mainly in the four holy cities, JERUSALEM, HEBRON, SAFAD, and TIBERIAS. Their presence in, and migration to, the Holy Land had persisted over the centuries under mainly religious inspiration since their last dispersion in the year 135 C.E. In 1882, these members of the "old" *yishuv* (community) numbered approximately 23,000 among a total population of some 400,000 to 500,000 Muslim and Christian Palestinians. Along with other ultra-Orthodox Jews around the world, they awaited divine intervention in the form of the coming of the Messiah, rather than the arrival of a European

TABLE 1
Changing Population Balance in Mandatory Palestine

	MUSLIMS	CHRISTIANS	TOTAL ARABS	JEWS	OTHER	TOTAL
1918 est.	512,000	60,880	572,880	66,100 (10.3%)	n.a.	638,980
1929	712,343	81,776	794,119	156,481 (16.3%)	9443	96 0,043
1936	848,342	106,474	954,816	370,483 (27.7%)	11,219	1,336,518
1939	927,133	116,958	1,044,091	445,457 (29.7%)	12,150	1,501,698
1946	1,076,783	145,063	1,221,846	608,225 (33.0%)	15,488	1,845,559

Sources: Palestine Blue Book (annual).

secular national movement, to usher in the redemption of the Jewish people.

The first organized group of modern Zionist immigrants who planned to create a self-contained Jewish nation was the Russian BILU society, whose first settlers arrived in Palestine in 1882. These began the "first *aliya*" (literally, "ascent" or "rising"; in this context, "wave of immigration"). They were followed by successive waves of Zionist immigrant-settlers of later *aliyot* (plural of *aliya*). Immigration from the first and second *aliyot* introduced both urban and rural elements and brought the Jewish population in the area to almost 80,000 by 1914.

In 1897, Zionism became an organized movement when various groups were united in a single World Zionist Organization (WZO) at the first Zionist Congress held at Basel, Switzerland. Theodor Herzl (1860–1904), who inspired and organized the congress, became the organization's first president. The program adopted at Basel in 1897 became the guiding manifesto of the Zionist movement. Ignoring the indigenous population in what one noted Palestinian historian called "a spirit characteristic of their age and continent," delegates defined the aim of Zionism as being "to create for the Jewish people a home in Palestine secured by public law" and indicated four means to the attainment of that end: colonization by Jewish workers, organizational unification of the Jewish people, fostering of "Jewish national sentiment," and steps toward obtaining "governmental consent" for the attainment of the aim of Zionism.

TABLE 2
Jewish Immigration to Palestine, estimated by *aliya*

First	(1882–1903) - 20–30,000
Second	(1904–1914) - 35,000–40,000
Third	(1919–1923) - 35,000
Fourth	(1924–1931) - 82,000 (1924–1928)*
Fifth	(1932–1944) - 265,000 (1933–1939)*

Source: S.N. Eisenstadt, *The Absorption of Immigrants* (London, 1954).

*E. Barnavi, ed. *A Historical Atlas of the Jewish People* (New York: Knopf, 1992), 220.

Initially, the Zionist Congress met annually, but after 1901 it met only every two years. For most of its history, the Zionist movement was dominated by "practical Zionists," whose approach emphasized achievements on the ground in Palestine—mainly immigration, land purchase, and building of settlements—rather than mobilization of political support from the international community. In Palestine, the separateness of Jewish settlers, rather than their assimilation or integration into Palestinian society, was the key to Zionist colonization. As Dr. Arthur Ruppin (1876–1943), who became known as "the father of Zionist settlement," described it during the 1913 Zionist Congress, the pattern of Jewish settlement and land purchase aimed at "the creation of a Jewish milieu and of a closed Jewish economy in which producers, consumers and middlemen shall all be Jewish." A company for purchasing land, the Jewish National Fund (JNF), was formed in 1901. Its statutes provided that lands acquired by the JNF became the inalienable property of the Jewish people.

In addition to trying to acquire Palestine "*dunum* by *dunum*," Zionist leaders became increasingly active in lobbying for support among the Jewish and Gentile public in the capitals of Europe. As an ideology, Zionism was slow to win the backing of the established elites of the Jewish communities in Eastern and Western Europe, creating periodic crises over its financial or ideological viability. During and immediately after World War I, an ailing WZO was taken over and rejuvenated by Dr. Chaim Weizmann (1874–1952), a Russian-born chemist who had emigrated to England in 1904. Weizmann teamed up with the veteran Zionist Nahum Sokolov (1860–1936), and together they succeeded in outmaneuvering anti-Zionist members of the Anglo-Jewish establishment in a battle for credibility in the eyes of influential British leaders.

The main fruit of the new Anglo-Zionist alliance was the BALFOUR DECLARATION of November 2, 1917, which one Palestinian historian has called "the document in which the Zionist myth became British policy and which constituted the first major step on the road to the Palestinian Arab Diaspora." Under the terms of the sixty-seven-word statement conveyed in a letter addressed by Foreign Secretary Arthur Balfour to the president of the English Zionist Federation, His Majesty's Government "view[ed] with favour the establishment in Palestine of a national home for the Jewish people" and would "use their best endeavours to facilitate the achievement of this object, it being clearly understood that nothing shall be done that may be done which may prejudice the civil and religious rights of existing non-Jewish communities."

This last-quoted phrase became the source of much controversy, as it signaled British intentions to bypass any national aspirations of the native Palestinian population, whom Europeans regarded in those days as "Muslim and Christian inhabitants," rather than "Arabs" or "Palestinians." The same Eurocentric and pro-Zionist wording was built into the text of the July 1922 League of Nations document, which endorsed the declaration and formally accorded the PALESTINE MANDATE to Great Britain.

Leaders of the Palestinians immediately recognized the Balfour Declaration's stifling effect on their own national aspirations, and they refused to acknowledge the right of Great Britain or the international community to award any special status to Jews inside or outside Palestine. This attitude was reflected in Palestinian leaders' frequent calls for rescinding the Balfour Declaration, their refusal to recognize the legality of the League of Nations Mandate, and their almost unanimous boycott of political dealings with representatives of official Zionist bodies.

The Anglo-Zionist alliance began showing its first signs of strain in the early 1920s, partly in response to expressions of Palestinian discontent and resistance in 1920 and 1921. During this period many Zionists grew impatient and disappointed with their new British patrons, despite the enactment of regulations favoring Jewish land purchase and immigration. The difficulties faced by British administrators in governing Palestine and implementing the Zionist policy against the wishes of its Arab inhabitants gradually ate away at the foundations of the Anglo-Zionist alliance.

Yet, despite such obstacles, further waves of Jewish immigration continued to increase the Jewish population of Palestine in both absolute and relative terms. During the British Mandate period (1922–48), almost 400,000 Jews arrived in Palestine, mainly from Europe and mainly after 1930. Land purchases by the JNF and other agencies gradually gave the Zionists a small but vital core of their future national territory. By 1947, these agencies had purchased around 7 percent of the land surface of the country: an estimated 12 percent of available arable lands and, by some accounts, the richest and most fertile parts of Palestine. Of the remaining 93 percent, 47 percent was under Palestinian ownership and 46 percent was classified as state land.

TABLE 3

Jewish Immigration to Palestine: selected years as recorded by the British mandatory administration

YEAR	IMMIGRATION	EMIGRATION	NET MIGRATION
1922	7,844	1,503	6,341
1924	12,856	2,073	10,783
1925	33,801	2,151	29,650
1927	2,713	5,071	-3,358
1928	2,178	2,168	10
1929	5,249	1,746	3,503
1932	9,553	n.a.	
1933	30,327	n.a.	

1934	42,757	n.a.	
1935	61,854	396	61,458
1936	29,727	773	28,954
1937	10,536	889	9,647
1939	16,405	1,019	15,386
1940	4,547	n.a.	
1943	8,507	n.a.	
194	14,464	n.a.	
1945	12,751	n.a.	
1946	7,851*	n.a.	
1947	n.a.*	n.a.	

Source: Palestine Blue Books (annual). According to various Israeli sources, the figure for 1946 should be 17,760 or 18,760, and that for 1947, 21,542 or 22,098.

Official Statements and Positions of the Zionist Organization In the final decades of Ottoman rule, the arrival of the first Zionist settlers corresponded with the awakening of Arab national feeling in the region. Observers such as Najib Azury predicted that two rival national movements were on an inevitable collision course. Indeed, Arab-Jewish relations in Palestine were soon marked by mutual segregation, rivalry, and deepening antagonism.

Zionist leaders were slow to react to the growing evidence that their intended homeland was not vacant but rather was populated by a relatively large population of Arabic-speaking Muslims and Christians whose own political consciousness was growing fast. From the arrival of the first settlers until the creation of the state of Israel in 1948, most of those Zionists who did perceive an "Arab question" saw it as a subsidiary issue to solving "the Jewish problem." Zionists wanted to

- correct the *yishuv*'s numerical and physical weakness
- ensure international diplomatic support for the Zionist endeavor
- exercise a certain isolationism and caution in dealing with the surrounding Arab population

Consistent with the tendency to downplay any Arab "question" or "problem," the WZO issued few official statements that dealt directly with the Arabs of Palestine. Partly as a result of Dr. Weizmann's first encounters with Palestinian leaders in 1918, Zionists developed the notion that it would be sufficient to develop healthy economic and social relations with the Palestinians while reserving political relations for the wider Arab world outside Palestine.

A common theme of official Zionist declarations was the lofty sentiment that Zionism intended to bring no harm, but only benefit, to the local inhabitants, and that the Jews desired to live together with the Arabs in peace and harmony. Thus, for example, the XIIth Zionist Congress meeting in Carlsbad in September 1921 passed a resolution declaring: "The two great Semitic peoples united of yore by the bonds of common creative civilisation will not fail in the hour of their national regeneration to comprehend the need of combining their vital interests in a common endeavour." The resolution further called upon the executive "to redouble its efforts to secure an honourable entente with the Arab people on the basis of this Declaration and in strict accordance with the Balfour Declaration," and ended by "emphatically" declaring "that the progress of Jewish colonisation will not affect the rights and needs of the working Arab nation." The 1921 resolution would be reaffirmed at subsequent biennial congresses. A noted Palestinian historian has decried such language as part of "the Zionist predilection for happy euphemisms" that covered more sinister intentions.

Another way in which the Palestinians appeared, although only indirectly, in official Zionist pronouncements was in Zionist Congress resolutions defining the organization's attitude to various crises in pre-1948 Palestine. Zionists frequently debated such questions as

- the appropriate response to outbreaks of Palestinian rioting and attacks, especially after 1921, 1929, and 1936
- whether the Palestinians were to be considered a "national movement"
- proposals by Vladimir (Zeev) Jabotinsky (1880–1940), leader of the Revisionist Party, for the creation of a visible Jewish military force—an "iron wall" that would protect Jewish settlements in Palestine better than the existing low-profile underground defense force known as the Haganah

Zionists were also called upon to define their positions on political proposals for the future of the country. In 1931, for example, the XVIIth Zionist Congress—meeting in the wake of the 1929 riots and the ensuing inquiry reports and white papers—rejected Jabotinsky's campaign to persuade the WZO to come out officially with the demand for a Jewish state in all of Palestine. Instead, it elected a leadership, under Nahum Sokolov, that endorsed the "basic principle that, without reference to numerical strength, neither of the two peoples shall dominate or be dominated by the other."

Several years later, when the British cabinet endorsed the PEEL COMMISSION's report calling for the partition of Palestine into a small, sovereign Jewish state and an Arab state to be joined to Transjordan, delegates to the XXth Zionist Congress meeting in Zurich voted by a two-thirds majority in favor of accepting the proposal in principle, although not in its details. The congress further reaffirmed previous declarations "expressing the readiness of the Jewish people to reach a peaceful settlement with the Arabs of Palestine, based on the free development of both peoples and the mutual recognition of their respective rights."

Driven by the crisis of European Jewry under Nazi persecution, an "Extraordinary Zionist Conference" held at New York's Biltmore Hotel in May 1942 redefined the official Zionist political goal as the making of Palestine into a sovereign "Jewish commonwealth"—that is, a Jewish state in all of Palestine. The Biltmore resolutions appeared to revoke the movement's recent endorsement of partition, while recalling earlier Zionist Congress resolutions "expressing the readiness and the desire of the Jewish people for full cooperation with their Arab neighbors."

Although the WZO officially supported the full Biltmore program even as late as the Basel Congress of 1947, members of the executive of the Jewish Agency for Palestine began hinting in early 1946 that Zionists would be ready to consider partition as a viable scenario for satisfying their aims in Palestine. Once the United Nations Special Committee on Palestine (UNSCOP) proposals to partition Palestine into separate Jewish and Arab states were on the table in late 1947, the WZO publicly favored acceptance.

Zionist Structures and Personalities The WZO opened its first official office in Palestine in Jaffa in 1908 under Arthur Ruppin and Dr. Yaacov Thon (1880–1950). Ruppin, who served for many years on the Zionist Executive, would later be a founding member of the Brit Shalom ("Covenant of Peace") society, which advocated a binational state as a way to achieve rapprochement with the Palestinians. Dr. Thon became a central member of the local leadership body of Palestine's Jewish community (the Vaad Leumi, or "National Council"), which often found itself in disagreement with the mainly "foreign" Zionist leaders who dominated the executive bodies of the world Zionist Organization until the mid-1930s.

Arriving behind the victorious British forces in 1918, a new body, the Zionist Commission for Palestine (ZC), superseded the WZO's Palestine office. The ZC was headed by Chaim Weizmann, and the fifth among its seven mandated tasks was "to help in establishing friendly relations with the Arabs and other non-Jewish communities." The ZC was soon replaced by the Palestine Zionist Executive (PZE), headed by Weizmann's personal appointee, an Anglo-Jewish career officer in the British army, Lt. Col. Frederick H. Kisch (1888–1943). Kisch served as director of the Political Department and chairman of the PZE from 1923 to 1931. In 1928, an important expansion of the WZO into the "Jewish Agency for Palestine" (JA) and its Executive (JAE) had the important effect of enlisting greater American Jewish commitment to the Zionist effort.

The "Arab policy" of Weizmann and Kisch had both an external and an internal dimension. Externally, it consisted of promoting friendly relations with the Hashemite princes Faysal and Abdullah in attempts to bypass the unwelcoming attitude of the Arabs of Palestine. The Weizmann-Faysal agreement, signed in London, January 3, 1919, was worked out with Col. T. E. Lawrence and had the immediate purpose of harmonizing the positions of all three parties before the Paris Peace Conference. The text of the agreement spelled out areas of cooperation between two mutually recognized entities: "the Arab State" (Faysal's independent kingdom in Damascus) and "Palestine" as envisaged in the Balfour Declaration.

Although this diplomatic document remained inoperative, it symbolized one of the recurring approaches of Zionists to the Arab question: namely, attempts to arrange what might be called an "exchange of services" with Arab leaders from outside Palestine. If these leaders could moderate Palestinian Arabs' objections to Zionism, the Zionists argued, then a Jewish Palestine and its worlwide Zionist supporters might place immense economic and political resources at the disposal of the Arab nation as a whole. After Faysal, it was only Emir (later King) Abdullah who showed any sustained interest in this "exchange of services" with the Zionists, but Abdullah's ability to influence Palestinians to agree to such a settlement was limited.

Inside Palestine, the PZE's "Arab policy" consisted of support for the attempts of people like the land-purchase agent Chaim Kalvariski (1867–1947) to create pro-Zionist Arab organizations and to influence Arab opinion through press subsidies. This activity was based on the assumption that some Palestinians took a "moderate" view of Zionism but needed encouragement against those who were seen as adopting "extremist" attitudes toward the Jews and the British presence.

During the early 1930s, when the Zionist dream of transforming Palestine quickly into a Jewish *Eretz Yisrael* seemed stalemated, Frederick Kisch was replaced by a new JAE leadership mainly from the dynamic Jewish labor sector in Palestine. These "socialist Zionists" had been dealing with an "Arab question" of their own for several decades, as the thrust of their brand of Zionism was to rebuild a new Jewish society by creating a strong, organized Jewish working-class movement. The impact of their *kibbush ha-avodah* ("conquest of labor") and *avodah ivrit* ("Hebrew labor") campaigns was to alienate those Palestinians who had previously enjoyed employment in the Jewish community. Yet, under the influence of their internationalist and socialist ideologies, some left-wing labor parties advocated the formation of mixed or joint labor unions, and also a binational state rather than partition or a purely Jewish state.

Chaim Arlosoroff (1899–1933), a young leader of the mainstream MAPAI labor party, headed the Political Department of the JAE in Jerusalem from 1931 until his assassination by unknown assailants in June 1933. In 1921 he had been among the first to recognize the reality of a Palestinian national movement, and in mid-1932 he reached the drastic conclusion that only a Jewish coup d'état in Palestine could save Zionism from imminent collapse. Despite the intellectual brilliance of his analysis of past and possible future stages of the Arab-Zionist conflict, his day-to-day "Arab policy" was hardly different from the futile approach of his predecessors. Relations between the JA and Abdullah were strengthened during his tenure, lending encouragement to those who wanted to see Transjordanian land opened up to Zionist settlement.

In late 1933, the new JAE included some fresh faces who would eventually shape Zionist policy even more than had the London- (and sometimes Rehovot-) based Chaim Weizmann: David Ben-Gurion (1886–1973) and Moshe Shertok (after 1949, Sharett, 1894–1965). Although their attitudes to Arabs were hard-line in contrast to those of members of Brit Shalom or other rapprochement groups, Ben-Gurion and Shertok were far more energetic in pursuit of some accommodation with Palestinian and neighboring Arabs than were most of their colleagues in leadership circles.

Within their own party, Ben-Gurion and Shertok argued for a greater appreciation of the Arab factor and rejected as futile previous political activity that had been based on the payment of *bakshish* ("bribes"), on sentimental racial-kinship theories, or on the maintaining of a low profile. Especially during 1934–36, Ben-Gurion sought meetings with representative Arab leaders whose patriotism was beyond reproach, hoping "to find a way to an understanding with the Arab national movement on the basis of what we and they want." During these years, he and Shertok met with Riyad al-Sulh, MUSA AL-ALAMI, AWNI ABD AL-HADI, GEORGE ANTONIUS, Ihsan al-Jabiri, and Amir Shakib Arslan.

Ben-Gurion's openness did little, however, to win the hearts of his Arab interlocutors; rather, they had the effect of drastically increasing Arab alarm at the extent of Zionist determination and the true scope of Zionist aims. Arab leaders found unacceptable Ben-Gurion's insistence on continued Jewish immigration and on eventual creation of a Jewish state on both sides of the Jordan. They even rejected his "parity" proposals for (transitional) constitutional relations inside Palestine, as well as his appeal to the pan-Arab framework as the route to a final answer to the Palestine dispute. Nevertheless, throughout these meetings, Ben-Gurion never found the Palestinian Arabs' case convincing enough to modify his own maximalist brand of Zionism.

Interpretation of Zionist Attitudes Despite attempts to portray the growing Arab-Zionist conflict over Palestine as a result of misunderstanding, or as an issue resolvable by eliminating outside interference and/or increasing the "good faith" displayed by the protagonists, several aspects of the conflict seemed to make it a "zero-sum game." The arrival of every new Zionist immigrant affected the population balance and whittled away at the preexisting Palestinian majority, leading to heightened Palestinian fears in the mid-1930s that the Jews might overtake them in a race for numerical supremacy and control of the country. Every *dunum* of land purchased by the JNF or similar agencies reduced the amount of land available for Palestinian agriculture as well as expanding the region's potential to absorb more Jewish immigrants.

The vast majority of Zionists did not consider Arab opposition to be a serious enough obstacle to deflect the ultimate advance of Zionism. Many believed instinctively in their own cultural superiority and in the beneficial impact Western "progress" would have on all the inhabitants of the area. Some deliberately chose, for tactical reasons, not to focus on the question of relations with the Palestinians. A minority, however, argued that, without resolving the "unseen question" of the contradictions between Arab and Zionist aims, there would be no guarantee of the Zionist project's success.

Among Zionists, there were many ideological outlooks on the Arabs and the Palestinians. On the right wing of the spectrum were the Zionist Revisionists. In 1925 they formed their own party, which in 1935 formally dissociated itself from the WZO headed by Weizmann and Ben-Gurion. Jabotinsky's Revisionists dissented from the Zionist mainstream in rejecting its gradualist approach and its cooperation with the Mandatory power. Another disputed area was the policy of *havlaga* ("self-restraint") practiced by the underground Haganah organization, which answered to the JAE leadership. Revisionists inspired the creation of dissident paramilitary organizations, mainly the Irgun Zvai Leumi (ETZEL, or "National Military Organization") and a more radical splinter group, the Lohamei Herut Yisrael (LEHI, or "Fighters for the Freedom of Israel," also known as the Stern Gang). These militant groups favored open rebellion against the British and also took more drastic action against Arab targets, whether in retaliation for attacks against Jews or in attempts to terrorize the Arab population into submission or flight.

Professing a more realistic and respectful attitude to the Palestinians, Revisionist politicians also laid claims to a Jewish state on both sides of the Jordan River (the full territory of the original British Mandate in 1922). Although they would have been willing to offer Palestinians the option of remaining an eventual minority in the future Jewish state, Zionist Revisionists believed that most Palestinians would have preferred to move to Iraq, Syria, or eastern Transjordan in order to live under Arab sovereignty. Although Revisionists were the main public advocates of the TRANSFER, or expulsion, of Palestinians to neighboring lands, recent research has shown that the concept of transfer was entertained by individuals across the Zionist spectrum. Prior to 1948 (and until 1977), proponents of the Revisionist philosophy (later incorporated into the Herut ["freedom"] and Likud ["Unity"] parties) remained in opposition to the dominant center-left labor party, Mapai.

If the Revisionists were maximalists, the left-wing minimalists advocated the conversion of Palestine into a binational, Arab-Jewish state in which both peoples would share equally in the government regardless of their relative proportions of the total population. Among the leading proponents of the binational idea were such idealists and humanists as Dr. Arthur Ruppin, the world-renowned philosopher Martin Buber, and Chaim Kalvariski. Another well-known supporter of binationalism was Dr. Judah L. Magnes, the American-born president and chancellor of the Hebrew University of Jerusalem. The most notable of the associations formed to advance binationalism during the Mandate period were Brit Shalom (f. 1925), the League for Jewish-Arab Rapprochement and Co-operation (f. 1939), and Ihud ("Unity," f. 1942). Two left-wing workers' parties, Poalei Tziyon Smol ("Left Faction, Workers of Zion") and Ha-shomer Ha-tzair ("the Young Watchman"), also took an active part in advocating a binational solution.

But binationalism never became a strong force among either Zionists or Arabs. The idea seems to have reached a high point in the year 1946, when the arguments advanced by Magnes and Buber before the ANGLO-AMERICAN COMMITTEE OF INQUIRY, 1945–1946, influenced the committee's report, which proposed that "Jew shall not dominate Arab and Arab shall not dominate Jew," and that "Palestine shall be neither a Jewish state nor an Arab state." But that committee's recommendations soon proved unworkable, and subsequently the UNITED NATIONS opted for the partition of Mandatory Palestine.

Occupying the middle of the Zionist spectrum was the Jewish labor movement, represented mainly by its party, Ahdut Ha-avodah ("Unity of Labor"; after 1931, Mapai, or "Workers' Party of Eret Yisrael"). This party advocated the goal of a Jewish majority and a Jewish state in Palestine, with the promise that the future Arab minority would enjoy full constitutional rights. Over the years, Ben-Gurion and other leading labor ideologists also proposed various formulae for cantons and national autonomy that would recognize the population's binational character. When the 1937 congress voted to accept, in principle, the Peel Commission proposal of a Jewish state in only part of Palestine, labor Zionists followed Ben-Gurion's lead and retreated (some only tactically) from the full Zionist program. Their hopes that this would be interpreted as a "compromise" and, as such, reciprocated by the Arabs, were highly unrealistic, as the Peel plan (including provision for the "forcible transfer of Arabs" from the proposed Jewish state) was rejected by Palestinians and by neighboring Arabs as "a nightmare come true."

Between 1882 and 1947, when the WZO officially accepted the United Nations proposal to partition Palestine, Zionist hopes were somewhat reduced in an attempt to adjust to some of the realities of rival Arab claims. At no time, however, did most Zionists renounce their vision of creating a Jewish state in at least a part of Palestine. Sooner or later, most came to realize that what they considered the historical necessity of building a Jewish national home was going to lead inexorably to a clash with the Palestinians. Where they differed was on the question of what concessions might be offered to minimize the destructiveness of that inevitable clash.

See also ZIONISM: IMPACT.

Neil Caplan

BIBLIOGRAPHY

Caplan, Neil. *Palestine Jewry and the Arab Question, 1917–1925.* London: Frank Cass, 1978.

——. *Futile Diplomacy,* 2 vols. London: Frank Cass, 1983 and 1986.

Gorny, Yosef. *Zionism and the Arabs, 1882–1948: A Study in Ideology.* Oxford: Clarendon Press, 1987.

Khalidi, Walid, ed. *From Haven to Conquest: Readings in Zionism and the Palestine Problem until 1948.* Washington, D.C.: Institute for Palestine Studies, 1971.

Lesch, Ann M. *Arab Politics in Palestine, 1917–1939: The Frustration of a Nationalist Movement.* Ithaca, N.Y. and London: Cornell University Press, 1979.

Porath, Yehoshua. *The Emergence of the Palestinian-Arab National Movement, 1918–1929.* London: Frank Cass, 1974.

——. *The Palestinian Arab National Movement, 1929–1939: From Riots to Rebellion.* London: Frank Cass, 1977.

Tessler, Mark. *A History of the Israeli-Palestinian Conflict,* Bloomington and Indianapolis: Indiana University Press, 1994.

Zionism: Impact

The Zionist movement has maintained a striking continuity in its aims and methods over the past century. From the start, the movement sought to achieve a Jewish majority in Palestine and to establish a Jewish state on as much of the LAND as possible. The methods included promoting mass Jewish immigration and acquiring tracts of land that would become the inalienable property of the Jewish people. This policy inevitably prevented the indigenous Arab residents from attaining their national goals and establishing a Palestinian state. It also necessitated displacing Palestinians from their lands and jobs when their presence conflicted with Zionist interests.

The Zionist movement—and subsequently the state of ISRAEL—failed to develop a positive approach to the Palestinian presence and aspirations. Although many Israelis recognized the moral dilemma posed by the Palestinians, the majority either tried to ignore the issue or to resolve it by *force majeure*. Thus, the Palestine problem festered and grew, instead of being resolved.

Historical Background The Zionist movement arose in late nineteenth-century Europe, influenced by the nationalist ferment sweeping that continent. Zionism acquired its particular focus from the ancient Jewish longing for the return to Zion and received a strong impetus from the increasingly intolerable conditions facing the large Jewish community in tsarist Russia. The movement also developed at the time of major European territorial acquisitions in Asia and Africa and benefited from the European powers' competition for influence in the shrinking Ottoman Empire.

One result of this involvement with European expansionism, however, was that the leaders of the nascent nationalist movements in the Middle East viewed Zionism as an adjunct of European colonialism. Moreover, Zionist assertions of the contemporary relevance of the Jews' historical ties to Palestine, coupled with their land purchases and immigration, alarmed the indigenous population of the Ottoman districts that Palestine comprised. The Jewish community (*yishuv*) rose from 6 percent of Palestine's population in 1880 to 10 percent by 1914. Although the numbers were insignificant, the settlers were outspoken enough to arouse the opposition of Arab leaders and induce them to exert counterpressure on the Ottoman regime to prohibit Jewish immigration and land buying.

As early as 1891, a group of Muslim and Christian notables cabled Istanbul, urging the government to prohibit Jewish immigration and land purchase. The resulting edicts radically curtailed land purchases in the *sanjak* (district) of JERUSALEM for the next decade. When a Zionist Congress resolution in 1905 called for increased colonization, the Ottoman regime suspended all land transfers to Jews in both the *sanjak* of Jerusalem and the *wilayat* (province) of Beirut.

After the coup d'etat by the Young Turks in 1908, the Palestinians used their representation in the central parliament and their access to newly opened local newspapers to press their claims and express their concerns. They were particularly vociferous in opposition to discussions that took place between the financially hard-pressed Ottoman regime and Zionist leaders in 1912–13, which would have let the world Zionist Organization purchase crown land (*jiftlik*) in the Baysan Valley, along the Jordan River.

The Zionists did not try to quell Palestinian fears, since their concern was to encourage colonization from Europe and to minimize the obstacles in their path. The only effort to meet to discuss their aspirations occurred in the spring of 1914. Its difficulties illustrated the incompatibility in their aspirations. The Palestinians wanted the Zionists to present them with a document that would state their precise political ambitions, their willingness to open their schools to Palestinians, and their intentions of learning Arabic and integrating with the local population. The Zionists rejected this proposal.

The British Mandate The proclamation of the BALFOUR DECLARATION on November 2, 1917, and the arrival of British troops in Palestine soon after, transformed the political situation. The declaration gave the Zionist movement its long-sought legal status. The qualification that "nothing shall be done which may prejudice the civil and religious rights of the existing non-Jewish communities in Palestine" seemed a relatively insignificant obstacle to the Zionists, especially since it referred only to those communities' "civil and religious rights," not to political or national rights. The subsequent British occupation gave Britain the ability to carry out that pledge and provide the protection necessary for the Zionists to realize their aims.

In fact, the British had contracted three mutually contradictory promises for the future of Palestine. The Sykes-Picot Agreement of 1916 with the French and Russian governments proposed that Palestine be placed under international administration. The HUSAYN-MCMAHON CORRESPONDENCE, 1915–1916, on whose basis the Arab revolt was launched, implied that Palestine would be included in the zone of Arab independence. In contrast, the Balfour Declaration encouraged the colonization of Palestine by Jews, under British protection. British officials recognized the irreconcilability of these pledges but hoped that a modus vivendi could be achieved, both between the competing imperial powers, France and Britain, and between the Palestinians and the Jews. Instead, these contradictions set the stage for the three decades of conflict-ridden British rule in Palestine.

Initially, many British politicians shared the Zionists' assumption that gradual, regulated Jewish immigration and settlement would lead to a Jewish majority in Palestine, whereupon it would become independent, with legal protection for the Arab minority. The assumption that this could be accomplished without serious resistance was shattered at the outset of British rule. Britain thereafter was caught in an increasingly untenable position, unable to persuade either Palestinians or Zionists to alter their demands and forced to station substantial military forces in Palestine to maintain security.

The Palestinians had assumed that they would gain some form of independence when Ottoman rule disintegrated, whether through a separate state or integration with neighboring Arab lands. These hopes were bolstered by the Arab revolt, the entry of Faysal ibn Husayn into Damascus in 1918, and the proclamation of Syrian independence in 1920. Their hopes were dashed, however, when Britain imposed direct colonial rule and elevated the *yishuv* to a special status. Moreover, the French ousted Faysal from Damascus in July 1920, and British compensation—in the form of thrones in Transjordan and Iraq for Abdullah and Faysal, respectively—had no positive impact on the Arabs in Palestine. In fact, the action underlined the different treatment accorded Palestine and its disadvantageous political situation. These concerns were exacerbated by Jewish immigration: the *yishuv* comprised 28 percent of the population by 1936 and reached 32 percent by 1947. The British umbrella was critically important to the growth and consolidation of the *yishuv,* enabling it to root itself firmly despite Palestinian opposition. Although British support diminished in the late 1930s, the *yishuv* was strong enough by then to withstand the Palestinians on its own. After World War II, the Zionist movement also was able to turn to the emerging superpower, the UNITED STATES, for diplomatic support and legitimization.

The Palestinians' responses to Jewish immigration, land purchases, and political demands were remarkably consistent. They insisted that Palestine remain an Arab country, with the same right of self-determination and independence as Egypt, Transjordan, and Iraq. Britain granted those countries independence without a violent struggle since their claims to self-determination were not contested by European settlers. The Palestinians argued that Palestinian territory could not and should not be used to solve the plight of the Jews in Europe, and that Jewish national aspirations should not override their own rights.

Palestinian opposition peaked in the late 1930s: the six-month general strike in 1936 was followed the next year by a widespread rural revolt. This rebellion welled up from the bottom of Palestinian society—unemployed urban workers, displaced peasants crowded into towns, and debt-ridden villagers. It was supported by most merchants and professionals in the towns, who feared competition from the *yishuv.* Members of the elite families acted as spokesmen before the British administration through the ARAB HIGHER COMMITTEE, which was formed during the 1936 strike. However, the British banned the committee in October 1937 and arrested its members, on the eve of the revolt.

Only one of the Palestinian political parties was willing to limit its aims and accept the principle of territorial partition. The NATIONAL DEFENSE PARTY, led by RAGHIB AL-NASHASHIBI (mayor of JERUSALEM from 1920 to 1934), was willing to accept partition in 1937 so long as the Palestinians obtained sufficient land and could merge with Transjordan to form a larger political entity. However, the British PEEL COMMISSION'S plan, announced in July 1937, would have forced the Palestinians to leave the olive- and grain- growing areas of Galilee, the orange groves on the Mediterranean coast, and the urban port cities of HAIFA and ACRE. That was too great a loss for even the National Defense Party to accept, and so it joined in the general denunciations of partition.

During the PALESTINE MANDATE period the Palestinian community was 70 percent rural, 75 to 80 percent illiterate, and divided internally between town and countryside and between elite families and villagers. Despite broad support for the national aims, the Palestinians could not achieve the unity and strength necessary to withstand the combined pressure of the British forces and the Zionist movement. In fact, the political structure was decapitated in the late 1930s when the British banned the Arab Higher Committee and arrested hundreds of local politicians. When efforts were made in the 1940s to rebuild the political structure, the impetus came largely from outside, from Arab rulers who were disturbed by the deteriorating conditions in Palestine and feared their repercussions on their own newly acquired independence.

The Arab rulers gave priority to their own national considerations and provided limited diplomatic and military support to the Palestinians. The Palestinian Arabs continued to demand a state that would reflect the Arab majority's weight—diminished to 68 percent by 1947. They rejected the UNITED NATIONS (U.N.) partition plan of November 1947, which granted the Jews statehood in 55 percent of Palestine, an area that included as many Arab residents as Jews. However, the Palestinian Arabs lacked the political strength and military force to back up their claim. Once Britain withdrew its forces in 1948 and the Jews proclaimed the state of Israel, the Arab rulers used their armed forces to protect those zones that the partition plans had allocated to the Arab state. By the time armistice agreements were signed in 1949, the Arab areas had shrunk to only 23 percent of Palestine. The Egyptian army held the GAZA STRIP, and Transjordanian forces dominated the hills of central Palestine. At least 726,000 of the 1.3 million Palestinian

Arabs fled from the area held by Israel. Emir Abdullah subsequently annexed the zone that his army occupied, renaming it the WEST BANK.

The Zionist Movement The dispossession and expulsion of a majority of Palestinians were the result of Zionist policies planned over a thirty-year period. Fundamentally, Zionism focused on two needs: to attain a Jewish majority in Palestine and to acquire statehood, irrespective of the wishes of the indigenous population. Nonrecognition of the political and national rights of the Palestinian people was a key Zionist policy.

Chaim Weizmann, president of the World Zionist Organization, placed maximalist demands before the Paris Peace Conference in February 1919. He stated that he expected 70,000 to 80,000 Jewish immigrants to arrive each year in Palestine. When they became the majority, they would form an independent government and Palestine and would become "as Jewish as England is English." Weizmann proposed that the boundaries should be the Mediterranean Sea on the west; Sidon, the Litani River, and Mount Hermon on the north; all of Transjordan west of the Hijaz railway on the east; and a line across Sinai from Aqaba to al-Arish on the south. He argued that "the boundaries above outlined are what we consider essential for the economic foundation of the country. Palestine must have its natural outlet to the sea and control of its rivers and their headwaters. The boundaries are sketched with the general economic needs and historic traditions of the country in mind." Weizmann offered the Arab countries a free zone in Haifa and a joint port at Aqaba.

Weizmann's policy was basically in accord with that of the leaders of the *yishuv*, who held a conference in December 1918 in which they formulated their own demands for the peace conference. The *yishuv* plan stressed that they must control appointments to the administrative services and that the British must actively assist their program to transform Palestine into a democratic Jewish state in which the Arabs would have minority rights. Although the peace conference did not explicitly allocate such extensive territories to the Jewish national home and did not support the goal of transforming all of Palestine into a Jewish state, it opened the door to such a possibility. More important, Weizmann's presentation stated clearly and forcefully the long-term aims of the movement.

These aims were based on certain fundamental tenets of Zionism. First, the movement was seen not only as inherently righteous, but also as meeting an overwhelming need among European Jews. Second, European culture was superior to indigenous Arab culture; the Zionists could help civilize the East. Third, external support was needed from a major power; relations with the Arab world were a secondary matter. Fourth, Arab nationalism was a legitimate political movement, but Palestinian nationalism was either illegitimate or nonexistent. Finally, if the Palestinians would not reconcile themselves to Zionism, *force majeure,* not compromise, was the only feasible response.

Adherents of Zionism believed that the Jewish people had an inherent and inalienable right to Palestine. Religious Zionists stated this in biblical terms, referring to the divine promise of the land to the tribes of Israel. Secular Zionists relied more on the argument that Palestine alone could solve the problem of Jewish dispersion and virulent anti-Semitism. Weizmann stated in 1930 that the needs of 16 million Jews had to be balanced against those of 1 million Palestinian Arabs: "The Balfour Declaration and the Mandate have definitely lifted [Palestine] out of the context of the Middle East and linked it up with the world-wide Jewish problem. . . . The rights which the Jewish people has been adjudged in Palestine do not depend on the consent, and cannot be subjected to the will, of the majority of its present inhabitants." This perspective took its most extreme form with the Revisionist movement. Its founder, Vladimir Jabotinsky, was so self-righteous about the Zionist cause that he justified any actions taken against the Arabs in order to realize Zionist goals.

Second, Zionists generally felt that European civilization was superior to Arab culture and values. Theodor Herzl, the founder of the World Zionist Organization, wrote in the *Jewish State* (1886) that the Jewish community could serve as "part of a wall of defense for Europe in Asia, an outpost of civilization against barbarism." Weizmann also believed that he was engaged in a fight of civilization against the desert. The Zionists would bring enlightenment and economic development to the backward Arabs. Similarly, David Ben-Gurion, the leading labor Zionist, could not understand why Arabs rejected his offer to use Jewish finance, scientific knowledge, and technical expertise to modernize the Middle East. He attributed this rejection to backwardness rather than to the affront that Zionism posed to the Arabs' pride and to their aspirations for independence.

Third, Zionist leaders recognized that they needed an external patron to legitimize their presence in the international arena and to provide them legal and military protection in Palestine. Great Britain played that role in the 1920s and 1930s, and the United States became the mentor in the mid-1940s. Zionist leaders realized that they needed to make tactical accommodations to that patron—such as downplaying their public statements about their political aspirations or accepting a state on a limited territory—while continuing to work toward their long-term goals. The presence and needs of the Arabs were viewed as secondary. The Zionist leadership never considered allying with the Arab world against the British and Americans. Rather, Weizmann, in particular, felt that the *yishuv* should bolster the British Empire and guard its strategic interests in the region. Later, the leaders of Israel perceived the Jewish state as a strategic asset to the United States in the Middle East.

Fourth, Zionist politicians accepted the idea of an Arab nation but rejected the concept of a Palestinian nation. They considered the Arab residents of Palestine as comprising a minute fraction of the land and people of the Arab world, and as lacking any separate identity and aspirations. Weizmann and Ben-Gurion were willing to negotiate with Arab rulers in order to gain those rulers' recognition of Jewish statehood in Palestine in return for the Zionists' recognition of Arab independence elsewhere, but they would not negotiate with the Arab politicians in Palestine for a political settlement in their common homeland. As early as 1918, Weizmann wrote to a prominent British politician, "The real Arab movement is developing in Damascus and Mecca . . . the so-called Arab question in Palestine would therefore assume only a purely local character, and in fact is not considered a serious factor." In line with that thinking, Weizmann met with Emir Faysal in the same year, in an attempt to win his agreement to Jewish statehood in Palestine in return for Jewish financial support for Faysal as ruler of Syria and Arabia.

Ben-Gurion, Weizmann, and other Zionist leaders met with prominent Arab officials during the 1939 LONDON CONFERENCE, which was convened by Britain to seek a compromise settlement in Palestine. The Arab diplomats from Egypt, Iraq, and Saudi Arabia criticized the exceptional position that the Balfour Declaration had granted the Jewish community and emphasized the estrangement between the Arab and Jewish residents that large-scale Jewish immigration had caused. In response, Weizmann insisted that Palestine remain open to all Jews who wanted to immigrate, and Ben-Gurion suggested that all of Palestine should become a Jewish state, federated with the surrounding Arab states. The Arab participants criticized these demands for exacerbating the conflict, rather than contributing to the search for peace. The Zionists' premise that Arab statehood could be recognized while ignoring the Palestinians was thus rejected by the Arab rulers themselves.

Finally, Zionist leaders argued that if the Palestinians could not reconcile themselves to Zionism, then *force majeure,* not a compromise of goals, was the only possible response. By the early 1920s, after violent Arab protests broke out in Jaffa and Jerusalem, leaders of the *yishuv* recognized that it might be impossible to bridge the gap between the aims of the two peoples. Building the national home would lead to an unavoidable clash, since the Arab majority would not agree to become a minority. In fact, as early as 1919 Ben-Gurion stated bluntly:

> Everybody sees a difficulty in the question of relations between Arabs and Jews. But not everybody sees that there is no solution to this question. No solution! There is a gulf, and nothing can fill this gulf. . . . I do not know what Arab will agree that Palestine should belong to the Jews. . . . We, as a nation, want this country to be *ours;* the Arabs, as a nation, want this country to be *theirs.*

As tensions increased in the 1920s and the 1930s Zionist leaders realized that they had to coerce the Arabs to acquiesce to a diminished status. Ben-Gurion stated in 1937, during the Arab revolt: "This is a national war declared upon us by the Arabs. . . . This is an active resistance by the Palestinians to what they regard as a usurpation of their homeland by the Jews. . . . But the fighting is only one aspect of the conflict, which is in its essence a political one. And politically we are the aggressors and they defend themselves." This sober conclusion did not lead Ben-Gurion to negotiate with the Palestinian Arabs: instead he became more determined to strengthen the Jewish military forces so that they could compel the Arabs to relinquish their claims.

Practical Zionism In order to realize the aims of Zionism and build the Jewish national home, the Zionist movement undertook practical steps in many different realms. They built political structures that could assume state functions, created a military force, promoted large-scale immigration, acquired land as the inalienable property of the Jewish people, and established and monopolistic concessions. The labor federation, Histadrut, tried to force Jewish enterprises to hire only Jewish labor, and the movement set up an autonomous Hebrew-language educational system. These measures created a self-contained national entity on Palestinian soil that was entirely separate from the Arab community.

The *yishuv* established an elected community council, executive body, administrative departments, and religious courts soon after the British assumed control over Palestine. When the PALESTINE MANDATE was ratified by the League of Nations in 1922, the World Zionist Organization gained the responsibility to advise and cooperate with the British administration not only on economic and social matters affecting the Jewish national home but also on issues involving the general development of the country. Although the British rejected pressure to give the World Zionist Organization an equal share in administration and control over immigration and land transfers, the *yishuv* did gain a privileged advisory position.

The Zionists were strongly critical of British efforts to establish a LEGISLATIVE COUNCIL in 1923, 1930, and 1936. They realized that Palestinians' demands for a legislature with a Palestinian majority ran counter to their own need to delay establishing representative bodies until the Jewish community was much larger. In 1923, the Jewish residents did participate in the elections for a Legislative Council, but they were relieved that the Palestinians' boycott compelled the British to cancel the results. In 1930 and 1936 the World Zionist Organization vigorously opposed British proposals for a legislature, fearing that, if the Palestinians received the majority status that proportional representation would require, then they would try to block Jewish immigration and the purchase of land by Zionist companies. Zionist opposition was couched indirectly in the assertion that Palestine was "not ripe" for self-rule, a code for "not until there's a Jewish majority."

To bolster this position, the *yishuv* formed defense forces (Haganah) in March 1920. They were preceded by the establishment of guards (*hashomer*) in Jewish rural settlements in the 1900s and the formation of a Jewish Legion in World War I. However, the British disbanded the Jewish Legion and allowed only sealed armories in the settlements and mixed Jewish-British area defense committees.

Despite its illegal status, the Haganah expanded to number 10,000 trained and mobilized men, and 40,000 reservists by 1936. During the 1937–38 Arab revolt, the Haganah engaged in "active defense" against Arab insurgents and cooperated with the British to guard railway lines, the oil pipeline to Haifa, and border fences. This cooperation deepened during World War II, when 18,800 Jewish volunteers joined the British forces. Haganah's special Palmach units served as scouts and sappers for the British army in Lebanon in 1941–42. This wartime experience helped to transform the Haganah into a regular fighting force. When Ben-Gurion became the World Zionist Organization's secretary of defense in June 1947, he accelerated mobilization as well as arms buying in the United States and Europe. As a result, mobilization leaped to 30,000 by May 1948, when statehood was proclaimed, and then doubled to 60,000 by mid-July—twice the number serving in the Arab forces arrayed against Israel.

A principal means for building up the national home was the promotion of large-scale immigration from Europe. Estimates of the Palestinian population demonstrate the dramatic impact of immigration. The first British census (December 31, 1922) counted 757,182 residents, of whom 83,794 were Jewish. The second census (December 31, 1931) enumerated 1,035,821, including 174,006 Jews. Thus, the absolute number of Jews had doubled and the relative number had increased from 11 percent to 17 percent. Two-thirds of this growth could be attributed to net immigration, and one-third to natural increase. Two-thirds of the *yishuv* was concentrated in Jerusalem and Jaffa and Tel Aviv, with most of the remainder in the north, including the towns of Haifa, SAFAD, and Tiberias.

The Mandate specified that the rate of immigration should accord with the economic capacity of the country to absorb the immigrants. In 1931, the British government reinterpreted this to take into account only the Jewish sector of the economy, excluding the Palestinian sector, which was suffering from heavy unemployment. As a result, the pace of immigration accelerated in 1932 and peaked in 1935–36. In other words, the absolute number of Jewish residents doubled in the five years from 1931 to 1936 to 370,000, so that they constituted 28 percent of the total population. Not until 1939 did the British impose a severe quota on Jewish immigrants. That restriction was resisted by the *yishuv* with a sense of desperation, since it blocked access to a key haven for the Jews whom Hitler was persecuting and exterminating in Germany and the rest of Nazi-occupied Europe. Net immigration was limited during the war years in the 1940s, but the government estimated in 1946 that there were about 583,000 Jews of nearly 1,888,000 residents, or 31 percent of the total. Seventy percent of them were urban, and they continued to be overwhelmingly concentrated in Jerusalem (100,000), the Haifa area (119,000), and the Tel Aviv and RAMLA districts (327,000). The remaining 43,000 were largely in Galilee, with a scattering in the Negev and almost none in the central highlands.

The World Zionist Organization purchasing agencies launched large-scale land purchases in order to found rural settlements and stake territorial claims. In 1920 the Zionists held about 650,000 *dunums* (one *dunum* equals approximately one-quarter of an acre). By 1930, the amount had expanded to 1,164,000 *dunums* and by 1936 to 1,400,000 *dunums*. The major purchasing agent (the Palestine Land Development Company) estimated that, by 1936, 89 percent had been bought from large landowners (primarily absentee owners from Beirut) and only 11 percent from peasants. By 1947, the *yishuv* held 1.9 million *dunums*. Nevertheless, this represented only 7 percent of the total land surface or 10 to 12 percent of the cultivable land.

According to Article 3 of the Constitution of the Jewish Agency, the land was held by the Jewish National Fund as the inalienable property of the Jewish people; only Jewish labor could be employed in the settlements. Palestinians protested bitterly against this inalienability clause. The moderate National Defense Party, for example, petitioned the British in 1935 to prevent further land sales, arguing that it was a "life and death [matter] to the Arabs, in that it results in the transfer of their country to other hands and the loss of their nationality."

The placement of Jewish settlements was often based on political considerations. The Palestine Land Development Company had four criteria for land purchase: the economic suitability of the tract, its contribution to forming a solid block of Jewish territory, the prevention of isolation of settlements, and the impact of the purchase on the political-territorial claims of the Zionists. The "stockade and watchtower" settlements constructed in 1937, for example, were designed to secure control over key parts of Galilee for the *yishuv* in case the British implemented the Peel partition plan. Similarly, eleven settlements were hastily erected in the Negev in late 1946 in an attempt to stake a political claim in that entirely Palestinian-populated territory.

In addition to making these land purchases, prominent Jewish businessmen won monopolistic concessions from the British government that gave the Zionist movement an important role in the development of Palestine's natural resources. In 1921, Pinhas Rutenberg's Palestine Electric Company acquired the right to electrify all of Palestine except Jerusalem. Moshe Novomeysky received the concession to develop the minerals in the Dead Sea in 1927. And the Palestine Land Development Company gained the concession to drain the Hula marshes, north of the Sea of Galilee, in 1934. In each case, the concession was contested by other serious non-Jewish claimants; Palestinian politicians argued that the government should retain control itself in order to develop the resources for the benefit of the entire country.

The inalienability clause in the Jewish National Fund contracts included provision that only Jews could work on Jewish agricultural settlements. The concepts of manual labor and the "return to the soil" were key to the Zionist enterprise. This "Jewish labor" policy was enforced by the General Foundation of Jewish Labor (Histadrut), founded in 1920 and headed by David Ben-Gurion. Since some Jewish builders and citrus growers hired Arabs, who worked for lower wages than Jews, the Histadrut launched a campaign in 1933 to remove those Arab workers. Histadrut organizers picketed citrus groves and evicted Arab workers from construction sites and factories in the cities. The strident propaganda by the Histradut increased the Arabs' fears for the future. George Mansur, a Palestinian labor leader, wrote angrily in 1937: "The Histadrut's fundamental aim is 'the conquest of labour' . . . No matter how many Arab workers are unemployed, they have no right to take any job which a possible immigrant might occupy. No Arab has the right to work in Jewish undertakings."

Finally, the establishment of an all-Jewish, Hebrew-language educational system was an essential component of building the Jewish national home. It helped to create a cohesive national ethos and a lingua franca among the diverse immigrants. However, it also entirely separated Jewish children from Palestinian children, who attended the governmental schools. The policy widened the linguistic and cultural gap between the two peoples. In addition, there was a stark contrast in their literacy levels: in 1931, 93 percent of Jewish males (above age seven) were literate, as were 71 percent of Christian males, but only 25 percent of Muslim males were literate. Overall, Palestinian literacy increased from 19 percent in 1931 to 27 percent by 1940, but only 30 percent of Palestinian children could be accommodated in government and private schools.

The practical policies of the Zionist movement created a compact and well-rooted community by the late 1940s. The *yishuv* had its own political, educational, economic, and military institutions, parallel to the governmental system. Jews minimized their contact with the Arab community and outnumbered the Arabs in certain key respects. Jewish urban dwellers, for example, greatly exceeded Arab urbanites, even though Jews constituted but one-third of the population. Many more Jewish children attended school than did Arab children, and Jewish firms employed seven times as many workers as Arab firms. Thus the relative weight and autonomy of the *yishuv* were much greater than sheer numbers would suggest. The transition to statehood was facilitated by the existence of the protostate institutions and a mobilized, literate public. But the separation from the Palestinian residents was exacerbated by these autarchic policies.

Policies Toward the Palestinians The main viewpoint within the Zionist movement was that the "Arab problem" would be solved by first solving the Jewish problem. In time, the Palestinians would be presented with the fait accompli of a Jewish majority. Settlements, land purchases, industries, and military forces were developed gradually and systematically so that the *yishuv* would become too strong to uproot. In a letter to his son, Weizmann compared the Arabs to the rocks of Judea, obstacles that had to be cleared to make the path smooth. When the Palestinians mounted violent protests in 1920, 1921, 1929, 1936–39, and the late 1940s, the *yishuv* sought to curb them by force, rather than seek a political accommodation with the indigenous people. Any concessions made to the Palestinians by the British government concerning immigration, land sales, or labor were strongly contested by the Zionist leaders. In fact, in 1936, Ben-Gurion stated that the Palestinians will only "acquiesce in a Jewish Eretz Israel" after they are in a state of "total despair."

Zionists viewed their acceptance of territorial partition as a temporary measure; they did not give up the idea of the Jewish community's right to all of Palestine. Weizmann commented in 1937, "In the course of time we shall expand to the whole country . . . this is only an arrangement for the next 15–30 years." Ben-Gurion stated in 1938, "After we become a strong force, as a result of the creation of a state, we shall abolish partition and expand to the whole of Palestine."

A few efforts were made to reduce Arab opposition. For example in the 1920s, Zionist organizations provided financial support to Palestinian political parties, newspapers, and individuals. This was most evident in the establishment and support of the National Muslim Societies (1921–23) and Agricultural Parties (1924–26). These parties were expected to be neutral or positive toward the Zionist movement, in return for which they would receive financial subventions and their members would be helped to obtain jobs and loans.

This policy was backed by Weizmann, who commented that "extremists and moderates alike were susceptible to the influence of money and honors." However, Leonard Stein, a member of the London office of the World Zionist Organization, denounced this practice. He argued that Zionists must seek "a permanent *modus vivendi*" with the Palestinians by hiring them in Jewish firms and admitting them to Jewish universities. He maintained that political parties in which "Arab moderates are merely Arab gramophones playing Zionist records" would collapse as soon as the Zionist financial support ended. In any event, the World Zionist Organization terminated the policy by 1927, as it was in the midst of a financial crisis and as most of the leaders felt that the policy was ineffective.

Some Zionist leaders argued that the Arab community had to be involved in the practical efforts of the Zionist movement. Chaim Kalvarisky, who initiated the policy of buying support, articulated in 1923 the gap between that ideal and the reality:

> Some people say . . . that only by common work in the field of commerce, industry and agriculture mutual understanding between Jews and Arabs will ultimately be attained. . . . This is, however, merely a theory. In practice we have not done and we are doing nothing for any work in common. How many Arab officials have we installed in our banks? Not even one. How many Arabs have we brought into our schools? Not one. What commercial houses have we established in company with Arabs? Not even one.

Two years later, Kalvarisky lamented: "We all admit the importance of drawing closer to the Arabs, but in fact we are growing more distant like a drawn bow. We have no contact: two separate worlds, each living its own life and fighting the other." Some members of the *yishuv* emphasized the need for political relations with the Palestinian Arabs, to achieve either a peacefully negotiated territorial partition (as Nahum Goldmann sought) or a binational state (as Brit Shalom and Hashomer Ha-tzair proposed). But few went as far as Dr. Judah L. Magnes, chancellor of The Hebrew University, who argued that Zionism meant merely the creation of a Jewish cultural center in Palestine rather than an independent state. In any case, the binationalists had little impact politically and were strongly opposed by the leadership of the Zionist movement.

Zionist leaders felt they did not harm the Palestinians by blocking them from working in Jewish settlements and industries or even by undermining their majority status. The Palestinians were considered a small part of the large Arab nation; their economic and political needs could be met in that wider context, Zionists felt, rather than in Palestine. They could move elsewhere if they sought land and could merge with Transjordan if they sought political independence.

This thinking led logically to the concept of population TRANSFER. In 1930 Weizmann suggested that the problems of insufficient land resources within Palestine and of the dispossession of peasants could be solved by moving them to Transjordan and Iraq. He urged the Jewish Agency to provide a loan of £1 million to help move Palestinian farmers to Transjordan. The issue was discussed at length in the Jewish Agency debates of 1936–37 on partition. At first, the majority proposed a voluntary transfer of Palestinians from the Jewish state, but later they realized that the Palestinians would never leave voluntarily. Therefore, key leaders such as Ben-Gurion insisted that compulsory transfer was essential. The Jewish Agency then voted that the British government should pay for the removal of the Palestinian Arabs from the territory allotted to the Jewish state.

The fighting from 1947 to 1949 resulted in a far larger transfer than had been envisioned in 1937. It "solved" the Arab problem by removing most of the Arabs and was the ultimate expression of the policy of *force majeure.*

✦ ✦ ✦

The land and people of Palestine were transformed during the thirty years of British rule. The systematic colonization undertaken by the Zionist movement enabled the Jewish community to establish separate and virtually autonomous political, economic, social, cultural, and military institutions. A state within a state was in place by the time the movement launched its drive for independence. The legal underpinnings for the autonomous Jewish community were provided by the British Mandate. The establishment of a Jewish state was first proposed by the British Royal Commission in July 1937 and then endorsed by the UNITED NATIONS in November 1947.

That drive for statehood ignored the presence of a Palestinian majority with its own national aspirations. The right to create a Jewish state—and the overwhelming need for such a state—were perceived as overriding Palestinian counterclaims. Few members of the *yishuv* supported the idea of binationalism. Rather, territorial partition was seen by most Zionist leaders as the way to gain statehood while according certain national rights to the Palestinians. Transfer of Palestinians to neighboring Arab states was also envisaged as a means to ensure the formation of a homogeneous Jewish territory. The implementation of those approaches led to the formation of independent Israel, at the cost of dismembering the Palestinian community and fostering long-term hostility with the Arab world. *See also* ZIONISM: ATTITUDES AND POLICIES.

Ann M. Lesch

BIBLIOGRAPHY

Abu Lughod, Janet L. "The Demographic Transformation of Palestine." In *The Transformation of Palestine,* ed. by Ibrahim Abu-Lughod. Evanston, Ill.: Northwestern University Press, 1971.

Caplan, Neil. *Palestine Jewry and the Arab Question, 1917–25.* London: Frank Cass, 1978.

Farsoun, Samih K., and Christina Zacharia. *Palestine and the Palestinians.* Boulder, Colo.: Westview Press, 1996.

Flapan, Simha. *Zionism and the Palestinians.* New York: Barnes & Noble, 1979.

Granott (Granovsky), Avraham. *The Land System in Palestine.* London: Frank Cass, 1978.

Hadawi, Sami. *Bitter Harvest: Palestine 1914–1979.* Rev. ed. Delmar, N.Y.: Caravan Books, 1979.

Hattis, Susan Lee. *The Bi-National Idea in Palestine during Mandatory Times.* Haifa: Shikmona Publishing Co., 1970.

Hertzberg, Arthur, ed. *The Zionist Idea.* New York: Atheneum, 1969.

Hurewitz, J. C. *The Struggle for Palestine.* Reprint. New York: Schocken Books, 1976.

Lesch, Ann Mosely. *Arab Politics in Palestine, 1917–1939.* Ithaca, N.Y.: Cornell University Press, 1979.

Mandel, Neville. "Attempts at an Arab-Zionist Entente, 1913–1914," *Middle Eastern Studies* 1 (1965).

———. "Turks, Arabs, and Jewish Immigration into Palestine, 1882–1914," *St. Antony's Papers* 17 (1965).

Mansur, George. *The Arab Worker under the Palestine Mandate.* Jerusalem: Commercial Press, 1937.

Porath, Yehoshua. *The Emergence of the Palestinian-Arab National Movement 1918–1929.* London: Frank Cass, 1974.

———. *Palestinian Arab National Movement, 1929–1939.* London: Frank Cass, 1977.

Ro'i, Yaacov. "The Zionist Attitude to the Arabs, 1908–1914." *Middle Eastern Studies* 4 (1968).

Ruedy, John. "Dynamics of Land Alienation." In *The Transformation of Palestine,* ed. by Ibrahim Abu-Lughod. Evanston, Ill.: Northwestern University Press, 1971.

Zu'aytir, Akram

activist, publicist, diplomat, and educator
1909– Nablus

Akram Zu'aytir was born in NABLUS. Through the JERUSALEM Arabic newspaper *Mir'at al-Sharq* (Mirror of the East), which he edited for a short period after the WESTERN (WAILING) WALL DISTURBANCES, 1929, and subsequently through the Jerusalem Arabic newspaper *al-Hayat* (established 1930), Akram encouraged Palestinian youth to oppose the British, who in his view should be the focus of the Palestinian struggle for independence because they were the main sponsors of the Zionist project. Akram expressed the same sentiment through his active membership in the ISTIQLAL PARTY (Hizb al-Istiqlal, "Independence Party"), formed in August 1932 under the leadership of AWNI ABD AL-HADI, a confidant of Emir Faysal in the early 1920s and a secretary of the ARAB EXECUTIVE after 1928. He was also involved in organizing a number of political fronts outside Palestine, most notably *Usbat al-Amal al-Qawmi* ("The League of Pan-Arab Action") (Syria) and *Nadi al-Muthanna* ("Muthanna Club") (Iraq); he also participated in numerous pan-Arab and Islamic conferences.

Akram's adoption of a hard line against British sponsorship of ZIONISM led to his arrest and detention in 1931 and 1936. He participated in Rashid Ali al-Kaylani's revolt in Iraq in 1941. His political activism forced him to spend many years (1937–51) in exile outside Palestine. Akram served in the Jordanian government as ambassador to Syria, Iran, Afghanistan, and Lebanon. After serving as Jordanian foreign minister for about one year in 1966, he was appointed in 1967 as member of the Jordanian Upper House of Parliament (Majlis al-A'yan) and as chief of the Royal Court. A firm believer in Palestinian and pan-Arab rights Akram strongly defended these rights in local, regional, and international forums.

Akram also wrote a number of important works based on personal experience and primary documents, including *Ta'rikhuna* (Our history), 1935; *al-Qadiyya al-Filastiniyya* (The Palestine cause), 1956. *Watha'iq al-Haraka al-Wataniyya al-Filastiniyya 1918–1939* (Documents on the Palestinian national movement 1918–1939), 1979; and *al-Haraka al-Wataniyya al-Filastiniyya, 1935–1939 Yawmiyyat Akram Zu'aytir* (The Palestinian national movement 1935–1939: The diaries of Akram Zu'aytir), 1980.

Muhammad Muslih

GLOSSARY

by Michael R. Fischbach

Abu: Followed by a personal name, means "father of." Often used by acquaintances in lieu of a man's name as a title of respect. Figures in the Palestinian national movement were often given the title *Abu* as pseudonyms or noms de guerre (e.g., Abu Iyad for SALAH KHALAF).

aliya: Hebrew term ("ascent") denoting Jewish immigration to Palestine/Israel.

Arab nationalism: Series of mid-twentieth-century political tendencies that stressed wider pan-Arab national identity, unity, and independence and reflected the belief in *qawmiyya* (wider pan-Arab nationalism) rather than *wataniyya* (local national patriotism). The most prominent Arab nationalist movements were those led by the Ba'th Party and the Egyptian president Jamal Abd al-Nasir, although the creation of the ARAB LEAGUE in 1945 indicated a general desire for cooperation even among Arab states not committed to unity.

al-Ard: "The Land," a pan-Arab nationalist movement among Palestinians in Israel, 1958–64.

awqaf: Plural of *waqf* [see *waqf*].

a'yan: Notables: prominent men who wielded socioeconomic and political influence.

Bedouin: Term usually denoting Arab pastoral nomads who migrate from locale to locale, in contrast to settled village cultivators or people living in towns.

Bethany: The Palestinian village of al-Ayzariyya near JERUSALEM.

bey: Title conferred on mid- to high-level ranks in the Ottoman administration and military, usually translated as "lord," "chief," or "master."

Bilad al-Sham: Greater Syria, or the regions of the eastern Mediterranean that include modern SYRIA, LEBANON, Palestine/Israel, and JORDAN.

Councilists [see *Majlisiyyun*].

Dead Sea: Palestine's largest body of water, this inland salty sea lies along its border with Jordan and is the lowest point on earth.

diaspora: A term by Jews (Hebrew, *galut*) to denote Jews living outside Israel and also (Arabic, *ghurba*) used by Palestinians to denote Palestinians in exile from Palestine.

dunum: Unit for measuring surface area. During late Ottoman times it equaled 919.3 square meters, or approximately 0.25 acre. During the PALESTINE MANDATE it was set at 1,000 square meters.

effendi: Title given to important Muslim clerics and lower-level Ottoman bureaucrats. Also, honorific title given to educated members of the urban elite.

Emergency Regulations: British PALESTINE MANDATE laws adopted in September 1945 granting authorities extremely wide powers of arrest, detention, and collective punishment in an effort to stem political violence in Palestine.

Fahd plan: Peace plan for resolving ARAB–ISRAELI CONFLICT proposed by the Saudi Crown Prince, Fahd, in August 1981, which called for establishment of a Palestinian state in the WEST BANK and the GAZA STRIP and implicitly recognized ISRAEL.

fallah: Usually denotes a subsistence-level peasant employing simple agricultural technology.

fatwa: Formal legal opinion issued by an Islamic jurist (mufti).

Fez Plan: Peace plan for resolving Arab–Israeli conflict proposed by September 1982 Arab summit meeting at Fez, Morocco. Similar to fahd plan, but called for more explicit role for Palestine Liberation Organization (PLO).

fida'iyyun: Fedayeen in English. Often rendered *fida'iyyin* (singular, *fida' i*), "those who sacrifice themselves." Palestinian irregular fighters who carried out commando-style raids against Israeli targets that often resulted in their death.

Galilee: Mountainous, northernmost region of Palestine.

Grand Mufti: Title bestowed by British authorities on the Ottoman era office of mufti (Islamic law expert) of Jerusalem during the tenure of Kamil al-HUSAYNI. The mufti's expanded role included control of *Shari'a* courts and *awqaf* (religious endowments).

Greater Israel: Term used in Israel to refer to historic "Land of Israel," including today's Israel and WEST BANK.

Green Line: Israel's 1948–67 boundaries. Derivation of term is from the green boundary line drawn on maps during Arab-Israeli armistice talks in Rhodes in 1949.

Hajj: Honorific title given to a Muslim who has made the pilgrimage to Mecca.

hamula: Usually translated as "clan," a kinship unit exercising important roles of social cohesion in the ARAB WORLD, especially in rural areas.

Holy Land: Term used by Westerners to denote the lands of the Bible, usually Palestine but, during the nineteenth century, parts of Jordan and other nearby regions as well.

Jewish national home: Terminology used in the 1917 BALFOUR DECLARATION, understood by British to mean a type of "home" for Jews but by Zionists to mean an eventually independent Jewish state.

jihad: "Holy Struggle" or "Holy War." The term generally refers to the religious duty to expand and defend Islamic territory.

Jordan River: The major river in Palestine, it runs from the Sea of Galilee (Lake Tiberias) to the Dead Sea along Palestine's border with Jordan.

Jordanian option: Israeli plan associated with the Labor Party by which Israel would reach a political settlement over the future of the West Bank and Gaza with Jordan instead of the Palestinians.

Judea and Samaria: Biblical names for region comprising today's West Bank. Used by many Israelis instead of West Bank.

khirba: Uninhabited ruins. Also denotes a satellite settlement, often a ruined site, temporarily inhabited by cultivators when farming fields far from the village.

Kilometer: Distance of 1,000 meters, or 0.62 miles

Kufr Qasim: Village in the Little Triangle region of what became Israel, site of an October 1956 massacre in which Israeli border guards killed forty-nine inhabitants who were unaware that a shoot-to-kill curfew order had been imposed on the village.

League of Nations: International association of nations from 1920 to 1946 that tried to promote world peace. Succeeded by the United Nations.

Majlisiyyun: "The Councilists." Followers of AL-HAJJ AMIN AL-HUSAYNI, whose power base was the SUPREME MUSLIM COUNCIL. Opponents of the *Mu'aridun*.

mamluk: slave soldier. Member of military oligarchy in Egypt and Syria that retained local power in some areas in the nineteenth century.

mandate: System after the First World War by which the League of Nations empowered Britain and France to administer territories liberated from the Central Powers, including Palestine, and prepare them for self-government.

Mount Carmel: Mountain range overlooking port city of HAIFA.

Mount of Olives: Hill outside the Old City of JERUSALEM venerated by Christians as the site of the ascension of Jesus Christ, it also contains an important Jewish cemetery.

millet system: Autonomy to regulate community affairs granted by the Ottoman Empire to certain non-Islamic sects, notably Christians and Jews.

miri: LAND for which the state technically owns the title but sells the heritable usufructuary rights to cultivators. Most cultivated land in Palestine was *miri*. Contrast with *mulk*.

Mu'aridun: "The Opposition." Followers of the NASHASHIBI FAMILY who opposed the policies of AL-HAJJ AMIN AL-HUSAYNI and the *Majlisiyyun*.

mufti: State-appointed jurist who issues a formal opinion (*fatwa*) on disputed interpretations of Islamic religious law.

mukhtar: Figure who represents a kinship unit or village in dealings with the government.

mulk: Land for which both title and usufructuary rights are privately owned. Contrast with *miri*.

musha: Agricultural land collectively owned and cultivated within a village.

naqib: Leader of a guild or other corporate body.

naqib al-ashraf: State-appointed leader of the descendants of the Prophet Muhammad in a particular area.

Negev (Arabic, Naqab): Huge, arid region of southern Palestine.

Occupied Territories: The Arab territories occupied by Israel in June 1967. Usually refers only to the WEST BANK and Gaza.

Opposition: [see *Mu'aridun*].

Ottoman Empire: An empire governed by a Turkish elite that by the sixteenth century ruled much of the Middle East, including Palestine, until the early twentieth century.

pasha: Title conferred on the highest ranks of the Ottoman administration and military.

Permanent Mandates Commission: Body of the League of Nations charged with ensuring that Britain and France complied with the terms of their respective Mandates, including the British PALESTINE MANDATE.

qadi: A religious or secular judge.

Revisionists: Zionist political organization formed in 1925 by Vladimir Jabotinsky, who advocated the establishment of a Jewish state on both sides of the Jordan River.

sanjak: Also called a *liwa,* an Ottoman subprovince, headed by an official called a *mutasarrif.*

shari'a courts: Islamic religious courts.

shaykh: Title of respect given to the venerable leader of a kinship unit. Also a title given to the leader of an Islamic *sufi* brotherhood or an instructor of Islamic religious sciences.

Shaykh al-Islam: Title given to the mufti (Islamic law expert) of Istanbul as the leading figure in the Ottoman Empire's Islamic religious establishment.

sijill: Ledger containing the rulings of a *shari'a* court.

sumud: "Steadfastness," a concept emphasized in Palestinian nationalism.

Tanzimat: Reforms of the Ottoman administration and military carried out from 1839 to 1878.

Templars: Protestants from southern Germany who began moving to Palestine beginning in 1868 to establish their vision of ideal Christian communities.

ulama: Plural of *alim,* a Muslim religious official or scholar who was often appointed to official positions.

Village Leagues: Association created by Israel in the WEST BANK from 1977 to 1983 with the aim of fostering a political alternative to the PLO.

wali: Governor of a province (*wilaya*) in the Ottoman Empire.

waqf: Landed property rendered permanently inalienable, the revenues of which finance a charitable endeavor in perpetuity. Some *waqf* lands benefited families rather than charities.

yishuv: Jewish community in Palestine prior to the establishment of Israel.

Zionist Commission: Body created by the World Zionist Organization in 1918 to represent Zionist interests before British authorities in Palestine. Replaced in 1921 by Palestine Zionist Executive.

CHRONOLOGY OF PALESTINIAN HISTORY

by Michael R. Fischbach

638		Umar ibn Khattab captures Jerusalem from the Byzantines, names it Jund (military district) Filastin. Arabization and Islamicization begins
688–91		Abd al-Malik builds Dome of the Rock shrine in Jerusalem
705–15		Al-Walid ibn Abd al-Malik builds al-Masjad al-Aqsa in Jerusalem, third holiest mosque in Islam
1099–1187		Crusaders invade Palestine, establish Latin Kingdom of Jerusalem
1187		Salah al-Din reconquers Palestine after Battle of Hittin
1260		Mamluks halt Mongol invasion at Battle of Ayn Jalut
1516		Ottoman rule begins in Palestine after Battle of Marj Dabiq
1746–1775		Rule of local leader Zahir al-Umar in northern Palestine
1799	**February–May**	French army under Napoleon Bonaparte captures portions of Palestine
1775–1804		Rule of local leader Ahmad Pasha al-Jazzar in northern Palestine
1830		Egyptian army under Ibrahim Pasha captures Palestine from Ottomans
1834		Anti-Egyptian revolt
1837		Severe earthquake in northern Palestine
1876		Palestinians representing Jerusalem sit in first Ottoman parliament
1878		First Jewish settlement of the Zionist era, Petah Tikva, established
1882–1903		First wave (Hebrew: *aliyah*) of Jewish immigration into Palestine
1892		Railroad line built from Jaffa to Jerusalem
	November	Ottoman government bans sale of certain categories of land to non-Ottoman Jews
1897	**August**	First congress of the World Zionist Organization held in Basel, Switzerland. Committee established in Palestine to study Zionist land-purchasing tactics
1900	**June**	Ottoman government dispatches commission to study effects of Zionist immigration, land purchases
1901	**July**	Concern mounts among Palestinian cultivators in Tiberias area over Zionist land purchases
1904–14		Second *aliyah*. Writer Najib Azuri warns of political claims of Zionists in Palestine and warns of future conflict between Arabs and Jews
	August–September	Conflict between Zionist settlers, Palestinian cultivators in Tiberias area
1907	**August**	Ottoman governor of Jerusalem circulates report on methods of Zionist land purchases and immigration outside the law.
1908		Delegates from several Palestinian cities sit in second Ottoman parliament. Establishment of newspaper *al-Karmil* in Haifa
	March 16	Zionist-Palestinian violence breaks out in Jaffa. One Palestinian killed, 13 Jews wounded

1909	**June**	Establishment of al-Dusturiyya School, first private secular school in Palestine
1911	**January**	Palestinian delegate to Ottoman parliament from Jaffa raises issue of Zionism
		Establishment of newspaper *Filastin* ("Palestine")
	May 16	Ottoman parliament conducts first major debate on Zionism
1912		Parliamentary elections return delegates from several Palestinian regions.
1915	**July 14, 1915–January 30, 1916**	Husayn-McMahon Correspondence between Britain, Sharif Husayn bin Ali of the Hashemite family of Mecca. Britain pledges to support an independent Arab state after the First World War in return for an Arab uprising against the Ottomans
1916		Sykes-Picot Agreement. Secret pact by which Britain and France agree to partition Arab provinces of the Ottoman Empire among themselves. Parts of Palestine to become an international zone
		Husayn bin Ali declares beginning of Arab revolt against the Ottomans
	June	Balfour Declaration published, by which Britain pledges support for a "Jewish national home" in Palestine
1917	**November 2:**	
		British Commonwealth forces occupy Jerusalem
	December 9	Establishment of the Arab Club literary association in Palestine
1918		Remainder of Palestine occupied by British forces
	September	Mudros Armistice ends Ottoman-Allied fighting
	October 30	First Muslim-Christian Association established in Jaffa
	November	Third *aliyah*
1919–23		Faysal-Weizmann correspondence signals willingness of Hashemite family to cooperate with Zionist movement
	January 3	
		Paris Peace Conference states that Ottomans will lose Arab provinces
	January 30	First Palestinian National Congress meets in Jerusalem. Sends declarations to Paris Peace Conference calling for independence, rejecting Balfour Declaration
	January 27–Febuary 10	
		National meeting of Muslim-Christian Associations in Palestine
	February	U.S. King-Crane Commission of Inquiry tours Middle East to determine popular wishes about political future of region
	June–July	
		General Syrian Congress in Damascus denounces Balfour Declaration
	July 8	King-Crane Commission issues report encouraging Paris Peace Conference to abandon Zionist goal of a Jewish state in Palestine
	August 28	
		General Syrian Conference in Damascus declares Syria (including Palestine) independent under Husayn bin Ali's son Faysal bin Husayn
1920	**March**	
		Palestinian attacks on Jews in Jerusalem following Islamic religious festival of al-Nabi Musa lead to deaths of five Jews, four Palestinians. British dismiss Musa Kazim al-Husayni, mayor of Jerusalem, for opposing Balfour Declaration; Raghib al-Nashashibi appointed
	April 4	
		San Remo Peace Conference awards Britain a "Mandate" to rule Palestine
	April 25	British authorities prevent convening of Second Arab National Congress in Palestine
	May	
		British establish civil government in Palestine under High Commissioner Sir Herbert Samuel
	July 1	
		French defeat Syrian kingdom of Faysal bin Husayn
	July	Palin Commission report on April 1920 disturbances issued, never published
	October 1	
		Third Arab National Congress meets in Haifa. Elects Executive Committee, known as the Arab Executive, headed by Musa Kazim al-Husayni
	December	
		Palestinian-Jewish violence in Jaffa kills forty-seven Jews, forty-eight Palestinians

	May 8	al-Hajj Amin al-Husayni, appointed by British to position of mufti of Jerusalem, takes office
	May–June	Fourth Arab National Congress in Jerusalem
	October	Haycroft Commission of Inquiry links Jaffa disturbances with Palestinian fear of Zionist immigration
1922	**January 9**	British establish Supreme Muslim Council with al-Hajj Amin al-Husayni as its president
	February 21	Second Palestinian delegation to London rejects Balfour Declaration
	June 3	Churchill White Paper details British understanding of Balfour Declaration. States Britain does not aim to allow all of Palestine to become a Jewish national home
	June 24	League of Nations confirms Britain's Mandate over Palestine
	August	Fifth Arab National Congress meets in Nablus, calls for economic boycott of Zionists.
	October	First British census in Palestine issued. Of 757,182 persons, 78 percent were Muslim, 11 percent Jewish, 9.6 percent Christian
1923		British propose Palestine legislative council. Plan rejected by Palestinians.
	September 29	Official onset of British Mandate for Palestine
	October	British government proposes creation of an Arab Agency; rejected by Palestinians
1924		1924–28. Fourth *aliyah*
1925		Palestine Arab Workers Society established
	October	Sixth Arab National Congress meets in Jaffa
1927	**July**	Earthquake kills 272 persons throughout Palestine
1928	**June**	Seventh Arab National Congress in Jerusalem
	September 23	Jewish attempts to amend traditional liberties of worship afforded Jews at the Western Wall in Jerusalem, an Islamic *waqf* property, causes Palestinian fear of Zionist takeover of the wall and al-Haram al-Sharif (Temple Mount)
	November	Islamic Conference meeting in Jerusalem calls for protection of Islamic rights to disputed area in Jerusalem
1929	**August 15**	Zionist demonstrations at Western Wall
	August 23–29	In wake of Jewish-Arab tension over the Western Wall, Palestinian attacks against Jews mount in Jerusalem, Hebron (where 64 Jews were massacred), other locales. A total of 133 Jews are killed. British forces suppress the disturbances. 116 Palestinians are killed, largely by security forces
	October	Palestinian conference on Western Wall controversy convenes in Jerusalem
	October	Arab women's congress
1930		Establishment of Arab Bank
	January 14	League of Nations forms commission to study Palestinian and Jewish rights to Western Wall
	March	British-established Shaw Commission of Inquiry attributes 1929 violence to Palestinian fear of Zionist takeover.
	March 30	Fourth Palestinian delegation sent to London
	October 20	Hope-Simpson Commission report into Jewish immigration and economic development in Palestine asserts country's inability to absorb large numbers of Zionist immigrants
	October 20	Passfield White Paper issued
	December	League of Nations commission on Western Wall upholds Islamic ownership rights to wall

1931		Arab National Fund established to assist Palestinian cultivators to retain their land in face of Zionist land purchasing efforts
	February 14	MacDonald Letter (called by Palestinians the "Black Letter") retracts Passfield White Paper
	November	Second British census of Palestine. Of 1,035,154 persons, 73.4 percent are Muslim, 16.9 percent Jewish, 8.6 percent Christian
	December	French Report on Palestine landlessness issued
	December 16	Pan-Islamic Congress in Jerusalem
1932		National Congress of Arab Youth held in Jaffa
	August 2	Establishment of Istiqlal Party, first major Palestinian political party formed during the Mandate
1933		Deepening of Haifa port
		Creation of Arab Agricultural Bank
		Meetings between Jewish Agency head David Ben-Gurion and Palestinian figures like Awni Abd al-Hadi, Musa al-Alami, and George Antonius on future of Palestine
	October	Arab Executive announcement of general strike leads to political unrest. Twenty-four persons killed
1933–39		Fifth *aliyah*
1934	**February**	Commission of inquiry headed by Sir William Murison issues report on 1933 violence
	March	Death of Musa Kazim al-Husayni, president of Arab Executive, leads to its demise
1935	**March 27**	Arab Party founded
	June 23	Reform Party founded
	October 5	National Bloc Party established
	November	Shaykh Izz al-Din al-Qassam and other guerrillas killed by British forces
1936	**April 21**	Representatives from the five major Palestinian parties call for a general strike
	April 25	Arab Higher Committee formed from major Palestinian political parties to guide general strike. Presided over by al-Hajj Amin al-Husayni
	May	Armed Palestinian insurrection commences
	August 25	Lebanese guerrilla leader Fawzi al-Qawuqji and 150 volunteers from surrounding Arab countries enter Palestine to assist insurrection
	October 11	Arab Higher Committee agrees to cease general strike following intervention by Arab monarchs. Violence wanes
	November 11	Royal Commission, also known as the Peel Commission, arrives to investigate causes of the uprising
1937	**July 7**	Royal (Peel) Commission report issued, marking first proposal to partition Palestine between Jews and Palestinians. British Statement of Policy issued simultaneously
	July 23	Arab Higher Committee rejects Peel Commission proposal. Rebellion resumes
	September 8	Congress of representatives from Arab countries begins in Bludan, Syria; rejects Peel Commission. Marks increasing involvement of surrounding Arab states in the affairs of Palestine
	October 1	British authorities ban Arab Higher Committee and other Palestinian political organizations. Al-Hajj Amin al-Husayni flees to Lebanon; other leaders arrested and deported to Seychelles Islands.
1938		Palestinian rebels control most of Palestine's major towns (Nablus, Ramallah, Tiberias, Old City of Jerusalem, Beersheba). Reinforced British troops defeat rebels and reoccupy the country

	November 9	Partition Commission established in January, also known as the Woodhead Commission, reports on its mission to study the possibilities of partitioning Palestine. States that the Peel Commission's proposals are unworkable. Recommends convening of a conference in London to discuss future of Palestine. Statement of Policy issued simultaneously.
1939	**February 7–March 27**	St. James Conference held in London. British, Arab, Zionist representatives attend. Conference ends inconclusively
	May 17	White Paper restricts Jewish immigration, land purchases, proposes eventual independent, unified Palestine after ten years. Both sides reject it
1940	**February 28**	Land Transfer Regulations restrict Jewish land purchases
1942		Federation of Arab Trade Unions formed out of dissension within Palestine Arab Workers Society
1945		Paramilitary youth organization al-Najjada established in Jaffa
	March 22	League of Arab States (Arab League) formed in Cairo
	November 22	(Second) Arab Higher Committee reconstituted
	November	Anglo-American Committee of Inquiry established
	December 2	Arab League organizes boycott of Jewish goods produced in Palestine
1946		First branch of the Muslim Brotherhood organized in Palestine (Jerusalem)
	May	Anglo-American Committee of Inquiry issues report calling for a binational state in Palestine
	May 28–29	Arab League summit in Anshas, Egypt, calls for Palestinian independence
	June	Fourth Arab Higher Committee constituted
	June 11–12	Arab League meeting in Bludan, Syria, adopts secret proposal to link shipment of Arab oil to Britain and the U.S. to their policies regarding Palestine
	July	Morrison-Grady Plan for a unified, federal government in Palestine issued
	July 31	Anglo-American Conference meets in London. Conference proposes implementation of the Morrison-Grady Plan
	September	Round Table Conference on Palestinian problem held in London; ends without agreement
1947		Paramilitary youth organization al-Futuwwa established
	January 26	Round Table Conference reconvenes but yields no progress
	February 18	In wake of failed Round Table Conference, Britain declares it will turn over future of Palestine to the United Nations
	April 28	Special session of United Nations General Assembly dealing with Palestine opens
	May 15	United Nations Special Committee on Palestine (UNSCOP) formed to suggest ways of resolving Jewish–Palestinian claims in Palestine
	September 8	UNSCOP report published; recommends partitioning Palestine into Jewish and Palestinian states, with area encompassing Jerusalem and Bethlehem to be an international zone
	September 26	Britain announces its intention to end the Mandate
	October 7–15	Arab League meeting in Alayh, Lebanon, decides to finance military operations to assist Palestinians
	November 29	U.N. General Assembly adopts UNSCOP partition plan as General Assembly Resolution 181 (II)
	December	Jewish–Palestinian violence erupts in Palestine. The Zionist militia Haganah implements Plan Gimel to capture strategic areas of the country in advance of British evacuation. Arab League forms Arab Liberation Army to assist in defense of Palestine; first units cross into Palestine
1948	**April 4**	Haganah initiates Plan Dalet to capture areas of Palestine assigned by U.N. to the proposed Arab state

	April 5	Abd al-Qadir al-Husayni, head of the Palestinian force called the Army of the Holy Struggle, killed in Battle of Qastil
	April 9	Zionist forces from Irgun and LEHI, with assistance from Haganah, attack village of Dayr Yasin. Some 100 Palestinians are killed in fighting and subsequent massacre
	May 13	U.N. appoints Count Folke Bernadotte as mediator in Palestine
	May 14	Last British high commissioner leaves Palestine; Zionist community declares independence under the name of "Israel"
	May 15	British Mandate ends. Units from Jordanian, Egyptian, Syrian, Lebanese, Iraqi, Saudi armies enter Palestine to combat Zionist forces
	May 19	Battle of Jerusalem begins between Haganah, Jordanian forces
	June 11–July 8	First truce
	July 19	UN-ordered second truce
	September–October	All-Palestine Government formed in Egyptian-controlled Gaza
	September 17	U.N. mediator Count Folke Bernadotte assassinated by LEHI in Jerusalem
	November	Pro-Jordanian notables at Jericho Conference call for Jordanian annexation of West Bank
	December 11	U.N. General Assembly adopts Resolution 194 (III) regarding the 726,000 Palestinian refugees from the fighting
		Formation in Beirut of Movement of Arab Nationalists by George Habash and others
1949	**January 12**	First Arab–Israeli armistice talks commence under U.N. supervision on Rhodes
	March	General Refugee Congress meets in Ramallah
	April 27–September 15	Lausanne peace talks
	July 27	U.N. mediator Ralph Bunche announces end to the fighting after completion of four Arab–Israeli armistice agreements
	December	Jordan annexes that part of Palestine controlled by its forces (known as the "West Bank"); U.N. establishes United Nations Relief and Works Agency for Palestine Refugees in the Near East (UNRWA)
1950	**January**	Israel imposes military law on its Palestinian citizens
	March 14	Israeli Absentee Property Law leads to Israel's seizure of vast area of land left behind by fleeing Palestinian refugees
	April 24	Jordanian parliament confirms annexation of West Bank
1951	**July 20**	Jordan's King Abdullah assassinated by a Palestinian in al-Aqsa Mosque in East Jerusalem
1953	**October 14**	Unit 101 of the Israeli army, commanded by Ariel Sharon, attacks village of Qibya in West Bank, killing fifty-three Palestinians
1956	**October 29**	Beginning of Suez War. Israel invades Gaza, Sinai Peninsula. France and Britain join the war on Egypt on October 31. Israeli border guards massacre forty-nine Palestinian citizens of Israel in Kufr Qasim
1958		Formation of Arab nationalist al-Ard movement in Israel
1959	**January**	Fatah formed by Yasir Arafat and others
1964		Al-Ard banned by Israeli authorities
	January	Formation of Palestine Liberation Organization (PLO) in Cairo. Ahmad Shuqayri becomes first chairman. Palestine Liberation Army, Palestinian National Fund also established.
	May	First meeting of the PLO's Palestine National Council (PNC) in East Jerusalem
1965	**January 1**	Fatah announces first raid into Israel from Jordanian territory

	May 31–June 4	Second PNC meeting held in Cairo
	August	Arab–Jewish split in Israeli Communist Party leads to formation of Rakah
1966	**November 13**	Israeli army attacks West Bank village of Sammu
	December 1	Israeli government lifts military law from its Palestinian citizens
1967	**June 5–10**	June War (also called Six-Day War) between Israel and the Arab world begins with Israeli air strikes on Arab air bases. Israel eventually captures Sinai Peninsula, Gaza, West Bank, and Golan Heights. East Jerusalem captured on June 7. All of Palestine now under Israeli control
	November 22	U.N. Security Council adopts Resolution 242, calling for Israeli withdrawal in return for right of all states to live in peace in the Middle East
	December	Formation of Popular Front for the Liberation of Palestine (PFLP) under George Habash. Beginning of U.N. peace mediation efforts through the efforts of Gunnar Jarring
	December 24	Third PNC meeting in Cairo. Ahmad Shuqayri resigns as PLO chairman
1968	**March 21**	Battle of al-Karama. Palestinian guerrillas, Jordanian troops inflict heavy losses on Israeli forces attacking guerrilla bases at al-Karama, Jordan
	July 10	Fourth PNC meeting in Cairo. PLO leadership organs taken over by guerrilla groups; Palestinian National Charter adopted in 1964 revised
	July 23	Israeli airliner hijacked to Algiers by PFLP; first example of Palestinian hijacking
1969	**November 2**	Cairo Agreement signed in Cairo between PLO, commander of Lebanese army, granting PLO operational independence in areas where Palestinian population predominates
	February	Democratic Front for the Liberation of Palestine (DFLP) formed by Nayif Hawatima and others following disputes within PFLP
	February 1–4	Fifth PNC meeting in Cairo elects Yasir Arafat, chairman of Fatah, as chairman of the PLO
	September 1–16	Sixth PNC meeting in Cairo
	December 9	U.S. presents Rogers Plan for ending War of Attrition between Egypt and Israel
1970	**May 30–June 4**	Seventh PNC meeting in Cairo
	September 17	Following multiple hijackings of international aircraft by PFLP that were flown to Jordan and destroyed, Jordanian army begins campaign against Palestinian forces in Jordan. Arab-brokered cease-fire leaves some Palestinian fighters in northern Jordan. Known by Palestinians as "Black September." PLO soon establishes new headquarters in Beirut
1971	**February 28–March 5**	Eighth PNC meeting in Cairo
	July	Jordanian army expels remaining Palestinian fighters from northern Jordan
	July 7–13	Ninth PNC meeting in Cairo
1972		Bir Zeit College assumes university status; first Palestinian university in Occupied Territories
	April 6–12	Tenth PNC meeting in Cairo
	September 5	Fatah faction known as Black September kills two Israeli athletes, takes nine others hostage during Olympic games in Munich. All nine, plus five Palestinians, die during gun battle with West German police. Israel bombs Palestinian refugee camps in Lebanon in reprisal, killing hundreds
1973	**January 6–12**	Eleventh PNC meeting in Cairo
	October 6	October War (also called Ramadan War, Yom Kippur War) begins with Egyptian-Syrian assault on Israeli positions in occupied Sinai, Golan
	October 22	U.N. Security Council passes Resolution 338 ending the war. Resolution reaffirms principles contained in Resolution 242

	December 21	Inconclusive Arab–Israeli peace conference takes place in Geneva
1974		Communist-dominated Palestinian National Front established to coordinate anti-Israeli resistance in occupied territories
	May 13	DFLP gunmen raid a school in the Israeli town of Ma'alot. Twenty-four schoolchildren die in resulting battle with Israeli forces
	June 1–9	Twelfth PNC meeting in Cairo. PLO adopts revised strategy from total liberation to one of establishing a "national authority" on any part of Palestine liberated from Israel, representing beginning of Palestinian acceptance of a "two-state solution"
	October	Iraqi-backed Rejection Front formed by PFLP, other groups, in opposition to new PLO strategy articulated in June
	October 14	U.N. General Assembly recognizes PLO as the representative of the Palestinian people
	October 29	Arab summit meeting in Rabat recognizes PLO as "sole, legitimate representative of the Palestinian people"
	November 13	PLO chairman Arafat addresses U.N. General Assembly
1975		Emergence of National Committee of Heads of Local Arab Councils in Israel, an important national organization among Palestinians in Israel
	April	Lebanese civil war begins
	September	U.S. government notifies Israel it will have no contact with PLO until it accepts U.N. Security Council Resolution 242 and renounces terrorism
	November 10	U.N. General Assembly Resolution 3379 equates Zionism with racism
	December 4	PLO allowed to participate in U.N. Security Council debate on Arab–Israeli-conflict
1976	**January**	Fatah joins Lebanese civil war on side of Lebanese National Movement
	March 30	Land Day protests against Israeli confiscation of Palestinian land in Israel leads to death of six Palestinians in Galilee
	April 12	Israeli occupation authorities allow first municipal elections in West Bank. Pro-PLO mayors sweep elections
	May 31	Syrian forces intervene in Lebanese Civil War, soon are engaged in action-against PLO-Lebanese National Movement fighters
	August 13	Lebanese Phalangist forces massacre Palestinians at Tall al-Za'tar refugee camp following fifty-three day siege
1977		Establishment of Arab Thought Forum in occupied West Bank Establishment of Rakah-led Democratic Front for Peace and Equality in Israel Emergence of Abna al-Balad movement in Israel
	March 12–22	Thirteenth PNC meeting in Cairo
	March 16	U.S. president Jimmy Carter affirms right of Palestinians to a "homeland," first U.S. president to do so
	November 19–20	Egyptian president Anwar Sadat visits Israel; first Arab leader to do so publicly
1978		Israeli military occupation in West Bank and Gaza replaced by "civil administration"
	March 14–June 13	Litani Operation. Israeli forces invade southern Lebanon, attack PLO forces there
	September 5–17	Camp David summit between U.S. president Jimmy Carter, Egyptian president Anwar Sadat, Israeli prime minister Menachem Begin. Camp David accords signed September 17 in Washington, laying foundation for Egyptian–Israeli peace
	November	Formation of National Guidance Committee in West Bank
1979		Arab Studies Society formed in Jerusalem

	January 15–22	Fourteenth PNC meeting in Damascus
	March 26	Egyptian–Israeli Peace Treaty signed in Washington, first peace treaty between Israel and an Arab state
	March 31	PLO, rest of Arab League break diplomatic relations with Egypt in wake of peace treaty
1980	**July 30**	Israeli Knesset resolution states Jerusalem is "eternal capital of Israel"
1981	**April 11–19**	Fifteenth PNC meeting in Damascus
	July	Severe PLO-Israeli fighting across Lebanese border. Israeli planes bomb Beirut, killing hundreds. PLO artillery fires from Lebanon into northern Israel, killing several Israelis.
	July 24	U.S. mediator Philip Habib arranges PLO-Israeli cease-fire indirectly, given that neither U.S. nor Israel recognizes the PLO
	August 8	Saudis announce Fahd Plan: implied Arab recognition of Israel in return for formation of Palestinian state
	November	Israel establishes "civil administration" in Occupied Territories in place of military administration
1982	**March**	Israeli authorities ban National Guidance Committee
	June 6	Beginning of Israeli invasion of Lebanon. Israeli forces invade Lebanon, attack PLO forces, eventually besiege West Beirut. Thousands of civilians are killed
	September 1	PLO chairman Arafat leads evacuation of Palestinian fighting forces from Beirut. PLO establishes new headquarters in Tunis
	September 1	Reagan Plan for Arab–Israeli peace announced by U.S. president Ronald Reagan. Proposes Palestinian autonomy in Occupied Territories, eventual Palestinian association with Jordan
	September 8	Fez Plan, similar to 1981 Fahd Plan, announced by Arab League
	Sepember 17–18	Sabra and Shatila massacres. Lebanese Phalangist forces operating in Israeli-controlled West Beirut massacre more than eight hundred Palestinians in two refugee camps
1983		Al-Hakawati Theater troupe establishes first theater–cultural center in Jerusalem
		First Palestinian Theater Festival held in Ramallah
	February 14–22	Sixteenth PNC meeting in Algiers
	May	Anti-Arafat uprising begins among certain Fatah units in Lebanon, led by Sa'id Musa Muragha (Abu Musa)
	December 20	Arafat and loyalist Fatah forces evacuate from Tripoli, Lebanon, following siege by Abu Musa, other pro-Syrian Palestinians
1984	**November**	Seventeenth PNC meeting in Amman
1985	**February 13**	Husayn-Arafat Agreement between Arafat and Jordan's King Husayn proposes joint Jordanian–Palestinian negotiating strategy
	February 22	Jordan, PLO issue peace plan
	March	Palestinian National Salvation Front established in Damascus by Palestinians opposed to Husayn-Arafat Agreement
	October 1	Israeli air force bombs PLO headquarters in Tunis
1986	**March**	King Husayn dissassociates himself from Husayn-Arafat Agreement
	October 1	Members of the Palestine Liberation Front faction seize control of Italian cruise ship *Achille Lauro* in the Mediterranean, murder a disabled Jewish–American passenger
1987		Eighteenth PNC meeting in Algiers
	December 9	Beginning of Intifada. Anti-Israeli demonstrations break out in Gaza, soon escalating into full-scale civil rebellion against occupation forces

1988		Establishment of Arab Democratic Party in Israel, first openly Arab legal political party in Israel
	February	Hamas issues first communique, publicly signaling its existence
	April 16	Israeli commandos assassinate PLO leader Khalil al-Wazir (Abu Jihad) near Tunis
	May 13	First communique of the United National Command of the Intifada, leadership cooperative directing the Intifada in coordination with PLO
	July 31	King Husayn cuts administrative ties between Jordan and the West Bank
	November 19	PNC meeting in Algiers declares existence of a Palestinian state
	December 13	Arafat addresses U.N. in Geneva, announces PLO recognition of U.N. Security Council Resolutions 242 and 338
	December 14	U.S. initiates dialogue with PLO in Tunis
1990	**June 20**	U.S. halts dialogue with PLO following raid by Palestine Liberation Front
	August 1990–February 1991	Iraqi occupation of Kuwait, subsequent Gulf War, leads to retaliatory expulsion of some 300,000 Palestinians from Arab Gulf countries in wake of Arafat's support of Iraq
	October 8	Israeli forces kill eighteen Palestinian demonstrators at al-Haram al-Sharif complex in Jerusalem
1991	**January 14**	Fatah official Salah Khalaf (Abu Iyad) assassinated in Tunis.
	April	U.S. Secretary of State James Baker initiates dialogue with Palestinian leaders in Jerusalem
	September	PNC meeting in Algiers
	October 30	Madrid Peace Conference begins
	December 10	Bilateral Arab–Israeli negotiations commence in Washington
	December 16	U.N. General Assembly adopts Resolution 4686 repealing 1975 "Zionism is Racism" decision
1992	**December 17**	Israeli government deports 417 Palestinians from Occupied Territories to southern Lebanon
	September	National Democratic and Islamic Front (also known as the "Damascus Ten") formed in Damascus by Palestinian groups opposed to peace talks
1993		Secret talks begin between Israeli, PLO representatives in Norway
	September 9	Yasir Arafat notifies Israeli prime minister Yitzhak Rabin of PLO's recognition of Israel after PLO executive committee vote
	September 12	Rabin notifies Arafat of Israeli recognition of PLO
	September 13	Israel, PLO sign Declaration of Principles in Washington
1994	**February 25**	Israeli settler opens fire in al-Ibrahimi Mosque in Hebron; twenty-nine Palestinians massacred
	April 4	First Israeli redeployments
	May 4	Israel, PLO sign Gaza Jericho Agreement ("Cairo Accord")
	May 12	Entrance of first units of Palestine Liberation Army into Jericho to serve as Palestinian police
	July 1	Yasir Arafat enters Gaza to head Palestinian Authority
	August 29	Israel, PLO sign Transfer of Powers accord
	October 30–November	First Middle East/North Africa Economic Summit in Casablanca leads to decision by Arab Gulf states to end aspects of the Arab boycott of Israel
	December 10	Arafat awarded Nobel Prize in Oslo along with Israeli prime minister Yitzhak Rabin, Israeli foreign minister Shimon Peres
1995	**September 28**	Israeli-PLO sign Interim Agreement and Elections accord (also called "Taba accords" and "Oslo II") in Washington
	October 29–30	Second Middle East/North Africa Economic Summit held in Amman
	November 4	Israeli prime minister. Rabin assassinated by Jewish militant in Tel Aviv

1996	**January 20**	First elections held for presidency and legislative council of the Palestinian Authority. Arafat elected president
	February–March	Four Hamas suicide bombings in Israel kill fifty-eight Israelis
	March 27	First meeting of Palestinian Legislative Council in Gaza
	April 22–26	Twenty-first Palestine National Council held in Gaza–first PNC meeting in Palestine since 1964. PNC votes to delete anti-Israel sections of 1968 Palestinian Charter on April 24
	May 15	Benjamin Netanyahu elected prime minister of Israel.
	September 25–26	Battles between Israel, PA security forces kill sixty-two Palestinians and fourteen Israelis
	November 12	Third Middle East/North Africa Economic Summit opens in Cairo
1997	**January 15**	Israel, PLO sign Hebron Protocol
	February 19	Israeli prime minister Netanyahu approves construction of Har Homa settlement in East Jerusalem. Israeli-PLO talks break down
1998	**October 23**	Israel, PLO sign "Wye River Memorandum"
	December 12	President Bill Clinton becomes first U.S. president to visit Palestinian Authority. Twenty-Charter once again in Clinton's presence on December 14
1999	**May 4**	End of five-year period by which Israel, PLO were to have resolved all final peace arrangements
	May 17	Labor Party candidate Ehud Barak elected prime minister of Israel
	September	Israeli Supreme Court bans torture of Palestinian prisoners
	September 9	Israel, PLO sign Sharm al-Shaykh Memorandum

ANNOTATED BIBLIOGRAPHY

by Don Peretz

BOOKS

Abed, George T. *The Economic Viability of a Palestinian State.* Washington, D.C.: Institute for Palestine Studies, 1990. Discussion of economic plans for Palestinian state.

——. *The Palestinian Economy: Studies in Development under Prolonged Occupation.* London: Routledge, 1988. Collection of papers on Palestinian economy with emphasis on West Bank and Gaza.

Abu-Amr, Ziad. *Islamic Fundamentalism in the West Bank and Gaza.* Bloomington: Indiana University Press, 1994. An analysis of fundamentalist influence on and competition with the PLO in occupied territories.

Abu-Ghazaleh, Adnan M. *Arab Cultural Nationalism in Palestine during the British Mandate.* Beirut: Institute for Palestine Studies, 1973. A short study of Palestinian Arab nationalist writing and writers to 1948.

Abu Iyad (Salah Khalaf), with Eric Rouleau. *My Home, My Land: A Narrative of the Palestinian Struggle.* New York: Times Books, 1981. Account of Arab–Israeli conflict by a former PLO leader.

Abu-Lughod, Ibrahim, ed. *The Transformation of Palestine: Essays on the Origin and Development of the Arab–Israeli Conflict.* 2d ed. Evanston, Ill.: Northwestern University Press, 1987. Collection of articles by diverse scholars from an Arab perspective.

Anabtawi, Sami N. *Palestinian Higher Education in the West Bank and Gaza.* London: KPI, 1986. Critique of Palestinian higher education in West Bank and Gaza.

Armstrong, Karen. *Jerusalem: One City, Three Faiths.* New York: Ballantine, 1997. Traces history of how Jews, Christians, and Muslims laid claim to Jerusalem as their holy city and how their conceptions have shaped and scarred the city.

Aronson, Geoffrey. *Israel, Palestinians, and the Intifada: Creating Facts on the West Bank.* Washington, D.C.: Institute for Palestine Studies, 1990. Critical examination of Israeli policy in West Bank.

Aruri, Naseer H. *The Obstruction of Peace: The United States, Israel, and the Palestinians.* Monroe, Maine: Common Courage, 1995. Critique of Oslo process.

Arzt, Donna. *Refugees Into Citizens: Palestinians and the End of the Arab–Israeli Conflict.* New York: Council on Foreign Relations, 1997. Blueprint for resolving Palestinian refugee problem.

Asali, K. J., ed. *Jerusalem in History.* New York: Olive Branch, 1990. Anthology of nine essays covering the Bronze Age until the 1980s.

Ashrawi, Hanan. *This Side of Peace: A Personal Account.* New York: Simon & Schuster, 1995. An account of peace negotiations in the early 1990s by spokeswoman of the Palestinian delegation.

Asmar, Fouzi el-. *To Be an Arab in Israel.* London: Institute for Palestine Studies, 1978. Autobiography illustrating discrimination against Israeli Palestinians.

Awaisi, Abdal-Fattah Muhammad al-. *The Muslim Brothers and the Palestine Question, 1928–1947.* New York: I. B. Tauris, 1998. Islamic fundamentalist involvement in Palestine.

Barakat, Halim. *Days of Dust.* Wilmette, IL.: Medina University, 1974. A Palestinian novel about the 1967 Six-Day War.

Beirut Massacre: The Complete Kahan Commission Report. Princeton, N.J.: Karz-Cohl, 1983. Report of Israeli investigation commission on the Sabra and Shatila massacre.

Bentwich, Norman, and Helen Bentwich. *Mandate Memoirs, 1918–1948.* New York: Schocken Books, 1965. Memoirs of a former high-ranking Anglo–Jewish Palestine official.

Benvenisti, Meron. *City of Stone. The Hidden History of Jerusalem.* Berkeley: University of California, 1997. Critical assessment of Israeli policies of planning, demography, administration and municipal politic by former deputy mayor.

———. *Jerusalem: The Torn City.* Minneapolis: University of Minnesota Press, 1976. Account of ethnic relations in city by Israeli former deputy mayor.

Benvenisti, Meron, with Ziad Abu-Zayed and Danny Rubinstein. *The West Bank Handbook: A Political Lexicon.* Boulder, Colo.: Westview, 1986. Collection of data on many aspects of the West Bank.

Bickerton, Ian J., and Carla L. Klausner. *A Concise History of the Arab–Israeli Conflict.* 2d ed. Englewood Cliffs, N.J.: Prentice Hall, 1995. Basic text containing maps, chronology, bibliography, documents.

Binur, Yoram. *My Enemy, My Self.* New York: Penguin, 1990. An Israeli Jewish journalist account of his experiences when disguised as an Arab worker during the late 1980s.

Boullata, Kamal, and Mirenne Ghossein, eds. *The World of Rashid Hussein: A Palestinian Poet in Exile.* Detroit: Association of Arab-American University Graduates, 1979. Essays on life and work of deceased Israeli Palestinian poet.

Brand, Laurie A. *Palestinians in Arab World: Institution Building and the Search for State.* New York: Columbia University Press, 1988. Pioneering study of Palestinians and their social and political organizations in Egypt, Kuwait, and Jordan after 1948.

Brynen, Rex. *Sanctuary and Survival: The PLO in Lebanon.* Boulder, Colo.: Westview Press, 1990. Study of the PLO's use of Lebanon as a base for armed activities.

Budeiri, Musa. *The Palestine Communist Party, 1919–1948: Arab and Jew in the Struggle for Internationalism.* London: Ithaca, 1979. Arab–Jewish relations in the Palestine communist movement before 1948.

Buehrig, Edward. *The U.N. and the Palestine Refugees: A Study in Nonterritorial Administration.* Bloomington: Indiana University Press, 1971. Study of the work and administration of UNRWA.

Caplan, Neil. *Futile Diplomacy.* 4 vols. Vol: 1 *Early Arab–Zionist Negotiation Attempts, 1913–1931;* Vol. 2: *Arab–Zionist Negotiations and the End of the Mandate;* Vol. 3: *The United Nations and the Great Powers in Middle East Peacemaking, 1948–1954;* and Vol. 4: *Operation Alpha and the Failure of Anglo-American Coercive Diplomacy in the Arab–Israeli Conflict 1954–1956.* London: Frank Cass, 1983, 1986, 1997. A fine study of Zionist–Arab contacts, including relevant documents.

———. *Palestine Jewry and the Arab Question, 1917–1925.* London: Frank Cass, 1978. The conflict during early British administration of Palestine.

Cattan, Henry. *The Palestine Question.* London: Croom Helm, 1988. A juridical analysis of Palestine question to 1982.

———. *The Question of Jerusalem.* New York: St. Martin's, 1981. History of Jerusalem with emphasis on illegal Israeli actions.

Chomsky, Noam. *The Fateful Triangle: The U.S., Israel and the Palestinians.* 2d ed. Boston: South End, 1999. Strong critique of U.S. pro-Israel policy.

Christison, Kathleen. *Perception of Palestine: Their Influence on U.S. Middle East Policy.* Berkeley, Calif.: University of California Press, 1999. Discussion of the assumptions that have shaped U. S. policy from the administration of Woodrow Wilson to Bill Clinton.

Ciment, James. *Palestine/Israel: The Long Conflict.* New York: Facts On File, 1997. Survey of the conflict through the peace process.

Cobban, Helena. *The Palestinian Liberation Organization: People, Power and Policies.* New York: Cambridge University Press, 1984. Sympathetic, scholarly study of Palestine resistance movement from 1948 to early 1980s conflicts in Lebanon.

Cohen, Amnon. *Palestine in the 18th Century: Patterns of Government and Administration.* Jerusalem: Magnes, 1973. Scholarly account of 18th-century Ottoman administration.

Cohen, Michael J. *The Origins and Evolution of the Arab–Zionist Conflict.* Berkeley: University of California Press, 1987. Interpretive examination of Arab–Zionist conflict to 1948, from a Zionist perspective.

Collins, Larry, and Dominique Lapierre. *O Jerusalem!* New York: Simon & Schuster, 1988. French journalist's account of battle for Jerusalem in 1948 war.

Cooley, John K. *Green March, Black September: The Story of the Palestinian Arabs*. London: Frank Cass, 1973. Discussion of mostly diaspora Palestinians, their organizations, literature, and supporters, and Israeli perceptions of them.

Corbin, Jane. *The Norway Channel: The Secret Talks That Led to the Middle East Peace Accord*. New York: Atlantic Monthly, 1994. Story behind secret negotiations leading to 1993 Oslo accords.

Cossali, Paul, and Clive Robson. *Stateless in Gaza*. London: Zed Books, 1986. Life in the Gaza Strip under Israeli occupation; position of women.

Cutting, Pauline. *Children of the Siege*. London: Heinemann, 1988. Account of British surgeon in Beirut Palestinian refugee camp, 1980s.

Darwish, Mahmoud. *Sand and Other Poems*. London: KPI, 1986. Translations of leading Palestinian nationalist poet.

Dimbleby, Johnathan. *The Palestinians*. New York: Quartet, 1980. Sympathetic account of Palestinian resistance with photos.

Divine, Donna Robinson. *Politics and Society in Ottoman Palestine: The Arab Struggle for Survival and Power*. Boulder, Colo.: Rienner, 1994. Survey of political, economic, and social developments among Palestinians in Ottoman era.

Doumani, Beshara. *Rediscovering Palestine: Merchants and Peasants in Jabal Nablus, 1700–1900*. Berkeley: University of California Press, 1995. Based on primary documents, revises both Arab and Western views of economic and political life in Ottoman Palestine.

Dumper, Michael. *Islam and Israel: Muslim Religious Endowments and the Jewish State*. Washington, D.C.: Institute for Palestine Studies, 1994. Discusses Waqf administration from Ottoman to Israeli times with focus on land question.

Elad-Bouskila. *Modern Palestinian Literature and Culture*. London: Frank Cass, 1999. An Israeli view of Palestinian literature with a focus on the intifada.

Elon, Amos. *Jerusalem: City of Mirrors*. Boston: Little, Brown, 1989. Israel's leading journalist's impressions and history of Jerusalem.

Emerson, Gloria. *Gaza: A Year in the Intifada. A Personal Account from an Occupied Land*. New York: Atlantic Monthly, 1991. Description of life under occupation.

ESCO Foundation for Palestine. *Palestine: A Study of Jewish, Arab and British Policies*. 2 vols. New Haven, Conn.: Yale University Press, 1947. Massive study of problem; sympathetic to Zionist position. Volume 1 covers emergence of Zionism, World War I to 1929; volume 2 covers up to 1946 Anglo-American committee.

Farsoun, Samih K., and Christina Zacharia. *Palestine and the Palestinians*. Boulder, Colo.: Westview, 1996. Pro-Palestinian examination of social, economic, and political development of the Palestinians from antiquity to the present.

Fernea, Elizabeth Warnock, and Mary Evelyn Hocking, eds. *The Struggle for Peace: Israelis and Palestinians*. Austin: University of Texas Press, 1992. Twelve essays that deal with issues from different perspectives and disciplines.

Flapan, Simha. *The Birth of Israel: Myth and Realities*. New York: Pantheon, 1988. Israeli revisionist account of 1948–51 period; presents series of conventional "myths" about Arab–Israel conflict.

——. *Zionism and the Palestinians*. New York: Barnes and Noble Books, 1979. Israeli revisionist history of Zionist–Arab relations in Palestine up to 1948; maintains peaceful solution was possible.

Frangi, Abdullah. *The PLO and Palestine*. London: Zed Books, 1983. Account of Palestine problem by former PLO/Arab League representative.

Fraser, T. G. *The Arab–Israel Conflict*. New York: St. Martin's, 1995. Reevaluation of Arab–Israel conflict in light of recent agreements between Israel and the PLO.

Freedman, Robert O., ed. *The Intifada: Its Impact on Israel, the Arab World, and the Superpowers*. Miami: Florida International University, 1991. Edited papers by diverse scholars.

Friedman, Isaiah. *The Question of Palestine, 1914–1918: British-Jewish-Arab Relations*. New York: Schocken Books, 1973. Detailed study of diplomacy, Balfour Declaration and Husayn-McMahon correspondence, from a Zionist perspective.

Friedman, Thomas L. *From Beirut to Jerusalem*. New York: Farrar, Straus & Giroux, 1991. Experiences and observations of *New York Times* correspondent covering Middle East and Arab–Israel conflict.

Furlonge, Sir Geoffrey. *Palestine Is My Country: The Story of Musa Alami*. New York: Praeger, 1969. Biography of leading Palestinian educational and political figure.

Gabbay, Rony E. *A Political Study of the Arab-Jewish Conflict.* New York: Lounz, 1959. One of the earliest studies, focuses on refugees, compensation, etc.

Geddes, Charles L., ed. *A Documentary History of the Arab-Israeli Conflict.* New York: Praeger, 1991. Annotated documentation collection with bibliography and sources.

Gerner, Deborah J. *One Land, Two Peoples: The Conflict Over Palestine.* 2d ed. Boulder, Colo.: Westview, 1994. Good introductory text to Arab-Israeli conflict.

Ghabra, Shafeeq N. *Palestinians in Kuwait: The Family and the Politics of Survival.* Boulder, Colo.: Westview, 1987. Study of Palestinian community and family networks in Kuwait.

Giacaman, Rita. *Life and Health in Three Palestinian Villages.* London: Ithaca, 1987. Examines health conditions with focus on women and children.

Giannou, Chris. *Beseiged: A Doctor's Story of Life and Death in Beirut.* New York: Olive Branch, 1992. Experiences of Canadian surgeon in Palestine Red Crescent hospital in Shatila refugee camp from 1985 to 1988.

Gilmour, David. *Dispossessed: The Ordeal of the Palestinians, 1917–1980.* London: Sphere Books, 1980. Sympathetic account of Palestinians in Palestine, Israel, occupied territories, diaspora, and refugee camps since 1917.

Glubb, Sir John Bagot. *Peace in the Holy Land: An Historical Analysis of the Palestine Problem.* London: Hodder & Stoughton, 1971. Former British commander of Arab Legion gives account of Arab-Israel conflict from ancient era to present; sympathetic to Palestinians.

Gorny, Yosef. *Zionism and the Arabs 1882–1948: A Study in Ideology.* New York: Oxford University, 1987. Study of early Zionist ideology toward the "Arab question."

Graham-Brown, Sarah. *Education, Repression & Liberation: Palestinians.* London: World University Service, 1984. Study of Palestinian education in relation to national liberation.

——. *Palestinians and Their Society, 1880–1946: A Photograpahic Essay.* London: Quartet Books, 1980. Collection of photographs with narrative covering rural and urban Palestinians.

Granott, A. *The Land System in Palestine: History and Structure.* London: Eyre & Spottiswoode, 1952. Detailed study of the land system during the mandate.

Gresh, Alain. *The PLO: The Struggle Within: Towards an Independent Palestinian State.* 2d ed. Totowa, N.J.: Zed Books, 1988. Account by French scholar of Palestinian national movement.

Grossman, David. *Sleeping on a Wire: Conversations with Palestinians in Israel.* New York: Farrar, Straus & Giroux, 1993. Israeli writer's meetings with country's Palestinians who describe their plight as second-class citizens.

——. *The Yellow Wind.* New York: Farrar, Straus & Giroux, 1988. Grossman's meetings and conversations with Palestinians in West Bank.

Habiby, Emile. *The Secret Life of Saeed: The Pessoptimist.* Columbia, La.: Readers International, 1989. Satirical novel about Arab minority in Israel by noted Israeli-Palestinian writer, a former leader of Communist Party.

Hadawi, Sami. *Bitter Harvest: A Modern History of Palestine.* 4th ed. Brooklyn, N.Y.: Interlink Publishing Group, 1991. Partisan history of Palestine conflict by Palestinian writer.

——. *Palestinian Rights and Losses in 1948: A Comprehensive Study.* Atlantic Highlands, U.K.: Saqi Books, 1988. Extensive study and evaluation of Palestinian property left in Israel, and work of UNCCP, by a former official of the UNCCP; maps, documents, tables.

Haidar, Aziz. *The Palestinians in Israeli Social Science Writings.* Washington, D.C.: International Center for Research & Public Policy, 1987. Study of what Israeli social scientists write about Arabs.

——. *Education, Empowerment and Control: The Case of the Arabs in Israel.* Albany: State University of New York Press, 1994. Part of study of status and condition of Israeli-Palestinians.

Halabi, Rafik. *The West Bank Story.* Rev. ed. San Diego, Calif.: Harcourt Brace Jovanovich, 1985. An account by Israeli Druze journalist of West Bank occupation.

Halsell, Grace. *Prophecy and Politics: Militant Evangelists on a Path to Nuclear War.* Westport, Conn.: Lawrence Hill, 1986. A critique of American militant evangelicals who support Israel.

Harkabi, Yehoshafat. *Israel's Fateful Hour.* New York: Harper & Row, 1988. Warning about Israel's dangerous policies vis-à-vis Palestinians.

Hart, Alan. *Arafat, a Political Biography.* Bloomington: Indiana University Press, 1989, Sympathetic account of Arafat and of Palestinian resistance.

Heiberg, Marianne, and Geir Ovensen. *Palestinian Society in Gaza, West Bank and Arab Jerusalem: A Survey of Living Conditions.* Oslo, Norway: FAFO (Institute for Applied Social Science), 1993. Extensive survey of 2,500 Palestinian households covering health, education, status of women, employment, and political views.

Heller, Mark. *A Palestinian State: The Implications for Israel.* Cambridge, Mass.: Harvard University Press, 1983. An Israeli proposal for Palestinian self-determination and its political, economic, and security implications for Israel.

Heller, Mark, and Sari Nusseibeh. *No Trumpets, No Drums: A Two-State Settlement of the Israeli–Palestinian Conflict.* New York: Hill and Wang, 1991. Compromise peace proposals of Israeli Jew and Palestinian Arab.

Hiltermann, Joost R. *Behind the Intifada: Labor and Women's Movements in the Occupied Territories.* Princeton, N.J.: Princeton University Press, 1991. Detailed discussion of diverse Palestinian women's organizations.

Hiro, Dilip. *Sharing the Promised Land: A Tale of Israelis and Palestinians.* New York: Olive Branch, 1999. Chronicle of Israeli–Palestinian relations by Indian-born journalist.

Hirst, David. *The Gun and the Olive Branch: The Roots of Violence in the Middle East.* New York: Harcourt Brace Jovanovich, 1977. British journalist's account of Palestine conflict, sympathetic to Palestinians, critical of Zionists and Israel.

Howard, Harry N. *The King-Crane Commission: An American Inquiry in the Middle East.* Beirut: Khayats, 1963. Scholarly study of commission sent by President Woodrow Wilson to Middle East after World War I to determine wishes of inhabitants.

Hunger, F. Robert. *The Palestinian Uprising: A War by Other Means.* Berkeley: University of California, 1991. Study of the first two-and-one-half years of the Intifada.

Hurewitz, J. C. *The Struggle for Palestine.* New York: Schocken Books, 1976. Detailed study of Palestine from 1936 to 1948 war and establishment of Israel.

Hyamson, Albert M. *Palestine under the Mandate.* London: Methuen, 1950. Account by Jewish former high-ranking British mandatory official.

Ingrims, Doreen, ed. *Palestine Papers, 1917–1922: Seeds of Conflict.* New York: Braziller, 1973. Excerpts from important documents with explanations.

Institute for Palestine Studies. *The Palestinian–Israeli Peace Agreement: A Documentary Record.* Washington, D.C.: Institute for Palestine Studies, 1994. Extensive collection of major documents from Camp David accords to 1993 Declaration of Principles.

———. *A Survey of Palestine.* Washington, D.C.: Institute for Palestine Studies, 1991. Reprint of two volumes and supplement prepared by Palestine mandatory government, 1945–47, for international investigation commission.

———. *United Nations Resolutions on Palestine and the Arab–Israeli Conflict, 1947–1998.* 4 vols. Washington, D.C.: Institute for Palestine Studies, 1988–99. Four volumes that include U.N. resolutions from 1947 to 1998.

———. *U.S. Official Statements.* 5 vols. Washington, D.C.: Institute for Palestine Studies, 1992–94. Official statements by U.S. government on conflict issues (the Palestinian refugees; status of Jerusalem; Israeli settlements/Fourth Geneva Convention; U.N. Resolution 242).

Jabra, Jabra I. *Hunters in a Narrow Street.* Washington, D.C.: Three Continents, n.d. Novel about diaspora Palestinians in Baghdad during 1940s.

———. *The Ship.* Washington, D.C.: Three Continents, 1985. Novel of post-1948 Palestinian exile in symbolic terms.

Jayyusi, Salma Khadra, ed. *Anthology of Modern Palestinian Literature.* New York: Columbia University Press, 1992. Largest and most comprehensive anthology of Palestinian literary writing in Western language with selections from some 100 20th-century Palestinian authors.

Jeffries, J. M. N. *Palestine: The Reality.* Westport, Conn.: Hyperion, 1976. Extensive presentation of Arab case; strongly condemns Britain.

Jiryis, Sabri. *The Arabs in Israel, 1948–1966.* 2d ed. New York: Monthly Review, 1976. Former Israeli Palestinian's examination of Israeli discrimination.

Joffe, Lawrence. *Keesing's Guide to the Mid-East Peace Process.* London: Cartermill, 1996. Useful reference of the Oslo peace process: its background, countries involved, and biographies of participants.

John, Robert, and Sami Hadawi. *The Palestine Diary.* 2d ed. 2 vols. New York: New World, 1971. Extensive documentation of Palestine question. Volume 1 covers British involvement from

World War I to 1945; Volume 2, from end of World War II to 1948.

Jureidini, Paul, and William E. Huzen. *The Palestinian Movement in Politics.* Lexington, Mass.: Lexington Books, 1976. Examines Palestinian movement from 1920s to 1975 with attention to guerrilla organizations and relations with Arab states.

Kaleh, Hala, and Simonetta Calderini. *The Intifada—The Palestinian Uprising in the West Bank and Gaza Strip: A Bibliography of Books and Articles 1987–1992.* Oxford, England: Middle East Libraries Committee, Oxford Middle East Centre, 1993. Index of major monographs and journal and magazine articles on first years of Intifada.

Kanafani, Ghassan. *Men in the Sun and Other Palestinian Stories.* Washington, D.C.: Three Continents, 1983. Fictional accounts of Palestinian condition by Palestinian author and political figure (assassinated by Israeli intellegence).

Kark, Ruth. *Jaffa: A City in Evolution, 1799–1917.* Jerusalem: Yad Izhak Ben-Zvi, 1990. Analysis of political, demographic, social, economic, and regional factors shaping Jaffa's development in 19th century.

The Karp Report: An Israeli Government Inquiry into Settler Violence Against Palestinians on the West Bank. Washington, D.C.: Institute for Palestine Studies, 1984. English translation from Hebrew of report by Israel's deputy attorney general.

Kassim, Anis F., ed. *The Palestine Yearbook of International Law.* Nicosia, Cyprus: Al-Shaybani Society of International Law, 1984–1995. Annual, including texts and documents on legal aspects of Palestine problem, from Palestinian perspective.

Kayyali, Abdul Wahhab. *Palestine: A Modern History.* London: Croom Helm, 1973. Chronological history of Palestine from 1881 to 1939.

Kazziha, Walid W. *Revolutionary Transformation in the Arab World: Habash and His Comrades from Nihilism to Marxism.* New York: St. Martin's, 1975. Study of how the Arab nationalist movement spawned the Popular Front for the Liberation of Palestine and other leftist Arab movements.

Kedourie, Elie, and Sylvia Haim, eds. *Zionism and Arabism in Palestine and Israel.* London: Frank Cass, 1982. Collection of papers on various aspects of Palestine problem, from a Zionist perspective.

Khalidi, Raja. *The Arab Economy in Israel: Dynamics of a Region's Development.* London: Croom Helm, 1988. Study of Israeli Arab economy; integration into Israeli economy.

Khalidi, Rashid. *British Policy towards Syria and Palestine, 1906–1914: A Study of the Antecedents of the Hussein-McMahon Correspondence, the Sykes-Picot Agreement, and the Balfour Declaration.* London: Ithaca, 1980. Study of Britain's conflicting commitments based on archives.

———. *Palestinian Identity: The Construction of Modern Nation as Consciousness.* New York: Columbia University Press, 1997. Critical assessment of the narrations that make up Palestinian history and identity.

———. *Under Siege: P.L.O. Decisionmaking during the 1982 War.* New York: Columbia University Press, 1986. PLO decisions during Beirut siege based on PLO and other documents.

Khalidi, Walid. *Before their Diaspora: A Photographic History of the Palestinians,1876–1948.* Washington, D.C.: Institute for Palestine Studies, 1984. Photo collection with a sympathetic text illustrating pre-1948 Palestinian life.

———. *Conflict and Violence in Lebanon.* Cambridge, Mass.: Harvard University Center for International Affairs, 1979. History of Lebanese Civil War and aftermath of Israeli 1978 invasion.

———. *From Haven to Conquest: Readings in Zionism and the Palestine Problem until 1948.* Beirut Institute for Palestine Studies, 1971. Collection of diverse documents, letters, and accounts critical of Zionism.

Khalidi, Walid, and Jill Khadduri, eds. *Palestine and the Arab-Israel Conflict: An Annotated Bibliography.* Beirut: Institute for Palestine Studies, 1974. Extensive bibliography of books and articles in several languages.

———. *Palestine Reborn.* New York: St. Martin's, 1992. Covers Israel–Arab relations and conflict and U.S. policy.

Khouri, Fred J. *The Arab-Israeli Dilemma.* 3d ed. Syracuse, N.Y.: Syracuse University Press, 1985. Detailed analysis of conflict with extensive coverage on United Nations.

Kimmerling, Baruch, and Joel S. Migdal. *Palestinians: The Making of a People.* New York: Free Press, 1993. Sociopolitical history of the Palestinians from 1834 revolt to 1987 Intifada.

King, John. *Handshake in Washington: The Beginning of Middle East Peace?* London: Ithaca, 1994. An optimistic assessment of the 1993 Oslo accords.

Kirkbride, Sir Alec Seath. *From the Wings: Amman Memoirs, 1947–1951.* London: Frank Cass, 1976. Account by former British diplomat of Jordan and 1948 war.

Korn, David A. *Assassination in Khartoum.* Bloomington: Indiana University Press, 1993. Covers Palestinian terrorism and kidnapping of U.S. diplomat in Sudan.

Kretzmer, David. *The Legal Status of the Arabs in Israel.* Boulder, Colo.: Westview, 1990. Published in cooperation with International Center for Peace in the Middle East.

Kuniholm, Bruce Robellet. *The Palestinian Problem and United States Policy: A Quick Guide to Issues and References.* Claremont, Calif.: Regina Books, 1986. Reference guide with extensive bibliography.

Kunstel, Marcia, and Joseph Albright. *Their Promised Land: Arab versus Jew in History's Cauldron: One Valley in the Jerusalem Hills.* New York: Crown, 1990. Jewish-Arab relations in Sorek Valley, 1917–49.

Kupferschmidt, Uri M. *Supreme Muslim Council: Islam Under the British Mandate for Palestine.* Leiden, Netherlands: Brill, 1987. Account of Palestine's Supreme Muslim Council and role of al-Hajj Amin al-Husayni.

Kurzman, Dan. *Genesis 1948: The First Arab-Israeli War.* New York: New American Library, 1970. Enthusiastic account of Israel's birth, based on interviews.

Kushner, David, ed. *Palestine in the Late Ottoman Period: Political, Social and Economic Transformation.* Leiden, Netherlands: Brill, 1986. Scholarly study of pre–World War I Palestine.

Kuttab, Jonathan, and Raja Shehadeh. *Civilian Administration in the Occupied West Bank: Analysis of Israeli Military Order No. 947.* Ramallah, West Bank: Law in the Service of Man, 1982. Legal analysis by two Palestinian lawyers of Israel's 1981 introduction of "civil administration."

Landau, Jacob. *The Arab Minority in Israel, 1967–1991: Political Aspects.* New York: Oxford University Press, 1993. Israeli scholar's study of Israeli Arabs. Critical of Palestinian nationalists but calls for Arab integration into Israel state.

Langer, Felicia. *With My Own Eyes: Israel and the Occupied Territories, 1967–1973.* London: Ithaca, 1975. Earlier account of Israeli lawyer's defense of Arab political prisoners.

Laqueur, Walter. *The Road to Jerusalem: Origin and Aftermath of the Arab-Israel Conflict, 1967/8.* Baltimore, Md.: Penguin Books, 1969. Account of 1967 war; sympathetic to Israel.

Laqueur, Walter, and Barry Rubin. *The Israel-Arab Reader: A Documentary History of the Middle East Conflict.* 4th ed. New York: Facts On File, 1985. Extensive collection of documents, speeches, etc., since 1880s.

Lehn, Walter, and Uri Davis. *The Jewish National Fund.* London: Kegan Paul, 1988. Critical study of Jewish National Fund land policies emphasizing discriminatory practices vis-à-vis Palestinians.

Lesch, Ann Mosely. *Arab Politics in Palestine, 1917–1939: The Frustration of a Nationalist Movement.* Ithaca, N.Y.: Cornell University Press, 1979. Fine scholarly account of Palestinian nationalist development.

——. *Political Perceptions of Palestinians on the West Bank and the Gaza Strip.* Washington, D.C.: Middle East Institute, 1980. Study of Palestinian attitudes after Camp David agreements.

——. *Transition to Palestinian Self-Government: Practical Steps Toward Israeli-Palestinian Peace.* Bloomington: Indiana University Press, 1992. Report of a study group convened by American Academy of Arts and Sciences in Cambridge, Massachusetts.

Lesch, Ann M., and Mark Tessler. *Israel, Egypt, and the Palestinians: From Camp David to Intifada.* Bloomington: Indiana University Press, 1989. Collection of essays by Lesch and Tessler on Israel, Egypt, and Palestinian relations—1980–88.

Lewis, William, and Robert W. Stookey, eds. *The End of the Palestine Mandate.* Austin: University of Texas Press, 1986. Essays on U.S., British, Arab, and Zionist attitudes on Mandates's end.

A License to Kill: Israeli Operations Against "Wanted" and Masked Palestinians. New York: Human Rights Watch, 1993. Israeli undercover operations against Palestinians in Gaza and West Bank.

Lockman, Zachary. *Comrades and Enemies: Arab and Jewish Workers in Palestine, 1906–1948.* Berkeley: University of California Press, 1996.

Explores the interaction between Palestinian and Jewish working classes, labor movement, and their parties.

Lockman, Zachary, and Joel Beinin, eds. *Intifada: The Palestinian Uprising Against Israeli Occupation.* Boston: South End, 1989. Collection of articles, impressions, documents, poetry of Intifada.

Lowi, Miriam R. *Water and Politics: The Politics of a Scarce Resource in the Jordan River Basin.* New York: Cambridge University Press, 1993. Analysis of history and current status of dispute between Israel and Arabs over Jordan River waters; various plans for development of Jordan River system.

Lukacs, Yehuda, ed. *The Israeli–Palestinian Conflict: A Documentary Record 1967–1990.* Cambridge, England: Cambridge University Press, 1992. Extensive documentation, including U.S., Israeli, Arab, and international documents, speeches, letters, pronouncements.

Lustick, Ian S. *Arabs in the Jewish State: Israel's Control of a National Minority.* Austin: University of Texas Press, 1980. Fine study of Israeli methods to control its citizens.

———. *For the Land and the Lord: Jewish Fundamentalism in Israel.* New York: Council on Foreign Relations, 1988. Study of Jewish fundamentalist and West Bank settlers, including their attitudes to Arabs.

Lustick, Ian S., ed. *Arab–Israeli Relations: A Collection of Contending Perspectives and Recent Research.* 10 vols. Hamden, Conn.: Garland, 1994. Useful collection of more than 170 articles by diverse authors covering Arab–Israel conflict from 19th century to 1991. Volumes 1–10, in order: *Arab–Israel Relations: Historical Background and Origins of the Conflict; Triumph and Catastrophe: The War of 1948, Israeli Independence, and the Refugee Problem; From War to War: Israel vs. the Arabs 1948–1967; From Wars Toward Peace in the Arab–Israeli Conflict 1969–1992; Religion, Culture, and Psychology in Arab Israeli Relations; Economic, Legal, and Demographic Dimensions of Arab–Israeli Relations; The Conflict With the Arabs in Israeli Politics and Society; The Conflict With Israel in Arab Politics and Society; Palestinians Under Israeli Rule;* and *Arab–Israeli Relations in World Politics.*

Lynd, Staughton, Sam Bahour, and Alice Lynd. *Homeland: Oral Histories of Palestine and Palestinians.* New York: Olive Branch, 1994. Interviews with diverse Palestinians in 1991–92.

MacBride, Sean, and Richard Falk, eds. *Israel in Lebanon: Report of the International Commission to Enquire into Reported Violations of International Law by Israel during Its Invasion of Lebanon.* London: Ithaca, 1983. Commission chaired by MacBride; strongly condemned Israel for crimes against humanity and occupation of Lebanon.

McCarthy, Justin. *The Population of Palestine: Population History and Statistics of the Late Ottoman Period and the Mandate.* Institute for Palestine Studies series. New York: Columbia University Press, 1990. Utilizes official statistics to establish facts about Palestinian population.

———. McDowall, David. *Palestine and Israel: The Uprising and Beyond.* Berkeley: University of California, 1989. Examines Israel-Palestinian relations and background of Intifada.

———. *The Palestinians: The Road to Nationhood.* Concord, Mass.: Minority Rights Publications, 1995. Describes the weak status of the Palestinians despite the recent peace accords.

McTague, John J. *British Policy in Palestine, 1917–1922.* Lanham, Md.: University Press of America, 1983. Covers period from Balfour Declaration to League of Nations mandate.

Magnes, Judah L., et al. *Palestine: Divided or United? The Case for a Bi-national Palestine Before the United Nations.* Westport, Conn: Greenwood, 1983. Reissue of 1947 testimony by Zionists (Ihud) before UNSCOP favoring binational state.

Makofvsky, David. *Making Peace with the PLO.* Boulder, Colo.: Westview, 1996. Detailed account of secret negotiations leading to Declaration of Principles.

Mallison, W. Thomas, and Sally Mallison. *An International Law Analysis if the Major United Nations Resolutions Concerning the Palestine Question.* New York: United Nations, 1979. Legal analysis of partition, refugees, Jerusalem, Palestinian status, critical of Israeli position.

———. *The Palestine Problem in International Law and World Order.* New York: Longman, 1983. Treatment of legal aspects of Balfour Declaration, U.N. Partition Resolution, Jerusalem, Israeli settlements, Palestinian rights; critical of Israel.

Mandel, Neville J. *The Arabs and Zionism before World War I.* Berkeley: University of California Press, 1976. Covers Arab reaction to Zionism from 1880s to 1914.

Manna, Adil. *Jerusalem and the Administered Territories, 1967–1976: A Select Bibliography.* Jerusalem: Hebrew University, Harry S. Truman Research Institute, 1977. Prepared for June 1977 seminar on Jerusalem and administered territories.

Ma'oz, Moshe. *Ottoman Reform in Syria and Palestine, 1840–1861: The Impact of the Tanzimat on Politics and Society.* Oxford, England: Clarendon, 1968. Covers Ottoman rule, including military, taxes, minorities, etc.

——. *Palestinian Arab Politics.* Jerusalem: Jerusalem Academic, 1975. Papers on Palestinian politics, parties, and literature under British and Jordanians.

——. *Palestinian Leadership on the West Bank: The Changing Role of the Mayors Under Jordan and Israel.* Totowa, N.J.: Frank Cass, 1984. An Israeli scholar's examination of Palestinian politics during occupation.

Ma'oz, Moshe, ed. *Studies on Palestine During the Ottoman Period.* Jerusalem: Magnes, 1975. Documented study of Ottoman era, from 1516 to 1917.

Mar'i, Sami K. *Arab Education in Israel.* Syracuse, N.Y.: Syracuse University Press, 1978. Critical account of Israeli Palestinian education in context of problems.

Marlowe, John. *The State of Pilate: An Account of the Palestine Mandate.* London: Cresset, 1959. Critical account of Britain in Palestine, 1917–48.

Masalha, Nur. *Expulsion of the Palestinians: The Concept of "Transfer" in Zionist Political Thought, 1882–1948.* Washington, D.C.: Institute for Palestine Studies, 1992. Analysis of Zionist ideas about and plans for Palestinian expulsion, which the author maintains were implemented in 1948 war.

Mattar, Philip. *The Mufti of Jerusalem: Al-Hajj Amin al-Husayni and the Palestinian Movement.* New York: Columbia University Press, 1992. Objective account of Mufti's life based on archival research.

Meinhertzhagen, Col. Richard. *Middle East Diary, 1917–1956.* London: Cresset, 1959. Diaries of British colonial official who became ardent Zionist.

Melman, Yossi, and Dan Raviv. *Beyond the Uprising: Israelis, Jordanians, and Palestinians.* Westport, Conn.: Greenwood, 1989. Covers Israel's relations with Jordan and Palestinians and U.S. involvement.

Mendelsohn, Everett, ed. *A Compassionate Peace: A Future for the Middle East.* New York: Hill and Wang, 1982. Report prepared for the American Friends Service Committee (Quakers).

Muslih, Muhammad Y. *The Origins of Palestinian Nationalism.* New York: Columbia University Press, 1988. Scholarly study of 1850s to 1920s based on archival research.

Najjar, Orayb Aref, and Kitty Warnock. *Portraits of Palestinian Women.* Salt Lake City: Utah University, 1992. Intimate interviews with women activists, intellectuals, homemakers, and professionals.

Nakleh, Emile. *The West Bank and Gaza: Toward the Making of a Palestinian State.* Washington, D.C.: American Enterprise Institute, 1979. Examination of West Bank and Gaza local government institutions.

Nakleh, Emile, ed. *A Palestinian Agenda for the West Bank and Gaza.* Washington, D.C.: American Enterprise Institute, 1980. Collection of papers about future education, agriculture, social work, local government, etc., by West Bank and Gaza Palestinians.

Nakleh, Khalil. *Indigenous Organizations in Palestine: Towards a Purposeful Societal Development.* Jerusalem: Arab Thought Forum, 1991. Emphasis on local and community development societies.

Nashif, Taysir N. *The Palestinian Arab and Jewish Political Leaderships: A Comparative Study.* New York: Asia, 1979. Based on quantitative comparisons of class, social background, education, occupation, etc.; covers 1920 to 1948.

Nazzal, Nafez. *The Palestinian Exodus from Galilee. 1948.* Beirut: Institute for Palestine Studies, 1978. Study of Palestinian 1948 exodus during the 1947–48 war.

Neff, Donald. *Fallen Pillars: U.S. Policy Towards Palestine and Israel, 1947–1994.* Washington, D.C.: Institute for Palestine Studies, 1995. Critique of American policy toward Israel–Palestine conflict.

Newman, David. *Population, Settlement, and Conflict: Israel and the West Bank.* Cambridge, England: Cambridge University Press, 1991. Importance of demography and population in solution of Arab–Israel conflict.

Newman, David, ed. *The Impact of Gush Emunim: Politics and Settlement in the West Bank.* New York: St. Martin's, 1985. Essays about militant Jewish West Bank settlers' movement.

O'Ballance, Edgar. *The Arab-Israeli War, 1948.* 1956. Reprint, Westport, Conn.: Hyperion, 1981. Account of 1948 war by British military analyst.

Ovendale, Ritchie. *The Origins of the Arab-Israeli Wars.* New York: Longman, 1984. Covers conflict since rise of Zionism; includes 1948, 1956, 1967, and 1973 wars.

Owen, Roger, ed. *Studies in the Economics and Social History of Palestine in the Nineteenth and Twentieth Centuries.* Carbondale: Southern Illinois University Press, 1982. Collection of studies by diverse authors covering economy, society, and government.

Palestine Royal Commission. *Report: Presented by the Secretary of State for the Colonies to Parliament by Command of His Majesty July, 1937.* London: HM Stationery Office, 1937. Detailed report on Palestine; also known as Peel Commission Report.

Palestinians in Profile: A Guide to Leading Palestinians in the Occupied Territories. East Jerusalem: Panorama-Center for the Dissemination of Alternative Information, 1993. Biographical data and interviews with 251 leading Palestinians.

Pappé, Illan. *Britain and the Arab-Israeli Conflict, 1948–51.* New York: St. Martin's, 1988. Detailed study based on archival materials of British policy.

——— . *The Israel-Palestine Question.* London: Routledge, 1999. Critical analysis of Zionism, Israel and the development of Palestinian-Israeli conflict.

——— . *The Making of the Arab-Israeli Conflict, 1947–51.* New York: I. B. Tauris, 1992. Diplomatic history of the 1948 war, background, and aftermath.

Peretz, Don. *The Arab-Israel Dispute.* New York: Facts On File, 1996. Reference work that includes overview, 100-page bibliography, maps, documents, etc.

——. *Intifada: The Palestinian Uprising.* Boulder, Colo.: Westview, 1990. Account of Intifada, background, causes, impact on Israel and Arabs.

——. *Israel and the Palestine Arabs.* Washington, D.C.: Middle East Institute, 1958. Israel's policy toward Arab minority and Palestine refugees.

——. *The West Bank: History, Politics, Society, and Economy.* Boulder, Colo.: Westview, 1986. Examination of West Bank from Ottoman era through Israeli occupation.

Peteet, Julie M. *Gender in Crisis: Women and the Palestinian Resistance Movement.* New York: Columbia University Press, 1991. Discusses Palestinian women's movements and women's plight from 1920s to 1982.

Peters, Joan. *From Time Immemorial: The Origins of the Arab-Israeli Conflict Over Palestine.* New York: Harper & Row, 1984. Highly controversial attempt to discredit Palestinian claims to Palestine.

Plascov, Avi. *Palestinian Refugees in Jordan, 1948–1957.* London: Frank Cass, 1981. Study of Palestinian refugees in Jordan after 1948.

Playfair, Emma, ed. *International Law and Administration of Occupied Territories: Two Decades of Israeli Occupation of the West Bank and Gaza Strip.* New York: Oxford University Press, 1992. Collection of essays from 1988 conference in East Jerusalem.

Polk, William, David Stamler, and Edmund Asfour. *Backdrop to Tragedy: The Struggle for Palestine.* Boston: Beacon Press, 1957. History of conflict; three perspectives from 19th century to creation of Israel; refugee problem, economic impact.

Porath, Yehoshua. *The Emergence of the Palestinian National Movement, 1918–1929.* London: Frank Cass, 1973. Scholarly study of the rise of the Palestinian national movement.

—— . *The Palestinian Arab National Movement, From Riots to Rebellion.* Vol. 2. London: Frank Cass, 1978. Continuation of Porath's study to end of Arab Rebellion, 1929–1939.

Prison Conditions in Israel and the Occupied Territories. New York: Human Rights Watch, 1991. Palestinian prison conditions, political prisoners, and civil rights.

Punishing a Nation: Human Rights Violations During the Palestinian Uprising, December 1987–December 1988. Ramallah, West Bank: al-Haq/Law in the Service of Man, 1988. Documented study of human violations by affiliate of the International Commission of Jurists from a Palestinian perspective.

Reiss, Nira. *The Health of the Arabs in Israel.* Boulder, Colo.: Westview, 1991. Examines Arab medical care, social conditions, and health services.

Reiter, Yitzhak. *Islamic Endowments in Jerusalem Under British Mandate.* London: Frank Cass, 1996. Comprehensive treatment of *waqf* institutions.

Richardson, John P. *The West Bank: A Portrait.* Washington, D.C.: Middle East Institute, 1984. Survey of the West Bank and its history from the Ottomans to occupation by Israel.

Rigby, Andrew. *Living the Intifada.* London: Zed Books, 1991. Detailed history of the Intifada through the Gulf War.

Roman, Michael, and Alex Wingrod. *Living Together Separately: Arabs and Jews in Contemporary Jerusalem.* Princeton, N.J.: Princeton University Press, 1991. Arab–Jewish ethnic relations since Israel's occupation of Jerusalem.

Rouhana, Nadim. *Palestinian Citizens in an Ethnic Jewish State.* New Haven, Conn.: Yale University Press, 1997. Analysis of the changing identity of the Palestinian citizens of Israel.

Roy, Sara. *The Gaza Strip: The Political Economy of De-Development.* Washington, D.C.: Institute for Palestine Studies, 1995. Detailed study of Gaza's political economy after Israeli occupation, and its deterioration.

Rubenberg, Cheryl A. *The Palestine Liberation Organization: Its Institutional Infrastructure.* Belmont, Mass.: Institute for Arab Studies, 1982. Study of PLO civilian welfare and educational and industrial institutions.

Rubinstein, Danny. *The Mystery of Arafat.* South Royalton, Vt.: Steerforth, 1995. Account of Arafat's problems by Israeli journalist.

——. *The People of Nowhere: The Palestinian Vision of Home.* New York: Times Books, 1991. Empathetic account by Israeli journalist of Palestinian insistence on "right of return."

Sahliyeh, Emile. *In Search of Leadership: West Bank Politics Since 1967.* Washington, D.C.: Brookings Institutions, 1988. West Bank politics under Israeli occupation; based on interviews.

——. *The PLO After the Lebanon War.* Boulder, Colo.: Westview, 1986. Describes impact of 1982 war on PLO.

Said, Edward W. *After the Last Sky: Palestinian Lives.* New York: Pantheon Books, 1986. Portrayal of Palestinian people's lives through photos and text.

——. *The Politics of Dispossession: The Struggle for Palestinian Self-Determination 1969–1994.* London: Chatto and Windus, 1994. Collection of essays by Palestinian–American intellectual critical of Western, Arab, and Palestinian policies.

——. *The Question of Palestine.* New York: Times Books, 1979. Presentation of Palestinian position; Zionist achievement of goals at expense of Palestinian people.

Said, Edward, and Christopher Hitchens, eds. *Blaming the Victims: Spurious Scholarship and the Palestinian Question.* New York: Verso, 1987. Collection of essays by diverse authors criticizing Middle East scholarship.

Sayigh, Rosemary. *Palestinians: From Peasants to Revolutionaries.* London: Zed Books, 1979. Sociological study of Palestinian displacement.

——. *Too Many Enemies: The Palestinian Experience in Lebanon.* London: Zed, 1994. Case study based on Shatila refugee camp on outskirts of Beirut.

Sayigh, Yezid. *Armed Struggle and the Search for State: The Palestinian National Movement, 1949–1993.* Oxford: Clarendon, 1997. A comprehensive history of the Palestinian national movement with a focus on the Palestinian armed struggle.

Schiff, Benjamin N. *Refugees unto the Third Generation: U.N. Aid to Palestinians.* Syracuse; N.Y.: Syracuse University Press, 1995. Detailed study of history and operations of UNRWA.

Schiff, Zeev, and Ehud Yaari. *Intifada: The Palestinian Uprising—Israel's Third Front.* New York: Simon & Schuster, 1990. A study of the revolt and its impact on Israel, the PLO, the region, and the United States.

Segev, Tom. *1949: The First Israelis.* New York: Free Press, 1986. Israeli journalist's account of Israeli confiscation of Palestinian property, early Palestinian policies, and initial mishandling of problems.

Shadid, Mohammed Khalil. *The United States and the Palestinians.* New York: St. Martin's, 1981. Critical analysis of U.S. policy from pre-1948 to President Carter.

Shafir, Gershon. *Land, Labor and the Origins of the Israeli–Palestinian Conflict, 1882–1914.* Cambridge, England: Cambridge University, 1989. Discussion of early causes of Arab-Jewish tension in Palestine.

Shalev, Carmel. *Collective Punishment in the West Bank and the Gaza Strip.* Jerusalem: B'tselem, 1990. Critique of Israeli human rights violations; by Israeli human rights group.

Shammas, Anton. *Arabesques.* New York: Harper & Row, 1988. Autobiographic novel by Israeli Palestinian; translated from Hebrew.

Shapira, Anita. *Land and Power: The Zionist Resort to Force, 1891–1948.* New York: Oxford University Press, 1992. Examines ideologies, myths, and symbols developed by Zionist settlers to justify confrontation with Palestine and other Arabs.

Sharabi, Hisham. *Palestine and Israel: The Lethal Dilemma.* New York: Pegasus, 1969. Palestinian scholar's discussion of the conflict and its ramifications.

Sharoni, Simona. *Gender and the Israel-Palestinian Conflict: The Politics of Women's Resistance.* Syracuse, N.Y.: Syracuse University Press, 1995. Feminist account of role played by Israeli and Palestinian women in the Arab–Israeli conflict.

Shehadeh, Raja. *Occupier's Law: Israel and the West Bank.* Washington, D.C.: Institute for Palestine Studies, 1989. Palestinian lawyer's documented study of human rights violations.

Shemesh, Moshe. *The Palestinian Entity, 1959–1974: Arab Politics and the PLO.* 2d ed. London: Frank Cass, 1996. Discussion of link between Arab politics and the evolution of the PLO.

Sherman, A. J. *Mandate Days: British Lives in Palestine 1918–1948.* New York: Thames and Hudson, 1997. Private lives of British officials who served in Palestine during British rule.

Shipler, David K. *Arab and Jew: Wounded Spirits in a Promised Land.* New York: Times Books, 1986; New York: Penguin, 1987. Pulitzer Prize–winning account of Arab and Jewish mutual perceptions by former *New York Times* correspondent.

Shlaim, Avi. *Collusion Across the Jordan: King Abdullah, the Zionist Movement, and the Partition of Palestine.* New York: Columbia University Press, 1988. Study of Jordan–Israel collaboration against Palestinian nationalists.

Smith, Barbara J. *The Roots of Separatism in Palestine: British Economic Policy, 1920–1929.* Syracuse, N.Y.: Syracuse University Press, 1993. British economic policy in mandatory Palestine and its impact on Palestinians.

Smith, Charles D. *Palestine and the Arab-Israeli Conflict.* 2d ed. New York: St. Martin's, 1992. Good overall introduction covering conflict from Ottomans to 1991.

Smooha, Sammy. *Arabs and Jews in Israel.* Vol. 1. *Conflicting and Shared Attitudes in a Divided Society.* Boulder, Colo.: Westview, 1992. Discussion of political and social attitudes based on survey research.

Stein, Kenneth W. *The Land Question in Palestine, 1917–1939.* Chapel Hill: University of North Carolina Press, 1984. Pro-Zionist discussion of Zionist land acquisition in mandatory Palestine.

Stone, Julius. *Israel and Palestine: Assault on the Law of Nations.* Baltimore, Md.: Johns Hopkins University Press, 1981. Analysis of international law favorable to Israel by international lawyer.

Storr, Ronald. *Orientations.* London: Nicholson & Wilson, 1945. First-hand account of the first military governor of Jerusalem under British rule.

Strum, Philippa. *The Women Are Marching: The Second Sex and the Palestinian Revolution.* New York: Lawrence Hill Books, 1992. Journal discussing women's emergence into leadership roles.

Sulaiman, Khalid A. *A Modern Arabic Poetry and Palestine.* London: Zed Books, 1984. Poems by Palestinian and other Arab poets with theme of Palestine.

Suleiman, Michael W. *U.S. Policy on Palestine from Wilson to Clinton.* Normal, Il.: Association of Arab-American University Graduates, 1995. Diverse Palestinian and American authors examine Palestine policies of U.S. administrations since World War I, from a pro-Palestinian perspective.

Sullivan, Anthony Thrall. *Palestinian Universities under Occupation.* Cairo: American University in Cairo, 1989. Analysis of Arab higher education in Occupied Territories.

Swedenburg, Ted. *Memories of Revolt.* Minneapolis: University of Minnesota Press, 1995. An account of Palestinians in the 1936–39 Arab revolt.

Sykes, Christopher. *Crossroads to Israel.* Cleveland, Ohio: World, 1965; Bloomington: Indiana University Press, 1973. Pro-Zionist account of British policy in Palestine 1917–1948.

Takenberg, Lex. *The Status of Palestinian Refugees in International Law.* Oxford: Clarendon, 1998. Useful and timely discussion of legal rights of the refugees.

Talhami, Ghada Hashem. *Palestine and Egyptian Nationalist Identity.* Westport, Conn.: Praeger, 1992. Surveys the range of Egyptian attitudes to Palestine in writings of diverse intellectuals.

Tamari, Salim ed. *Jerusalem 1948: The Arab Neighborhoods and Their Fate in the War.* Jerusalem: Institute for Jerusalem Studies, and Badil Resource Center, 1999. Useful study of the topic.

Tessler, Mark A. *A History of the Israeli-Palestinian Conflict.* Bloomington: Indiana University Press, 1994. Massive history, from Old Testament to Israel–PLO 1993 agreement.

Teveth, Shabtai. *Ben-Gurion and the Palestinian Arabs: From Peace to War.* Oxford, England: Oxford University, 1985. Ben-Gurion's perceptions, views, policies, and prescriptions vis-à-vis Palestinians and his changes in attitude from 1906 to 1939.

——. *The Cursed Blessing: The Story of Israel's Occupation of the West Bank.* New York: Random House, 1971. Critical account by leading Israeli journalist.

Tibawai, A. L. *Anglo-Arab Relations and the Question of Palestine, 1914–1921.* London: Luzac, 1978. An Arab interpretation, based on documents, of the critical issues, such as the McMahon pledge.

——. *Arab Education in Mandatory Palestine: A Study in Three Decades of British Administration.* London: Luzac, 1956. Account by former Palestinian educator.

——. *British Interests in Palestine, 1800–1901: A Study of Religious and Educational Enterprise.* London: Oxford University Press, 1961. Survey of British cultural and political interests in 19th-century Palestine.

——. *Jerusalem: Its Place in Islam and Arab History.* Beirut: Institute for Palestine Studies, 1969. Short account of Jerusalem's importance for Arabs and Islam.

Toye, Patricia ed. *Palestine Boundaries, 1833–1947.* 3 vols. Neuchâtel, Switzerland: Archive Editions, 1989. Reprinted documents from a number of archives preceded by a fine long introduction by J. C. Hurewitz and accompanied by fifteen maps.

U.S. Congress, House Committee on Foreign Affairs. Subcommittee on Near East. *Jerusalem: The Future of the Holy City for Three Monotheisms: Hearings before the House Committee on Foreign Affairs, Subcommittee on Near East.* 92d Cong., 1st sess., 28 July 1971. Washington, D.C.: U.S. Government Printing Office, 1972.

U.S. Congress. Senate Committee on the Judiciary. Subcommittee on Immigration and Naturalization. *The Colonization of the West Bank Territories by Israel: Hearings Before the Subcommittee on Immigration and Naturalization of the Committee of the Judiciary.* 95th Cong., 1st sess., 17 and 18 October 1977. Washington, D.C.: U.S. Government Printing Office, 1978. Discussion of Israeli settlements in West Bank.

Van Horn, Maj. Gen. Carl. *Soldiering for Peace.* New York: Mckay, 1967. Memoirs of former Swedish U.N. truce supervision officer in Middle East.

Van Leeuwen, Marianne. *Americans and the Palestinian Question: The U.S. Public Debate on Palestinian Nationhood, 1973–1988.* Atlanta, Ga.: Rodophi BV Editions, 1993. Comprehensive survey of American writing and discussion of Palestine question from 1973 war to Intifada.

Victor, Barbara. *A Voice of Reason: Hanan Ashrawi and Peace in the Middle East.* New York: Harcourt Brace, 1994. Biography of former spokesperson of Palestine delegation at Middle East peace negotiations.

Viorst, Milton. *Reaching for the Olive Branch: UNRWA and Peace in the Middle East.* Washington, D.C.: Middle East Institute, 1989. Monograph with history; work of U.N. Palestine refugee agency.

Waines, David. A. *A Sentence of Exile: The Palestinian/Israel Conflict, 1897–1977.* Wilmette, Il.: Medina University Press, 1977. Canadian historian's account of conflict sympathetic to Palestinians.

Wallach, Janet, and John Wallach. *Arafat in the Eyes of the Beholder.* Rocklin, Calif.: Prima, 1991. Biography of Arafat by two sympathetic American journalists.

——. *The New Palestinians: The Emerging Generation of Leaders.* Rocklin, Calif.: Prima, 1992. Life histories of 12 mostly West Bank and Gaza Palestinian leaders.

——. *Still Small Voices.* New York: Harcourt Brace Jovanovich, 1989. Portraits of West Bank and Gaza Arabs and Jewish settlers based on interviews.

Ward, Richard J., Don Peretz, and Evan M. Wilson. *The Palestinian State: A Rational Approach.* Rev. ed. Port Washington, N.Y.: Kennikat, 1977. Revision and updating of earlier edition with discussion of options for Palestinians.

Warnock, Kitty. *Land Before Honour: Palestinian Women in the Occupied Territories.* New York: Monthly Review, 1990. Discusses Palestinian women in society, work, and politics.

Wasserstein, Bernard. *The British in Palestine: The Mandatory Government and the Anglo-Jewish Conflict 1917–1929.* London: Royal Historical Society, 1978. Pro-Zionist detailed, documented study of British rule from 1917 to the Wailing Wall incident.

Weir, Shelagh. *Palestinian Costume.* Austin: University of Texas Press, 1989. Illustrated with 200 color and 100 black-and-white photos.

Wilson, Evan M. *Decision on Palestine: How the U.S. Came to Recognize Israel.* Stanford, Calif.: Hoover Institution, 1979. U.S. policy toward Palestine problem in 1940s and Palestine issue in Anglo-American diplomacy and U.S. politics.

Zureik, Elia. *The Palestinians in Israel: A Study in Internal Colonialism.* London: Routledge & Kegan Paul, 1979. Pro-Palestinian sociological study of Israeli Palestinian minority and its subordinate relationship to the Zionist state.

Zureik, Elia, and Fouad Moughrabi, eds. *Public Opinion and the Palestinian Question.* New York: St. Martin's, 1986. Several Studies of U.S. and Canadian public opinion on the conflict.

PERIODICALS

Arab Studies Quarterly. Normal, Il.: Association of Arab-American University Graduates and Institute of Arab Studies.

Challenge: A Magazine of the Israeli Left. Tel Aviv, Israel.

I & P: Israel and Palestine Political Report. Paris, France.

Israel Foreign Affairs. Sacramento, California.

Israel Horizons. New York: Americans for Progressive Israel.

Jerusalem Quarterly File, Jerusalem, Institute of Jerusalem Studies.

The Jerusalem Report. Jerusalem, Israel.

Journal of Palestine Studies: A Quarterly on Palestinian Affairs and the Arab-Israel Conflict. Washington, D.C.: Institute for Palestine Studies.

Jusoor: The Arab American Journal of Cultural Exchange. Washington, D.C.

The Link. New York: Americans for Middle East Understanding.

Middle Eastern Studies. London: Frank Cass.

Middle East Insight. Washington, D.C.: International Insight.

Middle East International. London and Washington, D.C.

The Middle East Journal. Washington, D.C.: Middle East Institute.

Middle East Policy. Washington, D.C.: Middle East Policy Council.

Middle East Quarterly. Philadelphia: Middle East Forum.

Middle East Report. Washington, D.C.: Middle East Research and Information Project (MERIP).

Middle East Watch Report. New York: Middle East Watch.

The Other Israel. Tel Aviv: Israel Council for Israeli-Palestinian Peace.

Palestine-Israel Journal. Jerusalem, Israel.

Report on Israeli Settlement in the Occupied Territories. Washington, D.C.: Foundation for Middle East Peace.

Tikkun: A Quarterly Jewish Critique of Politics, Culture and Society. Oakland, Calif.: Institute for Labor and Mental Health.

Washington Report on Middle East Affairs. Washington, D.C.: American Educational Trust.

LIST OF CONTRIBUTORS

Ziad Abu-Amr. Bir Zeit University member, Palestinian Legislative Council
As'ad AbuKhalil, California State University
sinan Antoon, Indiana University
Geoffrey Aronson, Director, Foundation for Middle East Peace
Issa J. Boullato, Artist, Menton, France
Laurie A. Brand, University of Southern California
Sarah Graham-Brown, Consultant and writer, London
Inea Bushnaq, Folklorist, New York
Neil Caplan, Vanier College, Montreal
Kathy Christison, Former CIA analyst, Santa Fe, New Mexico
Sharif Elmusa, American University of Cairo
Michael R. Fischbach, Randolph-Macon College; Director, Palestinian American Research Center
Fawwaz A. Gerges, Sarah Lawrence College
Albert Glock, Former director of the Albright Institute; founder of the Archaelolgical Institute, Bir Zeit University. (Lois Glock, wife of Albert Glock, updated the entry).
Galia Golan, Hebrew University
Eric Goldstein, Middle East Watch
Alain Gresh, *Le Monde Diplomatique*
Eric Hooglund, Editor, Critique: *Journal for Critical Studies of the Middle East*
George Irani, Washingto College
Rashid Khalidi, University of Chicago
Ann Mosely Lesch, Villanova University
F. T. Liu, International Peace Academy, New York
Ian Lustick, University of Pennsylvania
Sari Makdisi, Universtiy of Chicago
Adel Manna, Harry S. Truman Institute for Peasce, Jerusalem
Nur Masalha, The American International Universtiy, London
Philip Mattar, Director, Institute for Palestine Studies, Washington, D.C.
Muhammad Muslih, Long Island Universitiy
Justin McCarthy, University of Louisville
Benny Morris, Harry S. Truman Institute for Peace; Ben Gurion University
Fadle Naqib, University of Waterloo]
Robert Olson, Former U. S. diplomat, Hayward, Wisconsin
Don Perets, Professor emeritus, State Universtiy of New York, Binghamton
Julie Peteet, University of Louisville
Muin Rabbani, Oxford University
Cheryl Reubenberg, Florida International University
John Ruedy, Georgetown Universty
Sara Roy, Harvard University
Bernard Sabella, Bethlehem University
Muhammad Siddiq, Universtiy of California at Berkeley
Raja Shehadeh, Founder of al-Haq/Law in the Service of Man; lawyer, Ramalla
Avi Shlaim, Oxford University
Charles Smith, University of Arizona
Salim Tamari, Bir Zeit University; Director, Institute for Jerusalem Studies
Mark Tessler, University of Wisconsin
Janice J. Terry, East Michigan University
Shelagh G. Weir, Museum of Mankind, London

INDEX

Boldface page numbers denote main headings.

I

J

N

O

P

1 6/05
1 6/05
0 - 8/02
0 - 6/05